CRIMINAL LAW AND ITS PROCESSES

CASES AND MATERIALS

CRIMINAL LAW AND ITS PROCESSES

CASES AND MATERIALS

FOURTH EDITION

Sanford H. Kadish

Alexander F. and May T. Morrison Professor of Law
University of California, Berkeley

Stephen J. Schulhofer

Professor of Law
University of Pennsylvania

Monrad G. Paulsen

Late Dean
Cardozo School of Law, Yeshiva University

Little, Brown and Company
Boston   Toronto

Library of Congress Catalog Card No. 82-081495
ISBN 0-316-47812-1

Eighth Printing

MV

*Published simultaneously in Canada
by Little, Brown & Company (Canada) Limited*

Printed in the United States of America

SUMMARY OF CONTENTS

CONTENTS

CHAPTER 3

THE JUSTIFICATION OF PUNISHMENT   181

CHAPTER 4

DEFINING CRIMINAL CONDUCT — THE ELEMENTS OF JUST PUNISHMENT   249

CHAPTER 5

RAPE 371

CHAPTER 6

HOMICIDE   **407**

CHAPTER 7

THE SIGNIFICANCE OF RESULTING HARM 531

CHAPTER 8

GROUP CRIMINALITY   611

CHAPTER 9

EXCULPATION   721

CHAPTER 10

THEFT OFFENSES   913

CHAPTER 11

BUSINESS CRIMES   **987**

CHAPTER 12

Contents

PREFACE TO THE FOURTH EDITION

This edition, while preserving continuity with its predecessors, contains many significant changes in organization and content. The substantive criminal law sections retain their basic structure and purposes. However, the content, organization, and pedogogical objectives of the procedural material are essentially new. Instead of attempting a full coverage of the subject of criminal procedure, we have included in this edition only those aspects of procedural law that seemed to us especially helpful for understanding the substantive criminal law.

Why substantive criminal law? We conceive of a criminal law course as both serving the ends of legal training in general and training in the criminal law in particular. The chief value of the course as a part of a general legal education is to enlarge insight into and understanding of the potentialities and limitations of the law as an instrument of social control. We have in mind the variety of hard problems associated with the use of the law for the attainment of social ends: the difficulty of giving legal form to the compromises made necessary when goals are poised in conflict; the creation of institutional arrangements — judicial and administrative — appropriate to the goals sought; the limitations — moral and practical — on the use of the law as a means of social control; the relation of legal controls to other social processes. We regard the study of the substantive criminal law as an unusually suitable introduction to these pervasive problems of the law. The ends criminal law serves involve social and human values of the highest order. Its means, entailing the imposition of brute force on the lives of individuals, are potentially the most destructive and abusive to be found within the legal system. The issues it raises and the setting in which it raises them are compelling and vivid. Its institutions are acutely controversial and often controverted. And one of its underlying themes is the momentous issue of the reconciliation of authority and the individual. As Professor Herbert Wechsler has written: "Whatever views one holds about the penal law, no one will question its importance in society. This is the law on which men place their ultimate reliance for protection against all the deepest injuries that human conduct can inflict on individuals and institutions. By the same token penal law governs the strongest force that we permit official agencies to bring to bear on individuals. Its promise as an instrument of safety is matched only by its power to destroy. If penal law is weak or ineffective, basic human interests are in jeopardy. If it is harsh or arbitrary in its impact, it works a gross injustice on those caught within its toils. The law that carries such responsibilities should surely be as rational and just as law can be. Nowhere in the entire legal field is more at stake for the community or for the individual."[1]

1. Wechsler, The Challenge of a Model Penal Code, 65 Harv. L. Rev. 1097, 1097-1098 (1952).

What of the course's narrower purpose of training students in the criminal law in particular? Here there are two main pedagogic objectives. One is to furnish a solid foundation for those who will, in greater or lesser degree, participate directly in the processes of the criminal law, whether they will represent the state or the individual before or during the stages of trial and appeal or during the sentencing or correctional stages. This solid foundation does not require mastery of the full range of technical skills and information held by the practicing criminal lawyer or administrator but rather the development of power and confidence in the handling of principles and rules — judge-made or statutory — through the acquisition of knowledge about and insight into the larger implications of the doctrines and institutions of the criminal law. The second purpose is to create in law school graduates who will have little occasion to practice criminal law an interest in and an understanding of the profound problems of the criminal law and of its functioning. As influential members of their communities — and more directly as judges, legislators, or teachers — lawyers versed in the principles of criminal law will be in a position to bring an informed intelligence to the challenge of solving some of the most vexing problems of our times.[2]

Revisions for the fourth edition. In the substantive sections we have updated the cases, added Notes and Problems dealing with many issues of current concern, and in many areas wholly recast the presentation and organization. We have also added two new chapters, one dealing with business crimes and the other with rape.

As in previous editions, the substantive materials continue to focus on imparting an understanding of what is often called the "general part" of the criminal law — that is, those basic principles and doctrines that come into play across the range of specific offenses (for example, actus reus, mens rea, and the various justifications and excuses). We believe that mastery of the detailed elements of many particular crimes is a goal that is inappropriate for a basic criminal law course. Nevertheless, we have found that understanding of the basic principles is enhanced by testing their applications and interactions in the context of particular offenses. Accordingly, we now examine in detail four offense categories: rape (Chapter 5), homicide (Chapter 6), theft (Chapter 10), and business crimes (Chapter 11). The chapter on rape provides an opportunity to focus rigorously on the definitional elements of a major crime, examining the relationships among problems of actus reus, mens rea, and the rules of proof in a context that has become the focus of acute controversy because of changing perceptions and changing social values. The theme of the homicide chapter is the task of legislative grading of punishment in a particularly challenging area. The theft chapter explores the significance of the history and the continued impact of old doctrinal categories on the resolution of thoroughly modern difficulties in defining the boundaries of the criminal law. Finally, the chapter on business crimes focuses attention on the growing array of criminal statutes affecting the conduct of legitimate enterprise; the importance of assuring compliance with regulatory goals in a modern, highly interdependent society; and the special difficulties of effective enforcement in the context of complex business organizations.

---

2. For a fuller discussion of the role of the criminal law course in the law school curriculum, see Kadish, Why Substantive Criminal Law — A Dialogue, 29 Clev. St. L. Rev. 1 (1980).

The procedural sections of the third edition dealt comprehensively with the administration of the criminal process from the initial stages of police investigation and screening through trial, appeal, sentencing, and collateral attack. We believe that it is no longer feasible or desirable for the basic criminal law course to attempt to cover the ever-increasing intricacies of such subjects as search, electronic eavesdropping, arrest, interrogation, and line-ups. The issues in these areas are important enough to warrant detailed examination in their own right, and law teachers generally have concluded that this is best accomplished in a separate course devoted to criminal procedure. Accordingly, we have deleted virtually all of the previous treatment of procedure (Part Two in the third edition).

We continue to believe, however, that a sense of process is essential for appreciating the significance of issues in the substantive part of the course. Indeed, we have concluded that attention to the procedural framework ordinarily should precede the detailed examination of substantive criminal law and that this introduction is best provided not simply by some background reading or an opening lecture but rather by two to three weeks of sustained analysis of the fundamentals of the criminal process.

Which issues from the vast body of procedural doctrine warrant attention in a course primarily devoted to the substantive criminal law? The central objective is to impart understanding of the principles governing the proof of guilt. Students need to develop a sense of how "facts" and "elements of the offense" are actually established at trial; how testimony is presented and challenged in an adversary system; and how the process of proof is affected by the responsibilities assigned to the jury, to opposing counsel, and to the judge. Accordingly, many of the concerns that are central in criminal procedure courses are of only secondary importance for our purposes. We wanted to combine some of the classic topics in procedure — such as the right to counsel and the privilege against self-incrimination — with issues usually falling outside the bounds of the traditional procedure course — such as evidence-law materials dealing with the process of direct and cross-examination and the rules of relevancy and prejudicial effect. We also found it essential to focus on issues that fall somewhere between substantive criminal law, procedure, and evidence — issues such as the requirement of proof beyond a reasonable doubt, principles governing presumptions, jury nullification, and related questions concerning inconsistent or unsupported verdicts. Issues such as these, falling in a grey area between courses traditionally taught in law schools, sometimes fail to receive systematic attention anywhere in the curriculum; in any event, the student who will later study such matters in depth needs an introduction to these issues in order to have a perspective on problems that permeate the study of substantive criminal law.

Use of the materials in diverse teaching formats. Over the past decade, law schools have begun experimenting with a variety of formats for the basic criminal law course. Although the year-long five- or six-hour course remains common, some schools offer criminal law as a four- or even three-hour course, and some schedule the course in the second semester or even in the second or third years. Under these circumstances, a short book designed to be taught straight through, without adjustments or deletions, is bound to prove unsatisfactory for many users. In preparing the fourth edition we have sought to organize and edit the materials tightly enough to avoid significant surplusage for the average course, but we have not attempted to preempt all possible judgments about inclusion and exclusion. Rather, we thought it essential to preserve some freedom for teachers to select topics that accord with their own interests and with the curricular arrangements at their own schools. Thus, we have aspired to create a flexible teaching tool, one that reflects the rich diversity of its subject.

For the five- or six-hour, year-long course, the book can be taught straight through, perhaps with some minor deletions. For a four-hour course, and especially in the case of a three-hour course, substantial omissions will be necessary. Many teachers will have their own preferences, of course. We present here our own thoughts, based on our experience in structuring the material for use in shorter courses, both in the first semester and in the second and third years.

Chapter 1 (Structure of the Criminal Justice System). This text material lends itself to class discussion, but in a shorter course it should be assigned as background reading, and the first class can begin instead with discussion of material in Chapter 2.

Chapter 2 (How Guilt Is Established). In schools that require a criminal procedure course before the study of criminal law, this chapter can be largely omitted. It may be appropriate, however, to take up Section B4 (proof beyond a reasonable doubt). In addition, Section C (guilty pleas) focuses on relationships between plea bargaining and the substantive principles of penal law; the treatment differs from that typically given to the topic in criminal procedure courses, and one or two classes can usefully be devoted to exploring the continuing importance of substantive principles in a world now largely dominated by bargaining.

For students taking up criminal law in the first semester of their first year, Chapter 2 provides basic grounding in process. The teacher who is unable to cover the entire chapter can consider assigning Section A (overview), Sections B1 (counsel), B2 (evidence), B3 (self-incrimination), and B4 (assigning the burden-of-proof materials but omitting the material on presumptions), and Section C (guilty pleas). We believe that this material, which can be covered in roughly two weeks, provides a solid foundation for the subsequent study of substantive law. Teachers who skip Section B6 (role of counsel and judge) at the beginning of the course may wish to return to it later. This material raises provocative issues of pervasive importance for the study and practice of law; its themes can provide an appropriate and effective concluding topic for the course.

Chapter 3 (The Justification of Punishment) is basic to the substantive part of the course. Section A (Why Punish?) presents material that many teachers will wish to discuss directly and in depth in class. Others have found it useful, either because of time pressure or pedagogical taste, to assign Section A as background reading and then to bring those materials into focus by applying them to the concrete sentencing problems presented in Section B (Imposing Punishment). Section C (What to Punish?) raises basic problems that can be examined usefully either at this point or toward the end of the course.

Chapters 4 (Elements of Just Punishment), 6 (Homicide), 7 (Harm), 8 (Group Criminality), and *9 (Justification and Excuse)* will constitute the core of the typical substantive criminal law course and generally teachers will want to cover them in depth.

Chapter 5 (Rape) is important in its own right and as a complement to the materials on mens rea. It can be studied immediately after the mistake-of-fact cases in Chapter 4 or after all of Chapter 4 has been completed. Section C of the chapter on rape (problems of proof) can be used to pursue in more detail the themes studied in Chapter 2, or it can be used to introduce those themes when time does not permit full consideration of Chapter 2.

Chapters 10 (Theft), 11 (Business Crimes) and *12 (Disposition of the Convicted Offender)* pursue the general themes of the course in specific contexts. In a three- or four-hour course, one of these three chapters can be chosen for detailed treatment while the other two are omitted or deferred for study in advanced courses.

Collateral reading. Students wishing to pursue further the questions raised in the readings and Notes will find helpful six outstanding works: One is the text and Commentary of the American Law Institute's Model Penal Code. Much of the text is reproduced as an Appendix to this casebook, but space limitations preclude reprinting all but a few excerpts from the Commentary. In thirteen Tentative Drafts published over the period 1954-1961, the Code's reporters presented succinct analyses of existing law and the major issues it presented. Students will still find it useful to consult these earlier commentaries. For Part II of the Code (Definition of Specific Crimes), there is now available an expanded set of commentaries, including analysis of legislative developments through the 1970s. This more recent Commentary has been published in a three-volume set, Model Penal Code and Commentaries, Part II (1980). The revised commentaries for Part I of the Code are now in preparation and publication is expected in the near future.

The second resource consists of two works by Professor Glanville Williams. His treatise, Criminal Law: The General Part, appeared in its second edition in 1961. His Textbook of Criminal Law was published in 1978 and is primarily directed to the law student. While they are concerned with English law, the American student will find in these books a rich discussion of many of the issues raised in the casebook.

The third important recommended work is the late Professor Herbert Packer's The Limits of the Criminal Sanction, which appeared in 1968. This is a nontechnical but thoughtful analysis of the limitations of the use of the criminal law as a means of influencing conduct. In the course of his study, Professor Packer explores with freshness and clarity most of the fundamentally troubling issues and tensions of the criminal law, both substantive and administrative.

Fourth is Wayne LaFave & Austin Scott, Jr., Handbook on Criminal Law (1972), the best contemporary hornbook on American substantive criminal law, with the further advantage that its treatment of problems in many areas substantially parallels that in this casebook.

Fifth is the collection of essays by Professor H. L. A. Hart entitled Punishment and Responsibility (1968), now available in paperback. These short, powerful, and lucid essays have strongly influenced our own treatment of the subjects of punishment and responsibility, as well as contemporary thought generally on these issues.

The sixth collateral reading is Professor George Fletcher's Rethinking Criminal Law, published in 1978. This challenging book retraces many of the doctrines and problems of the course from a perspective that contrasts sharply with the pragmatism and utilitarianism of the Model Penal Code. Professor Fletcher's theoretical and comparative approach will prove provocative for many readers.

Style. Citations in the footnotes and text of extracted material have been omitted when they did not seem useful for pedagogical purposes, and we have not used ellipses or other signals to indicate such deletions. Ellipses are used, however, to indicate omitted text material. Where we have retained footnotes in readings and quotations, the original footnote numbers are preserved. Our own footnotes to excerpts and quotations from other works are designated by letters, while footnotes to our own Notes are numbered consecutively throughout each chapter.

Acknowledgments. Sanford H. Kadish wishes to express appreciation for the support provided by the Alexander F. and May T. Morrison Chair in Law at the Law School of the University of California, Berkeley; for the assistance of a number of students, including James Burke, Roger Dangerfield, Janet Hathaway, Lawrence R. Lincoln, Edwardo L. Quevedo, Lawrence Hajime Shinagawa and Alfredo L. Silva; for the excellent secretarial support of Tove Schalk and Joyce Millison; and, especially, for the aid and comfort of his wife, June. Stephen Schulhofer wishes to express his thanks for the research assistance of Maida Crane, J. Craig Fong, Joan Harrington, Kenneth Kress and Barry Temkin; for the excellent secretarial support of Maria Evangelou; and for the counsel of colleagues and associates who shared helpful comments on the manuscript: Peter Arenella, Mark Berger, Stephen Burbank, David Rudovsky, and James Strazzella. Stephen Schulhofer also wishes to express particular personal appreciation for support, professional and otherwise, to Laurie Wohl.

It was a source of profound regret that Monrad G. Paulsen's untimely death prevented his participating in the preparation of this edition. We dedicate it to his memory.

SHK
SJS

August 1982

ACKNOWLEDGMENTS

The authors would like to acknowledge the permissions kindly granted to reproduce excerpts from the following publications.

Allen, Francis, The Borderland of Criminal Justice (1964). Copyright © 1964 by The University of Chicago Press. Reprinted by permission of The University of Chicago Press.

Allen, Francis, The Criminal Law as an Instrument of Economic Regulation (International Institute for Economic Research, Original Paper #2, 1976). Reprinted by permission of the author.

Allen, Ronald, Structuring Jury Decisionmaking in Criminal Cases: A Unified Approach to Evidentiary Devices, 94 Harvard Law Review 321 (1980). Copyright © 1980 by the Harvard Law Review Association. Reprinted by permission of the Harvard Law Review Association and the author.

Alschuler, Albert W., The Prosecutor's Role in Plea Bargaining, 36 University of Chicago Law Review 50 (1968). Reprinted by permission.

Alschuler, Albert W., Book Review, 12 Criminal Law Bulletin 629 (1976). Reprinted by permission from the Criminal Law Bulletin, Volume 12, Number 5, September-October 1976. Copyright © 1976 by Warren, Gorham and Lamont, Inc., 210 South Street. Boston, MA. All rights reserved.

American Bar Association, Code of Professional Responsibility (1970). Copyright © 1970 by the American Bar Association, National Center for Professional Responsibility. Reprinted by permission.

American Bar Association, Minimum Standards for Criminal Justice (1967). Reprinted by permission.

American Bar Association, Standards for Criminal Justice (2d ed. 1980). Reprinted by permission of Little, Brown and Company.

American Bar Association, Commission on Evaluation of Professional Standards, Model Rules of Professional Conduct (1981). Copyright © 1981 by the American Bar Association, National Center for Professional Responsibility. Reprinted by permission.

American Bar Foundation, Criminal Justice in the United States (1967). Reprinted by permission.

American Friends Service Committee, The Struggle for Justice (1971). Reprinted by permission.

American Law Institute, Model Penal Code and Commentaries (Tentative Draft No. 1, 1953), Model Penal Code and Commentaries (Tentative Draft No. 4, 1955), Model Penal Code and Commentaries (Tentative Draft No. 8, 1958), Model Penal Code and Commentaries (Tentative Draft No. 9, 1959), Model Penal Code and Commentaries (Tentative Draft No. 10, 1960), Model

Penal Code and Commentaries (1980). Copyright © 1953, 1955, 1958, 1959, 1960, 1980 by The American Law Institute. Reprinted by permission of The American Law Institute.

Andenaes, Johannes, General Prevention, 43 Journal of Criminal Law, Criminology & Police Science 176 (1952). Reprinted by special permission. Copyright © 1952 by Northwestern University School of Law.

Arenella, Peter, Reforming the Federal Grand Jury and the State Preliminary Hearing to Prevent Conviction Without Adjudication, 78 Michigan Law Review 463 (1980). Reprinted by permission.

Austin, J. L., A Plea for Excuses, 57 Proceedings of the Aristotelian Society 1 (1956-1957). Copyright © 1956 by The Aristotelian Society. Reprinted by permission.

Barzun, Jacques, In Favor of Capital Punishment, 31 The American Scholar 181 (1962). Reprinted from The American Scholar, Volume 31, Number 2, Spring 1962. Copyright © 1962 by the United Chapters of Phi Beta Kappa. By the permission of the publisher and the author.

Bazelon, Honorable David L., The Defective Assistance of Counsel, 42 University of Cincinnati Law Review 1 (1973). Reprinted by permission.

Bazelon, Honorable David L., The Realities of *Gideon* and *Argersinger,* 64 Georgetown Law Journal 811 (1976). Copyright © 1976 by the Georgetown Law Journal. Reprinted by permission.

Bedau, Hugo Adam, The Death Penalty in America (1964). Copyright © 1964 by Hugo Adam Bedau. Reprinted by permission of Doubleday & Company, Inc.

Bedau, Hugo Adam, The Case Against the Death Penalty (1977). Reprinted by permission of the American Civil Liberties Union Capital Punishment Project.

Black, Charles, Capital Punishment: The Inevitability of Caprice and Mistake (2d ed. augmented 1981). Copyright © 1981, 1974 by W. W. Norton & Company, Inc.; copyright © 1977, 1978 by Charles L. Black, Jr., W. W. Norton, publisher. Reprinted by permission.

Brown, Sharon Morey, & Nicholas J. Wittner, Criminal Law (1978 Annual Survey of Michigan Law), 25 Wayne Law Review 335 (1979). Reprinted by permission.

Budd, M., & A. Lynch, Voluntariness, Causation and Strict Liability, [1978] Criminal Law Review 74. Reprinted by permission of Sweet & Maxwell Ltd.

Coffee, John, Corporate Crime and Punishment: A Non-Chicago View of the Economics of Criminal Sanctions, 17 American Criminal Law Review 419 (1980). Reprinted by permission of the author.

Cohen, Morris, Moral Aspects of the Criminal Law, 49 Yale Law Journal 987 (1940). Reprinted by permission of The Yale Law Journal Company and Fred B. Rothman & Company from the Yale Law Journal, Volume 49, pages 1012-1014.

Comment, [1979] Criminal Law Review 120. Reprinted by permission of Sweet & Maxwell Ltd.

Comment, The Law of Necessity as Applied in the Bisbee Deportation Case, 13 Arizona Law Review 264 (1961). Copyright © 1961 by the Arizona Board of Regents. Reprinted by permission.

Comment (on *Stephenson*), 31 Michigan Law Review 659 (1933). Reprinted by permission.

Damaška, Mirjan R., Evidentiary Barriers to Conviction and Two Models of Criminal Procedure, 121 University of Pennsylvania Law Review 506 (1973). Copyright © 1973 by the University of Pennsylvania Law Review. Reprinted by permission of the publisher and the author.

Denning, Alfred T., Freedom Under the Law (1949). Reprinted by permission of Sweet & Maxwell Ltd.

Denzer, R. G., & P. McQuillan, Supplementary Practice Commentary, McKinney's Consolidated Laws of New York, Book 39, §35.20 (Cum. Ann. Pkt. Pt. 1973-1974). Reprinted by permission of West Publishing Company.

Dershowitz, Alan, Abolishing the Insanity Defense: The Most Significant Feature of the Administration's Proposed Criminal Code — An Essay, 9 Criminal Law Bulletin 434 (1973). Published by Warren, Gorham and Lamont, Inc. Copyright © 1973 by The New York Times Company. Reprinted by permission.

Devlin, Sir Patrick, Criminal Responsibility and Punishment: Functions of Judge and Jury, [1954] Criminal Law Review 661. Reprinted by permission of Sweet & Maxwell Ltd.

Devlin, Sir Patrick, The Enforcement of Morals (1959). Copyright © 1959 by Oxford University Press. Reprinted by permission of Oxford University Press.

Durkheim, Emile, The Division of Labor in Society (George Simpson translator 1933). Reprinted by permission of The Free Press, a division of Macmillan Publishing Company.

Estey, John S., & David W. Marston, Pitfalls (and Loopholes) in the Foreign Bribery Law, 98 Fortune Magazine 182 (1978). Copyright © 1978 by Time Inc. All rights reserved. Reprinted by permission of Fortune Magazine and the authors.

Ewing, A. C., A Study of Punishment II: Punishment as Viewed by the Philosopher, 21 Canadian Bar Review 102 (1943). Reprinted by permission of the publisher.

Fletcher, George P., Rethinking Criminal Law (1978). Copyright © 1978 by George P. Fletcher. Reprinted by permission of Little, Brown and Company and the author.

Fletcher, George P., The Metamorphosis of Larceny, 89 Harvard Law Review 469 (1976). Copyright © 1976 by George P. Fletcher. Reprinted by permission of the author.

Frankel, Honorable Marvin E., Criminal Sentences: Law Without Order (1973). Copyright © 1972, 1973 by Marvin E. Frankel. Reprinted by permission of the author and Hill and Wang, a division of Farrar, Straus and Giroux, Inc.

Frankel, Honorable Marvin E., The Search for Truth: An Umpireal View, 123 University of Pennsylvania Law Review 1031 (1975). Reprinted by permission of the author.

Freedman, Monroe H., Lawyers' Ethics in an Adversary System (1975). Published by Michie, Bobbs-Merrill, Inc. Reprinted by permission of the author.

Friendly, Honorable Henry, The Fifth Amendment Tomorrow: The Case for

Constitutional Change, 37 University of Cincinnati Law Review 671 (1968). Reprinted by permission.

Galligan, D. J., Guidelines and Just Deserts: A Critique of Recent Trends in Sentencing Reform, [1981] Criminal Law Review 297. Reprinted by permission of Sweet & Maxwell Ltd.

Glazebrook, P. R., The Necessity Plea in English Criminal Law, 30 Cambridge Law Journal 87 (1972). Copyright © 1972 by Cambridge University Press. Reprinted by permission.

Goldstein, Joseph, & Jay Katz, Abolish the "Insanity Defense"—Why Not?, 72 Yale Law Journal 853 (1963). Reprinted by permission of The Yale Law Journal Company, Fred B. Rothman & Company, and the authors from the Yale Law Journal, Volume 69, pages 858-865.

Gustman, David C., The Foreign Corrupt Practices Act of 1977: A Transactional Analysis, 13 Journal of International Law & Economics 367 (1979). Reprinted by permission

Hall, Jerome, Theft, Law and Society (2d ed. 1952). Published by Michie, Bobbs-Merrill, Inc. Reprinted by permission of the publisher and the author.

Haney, Craig, & Michael J. Lowy, Bargain Justice in an Unjust World: Good Deals in the Criminal Courts, 13 Law & Society Review 633 (1979). Copyright © 1979 by the Law and Society Association. Reprinted by permission.

Hart, H. L. A., Book Review (Wootton, Crime and the Criminal Law (1963)), 74 Yale Law Journal 135 (1965). Reprinted by permission of The Yale Law Journal Company, Fred B. Rothman & Company, and the author from the Yale Law Journal, Volume 74, page 1328.

Hart, H. L. A., Intention and Punishment, Oxford Review No. 4 (Hilary 1967). Reprinted by permission of the author.

Hart, H. L. A., Law, Liberty and Morality (1963). Reprinted by permission of Stanford University Press.

Hart, H. L. A., Legal Responsibility and Excuses, reprinted by permission of the New York University Press from Determinism and Freedom in the Age of Modern Science, edited by Sidney Hook. Copyright © 1958, 1960 by New York University.

Hart, H. L. A., The Morality of the Criminal Law (1965). Published by Magnes Press. Reprinted by permission.

Hart, H. L. A., Punishment and Responsibility (1968). Copyright © 1968 by Oxford University Press. Reprinted by permission of Oxford University Press.

Hughes, Graham, Criminal Omissions, 67 Yale Law Journal 590 (1958). Reprinted by permission of The Yale Law Journal Company, Fred B. Rothman & Company, and the author from the Yale Law Journal, Volume 67, pages 599-600.

Jeffries, John Calvin, Jr., & Paul B. Stephan, Defense, Presumptions and Burdens of Proof in the Criminal Law, 88 Yale Law Journal 1325 (1979). Reprinted by permission of The Yale Law Journal Company, Fred B. Rothman & Company, and the authors from the Yale Law Journal, Volume 88, pages 1345-1347, 1389.

Johnson, Philip E., Importing Justice, 87 Yale Law Journal 406 (1977). Reprinted by permission of The Yale Law Journal Company, Fred B. Rothman &

Company, and the author from the Yale Law Journal, Volume 87, pages 410-414.

Johnson, Philip E., The Unnecessary Crime of Conspiracy, 61 California Law Review 1137 (1973). Copyright © 1973 by the California Law Review, Inc. Reprinted by permission of Fred B. Rothman & Company.

Junker, John M., Criminalization and Criminogenesis, 19 U.C.L.A. Law Review 697 (1972). Reprinted by permission.

Kadish, Sanford H., The Advocate and the Expert: Counsel in the Peno-Correctional Process, 45 Minnesota Law Review 803 (1961). Reprinted by permission.

Kadish, Sanford H., The Crisis of Overcriminalization, 374 Annals 157 (1967). Reprinted by permission of The American Academy of Political and Social Science.

Kadish, Sanford H., The Decline of Innocence, 26 Cambridge Law Journal 273 (1968). Copyright © 1968 by Cambridge University Press. Reprinted by permission.

Kadish, Sanford H., Legal Norm and Discretion in the Police and Sentencing Process, 75 Harvard Law Review 904 (1962). Copyright © 1962 by the Harvard Law Review Association. Used by permission.

Kadish, Sanford H., Respect for Life and Regard for Rights in the Criminal Law, 64 California Law Review 871 (1976). Copyright © 1976 by California Law Review, Inc. Reprinted by permission.

Kalven, Harry, & Hans Zeisel, The American Jury (1966). Reprinted by permission of Little, Brown and Company.

Kant, Immanuel, Metaphysical Elements of Justice (J. Ladd translator 1965). Copyright © 1965 by Bobbs-Merrill, Inc. Reprinted by permission of Bobbs-Merrill, Inc., Indianapolis, Ind.

Korn, Richard R., & Gregory B. Craig, Making It All Perfectly Legal, Washington Post (January 20, 1974). Reprinted by permission. Richard R. Korn is Professor of Sociology, John Jay College of Criminal Justice.

Korn, Richard R., & Gregory B. Craig, excerpts from an article appearing in the Washington Post (March 3, 1974). Reprinted by permission.

Langbein, John H., Torture and Plea Bargaining, 46 University of Chicago Law Review 3 (1978). Reprinted by permission.

Lee, Stephen, & Donald H. Zuckerman, Representing Parole Violators, 11 Criminal Law Bulletin 327 (1975). Reprinted by permission from the Criminal Law Bulletin, Volume 11, May-June 1975. Copyright © 1975 by Warren, Gorham and Lamont, Inc., 210 South Street, Boston MA. All rights reserved.

Levy, Leonard W., Origins of the Fifth Amendment (1968). Published by Oxford University Press. Reprinted by permission of the author.

Lewis, Anthony, excerpts from an article appearing in the International Herald Tribune (June 20, 1978). Copyright © 1978 by The New York Times Company. Reprinted by permission.

Lewis, Anthony, excerpts from an article appearing in the New York Times (August 7, 1963). Copyright © 1963 by The New York Times Company. Reprinted by permission.

Low, Peter W., Special Offender Sentencing, 8 American Criminal Law Quarterly 70 (1970). Reprinted by permission of the American Criminal Law Quarterly (now the American Criminal Law Review (the quarterly journal of the American Bar Association's Section on Criminal Justice) and the Georgetown University Law Center) and the author.

Mack, Eric, Bad Samaritanism and the Causation of Harm, 9 Philosophy & Public Affairs 230 (1980). Reprinted by permission of Princeton University Press from Philosophy & Public Affairs, Volume 9, Number 3 (Spring 1980). Excerpted from page 240.

Martinson, Robert, New Findings, New Views: A Note of Caution Regarding Sentencing Reform, 7 Hofstra Law Review 243 (1979). Reprinted by permission of the publisher.

Martinson, Robert, What Works? — Questions and Answers about Prison Reform, 36 The Public Interest 22 (1974). Reprinted by permission from The Public Interest, Number 35 (Spring 1974), pages 22-25. Copyright © 1974 by National Affairs, Inc.

Moore, Robert A., M.D., Legal Responsibility and Chronic Alcoholism, 122 American Journal of Psychiatry 748 (1966). Reprinted by permission of the publisher and the author.

Morris, Herbert, On Guilt and Innocence (1976). Copyright © 1976 by The Regents of the University of California. Reprinted by permission of the University of California Press.

Morris, Norval R., Somnambulistic Homicide: Ghosts, Spiders and North Koreans, 5 Res Judicatae 29 (1951). Reprinted by permission of the publisher.

Murphy, Jeffrie, G., Marxism and Retribution, 2 Philosophy & Public Affairs 217 (1973). Copyright © 1973 by Princeton University Press. Reprinted by permission from Philosophy & Public Affairs, Volume 2, Number 3 (Spring 1973).

National Research Council, Deterrence and Incapacitation: Estimating the Effects of Criminal Sanctions on Crime Rates (1978). Reprinted by permission of the National Academy Press, Washington, D.C.

New York Times, excerpts from articles appearing on February 17, 1980, March 14, 1980, February 7, 1968. Copyright © 1968, 1980 by The New York Times Company. Reprinted by permission.

1970 Sentencing Institute for California Superior Court Judges, 93 California Reporter, Appendix 25 (1970). Reprinted by permission of West Publishing Company.

1971 Sentencing Institute for California Superior Court Judges, 100 California Reporter 32 (1971). Reprinted by permission of West Publishing Company.

Noonan, John T., Book Review, 29 Stanford Law Review 363 (1977). Copyright © 1977 by the Board of Trustees of Leland Stanford Junior University. Reprinted by permission.

Note, Corporate Homicide: A New Assault on Corporate Decision-Making, 54 Notre Dame Lawyer 911 (1979). Copyright © 1979 by the Notre Dame Lawyer, University of Notre Dame. Reprinted by permission from Notre Dame Lawyer, Number 5 (1979).

Note, Developments in the Law — Corporate Crime: Regulating Corporate Behavior through Criminal Sanction, 92 Harvard Law Review 1227 (1979). Copyright © 1979 by the Harvard Law Review Association. Reprinted by permission of the Harvard Law Review Association.

Note, Developments in the Law — Criminal Conspiracy, 72 Harvard Law Review 920 (1959). Copyright © 1959 by the Harvard Law Review Association. Reprinted by permission of the Harvard Law Review Association.

Note, Due Process and Legislative Standards in Sentencing, 101 University of Pennsylvania Law Review 257 (1952). Copyright © 1952 by the University of Pennsylvania Law Review. Reprinted by permission.

Note, Individual Liability of Agents for Corporate Crimes under the Proposed Federal Criminal Code, 31 Vanderbilt Law Review 965 (1978). Reprinted by permission.

Note, A Rationale of the Law of Aggravated Theft, 54 Columbia Law Review 84 (1954). Reprinted by permission.

Nozick, R., Anarchy, State and Utopia (1974). Reprinted by permission of Basic Books, Inc.

Orkin, Mark M., Defence of One Known to Be Guilty, 1 Criminal Law Quarterly 170 (1958). Reprinted by permission of Canada Law Book, Ltd.

Pearce, Jack, Theft by False Promises, 101 University of Pennsylvania Law Review 967 (1953). Copyright © 1953 by the University of Pennsylvania Law Review. Reprinted by permission.

Posner, Richard A., Optimal Sentences for White-Collar Criminals, 17 American Criminal Law Review 409 (1980). Reprinted by permission of the author and the American Criminal Law Review (the quarterly journal of the American Bar Association's Section on Criminal Justice) and the Georgetown University Law Center.

Radzinowicz, Leon, & J. W. C. Turner, A Study of Punishment I: Introductory Essay, 21 Canadian Bar Review 91 (1943). Reprinted by permission.

Ross, Irwin, How Lawless Are Big Companies?, 103 Fortune Magazine 57 (1980). Copyright © 1980 by Time Inc. All rights reserved. Reprinted by permission of Fortune Magazine and the author.

San Francisco Chronicle, excerpts from article appearing on September 7, 1974, page 2. Reprinted by permission of the San Francisco Chronicle.

San Francisco Chronicle, excerpts from articles appearing on July 3, 1980, page 5, and November 14, 1964, page 4. Reprinted by permission of the Associated Press.

Sayre, Francis, Criminal Responsibility for the Acts of Another, 43 Harvard Law Review 689 (1930). Copyright © 1930 by the Harvard Law Review Association. Reprinted by permission of the Harvard Law Review Association.

Schlesinger, Rudolf, B., Comparative Criminal Procedure: A Plea for Utilizing Foreign Experience, 26 Buffalo Law Review 361 (1974). Reprinted by permission.

Schulhofer, Stephen, Due Process of Sentencing, 128 University of Pennsylvania Law Review 733 (1980). Copyright © 1980 by the University of Pennsylvania Law Review. Reprinted by permission of the publisher and the author.

Schulhofer, Stephen, Prosecutorial Discretion and Federal Sentencing Reform (1979). Reprinted by permission of the Federal Judicial Center and the author.

Schwartz, Louis, Reform of the Federal Criminal Laws, [1977] Duke Law Journal 171. Reprinted by permission.

Sellin, Johan Thorsten, The Death Penalty (1959). Copyright © 1959 by The American Law Institute. Reprinted by permission of The American Law Institute.

Smith, John Cyril, The Element of Chance in Criminal Liability, [1971] Criminal Law Review 63. Reprinted by permission of Sweet & Maxwell Ltd. and the author.

Solomon, Lewis D., & David C. Gustman, Questionable and Illegal Payments by American Corporations, 35 Journal of Business Law 67 (1980). Reprinted by permission of Sweet & Maxwell Ltd. and the authors.

Twentieth Century Fund, Task Force on Criminal Sentencing, Fair and Certain Punishment (1976). Reprinted by permission of McGraw-Hill Book Company.

Underwood, Barbara D., The Thumb on the Scales of Justice: Burdens of Persuasion in Criminal Cases, 86 Yale Law Journal 1299 (1977). Reprinted by permission of The Yale Law Journal Company and Fred B. Rothman & Company from the Yale Law Journal, Volume 86, pages 1299, 1312-1313, 1321-1324.

van den Haag, Ernest, On Deterrence and the Death Penalty, 60 Journal of Criminal Law, Criminology & Political Science 141 (1969). Copyright © 1969 by Northwestern University School of Law. Reprinted by permission.

van den Haag, Ernest, Punishing Criminals: Concerning a Very Old and Painful Question (1975). Copyright © 1975 by Basic Books, Inc. By permission of Basic Books, Inc., Publishers, New York, N.Y.

von Hirsch, Andrew, Doing Justice: The Choice of Punishments (1976). Reprinted by permission of Hill and Wang, a division of Farrar, Straus and Giroux, Inc.

Wasserstrom, Richard, Lawyers as Professionals: Some Moral Issues, 5 Human Rights 1 (1975). Reprinted by permission.

Wechsler, Herbert, The Challenge of a Model Penal Code, 65 Harvard Law Review 1097 (1952). Copyright © 1952 by the Harvard Law Review Association. Reprinted by permission of the Harvard Law Review Association and the author.

Wechsler, Herbert, Sentencing, Correction, and the Model Penal Code, 109 University of Pennsylvania Law Review 465 (1961). Copyright © 1961 by the University of Pennsylvania Law Review. Reprinted by permission.

Wheeler, Malcolm E., Products Liability: Manufacturers, Wrong Targets for Threat of Criminal Sanctions?, National Law Journal (December 22, 1980). Reprinted by permission of New York Law Publishing Company.

Wicker, Tom, A Penalty That Fits Mr. Chapin, New York Times (April 7, 1974). Copyright © 1974 by The New York Times Company. Reprinted by permission.

Williams, Glanville, Criminal Law: The General Part (2d edition 1961). Reprinted by permission of Sweet & Maxwell, Ltd. and the author.

Williams, Glanville, Euthanasia, 41 Medico-Legal Journal 14 (1973). Reprinted by permission of the publisher and the author.

Williams, Glanville, Police Control of Intending Criminals, [1955] Criminal Law Review 6. Reprinted by permission of Sweet & Maxwell Ltd. and the author.

William, Glanville, The Proof of Guilt (3d edition 1963). Reprinted by permission of Sweet & Maxwell Ltd. and the author.

Williams, Glanville, Provocation and the Reasonable Man, [1954] Criminal Law Review 740. Reprinted by permission of Sweet & Maxwell Ltd. and the author.

Wootton, Lady Barbara, Crime and the Criminal Law (1963). Reprinted by permission of Sweet & Maxwell Ltd.

Wyzanski, Honorable Charles E., A Trial Judge's Freedom and Responsibility, 65 Harvard Law Review 1281 (1952). Copyright © 1952 by the Harvard Law Review Association. Reprinted by permission of the Harvard Law Review Association and the author.

Zimring, Franklin E., Making the Punishment Fit the Crime: A Consumer's Guide to Sentencing Reform, Hastings Center Report (December 1976). Reprinted by permission of the author.

Zimring, Franklin E., & Gordon Hawkins, Deterrence: The Legal Threat in Crime Control (1973). Copyright © 1973 by The University of Chicago Press. Reprinted by permission of The University of Chicago Press.

CRIMINAL LAW AND ITS PROCESSES

CASES AND MATERIALS

CHAPTER

1

THE STRUCTURE OF THE CRIMINAL JUSTICE SYSTEM

PRESIDENT'S COMMISSION ON LAW ENFORCEMENT
AND THE ADMINISTRATION OF JUSTICE,
THE CHALLENGE OF CRIME IN A FREE SOCIETY
7-12, 91-107, 127-137, 141-150 (1967) [1]

Any criminal justice system is an apparatus society uses to enforce the standards of conduct necessary to protect individuals and the community. It operates by apprehending, prosecuting, convicting, and sentencing those members of the community who violate the basic rules of group existence. The action taken against lawbreakers is designed to serve three purposes beyond the immediately punitive one. It removes dangerous people from the community; it deters others from criminal behavior; and it gives society an opportunity to attempt to transform lawbreakers into law-abiding citizens. What most significantly distinguishes the system of one country from that of another is the extent and the form of the protections it offers individuals in the process of determining guilt and imposing punishment. Our system of justice deliberately sacrifices much in efficiency and even in effectiveness in order to preserve local autonomy and to protect the individual. . . .

The criminal justice system has three separately organized parts — the police, the courts, and corrections — and each has distinct tasks. However, these parts are by no means independent of each other. What each one does and how it does it has a direct effect on the work of the others. The courts must deal, and can only deal, with those whom the police arrest; the business of corrections is with those delivered to it by the courts. How successfully corrections reforms

1. For convenience of exposition, we have added some headings and altered the sequence of certain paragraphs in this excerpt. Though criminal justice problems have changed in many respects since the publication of this report, it provides a useful overview of the organization and functioning of the criminal justice system, and the passages excerpted here are still accurate as descriptions of current conditions. Where appropriate, we have provided more recent information in brackets and in the footnotes. Except as otherwise noted, current statistics were drawn from Sourcebook of Criminal Justice Statistics — 1980 (M. Hindelang, M. Gottfredson & T. Flanagan eds., U.S. Dept. Justice 1981), and Federal Bureau of Investigation, Uniform Crime Reports — 1979 (1980).

convicts determines whether they will once again become police business and influences the sentences the judges pass; police activities are subject to court scrutiny and are often determined by court decisions. And so reforming or reorganizing any part or procedure of the system changes other parts or procedures. . . . A study of the system must begin by examining it as a whole. . . .

I. AGENCIES AND OFFICIALS OF THE CRIMINAL JUSTICE SYSTEM

A. THE POLICE

At the very beginning of the process — or, more properly, before the process begins at all — something happens that is . . . seldom recognized by the public: law enforcement policy is made by the policeman. For policemen cannot and do not arrest all the offenders they encounter. It is doubtful that they arrest most of them. A criminal code, in practice, is not a set of specific instructions to policemen but a more or less rough map of the territory in which policemen work. How an individual policeman moves around that territory depends largely on his personal discretion.

That a policeman's duties compel him to exercise personal discretion many times every day is evident. Crime does not look the same on the street as it does in a legislative chamber. How much noise or profanity makes conduct "disorderly" within the meaning of the law? When must a quarrel be treated as a criminal assault: at the first threat or at the first shove or at the first blow, or after blood is drawn, or when a serious injury is inflicted? How suspicious must conduct be before there is "probable cause," the constitutional basis for an arrest? Every policeman, however complete or sketchy his education, is an interpreter of the law.

Every policeman, too, is an arbiter of social values, for he meets situation after situation in which invoking criminal sanctions is a questionable line of action. It is obvious that a boy throwing rocks at a school's windows is committing the statutory offense of vandalism, but it is often not at all obvious whether a policeman will better serve the interests of the community and of the boy by taking the boy home to his parents or by arresting him. Who are the boy's parents? Can they control him? Is he a frequent offender who has responded badly to leniency? Is vandalism so epidemic in the neighborhood that he should be made a cautionary example? With juveniles especially, the police exercise great discretion.

Finally, the manner in which a policeman works is influenced by practical matters: the legal strength of the available evidence, the willingness of victims to press charges and of witnesses to testify, the temper of the community, the time and information at the policeman's disposal. Much is at stake in how the policeman exercises this discretion. If he judges conduct not suspicious enough to justify intervention, the chance to prevent a robbery, rape, or murder may be lost. If he overestimates the seriousness of a situation or his actions are controlled by panic or prejudice, he may hurt or kill someone unnecessarily. His actions may even touch off a riot.

It is in the cities that . . . social tensions are the most acute, that riots occur, that crime rates are the highest, that the fear of crime and the demand for effective action against it are the strongest. It is in the cities that a large proportion of American policemen work and that a large proportion of police money is spent. Though there are 40,000 separate law enforcement agencies in the Nation, 55 of them, the police departments of the cities of more than 250,000 population, employ almost one-third of all police personnel. Policing a city of more than one million population costs $27.31 per resident per year; policing a city of less than 50,000 costs less than one-third as much, or $8.74. . . .

There is impressive evidence that in many cities there are too few policemen. The current police-population ratio of 1.7 policemen per thousand citizens obscures the many differences from city to city and region to region. Even the big-city ratio of 2.3 per thousand is misleading, for in San Diego there are 1.07 policemen per thousand citizens and in Boston 4.04.

There appears to be no correlation between the differing concentrations of police and the amount of crime committed, or the percentage of known crimes solved, in the various cities.[a]

At the same time it is apparent that, nationwide, the number of police has not kept pace with the relocation of the population and the attendant increases in crime and police responsibility. . . .

[By 1979 the national police-population ratio had risen to 2.1 police officers per thousand citizens and a total of 2.5 police employees, including civilian employees, per thousand. But there were still wide variations from city to city and from region to region. For cities over 250,000 population the average ratio was 3.4 police employees per thousand, but the ratios within this group varied from a high of 7.0 to a low of 1.7, and the average ratio for these large cities varied from 3.5 in the Middle Atlantic region to only 2.0 in the Pacific region. Boston, which had 4.04 police officers per thousand in 1966, had only 3.6 per thousand in 1979. Among smaller cities the average ratio of police employees to population was only 2.0 in cities of 25,000-50,000 population, and in this group the ratio varied from a high of 5.0 to a low of 0.1.]

B. PROSECUTORS

The key administrative officer in the processing of cases is the prosecutor. Theoretically the examination of the evidence against a defendant by a judge at a preliminary hearing, and its reexamination by a grand jury, are important parts of the process. Practically they seldom are because a prosecutor seldom has any difficulty in making a prima facie case against a defendant. In fact most defendants waive their rights to preliminary hearings and much more often than not grand juries indict precisely as prosecutors ask them to. The prosecutor wields almost undisputed sway over the pretrial progress of most cases. He decides whether to press a case or drop it. He determines the specific charge against a defendant. When the charge is reduced, as it is in as many as two-thirds of all cases in some cities, the prosecutor is usually the official who reduces it. . . .

The prosecutor's discretion to decide what charge to bring against, and what disposition to recommend for, an offender is indicative of his crucial position in the law enforcement system. The prosecutor is particularly able to influence police operations. He affects the development of legal rules by his arguments

a. An important study, based on experimental variations in Kansas City police patrol patterns, has provided substantial support for this hypothesis. See G. Kelling et al., The Kansas City Preventive Patrol Experiment: A Technical Report (1974). — EDS.

in court. He can help bring about needed reform by pressing for changes in bail practices, for example, or in procedures for the appointment of counsel. Except for the judge he is the most influential court official.

Yet many prosecutors in this country are part-time officers. They generally are elected or selected on a partisan political basis and serve for relatively short terms.[b] In many places the office traditionally has been a steppingstone to higher political office or the bench. Prosecutors in most places are so poorly paid that they must, and are expected to, engage in private law practice. This creates inevitable conflicts between the demands of the office and of private practice. It can lead to undesirable potential conflicts of interest in dealings with other attorneys, judges, and members of the community. As the participation of defense counsel in criminal cases grows, the need to improve the quality of the prosecution becomes increasingly urgent. . . .

C. THE JUDICIARY

The Magistrate

In direct contrast to the policeman, the magistrate before whom a suspect is first brought usually exercises less discretion than the law allows him. He is entitled to inquire into the facts of the case, into whether there are grounds for holding the accused. He seldom does. He seldom can. The more promptly an arrested suspect is brought into magistrate's court, the less likelihood there is that much information about the arrest other than the arresting officer's statement will be available to the magistrate. Moreover many magistrates, especially in big cities, have such congested calendars that it is almost impossible for them to subject any case but an extraordinary one to prolonged scrutiny. . . .

Judges

The quality of the judiciary in large measure determines the quality of justice. It is the judge who tries disputed cases and who supervises and reviews negotiated dispositions. Through sentencing the judge determines the treatment given to an offender. Through the exercise of his administrative power over his court he determines its efficiency, fairness, and effectiveness. No procedural or administrative reforms will help the courts, and no reorganizational plan will avail unless judges have the highest qualifications, are fully trained and competent, and have high standards of performance.

Selection of Judges. Methods for the selection of judges vary from jurisdiction to jurisdiction, and some States use different methods of selection for upper court judges than for lower court judges. In 11 States judges are appointed either by the Governor or the legislature; in some of these States they are first appointed and then must run for election on their records; in 15 States they are elected without party labels, and in 19 States they are elected on a partisan basis. In a number of States there is a professional or nonpartisan screening process that develops an identified group of professionally qualified persons from which all nominations or appointments are made, or that reviews

---

b. As of 1976, the chief local prosecutor was an elected official in at least 44 states. At that date, states and localities employed a total of roughly 29,000 attorneys in prosecution and other government legal work. (In many jurisdictions criminal litigation and other legal work are performed by a single governmental unit, and prosecutorial activity cannot be measured separately.) Of these attorneys, 8,300, or nearly 30 percent, were part-time employees. — Eds.

proposed nominations or appointments for professional competence. Sometimes this process is required by State constitution or statute; sometimes it is informal. Sometimes it is employed for all judges, sometimes only for certain kinds of judges. It is employed least often in the States in which judges are elected in partisan contests. . . .

The Lower Courts

In many big cities the congestion that produces both undue delay and unseemly haste is vividly exemplified in the lower courts — the courts that dispose of cases that are typically called "misdemeanors" or "petty offenses," and that process the first stages of felony cases. The importance of these courts in the prevention or deterrence of crime is incalculably great, for these are the courts that process the overwhelming majority of offenders. . . .

The Nation's court system was designed originally for small, rural communities. The basic unit of court organization in most States remains the county, and about two-thirds of the counties in this country still are predominantly rural in nature. But most Americans live in an urban environment, in large communities with highly mobile populations that are being subjected to particular stress. It is the urban courts that particularly need reform.

In a rural community the parties involved in a criminal case, the offender, the victim, the attorneys, the judge, and the jury, often know each other. What the trial does is to develop specific facts about the offense. In a city or large suburban community the parties in a case are likely to be strangers. One result is that prosecutors and judges seldom know anything at all about a defendant's background, character, or way of life either at first hand or by hearsay. Moreover, information of crucial importance to a magistrate when he fixes bail, to a prosecutor when he decides upon a charge, to a trial judge when he passes sentence is not always easy to obtain. Gathering such data requires trained personnel using time-consuming procedures. In city and suburban courts today these personnel and procedures are not adequate. [In many urban jurisdictions, computerized systems for storing and retrieving information, together with improvements in organization and staffing, now provide much better access to at least some kinds of data. Nevertheless, the procedures and personnel available in city and suburban courts frequently remain inadequate.]

 . . . [U]ntil legislation [in 1966] increased the number of judges, the District of Columbia Court of General Sessions had four judges to process the preliminary stages of more than 1,500 felony cases, 7,500 serious misdemeanor cases, and 38,000 petty offenses and an equal number of traffic offenses per year. An inevitable consequence of volume that large is the almost total preoccupation in such a court with the movement of cases. The calendar is long, speed often is substituted for care, and casually arranged out-of-court compromise too often is substituted for adjudication. Inadequate attention tends to be given to the individual defendant, whether in protecting his rights, sifting the facts at trial, deciding the social risk he presents, or determining how to deal with him after conviction. . . .

D. CORRECTIONS

The correctional apparatus to which guilty defendants are delivered is in every respect the most isolated part of the criminal justice system. Much of it is physically isolated; its institutions usually have thick walls and locked doors, and often they are situated in rural areas, remote from the courts where the institutions' inmates were tried and from the communities where they lived. The correctional apparatus is isolated in the sense that its officials do not have everyday working relationships with officials from the system's other branches, like those that commonly exist between policemen and prosecutors, or prosecutors and judges. . . . Finally, it is isolated from the public partly by its invisibility and physical remoteness; partly by the inherent lack of drama in most of its activities, but perhaps most importantly by the fact that the correctional apparatus is often used — or misused — by both the criminal justice system and the public as a rug under which disturbing problems and people can be swept.

The most striking fact about the correctional apparatus today is that, although the rehabilitation of criminals is presumably its major purpose, the custody of criminals is actually its major task. On any given day there are well over a million people being "corrected" in America, two-thirds of them on probation or parole and one-third of them in prisons or jails. However, prisons and jails are where four-fifths of correctional money is spent and where nine-tenths of correctional employees work.

[This situation has persisted. There are now roughly 300,000 prisoners in federal and state custody at any given time, but these account for only 17 percent of the total offenders subject to "correction"; nearly 1.5 million offenders are on probation or parole.[c] Nevertheless, as of 1978, states and localities assigned to parole and probation supervision only 7,000 of the roughly 253,000 employees involved in correctional activities, and state expenditures for probation and parole amounted to only $348 million, out of a total corrections budget of $2,855 million.[d]]

Furthermore, fewer than one-fifth of the people who work in State prisons and local jails have jobs that are not essentially either custodial or administrative in character. Many jails have nothing but custodial and administrative personnel. Of course many jails are crowded with defendants who have not been able to furnish bail and who are not considered by the law to be appropriate objects of rehabilitation because it has not yet been determined that they are criminals who need it.

What this emphasis on custody means in practice is that the enormous potential of the correctional apparatus for making creative decisions about its treatment of convicts is largely unfulfilled. This is true not only of offenders in custody but of offenders on probation and parole. Most authorities agree that while probationers and parolees need varying degrees and kinds of supervision, an average of no more than 35 cases per officer is necessary for effective attention; 97 percent of all officers handling adults have larger caseloads than that. [Although probation and parole supervision is relatively well staffed in the federal system, federal probation officers supervised an average of 147 probation and

c. As of the end of 1979, 314,000 convicted prisoners were in federal or state custody; 26,000 in federal institutions; and 288,000 in state institutions. In addition, roughly 158,000 prisoners (as of February 1978) were detained in local jails pending trial. Based on 1976 data, there were 1,252,000 state offenders subject to probation supervision and 210,000 state offenders released on parole. In the same year there were 35,000 federal offenders subject to supervision under some form of probation or parole. — EDS.

d. These expenditure figures, however, do not include expenditures by the county and municipal agencies that often bear much of the responsibility for probation and parole supervision. — EDS.

parole cases each in 1972. The number has declined sharply since then, but as of 1979 the average caseload was still 48 cases per officer.] . . .

II. CRIMINAL JUSTICE PROCEDURES

A. OVERVIEW OF THE STEPS IN THE CRIMINAL JUSTICE PROCESS

The popular, or even the lawbook, theory of everyday criminal process oversimplifies in some respects and overcomplicates in others what usually happens. That theory is that when an infraction of the law occurs, a policeman finds, if he can, the probable offender, arrests him and brings him promptly before a magistrate. If the offense is minor, the magistrate disposes of it forthwith; if it is serious, he holds the defendant for further action and admits him to bail. The case then is turned over to a prosecuting attorney who charges the defendant with a specific statutory crime. This charge is subject to review by a judge at a preliminary hearing of the evidence and in many places if the offense charged is a felony, by a grand jury that can dismiss the charge, or affirm it by delivering it to a judge in the form of an indictment. If the defendant pleads "not guilty" to the charge he comes to trial; the facts of his case are marshaled by prosecuting and defense attorneys and presented, under the supervision of a judge, through witnesses, to a jury. If the jury finds the defendant guilty, he is sentenced by the judge to a term in prison, where a systematic attempt to convert him into a law-abiding citizen is made, or to a term of probation, under which he is permitted to live in the community as long as he behaves himself.

Some cases do proceed much like that, especially those involving offenses that are generally considered "major": serious acts of violence or thefts of large amounts of property. However, not all major cases follow this course, and, in any event, the bulk of the daily business of the criminal justice system consists of offenses that are not major — of breaches of the peace, crimes of vice, petty thefts, assaults arising from domestic or street-corner or barroom disputes. These and most other cases are disposed of in much less formal and much less deliberate ways. . . .

B. THE INITIAL STAGES OF A CRIMINAL CASE

Investigation

When patrol fails to prevent a crime or apprehend the criminal while he is committing it, the police must rely upon investigation. Every sizable department has a corps of investigative specialists — detectives — whose job is to solve crimes by questioning victims, suspects, and witnesses, by accumulating physical evidence at the scene of the crime, and by tracing stolen property or vehicles associated with the crime. In practically every department the caseloads carried by detectives are too heavy to allow them to follow up thoroughly more than a small percentage of the cases assigned them. In other words, a great many cases are unsolved by default — or, at least, time will not permit a determination of whether or not they are solvable. The effects of this condition go far beyond lack of redress for many victims of crime. . . .

In the present state of police knowledge and organization many crimes are, in fact, not solvable. In the great majority of cases, personal identification by a victim or witness is the *only* clue to the identity of the criminal. The Commission analyzed 1,905 crimes reported during January of 1966 in Los Angeles, which has a notably well-trained and efficient police department. The police were furnished a suspect's name in 349 of these cases, and 301 were resolved either by arrest or in some other way — either the victim would not prosecute, subsequent investigation disclosed that the reported crime was not actually a crime, or a prosecutor declined to press the case. Of the 1,375 crimes for which no suspect was named, only 181 cases were cleared. Since crimes against the person are more likely to be named-suspect crimes than crimes against property, it is natural that a much higher proportion of them are solved. In 1965, 78 percent of reported serious crimes against property were never solved. . . .

[FBI statistics for 1979 indicate that of the violent crimes (murder, aggravated assault, forcible rape, and robbery) reported or otherwise known to the police, 44 percent were cleared by an arrest. Of the serious property crimes (burglary, motor vehicle theft, and other larceny-theft), only 17 percent of the offenses known to the police were cleared by an arrest. For cities over 250,000 population, only 38 percent of violent offenses and 15 percent of serious property offenses were cleared.] . . .

The Diversion of Cases before Charge

The limited statistics available indicate that approximately one-half of those arrested are dismissed by the police, a prosecutor, or a magistrate at an early stage of the case. Some of these persons are released because they did not commit the acts they were originally suspected of having committed, or cannot be proved to have committed them, or committed them on legally defensible grounds. The police can arrest on "probable cause," while conviction requires proof "beyond a reasonable doubt." Therefore, some justified arrests cannot lead to prosecution and conviction.

However, others who are released probably did commit the offenses for which they were arrested. In some instances offenders who could and should be convicted are released simply because of an overload of work, or inadequate investigation in the prosecutor's office. In other cases the police, or more often prosecutors, have exercised the discretion that is traditionally theirs to decline to prosecute offenders whose conduct appears to deviate from patterns of law-abiding conduct, or who present clear medical, mental, or social problems that can be better dealt with outside the criminal process than within it. First offenders are often dealt with in this way. So are persons whose offenses arise from drinking or mental problems, if the offenses are minor. So are many cases of assault or theft within families or among friends, of passing checks with insufficient funds, of shoplifting when restitution is made, of statutory rape when both boy and girl are young, of automobile theft by teenagers for the purpose of joyriding. . . .

Pretrial Release

One-half or more of the defendants who are brought into a police or magistrate's court are released or convicted and sentenced within 24 hours of their arrest. The cases of the remainder, including all those against whom the accusation of a serious crime can be maintained, await final disposition for days or weeks or sometimes months, depending on the prosecutor's caseload, the gravity and complexity of the case, and the condition of the calendar in the court that will hear it.

The magistrate is empowered to decide whether or not such defendants will be released pending trial. . . .

[Traditionally, the device most often used to free an untried defendant and at the same time assure his or her appearance for trial was money bail. In this system, still in use in many areas, the court fixes the amount of an appearance bond to be posted in cash or by a secured pledge; defendants able to post the required amount win their release and recover the sum upon appearance for trial. Defendants unable to raise the required amount usually attempt to secure the services of a bail-bond agency, which posts the necessary bond in return for a fixed fee, typically 10 percent of the total bail. In this system the bondsman's obligations are satisfied upon the defendant's appearance, but the 10 percent charge has to be paid by the defendant in any event.

[The money bail system has proved unsatisfactory in many respects. It results in confinement of large numbers of untried defendants, solely on account of inability to raise the required amounts. The bail figure often is set by a fixed schedule, without regard to the defendant's means, ties to the community, or likelihood of flight. For those who can raise funds to pay the bondsman's fee, the system provides release but no financial incentive to appear. And in many localities the relationships between bail-bond agencies and court officials have been a source of malfeasance and corruption.

[During the 1960s and 1970s bail-reform projects were initiated in numerous cities around the country. Broadly speaking, the principal aims of these projects were to ascertain the kinds of community ties that would make defendants safe candidates for release without financial guarantees, to establish procedures for expeditiously collecting and verifying the background information necessary to identify such defendants, and to develop a more effective system of financial guarantees for defendants who could not qualify for release on any other basis. The success of these projects in demonstrating the value of alternatives to money bail has led to widespread changes in legislation and administrative practice governing the release of defendants pending trial. Pretrial release projects now functioning in more than 100 cities assist the local magistrates in identifying defendants who can be released without money bail and often provide follow-up to help insure that the defendant returns for any scheduled appearances. Often defendants will simply be released "on recognizance" ("ROR"), that is, on their personal, unsecured promise to appear when scheduled. In many states (and in the federal system) when a defendant does not qualify for ROR, the magistrate is required to explore a variety of alternatives to money bail and to select the least restrictive option that will be adequate to assure the defendant's appearance. When money bail is used, many jurisdictions now follow a "10 percent plan," under which the defendant is permitted to post directly with the court 10 percent of the face amount of the bail bond, and most or all of this sum is refundable when the defendant appears for trial. This system eliminates the potential for corruption associated with bail-bond agencies, restores the financial incentive for appearance, and (because the sum to be raised is recuperable) makes it much easier for many defendants to obtain the necessary amounts.[e]

e. One such 10 percent plan is discussed (and its constitutionality upheld) in Schilb v. Kuebel, 404 U.S. 357 (1971). As of 1978, 24 states had established a statutory preference for using ROR where feasible, and 22 states had mandated release on the least restrictive conditions possible. At least 18 states had adopted 10 percent plans. See J. Goldkamp, Two Classes of Accused: A Study

[These reforms have led to dramatic increases in the proportion of defendants released without financial security and in the proportion of defendants who are released rather than detained for trial.[f] Nevertheless, traditional money bail survives in many localities as the primary or exclusive avenue of pretrial release. In addition, even where a strong preference for ROR or other nonfinancial release has been established, the ultimate decision about a defendant's eligibility for these programs remains in the hands of a magistrate, who must balance a variety of subjective factors in determining the risk of flight in a particular case. Concern persists about the fairness and accuracy of these judgments and particularly about the extent to which they are used as a screen for impermissible objectives. Defendants denied ROR and offered only a bail figure much higher than they can meet may be told that the decision is based on risk of flight, but the judgment often stems primarily from the magistrate's desire to insure immediate confinement for defendants perceived as dangerous to the community. In practice, this indirect form of preventive detention may prove very difficult to challenge.[g]]

C. THE GUILTY PLEA

Most defendants who are convicted — as many as 90 percent in some jurisdictions — are not tried. They plead guilty, often as the result of negotiations about the charge or the sentence. It is almost impossible to generalize about the extent to which pleas are negotiated or about the ways in which they are negotiated, so much does practice vary from jurisdiction to jurisdiction. A plea negotiation can be, and often is in a minor case, a hurried conversation in a courthouse hallway. In grave cases it can be a series of elaborate conferences over the course of weeks in which facts are thoroughly discussed and alternatives carefully explored. Most often the negotiations are between a prosecutor and defense counsel, but sometimes a magistrate or a police officer or the defendant himself is involved. In some courts there are no plea negotiations at all. There almost never are negotiations in the cases of petty offenders. And, of course, many guilty pleas are not the result of negotiations. . . .

---

of Bail and Detention in American Justice (1979). See also P. Wice, Bail and Its Reform: A National Survey (1973). — Eds.

f. For example, from 1962 to 1971, the percentage of felony defendants released on nonfinancial conditions rose from zero to 56 percent in Washington, D.C., and from zero to 33 percent in Philadelphia; the average percentage for 20 major cities rose from 5 percent to 23 percent for felony cases and from 10 percent to over 30 percent for misdemeanor cases. Meanwhile for the 20 cities, the percentage of all defendants who were detained throughout the period prior to trial dropped from 52 percent to 33 percent in felony cases and from 21 percent to only 12 percent in major misdemeanor cases. See W. Thomas, Bail Reform in America (1976). — Eds.

g. In the District of Columbia, legislation has expressly authorized preventive detention, on the ground of the defendant's threat to community safety, in certain situations and subject to various procedural safegrounds. See D.C. Code Ann. §23-1322. Although the constitutionality of the statute has been upheld in the local District of Columbia courts, see Blunt v. United States, 322 A.2d 579 (D.C. App. 1974), the Supreme Court has yet to decide whether preventive detention violates the Eighth Amendment prohibition against "excessive bail." In any event the procedural safeguards of the District of Columbia statute have made it unattractive to prosecutors, and it is seldom invoked. Preventive detention decisions probably continue to be made covertly, and without any safeguards at all, in the guise of judgments that "risk of flight" requires denying ROR and setting high money bail. — Eds.

A general view of The Criminal Justice System

This chart seeks to present a simple yet comprehensive view of the movement of cases through the criminal justice system. Procedures in individual jurisdictions may vary from the pattern shown here. The differing weights of line indicate the relative volumes of cases disposed of at various points in the system, but this is only suggestive since no nationwide data of this sort exists.

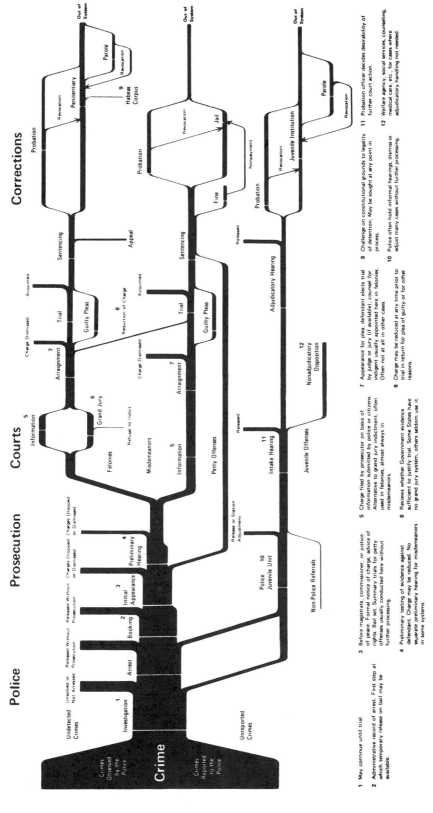

1 May continue until trial.

2 Administrative record of arrest. First step at which temporary release on bail may be available.

3 Before magistrate, commissioner, or justice of peace. Formal notice of charge, advice of rights. Bail set. Summary trials for petty offenses usually conducted here without further processing.

4 Preliminary testing of evidence against defendant. Charge may be reduced. No separate preliminary hearing for misdemeanors in some systems.

5 Charge filed by prosecutor on basis of information submitted by police or citizens. Alternative to grand jury indictment; often used in felonies, almost always in misdemeanors.

6 Reviews whether Government evidence sufficient to justify trial. Some States have no grand jury system; others seldom use it.

7 Appearance for plea, defendant elects trial by judge or jury (if available), counsel for indigent usually appointed here in felonies. Often not at all in other cases.

8 Charge may be reduced at any time prior to trial in return for plea of guilty or for other reasons.

9 Challenge on constitutional grounds to legality of detention. May be sought at any point in process.

10 Police often hold informal hearings, dismiss or adjust many cases without further processing.

11 Probation officer decides desirability of further court action.

12 Welfare agency, social services, counseling, medical care, etc., for cases where adjudicatory handling not needed.

D. THE TRIAL

. . . The cases decided at trial are only a small fraction of the total of cases, but they are most important to the process because they set standards for the conduct of all cases. The trial decides the hard legal issues, and reviews and rules on claims of official abuse. . . .

E. SENTENCING

There is no decision in the criminal process that is as complicated and difficult as the one made by the sentencing judge. A sentence prescribes punishment, but it also should be the foundation of an attempt to rehabilitate the offender, to insure that he does not endanger the community, and to deter others from similar crimes in the future. Often these objectives are mutually inconsistent, and the sentencing judge must choose one at the expense of the others. A man who has committed murder in a moment of extreme emotion may require no correctional program and may present no significant threat to the general safety, but few judges would be likely to respond to an offense so heinous by suspending the offender's sentence or granting him probation. . . .

Sentencing Procedures

Although the criminal trial on the issue of guilt is a strictly formal procedure, the determination of what is to be done with a convicted offender is often a rather informal one. A judge, when he sentences, needs facts about the offender and his offense. Both will be absent in those many instances when conviction has resulted from a plea of guilty and the court lacks, or has inadequate facilities for preparing, presentence reports. The judge then must rely on the necessarily incomplete and biased oral statements of the prosecutor, defense counsel, and defendant. Such statements may be supplemented by a "rapsheet," a 1-page record of the offender's prior criminal involvements. . . .

III. THE FLOW OF CASES THROUGH THE SYSTEM

[The chart presented above, taken from the report of the President's Commission at page 8, sets forth in simplified form the flow of cases through the criminal justice system and dramatically illustrates the filtering process through which the vast majority of all cases are winnowed out prior to trial.]

AMERICAN BAR FOUNDATION, CRIMINAL JUSTICE IN THE UNITED STATES 1-2 (1967):[2] Four general observations may be made about the system of criminal justice in the United States. First, the system deals with an enormous number of cases, so high indeed as to constitute a chronic condition of system overload.

Second, the system is pervaded by official discretion, that is, the power of individual judgment within general legal bounds. In part discretion is an administrative defense to system overload; in part it is an infusion of considerations of fairness or expediency into a system designed to assess guilt on formal legal premises; in part it is an inevitable feature of a criminal law system that must

2. This report, prepared by the staff of the American Bar Foundation, was based on a paper by Professor Geoffrey Hazard.

deal with conduct from first-degree murder to parking violations and all shades within these extremes.

Third, the administrative organization for dealing with crime and criminals is balkanized in the extreme. There are four functional components in the criminal law system: police, prosecution, judiciary, and corrections. In neither the United States as a whole nor in any single state is there common administrative supervision over these components, although there are points of common administration between some pairs of them in most states. Moreover, each one of these functional components may itself be divided jurisdictionally into parallel units. For example, in some localities there are county police (i.e., sheriffs' offices) and city police systems operating in the same geographical area; a county prosecutor and a city attorney prosecutor's office; a superior court for the trial of felonies, and a parallel, but independently operated, magistrate's court for hearing misdemeanors; and a division of correctional administration between local government, which handles probation and the administration of jail detention, and state government, which administers the prisons and parole supervision services.

And finally, the quality of the personnel and facilities serving the system varies enormously from jurisdiction to jurisdiction. Such states as California and Wisconsin are conspicuously above the average in these aspects. On the other hand, in many states, . . . the personnel and facilities for the administration of criminal justice show the effects of long-term inadequacy of public support.

CHAPTER

2

HOW GUILT IS ESTABLISHED

A. AN OVERVIEW OF CRIMINAL TRIAL PROCEDURE

We have described in Chapter 1 the general organization of the criminal justice system and the procedure typically followed at the pretrial stages of a criminal case. To introduce our examination of the trial stage itself, the present section briefly summarizes the typical course of a formal criminal trial. Naturally, the procedure followed in some jurisdictions or in particular cases may differ in points of detail from that set out in this preliminary overview.

A formal trial typically begins with the selection of the jury. A panel of prospective jurors (called a *venire*) enters the courtroom, and the judge briefly describes the nature of the case and the identity of the parties so that any prospective jurors who are personally involved in some way may be excused. Prospective jurors are then questioned individually by the judge or by opposing counsel to determine possible bias. On the basis of this questioning (called *voir dire*) prospective jurors may be excused *for cause,* and both prosecution and defense may remove a certain number of the panel, without showing cause, by exercising *peremptory challenges.* When the requisite number of acceptable jurors (usually 12) has been obtained by this procedure, the panel is sworn.

Now the presentation of the case begins. Usually the indictment is read to the jury; the prosecutor then makes an opening statement outlining the facts he or she plans to prove in the course of the trial. Defense counsel also may make an opening statement. Of course, claims made in these statements do not constitute *evidence;* they serve only to help the jury understand the formal testimony about to be presented. Various motions may be made at this time. In many jurisdictions, motions relating to the scope or validity of the indictment and motions to suppress evidence must be made a certain number of days prior to trial. In others, such motions can be made at the outset of the trial. Motions to limit the testimony or narrow the issues in some way also may be presented. If the judge grants a motion to dismiss the indictment, the case will terminate at this point. Otherwise the trial goes forward, although motions may be made or renewed as the trial proceeds.

Next the prosecution calls its witnesses. The presentation of their testimony often evokes objections from counsel, and the judge must decide the bounds of permissible testimony under complex rules of evidence. We examine some of these rules in the sections to follow. When the prosecution has completed the presentation of its evidence, the defense may choose to stand on the *presumption of innocence* and move for a *directed verdict* or *judgment of acquittal* on the ground that the charges have not been proved beyond a reasonable doubt. If such a motion is not made, or if the motion is made and denied, the defense may decide to offer its own evidence (through the defendant or other witnesses). The prosecution then will have an opportunity to present further evidence in rebuttal. When both sides have rested, having completed the presentation of their evidence, opposing counsel may make a closing argument to the jury. Ordinarily the prosecution's closing argument is presented first (because it bears the burden of proof), and the prosecutor is usually allowed an opportunity for rebuttal after the closing argument of the defense.

At this point the work of the opposing parties has been completed. The judge now intercedes with his or her most direct and by far most important contribution to the proceedings — the instructions to the jury. The judge's address to the jury may begin with a summary of the evidence; ordinarily, however, judicial comment on the evidence tends to be cautious and limited. Formal instructions on the law, however, are always given, and they are typically quite detailed. The instructions serve both as a guide for the jury's deliberations and as a focal point for challenges on appeal in the event of a conviction. Usually the instructions will cover formal procedures and responsibilities of the jurors in their deliberations (for example, how to elect a foreperson, when to refrain from discussing the case with other jurors or outsiders), matters related to the weight or relevance of particular kinds of testimony, and, above all, detailed explanations of the substantive criminal law applicable to the case, including specification of the elements necessary to establish the offense charged and definitions of legal concepts that the jury is called on to apply.

The jury at last retires to deliberate. Its verdict of guilty or not guilty on each offense charged must be reached by a substantial majority (and usually by unanimity). After a verdict of guilty and the imposition of sentence (usually by the judge), the trial terminates. There may of course be an appeal. If it finds trial errors, the reviewing court may reverse the conviction and order another trial, since American double jeopardy principles generally do not bar the retrial of a defendant who has successfully appealed his or her conviction.[1] A verdict of not guilty terminates the proceedings and is not subject to appeal or review of any kind, regardless of whether flagrant errors prejudicial to the prosecution occurred at trial.[2] When the jury is unable to agree by the requisite majority on a verdict of either guilty or not guilty (a hung jury case), a *mistrial* is declared, and the defendant then may be retried at the prosecutor's discretion.

Such, in rough outline, is the procedure by which guilt must be established when a criminal case is fully litigated through the formal trial stage. Of course,

---

1. United States v. Ball, 163 U.S. 662, 671-672 (1896); Burks v. United States, 437 U.S. 1 (1978). The English rule is to the contrary on this important issue. In that country, when a reviewing court finds prejudicial error, the conviction is "quashed," and no retrial is permitted. Criminal Appeal Act, 1968, ch. 19, §2(2)-(3); see M. Friedland, Double Jeopardy 221-228 (1969).

2. See Fong Foo v. United States, 369 U.S. 141 (1962). To avoid this difficulty many states provide for rulings prior to the start of trial on significant issues of law and permit the prosecutor to appeal an adverse ruling at that point.

as we have already seen, guilt can be (and very often is) established before the trial stage is ever reached by entry of a guilty plea.

Comprehensive treatment of all important aspects of trial and guilty plea procedure lies beyond the province of this book. Nevertheless, a book devoted primarily to the substantive law can and should explore some of the central features of the trial and guilty plea processes in order to illuminate the actual context in which criminal law is applied, the fundamental values that our procedural system serves or fails to serve, and the ways in which this system shapes (and in turn is shaped by) the substantive content of the criminal law. In the remaining sections of this chapter we undertake such an exploration.

B. THE ADVERSARY TRIAL PROCESS

INTRODUCTORY NOTE: THE SUPREME COURT AND STATE CRIMINAL PROCEDURE

The Bill of Rights of the United States Constitution contains a number of amendments bearing directly on the trial of criminal cases. The most important of these are as follows.

AMENDMENT IV: The right of the people to be secure in their persons, houses, papers, and effects, against unreasonable searches and seizures, shall not be violated, and no Warrants shall issue, but upon probable cause, supported by Oath or affirmation, and particularly describing the place to be searched, and the persons or things to be seized.

AMENDMENT V: No person shall be held to answer for a capital, or otherwise infamous crime, unless on a presentment or indictment of a Grand Jury, except in cases arising in the land or naval forces . . . ; nor shall any person be subject for the same offence to be twice put in jeopardy of life or limb; nor shall be compelled in any criminal case to be a witness against himself, nor be deprived of life, liberty, or property, without due process of law. . . .

AMENDMENT VI: In all criminal prosecutions, the accused shall enjoy the right to a speedy and public trial, by an impartial jury of the State and district wherein the crime shall have been committed, which district shall have been previously ascertained by law, and to be informed of the nature and cause of the accusation; to be confronted with the witnesses against him; to have compulsory process for obtaining witnesses in his favor, and to have the Assistance of Counsel for his defence.

AMENDMENT VIII: Excessive bail shall not be required, nor excessive fines imposed, nor cruel and unusual punishments inflicted.

Early in the history of the United States, the Supreme Court held that these and other provisions of the first eight amendments to the Constitution were binding only on the federal government and imposed no restrictions on the states. Barron v. Mayor of Baltimore, 32 U.S. (7 Pet.) 243 (1833). Thus, although most of those amendments were cast in general terms, they were not thought to affect procedure in the state courts. No federal restraint prevented a state from denying the right to counsel (to indigents or to everyone), from compelling self-incrimination, or even from imposing "cruel and unusual punishment." State constitutions often imposed comparable restrictions, but the interpretation of those restrictions was a matter for the state courts. Once a state supreme court had found no violation of state law in connection with a state criminal prosecution, the defendant generally could have no federal constitutional claim to present to the United States Supreme Court.

With the enactment of the Fourteenth Amendment after the Civil War in 1868, state criminal procedure for the first time potentially became subject to scrutiny under a federal standard — no state could "deprive any person of life, liberty, or property, without due process of law." It remained, however, to determine the content of the due process limitation that the states were obliged to respect.

Three schools of interpretation emerged. The first read "due process" to require *fundamental fairness.* Sometimes this meant that a procedural rule found in the Bill of Rights was also held binding on the states, because it was deemed "fundamental" or was "of the very essence of a scheme of ordered liberty." Palko v. Connecticut, 302 U.S. 319, 325 (1937).[3] Typically, however, the fundamental-fairness approach did not lead the Supreme Court to impose particular rules on the states. Rather, the Court focused on the question whether the proceedings in the particular case had been unfair under the "totality" of the circumstances.[4] This fundamental-fairness approach dominated Supreme Court interpretation of the due process clause for nearly 100 years after the adoption of the Fourteenth Amendment.

The second school of interpretation, usually referred to as that of *total incorporation,* read "due process" to include all of the first eight amendments. This approach, which received its fullest development in Justice Black's dissenting opinion in Adamson v. California, 332 U.S. 46 (1947), was based primarily on evidence from the legislative history of the Fourteenth Amendment, indicating that at least some of the amendment's sponsors intended the term due process to include or "incorporate" the Bill of Rights. The total-incorporation theory undoubtedly also attracted support because it was perceived as less subjective than the fundamental-fairness approach, it provided clearer guidance about the content of the due process requirement, and it promised broader and more effective protection for the accused. Nevertheless, the historical premises of the total-incorporation approach were sharply questioned,[5] and some of its practical consequences were most unwelcome. (Under the Seventh Amendment, for example, the states would have been required to provide a right to jury

3. Similarly in Twining v. New Jersey, 211 U.S. 78, 99 (1908), the Court had said that "it is possible that some of the personal rights safeguarded by the first eight Amendments against National action may also be safeguarded against state action, because a denial of them would be a denial of due process of law."

4. In Betts v. Brady, 316 U.S. 455, 462 (1942), for example, the Court had said, "Due process of law . . . formulates a concept less rigid and more fluid than those envisaged in other specific and particular provisions of the Bill of Rights. Its application is less a matter of rule. Asserted denial is to be tested by an appraisal of the totality of facts in a given case." See also Powell v. Alabama, 287 U.S. 45, 71 (1932).

5. See, e.g., **Fairman, Does the Fourteenth Amendment Incorporate the Bill of Rights?,** 2 Stan. L. Rev. 5 (1949).

trial in all *civil* suits at common law whenever the amount in controversy exceeded $20.) The total-incorporation approach won the votes of four justices in *Adamson*, supra, but it never commanded a majority of the Supreme Court.

The third school of interpretation, known as *selective incorporation*, reached ascendancy in the early 1960s, primarily as part of an effort to avoid the excessive subjectivity and uncertainty of the fundamental-fairness approach while also avoiding the excessive rigidity of total incorporation. Under the selective-incorporation approach, the Supreme Court examines a particular clause of the Bill of Rights (the right to counsel, the double jeopardy clause, etc.) in order to determine whether the rights protected by that clause are fundamental. If so, then that particular clause is "selectively incorporated" into the due process clause and becomes binding on the states. The selectivity and discretion afforded by this approach permit the Supreme Court to avoid applying certain Bill of Rights provisions to the states: the Fifth Amendment requirement of a grand jury indictment, for example, probably will never be held binding on the states. Once a clause is incorporated, however, further selectivity is (at least in theory) precluded; the scope and content of the clause as it applies to the states is identical to its scope and content with respect to the federal government. See, e.g., Malloy v. Hogan, 378 U.S. 1, 10-11 (1964); Benton v. Maryland, 395 U.S. 784, 795 (1969).

Selective incorporation is closely associated with the history of the Warren Court, which used this approach during the 1960s to extend procedural safeguards to defendants in state criminal prosecutions. Although the orientation of the Supreme Court probably has changed in recent years, the theory of selective incorporation continues to command a clear majority of the current Court.[6] Thus, the Court may in some cases adopt a narrow interpretation of a particular clause of the Bill of Rights, but the Court remains committed to the view that once this clause has been incorporated, due process requires the states to afford all the procedural safeguards that this clause imposes directly on the federal government.

Throughout this chapter we shall be exploring questions of criminal procedure, many of them of constitutional dimension. Our concern is not primarily to understand the proper role of the Supreme Court, for that task requires careful study of the relationship between the national and state governments, a problem that warrants detailed examination in connection with courses in criminal procedure and constitutional law.[7] Our principal concern, rather, is to understand the basic structure of the criminal process typical of most American states and the underlying values which that process reflects. Nevertheless, given the prevailing methodology of selective incorporation, Supreme Court decisions interpreting the meaning of "due process" often provide the essential starting point for consideration of which procedures are deemed fundamental in the American system — and why.

---

6. See, e.g., Crist v. Brest, 437 U.S. 28 (1978); Apodaca v. Oregon, 406 U.S. 404 (1972).

7. For further reading on the interpretation of the due process requirement in the context of criminal prosecutions, see Duncan v. Louisiana, 391 U.S. 145 (1968); id. at 171-193 (Harlan, J., dissenting); Friendly, The Bill of Rights as a Code of Criminal Procedure, 53 Calif. L. Rev. 929 (1965); Kadish, Methodology and Criteria in Due Process Adjudication — A Survey and Criticism, 66 Yale L.J. 319 (1957).

1. Representation by Counsel

a. The Right to Counsel

GIDEON v. WAINWRIGHT
Supreme Court of the United States
372 U.S. 335 (1963)

MR. JUSTICE BLACK delivered the opinion of the Court.

Petitioner was charged in a Florida state court with having broken and entered a poolroom with intent to commit a misdemeanor. This offense is a felony under Florida law. Appearing in court without funds and without a lawyer, petitioner asked the court to appoint counsel for him, whereupon the following colloquy took place:

The Court: Mr. Gideon, I am sorry, but I cannot appoint Counsel to represent you in this case. Under the laws of the State of Florida, the only time the Court can appoint Counsel to represent a Defendant is when that person is charged with a capital offense. I am sorry, but I will have to deny your request to appoint Counsel to defend you in this case.

The Defendant: The United States Supreme Court says I am entitled to be represented by Counsel.

Put to trial before a jury, Gideon conducted his defense about as well as could be expected from a layman. . . . The jury returned a verdict of guilty, and petitioner was sentenced to serve five years in the state prison. Later, petitioner filed in the Florida Supreme Court this habeas corpus petition attacking his conviction and sentence on the ground that the trial court's refusal to appoint counsel for him denied him rights "guaranteed by the Constitution and the Bill of Rights by the United States Government." . . . [T]he State Supreme Court . . . denied all relief. Since 1942, when Betts v. Brady, 316 U.S. 455, was decided by a divided Court, the problem of a defendant's federal constitutional right to counsel in a state court has been a continuing source of controversy and litigation in both state and federal courts. . . . [W]e granted certiorari. Since Gideon was proceeding in forma pauperis, we appointed counsel to represent him and requested both sides to discuss in their briefs and oral arguments the following: "Should this Court's holding in Betts v. Brady, 316 U.S. 455, be reconsidered?"

The facts upon which Betts claimed that he had been unconstitutionally denied the right to have counsel appointed to assist him are strikingly like the facts upon which Gideon here bases his federal constitutional claim. Betts was indicted for robbery in a Maryland state court. On arraignment, he told the trial judge of his lack of funds to hire a lawyer and asked the court to appoint one for him. Betts was advised that it was not the practice in that county to appoint counsel for indigent defendants except in murder and rape cases. He then pleaded not guilty, had witnesses summoned, cross-examined the State's witnesses, examined his own, and chose not to testify himself. He was found guilty by the judge, sitting without a jury, and sentenced to eight years in prison. Like Gideon, Betts sought release by habeas corpus, alleging that he had been denied the right to assistance of counsel in violation of the Fourteenth Amendment. Betts was denied any relief, and on review this Court affirmed. It was held that a refusal to appoint counsel for an indigent defendant charged with a felony did not necessarily violate the Due Process Clause of the Fourteenth Amendment, which for reasons given the Court deemed to be the only applicable federal constitutional provision. The Court said:

> Asserted denial [of due process] is to be tested by an appraisal of the totality of facts in a given case. That which may, in one setting, constitute a denial of fundamental fairness, shocking to the universal sense of justice, may, in other circumstances, and in the light of other considerations, fall short of such denial.

Treating due process as "a concept less rigid and more fluid than those envisaged in other specific and particular provisions of the Bill of Rights," the Court held that refusal to appoint counsel under the particular facts and circumstances in the *Betts* case was not so "offensive to the common and fundamental ideas of fairness" as to amount to a denial of due process. Since the facts and circumstances of the two cases are so nearly indistinguishable, we think the Betts v. Brady holding if left standing would require us to reject Gideon's claim that the Constitution guarantees him the assistance of counsel. Upon full reconsideration we conclude that Betts v. Brady should be overruled. . . .

We accept Betts v. Brady's assumption, based as it was on our prior cases, that a provision of the Bill of Rights which is "fundamental and essential to a fair trial" is made obligatory upon the States by the Fourteenth Amendment. We think the Court in *Betts* was wrong, however, in concluding that the Sixth Amendment's guarantee of counsel is not one of these fundamental rights. Ten years before Betts v. Brady, this Court, after full consideration of all the historical data examined in *Betts,* had unequivocally declared that "the right to the aid of counsel is of this fundamental character." Powell v. Alabama, 287 U.S. 45, 68 (1932). While the Court at the close of its *Powell* opinion did by its language, as this Court frequently does, limit its holding to the particular facts and circumstances of that case, its conclusions about the fundamental nature of the right to counsel are unmistakable. Several years later, in 1936, the Court reemphasized what it had said about the fundamental nature of the right to counsel in this language: "We conclude that certain fundamental rights, safeguarded by the first eight amendments against federal action, were also safeguarded against state action by the due process of law clause of the Fourteenth Amendment, and among them the fundamental right of the accused to the aid of counsel in a criminal prosecution." Grosjean v. American Press Co., 297 U.S. 233, 243-244 (1936). And again in 1938 this Court said: "[The assistance of counsel] is one of the safeguards of the Sixth Amendment deemed necessary to insure fundamental human rights of life and liberty. . . . The Sixth Amendment stands as a constant admonition that if the constitutional safeguards it provides be lost, justice will not 'still be done.'" Johnson v. Zerbst, 304 U.S. 458, 462 (1938). . . .

In light of these and many other prior decisions of this Court, it is not surprising that the *Betts* Court, when faced with the contention that "one charged with crime, who is unable to obtain counsel, must be furnished counsel by the state," conceded that "[e]xpressions in the opinions of this court lend color to the argument. . . ." The fact is that in deciding as it did — that "appointment of counsel is not a fundamental right, essential to a fair trial"— the Court in Betts v. Brady made an abrupt break with its own well-considered precedents. In returning to these old precedents, sounder we believe than the new, we but restore constitutional principles established to achieve a fair system of justice. Not only these precedents but also reason and reflection require us to recognize that in our adversary system of criminal justice, any person haled into court, who is too poor to hire a lawyer, cannot be assured a fair trial unless counsel is provided for him. This seems to us to be an obvious truth. Governments, both state and federal, quite properly spend vast sums of money to establish machinery to try defendants accused of crime. Lawyers to prosecute are everywhere deemed essential to protect the public's interest in an orderly society. Similarly, there are few defendants charged with crime, few indeed, who fail to hire the best lawyers they can get to prepare and present their defenses. That government hires lawyers to prosecute and defendants who have the money hire lawyers to defend are the strongest indications of the widespread belief that lawyers in criminal courts are necessities, not luxuries. The right of one charged with crime to counsel may not be deemed fundamental and essential to fair trials in some countries, but it is in ours. From the very beginning, our state and national constitutions and laws have laid great emphasis on procedural and substantive safeguards designed to assure fair trials before impartial tribunals in which every defendant stands equal before the law. This noble ideal cannot be realized if the poor man charged with crime has to face his accusers without a lawyer to assist him. A defendant's need for a lawyer is nowhere better stated than in the moving words of Mr. Justice Sutherland in Powell v. Alabama: "The right to be heard would be, in many cases, of little avail if it did not comprehend the right to be heard by counsel. Even the intelligent and educated layman has small and sometimes no skill in the science of law. If charged with crime, he is incapable, generally, of determining for himself whether the indictment is good or bad. He is unfamiliar with the rules of evidence. Left without aid of counsel he may be put on trial without a proper charge, and convicted upon incompetent evidence or evidence irrelevant to the issue or otherwise inadmissible. He lacks both the skill and knowledge adequately to prepare his defense, even though he may have a perfect one. He requires the guiding hand of counsel at every step in the proceedings against him. Without it, though he be not guilty, he faces the danger of conviction because he does not know how to establish his innocence." The Court in Betts v. Brady departed from the sound wisdom upon which the Court's holding in Powell v. Alabama rested. Florida, supported by two other States, has asked that Betts v. Brady be left intact. Twenty-two States, as friends of the Court, argue that *Betts* was "an anachronism when handed down" and that it should now be overruled. We agree.

The judgment is reversed and the cause is remanded to the Supreme Court of Florida for further action not inconsistent with this opinion.

Mr. Justice Harlan, concurring.

I agree that Betts v. Brady should be overruled, but consider it entitled to a more respectful burial than has been accorded, at least on the part of those of us who were not on the Court when that case was decided.

I cannot subscribe to the view that Betts v. Brady represented "an abrupt break with its own well-considered precedents." In 1932, in Powell v. Alabama,

287 U.S. 45, a capital case, this Court declared that under the particular facts there presented —"the ignorance and illiteracy of the defendants, their youth, the circumstances of public hostility . . . and above all that they stood in deadly peril of their lives"— the state court had a duty to assign counsel for the trial as a necessary requisite of due process of law. It is evident that these limiting facts were not added to the opinion as an afterthought; they were repeatedly emphasized, and were clearly regarded as important to the result.

Thus when this Court, a decade later, decided Betts v. Brady, it did no more than to admit of the possible existence of special circumstances in noncapital as well as capital trials, while at the same time insisting that such circumstances be shown in order to establish a denial of due process. The right to appointed counsel had been recognized as being considerably broader in federal prosecutions, see Johnson v. Zerbst, 304 U.S. 458, but to have imposed these requirements on the States would indeed have been "an abrupt break" with the almost immediate past. The declaration that the right to appointed counsel in state prosecutions, as established in Powell v. Alabama, was not limited to capital cases was in truth not a departure from, but an extension of, existing precedent.

The principles declared in *Powell* and in *Betts,* however, have had a troubled journey throughout the years that have followed first the one case and then the other. . . . [T]he "special circumstances" rule has continued to exist in form while its substance has been substantially and steadily eroded. In the first decade after *Betts,* there were cases in which the Court found special circumstances to be lacking, but usually by a sharply divided vote. However, no such decision has been cited to us, and I have found none, after Quicksall v. Michigan, 339 U.S. 660, decided in 1950. At the same time, there have been not a few cases in which special circumstances were found in little or nothing more than the "complexity" of the legal questions presented, although those questions were often of only routine difficulty. The Court has come to recognize, in other words, that the mere existence of a serious criminal charge constituted in itself special circumstances requiring the services of counsel at trial. In truth the Betts v. Brady rule is no longer a reality.

This evolution, however, appears not to have been fully recognized by many state courts, in this instance charged with the front-line responsibility for the enforcement of constitutional rights. To continue a rule which is honored by this Court only with lip service is not a healthy thing and in the long run will do disservice to the federal system. . . .

[The concurring opinions of Justices Douglas and Clark are omitted.][a]

---

a. The New York Times, August 7, 1963, page 56, col. 1, contained the following news report by Anthony Lewis: "Clarence Earl Gideon was acquitted by a jury of breaking and entering the Bay Harbor poolroom here. Two years and a day ago, on August 4, 1961, another jury convicted him of the same charge. He was given a five-year sentence. The difference between the two trials was that this time Mr. Gideon had a lawyer. The Florida courts . . . [had] ordered a new trial. A leading criminal lawyer here in Bay County, W. Fred Turner, was appointed to represent him. Mr. Turner found a new defense witness. He developed material to discredit the chief prosecution witness. He talked to the jury about 'reasonable doubt' and said that 'this country was not founded on a man having to prove his innocence — we're all thankful for that.' The trial began at 9 this morning and lasted most of the day. The jury took an hour and five minutes to decide on its verdict: Not guilty. The three prosecutors, who had thought it was an open-and-shut case, seemed surprised." For an absorbing account of the *Gideon* case, see A. Lewis, Gideon's Trumpet (1964).— EDS.

NOTES ON THE RIGHT TO COUNSEL AND OTHER ASSISTANCE

1. Foundations of the adversary system and the right to counsel. Consider the following comment on the sources of the government's obligation to afford assistance to indigent criminal defendants.

Report of the Attorney General's Committee on Poverty and the Administration of Criminal Justice 8-11 (1963): It should be understood that governmental obligation to deal effectively with problems of poverty in the administration of criminal justice does not rest or depend upon some hypothetical obligation of government to indulge in acts of public charity. It does not presuppose a general commitment on the part of the federal government to relieve impoverished persons of the consequences of limited means, whenever or however manifested. It does not even presuppose that government is always required to take into account the means of the citizen when dealing directly with its citizens. Few would maintain that in disposing of surplus property, for example, government is required to set prices at such levels that all citizens are rendered equally able to buy.

. . . The essential point is that the problems of poverty with which this Report is concerned arise in a process *initiated* by government for the achievement of basic governmental purposes. It is, moreover, a process that has as one of its consequences the imposition of severe disabilities on the persons proceeded against. Duties arise from action. When a course of conduct, however legitimate, entails the possibility of serious injury to persons, a duty on the actor to avoid the reasonably avoidable injuries is ordinarily recognized. When government chooses to exert its powers in the criminal area, its obligation is surely no less than that of taking reasonable measures to eliminate those factors that are irrelevant to just administration of the law but which, nevertheless, may occasionally affect determinations of the accused's liability or penalty. While government may not be required to relieve the accused of his poverty, it may properly be required to minimize the influence of poverty on its administration of justice.

The Committee, therefore, conceives the obligation of government less as an undertaking to eliminate "discrimination" against a class of accused persons and more as a broad commitment by government to rid its processes of all influences that tend to defeat the ends a system of justice is intended to serve. Such a concept of "equal justice" does not confuse equality of treatment with identity of treatment. We assume that government must be conceded flexibility in devising its measures and that reasonable classifications are permitted. The crucial question is, has government done all that can reasonably be required of it to eliminate those factors that inhibit the proper and effective assertion of grounds relevant to the criminal liability of the accused or to the imposition of sanctions and disabilities on the accused at all stages of the criminal process? . . .

It is not only the interests of accused persons that require attention be given to the problems of poverty in criminal-law administration. Other and broader social interests are involved. . . .

. . . The adversary system is the institution devised by our legal order for the proper reconciliation of public and private interests in the crucial areas of penal regulation. As such, it makes essential and invaluable contributions to the maintenance of the free society.

The essence of the adversary system is challenge. The survival of our system of criminal justice and the values which it advances depends upon a constant, searching, and creative questioning of official decisions and assertions of authority at all stages of the process. The proper performance of the defense function is thus as vital to the health of the system as the performance of the prosecuting and adjudicatory functions. It follows that insofar as the financial status of the accused impedes vigorous and proper challenges, it constitutes a threat to the viability of the adversary system. We believe that the system is imperiled by the large numbers of accused persons unable to employ counsel or to meet even modest bail requirements and by the large, but indeterminate, numbers of persons, able to pay some part of the costs of defense, but unable to finance a full and proper defense. . . . Persons suffering such disabilities are incapable of providing the challenges that are indispensable to satisfactory operation of the system. The loss to the interests of accused individuals, occasioned by these failures, are great and apparent. It is also clear that a situation in which persons are required to contest a serious accusation but are denied access to the tools of contest is offensive to fairness and equity. Beyond these considerations, however, is the fact that the conditions produced by the financial incapacity of the accused are detrimental to the proper functioning of the system of justice and that the loss in vitality of the adversary system, thereby occasioned, significantly endangers the basic interests of a free community.

2. The special circumstances rule. What is inherently unfair about a rule that provides free counsel to indigents only when the circumstances suggest some way that counsel could be helpful? In Betts v. Brady, 316 U.S. 455, 471-473 (1942), the Court had said:

> [I]n the great majority of the States, . . . appointment of counsel is not [considered] a fundamental right, essential to a fair trial. . . . [W]e are unable to say that the concept of due process incorporated in the Fourteenth Amendment obligates the States, whatever may be their own views, to furnish counsel in every criminal case. Every court has power, if it deems proper, to appoint counsel where that course seems to be required in the interest of fairness.
>
> . . . It is quite clear that in Maryland, if . . . it had appeared that the petitioner was, for any reason, at a serious disadvantage by reason of the lack of counsel, a refusal to appoint would have resulted in the reversal of a judgment of conviction. . . .
>
> . . . [W]e cannot say that the [Fourteenth A]mendment embodies an inexorable command that no trial for any offense, or in any court, can be fairly conducted and justice accorded a defendant who is not represented by counsel.

What, if anything, is wrong with the case-by-case approach approved in *Betts*? Is there *always* something significant that a defense lawyer can accomplish? If not, why not trust the trial judge or the appellate courts to identify the cases in which a lawyer might be needed? Are there reasons why these judges (as well as a defense lawyer appointed to handle an appeal after conviction) might fail to notice useful tactics that could have been pursued or defenses that might have been developed by an aggressive lawyer at or before trial?

3. Scope of the right to counsel. Although *Gideon* eliminated the vagaries of the special circumstances rule by establishing that indigents have an automatic right to appointed counsel in serious criminal cases, the decision raised almost as many questions as it answered. Consider these problems:

(a) In what *kinds of proceedings* does the automatic right to counsel apply? *Gideon* involved a felony case. Should the same rule apply in misdemeanor prosecutions? In Argersinger v. Hamlin, 407 U.S. 25 (1972), and Scott v. Illinois, 440 U.S. 367 (1979), the Court held that indigent misdemeanor defendants have an automatic right to counsel only if the proceedings actually result in imprisonment. A defendant prosecuted for an offense "punishable" by imprisonment can be tried and convicted without counsel if the judge in fact imposes only a fine or suspended sentence. Is this consistent with the reasoning of *Gideon*? With the Sixth Amendment language guaranteeing counsel "in all criminal prosecutions"? [8]

Suppose that defendant is tried and convicted without counsel and punished only by a fine but is subsequently prosecuted for another offense (this time with counsel) and convicted. Can the judge in the second prosecution give weight to the prior conviction when deciding how long a prison term to impose? In Baldasar v. Illinois, 446 U.S. 222 (1980), the Supreme Court answered this question in the negative, but a majority of the Court could not agree on a rationale. What should be the result and the rationale?

(b) Assuming that the case is one requiring counsel (a felony, for example), at what *stages of the case* does the right to counsel attach? *Gideon* involved a demand for counsel at the trial itself, but long before *Gideon* it was clear that where counsel was required for the trial, appointment early enough to permit adequate pretrial preparation was also required. See Powell v. Alabama, 287 U.S. 45 (1932). Determining how *early* in the case counsel must be made available nevertheless remains difficult and hotly debated. The Supreme Court now appears committed to the view that counsel is required only after the beginning of *formal* judicial proceedings, for example, by indictment, preliminary hearing, or arraignment.[9] Some state courts go further and interpret their state constitutions to require the presence of counsel for important stages in the case (such as lineups), whether or not they precede the initiation of formal proceedings. See, e.g., People v. Jackson, 391 Mich. 323, 217 N.W.2d 22 (1974). The problem is intimately connected with the broader debate over appropriate safeguards and restrictions for police investigation.

After trial and conviction, defendant retains the right to the assistance of counsel through sentencing, Mempa v. Rhay, 389 U.S. 128 (1967), and through any appeal afforded by the state as a matter of right, Douglas v. California, 372 U.S. 353 (1963). However, the Court has held that there is no right to counsel to pursue any further appeal available only as a matter of the reviewing court's discretion (such as review by the United States Supreme Court on writ of certiorari). Ross v. Moffitt, 417 U.S. 600 (1974). Nor is there an automatic right to the assistance of counsel for pursuing avenues of collateral attack on the conviction, such as the writ of habeas corpus. Cf. United States v. MacCollum,

---

8. Many states have gone further than *Argersinger* and *Scott* require and have extended the right to counsel to all misdemeanor prosecutions or to prosecutions for all offenses "punishable" by imprisonment. See, e.g., Alexander v. City of Anchorage, 490 P.2d 910 (Alaska 1971), and authorities collected in Scott v. Illinois, 440 U.S. 367, 385-388 (1979) (Brennan, J., dissenting).

9. See, e.g., Moore v. Illinois, 434 U.S. 220 (1977); Kirby v. Illinois, 406 U.S. 682 (1972).

426 U.S. 317 (1976).[10] Similarly, the Court has held that indigents do not have an automatic right to counsel either in proceedings to obtain release from prison on parole or in proceedings to commit a defendant to prison by revoking probation or parole. See Greenholtz v. Inmates of Nebraska Penal and Correctional Complex, 442 U.S. 1 (1979); Gagnon v. Scarpelli, 411 U.S. 778 (1973).

(c) What if defendant says that he or she does not *want* a lawyer? In Johnson v. Zerbst, 304 U.S. 458, 465 (1938), the Supreme Court said:

> The constitutional right of an accused to be represented by counsel invokes, of itself, the protection of a trial court. . . . This protecting duty imposes the serious and weighty responsibility upon the trial judge of determining whether there is an intelligent and competent waiver by the accused.

Elaborating on this standard, the Court held in Carnley v. Cochran, 369 U.S. 506, 516 (1962):

> Presuming waiver from a silent record is impermissible. The record must show, or there must be an allegation and evidence which show, that an accused was offered counsel but intelligently and understandingly refused the offer. Anything less is not waiver.

In the above situations defendant proceeded without counsel and later claimed the absence of a valid waiver. What if the accused makes clear his or her deliberate preference for proceeding without counsel but the trial judge insists on appointing a lawyer to represent the defendant? In Faretta v. California, 422 U.S. 806 (1975), the Supreme Court held that the state cannot *prevent* a defendant from waiving counsel if he or she knowingly and intelligently chooses to do so; defendant also has a constitutional right to proceed pro se. Can judges adequately fulfill their independent obligations to see justice done if they cannot provide attorneys to protect defendants' interests? Or is the interest in a substantively just result subordinate to the interest in permitting the opposing parties to decide for themselves how the adversary contest should be shaped? Most American courts have viewed self-determination by the parties as the paramount value. See, for example, United States v. Dougherty, 473 F.2d 1113, 1128 (D.C. Cir. 1972). But in countries that adopt "nonadversarial" systems of criminal procedure, this view is generally rejected. See pages 169-174 infra. How can the prevalent American attitude be justified?

4. Experts other than counsel. (a) The right to an appointed expert. Does the reasoning of *Gideon* suggest that under some circumstances the defense must be afforded the assistance of experts other than counsel in order to assure that the adversary system functions properly? If so, should the right to a court-appointed expert extend to any situation in which a defendant with adequate means would hire an expert? Or should the right be limited to situations in which the prosecution plans to use a similar expert? If the prosecution does plan to call an expert witness, must the judge appoint an expert for the defense even when such action appears unnecessary or too expensive? These problems frequently arise

---

10. Note, however, that prison authorities must provide inmates with access to a law library or to legally trained persons who can assist them in seeking postconviction relief. See Bounds v. Smith, 430 U.S. 817 (1977).

when the accused wishes to raise an insanity defense, but a wide range of other specialists, including pathologists, ballistics experts, handwriting experts, and so on, may be potentially useful as witnesses or as advisors to the defense attorney. In a variety of contexts courts have found it a violation of the Sixth and Fourteenth Amendments for a trial judge to refuse, regardless of the circumstances, to appoint an expert. See, e.g., Williams v. Martin, 618 F.2d 1021 (4th Cir. 1980). But if the judge rejects defendant's request for appointment of an expert on the ground that an appointed expert is not necessary to an effective defense in the particular case, the ruling may prove very difficult for the defendant to overturn. In effect defendant's right to expert assistance seems limited to "special circumstances," as determined by the trial judge. Is there any feasible alternative? See generally, Note, The Indigent's Right to an Adequate Defense: Expert and Investigational Assistance in Criminal Proceedings, 55 Cornell L. Rev. 632 (1970).

(b) *Extent of the required assistance.* In United States v. Chavis, 476 F.2d 1137 (D.C. Cir. 1973), a defense motion for a psychiatric examination had been granted but the accused had been found sane and competent to stand trial[11] after 15 days under examination at St. Elizabeths, a government-operated hospital. A defense motion for a second examination was later granted;[12] Dr. Maguigad, a psychiatrist not associated with St. Elizabeths, examined the accused in a 50-minute session and concluded that the accused was competent to stand trial but was suffering from a mental disease that had substantially affected his behavior at the time of the offense (a conclusion that afforded a basis for an insanity defense). The defense sought further examinations by Maguigad or another doctor on the ground that the 50-minute examination would carry little weight with the jury when compared with the 15 days' examination at St. Elizabeths. That request was denied. At trial Maguigad's testimony in support of an insanity defense was strongly challenged by the prosecution on the basis of his lack of familiarity with the case, and the jury rejected the insanity claim. The Court of Appeals reversed the conviction. The court refrained from holding that additional expert assistance was automatically required in such a case, but

---

11. For exploration of both legal insanity and incompetency to stand trial and discussion of the differences between these two concepts, see pages 821-824 infra.

12. 18 U.S.C. §3006A(e), applicable in federal prosecutions, provides:

"(e) SERVICES OTHER THAN COUNSEL. —

(1)*Upon request.* — Counsel for a person who is financially unable to obtain investigative, expert, or other services necessary for an adequate defense may request them in an ex parte application. Upon finding, after appropriate inquiry in an ex parte proceeding, that the services are necessary and that the person is financially unable to obtain them, the court, or the United States magistrate if the services are required in connection with a matter over which he has jurisdiction, shall authorize counsel to obtain the services.

(2) *Without prior request.* — Counsel appointed under this section may obtain, subject to later review, investigative, expert, or other services without prior authorization if necessary for an adequate defense. The total cost of services obtained without prior authorization may not exceed $150 and expenses reasonably incurred.

(3) *Maximum amounts.* — Compensation to be paid to a person for services rendered by him to a person under this subsection, or to be paid to an organization for services rendered by an employee thereof, shall not exceed $300, exclusive of reimbursement for expenses reasonably incurred, unless payment in excess of that limit is certified by the court, or by the United States magistrate if the services were rendered in connection with a case disposed of entirely before him, as necessary to provide fair compensation for services of an unusual character or duration, and the amount of the excess payment is approved by the chief judge of the circuit."

after a remand for an evidentiary hearing, the court found that Maguigad had not provided assistance sufficient for an adequate defense under all the circumstances. 486 F.2d 1290 (1973). Consider whether this approach goes far enough. Is it consistent with *Gideon's* rejection of the *Betts* "special circumstances" rule? Is it consistent with *Gideon's* reliance on the kinds of expenditures undertaken by the prosecution and by defendants of means? How much expert assistance *should* be afforded to the defense in a case like *Chavis*?

b. Implementing the Right to Counsel

BAZELON, THE DEFECTIVE ASSISTANCE OF COUNSEL
42 U. Cin. L. Rev. 1, 6-14 (1973)

Most of my own experience is in the District of Columbia, where representation for indigent defendants comes from a number of sources. About one-fourth of these cases are handled by a Public Defender Service. I am well aware that the quality of public defenders varies tremendously and that the one in the District of Columbia is certainly among the best. Our Public Defender Office controls its own caseload; with adequate support staff, one of its lawyers closes an average of about 160 felonies and misdemeanors each year. In contrast, with little control over their caseload and inadequate support staff, public defenders in other major American cities have annual felony caseloads of over 500 cases per attorney.

Our Public Defender is not directly governed by the local courts, but is accountable to a Board of Directors, the members of which are selected by the chief judges of the District's local and federal courts. The agency depends on Congress for appropriations. The danger always lurks that the agency will come under pressures inconsistent with the interests of its clients. In the District, but even more so where agencies operate under the direct control of trial judges, public defenders may be torn between their duty to the client and their duty to the court and its crowded calendar. I have been reliably informed that a director of one such agency periodically checked with trial judges to determine whether his staff attorneys were too aggressive or took too much of the courts' time. Criticism by a trial judge was passed on to the offending lawyers. Such practices may be conducive to rapid and efficient processing of cases but are not conducive to diligent and conscientious advocacy. . . .

Today, we in Washington are fortunate to have an unusually devoted, independent, and capable public defender office. But this has not always been the case, and there is a continuing awareness in the agency of the need to protect against subordinating the goal of criminal defense to the needs of the system.

The majority of the indigent defendants in Washington, as in other cities, are represented by private attorneys, who fall into three broad categories: the regulars, the uptown lawyers, and the neophytes.

The bulk of these cases are handled by a relatively small coterie of what are commonly called "courthouse regulars." These lawyers were depicted by the ABA Criminal Justice Project as "a cadre of mediocre lawyers who wait in the courtroom in the hopes of receiving an appointment" and have "more expertise at extracting a fee . . . than in defending a criminal case." [28] . . . Today in the District of Columbia, as well as in many states, these lawyers get their "modest fee" from public programs for compensation of appointed counsel such as the Federal Criminal Justice Act.[a] . . .

The Criminal Justice Act provides for payment on a per-hour basis with a statutory per case maximum. It is, in effect, a piece-work system of compensation. The more cases a "regular" handles, the more income he receives. The essential element in the regulars' practice is volume — . . .

Although the high-volume "regulars" are relatively few, they are assigned a percentage of appointed cases far out of proportion to their numbers. The result of their high-volume practice is that they often have little or no time to prepare a case or even to talk to their clients. Although the investigative services of the public defender are available to all appointed counsel, the "regulars" rarely bother. They often investigate a case by questioning the arresting officer for a few furtive minutes in the corridors of the courthouse, filling in the gaps through examination of witnesses during the trial.

Why do we tolerate this type of representation? Some argue that the "regulars" get better results for their clients than more zealous lawyers. A federal judge once warned me that the tenacious new breed of defense lawyers would only aggravate judges, resulting in fewer dismissals and longer sentences for their clients. The "regulars" probably justify their type of representation on the basis of just such a view.

Their rationalization, however, has serious implications. To the extent the quality of justice depends on an incestuous relationship between judges and attorneys, the adversary quality of the system is corrupted; but that alone is too simple a response. This rationalization is not necessarily a matter of bad faith; it may be a result of system maintenance pressures. When non-assertive lawyers get better deals for their clients, the system is rewarding them for saving the court's time. This is borne out by a recent study in Massachusetts showing that defendants who waive counsel generally get lower sentences than those who do not;[35] the system evidences its need for efficiency by pressuring defendants into not cluttering up the system with lawyers at all. That obviously strikes at the very heart of the adversary system, the sixth amendment and the right to trial itself. . . .

The District of Columbia has made efforts to circumvent some of these problems by assigning cases to the "uptown" lawyers — corporate, labor, securities, or patent attorneys — who are rarely seen in the vicinity of the courthouse. Most do not want anything to do with the criminal justice system; they may share the attitude of the Carl Sandburg character, who was asked whether there was a criminal lawyer in his town. "We think so," he replied, "but we haven't been able to prove it on him." [40] These attorneys accept appointments only as a matter of public duty and, on the whole, do fairly well, particularly if they

---

28. ABA Project on Minimum Standards for Criminal Justice, Providing Defense Services (app. draft 1971) [hereinafter cited as ABA Project].

a. 18 U.S.C. §3006A. — EDS.

35. See S. Bing & S. Rosenfeld, The Quality of Justice in the Lower Criminal Courts of Metropolitan Boston (1970); Harris, Annals of Law: In the Criminal Court 1, The New Yorker, April 14, 1973 at 45.

40. C. Sandburg, The People, Yes (1936).

have had some criminal law experience. But many others, including leaders of the bar in other fields of law, do not. In spite of the myth that all lawyers are generalists, criminal defense is a specialty. It requires a skilled trial advocate who is familiar with the criminal justice system, including not only the criminal code but also police and prosecutorial practices, the availability of local experts and private crime labs and the informal norms of the criminal courts. Certainly any self-respecting prosecutor would be familiar with these aspects of the system. Is it fair to saddle a defendant with counsel who is not? . . .

Another mode of providing counsel, one that is prevalent in many parts of the country, is assigning the most junior members of the bar to criminal appointments. This approach, too, is troublesome, as the ABA's Project on Standards for Criminal Justice has recognized.[41] Defense of an indigent is not an extension of law school. If criminal representation is too complex for the "uptown" practitioner, it is obviously beyond the grasp of a lawyer with no experience at all. You may have heard the familiar refrain: "I got experience — my client got jail." I, for one, would not like to be the defendant whose trial is the vehicle for some young lawyer to gain trial practice. The medical profession is often accused of letting new doctors get their training by practicing on the poor without the close supervision they need. The charge applies with equal force to our own profession.

Our inability to provide every defendant with an effective defense is also due to the failure of legal education. Law schools do not teach students how to try criminal cases. The ordinary law school graduate trying his first criminal case not only does not know what to do next; he does not know what to do first. Unlike his Wall Street counterpart, whose firm provides a closely supervised apprenticeship period, the neophyte criminal lawyer is not apt to find such on-the-job training programs. The Wall Street litigator may take three years to argue his first motion; he may never try a case entirely on his own. The criminal lawyer may have his first solo case a few weeks after passing the bar.

A common fear is that a neophyte will compensate for his inexperience by engaging in unnecessarily vigorous and hostile advocacy. But the supervisors of two of the leading legal internship programs believe that the opposite is the case; the unsupervised junior attorney is more apt to bury his anxiety by copping a plea or falling into the pattern of docility that he sees in the practice of the criminal court regulars. To their credit, the law schools have begun to deal with both of these dangers through clinical programs which provide the absolutely essential element of supervision at a critical juncture in the student's socialization process. Because of the need for close supervision, good clinical programs are expensive. As one would expect, some programs are good and some not so good. Without provision for careful supervision, they can become just another way of throwing the neophyte into the water where either he will swim or his client will sink.

PEOPLE v. PEREZ, 24 Cal. 3d 133, 594 P.2d 1 (1979): [The California Supreme Court upheld a state student-practice rule under which the defendant had been

41. ABA Project, supra note 28, at 28-29 (discussing recommendations for training the inexperienced attorney). . . . Problems with the neophyte appointment have often been presented to the courts. The typical treatment in the majority of courts has been to regard youth and inexperience as irrelevant to the determination of effective assistance of counsel. . . .

represented by a law student, acting under the supervision of a deputy public defender, at a jury trial for burglary (a felony). The court said:] We share defendant's concern over the risks posed by representation by inexperienced counsel. Every trial attorney, however, is inexperienced when he tries his first case; the real question . . . is whether the attorney should begin to acquire that experience as a student pursuant to rules which require close supervision by experienced counsel, or only after becoming a member of the bar when no such supervision is required. A doctrinaire adherence to the fiction that admission to the bar, and that alone, confers competence to appear on behalf of a criminal defendant would seriously impede progress toward the objective of providing defendants with counsel who are able in fact to provide a reasonably competent defense.

[In a dissenting opinion Justice Mosk noted that the supervising attorney had contributed virtually nothing of substance to the trial and stressed that an experienced supervisor cannot undo the harm that may be caused, for example, by inept handling of a difficult witness. He concluded: L]aw school clinical programs . . . are a useful adjunct to the classroom . . . [b]ut there are pragmatic limits to the professional services that students should be permitted to undertake. A felony trial transcends those limits.

NOTE ON METHODS FOR PROVIDING DEFENSE SERVICES[13]

The various approaches currently employed for providing representation to indigent criminal defendants in the United States can be grouped into four general categories:

(1) ad hoc appointment of counsel
(2) assigned-counsel programs
(3) defender offices
(4) mixed systems relying on both defender offices and assigned-counsel programs

The *ad hoc system* is the oldest method for providing defense services, and, although it has largely been abandoned in the large urban jurisdictions serving the bulk of the nation's population, 72 percent of all United States counties still utilize the ad hoc approach. Under this system appointments are made by the trial judges from lists compiled by the court or the local bar association. Often appointments are simply made from among the attorneys present in court when the case is called. The ad hoc approach has numerous drawbacks: It creates a strong potential for favoritism and discrimination in the assignment of cases; the dependency of attorneys on judicial favor for continued appointments jeopardizes the independence of counsel and the vigor of the adversary system; when lawyers are unavailable, defendants often are improperly pressured into

13. This Note is drawn primarily from the Report of the National Study Commission on Defense Services, Guidelines for Legal Defense Systems in the United States (1976), at, especially, 123-179, 462-484, and from these supplementary sources: American Bar Association, Standards for Criminal Justice, Providing Defense Services (2d ed. 1980); J. Casper, American Criminal Justice: The Defendant's Perspective (1972); Wilkerson, Public Defenders as Their Clients See Them, 1 Am. J. Crim. L. 141 (1972); Note, Client Service in a Defender Organization, 117 U. Pa. L. Rev. 448 (1969).

waiving the right to counsel; compensation provided is often inadequate or, at best, uneven; appointments typically are made much later than desirable; and investigative and other support services are normally unavailable or inadequate.

Under an *assigned-counsel program,* attorneys in private practice are appointed as cases arise, but in accordance with a systematic plan implemented by an administrator responsible to the court or the local bar association. This approach assures a more even distribution of the burdens and benefits of representation, better protects the independence of defense counsel, and eliminates much of the vulnerability of the assignment system to patronage and political influence. This method is generally considered more costly, however, than systems employing defenders who handle large numbers of cases for a fixed salary, and relatively few jurisdictions currently rely on assigned-counsel programs.

Defender systems rely on a staff of salaried lawyers who devote most or all of their time to representation of indigent defendants. Most defender organizations are governmental agencies, but roughly one-third of all metropolitan defenders and 50 percent of all rural defenders work for private, nonprofit corporations or associations which are run by an independent board of directors and which provide services under contract with the local government or court. Roughly 64 percent of the nation's population now resides in counties served by defender systems. Defender organizations afford the advantages of specialization and efficiency. Often, however, they are seen by defendants as part of "the system," the same governmental bureaucracy that is prosecuting and judging them.[14] Also, defender organizations often accept more cases than they can comfortably handle; as a result they may face heavy pressure to dispose of cases rapidly by plea or otherwise to cooperate with prosecutors and judges in expeditiously processing the daily workload.

A common response by defender organizations to the problems of heavy caseload is the system of sequential or stage representation, often called the "zone defense." Under this system an individual defender may spend a week or more assigned to a particular courtroom, handling (for example) a continual flow of bail applications, arraignments, or preliminary hearings. A defendant normally will see one attorney at the bail hearing and a new attorney at each subsequent stage of the case. This approach enables defenders to avoid the complexities of scheduling numerous appearances in different courtrooms (often in different parts of the city), greatly reduces travel and waiting time, permits a greater degree of specialization in the law and practice of particular litigation stages, and provides for more gradual training and advancement, so that the most complicated and important assignments (felony jury trials, for example) can be handled by the most experienced defenders.

Nevertheless, stage representation has been the target of much bitter criticism. Clients often report feeling buffeted from one lawyer to another or abandoned altogether;[15] in the end many feel that they have not been represented by counsel

14. At least one study, however, has found the same distrust in defendants' attitudes toward appointed counsel; like public defenders, appointed counsel are perceived as paid by and therefore beholden to the state. See J. Casper, supra page 32 footnote 13, at 31.

15. For an extreme example of a case in which stage representation "left petitioner to the most brutal and horrifying kind of isolation, effectively walled off for months from any genuine assistance by a facade of 'representation,' " see United States ex rel. Thomas v. Zelker, 332 F. Supp. 595, 599 (S.D.N.Y. 1971). See also Wallace v. Kern, 392 F. Supp. 834 (E.D.N.Y.), *rev'd on other grounds,* 481 F.2d 621 (2d Cir. 1973).

but only "processed" by the system. Poor client rapport not only damages client perceptions of the fairness of the judicial process but undermines the effectiveness of the services actually performed. Frank discussions between attorney and client can be impeded and the danger of serious failures of communication enhanced. Moreover, the division of labor may prevent the development of a unified trial strategy and may diffuse responsibility for the outcome of the case. These factors are even said to promote an assembly-line mentality among defenders themselves, thus diminishing job satisfaction and in turn impairing immediate effectiveness and aggravating the problem of overly rapid turnover of experienced defenders.

The principal national study commissions have strongly condemned stage representation and insisted on continuity in the attorney-client relationship (at least through the sentencing stage).[16] Reliance on the stage system nevertheless remains widespread.[17] If the heavy caseloads and relatively low budgets of many defender organizations are taken as given, stage representation may, for all its drawbacks, yield better results than could a system of continuous representation operating under the same constraints. Does this suggest that stage representation should be considered acceptable? Or that the heavy caseloads and low budgets should be considered unacceptable? Why should a defender agency, with a staff of perhaps 25 or 50 attorneys, consider itself obliged to accept all of the thousands of cases assigned to it by the court? Is there any feasible alternative?[18]

NOTE ON THE EFFECTIVENESS OF COUNSEL

The constitutional right to counsel would mean little if it could be satisfied by appointment of a totally incompetent attorney. Constitutional doctrines determining the level of competence required in criminal cases and establishing remedies for cases in which this minimal level is not reached are an important dimension of the Sixth Amendment and of the wider framework of principles governing the functioning of the adversary system. We take up the question of ineffective assistance, along with problems concerning ethical responsibilities of counsel, beginning at page 108 infra.

16. See, e.g., National Study Commission, page 32 footnote 13, at 477; American Bar Association, supra page 32 footnote 13, at §5-5.2.

17. Courts have questioned whether stage representation satisfies constitutional requirements but have stopped short of condemning that system per se. See, e.g., Moore v. United States, 432 F.2d 730 (3d Cir. 1970).

18. Although many defender agencies are obligated by their charters to accept all cases assigned, the American Bar Association recommends that agencies with an excessive workload refuse additional cases and, if necessary, insist that pending cases be transferred to assigned counsel. See American Bar Association, supra page 32 footnote 13, at §5-4.3 and Commentary at 5·48-50. For efforts by defendants to enjoin defender agencies from accepting additional cases, see Gardner v. Luckey, 500 F.2d 712 (5th Cir. 1974); Wallace v. Kern, 392 F. Supp. 834 (E.D.N.Y.), rev'd, 481 F.2d 621 (2d Cir. 1973). In Escambia County v. Behr, 384 So. 2d 147 (Fla. 1980), the Florida Supreme Court upheld the right of a public defender to withdraw from the case on the ground of excessive caseload, even though Florida statutes imposed on the defender a duty to provide representation to all indigent defendants.

2. *The Presentation of Evidence*

INTRODUCTORY NOTE

At trial the evidence is presented in accordance with a formally prescribed order. The prosecution first calls witnesses in an effort to prove the elements of the offense charged. As we have seen in Section A of this chapter, pages 15-17 supra, the case may terminate at this point if the prosecution fails to sustain its preliminary burden of proof. If not, the defense may then call witnesses in an effort to refute the prosecution's *case-in-chief* or to establish some *affirmative defense.* The prosecution then has an opportunity to recall witnesses or to call new witnesses solely for purposes of *rebuttal,* that is, to refute evidence offered by the defense. The defense in turn is afforded a chance to meet by *rejoinder* any matters introduced in the prosecutor's rebuttal.

Within these stages the examination of each witness follows a similar pattern. The witness is first questioned by the party that called the witness (*direct examination*), and afterward the opposing party has an opportunity to question that witness (*cross-examination*). Further questioning by the first party (*re-direct*) and by the opposing side (*re-cross*) may follow.

The rules governing the admissibility of evidence are extremely detailed and complex. For present purposes, it will be useful to begin by focusing on one obvious but deceptively simple requirement that has pervasive importance, the rule of relevancy. First, evidence is *never* admissible if it is irrelevant. The converse cannot be stated so categorically. Relevant evidence is *generally* admissible, but there are many exceptions to this principle. Before turning to these exceptions, we must first be clear about the meaning of *relevancy.*

Evidence is considered relevant for purposes of the rules of evidence only if it is both *probative* and *material,* and these are precise terms of art. Evidence is probative only if it tends to establish the proposition for which it is offered or — to be precise — if the proposition is more likely to be true given the evidence than it would be without the evidence. Thus, if the proposition to be proved is that *H* was the person who killed his wife *W,* evidence of a motive (that is, that *H* stood to inherit a substantial estate on *W*'s death) is probative. Of course, the existence of the motive does not, by itself, make it probable that *H* is the killer, but *H* is more likely to be the killer if he had a motive than if he did not; this greater likelihood is all that is required to establish probative value.

Probative value alone is often thought of as synonymous with relevancy. But relevancy for purposes of the rules of evidence requires in addition that the proposition that the evidence tends to prove be one that is legally material in the sense that proof of the proposition must affect the outcome of the case under applicable law. So, for example, evidence in a homicide prosecution that defendant acted in self-defense is material because under the substantive law self-defense is a defense. But evidence that the deceased consented to be killed is not material, because under the substantive law consent by the victim is not a defense to a homicide charge. Thus, evidence may be excluded as irrelevant for one of two distinct reasons — either because the evidence does not tend to establish the proposition in question or because that proposition is not material to the outcome of the case. The materiality requirement means that the first prerequisite for determining the relevancy and hence the admissibility of evidence is a command of the substantive law of crimes.

We may sum up what we have so far said about relevancy by quoting the formulation used in the Federal Rules of Evidence:

RULE 401
"Relevant evidence" means evidence having any tendency to make the existence of any fact that is of consequence to the determination of the action more probable or less probable than it would be without the evidence.

RULE 402
All relevant evidence is admissible, except as otherwise provided. . . . Evidence which is not relevant is not admissible.

Under what circumstances is relevant evidence *not* admissible? The law of evidence embodies dozens of distinct rules requiring the exclusion of relevant evidence. For example, the various rules relating to *privilege* give witnesses the right to withhold certain kinds of testimony, often in order to protect particular interests of the witness or specially important relationships with others. We examine one of the most important privileges, the privilege against self-incrimination, later in this chapter. See pages 49-64 infra. Some of the other important exclusionary rules will be considered in connection with the substantive crimes for which they have the greatest significance.[19] The present section explores one rather open-ended exclusionary rule of pervasive importance — the rule calling for exclusion of evidence whenever its probative value is outweighed by its *prejudicial effect*.

The term *prejudicial effect* possesses a rather technical meaning. To pursue the example previously mentioned, suppose that in *H*'s murder prosecution testimony is offered to the effect that shortly before the discovery of *W*'s bullet-ridden body, *H* was seen running from the scene carrying a smoking revolver. This testimony will undoubtedly be quite harmful to *H*'s chances for acquittal, but it will not be prejudicial, in the technical sense, because its harmfulness flows solely from its legitimate probative value. Evidence is considered prejudicial only when it is likely to affect the result in some *improper* way. Thus, prejudice is involved if the jury is likely to overestimate the probative value of the evidence or if the evidence will arouse undue hostility toward one of the parties.

The next case illustrates the application of these principles and their relationship to basic conceptions of criminal responsibility.

PEOPLE v. ZACKOWITZ
New York Court of Appeals
254 N.Y. 192, 172 N.E. 466 (1930)

[Defendant was convicted of first-degree murder and sentenced to death.]
CARDOZO, C.J. On November 10, 1929, shortly after midnight, the defendant

---

19. The hearsay rule and one of its important exceptions are explored in connection with conspiracy law, pages 643-654 infra. Special restrictions intended to protect the privacy of a witness are examined in connection with the materials on rape, pages 396-405 infra.

in Kings county shot Frank Coppola and killed him without justification or excuse. A crime is admitted. What is doubtful is the degree only.

Four young men, of whom Coppola was one, were at work repairing an automobile in a Brooklyn street. A woman, the defendant's wife, walked by on the opposite side. One of the men spoke to her insultingly, or so at least she understood him. The defendant, who had dropped behind to buy a newspaper, came up to find his wife in tears. He was told she had been insulted, though she did not then repeat the words. Enraged, he stepped across the street and upbraided the offenders with words of coarse profanity. He informed them, so the survivors testify, that "if they did not get out of there in five minutes, he would come back and bump them all off." Rejoining his wife, he walked with her to their apartment house located close at hand. He was heated with liquor which he had been drinking at a dance. Within the apartment he induced her to tell him what the insulting words had been. A youth had asked her to lie with him, and had offered her two dollars. With rage aroused again, the defendant went back to the scene of the insult and found the four young men still working at the car. In a statement to the police, he said that he had armed himself at the apartment with a twenty-five calibre automatic pistol. In his testimony at the trial he said that this pistol had been in his pocket all the evening. Words and blows followed, and then a shot. The defendant kicked Coppola in the stomach. There is evidence that Coppola went for him with a wrench. The pistol came from the pocket, and from the pistol a single shot, which did its deadly work. . . .

At the trial the vital question was the defendant's state of mind at the moment of the homicide. Did he shoot with a deliberate and premeditated design to kill? Was he so inflamed by drink or by anger or by both combined that, though he knew the nature of his act, he was the prey to sudden impulse, the fury of the fleeting moment? [a] If he went forth from his apartment with a preconceived design to kill, how is it that he failed to shoot at once? How reconcile such a design with the drawing of the pistol later in the heat and rage of an affray? These and like questions the jurors were to ask themselves and answer before measuring the defendant's guilt. Answers consistent with guilt in its highest grade can reasonably be made. Even so, the line between impulse and deliberation is too narrow and elusive to make the answers wholly clear. The sphygmograph records with graphic certainty the fluctuations of the pulse. There is no instrument yet invented that records with equal certainty the fluctuations of the mind. At least, if such an instrument exists, it was not working at midnight in the Brooklyn street when Coppola and the defendant came together in a chance affray. With only the rough and ready tests supplied by their experience of life, the jurors were to look into the workings of another's mind, and discover its capacities and disabilities, its urges and inhibitions, in moments of intense excitement. Delicate enough and subtle is the inquiry, even in the most favorable conditions, with every warping influence excluded. There must be no blurring

---

a. Under New York law, a deliberate and premeditated killing would be first-degree murder, while a killing provoked in "the fury of the fleeting moment" would be first-degree manslaughter (often called "voluntary manslaughter"). At the time of the *Zackowitz* decision the former offense was punishable by death and the latter by imprisonment for up to 20 years. N.Y. Penal Law §§1045, 1051 (1909). For current penalty provisions in New York and other representative states, see pages 410-415 infra. — EDS.

of the issues by evidence illegally admitted and carrying with it in its admission an appeal to prejudice and passion.

Evidence charged with that appeal was, we think, admitted here. . . . Almost at the opening of the trial the People began the endeavor to load the defendant down with the burden of an evil character. He was to be put before the jury as a man of murderous disposition. To that end they were allowed to prove that at the time of the encounter and at that of his arrest he had in his apartment, kept there in a radio box, three pistols and a tear-gas gun. There was no claim that he had brought these weapons out at the time of the affray, no claim that with any of them he had discharged the fatal shot. He could not have done so, for they were all of different calibre. The end to be served by laying the weapons before the jury was something very different. The end was to bring persuasion that here was a man of vicious and dangerous propensities, who because of those propensities was more likely to kill with deliberate and premeditated design than a man of irreproachable life and amiable manners. Indeed, this is the very ground on which the introduction of the evidence is now explained and defended. The District Attorney tells us in his brief that the possession of the weapons characterized the defendant as "a desperate type of criminal," a "person criminally inclined." The dissenting opinion, if it puts the argument less bluntly, leaves the substance of the thought unchanged. "Defendant was presented to the jury as a man having dangerous weapons in his possession, making a selection therefrom and going forth to put into execution his threats to kill." The weapons were not brought by the defendant to the scene of the encounter. They were left in his apartment where they were incapable of harm. In such circumstances, ownership of the weapons, if it has any relevance at all, has relevance only as indicating a general disposition to make use of them thereafter, and a general disposition to make use of them thereafter is without relevance except as indicating a "desperate type of criminal," a criminal affected with a murderous propensity. . . .

If a murderous propensity may be proved against a defendant as one of the tokens of his guilt, a rule of criminal evidence, long believed to be of fundamental importance for the protection of the innocent, must be first declared away. Fundamental hitherto has been the rule that character is never an issue in a criminal prosecution unless the defendant chooses to make it one (Wigmore, Evidence, vol. 1, §§55, 192). In a very real sense a defendant starts his life afresh when he stands before a jury, a prisoner at the bar. There has been a homicide in a public place. The killer admits the killing, but urges self-defense and sudden impulse. Inflexibly the law has set its face against the endeavor to fasten guilt upon him by proof of character or experience predisposing to an act of crime. . . . The principle back of the exclusion is one, not of logic, but of policy. There may be cogency in the argument that a quarrelsome defendant is more likely to start a quarrel than one of milder type, a man of dangerous mode of life more likely than a shy recluse. The law is not blind to this, but equally it is not blind to the peril to the innocent if character is accepted as probative of crime. "The natural and inevitable tendency of the tribunal — whether judge or jury — is to give excessive weight to the vicious record of crime thus exhibited, and either to allow it to bear too strongly on the present charge, or to take the proof of it as justifying a condemnation irrespective of guilt of the present charge" (Wigmore, Evidence, vol. 1, §194, and cases cited).

A different question would be here if the pistols had been bought in expectation of this particular encounter. They would then have been admissible as evidence of preparation and design. A different question would be here if they were so connected with the crime as to identify the perpetrator, if he had dropped them, for example, at the scene of the affray. They would then have been admissible as tending to implicate the possessor (if identity was disputed), no matter what the opprobrium attached to his possession. Different, also, would be the question if the defendant had been shown to have gone forth from the apartment with all the weapons on his person. To be armed from head to foot at the very moment of an encounter may be a circumstance worthy to be considered, like acts of preparation generally, as a proof of preconceived design. There can be no such implication from the ownership of weapons which one leaves behind at home.

The endeavor was to generate an atmosphere of professional criminality. It was an endeavor the more unfair in that, apart from the suspicion attaching to the possession of these weapons, there is nothing to mark the defendant as a man of evil life. . . . If his own testimony be true, he had gathered these weapons together as curios, a collection that interested and amused him. Perhaps his explanation of their ownership is false. There is nothing stronger than mere suspicion to guide us to an answer. Whether the explanation be false or true, he should not have been driven by the People to the necessity of offering it. Brought to answer a specific charge, and to defend himself against it, he was placed in a position where he had to defend himself against another, more general and sweeping. He was made to answer to the charge, pervasive and poisonous even if insidious and covert, that he was a man of murderous heart, of criminal disposition. . . .

The judgment of conviction should be reversed, and a new trial ordered.

POUND, J. (dissenting). . . .

The People may not prove against a defendant crimes not alleged in the indictment committed on other occasions than the crime charged as aiding the proofs that he is guilty of the crime charged unless such proof tends to establish (1) motive; (2) intent; (3) absence of mistake or accident; (4) a common scheme or plan embracing the commission of two or more crimes so related to each other that proof of the one tends to establish the other; (5) the identity of the person charged with the commission of the crime on trial. These exceptions are stated generally and not with categorical precision and may not be all-inclusive. None of them apply here nor were the weapons offered under an exception to the general rule. They were offered as a part of the transaction itself. The accused was tried only for the crime charged. The real question is whether the matter relied on has such a connection with the crime charged as to be admissible on any ground. If so, the fact that it constitutes another distinct crime does not render it inadmissible. . . .

As the District Attorney argues in his brief, if defendant had been arrested at the time of the killing and these weapons had been found on his person, the People would not have been barred from proving the fact, and the further fact that they were nearby in his apartment should not preclude the proof as bearing on the entire deed of which the act charged forms a part. Defendant was presented to the jury as a man having dangerous weapons in his possession, making a selection therefrom and going forth to put into execution his threats to kill; not as a man of a dangerous disposition in general, but as one who, having an opportunity to select a weapon to carry out his threats, proceeded to do so. . . .

The judgment of conviction should be affirmed.

NOTES ON ZACKOWITZ

1. On the facts of *Zackowitz,* we may assume that the killing was intentional. The principal issue at trial was whether the killing was "deliberate" (that is, whether the intent to kill was formulated before the shot, making the crime murder) or whether the killing was instead "impulsive" (that is, whether the intent to kill was formulated in a heat of passion during the final scuffle, making the crime manslaughter). Does defendant's possession of the weapons have some bearing on this issue? Recall that very slight probative value is usually sufficient to render evidence admissible; for example, evidence that Zackowitz stood to inherit money from the victim would undoubtedly be admissible as tending to show a motive for a deliberate killing. Does the evidence of weapons possession have at least that much probative value?

2. If the weapons evidence was relevant, as Judge (later Mr. Justice) Cardozo seems to assume, are there convincing reasons for excluding it? Cardozo stresses that the issue in the case was a "delicate" and "subtle" one. Under these circumstances was it not particularly important for the jury to have access to as much relevant evidence as possible? In which case will the trier of fact be better able to evaluate what actually happened: when it knows about the weapons, knows the defendant's explanation for them, and has a chance to judge the credibility of that explanation or when — as *Zackowitz* requires — all of this information is withheld?

The court's holding may be based in part on a concern that the probative value of the evidence will be outweighed by its prejudicial effect — that the jury will " 'allow it to bear too heavily on the present charge, or . . . take the proof of it as justifying condemnation irrespective of guilt of the present charge' [quoting Wigmore]." As applied to the facts of *Zackowitz,* is this concern really convincing? How great was the danger that the evidence would be given *improper* weight? Notice that Wigmore, from whom the court's quotation was taken, was referring to a "vicious record of crime." It is easy to see that a defendant charged with rape may suffer extreme prejudice of the kind described if the jury learns that he has already been convicted for rape on three or four prior occasions. Is there comparable danger of prejudice, of the jury's giving evidence *improper* weight, when (as in *Zackowitz*) the evidence shows that a defendant charged with first-degree murder is guilty of relatively minor offenses of weapons possession?

NOTES ON "OTHER-CRIMES" EVIDENCE UNDER CURRENT LAW

1. The general rule and its foundations. Subject to certain exceptions to be explored below, the basic principle invoked by the majority in *Zackowitz* appears to enjoy universal acceptance: Other crimes (and indeed any other kind of evidence designed to show "bad character") may not be introduced in order to show that the accused had an evil disposition and thus was more likely to have committed the offense charged.

What is the justification for this rule? McCormick states that such evidence "is not irrelevant, but in the setting of jury trial the danger of prejudice outweighs the probative value." C. McCormick, Evidence §190, at 447 (2d ed. 1972).[20] Undoubtedly, this statement holds true in a very wide range of contexts. But, as we saw in examining *Zackowitz*, there can be situations in which the danger of prejudice is arguably insufficient to justify the exclusion. And when a judge tries the case without a jury, the danger that the evidence will exert improper influence on the result, while not entirely absent, seems considerably less, as McCormick's statement itself implies. Should the rule of inadmissibility be abandoned when the case is tried to a judge?[21] Or are there other, perhaps more basic, reasons for restricting the admissibility of other-crimes evidence?

Consider how the criminal process would be affected if the prosecution were free to support its case by proving previous instances of criminal conduct by the accused. The defendant, who of course is contesting the charges of the present indictment, may deny having committed the other crimes as well. In particular, if the prosecution has not already obtained a formal conviction for the other crimes (that was the case in *Zackowitz*, for example), the entire focus of the trial could be diverted by the dispute about whether the other crimes were in fact committed.

Even if the defendant admits to committing other crimes or the other crimes are easily proved by a record of prior convictions, the defendant may feel called upon to explain the background of the other offenses or to claim extenuating circumstances. (This too happened in *Zackowitz*). The vice here is not simply that time and attention may be diverted from the main issue in the case. It is also that a defendant should not be forever obliged to explain prior transgressions in order to dispel suspicions of further misconduct. Thus, a person who has suffered conviction and sentence is said to have "paid his debt to society"; the slate should be wiped clean. Cardozo alludes to these concerns when he states: "In a very real sense a defendant starts his life afresh when he stands before a jury, a prisoner at the bar. . . . Whether the explanation [for Zackowitz's possession of the weapons] be true or false, he should not have been driven by the people to the necessity of offering it."

Whether or not a defendant has already "paid his debt" for the prior offense, basic assumptions about criminal responsibility are tested when the focus of the trial becomes centered on the defendant's general character rather than on his behavior in a discrete situation. To be sure, a trial designed to determine a defendant's responsibility for particular events often must explore many cir-

---

20. See also Michelson v. United States, 335 U.S. 469, 475-476 (1948): "The inquiry is not rejected because character is irrelevant; on the contrary it is said to weigh too much with the jury and to so overpersuade them as to prejudge one with a bad general record and deny him a fair opportunity to defend against a particular charge."

21. Courts have differed in their treatment of other-crimes evidence in nonjury trials. Compare United States v. Martinez, 333 F.2d 80 (2d Cir. 1964) (holding such evidence inadmissible), with State v. Garcia, 97 Ariz. 102, 397 P.2d 214 (1964) (treating admission of such evidence as technically improper but presuming that judge gave no weight to it). See generally Levin & Cohen, The Exclusionary Rules in Nonjury Criminal Cases, 119 U. Pa. L. Rev. 905 (1971); Note, Improper Evidence in Nonjury Trials: Basis for Reversal?, 79 Harv. L. Rev. 407 (1965).

cumstances of his life, but ultimately the events themselves are at issue, the concrete behavior precisely specified in the charges. The criminal trial usually is not viewed as a vehicle for passing judgment on the whole person. Again, Cardozo alludes to this principle: "Brought to answer a specific charge, [the defendant] had to defend himself against another, more general and sweeping[,] . . . pervasive and poisonous even if insidious and covert, that he was a man of murderous heart, of criminal disposition."

Consider whether the values described should be treated as fundamental to a just system of criminal law. Are they, for example, more important than the most accurate possible determination of the truth? Should they apply with as much force in proceedings to determine sentence (or the *degree* of the offense in *Zackowitz*) as they do when the issue is guilt versus innocence? [22] Consider the extent to which these values in fact *are* respected, or flouted, by the doctrines of criminal law examined in the remainder of this section and throughout this book.

2. Exceptions to the rule. Situations in which other-crimes evidence might be admissible are mentioned by the court in *Zackowitz,* and the dissenting opinion presents five specific "exceptions" to the rule of exclusion.[23] Thus, for example, if a defendant is prosecuted for the murder of *V,* evidence that the defendant previously committed a robbery witnessed by *V* will be admissible — not to show that the defendant was generally disposed to violence but rather to show his *motive* for this particular killing. Similarly, evidence that the defendant had previously stolen the pistol with which *V* was shot will be admissible — not to show the defendant's disposition to crime but to help *identify* him as the killer. Many other exceptions could be given. Treatises on evidence discuss the various possible categories in detail, and the categories themselves probably are not firm or all-inclusive.[24] The central point is that other-crimes evidence may be admissible if it is offered for some specific purpose *other than* that of suggesting that the defendant may have committed the crime because he or she has a bad character. Nevertheless it is not always easy to tell whether the evidence links the defendant to the crime in some legitimate way or whether it simply suggests a general criminal propensity. As a result, careless application of the exceptions can easily undermine the rule and the values it should protect. Consider these important exceptions:

(*a*) *The signature exception.* Evidence of other crimes committed by the defendant is admissible when the other crimes are "so nearly identical in method as to earmark them as the handiwork of the accused. . . . The device used must be so unusual and distinctive as to be like a signature." McCormick, page 41 supra, §190, at 449. The most famous illustration of this rule is the "brides in the bath" case, Rex v. Smith, 84 Cr. App. (K.B.) 137 (1915). The defendant's wife was found drowned in her bathtub shortly after she had executed a will in his

---

22. For exploration of the question whether punishment should be tailored to the character of the offender rather than the seriousness of the offense, see Chapter 3 infra.

23. Technically speaking, these situations do not involve exceptions to the rule of exclusion because, properly stated, that rule renders other-crimes evidence inadmissible only when offered "to prove the character of a person in order to show that he acted in conformity therewith." Fed. R. Evid. 404(b). In other words, the rule itself does not bar the use of other-crimes evidence for some purpose *other than* that of suggesting that he acted in conformity with a bad character.

24. See McCormick, page 41 supra, §190, at 447-454; 1 J. Wigmore, Evidence §§192-194 (3d ed. 1940).

favor. At his trial for her murder, the prosecution was allowed to prove that after this wife's death the defendant made two subsequent marriages, both of which had ended when the new bride, shortly after making a will in the defendant's favor, was found drowned in her bath. Here the uniqueness of the modus operandi gave the other crimes strong probative value as evidence of guilt.[25] However, courts have often had difficulty determining whether the pattern of criminality is sufficiently unusual. In the cases following, does the other-crimes evidence suggest a distinctive signature or at most only a propensity to commit offenses of some general type?

(i) *D* is charged with murdering a relative who had disappeared and was later found dead from a gunshot wound in the neck. Should the prosecution be permitted to prove that more than 20 years earlier, *D* had been convicted of murdering another relative who had disappeared and who also was later found dead from a gunshot wound in the neck? See People v. Peete, 28 Cal. 2d 306, 169 P.2d 924 (1946).

(ii) *H* and *M* are charged with committing a series of three robberies over a five-month period. In all three cases two armed men, wearing handkerchiefs over their faces, used an employees' entrance to enter stores shortly after closing time, forced some of the employees to lie down on the floor, and fled with large amounts of cash. Should the prosecution be permitted to prove that two years earlier *H* and *M* had robbed two restaurants in the same fashion? See People v. Haston, 69 Cal. 2d 233, 444 P.2d 91 (1969).

(iii) *S* is charged with picking up a woman in a bar, offering to drive her home, and then raping her in his car. *S* claims that the woman consented to intercourse. Should the prosecution be permitted to prove that a month earlier *S* had committed rape after picking up a victim in a bar under similar circumstances? See State v. Sauter, 125 Mont. 109, 232 P.2d 731 (1951).

(*b*) *The impeachment exception.* In all of the situations so far discussed, the question has been whether the prosecution can use evidence of other crimes as part of its case-in-chief. Even when the other-crimes evidence is clearly inadmissible for this purpose, if the accused chooses to testify in his own defense, then the prosecution generally will be permitted to ask about the other crimes in its cross-examination of the accused and to introduce other-crimes evidence in its rebuttal for purposes of impeaching the defendant's testimony. In theory, the other-crimes evidence may not be used to provide affirmative support for the prosecution's case. It may be considered only for purposes of judging the credibility of the defendant's testimony, and the jury will be so instructed.

The rationale of the impeachment exception appears to be that a person convicted of crime may be less trustworthy and more likely to give false testimony than a citizen with a "clean" record.[26] Whatever the soundness of this rationale

---

25. Notice the assumption that the two other incidents *were* crimes. In *Smith* the prosecution probably could not prove guilt beyond a reasonable doubt in any one incident taken by itself. But if there is a likelihood of guilt (that is, a 51 percent chance) in each instance, considered separately, and if the incidents can then be considered together, the jury might be convinced beyond a reasonable doubt of the defendant's guilt in all three of them. For a striking, recent example of other-crimes evidence used in this way, see United States v. Woods, 484 F.2d 127 (4th Cir. 1973).

26. At common law a person convicted of treason, felony, or other crime of infamy or dishonesty (crimen falsi) was disqualified from testifying as a witness. In the mid-1800s, when common law jurisdictions moved to remove the absolute disqualification, they generally provided by statute that prior convictions of the witness could be introduced for purposes of impeachment. See 2 J. Wigmore §§519-520 (3d ed. 1940); 3A J. Wigmore §§986-987 (Chadbourn rev. 1970).

when the previous misconduct involves perjury or other crimes of dishonesty, its invocation in the case of many crimes can border on the absurd. In a prosecution for rape, previous rape convictions are clearly inadmissible for the purpose of showing the defendant's disposition to commit this crime, but if the defendant claims to have been elsewhere at the time, the rape convictions will generally be held admissible to show a possibility that the defendant may be disposed to perjury! In recent years an increasing number of courts have recognized the injustice of this unqualified exception for impeachment use of prior offenses; these courts require admissibility to be determined on a case-by-case basis, weighing such factors as the recency of the prior offense, whether the crime involved dishonesty, and whether the crime was so similar to that charged as to enhance the danger of prejudice.[27] Even in these limited terms, the impeachment exception presents a striking anomaly. If the defendant is prosecuted for perjury, previous convictions for perjury or other dishonest behavior cannot be introduced as part of the prosecution's case-in-chief in order to show the defendant's propensity to lie under oath, but whenever a defendant chooses to testify, the prior convictions become admissible precisely for that purpose. In any event, most courts apparently still adhere to the exception in its broad, unqualified form: Once the defendant takes the stand, evidence of previous convictions for felony or other serious crimes becomes admissible almost automatically, for purposes of impeaching his credibility.[28]

Consider the consequences of this rule for the focus of the criminal trial and for the foundations of criminal liability. To what extent does the impeachment exception impair the values reflected in the general rule against use of other-crimes evidence? Does it matter whether these values are preserved only when the defendant chooses not to testify? [29]

Of course, the impeachment exception is premised on the assumption that the jury will take account of the other crimes *only* for the limited purpose of judging credibility and will obey the instructions cautioning it not to treat the other crimes as affirmative evidence of guilt. But is this a plausible assumption? Lawyers and social scientists have studied the question but have not reached definitive conclusions. The Note that follows explores the effectiveness of cautionary instructions and collects some of the available findings. The problem immediately at hand is to understand how the rules concerning other-crimes evidence actually function, but questions about the effectiveness of jury instructions are central to understanding the actual impact of all the elaborately crafted rules of criminal law and evidence that the jury is called upon to apply.

NOTE ON THE EFFECTIVENESS OF JURY INSTRUCTIONS

When other-crimes evidence has been introduced for impeachment purposes, a typical instruction to the jury might read as follows (1 E. Devitt & C. Blackmar, Federal Jury Practice and Instructions §12.09 (2d ed. 1970)):

27. See Gordon v. United States, 383 F.2d 936 (D.C. Cir. 1967) (Burger, J.); Luck v. United States, 348 F.2d 763 (D.C. Cir. 1965). See also Fed. R. Evid. 609.

28. E.g., Commonwealth v. West, 357 Mass. 245, 258 N.E.2d 22 (1970); see 3A J. Wigmore §987 (Chadbourn rev. 1970).

29. It is sometimes said that, by deciding to testify, a defendant *chooses* to put his character in issue. Is this convincing? See State v. Santiago, 53 Hawaii 254, 492 P.2d 657 (1971).

> Evidence of a defendant's previous conviction of a felony is to be considered by the jury, only insofar as it may affect the credibility of the defendant as a witness, and must never be considered as evidence of guilt of the crime for which the defendant is on trial.

Such an instruction calls on the jury to perform an intellectual task that is bound to run counter to the jury's natural inclinations. Indeed the rule generally excluding other-crimes evidence is premised on the assumption that such evidence *is* relevant to guilt and is very difficult for the jury to keep in perspective once it becomes known. Thus jurors may be strongly tempted to disregard the instruction, even if they are able to grasp the rather subtle distinction it asks them to draw. The problem of course arises over and over in the administration of the complex body of substantive and evidentiary principles that ostensibly govern the criminal process. Yet just as the jury creates the need for many of these complicated rules, the nature of the jury at the same time raises doubts about whether subtle or strongly counter-intuitive instructions actually have an impact on the outcome of the case.

Experienced judges confronting this question have expressed sharply divergent views about the effectiveness of jury instructions. Sometimes the courts suggest that there is no practical alternative to reliance on instructions and therefore that the effectiveness of such instructions must be assumed. In Spencer v. Texas, 385 U.S. 554, 565 (1967), the Supreme Court expressed its faith in "the ability of juries to approach their task responsibly and to sort out discrete issues given to them under proper instructions. . . ." [30] Others have been more skeptical. Chief Justice Warren once wrote that "it flouts human nature to suppose that a jury would not consider a defendant's previous trouble with the law in deciding whether he has committed the crime charged against him." Id. at 575 (dissenting opinion). Justice Jackson put the point even more strongly: "The naive assumption that prejudicial effects can be overcome by instructions to the jury . . . all practicing lawyers know to be unmitigated fiction." Krulewitch v. United States, 336 U.S. 440, 453 (1949) (concurring opinion), reprinted at pages 643-647 infra.

In recent years social scientists have undertaken studies to determine where the truth lies. Such efforts are at best problematical because the experimental method cannot be applied directly to actual juries deciding actual cases. A com-

---

30. *Spencer* involved a challenge to the procedure followed under Texas habitual criminal statutes. The statutes provided for enhanced punishment for those convicted of crime who were shown to have been convicted of other crimes in the past. When the prosecution sought to invoke the enhanced-punishment provisions, the prior offenses would be alleged in the indictment and proved at trial. Thus the jurors trying the current charge would learn of the prior offenses, even though they would be instructed that those offenses could not be considered in determining the defendant's guilt for the present offense. The Court held that the Texas procedure was consistent with due process, rejecting the defendant's argument that the state should be required to postpone all reference to the prior offenses until after a verdict of conviction is rendered.

In a few discrete areas, however, the Court has held that cautionary instructions are inadequate to eliminate particularly severe prejudicial effects. For example, in Jackson v. Denno, 378 U.S. 368 (1964), the Court held unconstitutional a New York procedure under which juries were required to determine the voluntariness of a confession and instructed that in passing on the question of guilt they should disregard the confession if it was found involuntary. The Court held that in order to insure that an involuntary (and hence constitutionally inadmissible) confession did not contribute to the verdict, the trial judge must make a preliminary determination outside the jury's presence and exclude any confession found involuntary. See also Bruton v. United States, 391 U.S. 123 (1968).

monly used research strategy has been to record or transcribe an actual case and then submit different versions of it to groups of volunteer research subjects (often college undergraduates). The research subjects are asked to record their verdicts, and the researchers can then compare the percentages of guilty verdicts obtained in different versions of the case (for example, with and without a cautionary instruction). Unfortunately, research results obtained in this way are at best only suggestive and at worst highly misleading: The "case" is not presented in realistic courtroom fashion, the "jurors" are not representative of those likely to serve on an actual jury, and the research subjects often cast their votes without the group deliberations that can affect the final ballot of jurors in real cases.[31]

A more reliable but far more expensive technique for discovering the impact of jury instructions is to use groups of "jurors" drawn at random from actual jury lists, to have each group observe a realistically staged version of the case, and to oblige the jurors to deliberate until they can reach a unanimous verdict. Very few researchers have attempted this approach, and for those that have, the cost of this method inhibits repeating each version of the trial often enough to insure statistically reliable conclusions. Moreover, many critics wonder whether even this relatively elaborate approach is sufficiently realistic. Mock jurors may behave differently from jurors in actual cases, either because they know that no real consequences for the defendant or the community turn on their decision (the *responsibility effect*); because they may be affected by awareness that their responses are being studied (*evaluation apprehension*); or because they may realize that a particular variable is being manipulated and thus may tailor their responses to the perceived expectations of the experimenter (*demand characteristics*).[32] Some researchers using a full-blown mock trial have reported that the recorded deliberations are quite serious and intense, and this observation tends to suggest that the behavior of those jurors was not skewed by the elements of artificiality.[33] Nevertheless, such studies must be approached with caution.[34]

A 1968 study used volunteer "jurors" who were culled from voter registration rolls but who decided individually rather than deliberating in groups. Before presenting them with the trial (by a taped transcript), researchers asked them to read either a sensationalistic or a much more conservative newspaper account of the case. Those exposed to the more sensational account were much more likely to convict, but among jurors instructed to disregard the newspaper accounts, the difference in conviction rates disappeared.[35]

31. There is some evidence, however, to the effect that jury verdicts tend to reflect the position favored by a majority on the first ballot. Kalven and Zeisel found that only in about 10 percent of the cases did a minority succeed in persuading the majority to change its mind. See H. Kalven & H. Zeisel, The American Jury 487-488 (1966).

32. See Gerbasi, Zuckerman & Reis, Justice Needs a New Blindfold: A Review of Mock Jury Research, 84 Psychological Bull. 323 (1977).

33. See, e.g., R. Simon, The Jury and the Defense of Insanity 213 (1967); Cornish & Sealy, Juries and the Rules of Evidence [London School of Economics Jury Project], [1973] Crim. L. Rev. 208, 210.

34. See generally, Gerbasi, Zuckerman & Reis, supra page 46 footnote 32; Bermant, McGuire, McKinley & Salo, The Logic of Simulation in Jury Research, 1 Crim. J. and Behavior 224 (1974). An alternative to using the formal experimental method with simulated cases is to use data from actual cases in an attempt (sometimes called an indirect experiment) to infer the significance of particular variables. The most important study of this kind, H. Kalven & H. Zeisel, supra page 46 footnote 31, did not explore the effect of cautionary instructions. On the uses and dangers of the indirect technique, see Zeisel, Reflections on Experimental Techniques in the Law, 2 J. Legal Stud. 107 (1973).

35. Simon, The Effects of Newspapers on the Verdicts of Potential Jurors, in R. Simon, The

In a 1973 experiment, conducted by circulating four-page case summaries to 107 freshman psychology students, researchers found that incriminating but legally inadmissible evidence (in that case a confession) significantly increased the likelihood of a guilty verdict when other evidence was weak. This study found, however, that the impact of the evidence was not eradicated by cautionary instructions; in fact, instructions to disregard the evidence had no significant effect on the likelihood of conviction.[36]

A 1973 English study [37] selected jurors in two ways: In one group, volunteers were solicited among London office workers; in the second group, interviewers recruited jurors in order to produce a broader sample representative of those actually eligible for jury service. Each jury (there were a total of 28 juries in each group) listened to a tape-recorded version of a trial and then deliberated in an effort to reach a unanimous verdict. Jury reactions to a record of prior convictions were tested by using four different versions of the case:

(1) mention was made of a previous record for offenses *similar* to that charged and *no instruction* to disregard the evidence was given
(2) mention was made of *dissimilar* offenses and *no instruction* to disregard the evidence was given
(3) mention was made of similar offenses and an *instruction* to disregard the evidence *was given*
(4) no previous record was mentioned

The researchers found that in one mock case (involving theft) the conviction rate was 57 percent in version (1), 33 to 35 percent in versions (2) and (3), and only 27 percent in version (4). In other words, evidence of previous similar offenses significantly increased the likelihood of conviction, but the cautionary instruction removed most of the prejudicial effect. Still, defendants afforded the cautionary instruction were more likely to be convicted than those whose prior record had not been mentioned at all. The instruction, in other words, failed to eliminate all of the prejudicial effect.[38]

To the extent that cautionary instructions do fail to eradicate prejudicial effects, the result could be due, at least in part, to jurors' inability to *understand* the subtle distinctions that such instructions sometimes require to be drawn. Several studies have produced disturbing evidence that jurors often do not follow the judge's explanations of legal concepts and that this may be due primarily to the phraseology used, rather than to the intrinsic complexity of the concepts

---

Sociology of Law 617-627 (1968). To the same effect, see Reed, Jury Simulation: The Impact of Judge's Instructions and Attorney Tactics on Decisionmaking, 71 J. Crim. L. and Criminology 68 (1980).

36. Sue, Smith & Caldwell, Effects of Inadmissible Evidence on the Decisions of Simulated Jurors: A Moral Dilemma, 3 J. Applied Soc. Psych. 345 (1973).

37. Cornish & Sealy, supra page 46 footnote 33.

38. In all of the case versions tested in this jury project, the other-crimes evidence was mentioned inadvertently or impermissibly, and the jury was then instructed to disregard the evidence completely. Are the project's conclusions applicable to a situation in which the other-crimes evidence is legitimately admitted and the jury is instructed to consider that evidence for *some* purposes but not for *other* purposes? How could the project have tested for the effect of that kind of instruction, and how do you suppose its findings would have been affected?

themselves.[39] Again, however, not all the evidence points in the same direction. Several studies of burden-of-proof problems have found that mock jurors do perceive a difference among various formulations of the burden of proof and that some formulations produce significantly higher conviction rates than others.[40]

QUESTIONS ON JURY INSTRUCTIONS

1. Methodology. To what extent should the above studies be considered reliable? Which of them seems least flawed? Consider how you would design a reliable, methodologically sound study of jury responses to cautionary instructions.

2. The impact of jury instructions. On the basis of existing information, what, if anything, can one conclude about the effectiveness of jury instructions? Is the viewpoint expressed by the Supreme Court in Spencer v. Texas, page 45 supra, a supportable one? If not, does Justice Jackson's position, page 45 supra, seem more accurate?

3. Implications. Whatever the available evidence may suggest about the usefulness of jury instructions, there clearly remain substantial doubts about whether instructions are as fully effective in practice as they are assumed to be in theory. What are the implications of this situation? Granted that jury instructions function imperfectly (at best), what is the alternative?

One pragmatic approach has been to consider changes in trial procedure that might enhance the effectiveness of instructions. For example, the wording of instructions could be improved so that their meaning is more clearly explained to the jury.[41] Beyond this, when a judge tells a jury to disregard evidence, why shouldn't he or she explain *why* the law considers the evidence inappropriate or misleading? The standard cautionary instructions tend to be rather perfunctory. For some provocative suggestions for expanding on such instructions in ways that would convey a far more forceful message, see Alschuler, Courtroom Misconduct by Prosecutors and Trial Judges, 50 Tex. L. Rev. 629, 652-654 (1972).

If such ameliorative reforms are successful, will they cure the difficulties of overly cumbersome jury instructions, or is the basic problem more fundamental? Note that jury instructions are necessary in the first place only because we want citizens without special training to participate and at the same time we want their decisions to conform to law. Do these partially inconsistent desires require a system that is simply too complex to function properly? This problem can be reconsidered in connection with the materials on other countries' approaches

39. See, e.g., Charrow & Charrow, Making Legal Language Understandable: A Psycholinguistic Study of Jury Instructions, 79 Colum. L. Rev. 1306 (1979); Strawn & Buchanan, Jury Confusion: A Threat to Justice, 59 Jud. 478 (1976); Forston, Judge's Instructions: A Quantitative Analysis of Juror's Listening Comprehension, 18 Today's Speech 34 (1970).

40. Simon & Mahan, Quantifying Burdens of Proof, 5 L. & Socy. Rev. 319 (1971); Kerr et al., Guilt Beyond a Reasonable Doubt, 34 J. Personality & Soc. Psych. 282 (1976). See also Cornish & Sealy, supra page 46 footnote 33, at 218-219. For discussion of the requirement of proof beyond a reasonable doubt, see pages 64-67 infra.

41. A proposal for clarifying jury instructions and translating them into plain English is developed in Schwartzer, Communicating with Juries: Problems and Remedies, 69 Calif. L. Rev. 731 (1981). See also B. Sales, A. Elwork & J. Alfini, Making Jury Instructions Understandable (1981).

to lay participation, pages 99-100 infra, and with the broader problems of adversary versus nonadversary procedure, pages 169-179 infra.

3.   The Privilege against Self-Incrimination

INTRODUCTORY NOTE

The development of the privilege against self-incrimination was complex and, in its earliest phases, quite obscure.[42] One of the important roots of the privilege can be traced to the practice of English ecclesiastical courts — the Court of High Commission and the Court of Star Chamber — down to the mid-seventeenth century. These courts, with increasing frequency toward the end of that period, used the device of the oath ex officio to examine clergymen or others suspected of religious and political crimes. The essence of this procedure was that before any evidence of guilt had been obtained against the suspect, he could be required to express opinions on a range of matters and thus in effect convict himself of heresy, for example. Opponents of this procedure invoked the maxim *nemo tenetur seipsum prodere* (no man is bound to accuse himself). The principle was itself of questionable legal force at the time, but at most it meant only that no one should be obliged to make the first accusation against himself. There was seemingly no objection to requiring testimony under oath from someone once he had been properly accused. In any event disputes over the ex officio oath were caught up in the larger debates over the jurisdiction of the ecclesiastical courts and the political and religious upheavals of the seventeenth century. When the Courts of High Commission and Star Chamber were abolished in 1641, one provision of the statutes forever forbade ecclesiastical courts from using the ex officio oath to require answers as to penal matters. By the end of the seventeenth century, this clause came to be interpreted as forbidding the ecclesiastical courts from insisting on answers from the accused, even after a proper accusation had been obtained from other sources.

All this had nothing to do with procedure in the common law courts, except that compulsory examination of the accused had acquired a very bad name. Down to the early 1600s there was no indication of a privilege not to be questioned in common law criminal cases. With the growing opposition to the ex officio oath, however, accused persons began asserting the *nemo tenetur* principle in common law trials, and judges increasingly came to acknowledge its validity. By the late 1600s it was generally accepted in common law courts that defendants could not be questioned against their will and, indeed, that other witnesses could not be compelled to give answers that would incriminate themselves.

By this time, too, other developments had led the common law courts to disqualify as witnesses not only the accused but all other party litigants and indeed any witness with an interest in the cause. Thus, the accused could not be forced to testify and could not testify even when he or she wished to do so. The privilege against self-incrimination remained important primarily as a

---

42. For thorough exploration of the topic, see L. Levy, Origins of the Fifth Amendment (1968); 8 J. Wigmore, Evidence §2250 (McNaughton rev. 1961). The capsule discussion in the text is drawn from these sources.

barrier to compulsory pretrial examination and to compulsory self-incrimination by nonparty witnesses in both civil and criminal cases. When the absolute disqualification of party witnesses was abolished by American and English statutes in the mid-1800s, the accused regained the *right* to testify, and the privilege against self-incrimination once again became important as a guarantee that the accused could not be *forced* to testify at his or her own trial.

The privilege against self-incrimination thus involves two related protections. First, and most important for our purposes, it forbids any questioning of the accused against his or her will in the criminal trial itself. Second, it forbids compelling any witness in any proceeding (civil, criminal, legislative, or administrative) to give a particular answer that might tend to incriminate him or her. The next case, Malloy v. Hogan, arises in connection with the latter requirement, but it focuses primarily on the question whether the basic principles underlying the privilege are fundamental to the American system of justice. The case that follows it, Griffin v. California, explores the application of the privilege in the context of the criminal trial itself.

MALLOY v. HOGAN
Supreme Court of the United States
378 U.S. 1 (1964)

MR. JUSTICE BRENNAN delivered the opinion of the Court.

In this case we are asked to reconsider prior decisions holding that the privilege against self-incrimination is not safeguarded against state action by the Fourteenth Amendment. Twining v. New Jersey, 211 U.S. 78; Adamson v. California, 332 U.S. 46.

The petitioner was arrested during a gambling raid in 1959 by Hartford, Connecticut, police. He pleaded guilty to the crime of pool selling, a misdemeanor, and was sentenced to one year in jail and fined $500. . . . About 16 months after his guilty plea, petitioner was ordered to testify before a referee appointed by the Superior Court of Hartford County to conduct an inquiry into alleged gambling and other criminal activities in the county. The petitioner was asked a number of questions related to events surrounding his arrest and conviction. He refused to answer any question "on the grounds it may tend to incriminate me." The Superior Court adjudged him in contempt, and committed him to prison until he was willing to answer the questions. Petitioner's application for a writ of habeas corpus was denied by the Superior Court, and the Connecticut Supreme Court of Errors affirmed . . . [, holding] that the Fifth Amendment's privilege against self-incrimination was not available to a witness in a state proceeding, that the Fourteenth Amendment extended no privilege to him, and that the petitioner had not properly invoked the privilege available under the Connecticut Constitution. . . .

We reverse. . . .

We hold today that the Fifth Amendment's exception from compulsory self-incrimination is also protected by the Fourteenth Amendment against abridgment by the States. Decisions of the Court since *Twining* and *Adamson* have departed from the contrary view expressed in those cases. We discuss first the decisions which forbid the use of coerced confessions in state criminal prosecutions.

Brown v. Mississippi, 297 U.S. 278, was the first case in which the Court held that the Due Process Clause prohibited the States from using the accused's coerced confessions against him. The Court in *Brown* felt impelled, in light of *Twining,* to say that its conclusion did not involve the privilege against self-incrimination. "Compulsion by torture to extort a confession is a different matter." 297 U.S., at 285. But this distinction was soon abandoned, and today the admissibility of a confession in a state criminal prosecution is tested by the same standard applied in federal prosecutions since 1897, when, in Bram v. United States, 168 U.S. 532, the Court held that "[i]n criminal trials, in the courts of the United States, wherever a question arises whether a confession is incompetent because not voluntary, the issue is controlled by that portion of the Fifth Amendment to the Constitution of the United States, commanding that no person 'shall be compelled in any criminal case to be a witness against himself.' " Under this test, the constitutional inquiry is not whether the conduct of state officers in obtaining the confession was shocking, but whether the confession was "free and voluntary: that is, [it] must not be extracted by any sort of threats or violence, nor obtained by any direct or implied promises, however slight, nor by the exertion of any improper influence. . . ." In other words the person must not have been compelled to incriminate himself. We have held inadmissible even a confession secured by so mild a whip as the refusal, under certain circumstances, to allow a suspect to call his wife until he confessed. Haynes v. Washington, 373 U.S. 503.

The marked shift to the federal standard in state cases . . . reflects recognition that the American system of criminal prosecution is accusatorial, not inquisitorial, and that the Fifth Amendment privilege is its essential mainstay. Governments, state and federal, are thus constitutionally compelled to establish guilt by evidence independently and freely secured, and may not by coercion prove a charge against an accused out of his own mouth. Since the Fourteenth Amendment prohibits the States from inducing a person to confess through "sympathy falsely aroused," Spano v. New York, [360 U.S. 315, 323], or other like inducement far short of "compulsion by torture," Haynes v. Washington, supra, it follows a fortiori that it also forbids the States to resort to imprisonment, as here, to compel him to answer questions that might incriminate him. The Fourteenth Amendment secures against state invasion the same privilege that the Fifth Amendment guarantees against federal infringement — the right of a person to remain silent unless he chooses to speak in the unfettered exercise of his own will, and to suffer no penalty, as held in *Twining,* for such silence.

This conclusion is fortified by our recent decision in Mapp v. Ohio, 367 U.S. 643, overruling Wolf v. Colorado, 338 U.S. 25, which had held "that in a prosecution in a State court for a State crime the Fourteenth Amendment does not forbid the admission of evidence obtained by an unreasonable search and seizure." *Mapp* held that the Fifth Amendment privilege against self-incrimination implemented the Fourth Amendment in such cases, and that the two guarantees of personal security conjoined in the Fourteenth Amendment to make the exclusionary rule obligatory upon the States. We relied upon the great case of Boyd v. United States, 116 U.S. 616, decided in 1886, which, considering the Fourth and Fifth Amendments as running "almost into each other," held that "Breaking into a house and opening boxes and drawers are circumstances of aggravation; but any forcible and compulsory extortion of a man's own testimony or of his private papers to be used as evidence to convict him of crime or to forfeit his goods, is within the condemnation of [those Amendments]. . . ." . . . In thus returning to the *Boyd* view that the privilege is one of the "principles of a free government," 116 U.S., at 632,[7] *Mapp* necessarily repudiated the *Twining* concept of the privilege as a mere rule of evidence "best defended not as an unchangeable principle of universal justice but as a law proved by experience to be expedient."

. . . The State urges, however, that the availability of the federal privilege to a witness in a state inquiry is to be determined according to a less stringent standard than is applicable in a federal proceeding. We disagree. We have held that the guarantees of the First Amendment, the prohibition of unreasonable searches and seizures of the Fourth Amendment, and the right to counsel guaranteed by the Sixth Amendment, are all to be enforced against the States under the Fourteenth Amendment according to the same standards that protect those personal rights against federal encroachment. . . . The Court thus has rejected the notion that the Fourteenth Amendment applies to the States only a "watered-down, subjective version of the individual guarantees of the Bill of Rights," Ohio ex rel. Eaton v. Price, 364 U.S. 263, 275 (dissenting opinion). . . .

We turn to the petitioner's claim that the State of Connecticut denied him the protection of his federal privilege. It must be considered irrelevant that the petitioner was a witness in a statutory inquiry and not a defendant in a criminal prosecution, for it has long been settled that the privilege protects witnesses in similar federal inquiries. We recently elaborated the content of the federal standard in Hoffman [v. United States, 341 U.S. 479 (1951)]: "The privilege afforded not only extends to answers that would in themselves support a conviction . . . but likewise embraces those which would furnish a link in the chain of evidence needed to prosecute. . . . [I]f the witness, upon interposing his claim, were required to prove the hazard . . . he would be compelled to surrender the very protection which the privilege is designed to guarantee. To sustain the privilege, it need only be evident from the implications of the question, in the setting in which it is asked, that a responsive answer to the question or an explanation of why it cannot be answered might be dangerous because injurious disclosure could result." We also said that, in applying that test, the judge must be " '*perfectly clear*, from a careful consideration of all the circumstances in the case, that the witness is mistaken, and that the answer[s] *cannot possibly* have such tendency' to incriminate." . . .

The investigation in the course of which petitioner was questioned . . . [involved] an inquiry into whether there was reasonable cause to believe that crimes, including gambling, were being committed in Hartford County. Petitioner appeared on January 16 and 25, 1961, and in both instances he was asked substantially the same questions about the circumstances surrounding his arrest and conviction for pool selling in late 1959. The questions which petitioner refused

---

7. *Boyd* had said of the privilege, ". . . any compulsory discovery by extorting the party's oath . . . to convict him of crime . . . is contrary to the principles of a free government. It is abhorrent to the instincts of an Englishman; it is abhorrent to the instincts of an American. It may suit the purposes of despotic power; but it cannot abide the pure atmosphere of political liberty and personal freedom."

Dean Griswold has said: "I believe the Fifth Amendment is, and has been through this period of crisis, an expression of the moral striving of the community. It has been a reflection of our common conscience, a symbol of the America which stirs our hearts." The Fifth Amendment Today 73 (1955).

to answer may be summarized as follows: (1) for whom did he work on September 11, 1959; (2) who selected and paid his counsel in connection with his arrest on that date and subsequent conviction; (3) who selected and paid his bondsman; (4) who paid his fine; (5) what was the name of the tenant of the apartment in which he was arrested; and (6) did he know John Bergoti. The Connecticut Supreme Court of Errors ruled that the answers to these questions could not tend to incriminate him because the defenses of double jeopardy and the running of the one-year statute of limitations on misdemeanors would defeat any prosecution growing out of his answers to the first five questions. As for the sixth question, the court held that petitioner's failure to explain how a revelation of his relationship with Bergoti would incriminate him vitiated his claim to the protection of the privilege afforded by state law.

The conclusions of the Court of Errors, tested by the federal standard, fail to take sufficient account of the setting in which the questions were asked. The interrogation was part of a wide-ranging inquiry into crime, including gambling, in Hartford. It was admitted on behalf of the State at oral argument — and indeed it is obvious from the questions themselves — that the State desired to elicit from the petitioner the identity of the person who ran the pool-selling operation in connection with which he had been arrested in 1959. It was apparent that petitioner might apprehend that if this person were still engaged in unlawful activity, disclosure of his name might furnish a link in a chain of evidence sufficient to connect the petitioner with a more recent crime for which he might still be prosecuted.

. . . We conclude, therefore, that as to each of the questions, it was "evident from the implications of the question, in the setting in which it [was] asked, that a responsive answer to the question or an explanation of why it [could not] be answered might be dangerous because injurious disclosure could result," Hoffman v. United States, 341 U.S., at 486-487.

Reversed.

[The dissenting opinions of Mr. Justice Harlan, which Mr. Justice Clark joined, and of Mr. Justice White, which Mr. Justice Stewart joined, are omitted.]

GRIFFIN v. CALIFORNIA
Supreme Court of the United States
380 U.S. 609 (1965)

Mr. Justice Douglas delivered the opinion of the Court.

Petitioner was convicted of murder in the first degree after a jury trial in a California court. He did not testify at the trial on the issue of guilt, though he did testify at the separate trial on the issue of penalty. The trial court instructed the jury on the issue of guilt, stating that a defendant has a constitutional right not to testify. But it told the jury:

> As to any evidence or facts against him which the defendant can reasonably be expected to deny or explain because of facts within his knowledge, if he does not testify or if, though he does testify, he fails to deny or explain such evidence, the jury may take that failure into consideration as tending to indicate the truth of such evidence and as indicating that among the inferences that may be reasonably drawn therefrom those unfavorable to the defendant are the more probable. . . .

Petitioner had been seen with the deceased the evening of her death, the evidence placing him with her in the alley where her body was found. The prosecutor made much of the failure of petitioner to testify:

> . . . He would know how she got down the alley. He would know how the blood got on the bottom of the concrete steps. He would know how long he was with her in that box. He would know how her wig got off. He would know whether he beat her or mistreated her. . . .
>
> These things he has not seen fit to take the stand and deny or explain.
>
> And in the whole world, if anybody would know, this defendant would know. Essie Mae is dead, she can't tell you her side of the story. The defendant won't.

The death penalty was imposed and the California Supreme Court affirmed. The case is here on a writ of certiorari. . . .

If this were a federal trial, reversible error would have been committed. Wilson v. United States, 149 U.S. 60, so holds. It is said, however, that the *Wilson* decision rested not on the Fifth Amendment, but on an Act of Congress, now 18 U.S.C. §3481. That indeed is the fact, as the opinion of the Court in the *Wilson* case states. But that is the beginning, not the end, of our inquiry. The question remains whether, statute or not, the comment rule, approved by California, violates the Fifth Amendment.

We think it does. It is in substance a rule of evidence that allows the State the privilege of tendering to the jury for its consideration the failure of the accused to testify. No formal offer of proof is made as in other situations; but the prosecutor's comment and the court's acquiescence are the equivalent of an offer of evidence and its acceptance. The Court in the *Wilson* case stated: ". . . It is not every one who can safely venture on the witness stand though entirely innocent of the charge against him. Excessive timidity, nervousness when facing others and attempting to explain transactions of a suspicious character, and offences charged against him, will often confuse and embarrass him to such a degree as to increase rather than remove prejudices against him. It is not every one, however honest, who would, therefore, willingly be placed on the witness stand. The statute, in tenderness to the weakness of those who from the causes mentioned might refuse to ask to be a witness, particularly when they may have been in some degree compromised by their association with others, declares that the failure of the defendant in a criminal action to request to be a witness shall not create any presumption against him."

If the words "Fifth Amendment" are substituted for . . . "statute," the spirit of the Self-Incrimination Clause is reflected. For comment on the refusal to testify is a remnant of the "inquisitorial system of criminal justice," Murphy v. Waterfront Comm'n, 378 U.S. 52, 55, which the Fifth Amendment outlaws. It is a penalty imposed by courts for exercising a constitutional privilege. It cuts down on the privilege by making its assertion costly. It is said, however, that the inference of guilt for failure to testify as to facts peculiarly within the accused's knowledge is in any event natural and irresistible, and that comment on the failure does not magnify that inference into a penalty for asserting a constitutional privilege. People v. Modesto, 62 Cal. 2d 436, 452-453, 398 P.2d 753, 762-763. What the jury may infer, given no help from the court is one thing. What it may infer when the court solemnizes the silence of the accused into evidence against him is quite another. That the inference of guilt is not always so natural or irresistible is brought out in the *Modesto* opinion itself: "Defendant contends that the reason a defendant refuses to testify is that his prior convictions will be introduced in evidence to impeach him and not that he is unable to deny the accusations. It is true that the defendant might fear that his prior convictions will prejudice the jury, and therefore another possible inference can be drawn from his refusal to take the stand."

We said in Malloy v. Hogan that "the same standards must determine whether an accused's silence in either a federal or state proceeding is justified." We take that in its literal sense and hold that the Fifth Amendment, in its direct application to the Federal Government, and in its bearing on the States by reason of the Fourteenth Amendment, forbids either comment by the prosecution on the accused's silence or instructions by the court that such silence is evidence of guilt.

Reversed.

MR. JUSTICE STEWART, with whom MR. JUSTICE WHITE joins, dissenting. . . .

We must determine whether the petitioner has been "compelled . . . to be a witness against himself." Compulsion is the focus of the inquiry. Certainly, if any compulsion be detected in the California procedure, it is of a dramatically different and less palpable nature than that involved in the procedures which historically gave rise to the Fifth Amendment guarantee. When a suspect was brought before the Court of High Commission or the Star Chamber, he was commanded to answer whatever was asked of him, and subjected to a far-reaching and deeply probing inquiry in an effort to ferret out some unknown and frequently unsuspected crime. He declined to answer on pain of incarceration, banishment, or mutilation. And if he spoke falsely, he was subject to further punishment. Faced with this formidable array of alternatives, his decision to speak was unquestionably coerced.

Those were the lurid realities which lay behind enactment of the Fifth Amendment, a far cry from the subject matter of the case before us. I think that the Court in this case stretches the concept of compulsion beyond all reasonable bounds, and that whatever compulsion may exist derives from the defendant's choice not to testify, not from any comment by court or counsel. In support of its conclusion that the California procedure does compel the accused to testify, the Court has only this to say: "It is a penalty imposed by courts for exercising a constitutional privilege. It cuts down on the privilege by making its assertion costly." Exactly what the penalty imposed consists of is not clear. . . .

It is not at all apparent to me, on any realistic view of the trial process, that a defendant will be at more of a disadvantage under the California practice than he would be in a court which permitted no comment at all on his failure to take the witness stand. How can it be said that the inferences drawn by a jury will be more detrimental to a defendant under the limiting and carefully controlling language of the instruction here involved than would result if the jury were left to roam at large with only its untutored instincts to guide it, to draw from the defendant's silence broad inferences of guilt? . . .

Moreover, no one can say where the balance of advantage might lie as a result of the attorneys' discussion of the matter. No doubt the prosecution's argument will seek to encourage the drawing of inferences unfavorable to the defendant. However, the defendant's counsel equally has an opportunity to explain the various other reasons why a defendant may not wish to take the stand, and thus rebut the natural if uneducated assumption that it is because the defendant cannot truthfully deny the accusations made.[a]

I think the California comment rule is not a coercive device which impairs the right against self-incrimination but rather a means of articulating and bringing into the light of rational discussion a fact inescapably impressed on the jury's consciousness. . . .

. . . No constitution can prevent the operation of the human mind. Without limiting instructions, the danger exists that the inferences drawn by the jury may be unfairly broad. Some States have permitted this danger to go unchecked, by forbidding any comment at all upon the defendant's failure to take the witness stand. Other States have dealt with this danger in a variety of ways, as the Court's opinion indicates. Some might differ, as a matter of policy, with the way California has chosen to deal with the problem, or even disapprove of the judge's specific instructions in this case. But, so long as the constitutional command is obeyed, such matters of state policy are not for this Court to decide.

I would affirm the judgment.

NOTES ON THE SCOPE OF THE PRIVILEGE

The power of government to compel testimony, subject only to narrowly limited privileges and exceptions, has been considered essential to the effective functioning of courts and thus to orderly resolution of disputes under the rule of law. The Fifth Amendment embodies one of these narrow privileges: "[N]o person . . . shall be compelled in any criminal case to be a witness against himself." Thus, the amendment protects only against *incrimination* ("in a criminal case"); the incrimination must result from *testimony* ("to be a witness"); the testimony must be obtained by *compulsion;* and the testimony compelled must lead to *self*-incrimination ("against himself"). These Notes briefly examine the meaning, often quite technical, that these terms have acquired over time.

1. Testimony. Suppose that the police obtain a valid search warrant and use it to seize and take from the defendant a murder weapon hidden in the defendant's pocket. Have they not compelled the defendant to incriminate himself or herself? One answer has been that the Fifth Amendment prohibits only compulsion to be a "witness." Hence, the government may (within Fourth Amendment limits) use force to obtain physical evidence (often called *real evidence*). Fifth Amendment restrictions apply only to evidence deemed *testimonial.*

In Schmerber v. California, 384 U.S. 757 (1966), the Court held that a blood sample could be forcibly extracted from a defendant since the evidence was not "testimonial." On the same ground, the Court has held that defendants can be compelled to exhibit their bodies, their handwriting, and even their voices: All are deemed personal characteristics (real evidence) rather than communications of knowledge or information (testimonial evidence). See United States v. Wade, 388 U.S. 218 (1967), and Gilbert v. California, 388 U.S. 63 (1967).

a. Is this position realistic? How is Justice Stewart's argument affected by the rule that prior convictions become admissible, for impeachment purposes, if defendant chooses to testify? — Eds.

Can a defendant raising the insanity defense be compelled (on pain of either contempt or summary rejection of the defense) to submit to a government psychiatrist's searching exploration of his or her thoughts, dreams, and desires? Suppose that the defendant's statements are used only for diagnosis and cannot be introduced as evidence of the matters discussed. Is it then clear that the psychiatric interview compels disclosure only of "personal characteristics" and that the Fifth Amendment should therefore be inapplicable? [43]

2. *Compulsion.* (*a*) *Searches.* Suppose that among the items seized during a valid search are letters and other personal papers in which the accused makes incriminating admissions. It should be clear that this kind of evidence, at least, is testimonial. Does the Fifth Amendment forbid the forcible seizure and use of the evidence? In Boyd v. United States, 116 U.S. 616 (1886), the Court stated that "we are unable to perceive that the seizure of a man's private books and papers to be used in evidence against him is substantially different from compelling him to be a witness against himself." 116 U.S. at 633. For years after *Boyd,* the cases assumed that seizure from a defendant of his or her private papers was barred by the Fifth Amendment, even if Fourth Amendment requirements had been satisfied. However, in Andresen v. Maryland, 427 U.S. 463 (1976), the Court characterized the *Boyd* statement as dictum and rejected it. Mr. Justice Blackmun, writing for seven members of the Court, held (427 U.S. at 473-476):

> . . . [T]he Fifth Amendment may protect an individual from complying with a subpoena for the production of his personal records in his possession because the very act of production may constitute a compulsory authentication of incriminating information. [But] a seizure of the same materials by law enforcement officers differs in a crucial respect — the individual against whom the search is directed is not required to aid in the discovery, production or authentication of incriminating evidence. . . .
>
> In this case, petitioner, at the time he recorded his communication, at the time of the search, and at the time the records were admitted at trial, was not subjected to "the cruel trilemma of self-accusation, perjury or contempt." Indeed, he was never required to say or to do anything under penalty of sanction. . . .

In a dissenting opinion Mr. Justice Brennan wrote (id. at 486-487):

> The matter cannot be resolved on any simplistic notion of compulsion. . . . The door to one's house, for example, is as much the individual's resistance to the intrusion of outsiders as his personal physical efforts to prevent the same. To refuse recognition to the sanctity of that door and, more generally, to confine

---

43. See Aronson, Should the Privilege against Self-Incrimination Apply to Compelled Psychiatric Examinations?, 26 Stan. L. Rev. 55 (1973); Wesson, The Privilege against Self-Incrimination in Civil Commitment Proceedings, [1980] Wis. L. Rev. 697. The issue was left open in Estelle v. Smith, 451 U.S. 454 (1981). In that case the defendant had been compelled to submit to a psychiatric interview that was used by the prosecution to establish "dangerousness," an issue that was relevant at the penalty phase of the defendant's trial on a capital murder charge. The Court held that this procedure violated the Fifth Amendment. The Court stressed that the psychiatrist based his evaluation on the defendant's statements reciting the details of the crime and that the state had used "the substance of his disclosures" rather than testimony about nontestimonial personal characteristics. The applicability of the Fifth Amendment privilege in the context of the insanity defense was not reached by the Court.

the dominion of privacy to the mind . . . den[ies] to the individual a zone of physical freedom necessary for conducting one's affairs.

(*b*) *Police interrogation.* Before the Fifth Amendment was held applicable to the states, the Court had reviewed (under the due process clause of the Fourteenth Amendment) the admissibility of out-of-court confessions elicited by police interrogation. The prevailing requirement of "voluntariness," though similar to the "no-compulsion" requirement of the Fifth Amendment, had in practice been construed to allow some degree of pressure in the interrogation process. After *Malloy* the focus in confession cases shifted from voluntariness to compulsion, but some interrogation tactics continued to be considered permissible; not all pressure amounted to "compulsion."

Finally, in Miranda v. Arizona, 384 U.S. 486 (1966), the Court held that in-custody interrogation was "inherently compelling" and, accordingly, that the Fifth Amendment barred the use of any confession obtained by custodial interrogation in the absence of a series of warnings designed to "dispel the compulsion inherent in custodial surroundings." 384 U.S. at 458. The scope and implications of *Miranda* warrant detailed examination in connection with the study of police practices and criminal procedure. For present purposes it is sufficient to note that while *Miranda* sought to effect a marked reduction in the permissible level of pressure, the decision did not equate all forms of pressure with compulsion. In fact, if proper warnings are given and the suspect then agrees to talk in the absence of an attorney (as many suspects apparently continue to do), police interrogation (including the use of many subtle tactics and inducements) remains permissible. For Fifth Amendment purposes, "compulsion" is no longer limited to the formal compulsion of a legal *obligation* to speak, enforceable by formal process: Informal pressures or inducements to speak will trigger the Fifth Amendment, but only when the courts are prepared to characterize them as "excessive" or "unfair."

(*c*) *Inferences from the failure to testify.* Does comment on the defendant's silence "compel" the defendant to testify? If so, doesn't the prosecution "compel" testimony every time it introduces evidence highly probative of guilt? One answer may be that the inference of guilt from silence is not rational and, accordingly, that this kind of pressure to testify is unfair. But why is the inference not a rational one? If a defendant is exposed to impeachment use of prior convictions, we probably cannot infer from the defendant's decision not to testify that he or she has no explanation to offer. But consider the situation that would obtain in a state that decided to prohibit the use of prior convictions for impeachment purposes in most situations. In such a jurisdiction, would an inference of guilt from silence still be irrational? If not, should comment on silence become permissible? Or should *Griffin* still apply, on the ground that the state should not be allowed, as Justice Douglas puts it, to "solemnize the silence of the accused into evidence against him"? 380 U.S. at 614.

For an analysis highly critical of *Griffin*, see Ayer, The Fifth Amendment and the Inference of Guilt From Silence: Griffin v. California after Fifteen Years, 78 Mich. L. Rev. 841 (1980). Compare Bradley, Griffin v. California: Still Viable after All These Years, 79 Mich. L. Rev. 1290 (1981).

3. Incrimination. The privilege may be asserted in proceedings that are not themselves criminal (civil suits and legislative investigations are common settings for the assertion of the privilege), but in all instances witnesses must have a plausible claim that the testimony sought could be used against them in a criminal prosecution. *Malloy* itself involves the application of this principle in a situation in which there was a *possibility* of incrimination, even though only a rather speculative one.

Because *incrimination* is required, a party in a civil suit has no privilege to withhold nonincriminating testimony, regardless of the importance of the money or property at stake and regardless of how personally embarrassing the testimony might be. A witness may even be compelled to testify about his or her own criminal behavior, if all danger of incrimination has been removed by previous conviction on the only possible charges (this was the state's claim in *Malloy*, for example) or by a grant of immunity from prosecution.[44]

4. Self-incrimination and required records. The privilege does not of course permit the withholding of testimony that may incriminate *others*. Strict application of this requirement, however, has produced some less obvious results. For example, officers or agents of a corporation may be compelled to produce corporate documents that may incriminate them. It is said that the documents belong to the corporation and it is the *corporation* that is being compelled to incriminate another party — the individual.[45] When the individual produces the documents, he or she is said to be acting on behalf of the corporation, and thus the individual's act leads to incrimination of one party by another, not to *self*-incrimination.

Since an individual serving as an "agent" can be compelled to make disclosures that are personally incriminating, can the government require individuals to record incriminating information by simply treating them as agents and by claiming that the records belong to the government from the outset? In Shapiro v. United States, 335 U.S. 1, 33 (1948), the Supreme Court, in a 5–4 decision, held that the constitutional privilege did not extend to "records required by law to be kept in order that there may be suitable information of transactions which are the appropriate subject of governmental regulation. . . ." Justices Frankfurter, Jackson, Murphy, and Rutledge dissented. Justice Jackson stated (335 U.S. at 70-71):

> The protection against compulsory self-incrimination, guaranteed by the Fifth Amendment, is nullified to whatever extent this Court holds that Congress may require a citizen to keep an account of his misdeeds and turn over or exhibit the record on demand of government inspectors, who then can use it to convict him. . . . It would, no doubt, simplify enforcement of all criminal laws if each citizen were required to keep a diary that would show where he was at all times, with whom he was, and what he was up to. The decision of today, applying this rule not merely to records specially required under the Act but also to records "customarily kept," invites and facilitates that eventuality.

In Marchetti v. United States, 390 U.S. 39 (1968), and Grosso v. United States, 390 U.S. 62 (1968), the Court limited the reach of *Shapiro* and held that the privilege against self-incrimination could be asserted as a defense to criminal

---

44. Kastigar v. United States, 406 U.S. 441 (1972).

45. Wilson v. United States, 221 U.S. 361 (1911). Note also that the corporation itself cannot invoke the Fifth Amendment, because the Court has held that the privilege against self-incrimination is available only to individuals, not to impersonal organizations such as corporations or labor unions. See United States v. White, 322 U.S. 694 (1944).

prosecutions for violation of both the registration and taxing provisions of federal wagering tax statutes. The Court concluded that "the statutory obligations are directed almost exclusively to individuals inherently suspect of criminal activities [bookies]" and that "the information demanded lacks every characteristic of a public document." Grosso v. United States, 390 U.S. at 68. The obligation to pay the taxes, it declared, could not be separated from the informational and incriminatory purposes of the statutes.

PROBLEM

A provision of the California Vehicle Code requires the driver of a motor vehicle involved in an accident to stop at the scene and give his name and address. Can a driver who refuses to comply be prosecuted for failure to stop or for failure to give his name? Or would enforcement of these obligations violate the Fifth Amendment? Which Fifth Amendment doctrines could the prosecution most convincingly invoke in an effort to sustain this statute? See California v. Byers, 402 U.S. 424 (1971).

NOTES AND QUESTIONS ON THE POLICIES SERVED BY THE PRIVILEGE

1. The Court in *Malloy,* supra, refers to the privilege as "one of the 'principles of a free government' " (quoting Boyd v. United States, 116 U.S. 616, 632 (1886)) and as " 'a symbol of America which stirs our hearts' " (quoting E. Griswold, The Fifth Amendment Today 73 (1955)). Why is the privilege so important? Consider the following viewpoints.

Murphy v. Waterfront Commission, 378 U.S. 52, 55 (1964), Goldberg, J.: [The privilege] reflects many of our fundamental values and most notable aspirations: our unwillingness to subject those suspected of crime to the cruel trilemma of self-accusation, perjury or contempt; our preference for an accusatorial rather than an inquisitorial system of criminal justice; our fear that self-incriminating statements will be elicted by inhumane treatment and abuses; our sense of fair play which dictates "a fair state-individual balance by requiring the government to leave the individual alone until good cause is shown for disturbing him and by requiring the government in its contest with the individual to shoulder the entire load," our respect for the inviolability of the human personality and the right of each individual "to a private enclave where he may lead a private life," our distrust of self-deprecatory statements; and our realization that the privilege, while sometimes "a shelter to the guilty," is often a "protection to the innocent."

Tehan v. Schott, 382 U.S. 406, 415-416 (1966), Stewart, J.: The basic purposes that lie behind the privilege against self-incrimination do not relate to protecting the innocent from conviction, but rather to preserving the integrity of a judicial system in which even the guilty are not to be convicted unless the prosecution "shoulder the entire load.". . . [T]he Fifth Amendment's privilege against self-incrimination is not an adjunct to the ascertainment of truth. That privilege, like the guarantees of the Fourth Amendment, stands as a protection of quite different constitutional values — values reflecting the concern of our society for the right of each individual to be let alone.

L. Levy, Origins of the Fifth Amendment 331-332 (1968): [The privilege] was at first a privilege of the guilty, given the nature of the substantive law of religious and political crimes. It was also a protection of the innocent. But the right became neither a privilege of the guilty nor a protection of the innocent. It became merely one of the ways of fairly determining guilt or innocence, like trial by jury itself; it became part of the due process of the law, a fundamental principle of the accusatorial system. The right implied a humane or ethical standard in judging a person accused of crime, regardless how heinous the crime or strong the evidence of his guilt. . . .

Above all, the right was most closely linked to freedom of religion and speech. It was, in its origins, unquestionably the invention of those who were guilty of religious crimes, like heresy, schism, and nonconformity, and, later, of political crimes like treason, seditious libel, and breach of parliamentary privilege — more often than not, the offense was merely criticism of the government, its policies, or its officers. The right was associated then with guilt for crimes of conscience, of belief, and of association. In the broadest sense it was a protection not of the guilty, or of the innocent, but of freedom of expression, of political liberty, of the right to worship as one pleased.

2. *Questions.* Do the foregoing defenders of the privilege satisfactorily explain its basis? Can they adequately account for the various limitations on its scope? Note the following problems:

(a) If the privilege is intended to prevent cruel methods of extracting testimony, why should it protect against formal legal compulsion by a contempt citation? We are perfectly willing to use this kind of compulsion against witnesses other than the criminal defendant. The Court in *Malloy* reasons that since subtle pressure in the police station is prohibited, actual imprisonment for refusal to testify in court should be barred "a fortiori." Does this follow?

(b) If the privilege is intended to protect individual privacy and freedom from governmental intrusion, how can the strict insistence upon *incrimination* be explained?

(c) If the privilege is designed to protect freedom of conscience and freedom of expression, should it have any application in prosecutions for murder, kidnapping, or theft?

(d) If the privilege is intended to force the government to "shoulder the entire load" in an accusatorial system, how can one explain the strict limitation to *testimonial* incrimination, reflected in cases like *Wade* and *Schmerber,* page 56 supra?

3. Judge Henry J. Friendly has sharply questioned the value of the privilege. An exposition of his views follows.

Friendly, The Fifth Amendment Tomorrow: The Case for Constitutional Change, 37 U. Cin. L. Rev. 671, 679-694 (1968): A good way to start dissipating the lyricism now generally accompanying any reference to the privilege is to note how exceptional it is in the general setting of jurisprudence and morality. Most other [testimonial] privileges — for communications between husband and wife, attorney and client, doctor and patient, priest and penitent — promote and preserve relationships possessing social value. Yet the law has rather steadfastly resisted their expansion, even to a profession having such strong claims as accountancy. In contrast the Fifth Amendment privilege extends, by hypothesis, only to persons who have been breakers of the criminal law or reasonably believe they may be charged as such.

Again while the other privileges accord with notions of decent conduct generally accepted in life outside the court room, the privilege against self-incrimination defies them. No parent would teach such a doctrine to his children; the lesson parents preach is that while a misdeed, even a serious one, will generally be forgiven, a failure to make a clean breast of it will not be. Every hour of the day people are being asked to explain their conduct to parents, employers and teachers. Those who are questioned consider they are morally bound to respond, and the questioners believe it proper to take action if they don't.

Finally, the privilege, at least in its pre-trial application, seriously impedes the state in the most basic of all tasks, "to provide for the security of the individual and his property.". . . In contrast to the rare case where it may protect an innocent person, it often may do the contrary. . . .

[Referring to Justice Goldberg's "market basket" of explanations in *Murphy*, Judge Friendly dismissed several as "mere rhetoric" and then continued:]

Let me deal with the privacy argument . . . in some detail, since privacy is an extremely "in" legal principle today. . . . Surely, it is a far graver violation of privacy for a defendant in an annulment suit to be obliged to testify as to inability or unwillingness to engage in intercourse . . . , or for a mother to have to reveal her son's possession of a murder weapon, than for a motorist to be required to admit he exceeded the speed limit. Furthermore, as privacy proponents concede, it is "not easy to square the privacy interest as a prime purpose of the privilege with immunity statutes that require surrender of privacy." "Impossible" would be a more candid and accurate adjective. . . .

. . . [O]ne of the charms of the "fair state-individual balance" argument for proponents of the privilege is that it can be summoned to justify almost any extension. Moreover, the privilege is a long way from being the only factor entering into the balance. How can one tell, for example, whether the desired balance would be better achieved by relaxing the stated requirement of compulsion as a condition to the privilege, as the Supreme Court has been doing in a variety of areas, or by such other measures as greater discovery against the government, freer disclosure of grand jury minutes, stiffer requirements for the corroboration of accomplice testimony, or by modification of the rule that by taking the stand a defendant allows the government to open up his entire criminal record as impeaching his credibility?

4. Despite the claim that the privilege is one of the "principles of a free government," Boyd v. United States, 116 U.S. 616, 632 (1886), other democratic countries adopt quite a different approach to the self-incrimination problem.

Damaška, Evidentiary Barriers to Conviction and Two Models of Criminal Procedure, 121 U. Pa. L. Rev. 506, 526-529 (1973): It is sometimes said that there is no privilege against self-incrimination in the continental system of criminal procedure. If, parochially oriented, we expect to find in the civil law system exactly the same procedural arrangements which in the American variant of the common law system are classified under this rubric, the above statement is obviously true. If, however, we assume that the minimum content of the privilege reduces to the idea that no person should be compelled to cause his own conviction by testifying, then the statement is generally false. Differences between the two systems appear only if we go beyond the minimum content and explore the technical implementation of the privilege. . . .

In contrast to the common law concept of the privilege, the continental defendant is not free to decide whether to take the stand and submit to the interrogation process. Questions can always be asked of him. He only has the right to refuse to answer at all, or refuse to respond to particular questions. Although, as a matter of formal doctrine, the trier of fact is usually not permitted to draw unfavorable inferences from his silence, the defendant's quite realistic concern that such inferences will, consciously or unconsciously, in fact be drawn, acts in a typical case as a psychological pressure to speak and respond to questions. Thus, it should occasion no surprise that almost all continental defendants choose to testify. The pressure to speak is, I believe, somewhat stronger than the parallel pressure in the common law trial on the defendant to take the stand, as more immediate inferences can be drawn from refusal to answer specific questions than from the general refusal to submit to the questioning process. . . .

. . . The proper dimensions of the difference in the approach of the two systems to the use of the defendant's testimony at trial can, however, not be ascertained if one ignores the time sequence. In the common law trial, of course, the defendant cannot take the stand, even if he wishes to do so, before the prosecution has established a prima facie case. Before he is given a chance to submit to questioning, he has already heard the witnesses for the prosecution. Consider the defendant's position in the continental courtroom. As there is no requirement here that the prosecution establish a credible case before the defense introduces its evidence, there is no obstacle to beginning the proof-taking stage by the interrogation of the defendant, and this in fact is the rule in continental systems. . . . While the strategic value of this arrangement for the defense is a matter of some dispute, there is little doubt that it is advantageous to the prosecution.

Schlesinger, Comparative Criminal Procedure: A plea for utilizing foreign experience, 26 Buff. L. Rev. 361, 378-381, 384 (1977): In . . . encouraging the accused to remain silent, our legal system stands virtually alone. In England, defendants rarely opt for silence, because English law differs from ours in two crucial respects. If the accused takes the stand, the English rule is to the effect that he cannot by reason of that alone be cross-examined as to previous convictions. And if he remains silent, the judge is authorized by English law to "suggest to the jury that it draw an adverse inference from the defendant's failure to explain away the evidence against him."

Implementing a similar policy by partly different techniques, the continental systems likewise discourage the accused from standing mute. . . . Thus, by combining unlimited discovery for the benefit of the defense with rules making it advantageous for the accused to talk, the continental systems have fashioned a highly efficient vehicle for the ascertainment of truth. . . .

I realize, of course, that other values may compete with the value of truth.

The truth may have to remain hidden if it can be brought out into the open only at the expense of human dignity or of other values held sacred in our society. But, as English and continental experience shows, the defendant's dignity is not diminished, and no other basic values are seriously jeopardized, by rules which in a civilized manner discourage silence, for example, by a rule permitting the trier of the facts to draw whatever inferences may be dictated by logic and reason.

5. For other useful discussions of the origins of and justifications for the privilege, see E. Griswold, The Fifth Amendment Today (1955): L. Levy, Origins of the Fifth Amendment (1968); L. Mayers, Shall We Amend the Fifth Amendment? (1959); McKay, Self-Incrimination and the New Privacy, [1967] Sup. Ct. Rev. 193.

NOTE ON THE CONSEQUENCES OF THE PRIVILEGE

Whatever doubts there may be about the justifications for the privilege, it remains a definite given in the American procedural system. Even if the scope of the privilege should be interpreted less expansively by the Supreme Court in years ahead, the government undoubtedly will continue to be denied formal power to compel the criminal defendant to take the stand. This fact plainly makes the prosecutor's task more difficult than it otherwise would be, particularly if the defendant's own frame of mind is an essential part of what the prosecutor must prove and if this proof must be made beyond a reasonable doubt. Consider how the existence of the privilege may affect legislative and judicial decisions about what facts have to be proved (Chapter 4 infra) or about when the prosecution should shoulder the burden of proving them (Chapter 2, pages 67-82 infra). Is it clear that easing the government's task in these ways is less dangerous than modifying some applications of the privilege?

4. *Proof beyond a Reasonable Doubt*

INTRODUCTORY NOTES

1. The constitutional rule and its foundations. In In re Winship, 397 U.S. 358, 364 (1970), the Supreme Court held that "the Due Process Clause protects the accused against conviction except upon proof beyond a reasonable doubt of every fact necessary to constitute the crime charged." The Court explained the fundamental importance of this standard of proof as follows (id. at 363-364):

> The reasonable-doubt standard plays a vital role in the American scheme of criminal procedure. It is a prime instrument for reducing the risk of convictions resting on factual error. The standard provides concrete substance for the presumption of innocence — that bedrock "axiomatic and elementary" principle whose "enforcement lies at the foundation of the administration of our criminal law.". . .

. . . The accused during a criminal prosecution has at stake interests of immense importance, both because of the possibility that he may lose his liberty upon conviction and because of the certainty that he would be stigmatized by the conviction. Accordingly, a society that values the good name and freedom of every individual should not condemn a man for commission of a crime when there is reasonable doubt about his guilt. . . .

Moreover, use of the reasonable-doubt standard is indispensable to command the respect and confidence of the community in applications of the criminal law. It is critical that the moral force of the criminal law not be diluted by a standard of proof that leaves people in doubt whether innocent men are being condemned. It is also important in our free society that every individual going about his ordinary affairs have confidence that his government cannot adjudge him guilty of a criminal offense without convincing a proper factfinder of his guilt with utmost certainty.

In a concurring opinion Mr. Justice Harlan added (id. at 371-372):

If . . . the standard of proof for a criminal trial were a preponderance of the evidence rather than proof beyond a reasonable doubt, there would be a smaller risk of factual errors that result in freeing guilty persons, but a far greater risk of factual errors that result in convicting the innocent. Because the standard of proof affects the comparative frequency of these two types of erroneous outcomes, the choice of the standard to be applied in a particular kind of litigation should, in a rational world, reflect an assessment of the comparative social disutility of each.

When one makes such an assessment, the reason for different standards of proof in civil as opposed to criminal litigation becomes apparent. In a civil suit between two private parties for money damages, for example, we view it as no more serious in general for there to be an erroneous verdict in the defendant's favor than for there to be an erroneous verdict in the plaintiff's favor. . . .

In a criminal case, on the other hand, we do not view the social disutility of convicting an innocent man as equivalent to the disutility of acquitting someone who is guilty. . . . In this context, I view the requirement of proof beyond a reasonable doubt in a criminal case as bottomed on a fundamental value determination of our society that it is far worse to convict an innocent man than to let a guilty man go free.

2. How burden-of-proof problems arise. Problems relating to the reasonable-doubt standard can surface in many different ways. The issue normally arises first at the close of the prosecution's case. If the judge decides that the evidence raises a reasonable doubt about guilt *as a matter of law* (an elusive concept explored in the next paragraph), the judge must direct a verdict for the defendant. The same problem of assessing the sufficiency of the evidence may be presented to the judge again at the close of all the evidence (when the defendant may again move for a directed verdict); it will be a central concern of the jurors in their deliberations; and it may arise again on appeal (when the defendant may seek reversal on the basis of insufficient evidence).

Courts have often had difficulty articulating the standard that judges should apply in determining whether the evidence is insufficient as a matter of law. In a sense the judges must give the defendant the *benefit of the doubt.* If there is a reasonable doubt, then a guilty verdict would seem improper. On the other hand, before taking a case away from the jury (or reversing a jury's verdict), judges must resolve all evidentiary doubts against the proponent of the motion; in this sense the courts must give the *prosecution* the benefit of the doubt on the question whether its evidence does prove guilt beyond a reasonable doubt. The following comment from the opinion in Curley v. United States, 160 F.2d 229, 232-233 (D.C. Cir. 1947), helps clarify this elusive problem and provides a relatively precise statement of the test that judges apply in passing on questions of evidentiary sufficiency:

> [It is sometimes said] that unless the evidence excludes the hypothesis of innocence, the judge must direct a verdict . . . [and] that if the evidence is such that a reasonable mind might fairly conclude either guilt or innocence, a verdict of guilt must be reversed on appeal. But obviously neither of those translations is the law. Logically the ultimate premise of that thesis is that if a reasonable mind might have a reasonable doubt, there is, therefore, a reasonable doubt. That is not true. . . .
>
> The functions of the jury include the determination of the credibility of witnesses, the weighing of the evidence, and the drawing of justifiable inferences of fact from proven facts. It is the function of the judge to deny the jury any opportunity to operate beyond its province: The jury may not be permitted to conjecture merely, or to conclude upon pure speculation or from passion, prejudice or sympathy. The critical point in this boundary is the existence or non-existence of a reasonable doubt as to guilt. If the evidence is such that reasonable jurymen must necessarily have such a doubt, the judge must require acquittal, because no other result is permissible within the fixed bounds of jury consideration. But if a reasonable mind might fairly have a reasonable doubt or might fairly not have one, the case is for the jury, and the decision is for the jurors to make. . . .
>
> The true rule, therefore, is that a trial judge, in passing upon a motion for directed verdict of acquittal, must determine whether upon the evidence, giving full play to the right of the jury to determine credibility, weigh the evidence, and draw justifiable inferences of fact, a reasonable mind might fairly conclude guilt beyond a reasonable doubt. . . . If he concludes that either of the two results, a reasonable doubt or no reasonable doubt, is fairly possible, he must let the jury decide the matter. In a given case, particularly one of circumstantial evidence, that determination may depend upon the difference between pure speculation and legitimate inference from proven facts. The task of the judge in such case is not easy, for the rule of reason is frequently difficult to apply, but we know of no way to avoid that difficulty.

The problem of evidentiary sufficiency arises not only for judges but for the jury, and the instructions accordingly must tell the jury how it should evaluate the evidence. A conviction could be reversed for error in explaining the reasonable doubt standard to the jury, even though the appellate court might not consider the evidence insufficient as a matter of law. A typical definition of *reasonable doubt* is the following (Cal. Jury Instructions — Criminal §2.90 (4th ed. 1979)): [46]

46. Empirical studies tend to show that jurors do convict more readily when intructed under a more-likely-than-not standard than when instructed under the reasonable-doubt standard. See Underwood, The Thumb on the Scales of Justice: Burdens of Persuasion in Criminal Cases, 86 Yale L.J. 1299, 1309-1311 (1977); Simon & Mahan, Quantifying Burdens of Proof, 5 L. & Soc. Rev. 319 (1971); Cornish & Sealy, Juries and the Rules of Evidence, [1973] Crim. L. Rev. 208. There are relatively few studies of whether juries distinguish among different ways of formulating the reasonable-doubt standard. However, Cornish & Sealy, supra, at 216-217, found jurors even less likely to convict when instructed that they must "feel sure and certain" than they were when instructed that they must be "sure beyond a reasonable doubt." For exploration of the impact of jury instructions generally, see pages 44-48 supra.

Reasonable doubt is . . . not a mere possible doubt; because everything relating to human affairs, and depending on moral evidence, is open to some possible or imaginary doubt. It is that state of the case which, after the entire comparison and consideration of all the evidence, leaves the minds of the jurors in that condition that they cannot say they feel an abiding conviction, to a moral certainty, of the truth of the charge.

The foregoing problems of evidentiary sufficiency are distinct from questions concerning the *allocation* of the burden of proof. As we shall see, even though the ultimate finding of guilt must be made *beyond reasonable doubt,* it is sometimes permissible for the burden of proof on particular subsidiary issues to be imposed on the defendant. Finally, the prosecution may, while technically retaining the burden of proof, seek to invoke a *presumption.* Through this device the burden of establishing some essential fact can be met through proof of some other fact (from which the existence of the essential fact can be "presumed"). Like problems of evidentiary sufficiency, these problems of allocating the burden of proof and invoking presumptions can arise in the context of a challenge to jury instructions dealing with these matters or a challenge for failure to grant a directed verdict. The difference is that in situations involving allocation issues or presumptions, the prosecution normally will concede that it has not proved a particular point beyond a reasonable doubt; the question will be whether it must do so.

The materials in this section explore these last two aspects of the burden of proof — the allocation of the burden and the use of presumptions.

a. Allocating the Burden of Proof

<u>PATTERSON v. NEW YORK</u>
Supreme Court of the United States
432 U.S. 197 (1977)

MR. JUSTICE WHITE delivered the opinion of the Court. . . .

After a brief and unstable marriage, the appellant, Gordon Patterson, Jr., became estranged from his wife, Roberta. Roberta resumed an association with John Northrup, a neighbor to whom she had been engaged prior to her marriage to appellant. On December 27, 1970, Patterson borrowed a rifle from an acquaintance and went to the residence of his father-in-law. There, he observed his wife through a window in a state of semiundress in the presence of John Northrup. He entered the house and killed Northrup by shooting him twice in the head.

Patterson was charged with second-degree murder. In New York there are two elements of this crime: (1) "intent to cause the death of another person"; and (2) "caus[ing] the death of such person or of a third person." Malice aforethought is not an element of the crime. In addition, the State permits a person accused of murder to raise an affirmative defense that he "acted under the influence of extreme emotional disturbance for which there was a reasonable explanation or excuse." [a]

a. The relevant provisions of the New York Penal Code may be found at pages 413-415 infra. — EDS.

New York also recognizes the crime of manslaughter. A person is guilty of manslaughter if he intentionally kills another person "under circumstances which do not constitute murder because he acts under the influence of extreme emotional disturbance." Appellant confessed before trial to killing Northrup, but at trial he raised the defense of extreme emotional disturbance.

The jury was instructed as to the elements of the crime of murder. Focusing on the element of intent, the trial court charged:

> Before you, considering all of the evidence, can convict this defendant or anyone of murder, you must believe and decide that the People have established beyond a reasonable doubt that he intended, in firing the gun, to kill either the victim himself or some other human being. . . .
>
> Always remember that you must not expect or require the defendant to prove to your satisfaction that his acts were done without the intent to kill. Whatever proof he may have attempted, however far he may have gone in an effort to convince you of his innocence or guiltlessness, he is not obliged, he is not obligated to prove anything. It is always the People's burden to prove his guilt, and to prove that he intended to kill in this instance beyond a reasonable doubt.

The jury was further instructed, consistently with New York law, that the defendant had the burden of proving his affirmative defense by a preponderance of the evidence. The jury was told that if it found beyond a reasonable doubt that appellant had intentionally killed Northrup but that appellant had demonstrated by a preponderance of the evidence that he had acted under the influence of extreme emotional disturbance, it had to find appellant guilty of manslaughter instead of murder.

The jury found appellant guilty of murder. Judgment was entered on the verdict, and the Appellate Division affirmed. While appeal to the New York Court of Appeals was pending, this Court decided Mullaney v. Wilbur, 421 U.S. 684 (1975), in which the Court declared Maine's murder statute unconstitutional. Under the Maine statute, a person accused of murder could rebut the statutory presumption that he committed the offense with "malice aforethought" by proving that he acted in the heat of passion on sudden provocation. The Court held that this scheme improperly shifted the burden of persuasion from the prosecutor to the defendant and was therefore a violation of due process. In the Court of Appeals appellant urged that New York's murder statute is functionally equivalent to the one struck down in *Mullaney* and that therefore his conviction should be reversed.

The Court of Appeals rejected appellant's argument, . . . distinguish[ing] *Mullaney* on the ground that the New York statute involved no shifting of the burden to the defendant to disprove any fact essential to the offense charged since the New York affirmative defense of extreme emotional disturbance bears no direct relationship to any element of murder. This appeal ensued. . . . We affirm. . . .

In determining whether New York's allocation to the defendant of proving the mitigating circumstances of severe emotional disturbance is consistent with due process, it is . . . relevant to note that this defense is a considerably expanded version of the common-law defense of heat of passion on sudden provocation and that at common law the burden of proving the latter, as well as other affirmative defenses — indeed, "all . . . circumstances of justification, excuse or alleviation"— rested on the defendant. 4 W. Blackstone, Commentaries *201. This was the rule when the Fifth Amendment was adopted, and it was the American rule when the Fourteenth Amendment was ratified. Commonwealth v. York, 50 Mass. 93 (1845).

In 1895 the common-law view was abandoned with respect to the insanity defense in federal prosecutions. Davis v. United States, 160 U.S. 469 (1895). This ruling had wide impact on the practice in the federal courts with respect to the burden of proving various affirmative defenses, and the prosecution in a majority of jurisdictions in this country sooner or later came to shoulder the burden of proving the sanity of the accused and of disproving the facts constituting other affirmative defenses, including provocation. *Davis* was not a constitutional ruling, however, as Leland v. Oregon, [343 U.S. 790 (1952)], made clear.

At issue in Leland v. Oregon was the constitutionality under the Due Process Clause of the Oregon rule that the defense of insanity must be proved by the defendant beyond a reasonable doubt. Noting that *Davis* "obviously establish[ed] no constitutional doctrine," the Court refused to strike down the Oregon scheme, saying that the burden of proving all elements of the crime beyond reasonable doubt, including the elements of premeditation and deliberation, was placed on the State under Oregon procedures and remained there throughout the trial. To convict, the jury was required to find each element of the crime beyond a reasonable doubt, based on all the evidence, including the evidence going to the issue of insanity. Only then was the jury "to consider separately the issue of legal sanity per se. . . ." This practice did not offend the Due Process Clause even though among the 20 States then placing the burden of proving his insanity on the defendant, Oregon was alone in requiring him to convince the jury beyond a reasonable doubt. . . .

[After the decision in *Mullaney,* supra,] the Court confirmed that it remained constitutional to burden the defendant with proving his insanity defense when it dismissed, as not raising a substantial federal question, a case in which the appellant specifically challenged the continuing validity of Leland v. Oregon. . . . Rivera v. Delaware, 429 U.S. 877 (1976). . . .

We cannot conclude that Patterson's conviction under the New York law deprived him of due process of law. The crime of murder is defined by the statute, which represents a recent revision of the state criminal code, as causing the death of another person with intent to do so. The death, the intent to kill, and causation are the facts that the State is required to prove beyond a reasonable doubt if a person is to be convicted of murder. No further facts are either presumed or inferred in order to constitute the crime. . . . It seems to us that the State satisfied the mandate of *Winship* [, 397 U.S. 358 (1970), page 64 supra,] that it prove beyond a reasonable doubt "every fact necessary to constitute the crime with which [Patterson was] charged."

In convicting Patterson under its murder statute, New York did no more than *Leland* and *Rivera* permitted it to do without violating the Due Process Clause. Under those cases, once the facts constituting a crime are established beyond a reasonable doubt, based on all the evidence including the evidence of the defendant's mental state, the State may refuse to sustain the affirmative defense of insanity unless demonstrated by a preponderance of the evidence.[b]

The New York law on extreme emotional disturbance follows this pattern. This affirmative defense . . . does not serve to negative any facts of the crime which the State is to prove in order to convict of murder. It constitutes a separate issue on which the defendant is required to carry the burden of persuasion; and unless we are to overturn *Leland* and *Rivera*, New York has not violated the Due Process Clause, and Patterson's conviction must be sustained.

We are unwilling to reconsider *Leland* and *Rivera*. But even if we were to hold that a State must prove insanity to convict once that fact is put in issue, it would not necessarily follow that a State must prove beyond a reasonable doubt every fact, the existence or nonexistence of which it is willing to recognize as an exculpatory or mitigating circumstance affecting the degree of culpability or the severity of the punishment. Here, in revising its criminal code, New York provided the affirmative defense of extreme emotional disturbance, a substantially expanded version of the older heat-of-passion concept; but it was willing to do so only if the facts making out the defense were established by the defendant with sufficient certainty. The State was itself unwilling to undertake to establish the absence of those facts beyond a reasonable doubt, perhaps fearing that proof would be too difficult and that too many persons deserving treatment as murderers would escape that punishment if the evidence need merely raise a reasonable doubt about the defendant's emotional state. It has been said that the new criminal code of New York contains some 25 affirmative defenses which exculpate or mitigate but which must be established by the defendant to be operative.[10] The Due Process Clause, as we see it, does not put New York to the choice of abandoning those defenses or undertaking to disprove their existence in order to convict of a crime which otherwise is within its constitutional powers to sanction by substantial punishment.

The requirement of proof beyond a reasonable doubt in a criminal case is "bottomed on a fundamental value determination of our society that it is far worse to convict an innocent man than to let a guilty man go free." *Winship,*

---

b. Is the Court implying that when a state treats an issue as an affirmative defense, allocating the burden of proof to the defendant, it is *not* permitted to require the defendant's proof to meet a standard higher than that of "the preponderance of the evidence"? Would such a safeguard be consistent with the Court's reasoning? Note that under the Oregon procedure upheld in *Leland,* the defendant was required to prove insanity *beyond a reasonable doubt.* The Delaware statute upheld in *Rivera* called only for proof by a preponderance, and apparently no state now requires the defense to meet the stringent *Leland* standard. But under the Court's analysis, would a state not be permitted to insist that all affirmative defenses be established beyond a reasonable doubt? — Eds.

10. The State of New York is not alone in this result: "Since the Model Penal Code was completed in 1962, some 22 states have codified and reformed their criminal laws. At least 12 of these jurisdictions have used the concept of an 'affirmative defense' and have defined that phrase to require that the defendant prove the existence of an 'affirmative defense' by a preponderance of the evidence. Additionally, at least six proposed state codes and each of the four successive versions of a revised federal code use the same procedural device. Finally, many jurisdictions that do not generally employ this concept of 'affirmative defense' nevertheless shift the burden of proof to the defendant on particular issues." Low & Jeffries, DICTA: Constitutionalizing the Criminal Law?, 29 Va. Law Weekly, No. 18, p. 1 (1977). Even so, the trend over the years appears to have been to require the prosecution to disprove affirmative defenses beyond a reasonable doubt. The split among the various jurisdictions varies for any given defense. Thus, 22 jurisdictions place the burden of proving the affirmative defense of insanity on the defendant, while 28 jurisdictions place the burden of disproving insanity on the prosecution. . . .

397 U.S., at 372 (Harlan, J., concurring). . . . While it is clear that our society has willingly chosen to bear a substantial burden in order to protect the innocent, it is equally clear that the risk it must bear is not without limits; and Mr. Justice Harlan's aphorism provides little guidance for determining what those limits are. Due process does not require that every conceivable step be taken, at whatever cost, to eliminate the possibility of convicting an innocent person. Punishment of those found guilty by a jury, for example, is not forbidden merely because there is a remote possibility in some instances that an innocent person might go to jail.

. . . It is . . . very likely true that fewer convictions of murder would occur if New York were required to negative the affirmative defense at issue here. But in each instance of a murder conviction under the present law, New York will have proved beyond a reasonable doubt that the defendant has intentionally killed another person, an act which it is not disputed the State may constitutionally criminalize and punish. If the State nevertheless chooses to recognize a factor that mitigates the degree of criminality or punishment, we think the State may assure itself that the fact has been established with reasonable certainty. To recognize at all a mitigating circumstance does not require the State to prove its nonexistence in each case in which the fact is put in issue, if in its judgment this would be too cumbersome, too expensive, and too inaccurate.[11] . . .

This view may seem to permit state legislatures to reallocate burdens of proof by labeling as affirmative defenses at least some elements of the crimes now defined in their statutes. But there are obviously constitutional limits beyond which the States may not go in this regard. "[I]t is not within the province of a legislature to declare an individual guilty or presumptively guilty of a crime." McFarland v. American Sugar Rfg. Co., 241 U.S. 79, 86 (1916). The legislature cannot "validly command that the finding of an indictment, or mere proof of the identity of the accused, should create a presumption of the existence of all the facts essential to guilt." Tot v. United States, 319 U.S. 463, 469 (1943). . . .

It is urged that Mullaney v. Wilbur necessarily invalidates Patterson's conviction. In *Mullaney* the charge was murder, which the Maine statute defined as the unlawful killing of a human being "with malice aforethought, either express or implied." The trial court instructed the jury that the words "malice aforethought" were most important because "malice aforethought is an essential and indispensable element of the crime of murder." Malice, as the statute indicated and as the court instructed, could be implied and was to be implied from "any deliberate, cruel act committed by one person against another suddenly

11. The drafters of the Model Penal Code would, as a matter of policy, place the burden of proving the nonexistence of most affirmative defenses, including the defense involved in this case, on the prosecution once the defendant has come forward with some evidence that the defense is present. The drafters recognize the need for flexibility, however, and would, in "some exceptional situations," place the burden of persuasion on the accused. "Characteristically these are situations where the defense does not obtain at all under existing law and the Code seeks to introduce a mitigation. Resistance to the mitigation, based upon the prosecution's difficulty in obtaining evidence, ought to be lowered if the burden of persuasion is imposed on the defendant. Where that difficulty appears genuine and there is something to be said against allowing the defense at all, we consider it defensible to shift the burden in this way." ALI, Model Penal Code §1.13, Comment, p. 113 (Tent. Draft No. 4, 1955). . . .

. . . or without a considerable provocation," in which event an intentional killing was murder unless by a preponderance of the evidence it was shown that the act was committed "in the heat of passion, on sudden provocation." The instructions emphasized that " 'malice aforethought and heat of passion on sudden provocation are two inconsistent things'; thus, by proving the latter the defendant would negate the former.". . . This Court, accepting the Maine court's interpretation of the Maine law, unanimously agreed with the Court of Appeals that Wilbur's due process rights had been invaded by the presumption casting upon him the burden of proving by a preponderance of the evidence that he had acted in the heat of passion upon sudden provocation.

Mullaney's holding, it is argued, is that the State may not permit the blameworthiness of an act or the severity of punishment authorized for its commission to depend on the presence or absence of an identified fact without assuming the burden of proving the presence or absence of that fact, as the case may be, beyond a reasonable doubt. In our view, the *Mullaney* holding should not be so broadly read. . . .

Mullaney surely held that a State must prove every ingredient of an offense beyond a reasonable doubt, and that it may not shift the burden of proof to the defendant by presuming that ingredient upon proof of the other elements of the offense. This is true even though the State's practice, as in Maine, had been traditionally to the contrary. Such shifting of the burden of persuasion with respect to a fact which the State deems so important that it must be either proved or presumed is impermissible under the Due Process Clause.

It was unnecessary to go further in *Mullaney.* The Maine Supreme Judicial Court made it clear that . . . malice, in the sense of the absence of provocation, was part of the definition of that crime. Yet malice, i.e., lack of provocation, was presumed and could be rebutted by the defendant only by proving by a preponderance of the evidence that he acted with heat of passion upon sudden provocation. In *Mullaney* we held that however traditional this mode of proceeding might have been, it is contrary to the Due Process Clause as construed in *Winship.*

As we have explained, nothing was presumed or implied against Patterson; and his conviction is not invalid under any of our prior cases. The judgment of the New York Court of Appeals is affirmed.

MR. JUSTICE POWELL, with whom MR. JUSTICE BRENNAN and MR. JUSTICE MARSHALL join, dissenting. . . .

Mullaney held invalid Maine's requirement that the defendant prove heat of passion. The Court today, without disavowing the unanimous holding of *Mullaney*, approves New York's requirement that the defendant prove extreme emotional disturbance. The Court manages to run a constitutional boundary line through the barely visible space that separates Maine's law from New York's. It does so on the basis of distinctions in language that are formalistic rather than substantive. . . .

Maine's statute was invalid, the Court reasons, because it "defined [murder] as the unlawful killing of a human being 'with malice aforethought, either express or implied.' ". . . *Winship* was violated only because this "fact"— malice — was "presumed" unless the defendant persuaded the jury otherwise by showing that he acted in the heat of passion. New York, in form presuming no affirmative "fact" against Patterson, and blessed with a statute drafted in the leaner language of the 20th century, escapes constitutional scrutiny unscathed even though the effect on the defendant of New York's placement of the burden of persuasion is exactly the same as Maine's.

This explanation of the *Mullaney* holding bears little resemblance to the basic rationale of that decision. But this is not the cause of greatest concern. The test the Court today establishes allows a legislature to shift, virtually at will, the burden of persuasion with respect to any factor in a criminal case, so long as it is careful not to mention the nonexistence of that factor in the statutory language that defines the crime. The sole requirement is that any references to the factor be confined to those sections that provide for an affirmative defense. . . .

. . . [T]he Court scarcely could distinguish this case from *Mullaney* without closing its eyes to the constitutional values for which *Winship* stands. . . . Explaining *Mullaney,* the Court says today, in effect, that society demands full confidence before a Maine factfinder determines that heat of passion is missing — a demand so insistent that this Court invoked the Constitution to enforce it over the contrary decision by the State. But we are told that society is willing to tolerate far less confidence in New York's factual determination of precisely the same functional issue. . . .

With all respect, this type of constitutional adjudication is indefensibly formalistic. A limited but significant check on possible abuses in the criminal law now becomes an exercise in arid formalities. What *Winship* and *Mullaney* had sought to teach about the limits a free society places on its procedures to safeguard the liberty of its citizens becomes a rather simplistic lesson in statutory draftsmanship. Nothing in the Court's opinion prevents a legislature from applying this new learning to many of the classical elements of the crimes it punishes.[8] It would be preferable, if the Court has found reason to reject the rationale of *Winship* and *Mullaney,* simply and straightforwardly to overrule those precedents.

The Court understandably manifests some uneasiness that its formalistic approach will give legislatures too much latitude in shifting the burden of persuasion. And so it issues a warning that "there are obviously constitutional limits beyond which the States may not go in this regard." The Court thereby concedes that legislative abuses may occur and that they must be curbed by the judicial branch. But if the State is careful to conform to the drafting formulas articulated today, the constitutional limits are anything but "obvious." This decision simply leaves us without a conceptual framework for distinguishing abuses from legitimate legislative adjustments of the burden of persuasion in criminal cases.

It is unnecessary for the Court to retreat to a formalistic test for applying *Winship.* Careful attention to the *Mullaney* decision reveals the principles that should control in this and like cases. *Winship* held that the prosecution must

---

8. For example, a state statute could pass muster under the only solid standard that appears in the Court's opinion if it defined murder as mere physical contact between the defendant and the victim leading to the victim's death, but then set up an affirmative defense leaving it to the defendant to prove that he acted without culpable mens rea. The State, in other words, could be relieved altogether of responsibility for proving *anything* regarding the defendant's state of mind, provided only that the face of the statute meets the Court's drafting formulas.

To be sure, it is unlikely that legislatures will rewrite their criminal laws in this extreme form. The Court seems to think this likelihood of restraint is an added reason for limiting review largely to formalistic examination. But it is completely foreign to this Court's responsibility for constitutional adjudication to limit the scope of judicial review because of the expectation — however reasonable — that legislative bodies will exercise appropriate restraint.

bear the burden of proving beyond a reasonable doubt " 'the existence of every fact necessary to constitute the crime charged.' " In *Mullaney* we concluded that heat of passion was one of the "facts" described in *Winship* — that is, a factor as to which the prosecution must bear the burden of persuasion beyond a reasonable doubt. We reached that result only after making two careful inquiries. First, we noted that the presence or absence of heat of passion made a substantial difference in punishment of the offender and in the stigma associated with the conviction. Second, we reviewed the history, in England and this country, of the factor at issue. Central to the holding in *Mullaney* was our conclusion that heat of passion "has been, almost from the inception of the common law of homicide, the single most important factor in determining the degree of culpability attaching to an unlawful homicide."

Implicit in these two inquiries are the principles that should govern this case. The Due Process Clause requires that the prosecutor bear the burden of persuasion beyond a reasonable doubt only if the factor at issue makes a substantial difference in punishment and stigma. The requirement of course applies a fortiori if the factor makes the difference between guilt and innocence. But a substantial difference in punishment alone is not enough. It also must be shown that in the Anglo-American legal tradition the factor in question historically has held that level of importance. If either branch of the test is not met, then the legislature retains its traditional authority over matters of proof. . . .

I hardly need add that New York's provisions allocating the burden of persuasion as to "extreme emotional disturbance" are unconstitutional when judged by these standards. "Extreme emotional disturbance" is, as the Court of Appeals recognized, the direct descendant of the "heat of passion" factor considered at length in *Mullaney*. . . . The presence or absence of extreme emotional disturbance makes a critical difference in punishment and stigma, and throughout our history the resolution of this issue in fact, although expressed in somewhat different terms, has distinguished manslaughter from murder. See 4 W. Blackstone, Commentaries *190-193, 198-201.

The Court beats its retreat from *Winship* apparently because of a concern that otherwise the federal judiciary will intrude too far into substantive choices concerning the content of a State's criminal law. The concern is legitimate, but misplaced. . . .

The *Winship/Mullaney* test identifies those factors of such importance, historically, in determining punishment and stigma that the Constitution forbids shifting to the defendant the burden of persuasion when such a factor is at issue. *Winship* and *Mullaney* specify only the procedure that is required when a State elects to use such a factor as part of its substantive criminal law. They do not say that the State must elect to use it. For example, where a State has chosen to retain the traditional distinction between murder and manslaughter, as have New York and Maine, the burden of persuasion must remain on the prosecution with respect to the distinguishing factor, in view of its decisive historical importance. But nothing in *Mullaney* or *Winship* precludes a State from abolishing the distinction between murder and manslaughter and treating all unjustifiable homicide as murder.[13] In this significant respect, neither *Winship* nor *Mullaney* eliminates the substantive flexibility that should remain in legislative hands.

13. Perhaps under other principles of due process jurisprudence, certain factors are so fundamental that a State could not, as a substantive matter, refrain from recognizing them so long as it

Moreover, it is unlikely that more than a few factors — although important ones — for which a shift in the burden of persuasion seriously would be considered will come within the *Mullaney* holding. . . . New ameliorative affirmative defenses, about which the Court expresses concern, generally remain undisturbed by the holdings in *Winship* and *Mullaney* — and need not be disturbed by a sound holding reversing Patterson's conviction.

Furthermore, as we indicated in *Mullaney,* even as to those factors upon which the prosecution must bear the burden of persuasion, the State retains an important procedural device to avoid jury confusion and prevent the prosecution from being unduly hampered. The State normally may shift to the defendant the burden of production, that is, the burden of going forward with sufficient evidence "to justify [a reasonable] doubt upon the issue." ALI, Model Penal Code §1.13, Comment, p. 110 (Tent. Draft No. 4, 1955). If the defendant's evidence does not cross this threshold, the issue — be it malice, extreme emotional disturbance, self-defense, or whatever — will not be submitted to the jury. See Sansone v. United States, 380 U.S. 343, 349 (1965); Stevenson v. United States, 162 U.S. 313, 314-316 (1896). . . .

NOTES AND QUESTIONS

1. The burden of production versus the burden of persuasion. Rules allocating the burden of proof deal with two distinct problems. The first concerns allocating the burden of coming forward with enough evidence to put a certain fact in issue. This is commonly referred to as the burden of *production.* The second problem concerns allocating the burden of convincing the trier of fact. This is commonly referred to as the burden of *persuasion.* With respect to most elements of most crimes, the prosecution bears *both* burdens. That is, the prosecution must introduce enough evidence not only to put the facts in issue but also to persuade the trier of fact beyond a reasonable doubt. In some instances state law may require the defense to bear both burdens, and *Patterson* deals with the question of when this is constitutionally permissible. But note that an intermediate position is possible: State law might allocate the burden of *production* to the defense but the burden of *persuasion* to the prosecution. For example, the state might provide that a defendant seeking acquittal on grounds of duress must introduce some evidence of duress,[47] but that once this is done, the prosecu-

---

chooses to punish given conduct as a crime. . . . But substantive limits were not at issue in *Winship* or *Mullaney,* and they are not at issue here.

Even if there are no constitutional limits preventing the State, for example, from treating all homicides as murders punishable equally regardless of mitigating factors like heat of passion or extreme emotional disturbance, the *Winship/Mullaney* rule still plays an important role. The State is then obliged to make its choices concerning the substantive content of its criminal laws with full awareness of the consequences, unable to mask substantive policy choices by shifts in the burden of persuasion. See Fletcher, Two Kinds of Legal Rules: A Comparative Study of Burden-of-Persuasion Practices in Criminal Cases, 77 Yale L.J. 880, 894 (1968) ("The burden of persuasion has proved to be a subtle, low-visibility tool for adjusting the interests of competing classes of litigants"). The political check on potentially harsh legislative action is then more likely to operate. . . .

47. With respect to certain special defenses, notably alibi and insanity, states sometimes require that the defendant give notice of the claim by pleading it prior to trial. Typically, however, the defendant need not raise the defense by a formal pleading, even when he has the burden of production. Note also that the prosecutor's case may itself contain evidence sufficient to put some defense in issue. For example, testimony that defendant shot the deceased during a quarrel may include at least some evidence supportive of a self-defense claim. The burden of production is then satisfied

tion must prove the absence of duress beyond a reasonable doubt. In this situation it is sometimes said (confusingly) that the defendant bears the initial burden of proof and that, once duress is at issue, the burden *shifts* to the prosecution. Or it may be said that absence of duress is *presumed,* but that when evidence of duress is introduced the presumption is *rebutted* or simply *disappears.* All these expressions are equivalent to the more straightforward statement that the defendant bears the burden of production and the prosecution the burden of proof.

Under what circumstances should the burden of production be placed upon the defendant? There appears to be relatively little case law concerning the constitutionality of assigning this burden (as distinguished from the burden of persuasion) to the defense, and in practice the essential considerations are largely pragmatic (Model Penal Code §1.13, Comment at 110-111 (Tent. Draft No. 4, 1955)):

> No single principle can be conscripted to explain when these shifts of burden to defendants are defensible, even if the burden goes no further than to call for the production of some evidence. Neither the logical point that the prosecution would be called upon to prove a negative, nor the grammatical point that the defense rests on an exception or proviso divorced from the definition of the crime is potently persuasive, although both points have been invoked. . . . What is involved seems rather a more subtle balance which acknowledges that a defendant ought not be required to defend until some solid substance is presented to support the accusation but, beyond this, perceives a point where need for narrowing the issues, coupled with the relative accessibility of evidence to the defendant, warrants calling upon him to present his defensive claim. No doubt this point is reached more quickly if, given the facts the prosecution must establish, the normal probabilities are against the defense, but this is hardly an essential factor. Given the mere fact of an intentional homicide, no one can estimate the probability that it was or was not committed in self-defense. The point is rather that purposeful homicide is an event of such gravity to society, and the basis for a claim of self-defense is so specially within the cognizance of the defendant, that it is fair to call on him to offer evidence if the defense is claimed. . . .

When the defendant does bear the burden of production, how much evidence is necessary to satisfy that burden so that the prosecution will be required to disprove the claim beyond a reasonable doubt? Courts have used a variety of formulas to describe the amount of evidence required; some refer to evidence that "fairly raises the issue" or even to "slight evidence." Howard v. United States, 232 F.2d 274, 276 (5th Cir. 1956). One court has spoken in terms of "some" evidence but "more than a mere scintilla." Kadis v. United States, 373 F.2d 370, 374 (1st Cir. 1967). There appears to be a trend toward requiring that the evidence be sufficient to raise at least a reasonable doubt on the matter. See Frazier v. Weatherholtz, 572 F.2d 994 (4th Cir. 1978). In any event, once the defense has produced evidence sufficient to satisfy the applicable threshold requirement, it becomes necessary to determine which party must bear the burden of persuading the trier of fact.

---

even if the evidence is not offered by the defense itself. When we say that the defendant bears the burden of production we mean not that the defendant himself or other defense witnesses must produce the evidence directly but only that the defense will lose on the issue if some evidence is not produced.

2. *Allocating the burden of persuasion: the basis of* Patterson. Which of the various considerations invoked by the Court in *Patterson* is central to its decision? Does the Court hold that the states may allocate a burden of persuasion to the defendant whenever they choose to do so or only when the considerations specifically relied on in *Patterson* are applicable? Consider these problems:

(*a*) *The formal structure of the statute.* Suppose that (as is commonly the case) state law defines murder as an "unlawful killing with malice aforethought." Under such a statutory scheme a justification like self-defense presumably renders a killing lawful and thus negates one of the definitional elements of murder. Does this mean that the constitution forbids imposing the burden of persuasion on the defendant on the self-defense issue? Should the result be different if state law explicitly describes self-defense as an affirmative defense; if state law expressly imposes the burden of persuasion on the defendant, or only if the word *unlawful* is absent from the language defining murder? Why should constitutional requirements turn on distinctions of this kind? Compare Wynn v. Mahoney, 600 F.2d 448 (4th Cir. 1979) (placing burden on defendant is unconstitutional because in North Carolina "unlawfulness" is an element of murder), with Williams v. Mohn, 462 F. Supp. 756 (N.D.W. Va. 1978) (opposite result because in West Virginia "unlawfulness" not an element of murder). See also Berrier v. Egeler, 583 F.2d 515 (6th Cir. 1978) (court splits because in Michigan murder is defined by common law rather than by statute; majority and dissent disagree about whether common law cases make the absence of self-defense an element of murder).

(*b*) *The alibi defense.* Suppose that a state judge charges the jury that (1) the state must prove beyond a reasonable doubt all the elements of robbery and must prove beyond a reasonable doubt that the robbery was committed by this defendant and (2) as for the defendant's claim "that he was not present at the time . . . this is known as the affirmative defense of alibi. . . . [I]t is the defendant's burden to prove to your satisfaction the defense of alibi . . . by a preponderance of the evidence. . . ." Does this charge fit the pattern of cases like *Leland, Rivera,* and *Patterson,* or is it impermissible under *Mullaney?* See Rogers v. Redman, 457 F. Supp. 929, 931 (D. Del. 1978). See also Wright v. Smith, 569 F.2d 1188 (2d Cir. 1978).

(*c*) *Liberalizing and nonliberalizing changes in the law.* In *Patterson* the affirmative defense involved "a substantially expanded version of the older heat-of-passion concept," and the Court stressed the need for permitting the states flexibility in this situation. But what if, after *Patterson*, a state decides to shift to the defendant a burden of persuasion that had previously been imposed on the prosecution and does not in any way enlarge the scope of the traditionally sanctioned defense? See Novosel v. Helgemore, 384 A.2d 124 (N.H. 1978) (insanity); State v. King, 39 Wash. 2d 541, 599 P.2d 522 (1979) (self-defense). Should it matter whether the traditional defense might otherwise have been restricted or repealed? Would it be feasible (and seemly) for courts to resolve the constitutional issues on that basis?

3. *An alternative approach: limitations based on substance rather than procedural structure.* (*a*) *Should the greater power include the lesser?* The *Patterson* majority assumed that New York could choose to eliminate the "extreme emotional disturbance" defense altogether, a point conceded by Justice Powell's dissent. If this is so, how can there be any serious challenge to the constitutionality of recognizing

the defense only in diluted form, that is, when the defendant can prove it? Several commentators argue that "the greater power should include the lesser." [48] Under this analysis the constitutionality of imposing a burden of persuasion on the defendant would not depend on either the formal structure of the statute or the kind of historical analysis emphasized in the dissenting opinion. Rather, the states would be left free to reallocate burdens of persuasion relating to any fact that is not a constitutionally mandated prerequisite to just punishment, but, conversely, the states would be required to prove a fact beyond a reasonable doubt if punishment would be impermissible (or constitutionally excessive, violating Eight Amendment proportionality requirements) as applied to conduct not involving that fact. See, e.g., Allen, The Restoration of In re Winship: A Comment on Burdens of Persuasion in Criminal Cases after Patterson v. New York, 76 Mich. L. Rev. 30 (1977); Jeffries & Stephan, Defenses, Presumptions and Burdens of Proof in Criminal Law, 88 Yale L.J. 1325 (1979). Is the greater-includes-the-lesser analysis satisfactory? Consider these comments.

Jeffries & Stephan, Defenses, Presumptions and Burdens of Proof in the Criminal Law, 88 Yale L.J. 1325, 1345-1347 (1979): The procedural interpretation of *Winship* would allow the government to abolish a given ground of exculpation, but not to retain it as an affirmative defense. . . . [T]he procedural approach to burden of proof would force the state to choose between the extremes of proving more or proving less. On the face of it, we find it hard to believe that this incongruity is constitutionally mandated.

. . . [A] purely procedural interpretation of *Winship* — one that is wholly illogical as a statement of substantive policy — must find its justification in an exclusively procedural concern that exists no matter what the content of the underlying substantive issue. . . . The chief justification for proof beyond a reasonable doubt in general has always been thought to be that it enhances the certainty of the factual findings needed for criminal conviction. . . . The trouble is that this rationale does not justify the rule for which it is offered. Implementing the presumption of innocence — whether on an actual or a symbolic level — requires that *something* be proved beyond a reasonable doubt. It does not, however, speak to the question of *what* that something must be. . . . In our view, these rationales extend only so far as the substantive issue at stake is thought to be an essential ingredient of the state's case. When, in contrast, the state considers a gratuitous defense, that is, one that it may grant or deny as it sees fit, a constitutional insistence on proof beyond a reasonable doubt no longer makes sense. Such a rule would purport to preserve individual liberty and the societal sense of commitment to it by forcing the government *either* to disprove the defense beyond a reasonable doubt *or* to eliminate the defense altogether. The latter solution results in an extension of penal liability despite the presence of mitigating or exculpatory facts. It is difficult to see this result as constitutionally compelled and harder still to believe that it flows from a general policy, whether actual or symbolic, in favor of individual liberty.[62] . . .

48. The originator of the greater-includes-the-lesser argument in this context is generally thought to be Justice Holmes, who advanced it in his opinion for the Court in Ferry v. Ramsey, 277 U.S. 88 (1928).

62. There is no apparent reason to believe that the symbolic value of society's commitment to proof beyond a reasonable doubt is in any way impaired by the existence of presumptions and

The trouble lies in trying to define justice in exclusively procedural terms. *Winship*'s insistence on the reasonable doubt standard is thought to express a preference for letting the guilty go free rather than risking conviction of the innocent. This value choice, however, cannot be implemented by a purely procedural concern with burden of proof. Guilt and innocence are substantive concepts. Their content depends on the choice of facts determinative of liability. If this choice is remitted to unconstrained legislative discretion, no rule of constitutional procedure can restrain the potential for injustice. . . . This doctrine would force a legislative election between proving more or proving less, but it would not reduce the risk of convicting the "innocent" in any save a cruelly formal sense.

Underwood, The Thumb on the Scales of Justice: Burdens of Persuasion in Criminal Cases, 86 Yale L.J. 1299, 1312-1313, 1321-1324 (1977): Some commentators . . . [argue that] if the legislature has the power to make a fact irrelevant to guilt, then the legislature must also have the power to choose its own rules for proving that fact. In particular, when the law provides a defense that turns on proof of such a fact, that defense may be characterized as gratuitous, and therefore exempt from the requirement of proof by the government beyond a reasonable doubt. . . .

[Professor Underwood challenges the "gratuitous defense" argument on several grounds. Two are particularly relevant for present purposes. First, she argues, adjusting burdens of proof is an inappropriate way of compromising disputes over the proper reach of substantive law. Second, this approach tends to obscure the substantive commands of the law. Excerpts from the discussion of these two points follow.]

[First, s]uppose that a legislature has decided to prohibit the possession of certain narcotic drugs. Suppose further that there is a controversy over a proposal to exempt from punishment those who possess narcotics solely for their personal use. Proponents and opponents of the defense might well seek an intermediate position that would recognize a defense for some, but not all, of those who possess for personal use. One possibility for substantive compromise would be to exempt from punishment only those who possess specified small quantities for personal use. Another possibility would be to exempt only those who possess for personal use in the privacy of their homes. Each of these compromises, by redefining the prohibited conduct, seeks to accommodate differing views about the harm caused, or the harm threatened, or the culpability of the actor in various situations. This substantive compromise attempts to limit the defense to those who are least culpable, or least harmful, or otherwise least suitable for criminal sanctions in the view of opponents of the defense, and at the same time most centrally deserving of the defense in the view of its proponents.[77]

---

affirmative defenses. These devices have existed for a long time and have not been widely perceived or popularly condemned as invasions of the presumption of innocence.

77. A compromise that takes the form of redefining the crime may of course be motivated by evidentiary considerations. In each of the examples in text, the group might be singled out for the defense precisely because their claim of possession for personal use is thought most likely to be true. Nevertheless, if the compromise is forced into the form of an intermediate position on substantive liability, then it avoids two of the principal targets of the reasonable doubt rule: the opportunity for arbitrariness in the decision of individual cases by prosecutor or factfinder, and the low visibility of a compromise framed in procedural terms.

A substantive disagreement about whether to recognize a defense [of possession solely for personal use] amounts to a disagreement about whether the person with the proposed defense is less suitable than other offenders for specified criminal sanctions. By shifting the burden of persuasion [on the personal-use issue] to the defendant, a legislature limits the defense to those for whom the evidence is most abundant. That group, however, is not necessarily the least culpable, least harmful, or least deterrable. . . . An exception [to the reasonable-doubt rule] designed solely for the purpose of compromise would subvert the policies of the rule, without accomplishing an appropriate compromise of substantive disagreements. . . .

[Second, a]lthough popular understanding of the substantive law is notoriously deficient, rules about proof at trial are even less accessible to popular understanding than rules about conduct in society. One consequence of that fact is that it is somewhat more reasonable in the case of substantive law than in the case of rules of proof to rely on political processes to evaluate and revise the law. Another consequence is that unusual rules of proof, even more than unusual substantive laws, are likely to trap an unsuspecting public into reliance on a false idea of the law. . . .

This is an argument for truth-in-labeling.[a]

(*b*) *Questions.* Under a greater-includes-the-lesser analysis, a court passing on a burden-of-proof question would necessarily have to determine first whether the fact at issue was a constitutionally necessary prerequisite to punishment. The implications of such a requirement will be better appreciated after the constitutional principles applicable to substantive criminal law have been explored.[49] It will be important to consider whether *Patterson,* so interpreted, would fulfill the Court's desire to reduce federal judicial intervention in questions of state substantive criminal law. Conceivably *Patterson,* so interpreted, might even lead to greater "constitutionalization" of the law of crimes. Is this in itself undesirable?

Note also that under this interpretation of *Patterson,* once the Court does uphold shifting the burden to the defendant on a particular fact, its decision would necessarily imply that this fact is *not* a constitutionally necessary element of just punishment. Recall, for example, the *Rivera* decision, discussed in *Patterson,* page 69 supra, summarily dismissing, for want of a substantial federal question, a challenge to a Delaware law that required the defendant to bear the burden of proving insanity. Should *Rivera* be read as settling, by implication, the long-standing debate (see pages 901-909 infra) over the question whether some form of an insanity defense is constitutionally mandated? Consider also the status of self-defense claims. The lower courts seem to assume that a state can, if its statutes are properly cast (see Note 2(a) supra), require the defendant to bear the burden of persuasion on the self-defense issue. Does this mean that a state could constitutionally convict of a crime and — without excessive

a. For comment on Professor Underwood's analysis, see Allen, The Restoration of In re Winship: A Comment on Burdens of Persuasion after Patterson v. New York, 76 Mich. L. Rev. 30, 43-45 & n. 60 (1977); Jeffries & Stephan, Defenses, Presumptions, and Burden of Proof in the Criminal Law, 88 Yale L.J. 1325, 1345-1353 (1979). — Eds.

49. See pages 340-350 (proportionality), 350-370 (notice), 251-257 (voluntary act), and 267-282 (mens rea).

severity — could punish as a murderer, someone who kills under circumstances making the act immediately necessary to save his own life? If self-defense and insanity cannot be regarded as "gratuitous" defenses, should it follow that a shift in the burden of persuasion is necessarily improper?

(*c*) *Summary and comment on substantive approaches.* There is surely great appeal to the notion that if a fact is so important that the constitution mandates consideration of it, then once the fact is in issue the state should be required to negate its existence beyond a reasonable doubt. But this notion must be tested carefully in the context of the specific justifications and excuses that are most often the focus of burden-of-proof debates. The insanity defense poses unique dilemmas because of the rules affecting disposition of persons acquitted by reason of insanity. See pages 843-855 infra. Self-defense involves different problems. The traditional right of self-defense is rather narrow, and a state might wish to expand it. But a legislature might be willing to do this only if it could shift the burden of persuasion to the defendant on the expanded defense. If this shift of burden is constitutional, doesn't the state avoid proving beyond a reasonable doubt a fact essential to substantive guilt? But if this shift of burden is not constitutional, won't the state be induced to retain the narrowly defined defense and forego the kinds of ameliorative reform that the greater-includes-the-lesser advocates seek to encourage?[50]

If it seems inappropriate to limit burden-of-proof analysis solely to the question whether a particular fact is a constitutionally mandated element of just punishment, what alternatives are feasible? Can a balancing approach (considering whatever historical traditions and substantive problems may be pertinent in a given case) afford a workable basis for constitutional adjudication? The problem should be reconsidered after the various doctrines of substantive law have been studied in depth.

4. How should a state exercise its discretion? Patterson deals only with the question of a state's *minimum* obligations under the constitution. Even where *Patterson* leaves a state free to impose a burden of persuasion on the defendant, the decision does not of course imply that the state must do so or even that the state preferably should do so. State legislatures (or state courts, when statutes do not control) must decide what is desirable, as a matter of policy, with respect to each defense of this kind. Those making the choice will usually want to consider whether the defendant would have much more ready access to the relevant evidence, whether a defendant's claim would be intrinsically difficult to refute beyond a reasonable doubt, and whether a refusal to shift the burden of persuasion to the defendant on the specific issue would prevent recognition of a new or expanded substantive defense. Burden-of-proof questions therefore should be reconsidered in light of specific problems associated with particular substantive law doctrines.

5. Further reading. For a useful analysis of the early American decisions concerning the allocation problem and a comparison of them to French and German approaches, see Fletcher, Two Kinds of Legal Rules: A Comparative Study of Burden-of-Persuasion Practices in Criminal Cases, 77 Yale L.J. 880 (1968).

---

50. In theory, the prosecution could be required to negate those minimal elements of the defense that are constitutionally mandated, while the defendant would bear the burden of proving the aspects of an expanded defense that are constitutionally optional; in practice this cumbersome approach could not realistically be implemented.

See also Dutile, The Burden of Proof in Criminal Cases: A Comment on the *Mullaney-Patterson* Doctrine, 55 Notre Dame Law. 380 (1980); McLane, The Burden of Proof in Criminal Cases: *Mullaney* and *Patterson* Compared, 15 Crim. L. Bull. 346 (1979); Angel, Substantive Due Process and the Criminal Law, 9 Loy. Chi. L.J. 61, 93-111 (1977); Ashford & Risinger, Presumptions, Assumptions, and Due Process in Criminal Cases: A Theoretical Overview, 79 Yale L.J. 165 (1969); Comment, The Constitutionality of Affirmative Defenses after Patterson v. New York, 78 Colum. L. Rev. 655 (1978).

b.   Presumptions

LEARY v. UNITED STATES
Supreme Court of the United States
395 U.S. 6 (1969)

MR. JUSTICE HARLAN delivered the opinion of the Court.

This case presents constitutional questions arising out of the conviction of the petitioner, Dr. Timothy Leary, for violation of two federal statutes governing traffic in marihuana.

. . . On December 20, 1965, petitioner left New York by automobile, intending a vacation trip to Yucatan, Mexico. He was accompanied by his daughter and son, both teenagers, and two other persons. On December 22, 1965, the party drove across the International Bridge between the United States and Mexico at Laredo, Texas. They stopped at the Mexican customs station and, after apparently being denied entry, drove back across the bridge. They halted at the American secondary inspection area, explained the situation to a customs inspector, and stated that they had nothing from Mexico to declare. The inspector asked them to alight, examined the interior of the car, and saw what appeared to be marihuana seeds on the floor. The inspector then received permission to search the car and passengers. Small amounts of marihuana were found on the car floor and in the glove compartment. A personal search of petitioner's daughter revealed a silver snuff box containing semi-refined marihuana and three partially smoked marihuana cigarettes. . . .

Leary was convicted on a charge of that he had knowingly transported and facilitated the transportation and concealment of marihuana which had been illegally imported or brought into the United States, with knowledge that it had been illegally imported or brought in, . . . in violation of [21 U.S.C.] §176a. . . .

Insofar as here relevant, §176a imposes criminal punishment upon every person who: . . .

> receives, conceals, buys, sells, or in any manner facilitates the transportation, concealment, or sale of such marihuana after being imported or brought in, knowing the same to have been imported or brought into the United States contrary to law. . . .

A subsequent paragraph establishes the presumption now under scrutiny:

> Whenever on trial for a violation of this subsection, the defendant is shown to have or to have had the marihuana in his possession, such possession shall be

deemed sufficient evidence to authorize conviction unless the defendant explains his possession to the satisfaction of the jury. . . .

By what criteria is the constitutionality of the §176a presumption to be judged?

Early decisions of this Court set forth a number of different standards by which to measure the validity of statutory presumptions. However, in Tot v. United States, 319 U.S. 463 (1943), the Court . . . held that the "controlling" test for determining the validity of a statutory presumption was "that there be a rational connection between the facts proved and the fact presumed." The Court stated: ". . . [W]here the inference is so strained as not to have a reasonable relation to the circumstances of life as we know them, it is not competent for the legislature to create it as a rule governing the procedure of courts."

The Tot Court reduced to the status of a "corollary" another test which had some support in prior decisions: whether it was more convenient for the defendant or for the Government to supply proof of the ultimate fact which the presumption permitted to be inferred. The Court stated that "[t]he argument from convenience is admissible only where the inference is a permissible one. . . ." The Court rejected entirely another suggested test with some backing in the case law, according to which the presumption should be sustained if Congress might legitimately have made it a crime to commit the basic act from which the presumption allowed an inference to be drawn. The Tot Court stated simply that "for whatever reason" Congress had not chosen to make the basic act a crime. . . .

The upshot of Tot . . . is, we think, that a criminal statutory presumption must be regarded as "irrational" or "arbitrary," and hence unconstitutional, unless it can at least be said with substantial assurance that the presumed fact is more likely than not to flow from the proved fact on which it is made to depend.[64] And in the judicial assessment the congressional determination favoring the particular presumption must, of course, weigh heavily.

How does the §176a presumption fare under these standards?

So far as here relevant, the presumption, quoted supra, authorizes the jury to infer from a defendant's possession of marihuana two necessary elements of the crime: (1) that the marihuana was imported or brought into the United States illegally; and (2) that the defendant knew of the unlawful importation or bringing in. . . . For reasons that follow, we hold unconstitutional that part of the presumption which relates to a defendant's knowledge of illegal importation. Consequently, we do not reach the question of the validity of the "illegal importation" inference. . . .

[T]o determine the constitutionality of the "knowledge" inference, one must have direct or circumstantial data regarding the beliefs of marihuana users generally about the source of the drug they consume. . . . Written material inserted in the record of the Senate hearings included [a statement] of an experienced federal customs agent . . . to the effect that high-quality marihuana was being grown near the Texas cities of Laredo and Brownsville. A written report of the Ohio Attorney General recited that marihuana "may grow unnoticed along

---

64. Since we find that the §176a presumption is unconstitutional under this standard, we need not reach the question whether a criminal presumption which passes muster when so judged must also satisfy the criminal "reasonable doubt" standard if proof of the crime charged or an essential element thereof depends upon its use. . . .

roadsides and vacant lots in many parts of the country," and a Philadelphia Police Academy bulletin stated that: "Plenty of [marihuana] is found growing in this city.". . . [Nevertheless] the materials which we have examined point quite strongly to the conclusion that most domestically consumed marihuana is still of foreign origin . . . [But] it by no means follows that a majority of marihuana possessors "know" that their marihuana was illegally imported. . . .

Once it is established that a significant percentage of domestically consumed marihuana may not have been imported at all, then it can no longer be postulated, without proof, that possessors will be even roughly aware of the proportion actually imported. We conclude that in order to sustain the inference of knowledge we must find on the basis of the available materials that a majority of marihuana possessors either are cognizant of the apparently high rate of importation or otherwise have become aware that *their* marihuana was grown abroad. . . .

With respect to packaging, there is evidence that Mexican marihuana is commonly compressed into distinctive "bricks" and then wrapped in characteristically Mexican paper. Yet even if it is assumed that most Mexican marihuana bears such distinguishing marks when first brought into this country, there is no indication that they normally are still present when it reaches the consumer. . . .

With respect to taste, the Senate hearing record contains the statement of a federal customs agent that: "A good marihuana smoker can probably tell good marihuana from bad." As has been seen, there is a preponderance of opinion to the effect that Mexican marihuana is more potent than domestic. One authority states that purchasers of marihuana commonly sample the product before making a "buy." However, the agent quoted above also asserted that some "good" marihuana was grown in Texas. And the account of the sampling custom further states that tasting is merely a ritual since "[u]sually the intoxication will not differ much from one cigarette to another. . . ." Once again, we simply are unable to estimate what proportion of marihuana possessors are capable of "placing" the marihuana in their possession by its taste, much less what proportion actually have done so by the time they are arrested.

We conclude that the "knowledge" aspect of the §176a presumption cannot be upheld. . . .

Reversed and remanded.

[The concurring opinions of the CHIEF JUSTICE and JUSTICES BLACK and STEWART are omitted.]

NOTES AND QUESTIONS

1. The terminology of presumptions. The term *presumption* is used in different and often inconsistent ways. McCormick writes (Evidence §342, at 802-803 (2d ed. 1972)): "One ventures the assertion that 'presumption' is the slipperiest member of the family of legal terms, except its first cousin, 'burden of proof.' One author has listed no less than eight senses in which the term has been used by the courts." To add further variety, courts may refer to *mandatory, permissive, conclusive,* and *rebuttable* presumptions, as well as use terms like *inference* or even *assumption*. To understand the significance of a presumption, one cannot simply resort to a dictionary but must focus on the precise effect of the presumption at trial. Some presumptions concern an inference of fact to be drawn from some other fact in evidence, but such common presumptions as the *presumption of innocence* and the *presumption of sanity* do not function in this evidentiary sense at all. We shall call them *misnamed presumptions*. The inferences of fact drawn from some other fact in evidence are the *true* presumptions subject to the constitutional principles discussed in *Leary*. As we indicate below, however, the presumptions within this category are not all of a piece; inferences of varying force may be drawn and hence the governing constitutional principles may themselves vary.

(a) *Misnamed presumptions.* It is commonly said that a defendant in a criminal case is "presumed innocent until proven guilty." Is this because there is some "rational connection," a "more-often-than-not" relationship between being charged as defendant and being innocent? Obviously not: The vast majority of criminal defendants are ultimately found guilty, and indeed the filing of an indictment requires a formal finding of probable guilt. The presumption of innocence does not concern the drawing of rational inferences from facts in evidence but rather is simply a traditional way of stating that the prosecution bears the burden of proving guilt beyond a reasonable doubt.

Some of the important misnamed presumptions are unfavorable to the defendant. It is common, for example, to state that defendants are "presumed sane" unless some evidence of insanity is introduced or to say that an intentional killing is "presumed to be unlawful," unless the defendant produces evidence of some justification. What is normally meant is that the defendant has the burden of production (and possibly the burden of persuasion) on the issues of insanity or justification. As we have seen earlier in this chapter, in Section B4a, pages 67-82 supra, there are constitutional limitations applicable here, very weak ones for burdens of production and stronger ones governing the burden of persuasion. But the applicable tests in any event are not those discussed in *Leary*. It could be that intentional killings are often, even half the time, committed in self-defense: A true presumption — an evidentiary inference of no self-defense — would surely be unconstitutional, but a presumption that serves only to allocate the burden of production almost surely is constitutional.

(b) *True presumptions.* True presumptions deal with inferences drawn from a fact actually proved (the *basic fact*) to some other critical fact (the *presumed fact*). Typically the presumed fact is one on which the prosecution bears the burden of persuasion. The presumption serves, however, to make this burden somewhat easier to carry.

Note that a presumption may ease the prosecution's burden in several distinct ways. For example, a presumption might allow the jury to draw the inference from basic to presumed fact, or instead the presumption might *require* the jury to draw the inference. The former are often called *permissive* presumptions or permissive inferences; the latter are often called *mandatory* presumptions. Presumptions may also differ in the extent to which they remain effective after the defense offers rebuttal evidence to negate the presumed fact.[51] At one extreme a presumption requiring an inference to be drawn might remain in effect no matter how much evidence was offered to refute the presumed fact. A pre-

---

51. Note that the defense also may offer evidence to challenge the existence of the basic fact. Since the presumption cannot come into play until the trier of fact is satisfied that the *basic* fact exists, refuting the basic fact will always render the presumption inoperative.

sumption of this kind is often called a *conclusive presumption:* In effect it is not a presumption at all because it establishes a substantive rule rendering the basic fact determinative and the presumed fact legally irrelevant. (Do you see why?) At the other extreme, the effect of a presumption might be entirely eliminated once the defense produces a rather small quantum of evidence. A presumption of this kind has precisely the same effect as a rule allocating the burden of production (do you see why?), and once that production burden is satisfied, the so-called presumption has no impact at all on the burden of persuasion.

Other presumptions retain some force even after rebuttal evidence is introduced, but the range of possible variations is wide. State law might provide that upon proof of a basic fact the jury will be required to find the presumed fact, unless the defendant introduces in rebuttal "slight" evidence or "some" evidence or "substantial" evidence. For situations in which the jury is not *required* to find the presumed fact, it may be instructed that it is *permitted* to do so, and the jury also might be informed (with varying degrees of emphasis) about the legislature's or judge's view that the basic fact sometimes (or often or usually) is sufficient to warrant finding the presumed fact. For the sake of convenience we will divide the true presumptions into two major categories: First are the *mandatory-but-rebuttable presumptions.* Here the jury will be told that upon proof of the basic fact, it *must* find the presumed fact, unless a given quantum of rebuttal evidence is forthcoming. There will be variations in the amount of rebuttal evidence required to satisfy this condition.

Second, we have *permissive inferences.* Here the jury will be told that upon proof of the basic fact it *may* (but is not required) to find the presumed fact. Thus, the jury may reject the presumed fact even if no rebuttal is offered, and it may find the presumed fact even if extensive rebuttal is offered. There will be variations in the degree to which the jury is encouraged to find the presumed fact. The cases in this section are concerned with the question whether different constitutional standards should govern permissive, as distinguished from mandatory-but-rebuttable presumptions, and with the question of what those standards should be.

2. The constitutional concerns raised by presumptions. Because a presumption (whether permissive or mandatory-but-rebuttable) can ease the prosecutor's burden of proof, use of this device naturally raises concerns about diluting or evading the constitutional requirement of proof beyond a reasonable doubt. Are concerns of that kind central to the Court's decision in *Leary?* Observe that the reasonable-doubt concept is never relied on in the Court's analysis and that *Winship* was yet to be decided at the time of *Leary.* In the background of judicial sensitivity to presumptions are a variety of broader concerns. Thus, a portion of the *Tot* opinion quoted in *Leary* bases the objection in part on a perception of legislative interference with the rules of procedure governing courts (see page 83 supra), and the Court has held that an irrational presumption is unconstitutional even in a civil case.[52] The notion here seems to be that an irrational presumption intrudes on the factfinding process and thus violates separation of powers

---

52. Western & Atl. R.R. v. Henderson, 279 U.S. 639 (1929). See also Mobile J. & K.C.R.R. v. Turnipseed, 219 U.S. 35 (1910).

principles.[53] In addition, in criminal cases at least three other constitutional rights are implicated:

(a) *The right to jury trial.* To the extent that presumptions influence or even direct the course of jury decisionmaking (and especially when they do so "irrationally"), they may interfere with the right under the Sixth Amendment to have a jury find the facts. We explore the dimensions of this right in Section B5 of this chapter, pages 94-108 infra.

(b) *The right to confront adverse witnesses.* To the extent that a presumption draws its validity either from specialized research or from intuitive judgments debated in the legislature but not made explicit in court, the defendant is in effect denied the opportunity to confront and cross-examine his accusers with respect to the presumed fact.

(c) *The privilege against self-incrimination.* A presumption creates a strong inducement for the defense to offer rebuttal evidence. Sometimes this rebuttal evidence can be provided through witnesses other than the defendant, but in practice the kind of evidence required (in *Leary,* for example, the evidence of defendant's personal knowledge about the origin of the marijuana) is most unlikely to be available from any witness other than the defendant himself. The presumption thus tends to put pressure on the defendant to testify.[54] The very existence of the privilege against self-incrimination goes far toward explaining the need for presumptions (especially those bearing on knowledge and intent) at the same time that it raises concern about their legitimacy.

Combined with all of the above interests is the special concern in criminal cases to insure respect for the requirement of proof beyond a reasonable doubt. To the extent that a presumption is rational (more likely than not to be true), the other concerns are largely and perhaps wholly satisfied, but the reasonable-doubt concern persists, does it not? If a presumption is no better than rational, is the presumed fact supported by anything more than a preponderance of the evidence (out-of-court "evidence" at that)? If not (and if the presumed fact is an element of the offense), how can such a presumption be reconciled with the dictates of *Winship* and *Mullaney?*

3. *Questions about* Leary. (a) *The facts.* Suppose that federal drug authorities succeed in publicizing the relative scarcity of domestically grown marijuana so that nearly all users become aware of the foreign source of the drug. Could the government then invoke the §176a presumption? Or suppose that marijuana from a particular foreign source (Colombia, for example) had a distinctive taste recognizable by all users? Could the government then invoke the §176a presumption at least in prosecutions involving marijuana from that source? In such a case, the defendant is very likely (if he has tasted the drug) to know of its

---

53. See generally Crowell v. Benson, 285 U.S. 22, 56-57, 63-64 (1932). In its specific application in the field of administrative law, the principle illustrated by *Crowell* has, however, undergone considerable evolution. See K. Davis, Administrative Law §29.08, at 539-540 (3d ed. 1972); L. Jaffe, Judicial Control of Administrative Action 87-94 (1965).

54. Of course, not all pressure amounts to compulsion within the meaning of the privilege. But doesn't a presumption like that in *Leary* generate at least as much pressure as did the comment on the defendant's silence held impermissible in Griffin v. California, pages 53-56 supra? If so, should such a presumption be held to violate the privilege against self-incrimination even when it satisfies a more-likely-than-not standard? Or should the rationality of the inference drawn have some bearing on the fairness of the resulting pressure to testify?

source. But if he can raise a reasonable doubt on this question, he should be entitled to an acquittal, should he not? Section 176a requires a defendant to show much more than this, does it not? In other words, doesn't §176a conflict with *Winship even if* the presumption itself satisfies a reasonable-doubt test? If the answer is yes, then the Court's detailed analysis of taste, packaging, and so on was completely unnecessary. But given the Court's approach, a strong presumption structured like §176a might be upheld if it passes the reasonable-doubt test. How can use of that kind of presumption ever be reconciled with *Winship* and *Mullaney*?

(b) *Does the greater power include the lesser?* There is little doubt that Congress could punish possession of illegally imported marijuana without regard to the defendant's knowledge of the importation. See, e.g., United States v. Dotterweich, 320 U.S. 277 (1943), page 1029 infra. Accordingly, the argument goes, a statute using a presumption (however tenuous) to infer knowledge cannot possibly be worse for the defendant than a statute that eliminates the knowledge requirement altogether. In *Leary* the Court dismisses this argument with the simple statement that Congress did choose to make knowledge relevant. Is this an adequate answer? Consider Jeffries & Stephan, page 78 supra, at 1389:

> The *Tot-Leary* approach to the constitutionality of presumptions is conceptually consistent with the *Mullaney* condemnation of affirmative defenses. Both approaches would focus on procedural formality without reference to substantive impact. Both would disallow legislative crime definition for reasons not related to the legitimate scope of legislative authority over the issue in question or to the government's proof of a constitutionally adequate basis for punishment. Both would force the legislature to the incongruous choice of proving either more or less, and both would therefore raise the specter of retrogressive rules of penal liability adopted by reluctant legislatures in order to comply with a supposedly constitutional command of fairness to criminal defendants.

The ramifications of this greater-includes-the-lesser analysis with respect to affirmative defenses are explored at pages 77-81 supra. In the context of presumptions, the analysis raises additional questions. Should a court uphold a wholly irrational presumption (one that is rarely if ever true), whenever the defense in question is constitutionally "gratuitous"? What if the legislature itself thought (or might have thought) that the presumption was rational, but a court's careful focus on the factual relationship suggests that the legislature's premise was false? What if, instead, the legislature makes clear that it does not *care* whether the presumption is rational or not? If there is something about the concept of the judicial function, about the concept of case-by-case adjudication of guilt, that renders such a presumption offensive — even when it relates to a substantive defense that the legislature remains free to abolish completely?

4. Developments following Leary. For many years after the *Leary* decision, the Court continued to leave unresolved the question reserved in footnote 64 of the opinion (see page 83 supra) — whether a valid presumption must not only satisfy the more-likely-than-not standard but also the beyond-a-reasonable-doubt test. But cases reaching the Court also indicated that the choice of a standard might be less important than the way the standard was applied. See, e.g., Turner v. United States, 396 U.S. 398 (1970)(holding that a presumption that the possessor of cocaine knows of its illegal importation could not pass the more-likely-than not test, but that a similar presumption relating to heroin was valid even under the reasonable-doubt standard); Barnes v. United States, 412 U.S. 837 (1973)(upholding under the reasonable-doubt test an instruction that "[p]osses-sion of recently stolen property, if not satisfactorily explained, is ordinarily a circumstance from which [the jury may infer] . . . that the person in possession knew the property had been stolen").

COUNTY COURT OF ULSTER COUNTY v. ALLEN
Supreme Court of the United States
442 U.S. 140 (1979)

[Four persons, three adult males and a 16-year-old girl, riding in a Chevrolet were stopped for speeding on the New York Thruway. Two large-caliber hand-guns were seen through the window of the car by the investigating police officer. The weapons were in an open handbag on either the front floor or the front seat of the car on the passenger side where the girl was sitting, and she admitted that the handbag was hers. All four people in the car were charged with illegal possession of the handguns, and at trial the judge instructed the jurors that upon proof of the presence of a firearm in an automobile, they were entitled to infer illegal possession by all persons then occupying the vehicle. All four defendants were convicted.

[After the convictions were affirmed by the state courts, the defendants initiated federal postconviction proceedings, and the United States Supreme Court granted review. In a complex opinion drawing several important distinctions, the Supreme Court resolved the issue left open in *Leary* and then upheld the convictions. The Court said that in testing a mandatory presumption — one that the jury was *required* to accept in the absence of defense rebuttal — two principles were to be followed: (1) the rationality of the presumption would be examined over the general run of possible situations, without regard to the facts of the particular case and (2) the presumption would pass muster only if, over that generality of cases, it held true beyond a reasonable doubt.

[In contrast, the Court held that in testing a permissive presumption — one that the jury was free to reject even in the absence of defense rebuttal — the principles to be applied were that (1) the rationality of the presumption would be examined in light of the facts of the particular case and (2) the presumption would pass muster if it was "more likely that not" to hold true in the particular case.

[Excerpts from the principal opinions follow.]

MR. JUSTICE STEVENS delivered the opinion of the Court. . . .

. . . Because [a] permissive presumption leaves the trier of fact free to credit or reject the inference and does not shift the burden of proof, it affects the application of the "beyond a reasonable doubt" standard only if, under the facts of the case, there is no rational way the trier could make the connection permitted by the inference. For only in that situation is there any risk that an explanation of the permissible inference to a jury, or its use by a jury, has caused the presumptively rational factfinder to make an erroneous factual deter-mination.

A mandatory presumption is a far more troublesome evidentiary device. For it may affect not only the strength of the "no reasonable doubt" burden but also the placement of that burden; it tells the trier that he or they *must* find the elemental fact upon proof of the basic fact, at least unless the defendant has come forward with some evidence to rebut the presumed connection between the two facts. . . . To the extent that the trier of fact is forced to abide by the presumption, and may not reject it based on an independent evaluation of the particular facts presented by the State, the analysis of the presumption's constitutional validity is logically divorced from those facts and based on the presumption's accuracy in the run of cases.[17]

The trial judge's instructions [in this case] make it clear that the presumption was merely a part of the prosecution's case, that it gave rise to a permissive inference available only in certain circumstances, rather than a mandatory conclusion of possession, and that it could be ignored by the jury even if there was no affirmative proof offered by defendants in rebuttal. . . . In short, the instructions plainly directed the jury to consider all the circumstances tending to support or contradict the inference that all four occupants of the car had possession of the two loaded handguns and to decide the matter for itself without regard to how much evidence the defendants introduced. . . .

As applied to the facts of this case, the presumption of possession is entirely rational..[R]espondents were not "hitch-hikers or other casual passengers," and the guns were neither "a few inches in length" or "out of [respondents'] sight." . . . The argument against possession by any of the respondents was predicated solely on the fact that the guns were in Jane Doe's pocketbook. But several circumstances . . . made it highly improbable that she was the sole custodian of those weapons.

. . . As a 16-year-old girl in the company of three adult men she was the least likely of the four to be carrying one, let alone two, heavy handguns. It is far more probable that she relied on the pocket-knife found in her brassiere for any necessary self-protection. Under these circumstances, it was not unreasonable for her counsel to argue and for the jury to infer that when the car was halted for speeding, the other passengers in the car anticipated the risk of search and attempted to conceal their weapons in a pocketbook in the front seat. The inference is surely more likely than the notion that these weapons were the sole property of the 16-year-old girl.

. . . The application of the statutory presumption in this case therefore com-

17. . . . [T]his point is illustrated by Leary v. United States, supra. . . . [The statute involved there included] a mandatory presumption: "possession shall be deemed sufficient evidence to authorize conviction [for importation] unless the defendant explains his possession to the satisfaction of the jury." Leary admitted possession of the marihuana and claimed that he had carried it from New York to Mexico and then back.

Justice Harlan for the Court noted that under one theory of the case, the jury could have found direct proof of all the necessary elements of the offense without recourse to the presumption. But he deemed that insufficient reason to affirm the conviction because under another theory the jury might have found knowledge of importation on the basis of either direct evidence or the presumption, and there was accordingly no certainty that the jury had not relied on the presumption. The Court therefore found it necessary to test the presumption against the Due Process Clause. . . . Despite the fact that the defendant was well educated and had recently traveled to a country that is a major exporter of marihuana to this country, the Court found the presumption of knowledge of importation from possession irrational. It did so not because Dr. Leary was unlikely to know the source of the marihuana but instead because "a majority of possessors" were unlikely to have such knowledge. . . .

ports with the standard laid down in Tot v. United States, 319 U.S. 463, 467, and restated in Leary v. United States, supra. For there is a "rational connection" between the basic facts that the prosecution proved and the ultimate fact presumed, and the latter is "more likely than not to flow from" the former.

Respondents argue, however, that the validity of the New York presumption must be judged by a "reasonable doubt" test rather than the "more likely than not" standard employed in *Leary*. Under the more stringent test, it is argued that a statutory presumption must be rejected unless the evidence necessary to invoke the inference is sufficient for a rational jury to find the inferred fact beyond a reasonable doubt. Respondents' argument again overlooks the distinction between a permissive presumption on which the prosecution is entitled to rely as one not-necessarily-sufficient part of its proof and a mandatory presumption which the jury must accept even if it is the sole evidence of an element of the offense.

In the latter situation, since the prosecution bears the burden of establishing guilt, it may not rest its case entirely on a presumption unless the fact proved is sufficient to support the inference of guilt beyond a reasonable doubt. But in the former situation, the prosecution may rely on all of the evidence in the record to meet the reasonable doubt standard. There is no more reason to require a permissive statutory presumption to meet a reasonable doubt standard before it may be permitted to play any part in a trial than there is to require that degree of probative force for other relevant evidence before it may be admitted. As long as it is clear that the presumption is not the sole and sufficient basis for a finding of guilt, it need only satisfy the test described in *Leary*. . . .

Mr. Justice Powell, with whom Mr. Justice Brennan, Mr. Justice Stewart, and Mr. Justice Marshall join dissenting. . . .

. . . [T]here are countless situations in which individuals are invited as guests into vehicles the contents of which they know nothing about, much less have control over. . . . Because the specific factual inference recommended to the jury in this case is not one that is supported by the general experience of our society, I cannot say that the presumption charged is "more likely than not" to be true. Accordingly, respondents' due process rights were violated by the presumption's use.

As I understand it, the Court today does not contend that in general those who are present in automobiles are more likely than not to possess any gun contained within their vehicles. It argues, however, that the nature of the presumption here involved requires that we look, not only to the immediate facts upon which the jury was encouraged to base its inference, but to the other facts "proved" by the prosecution as well. The Court suggests that this is the proper approach when reviewing what it calls "permissive" presumptions because the jury was urged "to consider all the circumstances tending to support or contradict the inference." . . . But the jury was told that it could conclude that respondents possessed the weapons found therein from proof of the mere fact of respondents' presence in the automobile. For all we know, the jury rejected all of the prosecution's evidence concerning the location and origin of the guns, and based its conclusion that respondents possessed the weapons solely upon its belief that respondents had been present in the automobile. For purposes of reviewing the constitutionality of the presumption at issue here, we must assume that this was the case. . . .

. . . Under the Court's analysis, whenever it is determined that an inference is "permissive," the only question is whether, in light of all of the evidence adduced at trial, the inference recommended to the jury is a reasonable one. The Court has never suggested that the inquiry into the rational basis of a permissible inference may be circumvented in this manner. Quite the contrary, the Court has required that the "evidence *necessary to invoke the inference* [be] sufficient for a rational juror to find the inferred fact. . . ." Barnes v. United States, 412 U.S. 843 (1973) (emphasis supplied). Under the presumption charged in this case, the only evidence necessary to invoke the inference was the presence of the weapons in the automobile with respondents — an inference that is plainly irrational.

. . . [T]he Court in effect . . . construct[s] a rule that permits the use of any inference — no matter how irrational in itself — provided that otherwise there is sufficient evidence in the record to support a finding of guilt. Applying this novel analysis to the present case, the Court upholds the use of a presumption that it makes no effort to defend in isolation. . . . I dissent.

NOTES

1. Sandstrom v. Montana, 442 U.S. 510 (1979), involved a prosecution for "deliberate homicide." Under Montana law one element of the offense was an intent to kill. The defendant admitted the act of killing but introduced evidence suggesting that the act was not intentional. The jury was instructed that "[t]he law presumes that a person intends the ordinary consequences of his voluntary acts." On appeal from the conviction, the prosecution contended that the quoted language (which was not otherwise explained to the jury) established either a permissive inference or at most only a mandatory presumption rebuttable by "some" evidence and that under either interpretation the presumption satisfied applicable standards. The Supreme Court unanimously reversed. The Court held that the jurors might have understood the instruction either as establishing a conclusive presumption (that is, that intent was deemed to be established regardless of the defendant's proof) or as shifting the burden of persuasion (that is, requiring the defendant to prove the lack of intent by at least a preponderance of the evidence). In either event the presumption violated *Winship*, page 64 supra, and *Mullaney*, page 68 supra, because state law specifically made intent an element of the offense. The Court accordingly did not reach the question whether the instruction would pass muster, if coupled with language clearly rendering its effect permissive or mandatory-but-rebuttable.

2. Does the Court in the *Ulster County* case persuasively explain its choice of a standard for testing permissive presumptions? For that matter, does the Court persuasively explain why permissive presumptions differ significantly, and not merely in degree, from mandatory presumptions? For that matter, has the Court persuasively explained why the various presumptions differ significantly, and not merely in degree, from shifts in the burdens of production and persuasion? Consider the following comment.

Allen, Structuring Jury Decisionmaking in Criminal Cases: A Unified Constitutional Approach to Evidentiary Devices, 94 Harv. L. Rev. 321, 338 (1980), id. at 330-331,

335-337, 362: [T]he superficially distinct evidentiary devices employed in criminal trials — affirmative defenses, placement of burdens of production and the concomitant possibility of a directed verdict on an issue, judicial comment on the evidence, and instructions on presumptions and inferences — are actually very similar. Their primary unifying trait is that they all modify the evidentiary relationship of the parties at trial by manipulating burdens of persuasion. . . .

Moreover, these devices cannot be distinguished on the basis of the magnitude of their effect on the burden of persuasion, for that effect unmistakably varies within each category. . . .

. . . [T]he Supreme Court has upheld the power of the trial judge to express his views on the weight of the evidence, although there have been occasional cases where the trial judge has gone too far.[a] The conventional view of the purpose of such comment, as stated by the Supreme Court, is "to assist [the jury] in arriving at a just conclusion."[37] . . . By commenting on the weight of the evidence as he sees it, the judge attempts to guide the jurors toward a more rational verdict by bringing to their attention implications that may otherwise have eluded them.

. . . Whereas explicit judicial comment attempts to inform the jury of the factors that may be relevant to its decision, and why they may be relevant, presumptive instructions merely inform the jury of a permissible outcome. Judges make little or no effort to explain to the jury why a particular result might be appropriate. Consequently, presumptive instructions may tend to promote irrational decisionmaking, even though they may also enhance the probability of a more accurate result. . . .

Similarly, irrationality is fostered by instructions that allow but do not require an inference to be drawn. . . . Knowing only that it may, but need not, draw an inference, the jury will make a decision that "can only be arbitrary, no matter which way it finds."[57] The problem is exacerbated by the restrictions imposed on judicial comment by many states and by the lack of satisfactory legislative history in many states that authorize these instructions by statute. . . . The resulting dilemma was aptly stated by one trial court:

> [A]ssuming in the instant case that defendant introduced no evidence at trial, the jury would be told of the statutory presumption and that it could find the existence of the presumed fact from proof of the basic fact if it choose [sic] to do so. . . . Should the jury request clarification or illumination from the court as to how and why it should make this choice, this court would be hard-pressed to provide any.[58]

. . . The rational relationship test surely was an effort by the Court to ameliorate these difficulties, but that test cannot remove the enhanced risk of arbitrary decisionmaking by a jury instructed on an inference or a presumption. Regardless of how "rational" an inference may be in a particular case, the jury's decision

---

a. In the United States, judicial comment on the evidence has generally been questioned not so much in terms of the reasonable-doubt rule but primarily in terms of its potential for interference with the right to jury trial. The problem is explored at page 100 and footnote a infra. — EDS.

37. Vicksburg & M.R.R. v. Putman, 118 U.S. 545, 553 (1886). . . .

57. [Note, The Unconstitutionality of Statutory Criminal Presumptions, 22 Stan. L. Rev. 341, 351 (1970).]

58. People v. Thomas, 95 Misc. 2d 289, 291, 407 N.Y.S.2d 812, 814 (Crim. Ct. N.Y. 1978) (citation omitted).

must be arbitrary if all it knows is that it "may but need not" draw the inference. Accordingly, the Court should simply require that these instructions be unmasked. If guidance is to be given to the jury, it should be done directly and in a manner that furthers rather than detracts from the values secured by the right to a jury trial. In short, the Court should require that these instructions be given in the form of accurate comment on the evidence.

3. For further analysis of these problems, see Nesson, Reasonable Doubt and Permissive Inferences: The Value of Complexity, 92 Harv. L. Rev. 1187 (1979).

5. *The Role of the Jury*

DUNCAN v. LOUISIANA
Supreme Court of the United States
391 U.S. 145 (1968)

MR. JUSTICE WHITE delivered the opinion of the Court.

Appellant, Gary Duncan, was convicted of simple battery in the Twenty-fifth Judicial District Court of Louisiana. Under Louisiana law simple battery is a misdemeanor, punishable by two years' imprisonment and a $300 fine. Appellant sought trial by jury, but because the Louisiana Constitution grants jury trials only in cases in which capital punishment or imprisonment at hard labor may be imposed, the trial judge denied the request. Appellant was convicted and sentenced to serve 60 days in the parish prison and pay a fine of $150. Appellant sought review in the Supreme Court of Louisiana, asserting that the denial of jury trial violated rights guaranteed to him by the United States Constitution. The Supreme Court [of Louisiana denied review.] We noted probable jurisdiction. . . .

. . . While driving on Highway 23 in Plaquemines Parish on October 18, 1966, [appellant] saw two younger cousins engaged in a conversation by the side of the road with four white boys. Knowing his cousins, Negroes who had recently transferred to a formerly all-white high school, had reported the occurrence of racial incidents at the school, Duncan stopped the car, got out, and approached the six boys. . . . The testimony was in dispute on many points, but the witnesses agreed that appellant and the white boys spoke to each other, that appellant encouraged his cousins to break off the encounter and enter his car, and that appellant was about to enter the car himself for the purpose of driving away with his cousins. The whites testified that just before getting in the car appellant slapped Herman Landry, one of the white boys, on the elbow. The Negroes testified that appellant had not slapped Landry, but had merely touched him. The trial judge concluded that the State had proved beyond a reasonable doubt that Duncan had committed simple battery, and found him guilty.

. . . Because we believe that trial by jury in criminal cases is fundamental to the American scheme of justice, we hold that the Fourteenth Amendment guarantees a right of jury trial in all criminal cases which — were they to be tried in a federal court — would come within the Sixth Amendment's guarantee. Since we consider the appeal before us to be such a case, we hold that the

Constitution was violated when appellant's demand for jury trial was refused.

The history of trial by jury in criminal cases has been frequently told. It is sufficient for present purposes to say that by the time our Constitution was written, jury trial in criminal cases had been in existence in England for several centuries and carried impressive credentials traced by many to Magna Carta. Its preservation and proper operation as a protection against arbitrary rule were among the major objectives of the revolutionary settlement which was expressed in the Declaration and Bill of Rights of 1689. . . .

The guarantees of jury trial in the Federal and State Constitutions reflect a profound judgment about the way in which law should be enforced and justice administered. A right to jury trial is granted to criminal defendants in order to prevent oppression by the Government. Those who wrote our constitutions knew from history and experience that it was necessary to protect against unfounded criminal charges brought to eliminate enemies and against judges too responsive to the voice of higher authority. The framers of the constitutions strove to create an independent judiciary but insisted upon further protection against arbitrary action. Providing an accused with the right to be tried by a jury of his peers gave him an inestimable safeguard against the corrupt or overzealous prosecutor and against the compliant, biased, or eccentric judge. If the defendant preferred the common-sense judgment of a jury to the more tutored but perhaps less sympathetic reaction of the single judge, he was to have it. Beyond this, the jury trial provisions in the Federal and State Constitutions reflect a fundamental decision about the exercise of official power — a reluctance to entrust plenary powers over the life and liberty of the citizen to one judge or to a group of judges. . . . The deep commitment of the Nation to the right of jury trial in serious criminal cases as a defense against arbitrary law enforcement qualifies for protection under the Due Process Clause of the Fourteenth Amendment, and must therefore be respected by the States. . . .

We are aware of the long debate, especially in this century, among those who write about the administration of justice, as to the wisdom of permitting untrained laymen to determine the facts in civil and criminal proceedings. . . . [M]ost of the controversy has centered on the jury in civil cases. . . . [A]t the heart of the dispute have been express or implicit assertions that juries are incapable of adequately understanding evidence or determining issues of fact and that they are . . . little better than a roll of dice. Yet, the most recent and exhaustive study of the jury in criminal cases concluded that juries do understand the evidence and come to sound conclusions in most of the cases presented to them and that when juries differ with the result at which the judge would have arrived, it is usually because they are serving some of the very purposes for which they were created and for which they are now employed.[26]

The State of Louisiana urges that holding that the Fourteenth Amendment assures a right to jury trial will cast doubt on the integrity of every trial conducted without a jury. . . . We would not assert, however, that every criminal trial — or any particular trial — held before a judge alone is unfair or that a defendant may never be as fairly treated by a judge as he would be by a jury. Thus we hold no constitutional doubts about the practices, common in both federal and state courts, of accepting waivers of jury trial and prosecuting petty crimes with-

---

26. Kalven & Zeisel, [The American Jury (1966)].

out extending a right to jury trial. However, the fact is that in most places more trials for serious crimes are to juries than to a court alone; a great many defendants prefer the judgment of a jury to that of a court. Even where defendants are satisfied with bench trials, the right to a jury trial very likely serves its intended purpose of making judicial or prosecutorial unfairness less likely.

Louisiana's final contention is that even if it must grant jury trials in serious criminal cases, the conviction before us is valid and constitutional because here the petitioner was tried for simple battery and was sentenced to only 60 days in the parish prison. We are not persuaded. It is doubtless true that there is a category of petty crimes or offenses which is not subject to the Sixth Amendment jury trial provision and should not be subject to the Fourteenth Amendment jury trial requirement here applied to the States. . . .

. . . We need not, however, settle in this case the exact location of the line between petty offenses and serious crimes. It is sufficient for our purpose to hold that a crime punishable by two years in prison is, based on past and contemporary standards in this country, a serious crime and not a petty offense. Consequently, appellant was entitled to a jury trial and it was error to deny it. . . .

Reversed and remanded.

[The concurring opinion of MR. JUSTICE BLACK, which MR. JUSTICE DOUGLAS joined, and the concurring opinion of MR. JUSTICE FORTAS are omitted.]

MR. JUSTICE HARLAN, which MR. JUSTICE STEWART joins, dissenting. . . .

[There] is a wide range of views on the desirability of trial by jury, and on the ways to make it most effective when it is used; there is also considerable variation from State to State in local conditions such as the size of the criminal caseload, the ease or difficulty of summoning jurors, and other trial conditions bearing on fairness. We have before us, therefore, an almost perfect example of a situation in which the celebrated dictum of Mr. Justice Brandeis should be invoked. It is, he said, "one of the happy incidents of the federal system that a single courageous state may, if its citizens choose, serve as a laboratory. . . ." New State Ice Co. v. Liebmann, 285 U.S. 262, 280, 311 (dissenting opinion). This Court, other courts, and the political process are available to correct any experiments in criminal procedure that prove fundamentally unfair to defendants.

NOTES

1. The scope of the right to jury trial. Mr. Justice Frankfurter once wrote that "[n]o changes or chances can alter the content of the verbal symbol of 'jury'— a body of twelve men who must reach a unanimous conclusion if the verdict is to go against the defendant." Rochin v. California, 342 U.S. 165, 170 (1952). Except for the limitation to males, which had passed away long before Frankfurter reiterated it, this statement expressed a nearly universal view about what was meant by a jury. Nevertheless, in Williams v. Florida, 399 U.S. 78, 86 (1970), the Court said that the decision to fix the size of the jury at twelve "appears to have been a historical accident, unrelated to the great purposes that gave rise to the jury" and held that a six-member jury satisfied the constitutional requirement.[55] In Apodaca v. Oregon, 406 U.S. 404 (1972), the Court held that unanimity was not required in state criminal trials, so long as a substantial majority of the jury supports the verdict. The Court in that case upheld guilty verdicts obtained by 11 – 1 and 10 – 2 votes, without ruling explicitly on whether a smaller majority could also be sufficiently substantial.[56]

Duncan had raised, but not resolved, the question of what may be deemed a "petty offense," for which the Sixth Amendment jury trial guarantee would be inapplicable. In Baldwin v. New York, 399 U.S. 66 (1970), the Court held that no offense may be deemed petty where imprisonment for more than six months is authorized. In such cases a defendant has a constitutional right to jury trial, whether or not imprisonment is in fact likely to be imposed.[57]

2. *The policies served (and disserved) by jury trial.* The existence of the jury has a profound effect on the administration of American criminal law.

(1) Because lay people may not assess items of proof as carefully as the law-trained, the Anglo-American law includes an elaborate structure of rules providing for the exclusion of certain evidence at the trial.

(2) The existence of the jury creates a great range of legal issues that engage much attention, for example:

(a) The judge is judge of the law; the jury decides questions of fact. The legal system must characterize the nature of a given question: Is it a question of law or of fact?

(b) The judge and the jury may take different views of a case, thus putting them into a kind of contest resolved in the common law by rules respecting directed verdicts, motions to set aside verdicts, and judgments notwithstanding verdicts.

(c) The very presence of 12 lay people participating in a trial gives rise to a great many possible errors in respect to their conduct or in respect to their mode of reaching a decision.

(d) Judges must instruct juries on the law. They are required to formulate for jurors' use an acceptable statement of applicable legal rules, though these rules may be the most difficult imaginable. Obviously a great many errors in statements are made that require reversal.

(3) The entire texture and coloration of the trial is influenced by the existence of the jury. Instead of addressing arguments to one law-trained person, the lawyers address themselves to 12 lay people. Obviously lawyers believe that nonlegal factors will influence a jury and attempt, with some success, to put such matters before it.

---

55. In Ballew v. Georgia, 435 U.S. 223 (1978), the Court held that a five-person jury did not fulfill the constitutional jury trial requirement.

56. In Burch v. Louisiana, 441 U.S. 130 (1979), the Court held that a 5 – 1 vote did not satisfy constitutional requirements. Thus, where states elect to use a six-person jury, the verdict must be unanimous. The opinions in *Apodaca* suggest that for *federal* criminal trials, a majority of the Court would continue to view unanimity as constitutionally mandated; in any event Rule 31(a) of the Federal Rules of Criminal Procedure requires a unanimous verdict in federal prosecutions.

57. Compare the Sixth Amendment right to counsel, which normally comes into play only in cases in which imprisonment is actually imposed. See page 26 supra. A defendant thus may have a right to counsel but not a right to jury trial. Are there cases in which a defendant would have a right to jury trial but not a right to counsel?

The Court in *Duncan* summarizes the principal reasons why it regards the availability of trial by jury as an essential component of fair procedure. Is it clear that the advantages of jury trial outweigh its costs or that experimentation with different kinds of factfinding procedures should be considered intolerable? Consider the following comments.

G. Williams, The Proof of Guilt 271-272 (3d ed. 1963): [I]t is an understatement to describe a jury, with Herbert Spencer, as a group of twelve people of average ignorance. There is no guarantee that members of a particular jury may not be quite unusually ignorant, credulous, slow-witted, narrow-minded, biased or temperamental. The danger of this happening is not one that can be removed by some minor procedural adjustment; it is inherent in the English notion of a jury as a body chosen from the general population at random.

Broeder, The Functions of the Jury — Facts or Fictions?, 21 U. Chi. L. Rev. 386, 413-417 (1947): From the time of the Alien and Sedition Acts, the government's attempted inroads on civil rights seem to have received the enthusiastic support of jurors. . . .

. . . But the case against the criminal jury as a protector of individual liberty extends further than to contests between government and citizens opposed to its policies. Minority groups have often suffered at the hands of jurymen. Wholesale acquittals of lynch-law violators, convictions of Negroes on the slightest evidence, and numerous other occurrences which have now almost become a part of the jury tradition might be instanced as examples. . . .

Aside from the incidental psychological functions which the criminal jury is alleged to perform, the sole remaining virtue claimed for it lies in its ability to make allowances for the circumstances of the particular case — to dispense with a rule of law. As noted previously, however, law-dispensing is a two-edged sword, and there is no current means of ascertaining which way it more often swings. It may seriously be doubted whether entrusting the jury with law-dispensing powers is justified. While flexibility of legal administration is desirable, it would seem that the necessary exceptions to the normal rules could with better reason be fashioned by the legislature or court.

H. Kalven & H. Zeisel, The American Jury 7-9 (1966): The [jury] controversy centers around three large issues. First, there is a series of collateral advantages and disadvantages that are often charged against, or pointed to on behalf of, the jury as an institution. In this realm fall such positive points as that the jury provides an important civic experience for the citizen; that, because of popular participation, the jury makes tolerable the stringency of certain decisions; that, because of its transient personnel, the jury acts as a sort of lightning rod for animosity and suspicion which otherwise might center on the more permanent judge; and that the jury is a guarantor of integrity, since it is said to be more difficult to reach twelve men than one. Against such affirmative claims, serious collateral disadvantages have been urged, chiefly that the jury is expensive; that it contributes to delay in civil litigation; that jury service imposes an unfair tax and social cost on those forced to serve; and that, in general, exposure to jury duty disenchants the citizen and causes him to lose confidence in the administration of justice.

Second, there is a group of issues that touch directly on the competence of the jury. Here the debate has been fascinating but bitter. On the one hand, it is urged that the judge, as a result of training, discipline, recurrent experience, and superior intelligence, will be better able to understand the law and analyze the facts than laymen, selected from a wide range of intelligence levels, who have no particular experience with matters of this sort, and who have no durable official responsibility. On the other hand, it is argued that twelve heads are inevitably better than one; that the jury as a group has wisdom and strength which need not characterize any of its individual members; that it makes up in common sense and common experience what it may lack in professional training, and that its very inexperience is an asset because it secures a fresh perception of each trial, avoiding the stereotypes said to infect the judicial eye.

The third group of issues about the jury goes to what is perhaps the most interesting point. The critics complain that the jury will not follow the law, either because it does not understand it or because it does not like it, and that thus only a very uneven and unequal administration of justice can result from reliance on the jury; indeed, it is said that the jury is likely to produce that government by man, and not by rule of law, against which Anglo-American political tradition is so steadfastly set.

This same flexibility of the jury is offered by its champions as its most endearing and most important characteristic. The jury, it is said, is a remarkable device for insuring that we are governed by the spirit of the law and not by its letter; for insuring that rigidity of any general rule of law can be shaped to justice in the particular case. One is tempted to say that what is one man's equity is another man's anarchy.

3. Lay adjudicators in other countries. Other legal systems use different means to provide for lay participation. Consider the following comment.

G. Williams, The Proof of Guilt 254-256, 307 (3d ed. 1963): So great was the prestige of the British jury that it was transplanted to one Continental country after another as a symbol of new-found political freedom. . . .

[E]fforts to acclimatise jury trial have generally met with indifferent success, partly because of a failure to settle satisfactorily the relative provinces of judge and jury. Perhaps another contributing factor was the failure to apply the restrictive rules of the law of evidence (particularly in respect of the character of the accused) which English experience had shown to be necessary. . . . The strong tendency on the Continent of late years has been to replace the jury by lay justices or assessors, sitting with the judges and sharing with them the responsibility of deciding both fact and law and determining sentence. These lay justices may, as in France since 1941, bear the name of a jury and be very close to the English jury in being chosen at random from the community, differing, however, in that they sit on the Bench for a whole session and constitute a joint tribunal with the professional judges; or they may, as in Sweden, be somewhat similar to the English justices of the peace, being lay magistrates specially chosen to serve for a period of office and not merely for a particular case or short series of cases; in Sweden the choice of magistrates is made by election. . . .

Looking at these strains and stresses of the jury system in other countries, we may find the comparative success of the English jury not in its ability to nullify unpopular laws, nor in its superior ability to ascertain facts, but in the fact that our system of summing up enables the judge to give the jury a lead,[a] which the jury follow sufficiently often to give an appearance of reliability to the mode of trial. It need hardly be pointed out that this explanation of the jury's success is not one that yields any very strong argument for a continuation of the system.

4. *The behavior of the jury in the United States.* The empirical study referred to by the Court in *Duncan,* H. Kalven & H. Zeisel, The American Jury (1966), represents an effort to determine the extent to which juries decide cases differently from the way judges would and to determine the sources of such differences. The entire book warrants careful reading in connection with efforts to understand the impact of jury trial in American criminal cases.[58] The authors find that judges and juries disagree in roughly 25 percent of jury trial cases. In a small portion of these (2 percent of the total cases), the jury convicts when the judge would acquit; in 17 percent of all cases the jury acquits when the judge would convict; in roughly 6 percent of the cases the jury "hangs" (fails to agree on a verdict). Id. at 56-57.

The authors examine in great depth the possible reasons for judge-jury disagreement. They conclude that of the various factors apparently involved (disagreements could not be explained in only 10 percent of the cases), differences in assessing the evidence in close cases played a significant role. They attributed 79 percent of the disagreements to this source. The other major factors that helped account for disagreement were jury sentiments about the law (50 percent of the cases), jury sentiments about the defendant (22 percent), facts only the judge knew (5 percent), and disparity of counsel (8 percent). Id. at 111. It will be noted that there was often more than one reason for disagreement in a case. In fact, the closeness of the evidence usually appeared with one of the other reasons, so that this factor apparently "liberated the jury to respond to non-evidentiary factors." Id. at 106. It thus appeared that jury sentiment about the law was one of the most significant considerations, and this factor of course lies close to the heart of the jury's function as a guarantor of lenity and equity in dispensing criminal justice. The study suggests that "in cases having a de minimus cast or a note of contributory fault or provocation . . . the jury will exercise its de facto powers to write these equities into the criminal law." Id. at 285. Other sentiments about the law that appeared to have significant impact included "impatience with the nicety of the law's boundaries hedging the privilege of self-defense" (id. at 241) and resistance to the enforcement of a few unpopular laws, primarily hunting, liquor, gambling, and drunken-driving laws. While the study provides extensive evidence of jury nullification, it also should

---

a. This role for the judge is generally not seen in the United States. Judicial commentary of the kind described by Prof. Williams is often viewed as a violation of state constitutional provisions making the jury the exclusive trier of fact. Nearly 20 states permit the judge to summarize the evidence but prohibit comment on its weight, credibility, and persuasiveness. Another 20 states prohibit both summary and comment. Only the federal courts and about 11 states permit both summary and comment, and even in these jurisdictions the judge often declines to make use of this prerogative. See H. Kalven & H. Zeisel, The American Jury 418-425 (1966). The problem of judicial summary and comment is examined in depth in Saltzburg, The Unnecessarily Expanding Role of the American Trial Judge, 64 Va. L. Rev. 1, 22-52 (1978). — Eds.

58. For a critique of the methodology employed in this ground-breaking study, see Walsh, The American Jury: A Reassessment, 79 Yale L.J. 142 (1969).

be noted that judge and jury *agreed* in 75 percent of the cases, that only half the disagreement cases involved jury sentiments about the law, and that these sentiments usually (78 percent of the time, id. at 113) emerged in combination with other factors, principally the closeness of the evidence. The authors thus observe that the "jury's war with the law is now a polite one" (id. at 76) and conclude (at 498):

> The jury thus represents a uniquely subtle distribution of official power, an unusual arrangement of checks and balances. It represents also an impressive way of building discretion, equity and flexibility into a legal system. Not the least of the advantages is that the jury, relieved of the burdens of creating precedent, can bend the law without breaking it.

Notice that in *Duncan* the Court, referring to Kalven and Zeisel, says that when juries differ from the judge "it is usually because they are serving some of the very purposes for which they were created." Does this mean that the jury's equity-dispensing function is constitutionally protected and that procedures designed to minimize nullification would be unconstitutional?

UNITED STATES v. DOUGHERTY
United States Court of Appeals, District of Columbia Circuit
473 F.2d 1113 (1972)

LEVENTHAL, J. Seven of the so-called "D.C. Nine" bring this joint appeal from convictions arising out of their unconsented entry into the Washington offices of the Dow Chemical Company, and their destruction of certain property therein.[a] . . . [A]fter a six-day trial, the seven were each convicted of two counts of malicious destruction. . . .

. . . Appellants urge . . . [that] the judge erroneously refused to instruct the jury of its right to acquit appellants without regard to the law and the evidence, and refused to permit appellants to argue that issue to the jury. . . .

. . . [Appellants] say that the jury has a well-recognized prerogative to disregard the instructions of the court even as to matters of law, and that they accordingly have the legal right that the jury be informed of its power. . . .

There has evolved in the Anglo-American system an undoubted jury prerogative-in-fact, derived from its power to bring in a general verdict of not guilty in a criminal case, that is not reversible by the court. The power of the courts to punish jurors for corrupt or incorrect verdicts, which persisted after the medieval system of attaint by another jury became obsolete, was repudiated in 1670 when Bushell's Case, 124 Eng. Rep. 1006 (C.P. 1670), discharged the jurors who had acquitted William Penn of unlawful assembly. Juries in civil cases became

---

a. The background of the case is capsulated in the separate opinion of Judge Adams: "Here, the defendants, by interrupting the business of a large chemical company, attempted to publicize their dissenting views regarding the morality of the American involvement in the Vietnam War. It is apparent that the defendants attempted to exploit their criminal trial by using it as a platform for further exposition of their beliefs. . . . In furtherance of their efforts to transform what would otherwise be an ordinary criminal trial into a "political" fray, defendants wished to represent themselves, to deviate from the usual mode of conducting a criminal trial, and to argue to the jury that although they were in violation of the applicable statutes, they should be acquitted because their actions were morally justified."— EDS.

subject to the control of ordering a new trial; no comparable control evolved for acquittals in criminal cases.

The pages of history shine on instances of the jury's exercise of its prerogative to disregard uncontradicted evidence and instructions of the judge. Most often commended are the 18th century acquittal of Peter Zenger of seditious libel, on the plea of Andrew Hamilton, and the 19th century acquittals in prosecutions under the fugitive slave law. The values involved drop a notch when the liberty vindicated by the verdict relates to the defendant's shooting of his wife's paramour, or purchase during Prohibition of alcoholic beverages. . . .

The existence of an unreviewable and unreversible power in the jury, to acquit in disregard of the instructions on the law given by the trial judge, has for many years co-existed with legal practice and precedent upholding instructions to the jury that they are required to follow the instructions of the court on all matters of law. . . .

The rulings [in the early cases] did not run all one way, but rather precipitated "a number of classic exchanges on the freedom and obligations of the criminal jury." [36] This was, indeed, one of the points of clash between the contending forces staking out the direction of the government of the newly established Republic, a direction resolved in political terms by reforming but sustaining the status of the courts, without radical change. As the distrust of judges appointed and removable by the king receded, there came increasing acceptance that under a republic the protection of citizens lay not in recognizing the right of each jury to make its own law, but in following democratic processes for changing the law. . . .

Since the jury's prerogative of lenity . . . introduces a "slack into the enforcement of law, tempering its rigor by the mollifying influence of current ethical conventions," it is only just, say appellants, that the jurors be so told. It is unjust to withhold information on the jury power of "nullification," since conscientious jurors may come, ironically, to abide by their oath as jurors to render verdicts offensive to their individual conscience, to defer to an assumption of necessity that is contrary to reality.

This so-called right of jury nullification is put forward in the name of liberty and democracy, but its explicit avowal risks the ultimate logic of anarchy. This is the concern voiced by Judge Soboloff in United States v. Moylan, 417 F.2d 1002, 1009 (4th Cir. 1969): "To encourage individuals to make their own determinations as to which laws they will obey and which they will permit themselves as a matter of conscience to disobey is to invite chaos. No legal system could long survive if it gave every individual the option of disregarding with impunity any law which by his personal standard was judged morally untenable. Toleration of such conduct would not be democratic, as appellants claim, but inevitably anarchic." [T]he advocates of jury "nullification" apparently assume that the articulation of the jury's power will not extend its use or extent, or will not do so significantly or obnoxiously. Can this assumption fairly be made? . . .

The way the jury operates may be radically altered if there is alteration in the way it is told to operate. The jury knows well enough that its prerogative is not limited to the choices articulated in the formal instructions of the court.

36. M. R. Kadish and S. H. Kadish, On Justified Rule Departures by Officials, 59 Calif. L. Rev. 905, 914 (1971).

The jury gets its understanding as to the arrangements in the legal system from more than one voice. . . .

When the legal system relegates the information of the jury's prerogative to an essentially informal input, it is not being duplicitous, chargeable with chicane and intent to deceive. The limitation to informal input is, rather, a governor to avoid excess: the prerogative is reserved for the exceptional case, and the judge's instruction is retained as a generally effective constraint. We "recognize a constraint as obligatory upon us when we require not merely reason to defend our rule departures, but damn good reason." [49] The practicalities of men, machinery and rules point up the danger of articulating discretion to depart from a rule, that the breach will be more often and casually invoked. We cannot gainsay that occasionally jurors uninstructed as to the prerogative may feel themselves compelled to the point of rigidity. The danger of the excess rigidity that may now occasionally exist is not as great as the danger of removing the boundaries of constraint provided by the announced rules. . . .

Moreover, to compel a juror involuntarily assigned to jury duty to assume the burdens of mini-legislator or judge, as is implicit in the doctrine of nullification, is to put untoward strains on the jury system. It is one thing for a juror to know that the law condemns, but he has a factual power of lenity. To tell him expressly of a nullification prerogative, however, is to inform him, in effect, that it is he who fashions the rule that condemns. That is an overwhelming responsibility, an extreme burden for the jurors' psyche. And it is not inappropriate to add that a juror called upon for an involuntary public service is entitled to the protection, when he takes action that he knows is right, but also knows is unpopular, either in the community at large or in his own particular grouping, that he can fairly put it to friends and neighbors that he was merely following the instructions of the court. . . .

. . . [W]hat is tolerable or even desirable as an informal, self-initiated exception, harbors grave dangers to the system if it is opened to expansion and intensification through incorporation in the judge's instruction. . . .

BAZELON, C.J., concurring in part and dissenting in part. . . .

[T]he Court apparently concedes — although in somewhat grudging terms — that the power of nullification is a "necessary counter to case-hardened judges and arbitrary prosecutors," and that exercise of the power may, in at least some instances, "enhance the over-all normative effect of the rule of law." We could not withhold that concession without scoffing at the rationale that underlies the right to jury trial in criminal cases, and belittling some of the most legendary episodes in our political and jurisprudential history.

The sticking point, however, is whether or not the jury should be told of its power to nullify the law in a particular case. Here, the trial judge not only denied a requested instruction on nullification, but also barred defense counsel from raising the issue in argument before the jury. The majority affirms that ruling. I see no justification for, and considerable harm in, this deliberate lack of candor.

. . . [T]he justification for this sleight-of-hand lies in a fear that an occasionally

---

49. Kadish and Kadish, supra, note 36, 59 Calif. L. Rev. at 926. [The "damn-good-reason" position is criticized in Scheflin & Van Dyke, Jury Nullification: The Contours of a Controversy, 43 L. & Contemp. Prob. 51, 98-108 (1980). — EDS.]

noble doctrine will, if acknowledged, often be put to ignoble and abusive purposes — or, to borrow the Court's phrase, will "run the risk of anarchy.". . .
The Court assumes that these abuses are most likely to occur if the doctrine
is formally described to the jury by argument or instruction. . . . It seems substantially more plausible to me to assume that the very opposite is true. . . .

   . . . [T]he Court takes comfort in the fact that informal communication to
the jury "generally convey[s] adequately enough the idea of prerogative, of
freedom in an occasional case to depart from what the judge says.". . . [But
if] awareness is preferable to ignorance, then I simply do not understand the
justification for relying on a haphazard process of informal communication whose
effectiveness is likely to depend, to a large extent, on whether or not any of
the jurors are so well-educated and astute that they are able to receive the
message. If the jury should know of its power to disregard the law, then the
power should be explicitly described by instruction of the court or argument
of counsel. . . .

NOTES AND QUESTIONS ON NULLIFICATION INSTRUCTIONS

1. Nearly all American states follow the federal rule reflected in *Dougherty*
and refuse to permit instructions officially informing the jury of its nullification
power. In State v. McClanahan, 212 Kan. 208, 510 P.2d 153, 154-155 (1973),
the court held improper the following cautiously worded nullification instruction:

> [J]udges are presumed to be the best judges of the law. Accordingly, you must
> accept my instructions as being correct statements of the generally accepted legal
> principles that apply in a case of the type you have heard. . . .
> Even so, it is difficult to draft legal statements that are so exact that they are
> right for all conceivable circumstances. Accordingly, you are entitled to act upon
> your conscientious feeling about what is a fair result in this case and acquit the
> defendant if you believe that justice requires such a result.
> Exercise your judgment without passion or prejudice, but with honesty and under-
> standing. Give respectful regard to my statements of the law for what help they
> may be in arriving at a conscientious determination of justice in this case.

2. In three states the approach rejected in *Dougherty* still survives through
constitutional provisions that the jury shall be the judge of the law as well as
the facts. Ga. Const. 2-108; Ind. Const. arts. 1, 8, 19; Md. Const. art. 27, §593.
In Georgia, however, courts have tended to confine the effect of the provision,
for example by upholding a charge that the jurors are the judges of the law
but are obliged to apply the court's instructions to the facts and by forbidding
defense counsel to argue to the jury that it should disregard the law. See Brown
v. State, 262 S.E.2d 497 (Ga. App. 1979); Jones v. State, 235 Ga. 103, 218
S.E.2d 899 (1975). Current practice in Indiana and Maryland is summarized
in Scheflin & Van Dyke, Jury Nullification: The Contours of a Controversy, 43
L. & Contemp. Prob. 51, 79-85 (1980).

3. Suppose that the jurors are instructed, over the defendant's *objection,* that
they are the judges of the law as well as the facts. Does such an instruction
subject the defendant to capricious judgment and violate his right to be tried
in accordance with ascertainable law? See Isaacs v. State, 31 Md. App. 604,
358 A.2d 273 (1976); Wyley v. Warden, 372 F.2d 742 (4th Cir. 1967).

4. For further exploration of the issues posed by *Dougherty,* see M. Kadish & S. Kadish, Discretion to Disobey 37-94 (1973); Simpson, Jury Nullification in the American System: A Skeptical View, 64 Tex. L. Rev. 488 (1976); Scheflin, Jury Nullification: The Right to Say "No," 45 S. Cal. L. Rev. 168 (1972). The historical background of the jury's role as judge of both law and fact is explored (and its continuing relevance advocated) in Van Dyke, The Jury as a Political Institution, The Center Magazine 17-26 (Mar.-Apr. 1970). See also Scheflin & Van Dyke, Note 2 supra; Comment, Jury Nullification in Historical Perspective: Massachusetts as a Case Study, 12 Suffolk U.L. Rev. 968 (1978).

NOTES AND QUESTIONS ON SPECIAL VERDICTS

1. The Spock *case.* United States v. Spock, 416 F.2d 165 (1st Cir. 1969), involved the prosecution of Dr. Benjamin Spock, Reverend William Sloane Coffin, Jr., and several others who had helped organize protests against the Vietnam war and the draft to support it. The defendants were charged with conspiring to "counsel, aid and abet diverse Selective Service registrants to . . . neglect, fail, refuse and evade service in the armed forces." At trial, the district judge put to the jury, in addition to the general issue of guilt, ten special questions to be answered yes or no. One question, for example, asked the jury to consider whether the defendants had conspired to "counsel" draft evasion; a second question substituted for the word *counsel* the word *aid;* a third substituted the word *abet.* Four defendants were convicted, but the United States Court of Appeals held that the submission of these special questions required reversal. The court noted that although such special verdicts are an everyday occurrence in civil cases, they pose special dangers in a criminal case (id. at 181-182):

> [N]ot only must the jury be free from direct control in its verdict, but it must be free from judicial pressure, both contemporaneous and subsequent. . . . There is no easier way to reach, and perhaps force, a verdict of guilty than to approach it step by step. A juror, wishing to acquit, may be formally catechized . . . [and] led to vote for a conviction which, in the large, he would have resisted. . . . The constitutional guarantees of due process and trial by jury require that a criminal defendant be afforded the full protection of a jury unfettered, directly or indirectly.

The court added that although some courts had upheld convictions where the use of a special verdict did not appear prejudicial, "we do not think it desirable to treat this issue by weighing subjective prejudice; to some extent the pressure is always present." Id. at 183 n. 41½.

Queries: If the questions put to the *Spock* jurors fairly focused their attention on the proper issues, then didn't the questions serve to enhance the probability that the jury would follow the judge's instructions on the law? Was the court saying that this is undesirable? Can the approach to special verdicts taken in *Spock* be reconciled with the approach to nullification instructions taken in *Dougherty?*

2. Current status of the Spock *rule.* Although the *Spock* decision appeared to treat the use of special verdicts as erroneous per se, regardless of whether they would tend to "lead" the jury to a particular result, most of the recent decisions appear to uphold the use of special verdicts where the appellate court concludes that under all the circumstances there is "no indication that judicial pressure was brought to bear." United States v. Looney, 544 F.2d 385, 392 (9th Cir. 1976).[59] Can such decisions be reconciled with *Spock?* Will even a noncoercive special verdict tend to constrain the jury in exercising its privilege to acquit against the weight of the evidence? Since leading or coercive special verdicts presumably would be improper even in a civil case, are the special prerogatives of the criminal jury adequately protected by this approach?

3. *Defense requests for a special verdict.* Suppose that a defendant seeks to clarify the issues in a complex case by asking the jury to return a special verdict. Most courts appear to uphold the denial of such defense requests, often with broad statements about the impropriety of special verdicts.[60] Is the rationale of *Spock* really applicable when the defendant *wants* a special verdict? Is there any good reason for restricting *defense* efforts to insure that the jury faithfully follows judicial instructions on the law?

NOTES AND QUESTIONS ON INCONSISTENT VERDICTS

1. *The problem and the prevailing solutions.* When a prosecution involves several separate counts, it sometimes happens that the jury's verdict on one count will be irreconcilably in conflict with its verdict on another count. Consider, for example, DeSacia v. State, 469 P.2d 369 (Alaska 1970). Defendant's reckless driving forced another vehicle off the road, and both the driver (Hogan) and passenger (Evangelista) in the other vehicle were killed. Defendant was prosecuted on two counts of manslaughter; the jury convicted on the count charging manslaughter of Evangelista but acquitted on the count charging manslaughter of Hogan. Since the defendant's conduct had endangered the two victims in precisely the same way, he was in principle guilty of manslaughter either in both cases or in neither. Should the inconsistent verdicts nevertheless be allowed to stand?

In the *DeSacia* case, the court noted that the verdict of acquittal was final; any relitigation of that count would violate the double jeopardy clause. But the court set aside the conviction on the other count, explaining that such action was necessary to assure that the conviction was not the product of jury confusion or irrationality. The court therefore remanded for a new trial on the count relating to the death of Evangelista. Only a minority of American jurisdictions appear to follow this approach, however. The federal courts and most of the states would allow the inconsistent conviction to stand.[61]

Which approach seems more faithful to the premises of jury trial? If the jury is expected to give voice to the rough common sense of the community, isn't the *DeSacia* court's desire for logic out of place? [62] Consider whether inconsistent

59. See also Heald v. Mullaney 505 F.2d 1241, 1246 (1st Cir. 1974) (special verdict did not "coerce the jury's decision-making"); Commonwealth v. Beneficial Finance Co., 360 Mass. 188, 275 N.E.2d 33, 97 (1971) (special verdict did not "lead the jurors down the guilty trail").

60. See, e.g., United States v. McCracken, 488 U.S. 406 (5th Cir. 1974); United States v. Frezzo Bros., Inc., 602 F.2d 1123 (3d Cir. 1979).

61. See Comment, Inconsistent Verdicts in a Federal Criminal Trial, 60 Colum. L. Rev. 999, 1002-1004 n. 18 (1960). See also Wax, Inconsistent and Repugnant Verdicts in Criminal Trials, 24 N.Y.L. Sch. L. Rev. 713 (1979).

62. "The verdict of the jurors is not just the verdict of twelve men; it is the verdict of a *pays,* a 'country,' a neighborhood, a community. . . . The justices seem to feel that if they analyzed the verdict they would miss the very thing for which they are looking, the opinion of the country." 2 F. Pollock & F. Maitland, History of English Law 624, 626 (2d ed. 1952).

verdicts facilitate the exercise of the jury's leniency or whether they encourage compromise *convictions* on counts about which the jury may not really be persuaded beyond a reasonable doubt.

2. Constitutional implications. Do decisions like *DeSacia,* which bar inconsistent verdicts, violate the constitutional right to jury trial, by impairing the jury's function as a safety valve for tempering the law's rigid logic? One answer may simply be that the defendant will not complain, because the rule leads only to reversal of the illogical conviction. But what if the prosecution seeks an instruction, in a case like *DeSacia,* that the jury must either acquit on both counts or convict on both counts? The result in *DeSacia* in effect requires such an instruction in future cases, does it not? If so, would the defendant then be justified in claiming that the instruction improperly constrained the jury's equity-dispensing function?

In connection with the constitutional problems, consider whether it was entirely a coincidence that the *DeSacia* jury convicted for the death of Evangelista, who was a passenger, but acquitted for the death of Hogan, the other driver. As we shall see, contributory negligence ordinarily is not a defense in a criminal prosecution, see page 443 infra, but the Kalven and Zeisel study, page 104 supra, at 242-257, showed that jury nullification often occurred when contributory fault by the victim was involved. If this factor played a role in the acquittal with respect to Hogan, then wasn't the jury — to quote from Duncan v. Louisiana, page 95 supra — "serving some of the very purposes for which [it was] created"?

3. Inconsistency in nonjury trials. Jurisdictions that permit inconsistent verdicts in jury trials must decide whether to follow the same approach when an inconsistent acquittal and conviction are rendered in a bench trial. In United States v. Maybury, 274 F.2d 899 (2d Cir. 1960), the court, in an opinion by Judge Friendly, held such inconsistency unacceptable in a bench trial and reversed the conviction. But several other state and federal courts have rejected *Maybury.*[63] Are the reasons for tolerating inconsistent jury verdicts applicable in trials before a judge? If it is sound to protect the jury's equity-dispensing power, why should a judge not have the same power?

4. Unsupported lesser offenses. Closely related to the above problems is the question whether the defendant should be entitled to have the jury instructed about a lesser included offense, even when the evidence could not logically support a guilty verdict on that charge. The issue arises in many diverse contexts; homicide prosecutions are illustrative. As we shall see in Chapter 6 infra, unlawful homicide can be of four or more kinds. The most serious, first-degree murder, typically applies to an intentional killing; the least serious, involuntary manslaughter, typically applies to a killing committed unintentionally by culpable negligence. In some situations the evidence could rationally support either verdict: If, for example, the defendant shot a business partner in the course of a hunting trip, the jury might find that the killing was deliberate or, if not, culpably negligent. But suppose that the defendant claims to have shot an intruder in self-defense, or suppose that the defendant admits killing a friend as an act of mercy, to terminate a painful and prolonged illness. In cases like these, the

---

63. See, e.g., United States v. West, 549 F.2d 545 (8th Cir. 1977); Commonwealth v. Harris, 239 Pa. Super. 603, 360 A.2d 728 (1976). The Supreme Court has held that the due process clause does not bar inconsistency in state bench trials, nor does the constitution require state judges to give reasons for rendering facially inconsistent judgments. See Harris v. Rivera, 102 S. Ct. 460 (1981).

killing is plainly intentional; it might or might not be considered unlawful but under no circumstances would these situations involve negligent, involuntary manslaughter. Should the jury nevertheless be offered the option of convicting for involuntary manslaughter?

All courts agree that when the evidence is consistent with a negligent killing, involuntary manslaughter instructions must be given at the request of either the prosecution or the defense.[64] But when the killing was clearly intentional (or when, in other situtations, the evidence cannot logically support a conviction on a related-but-less-serious charge), virtually all courts hold it improper to instruct the jury on the lesser included offense.[65] In such a situation the jury will be afforded only the options of convicting on one of the more serious charges or acquitting altogether.

How can this approach be reconciled with the willingness of most courts to accept inconsistent jury verdicts in a context like that of the *De Sacia* case? Is it undesirable (and should it be unconstitutional under Duncan v. Louisiana) for the jury instructions to foreclose an intuitively attractive, though legally "irrational" compromise? Or, if the categories of an offense like homicide do not accord with common sense and community sentiment, is it better to rely on the legislative process to change them?

6. The Role of Counsel and the Judge

a. The Competence of Counsel

BAZELON, THE REALITIES OF *GIDEON* AND *ARGERSINGER,* 64 Geo. L.J. 811, 818-824 (1976): For too long now, courts have shied away from reversing convictions in order to enforce the plain words of the sixth amendment. The history of the application of the sixth amendment has been one of tiny steps forward followed by long periods without any movement. The first plateau was reached over 40 years ago when the Supreme Court recognized that the sixth amendment demands more than placing a warm body with a legal pedigree next to an indigent defendant. The Supreme Court proclaimed at that time that defendants are entitled to "effective and substantial aid" from counsel.[38] The Court failed to define "effective aid," however, and the lower courts defined away the problem of ineffective representation. Ineffectiveness, they concluded, exists "only when the trial was a farce, or a mockery of justice, or was shocking

64. See Beck v. Alabama, 447 U.S. 625, 636 & n. 12 (1980). In *Beck* the Supreme Court held this rule to be constitutionally mandated, at least in the context of a capital case. Thus, although a prosecutor ordinarily is free to withhold charges that are fully supported by evidence, once the prosecutor presses a serious charge, the defendant can insist that less serious included offenses also be presented to the jury if they are supported by sufficient evidence.

65. See, e.g., State v. Williams, 270 Or. 152, 526 P.2d 1384 (1974); Day v. United States, 390 A.2d 957 (D.C. App. 1978). Florida may be the lone exception; statutory provisions there have been interpreted to require the submission of lesser included offenses even when not supported by any evidence. See Robinson v. State, 338 So. 2d 1309 (Fla. App. 1976). In Pennsylvania the applicable rule has long wavered so elusively that federal courts have held the absence of a governing standard to constitute in itself a denial of due process. See United States ex rel. Matthews v. Johnson, 503 F.2d 339 (3d Cir. 1974) (voluntary manslaughter instructions); Bishop v. Mazurkiewicz, 484 F. Supp. 871 (W.D. Pa. 1980) (involuntary manslaughter instructions). The state supreme court now appears to have aligned itself with the majority view. See Commonwealth v. White, 490 Pa. 179, 415 A.2d 399 (1980).

38. Powell v. Alabama, 287 U.S. 45, 53 (1932). . . .

to the conscience of the reviewing court, or the purported representation was only perfunctory, in bad faith, a sham, a pretense. . . ." [39] The farce or mockery test and its successor in our circuit, the "gross incompetence . . . [that has] blotted out the essence of a substantial defense" test,[40] require such a minimal level of performance that the tests themselves mock the sixth amendment. . . . Who would be content with their doctor because he did not make a mockery of medicine, or was not grossly incompetent?

The second step forward in the implementation of the sixth amendment has been taken only within the past five years, and has not yet been taken by all jurisdictions. In two recent cases involving collateral attacks on guilty pleas, the Supreme Court broached the issue of ineffective assistance of counsel and asked whether counsel's advice fell "within the range of competence demanded of attorneys in criminal cases." [44] Adopting this approach, a majority of the United States Court of Appeals have rejected the mockery test and now require that counsel "exercise . . . the customary skill and knowledge which normally prevails at the time and place," or "a minimum standard of professional representation," or "reasonably effective assistance." Approximately half the state courts recently have adopted similar-sounding tests.

Although the second plateau appears to mark an improvement, there is, in Dorothy Parker's phrase, "*less* here than meets the eye"; the new test is built on words like "customary" or "reasonable," which are themselves empty vessels into which content must be poured. Such standards beg the question of what is customary or reasonable for a lawyer to do prior to or at arraignment, plea bargaining, trial, or sentencing. Thus far the courts have failed to address these questions, with the result that the new test has made little change. In some jurisdictions where courts have rejected the mockery test as much as five years ago, there are still only a handful of cases in which the courts have found ineffective assistance. In jurisdictions that recently rejected the mockery test, the courts already have shown such a jaded view of what is "customary" or "reasonable" as to remove all bite from the new formulations.[49] The mockery language may have been discarded officially, but its spirit, the spirit of papering over, lives on.

The reasons that judges have papered over the problem for so long are manifold. The root cause is not venality but timidity. . . . [I]f the courts gave the sixth amendment real bite, we judges would have to swallow the bitter pill of reversing an uncomfortably large number of convictions and releasing large numbers of defendants from their guilty pleas.[a] Even if reversals and releases would not be that frequent, the spectre of a flood of frivolous ineffectiveness claims haunts many judges.

These judicial concerns are understandable, but they cannot excuse inaction. That the problem is so difficult and widespread makes our responsibility to confront it all the more urgent. . . .

39. Williams v. Beto, 354 F.2d 698, 704 (5th Cir. 1965). . . .

40. Bruce v. United States, 379 F.2d 113, 116-17 (D.C. Cir. 1967).

44. Tollett v. Henderson, 411 U.S. 258, 266 (1973); McMann v. Richardson, 397 U.S. 759, 771 (1970).

49. See, e.g., . . . State v. Harper, 57 Wis. 2d 543, 550-57, 205 N.W.2d 1, 6-9 (1973) (failure to interview client before trial, to conduct independent investigation, to give timely notice of alibi, and to seek suppression of illegally seized evidence not ineffective assistance).

a. See also Bazelon, The Defective Assistance of Counsel, 42 U. Cin. L. Rev. 1, 70-71 (1973): "I have often been told that if my court were to reverse every case in which there was inadequate counsel, we would have to send back half the convictions in my jurisdiction."— EDS.

NOTE

Another outspoken critic of current levels of performance by the trial bar is Chief Justice Warren Burger. The Chief Justice sees the primary source of the problem in the lack of specialized training in the skills of trial advocacy, and he is a vigorous proponent of reform through modifications in law school curricula and special certification for trial lawyers. See Burger, The Special Skills of Advocacy: Are Specialized Training and Certification of Advocates Essential to Our System of Justice?, 42 Fordham L. Rev. 227 (1973); Burger, Some Further Reflections on the Problem of Adequacy of Trial Counsel, 49 Fordham L. Rev. 1 (1980).

UNITED STATES v. KATZ, 425 F.2d 928, 930-931 (2d Cir. 1970), Friendly, J.: The sole ground of Katz' appeals is ineffective representation by counsel. Murry Boxer, Esq., had been retained by him in both cases; when it was demonstrated that Katz would be unable to pay, Boxer was assigned under the Criminal Justice Act, 18 U.S.C. §3006A. . . .

We find it difficult to see what mode of defense could have helped Katz on the first indictment. . . . The claim with respect to the second indictment, where Katz did have the semblance of a defense, namely, to put the blame on Weiss, is a shade more impressive, but not sufficiently so. Counsel stresses statements by Mr. Boxer to the judge outside the presence of the jury early in the trial that he "would rather walk out on this case and not be on it," was "not very happy about the entire thing," and was "just doing a duty," and that on two occasions he was observed to be sleeping while Weiss' counsel was examining a witness. But this attitude and conduct did not require the trial judge to set aside the conviction unless it prevented Katz from receiving a fair trial. She was justified in concluding that Mr. Boxer did not in fact fail in his duty of loyalty or in elementary skill. Mr. Boxer went after Weiss with vigor. . . .

That these endeavors were not without success is evidenced by the acquittal of both defendants on the first count. In denying the motion for a new trial, Judge Motley stated that the testimony during the periods of counsel's somnolence was not central to Katz' case and that, if it had been, she would have awakened him rather than have waited for the luncheon recess to warn him. It is claimed that while Mr. Boxer was too sleepy on these occasions, he was too aggressive on others, notably in a totally unwarranted attack on the qualifications of an FBI handwriting expert. Much as we deplore such methods, Mr. Boxer was not the first attorney to use them and doubtless will not be the last. Having reviewed all the specifications, we cannot find, especially in light of the considered opinion of the trial judge, that individually or in the aggregate they suffice to constitute a denial of effective representation.

UNITED STATES v. DECOSTER
United States Court of Appeals, District of Columbia Circuit
624 F.2d 196 (1979)

[Decoster and two accomplices allegedly attacked one Crump, rifled his pockets, and took a wallet containing over $100 in cash. Two plainclothes police officers saw the robbery in progress and gave chase. One of them testified that he followed Decoster from the scene into the D.C. Annex Hotel, where he arrested him at the lobby desk. The officer testified that he had never lost sight of Decoster and that Crump had immediately identified Decoster as one of the robbers. A search of Decoster failed to turn up any money, and the wallet was never recovered.

[At the trial Decoster testified that he had had a few drinks with Crump at a bar but had left Crump in the bar, walked back to his hotel and was getting his key from the desk clerk when he was arrested. The defense also called one of the accomplices, one Eley, who had already pleaded guilty to participation in the robbery of Crump. Eley confirmed that Decoster had met Crump in the bar, but he also testified that he had seen Decoster and Crump fighting outside the bar, thus contradicting Decoster's claim that he had left the bar alone. Decoster was convicted of aiding and abetting an armed robbery, and sentenced to two to eight years in prison.

[The claim of ineffective assistance centered on the failure of Decoster's counsel to contact potential witnesses. Counsel made no effort to interview the victim, the two police officers, the hotel desk clerk, any of those in the bar, or any potential eyewitnesses to the robbery. Counsel also failed to interview the two alleged accomplices prior to trial, but he did interview Eley shortly before Eley was called to the stand at trial. Counsel claimed that at this interview Eley had corroborated Decoster's alibi, although Eley's testimony on the stand later that day contradicted Decoster's alibi claim.

[On appeal a panel of the District of Columbia Circuit, in an opinion by Judge Bazelon, found a prima facie violation of the defendant's right to "reasonably competent assistance." United States v. DeCoster, 487 F.2d 1197, 1202 (1973) (hereafter *DeCoster I*).[a] The panel ruled that counsel must be guided by the American Bar Association's Standards Relating to the Defense Function (App. Draft 1971) (hereinafter cited as ABA Standards) and, specifically, must confer with the client as often as necessary to elicit matters of defense and to discuss tactical choices; must advise the client of his rights and take all actions necessary to preserve them; and must conduct appropriate investigations, both factual and legal, to determine what matters of defense can be developed. The panel also held that once a substantial violation of these duties was shown, relief must be granted unless the government can establish lack of prejudice. The panel remanded for an evidentiary hearing to determine compliance with these principles.

[After remand, a panel of the District of Columbia Circuit found that ineffective assistance had been established under the standards laid down in *DeCoster I* and thus reversed the conviction. United States v. Decoster, 20 Crim. L. Rptr. 2080 (1976) (*Decoster II*). Subsequently, however, the District of Columbia Circuit vacated the panel opinion in *Decoster II* and ordered rehearing en banc.]

LEVENTHAL, J. . . . The Sixth Amendment guarantees that "in all criminal prosecutions, the accused shall have the Assistance of Counsel for his defense." In giving content to this provision, the courts have recognized the need for

a. In subsequent opinions the Court of Appeals changed the spelling of defendant's name to "Decoster," but the court continued to use the spelling "DeCoster" when referring to the first opinion. — EDS.

differing approaches depending on the nature of the particular claim of denial of assistance in each case. . . .

The cases present a continuum. At one end are cases of structural or procedural impediments by the state that prevent the accused from receiving the benefits of the constitutional guarantee. The most obvious example is, of course, the failure of the state to provide any counsel whatever. . . .

The right to have counsel provided is so fundamental that . . . the violation of the constitutional right mandates reversal "even if no particular prejudice is shown and even if the defendant was clearly guilty." [11]

"Effective" assistance of counsel is denied by a statute that, while permitting a defendant to make an unsworn statement, bars the defendant from having his testimony elicited by counsel through direct examination [14]; by a statute that restricts counsel in deciding when to put the defendant on the stand [15]; by a statute that gives the judge in a non-jury trial the power to deny defense counsel closing summation [16]; and by a trial court order directing a defendant not to consult with his attorney during an overnight recess that falls between direct and cross examination.[17] . . . Because these impediments constitute direct state interference with the exercise of a fundamental right, and because they are susceptible to easy correction by prophylactic rules, a categorical approach is appropriate. . . .

The problem of late appointment moves us farther along the continuum. The Supreme Court has long recognized that sufficient time to prepare a defense is a vital element of effective assistance. . . . Yet in its 1970 *Chambers* opinion,[22] the Supreme Court indicated that categorical rules were not appropriate in this area. Although the Court's treatment was cursory, it made clear that determining whether counsel was ineffective due to late appointment turned on the facts of the case. The Court emphasized, "we are not disposed to fashion a per se rule requiring reversal of every conviction following tardy appointment of counsel."

At the other end of the continuum are cases, including the present one, in which the issue is counsel's performance when he is "untrammelled and unimpaired" by state action. The Supreme Court has never addressed this issue frontally, though it has indicated — albeit in abbreviated fashion — that it does not contemplate simplistic or categorical approaches. . . . [T]he reasons for a non-categorical approach . . . are not difficult to discern. The defense attorney's function consists, in large part, of the application of professional judgment to an infinite variety of decisions in the development and prosecution of the case. A determination whether any given action or omission by counsel amounted to ineffective assistance cannot be divorced from consideration of the peculiar facts and circumstances that influenced counsel's judgment. In this fact-laden atmosphere, categorical rules are not appropriate. . . .

The task remains of delineating the non-categorical criteria that are to be

11. Chapman v. California, 386 U.S. 18, 43 (1967) (Stewart, J., concurring).
14. Ferguson v. Georgia, 365 U.S. 570 (1961).
15. Brooks v. Tennessee, 406 U.S. 605 (1972).
16. Herring v. New York, 422 U.S. 853 (1975).
17. Geders v. United States, 425 U.S. 80 (1976).
22. Chambers v. Maroney, 339 U.S. 42 (1970).

applied in evaluating claims of inadequate performance by counsel. . . . Some circuits have attempted to give content to their standards by adopting, explicitly or by implication, specific duties the violation of which amounts to ineffective assistance. The panel of this court that wrote *DeCoster I* employed — with some embellishment — the standards for the defense function promulgated by the American Bar Association. The ABA Standards, however, were not put forward by the ABA as either exclusively "minimum" standards or as "a set of per se rules applicable to post-conviction procedures." [52] Rather, they constitute a "blend of description of function, functional guide-lines, ethical guidelines and recommended techniques," [53] a mixture of the aspirational and the obligatory. . . .

This brief survey underscores that generalized standards may be little more than a "semantic merry-go-round." . . . [I]n the last analysis they are necessarily limited efforts to describe that courts will condemn only a performance that is egregious and probably prejudicial. . . . The claimed inadequacy must be a serious incompetency that falls measurably below the performance ordinarily expected of fallible lawyers. And the accused must bear the initial burden of demonstrating a likelihood that counsel's inadequacy affected the outcome of the trial. Once the appellant has made this initial showing, the burden passes to the government, and the conviction cannot survive unless the government demonstrates that it is not tainted by the deficiency, and that in fact no prejudice resulted. . . .

The court's appraisal requires a judgmental rather than a categorical approach. It must be wary lest its inquiry and standards undercut the sensitive relationship between attorney and client and tear the fabric of the adversary system. . . . A shortfall by defense counsel that is perceptible but is modest rather than egregious is no basis for judicial interposition. . . . This limitation, preserves the freedom of counsel to make quick judgments, and avoids the possibility that there will be frequent and wide-ranging inquiries into the information and reasoning that prompted counsel to pursue a given course. . . .

For the law to encourage a wide-ranging inquiry, even after trial, into the conduct of defense counsel would undercut the fundamental premises of the trial process and transform its essential nature. The resulting upheaval in the role of the trial judge, widely recognized as a serious difficulty, would in itself call into question any broad doctrine of ineffective assistance. And the prosecution in a criminal case would in turn ask to oversee defense counsel's conduct at trial — to ensure against reversal.

An even more difficult problem would be posed by the supervision of defense counsel's development of the case before trial. Even if we had the authority, it would be unwise to embark upon a doctrine that would open the door to a fundamental reordering of the adversary system into a system more inquisitorial in nature. . . .

Our reflections on this point are congruent with the standard applicable when counsel for an indigent defendant seeks funds to obtain investigative services to assist in the preparation of the defense. While in general effective assistance of counsel embraces such an allowance it is far from automatic and "depends

---

52. ABA Standards, supra, at 11. . . .
53. Id. at 11.

on the facts and circumstances of a particular case," with funds provided when counsel makes a showing of necessity, of the specific subjects to be explored and of their likely materiality.

Finally, claims based on a duty to investigate must be considered in light of the strength of the government's case. . . . It is all well and good for a millionaire to retain counsel with the instruction to "leave not the smallest stone unturned." But it goes too far to insist that such a course is a general constitutional mandate.

We turn from general questions of principle and approach to the matter of application to the case at hand. . . .

Appellant attacks defense counsel's failure to interview the desk clerk at the D.C. Annex Hotel, and his failure to make an effort to locate and interview potential eyewitnesses that might have been in the hotel at the time appellant entered and was apprehended. These are abstractions without context. Appellant himself testified at trial that he had just entered the lobby when he was arrested. Counsel was aware that there would be, as indeed there was, testimony of the police officer that he had not lost sight of appellant from the time of the robbery to the time of his apprehension. Appellant makes no claim that he advised counsel of any occurrence that would generate a significant issue as to his entry into the hotel.

If given an unrestricted budget and freed of any constraints as to probable materiality or accountability, a lawyer might have cheerfully logged in many hours looking for the legal equivalent of a needle in a haystack. . . . However, a defendant is not entitled to perfection but to basic fairness. In the real world, expenditure of time and effort is dependent on a reasonable indication of materiality. In the circumstances of this case, appellant has singularly failed to make a meaningful demonstration that counsel's omission probably affected the outcome of the trial. It is argued that potential witnesses might have testified to appellant's demeanor as he entered the lobby. This abstract possibility is not only speculative but remote in the extreme. It cannot fairly be said to undercut materially the positive police testimony. . . .

As already indicated, we do not approve the belated effort to interview the co-defendants. However, appellant has not demonstrated a likelihood that counsel's omission affected the outcome of trial. . . .

The several claims, both seriatim and in combination, do not raise in our minds serious misgivings as to whether justice was done. . . . In the absence of a governmental impediment to effective assistance of counsel, the court cannot lightly vacate a conviction on the basis of its own appraisal of the performance of defense counsel. The door is open, but only for cases of grievous deficiency and where the court has serious misgivings that justice has not been done. . . .

We support efforts to upgrade performance of defense trial counsel. We commend the programs of the last decade in clinical education for law students. We approve the American Bar Association's efforts to clarify the defense and prosecution functions. More should be done. But more is not better if it undercuts the adversary system. . . .

Judge Bazelon recognizes that the government can always defend by showing beyond a reasonable doubt that the violation was harmless — a rule prescribed by *Chapman* [101] even for established constitutional violations. The realistic thrust

---

101. Chapman v. California, 386 U.S. 18 (1967).

of Judge Bazelon's approach, however, is a rule structured toward a conclusion of prejudice from any deviation from the checklist of standards concerning preparation, whatever the likely or actual consequence. Omissions of investigation lead to new trials on the rationale that one can never be certain what might have happened had counsel performed better. A new trial is needed if exculpatory information might have been turned up (obviously), and also if the fruits of the investigation would have proved neutral or even inculpatory, for defense counsel could have been in a stronger position to lead his client to plead guilty. This kind of speculation renders no error harmless. . . .

Judge Bazelon is animated by a view of the adversary system as so impaired in practice as to warrant a thorough reordering, with extensive supervision by the trial judge through a pretrial "checklist" to ensure that counsel has met his duties of preparation, and oversight of the conduct of the trial. The manifest consequence would be inevitable and increasing intrusion into the development and presentation of the defense case by the trial judge, and (out of self-protection) by the prosecution.

The adversary system is neither sacrosanct nor impervious to change. But Judge Bazelon has not pointed to any system — let alone the inquisitorial system of the Continent — that guarantees better protection against injustice. We do not think he has made a case for the drastic overhaul of a system that historically has heightened protection of the accused. Perhaps the spectre of disruption will lead to increased appropriations to the criminal justice system, but such a tactical approach to the judicial function would be perilous. . . . Certainly there is need for the allocation of additional resources. . . . Responses are primarily required from the bodies that can supply resources — the legislature and the bar. Judge Bazelon's bold but single-valued approach would tolerate disruption of the administration of justice and a reordering of the adversary system, with little guarantee of improved performance and impassivity as to the uncharted and likely noxious consequences.

Our approach toward the minimum legal obligations of our democratic society to ward off injustice may be more earthbound, but in our view it is more salutary.

Affirmed.

MACKINNON, J. . . . [Judge MacKinnon agreed with much of Judge Leventhal's opinion but argued that a defendant who claims ineffective assistance "must show that substantial prejudice to his defense resulted from the alleged violation of duty." Judge MacKinnon added:]

. . . Decoster's counsel knew from the information available to him that his client was guilty. This knowledge was confirmed after the trial when Decoster admitted his guilt. Thus, without speculating at all, it can be said that no investigation, however exhaustive, could have discovered evidence that would have helped Decoster. When as here a defense attorney knows his client is guilty, I wholeheartedly agree with then Judge (now Justice) Stevens' statement that "counsel ha[s] no duty to search for witnesses, expert or otherwise, who might falsely testify to the contrary." Matthews v. United States, 518 F.2d 1245, 1246 (7th Cir. 1975). . . .

The dissent states:

> The suggestion that a client whose lawyer believes him to be guilty deserves less pretrial investigation is simply wrong. An attorney's duty to investigate is not relieved by his own perception of his client's guilt or innocence.

This pronouncement is foreign to a lawyer's basic obligation to the court and his profession. . . . While the quality of counsel's performance may not depend on the guilt or innocence of his client, that does not contradict the principle that in determining whether a counsel has breached a duty, the guilt or innocence of his client may affect what he was required to do to satisfy the requirement of a reasonably competent lawyer.

Defense counsel are not required to close their eyes to the obvious and search for alibis for defendants who would like assistance in the fabrication of a defense, for that would be a violation of the ethical standards of the legal profession. . . .

[ROBINSON, J., concurring only in the result, rejected the view that either "likely prejudice" (the Leventhal approach) or "actual prejudice" (the MacKinnon approach) should be an element of the defendant's ineffective assistance claim. He argued that once a defendant shows that counsel defaulted on an obligation owed to the accused, the government should bear the burden of proving that the default was harmless beyond a reasonable doubt. But Judge Robinson found that this stringent test of harmlessness was satisfied on the facts of the case.]

BAZELON, J. . . . dissenting: Willie Decoster was denied the effective assistance of counsel guaranteed by the Sixth Amendment because he could not afford to hire a competent and conscientious attorney. His plight is an indictment of our system of criminal justice, which promises "Equal Justice Under Law," but delivers only "Justice for Those Who Can Afford It." Though purporting to address the problem of ineffective assistance, the majority's decision ignores the sordid reality that the kind of slovenly, indifferent representation provided Willie Decoster is uniquely the fate allotted to the poor. . . . Like Justice Black, I believe that "[t]here can be no equal justice where the kind of trial a man gets depends on the amount of money he has." [1] . . .

The duties set forth in *DeCoster I* were derived from the American Bar Association's Standards for the Defense Function. These ABA Standards summarize the consensus of the practicing Bar on the crucial elements of defense advocacy in our adversary system. Even though these standards were not intended by their drafters to serve "as criteria for judicial evaluation of effectiveness[,]" this court noted that "they are certainly relevant guideposts in this largely uncharted area." Naturally, given the complexities of each case and the constant call for professional discretion, it would be a misguided endeavor to engrave in stone any rules for attorney performance. . . .

In *DeCoster I* this court was sensitive to these concerns and so did not attempt to prescribe categorical standards of attorney performance. . . . We recognized, however, that there were certain tasks, such as the ones we enumerated in our decision, that can never be ignored: conferring with the client without delay and as often as necessary; fully discussing potential strategies and tactical choices; advising the client of his rights and taking all actions necessary to preserve them; and conducting appropriate factual and legal investigations. I submit that no one can dispute that a reasonably competent lawyer, absent good cause, would or should do less. . . .

Prominent among the duties of defense counsel is the obligation to "conduct appropriate investigations, both factual and legal, to determine what matter of

1. Griffin v. Illinois, 351 U.S. 12, 19 (1956).

defense can be developed.". . . Investigation is crucial for several reasons. First, the proper functioning of our adversary system demands that both sides prepare and organize their case in advance of trial. There can be no justice where one party to the battle has made no effort to arm itself with the pertinent facts and law. Second, in a very practical sense, cases are won on the facts. Proper investigation is critical not only in turning up leads and witnesses favorable to the defense, but in allowing counsel to take full advantage of trial tactics such as cross-examination and impeachment of adverse witnesses. . . . "[I]t is axiomatic among trial lawyers and judges that cases are not won in the courtroom but by the long hours of laborious investigation and careful preparation and study of legal points which precede the trial.". . .

. . . Although the failure to interview a particular witness, by itself, may not rise to the level of inadequate assistance, defense counsel's investigation and preparation for this case was so perfunctory that it clearly violated his duties to his client. . . . [D]efense counsel made absolutely no effort to discover, contact, or interview a *single witness* prior to trial. Apparently, he was willing to go to trial without having made any real effort to determine what could be elicited by way of defense or to evelute the strengths and weaknesses of his client's case.

Moreover, defense counsel's violations of the duties owed to his client were not limited to an egregious failure to investigate. There are several indications that counsel did not "confer with his client . . . as often as necessary to elicit matters of defense, or to ascertain that potential defenses are unavailable." . . .[89] In this case, the frequency and pervasiveness of defense counsel's omissions and failures certainly belie any notion that these actions were isolated and excusable events. . . . The record reveals that counsel conducted almost no investigation whatsoever in the 17 months preceeding trial. . . .

Nor do any special circumstances justify counsel's breach of his obligations. In some cases prudential judgments or tactical considerations may be involved in counsel's decision about whom to interview. In the present case, however, there simply is no possible justification for counsel's near-total lack of investigation and preparation.

Defense counsel's failure to investigate cannot be justified on the basis that he felt he was familiar enough with the facts of this case to judge for himself that his client was guilty. . . . [D]efense counsel's total knowledge of the case in fact consisted entirely of two conflicting versions of the events — one from a police officer and the other from his own client. Perhaps counsel concluded from this limited information that his client had no abili defense and was guilty, and that therefore counsel was excused from conducting any investigation.[102]

89. Counsel's failure to investigate and confer with his client more frequently may have resulted from his inability to devote sufficient time to each of his cases. The records of the Administrative Office of the United States Courts reveal that in 1972, the year that Decoster went to trial, his attorney received payments under the Criminal Justice Act totalling $51,098.47 for handling 284 different cases — more than one case for every working day. This total, of course, does not include any criminal and civil cases that Decoster's attorney may have handled on a retained basis. . . .

102. Judge MacKinnon apparently would go one step further and *require* an attorney to refrain from investigation if he believes his client to be guilty. . . . But an attorney's duty not to present perjured testimony is not a mandate to abjure investigation on behalf of his client, as appears to have happened here. . . . And, even in those cases where a defendant admits guilt to his attorney, the attorney must conscientiously gather information to protect the defendant's interests at all stages of the criminal process.

But the suggestion that a client whose lawyer believes him to be guilty deserves less pretrial investigation is simply wrong. . . . I can think of nothing more destructive of the adversary system than to excuse inadequate investigation on the grounds that defense counsel — the accused's only ally in the entire proceedings — disbelieved his client and therefore thought that further inquiry would prove fruitless.[104] The Constitution entitles a criminal defendant to a trial in court by a jury of his peers — not to a trial by his court-appointed defense counsel.[105]

To satisfy its burden of establishing lack of prejudice, it is not enough for the government simply to point to the evidence of guilt adduced at trial, no matter how overwhelming such evidence may be. In the first place, "proof of prejudice may well be absent from the record precisely because counsel has been ineffective." When, as in this case, ineffectiveness is founded upon gross omissions of counsel rather than specific errors, counsel's violations so permeate the trial that they necessarily cast doubt on the entire adjudicative process. Even where the consequences of counsel's omissions are less pervasive, it will generally be impossible to know precisely how the proceedings were affected, and the resulting prejudice will be "incapable of any sort of measurement." . . .

Moreover, "prejudice" to the defendant may take many forms. The likelihood of acquittal at trial is not the only touchstone against which the consequence of counsel's failures is to be measured. . . . [I]nadequate investigation and preparation may prejudice the defendant not only *at* trial but *before* trial — in counsel's inability to offer informed, competent advice on whether to plead guilty and whether to demand a jury trial — as well as *after* trial — in providing ineffective representation at sentencing. . . .

104. Such attitudes can only exacerbate what is already a serious problem of defendant mistrust of court-appointed counsel. See, e.g., J. Casper, American Criminal Justice: The Defendant's Perspective 106-15 (1972); ABA Standards at 197-98; Wice & Suwak, [Current Realities of Public Defender Programs, 10 Crim. L. Bull. 161 (1974)], at 171.

105. The dangers that can result from excusing counsel's inadequate representation on the ground that his client's "guilt is obvious" are vividly illustrated by a series of events occurring shortly after appellant's trial involving the same attorney whose performance is challenged in the present case. In December 1971, Decoster's lawyer was appointed to represent another indigent defendant, Samuel A. Saunders, who was accused of purse snatching. . . .

Saunders, who spent over 9 years in an institution for the mentally retarded and is half-blind, maintained that he was innocent and that he had been working on the day of the robbery. Decoster's lawyer evidently did not believe him; as in the present case, the lawyer apparently conducted no investigation whatsoever. At trial, Saunders' entire defense consisted of his own testimony . . . that he had not stolen the purse. Decoster's lawyer made no attempt to develop the defense beyond this single denial. . . . The most critical dereliction, however, was the lawyer's failure to pursue either in redirect examination or through post-trial investigation, Saunders' assertion during cross-examination that he had been working for the D. C. Employment Service on the day of the robbery and that "they will verify that date."

Not surprisingly, Saunders was convicted and sentenced to 2-6 years. Fortunately, this court appointed a conscientious attorney to represent Saunders on appeal. This lawyer . . . had her secretary call the U.S. Employment Service, . . . and found indisputable documentary proof that Saunders had been working on a Washington Star delivery truck on that day and was nowhere near the scene of the crime. . . . The district court granted a motion for a new trial based on the newly-discovered evidence and the charges against Saunders were dismissed. In the meantime, Saunders had spent a year in jail for a crime he had not committed.

Saunders, of course, could demonstrate prejudice, even under the majority's proposed analyses. But there are undoubtedly countless other indigent defendants, like Decoster himself, who are represented with the same callous indifference by court-appointed trial counsel, and who are not fortunate enough to have indisputable evidence, preserved in documentary form, attesting to the prejudice they have suffered. . . .

On the record before us in the present case, I would conclude that the government has failed to discharge its burden of proving that no adverse consequences resulted from counsel's gross violations of his duties to his client. Several important questions on the matter of prejudice remain unanswered, and in the absence of any evidence on these critical issues, I am unable to find that counsel's violations were "so unimportant and insignificant" that reversing appellant's conviction would be a futile exercise. No inquiry was made, for example, on the relationship between counsel's failure to investigate and Decoster's decision to go to trial rather than to seek and possibly accept a plea bargain comparable to that of his codefendants.[151]

The real battle for equal justice . . . must be waged in the trenches of the trial courts. Although reversing criminal convictions can have a significant deterrent effect, an appellate court necessarily depends upon the trial courts to implement the standards it announces. . . . [A] first step that a trial judge can take is to refuse to allow a trial to begin until he is assured that defense counsel has conducted the necessary factual and legal investigation. The simple question, "Is defense ready?" may be insufficient to provide that assurance. Instead, we should consider formalizing the procedure by which the trial judge is informed about the extent of counsel's preparation. Before the trial begins — or before a guilty plea is accepted — defense counsel could submit an investigative checklist certifying that he has conducted a complete investigation and reviewing the steps he has taken in pretrial preparation, including what records were obtained, which witnesses were interviewed, when the defendant was consulted, and what motions were filed. Although a worksheet alone cannot assure that adequate preparation is undertaken, it may reveal gross violations of counsel's obligations; at a minimum, it should heighten defense counsel's sensitivity to the need for adequate investigation and should provide a record of counsel's asserted actions for appeal.

The trial judge's obligation does not end, however, with a determination that counsel is prepared for trial. Whenever during the course of the trial it appears that defense counsel is not properly fulfilling his obligations, the judge must take appropriate action to prevent the deprivation of the defendant's constitutional rights. "It is the judge, not counsel, who has the ultimate responsibility for the conduct of a fair and lawful trial." [161]

My colleagues fear that judicial "inquiry and standards . . . [may] tear the fabric of our adversary system." *But for so very many indigent defendants, the adversary system is already in shreds.* . . . The adversary system can "provide salutory protection for the rights of the accused" [164] only if both sides are equally prepared for the courtroom confrontation.[165]

---

151. . . . Decoster's codefendants pleaded guilty to one robbery count and received suspended sentences and 5-years probation. Decoster was convicted of armed robbery and was sentenced to 2-8 years. . . .

161. Lakeside v. Oregon, 435 U.S. 333, 341 (1978). . . .

164. Opinion of Leventhal, J.

165. Some commentators have questioned the propriety of the adversary system as the "engine of truth" in the criminal process. See, e.g., Frankel, The Search for Truth: An Umpireal View, 123 U. Pa. L. Rev. 1031 (1975). Many of their criticisms are well taken. But many of the failings of the adversary system do not stem from inherent defects in the adversary process. Rather, they result from the imbalance between the opposing parties that is a by-product of the inferior representation available to the poor. A serious commitment to eliminate the gross disparities in representation would go a long way toward bringing the realities of the adversary system into line with the model on which much of Anglo-American jurisprudence is based.

Some of my colleagues are also concerned that a wide-ranging inquiry into the conduct of defense counsel would transform the role of the trial judge. . . . Yet [the trial judge has] the ultimate responsibility for ensuring that the accused receives a fair trial, with all the attendant safeguards of the Bill of Rights. . . . The trial judge simply cannot "stand idly by while the fundamental rights of a criminal defendant are forfeited through the inaction of ill-prepared counsel. . . ."

However vigilant the judge, the problem of inadequate representation of the indigent cannot be solved by the courts alone. The bench, bar and public must jointly renew our commitment to equal justice.[169] The bar certainly must increase its efforts to monitor the performances of its members and to take appropriate disciplinary action against those attorneys who fail to fulfill their obligations to their clients.[170] . . .

That the ultimate solution does not lie exclusively within the province of the courts does not justify our ignoring the situation nor our accepting it as immutable. The people have bestowed upon the courts a trust: to ensure that the awesome power of the State is not invoked against anyone charged with a crime unless that individual has been afforded all the rights guaranteed by the Constitution. We fail that trust if we sit by silently while countless indigent defendants continue to be deprived of liberty without the effective assistance of counsel.

[A separate statement by WRIGHT, J., is omitted.]

NOTES

1. *Effective assistance and the responsibilities of the trial judge.* Suppose that during the course of a trial, the judge develops strong doubts about whether defense counsel has adequately prepared the case. The prevailing opinions in *Decoster* appear to hold that the judge is not invariably *obligated* to intervene to protect the defendant's rights. Does the judge nevertheless have *discretion* to intervene (for example, by questioning defense trial strategy or by requiring further investigation), or would such intervention itself impair the effective assistance of counsel? For a federal judge's thoughtful discussion of the dilemma, see Schwartzer, Dealing with Incompetent Counsel — The Trial Judge's Role, 93 Harv. L. Rev. 633 (1980).

The proper course for the trial judge may not be clear even when the judge becomes convinced that defense counsel is incompetent. Should the judge have discretion (or the obligation) to remove the lawyer and appoint new counsel? If so, should the judge be permitted to exercise that power even when the defendant prefers to continue with the first attorney? Compare United States

---

169. . . . Efforts to raise the overall level of lawyers' skills are commendable, but none of these proposals even begins to address the unique problems of providing adequate representation for the poor. None of these suggested reforms attempts to deal with the most frequent causes of ineffective assistance for the poor defendant — attorney indifference and overwork. . . .

170. To date, the bar has been notably lax in disciplining those attorneys who shirk their obligations. . . . In the *Saunders* case, see note 105 supra, appellate counsel was so outraged by trial counsel's failure to carry out his obligations as an attorney that she filed a grievance with the D.C. Bar Association. The results of that complaint are not public, but it is significant that Decoster's attorney continued to receive appointments in the D.C. courts. . . .

v. Rogers, 471 F. Supp. 847 (E.D.N.Y. 1979) (removal of incompetent attorney, over defendant's objection, held proper), with Smith v. Superior Court, 68 Cal. 2d 547, 440 P.2d 65 (1968) (removal of incompetent attorney, over defendant's objection, held to violate defendant's constitutional right to counsel).

For further exploration of the extent to which the judge in an adversary system should be conceived as a passive, neutral arbiter or instead as a person actively seeking to ascertain the truth, see pages 145-147 infra.

2. Effective assistance and the ethical responsibilities of defense counsel. The prevailing opinions in *Decoster* hold that defense counsel's failure to investigate the alibi claim was not constitutionally "ineffective" under the circumstances, but Judge Leventhal's opinion implies that a vigorous defense attorney might properly have done so. How far may defense counsel go in developing and presenting a defense that he or she believes (or "knows") to be unfounded? This problem is explored at pages 121-141 infra.

b. Ethical Responsibilities of Defense Counsel

AMERICAN BAR ASSOCIATION, CODE OF PROFESSIONAL RESPONSIBILITY
(1970)

CANON 7

A LAWYER SHOULD REPRESENT A CLIENT ZEALOUSLY WITHIN THE BOUNDS OF THE LAW

Ethical Considerations
EC 7-1 The duty of a lawyer, both to his client and to the legal system, is to represent his client zealously within the bounds of the law, which includes Disciplinary Rules and enforceable professional regulations. . . .

EC 7-26 The law and Disciplinary Rules prohibit the use of fraudulent, false, or perjured testimony or evidence. A lawyer who knowingly participates in introduction of such testimony or evidence is subject to discipline. A lawyer should, however, present any admissible evidence his client desires to have presented unless he knows, or from facts within his knowledge should know, that such testimony or evidence is false, fraudulent, or perjured.

Disciplinary Rules
DR 7-101 REPRESENTING A CLIENT ZEALOUSLY.
(A) A lawyer shall not intentionally:
    (1) Fail to seek the lawful objectives of his client through reasonably available means permitted by law and the Disciplinary Rules, except as provided by DR 7-101(B). . . .
    (3) Prejudice or damage his client during the course of the professional relationship, except as required under DR 7-102 (B).
(B) In his representation of a client, a lawyer may:
    (1) Where permissible, exercise his professional judgment to waive or fail to assert a right or position of his client.

(2) Refuse to aid or participate in conduct that he believes to be unlawful, even though there is some support for an argument that the conduct is legal.

DR 7-102 REPRESENTING A CLIENT WITHIN THE BOUNDS OF THE LAW.

(A) In his representation of a client, a lawyer shall not: . . .

(4) Knowingly use perjured testimony or false evidence.

(5) Knowingly make a false statement of law or fact.

(6) Participate in the creation or preservation of evidence when he knows or it is obvious that the evidence is false.

(7) Counsel or assist his client in conduct that the lawyer knows to be illegal or fraudulent.

(8) Knowingly engage in other illegal conduct or conduct contrary to a Disciplinary Rule.

(B) A lawyer who receives information clearly establishing that:

(1) His client has, in the course of the representation, perpetrated a fraud upon a person or tribunal shall promptly call upon his client to rectify the same, and if his client refuses or is unable to do so, he shall reveal the fraud to the affected person or tribunal, except when the information is protected as a privileged communication.[a] . . .

(2) A person other than his client has perpetrated a fraud upon a tribunal shall promptly reveal the fraud to the tribunal.

M. FREEDMAN, LAWYERS' ETHICS IN AN ADVERSARY SYSTEM
3-4, 27-42 (1975)

[T]he adversary process has its foundations in respect for human dignity, even at the expense of the search for truth[.] I do not mean to deprecate the search for truth or to suggest that the adversary system is not concerned with it. On the contrary, truth is a basic value, and the adversary system is one of the most efficient and fair methods designed for determining it. . . . Nevertheless, the point that I now emphasize is that in a society that honors the dignity of the individual, the high value that we assign to truth-seeking is not an absolute, but may on occasion be subordinated to even higher values. . . .

Is it ever proper for a criminal defense lawyer to present perjured testimony? One's instinctive response is in the negative. On analysis, however, it becomes

---

a. The provisions of the ABA Code relevant to privileged communications are as follows:

"DR 4-101. PRESERVATION OF CONFIDENCES AND SECRETS OF A CLIENT.

(A) 'Confidence' refers to information protected by the attorney-client privilege under applicable law, and 'secret' refers to other information gained in the professional relationship that the client has requested be held inviolate or the disclosure of which would be embarrassing or would be likely to be detrimental to the client.

(B) Except when permitted under DR 4-101(C), a lawyer shall not knowingly:

(1) Reveal a confidence or secret of his client.

(2) Use a confidence or secret of his client to the disadvantage of the client. . . .

(C) A lawyer may reveal:

(1) Confidences or secrets with the consent of the client or clients affected, but only after a full disclosure to them.

(2) Confidences or secrets when permitted under Disciplinary Rules or required by law or court order.

(3) The intention of his client to commit a crime and the information necessary to prevent the crime. . . ." — EDS.

apparent that the question is an exceedingly perplexing one. My own answer is in the affirmative.

At the outset, we should dispose of some common question-begging responses. The attorney, we are told, is an officer of the court, and participates in a search for truth. Those propositions, however, merely serve to state the problem in different words: As an officer of the court, participating in a search for truth, what is the attorney obligated to do when faced with perjured testimony? That question cannot be answered properly without an appreciation of the fact that the attorney functions in an adversary system of criminal justice which . . . imposes special responsibilities upon the advocate.

First, the lawyer is required to determine "all relevant facts known to the accused," because "counsel cannot properly perform their duties without knowing the truth." The lawyer who is ignorant of any potentially relevant fact "incapacitates himself to serve his client effectively," because "an adequate defense cannot be framed if the lawyer does not know what is likely to develop at trial."

Second, the lawyer must hold in strictest confidence the disclosures made by the client in the course of the professional relationship. . . . If this were not so, the client would not feel free to confide fully, and the lawyer would not be able to fulfill the obligation to ascertain all relevant facts. . . .

Third, the lawyer is an officer of the court, and his or her conduct before the court "should be characterized by candor."

As soon as one begins to think about those responsibilities, it becomes apparent that the conscientious attorney is faced with what we may call a trilemma — that is, the lawyer is required to know everything, to keep it in confidence, and to reveal it to the court. . . .

Before addressing the issue of the criminal defense lawyer's responsibilities when the client indicates to the lawyer the intention to commit perjury in the future, we might note the somewhat less difficult question of what the lawyer should do when knowledge of the perjury comes after its commission rather than before it. Although there is some ambiguity in the most recent authorities, the rules appear to require that the criminal defense lawyer should urge the client to correct the perjury, but beyond that, the obligation of confidentiality precludes the lawyer from revealing the truth. . . .

With respect to the case where the lawyer has foreknowledge of the perjury, . . . the Code appears, at first reading, to be unambiguous. According to DR 7-102(A)(4), a lawyer must not "knowingly use perjured testimony or false evidence." The difficulty, however, is that the Code does not indicate how the lawyer is to go about fulfilling that obligation. What if the lawyer advises the client that perjury is unlawful and, perhaps, bad tactics as well, but the client nevertheless insists upon taking the stand and committing perjury in his or her own defense? What steps, specifically, should the lawyer take? Just how difficult it is to answer that question becomes apparent if we review the relationship between lawyer and client as it develops, and consider the contexts in which the decision to commit perjury may arise.

If we recognize that professional responsibility requires that an advocate have full knowledge of every pertinent fact, then the lawyer must seek the truth from the client, not shun it. That means that the attorney will have to dig and pry and cajole, and, even then, the lawyer will not be successful without convincing the client that full disclosure to the lawyer will never result in prejudice to the client by any word or action of the attorney. That is particularly true in the case of the indigent defendant, who meets the lawyer for the first time in the cell block or the rotunda of the jail. The client did not choose the lawyer, who comes as a stranger sent by the judge, and who therefore appears to be part of the system that is attempting to punish the defendant. It is no easy task to persuade that client to talk freely without fear of harm. . . . [T]he truth can be obtained only by persuading the client that it would be a violation of a sacred obligation for the lawyer ever to reveal a client's confidence. Of course, once the lawyer has thus persuaded the client of the obligation of confidentiality, that obligation must be respected scrupulously.

Assume the following situation. Your client has been falsely accused of a robbery committed at 16th and P Streets at 11:00 P.M. He tells you at first that at no time on the evening of the crime was he within six blocks of that location. However, you are able to persuade him that he must tell you the truth and that doing so will in no way prejudice him. He then reveals to you that he was at 15th and P Streets at 10:55 that evening, but that he was walking east, away from the scene of the crime, and that, by 11:00 P.M., he was six blocks away. At the trial, there are two prosecution witnesses. The first mistakenly, but with some degree of persuasiveness, identifies your client as the criminal. At that point the prosecution's case depends upon that single witness, who might or might not be believed. The second prosecution witness is an elderly woman who is somewhat nervous and who wears glasses. She testifies truthfully and accurately that she saw your client at 15th and P Streets at 10:55 P.M. She has corroborated the erroneous testimony of the first witness and made conviction extremely likely. However, on cross-examination her reliability is thrown into doubt through demonstration that she is easily confused and has poor eyesight. Thus, the corroboration has been eliminated, and doubt has been established in the minds of the jurors as to the prosecution's entire case.

The client then insists upon taking the stand in his own defense, not only to deny the erroneous evidence identifying him as the criminal, but also to deny the truthful, but highly damaging, testimony of the corroborating witness who placed him one block away from the intersection five minutes prior to the crime. Of course, if he tells the truth and thus verifies the corroborating witness, the jury will be more inclined to accept the inaccurate testimony of the principal witness, who specifically identified him as the criminal.

In my opinion, the attorney's obligation in such a situation would be to advise the client that the proposed testimony is unlawful, but to proceed in the normal fashion in presenting the testimony and arguing the case to the jury if the client makes the decision to go forward. Any other course would be a betrayal of the assurances of confidentiality given by the attorney in order to induce the client to reveal everything, however damaging it might appear. . . .

In a criticism of my position, Professor John Noonan of Boalt Hall argued that the true function of the advocate is to assist the trier of fact to reach a "wise and informed decision." [19] [However,] Professor Noonan's general proposition does not decide specific cases. Like other critics who express disapproval of the idea that a lawyer might knowingly present perjured testimony, Professor

19. Noonan, The Purposes of Advocacy and the Limits of Confidentiality, 64 Mich. L. Rev. 1485 (1966). . . .

Noonan does not suggest what a lawyer should do, as a practical matter, in the course of conferring with the client and presenting the case in court. . . .

The most obvious way to avoid the ethical difficulty is for the lawyer to withdraw from the case, at least if there is sufficient time before trial for the client to retain another attorney. The client will then go to the nearest law office, realizing that the obligation of confidentiality is not what it has been represented to be, and withhold incriminating information or the fact of guilt from the new attorney. In terms of professional ethics, the practice of withdrawing from a case under such circumstances is difficult to defend, since the identical perjured testimony will ultimately be presented. Moreover, the new attorney will be ignorant of the perjury and therefore will be in no position to attempt to discourage the client from presenting it. Only the original attorney, who knows the truth, has that opportunity, but loses it in the very act of evading the ethical problem.

The difficulty is all the more severe when the client is indigent. In that event, the client cannot retain other counsel, and in many jurisdictions it is impossible for appointed counsel or a public defender to withdraw from a case except for extraordinary reasons. Thus, the attorney can successfully withdraw only by revealing to the judge that the attorney has received knowledge of the client's guilt,* or by giving the judge a false or misleading reason for moving for leave to withdraw. However, for the attorney to reveal knowledge of the client's guilt would be a gross violation of the obligation of confidentiality, particularly since it is entirely possible in many jurisdictions that the same judge who permits the attorney to withdraw will subsequently hear the case and sentence the defendant. Not only will the judge then have personal knowledge of the defendant's guilt before the trial begins, but it will be knowledge of which the newly appointed counsel for the defendant will very likely be ignorant. . . .

Another solution that has been suggested is that the attorney move for leave to withdraw and that, when the request is denied, the attorney then proceed with the case, eliciting the defendant's testimony and arguing the case to the jury in the ordinary fashion. Since that proposal proceeds on the assumption that the motion will be denied, it seems to me to be disingenuous. If the attorney avoids the ethical problem, it is only by passing it on to the judge. Moreover, the client in such a case would then have grounds for appeal on the basis of deprivation of due process and denial of the right to counsel, since the defendant would have been tried before, and sentenced by, a judge who had been informed by the defendant's own lawyer that the defendant is guilty both of the crime charged and of perjury. . . .

Another unsuccessful effort to deal with the problem appears in the ABA Standards Relating to the Defense Function. . . . Section 7.7 of the Standards requires that the lawyer "must confine his examination to identifying the witness as the defendant and permitting him to make his statement." That is, the lawyer "may not engage in direct examination of the defendant . . . in the conventional manner." Thus, the client's story will become part of the record, although without the attorney's assistance through direct examination. The general rule, of course, is that in closing argument to the jury "the lawyer may argue all reason-

---

* The typical formula is for the attorney to advise the judge of "an ethical problem." The judge understands that to mean that the client is insisting upon a perjured alibi over the lawyer's objections. In one case, the judge incorrectly drew that inference when the lawyer's ethical concern was with the fact that the client wanted to enter a guilty plea despite the fact that he was innocent.

able inferences from the evidence in the record." Section 7.7 also provides, however, that the defense lawyer is forbidden to make any reference in closing argument to the client's testimony.

There are . . . critical flaws in that proposal. . . . [E]xperienced trial attorneys have often noted that jurors assume that the defendant's lawyer knows the truth about the case, and that the jury will frequently judge the defendant by drawing inferences from the attorney's conduct in the case. There is, of course, only one inference that can be drawn if the defendant's own attorney turns his or her back on the defendant at the most critical point in the trial, and then, in closing argument, sums up the case with no reference to the fact that the defendant has given exculpatory testimony. . . . Ironically, the Standards reject any solution that would involve informing the judge, but then propose a solution that, as a practical matter, succeeds in informing not only the judge but the jury as well.

It would appear that the ABA Standards have chosen to resolve the trilemma by maintaining the requirements of complete knowledge and of candor to the court, and sacrificing confidentiality. Interestingly, however, that may not in fact be the case. I say that because the Standards fail to answer a critically important question: Should the client be told about the obligation imposed by Section 7.7? That is, the Standards ignore the issue of whether the lawyer should say to the client at the outset of their relationship: "I think it's only fair that I warn you: If you should tell me anything incriminating and subsequently decide to deny the incriminating facts at trial, I would not be able to examine you in the ordinary manner or to argue your untrue testimony to the jury.". . . Obviously, any other course would be a betrayal of the client's trust, since everything else said by the attorney in attempting to obtain complete information about the case would indicate to the client that no information thus obtained would be used to the client's disadvantage. On the other hand, the inevitable result of [this] position would be to caution the client not to be completely candid with the attorney. That, of course, returns us to resolving the trilemma by maintaining confidentiality and candor, but sacrificing complete knowledge. . . . I continue to stand with those lawyers who hold that "the lawyer's obligation of confidentiality does not permit him to disclose the facts he has learned from his client which form the basis for his conclusion that the client intends to perjure himself." What that means — necessarily, it seems to me — is that the criminal defense attorney, however unwillingly in terms of personal morality, has a professional responsibility as an advocate in an adversary system to examine the perjurious client in the ordinary way and to argue to the jury, as evidence in the case, the testimony presented by the defendant.

NOONAN, BOOK REVIEW, 29 Stan. L. Rev. 363-366 (1977): Can an honest person practice regularly as a criminal defense lawyer in the United States? . . . Dean Freedman's implicit answer to [this question] is "no.". . .

Under our constitutional system, the right to counsel in a criminal case cannot be denied. The right to counsel includes the right to give one's lawyer in confidence all of the facts that one subjectively believes are relevant to one's defense. These two propositions are incontestable. From them, Dean Freedman concludes that one has a right to appear as a witness for oneself and to be examined by one's counsel, whether the story one is telling is true or false. The attorney who is unable to dissuade his client from perjury must proceed by presenting the testimony and arguing the case to the jury in the normal fashion. To say that counsel must or even may withdraw or not conduct the examination if his client insists on perjuring himself is, Dean Freedman contends, to deny the constitutional right. To support his contention he has the authority of Johns v. Smyth,[1] a case decided by Walter Hoffman, a federal judge in Norfolk, Virginia, and the proclaimed practice of 90 percent of the lawyers answering a survey in the District of Columbia.

Dean Freedman is very American in implying that what is required by the Constitution of the United States must be morally good, and his use of common practice to establish morality only transfers to the field of legal ethics an argument frequently used as to sexual morality. Both standards, however, are parochial. The Constitution of the United States once required the return of fugitive slaves. Dean Freedman himself is not at all happy with common practice as the criterion when he discusses the practices of prosecutors. . . . Rejecting the criteria Dean Freedman uses here, I continue to believe that the presentation of perjury to a court is fraud whether it is done by concocting a document, hiring a witness, or presenting one's own lying client as a truthteller. If, as Dean Freedman maintains, criminal law practice cannot be carried on otherwise, then honest persons cannot engage in it.

Yet ours, Dean Freedman might point out, is not an ordinary trade. It is socially indispensable. Moreover, it is indispensable to the defense of human dignity. Without counsel, the defendant in a criminal case stands naked before the power of the state. Is not the object of criminal trial procedure as much the preservation of the dignity of the defendant as the discovery of the truth? If it is, counsel performs a noble role, and if those who do in fact perform this role assert that only by cooperating in perjury can they accomplish it, should not their noble role justify their aid to falsehood?

The importance of preserving human dignity, which Dean Freedman puts so eloquently at the beginning of his book as a fundamental purpose in criminal trials, I willingly grant. But it seems strange to me to build on this foundation a defense of lying. "Only if I can tell my shabby falsehood with your help can I retain my sense of human worth" is what we must take to be the plea of each incriminated defendant who wants to testify falsely. I have difficulty grasping how accepting such an appeal preserves the dignity of the accused. . . .

Dean Freedman rightly points out that the attorney's difficulty is particularly acute when the client is indigent, since he cannot retain other counsel. Moreover, in many jurisdictions appointed counsel or the public defender may only withdraw from a case for extraordinary reasons, which would necessarily require revealing the client's perjurious intent to the very judge before whom he will be tried and sentenced. But Dean Freedman ignores an alternative to the problem: allow the attorney to withdraw without breaching the confidence and if prejudicial inferences are likely to be drawn, assign both a new judge and a new attorney. Clearly if we must choose between a rule based on administrative convenience and the presentation of perjury, let us do away with the rule.

Yet the problem remains, says Freedman, since the client, "realizing that the obligation of confidentiality is not what it has been represented to be,"

1. Johns v. Smyth, 176 F. Supp. 949 (E.D. Va. 1959). . . .

will withhold incriminating information or the fact of guilt from the new attorney and perjured testimony will be presented by an unwitting attorney. That may be true, but there is a crucial difference this time around: neither the first nor the second attorney has knowingly acquiesced in perjury, a result of no small importance in preserving the integrity of a truth-seeking system. . . .

. . . Dean Freedman [argues that] "Professor Noonan's general proposition does not decide specific cases." I am at a loss to understand this statement. The principle I espouse excludes the use of perjury even in the "hard cases" that Dean Freedman has appealingly constructed. Consequently I answer the first question in this review differently from the answer implicit in Lawyers' Ethics in an Adversary System.

NOTES

1. The ABA has established a Commission on Evaluation of Professional Standards to undertake a revision of the Code of Professional Responsibility. The Commission's Model Rules of Professional Conduct (Prop. Final Draft, May 30, 1981) appear to adopt a view similar to that espoused by Professor Noonan. Rule 3.3 of the draft (not yet approved by the ABA House of Delegates) provides:

RULE 3.3   CANDOR TOWARD THE TRIBUNAL

(a) A LAWYER SHALL NOT KNOWINGLY: . . .
(4) OFFER EVIDENCE THAT THE LAWYER KNOWS TO BE FALSE. IF A LAWYER HAS OFFERED MATERIAL EVIDENCE AND COMES TO KNOW OF ITS FALSITY, THE LAWYER SHALL TAKE REASONABLE REMEDIAL MEASURES. . . .

CAVEAT: CONSTITUTIONAL LAW DEFINING THE RIGHT TO ASSISTANCE OF COUNSEL IN CRIMINAL CASES MAY SUPERSEDE THE OBLIGATIONS STATED IN THIS RULE.

The Commentary to the draft Rule states (id. at 126):

While it is agreed that the lawyer should seek to persuade the client to refrain from perjurious testimony, there has been dispute concerning the lawyer's duty when that persuasion fails [and if it is not possible for the lawyer to withdraw]. . . . Three resolutions of this dilemma have been proposed. One is to permit the accused to testify by a narrative without guidance through the lawyer's questioning. This compromises both contending principles; it exempts the lawyer from the duty to disclose false evidence but subjects the client to an implicit disclosure of information imparted to counsel. Another suggested resolution, of relatively recent origin, is that the advocate be entirely excused from the duty to reveal perjury if the perjury is that of the client. This is a coherent solution but makes the advocate a knowing instrument of perjury.

The other resolution of the dilemma is that the lawyer must reveal the client's perjury if necessary to rectify the situation. A criminal accused has a right to the assistance of an advocate, a right to testify on his own behalf and a right of confidential communication with counsel. However, an accused should not have a right to assistance of counsel in committing perjury. Furthermore, an advocate has an obligation, not only in professional ethics but under the law as well, to avoid implication in the commission of perjury or other falsification of evidence. . . . The advocate accordingly must disclose a client's perjury if efforts to prevent commission of perjury have failed.

2. Should it follow under the draft Code that the attorney must, at the outset of the representation, advise the client of the limitation on the confidentiality of attorney-client communications? Professor Norman Lefstein, the reporter for a related ABA Committee on Standards Relating to the Defense Function, urges that such disclosure be made. See Lefstein, The Criminal Defendant Who Proposes Perjury, 6 Hofstra L. Rev. 665, 687-691 (1978). What effect would such disclosure have on effective communication between attorney and client? Plainly such warning would prevent frank discussion by the guilty defendant who has decided in advance to commit perjury. But could it also inhibit full disclosure and effective defense planning for the defendant who may have a legitimate defense?

3. What is the significance of the ABA's caveat to Rule 3.3? Consider the case that follows.

LOWERY v. CARDWELL

United States Court of Appeals, 9th Circuit

575 F.2d 727 (1978)

MERRILL, J. . . . Appellant was charged by the State of Arizona with first degree murder. She pleaded not guilty and trial was had to the court without a jury. Testimony established that the victim's body had been found seated in his car, parked in front of a cafe. He had been shot twice at close range. The state's principal witness testified that he had seen appellant walk to the car with the deceased and stand on the far side of the car — the driver's side — while the deceased entered the car. Sounds similar to those of the popping of fire crackers had then been heard. . . .

The appellant took the stand and testified [that she did not walk to the car with the deceased and did not shoot him.] . . . Counsel then requested a recess which was granted. The trial transcript discloses that in chambers, without appellant being present, the following occurred:

Mr. Lyding: I'd like to put on the record that I move to withdraw.
The Court: State your reason.
Mr. Lyding: I cannot state the reason.
The Court: Okay. The motion will be denied. . . .

Back in court counsel stated that he had no further questions of appellant. In closing argument to the court he made no reference to appellant's testimony to the effect that she had not accompanied the deceased to his car and had not shot him. Instead counsel argued that the state's case was subject to reasonable doubt and that if the court should find that appellant had pulled the trigger, still the case was not one of first degree murder.

The court found appellant guilty of second degree murder. The Supreme Court of Arizona affirmed. After exhausting state remedies appellant sought habeas corpus in the District Court for the District of Arizona. The writ was denied. . . . [It] was established that counsel had sought to withdraw because he believed appellant was lying; that for the same reason he had failed further to interrogate appellant or to argue her assertion that she had not shot the deceased. . . .

The problem presented is that which arises when defense counsel, in the course of a criminal trial, forms the belief that his client's defense is based on false testimony. We start with the basic proposition that if, under these circumstances, counsel informs the fact finder of his belief he has, by that action, disabled the fact finder from judging the merits of the defendant's defense. Further, he has by his action openly placed himself in opposition to his client upon her defense. The consequences of such action on the part of counsel, in our judgment, are such as to deprive the defendant of a fair trial. If in truth the defendant has committed perjury (a fact we do not know in this case) she does not by that falsehood forfeit her right to fair trial.

The question presented, then, is whether what here occurred amounted to such an unequivocal announcement to the fact finder as to deprive appellant of due process. In our judgment it must be said that it did. The judge, and not a jury, was the fact finder. From the testimony of appellant that we have quoted, from the fact that the examination of appellant ceased abruptly at that point with a request for a recess, from the making of the motion to withdraw and counsel's statement to the court that he could not state the reason for his motion, the only conclusion that could rationally be drawn by the judge was that in the belief of her counsel appellant had falsely denied shooting the deceased.

The result on these unusual facts is not inconsistent with the principles of professional responsibility under ethical standards as they are generally recognized today and does not expose counsel to a charge of subornation of perjury. The American Bar Association Code of Professional Responsibility states only that "In his representation of a client, a lawyer shall not . . . knowingly use perjured testimony or false evidence." Disciplinary Rule 7-102(A)(4). The ABA Defense Function Standards [§7.7] . . . would appear to require that when, in the course of trial, counsel is surprised by his client's perjury he should not act to advance it. However, there is no requirement that he seek to withdraw, since, during trial, that course is likely not to be feasible. The Standards seem quite sensibly to assume that counsel will not be expected to act in such a fashion as to disclose his quandary to the fact finder.

Thus it does not follow from our holding that a passive refusal to lend aid to what is believed to be perjury in accordance with the Defense Function Standards would violate due process. In our view, mere failure to pursue actively a certain course of defense, which counsel ethically is precluded from actively pursuing, cannot be said to constitute denial of fair trial. While a knowledgeable judge or juror, alert to the ethical problems faced by attorneys and the manner in which they traditionally are met, might infer perjury from inaction, counsel's belief would not appear in the clear and unequivocal manner presented by the facts here. There may be many reasons for failure actively to pursue a particular line of defense. And in the weighing of competing values in which we are engaged — the accommodation we specified at the outset of this opinion — the integrity of the judicial process must be allowed to play a respectable role; the concept of due process must allow room for it.

The distinction we draw is between a passive refusal to lend aid to perjury and such direct action as we find here — the addressing of the court in pursuit of court order granting leave to withdraw. By calling for a judicial decision upon counsel's motion in a case in which the judge served as fact finder, this conduct affirmatively and emphatically called the attention of the fact finder to the problem counsel was facing.[5]

. . . We are acutely aware of the anomaly presented when mistrial must result from counsel's bona fide efforts to avoid professional irresponsibility. We find no escape, however, from the conclusion that fundamental requisites of fair trial have been irretrievably lost. Whether a just result nevertheless was reached would be a futile and irrelevant inquiry.

Reversed. . . .

HUFSTEDLER, J., specially concurring:

Although I do not disagree with the majority's due process analysis, I would rest the decision on the petitioner's Sixth Amendment right to effective assistance of counsel. . . . Under the circumstances that Judge Merrill describes, when defense counsel moved to withdraw, he ceased to be an active advocate of his client's interests. . . . No matter how commendable may have been counsel's motives, his interest in saving himself from potential violation of the canons was adverse to his client, and the end product was his abandonment of a diligent defense. . . .

NOTES

1. Explicit disclosure of client confidences. Some courts have held that when the defendant proposes to commit perjury, the lawyer may disclose this fact explicitly to the trial judge, at least if the judge is not the trier of fact. See, e.g., State v. Maddox, 613 S.W.2d 275, 283–284 (Tex. Crim. App. 1981). *Lowery* deals with the more limited situation in which the judge is the trier of fact. Does *Lowery* hold that no explicit disclosure should be made in this situation or instead that the attorney should make the disclosure, move to withdraw from the case, and move to disqualify the trial judge as well? Which approach is preferable? Consider again the danger of tacit disclosure signaled by the attorney's passive trial tactics. Isn't this danger even more serious when the trier of fact is a judge?

2. "Passive refusal to lend aid" and the effective assistance of counsel. Is there any significant difference, in practice, between the due process theory relied on by the *Lowery* majority and the Sixth Amendment rationale advanced in Judge Hufstedler's concurrence? Notice that the majority apparently would have upheld the conviction if the attorney had passively refused to aid in the supposed perjury, so long as he or she did not explicitly reveal a confidence to the trier of fact. But would that approach have satisfied Judge Hufstedler's conception of the rights to an "active advocate of [the] client's interests" and to a "diligent de-

---

5. The attorney may justifiably desire to establish a record for his own protection in the event that his professional conduct is later questioned. Especially in a case tried to the court, and even in a jury trial: ". . . if the trial judge is informed of the situation, the defendant may be unduly prejudiced . . . and the lawyer may feel he is caught in a dilemma between protecting himself by making such a record and prejudicing his client's case by making it with the court. The dilemma can be avoided in most instances by making the record in some other appropriate manner, for example, by having the defendant subscribe to a file notation, witnessed, if possible, by another lawyer." ABA Defense Function Standards §7.7 Commentary at 277.

fense"? If not, the compromise approach reflected in §7.7 of the ABA Standards would presumably be unconstitutional; the only permissible alternatives would be for the lawyer actively to argue the defendant's version of the facts (as urged by Professor Freedman) or to withdraw so that another attorney (presumably one ignorant of the true facts) could do so.

In several recent decisions, courts have held that the passive approach does not in itself deny the effective assistance of counsel. See State v. Maddox, 613 S.W.2d 275, 284 (Tex. Crim. App. 1981); State v. Robinson, 290 N.C. 56, 224 S.E.2d 174 (1976). This viewpoint, however, does not necessarily permit escape from all difficulties. In both *Maddox* and *Robinson,* for example, the attorney's passive strategy, though ultimately approved by the appellate court, had been strongly condemned by an infuriated client, who insisted that the attorney be removed from the case. What should the trial judge do in such a situation? Since counsel's behavior is viewed as quite proper, it seems inappropriate to grant the defendant a mistrial and appoint a new attorney (who, in any event, might quickly precipitate precisely the same dilemma). On the other hand, it appears inappropriate to force the defendant to proceed with the original lawyer after a complete breakdown of trust has occurred. That approach, followed by the trial judge in *Robinson,* supra, was held to deny the consitutional right to a fair trial.

The proper solution, apparently, is to advise the defendant that he or she is not entitled to new counsel under the circumstances but that he or she can choose either to retain the original attorney or to discharge that attorney and proceed pro se. This course was followed in *Maddox,* and the defendant conducted the rest of the trial himself, with some advice and limited participation by the original attorneys. Nevertheless, the conviction in *Maddox* was sustained only by a narrow margin. Four dissenting judges argued that the defendant had in effect waived his right to counsel and that the waiver was invalid because it had been made without a full appreciation of the dangers of pro se representation. The five-judge majority concluded that Maddox was not really deprived of the assistance of counsel because his defense attorneys had remained sufficiently active in this particular case. In other situations this form of "hybrid representation" may not be viewed as adequate to meet Sixth Amendment requirements, and in any event when a defendant elects to proceed without any assistance from the original attorney, the conviction is likely to remain vulnerable unless the requirements for a "knowing and intelligent" waiver of counsel have been scrupulously satisfied.

NOTE ON COUNSELING PROBLEMS

In all the foregoing situations the defense attorney "knew" that the client's testimony would be false. Can the attorney obviate the ethical problem by simply avoiding too much knowledge? Consider the following comment.

M. Freedman, Lawyers' Ethics in an Adversary System 69-77 (1975): Particularly effective in illustrating the difficulty is the so-called Anatomy of a Murder situation.[44]

---

44. See J. Voelker (R. Traver, pseudonym), Anatomy of a Murder (1958).

The lawyer who has received from his client an incriminating story of murder in the first degree, says, in effect: "If the facts are as you have stated them, you have no legal defense, and you will probably be electrocuted. On the other hand, if you acted in a blind rage, there is a possibility of saving your life. Think it over, and we will talk about it tomorrow." A number of lawyers have sought to avoid the implications of that case by arguing that the lawyer's principal fault was in not counselling the client in a manner that would have avoided the lawyer's knowing too much too soon. That is, the criticism is that the attorney could have given the legal advice (which ultimately prompted the perjurious defense) at a significantly earlier point, so that the lawyer would have been in a more effective position to claim that he did not really "know" the incriminating facts before channelling the client's story in the desired direction. Most of those same lawyers would recognize, however, the tactical importance of getting a substantial part of the client's narrative version of the facts before any suggestive or directive prompting by the lawyer begins. Otherwise, as we have seen in reviewing the psychological literature, the lawyer may well close off information that would be essential to developing a sound tactical position. Can the lawyer, then, have it both ways? Is it possible to know enough of the incriminating truth for tactical purposes and not, at the same time, come to know enough to be placed upon moral notice that the lawyer's advice about the law is likely to do more than simply prompt remembering-reconstructing in accordance with self-interest, and enter the area of prompting a conscious decision to commit perjury?

Before attempting to deal directly with the Anatomy of a Murder situation, in which the facts are unambiguous and the lawyer is suggesting a defense based upon radically different facts from those related by the client, let us deal with some situations in which there is necessarily a degree of ambiguity about facts that are relevant under applicable law. . . . [In] an ambiguous situation . . . it would be absurd for the lawyer to insist that the client state a conclusion . . . without first explaining to the client what the applicable law is and what the significance would be of each of the possible responses. . . . For example, assume that your client, on trial for his life in a first-degree murder case, has killed another man with a penknife but insists that the killing was in self-defense. You ask him: "Do you regularly carry the penknife in your pocket, do you carry it frequently or infrequently, or did you take it with you only on that particular occasion?" He replies: "Why do you ask me a question like that?" It is entirely appropriate to inform him that his carrying the knife only on that occasion, or infrequently, might support an inference of premeditation, while if he carried the knife invariably, or frequently, the inference of premeditation would be negated. . . . Despite the possibility that the client or a third party might infer that the lawyer was prompting the client to lie, the lawyer must apprise the defendant of the significance of his answer. There is no conceivable ethical requirement that the lawyer trap the client into a hasty and ill-considered answer before telling him the significance of the question. . . .

Up to this point, the analysis presented in this chapter parallels that in my earliest article, in the Michigan Law Review.[47] I now believe, however, that I

---

47. Freedman, [Professional Responsibility of the Criminal Defense Lawyer: The Three Hardest Questions, 64 Mich. L. Rev. 1469, 1478-1480 (1966)].

erred in going on to conclude that the Anatomy of a Murder situation is "essentially no different" from those just discussed. . . . [I suggested that information] about a factual defense that would have more chance of success than the facts narrated by the client . . . is information which the lawyer would have, without advice, were the lawyer in the client's position, and that the client is entitled to have that information about the law and to make his own decision as to whether to act upon it. To withhold the advice, I said, would not only penalize the less well-educated defendant, but would also prejudice the client because of his initial truthfulness in telling his story in confidence to the attorney.

The fallacy in that argument is that the lawyer is giving the client more than just "information about the law," but is actively participating in — indeed, initiating — a factual defense that is obviously perjurious. To suggest that the less well-educated defendant is entitled to that extent of participation by the attorney in manufacturing perjury carries the "equalizer" concept of the lawyer's role too far. Moreover, even though the client has initially been truthful in telling his story to the attorney in confidence, it does not follow that there is any breach of confidentiality if the lawyer simply declines to create a false story for the client.* . . .

In interviewing, therefore, the attorney must take into account the practical psychological realities of the situation. That means, at least at the earlier stages of eliciting the client's story, that the attorney should assume a skeptical attitude, and that the attorney should give the client legal advice that might help in drawing out useful information that the client, consciously or unconsciously, might be withholding. To that extent — but on a different, and more limiting, rationale — I adhere to my earlier position that there are situations in which it may be proper for the attorney to give the client legal advice even though the attorney has reason to believe that the advice may induce the client to commit perjury. There does come a point, however, where nothing less than "brute rationalization" can purport to justify a conclusion that the lawyer is seeking in good faith to elicit truth rather than actively participating in the creation of perjury.

NOTE ON PROBLEMS ARISING "WITHIN THE BOUNDS OF THE LAW"

Despite the wide range of disagreement reflected in the preceding materials, all participants in the debate accept that in principle an attorney should not use illegal means to further a client's interests. No one would argue that a zealous defense attorney should attempt to shoot (or even bribe) the prosecution's chief witness. Professor Freedman stresses that defense counsel should always attempt to dissuade his or her client from perjury. Disagreement arises when the attorney can avoid illegality only by compromising some other contending principle; putting this somewhat special problem to one side, all agree that zealous representation must remain "within the bounds of the law."

Does it follow that ethical counsel may (and indeed *must*, to be truly effective)

---

* That is a very different matter from accepting a client's decision to commit perjury, and presenting that perjury to the court, recognizing that to do otherwise would undermine the confidential relationship. . . .

use all helpful tactics that *are* within the bounds of the law? Even after we have ruled out illegal means, is it not still troublesome for an attorney to exercise his special training and skills, to use all of his best effort, in order to promote a result that he knows to be socially harmful? Consider the following comments.

ORKIN, DEFENCE OF ONE KNOWN TO BE GUILTY
1 Crim. L.Q. 170, 172-175 (1958)

Dr. Johnson, as usual, resumed the question with judicial finality: "We asked of the practice of law. Sir William Forbes said he thought an honest lawyer should never undertake a cause which he was satisfied was not a just one. Sir (said Mr. Johnson), a lawyer has no business with the justice or injustice of the cause which he undertakes, unless his client asks his opinion and then he is bound to give it honestly. The justice or injustice of the cause is to be decided by the judge. Consider, Sir, what is the purpose of courts of justice? It is, that every man may have his cause fairly tried, by men appointed to try causes. A lawyer is not to tell what he knows to be a lie: he is not to produce what he knows to be a false deed; but he is not to usurp the province of the jury and of the judge, and determine what shall be the effect of evidence — what shall be the result of legal argument. . . . If lawyers were to undertake no causes till they were sure they were just, a man might be precluded altogether from a trial of his claim, though, were it judicially examined, it might be found a very just claim." [1] . . .

The most famous illustration of this principle occurred at the trial in 1840 of the Swiss valet, Courvoisier, who was convicted and executed for the atrocious murder of his master, Lord William Russell. This case was tried by Chief Justice Tindal, with Baron Parke sitting on the bench beside him. In the course of the trial Courvoisier confessed his guilt to Charles Phillips, his counsel, and asked that Phillips continue to defend him. Phillips, much perturbed by this confidence, consulted with Baron Parke as to his duty under the circumstances. Baron Parke asked whether the accused still wanted Phillips to defend him and, on being informed that he did, advised Phillips that he was bound to do so *and to use all fair arguments arising out of the evidence.* Subsequently Phillips was taxed with having retained the brief and also with having set up a defence by endeavouring to cast the guilt on another person. So far as the latter charge is concerned, it was not warranted by the facts, and Phillips himself vehemently denied it after the trial.

The *Courvoisier* case may be taken as authority for the following principles: (a) Counsel is bound to retain a case even though he may learn during the course of the trial that his client is guilty; (b) it is his duty, in defense of his client, to use all fair arguments arising on the evidence; (c) counsel may not, under the circumstances, try to cast suspicion of guilt upon another person.

In England, the General Council of the Bar has dealt at length with the propriety of counsel defending on a plea of not guilty a prisoner charged with an offence who has confessed to counsel the fact that he did commit the offence charged. . . .

1. Boswell's Life of Johnson, vol. 5, pp. 28-9.

A confession of guilt by the accused to his counsel does not ". . . release the advocate from his imperative duty to do all he honourably can do for his client. But such a confession imposes very strict limitations on the conduct of the defence. An advocate 'may not assert that which he knows to be a lie. He may not connive at, much less attempt to substantiate, a fraud.' While therefore, it would be right to take any objection to the competency of the Court, to the form of the indictment, to the admissibility of any evidence, or to the sufficiency of the evidence admitted, it would be absolutely wrong to suggest that some other person had committed the offence charged, or to call any evidence which he must know to be false having regard to the confession, such, for instance, as evidence in support of an alibi; which is intended to show that the accused could not have done, or in fact had not done the act; that is to say an advocate must not (whether by calling the accused or otherwise) set up an affirmative case inconsistent with the confession made to him. A more difficult question is within what limits, in the case supposed, may an advocate attack the evidence for the prosecution by cross-examination or in his speech to the tribunal charged with the decision of the facts. No clearer rule can be laid down than this, that he is entitled to test the evidence given by each individual witness, and to argue that the evidence as a whole is insufficient to amount to proof that the accused is guilty of the offence charged. Further than this he ought not to go."

BRESS, PROFESSIONAL ETHICS IN CRIMINAL TRIALS: A VIEW OF DEFENSE COUNSEL'S RESPONSIBILITY, 64 Mich. L. Rev. 1493, 1494 (1966): [A]bsent some unusual circumstances, every witness presented by one's adversary should be subjected to searching cross-examination. Once a defendant has exercised his constitutional right to put the government to its proof, the question of his guilt or innocence is to be determined by the trier of fact. Accordingly, the advocate should not rely on his own opinion of the witness' veracity, but rather must present to the jury all of the factors relevant to the witness' perceptual ability, his bias, and the consistency of his testimony.

M. FREEDMAN, LAWYERS' ETHICS IN AN ADVERSARY SYSTEM
43-49 (1975)

More difficult than the question of whether the criminal defense lawyer should present known perjury, is the question of whether the attorney should cross-examine a witness who is testifying accurately and truthfully, in order to make the witness appear to be mistaken or lying. The issue was raised effectively in a symposium on legal ethics through the following hypothetical case.

The accused . . . is charged with rape. . . . The alleged victim is the twenty-two-year-old daughter of a local bank president. She is engaged to a promising young minister in town. The alleged rape occurred in the early morning hours at a service station some distance from town, where the accused was employed as an attendant. That is all you know about the case when you have your first interview with your client.

At first the accused will not talk at all. You assure him that you cannot help him unless you know the truth and that he can trust you to treat what he says as confidential. He then says that he had intercourse with the young woman, but that she "consented in every way.". . . . He says that on the night in question she came in for gas; they talked; and she invited him into the car. One thing led to another and, finally, to sexual intercourse. . . . .

The accused tells you he was tried for rape in California four years ago and acquitted. He has no previous convictions. . . .

You learn that the victim has had affairs with two local men from good families. . . . Jones, apparently a bitterly disappointed and jealous suitor, readily states that he frequently had intercourse with the victim, and describes her behavior toward strange men as scandalous. He once took her to a fraternity dance, he says, and, having noticed she had been gone for some time, discovered her upstairs with Smith, a fraternity brother, on a bed in a state of semi-undress. He appears eager to testify and he states that the girl got what she'd always been asking for. You believe Jones, but are somewhat repelled by the disappointed suitor's apparent willingness to smear the young woman's reputation.

Suppose the accused, after you press him, admits that he forced himself on the victim and admits that his first story was a lie. He refuses to plead guilty to the charge or any lesser charge. He says that he can get away with his story, because he did once before in California.

Should the defense lawyer use the information supplied by Jones to impeach the young woman and, if necessary, call Jones as a witness?

One of the panelists who spoke to that question was Chief Justice (then Judge) Burger. The Chief Justice first discussed the question in terms of "basic and fundamental rules." One of those rules, which he characterized as "clear-cut and unambiguous," is that "a lawyer may never, under any circumstances, knowingly . . . participate in a fraud on the court." That rule, he said, "can never admit of any exception, under any circumstances," and no other consideration "can ever justify a knowing and conscious departure" from it. . . . Indeed, the Chief Justice held any other view to be "so utterly absurd that one wonders why the subject need even be discussed among persons trained in the law."[2]

After that powerful rhetoric, Chief Justice Burger's response to the question posed is a matter of some astonishment. The function of an advocate, and "particularly the defense advocate in the adversary system," is to use "all the legitimate tools available to test the truth of the prosecution's case." Therefore, he concluded, "the testimony of bad repute of the complaining witness, being recent and not remote in point of time, is relevant to her credibility." The Chief Justice was even more explicit in the question period following the panel discussion: he considers it ethical to cast doubt on the woman's credibility by destroying her reputation, even though the lawyer knows that she is telling the truth.

That, of course, is sanction for nothing less than a deliberate attempt to perpetrate a fraud upon the finder of fact. The lawyer knows that the client is guilty and that the prosecutrix is truthful. In cross-examining, the lawyer has one purpose, and one purpose only: to make it appear, contrary to fact, that the prosecutrix is lying in testifying that she was raped.

There is only one difference in practical effect between presenting the defendant's perjured alibi — which the Chief Justice considers to be clearly im-

2. Burger, Standards of Conduct for Prosecution and Defense Personnel: A Judge's Viewpoint, 5 Am. Crim. L.Q. 11, 12 (1966).

proper — and impeaching the truthful prosecutrix. In both cases, the lawyer participates in an attempt to free a guilty defendant. In both cases, the lawyer participates in misleading the finder of fact. In the case of the perjured witness, however, the attorney asks only nonleading questions, while in the case of impeachment, the lawyer takes an active, aggressive role, using professional training and skills, including leading questions, in a one-on-one attack upon the client's victim. The lawyer thereby personally and directly adds to the suffering of the prosecutrix, her family, and the minister to whom she is engaged. In short, under the euphemism of "testing the truth of the prosecution's case," the lawyer communicates, to the jury and to the community, the most vicious of lies.

That case takes us to the heart of my disagreement with the traditional approach to dealing with difficult questions of professional responsibility. That approach has two characteristics. First, in a rhetorical flourish, the profession is committed in general terms to all that is good and true. Then, specific questions are answered by uncritical reliance upon legalistic norms, regardless of the context in which the lawyer may be acting, and regardless of the motive and the consequences of the act. Perjury is wrong, and therefore no lawyer, in any circumstance, should knowingly present perjury. Cross-examination, however, is good, and therefore any lawyer, under any circumstances and regardless of the consequences, can properly impeach a witness through cross-examination. The system of professional responsibility that I have been advancing, on the other hand, is one that attempts to deal with ethical problems in context. . . .

Let us return, then, to the case involving the street robbery at 16th and P Streets, in which the defendant has been wrongly identified as the criminal, but correctly identified by the nervous, elderly woman who wears eyeglasses, as having been only a block away five minutes before the crime took place.[a] If the woman is not cross-examined vigorously and her testimony shaken, it will serve to corroborate the erroneous evidence of guilt. On the other hand, the lawyer could take the position that since the woman is testifying truthfully and accurately, she should not be made to appear to be mistaken or lying. But if a similar course were to be adopted by every lawyer who learned the truth through confidential disclosures from the client, such disclosures would soon cease to be made. . . .

Obviously, however, the rape case is a much harder one, because the injury done to the prosecutrix is far more severe than the more limited humiliation of the public-spirited and truthful witness in the case of the street robbery. In addition, in the rape case, the lawyer is acting pursuant to a manifestly irrational rule, that is, one that permits the defense to argue that the prosecutrix is the kind of person who would have sexual intercourse with a stranger because she has had sexual relations with two men whom she knew in wholly different social circumstances. Irrational or not, however, in those jurisdictions in which the defense of unchastity is still the law, the attorney is bound to provide it on the client's behalf.[6] For the lawyer who finds the presentation of that defense, and perhaps others in rape cases, to go beyond what he or she can in good conscience do, there are two courses that should be followed. The first is to be active in efforts to reform the law in that regard; the second is to decline

a. See page 124 supra. — EDS.
6. DR 7-101(A)(1).

to accept the defense of rape cases, on the grounds of a conflict of interest (a strong personal view) that would interfere with providing the defendant with his constitutional right to effective assistance of counsel.

WASSERSTROM, LAWYERS AS PROFESSIONALS: SOME MORAL ISSUES
5 Human Rights 1, 5-15 (1975)

Conventional wisdom has it that where the attorney-client relationship exists, . . . it is often appropriate and many times even obligatory for the attorney to do things that, all other things being equal, an ordinary person need not, and should not do. What is characteristic of this role of a lawyer is the lawyer's required indifference to a wide variety of ends and consequences that in other contexts would be of undeniable moral significance. . . . Provided that the end sought is not illegal, the lawyer is, in essence, an amoral technician whose peculiar skills and knowledge in respect to the law are available to those with whom the relationship of client is established. The question, as I have indicated, is whether this particular and pervasive feature of professionalism is itself justifiable. At a minimum, I do not think any of the typical, simple answers will suffice.

. . . The received view within the profession (and to a lesser degree within the society at large) is that having once agreed to represent the client, the lawyer is under an obligation to do his or her best to defend that person at trial, irrespective, for instance, even of the lawyer's belief in the client's innocence. . . . [I]t is thought both appropriate and obligatory for the attorney to put on as vigorous and persuasive a defense of a client believed to be guilty as would have been mounted by the lawyer thoroughly convinced of the client's innocence. I suspect that many persons find this an attractive and admirable feature of the life of a legal professional. I know that often I do. . . .

But part of the difficulty is that the irrelevance of the guilt or innocence of an accused client by no means exhausts the altered perspective of the lawyer's conscience, even in criminal cases. For in the course of defending an accused, an attorney may have, as a part of his or her duty of representation, the obligation to invoke procedures and practices which are themselves morally objectionable and of which the lawyer in other contexts might thoroughly disapprove. . . . For example, in California, the case law permits a defendant in a rape case to secure in some circumstances an order from the court requiring the complaining witness, that is the rape victim, to submit to a psychiatric examination before trial. For no other crime is such a pretrial remedy available. . . . I think such a rule is wrong and is reflective of the sexist bias of the law in respect to rape. . . . Nonetheless, it appears to be part of the role-differentiated obligation of a lawyer for a defendant charged with rape to seek to take advantage of this particular rule of law — irrespective of the independent moral view he or she may have of the rightness or wrongness of such a rule.

Nor, it is important to point out, is this peculiar, strikingly amoral behavior limited to the lawyer involved with the workings of the criminal law. . . . Suppose that a client desires to make a will disinheriting her children because they opposed the war in Vietnam. Should the lawyer refuse to draft the will because the lawyer thinks this a bad reason to disinherit one's children? . . . [T]he accepted view within the profession is that these matters are just of no concern to the lawyer qua lawyer. The lawyer need not of course agree to represent the client (and that is equally true for the unpopular client accused of a heinous crime), but there is nothing wrong with representing a client whose aims and purposes are quite immoral. And having agreed to do so, the lawyer is required to provide the best possible assistance, without regard to his or her disapproval of the objective that is sought.

. . . In this way, the lawyer as professional comes to inhabit a simplified universe which is strikingly amoral — which regards as morally irrelevant any number of factors which nonprofessional citizens might take to be important, if not decisive, in their everyday lives. And the difficulty I have with all of this is that the arguments for such a way of life seem to be not quite so convincing to me as they do to many lawyers. . . .

. . . [O]ne feature of this simplified, intellectual world is that it is often a very comfortable one to inhabit. To be sure, on occasion, a lawyer may find it uncomfortable to represent an extremely unpopular client. On occasion, too, a lawyer may feel ill at ease invoking a rule of law or practice which he or she thinks to be an unfair or undesirable one. Nonetheless, for most lawyers, most of the time, pursuing the interests of one's clients is an attractive and satisfying way to live in part just because the moral world of the lawyer is a simpler, less complicated, and less ambiguous world than the moral world of ordinary life. There is, I think, something quite seductive about being able to turn aside so many ostensibly difficult moral dilemmas and decisions with the reply: but that is not my concern; my job as a lawyer is not to judge the rights and wrong of the client or the cause; it is to defend as best I can my client's interests. . . .

But there is, of course, also an argument which seeks to demonstrate that it is good and not merely comfortable for lawyers to behave this way.

It is good, so the argument goes, that the lawyer's behavior and concomitant point of view are role-differentiated because the lawyer qua lawyer participates in a complex institution which functions well only if the individuals adhere to their institutional roles. . . .

When an individual is charged with having committed a crime, the trial is the mechanism by which we determine in our society whether or not the person is in fact guilty. Just imagine what would happen if lawyers were to refuse, for instance, to represent persons whom they thought to be guilty. . . . The private judgment of individual lawyers would in effect be substituted for the public, institutional judgment of the judge and jury. The amorality of lawyers helps to guarantee that every criminal defendant will have his or her day in court. . . .

Now, all of this certainly makes some sense. . . . Nonetheless, it seems to me that one dilemma which emerges is that if this line of argument is sound, it also appears to follow that the behavior of the lawyers involved in Watergate was simply another less happy illustration of lawyers playing their accustomed institutional role. . . . I am not, let me hasten to make clear, talking about the easy cases — about the behavior of the lawyers that was manifestly illegal. . . . What I am interested in is all of the Watergate behavior engaged in by the Watergate lawyers that was not illegal, but that was, nonetheless, behavior of which we quite properly disapprove. I mean lying to the public; dissembling; stonewalling; tape-recording conversations; playing dirty tricks.

. . . [A]rguments that support the role-differentiated amorality of the lawyer on institutional grounds can succeed only if the enormous degree of trust and confidence in the institutions themselves is itself justified. . . . But the less certain we are entitled to be of either the rightness or the self-corrective nature of the larger institutions of which the professional is a part, the less apparent it is that we should encourage the professional to avoid direct engagement with the moral issues as they arise. And we are, today, I believe, certainly entitled to be quite skeptical both of the fairness and of the capacity for self-correction of our larger institutional mechanisms, including the legal system. . . .

Second, it is clear that there are definite character traits that the professional such as the lawyer must take on if the system is to work. What is less clear is that they are admirable ones. Even if the role-differentiated amorality of the professional lawyer is justified by the virtues of the adversary system, this also means that the lawyer qua lawyer will be encouraged to be competitive rather than cooperative; aggressive rather than accommodating; ruthless rather than compassionate; and pragmatic rather than principled. This is, I think, part of the logic of the role-differentiated behavior of lawyers in particular, and to a lesser degree of professionals in general. . . .

Third, there is a special feature of the role-differentiated behavior of the lawyer that distinguishes it from the comparable behavior of other professionals. What I have in mind can be brought out through the following question: Why is it that it seems far less plausible to talk critically about the amorality of the doctor, for instance, who treats all patients irrespective of their moral character than it does to talk critically about the comparable amorality of the lawyer? Why is it that it seems so obviously sensible, simple and right for the doctor's behavior to be narrowly and rigidly role-differentiated, i.e., just to try to cure those who are ill? And why is it that at the very least it seems so complicated, uncertain, and troublesome to decide whether it is right for the lawyer's behavior to be similarly role-differentiated? [a]

The answer, I think, is twofold. To begin with . . . it is, so to speak, intrinsically good to try to cure disease, but in no comparable way is it intrinsically good to try to win every lawsuit or help every client realize his or her objective.[b] In addition . . . , the lawyer's behavior is different in kind from the doctor's. The lawyer — and especially the lawyer as advocate — directly says and affirms things. The lawyer makes the case for the client. He or she tries to explain, persuade and convince others that the client's cause should prevail. . . . If the lawyer actually believes everything that he or she asserts on behalf of the client, then it appears to be proper to regard the lawyer as in fact embracing and endorsing

a. Consider J. Kaplan & J. Waltz, The Trial of Jack Ruby 5 (1965): "Oswald slumped, moaning, to the floor while policemen piled in from all sides to drag down his assailant. . . . Within four minutes of the shooting an ambulance arrived, and . . . rushed Oswald to the Parkland Memorial Hospital. There, in an emergency room just across the hall from the one in which President Kennedy had been pronounced dead two days before, a twelve-man surgical team — the majority of whom would probably have considered as somehow immoral any lawyer who attempted to save Oswald's life by defending him in court — opened Oswald's chest and massaged his heart in relays. . . . Two of the doctors who struggled to preserve Oswald's life had rendered similar service to the expiring President."— EDS.

b. See also Simon, Homo Psychologicus: Notes on a New Legal Formalism, 32 Stan. L. Rev. 487, 501-502 (1980): "The analogies to such roles as doctor and priest are fundamentally misleading. For unlike the relations defined by these roles, the lawyer-client relation is fundamentally impersonal and other-regarding. . . . In the case of doctors and priests, the principal impact of the professional's activity occurs within the professional relation in the form of the change which the patient or penitent undergoes. But in the case of lawyers, the principal impact occurs *outside* the professional relation. The client benefits only to the extent that outsiders are affected." — EDS.

the points of view that he or she articulates. If the lawyer does not in fact believe what is urged by way of argument, if the lawyer is only playing a role, then it appears to be proper to tax the lawyer with hypocrisy and insincerity. To be sure, actors in a play take on roles and say things that the characters, not the actors, believe. But we know it is a play and that they are actors. The law courts are not, however, theaters, and the lawyers both talk about justice and they genuinely seek to persuade. . . . [T]he lawyer's words, thoughts, and convictions are, apparently, for sale. . . . The verbal, role-differentiated behavior of the lawyer qua advocate puts the lawyer's integrity into question in a way that distinguishes the lawyer from the other professionals.

Fourth, . . . even if on balance the role-differentiated character of the lawyer's way of thinking and acting is ultimately deemed to be justifiable within the system on systemic instrumental grounds, it still remains the case that we do pay a social price for that way of thought and action. For to become and to be a professional, such as a lawyer, is to incorporate within oneself ways of behaving and ways of thinking that shape the whole person. . . .

NOTE

For contrasting perspectives on these issues, see Goldman, The Moral Foundations of Professional Ethics (1980) (attacking the highly role-differentiated standards of prevailing legal ethics); Simon, The Ideology of Advocacy, [1978] Wis. L. Rev. 29 (also sharply challenging role differentiation); Kaufman, Book Review, 94 Harv. L. Rev. 1504 (1981) (criticizing Goldman); Fried, The Lawyer as Friend: The Moral Foundations of the Lawyer-Client Relation, 85 Yale L.J. 1060 (1976) (generally supporting a highly role-differentiated standard); Dauer & Leff, Correspondence: The Lawyer as Friend, 86 Yale L.J. 573 (1977) (criticizing Fried).

c.   Ethical Responsibilities of the Prosecutor

INTRODUCTORY NOTE

An inscription over the doors of the United States Department of Justice states, "The United States wins its point whenever justice is done its citizens in the courts." [66] As a corollary of this principle, prosecutors are considered ethically bound to seek a just result in the individual case, even if this means "losing" to the adversary. The ABA Code of Professional Responsibility expresses this notion as follows:

> **EC 7-13**   The responsibility of a public prosecutor differs from that of the usual advocate; his duty is to seek justice, not merely to convict. This special duty exists because: (1) the prosecutor represents the sovereign and therefore should use

---

66. See Brady v. Maryland, 373 U.S. 83, 87 (1963). See also Berger v. United States, 295 U.S. 78, 88 (1935): "The United States Attorney is the representative not of an ordinary party to a controversy, but of a sovereignty whose obligation [is] to govern impartially . . . ; and whose interest, therefore, in a criminal prosecution is not that it shall win a case, but that justice shall be done."

restraint in the discretionary exercise of governmental powers, such as in the selection of cases to prosecute; (2) during trial the prosecutor is not only an advocate but he also may make decisions normally made by an individual client, and those affecting the public interest should be fair to all; and (3) in our system of criminal justice the accused is to be given the benefit of all reasonable doubts. With respect to evidence and witnesses, the prosecutor has responsibilities different from those of a lawyer in private practice: the prosecutor should make timely disclosure to the defense of available evidence, known to him, that tends to negate the guilt of the accused, mitigate the degree of the offense, or reduce the punishment. Further, a prosecutor should not intentionally avoid pursuit of evidence merely because he believes it will damage the prosecution's case or aid the accused.

Are you persuaded that the normal obligations of "zealous advocacy" should be tempered, in the case of a prosecutor, by concern for the broader public interest? It is customary to argue (at least in the case of defense counsel and other private attorneys) that "fairness," "justice," and "the public interest" are best determined by a neutral arbiter presented with opposing arguments vigorously developed by contending parties. Is there a danger that the prosecutor may, through excessive concern for fairness, undermine the proper functioning of the adversary system? If that danger seems remote, do we need to reexamine more generally the axiom that justice is best promoted by the zealous advocacy of attorneys who rigorously disregard their personal opinion of the merits of their client's case? Consider how these tensions are most appropriately resolved in the context of the specific doctrinal issues explored in the Note that follows.

NOTES AND QUESTIONS ON THE PROSECUTOR'S DUTY OF DISCLOSURE

1. Background and constitutional limitations. We have already noted that defense counsel is ethically bound to avoid introduction of perjured testimony, if possible. In Mooney v. Holohan, 294 U.S. 103 (1935), the Supreme Court held that a state prosecutor's knowing use of perjured testimony was not only unethical but a violation of the constitutional right to a fair trial. *Mooney* was extended a step in Napue v. Illinois, 360 U.S. 264 (1959). In the latter case, a witness gave a false answer in response to a question by the prosecutor. Although the prosecutor had not expected the answer, he knew it to be false and nevertheless made no effort to correct it. The Court held that the prosecutor's failure to correct the false testimony also violated due process.

Although *Napue* created a right to disclosure by the prosecutor of information favorable to the defense under very special circumstances, it remained true (and remains true today) that there is no general right of "discovery" in criminal cases. In civil litigation, a plaintiff or defendant ordinarily can obtain access before trial to a very broad range of information under the control of the opposing party. Possibilities for unfair surprise at trial are thus greatly reduced. In criminal cases, wide-ranging discovery rights of this kind are generally unknown. The Fifth Amendment has been thought to limit most discovery directed against the defendant, and considerations of parity, together with a mix of other concerns, long led most states to deny virtually all discovery directed against the prosecution. In recent years many states have begun to recognize rights to discovery by the defense for various categories of information, but criminal discovery remains extremely limited by comparison to the pretrial discovery available in civil cases.[67]

Against this background it can be seen that the right to disclosure created by *Napue* was an extremely limited one. The prosecution was still entitled to deny pretrial access to all evidence, both exculpatory and inculpatory, that was in its possession, so long as no perjured testimony was actually used. A prosecutor refusing to provide discovery in such a situation was, in a sense, abiding by the usual norms of the adversary system. Believing the defendant to be guilty, the prosecutor was attempting in good faith to convict by zealously advancing his or her own tactical interests within the bounds of the law. Does it follow that prosecutors are never ethically (or constitutionally) obliged to turn over information that may be helpful to the defense (provided, of course, that they believe the defendant to be guilty)? Consider the situation presented in the next Note.

2. *The* Brady *case.* In Brady v. Maryland, 373 U.S. 83 (1963), defendant and one Boblit, a coconspirator, were charged with first-degree murder and prosecuted in separate trials. Prior to Brady's trial his counsel requested access to Boblit's statements and was shown several, but the prosecutor withheld a statement in which Boblit admitted being the actual killer. At Brady's trial, his counsel admitted Brady's participation in the killing but argued against the death sentence on the ground that Boblit was the actual killer. Nevertheless, the jury convicted and sentenced Brady to death. Only after trial did defense counsel learn of the statement in which Boblit had confirmed the basis for Brady's plea in mitigation. Under these circumstances, the Supreme Court found a violation of due process in the penalty portion of Brady's trial. The Court held that (id. at 87-88) "the suppression by the prosecution of evidence favorable to an accused upon request violates due process where the evidence is material either to guilt or to punishment, irrespective of the good faith or bad faith of the prosecution." The Court explained:

> The principle of Mooney v. Holohan is not punishment of society for misdeeds of a prosecutor but avoidance of an unfair trial to the accused. Society wins not only when the guilty are convicted but when criminal trials are fair. . . . A prosecution that withholds evidence on demand of an accused which, if made available, would tend to exculpate him or reduce the penalty . . . [plays] the role of an architect of a proceeding that does not comport with standards of justice, even though, as in the present case, [its] action is not "the result of guile." . . .

3. *Questions.* How far should the courts extend the constitutional principle reflected in *Brady*? Assuming, for example, that a prosecutor obtains material evidence favorable to the accused, why should his or her duty to disclose depend on whether defense counsel happened to request it? Should the answer depend on how clearly "material" and how clearly "exculpatory" the evidence is? Or would it be simpler (and fairer) for the prosecutor to disclose to the defense (without request) any evidence that *might* be helpful to the defense?

Should the prosecutor ever be required to disclose evidence *unfavorable* to

---

67. See generally American Bar Association, Standards for Criminal Justice, Discovery and Procedure before Trial, §§11-1.1 et seq. (2d ed. 1980).

the accused? In civil cases, advance disclosure of both favorable and unfavorable evidence (and information not necessarily admissible in evidence) is thought to promote prospects for a fair trial. Why should the duty of disclosure recognized in *Brady* be confined to "exculpatory" evidence?

For exploration of these problems, see United States v. Agurs, 427 U.S. 97 (1976); Note, 69 J. Crim. L. & C. 197 (1978).

d. The Judge's Role

INTRODUCTORY NOTE

Given the principles of the adversary system examined in the preceding sections, and in particular the premise that the justice of a cause will best be determined by a neutral arbiter after vigorous development of opposing arguments by attorneys committed to the interests of their clients, does it follow that the judge should be a passive listener who must refrain from efforts to ferret out facts or refine the available arguments? What should the judge do if he or she becomes convinced that a witness has deliberately misled the jury or has become confused by vigorous cross-examination or has simply never been asked the critically important questions? What if opposing counsel fails to step in to rectify these difficulties? Should the judge intervene to expose the misleading testimony, to demand clarification of confusing statements, or to probe for essential but undisclosed details?

American judges do have the power, in appropriate cases, to question witnesses and even to call witnesses not summoned by either party.[68] In some jurisdictions they are also permitted to intervene by summing up the evidence and commenting on its persuasiveness.[69] The problem is to determine when, in an adversary system, it becomes appropriate for judges to use these powers. How can a judge relatively unfamiliar with the background of a controversy know whether his or her intervention will in fact help to sharpen the facts or the issues in dispute? Is it proper for the judge to bring out facts helpful to one party if that party prefers (even at the price of tactical disadvantage) to keep those facts out of the case? Generally speaking, American judges resolve these doubts by adopting a passive conception of their proper role. But what is the effect of such attitudes on the quality of justice rendered in the adversary system? Consider these comments.

WYZANSKI, A TRIAL JUDGE'S FREEDOM AND RESPONSIBILITY, 65 Harv. L. Rev. 1281, 1290-1293 (1952): In nonjury as in jury cases, a substantial part. of the bar prefers to have the judge sit patiently while the evidence comes in and then at the end of the trial summarize the testimony which he believes. This seems the sounder practice in the great bulk of trials. But in cases of public significance, Edmund Burke admonished us: "It is the duty of the Judge to receive every offer of evidence, apparently material, suggested to him, though

---

68. See Saltzburg, The Unnecessarily Expanding Role of the American Trial Judge, 64 Va. L. Rev. 1, 52-80 (1978).

69. See supra page 100 footnote a.

the parties themselves through negligence, ignorance, or corrupt collusion, should not bring it forward. A judge is not placed in that high situation merely as a passive instrument of parties. He has a duty of his own, independent of them, and that duty is to investigate the truth."

. . . [But in those federal criminal] cases which come to trial . . . , the preliminary investigation by the FBI and other agencies of detection has reduced to a small compass the area of doubt. Often the only remaining substantive issue of significance is whether the defendant acted "knowingly." Indeed, the usual federal criminal trial is as apt to turn on whether the prosecution has procured its evidence in accordance with law and is presenting it fairly, as on whether the defendant is guilty as charged. All these factors combine to concentrate the judge's attention upon the avoidance of prejudicial inquiries, confusion of proof and inflammatory arguments. Counsel can aid the judge to maintain the proper atmosphere. . . . But if cooperation is not forthcoming, the judge should hesitate to fill the gap by becoming himself a participant in the interrogation or to indicate any view of the evidence. For the criminal trial is as much a ceremony as an investigation. Dignity and forbearance are almost the chief desiderata.

FRANKEL, THE SEARCH FOR TRUTH: AN UMPIREAL VIEW, 123 U. Pa. L. Rev. 1031, 1041-1042, 1045 (1975):

> In a trial by jury in a federal court, the judge is not a mere moderator, but is the governor of the trial for the purpose of assuring its proper conduct and of determining questions of law.[21]

This observation has a clarion ring to the judicial ear. It is not inspiring to be a "mere" anything. The role of moderator is not heady. The invitation from the highest court to play a doughtier part is instantly attractive. It has proved, however, to be a siren's call. The "not a mere moderator" slogan is cited as often as not in cases reversing trial judges for being less "mere" or moderate than they should be. The fountainhead case from which the quotation comes was itself such a decision. The reversals seem, even to a trial judge, to be warranted most of the time.

The fact is that our system does not allow much room for effective or just intervention by the trial judge in the adversary fight about the facts. The judge views the case from a peak of Olympian ignorance. His intrusions will in too many cases result from partial or skewed insights. He may expose the secrets one side chooses to keep while never becoming aware of the other's. He runs a good chance of pursuing inspirations that better informed counsel have considered, explored, and abandoned after fuller study. He risks at a minimum the supplying of more confusion than guidance by his sporadic intrusions.

The ignorance and unpreparedness of the judge are intended axioms of the system. The "facts" are to be found and asserted by the contestants. The judge is not to have investigated or explored the evidence before trial. No one is to have done it for him. The judicial counterpart in civil law countries, with the file of the investigating magistrate before him, is a deeply "alien" conception.

---

21. Quercia v. United States, 289 U.S. 466, 469 (1933).

. . . Without an investigative file, the American trial judge is a blind and blundering intruder, acting in spasms as sudden flashes of seeming light may lead or mislead him at odd times.

. . . [T]he judge as a participant is likely to impair the adversary process as frequently as he improves it. . . . [T]he critical flaw of the system, the low place it assigns to truth-telling and truth-finding, is not cured to any perceptible degree by such participation.

C. CONVICTION BY GUILTY PLEA

BRADY v. UNITED STATES
Supreme Court of the United States
397 U.S. 742 (1970)

Mr. Justice White delivered the opinion of the Court.

In 1959, petitioner was charged with kidnaping in violation of 18 U.S.C. §1201(a).[1] Since the indictment charged that the victim of the kidnaping was not liberated unharmed, petitioner faced a maximum penalty of death if the verdict of the jury should so recommend. Petitioner, represented by competent counsel throughout, first elected to plead not guilty. Apparently because the trial judge was unwilling to try the case without a jury, petitioner made no serious attempt to reduce the possibility of a death penalty by waiving a jury trial. Upon learning that his codefendant, who had confessed to the authorities, would plead guilty and be available to testify against him, petitioner changed his plea to guilty. His plea was accepted after the trial judge twice questioned him as to the voluntariness of his plea. Petitioner was sentenced to 50 years' imprisonment, later reduced to 30.

In 1967, petitioner sought [postconviction] relief . . . , claiming that his plea of guilty was not voluntarily given because §1201(a) operated to coerce his plea. . . . [The lower courts denied relief and the Supreme Court granted certiorari].

In United States v. Jackson, [390 U.S. 570 (1968)], the defendants were indicted under §1201(a). The District Court dismissed the §1201(a) count of the indictment, holding the statute unconstitutional because it permitted imposition of the death sentence only upon a jury's recommendation and thereby made the risk of death the price of a jury trial. This Court held the statute valid, except for the death penalty provision; with respect to the latter, the Court agreed with the trial court "that the death penalty provision . . . imposes an impermissible burden upon the exercise of a constitutional right. . . ." . . . The inevitable effect of the provision was said to be to discourage assertion of the Fifth Amendment right not to plead guilty and to deter exercise of the Sixth Amendment right to demand a jury trial. Because the legitimate goal of limiting the death penalty to cases in which a jury recommends it could be

1. "Whoever knowingly transports in interstate or foreign commerce, any person who has been unlawfully . . . kidnaped . . . shall be punished (1) by death if the kidnaped person has not been liberated unharmed, and if the verdict of the jury shall so recommend, or (2) by imprisonment for any term of years or for life, if the death penalty is not imposed."

achieved without penalizing those defendants who plead not guilty and elect a jury trial,[a] the death penalty provision "needlessly penalize[d] the assertion of a constitutional right," and was therefore unconstitutional.

Since the "inevitable effect" of the death penalty provision of §1201(a) was said by the Court to be the needless encouragement of pleas of guilty and waivers of jury trial, Brady contends that *Jackson* requires the invalidation of every plea of guilty entered under that section, at least when the fear of death is shown to have been a factor in the plea. Petitioner, however, has read far too much into the *Jackson* opinion. . . . [T]hat decision neither fashioned a new standard for judging the validity of guilty pleas nor mandated a new application of the test theretofore fashioned by courts. . . . Waivers of constitutional rights not only must be voluntary but must be knowing, intelligent acts done with sufficient awareness of the relevant circumstances and likely consequences. On neither score was Brady's plea of guilty invalid. . . .

The voluntariness of Brady's plea can be determined only by considering all of the relevant circumstances surrounding it. . . . It may be that Brady, faced with a strong case against him and recognizing that his chances for acquittal were slight, preferred to plead guilty and thus limit the penalty to life imprisonment rather than to elect a jury trial which could result in a death penalty. But even if we assume that Brady would not have pleaded guilty except for the death penalty provision of §1201(a), this assumption merely identifies the penalty provision as a "but for" cause of his plea. That the statute caused the plea in this sense does not necessarily prove that the plea was coerced and invalid as an involuntary act.

The State to some degree encourages pleas of guilty at every important step in the criminal process. . . . [A]pprehension and charge, [or] the post-indictment accumulation of evidence may convince the defendant and his counsel that a trial is not worth the agony and expense to the defendant and his family. All these pleas of guilty are valid in spite of the State's responsibility for some of the factors motivating the pleas. . . .

Of course, the agents of the State may not produce a plea by actual or threatened physical harm or by mental coercion overbearing the will of the defendant. But nothing of the sort is claimed in this case; nor is there evidence that Brady was so gripped by fear of the death penalty or hope of leniency that he did not or could not, with the help of counsel, rationally weigh the advantages of going to trial against the advantages of pleading guilty. Brady's claim is of a different sort: that it violates the Fifth Amendment to influence or encourage a guilty plea by opportunity or promise of leniency and that a guilty plea is coerced and invalid if influenced by the fear of a possibly higher penalty for the crime charged if a conviction is obtained after the State is put to its proof.

Insofar as the voluntariness of his plea is concerned, there is little to differentiate Brady from (1) the defendant, in a jurisdiction where the judge and jury have the same range of sentencing power, who pleads guilty because his lawyer advises him that the judge will very probably be more lenient than the jury; (2) the defendant, in a jurisdiction where the judge alone has sentencing power, who is advised by counsel that the judge is normally more lenient with defendants

a. For example, the choice between life imprisonment and death could be left to a jury in every case, regardless of how the defendant's guilt has been determined. See United States v. Jackson, supra, at 582. — EDS.

who plead guilty than with those who go to trial; (3) the defendant who is permitted by prosecutor and judge to plead guilty to a lesser offense included in the offense charged; and (4) the defendant who pleads guilty to certain counts with the understanding that other charges will be dropped. In each of these situations,[8] as in Brady's case, the defendant might never plead guilty absent the possibility or certainty that the plea will result in a lesser penalty than the sentence that could be imposed after a trial and a verdict of guilty. We decline to hold, however, that a guilty plea is compelled and invalid under the Fifth Amendment whenever motivated by the defendant's desire to accept the certainty or probability of a lesser penalty rather than face a wider range of possibilities extending from acquittal to conviction and a higher penalty authorized by law for the crime charged.

The issue we deal with is inherent in the criminal law and its administration because guilty pleas are not constitutionally forbidden, because the criminal law characteristically extends to judge or jury a range of choice in setting the sentence in individual cases, and because both the State and the defendant often find it advantageous to preclude the possibility of the maximum penalty authorized by law. For a defendant who sees slight possibility of acquittal, the advantages of pleading guilty and limiting the probable penalty are obvious — his exposure is reduced, the correctional processes can begin immediately, and the practical burdens of a trial are eliminated. For the State there are also advantages — the more promptly imposed punishment after an admission of guilt may more effectively attain the objectives of punishment; and with the avoidance of trial, scarce judicial and prosecutorial resources are conserved for those cases in which there is a substantial issue of the defendant's guilt or in which there is substantial doubt that the State can sustain its burden of proof. It is this mutuality of advantage that perhaps explains the fact that at present well over three-fourths of the criminal convictions in this country rest on pleas of guilty,[10] a great many of them no doubt motivated at least in part by the hope or assurance of a lesser penalty than might be imposed if there were a guilty verdict after a trial to judge or jury.

Of course, that the prevalence of guilty pleas is explainable does not necessarily validate those pleas or the system which produces them. But we cannot hold that it is unconstitutional for the State to extend a benefit to a defendant who in turn extends a substantial benefit to the State and who demonstrates by his plea that he is ready and willing to admit his crime and to enter the correctional system in a frame of mind that affords hope for success in rehabilitation over a shorter period of time than might otherwise be necessary. . . .

Bram v. United States, 168 U.S. 532 (1897), held that the admissibility of a confession depended upon whether it was compelled within the meaning of the Fifth Amendment. To be admissible, a confession must be " 'free and volun-

8. We here make no reference to the situation where the prosecutor or judge, or both, deliberately employ their charging and sentencing powers to induce a particular defendant to tender a plea of guilty. In Brady's case there is no claim that the prosecutor threatened prosecution on a charge not justified by the evidence or that the trial judge threatened Brady with a harsher sentence if convicted after trial in order to induce him to plead guilty.

10. It has been estimated that about 90%, and perhaps 95%, of all criminal convictions are by pleas of guilty; between 70% and 85% of all felony convictions are estimated to be by guilty plea. D. Newman, Conviction, The Determination of Guilt or Innocence Without Trial 3 and n. 1 (1966).

tary: that is, must not be extracted by any sort of threats or violence, nor obtained
by any direct or implied promises, however slight, nor by the exertion of any
improper influence.' ". . . . *Bram* is not inconsistent with our holding that Brady's
plea was not compelled even though the law promised him a lesser maximum
penalty if he did not go to trial. *Bram* dealt with a confession given by a defendant
in custody, alone and unrepresented by counsel. In such circumstances, even
a mild promise of leniency was deemed sufficient to bar the confession, not
because the promise was an illegal act as such, but because defendants at such
times are too sensitive to inducement and the possible impact on them too
great to ignore and too difficult to assess. . . .

Brady's situation bears no resemblance to Bram's. . . . He had competent
counsel and full opportunity to assess the advantages and disadvantages of a
trial as compared with those attending a plea of guilty; there was no hazard
of an impulsive and improvident response to a seeming but unreal advantage.
His plea of guilty was entered in open court and before a judge obviously sensitive
to the requirements of the law with respect to guilty pleas. Brady's plea, unlike
Bram's confession, was voluntary.

The standard as to the voluntariness of guilty pleas must be essentially that
defined by Judge Tuttle of the Court of Appeals for the Fifth Circuit: " '[A]
plea of guilty entered by one fully aware of the direct consequences, including
the actual value of any commitments made to him by the court, prosecutor,
or his own counsel, must stand unless induced by threats (or promises to discontinue improper harassment), misrepresentation (including unfulfilled or unfulfill-
able promises), or perhaps by promises that are by their nature improper as
having no proper relationship to the prosecutor's business (e.g. bribes).' " [13]
Under this standard, a plea of guilty is not invalid merely because entered to
avoid the possibility of a death penalty.

The record before us also supports the conclusion that Brady's plea was intelligently made. He was advised by competent counsel, he was made aware of
the nature of the charge against him, and there was nothing to indicate that
he was incompetent or otherwise not in control of his mental faculties. . . .

It is true that Brady's counsel advised him that §1201(a) empowered the
jury to impose the death penalty and that nine years later in United States v.
Jackson, supra, the Court held that the jury had no such power as long as the
judge could impose only a lesser penalty if trial was to the court or there was
a plea of guilty. But . . . [a] defendant is not entitled to withdraw his plea
merely because he discovers long after the plea has been accepted that his
calculus misapprehended the quality of the State's case or the likely penalties
attached to alternative courses of action. More particularly, absent misrepresentation or other impermissible conduct by state agents, a voluntary plea of guilty
intelligently made in the light of the then applicable law does not become vulnerable because later judicial decisions indicate that the plea rested on a faulty
premise. . . .

The fact that Brady did not anticipate United States v. Jackson, supra, does
not impugn the truth or reliability of his plea. We find no requirement in the
Constitution that a defendant must be permitted to disown his solemn admissions

---

13. Shelton v. United States, 246 F.2d 571, 572 n. 2 (C.A. 5th Cir. 1957) (en banc), *rev'd on
confession of error on other grounds*, 356 U.S. 26 (1958).

in open court that he committed the act with which he is charged simply because it later develops that the State would have had a weaker case than the defendant had thought or that the maximum penalty then assumed applicable has been held inapplicable in subsequent judicial decisions.

This is not to say that guilty plea convictions hold no hazards for the innocent or that the methods of taking guilty pleas presently employed in this country are necessarily valid in all respects. This mode of conviction is no more foolproof than full trials to the court or to the jury. Accordingly, we take great precautions against unsound results, and we should continue to do so, whether conviction is by plea or by trial. We would have serious doubts about this case if the encouragement of guilty pleas by offers of leniency substantially increased the likelihood that defendants, advised by competent counsel, would falsely condemn themselves. But our view is to the contrary and is based on our expectations that courts will satisfy themselves that pleas of guilty are voluntarily and intelligently made by competent defendants with adequate advice of counsel and that there is nothing to question the accuracy and reliability of the defendants' admissions that they committed the crimes with which they are charged. . . .

Although Brady's plea of guilty may well have been motivated in part by a desire to avoid a possible death penalty, we are convinced that his plea was voluntarily and intelligently made and we have no reason to doubt that his solemn admission of guilt was truthful.

Affirmed.

[The concurring opinions of JUSTICES BLACK and BRENNAN are omitted.]

ALSCHULER, THE SUPREME COURT, THE DEFENSE ATTORNEY, AND THE GUILTY PLEA, 47 U. Colo. L. Rev. 1, 55-58 (1975): [I]t may be reasonable to equate a competently counseled guilty plea with a knowing guilty plea. . . . In *Brady*, however, the Supreme Court seemed to conclude that a competently counseled guilty plea would ordinarily be, not only a knowing plea, but a voluntary plea as well. I believe that this second equation was unsound, and, indeed, that the presence of counsel has little relevance to the question of voluntariness. A guilty plea entered at gunpoint is no less involuntary because an attorney is present to explain how the gun works.

Under today's guilty-plea system, the basic function of the defense attorney is indeed to explain "how the gun works"— something that was illustrated by the record in *Brady*. . . . The defense attorney had two allies in his effort to persuade the defendant to plead guilty. The trial judge announced from the bench that he thought the defendant "might get the death penalty." Moreover, when the defense attorney told the judge in chambers that he thought that a guilty plea would probably be entered at a later date, the judge replied, "Well, I think you are very wise, because I was certainly going to submit the death penalty to the jury." The attorney dutifully reported this comment to the defendant.

The defendant's mother may also have been influential in altering the defendant's choice of plea. She attempted to visit the defendant in jail but found that "it wasn't visiting hours." She testified:

I went through the alley of the city jail where he was being held and I kept yelling, "Brady. Brady." Then — then there was somebody, some fellow up there that yelled,

"Is there a Brady here?" So then Brady came to the window. It was upstairs. I don't know how many floors. Brady came to the window and he said, "Mom what are you doing? You are going to get yourself in trouble," and I just said, "For God's sake, plead guilty. They are going to give you the death sentence."

When it became apparent that a co-defendant would probably testify against him, the defendant agreed to plead guilty. The defense attorney reported that he "felt very gratified when [the defendant] decided to change his plea in that we saved him from a death penalty in my opinion."

The defense attorney was, I think, entitled to feel gratified; he had done a capable job and may indeed have saved the defendant from a death sentence. The defendant's principal complaint did not, however, concern his attorney's performance; it was directed to the fact that exercise of the right to trial might have incurred an awesome penalty. This underlying reality was beyond the defense attorney's control but not beyond the control of the Supreme Court.

Contrary to the Supreme Court's suggestion, the presence of the defense attorney in *Brady* did not "dissipate" the "possibly coercive impact" of this reality. Indeed, the record in *Brady* suggests that the principal function of a competent attorney in the guilty-plea system is exactly the opposite of the function suggested by the Supreme Court. Rather than dispel the coercive impact of a promise of leniency, the attorney must make the defendant realize with full clarity the coercive power of the alternatives that he faces. In that way, the attorney may persuade the defendant to choose the course that within the confines of a cynical system, is likely to injure him least.

FEDERAL RULES OF CRIMINAL PROCEDURE
(As amended, 1979)

RULE 11 PLEAS

(a) ALTERNATIVES. A defendant may plead not guilty, guilty, or nolo contendere. If a defendant refuses to plead or if a defendant corporation fails to appear, the court shall enter a plea of not guilty.

(b) NOLO CONTENDERE. A defendant may plead nolo contendere only with the consent of the court. Such a plea shall be accepted by the court only after due consideration of the views of the parties and the interest of the public in the effective administration of justice.

(c) ADVICE TO DEFENDANT. Before accepting a plea of guilty or nolo contendere, the court must address the defendant personally in open court and inform him of, and determine that he understands, the following:

(1) the nature of the charge to which the plea is offered, the mandatory minimum penalty provided by law, if any, and the maximum possible penalty provided by law; and

(2) if the defendant is not represented by an attorney, that he has the right to be represented by an attorney at every stage of the proceeding against him and, if necessary, one will be appointed to represent him; and

(3) that he has the right to plead not guilty or to persist in that plea if it has already been made, and that he has the right to be tried by a jury and at that trial has the right to the assistance of counsel, the right to confront

and cross-examine witnesses against him, and the right not to be compelled to incriminate himself; and

(4) that if he pleads guilty or nolo contendere there will not be a further trial of any kind, so that by pleading guilty or nolo contendere he waives the right to a trial; and

(5) that if he pleads guilty or nolo contendere, the court may ask him questions about the offense to which he has pleaded, and if he answers these questions under oath, on the record, and in the presence of counsel, his answers may later be used against him in a prosecution for perjury or false statement.

(d) INSURING THAT THE PLEA IS VOLUNTARY. The court shall not accept a plea of guilty or nolo contendere without first, by addressing the defendant personally in open court, determining that the plea is voluntary and not the result of force or threats or of promises apart from a plea agreement. The court shall also inquire as to whether the defendant's willingness to plead guilty or nolo contendere results from prior discussions between the attorney for the government and the defendant or his attorney.

(e) PLEA AGREEMENT PROCEDURE

(1) *In general.* The attorney for the government and the attorney for the defendant or the defendant when acting pro se may engage in discussions with a view toward reaching an agreement that, upon the entering of a plea of guilty or nolo contendere to a charged offense or to a lesser or related offense, the attorney for the government will do any of the following:

(A) move for dismissal of other charges; or

(B) make a recommendation, or agree not to oppose the defendant's request, for a particular sentence, with the understanding that such recommendation or request shall not be binding upon the court; or

(C) agree that a specific sentence is the appropriate disposition of the case.

The court shall not participate in any such discussions.

(2) *Notice of such agreement.* If a plea agreement has been reached by the parties, the court shall, on the record, require the disclosure of the agreement in open court or, on a showing of good cause, in camera, at the time the plea is offered. If the agreement is of the type specified in subdivision (e) (1) (A) or (C), the court may accept or reject the agreement, or may defer its decision as to the acceptance or rejection until there has been an opportunity to consider the presentence report. If the agreement is of the type specified in subdivision (e) (1) (B), the court shall advise the defendant that if the court does not accept the recommendation or request the defendant nevertheless has no right to withdraw his plea.

(3) *Acceptance of a plea agreement.* If the court accepts the plea agreement, the court shall inform the defendant that it will embody in the judgment and sentence the disposition provided for in the plea agreement.

(4) *Rejection of a plea agreement.* If the court rejects the plea agreement, the court shall, on the record, inform the parties of this fact, advise the defendant personally in open court or, on a showing of good cause, in camera, that the court is not bound by the plea agreement, afford the defendant the opportunity to then withdraw his plea, and advise the defendant that if he persists in his guilty plea or plea of nolo contendere the disposition of the case may

be less favorable to the defendant than that contemplated by the plea agreement.

(5) *Time of plea agreement procedure.* Except for good cause shown, notification to the court of the existence of a plea agreement shall be given at the arraignment or at such other time, prior to trial, as may be fixed by the court.

(6) *Inadmissibility of pleas, plea discussions, and related statements.* Except as otherwise provided in this paragraph, evidence of the following is not, in any civil or criminal proceeding, admissible against the defendant who made the plea or was a participant in the plea discussions:

(A) a plea of guilty which was later withdrawn;

(B) a plea of nolo contendere;

(C) any statement made in the course of any proceedings under this rule regarding either of the foregoing pleas; or

(D) any statement made in the course of plea discussions with an attorney for the government which do not result in a plea of guilty or which result in a plea of guilty later withdrawn. However, such a statement is admissible (i) in any proceeding wherein another statement made in the course of the same plea or plea discussions has been introduced and the statement ought in fairness be considered contemporaneously with it, or (ii) in a criminal proceeding for perjury or false statement if the statement was made by the defendant under oath, on the record, and in the presence of counsel.

(f) Determining Accuracy of Plea. Notwithstanding the acceptance of a plea of guilty, the court should not enter a judgment upon such plea without making such inquiry as shall satisfy it that there is a factual basis for the plea.

(g) Record of Proceedings. A verbatim record of the proceedings at which the defendant enters a plea shall be made and, if there is a plea of guilty or nolo contendere, the record shall include, without limitation, the Court's advice to the defendant, the inquiry into the voluntariness of the plea including any plea agreement, and the inquiry into the accuracy of a guilty plea.

NOTES

1. The extent of plea bargaining. The Court states in *Brady* that well over three-fourths of all criminal convictions are obtained by guilty plea. More recently, however, research has disclosed wide variations in guilty plea rates, both among states and among jurisdictions within states. Moreover, the variations do not seem to correlate well with population size or other factors indicative of caseload pressure. In some states, for example, guilty pleas appear to be more prevalent in rural than in urban jurisdictions. And the dependence on guilty pleas appears to be much greater in some large cities than in others; for cities with a population over 500,000, the mean guilty plea rate was found to be 92.7 percent in New York State but only 65.5 percent in Pennsylvania. See H. Miller, W. McDonald & J. Cramer, Plea Bargaining in the United States 16-24 (Georgetown U. Law Center 1977). Although it remains undeniable that a substantial portion of all criminal convictions are obtained by guilty plea, these data raise serious questions about the relationship between costs, caseload pressure, and guilty pleas.

The extent of guilty pleas should not, of course, be equated with the extent of plea *bargaining.* It is normally useful to treat bargaining as including not only overt negotiations for specific concessions but also situations in which a defendant pleads guilty with tacit expectations of leniency. Some defendants, however, may plead guilty without any hope of more lenient treatment; some such pleas might continue to be tendered even if all forms of guilty plea concessions were abolished. In this sense the guilty plea rate may overstate the *bargaining* rate and exaggerate the need for bargaining. On the other hand, it is customary in some jurisdictions for defendants to plead not guilty, waive a jury, and then present only a perfunctory defense before the judge; typically, the defendant who has saved the court's time in this way is treated much more leniently than one who presents a full-blown defense. These "slow pleas" are in some ways the functional equivalent of guilty pleas and, where they are common, the official guilty plea rates may in effect understate the importance of plea bargaining.

2. *Guilty pleas and sentencing concessions.* Most defendants probably plead guilty in response to tacit or express offers of leniency in sentencing. In Santobello v. New York, 404 U.S. 257 (1971), the Court held that if the prosecution fails to honor commitments made to the defendant in exchange for his or her plea, then the defendant must be given an opportunity to withdraw the plea. This holding does not mean, however, that the defendant who pleads guilty will receive precisely the sentence he or she expects. The prosecutor's commitment might take the form of a promise to dismiss certain counts or to "recommend" a certain sentence to the judge. In *Santobello* the prosecution had promised only that it would *not* make any recommendation; its promise had been broken because a prosecutor later did recommend a prison sentence. In these situations the prosecution's bargain is fulfilled if it takes precisely the action promised, even though this action may not prevent the judge from imposing a different sentence from the one the defendant (and perhaps even the prosecutor) expected. The implications of a plea bargain for the sentence ultimately imposed are thus problematic. The complexities of sentencing in the guilty plea context are explored in more detail in Chapter 12 infra.

How large are the concessions typically given to defendants pleading guilty? (Or, to put it another way, how large is the penalty imposed on those who stand trial?) It is difficult to obtain precise information about the sentence that a guilty plea defendant would have received after conviction at trial. Some large-scale statistical studies have suggested that the sentencing concession actually received in exchange for a guilty plea is very small or nonexistent in the average case. See Schulhofer, Due Process of Sentencing, 128 U. Pa. L. Rev. 733, 757 & n. 97 (1980). These studies suffer various methodological flaws, however, and, in any event, the individual defendants may *think* they face a substantial penalty for insisting on trial. See Alschuler, The Changing Plea-Bargaining Debate, 69 Calif. L. Rev. 652, 653-657 & n. 7 (1981).

In one study that compared sentences imposed after trial in New York City to actual concessions that those individuals would have received for pleading guilty, Professor Hans Zeisel found that the average increase over the sentence offered for a plea was 136 percent; in other words, the sentence imposed after trial was, on the average, more than double the proposed guilty plea sentence. Professor Zeisel noted, moreover, that these figures are likely to *understate* the average sentencing differential for all cases. The sample included only defendants who did go to trial, and some of them presumably chose to do so because they considered the proposed concession *too small;* cases in which the defendants accepted the plea proposal and waived trial could well have involved even more substantial concessions. See Zeisel, The Offer That Cannot Be Refused, in F. Zimring & R. Frase, The Criminal Justice System 558-561 (1980).

Should there be limits on the size of the guilty plea concessions (that is, trial penalties) that are permitted? Note that in *Brady* the Court said that it would "have serious doubts about this case if the encouragement of guilty pleas by offers of leniency substantially increased the likelihood that defendants . . . would falsely condemn themselves." But why did *Brady* itself not involve a plea concession large enough to create such a possibility? Or consider Bordenkircher v. Hayes, 434 U.S. 357 (1978). There, a defendant who had two prior convictions was charged with forging a check in the amount of $88.30, an offense punishable by a term of 2 to 10 years in prison. The prosecutor offered to recommend a five-year sentence but also said that if the defendant did not plead guilty, he would seek a habitual criminal indictment, under which the defendant would face a mandatory sentence of life imprisonment. The defendant rejected the offer, and after trial and conviction, the life sentence was imposed. The Court upheld both the prosecutor's bargaining tactics and this particularly large penalty. Thus, although the Court has implied that plea concessions are subject to some limitations, in practice very large concessions seem to be permissible, at least as a constitutional matter.

Will courts inevitably prove incapable of articulating workable limits on the extent of the allowable plea inducements? Or should judges simply say that some sentencing concessions are "just too much"? These problems should be reexamined in connection with the study of sentencing decisions in Chapter 3 infra and sentencing procedures in Chapter 12 infra.

3. Justifications and objections. Despite the uncertainties concerning the precise extent of either the average sentencing differential or the maximum permissible concession, plea bargaining plainly imposes some price on the exercise of the right to trial. This fact in itself seems to offend the notion of a constitutionally protected right.[70] And even if concessions for pleading guilty seem acceptable in theory, the concession system is in practice vulnerable to serious problems of administration: Negotiated agreements can be inconsistent, skewed by conflicts of interest, and tainted by the influence of irrelevant or even invidious considerations. The dangers are vividly documented in Alschuler, The Defense Attorney's Role in Plea Bargaining, 84 Yale L.J. 1179 (1975); Alschuler, The Prosecutor's Role in Plea Bargaining, 36 U. Chi. L. Rev. 50 (1968).

Do the asserted efficiency advantages of plea bargaining justify these costs? Are there other convincing justifications for plea bargaining? Consider whether the following are persuasive:

President's Commission on Law Enforcement and the Administration of Justice, The Challenge of Crime in a Free Society 135 (1967): It would be a serious mistake . . . to assume that the guilty plea is no more than a means of disposing of criminal cases at

---

70. The validity of penalties that burden the exercise of constitutional rights (whether directly or indirectly, whether purposely or unintentionally) is a complex subject warranting careful consideration in connection with the study of constitutional law and the constitutional aspects of criminal procedure. The problem is explored in North Carolina v. Pearce, 395 U.S. 711 (1969); Van Alstyne, The Demise of the Right — Privilege Distinction in Constitutional Law, 81 Harv. L. Rev. 1439 (1968); Note, The Unconstitutionality of Plea Bargaining, 83 Harv. L. Rev. 1387 (1970).

minimal cost. It relieves both the defendant and the prosecution of the inevitable risks and uncertainties of trial. It imports a degree of certainty and flexibility into a rigid, yet frequently erratic system. The guilty plea is used to mitigate the harshness of mandatory sentencing provisions and to fix a punishment that more accurately reflects the specific circumstances of the case than otherwise would be possible under inadequate penal codes. It is frequently called upon to serve important law enforcement needs by agreements through which leniency is exchanged for information, assistance, and testimony about other serious offenders.

Enker, Perspectives on Plea Bargaining, in President's Commission on Law Enforcement and the Administration of Justice, Task Force Report: The Courts 112 (1967): [A] substantial increase in criminal trials would entail an equally substantial increase in the burden of jury duty on citizens. Many citizens prefer to avoid jury service because it interferes with their private and business lives. Would a disproportionate increase in this burden produce resentment against or a sense of alienation from the criminal process that might be directed against defendants and make other "pro-defendant" reforms less politically acceptable? Probably the best that we can say is that we do not know the answer to this question, but it should cause us to pause before throwing administrative considerations to the winds.

Maximization of adjudication by trial may actually result in more inaccurate verdicts. So long as trials are the exception rather than the rule and are limited, by and large, to cases in which the defense offers a substantial basis for contesting the prosecutor's allegations, the defendant's presumption of innocence and the requirement of proof beyond a reasonable doubt are likely to remain meaningful to a jury. The very fact that the defendant contests the charges impresses upon the jurors the seriousness of their deliberations and the need to keep an open mind about the evidence and to approach the testimony of accusing witnesses with critical care and perhaps even a degree of skepticism. If contest becomes routine, jurors may likely direct their skepticism at the defense. Prosecutors too readily apply the overall, and overwhelming, statistical probability of guilt to individual cases; we do not want jurors to do the same. It makes some sense, then, to screen out those cases where there is no real dispute and encourage their disposition by plea, leaving for trial to the extent possible only those cases where there exists a real basis for dispute.[a]

H. Miller, W. McDonald & J. Cramer, Plea Bargaining in the United States at p. vi (Georgetown U. Law Center 1977): Proponents believe in the legitimization of plea bargaining through standards and judicial oversight. They assume that under no circumstances can there be a rigid prohibition of plea bargaining in the real world. They reason that the abolishment of plea bargaining will create pressure for hidden negotiations, thus causing a regression to those days where the process was completely hidden from view — with no safeguards. Thus, plea bargaining, subject to standards, becomes essential to the operation of the system.

a. Is it clear that plea bargaining serves primarily to screen out cases of this kind? Or is its function more often to screen out cases precisely because they do involve debatable issues and uncertainties that the parties prefer to avoid? Which view is taken in the excerpt preceding the Enker article? — EDS.

Schulhofer, Due Process of Sentencing, 128 U. Pa. L. Rev. 733, 790 n. 223 (1980): Commentators and reformers often seem to assume that formal rules to regulate or prohibit plea bargaining inevitably would be circumvented by resourceful courthouse regulars. For example, Milton Heumann . . . [in Plea Bargaining 157, 162 (1978) asserts flatly:] "abolition [of plea bargaining] is an impossibility. . . . [T]o speak of a plea bargaining-free criminal justice system is to operate in a land of fantasy." The manipulation and the "no threats or promises" charade of past years occurred, though, in a system that never explicitly addressed the relationship of negotiated pleas to the acknowledged principle of voluntariness and that, for the most part, attempted to ignore the bargaining system entirely. We have no basis for assuming that attorneys would systematically pursue an unethical and dishonest course in a system that imposed clear bargaining restrictions and at the same time made realistic provision for processing all cases within the formal rules.

Enker, Perspectives on Plea Bargaining, in President's Commission on Law Enforcement and the Administration of Justice, Task Force Report: The Courts 112 (1967): It is easy to minimize administrative convenience and need. Simply increase the staff of prosecutors, judges, defense counsel, and probation officers if the present complement is insufficient to handle the task, it is said. Even if the money were readily available, it would still not be clear that we could call upon sufficient numbers of competent personnel. A lowering of standards in order to man the store adequately may well result in poorer justice. It may also divert both funds and personnel from other segments of the criminal process, such as corrections work, where they are arguably more needed.

Alschuler, Book Review, 12 Crim. L. Bull. 629, 632 (1976): [T]he most pernicious of the myths with which the apologists for plea bargaining have surrounded the process [is] the notion that, absent a radical restructuring of the criminal justice system, plea bargaining will remain a "practical necessity." Contrary to this widespread belief, the best estimate is that fewer than 350,000 people are charged with felonies each year in the United States, and if society were to provide each of them with the kind of trial that, say, $1,000 could buy, the total cost of $350 million would be about one-fourteenth of Lockheed's cost overrun on the C5-A aircraft.

The prospect of multiplying current criminal-court resources several times over may seem unthinkable until one realizes how limited these resources are. The situation in my own jurisdiction, however, seems typical. (Those familiar with criminal courts elsewhere can make their own rough calculations.) In Travis County, Texas, a county of more than 250,000 people, one judge hears felony cases full-time, and another hears felony cases part-time. To multiply these resources five times, or ten, or fifteen would require no more than the building and staffing of a single new courthouse, a task that might be almost as difficult as the building and staffing of a new hospital or a new high school. If the need were in the area of medicine or education, however, responsible citizens would at least talk about meeting it. They would not insist that "practical necessity" required bargaining with patients to "waive" their operations or with students to "waive" their classes.

4. *Abolition of plea bargaining: the Alaska experience.* In 1975 the Alaska attorney general announced a policy forbidding prosecutors from engaging in plea bargaining. Thereafter, some bargaining continued in the form of negotiations between defense counsel and the judge, but in 1977 the Alaska Supreme Court barred trial judges from engaging in either charge or sentence bargaining. See State v. Buckalew, 561 P.2d 289 (Alaska 1977). Preliminary studies of the plea bargaining ban revealed, somewhat surprisingly to some observers, that a massive logjam in the processing of cases did not occur. Comparing the year before the attorney general's ban to the year after it, the number of felony trials increased only 25 percent in Fairbanks (from 72 to 90 cases). In Anchorage the number of trials did increase by 97 percent, but the total after the ban, only 57 trials, was readily handled by the system. In fact in all the major cities the mean disposition time (that is, the period cases were pending) actually declined after the ban, primarily as a result of administrative and calendaring changes not directly related to plea bargaining. See Rubenstein & White, Plea Bargaining: Can Alaska Live Without It?, 62 Judicature 266 (1979).

If plea bargaining really had been eliminated, why did more defendants *not* insist on a trial? Conversely, since the number of trials did not grow enormously, must there not have remained some forms of plea bargaining? Rubenstein & White, supra, found that prosecutors generally (though not exclusively) complied with the ban. But some judges circumvented it (the comparisons were made before the Alaska Supreme Court's ban on judicial bargaining), and there also was evidence that in some categories of offenses, defendants pleading guilty tended to receive lower sentences than those going to trial, thus suggesting that tacit inducements to plead guilty persisted. In addition, of course, even if total abolition of plea bargaining does prove feasible for Alaska, it would not follow that similar results could be expected in New York City or Chicago. The practical impact of a plea bargaining ban remains a subject for careful study.

NORTH CAROLINA v. ALFORD
Supreme Court of the United States
400 U.S. 25 (1970)

Mr. Justice White delivered the opinion of the Court.

On December 2, 1963, Alford was indicted for first-degree murder, a capital offense under North Carolina law. The court appointed an attorney to represent him, and this attorney questioned all but one of the various witnesses who appellee said would substantiate his claim of innocence. The witnesses, however, did not support Alford's story but gave statements that strongly indicated his guilt. Faced with strong evidence of guilt and no substantial evidentiary support for the claim of innocence, Alford's attorney recommended that he plead guilty, but left the ultimate decision to Alford himself. The prosecutor agreed to accept a plea of guilty to a charge of second-degree murder, and on December 10, 1963, Alford pleaded guilty to the reduced charge.

Before the plea was finally accepted by the trial court, the court heard the sworn testimony of a police officer who summarized the State's case. Two other witnesses besides Alford were also heard. Although there was no eyewitness to the crime, the testimony indicated that shortly before the killing Alford took his gun from his house, stated his intention to kill the victim, and returned home with the declaration that he had carried out the killing. After the summary presentation of the State's case, Alford took the stand and testified that he had not committed the murder but that he was pleading guilty because he faced the threat of the death penalty if he did not do so.[2] In response to the questions of his counsel, he acknowledged that his counsel had informed him of the difference between second- and first-degree murder and of his rights in case he chose to go to trial. The trial court then asked appellee if, in light of his denial of guilt, he still desired to plead guilty to second-degree murder and appellee answered, "Yes, sir. I plead guilty on — from the circumstances that he [Alford's attorney] told me." After eliciting information about Alford's prior criminal record, which was a long one, the trial court sentenced him to 30 years' imprisonment, the maximum penalty for second-degree murder.

[Alford petitioned for his release in habeas corpus proceedings, on the ground that his guilty plea was invalid. The United States Court of Appeals for the Fourth Circuit granted relief, and the prosecution appealed to the Supreme Court]. . . .

State and lower federal courts are divided upon whether a guilty plea can be accepted when it is accompanied by protestations of innocence and hence contains only a waiver of trial but no admission of guilt. Some courts, giving expression to the principle that "[o]ur law only authorizes a conviction where guilt is shown," require that trial judges reject such pleas. But others have concluded that they should not "force any defense on a defendant in a criminal case," particularly when advancement of the defense might "end in disaster. . . ." . . .

This Court has not confronted this precise issue, but prior decisions do yield relevant principles. . . . The issue in Hudson v. United States, 272 U.S. 451 (1926), was whether a federal court has power to impose a prison sentence after accepting a plea of nolo contendere, a plea by which a defendant does not expressly admit his guilt, but nonetheless waives his right to a trial and authorizes the court for purposes of the case to treat him as if he were guilty. The Court held that a trial court does have such power, and, except for the cases which were rejected in *Hudson*, the federal courts have uniformly followed this rule, even in cases involving moral turpitude. Implicit in the nolo contendere cases is a recognition that the Constitution does not bar imposition of a prison sentence upon an accused who is unwilling expressly to admit his guilt but who, faced with grim alternatives, is willing to waive his trial and accept the sentence.

2. After giving his version of the events of the night of the murder, Alford stated: "I pleaded guilty on second degree murder because they said there is too much evidence, but I ain't shot no man, but I take the fault for the other man. We never had an argument in our life and I just pleaded guilty because they said if I didn't they would gas me for it, and that is all." In response to questions from his attorney, Alford . . . reaffirmed his decision to plead guilty to second-degree murder:

Q. [by Alford's attorney]. And you authorized me to tender a plea of guilty to second degree murder before the court?
A. Yes, sir.
Q. And in doing that, that you have again affirmed your decision on that point?
A. Well, I'm still pleading that you all got me to plead guilty. I plead the other way, circumstantial evidence; that the jury will prosecute me on — on the second. You told me to plead guilty, right. I don't — I'm not guilty but I plead guilty.

These cases would be directly in point if Alford had simply insisted on his plea but refused to admit the crime. The fact that his plea was denominated a plea of guilty rather than a plea of nolo contendere is of no constitutional significance with respect to the issue now before us, for the Constitution is concerned with the practical consequences, not the formal categorizations, of state law. Thus, while most pleas of guilty consist of both a waiver of trial and an express admission of guilt, the latter element is not a constitutional requisite to the imposition of criminal penalty. An individual accused of crime may voluntarily, knowingly, and understandingly consent to the imposition of a prison sentence even if he is unwilling or unable to admit his participation in the acts constituting the crime.

. . . Here the State had a strong case of first-degree murder against Alford. Whether he realized or disbelieved his guilt, he insisted on his plea because in his view he had absolutely nothing to gain by a trial and much to gain by pleading. . . . When his plea is viewed in light of the evidence against him, which substantially negated his claim of innocence and which further provided a means by which the judge could test whether the plea was being intelligently entered, its validity cannot be seriously questioned. In view of the strong factual basis for the plea demonstrated by the State and Alford's clearly expressed desire to enter it despite his professed belief in his innocence, we hold that the trial judge did not commit constitutional error in accepting it.[11] . . .

[A concurring statement by JUSTICE BLACK is omitted.]

MR. JUSTICE BRENNAN, with whom MR. JUSTICE DOUGLAS and MR. JUSTICE MARSHALL join, dissenting. . . .

. . . [W]ithout reaching the question whether due process permits the entry of judgment upon a plea of guilty accompanied by a contemporaneous denial of acts constituting the crime, I believe that at the very least such a denial of guilt is also a relevant factor in determining whether the plea was voluntarily and intelligently made. With these factors in mind, it is sufficient in my view to state that the facts set out in the majority opinion demonstrate that Alford was "so gripped by fear of the death penalty" that his decision to plead guilty was not voluntary. . . . Accordingly, I would affirm the judgment of the Court of Appeals.

NOTES ON NEGOTIATING THE FACTS

Does the guilty plea system produce results different from those that would occur at trial? To be more specific, does it convict defendants who are in fact innocent (*and* would be acquitted) or convict defendants who committed the

---

11. Our holding does not mean that a trial judge must accept every constitutionally valid plea merely because a defendant wishes so to plead. A criminal defendant does not have an absolute right under the Constitution to have his guilty plea accepted by the court, although the States may by statute or otherwise confer such a right. Likewise, the States may bar their courts from accepting guilty pleas from any defendants who assert their innocence. Cf. Fed. Rule Crim. Proc. 11, which gives a trial judge discretion to "refuse to accept a plea of guilty. . . ." We need not now delineate the scope of that discretion.

offense but (for a variety of reasons) could not be found guilty beyond a reasonable doubt at trial or convict defendants who are guilty of some offense significantly different from the charge to which the plea of guilty is formally entered? For the many observers who are inclined to give affirmative answers to these questions, the entire body of substantive criminal law may even seem a supreme irrelevance; up to 90 percent of all convictions are obtained by guilty pleas, and these convictions in turn are seen as the outcome of open-ended, often hurried horsetrading rather than the thoughtful application of complex legal principles to the known facts. What is the practical significance of substantive law in a world dominated by plea bargaining? This Note explores two aspects of this issue:

(1) Do the formal rules of law have *any* impact on the outcome of negotiated cases?

(2) If so, do formal rules nevertheless function differently in negotiation than they do in the setting of adjudication by trial? Are the differences observed in negotiation desirable or undesirable?

1. Do formal rules have any impact on plea negotiation? In an important and influential study, Professor Milton Heumann reported the results of over a year's field research on the experiences of prosecutors, defense counsel, and judges learning to adapt to the plea bargaining environment in the Connecticut courts. M. Heumann, Plea Bargaining (1978). Heumann found that defense attorneys initially expected that many of their clients would be innocent. They discovered, however, that most of their clients were factually guilty. Moreover, the attorneys initially expected that many of their cases would involve difficult legal issues, and they believed "that cases can be won or lost on the basis of their own legal acumen." Id. at 60. But they learned that "of the approximately 90 percent of the defendants who are factually guilty, most have cases devoid of any legally disputable issue. These cases, as one defense attorney phrased it, are 'born dead.' " Id. Similarly, prosecutors expected their efforts to be largely centered on the difficulties of proving guilt, but they learned that "in most cases the evidence in the file is sufficient to conclude (and prove) that the defendant is factually guilty. . . . [M]ost cases are simply barren of any contestable legal issue. . . ." Id. at 100-101.

For contrasting viewpoints, consider these comments:

Haney & Lowy, Bargain Justice in an Unjust World: Good Deals in the Criminal Courts, 13 L. & Socy. Rev. 633, 641-642 (1979): [Heumann argues that] plea bargaining has become the "preferred, ubiquitous, and inevitable form of justice in this country" . . . because nearly all defendants are guilty! How does he know? Because the lawyers he interviewed told him so. . . . We simply do not know how many [defendants] cop a plea to a crime they did not commit because they were offered an attractive deal, or because they had no faith in the capacity of the defense attorney to secure an acquittal at trial. The point is, however, Heumann does not know this either, nor do the lawyers he uncritically cites. The rest of his book and our own experience offer ample grounds to suspect that the number is not small.

A prosecutor tells Heumann how he "knows" that most defendants are guilty. In a typical case, he says, after some inconclusive preliminary negotiations:

. . . you come back and say "Well, we'll take a suspended sentence and probation," suddenly [the defendant] says, "Yes, I'm guilty." So it leads you to conclude that, well, all these people who are proclaiming innocence really are not innocent. . . .

Such "evidence" might have been enough for the prosecutor, but it should not have satisfied Heumann. . . .[7]

D. Newman, Conviction 216 (1966): A charge reduction or sentence promise is not ordinarily a result of personal influence of the lawyer with the prosecutor or judge. The strength of a lawyer's argument for a charge reduction depends in good part on how strong a professional case he can make for the appropriateness of the lesser charge and doubtful convictability on the higher count. . . . In short, the full-blown negotiated plea is not merely an appeal for mercy; it is an adversary process and the lawyer serves the function of the guilty defendant's advocate.

2. *Do the rules of law function differently in the bargaining than they do in formal adjudication?*[71] Consider these comments:

Enker, Perspectives on Plea Bargaining, in President's Commission on Law Enforcement and the Administration of Justice, Task Force Report: The Courts 113-114 (1967): [C]oncern over the possibility that a negotiated plea can result in an erroneous judgment of conviction assumes a frame of reference by which the accuracy of the judgment is to be evaluated. It assumes an objective truth existing in a realm of objective historical fact which it is the sole function of our process to discover. Some, but by no means all, criminal cases fit this image. For example, this is a relatively accurate description of the issues at stake in a case in which the defendant asserts a defense of mistaken identity. . . .

But not all criminal cases fit the above picture. . . . Much criminal adjudication concerns the passing of value judgments on the accused's conduct as is obvious where negligence, recklessness, reasonable apprehension of attack, use of unnecessary force, and the like are at issue. Although intent is thought of as a question of fact, it too can represent a judgment of degrees of fault, for example, in cases where the issue is whether the defendants entertained intent to defraud or intent to kill. In many of these cases, objective truth is more ambiguous, if it exists at all. Such truth exists only as it emerges from the fact-determining process, and accuracy in this context really means relative equality of results as between defendants similarly situated and relative congruence between the formal verdict and our understanding of society's less formally expressed evaluation of such conduct.

7. Heumann is in no position to evaluate the factual guilt of defendants in the cases he examined, and the attorneys who provided him with the "facts" are obviously not objective analysts. Anyone who works on a legal case knows that evidence means different things to different people, and much of it can be interpreted in many ways. Indeed, whole categories of evidence, once perceived as credible and trustworthy, are now regarded as questionable by many attorneys and judges. A suspect picked out of a line-up by an eyewitness was once viewed as factually guilty; in light of much recent research, we are no longer so sure. . . .

71. For general perspectives on differences between negotiation and adjudication, see Eisenberg, Private Ordering through Negotiation: Dispute-Settlement and Rulemaking, 89 Harv. L. Rev. 637 (1976).

The negotiated plea can, then, be an accurate process in this sense. So long as the judgment of experienced counsel as to the likely jury result is the key element entering into the bargain, substantial congruence is likely to result. Once we recognize that what lends rationality to the factfinding process in these instances lies not in an attempt to discover objective truth but in the devising of a process to express intelligent judgment, there is no inherent reason why plea negotiation need be regarded any the less rational or intelligent in its results.

Indeed, it may be that in some instances plea negotiation leads to more "intelligent" results. A jury can be left with the extreme alternatives of guilty of a crime of the highest degree or not guilty of any crime, with no room for any intermediate judgment. And this is likely to occur in just those cases where an intermediate judgment is the fairest and most "accurate" (or most congruent).

Clearly, the line between responsibility and irresponsibility due to insanity is not as sharp as the alternatives posed to a jury would suggest. . . . The very visibility of the trial process may be one factor that prevents us from offering the jury [a] compromise in order to preserve the symbolism of uniform rules evenly applied. The low visibility of the negotiated plea allows this compromise which may be more rational and congruent than the result we are likely to arrive at after a trial. While the desire to protect the symbolism of legality and the concern over lay compromises may warrant limiting the jury to extreme alternative[s], it does not follow that to allow the defendant to choose such a compromise is an irrational or even a less rational procedure.

Schulhofer, Due Process of Sentencing, 128 U. Pa. L. Rev. 733, 793 n. 234 (1980): One reason for regarding a trial as the most reliable procedure is the structure of the process, including its visibility and the neutrality of the decisionmaker. Commentary defending compromise in close cases often rests on thinly disguised distrust of the jury system. Although such distrust is of course justified in some instances, our system's preference for open decision by disinterested officials is, on balance, a sound one.

Another, more fundamental factor is that only trial procedure requires full development of the available facts prior to judgment. Even if one had confidence in the guilty plea decisionmakers, their judgments still would be based on preliminary investigations, cold files, and statements not tested by cross-examination. Under these conditions, bargains in close cases cannot be regarded as plausible compromises by fully informed decisionmakers confronting the "unknowable." The difficulty, moreover, is not a curable one, but rather an inevitable characteristic of a system that depends for its efficiency upon short-circuiting the available techniques for careful evidentiary development; a pre-plea hearing procedure that provided all appropriate factual safeguards would simply reinvent the trial under another name. . . .

Alschuler, The Prosecutor's Role in Plea Bargaining, 36 U. Chi. L. Rev. 50, 71-79 (1968): Professor Enker suggests that the insanity defense raises problems that frequently merit a compromise solution. Such a solution was provided in the publicized case of William Heirens, a seventeen-year-old college student who pleaded guilty to three separate murders and was sentenced to three consecutive life terms. . . . It was obvious that Heirens suffered from a severe mental abnormality, but it was not clear that his attorneys could establish a legal defense of insanity. . . .

William Heirens' culpability under traditional legal standards was doubtful, yet both the defendant and society were deprived of an authoritative resolution of this issue. Heirens is today an inmate of the Stateville Penitentiary, although no one has determined on the basis of the evidence that a prison is where Heirens belongs. Society devised the insanity defense precisely to avoid such distressing spectacles. Like other legal issues, the defense was designed to be tried, not compromised; and I fail to see how it can serve its purpose in any other way.

Finally, consider the case that District Attorney Specter advances to illustrate his concept of "variable guilt." . . . :

> The dictum that "justice and liberty are not the subjects of bargaining and barter" does not fit the realities of a typical barroom killing. . . .
>
> There is ordinarily sufficient evidence of malice and deliberation in such cases for the jury to find the defendant guilty of murder in the first degree, which [in Pennsylvania] carries either life imprisonment or death in the electric chair. Or, the conceded drinking by the defendant may be sufficient to nullify specific intent or malice to make the case second degree murder, which calls for a maximum of 10 to 20 years in jail. From all the prosecutor knows by the time the cold carbon copies of the police reports reach the District Attorney's office, the defendant may have acted in "hot blood," which makes the offense only voluntary manslaughter with a maximum penalty of 6 to 12 years. And, the defense invariably produces testimony showing that the killing was pure self-defense.
>
> When such cases are submitted to juries, a variety of verdicts are returned, which leads to the inescapable conclusion of variable guilt. Most of those trials result in convictions for second degree murder or voluntary manslaughter. The judges generally impose sentences with a minimum range of 5 to 8 years and a maximum of 10 to 20 years. That distilled experience enables the assistant district attorney and the defense lawyer to bargain on the middle ground of what experience has shown to be "justice" without the defense running the risk of the occasional first degree conviction . . . and without the Commonwealth tying up a jury room for 3 to 5 days and running the risk of acquittal.[62]

This argument seems to rest on the notion that when a man has seen one barroom killing, he has seen them all. . . . It would be easy to dismiss this sort of analysis with the observation that prosecutors may be too ready to seek quick, comfortable pigeonholes for every case. . . . Nevertheless, Specter's argument is a forceful one. In the homicide area particularly, . . . the distinctions drawn by the criminal code . . . sometimes prove too fine for workable, everyday application. . . .

. . . If the perspective of these practitioners is sound, the best solution to the defects they perceive in the trial system does not lie in a shift from trial procedures to off-stage compromises. It lies instead in a simplification of the criminal code to reflect "everyday reality" rather than common-law refinement. . . . [Moreover,] it seems doubtful that plea negotiation can eliminate the irrationalities of the criminal code without substituting more serious irrationalities of its own. It might make sense to establish a new crime called "barroom killing," with a minimum penalty of five to eight years imprisonment and a maximum

---

62. Specter, Book Review, 76 Yale L.J. 604, 606-07 (1967) (D. Newman, Conviction).

penalty of ten to twenty years imprisonment. (Frankly, of course, I doubt it.) Plea negotiation, however, does not effectively establish this new crime category. Most barroom killings seem to end in bargained pleas to voluntary manslaughter; but some end in bargained pleas to second degree murder; some end in bargained pleas to various categories of felonious assault; and I know of one barroom shooting that was resolved by a guilty plea to the crime of involuntary manslaughter, which, under the circumstances, seemed to be the last crime in the code of which the defendant might be guilty. It is therefore not clear that plea negotiation leads to greater uniformity of result than trial by jury.

Juries, of course, have biases, but the rules of evidence attempt to direct their attention to relevant issues. There are no rules of evidence in plea negotiation; individual prosecutors may be influenced not only by a desire to smooth out the irrationalities of the criminal code but by thoroughly improper considerations that no serious reformer of the penal code would suggest. Moreover, there is a basic difference between the personal biases of juries and the institutional biases of prosecutors. Juries may react differently to the circumstances of indistinguishable crimes, but at least they react to the circumstances of the crimes. A jury is unlikely to seek conviction for the sake of conviction, to respond to a defense attorney's tactical pressures, to penalize a defendant because he has taken an inordinate share of the court's and the prosecutor's time, to do favors for particular defense attorneys in the hope of future cooperation, or to attempt to please victims and policemen for political reasons.

PEOPLE v. FOSTER
New York Court of Appeals
19 N.Y.2d 150, 225 N.E.2d 200 (1967)

SCILEPPI, J. Defendant was charged with manslaughter in the first degree for the killing of one Thomas Hicks. Defendant was permitted to withdraw his original plea of not guilty and plead guilty to attempted manslaughter in the second degree.

On this appeal, defendant's principal argument is that he pleaded guilty to a nonexistent crime; therefore, his plea of guilty to such a charge, i.e., attempted manslaughter in the second degree, is a nullity, and that the judgment of conviction has no basis in law and violates due process. . . .

Sections 1050 and 1052 of the Penal Law provide that the crimes of manslaughter in the first degree and in the second degree respectively are homicides committed "without a design to effect death."

Section 2 of the Penal Law defines an attempt to commit crime as "An act done with intent to commit a crime, and tending but failing to effect its commission."

Defendant argues that, since no intent is required in the crime of manslaughter and since an attempt to commit a crime requires an intent to commit the crime, a plea of guilty to attempted manslaughter is logically and legally impossible. The defendant relies upon People v. Brown (21 A.D.2d 738, 249 N.Y.S.2d 922) in support of his position. In *Brown* the defendant was convicted, *pursuant to a jury verdict,* of the crime of attempted manslaughter, having been indicted for attempted murder in the first degree. The Appellate Division modified, holding:

"An attempt to commit a crime consists of (1) the intent to commit the crime; (2) the performance of an act toward the commission and (3) failure to consummate. There must be an intent to commit a specific crime in order to constitute an attempt. An attempt to commit manslaughter is apparently a contradiction because the specific crime of manslaughter involves no intent and, accordingly, an intention to commit a crime whose distinguishing element is lack of intent is logically repugnant." There is no doubt that the above case would be dispositive of this appeal if we were faced with an appeal from a jury verdict.

In our case, however, the charge in the indictment is manslaughter in the first degree and a *plea* was taken to attempted manslaughter in the second degree as a lesser included crime. This presents an entirely different situation. . . . We hold that . . . when a defendant knowingly accepts a plea to attempted manslaughter as was done in this case in satisfaction of an indictment charging a crime carrying a heavier penalty . . . , there is no violation of defendant's right to due process. The defendant declined to risk his chances with a jury. He induced the proceeding of which he now complains. He made no objection or complaint when asked in the presence of his counsel whether he had any legal cause to show why judgment should not be pronounced against him, and judgment was thereafter pronounced. As a result, the range of sentence which the court could impose was cut in half — a substantial benefit to defendant. . . .

In People v. Griffin (7 N.Y.2d 511, 166 N.E.2d 684), Judge Van Voorhis addressed himself to the question of accepting pleas in criminal cases, saying: "Moreover, the practice of accepting pleas to lesser crimes is generally intended as a compromise in situations where conviction is uncertain of the crime charged. The judgment entered on the plea in such situation may be based upon no objective state of facts. *It is often a hypothetical crime,* and the procedure — authorized by statute — is justified for the reason that it is in substitution for a charge of crime of a more serious nature which has been charged but perhaps cannot be proved . . . his plea may relate to a *hypothetical situation without objective basis.*" (emphasis added).

We agree with this reasoning in dealing with acceptance of guilty pleas. While there may be question whether a plea to attempted manslaughter is technically and logically consistent, such a plea should be sustained on the ground that it was sought by defendant and freely taken as part of a bargain which was struck for the defendant's benefit. . . .

Accordingly, the judgment of conviction should be affirmed.

NOTES ON THE FACTUAL BASIS FOR THE PLEA

1. Factual-basis requirements under current law. In the federal courts and in most of the states, a guilty plea may not be accepted until the judge determines that there is a "factual basis" for the plea.[72] But the question arises — a factual basis with respect to what? The most extreme position, reflected in cases like *Foster,* allows a plea even to a nonexistent crime, at least where the defendant appears to have committed a more serious, actual offense. Other courts have

---

72. For the federal courts, the requirement is embodied in Fed. R. Crim. P. 11(f), page 154 supra. Many other jurisdictions have adopted similar requirements by statute or court rule.

attempted to require some nexus between the offense pleaded to and the offense actually committed. Some require that the former be a lesser included offense of the latter. See, e.g., State v. Fletchinger, 51 Ohio App. 2d 73, 366 N.E.2d 300 (1977) (plea to corruption of minor invalid where original indictment was for rape). An alternative, less technical approach is suggested in the American Bar Association, Standards for Criminal Justice, Pleas of Guilty, §14-3.1(b)(ii) (2d ed. 1980): The offense pleaded to must be "reasonably related" to the actual offense. Adopting this approach, the California Supreme Court upheld a plea to maintaining a place for the sale of narcotics in a case in which the defendant had been charged with (and apparently had committed) the offense of possession of marijuana. The court held that the two charges were sufficiently similar since both involved offenses relating to restricted drugs. People v. West, 3 Cal. 3d 595, 477 P.2d 409 (1970).

How broadly should the "reasonable relationship" concept be stretched? Are there not significant differences between the two charges in *West* — possession of marijuana and "maintaining a place for the sale" of drugs? Reflecting the difficulty of applying the ABA test, some courts simply require that there be a factual basis for the precise charge to which the defendant pleads. State v. Page, 115 Ariz. 156, 564 P.2d 379 (1977); United States v. Davis, 493 F.2d 502 (5th Cir. 1974). But generally speaking, relatively few jurisdictions insist on a factual basis for the offense to which the defendant actually pleads (and on which conviction will be entered).

2. Relationships to rules for contested cases. Despite the variations just noted, nearly all courts will accept a guilty plea to a lesser included offense or some other closely related charge. Thus, for example, if the facts clearly establish an intentional killing, a guilty plea to involuntary manslaughter generally will be accepted. E.g., State v. Gustafson, 298 Minn. 200, 214 N.W.2d 341 (1974). Yet, as we have seen (page 108 supra), nearly all courts will refuse to submit an involuntary manslaughter instruction to a jury under similar circumstances in a contested case. Rather, in contested trials, a lesser included offense will not be submitted, even when the prosecution and defense mutually agree, unless there is some evidence for all the elements of the lesser offense.

How can this difference in the treatment of contested and uncontested cases be justified? Is there not at least as much (or even more) reason to permit irrational compromise by a jury expressing an intuitive community judgment? Or does a plea bargaining system, once instituted, generate its own pressures for ways to facilitate compromise so that cases will not have to be tried?

If there is a perceived need for a smoothly functioning negotiation system, are there better ways to meet this need? Now that plea bargaining has "come out into the open," courts may become more comfortable with explicit sentencing concessions and accordingly may feel less need to tolerate the kind of artificial charging agreements approved in *Foster* and *West*. Where courts continue to follow the approach of such cases, do the principles of substantive criminal law have any role to play in assessing the validity of a conviction to which the defendant consents? Do the principles of substantive criminal law nevertheless continue to play some role behind the scenes, as a means of leverage in negotiation?

D. PERSPECTIVES ON THE ADVERSARY SYSTEM

DAMAŠKA, EVIDENTIARY BARRIERS TO CONVICTION AND TWO MODELS OF CRIMINAL PROCEDURE
121 U. Pa. L. Rev. 506, 563-564, 571-573, 583-584 (1973)

. . . [Let] me quickly outline the sequence of procedural ideas inherent in the adversary model. The fundamental matrix is based upon the view that proceedings should be structured as a dispute between two sides in a position of theoretical equality before a court which must decide on the outcome of the contest. The procedural aim is to settle the conflict stemming from the allegation of commission of crime. Since the proceeding is essentially a contest, devices such as pleadings and stipulations are not only acceptable but, indeed, essential because they establish the existence of a contest and delineate its borders. The protagonists of the model have definite, independent, and conflicting functions: the prosecutor's role is to obtain a conviction; the defendant's role is to block this effort. In his charge the prosecutor determines which factual propositions he will attempt to prove and must marshal evidence in support of his factual contentions. Not only does he have the burden of persuasion with respect to the latter, but also the burden of presenting evidence in court. In doing so he is expected to be partisan. The defendant decides which facts favorable to his theses he will attempt to prove, and must adduce evidence in support of all his factual contentions. . . . The role of the adjudicator becomes that of an umpire who sees to it that the parties abide by the rules regulating their contest. Even here his basic attitude is one of passivity: he is to rule on the propriety of conduct only upon the objection of the side adversely affected. When the contest is over the adjudicator must, of course, decide on the outcome. An important outgrowth of the fundamental matrix is a great number of technical rules regarding proper conduct of the protagonists. Proceedings tend to become "over-lawyered."

Many features of actual criminal procedures in common law countries are not essential characteristics of this model. Judgment by one's peers, ambushes as a result of lack of discovery, publicity, emphasis on oral testimony — these and many other features are not indispensable to the adversary model. Yet, as we shall see, the ideological assumptions underlying the model make many of these non-essential features a matter of natural choice. . . .

Non-adversary proceedings emerge from the following central structural idea. Rather than being conceived of as a dispute, they are considered an official and thorough inquiry, triggered by the initial probability that a crime has been committed. The procedural aim is to establish whether this is in fact the case, and whether the imposition of criminal sanctions is justified. Of course, the matrix of an official investigation is incompatible with formal pleadings and stipulations: the court-controlled pursuit of facts cannot be limited by mutual consent of the participants. "Parties" in the sense of independent actors are not needed. . . . Factfinding is "unilateral" and detached. . . . Obviously, then, this much simpler structure of proceedings leads to fewer technicalities. The non-adversary model is, thus, "under-lawyered."

Many historically-determined features of continental procedures are not essential to the model. It is, moreover, theoretically possible that the presentation of evidence could outwardly proceed in an adversary fashion, as long as the adjudicators were at least subsidiarily authorized to raise new issues, examine proof sua sponte, and hear evidence themselves whenever necessary to advance the official inquiry. But, once again, the ideological assumptions behind the model make many features of real-life continental proceedings a matter of natural choice. . . .

More than two decades ago, . . . Karl Llewellyn contrasted the "parental" and the "arm's length" systems of criminal justice.[157] The keynote of the first is attitudinal: it resides in a feeling of togetherness, or "We-ness," in Llewellyn's idiom, between the miscreant and the group-management. The defendant is viewed as an integral part of the community, a member of a going team. There is no distrust of officials, who harbor parental emotions, even feelings of love. The goal of any activity directed toward the miscreant is to reintegrate him into the community, through repentance and open confession. Thus, punishment, when imposed, is not thought of as merely a deterrent or simple vengeance; it becomes an educational tool. Official action finds broad popular support and procedures are simple.

The "arm's length" system of criminal justice is the antipode of the "parental" type just described. The defendant is not viewed as a member of a team here, but rather as a "person quite outside," whom the officials are to take hold of only if they can pin upon him some specific act. One of the basic characteristics of the system dictating policy choices is distrust of officials. In keeping with the fundamental "detached" tone, the goal of the official activity towards miscreants is a narrow one: if it were to go beyond punishment, too momentous an invasion of the culprit's personality would occur.

Implications flowing from these two "ideologies" were only outlined by Llewellyn, but no doubt remains that, in the procedural domain, opposing policy choices result in two technical-legal models strikingly resembling the opposition between non-adversary and adversary proceedings. . . .

More recently, John Griffiths has constructed two diametrically opposed ideological models of the criminal process along almost identical lines.[164] One he calls the "family" model, the other the "battle" model. While the latter is predicated on the idea that there is in the domain of the criminal process an irreconcilable conflict between the individual and the state, the former is based on the proposition of reconciliable interests, even a state of love. While the family model implies a basic trust in public officials, the battle model is characterized by a lack of faith in them. The family approach prevents fractionalization and a narrow view of the functions to be fulfilled by the criminal process; its antipode leads to "conceptual compartmentalization" and the blacking out of possible educational purposes of the trial besides the "meting out of deterrence.". . . In sum, what Llewellyn and Griffiths seem to have done is to present two possible ideological justifications for the rival adversary and non-adversary models of the criminal process.

. . . [T]he adversary system in its modern variant is inspired to a great extent by an attitude of distrust of public officials and its complementary demand for

157. See his article on the anthropology of criminal guilt, reprinted in K. Llewellyn, Jurisprudence 439, 444-50 (1962). . . .

164. Griffiths, Ideology in Criminal Procedure or A Third "Model" of the Criminal Process, 79 Yale L.J. 359 (1970).

safeguards against abuse. Accordingly, the adversary system is quite tolerant of evidentiary barriers limiting the search for the truth for fear of abuse of governmental power. Moreover, it does not view as unnatural the use of the criminal process itself "as the appropriate forum for correcting its own abuses," thus making possible the reversal of "substantively" just decisions on "technical-procedural" grounds. It stands to reason that as a result of greater hospitality toward such ideas, the factfinding potential of the system must somehow be decreased . . . ; guilt and innocence are not paramount.

By contrast, the ideology supporting modern non-adversary procedure, be it in the "family" or some other variant, while not ignoring the potential danger of abuse, exhibits much less distrust of police, prosecutors, judges, and public officials in general. Accordingly, many procedural safeguards and technical rules, acceptable to the ideology of adversary procedure, are dismissed as unjustified loopholes, "unnecessary obstacles of pendant legal etiquette," or impermissible injections of collateral issues into the search for guilt or innocence.

FRANKEL, THE SEARCH FOR TRUTH: AN UMPIREAL VIEW
123 U. Pa. L. Rev. 1031, 1032-1041, 1052-1054 (1975)

My theme, to be elaborated at some length, is that our adversary system rates truth too low among the values that institutions of justice are meant to serve. . . .

This is a topic on which our profession has practiced some self-deception. We proclaim to each other and to the world that the clash of adversaries is a powerful means for hammering out the truth. Sometimes, less guardedly, we say it is "best calculated to getting out all the facts. . . ." [a] That the adversary technique is useful within limits none will doubt. That it is "best" we should all doubt if we were able to be objective about the question. Despite our untested statements of self-congratulation, we know that others searching after facts — in history, geography, medicine, whatever — do not emulate our adversary system. We know that most countries of the world seek justice by different routes. What is much more to the point, we know that many of the rules and devices of adversary litigation as we conduct it are not geared for, but are often aptly suited to defeat, the development of the truth.

We are unlikely ever to know how effectively the adversary technique would work toward truth if that were the objective of the contestants. Employed by interested parties, the process often achieves truth only as a convenience, a byproduct, or an accidental approximation. The business of the advocate, simply stated, is to win if possible without violating the law. (The phrase "if possible" is meant to modify what precedes it, but the danger of slippage is well known.) His is not the search for truth as such. To put that thought more exactly, the truth and victory are mutually incompatible for some considerable percentage of the attorneys trying cases at any given time.

Certainly, if one may speak the unspeakable, most defendants who go to trial in criminal cases are not desirous that the whole truth about the matters

a. See also J. Wigmore, Evidence §1367, at 29 (3d ed. 1940): "[C]ross-examination is the greatest legal engine ever invented for the discovery of truth." — EDS.

in controversy be exposed to scrutiny. . . . Whatever doctrine teaches, it is a fact of interest here that most criminal defense counsel are not at all bent upon full disclosure of the truth. To a lesser degree, but stemming from the same ethos, we know how fiercely prosecutors have resisted disclosure, how often they have winked at police lapses, how mixed has been their enthusiasm for the principle that they must seek justice, not merely convictions. While the patterns of civil cases are different, and variable, we may say that it is the rare case in which either side yearns to have the witnesses, or anyone, give *the whole truth*. And our techniques for developing evidence feature devices for blocking and limiting such unqualified revelations.

The devices are too familiar to warrant more than a fleeting reminder. To begin with, we leave most of the investigatory work to paid partisans, which is scarcely a guarantee of thorough and detached exploration. Our courts wait passively for what the parties will present, almost never knowing — often not suspecting — what the parties have chosen not to present. The ethical standards governing counsel command loyalty and zeal for the client, but no positive obligation at all to the truth. Counsel must not knowingly break the law or commit or countenance fraud. Within these unconfining limits, advocates freely employ time-honored tricks and stratagems to block or distort the truth.

. . . To be sure, honest people may honestly differ, and we mere lawyers cannot — actually, must not — set ourselves up as judges of the facts. That is the great release from effective ethical inhibitions. We are not to pass judgment, but only to marshal our skills to present and test the witnesses and other evidence — the skills being to make the most of these for our side and the least for the opposition. What will out, we sometimes tell ourselves and often tell others, is the truth. And, if worse comes to worst, in the end who really knows what is truth?

There is much in this of cant, hypocrisy, and convenient overlooking. As people, we know or powerfully suspect a good deal more than we are prepared as lawyers to admit or explore further. The clearest cases are those in which the advocate has been informed directly by a competent client, or has learned from evidence too clear to admit of genuine doubt, that the client's position rests upon falsehood. It is not possible to be certain, but I believe from recollection and conversation such cases are far from rare. Much more numerous are the cases in which we manage as counsel to avoid too much knowledge. The sharp eye of the cynical lawyer becomes at strategic moments a demurely averted and filmy gaze. . . . Unfettered by the clear prohibitions actual "knowledge" of the truth might impose, lawyers may be effective and exuberant in employing the familiar skills: techniques that make a witness look unreliable although the look stems only from counsel's artifice, cunning questions that stop short of discomfiting revelations, complaisant experts for whom some shopping may have been necessary. The credo that frees counsel for such arts is not a doctrine of truth-seeking.

The litigator's devices, let us be clear, have utility in testing dishonest witnesses, ferreting out falsehoods, and thus exposing the truth. But to a considerable degree these devices are like other potent weapons, equally lethal for heroes and villains. It is worth stressing, therefore, that the gladiator using the weapons in the courtroom is not primarily crusading after truth, but seeking to win. . . .

Two means for controlling adversary excesses in the trial process are intervention by the judge and better training and regulation of counsel. . . . Neither of the two approaches, at least as they have been formulated thus far, contemplates any basic changes in the existing standards and procedures. For this central reason, neither seems to me to hold much promise.[b] . . .

We should begin, as a concerted professional task, to question the premise that adversariness is ultimately and invariably good. . . .

In considering the possibility of change, we must open our minds to the variants and alternatives employed by other communities that also aspire to civilization. Without voting firmly, I raise the question whether the virginally ignorant judge is always to be preferred to one with an investigative file. We should be prepared to inquire whether our arts of examining and cross-examining, often geared to preventing excessive outpourings of facts, are inescapably preferable to safeguarded interrogation by an informed judicial officer. It is permissible to keep asking, because nobody has satisfactorily answered, why our present system of confessions in the police station versus no confessions at all is better than an open and orderly procedure of having a judicial official question suspects. . . .

To propose only one other topic for illustration, we need to study whether our elaborate struggles over discovery, especially in criminal cases, may be incurable symptoms of pathology. . . . Central in the debates on discovery is the concern of the ungenerous that the evidence may be tainted or alchemized between the time it is discovered and the time it is produced or countered at the trial. The concern, though the debaters report it in differing degrees, is well founded. It is significant enough to warrant our exploring alternative arrangements abroad where investigation "freezes" the evidence (that is, preserves usable depositions and other forms of relatively contemporaneous evidence) for use at trial, thus serving both to inhibit spoilage and to avoid pitfalls and surprises that may defeat justice.[64]

NOTE

For further exploration of the relative advantages of adversary and nonadversary methods of developing evidence, see Damaška, Presentation of Evidence and Factfinding Precision, 123 U. Pa. L. Rev. 1083, 1095 (1975). Professor Damaška concludes that "it is treacherous to make definitive pronouncements about which of the two manners of presenting evidence is a more effective tool in the search for truth." He continues (id. at 1103-1105):

b. Judge Frankel's reasons for pessimism about the value of more active judicial intervention are developed in another portion of this article, reprinted at pages 146-147 supra. — EDS.

64. In the depths of the cold war, Mr. Justice Jackson reported a comparison that should be no more offensive in a time of even tremulous détente: "[T]he Soviet Delegation objected to our practice on the ground that it is not fair to defendants. Under the Soviet System when an indictment is filed every document and the statement of every witness which is expected to be used against the defendant must be filed with the court and made known to the defense. It was objected that under our system the accused does not know the statements of accusing witnesses nor the documents that may be used against him, that such evidence is first made known to him at the trial too late to prepare a defense, and that this tends to make the trial something of a game instead of a real inquest into guilt. It must be admitted that there is a great deal of truth in this criticism. We reached a compromise by which the Nurnberg indictment was more informative than in English or American practice but less so than in Soviet and French practice." Bull, Nurnburg Trial, 7 F.R.D. 175, 178 (n.d.) (quoting Justice Jackson, source not indicated).

Quite unrealistically, let me assume that experimentation has proven conclusively that one manner of presenting evidence leads to more precise factual findings than the other. What would be the significance of such an empirical datum for the question of which evidentiary arrangement is preferable? . . . Anglo-American decisionmakers are traditionally strongly attached to individualized justice and strive to arrive at the just result in the light of concrete circumstances of the case: Justice to them can hardly be separated from details. The continental decisionmakers are relatively more concerned about uniformity and predictability: they are much more ready than the common-law adjudicator to neglect the details of the case in order to organize the world of fluid social reality into a system. . . .

If I am right, and there is indeed a subtle discrepancy in the "realities" constituting the object of proof in the two systems, then it is only natural that methods of inquiry into such different realities need not be exactly the same. The continental system would tend to embrace a paradigm closer to that of scientific investigation. The Anglo-American system, where truth is so much a matter of perspective, would tend to espouse a variation of the dialectic method for the divination of the elusive truth.

LANGBEIN, TORTURE AND PLEA BARGAINING
46 U. Chi. L. Rev. 3, 3-14, 19-22 (1978)

For about half a millennium, from the middle of the thirteenth century to the middle of the eighteenth, a system of judicial torture lay at the heart of Continental criminal procedure. . . . The medieval law of proof was designed in the thirteenth century to replace an earlier system of proof, the ordeals, which the Roman Church effectively destroyed in the year 1215. The ordeals purported to achieve absolute certainty in criminal adjudication through the happy expedient of having the judgments rendered by God, who could not err. The replacement system of the thirteenth century aspired to achieve the same level of safeguard — absolute certainty — for human adjudication.

Although human judges were to replace God in the judgment seat, they would be governed by a law of proof so objective that it would make that dramatic substitution unobjectionable — a law of proof that would *eliminate human discretion* from the determination of guilt or innocence. Accordingly, the Italian Glossators who designed the system developed and entrenched the rule that conviction had to be based upon the testimony of two unimpeachable eyewitnesses. . . . Only if the accused *voluntarily* confessed the offense could the court convict him without the eyewitness testimony. . . .

In the history of Western culture no legal system has ever made a more valiant effort to perfect its safeguards and thereby to exclude completely the possibility of mistaken conviction. But the Europeans . . . had set the level of safeguard too high. . . . Because society cannot long tolerate a legal system that lacks the capacity to convict unrepentant persons who commit clandestine crimes, something had to be done to extend the system to those cases. The two-eyewitness rule was hard to compromise or evade, but the confession rule seemed to invite the "subterfuge" that in fact resulted. To go from accepting a voluntary confession to coercing a confession from someone against whom there was already strong suspicion was a step that began increasingly to be taken. The law of torture grew up to regulate this process of generating confessions.

The spirit of safeguard that had inspired the unworkable formal law of proof also permeated the subterfuge. The largest chapter of the European law of torture concerned the prerequisites for examination under torture. The European jurists devised what Anglo-American lawyers would today call a rule of probable cause, designed to assure that only persons highly likely to be guilty would be examined under torture. Thus, torture was permitted only when a so-called "half proof" had been established against the suspect. That meant either one eyewitness, or circumstantial evidence of sufficient gravity, according to a fairly elaborate tariff. . . .

In order to achieve a verbal or technical reconciliation with the requirement of the formal law of proof that the confession be voluntary, the medieval lawyers treated a confession extracted under torture as involuntary, hence ineffective, unless the accused repeated it free from torture at a hearing that was held a day or so later. Often enough the accused who had confessed under torture did recant when asked to confirm his confession. But seldom to avail: the examination under torture could thereupon be repeated. An accused who confessed under torture, recanted, and then found himself tortured anew, learned quickly enough that only a "voluntary" confession at the ratification hearing would save him from further agony in the torture chamber. . . .

In our day, jury trial continues to occupy its central place both in the formal law and in the mythology of the law. . . . In truth, criminal jury trial has largely disappeared in America. The criminal justice system now disposes of virtually all cases of serious crime through plea bargaining. . . .

Why? . . .

In eighteenth-century England jury trial was still a *summary proceeding.* In the Old Bailey in the 1730s we know that the court routinely processed between twelve and twenty jury trials for felony in a single day. . . . Lawyers were not employed in the conduct of ordinary criminal trials, either for the prosecution or the defense. The trial judge called the witnesses (whom the local justice of the peace had bound over to appear), and the proceeding transpired as a relatively unstructured "altercation" between the witnesses and the accused. In the 1790s, when the Americans were constitutionalizing English jury trial, it was still rapid and efficient. "The trial of Hardy for high treason in 1794 was the first that ever lasted more than one day, and the court seriously considered whether it had any power to adjourn. . . ." By contrast, we may note that the trial of Patricia Hearst for bank robbery in 1976 lasted forty days and that the average felony jury trial in Los Angeles in 1968 required 7.2 days of trial time. . . .

Nobody should be surprised that jury trial has undergone great changes over the last two centuries. It desperately needed reform. The level of safeguard against mistaken conviction was in several respects below what civilized peoples now require. What we will not understand until there has been research directed to the question is why the pressure for greater safeguard led in the Anglo-American procedure to the law of evidence and the lawyerization of the trial, reforms that ultimately destroyed the system in the sense that they made jury trial so complicated and time-consuming that they rendered it unworkable as the routine dispositive procedure. Similar pressures for safeguard were being felt on the Continent in the same period, but they led to reforms in nonadversarial procedure that preserved the institution of trial. . . .

In twentieth-century America we have duplicated the central experience of medieval European criminal procedure: we have moved from an adjudicatory to a concessionary system. We coerce the accused against whom we find probable cause to confess his guilt. . . .

I have said that European law attempted to devise safeguards for the use of torture that proved illusory; these measures bear an eerie resemblance to the supposed safeguards of the American law of plea bargaining. Foremost among the illusory safeguards of both systems is the doctrinal preoccupation with characterizing the induced waivers as voluntary. The Europeans made the torture victim repeat his confession "voluntarily," but under the threat of being tortured anew if he recanted. The American counterpart is Rule 11(d) of the Federal Rules of Criminal Procedure, which forbids the court from accepting a guilty plea without first "addressing the defendant personally in open court, determining that the plea is voluntary and not the result of force or threats or of promises *apart from a plea agreement.*" Of course, the plea agreement is the *source* of the coercion and already embodies the involuntariness. . . .

. . . The law of torture endured for half a millennium although its dangers and defects had been understood virtually from the outset; and plea bargaining lives on although its evils are quite familiar to us all. . . .

Why is it so hard for a legal system to reform a decadent system of proof? I think that there are two main reasons. One is in a sense practical: nothing is quite so imbedded in a legal system as the procedures for proof and trial, because most of what a legal system does is to decide matters of proof — what we call fact-finding. . . .

The inertia, the resistance to change that is associated with such deep-seated interests, is inevitably reinforced by the powerful ideological component that underlies a system of proof and trial. Adjudication, especially criminal adjudication, involves a profound intrusion into the lives of affected citizens. Consequently, in any society the adjudicative power must be rested on a theoretical basis that makes it palatable to the populace. Because the theory of proof purports to govern and explain the application of the adjudicative power, it plays a central role in legitimating the entire legal system. The medieval European law of proof assured people that the legal system would achieve certainty. The Anglo-American jury system invoked the inscrutable wisdom of the folk to justify its results. Each of these theories was ultimately untenable. . . . Yet the ideological importance of these theories prevented either legal system from recanting upon them. . . .

The medieval Europeans insisted on two eyewitnesses and wound up with a law of torture that allowed condemnation with no witnesses at all. American plea bargaining, in like fashion, sacrifices just those values that the unworkable system of adversary jury trial is meant to serve: lay participation in criminal adjudication, the presumption of innocence, the prosecutorial burden of proof beyond reasonable doubt, the right to confront and cross-examine accusers, the privilege against self-incrimination. . . .

Furthermore, the sacrifice of our fundamental values through plea bargaining is needless. In its sad plea bargaining opinions of the 1970s, the Supreme Court has effectively admitted that for reasons of expediency American criminal justice cannot honor its promise of routine adversary criminal trial, but the Court has simply assumed that the present nontrial plea bargaining procedure is the inevitable alternative. There is, however, a middle path between the impossible system of routine adversary jury trial and the disgraceful nontrial system of plea bargaining. That path is a streamlined nonadversarial trial procedure.

The contemporary nonadversarial criminal justice systems of countries like West Germany have long demonstrated that advanced industrial societies can institute efficient criminal procedures that nevertheless provide for lay participation and for full adjudication in every case of serious crime. . . . Not the least of its achievements is that in cases of serious crime it functions with no plea bargaining whatsoever.[47] Confessions are still tendered in many cases (41 percent in one sample), but they are not and cannot be bargained for; nor does a confession excuse the trial court from hearing sufficient evidence for conviction on what amounts to a beyond-reasonable-doubt standard of proof. . . .

I hope that over the coming decades we who still live under criminal justice systems that engage in condemnation without adjudication will face up to the failure of adversary criminal procedure. I believe that we will find in modern Continental criminal procedure an irresistible model for reform. . . .

. . . Today in lands where the law of torture once governed, peoples who live in contentment with their criminal justice systems look out across the sea in disbelief[51] to the spectacle of plea bargaining in America, while American tourists come by the thousands each year to gawk in disbelief at the decaying torture chambers of medieval castles.

ARENELLA, REFORMING THE FEDERAL GRAND JURY AND THE STATE PRELIMINARY HEARING TO PREVENT CONVICTION WITHOUT ADJUDICATION, 78 Mich. L. Rev. 463, 525-528 (1980): Proponents of the inquisitorial model suggest that we explicitly abandon the adversarial system and replace it with some of the best features of continental criminal procedure. Professor Weinreb has proposed that we strip the police of all investigatory powers beyond those incidental to their peace-keeping and emergency functions.[322] He would also divest the prosecutor of all investigatory, accusatory, and adjudicative duties. A judicial officer, the investigatory magistrate, would assume all of those powers. Patterned after France's juge d' instruction, the investigating magistrate would conduct an official inquiry to determine whether the accused is guilty, considering any probative evidence and questioning the accused in a noncoercive manner. A defense attorney and the prosecutor would suggest witnesses or lines of inquiry. Thus, instead of two partisan investigations designed to produce evidence favorable to a particular party, one official investigation would determine the truth. The magistrate would prepare a complete evidentiary record (a dossier) to substantiate all findings. Prosecutorial discretion in filing charges would be eliminated as the magistrate would make all charging decisions. Instead of a

47. For recent discussion see Langbein & Weinreb, Continental Criminal Procedure: "Myth" and Reality, 87 Yale L.J. 1549, 1561-65 (1978). For the observation that modern Continental nonadversarial procedure confers more safeguards upon the accused than does American plea bargaining, see Damaška, Evidentiary Barriers to Conviction and Two Models of Criminal Procedure: A Comparative Study, 121 U. Pa. L. Rev. 506, 552 (1973).

51. In the German press the judicial procedure surrounding the resignation of Vice President Agnew was viewed with the sort of wonder normally inspired by reports of the customs of primitive tribes. "The resignation occurred as part of a 'cow-trade,' as it can only in the United States be imagined." Badische Zeitung, Oct. 12, 1973, at 3, col. 2.

322. L. Weinreb, [Denial of Justice: Criminal Process in the United States (1977)], at 118-19.

prosecutor bringing the most serious charges that could possibly apply, the magistrate would formally accuse only if convinced beyond a reasonable doubt of the defendant's guilt for the specific crime charged.

Once the magistrate concluded the investigation and filed charges, Weinreb and Langbein suggest that the case should proceed quickly to a nonadversarial trial. Plea-bargaining would be abolished. The charge would reflect the crimes for which the state sought conviction, and a defendant's confession would not negate the state's obligation to adjudicate guilt fairly and carefully at trial. A presiding judge would direct the presentation of evidence. The defense attorney and the prosecutor would advise the court by suggesting witnesses, lines of inquiry, and ways to interpret the evidence. A mixed panel of professional and lay members would then adjudicate the defendant's guilt.

If such inquisitorial safeguards function as advertised, they are attractive because they provide for lay participation in a neutral body that adjudicates the defendant's guilt. However, . . . [a]t the very least, proponents of such radical change bear the burden of persuading the body politic that the inquisitorial safeguards function as described. The current academic controversy over those safeguards' effectiveness in controlling police investigations and limiting prosecutorial discretion suggests that this burden has not yet been met.[335] While proponents insist that their description of inquisitorial procedures is not idealized, other scholars have concluded that the pure inquisitorial model describes the continental systems' processing of most cases no more accurately than the due process, accusatorial model describes our system's performance.[337]

JOHNSON, IMPORTING JUSTICE, 87 Yale L.J. 406, 410-414 (1977): Even if Weinreb's highly critical assessment of the American criminal justice system were entirely justified, he would still have failed to establish that the faults of our system are the result of our refusal to adopt European models of investgation and trial. To do so he would have to examine the extent to which the failings of criminal justice in the United States are also to be found in Great Britain, Canada, Australia, and New Zealand: countries that share with us a common legal tradition and have in many respects similar institutions. If these countries have police forces that behave in a reasonably lawful and civilized manner, if they can bring cases to trial without months and years of pointless delay, if they are not forced to rely on assembly line plea bargaining, and if they hold members of the Bar to standards of honesty and candor at least as high as those practiced by encyclopedia salesmen, then perhaps our faults flow from

---

335. Compare Goldstein & Marcus, The Myth of Judicial Supervision in Three "Inquisitorial" Systems: France, Italy, and Germany, 87 Yale L.J. 240 (1977), with Langbein & Weinreb, [Continental Criminal Procedure: "Myth" and Reality, 87 Yale L.J. 1549 (1978].

337. See Goldstein & Marcus, supra note 335. The authors contend that the pure inquisitorial model greatly exaggerates the role of judicial supervision in the pretrial process for most cases. . . .

Goldstein and Marcus also argue that the absence of careful judicial pretrial screening is not cured by the nonadversarial trial that follows. While the inquisitorial model assumes that the court will aggressively pursue the truth, "genuinely probing trials take place only in those few cases in which the defendant actively contests the charges against him." For the majority of cases where the defendant admits guilt or does not contest culpability, the nonadversarial trial offers a public recapitulation of the dossier's findings. . . . In other words, implicit bargaining can and does occur because defendants know that they can receive more lenient treatment when their cooperation enables the prosecutor to handle the case summarily. . . . Langbein argues that the analogy [to] American plea-bargaining . . . is exceedingly misleading. . . .

something other than our failure to imitate the institutions of France. Unless this comprehensive comparison is made, it is impossible to be sure that the glaring defects of American criminal process are not better explained by such factors as our ethnic and racial differences, the traditional lawlessness of our people and our officials, and our insistence on using the criminal law to combat every form of socially disapproved conduct. A change in the form of our institutions is not going to help anything very much if the real problem is one of cultural traditions and unrealistic objectives. . . . As Mirjan Damaška explained . . . ,[10] European and Anglo-American attitudes toward authority and structures of government differ profoundly in ways that have the greatest significance in shaping legal institutions and practices. Europeans tend to value theory, hierarchical organization, and central authority; we stress pragmatism, checks and balances, and decentralization. As Damaška explains, the basic differences in the criminal justice systems reflect those underlying societal values. Given these differences in philosophy, there is simply no way that the institutions of one system can be transported to the other without undergoing profound and possibly self-defeating change.

As an example consider the office of investigating magistrate, the creation of which is the principal proposal of Weinreb's book. . . .

Whatever the title of the investigator, he would of course be an American sharing the attitudes and prejudices of his countrymen. He would not be perceived as "neutral" or "disinterested" by the defendant or defense lawyer because he would represent the authority of the state, and we perceive the criminal process as a contest between the individual and the state. He would be tempted to take short cuts and abridge rights to satisfy the public demand that he solve crimes and see to it that the guilty are punished. Defendants would constantly try to hamstring him with time-consuming motions and hearings, and they would sometimes obtain support from higher court judges who are themselves former practicing lawyers distrustful of governmental authority. The political and cultural conflicts that have made our criminal process what it is would not go away, and they would go to work to transform the alien system. . . .

. . . We cannot expect to conduct trials promptly and efficiently as long as we give criminal defendants so many legally protected rights, including the right to inquire at length into the legality of every aspect of the criminal investigation. Our problems are largely home grown; they result both from the conflicting demands we place on the criminal justice system and from our conflicting attitudes about governmental authority. We can no more import our solutions than we can export our problems.

---

10. Damaška, Structures of Authority and Comparative Criminal Procedure, 84 Yale L.J. 480 (1975).

CHAPTER
3

THE JUSTIFICATION OF PUNISHMENT

A. WHY PUNISH?

1. Introduction

MODEL PENAL CODE: *Section 1.02.* (1) The general purposes of the provisions governing the definition of offenses are: (a) to forbid and prevent conduct that unjustifiably and inexcusably inflicts or threatens substantial harm to individual or public interests; (b) to subject to public control persons whose conduct indicates that they are disposed to commit crimes; . . . (e) to differentiate on reasonable grounds between serious and minor offenses.

(2) The general purposes of the provisions governing the sentencing and treatment of offenders are: (a) to prevent the commission of offenses; (b) to promote the correction and rehabilitation of offenders; (c) to safeguard offenders against excessive, disproportionate or arbitrary punishment. . . .

NEW YORK PENAL LAW: *Section 1.05.* The general purposes of the provisions of this chapter are: . . .

5. To insure the public safety by preventing the commission of offenses through the deterrent influence of the sentences authorized, the rehabilitation of those convicted, and their confinement when required in the interests of public protection.

CALIFORNIA PENAL CODE (1976 amend.): *Section 1170.* The Legislature finds and declares that the purpose of imprisonment for crime is punishment. This purpose is best served by terms proportionate to the seriousness of the offense with provision for uniformity in the sentences of offenders committing the same offense under similar circumstances. The Legislature further finds and declares that the elimination of disparity and the provision of uniformity of sentences can best be achieved by determinate sentences fixed by statute in proportion to the seriousness of the offense as determined by the Legislature to be imposed by the court with specified discretion.

REGINA v. DUDLEY AND STEPHENS
Queen's Bench Division
14 Q.B.D. 273 (1884)

LORD COLERIDGE, C.J. The two prisoners, Thomas Dudley and Edwin Stephens, were indicted for the murder of Richard Parker on the high seas on the 25th of July in the present year. They were tried before my Brother Huddleston at Exeter on the 6th of November, and, under the direction of my learned Brother, the jury returned a special verdict, the legal effect of which has been argued before us, and on which we are now to pronounce judgment.

The special verdict as, after certain objections by Mr. Collins to which the Attorney General yielded, it is finally settled before us is as follows.

That on July 5, 1884, the prisoners, Thomas Dudley and Edward [sic] Stephens, with one Brooks, all able-bodied English seamen, and the deceased also an English boy, between seventeen and eighteen years of age, the crew of an English yacht, a registered English vessel, were cast away in a storm on the high seas 1,600 miles from the Cape of Good Hope, and were compelled to put into an open boat belonging to the said yacht. That in this boat they had no supply of water and no supply of food, except two 1 lb. tins of turnips, and for three days they had nothing else to subsist upon. That on the fourth day they caught a small turtle, upon which they subsisted for a few days, and this was the only food they had up to the twentieth day when the act now in question was committed. That on the twelfth day the remains of the turtle were entirely consumed, and for the next eight days they had nothing to eat. That they had no fresh water, except such rain as they from time to time caught in their oilskin capes. That the boat was drifting on the ocean, and was probably more than 1,000 miles away from land. That on the eighteenth day, when they had been seven days without food and five without water, the prisoners spoke to Brooks as to what should be done if no succour came, and suggested that some one should be sacrificed to save the rest, but Brooks dissented, and the boy, to whom they were understood to refer, was not consulted. That on the 24th of July, the day before the act now in question, the prisoner Dudley proposed to Stephens and Brooks that lots should be cast who should be put to death to save the rest, but Brooks refused to consent, and it was not put to the boy, and in point of fact there was no drawing of lots. That on the day the prisoners spoke of their families, and suggested it would be better to kill the boy that their lives should be saved, and Dudley proposed that if there was no vessel in sight by the morrow morning the boy should be killed. That next day, the 25th of July, no vessel appearing, Dudley told Brooks that he had better go and have a sleep, and made signs to Stephens and Brooks that the boy had better be killed. The prisoner Stephens agreed to the act, but Brooks dissented from it. That the boy was then lying at the bottom of the boat quite helpless and extremely weakened by famine and by drinking sea water, and unable to make any resistance, nor did he ever assent to his being killed. The prisoner Dudley offered a prayer asking forgiveness for them all if either of them should be tempted to commit a rash act, and that their souls might be saved. That Dudley, with the assent of Stephens, went to the boy, and telling him that his time was come, put a knife into his throat and killed him then and there; that the three men fed upon the body and blood of the boy for four days; that on the fourth day after the act had been committed the boat was picked up by a passing vessel, and the prisoners were rescued, still alive, but in the lowest state of prostration. That they were carried to the port of Falmouth, and committed for trial at Exeter.

That if the men had not fed upon the body of the boy they would probably not have survived to be so picked up and rescued, but would within four days have died of famine. That the boy, being in a much weaker condition, was likely to have died before them. That at the time of the act in question there was no sail in sight, nor any reasonable prospect of relief. That under these circumstances there appeared to the prisoners every probability that unless they then fed or very soon fed upon the boy or one of themselves they would die of starvation. That there was no appreciable chance of saving life except by killing some one for the others to eat. That assuming any necessity to kill anybody, there was no greater necessity for killing the boy than any of the other three men. But whether upon the whole matter by the jurors found the killing of Richard Parker by Dudley and Stephens be felony and murder the jurors are ignorant, and pray the advice of the Court thereupon, and if upon the whole matter the Court shall be of opinion that the killing of Richard Parker be felony and murder, then the jurors say that Dudley and Stephens were each guilty of felony and murder as alleged in the indictment. . . .

From these facts, stated with the cold precision of a special verdict, it appears sufficiently that the prisoners were subject to terrible temptation, to sufferings which might break down the bodily power of the strongest man, and try the conscience of the best. Other details yet more harrowing, facts still more loathsome and appalling, were presented to the jury, and are to be found recorded in my learned Brother's notes. But nevertheless this is clear, that the prisoners put to death a weak and unoffending boy upon the chance of preserving their own lives by feeding upon his flesh and blood after he was killed, and with the certainty of depriving *him* of any possible chance of survival. The verdict finds in terms that "if the men had not fed upon the body of the boy they would *probably* not have survived," and that "the boy being in a much weaker condition was *likely* to have died before them." They might possibly have been picked up next day by a passing ship; they might possibly not have been picked up at all; in either case it is obvious that the killing of the boy would have been an unnecessary and profitless act. It is found by the verdict that the boy was incapable of resistance, and, in fact, made none; and it is not even suggested that his death was due to any violence on his part attempted against, or even so much as feared by, those who killed him. Under these circumstances the jury say that they are ignorant whether those who killed him were guilty of murder, and have referred it to this Court to determine what is the legal consequence which follows from the facts which they have found. . . .

. . . [T]he real question in the case [is] whether killing under the circumstances set forth in the verdict be or not be murder. The contention that it could be anything else was, to the minds of us all, both new and strange, and we stopped the Attorney General in his negative argument in order that we might hear what could be said in support of a proposition which appeared to us to be at once dangerous, immoral, and opposed to all legal principle and analogy. . . . First it is said that it follows from various definitions of murder in books of authority, which definitions imply, if they do not state, the doctrine, that in order to save you own life you may lawfully take away the life of another, when that other is neither attempting nor threatening yours, nor is guilty of any illegal act whatever towards you or any one else. But if these definitions be looked at they will not be found to sustain this contention. . . .

It is . . . clear . . . that the doctrine contended for receives no support from the great authority of Lord Hale. It is plain that in his view the necessity which justified homicide is that only which has always been and is now considered a justification. . . . Lord Hale regarded the private necessity which justified, and alone justified, the taking the life of another for the safeguard of one's own to be what is commonly called "self-defence." (Hale's Pleas of the Crown, i. 478.)

But if this could be even doubtful upon Lord Hale's words, Lord Hale himself has made it clear. For in the chapter in which he deals with the exemption created by compulsion or necessity he thus expresses himself: —"If a man be desperately assaulted and in peril of death, and cannot otherwise escape unless, to satisfy his assailant's fury, he will kill an innocent person then present, the fear and actual force will not acquit him of the crime and punishment of murder, if he commit the fact [sic], for he ought rather to die himself than kill an innocent; but if he cannot otherwise save his own life the law permits him in his own defence to kill the assailant, for by the violence of the assault, and the offence committed upon him by the assailant himself, the law of nature, and necessity, hath made him his own protector *cum debito moderamine inculpatae tutelae.*" (Hale's Pleas of the Crown, vol. i. 51.)

But, further still, Lord Hale in the following chapter deals with the position asserted by the casuists, and sanctioned, as he says, by Grotius and Puffendorf, that in a case of extreme necessity, either of hunger or clothing; "theft is no theft, or at least not punishable as theft, as some even of our own lawyers have asserted the same." "But," says Lord Hale, "I take it that here in England, that rule, at least by the laws of England, is false; and therefore, if a person, being under necessity for want of victuals or clothes, shall upon that account clandestinely and animo furandi steal another man's goods, it is felony, and a crime by the laws of England punishable with death." (Hale, Pleas of the Crown, i. 54). If, therefore, Lord Hale is clear — as he is — that extreme necessity of hunger does not justify larceny, what would he have said to the doctrine that it justified murder? [The opinion then reviewed other early text writers and found that none of them supported the defendants' contentions.]

Is there, then, any authority for the proposition which has been presented to us? Decided cases there are none. . . . The American case cited by my Brother Stephen in his Digest, from Wharton on Homicide, in which it was decided, correctly indeed, that sailors had no right to throw passengers overboard to save themselves, but on the somewhat strange ground that the proper mode of determining who was to be sacrificed was to vote upon the subject by ballot, can hardly, as my Brother Stephen says, be an authority satisfactory to a court in this country. . . .

The one real authority of former time is Lord Bacon, who, in his commentary on the maxim, *necessitas inducit privilegium quoad jura privata,* lays down the law as follows: —"Necessity carrieth a privilege in itself. Necessity is of three sorts — necessity of conservation of life, necessity of obedience, and necessity of the act of God or of a stranger. First of conservation of life; if a man steal viands to satisfy his present hunger, this is no felony nor larceny. So if divers be in danger of drowning by the casting away of some boat or barge, and one of them get to some plank, or on the boat's side to keep himself above water, and another to save his life thrust him from it, whereby he is drowned, this is

neither se defendendo nor by misadventure, but justifiable." [a] . . . Lord Bacon
was great even as a lawyer; but it is permissible to much smaller men, relying
upon principle and on the authority of others, the equals and even the superiors
of Lord Bacon as lawyers, to question the soundness of his dictum. There are
many conceivable states of things in which it might possibly be true, but if
Lord Bacon meant to lay down the broad proposition that man may save his
life by killing, if necessary, an innocent and unoffending neighbour, it certainly
is not law at the present day. . . .

Now, except for the purpose of testing how far the conservation of a man's
own life is in all cases and under all circumstances, an absolute, unqualified,
and paramount duty, we exclude from our consideration all the incidents of
war. We are dealing with a case of private homicide, not one imposed upon
men in the service of their Sovereign and in the defence of their country. Now
it is admitted that the deliberate killing of this unoffending and unresisting
boy was clearly murder, unless the killing can be justified by some well-recognised
excuse admitted by the law. It is further admitted that there was in this case
no such excuse, unless the killing was justified by what has been called "necessity." But the temptation to the act which existed here was not what the law
has ever called necessity. Nor is this to be regretted. Though law and morality
are not the same, and many things may be immoral which are not necessarily
illegal, yet the absolute divorce of law from morality would be of fatal consequence; and such divorce would follow if the temptation to murder in this case
were to be held by law an absolute defence of it. It is not so. To preserve
one's life is generally speaking a duty, but it may be the plainest and the highest
duty to sacrifice it. War is full of instances in which it is a man's duty not to
live, but to die. The duty, in case of shipwreck, of a captain to his crew, of
the crew to the passengers, of soldiers to women and children, as in the noble
case of the *Birkenhead;* these duties impose on men the moral necessity, not of
the preservation, but of the sacrifice of their lives for others, from which in
no country, least of all, it is to be hoped, in England, will men ever shrink, as
indeed, they have not shrunk. It is not correct, therefore, to say that there is
any absolute or unqualified necessity to preserve one's life. *Necesse est ut eam,
non ut vivam,* is a saying of a Roman officer quoted by Lord Bacon himself
with high eulogy in the very chapter on necessity to which so much reference
has been made. It would be a very easy and cheap display of commonplace
learning to quote from Greek and Latin authors, from Horace, from Juvenal,
from Cicero, from Euripides, passage after passage, in which the duty of dying
for others has been laid down in glowing and emphatic language as resulting
from the principles of heathen ethics; it is enough in a Christian country to
remind ourselves of the Great Example whom we profess to follow. It is not
needful to point out the awful danger of admitting the principle which has
been contended for. Who is to be the judge of this sort of necessity? By what
measure is the comparative value of lives to be measured? Is it to be strength,

a. The omitted first sentence with which Bacon introduced the passage quoted read as follows:
"The law chargeth no man with default where the act is compulsory and not voluntary, and where
there is not a consent and election: and therefore, if either there be an impossibility for a man to
do otherwise, or so great a perturbation of the judgment and reason as in presumption of law
man's nature cannot overcome, such necessity carrieth a privilege in itself." Shedding, Ellis & Heath,
The Works of Francis Bacon 343 (1859). — Eds.

or intellect, or what? It is plain that the principle leaves to him who is to profit by it to determine the necessity which will justify him in deliberately taking another's life to save his own. In this case the weakest, the youngest, the most unresisting, was chosen. Was it more necessary to kill him than one of the grown men? The answer must be "No"—

> So spake the Fiend, and with necessity,
> The tyrant's plea, excused his devilish deeds.

It is not suggested that in this particular case the deeds were "devilish," but it is quite plain that such a principle once admitted might be made the legal cloak for unbridled passion and atrocious crime. There is no safe path for judges to tread but to ascertain the law to the best of their ability and to declare it according to their judgment; and if in any case the law appears to be too severe on individuals, to leave it to the Sovereign to exercise that prerogative of mercy which the Constitution has intrusted to the hands fittest to dispense it.

It must not be supposed that in refusing to admit temptation to be an excuse for crime it is forgotten how terrible the temptation was; how awful the suffering; how hard in such trials to keep the judgment straight and the conduct pure. We are often compelled to set up standards we cannot reach ourselves, and to lay down rules which we could not ourselves satisfy. But a man has no right to declare temptation to be an excuse, though he might himself have yielded to it, nor allow compassion for the criminal to change or weaken in any manner the legal definition of the crime. It is therefore our duty to declare that the prisoners' act in this case was wilful murder, that the facts as stated in the verdict are no legal justification of the homicide; and to say that in our unanimous opinion the prisoners are upon this special verdict guilty of murder.[1]

The Court then proceeded to pass sentence of death upon the prisoners.[2]

NOTE

For discussions of the historical background of the principal case, see Mallin, In Warm Blood: Some Historical and Procedural Aspects of Regina v. Dudley and Stephens, 34 U. Chi. L. Rev. 387 (1967); Simpson, Cannibals at Common Law, 77 U. Chi. Law School Rec. 3 (1981).

There is a large literature on the subject of punishment. Bibliographies may be found in E. Pincoffs, The Rationale of Legal Punishment 139 et seq. (1966); Freedom and Responsibility 546-547 (H. Morris ed. 1961); Gerber & McAnany, Punishment: Current Survey of Philosophy and Law, 11 St. Louis U.L.J. 491 (1967). There are several useful anthologies of readings: R. Gerber & P. McAnany, Contemporary Punishment: Views, Explanations and Justifications (1972); G. Ezorsky, Philosophical Perspectives on Punishment (1972); H. B. Acton, The Philosophy of Punishment (1969).

---

1. My brother Grove has furnished me with the following suggestion, too late to be embodied in the judgment but well worth preserving: "If the two accused men were justified in killing Parker, then if not rescued in time, two of the three survivors would be justified in killing the third, and of the two who remained the stronger would be justified in killing the weaker, so that three men might be justifiably killed to give the fourth a chance of surviving."— C.

2. This sentence was afterwards commuted by the Crown to six months' imprisonment.

The ideas of Professor H. L. A. Hart have been highly influential in recent years. His essays on punishment are contained in Punishment and Responsibility (1968), available in paperback. For a retributive justification of punishment, see Mabbot, Punishment, 48 Mind 152 (1939); Armstrong, The Retributivist Hits Back, 70 Mind 471 (1961); Morris, Persons and Punishment, 52 Monist 475 (1968). For a critical analysis of retribution, see A. C. Ewing, The Morality of Punishment (1929).

Two recent examinations of the issues find no existing theory fully satisfactory. R. Wasserstrom, Philosophy and Social Issues 112-151 (1980); Walker, Punishing, Denouncing or Reducing Crime?, in Reshaping the Criminal Law 391 (P. R. Glazebrook ed. 1978), republished as The Efficacy and Morality of Deterrents, [1979] Crim. L. Rev. 129.

2. Retribution and Related Themes

I. KANT, THE METAPHYSICAL ELEMENTS OF JUSTICE 99-102 (J. Ladd trans. 1965): The right to punish contained in the penal law [*das Strafrecht*] is the right that the magistrate has to inflict pain on a subject in consequence of his having committed a crime. . . .

Judicial punishment (*poena forensis*) is entirely distinct from natural punishment (*poena naturalis*). In natural punishment, vice punishes itself, and this fact is not taken into consideration by the legislator. Judicial punishment can never be used merely as a means to promote some other good for the criminal himself or for civil society, but instead it must in all cases be imposed on him only on the ground that he has committed a crime; for a human being can never be manipulated merely as a means to the purposes of someone else and can never be confused with the objects of the Law of things [*Sachenrecht*]. His innate personality [that is, his right as a person] protects him against such treatment, even though he may indeed be condemned to lose his civil personality. He must first be found to be deserving of punishment before any consideration is given to the utility of this punishment for himself or for his fellow citizens. The law concerning punishment is a categorical imperative, and woe to him who rummages around in the winding paths of a theory of happiness looking for some advantage to be gained by releasing the criminal from punishment or by reducing the amount of it — in keeping with the Pharisaic motto: "It is better that one man should die than that the whole people should perish." If legal justice perishes, then it is no longer worth while for men to remain alive on this earth. If this is so, what should one think of the proposal to permit a criminal who has been condemned to death to remain alive, if, after consenting to allow dangerous experiments to be made on him, he happily survives such experiments and if doctors thereby obtain new information that benefits the community? Any court of justice would repudiate such a proposal with scorn if it were suggested by a medical college, for [legal] justice ceases to be justice if it can be bought for a price.

What kind and what degree of punishment does public legal justice adopt as its principle and standard? None other than the principle of equality (illustrated by the pointer on the scales of justice), that is, the principle of not treating one side more favorably than the other. Accordingly, any undeserved evil that you inflict on someone else among the people is one that you do to yourself. If you vilify him, you vilify yourself; if you steal from him, you steal from yourself; if you kill him, you kill yourself. Only the Law of retribution (*jus talionis*) can determine exactly the kind and degree of punishment; it must be well understood, however, that this determination [must be made] in the chambers of a court of justice (and not in your private judgment). All other standards fluctuate back and forth and, because extraneous considerations are mixed with them, they cannot be compatible with the principle of pure and strict legal justice. . . .

If [the offender] has committed a murder, he must die. In this case, there is no substitute that will satisfy the requirements of legal justice. There is no sameness of kind between death and remaining alive even under the most miserable conditions, and consequently there is also no equality between the crime and the retribution unless the criminal is judicially condemned and put to death. But the death of the criminal must be kept entirely free of any maltreatment that would make an abomination of the humanity residing in the person suffering it. Even if a civil society were to dissolve itself by common agreement of all its members (for example, if the people inhabiting an island decided to separate and disperse themselves around the world), the last murderer remaining in prison must first be executed, so that everyone will duly receive what his actions are worth and so that the bloodguilt thereof will not be fixed on the people because they failed to insist on carrying out the punishment; for if they fail to do so, they may be regarded as accomplices in this public violation of legal justice.

H. MORRIS, ON GUILT AND INNOCENCE 33-34 (1976): I want to . . . set . . . out two complex types of institutions both of which are designed to maintain some degree of social control. In the one a central concept is punishment for wrongdoing and in the other the central concepts are control of dangerous individuals and treatment of disease.

Let us first turn attention to the institutions in which punishment is involved. The institutions I describe will resemble those we ordinarily think of as institutions of punishment; they will have, however, additional features we associate with a system of just punishment.

Let us suppose that men are constituted roughly as they now are, with a rough equivalence in strength and abilities, a capacity to be injured by each other and to make judgments that such injury is undesirable, a limited strength of will, and a capacity to reason and to conform conduct to rules. Applying to the conduct of these men are a group of rules, ones I shall label "primary," which closely resemble the core rules of our criminal law, rules that prohibit violence and deception and compliance with which provides benefits for all persons. These benefits consist of noninterference by others with what each person values, such matters as continuance of life and bodily security. The rules define a sphere for each person then, which is immune from interference by others. Making possible this mutual benefit is the assumption by individuals of a burden. The burden consists in the exercise of self-restraint by individuals over inclinations that would, if satisfied, directly interfere or create a substantial risk of interference with others in proscribed ways. If a person fails to exercise self-restraint even though he might have and gives in to such inclinations, he renounces a burden which others have voluntarily assumed and thus gains an advantage which others, who have restrained themselves, do not possess. This system, then, is one in which the rules establish a mutuality of benefit and burden and in which the benefits of noninterference are conditional upon the assumption of burdens.

Connecting punishment with the violation of these primary rules, and making public the provision for punishment, is both reasonable and just. First, it is only reasonable that those who voluntarily comply with the rules be provided some assurance that they will not be assuming burdens which others are unprepared to assume. Their disposition to comply voluntarily will diminish as they learn that others are with impunity renouncing burdens they are assuming. Second, fairness dictates that a system in which benefits and burdens are equally distributed have a mechanism designed to prevent a maldistribution in the benefits and burdens. Thus, sanctions are attached to noncompliance with the primary rules so as to induce compliance with the primary rules among those who may be disinclined to obey. In this way the likelihood of an unfair distribution is diminished.

Third, it is just to punish those who have violated the rules and caused the unfair distribution of benefits and burdens. A person who violates the rules has something others have — the benefits of the system — but by renouncing what others have assumed, the burdens of self-restraint, he has acquired an unfair advantage. Matters are not even until this advantage is in some way erased. Another way of putting it is that he owes something to others, for he has something that does not rightfully belong to him. Justice — that is punishing such individuals — restores the equilibrium of benefits and burdens by taking from the individual what he owes, that is, exacting the debt. It is important to see that the equilibrium may be restored in another way. Forgiveness — with its legal analogue of a pardon — while not the righting of an unfair distribution by making one pay his debt is, nevertheless, a restoring of the equilibrium by forgiving the debt. Forgiveness may be viewed, at least in some types of cases, as a gift after the fact, erasing a debt, which had the gift been given before the fact, would not have created a debt. But the practice of pardoning has to proceed sensitively, for it may endanger in a way the practice of justice does not, the maintenance of an equilibrium of benefits and burdens. If all are indiscriminately pardoned less incentive is provided individuals to restrain their inclinations, thus increasing the incidence of persons taking what they do not deserve.

BENTHAM, AN INTRODUCTION TO THE PRINCIPLES OF MORALS AND LEGISLATION, in Bentham & Mill, The Utilitarians 162, 166 (Dolphin Books 1961): The general object which all laws have, or ought to have, in common, is to augment the total happiness of the community; and therefore, in the first place, to exclude, as far as may be, every thing that tends to subtract from that happiness: in other words, to exclude mischief.

But all punishment is mischief: all punishment in itself is evil. Upon the principle of utility, if it ought at all to be admitted, it ought only to be admitted in as far as it promises to exclude some greater evil.

It is plain, therefore, that in the following cases punishment ought not to be inflicted.

1. Where it is *groundless:* where there is no mischief for it to prevent; the act not being mischievous upon the whole.

2. Where it must be *inefficacious:* where it cannot act so as to prevent the mischief.

3. Where it is *unprofitable;* or too expensive: where the mischief it would produce would be greater than what it prevented.

4. Where it is *needless:* where the mischief may be prevented, or cease of itself, without it: that is, at a cheaper rate. . . .

2 J. F. STEPHEN, A HISTORY OF THE CRIMINAL LAW OF ENGLAND 81-82 (1883): [T]he sentence of the law is to the moral sentiment of the public in relation to any offence what a seal is to hot wax. It converts into a permanent final judgment what might otherwise be a transient sentiment. The mere general suspicion or knowledge that a man has done something dishonest may never be brought to a point, and the disapprobation excited by it may in time pass away, but the fact that he has been convicted and punished as a thief stamps a mark upon him for life. In short, the infliction of punishment by law gives definite expression and a solemn ratification and justification to the hatred which is excited by the commission of the offence, and which constitutes the moral or popular as distinguished from the conscientious sanction of that part of morality which is also sanctioned by the criminal law. The criminal law thus proceeds upon the principle that it is morally right to hate criminals, and it confirms and justifies that sentiment by inflicting upon criminals punishments which express it. . . . I am also of opinion that this close alliance between criminal law and moral sentiment is in all ways healthy and advantageous to the community. I think it highly desirable that criminals should be hated, that the punishments inflicted upon them should be so contrived as to give expression to that hatred, and to justify it so far as the public provision of means for expressing and gratifying a healthy natural sentiment can justify and encourage it. . . . No doubt they are peculiarly liable to abuse, and in some states of society are commonly in excess of what is desirable, and so require restraint rather than excitement, but unqualified denunciations of them are as ill-judged as unqualified denunciations of sexual passion. The forms in which deliberate anger and righteous disapprobation are expressed, and the execution of criminal justice is the most emphatic of such forms, stand to the one set of passions in the same relation in which marriage stands to the other.

ROYAL COMMISSION ON CAPITAL PUNISHMENT, Minutes of Evidence, Ninth Day, Dec. 1, 1949, Memorandum Submitted by the Rt. Hon. Lord Justice Denning, 207: Whilst everyone agrees that crimes must be punished, there is profound disagreement as to the form which punishment should take. Many are inclined to test the efficacy of punishment solely by its value as a deterrent: but this is too narrow a view. Punishment is the way in which society expresses its denunciation of wrong doing: and, in order to maintain respect for law, it is essential that the punishment inflicted for grave crimes should adequately reflect the revulsion felt by the great majority of citizens for them. It is a mistake to consider the objects of punishment as being deterrent or reformative or preventive and nothing else. If that were so, we should not send to prison a man who was guilty of motor manslaughter, but only disqualify him from driving;

but would public opinion be content with this? The truth is that some crimes are so outrageous that society insists on adequate punishment, because the wrong-doer deserves it, irrespective of whether it is a deterrent or not. . . . Some cases are so outrageous that, irrespective of the value of the death penalty as a deterrent, the great bulk of the community consider that the only fitting penalty is death. In my view the ultimate justification of any punishment is, not that it is a deterrent, but that it is the emphatic denunciation by the community of a crime: and from this point of view, there are some murders which, in the present state of public opinion, demand the most emphatic denunciation of all, namely the death penalty.

E. DURKHEIM, THE DIVISION OF LABOR IN SOCIETY 108-109 (Simpson trans. 1933): Although [punishment] proceeds from a quite mechanical reaction, from movements which are passionate and in great part non-reflective, it does play a useful role. Only this role is not where we ordinarily look for it. It does not serve, or else only serves quite secondarily, in correcting the culpable or in intimidating possible followers. From this point of view, its efficacy is justly doubtful and, in any case, mediocre. Its true function is to maintain social cohesion intact, while maintaining all its vitality in the common conscience. Denied so categorically, it would necessarily lose its energy, if an emotional reaction of the community did not come to compensate its loss, and it would result in a breakdown of social solidarity. It is necessary, then, that it be affirmed forcibly at the very moment when it is contradicted, and the only means of affirming it is to express the unanimous aversion which the crime continues to inspire, by an authentic act which can consist only in suffering inflicted upon the agent. Thus, while being the necessary product of the causes which engender it, this suffering is not a gratuitous cruelty. It is the sign which witnesses that collective sentiments are always collective, that the communion of spirits in the same faith rests on a solid foundation, and accordingly, that it is repairing the evil which the crime inflicted upon society. That is why we are right in saying that the criminal must suffer in proportion to his crime, why theories which refuse to punishment any expiatory character appear as so many spirits subversive of the social order. It is because these doctrines could be practiced only in a society where the whole common conscience would be nearly gone. Without this necessary satisfaction, what we call the moral conscience could not be conserved. We can thus say without paradox that punishment is above all designed to act upon upright people, for, since it serves to heal the wounds made upon collective sentiments, it can fill this role only where these sentiments exist, and commensurately with their vivacity. Of course, by warning already disturbed spirits of a new enfeeblement of the collective soul, it can even stop attacks from multiplying, but this result, however useful, is only a particular counter blow. In short, in order to form an exact idea of punishment, we must reconcile the two contradictory theories which deal with it: that which sees it as expiation, and that which makes it a weapon for social defense. It is certain that it functions for the protection of society, but that is because it is expiatory. Moreover, if it must be expiatory, that does not mean that by some mystical virtue pain compensates for the error, but rather that it can produce a socially useful effect only under this condition.

QUESTIONS

Bentham sees punishment as the deliberate infliction of pain and suffering but justifies it as a necessary evil when the good it produces overall outweighs its harmful effects. Kant justifies punishment as a positive good regardless of what effects it produces. What underlying perspectives explain those radically different conclusions? How would Kant respond to Bentham's arguments? How would Bentham respond to Kant's?

In the pure retributive view that Kant espouses, why is it thought to be a good that offenders be made to suffer for their wrongs? If Kant's position seems extravagant, how might one account for commonly held views about the rightness of punishing particularly egregious offenders, such as the Nazis who perpetrated the holocaust?

What does it mean to say that offenders *deserve* punishment? If we can agree that individuals deserve to be rewarded for their good acts, does it follow that they deserve to be punished for their evil ones?

Morris argues that punishment fairly imposes on offenders the burden assumed voluntarily by the rest of society and deprives them of the benefit they unfairly obtained by violating the law. The argument works plausibly in cases of theft or tax evasion (though, on this theory, restitution and a tax lien on the offender's property may be more appropriate than punishment). Does Morris's argument work in cases such as rape? More generally, does it rest on a view of human nature that is not necessarily correct? For a discriminating critique, see R. Wasserstrom, Philosophy and Social Issues 139-146 (1980).

Consider the denunciatory theory of justification in the Stephen and Denning excerpts. In its basic rationale, is this view more compatible with Bentham or with Kant and Morris? Why should the law formally express the popular hatred of the offender? Is it because it is just to do so or because it is useful? For a critique of the denunciatory theory, see H. L. A. Hart, Punishment and Responsibility 170-172 (1968).

Durkeim sees the function of punishment as the maintenance of social cohesion. How does his view differ from that of Stephen and Denning? Consider the extent to which Durkeim's arguments support reformation rather than the infliction of pain and condemnation as the appropriate response to law violation.

MURPHY, MARXISM AND RETRIBUTION
2 Philosophy & Pub. Aff. 217 (1973)

> Is it not a delusion to substitute for the individual with his real motives, with multifarious social circumstances pressing upon him, the abstraction of "free will"— one among the many qualities of man for man himself? . . . Is there not a necessity for deeply reflecting upon an alteration of the system that breeds these crimes, instead of glorifying the hangman who executes a lot of criminals to make room only for the supply of new ones?
>
> KARL MARX, Capital Punishment,
> N.Y. Daily Tribune, Feb. 18, 1853

In outline . . . I want to argue that when Marx challenges the material adequacy of the retributive theory of punishment, he is suggesting that it presupposes a certain view of man and society that is false. . . .

In trying to develop this case, I shall draw primarily upon Willem Bonger's Criminality and Economic Conditions (1916), one of the few sustained Marxist analyses of crime and punishment. . . .

. . . Put bluntly, his theory is as follows. Criminality has two primary sources: (1) need and deprivation on the part of disadvantaged members of society, and (2) motives of greed and selfishness that are generated and reinforced in competitive capitalistic societies. Thus criminality is economically based — either directly in the case of crimes from need, or indirectly in the case of crimes growing out of motives or psychological states that are encouraged and developed in capitalistic society. In Marx's own language, such an economic system alienates men from themselves and from each other. It alienates men from themselves by creating motives and needs that are not "truly human." It alienates men from their fellows by encouraging a kind of competitiveness that forms an obstacle to the development of genuine communities to replace mere social aggregates. And in Bonger's thought, the concept of community is central. He argues that moral relations and moral restraint are possible only in genuine communities characterized by bonds of sympathetic identification and mutual aid resting upon a perception of common humanity. All this he includes under the general rubric of reciprocity. In the absence of reciprocity in this rich sense, moral relations among men will break down and criminality will increase. Within bourgeois society, then, crimes are to be regarded as normal, and not psychopathological, acts. That is, they grow out of need, greed, indifference to others, and sometimes even a sense of indignation — all, alas, perfectly typical human motives. . . .

No doubt this claim will strike many as extreme and intemperate — a sample of the old-fashioned Marxist rhetoric that sophisticated intellectuals have outgrown. Those who are inclined to react in this way might consider just one sobering fact: of the 1:3 million criminal offenders handled each day by some agency of the United States correctional system, the vast majority (80 percent on some estimates) are members of the lowest 15-percent income level — that percent which is below the "poverty level" as defined by the Social Security Administration. Unless one wants to embrace the belief that all these people are poor because they are bad, it might be well to reconsider Bonger's suggestion that many of them are "bad" because they are poor. At any rate, let us suppose for purposes of discussion that Bonger's picture of the relation between crime and economic conditions is generally accurate. At what points will this challenge the credentials of the contractarian retributive theory . . . ?

. . . The retributive theory claims to be grounded on justice; but is it just to punish people who act out of those very motives that society encourages and reinforces? If Bonger is correct, much criminality is motivated by greed, selfishness, and indifference to one's fellows; but does not the whole society encourage motives of greed and selfishness ("making it," "getting ahead"), and does not the competitive nature of the society alienate men from each other and thereby encourage indifference — even, perhaps, what psychiatrists call psychopathy? . . . There is something perverse in applying principles that presuppose a sense of community in a society which is structured to destroy genuine community.

Related to this is the whole allocation of benefits in contemporary society. The retributive theory really presupposes what might be called a "gentlemen's club" picture of the relation between man and society — i.e., men are viewed as being part of a community of shared values and rules. The rules benefit all concerned and, as a kind of debt for the benefits derived, each man owes obedience to the rules. In the absence of such obedience, he deserves punishment in the sense that he owes payment for the benefits. For, as a rational man, he can see that the rules benefit everyone (himself included) and that he would have selected them in the original position of choice. . . .

. . . But to think that [this] applies to the typical criminal, from the poorer classes, is to live in a world of social and political fantasy. . . . [T]hey certainly would be hard-pressed to name the benefits for which they are supposed to owe obedience. If justice, as both Kant and Rawls suggest, is based on reciprocity, it is hard to see what these persons are supposed to reciprocate for. . . .

Consider one example: a man has been convicted of armed robbery. On investigation, we learn that he is an impoverished black whose whole life has been one of frustrating alienation from the prevailing socio-economic structure — no job, no transportation if he could get a job, substandard education for his children, terrible housing and inadequate health care for his whole family, condescending-tardy-inadequate welfare payments, harassment by the police but no real protection by them against the dangers in his community, and near total exclusion from the political process. Learning all this, would we still want to talk — as many do — of his suffering punishment under the rubric of "paying a debt to society"? Surely not. Debt for what? I do not, of course, pretend that all criminals can be so described. But I do think that this is a closer picture of the typical criminal than the picture that is presupposed in the retributive theory — i.e., the picture of an evil person who, of his own free will, intentionally acts against those just rules of society which he knows, as a rational man, benefit everyone including himself.

But what practical help does all this offer, one may ask. How should we design our punitive practices in the society in which we now live? This is the question we want to ask, and it does not seem to help simply to say that our society is built on deception and inequity. How can Marx help us with our real practical problem? The answer, I think, is that he cannot and obviously does not desire to do so. For Marx would say that we have not focused (as all piecemeal reform fails to focus) on what is truly the real problem. And this is changing the basic social relations. Marx is the last person from whom we can expect advice on how to make our intellectual and moral peace with bourgeois society. And this is surely his attraction and his value.

What does Bonger offer? He suggests, near the end of his book, that in a properly designed society all criminality would be a problem "for the physician rather than the judge." But this surely will not do. The therapeutic state, where prisons are called hospitals and jailers are called psychiatrists, simply raises again all the old problems about the justification of coercion and its reconciliation with autonomy that we faced in worrying about punishment. The only difference is that our coercive practices are now surrounded with a benevolent rhetoric which makes it even harder to raise the important issues. Thus the move to therapy, in my judgment, is only an illusory solution — alienation remains and the problem of reconciling coercion with autonomy remains unsolved. Indeed, if the alternative is having our personalities involuntarily restructured by some state psychiatrist, we might well want to claim the "right to be punished" that Hegel spoke of.

Perhaps, then, we may really be forced seriously to consider a radical proposal. If we think that institutions of punishment are necessary and desirable, and if we are morally sensitive enough to want to be sure that we have the moral right to punish before we inflict it, then we had better first make sure that we have restructured society in such a way that criminals genuinely do correspond to the only model that will render punishment permissible — i.e., make sure that they are autonomous and that they do benefit in the requisite sense. Of course, if we did this then — if Marx and Bonger are right — crime itself and the need to punish would radically decrease if not disappear entirely.

QUESTIONS

A major theme of Murphy's article appears to be that the practice of punishment becomes morally indefensible when it takes place in a society characterized by prejudice against particular groups, gross inequalities in wealth distribution, disparate access to positions of power and attainment, and cultural influences that lead individuals to commit crimes. On what theory is punishment made wrong by these factors? Is it because the offenders in such a society are so completely the products of pervasive social evils that they are not individually responsible? But then how account for the vast majority of deprived people who remain law-abiding? If social (or psychological) conditions contribute to crime, does it follow that all crime is determined solely by those conditions and not at all by the chosen actions of the offender?

Or is it the author's theory that, even assuming people retain a choice to commit crime, such a society, by the immoralities it itself has perpetrated, has forfeited its moral right to punish? Would this proposition mean that retribution against a murderer or a rapist would be morally indefensible? Suppose a sentencing judge rejects probation for a convicted rapist on the ground that the offender *deserves* a more severe punishment. Would this action be morally indefensible?

3. Deterrence

INTRODUCTORY NOTE

Deterrence theories furnish a widely accepted rationale of the practice of punishment. According to these theories, punishment should not be designed to exact retribution on convicted offenders but to deter the commission of future offenses. Deterrence theorists distinguish between the effect of punishment as a general deterrent and its effect as a special deterrent. Punishment acts as a *general deterrent* insofar as the threat of punishment deters potential offenders in the general community. It acts as a *special deterrent* insofar as the infliction of punishment on convicted defendants leaves them less likely to engage in crime.

Attacks on deterrence theories have concentrated on the empirical claim that criminals and would-be criminals are dissuaded from crime by an assessment of the risks of conviction and the unpleasantness of imprisonment. Defenses of the deterrent position have likewise concentrated on this claim, although modern deterrence theories have also emphasized the broader effects of punishment in maintaining law-abiding conduct. A fundamental issue of deterrence is the morality of punishing some offenders in order to deter others.

The following selections exhibit aspects of these themes.

BENTHAM, PRINCIPLES OF PENAL LAW, Pt. II, bk. 1, ch. 3, in J. Bentham's Works 396, 402 (J. Bowring ed. 1843): Pain and pleasure are the great springs of human action. When a man perceives or supposes pain to be the consequence of an act, he is acted upon in such a manner as tends, with a certain force, to withdraw him, as it were, from the commission of that act. If the apparent magnitude, or rather value of that pain be greater than the apparent magnitude or value of the pleasure or good he expects to be the consequence of the act, he will be absolutely prevented from performing it. The mischief which would have ensued from the act, if performed, will also by that means be prevented. . . .

The observation of rules of proportion between crimes and punishments has been objected to as useless, because they seem to suppose, that a spirit of calculation has place among the passions of men, who, it is said, never calculate. But dogmatic as this proposition is, it is altogether false. In matters of importance every one calculates. Each individual calculates with more or less correctness, according to the degrees of his information, and the power of the motives which actuate him, but all calculate. It would be hard to say that a madman does not calculate. Happily, the passion of cupidity, which on account of its power, its constancy, and its extent, is most formidable to society, is the passion which is most given to calculation. This, therefore, will be more successfully combated, the more carefully the law turns the balance of profit against it.

ANDENAES, GENERAL PREVENTION, 43 J. Crim. L.C. & P.S. 176, 179-180 (1952): By general prevention we mean the ability of criminal law and its enforcement to make citizens law-abiding. If general prevention were 100 percent effective there would be no crime at all. General prevention may depend on the mere frightening or deterrent effect of punishment — the risk of discovery and punishment outweighing the temptation to commit crime. This was what Feuerbach had in mind when he designed his famous theory of punishment as psychological coercion directed against the citizen. Later theory puts much stress on the ability of penal law to arouse or strengthen inhibitions of another sort. In Swedish discussion the *moralizing* — in other words the *educational* — function has been greatly stressed. The idea is that punishment as a concrete expression of society's disapproval of an act helps to form and to strengthen the public's moral code and thereby creates conscious and unconscious inhibitions against committing crime. Unconscious inhibitions against committing forbidden acts can also be aroused without appealing to the individual's concepts of morality. Purely as a matter of habit, with fear, respect for authority or social imitation as connecting links, it is possible to induce favorable attitudes toward this or that action and unfavorable attitudes toward another action. . . .

We can say that punishment has three sorts of general-preventive effects: it may have a *deterrent* effect, it may strengthen *moral inhibitions* (a *moralizing* effect), and it may stimulate habitual *law-abiding conduct.* I have reason to emphasize this, since many of those who are most skeptical of general prevention think only of the deterrent effect. Even if it can be shown that conscious fear of punishment is not present in certain cases, this is by no means the same as showing that the secondary effects of punishment are without importance. To the lawmaker, the achievement of inhibition and habit is of greater value than mere deterrence. For these apply in cases where a person need not fear detection and punishment, and they can apply without the person even having knowledge of the legal prohibition.

NOTE AND QUESTIONS ON CERTAINTY AND SEVERITY OF PUNISHMENT

The two plausible ways to increase the deterrent effect of punishment are, first, to increase the risk of conviction, and second, to increase the severity of punishment. The first of these alternatives appears to be the more effective, although it is also the more difficult to implement.

The evidence supporting a correlation between effective enforcement and deterrence is anecdotal. See F. Zimring & G. Hawkins, Deterrence: The Legal Threat in Crime Control 158-172 (1973). Where enforcement has been weak or nonexistent, certain crime has increased dramatically. In Liverpool in 1919, a police strike preceded widespread looting; in Copenhagen in 1944, arrest of the police by the German occupying forces was followed by a tenfold increase in robberies and larcenies. Conversely, where the likelihood of conviction has increased, the crime rate has dropped. Improvements in chemical and toxicological techniques for investigating poisoning were followed by a decrease in this type of crime. Likewise, bank robberies and kidnappings decreased following enactment of legislation making these offenses federal crimes. See Andenaes, The General Preventive Effects of Punishment, 114 U. Pa. L. Rev. 949, 961-962 (1960). A study in New York reports that the crime rate in one precinct fell sharply after the number of police stationed there was more than doubled. Sellin, The Law and Some Aspects of Criminal Conduct, in Aims and Methods of Legal Research 113, 119-120 (A. Conard ed. 1955).

It is important to note, however, that increased enforcement does not by itself result directly in increased general deterrence. Since the effectiveness of the threat of punishment must be judged from the viewpoint of the potential criminal, certainty of punishment is important only as it contributes to the appearance of certainty.

Increased severity of punishment has a more doubtful deterrent effect. Some studies have gone so far as to question whether increased severity has any correlation at all with increased deterrence. A California study, for instance, concludes (California Assembly Committee on Criminal Procedure, Progress Report, Deterrent Effects of Criminal Sanctions 7 (May 1968)):

[A]dult prison inmates had the highest degree of knowledge of penalties, yet at least half had not been restrained in their actions because of this knowledge. Furthermore, it was known that California ranked fifth among all states in the length of time it held people in prison — almost 10 times longer than the national average. Yet our crime rate is higher and as many men fail on parole here as in other states where prison time was considerably less.

Query: What problems do you see in this reasoning? Other studies have been more equivocal, largely because of the absence of extensive empirical evidence. See F. Zimring & G. Hawkins, Deterrence: The Legal Threat in Crime Control 194-208 (1973).

Consider Andenaes, The General Preventive Effects of Punishment, 114 U. Pa. L. Rev. 949, 965-970 (1966):

It seems reasonable to conclude that as a general rule, though not without exceptions, the general preventive effect of the criminal law increases with the growing severity of penalties. Contemporary dictatorships display with almost frightening clarity the conformity that can be produced by a ruthlessly severe justice.[a]

However, it is necessary to make two important reservations. In the first place, as we indicated when discussing the risk of detection, what is decisive is not the actual practice but how this practice is conceived by the public. Although little research has been done to find out how much the general public knows about the penal system, presumably most people have only vague and unspecified notions. Therefore, only quite substantial changes will be noticed. Only rarely does a single sentence bring about significant preventive effects.

In the second place, the prerequisite of general prevention is that the law be enforced. Experience seems to show that excessively severe penalties may actually reduce the risk of conviction, thereby leading to results contrary to their purpose.

NATIONAL RESEARCH COUNCIL, DETERRENCE AND INCAPACITATION: ESTIMATING THE EFFECTS OF CRIMINAL SANCTIONS ON CRIME RATES
4-7 (1978)

ASSESSMENT OF THE EVIDENCE ON DETERRENCE

The hypothesis underlying deterrence derives from the general proposition that human behavior can be influenced by incentives. This leads to the specific prediction that increases in the severity of the penalties or the certainty of their imposition on offenders who are detected will reduce crime by those who are not directly sanctioned. It is argued that, in response to the resulting perceived risk of sanctions, at least part of the population is dissuaded from committing some criminal acts. Thus, all theories of deterrence predict a negative association between aggregate crime rates and sanctions, with levels of sanctions measured either by severity or by risk. The sanction risks usually studied in analyses of

---

a. The lower crime rates in dictatorships might also be attributed to the unusually large police forces maintained by such governments. Hence the risk of apprehension and conviction is also higher in dictatorships than in democracies. See MacNamara, Crime Patterns in Democratic and Totalitarian Society, 1 J.A. Psych. Treatment Offenders 4 (Oct. 1957). — EDS.

deterrence are apprehension, conviction, imprisonment, or execution (all conditional on committing a crime), and sanction severity is usually measured by prison sentence length or time served.

There are three major kinds of research designs for estimating the magnitude and statistical significance of the deterrent effect: experiments, quasi-experiments, and analyses of natural variation. Because of practical, scientific, and ethical constraints, the opportunities for experiments are rare. Quasi-experiments are more common; typically, such studies have examined statutory changes in sanctions (e.g., the abolition of capital punishment) or a clearly defined change in enforcement policy (e.g., a crackdown on speeding violators). The most commonly used approach for measuring deterrent effects is the analysis of the natural variation in crime rates and sanction levels across different units of observation. These analyses interpret a negative association between sanction levels and crime rates (i.e., when sanction levels are high, crime rates are low, and vice versa) as an indication of a possible deterrent effect.

THE EVIDENCE ON NONCAPITAL SANCTIONS: ANALYSES OF NATURAL VARIATION
Taken as a whole, the reported evidence consistently finds a negative association between crime rates and the risks of apprehension, conviction, or imprisonment. The Panel's task is to assess the degree to which the observed association is found *because* the higher sanction levels reduced the amount of crime committed. If the association is found to reflect deterrence, the Panel's task is then to assess the accuracy of the magnitude of the estimated effect.

Sources of Bias

There are three primary obstacles to interpreting the finding of a negative association in analyses of natural variation as valid evidence that sanctions indeed deter crime: (1) the error in measuring crimes; (2) the confounding of incapacitation and deterrence; and (3) the possibility that the level of crime affects sanctions in addition to sanctions deterring crime, which is known as a simultaneous relationship.

Error in Measuring Crimes The sanction measure most commonly used in studies of deterrence is the risk of being sanctioned for a crime, for example, the risk of apprehension or of imprisonment. In most analyses, these measures are defined as the ratio of the number of times the sanction is imposed to the number of offenses known to the police (e.g., the number of arrests divided by the number of offenses). The number of offenses then appears in both the numerator of the crime rate (offenses per population) and the denominator of the sanction variable.

Data on known offenses are the result of citizens' reports to the police or of the police discovering offenses on their own and of those reports then being recorded in official crime statistics. Because of the way the sanction risk and the crime rate are defined, any variation in the reporting or recording rates in different jurisdictions could cause a negative association, even in the absence of a deterrent effect.

Confounding of Deterrence and Incapacitation Imprisoning offenders produces an incapacitative effect as well as a deterrent effect. The incapacitation of those offenders who are imprisoned will thereby reduce crime even in the absence of any deterrent effect. For sanctions having incapacitative effects, then, a negative association between crimes and sanctions reflects the combined effects of, deterrence and incapacitation, rather than a deterrent effect alone.

Simultaneous Effects   Any negative association between crime and sanctions could also be interpreted as reflecting an inverse causal effect, whereby jurisdictions impose lower sanctions because they have higher crime rates. Such an inverse causal effect of crimes on sanctions may arise because the criminal justice system resources (e.g., police, prosecutors, prisons) become overburdened by the increased amount of crime and hence less able to deal with new offenders. Another explanation for such an inverse effect may be an increased tolerance for criminality in those jurisdictions where crime is more common, as reflected, for example, in a reduction in the average sanctions imposed for a particular type of crime. In either case, crimes and sanctions are then simultaneously related.

The statistical procedures for isolating the deterrent effect in a simultaneous relationship require critical prior assumptions called "identification restrictions." These generally involve assuming that certain factors *do not* influence the crime rate directly, but *do* affect one or more of the other simultaneously related variables (such as sanction levels). If these assumptions are seriously in error, the estimated effect may contain large errors reflecting contamination by the simultaneous effects.

The arguments for and against simultaneity differ appreciably, both in substance and persuasiveness, for different sanctions. Thus, in assessing the evidence, the Panel examined the different sanctions separately and examined each from the perspectives of both the assumption of simultaneity and the assumption of nonsimultaneity. Those assessments involved both the validity of the alternative assumptions and our assessment of the research results under each assumption.

Summary of the Evidence

Analyses of natural variation, with few exceptions, find a negative association between crime rates and noncapital sanction risks, controlling for other presumably causal determinants of crime. Any conclusion that these negative associations reflect a deterrent effect, however, is limited principally by the inability to eliminate other factors that could account for the observed relationship, even in the absence of a deterrent effect.

The most important such factor is the possibility that crime rates influence sanctions as well as vice versa; that is, that there is a simultaneous relationship between crimes and sanctions. If this is so, simultaneous estimation methods are required to isolate the deterrent effect. If simultaneous effects are appreciable, then substantial questions remain about whether the simultaneous analyses have successfully isolated the deterrent effect in the simultaneous relationships.

The extent to which simultaneity is an issue may vary with the kind of sanction employed. The likelihood that sanctions and crime are simultaneously determined is probably greatest for imprisonment, less for conviction, and least for arrest. The extent to which simultaneity does exist has rarely been investigated. Until we have a clearer understanding of simultaneity, however, we believe that caution should be exercised in interpreting the available results as establishing a deterrent effect, and especially so for the sanction of imprisonment.

For those sanctions for which simultaneous effects are probably not appreciable, the deterrence estimates resulting from the nonsimultaneous analyses suffer from the bias introduced by error in measuring crimes; this bias forces a negative association even in the absence of deterrent effects. However, since it is unlikely that the observed negative association can be wholly attributed to measurement error for all crime types, the analyses based on an assumption of nonsimultaneity do offer some credible evidence of the existence of a deterrent effect. The estimates of the magnitude of that effect, however, are likely to be seriously in error because of the bias.

In summary, therefore, we cannot yet assert that the evidence warrants an affirmative conclusion regarding deterrence. We believe scientific caution must be exercised in interpreting the limited validity of the available evidence and the number of competing explanations for the results. Our reluctance to draw stronger conclusions does not imply support for a position that deterrence does not exist, since the evidence certainly favors a proposition supporting deterrence more than it favors one asserting that deterrence is absent. The major challenge for future research is to estimate the magnitude of the effects of different sanctions on various crime types, an issue on which none of the evidence available thus far provides very useful guidance. The research program developed in this report is intended to facilitate these efforts.

THE EVIDENCE ON NONCAPITAL SANCTIONS: EXPERIMENTS AND QUASI-EXPERIMENTS

Controlled experiments are relatively rare; quasi-experiments are far more common, usually taking advantage of abrupt changes in the law or in the actual application of sanctions when these occur. The best examples of controlled experiments in deterrence are the test of the crime-control effectiveness of preventive patrol by police in Kansas City, the San Diego field-interrogation experiment, and the study of the effectiveness of different strategies to reduce income tax evasion. Quasi-experimental studies are available on the effect of changes in penalties for drunk driving, drug use and sales, bad checks, and abortion. The deterrent effects of changes in enforcement or patrol practice have also been examined for speeding, for crime on the subway in New York City, and for crime in general.

The results of the experimental and quasi-experimental studies are mixed: some find evidence of significant deterrent effects and others find no evidence of measurable changes in crime rates. In most cases, however, the research designs suffer from a variety of remediable flaws, which undermine confidence in the results; all too often, other factors can be identified to account for findings of either an effect or of no effect.

When the flaws in a particular study have been identified, that line of research is much more likely to be dropped rather than to be replicated with the flaws corrected. As a result, there is a proliferation of unique studies examining a wide variety of intervention strategies. Because most of the studies are not comparable, the results are usually limited to the specific crime types examined and the specific crime control tactics invoked, and they are often restricted to the particular experimental locale. Therefore, no general conclusions can be drawn from the evidence available at this time from experimental and quasi-experimental studies on deterrence.

F. ZIMRING & G. HAWKINS, DETERRENCE: THE LEGAL THREAT IN CRIME CONTROL 35-37 (1973): One of the most familiar and influential statements of objection [to punishment for deterrent purposes] is contained in a passage from Immanuel Kant's Philosophy of Law. "Punishment," says Kant, "can never be administered merely as a means for promoting another good. . . . For one man ought never be dealt with merely as a means subservient to the purpose of another." Now Professor Andenaes in a recent article on The Morality of Deterrence [44] deals with this objection, and what we have to say on this point can conveniently be stated by reference to his treatment of it.

Andenaes states Kant's principle as being "that man should always be treated as an end in himself, not only as a means for some other end." He goes on to say that "realistically, societies often treat people in ways designed to promote the good of society at the expense of the individual concerned." By way of example he cites military conscription, quarantine regulations, the confinement of dangerous mentally ill patients and the detention of enemy citizens in wartime. And he concludes that "the Kantian principle, in practical application, is of doubtful value."

Nevertheless, Professor Andenaes admits that the Kantian principle "lends itself to different interpretations." And it seems to us that a different interpretation both preserves what is valuable in the Kantian position and at the same time does not constitute an irrebuttable objection to deterrence. The point is a very simple one. It is that Kant did not say we must never treat men as means. He said that men should never be treated *merely as a means* or, as Andenaes puts it, *only as a means.* This interpretation is favored by Professor H. L. A. Hart in his discussion of Chief Justice Holmes's theory of objective liability.[48]

Kant, Hart maintains, insisted that we should never treat men *only* as means "but in every case as ends also." Hart goes on to say that this means "we are justified in requiring sacrifices from some men for the good of others only in a social system which also recognizes their rights and their interests. In the case of punishment, the right in question is the right of men to be left free and not punished for the good of others, unless they have broken the law where they had the capacity and a fair opportunity to conform to its requirements." Insofar as this interpretation is valid, the Kantian principle does not necessarily imply the rejection of punishment based on deterrence; but it manifestly implies some limitations upon its use.

QUESTIONS

Would one of the limitations of the Kantian principle suggested by Zimring and Hawkins have to do with the effectiveness of deterrence? If punishment of offenders had no deterrent effect in fact, would it then not only be futile but also unjust as a gratuitous infliction of suffering? How much proof is needed

44. [1970] U. Chi. L. Rev. 649.
48. H. L. A. Hart, Punishment and Responsibility (1968) 242-44.

to establish the injustice? Who should bear the burden of proof, the proponents or opponents? What is the moral case for punishment in a situation of uncertainty?

Consider, as well, the implications of (1) punishment in excess of what is needed to deter; (2) punishment that is more severe than usual in periods in which the crimes offenders commit are sharply increasing in frequency; (3) singling out for exemplary punishment only offenders of a particular kind, for example, those whose offenses are most likely to capture public attention because they involve public figures or newsworthy circumstances, thus enabling the criminal justice system to minimize the amount of total punishment while attaining the maximum deterrent impact. See F. Zimring & G. Hawkins, supra, at 37-50.

4. Reform

RADZINOWICZ & TURNER, A STUDY OF PUNISHMENT I: INTRODUCTORY ESSAY
21 Canadian B. Rev. 91, 91-97 (1943)

. . . [I]n the past 150 years . . . our penal policy is seen to move in three main stages. In the earliest the salient feature is a crude utilitarianism aiming at the reduction of crime through the weapon of terror. The following passage indicates how this doctrine inspired the legislator.

"If a man injured Westminster Bridge, he was hanged. If he appeared disguised on a public road, he was hanged. If he cut down young trees; if he shot rabbits; if he stole property valued at five shillings; if he stole anything at all from a bleach field; if he wrote threatening letters to extort money; if he returned prematurely from transportation; for any of these offenses he was immediately hanged."

The attitude of the contemporary moralist is well illustrated by the views expressed by the Reverend Sydney Smith, Editor of the Edinburgh Review in the eighteen-thirties, in the following quotations:

"The real and only test, in short, of a good prison system is the diminution of offences by the terror of the punishment.

"Mrs. Fry is an amiable excellent woman, and a thousand times better than the infamous neglect that preceded her; but hers is not the method to stop crimes. In prisons which are really meant to keep the multitude in order, and to be a terror to evil-doers, there must be no sharing of profits — no visiting friends — no education but religious education — no freedom of diet — no weavers' looms or carpenters' benches. There must be a great deal of solitude; coarse food; a dress of shame; hard, incessant, irksome, eternal labour; a planned and regulated and unrelenting exclusion of happiness and comforts.". . .

Speaking generally, the study of this first stage of our criminal policy establishes the conclusion that there was no acceptance of any principle that the severity of punishment should be equated to the gravity of the offence. This principle became prominent in the second stage, when the doctrine of retribution took a leading place in contemporary thought on penal questions and therefore the crimes have to be graded according to their gravity and the punishments corre-

spondingly graded so as to fit the crime in each case. The major assumption
on which this conception rests is that every individual in the State has certain
fundamental rights as a human being, which should not be forfeited by the
fact that he may have committed a crime.

Certain thinkers in Europe had drawn attention to the evils which resulted
from the policy of terror, especially when, as often, it allowed too great a discretion to the tribunals and also too great freedom to those who carried out the
sentences of the tribunals. As a safeguard against this danger it was felt that
the individual should be protected by the establishment of legal rules which
would closely define the nature and the amount of punishment which should
be administered for each crime. . . .

If it is to be granted that all individuals have equal fundamental rights it
seemed naturally to follow that they all must bear equal responsibilities; and
the result was that whereas the liberal doctrine of equality protected the individual against the arbitrary cruelties of the policy of terror, it tended to assume
that all individuals have the same powers of resistance to temptation and that
each will deserve the same punishment for the same crime, and moreover will
react in the same way to that punishment. Thus it may be said that the liberal
theory standardised individuals and concerned itself little or not at all with
what at the present day is so closely studied, namely the variations of individual
personality. According to this idea the primary consideration in determining
the punishment to be imposed is the intrinsic nature of the particular crime
which the delinquent has committed.

This development marks a revulsion against the defects which were detected
in the brutality of the earlier period but in its turn it was found to be insufficiently
effective to reduce adequately the volume of crime. The volume of crime was
a fact to cause concern to the least speculative observer but there were other
forces at work in the second half of the nineteenth century which helped to
create a general consciousness that our penal system needed overhauling. In
all branches of science there arose a desire to enquire into origins, and this
tendency affected those thinkers who were interested in the problem of crime.
Investigations (largely stimulated by the writers of the Italian school) into the
social and biological causes of crime produced results which cast doubts on
many of the established theories concerning free will, and the efficacy of basing
criminal policy on deterrence and retribution. Advances in medical science drew
attention to varieties of mental abnormality hitherto not properly appreciated.
Developments in educational science also brought about a realisation that children and adolescents have their own special difficulties in life and that there
was needed a new approach to their problems. Again, more attention was paid
to the publication of the official criminal statistics which, to take only two features,
revealed the very large percentage of juvenile offenders and recidivists. Investigations showed the ineffectiveness of the practice of short term detention, and
on the other hand the corruptive effect of unscientific and antiquated prison
organization. . . .

The new approach which characterises the third period involved a fuller appreciation of the necessity of studying the personality of the offender if the disease
of crime was to be successfully attacked. This led to the introduction of measures
which adopted and regulated the punishment deemed appropriate for defined
groups of offenders, in general without any special regard to the particular

character of the crimes which they might commit. This appreciation is shown in the Report from the Departmental Committee on Prisons which, speaking of persistent offenders states: "To punish them for the particular offence in which they are detected is almost useless . . . the real offence is the willful persistence in the deliberately acquired habit of crime. We venture to offer the opinion formed during the inquiry that a new form of sentence should be placed at the disposal of the judges by which those offenders might be segregated for long periods of detention." In 1908 an Act of Parliament singled out two special groups of delinquents for one of which, now known as the "Young Adults," is prescribed a special treatment, namely, the Borstal sanction, and for the other group, being adult habitual offenders, the sanction of prolonged detention. It is significant that this statute was called the "Prevention of Crime Act." The same idea of prevention had inspired the Probation Act of 1907, which in its main provisions, rejecting the doctrine that a retributory punishment must follow crime, has concentrated on the personality of the delinquent and on the external circumstances affecting his past and future conduct. When it is remembered that in the period immediately preceding the present war out of every ten offenders found guilty of indictable offences more than five were dealt with under the provisions of this Act it will be realized how far our criminal policy has moved away from the position it had taken up in the nineteenth century.

NOTE ON THE REHABILITATIVE IDEAL

The development of the rehabilitative ideal, summarized in the excerpt from Radzinowicz and Turner, had great influence on American penology and corrections policies. In recent years, however, its influence has gone into eclipse, an eclipse exemplified most dramatically by what has happened in California. California pioneered with an indeterminate-sentence law in 1917. This law was grounded on a commitment to individualized correction, with prison sentences statutorily set over a broad span of years and the time and conditions of release administratively determined by the progress of the prisoner. In 1976, however, the state rejected this arrangement by enacting a determinate-sentence law that declared that "the purpose of imprisonment for crime is punishment" and that accordingly set the punishment for each crime at a fixed number of years of imprisonment, with only narrow judicial authority to vary the statutory sentence. For an analysis of the forces that produced this situation, see F. A. Allen, The Decline of the Rehabilitative Ideal — Penal Policy and Social Policy (1981).

H. L. A. HART, PUNISHMENT AND RESPONSIBILITY 25-27 (1968): It is . . . important to see precisely what the relation of Reform to punishment is because its advocates too often misstate it. "Reform" as an objective is no doubt very vague; it now embraces any strengthening of the offender's disposition and capacity to keep within the law, which is intentionally brought about by human effort otherwise than through fear of punishment. Reforming methods include the inducement of states of repentance, or recognition of moral guilt, or greater awareness of the character and demands of society, the provision of education in a broad sense, vocational training and psychological treatment.

Many seeing the futility and indeed harmful character of much traditional punishment speak as if Reform could and should be the General Aim of the whole practice of punishment or the dominant objective of the criminal law:

> The *corrective theory* based upon a conception of multiple causation and curative-rehabilitative treatment, should clearly predominate in legislation and in judicial and administrative practices.[26]

Of course this is a possible ideal but is not an ideal for punishment. Reform can only have a place within a system of punishment as an exploitation of the opportunities presented by the conviction or compulsory detention of offenders. It is not an alternative General Justifying Aim of the practice of punishment but something the pursuit of which within a system of punishment qualifies or displaces altogether recourse to principles of justice or proportion in determining the amount of punishment. This is where both Reform and individualized punishment have run counter to the customary morality of punishment.

There is indeed a paradox in asserting that Reform should "predominate" in a system of Criminal Law, as if the main purpose of providing punishment for murder was to reform the murderer not to prevent murder; and the paradox is greater where the legal offence is not a serious moral one: e.g., infringing a state monopoly of transport. The objection to assigning to Reform this place in punishment is not merely that punishment entails suffering and Reform does not; but that Reform is essentially a remedial step for which ex hypothesi there is an opportunity only at the point where the criminal law has failed in its primary task of securing society from the evil which breach of the law involves. Society is divisible at any moment into two classes (i) those who have actually broken a given law and (ii) those who have not yet broken it but may. To take Reform as the dominant objective would be to forgo the hope of influencing the second and — in relation to the more serious offences — numerically much greater class. We should thus subordinate the prevention of first offences to the prevention of recidivism.

Consideration of what conditions or beliefs would make this appear a reasonable policy brings us to the topic to which this paper is a mere prolegomenon: modern sceptical doubt about the whole institution of punishment. If we believed that nothing was achieved by announcing penalties or by the example of their infliction, either because those who do not commit crimes would not commit them in any event or because the penalties announced or inflicted on others are not among the factors which influence them in keeping the law, then some dramatic change concentrating wholly on actual offenders, would be necessary. Just because at present we do not entirely believe this, we have a dilemma and an uneasy compromise. Penalties which we believe are required as a threat to maintain conformity to law at its maximum may convert the offender to whom they are applied into a hardened enemy of society; while the use of measures of Reform may lower the efficacy and example of punishment on others. At present we compromise on this relatively new aspect of punishment as we do over its main elements. What makes this compromise seem tolerable is the belief that the influence which the threat and example of punishment extracts is often

26. Hall and Glueck, Cases on Criminal Law and its Enforcement (1951), p. 14.

independent of the severity of the punishment, and is due more to the disgrace attached to conviction for crime or to the deprivation of freedom which many reforming measures at present used in any case involve.

COHEN, MORAL ASPECTS OF THE CRIMINAL LAW, 49 Yale L.J. 987, 1012-1014 (1940): The most popular theory today is that the proper aim of criminal procedure is to reform the criminal so that he may become adjusted to the social order. A mixture of sentimental and utilitarian motives gives this view its great vogue. With the spread of humane feeling and the waning of faith in the old conception of the necessity for inflicting pain in the treatment of children and those suffering from mental disease, there has come a revulsion at the hardheartedness of the old retributive theory. The growing belief in education and in the healing powers of medicine encourages people to suppose that the delinquent may be re-educated to become a useful member of society. Even from the strictest economic point of view, individual men and women are the most valuable assets of any society. Is it not better to save them for a life of usefulness rather than punish them by imprisonment which generally makes them worse after they leave than before they entered?

There are, however, a number of highly questionable assumptions back of this theory which need to be critically examined.

We have already had occasion to question the assumption that crime is a physical or mental disease. We may now raise the question whether it is curable and if so at what cost to society? Benevolent social reformers are apt to ignore the amount of cold calculating business shrewdness among criminals. Some hot-blooded ones may respond to emotional appeal; but they are also likely to backslide when opportunity or temptation comes along. Human beings are not putty that can be remolded at will by benevolent intentions. The overwhelming majority of our criminals have been exposed to the influence of our school system which we have at great cost tried to make as efficient as possible. Most criminals are also religious, as prison chaplains can testify. Yet with all our efforts school education and religion do not eliminate crime. It has not even been demonstrated that they are progressively minimizing it. Nor does the record of our special reformatories for young offenders prove that it is always possible to reform even young people so that they will stay reformed for any length of time. The analogy of the criminal law to medicine breaks down. The surgeon can determine with a fair degree of accuracy when there is an inflamed appendix or cancerous growth, so that by cutting it out he can remove a definite cause of distress. Is there in the complex of our social system any one cause of crime which any social physician can as readily remove on the basis of similarly verifiable knowledge?

Let us abandon the light-hearted pretension that any of us know how all cases of criminality can be readily cured, and ask the more modest and serious question: to what extent *can* criminals be re-educated or reconditioned so that they can live useful lives? It would indeed be illiberal dogmatism to deny all possibility and desirability of effort along this line. Yet we must keep in mind our human limitations.

If the causes of crime are determined by the life of certain groups, it is foolish to deal with the individual as if he were a self-sufficient and self-determining system. We must deal with the whole group to which he naturally belongs or gravitates and which determines his morale. Otherwise we have to adapt him completely to some other group or social condition, which is indeed a very difficult problem in social engineering.

And here we must not neglect the question of cost. When we refer to any measure as impracticable, we generally mean that the cost is too great. There is doubtless a tremendous expense in maintaining our present system of punishment. But this expense is not unlimited. Suppose that fiendish perpetrators of horrible crimes on children could be reformed by being sent first for several years to a special hospital. Will people vote large funds for such purposes when honest law-abiding citizens so often cannot get adequate hospital facilities? Suppose that we find that a certain social environment or that an elaborate college course will reform a burglar or gunman, would our community stand for the expense when so many worthy young people cannot afford to go to college because they have to go to work? We certainly should not give even the appearance of reward for criminality. Let us not forget that there is always a natural resentment in any society against those who have attacked it. Will people be satisfied to see one who is guilty of horrible crimes simply reformed, and not give vent to the social horror and resentment against the miscreant?

MARTINSON, WHAT WORKS? — QUESTIONS AND ANSWERS ABOUT PRISON REFORM, 36 Pub. Interest 22, 22-25 (1974): One of the problems in the constant debate over "prison reform" is that we have been able to draw very little on any systematic empirical knowledge about the success or failure that we have met when we *have* tried to rehabilitate offenders, with various treatments and in various institutional and non-institutional settings. The field of penology has produced a voluminous research literature on this subject, but until recently there has been no comprehensive review of this literature and no attempt to bring its findings to bear, in a useful way, on the general question of "What works?" My purpose in this essay is to sketch an answer to that question. . . .

What we set out to do in this study was fairly simple, though it turned into a massive task. First we undertook a six-month search of the literature for any available reports published in the English language on attempts at rehabilitation that had been made in our corrections systems and those of other countries from 1945 through 1967. We then picked from that literature all those studies whose findings were interpretable — that is, whose design and execution met the conventional standards of social science research. . . . [W]e drew from the total number of studies 231 acceptable ones, which we not only analyzed ourselves but summarized in detail so that a reader of our analysis would be able to compare it with his independent conclusions.

These treatment studies use various measures of offender improvement: recidivism rates (that is, the rates at which offenders return to crime), adjustment to prison life, vocational success, educational achievement, personality and attitude change, and general adjustment to the outside community. We included all of these in our study; but in these pages I will deal only with the effects of rehabilitative treatment on recidivism, the phenomenon which reflects most directly how well our present treatment programs are performing the task of rehabilitation. The use of even this one measure brings with it enough methodological complications to make a clear reporting of the findings most difficult. The groups that are studied, for instance, are exceedingly disparate, so that it is hard to tell whether what "works" for one kind of offender also works for others. In addition, there has been little attempt to replicate studies; therefore one cannot be certain how stable and reliable the various findings are. Just as important, when the various studies use the term "recidivism rate," they may in fact be talking about somewhat different measures of offender behavior — i.e., "failure" measures such as arrest rates or parole violation rates, or "success" measures such as favorable discharge from parole or probation. And not all of these measures correlate very highly with one another. These difficulties will become apparent again and again in the course of this discussion.

With these caveats, it is possible to give a rather bald summary of our findings: *With few and isolated exceptions, the rehabilitative efforts that have been reported so far have had no appreciable effect on recidivism.* Studies that have been done since our survey was completed do not present any major grounds for altering that original conclusion.

NOTE

It is indicative of the primitive state of our understanding of these matters that the findings of subsequent research led Martinson to recant. In Martinson, New Findings, New Views: A Note of Caution Regarding Sentencing Reform, 7 Hofstra L. Rev. 243, 252-254 (1979), he wrote:

> Any conclusion in scientific inquiry is held provisionally, subject to further evidence. . . . [N]ew evidence from our current study leads me to reject my original conclusion and suggest an alternative more adequate to the facts at hand. . . .
>
> Different procedures were used in the two surveys. ECT [The Effectiveness of Correctional Treatment, Martinson's earlier book] is based primarily on the findings of evaluation research — a special kind of research which was applied to criminal justice on a wide scale for the first time in California during the period immediately following World War II. This research is experimental — that is, offenders are often randomly allocated to treatment and nontreatment groups so that comparison can be made of outcome. Our current study, however, compares the reprocessing rates of groups receiving treatment with roughly comparable groups who receive the "standard processing" given to most offenders across the United States. . . .
>
> In brief, ECT focused on summarizing evaluation research which purported to uncover *causality;* in our current study we reject this perspective as premature and focus on uncovering *patterns* which can be of use to policymakers in choosing among available treatment programs. . . .
>
> . . . More precisely, treatments will be found to be "impotent" under certain conditions, beneficial under others, and detrimental under still others. The current study, by enabling us to uncover a major category of *harmful treatment,* is an advance on ECT. It enables us to indicate, at least roughly, the conditions under which a treatment program will fall into one of three categories: (1) beneficial (the program *reduces* reprocessing rates); (2) neutral (*no impact,* positive or negative, can be determined); and (3) deterimental (the program *increases* reprocessing rates).
>
> The most interesting general conclusion is that no treatment program now used

in criminal justice is inherently either substantially helpful or harmful. The critical fact seems to be the *conditions* under which the program is delivered.[29] For example, our results indicate that a widely-used program, such as formal education, is deterimental when given to juvenile sentenced offenders in a group home, but is beneficial (decreases reprocessing rates) when given to juveniles in juvenile prisons. Such startling results are found again and again in our study, for treatment programs as diverse as individual psychotherapy, group counseling, intensive supervision, and what we have called "individual/help" (aid, advice, counseling).

B.   IMPOSING PUNISHMENT

INTRODUCTORY NOTE

The preceding section suggested various purposes that could or should be served by punishment and introduced the continuing debate over the moral legitimacy and pragmatic effectiveness of using penal sanctions to pursue each of those purposes. The present section explores the implications of that debate and its many remaining uncertainties for the concrete decision that must be made now, while the scientific and philosophical inquiries proceed: What sentence should be imposed in this case, today?

A few words are necessary about the institutional setting in which this question arises. Until very recently, the punishment decision was for practical purposes entrusted largely to the discretion of the trial judge. Statutory limits on sentences, the charging authority of the prosecutor, and the releasing authority of the parole board qualified the trial judge's power in important ways, but the individual judge retained primary control over the penalty to be inflicted. That situation probably still prevails today in a majority of the states, but a significant and growing minority have moved to limit the trial judge's power (1) by narrowing the range of penalties authorized by statute, (2) by establishing an administrative agency to promulgate guidelines channeling the choice of sentence in particular cases, (3) by providing for appellate review of trial court sentencing, or (4) by some combination of these measures. Authority to determine the actual punishment has always been divided to some degree, and today the divisions are perhaps more complex and less uniform among the states than in the past.

For present purposes we put to one side these complex questions about how sentencing authority should be distributed and focus solely on the question of what punishment ought to be imposed in given cases by society's authorized decisionmaking body, whoever or whatever it may be. Since, in practice, that authority usually has been the trial judge, we choose cases, some typical and some not-so-typical, in which the decision about punishment lies essentially in the judge's hands. We want to examine what factors the judge should or should not consider, what arguments and what factual matters should be developed by the prosecutor and the defense, and what decision should be reached on

29. Controlling for these conditions in a regression analysis indicates that some treatments added to criminal justice do have overall effects. These effects are not large and many of them are unstable. In general, treatments added account for less than three percent of the variance in reprocessing rates. It is the effect of treatment given at certain "locations" that prompts me to withdraw my previous conclusion.

the merits. Exploration of these problems provides an essential foundation for considering the related issues of how crimes should be defined and graded (the subject of Chapters 4 to 11) as well as for examining the intricate institutional questions of whether sentencing authority should be distributed in different fashion or subjected to more extensive controls (the subject of Chapter 12).

UNITED STATES v. BERGMAN
United States District Court, S.D.N.Y.
416 F. Supp. 496 (1976)

FRANKEL, J. Defendant is being sentenced upon his plea of guilty to two counts of an 11-count indictment. The sentencing proceeding is unusual in some respects. It has been the subject of more extensive submissions, written and oral, than this court has ever received upon such an occasion. The court has studied some hundreds of pages of memoranda and exhibits, plus scores of volunteered letters. A broad array of issues has been addressed. Imaginative suggestions of law and penology have been tendered. A preliminary conversation with counsel, on the record, preceded the usual sentencing hearing. Having heard counsel again and the defendant speaking for himself, the court postponed the pronouncement of sentence for further reconsideration of thoughts generated during the days of studying the briefs and oral pleas. It seems fitting now to report in writing the reasons upon which the court concludes that defendant must be sentenced to a term of four months in prison.

DEFENDANT AND HIS CRIMES

Defendant appeared until the last couple of years to be a man of unimpeachably high character, attainments, and distinction. A doctor of divinity and an ordained rabbi, he has been acclaimed by people around the world for his works of public philanthropy, private charity, and leadership in educational enterprises. Scores of letters have come to the court from across this and other countries reporting debts of personal gratitude to him for numerous acts of extraordinary generosity. (The court has also received a kind of petition, with fifty-odd signatures, in which the signers, based upon learning acquired as newspaper readers, denounce the defendant and urge a severe sentence. Unlike the pleas for mercy, which appear to reflect unquestioned facts inviting compassion, this document should and will be disregarded.) In addition to his good works, defendant has managed to amass considerable wealth in the ownership and operation of nursing homes, in real estate ventures, and in a course of substantial investments.

Beginning about two years ago, investigations of nursing homes in this area, including questions of fraudulent claims for Medicaid funds, drew to a focus upon this defendant among several others. The results that concern us were the present indictment and two state indictments. After extensive pretrial proceedings defendant embarked upon elaborate plea negotiations with both state and federal prosecutors. A state guilty plea and the instant plea were entered in March of this year. (Another state indictment is expected to be dismissed after defendant is sentenced on those to which he has pled guilty.) As part of the detailed plea arrangements, it is expected that the prison sentence imposed by this court will comprise the total covering the state as well as the federal convictions.

For purposes of the sentence now imposed, the precise details of the charges, and of defendant's carefully phrased admissions of guilt, are not matters of prime importance. Suffice it to say that the plea on Count One (carrying a maximum of five years in prison and a $10,000 fine) confesses defendant's knowing and wilful participation in a scheme to defraud the United States in various ways, including the presentation of wrongfully padded claims for payments under the Medicaid program to defendant's nursing homes. Count Three, for which the guilty plea carries a theoretical maximum of three more years in prison and another $5,000 fine, is a somewhat more "technical" charge. Here, defendant admits to having participated in the filing of a partnership return which was false and fraudulent in failing to list people who had bought partnership interests from him in one of his nursing homes, had paid for such interests, and had made certain capital withdrawals.

The conspiracy to defraud, as defendant has admitted it, is by no means the worst of its kind; it is by no means as flagrant or extensive as has been portrayed in the press; it is evidently less grave than other nursing-home wrongs for which others have been convicted or publicized. At the same time, the sentence, as defendant has acknowledged, is imposed for two federal felonies including, as the more important, a knowing and purposeful conspiracy to mislead and defraud the Federal Government.

The Guiding Principles of Sentencing

Proceeding through the short list of the supposed justifications for criminal sanctions, defense counsel urge that no licit purpose could be served by defendant's incarceration. Some of these arguments are plainly sound; others are not.

The court agrees that this defendant should not be sent to prison for "rehabilitation." Apart from the patent inappositeness of the concept to this individual, this court shares the growing understanding that no one should ever be sent to prison *for rehabilitation.* That is to say, nobody who would not otherwise be locked up should suffer that fate on the incongruous premise that it will be good for him or her. Imprisonment is punishment. Facing the simple reality should help us to be civilized. It is less agreeable to confine someone when we deem it an affliction rather than a benefaction. If someone must be imprisoned — for other, valid reasons — we should seek to make rehabilitative resources available to him or her. But the goal of rehabilitation cannot fairly serve in itself as grounds for the sentence to confinement.[3]

Equally clearly, this defendant should not be confined to incapacitate him. He is not dangerous. It is most improbable that he will commit similar, or any, offenses in the future. There is no need for "specific deterrence."

---

3. This important point, correcting misconceptions still widely prevalent, is developed more fully by Dean Norval Morris in The Future of Imprisonment (1974).

Contrary to counsel's submissions, however, two sentencing considerations demand a prison sentence in this case:

First, the aim of *general deterrence,* the effort to discourage similar wrongdoing by others through a reminder that the law's warnings are real and that the grim consequence of imprisonment is likely to follow from crimes of deception for gain like those defendant has admitted.

Second, the related, but not identical, concern that any lesser penalty would, in the words of the Model Penal Code, §7.01(1)(c), "depreciate the seriousness of the defendant's crime."

Resisting the first of these propositions, defense counsel invoke Immanuel Kant's axiom that "one man ought never to be dealt with merely as a means subservient to the purposes of another." [4] In a more novel, but equally futile, effort, counsel urge that a sentence for general deterrence "would violate the Eighth Amendment proscription against cruel and unusual punishment." Treating the latter point first, because it is a short subject, it may be observed simply that if general deterrence as a sentencing purpose were now to be outlawed, as against a near unanimity of views among state and federal jurists, the bolt would have to come from a place higher than this.

As for Dr. Kant, it may well be that defense counsel mistake his meaning in the present context.[6] Whether or not that is so, and without pretending to authority on that score, we take the widely accepted stance that a criminal punished in the interest of general deterrence is not being employed "*merely* as a means. . . ." Reading Kant to mean that every man must be deemed *more* than the instrument of others, and must "always be treated as an end in himself," [7] the humane principle is not offended here. Each of us is served by the enforcement of the law — not least a person like the defendant in this case, whose wealth and privileges, so long enjoyed, are so much founded upon law. More broadly, we are driven regularly in our ultimate interests as members of the community to use ourselves and each other, in war and in peace, for social ends. One who has transgressed against the criminal laws is certainly among the more fitting candidates for a role of this nature. This is no arbitrary selection. Warned in advance of the prospect, the transgressor has chosen, in the law's premises, "between keeping the law required for society's protection or paying the penalty." [8]

But the whole business, defendant argues further, is guesswork; we are by no means certain that deterrence "works." The position is somewhat overstated; there is, in fact, some reasonably "scientific" evidence for the efficacy of criminal sanctions as deterrents, at least as against some kinds of crimes.[9] Moreover, the time is not yet here when all we can "know" must be quantifiable and digestible by computers. The shared wisdom of generations teaches meaningfully, if somewhat amorphously, that the utilitarians have a point; we do, indeed, lapse often into rationality and act to seek pleasure and avoid pain. It would be better, to be sure, if we had more certainty and precision. Lacking these

---

4. Quoting from I. Kant, Philosophy of Law 1986 (Hastie Trans. 1887).
6. See H. L. A. Hart, Punishment and Responsibility 243-44 (1968).
7. Andenaes, The Morality of Deterrence, 37 U. Chi. L. Rev. 649 (1970). See also O. Holmes, Common Law 43-44, 46-47 (1881).
8. H. L. A. Hart, supra note 6, at 23.
9. See, e.g., F. Zimring and G. Hawkins, Deterrence 168-71, 282 (1973).

comforts, we continue to include among our working hypotheses a belief (with some concrete evidence in its support) that crimes like those in this case — deliberate, purposeful, continuing, non-impulsive, and committed for profit — are among those most likely to be generally deterrable by sanctions most shunned by those exposed to temptation.

The idea of avoiding depreciation of the seriousness of the offense implicates two or three thoughts, not always perfectly clear or universally agreed upon, beyond the idea of deterrence. It should be proclaimed by the court's judgment that the offenses are grave, not minor or purely technical. Some attention must be paid to the demand for equal justice; it will not do to leave the penalty of imprisonment a dead letter as against "privileged" violators while it is employed regularly, and with vigor, against others. There probably is in these conceptions an element of retributiveness, as counsel urge. And retribution, so denominated, is in some disfavor as a reason for punishment. It remains a factor, however, as Holmes perceived, and as is known to anyone who talks to judges, lawyers, defendants, or people generally. It may become more palatable, and probably more humanely understood, under the rubric of "deserts" or "just deserts." [13] However the concept is formulated, we have not yet reached a state, supposing we ever should, in which the infliction of punishments for crime may be divorced generally from ideas of blameworthiness, recompense, and proportionality.

AN ALTERNATIVE, "BEHAVIORAL SANCTION"

Resisting prison above all else, defense counsel included in their thorough memorandum on sentencing two proposals for what they call a "constructive," and therefore a "preferable" form of "behavioral sanction." One is a plan for Dr. Bergman to create and run a program of Jewish vocational and religious high school training. The other is for him to take charge of a "Committee on Holocaust Studies," again concerned with education at the secondary school level.

A third suggestion was made orally at yesterday's sentencing hearing. It was proposed that Dr. Bergman might be ordered to work as a volunteer in some established agency as a visitor and aide to the sick and the otherwise incapacitated. The proposal was that he could read, provide various forms of physical assistance, and otherwise give comfort to afflicted people.

No one can doubt either the worthiness of these proposals or Dr. Bergman's ability to make successes of them. But both of the carefully formulated "sanctions" in the memorandum involve work of an honorific nature, not unlike that done in other projects to which the defendant has devoted himself in the past. It is difficult to conceive of them as "punishments" at all. The more recent proposal is somewhat more suitable in character, but it is still an insufficient penalty. The seriousness of the crimes to which Dr. Bergman has pled guilty demands something more than "requiring" him to lend his talents and efforts to further philanthropic enterprises. It remains open to him, of course, to pursue the interesting suggestions later on as a matter of unforced personal choice.

13. See A. von Hirsch, Doing Justice 45-55 (1976); see also N. Morris, The Future of Imprisonment 73-77 (1974).

"Measuring" the Sentence

In cases like this one, the decision of greatest moment is whether to imprison or not. As reflected in the eloquent submissions for defendant, the prospect of the closing prison doors is the most appalling concern; the feeling is that the length of the sojourn is a lesser question once that threshold is passed. Nevertheless, the setting of a term remains to be accomplished. And in some respects it is a subject even more perplexing, unregulated, and unprincipled.

Days and months and years are countable with a sound of exactitude. But there can be no exactitude in the deliberations from which a number emerges. Without pretending to a nonexistent precision, the court notes at least the major factors.

The criminal behavior, as has been noted, is blatant in character and unmitigated by any suggestion of necessitous circumstance or other pressures difficult to resist. However metaphysicians may conjure with issues about free will, it is a fundamental premise of our efforts to do criminal justice that competent people, possessed of their faculties, make choices and are accountable for them. In this sometimes harsh light, the case of the present defendant is among the clearest and least relieved. Viewed against the maxima Congress ordained, and against the run of sentences in other federal criminal cases, it calls for more than a token sentence.[14]

On the other side are factors that take longer to enumerate. Defendant's illustrious public life and works are in his favor, though diminished, of course, by what this case discloses. This is a first, probably a last, conviction. Defendant is 64 years old and in imperfect health, though by no means so ill, from what the court is told, that he could be expected to suffer inordinately more than many others of advanced years who go to prison. . . .

How, then, the particular sentence adjudged in this case? As has been mentioned, the case calls for a sentence that is more than nominal. Given the other circumstances, however — including that this is a first offense, by a man no longer young and not perfectly well, where danger of recidivism is not a concern — it verges on cruelty to think of confinement for a term of years. We sit, to be sure, in a nation where prison sentences of extravagant length are more common than they are almost anywhere else. By that light, the term imposed today is not notably long. For this sentencing court, however, for a nonviolent first offense involving no direct assaults or invasions of others' security (as in bank robbery, narcotics, etc.), it is a stern sentence. For people like Dr. Bergman, who might be disposed to engage in similar wrongdoing, it should be sufficiently frightening to serve the major end of general deterrence. For all but the profoundly vengeful, it should not depreciate the seriousness of his offenses.

---

14. Despite Biblical teachings concerning what is expected from those to whom much is given, the court has not, as his counsel feared might happen, held Dr. Bergman to a higher standard of responsibility because of his position in the community. But he has not been judged under a lower standard either.

Much of defendant's sentencing memorandum is devoted to the extensive barrage of hostile publicity to which he has been subjected during the years before and since his indictment. He argues, and it appears to be undisputed, that the media (and people desiring to be featured in the media) have vilified him for many kinds of evildoing of which he has in fact been innocent. Two main points are made on this score with respect to the problem of sentencing.

First, as has been mentioned, counsel express the concern that the court may be pressured toward severity by the force of the seeming public outcry. That the court should not allow itself to be affected in this way is clear beyond discussion. . . .

Defendant's second point about his public humiliation is the frequently heard contention that he should not be incarcerated because he "has been punished enough." The thought is not without some initial appeal. If punishment were wholly or mainly retributive, it might be a weighty factor. In the end, however, it must be a matter of little or no force. Defendant's notoriety should not in the last analysis serve to lighten, any more than it may be permitted to aggravate, his sentence. The fact that he has been pilloried by journalists is essentially a consequence of the prestige and privileges he enjoyed before he was exposed as a wrongdoer. The long fall from grace was possible only because of the height he had reached. The suffering from loss of public esteem reflects a body of opinion that the esteem had been, in at least some measure, wrongly bestowed and enjoyed. It is not possible to justify the notion that this mode of nonjudicial punishment should be an occasion for leniency not given to a defendant who never basked in such an admiring light at all. The quest for both the appearance and the substance of equal justice prompts the court to discount the thought that the public humiliation serves the function of imprisonment.

Writing, as judges rarely do, about a particular sentence concentrates the mind with possibly special force upon the experience of the sentencer as well as the person sentenced. Consigning someone to prison, this defendant or any other, "is a sad necessity." There are impulses of avoidance from time to time — toward a personally gratifying leniency or toward an opposite extreme. But there is, obviously, no place for private impulse in the judgment of the court. The course of justice must be sought with such objective rationality as we can muster, tempered with mercy, but obedient to the law, which, we do well to remember, is all that empowers a judge to make other people suffer.

WICKER, A PENALTY THAT FITS MR. CHAPIN
N.Y. Times, Apr. 7, 1974, at E17

Richard Nixon's former appointments secretary, Dwight Chapin, has been found guilty of lying to a grand jury and on May 16 he will be sentenced to what could be ten years in prison and a $20,000 fine. Judge Gerhard A. Gesell, a humane and sensible man, probably will not impose a penalty as severe as that, but if he were another judge, he could.

What is the point of such Draconian provisions in the law? Mr. Chapin's offense — that he lied to a grand jury about the kind of instructions and direction he gave Donald H. Segretti in Mr. Segretti's 1972 "dirty tricks" campaign — is of course a serious one, the more so in that Mr. Chapin was a high and privileged Government official at the time he committed it. But does locking him up in a prison, for whatever period, really make any sense?

Mr. Chapin is not dangerous or violent. He is not a habitual lawbreaker or a chattel of organized crime. Putting him behind bars would chasten, humiliate and severely punish him, but what other purpose would it serve? Isn't there something more useful to be done in his and thousands of other cases?

Since United Air Lines has said it would ask Mr. Chapin to resign his executive position if he was convicted, probably the imposition of a heavy fine also would be a severe penalty for Mr. Chapin. In general, the fine as appropriate punishment is not often enough used in the United States; in Britain, the installment payment of heavy fines has been instituted, enabling offenders to remain at their jobs and several prisons to be closed.

This is not intended as an argument that a white-collar lawbreaker or an affluent offender with good political connections ought to be let off more lightly than, say, a ghetto street mugger. Rather, it is to raise the question whether incarceration makes sense for either kind of offender, unless he or she is known to be so violent or so habitually criminal that society can be protected only by physical separation.

It is a singular circumstance that the United States has the most severe criminal sentences of any Western nation, imposes the most prison terms, and still has more crime and more violence than any other. In startling contrast is the fact that since the early nineteen-sixties, the prison population of the Netherlands has been cut in half, while the crime rate rose only 10 percent. In the same period in this country, the annual rate of violent crime more than doubled, from less than 200 to about 400 per 100,000 population. Serious property crime almost tripled in the same years.

There is little logic, therefore, in the automatic assumption of American society that people convicted of crimes should be sent to prison; or in the nearly automatic workings of the criminal justice system — save in the case of white-collar offenders — to see that those convicted go to prison. Parole, moreover, while aimed at getting people out of prison, is so fearfully and punitively administered as to keep many inmates behind the walls far longer than necessary, and to send many others back for the slightest offense.

A system that worked the other way around would make far more sense. The assumption should be that people go to prison only as a final resort, when there appears no alternative for the protection of society; and the system should be so designed as to give judges great latitude in deciding upon an appropriate penalty, and sufficient resources to aid them in reaching a decision useful to the offender and to society alike.

A letter-writer to The New York Times proposed, for a somewhat analogous example, that the State of Maryland should not disbar Spiro T. Agnew from the practice of law; rather it should require him to devote a certain portion of his practice, for a considerable length of time, to community service legal work — that his penalty should be the devotion of part of his talents and profession to the good of society.

Would something of that kind not make more sense in the case of Dwight Chapin? In addition to a severe fine, Judge Gesell might require him to use his undoubted abilities and knowledge of government in some public service capacity until he made adequate restitution to society for having broken its trust.

For that matter, a young street mugger could well be treated in the same way; if work and training were provided so that he might repay his victims and find a useful place for himself, there would be a reasonable chance that he would not revert to a criminal life.

In some instances, the criminal justice system does seem to be moving slowly away from automatic imprisonment; but the case of Dwight Chapin suggests how heavily the law leans toward locking up offenders, whether or not it makes sense.

NOTES

1. Judge Gesell sentenced Chapin to a prison term of not less than 10 nor more than 30 months, commenting that he had imposed "a punishment sentence for a man who is not likely to repeat and needs no rehabilitation." N.Y. Times, May 16, 1974, at 1. Later the judge reduced the sentence to a 6-18 month term, with a recommendation that Chapin be paroled as soon as the minimum term was served. N.Y. Times, Dec. 23, 1975, at 31. Chapin was eventually released on parole after serving 7 months and 22 days. N.Y. Times, Apr. 3, 1976, at 20.

2. An approach similar to that favored by Wicker, "that people go to prison only as a final resort," is endorsed by the Model Penal Code, which adopts a formal preference for sentences other than imprisonment. See §7.01, Appendix to this casebook. The American Bar Association has approved a similar presumption against incarceration. See American Bar Association, Standards for Criminal Justice, Sentencing Alternatives and Procedures, §18-2.5(c) (2d ed. 1980).

The reasons underlying the Model Penal Code approach are set forth in Wechsler, Sentencing, Correction and the Model Penal Code, 109 U. Pa. L. Rev. 465, 471-472 (1961):

> The grounds of policy that warrant thus according a priority to dispositions which forego an institutional commitment by conditional suspension or probation are not difficult to state. No other mode of sentence serves as many of the values that are relevant on the analysis set forth above. The judgment and the order give expressive voice to the community's collective condemnation of the conduct constituting the defendant's crime and the insensitivity to the demands of social life that it implies upon his part. It is made clear that he has forfeited his independence and subjected himself to direction and control of the sort that the immature must have. At the same time, as Henry Hart has said, the regime thus established "can provide an environment favorable to rehabilitation, both by conveying to the defendant a sense of the community's confidence in his ability to live responsibly and by giving him a special incentive to do so." A well equipped probation service, drawing on community resources, can supply both help and guidance of the sort that it is difficult to give in institutions. The inevitable negative results of a commitment in terms of poor associations, on the one hand, and the loss of usefulness, upon the other, are of course avoided. Finally, but certainly not least important, the burden upon public budgets is reduced to a small fraction of the cost of an imprisonment.

Were it not for the accident of history that prisons emerged as a humane substitute for death or transportation, which had previously been the normal fate of criminals, would the sense that imprisonment is somehow the right penal sanction, rather than the grave exception, ever have attained the influence it has? Practice has now come close to the correction of this most unfortunate inversion. The Code provision would articulate and ratify what the best practice already has achieved.

3. The trend referred to by Professor Wechsler appears to be accelerating. Of 1.2 million offenders in American correctional systems on an average day in 1965, 53 percent were on probation. President's Commission on Law Enforcement and the Administration of Justice, Task Force Report: Corrections 27 (1967). The Commission projected that by 1975, 58 percent of all offenders would be sentenced to probation. But a 1974 study found that in four localities surveyed, on the average 77 percent of all adult offenders were sentenced to probation. See American Bar Association, Standards for Criminal Justice, Sentencing Alternatives and Procedures, Standard 18-2.3, Commentary at 18-77 (2d ed. 1980).

PROBLEM

Would a sentence of imprisonment have been justified in the Chapin case if the specific standards of Model Penal Code §7.01 had been applicable? How helpful is statutory guidance of this kind? How could a statutory presumption against imprisonment be drafted in order to reflect more closely the kind of approach favored, for example, by Wicker?

BROWDER v. UNITED STATES, 398 F. Supp. 1042 (D. Or. 1975): [Browder pleaded guilty to a series of indictments charging that he had transported and pledged stolen securities worth over $500,000. He was sentenced to four 10-year terms and one 5-year term, with a total of 25 years to run consecutively. Subsequently he filed a petition seeking to have the sentence set aside as cruel and unusual punishment and as a violation of the equal protection clause. Rejecting the petition, the court wrote:]

Edward Browder is a 53 year old man with extensive business experience in promotion and sales. He has a college background in aeronautical engineering. His testimony on the witness stand revealed a degree of intelligence and a facility with the English language that would be the pride of most attorneys. The quality of his in forma pauperis brief enhances that observation.

In 1958 Mr. Browder somehow became involved with organized crime. A crime syndicate apparently stole the bonds which he was indicted for transporting and pledging. Browder alleges that in 1967 or 1968 he attempted to sever his connections with the syndicate. . . .

The basis for petitioner's claim is a study he conducted of 100 cases involving similar white collar crimes. If accurate, his study contains startling statistics. Of the 100 defendants studied, 20% received fines, probation, or suspended sentences only for acts involving $350,000,000 or more. The others studied received light sentences for a variety of swindles in which the public became victim to members of the Mafia, labor union officials, mayors, attorneys, stock brokers, business executives, bankers, a former state Attorney General, a governor, a federal judge, and others.

I can only speculate on the motivations for sentences rendered in the individual cases listed. As Mr. Browder observes, "wherein the greater the offense against capital, the lesser the punishment imposed by the sentencing court." If Mr. Browder's study is accurate, the pattern of sentencing revealed is deplorable.

If there is a logic to this paradox, it eludes me. I cannot reconcile a policy of sending poorly educated burglars from the ghetto to jail when men in the highest positions of public trust and authority receive judicial coddling when they are caught fleecing their constituencies. Penology's recent enchantment with rehabilitation as a wholesale justification for imprisonment has dissolved in the face of numerous studies proving that rehabilitation rarely occurs. A minority of the prison population are rightfully locked up because they are too dangerous to release. If we are to justify imprisonment for the rest, it must be on the grounds of punishment or deterrence. And if this is our premise, the white collar criminal must come to expect equal or greater treatment than the common, non-violent thief. The consequences of a white collar property crime tend to reach a higher magnitude in direct proportion to the level of status and power held by the criminal involved. The men Browder studied abused their influence to defraud thousands of people throughout the country out of millions of dollars. Apparently this has been tolerated through light sentencing because of the staggering proportions of the crime.

The defect in Browder's reasoning is his conclusion that because other white collar criminals have been receiving disparate treatment, he should too. As a matter of law, I cannot review the propriety of the sentence he received. The sentence was within statutory limits. Therefore it was a constitutional product of the trial court's discretion. . . . The sentencing judge may have shared my dismay, and Browder's, at the pattern of white collar crime sentences. White collar crime pays. It will continue to do so as long as judges endorse it through their sentencing policy. . . .

Edward Browder was convicted of pledging over $500,000 worth of stolen securities. He concedes his guilt for those crimes. The fact that they were accomplished by means of wit and charm rather than a burglar's tool does not minimize the damage done to the public. The judge who sentenced Browder obviously shared that view. It is a tragedy, if Browder's study is accurate, that fewer judges — and not more of them — subscribe to it also.

1970 SENTENCING INSTITUTE FOR CALIFORNIA SUPERIOR COURT JUDGES,[1] CASE NO. 1

93 Cal. Rptr., Appendix at 25-36 (1970)

OFFENSE: BURGLARY SECOND. Defendant broke into a pharmacy and removed several containers of drugs from a locked cabinet. He was apprehended

---

1. This conference provides state trial judges an opportunity to discuss and compare their approaches to sentencing problems. The discussion is based on the actual file of a recent case, but the viewpoints of the participants and the "vote" taken by them do not affect the sentence imposed; a single judge (often one of the participants) has already made a definitive decision for the actual case. — EDS.

shortly thereafter and readily admitted the offense, and two others of a similar nature.

PRIOR CRIMINAL HISTORY:

1955-57	County X	Juvenile offenses	Probation
8/59	County X	Battery	5 days county jail
3/61	County X	Burglary	2 years probation
4/62	County X	Burglary	2 additional years probation, 60 days county jail
1/63	County X	11501 H. & S. Code [transportation or sale of narcotics]	Sent to California Rehabilitation Center
4/64	CRC	Released on parole	Discharged from parole in April 1967
3/70	County X	PRESENT OFFENSE	

CASE HISTORY INFORMATION: This 29-year-old man of Latin-American laboring class ancestry was born and raised in a large urban community in Southern California, the oldest of three children. He was 12 years old when his father died, and his mother subsequently supported the family by performing domestic labor, unskilled factory work and by welfare. One sister had been institutionalized in a mental hospital, while his youngest sister, now age 24, has become a nurse.

Defendant has an exceptionally high IQ and has done very well in high school and in college which he is currently attending during the day. As a youngster, he had a series of offenses as part of a juvenile gang including petty theft and burglary, for which he was made a ward of the court. He began using marijuana at the age of 15 and later graduated to using heroin. His offenses as a young adult were related to his narcotic addiction since he was stealing to try to finance his drug habit. Finally in 1963, he was committed to the California Rehabilitation Center where he spent the ensuing 15 months in treatment. Institutional officials at CRC commented favorably about his active involvement in the treatment program and he was paroled to a job in Northern California. Significantly he managed to refrain from the use of drugs for a three-year period, which led to his successful discharge from parole in 1967. Furthermore, in the almost two years since his discharge from parole there was no record of any offenses except the present ones.

He was married at the age of 19 and one child was born to that union. The marriage was dissolved after his son was born and he assumes full responsibility for not having sufficient maturity at the time to adequately act as a husband and father. When he has not been institutionalized, he has made efforts to contribute to the support of his child.

For the past three years, he has been working nights at a semiskilled job while attending college during the daytime. He has completed three and one-half years of college in business administration and his verified academic record is excellent. He hopes to become a business executive.

CASE EVALUATION: This is a young adult who, despite a poor start, has striven in recent years to assume a productive role in society. His present offense is related to narcotics which he started using again approximately three months ago. He is very bright and verbal and attributes his present predicament to an exceptionally stressful situation caused by the pressures of working full time coupled with keeping up with a demanding college program. He does not have a heavy drug habit at this time since he attempted to limit his drug use in his most recent encounter. His return to the CRC program is not recommended by the probation officer who prepared the court report on the grounds that he has derived all the benefits that their program has to offer. The District Attorney and arresting narcotics officer feel he is a menace to society and should be sent to prison. They note that he committed several offenses and would have committed more if he hadn't been caught. . . .

JUDGE WOODMANSEE: This is rather an extraordinary case history of a man who has a very high IQ and who has finished three and a half years of college. The present offense appears to be second-degree burglary.

He was apprehended and admitted everything and confessed to a couple of other similar burglaries. It is stated that he is not heavily addicted. But it would appear that he is rather desperate because he is knocking over these drugstores to get drugs.

I would place him on probation under intensive care and supervision with special antinarcotic conditions if such a program were available. If not, I would return him to the California Rehabilitation Center. I would not send him to state prison at this time.[a]

The probation officer recommended against a return to the California Rehabilitation Center; but it seems to me that worked for him initially. He was drug free for seven years. Obviously, if his drug problem can be controlled, society will be protected and he will be rehabilitated. The question is how best to accomplish those ends. If he were sent to state prison, with that record he would probably be released on parole in a relatively short period. I think the California Rehabilitation Center facility would probably keep him just as long, retain him on parole just as long, and would probably cope with his problems better. But if there was an intensive care unit of the probation department in

a. Under the California sentencing system in effect at the time (since superseded by a determinate-sentence system), the trial judge could not fix the term of incarceration for offenders sent to state prison after conviction for a felony. The offender was deemed to be serving the maximum sentence authorized by statute, usually a very long term. The California Adult Authority would then determine the period that the offender would serve in confinement and on parole, with the total time falling anywhere within the statutory maximum.

In order to avoid remitting an offender to the discretion of the Adult Authority and thus exposing him to the possibility of an extremely severe sentence, the state trial judges could resort principally to two devices. First, they could acquit the offender of the felony charge but find him guilty of some lesser included misdemeanor. For a misdemeanor the judge was permitted to grant probation, fix a specific period of incarceration (usually not to exceed one year) to be served in the county jail, or impose some combination of county jail time, followed by probation. Second, the judge could convict on the felony charge but grant probation rather than a state prison sentence. The judge could then require as a "condition of probation" that the offender serve a fixed period (up to one year) in the county jail. By this device the judge could insure a felony conviction and a substantial period of incarceration, while at the same time circumventing the control of the Adult Authority. — EDS.

the county, I believe I would place him on probation under certain specified terms and conditions to see if he could make it on the outside. . . .

As a term of probation I would commit him to the county jail for probably 120 days to dry him out so that he would get over his present craving for narcotics and then I would impose the usual terms of probation. In this case I would make a condition of probation that he consent to searches of his person and property by any peace officer at any time without warrant and without probable cause. I would explain carefully my reasons for this. I do not do this routinely in all narcotic cases but I would state to him that I felt it would help him in his rehabilitation if he knew that his person and property were subject to search at any time and therefore I thought he would be less likely to hold or possess narcotics.

This type of condition of probation is not very popular with probation officers or with defense attorneys. The first time I used it where I thought it was justified, the defense attorney hit the ceiling. But I would refer him to the *Kern* case and to the *Fitzpatrick* case, which is a recent case in 3 Cal. App. 3d 824, and I would explain exactly what my motive was. I would also tell him that if he feels he has been harassed at any time by law enforcement officers he could petition the court for modification.[b]

And, of course, one of the conditions of probation to provide intensive care and treatment would be that he be subjected to periodic and unannounced nalline tests.

I think that under such a probationary order the court would then have ample options left. If the defendant failed on probation you could still do anything you wanted. You would probably find out about any lapses if you would require the probation officer to make periodic progress reports in this case.

JUDGE DREIZEN: As I analyze the facts, we've got a man who has committed his third burglary; he's been placed on probation twice. He has a background of juvenile problems having received probation then. He has also been sent to the California Rehabilitation Center and with all due respect to their rehabilitation programs, that did not succeed.

I feel that it's just a question of whether or not you're going to send him to state prison or give him county jail time. I don't think that probation has helped this man and I don't think the crime, burglary second, based on his background and his present case history, is serious enough to send him to prison. But I would not put him on probation. I would give him probably a year in the county jail.

JUDGE NIELSEN: I think he's gotten a lot from the original California Rehabilitation Center commitment and he's come awfully close to making it under very adverse conditions. He's been working full time and has exceptional grades in college during this period. I agree with Judge Woodmansee. . . .

---

b. Most courts continue to uphold the legality of subjecting probationers to searches without probable cause and without a warrant, even though such searches plainly would be illegal if not for the probationary status of the person searched. See, e.g., Latta v. Fitzharris, 521 F.2d 246 (9th Cir. 1975) (search must be conducted by parole officer, not by police, but may be based on mere "hunch"); People v. Mason, 5 Cal. 3d 759, 488 P.2d 630 (1971) (search by police officer upheld without probable cause or warrant). A few recent decisions are to the contrary. E.g., United States v. Bradley, 571 F.2d 787 (4th Cir. 1978) (warrant required for search of parolee's room). See generally White, The Fourth Amendment Rights of Parolees and Probationers, 31 U. Pitt. L. Rev. 167 (1969). — EDS.

JUDGE ARNASON: For whatever it may be worth I wouldn't reward this guy with a misdemeanor. I would put him on felony probation. I would put him in the county jail for a period of time and I would require him to participate in our narcotic treatment program, which while it is not altogether effective at least provides some semblance of support. I would want him to be on probation for about three years and if he didn't make it on probation then he would at least be faced with a felony. He's been dealt with, I think, very leniently since 1957 when he obviously was about fourteen years of age. . . .

JUDGE DREIZEN: . . . My opposition to using probation in itself is that it has been a failure. I think the facts make that plain. If I were going to go the straight felony route I would sentence him to prison and suspend it for a period of three to five years. You could add conditions with respect to treatment and with respect to confinement in the county jail, say six months or a year. I think he has not really been sentenced for the previous crimes that he has committed, and this might in some way rehabilitate him. The judges who have commented they want further treatment for this man believe in it, which is very good. But the prognosis is poor.

JUDGE WILSON: I disagree with the finding that probation has been a failure. If you look at his history, you'll see that probation has been given at a time when he was very young. On the other hand, after he left the California Rehabilitation Center program, where he was on parole for a period of about three years, he did very well under supervision. He also did well without supervision and, it seems to me this man came very close to succeeding. He seems to do well, especially since he's become an adult, under supervision. In view of the stress he's been under just prior to this most recent offense, perhaps an additional period of probation might be just enough to really take him over the hump.

JUDGE SMITH: This man needs someone with whom he can identify. He has to improve his self-image; that's the central problem here. It may well be the probation officer didn't have the time to do that, and this raises a pretty critical problem. I agree that he should be under intensive supervision, but the question is how intensive is the intensive care unit? Actually, their case load is greater than it should be and the case load of the regular probation officer is greater than it should be. It seems to me here is an individual who could be helped, say, by the aid of a citizen group or by having some citizen working with the probation officer in the intensive care unit. If we could have the assistance of volunteer citizens in our community to help with these problems we would be able to do something about preventing an individual like this from coming before us in the criminal courts.

JUDGE McCOURTNEY: I feel this particular individual epitomizes a good many of the defendants and the type of offenses we have coming before us. As far as I can see, every offense here is in relation to his drug habit with the possible exception of one battery. I don't know what that involved but he only got five days in the county jail, so it must not have been too aggravated.

I feel strongly that this is the type of individual that you try to help rather than rely only on punishment. In so saying, I'm not condoning his offenses. I would be very opposed to giving a felony sentence. He's been working nights and he's within one-half year of getting a degree. This is a man who's really trying to help himself, and we want to give him all the assistance we can to become a productive member of society. I don't think that you do it by pinning a felony record on him. This is the type of person that you should give six months in the county jail to, to really dry him out, and then give him probation so that he could possibly rehabilitate himself. The only limiting factor I might have on the sentence would be to determine when he could best return to college to finish his education. I would presume that his education would have been interrupted by the time we got to trial. But we ought to get him back as soon as he is psychologically and emotionally able to resume the burdens. . . .

JUDGE GOLDSTEIN: . . . We had a meeting only yesterday with the head of the department of pharmacology at Stanford, who is very much interested in the use of this drug methadone, which permits people to work and function in society. It's an addictive drug that replaces heroin in the system and destroys the desire for heroin. But this drug seems to have a remarkable effect on heroin addicts. . . . I think this fellow's basic problem is simply drug addiction. He has never been able to keep it in remission very long. He is off for a few years but goes back to it again. He hasn't been cured.

MR. STUTSMAN (Chief Deputy Director, Department of Corrections): Now, I would agree that this man needs some more control. And when we evaluate our California Rehabilitation Center program we're becoming more aware that it's not so important what we do inside the institution as what we do when he gets back out in the community. And we make efforts to provide some support in the community and get people involved to help. If you have a probation department that has this kind of a program, I'd go right along with giving him probation. I believe the only reason this man stayed out is because someone was looking down his throat and controlling him for three or four years out there. When that crutch was taken away from him, he could not make it. . . .

Methadone is a very controversial program, as you are well aware. . . . We think one of the keys to success with methadone is selection. If you're going to addict a person — and this is really what you do with methadone — if you do it to some guy who has been on drugs for five or six years, I don't think it's any great problem. Of course, if you have somebody who hasn't had a lot of drug experience, you might want to think twice, and at least try some other things first. We're going to get some experience with this and we have some research set up to follow it. But there are a lot of people in our narcotics evaluation authority, which is the group that handles CRC releases, who won't go with this program. . . .

JUDGE HOLMES: Out of the dozens of probation reports that I've read in recent weeks I would say this is probably the most affirmative and most favorable that I've seen. In other words, to me this man has a great deal of potentiality. There is apparently a history of mental illness in this family. His sister is in a mental hospital. Before you undertook to pass judgment upon this man, would it not be desirable to have some kind of diagnostic study made to determine whether perhaps what is standing in his way may be some kind of a surmountable mental block? He comes so close to being a useful and productive citizen that I think jail is the wrong place for him. The CRC program has not been able to accomplish its purpose. Is there possibly some other and unrelated area that can be investigated in the field of his mental condition?

JUDGE ARNASON: What are you suggesting, a P.C. Section 1203.03 referral,[c] or something like that?

c. Cal. Penal Code §1203.03 provides that whenever a defendant is convicted of an offense punishable by a state prison sentence, if the court "concludes that a just disposition of the case requires such diagnosis and treatment services as can be provided at a diagnostic facility of the Department

JUDGE HOLMES: That's right. . . .

JUDGE DREIZEN: . . . [I]f you put this man on probation I think you're overlooking one important aspect and that is, what deterrent is this to the public generally. How does it reflect on the judiciary to put a man on probation who has committed three burglaries within a period of nine years?

I agree we should try to rehabilitate him. But I think you've got a hopeless case. I really think that when you're sentencing such a case you should keep in mind what deterrent is it going to be to the public to have the papers print that a man who has been convicted of three burglaries is still being granted probation. . . .

JUDGE ARNASON: Why don't we take a vote? Is there anybody here in favor of the state prison sentence outright? Nobody is in favor of state prison, in this case.

How many are in favor of straight county jail sentence as distinguished from felony probation with county jail? Any people favor that straight county jail, which means giving him a misdemeanor? One.

How many are in favor of felony probation with no jail?

How many in favor of felony probation with county jail, various times? Eleven.

How many for CRC? . . . Two.

JUDGE WOODMANSEE: As I indicated, intensive care and supervision probation if available; otherwise, CRC.

JUDGE ARNASON: All right, we'll give it three. . . .

JUDGE ARNASON: The point raised at the very end here is an extremely important one. I think you would have a hard time in a lot of communities were the paper to pick up a case of burglary of a drugstore by a three-time burglary and narcotic addict who was granted probation. If you appeared before the PTA group or any other organization, that would be the first case they would want to ask you questions about. I think that the public interest here is something you can't ignore.

JUDGE NIELSEN: This, to my mind, would be the perfect case. I think I could give a perfectly logical and convincing explanation of why I'm using probation. . . .

1971 SENTENCING INSTITUTE FOR CALIFORNIA SUPERIOR COURT JUDGES, CASE NO. 3

100 Cal. Rptr., Appendix at 32-37 (1971)

OFFENSE: BURGLARY 2ND. During the night a woman noticed that a strange man was in her neighbors' house while they were away on vacation. She called the police and they apprehended defendant as he was leaving the house. Arresting officers found in his possession jewelry and coins, valued at $500, belonging to the homeowners.

---

of Corrections," the court may commit the defendant to the diagnostic facility for a 90-day period, after which the Director of the Department of Corrections must report to the court his or her diagnosis and recommendations concerning the further disposition and treatment of the defendant. — EDS.

PRIOR CRIMINAL HISTORY:

6/61	County Z	Petty theft/truancy	Informal probation
3/62	County Z	Petty theft/mal. mischief	Ward, juvenile ct., placed with aunt
5/64	County Z	Burglary	Boys camp-probation, released 12/64
4/66	County Y	Drunk/disorderly conduct	Fined and released
10/66	County Z	Petty theft/susp. of burg.	Co. jail 3 mos., 1 yr. probation
2/68	County Y	Petty theft	Co. jail 10 days
4/69	County Z	Burglary	Co. jail 6 mos., 2 yrs. probation
2/70	County Z	Drunk/disorderly conduct	Fined
3/71	County Z	PRESENT OFFENSE	

CASE HISTORY INFORMATION: Defendant, age 23, is the youngest of five children born to a rural Louisiana Negro family. His natural father was unknown to him but when the defendant began getting into trouble, his aunts often suggested to him that he took after his "jailbird" father. An older brother also has an extensive criminal record. His mother remarried (common-law relationship) when the defendant was four years old, and he says his stepfather was a very severe disciplinarian who was a churchgoing, devoutly religious fanatic. Defendant admits he frequently exploited existing conflict between his mother and stepfather, playing one against the other, to divert attention from his own misbehavior. The family moved in 1952 to central California where they settled in an area housing predominantly agricultural laborers. His education is limited, having dropped out of school at the age of 16 while in the ninth grade. Verified reports from school indicate that he was never a disciplinary problem, but he was a poor student and was often truant.

His record as a juvenile delinquent includes arrests for petty theft, malicious mischief, truancy, and running away from home.

He was made a juvenile court ward in 1962 at age 14, and was placed with an aunt and uncle because the court felt that his parents were unable to control him; however, he kept running away from these placements to return home. At the age of 16 he was sent to a boys' camp for violating probation, as a result of a burglary.

More recently, as an adult, he has had a number of arrests for burglary, petty theft, and drunk and disorderly conduct. While he has had several arrests, he has only served two terms in county jails, one a six-month county jail sentence for burglarizing a grocery store, and the other a three-month sentence for petty theft.

His employment record is quite spotty and largely includes short, seasonal unskilled jobs as a farm laborer and as a winery worker. He says he preferred working in the winery, but his employer dismissed him for stealing bottles of wine and for being drunk. He has had several drunk arrests and shows signs of a drinking problem, despite his youth.

He has been legally married once and blames his in-laws for the failure of the marriage. One child was born of that union and on one occasion defendant was prosecuted for failure to provide for his child. He responds that he refused to pay child support because his wife would not allow him to visit the child and therefore he took matters in his own hands. His wife and child are supported by public assistance. About six months prior to the present offense, defendant was living in a common-law relationship but declines to discuss it except to say that it terminated when he was arrested.

He says that although his mother is quite disconcerted at his repeated antisocial behavior, he nevertheless feels that she would offer him assistance if he was placed on probation. He also says he has a job offer and that he realizes his offense was foolish. He tends to blame the present offense on feeling sorry for himself, drinking and being out of work. He asserts this an isolated offense and denies any other burglaries.

CASE EVALUATION: The examining psychologist observed that defendant makes an ineffectual and inadequate response to emotional, social, intellectual and vocational demands placed upon him. While he is not mentally deficient, he does exhibit considerable ineptness, poor judgment and inadaptability. Coupled with his inadequate orientation and antisocial traits, he appears irresponsible, impulsive and hedonistic and finds it difficult to learn either from life, experience or punishment. His frustration tolerance appears low.

While he confesses to misuse of alcohol, there is no evidence that he has used drugs despite arresting officers' suspicions that his burglaries were connected with efforts to get money for drug use.

The prognosis for this individual is that of a marginal social adjustment. His criminal history has largely revolved around crimes against property rather than crimes against persons. He adjusted well to institutional life in past occasions as a juvenile and during his two county jail sentences. He also has had reasonably long intervals in which he does not get involved in serious crimes. The district attorney urges his commitment to the Department of Corrections because of his criminal record, while his mother and the public defender who represented him urge that he be given a jail term, continued on probation and placed in a specialized, close supervision caseload in order that he can be given vocational and social guidance. He was referred to the Department of Corrections for a P.C. §1203.03 study and they recommended that he be handled on the local level.[a]

JUDGE DELL: This is one of my typical cases. I don't hold out very much hope for this guy. The facts say he has had some periods where he hasn't committed any crimes. He's only 23, and I'm just not very optimistic on anything about him. He doesn't seem to be particularly a hazard, with the only exception that he was involved in at least one residential burglary.

I don't know what kind of burglaries the others were. It may be that he's

a. On the §1203.03 referral, see supra page 225 footnote c. The recommendation in this case seems to imply that the Department of Corrections did not consider any of the state-run training or treatment facilities suitable for this defendant and that he should therefore be committed to a locally run treatment program, if available, or receive a county jail sentence. — EDS.

careful to burglarize places that are vacant, but I think that any kind of residential burglary is a potential assault. The possibility of a burglar being surprised in a residence does cause some sort of a hazard, and does cause me some concern. There isn't anything here, though, that indicates any violent conduct. The guy is a nuisance, and I hate to send this kind of person to state prison. The Department of Corrections recommended confinement at the local level, and I certainly would go for it.

The only question is whether it might be advisable to put him on probation really more as a threat than anything else. Frankly, I think I'd use probation if proceedings are suspended and the fellow is left with a felony, with the possibility of a more punitive sanction later on. Perhaps this will be a deterrent. I don't know, however, since he still is on probation for the 1969 burglary. He was placed on two years' probation then, and this is less than two years after that. I expect that I would take into consideration perhaps the amount of time he's been in custody and give him somewhere from six months to a year in the county jail.

JUDGE NIELSEN: My problem with this case is that the jail isn't going to do anything for him in the long run. The only hope I see for him is to get a trade, get some skills by which he can make a living. We have no local facilities where he can learn a trade under these circumstances, and I'd be inclined to send him to state prison just for that purpose.

JUDGE LOW: I'm inclined to agree because everything else has been tried and hasn't been successful. . . .

JUDGE KONGSGAARD: We get a lot of cases like this. You kind of throw up your hands; what do you do?

JUDGE DELL: Well, in this case, we have a 1203.03 study which, presumably, evaluated his vocational needs. And they recommended handling him at the local level which is one of the factors that I took into consideration.

JUDGE KONGSGAARD: Many of us don't have the facility at the local level to do anything; that's our problem. . . .

JUDGE FITTS: I note the guy is 23 years old. It seems to me that somewhere down the line somebody could have sent him to the California Youth Authority. I'm impressed with those who want to learn a trade. He never had that opportunity. . . . I'm sorry that he isn't younger so that we could send him to the Youth Authority. And I sure agree that state prison is probably the only place with facilities available right now to give him something that he needs. . . .

JUDGE DELL: . . . I'm assuming the defendant is a rather poor subject to work with. This is a case where some judges might suspend proceedings and sentence him to a year in the county jail, conditional on a number of things, including his completing his high school education.

I doubt very much that this fellow would qualify, but we've tried it with people who have a little bit more promise. We have a facility where a man can finish his high school, he can finish three years in about 10 months if he applies himself enough, or correspondingly, he can finish one year in a very short period of time.

JUDGE KONGSGAARD: While he's an inmate?

JUDGE DELL: While he's an inmate. And once he gets his certificate, then we will release him on intensive supervision. But I just don't think he is a candidate for it.

JUDGE ROSSON: It really is a shame, I think, if this chap is sent to prison because he needs vocational training. He might respond or might not. It really is a waste to have to send a guy to prison to get vocational training. . . .

JUDGE FITTS: One of the nice things about this is that you don't have to keep him very long.

JUDGE ROSSON: Probably a year by the time he's out; not because we have a lot of hope, but because we're dealing with imperfect solutions. But one of the first parts of the imperfect solution is the longer a person spends in jail the less his chances to improve. . . .

JUDGE KONGSGAARD: Well, let's take a consensus on this fellow.

How many for prison on case three? Ten.

How many for county jail with probation? Eight.

C.   WHAT TO PUNISH?

INTRODUCTORY NOTE

It is obvious that our society does not subject to criminal punishment all conduct that is antisocial or otherwise undesirable. Criminal punishment is only one of many sanctions available to induce compliance with preferred norms of conduct. A society may make undesired conduct more costly by taxing it or exposing it to high risk; it may provide for civil liability, including injunctive relief, at the behest of a public agency or a private person; it may establish an agency to govern such behavior through licenses, rules, and regulations; or it may leave it to be dealt with by private social pressures. When, then, is criminal punishment the appropriate sanction? What is there about the practice of punishment that makes it improper or wrong or costly or dangerous to use for certain kinds of conduct? At least when we pass beyond the major forms of invasion of personal security and property and community security, as all modern penal codes have, to the numerous and varied lesser forms of conduct that are thought for one reason or another to be undesirable, the issues are of great consequence.

It is not easy to grapple with these questions, particularly so early in a criminal law course. They concern the fundamental features of a criminal-punishment system — the principles of culpability and legality and the inevitable practical realities of administering the criminal law — which much of this casebook is designed to deal with. But the importance of the subject matter makes an early start worthwhile. Professor Packer has written a classic treatment of these issues which the student is encouraged to consult. H. Packer, The Limits of the Criminal Sanction (1968).

For an introduction to the problems of the reach of the criminal law, we have chosen as an example the use of the criminal law to deal with sexual misconduct.[2] This area has witnessed revolutionary changes over the past 20 years. Criminal prohibitions long imbedded in American laws — on sex out of

2. Other discussion of issues concerning how far the criminal law should reach is presented elsewhere in this casebook, notably in Chapter 10, Theft Offenses, pages 913-986 infra, and Chapter 11, Business Crimes, pages 986-1006 infra.

marriage, marital infidelity, unconventional sex practices, and homosexuality (though not prostitution) — have begun to fall in many jurisdictions. Following the lead of the Model Penal Code §17, recently revised state penal codes have omitted adultery and fornication statutes. American Law Institute, Model Penal Code and Commentaries, Pt. II, Note to Article 213 at 439 (1980). More than one-half of the states now exclude criminal sanctions for any form of sexual intimacy between husband and wife. Id., Comment to §213.2 at 364. Laws prohibiting adult consensual homosexuality have also changed, though more slowly. The Model Penal Code Commentary states (id. at 372-373):

> As of that date [1955], the Model Penal Code exclusion of criminal penalties for consensual sodomy was without precedent in this country.
> Many European nations had excepted private sexual behavior from their penal laws and Great Britain has since followed suit by enacting the recommendations of the Wolfenden Commission in 1967. In 1961, Illinois became the first American jurisdiction to adopt the Model Code position. A number of other states have taken this step in recent revisions, and . . . even though many states still punish consensual sodomy, most modern revision efforts effect a substantial reduction in the gravity of sanctions authorized for such behavior.

NEW YORK REVISED PENAL LAW: *Section 1.05.* The general purposes of the provisions of this chapter: 1. To proscribe conduct which unjustifiably and inexcusably causes or threatens substantial harm to individual or public interests.

CRIMINAL JUSTICE REFORM ACT OF 1973, S. 1, 93d Cong., 1st Sess.: *Section 1-1A.2.* General Purposes: The purpose of this code is to establish order with justice so that the nation and its people may be secure in their persons, property, relationships, and other interests. This code aims at the articulation of the nation's fundamental system of values and its vindication through the imposition of merited punishment.

L. B. SCHWARTZ, THE PROPOSED FEDERAL CRIMINAL CODE, COMPARISON OF S. 1 AND THE RECOMMENDATIONS OF THE NATIONAL COMMISSION ON REFORM OF FEDERAL CRIMINAL LAWS 10 (Feb. 19, 1973) (mimeo): S. 1 injects a new, false, and dangerous notion that the criminal code "aims at the articulation of the nation's fundamental system of public values" and its vindication through punishment. A criminal code necessarily falls far short of expressing the nation's morality. Many things are evil or undesirable without being at all appropriate for imprisonment: lying, overcharging for goods and services, marital infidelity, lack of charity or patriotism. Nothing has been more widely recognized in modern criminal law scholarship than the danger of creating more evil by ill-considered use of the criminal law than is caused by the target misconduct. Accordingly, the failure to put something under the ban of the penal code is not an expression of a favorable "value" of the non-penalized behavior. It is a fatal confusion of values to see the Criminal Code as anything but a list of those most egregious misbehaviors, which, according to a broad community consensus, can be usefully dealt with by social force.

PEOPLE v. ONOFRE
New York Court of Appeals
51 N.Y.2d 476, 415 N.E.2d 936 (1980)

JONES, J. These appeals, argued together, present a common question — viz., whether the provision of our State's Penal Law that makes consensual sodomy a crime is violative of rights protected by the United States Constitution. We hold that it is. . . .

[Defendants were each convicted of "consensual sodomy" under the New York statute and each appealed to the Appellate Division, which reversed their convictions on a finding that the sodomy law was unconstitutional. The state appealed.]

The statutes under which these defendants were charged and convicted provide as follows:

§130.38 CONSENSUAL SODOMY

A person is guilty of consensual sodomy when he engages in deviate sexual intercourse with another person.

§130.00. SEX OFFENSES; DEFINITIONS OF TERMS

The following definitions are applicable to this article: . . .

2. Deviate sexual intercourse means sexual conduct between persons not married to each other consisting of contact between the penis and the anus, the mouth and penis, or the mouth and the vulva.

Because the statutes are broad enough to reach noncommercial, cloistered personal sexual conduct of consenting adults and because it permits the same conduct between persons married to each other without sanction, we agree with defendants' contentions that it violates both their right of privacy and the right to equal protection of the laws guaranteed them by the United States Constitution.

As to the right of privacy. At the outset it should be noted that the right addressed in the present context is not, as a literal reading of the phrase might suggest, the right to maintain secrecy with respect to one's affairs or personal behavior; rather, it is a right of independence in making certain kinds of important decisions, with a concomitant right to conduct oneself in accordance with those decisions, undeterred by governmental restraint — what we referred to in People v. Rice (41 N.Y.2d 1018, 1019) as "freedom of conduct." . . .

[The court reviewed a number of Supreme Court decisions that found the constitutional right of privacy invaded by laws against contraception, Griswold v. Connecticut, 381 U.S. 479 (1965), and Eisenstadt v. Baird, 405 U.S. 438 (1972); prohibiting abortion, Roe v. Wade, 410 U.S. 113 (1973); prohibiting marriage between people of certain races, Loving v. Virginia, 388 U.S. 1 (1967); compelling sterilization of twice-convicted felons, Skinner v. Oklahoma, 316 U.S. 535 (1942); requiring parents to send their children to public schools rather than to private or parochial schools, Pierce v. Society of Sisters, 268 U.S. 510 (1925); prohibiting teaching a foreign language to children, Meyer v. Nebraska, 262 U.S. 390 (1923); prohibiting possession of obscene material, Stanley v. Georgia, 394 U.S. 557 (1969).]

The People are in no disagreement that a fundamental right of personal decision exists; the divergence of the parties focuses on what subjects fall within
its protection, the People contending that it extends to only two aspects of
sexual behavior — marital intimacy (by virtue of the Supreme Court's decision
in Griswold v. Connecticut) and procreative choice (by reason of Eisenstadt v.
Baird and Roe v. Wade). Such a stance fails however adequately to take into
account the decision in Stanley v. Georgia and the explication of the right of
privacy contained in the court's opinion in *Eisenstadt*. In *Stanley* the court found
violative of the individual's right to be free from governmental interference in
making important, protected decisions a statute which made criminal the possession of obscene matter within the privacy of the defendant's home. Although
the material itself was entitled to no protection against government proscription
the defendant's choice to seek sexual gratification by viewing it and the effectuation of that choice within the bastion of his home, removed from the public
eye, was held to be blanketed by the constitutional right of privacy. That the
right enunciated in Griswold v. Connecticut to make decisions with respect to
the consequence of sexual encounters and, necessarily, to have such encounters,
was not limited to married couples was made clear by the language of the court
in Eisenstadt v. Baird: "It is true that in *Griswold* the right of privacy in question
inhered in the marital relationship. Yet the marital couple is not an independent
entity with a mind and heart of its own, but an association of two individuals
each with a separate intellectual and emotional makeup. If the right of privacy
means anything, it is the right of the *individual,* married or single, to be free
from unwarranted governmental intrusion into matters so fundamentally affecting a person as the decision whether to bear or beget a child. See Stanley v.
Georgia, 394 U.S. 557 (1969)." In a footnote appended to the *Stanley* citation
the court set out the following quotation from that decision (p. 453, n. 10):
" '[A]lso fundamental is the right to be free, except in very limited circumstances,
from unwanted governmental intrusions into one's privacy.

" ' "The makers of our Constitution undertook to secure conditions favorable
to the pursuit of happiness. They recognized the significance of man's spiritual
nature, of his feelings and of his intellect. They knew that only a part of the
pain, pleasure and satisfactions of life are to be found in material things. They
sought to protect Americans in their beliefs, their thoughts, their emotions and
their sensations. They conferred, as against the Government, the right to be
let alone — the most comprehensive of rights and the right most valued by
civilized man.' Olmstead v. United States, 277 U.S. 438, 478 (1928) (Brandeis,
J., dissenting)." ' "

In light of these decisions, protecting under the cloak of the right of privacy
individual decisions as to indulgence in acts of sexual intimacy by unmarried
persons and as to satisfaction of sexual desires by resort to material condemned
as obscene by community standards when done in a cloistered setting, no rational
basis appears for excluding from the same protection decisions — such as those
made by defendants before us — to seek sexual gratification from what at least
once was commonly regarded as "deviant" conduct,[3] so long as the decisions

3. We express no view as to any theological, moral or psychological evaluation of consensual
sodomy. These are aspects of the issue on which informed, competent authorities and individuals
may and do differ. Contrary to the view expressed by the dissent, although on occasion it does

are voluntarily made by adults in a noncommercial, private setting. Nor is any such basis supplied by the claims advanced by the prosecution — that a prohibition against consensual sodomy will prevent physical harm which might otherwise befall the participants, will uphold public morality and will protect the institution of marriage. Commendable though these objectives clearly are, there is nothing on which to base a conclusion that they are achieved by section 130.38 of the Penal Law. No showing has been made, even in references tendered in the briefs, that physical injury is a common or even occasional consequence of the prohibited conduct. . . .

Any purported justification for the consensual sodomy statute in terms of upholding public morality is belied by the position reflected in the *Eisenstadt* decision in which the court carefully distinguished between public dissemination of what might have been considered inimical to public morality and individual recourse to the same material out of the public arena and in the sanctum of the private home. There is a distinction between public and private morality and the private morality of an individual is not synonymous with nor necessarily will have effect on what is known as public morality. . . .

Finally, the records and the written and oral arguments of the District Attorneys as well are devoid of any support for the statement that a prohibition against consensual sodomy will promote or protect the institution of marriage, venerable and worthy as is that estate. Certainly there is no suggestion that the one is a substitute or alternative for the other nor is any empirical data submitted which demonstrates that marriage is nothing more than a refuge for persons deprived by legislative fiat of the option of consensual sodomy outside the marital bond.

In sum, there has been no showing of any threat, either to participants or the public in general, in consequence of the voluntary engagement by adults in private, discreet, sodomous conduct. Absent is the factor of commercialization with the attendant evils commonly attached to the retailing of sexual pleasures; absent the elements of force or of involvement of minors which might constitute compulsion of unwilling participants or of those too young to make an informed choice, and absent too intrusion on the sensibilities of members of the public, many of whom would be offended by being exposed to the intimacies of others. Personal feelings of distaste for the conduct sought to be proscribed by section 130.38 of the Penal Law and even disapproval by a majority of the populace, if that disapproval were to be assumed, may not substitute for the required demonstration of a valid basis for intrusion by the State in an area of important

---

serve such ends, it is not the function of the Penal Law in our governmental policy to provide either a medium for the articulation or the apparatus for the intended enforcement of moral or theological values. Thus, it has been deemed irrelevant by the United States Supreme Court that the purchase and use of contraceptives by unmarried persons would arouse moral indignation among broad segments of our community or that the viewing of pornographic materials even within the privacy of one's home would not evoke general approbation (Stanley v. Georgia, supra). We are not unmindful of the sensibilities of many persons who are deeply persuaded that consensual sodomy is evil and should be prohibited. That is not the issue before us. The issue before us is whether, assuming that at least at present it is the will of the community (as expressed in legislative enactment) to prohibit consensual sodomy, the Federal Constitution permits recourse to the sanctions of the criminal law for the achievement of that objective. The community and its members are entirely free to employ theological teaching, moral suasion, parental advise, psychological and psychiatric counseling and other noncoercive means to condemn the practice of consensual sodomy. The narrow question before us is whether the Federal Constitution permits the use of the criminal law for that purpose.

personal decision protected under the right of privacy drawn from the United States Constitution — areas, the number and definition of which have steadily grown but, as the Supreme Court has observed, the outer limits of which it has not yet marked.

The assertion in the dissent that validation of the consensual sodomy statute is mandated by our recent decision in People v. Shepard (50 N.Y.2d 640) proceeds from a misconception of our holding in *Shepard*. In that case we upheld the constitutionality of the statutory proscription against the possession of marihuana as applied to possession by an individual in the privacy of his home, noting the existence of a legitimate controversy with respect to whether marihuana is a dangerous substance.[a] The concurring opinion assembled the impressive evidence of the harmfulness which attends the use of marihuana. On such a record we sustained the right of the Legislature to reach the substantive conclusion that the use of marihuana was indeed harmful and accordingly to impose a criminal proscription based on that predicate. . . . By critical contrast neither the People nor the dissent has cited any authority or evidence for the proposition that the practice of consensual sodomy in private is harmful either to the participants or to society in general; indeed, the dissent's appeal is only to the historical, conventional characterization which attached to the practice of sodomy.[5] It surely does not follow that, because it is constitutionally permissible to enter the privacy of an individual's home to regulate conduct justifiably found to be harmful to him, the Legislature may also intrude on such privacy to regulate individual conduct where no basis has been shown for concluding that the conduct is harmful.

As to the denial of defendants' right to equal protection. Section 130.38 of the Penal Law on its face discriminates between married and unmarried persons, making criminal when done by the latter what is innocent when done by the former. With that distinction drawn, we look to see whether there is, as a minimum, "some ground of difference that rationally explains the different treatment accorded married and unmarried persons" under the statute. In our view, none has been demonstrated or identified by the People in any of the cases before us. In fact, the only justifications suggested are a societal interest in protecting and nurturing the institution of marriage and what are termed "rights accorded married persons." As has been indicated, however, no showing has been made as to how, or even that, the statute banning consensual sodomy between persons not married to each other preserves or fosters marriage. . . . The statute therefore must fall as violative of the right to equal protection enjoyed by persons not married to each other. . . .

Finally, we do not plow new ground in the result we reach today. Most recently, the Supreme Court of Pennsylvania, for some of the same reasons that underlie our decision, has reached a similar conclusion even in a case in which the defendants were charged with commission of deviant acts of sexual conduct with members of the audience at performances in a public theatre for which an admis-

---

a. Compare Ravin v. State, 537 P.2d 494 (Alaska 1975), in which the Alaska Supreme Court found a state constitutional provision guaranteeing the right to privacy to be violated by a state law criminalizing the possession of marijuana by adults at home for personal use. — EDS.

5. Twenty-two States have now decriminalized consensual sodomy between adults in private (Rivera, Our Straight-Laced Judges: The Legal Position of Homosexual Persons in the United States, 30 Hastings L.J. 799, 950-951; N.J. Stats. Ann., §2C:98-2).

sion fee had been charged (Commonwealth v. Bonadio, [490] Pa. [91], 415 A.2d
47 [Pa.]). [See also] State v. Pilcher (242 N.W.2d 348 [Iowa]) and State v. Ciuffini
(164 N.J. Super. 145). . . . Nor is any contrary result compelled by Doe v.
Commonwealth's Attorney for City of Richmond (403 F. Supp. 1199, affd 425
U.S. 901), a civil action in which prayers for a declaratory judgment invalidating
and an injunction precluding prosecution under a Virginia sodomy statute, which
expressly included consensual sodomy, were denied. Although the District Court
in its opinion addressed the constitutionality of the statute and concluded that
it was not invalid, its disposition included no declaration of constitutionality,
but merely denied the relief requested and dismissed the complaint. [The] summary affirmance . . . by the Supreme Court does not necessarily signify approval
of the reasoning by which the lower court resolved the case. . . .

That difficult question, to the extent that it is posed by these appeals, is
before us now. For the reasons given above, we conclude that the imposition
of criminal sanctions such as those contained in section 130.38 of the Penal
Law is proscribed by the Constitution of the United States. . . .

GABRIELLI, J. (dissenting). . . . Under the analysis utilized by the majority,
all private, consensual conduct would necessarily involve the exercise of a constitutionally protected "fundamental right" unless the conduct in question jeopardizes the physical health of the participant. In effect, the majority has held that
a State statute regulating private conduct will not pass constitutional muster if
it is not designed to prevent physical harm to the individual. Such an analysis,
however, can only be based upon an unnecessarily restrictive view of the scope
of the State's power to regulate the conduct of its citizens. In my view, the
so-called "police powers" of the State must include the right of the State to
regulate the moral conduct of its citizens and "to maintain a decent society.". . .
[A]lthough the Legislature may not exercise this power in a manner that would
impair a constitutionally protected "fundamental right," it begs the question
to suggest, as the majority has, that such a right is necessarily involved whenever
the State seeks to regulate conduct pursuant only to its interest in the moral
well-being of its citizenry.

We may avoid the circularity in the majority's reasoning in cases such as
this only if we utilize a two-tiered approach, taking care to ascertain at the
outset whether a "fundamental right" is actually implicated without regard to
the nature of the governmental interest involved in the challenged statute. If
no such right is found to exist, we must refrain from interfering with the choice
made by the Legislature and rest content upon the assurance that when the
challenged statute is no longer palatable to the moral sensibilities of a majority
of our State's citizens, it will simply be repealed.

Although our decision to sustain the statute challenged in *Shepard* under settled
principles of judicial restraint would seem dispositive of the issue in this case,
the majority has nonetheless adopted a contrary view. . . . I cannot agree, however, that the right of an individual to select his own form of sexual gratification
should stand on any better footing than does the right of an individual to choose
his own brand of intoxicant without governmental interference. Admittedly, the
issue in this case is superficially distinguishable from the issue in *Shepard*, in
that here we are concerned with a claim involving freedom of sexual expression,
and it is therefore tempting to equate the "right" asserted by defendants with
other well-established sexually related rights such as the right of an individual

to obtain contraceptives (Griswold v. Connecticut), the right of a woman to terminate an unwanted pregnancy (Roe v. Wade) and the right of a citizen to consume printed pornographic material in the privacy of his own home (Stanley v. Georgia). But the decisions in *Griswold, Roe* and *Stanley* cannot fairly be interpreted as collectively establishing an undifferentiated right to unfettered sexual expression (see Note, Constitutionality of Sodomy Statutes, 45 Fordham L. Rev. 553, 575). . . .

The majority impliedly recognizes that the Supreme Court has to date limited the protection of the Constitution to decisions relating to the traditionally protected areas of family life, marital intimacy and procreation. Yet the majority has also concluded that there exists "no rational basis . . . for excluding from the same protection decisions . . . to seek sexual gratification from what at least once was commonly regarded as 'deviant' conduct." I must disagree, however, because my reading of the recent Supreme Court cases leads me to the conclusion that the distinction repeatedly drawn in those cases between freedom of choice in the historically insulated areas of procreation, family life and marital relationships on the one hand and the general freedom of unfettered sexual choice on the other is more than just a temporary or artificial one. . . .

In contrast to decisions relating to family life, matrimony and procreation, decisions involving pure sexual gratification have been subject to State intervention throughout the history of western civilization. . . . Consequently, it simply cannot be said that such freedom is an integral part of our concept of ordered liberty as embodied in the due process clauses of the Fifth and Fourteenth Amendments.

In view of the continuous and unbroken history of antisodomy laws in the United States, the majority's decision to strike down New York's statute prohibiting consensual sodomy can only be regarded as an act of judicial legislation creating a "fundamental right" where none has heretofore existed.[3] . . .

HOME OFFICE, SCOTTISH HOME DEPARTMENT, REPORT OF THE COMMITTEE ON HOMOSEXUAL OFFENSES AND PROSTITUTION (WOLFENDEN REPORT)
9-10, 20-21, 79-80 (1957)

48. . . . [W]e have reviewed the existing provisions of the law in relation to homosexual behaviour between male persons. We have found that with the great majority of these provisions we are in complete agreement. We believe that it is part of the function of the law to safeguard those who need protection by reason of their youth or some mental defect, and we do not wish to see any change in the law that would weaken this protection. Men who commit

---

3. Without intending to sound a general alarm, I cannot help but wonder what the limits of the majority's new doctrine of "personal autonomy" might be. If, for example, the freedom of an individual to engage in acts of consensual sodomy is truly a "fundamental right," it would seem fairly clear that, absent a "compelling state interest," the State cannot impose a burden upon the free exercise of that right by limiting the individual's access to government jobs (cf. Shapiro v. Thompson, 394 U.S. 618). Moreover, if the only criterion for determining when particular conduct should be deemed to be constitutionally protected is whether the conduct affects society in a direct and tangible way, then it is difficult to perceive how a State may lawfully interfere with such consensual practices as euthanasia, marihuana smoking, prostitution and homosexual marriage. . . .

offences against such persons should be treated as criminal offenders. Whatever may be the causes of their disposition or the proper treatment for it, the law must assume that the responsibility for the overt acts remains theirs, except where there are circumstances which it accepts as exempting from accountability. Offences of this kind are particularly reprehensible when the men who commit them are in positions of special responsibility or trust. We have been made aware that where a man is involved in an offence with a boy or youth the invitation to the commission of the act sometimes comes from him rather than from the man. But we believe that even when this is so that fact does not serve to exculpate the man.

49. It is also part of the function of the law to preserve public order and decency. We therefore hold that when homosexual behavior between males takes place in public it should continue to be dealt with by the criminal law. . . .

52. . . . [W]e have reached the conclusion that legislation which covers acts [committed between adults in private] goes beyond the proper sphere of the law's concern. We do not think that it is proper for the law to concern itself with what a man does in private unless it can be shown to be so contrary to the public good that the law ought to intervene in its function as the guardian of that public good. . . .

61. . . . There remains one additional . . . argument which we believe to be decisive, namely, the importance which society and the law ought to give to individual freedom of choice and action in matters of private morality. Unless a deliberate attempt is to be made by society, acting through the agency of the law, to equate the sphere of crime with that of sin, there must remain a realm of private morality and immorality which is, in brief and crude terms, not the law's business. To say this is not to condone or encourage private immorality. On the contrary, to emphasise the personal and private nature of moral or immoral conduct is to emphasise the personal and private responsibility of the individual for his own actions, and that is a responsibility which a mature agent can properly be expected to carry for himself without the threat of punishment from the law. . . .[a]

P. DEVLIN, THE ENFORCEMENT OF MORALS [3]
4, 6-18, 20, 20-23 (1959)

What is the connection between crime and sin and to what extent, if at all, should the criminal law of England concern itself with the enforcement of morals and punish sin or immorality as such?

The statements of principle in the Wolfenden Report provide an admirable and modern starting-point for such an inquiry. . . .

. . . I must admit that I begin with a feeling that a complete separation of crime from sin (I use the term throughout this lecture in the wider meaning)

a. Ten years after the publication of the recommendations of the Wolfenden Report, Parliament repealed criminal penalties for homosexual acts committed in private by consenting adults in England. Sexual Offenses Act, Pt. II, ch. 60 (1967). A more recent study of related issues is contained in the Working Party Report of the Sexual Law Reform Society. A shortened version of this report may be found in [1975] Crim. L. Rev. 323. — Eds.

3. Maccabaian Lecture in Jurisprudence of the British Academy. This lecture appears also as a chapter in P. Devlin, The Enforcement of Morals (1965).

would not be good for the moral law and might be disastrous for the criminal. But can this sort of feeling be justified as a matter of jurisprudence? And if it be a right feeling how should the relationship between the criminal and the moral law be stated? Is there a good theoretical basis for it, or is it just a practical working alliance, or is it a bit of both? That is the problem which I want to examine. . . .

. . . The criminal law of England has from the very first concerned itself with moral principles. A simple way of testing this point is to consider the attitude which the criminal law adopts towards consent.

Subject to certain exceptions inherent in the nature of particular crimes, the criminal law has never permitted consent of the victim to be used as a defence. In rape, for example, consent negatives an essential element. But consent of the victim is no defence to a charge of murder. It is not a defence to any form of assault that the victim thought his punishment well deserved and submitted to it; to make a good defence the accused must prove that the law gave him the right to chastise and that he exercised it reasonably. Likewise, the victim may not forgive the aggressor and require the prosecution to desist; the right to enter a nolle prosequi belongs to the Attorney-General alone.

Now, if the law existed for the protection of the individual, there would be no reason why he should avail himself of it if he did not want it. The reason why a man may not consent to the commission of an offence against himself beforehand or forgive it afterwards is because it is an offence against society. . . .

Thus, if the criminal law were to be reformed so as to eliminate from it everything that was not designed to preserve order and decency or to protect citizens (including the protection of youth from corruption), it would overturn a fundamental principle. It would also end a number of specific crimes. Euthanasia, or the killing of another at his own request, suicide, attempted suicide and suicide pacts,[a] duelling, abortion, incest between brother and sister, are all acts which can be done in private and without offence to others and need not involve the corruption or exploitation of others. . . .

I think it is clear that the criminal law as we know it is based upon moral principle. In a number of crimes its function is simply to enforce a moral principle and nothing else. . . .

In jurisprudence, as I have said, everything is thrown open to discussion and, in the belief of that they cover the whole field, I have framed three interrogatories addressed to myself to answer:

1. Has society the right to pass judgement at all on matters of morals? Ought there, in other words, to be a public morality, or are morals always a matter for private judgement?
2. If society has the right to pass judgement, has it also the right to use the weapon of the law to enforce it?
3. If so, ought it to use that weapon in all cases or only in some; and if only in some, on what principles should it distinguish? . . .

---

a. The crime of attempted suicide was abolished by the Suicide Act, 9 & 10 Eliz. 2, ch. 60 (1961). Cf. Crime of Suicide, 196 Economist 871-872 (Sept. 3, 1960). The great majority of American jurisdictions now provide no criminal punishment for suicide or attempted suicide. See American Law Institute, Model Penal Code and Commentaries, Pt. II Comment to §210.5 at 94 (1980). — EDS.

The language used in . . . the Wolfenden Report suggest[s] the view that there ought not to be a collective judgment about immorality per se. Is this what is meant by "private morality" and "individual freedom of choice and action"? . . . In truth, the Report takes it for granted that there is in existence a public morality which condemns homosexuality and prostitution. What the Report seems to mean by private morality might perhaps be better described as private behaviour in matters of morals.

This view — that there is such a thing as public morality — can also be justified by a priori argument. What makes a society of any sort is community of ideas, not only political ideas but also ideas about the way its members should behave and govern their lives; these latter ideas are its morals. Every society has a moral structure as well as a political one: or rather, since that might suggest two independent systems, I should say that the structure of every society is made up both of politics and morals. . . .

. . . [W]ithout shared ideas on politics, morals, and ethics no society can exist. Each one of us has ideas about what is good and what is evil; they cannot be kept private from the society in which we live. If men and women try to create a society in which there is no fundamental agreement about good and evil they will fail; if having based it on common agreement, the agreement goes, the society will disintegrate. For society is not something that is kept together physically; it is held by the invisible bonds of common thought. If the bonds were too far relaxed the members would drift apart. A common morality is part of the bondage. The bondage is part of the price of society; and mankind, which needs society, must pay its price. . . .

. . . Society is entitled by means of its laws to protect itself from dangers, whether from within or without. Here again I think that the political parallel is legitimate. The law of treason is directed against aiding the king's enemies and against sedition from within. The justification for this is that established government is necessary for the existence of society and therefore its safety against violent overthrow must be secured. But an established morality is as necessary as good government to the welfare of society. Societies disintegrate from within more frequently than they are broken up by external pressures. There is disintegration when no common morality is observed and history shows that the loosening of moral bonds is often the first state of disintegration, so that society is justified in taking the same steps to preserve its moral code as it does to preserve its government and other essential institutions. The suppression of vice is as much the law's business as the suppression of subversive activities; it is no more possible to define a sphere of private morality than it is to define one of private subversive activity. . . .

. . . Nothing should be punished by the law that does not lie beyond the limits of tolerance. It is not nearly enough to say that a majority dislike a practice; there must be a real feeling of reprobation. Those who are dissatisfied with the present law on homosexuality often say that the opponents of reform are swayed simply by disgust. If that were so it would be wrong, but I do not think one can ignore disgust if it is deeply felt and not manufactured. Its presence is a good indication that the bounds of toleration are being reached. Not everything is to be tolerated. No society can do without tolerance, indignation, and disgust; they are the forces behind the moral law, and indeed it can be argued that if they or something like them are not present the feelings of society cannot be weighty enough to deprive the individual of freedom of choice. . . . Every moral judgement, unless it claims a divine source, is simply a feeling that no right-minded man could behave in any other way without admitting that he was doing wrong. . . . There is, for example, a general abhorrence of homosexuality. We should ask ourselves in the first instance whether looking at it calmly and dispassionately, we regard it as a vice so abominable that its mere presence is an offence. If that is the genuine feeling of the society in which we live, I do not see how society can be denied the right to eradicate it. . . .[b]

NOTES

1. While consent to a physical assault, particularly a violent one, is uniformly held to constitute no defense for the accused, the courts have tended to make certain exceptions. For example, see Rex v. Donovan [1934] 2 K.B. 498, 508 (consent no defense for sadistic caning, but otherwise for such "manly diversions" as "cudgels, foils, or wrestling"); People v. Samuels, 250 Cal. App. 2d 501, 58 Cal. Rptr. 439 (Dist. Ct. App. 1967) (consent to sado-masochistic beating no defense, but otherwise "in a situation involving ordinary physical contact or blows incident to sports such as football, boxing or wrestling"). See the comment on the latter case in 81 Harv. L. Rev. 1339, 1340 (1968), where it is observed:

> Surgeons who perform an operation at the request of a patient as well as sports participants who injure opponents in the course of competition appear to be in no danger of conviction. On the other hand, assaults involving aberrant behavior or conduct with no apparent social utility are often held to be criminal without regard to the consent of the victim if the force used has as its probable result bodily injury.

Query: Is the distinction between boxing and consensual sado-masochistic beatings a tenable one? Would it be tenable under the reasoning of decisions like *Onofre?*

See generally, Beale, Consent in the Criminal Law, 8 Harv. L. Rev. 317 (1895); Puttkamer, Consent in Criminal Assault, 19 Ill. L. Rev. 617 (1925); Williams, Consent and Public Policy, [1962] Crim. L. Rev. 74; Annot., Consent as defense to charge of mayhem, 86 A.L.R.2d 268 (1962).

2. Professor H. L. A. Hart in Law, Liberty, and Morality (1963) replies to Devlin's argument founded on the law's acceptance of the principle that consent of the victim is no defense. Devlin argued that the function of disallowing this defense is "to enforce a moral principle and nothing else"— the moral principle

---

b. For a similar view from a sociologist, see E. Durkheim, The Division of Labor in Society 93-107 (Simpson trans. 1933). E.g., at 105-106: "Thus we see what type of solidarity penal law symbolizes. Everybody knows that there is a social cohesion whose cause lies in a certain conformity of all particular consciences to a common type which is none other than the psychic type of society. In these conditions, not only are all the members of the group individually attracted to one another because they resemble one another, but also because they are joined to what is the condition of existence of this collective type; that is to say, to the society that they form by their union. Not only do citizens love each other and seek each other out in preference to strangers, but they love their country. . . . It is this solidarity which repressive law expresses, at least whatever there is vital in it. . . ."— Eds.

being the sanctity of human life and physical integrity of the person. Hart disagrees, stating (id. at 31) that the

> rules excluding the victim's consent as a defense to charges of murder or assault may perfectly well be explained as a piece of paternalism, designed to protect individuals against themselves. Mill no doubt might have protested against a paternalistic policy of using the law to protect even a consenting victim from bodily harm nearly as much as he protested against laws used merely to enforce positive morality; but this does not mean that these two policies are identical.

To what extent can the distinctions that courts have made as to when to recognize consent as a defense (discussed in the preceding note) be explained on grounds of paternalism rather than legal moralism? Is it physical injury to persons, even consenting persons, that the courts are protecting against or physical harm in the course of immoral behavior?

3. Consider the connection between the criminalization of immoral conduct and the theory that justifies the practice of punishment in terms of its expression of reprobation against wrongdoing (see, for example, the excerpts from Stephen and Denning, supra pages 190-191). See Cohen, Moral Aspects of the Criminal Law, 49 Yale L.J. 987, 1017 (1940):

> It is one of the functions of the criminal law to give expression to the collective feeling of revulsion toward certain acts, even when they are not very dangerous — for example, buggery. There are, of course, various forms and degrees of social disapproval and it is not always necessary to bring the legal machinery into operation. But at some point or other the collective feeling must be embodied in some objective communal act. By and large such expression of disapproval is a deterrent. But deterrence here is secondary. Expression is primary. Such disapproval need not be cruel or take extreme forms. An enlightened society will recognize the futility of severely punishing unavoidable retrogression in human dignity. But it is vain to preach to any society that it must suppress its feelings. In all our various social relations, in business, in public life, in our academic institutions and even in a church, people are rewarded for being attractive and therefore penalized for not being so.
>
> The reprobative theory will explain why it is difficult to repeal penal statutes where no one believes that the punishment will have any reformatory effect on the offender or any deterrent effect on others and consequent diminution of the number of offenses. An example of this is the law against suicide. There are also statutes such as those making adultery a crime which the community does not want to see enforced. For the publicity in the matter would do more harm than good. Yet people will not vote to repeal it; for such repeal would look like removing the social disapproval.[a]

a. Professor Hart develops a full-dress reply to Devlin in his Law, Liberty, and Morality (1962). See also his later article, Social Solidarity and the Enforcement of Morality, 35 U. Chi. L. Rev. 1 (1967). For other treatment of the issues, see B. Mitchell, Law, Morality and Religion in a Secular Society (1967); E. Rostow, The Sovereign Prerogative 45-80 (1962); Hughes, Morals and the Criminal Law, 71 Yale L.J. 662 (1962); Dworkin, Lord Devlin and the Enforcement of Morals, 75 Yale L.J. 986 (1966). — Eds.

4. On the issue of the consensus on moral standards, which Lord Devlin argues is legitimately expressed by criminal prohibitions, Professor Gussfield contributes the insight that in many situations it is not consensus that is expressed but rather the symbolic interim victory of one set of contending forces or interests over another. See Gussfield, On Legislating Morals: The Symbolic Process of Designating Deviancy, 56 Calif. L. Rev. 54, 58-59 (1968):

> Affirmation through law and governmental acts expresses the public worth of one subculture's norms relative to those of others, demonstrating which cultures have legitimacy and public domination. Accordingly it enhances the social status of groups carrying the affirmed culture and degrades groups carrying that which is condemned as deviant. . . . My analysis of the American temperance movement has shown how the issue of drinking and abstinence became a politically significant focus for the conflicts between Protestant and Catholic, rural and urban, native and immigrant, middle class and lower class in American society, as an abstinent Protestant middle class attempted to control the public affirmation of morality in drinking. Victory or defeat thus symbolized the status and power of the opposing cultures, indicating that legal affirmation or rejection can have symbolic as well as instrumental importance.

5. To what extent can the problem of determining whether certain conduct should be made criminal be resolved by an assessment of the practical consequences of doing so, without resolving the larger value choices involved in criminalizing the immoral? The following excerpts are addressed to this question, which presents itself not only in connection with sexual conduct but also in a variety of other contexts.

KADISH, THE CRISIS OF OVERCRIMINALIZATION
374 Annals 157 (1967)

. . . My objective is to call attention to matters of the hardest concreteness and practicality, which should be of as much concern in reaching final judgment to a Devlin as to the staunchest libertarian; namely, the adverse consequences to effective law enforcement of attempting to achieve conformity with private moral standards through use of the criminal law.

The classic instance of the use of the criminal law purely to enforce a moral code is the laws prohibiting extra-marital and abnormal sexual intercourse between a man and a woman. . . . [It is not] disputed that there is no effort to enforce these laws. The traditional function of the criminal law, therefore — to curtail socially threatening behavior through the threat of punishment and the incapacitation and rehabilitation of offenders — is quite beside the point. Thurman Arnold surely had it right when he observed that these laws "are unenforced because we want to continue our conduct, and unrepealed because we want to preserve our morals."

But law enforcement pays a price for using the criminal law in this way. First, the moral message communicated by the law is contradicted by the total absence of enforcement; for while the public sees the conduct condemned in words, it also sees in the dramatic absence of prosecutions that it is not condemned in deed. Moral adjurations vulnerable to a charge of hypocrisy are self-defeating no less in law than elsewhere. Second, the spectacle of nullification of the legislature's solemn commands is an unhealthy influence on law enforcement generally. It tends to breed a cynicism and an indifference to the criminal-law processes which augment tendencies toward disrespect for those who make and enforce the law, a disrespect which is already widely in evidence. . . .

Finally, these laws invite discriminatory enforcement against persons selected for prosecution on grounds unrelated to the evil against which these laws are purportedly addressed, whether those grounds be "the prodding of some reform group, a newspaper-generated hysteria over some local sex crime, a vice drive which is put on by the local authorities to distract attention from defects in their administration of the city government.". . .

On the other hand, the use of the criminal law has been attended by grave consequences. A commonly noted consequence is the enhanced opportunities created for extortionary threats of exposure and prosecution. . . . But, of more significance for the administration of justice, enforcement efforts by police have created problems both for them and for the community. Opportunities for enforcement are limited by the private and consensual character of the behavior. . . . To obtain evidence, police are obliged to resort to behavior which tends to degrade and demean both themselves personally and law enforcement as an institution. However one may deplore homosexual conduct, no one can lightly accept a criminal law which requires for its enforcement that officers of the law sit concealed in ceilings, their eyes fixed to "peepholes," searching for criminal sexuality in the lavatories below, or that they loiter suggestively around public toilets or in corridors hopefully awaiting a sexual advance. Such conduct corrupts both citizenry and police and reduces the moral authority of the criminal law, especially among those portions of the citizenry — the poor and subcultural — who are particularly liable to be treated in an arbitrary fashion. The complaint of the critical that the police have more important things to do with their time is amply attested by the several volumes of the National Crime Commission's reports.

The offense of prostitution creates similar problems. Although there are social harms beyond private immorality in commercialized sex — spread of venereal disease, exploitation of the young, and the affront of public solicitation, for example — the blunt use of the criminal prohibition has proven ineffective and costly. . . . The costs . . . are similar to those entailed in enforcing the homosexual laws — diversion of police resources; encouragement of use of illegal means of police control (which, in the case of prostitution, take the form of knowingly unlawful harassment arrests to remove suspected prostitutes from the streets; and various entrapment devices, usually the only means of obtaining convictions); degradation of the image of law enforcement; discriminatory enforcement against the poor; and official corruption.

To the extent that spread of venereal disease, corruption of the young, and public affront are the objects of prostitution controls, it would require little ingenuity to devise modes of social control short of the blanket criminalization of prostitution which would at the same time prove more effective and less costly for law enforcement. Apparently, the driving force behind prostitution laws is principally the conviction that prostitution is immoral. Only the judgment that the use of the criminal law for verbal vindication of our morals is more important than its use to protect life and property can support the preservation of these laws as they are. . . .

Laws against gambling and narcotics present serious problems for law enforcement. Despite arrests, prosecutions and convictions, and increasingly severe penalties, the conduct seems only to flourish. The irrepressible demand for gambling and drugs, like the demand for alcohol during Prohibition days, survives the condemnation of the criminal law. Whether or not the criminal restriction operates paradoxically, as some have thought, to make the conduct more attractive, it is clear that the prohibitions have not substantially eliminated the demand.

Nor have the laws and enforcement efforts suppressed sources of supply. No one with an urge to gamble in any fair-sized city of this country has far to go to place an illegal bet. And in the case of narcotics, illicit suppliers enter the market to seek the profits made available by the persistence of the demand and the criminal law's reduction of legitimate sources of supply, while "pusher"-addicts distribute narcotics as a means of fulfilling their own needs. Risk of conviction, even of long terms of imprisonment, appears to have little effect. Partly, this is because the immediate and compelling need of the "pusher"-addict for narcotics precludes any real attention to the distant prospect of conviction and imprisonment. For large-scale suppliers, who may not be addicts, the very process of criminalization and punishment serves to raise the stakes — while the risk becomes greater, so do the prospects of reward.[31]. . .

Our indiscriminate policy of using the criminal law against selling what people insist on buying has spawned large-scale, organized systems, often of national scope, comprising an integration of the stages of production and distribution of the illicit product on a continuous and thoroughly business-like basis. Not only are these organizations especially difficult for law enforcement to deal with; they have the unpleasant quality of producing other crimes as well. . . . . To enhance their effectiveness, these organized systems engage in satellite forms of crime, of which bribery and corruption of local government are the most far-reaching in their consequences. Hence the irony that, in some measure, crime is encouraged and successful modes of criminality are produced by the criminal law itself.

Another significant cost of our policy is that the intractable difficulties of enforcement, produced by the consensual character of the illegal conduct and the typically organized methods of operation, have driven enforcement agencies to excesses in pursuit of evidence. These are not only undesirable in themselves, but have evoked a counterreaction in the courts in the form of restrictions upon the use of evidence designed to discourage these police practices. . . . Decisions involving the admissibility of evidence arising out of illegal arrests have, for the most part, been rendered in gambling, alcohol, and narcotics prosecutions. Legal restraints upon unlawful search and seizure have largely grown out of litigation over the last five decades concerning a variety of forms of physical intrusion by police in the course of obtaining evidence of violations of these same laws. . . .

There is, finally, a cost of inestimable importance, one which tends to be a product of virtually all the misuses of the criminal law discussed in this paper. That is the substantial diversion of police, prosecutorial, and judicial time, personnel, and resources. At a time when the volume of crime is steadily increasing, the burden on law-enforcement agencies is becoming more and more onerous,

31. Packer, The Crime Tariff, 33 American Scholar 551 (1964).

and massive efforts are being considered to deal more effectively with threats to the public of dangerous and threatening conduct, releasing enforcement resources from the obligation to enforce the vice laws must be taken seriously. Indeed, in view of the minimal effectiveness of enforcement measures in dealing with vice crimes and the tangible costs and disadvantages of that effort, the case for this rediversion of resources to more profitable purposes becomes commanding. It seems fair to say that in few areas of the criminal law have we paid so much for so little.

JUNKER, CRIMINALIZATION AND CRIMINOGENESIS
19 U.C.L.A.L. Rev. 697, 697-698, 699-700, 702, 704, 705-706, 709-710, 713-714 (1972)

The analysis, subsumed within the idiom of "criminalization," purports to be a "practical," non-philosophic approach to the question of the limits of the criminal law. Its spokesmen acknowledge the contributions of their predecessors — Mill, Stephen, Devlin and Hart — but do not consider themselves obliged to seek for or justify the limits of criminalization according to the terms provided by that legacy. The most prominent of these spokesmen include Professors Sanford Kadish,[4] Norval Morris and Gordon Hawkins,[5] and Herbert Packer.[6]

What these four academic lawyers have in common, and what distinguishes them from those who have previously grappled with the issue of the proper scope of the criminal law, is allegiance to the proposition, implied or explicit in their writings, that this issue can be resolved or at least greatly explicated by reference to the effects of a given criminal law on the operation of the criminal justice system itself. . . .

The general thesis of those who urge the exclusion from the criminal code of private offenses because of their effects on the criminal justice system is that such offenses are, for a variety of reasons, themselves criminogenic and cause an increase in criminal behavior. It is the purpose of this Article to examine the four distinct arguments most commonly advanced in support of this general thesis. They are identified here as: (1) diminished respect for law; (2) unenforceability, corruption, and discrimination; (3) the crime tariff; and (4) misallocation of enforcement resources.

It is the general conclusion of this analysis that the proffered arguments are parasites in search of a host: they derive the persuasive power they seem to possess from the unstated and unproved proposition that private behavior ought not to be prohibited by the criminal law. What is missing is the principle or set of principles from which this latter proposition may be derived. For if it cannot be shown that the laws in question are, on principle, inappropriate uses of the criminal sanction, neither can it be shown that their criminogenic effects ought not to be borne, as they must be borne for all other criminal offenses, as the price for prohibition. . . .

. . . [W]hereas [underenforcement] is offered as a basis for retrenching the criminal law applicable to adults, it is entirely dismissed when the discussion

---

4. Kadish, The Crisis of Overcriminalization, 374 Annals 157, 159 (1967) [hereinafter cited as Kadish].

5. N. Morris & G. Hawkins, The Honest Politician's Guide to Crime Control 4 (1970).

6. H. Packer, The Limits of the Criminal Sanction 266 (1968) [hereinafter cited as Packer].

turns to young people. . . . There is no reason to expect that underenforcement, corruption and discriminatory application of the law will not attend enforcement of the young people's criminal code. There is reason to believe, of course, that such costs ought perhaps to be accepted as the price of such protection. But that judgment does not deny — indeed it reinforces — the central point that criminogenic effects are only attractive makeweights that permit their proponent to indulge his moral or ideological preference for a less pervasive use of the criminal law. . . .

It is ironic that the most rigorously urged reason for repeal of the laws forbidding private offenses — that their existence diverts resources from the enforcement of other offenses — is also the most vacuous of the arguments for decriminalization. . . .

Professor Kadish illustrates "the diversion of resources from genuine threatening criminality" [50] by reference to the insufficient-fund bad check laws.

> Merchants, of course, are aware of the risk of accepting payment in checks [from a person who draws a check on his own account knowing he has insufficient funds to cover it], but expectedly prefer not to discourage sales. The effect of the . . . laws, therefore, is to enable them to make use of the resources of the criminal law to reduce what, in a sense, are voluntarily assumed business risks.[51]

The same could be said of shoplifting from a self-service store: To maximize profit the merchant displays his wares in the most attractive and accessible way, and to reduce costs he relies on the customer to get them from the shelf to the door without succumbing to the temptation to bypass the cash register. Similarly, inn-keepers rely on the law to deter those who would defraud them, in preference to the reduction in revenue that would likely result from a policy of payment in advance. Indeed, does not every citizen rely upon the laws against burglary and assault in preference to the economic and psychic costs involved in maintaining a fortress residence and constant bodyguard? How far must the private citizen or merchant be required to "crime-proof" his activities in order to be entitled to the protection and services of the law enforcement system? Assumption of the risk, here as elsewhere, merely expresses a conclusion as to who should bear a particular loss, but it provides no principle from which that conclusion may be inferred. . . .

In the absence of a fundamental moral basis for limiting the scope of the criminal law, analysts have sought to withdraw the criminal sanction from the area of private offenses (1) by defining the functions of the criminal law so as arguably to exclude the functions served by criminalization of private offenses, and (2) by stressing the criminogenic consequences of criminalizing such offenses. If the thesis of this Article has been demonstrated, the latter attempt must be counted a failure because "criminogenesis" cannot adequately distinguish between offenses marked for repeal, such as prostitution, gambling and drug use, and offenses sought to be preserved, such as bribery, weapons offenses and indecent affronts. The defect in the "function" argument is that the ascription of only a narrow set of functions to the criminal law is essentially an ipse dixit. According to what set of principles is it improper, as Kadish asserts, to

50. Kadish 167.
51. Id. at 166.

"use . . . the criminal law for verbal vindication of our morals [as well as] to protect life and property," even if only symbolic, and not instrumental, vindication of positive morality is all that is achieved by the prohibition of private offenses? And in the absence of such principles, on what basis can the citizenry be told that its legislatively expressed preference for the prohibition of private offenses must give way to a new, narrower conception of the role of the criminal law? [a]

a. For further readings on these issues, see Kadish, More on Overcriminalization: A Reply to Professor Junker, 19 U.C.L.A.L. Rev. 719 (1972); Skolnick, Criminalization and Criminogenesis: A Reply to Professor Junker, 19 U.C.L.A.L. Rev. 715 (1972). — Eds.

CHAPTER

4

DEFINING CRIMINAL CONDUCT — THE ELEMENTS OF JUST PUNISHMENT

A. INTRODUCTION

In Chapter 3 we were essentially concerned, particularly in Section A, with the justification for a system of punishment, that is, why do we develop systems characterized by the visitation of pain and deprivation on those who break the law? The material in this chapter addresses the other central question we may ask about punishment: What principles justify the selection of persons to be punished? Professor H. L. A. Hart develops this distinction in his Prolegomenon to the Principles of Punishment (Chapter 1 of his Punishment and Responsibility (1968)). He refers to the first question as raising the general justifying aim of the practice of punishment, in contrast to the second which raises issues concerning the distribution of punishment.

This distinction is useful because it helps us to avoid erroneously assuming that answers to the latter kind of question (whom may and whom may we not punish?) necessarily follow from the former (why do we have punishment?). Of course, the answers *may* follow logically. For example, suppose we view punishment as justified by virtue of its prevention of criminal conduct through deterrent threat. This view should lead us to find it inappropriate to punish persons in circumstances where the deterrent threat cannot reach, for example, where the defendant is legally insane. But suppose we could be persuaded that convicting the legally insane *would* assist deterrence against the *deterrable,* who otherwise might on some occasions be inclined to think that they could escape punishment by feigning insanity. If we wanted to resist the conclusion that insane persons should be punished, we should be obliged to adduce a justification from principles governing the distribution of punishment rather than from those governing the general justifying aim of punishment.

Now suppose we articulate a principle of punishment distribution to the effect that persons who are unable to make choices and, hence, cannot be blamed for their actions should not be punished. Despite our protestations that the purpose of the practice of punishment is prevention, would we necessarily have revealed ourselves to be retributivists? After all, not punishing the blameless is a principle for the distribution of punishment that does follow from the principle that punishing the blameworthy (retribution) is the justifying aim of the practice of punishment. Hart's distinction is helpful here in revealing an answer to this challenge. It is perfectly logical to reply that the fact that we do not punish the blameless does not necessarily imply that we punish the blameworthy because it is a good thing to visit pain on the blameworthy. We may say that the general justifying aim of punishment is prevention of violations of the criminal law but that other principles enter to lead us to choose to give up some efficiency in prevention in order to further the general and independently derived principle that only those who have chosen to violate the law may be punished. In other words, as Hart puts it, a person can be a retributivist in distribution without being a retributivist in general justifying aim.

It will be seen, therefore, that how we justify a system of punishment need not determine which persons should and should not be punished. The latter question is the subject of this chapter. (It is also the subject of Chapter 9, Conditions of Exculpation, which is deferred only for pedagogical reasons.) The material is here presented with the view that our law reflects three principles that function to limit the distribution of punishment: culpability, proportionality, and legality. These principles correspond to three of the general purposes stated in §1.02(1) of the Model Penal Code governing the definition of offenses: "to safeguard conduct that is without fault from condemnation as criminal" (culpability), "to give fair warning of the nature of the conduct declared to constitute an offense" (legality), and "to differentiate on reasonable grounds between serious and minor offenses" (proportionality).

How faithful is the system of justice in the United States to the three principles identified here? When departures from them occur, what are the circumstances that are said to justify them and are they adequate?

B. CULPABILITY

1. Actus Reus — Culpable Actions

MARTIN v. STATE

Alabama Court of Appeals
31 Ala. App. 334, 17 So. 2d 427 (1944)

SIMPSON, J. Appellant was convicted of being drunk on a public highway, and appeals. Officers of the law arrested him at his home and took him onto the highway, where he allegedly committed the proscribed acts, viz., manifested a drunken condition by using loud and profane language.

The pertinent provisions of our statute are: "Any person who, while intoxicated or drunk, appears in any public place where one or more persons are present, . . . and manifests a drunken condition by boisterous or indecent conduct, or loud and profane discourse, shall, on conviction, be fined," etc. Code 1940, Title 14, Section 120.

Under the plain terms of this statute, a voluntary appearance is presupposed. The rule has been declared, and we think it sound, that an accusation of drunkenness in a designated public place cannot be established by proof that the accused, while in an intoxicated condition, was involuntarily and forcibly carried to that place by the arresting officer. . . .

Conviction of appellant was contrary to this announced principle and, in our view, erroneous. . . .

Reversed and rendered.

NOTES

1. Suppose appellant Martin had become drunk and boisterous in a private place (a public bar, a club, another's home) and had been ejected therefrom by reasonable and lawful force. Then, found drunk and boisterous in the street by a policeman, could he have been convicted? See Lanham, Larsonneur Revisited, [1976] Crim. L. Rev. 276, 278.

2. See Morris, An Australian News Letter, [1955] Crim. L. Rev. 290, 295:

Since first reading criminal law I have had the greatest sympathy with Miss Larsonneur who, in 1933, was held by the Court of Criminal Appeal (1933) 24 Cr. App. R. 74, to have offended against Article 18(1)(b) of the Aliens Order, 1920, by being an alien who was "found" in the United Kingdom without permission. Miss Larsonneur was a French woman who, it is said, worked more by night than by day. She decided to come to England, possibly in an endeavour to acquire a sufficient dowry to return to a happy Continental marriage. She was given permission to land in England. Later, the propriety of her means of livelihood being doubted, she was required to leave. Anxious not to commit an offence, she promptly travelled to the Irish Free State. Far from being welcomed there, she was arrested and handed back in custody to the English police. She was then, by skilful detection, "found" in the United Kingdom — in a cell. The Court of Criminal Appeal held her offence to be complete. How far must one go to avoid committing a crime?

PEOPLE v. NEWTON
California District Court of Appeal
8 Cal. App. 3d 359, 87 Cal. Rptr. 394 (1970)

RATTIGAN, J. Huey P. Newton appeals from a judgment convicting him of voluntary manslaughter.

[Newton was charged with the murder of John Frey, a police officer who died of bullet wounds received in a struggle with defendant. A jury found him guilty of voluntary manslaughter.

[Frey stopped a car driven by Newton and ordered him out of the car and an altercation ensued. From the testimony of the prosecution's witnesses, it appeared that Newton had drawn a gun and, in the struggle for its possession, the gun went off and wounded Heanes, another police officer. The struggle continued and Heanes fired a shot at Newton's midsection. At some point, Newton wrested the gun away, and fired several shots point blank at Frey. He then ran away. Shortly afterward, Newton appeared at a hospital emergency room, seeking treatment for a bullet wound in the abdomen.

[Newton testified that he had carried no gun. According to his account, the struggle began when Frey struck him for protesting his arrest. As he stumbled backwards, Frey drew a revolver. At this point, he felt a "sensation like . . . boiling hot soup had been spilled on my stomach," and heard an "explosion," then a "volley of shots." He remembered "crawling . . . a moving sensation," but nothing else until he found himself at the entrance of Kaiser Hospital with no knowledge of how he arrived there. He expressly testified that he was "unconscious or semiconscious" during this interval, that he was "still only semiconscious" at the hospital entrance, and that — after recalling some events at Kaiser Hospital — he later "regained consciousness" at another hospital.]

The defense called Bernard Diamond, M.D., who testified that defendant's recollections were "compatible" with the gunshot wound he had received; and that

> [a] gunshot wound which penetrates in a body cavity, the abdominal cavity or the thoracic cavity is very likely to produce a profound reflex shock reaction, that is quite different than a gunshot wound which penetrates only skin and muscle and it is not at all uncommon for a person shot in the abdomen to lose consciousness and go into this reflex shock condition for short periods of time up to half an hour or so.

Defendant asserts prejudicial error in the trial court's failure to instruct the jury on the subject of *unconsciousness* as a defense to a charge of criminal homicide. . . .

Although the evidence of the fatal affray is both conflicting and confused as to who shot whom and when, some of it supported the inference that defendant had been shot in the abdomen before he fired any shots himself. Given this sequence, defendant's testimony of his sensations when shot — supplemented to a degree, as it was, by Dr. Diamond's opinion based upon the nature of the abdominal wound — supported the further inference that defendant was in a state of unconsciousness when Officer Frey was shot.

Where not self-induced, as by voluntary intoxication or the equivalent (of which there is no evidence here, . . .) unconsciousness is a complete defense to a charge of criminal homicide. (Pen. Code, §26, subd. 5; . . .) "Unconsciousness," as the term is used in the rule just cited, need not reach the physical dimensions commonly associated with the term (coma, inertia, incapability of locomotion or manual action, and so on); it can exist — and the above-stated rule can apply — where the subject physically acts in fact but is not, at the time, conscious of acting. The statute underlying the rule makes this clear,[11] as does one of the unconsciousness instructions originally requested by defendant.[12] Thus, the rule has been invoked in many cases where the actor fired multiple gunshots while inferably in a state of such "unconsciousness". . . . including some in which the only evidence of "unconsciousness" was the actor's own testimony that he did not recall the shooting. . . .

Where evidence of involuntary unconsciousness had been produced in a homi-

11. Penal Code section 26 provides in pertinent part that "All persons are capable of committing crimes except those belonging to the following classes: . . . Five — Persons who *committed the act charged without being conscious thereof.*" (Italics added.)

12. CALJIC 71-C, which read in pertinent part as follows:

"Where a person *commits an act without being conscious thereof,* such act is not criminal even though, if committed by a person who was conscious, it would be a crime. . . ." (Italics added.)

cide prosecution, the refusal of a requested instruction on the subject, and its effect as a complete defense if found to have existed, is prejudicial error. . . .

NOTES AND QUESTIONS

1. The Model Penal Code approach. Consider at this point Model Penal Code §2.01(1), Appendix to this casebook. The Code excludes liability in the absence of a voluntary act, but does the Code define what voluntary action is? How would the *Martin* and *Newton* cases be decided under the Code?

The theory behind excluding liability in the absence of a voluntary action is explained in the Comment as follows ((Tent. Draft No. 4, 1955) at 119):

> That penal sanctions can not be employed with justice unless these requirements are satisfied seems wholly clear. The law can not hope to deter involuntary movement or to stimulate action that can not physically be performed; the sense of personal security would be short-lived in a society where such movement or inactivity could lead to formal social condemnation of the sort that a conviction necessarily entails. People whose involuntary movements threaten harm to others may present a public health or safety problem, calling for therapy or even for custodial commitment; they do not present a problem of correction.
>
> These are axioms under the present law, though dealt with only indirectly by our penal legislation in the states where legislation touches the subject at all.

2. Distinguishing between voluntary and involuntary acts. The question of what it means to say that an act is involuntary, in situations other than the paradigmatic ones in which a person physically forces the movements of another or in which one's body is in the grip of a spasm or reflex, is problematic. In Bratty v. Attorney-General [1963] A.C. 386, 409-410 (H.L. 1961), Lord Denning commented as follows:

> No act is punishable if it is done involuntarily: and an involuntary act in this context — some people nowadays prefer to speak of it as "automatism"— means an act which is done by the muscles without any control by the mind such as a spasm, a reflex action or a convulsion; or an act done by a person who is not conscious of what he is doing such as an act done whilst suffering from concussion or whilst sleep-walking. The point was well put by Stephen, J., in 1889: "Can anyone doubt that a man who, though he might be perfectly sane, committed what would otherwise be a crime in a state of somnambulism, would be entitled to be acquitted? And why is this? Simply because he would not know what he was doing.". . . The term "involuntary act" is, however, capable of wider connotations: and to prevent confusion it is to be observed that in the criminal law an act is not to be regarded as an involuntary act simply because the doer does not remember it. . . . Nor is an act to be regarded as an involuntary act simply because the doer could not control his impulse to do it. When a man is charged with murder, and it appears that he knew what he was doing, but he could not resist it, then his assertion "I couldn't help myself" is no defence in itself. . . . Nor is an act to be regarded as an involuntary act simply because it is unintentional or its consequences are unforeseen. When a man is charged with dangerous driving, it is no defence for him to say, however truly, "I did not mean to drive dangerously."

Consider the following problems:

(a) *Habitual acts.* The Model Penal Code expressly declares that a habitual action done without thought is to be treated as a voluntary action. Why should this be so? Consider, for example, a person who, immediately after announcing to her husband that she plans to drive downtown before going to her office, gets into her car and starts driving her habitual route to the office instead of heading downtown. Or consider a person who continues to say "You know" before every other sentence, despite having firmly resolved never again to use that abominable locution. Why should these habits be treated as voluntary acts?

(b) *Hypnosis.* Are actions taken while a person is in a hypnotic trance voluntary actions? There are few decisions on the subject. See People v. Marsh, 170 Cal. App. 2d 284, 338 P.2d 495 (1959), where the defense was rejected by the jury.

The Model Penal Code took the position that the acts of a hypnotized subject are not voluntary, stating (§2.01, Comment at 122 (Tent. Draft No. 4, 1955)):

> The view that the hypnotized subject will not follow suggestions which are repugnant to him, which is widely held . . . does not suffice, in our view, to warrant treating his conduct as voluntary; his dependency and helplessness are too pronounced.

Consider the following observations of Dr. Martin Orne in his review of Reiter, Antisocial or Criminal Acts and Hypnosis: A Case Study, 46 A.B.A.J. 81, 83 (1960). The book describes a prolonged personal relationship between two cellmates in which one, the hypnotist, established an ability to control the actions of the other, the subject, to a surprising extent. After his release, the hypnotist suggested to the subject who was in a hypnotic state that he rob a bank to obtain funds for some fantastic political movement. The subject did so and in the process killed several people. To the conclusion of Dr. Reiter that this demonstrated that a person can be impelled to perform criminal acts in hypnosis, Dr. Orne retorts:

> As in any intense relationship the motivations of the individuals involved are extremely complex and the behavior of each with regard to the other must be understood in the context of the total relationship. An explanation which purports to account for such behavior by singling out one aspect of the relationship — i.e., hypnosis — must be viewed with skepticism.
>
> With regard to criminal behavior it is not extraordinary for one individual to perform antisocial behavior which benefits another. The only unusual feature of the Reiter case is that hypnosis played some role. We would not ascribe the subject's motivation to hypnotic influence, as Dr. Reiter seems to do, but would relate it to the kind of relationship which existed between *H* and *N*. In this case the relationship seems to have been characterized by a shared psychotic system and there are some indications of latent homosexuality. The role that hypnosis plays is to disguise for the subject his own motivation and to create a situation which allows the subject to, at some level, disclaim responsibility for his actions. We will refrain from committing ourselves on the question of legal or moral responsibility which, in any case, is not for a psychiatrist to settle. In our view antisocial behavior such as *H*'s could have been performed without the introduction of hypnosis.

See generally Note, Hypnotism and the Law, 14 Vand. L. Rev. 1509 (1961).

(c) *Somnambulism.* Should acts done during sleepwalking be treated as involuntary? Consider Morris, Somnambulistic Homicide: Ghosts, Spiders, and North Koreans, 5 Res Judicatae 29, 29-30 (1951):

> Mrs. Cogdon was charged with the murder of her only child, a daughter called Pat, aged nineteen. . . . Describing the relationship between Pat and her mother, Mr. Cogdon testified: "I don't think a mother could have thought any more of her daughter. I think she absolutely adored her." On the conscious level, at least, there was no reason to doubt Mrs. Cogdon's deep attachment to her daughter.
>
> To the charge of murdering Pat, Mrs. Cogdon pleaded not guilty. Her story, though somewhat bizarre, was not seriously challenged by the Crown, and led to her acquittal. She told how, on the night before her daughter's death she had dreamt that their house was full of spiders and that these spiders were crawling all over Pat. In her sleep, Mrs. Cogdon left the bed she shared with her husband, went into Pat's room and awakened to find herself violently brushing at Pat's face, presumably to remove the spiders. This woke Pat. Mrs. Cogdon told her she was just tucking her in. At the trial, she testified that she still believed, as she had been told, that the occupants of a nearby house bred spiders as a hobby, preparing nests for them behind the pictures on their walls. It was these spiders which in her dreams had invaded their home and attacked Pat. There had also been a previous dream in which ghosts had sat at the end of Mrs. Cogdon's bed and she had said to them, "Well, you have come to take Pattie." It does not seem fanciful to accept the psychological explanation of these spiders and ghosts as the projections of Mrs. Cogdon's subconscious hostility towards her daughter; a hostility which was itself rooted in Mrs. Cogdon's own early life and marital relationship.
>
> The morning after the spider dream she told her doctor of it. He gave her a sedative and, because of the dream and certain previous difficulties she had reported, discussed the possibility of psychiatric treatment. That evening Mrs. Cogdon suggested to her husband that he attend his lodge meeting, and asked Pat to come with her to the cinema. After he had gone Pat looked through the paper, not unusually found no tolerable programme, and said that as she was going out the next evening she thought she would rather go to bed early. Later while Pat was having a bath preparatory to retiring, Mrs. Cogdon went into her room, put a hot water bottle in the bed, turned back the bedclothes, and placed a glass of hot milk beside the bed ready for Pat. She then went to bed herself. There was some desultory conversation between them about the war in Korea, and just before she put out her light Pat called out to her mother, "Mum, don't be so silly worrying about the war, it's not on our front door step yet."
>
> Mrs. Cogdon went to sleep. She dreamt that "the war was all around the house," that the soldiers were in Pat's room, and that one soldier was on the bed attacking Pat. This was all of the dream that she could later recapture. Her first "waking" memory was of running from Pat's room, out of the house to the home of her sister who lived next door. When her sister opened the front door Mrs. Cogdon fell into her arms crying, "I think I've hurt Pattie."
>
> In fact Mrs. Cogdon had, in her somnambulistic state, left her bed, fetched an axe from the woodheap, entered Pat's room, and struck her two accurate forceful blows on the head with the blade of the axe, thus killing her.
>
> Mrs. Cogdon's story was supported by the evidence of her physician, a psychiatrist, and a psychologist. The burden of the evidence of all three, which was not contested by the prosecution, was that Mrs. Cogdon was suffering from a form of hysteria with an overlay of depression, and that she was of a personality in which such dissociated states as fugues, amnesias, and somnambulistic acts are to be expected. They agreed that she was not psychotic, and that if she had been

awake at the time of the killing no defence could have been spelt out under the
M'Naughten Rules. They hazarded no statement as to her motives, the idea of defence
of the daughter being transparently insufficient. However, the psychologist and
the psychiatrist concurred in hinting that the emotional motivation lay in an acute
conflict situation in her relations with her own parents; that during marital life
she suffered very great sexual frustration; and that she over-compensated for her
own frustration by over-protection of her daughter. Her exaggerated solicitude
for her daughter was a conscious expression of her subconscious emotional hostility
to her, and the dream ghosts, spiders, and Korean soldiers were projections of
that aggression. . . .

At all events the jury believed Mrs. Cogdon's story. . . . [S]he was acquitted
because the act of killing itself was not, in law, regarded as her act at all.

3. Problem. Can there be any situations in which the defendant may be held
criminally liable even though the action causing the harm was clearly involuntary — for example, epileptic reflexes? Consider People v. Decina, 2 N.Y.2d
133, 139-140, 138 N.E.2d 799, 803-804 (1956):

The indictment states essentially that defendant, *knowing* "that he was subject to
epileptic attacks or other disorder rendering him likely to lose consciousness for
a considerable period of time," was culpably negligent "in that he consciously
undertook to and *did operate* his Buick sedan on a public highway" (emphasis supplied) and "while so doing" suffered such an attack which caused said automobile
"to travel at a fast and reckless rate of speed, jumping the curb and driving over
the sidewalk" causing the death of 4 persons. In our opinion, this clearly states a
violation of section 1053-a of the Penal Law. . . . ["A person who operates or
drives any vehicle of any kind in a reckless or culpably negligent manner, whereby
a human being is killed is guilty of criminal negligence in the operation of a vehicle
resulting in death."]

Assuming the truth of the indictment, as we must on a demurrer, this defendant
knew he was subject to epileptic attacks and seizures that might strike at any time.
He also knew that a moving motor vehicle uncontrolled on a public highway is a
highly dangerous instrumentality capable of unrestrained destruction. With this
knowledge, and without anyone accompanying him, he deliberately took a chance
by making a conscious choice of a course of action, in disregard of the consequences
which he knew might follow from his conscious act, and which in this case did
ensue. How can we say as a matter of law that this did not amount to culpable
negligence within the meaning of section 1053-a?

To hold otherwise would be to say that a man may freely indulge himself in
liquor in the same hope that it will not affect his driving, and if it later develops
that ensuing intoxication causes dangerous and reckless driving resulting in death,
his unconsciousness or involuntariness at that time would relieve him from prosecution under the statute. His awareness of a condition which he knows may produce
such consequences as here, and his disregard of the consequences, renders him
liable for culpable negligence, as the courts below have properly held. To have a
sudden sleeping spell, an unexpected heart or other disabling attack, without any
prior knowledge or warning thereof, is an altogether different situation.

4. Courts have reached different conclusions on whether the prosecution or
the defense carries the burden of proving unconsciousness. The authorities
are reviewed in State v. Caddell, 287 N.C. 266, 215 S.E.2d 348 (1975). Under
the decisions of the United States Supreme Court, pages 67-82 supra, does

the Constitution now require that the prosecution carry the burden of proof beyond a reasonable doubt?

5. What distinguishes nonactions and excused actions, and why does the law distinguish between them? Professor J. G. Murphy, in Involuntary Acts and Criminal Liability, 51 Ethics 332 (1971), points out that there are two basic situations in which human actions "misfire." One is the instance when actions are done in ignorance, accidentally, compulsorily, or under duress. The other encompasses misfiring in a more basic way — such as in cases of seizures, convulsions, reflex movements, and somnambulism. In the first group of cases, we speak of mitigating the actor's responsibility or of excusing his or her act. In the second group of cases, however, we do not think of excuse but rather that no human action occurred at all — "talk of excuse here seems to make no more sense than would talk of excusing a rock for falling on one's head." Indeed, this dichotomy is reflected in the organization of this casebook. The second group of cases is at issue here; problems of accident are dealt with in the section on mens rea that follows, and problems of excuse generally are dealt with in Chapter 9 Section B.

The distinction between these two categories of actions misfiring can have important legal consequences. As we shall see, it may make a difference in cases of strict liability, where ignorance or accident is ruled out as a defense but where the defense of no action (or no voluntary action) may serve as a defense. See pages 332-336 infra. The distinction may also matter in cases involving severe mental disturbance: if the action can be said not to have been a true action, the defendant may be entitled to outright acquittal instead of to a verdict of "not guilty by reason of insanity," which verdict differs from an outright acquittal in its implications for mandatory commitment. For further discussion of the relation between the defense of absence of an act and the defense of legal insanity, see pages 856-862 infra.

Query: Is there a rational explanation for distinguishing these two classes of cases? Compare the responses of Professor Murphy in the article just cited and of Professor Hart in Punishment and Responsibility 90-112 (1968).

NOTE ON OBJECTIVELY INNOCENT ACTS, EVIL THOUGHTS, AND OMISSIONS TO ACT

As we have seen, the absence of an *act* precludes culpability. In such a case, there is physical action, but it is discounted because there is no mental disposition to take such action, let alone a criminal disposition. Now consider two other situations in which the absence of an appropriate action is sometimes said to preclude criminality but which are actually distinguishable.

1. First, consider the case in which there is external behavior accompanied by a criminal disposition, but the external behavior is, looked at from an objective view, wholly innocent. Consider these examples:

A soldier during battle shoots and kills an enemy soldier believing that his victim is his own sergeant.

A man has sexual intercourse with a woman over the age of consent, though he believes that she is underage.

A man deliberately shoots and kills deceased unaware that at that very instant deceased was about to kill him.

Does the principle that requires a voluntary act or any other principle preclude imposing punishment in these cases? These problems are discussed more fully at page 594 infra in connection with the defense of impossibility to a charge of an attempt to commit a crime.

For a discussion of these and related questions, see G. Williams, Criminal Law: The General Part 22-27 (2d ed. 1961).

2. Second, consider the case in which there is no external behavior, but there is a criminal disposition. An example is the situation in which a person, who conceives a criminal plot in his or her mind, takes no action to further the plot. In such a case, is it the principle that conditions criminality on a voluntary act that precludes criminality, or is it some other principle? Criminality is said to be precluded in this case by the maxim *cogitationis poenam nemo patitur* (no one is punishable solely for his thoughts). What is the root justification of this principle? Consider the following:

*4 W. Blackstone, Commentaries *21:* Indeed, to make a complete crime, cognizable by human laws, there must be both a will and an act. For though, in *foro conscientiae*, a fixed design or will to do an unlawful act is almost as heinous as the commission of it, yet, as no temporal tribunal can search the heart, or fathom the intentions of the mind, otherwise than as they are demonstrated by outward actions, it therefore cannot punish for what it cannot know. For which reason in all temporal jurisdictions an overt act, or some open evidence of an intended crime, is necessary, in order to demonstrate the depravity of the will, before the man is liable-to-punishment.

2 J. F. Stephen, A History of the Criminal Law of England 78 (1833): Sinful thoughts and dispositions of mind might be the subject of confession and of penance, but they were never punished in this country by ecclesiastical criminal proceedings. The reasons for imposing this great leading restriction upon the sphere of criminal law are obvious. If it were not so restricted it would be utterly intolerable; all mankind would be criminals, and most of their lives would be passed in trying and punishing each other for offences which could never be proved.

G. Dworkin & G. Blumenfeld, Punishment for Intentions, 75 Mind 396, 401 (1966): What would a system of laws embodying a rule providing for the punishment of intentions look like? When would punishment be administered? As soon as we find out the agent's intentions? But how do we know he will not change his mind? Furthermore, isn't the series — fantasying, wishing, desiring, wanting, intending — a continuum, making it a rather hazy matter to know just when a person is intending rather than wishing? This last objection has two aspects, the difficulty of the authorities distinguishing between fantasying, wishing, etc. and even more importantly the difficulties the individual would have in identifying the nature of his emotional and mental set. Would we not be constantly worried about the nature of our mental life? Am I only wishing my mother-in-law were dead? Perhaps I have gone further. The resultant guilt would tend to impoverish and stultify the emotional life.

G. Williams, Criminal Law: The General Part 2 (2d ed. 1961): Better reasons for the rule would be (1) the difficulty of distinguishing between daydream and fixed intention in the absence of behavior tending towards the crime intended, and (2) the undesirability of spreading the criminal law so wide as to cover a mental state that the accused might be too irresolute even to begin to translate into action.

Goldstein, Conspiracy to Defraud the United States, 68 Yale L.J. 405, 405-406 (1959): It [the maxim that we do not punish an evil intent alone] expresses today, as it did three centuries ago, the feeling that the individual thinking evil thoughts must be protected from a state which may class him as a threat to its security. Rooted in skepticism about the ability either to know what passes through the minds of men or to predict whether antisocial behavior will follow from antisocial thoughts, the act requirement serves a number of closely-related objectives: it seeks to assure that the evil intent of the man branded a criminal has been expressed in a manner signifying harm to society; that there is no longer any substantial likelihood that he will be deterred by the threat of sanction; and that there has been an identifiable occurrence so that multiple prosecution and punishment may be minimized.

It should be remembered that while the common law requires an act as well as an accompanying state of mind (mens rea) and does not generally consider a verbal declaration of the mens rea a sufficient act in itself, words are a kind of act and are treated as such for some purposes. In cases of treason, seditious utterance, solicitation, conspiracy, or aiding and abetting another to commit a crime through instruction or encouragement, for example, words are sufficient to constitute the actus reus of the crime. Is this consistent with the doctrine that a person is not criminally liable for his or her thoughts alone?

3. The foregoing Note is addressed to the question of punishing people solely for their evil thoughts. Compare the question of punishment for a failure to act. Are the two questions the same? Do the reasons for not punishing for evil thoughts also support the policy of not punishing for failing to act? Are there other reasons why punishing for failing to act may be problematic? Consider the following material in this connection.

JONES v. UNITED STATES

United States Court of Appeals, District of Columbia Circuit
308 F.2d 307 (1962)

WRIGHT, J. [Defendant was found guilty of involuntary manslaughter through failure to provide for Anthony Lee Green, which failure resulted in his death. The deceased was the 10-month-old illegitimate baby of Shirley Green. He was placed with the defendant, a family friend. Shirley Green lived in the house with defendant for some of the time, but there was conflict in the evidence as to how long. There was also conflict as to whether or not the defendant was paid for taking care of the baby. The medical evidence was clear that the baby was shockingly neglected and died of malnutrition. It was uncontested that the defendant had ample means to provide food and medical care.]

Appellant . . . takes exception to the failure of the trial court to charge that the jury must find beyond a reasonable doubt, as an element of the crime, that appellant was under a legal duty to supply food and necessities to Anthony Lee. . . .

The problem of establishing the duty to take action which would preserve the life of another has not often arisen in the case law of this country. The most commonly cited statement of the rule is found in People v. Beardsley, 150 Mich. 206, 113 N.W. 1128, 1129: "The law recognizes that under some circumstances the omission of a duty owed by one individual to another, where such omission results in the death of the one to whom the duty is owing, will make the other chargeable with manslaughter. . . . This rule of law is always based upon the proposition that the duty neglected must be a legal duty, and not a mere moral obligation. It must be a duty imposed by law or by contract, and the omission to perform the duty must be the immediate and direct cause of death. . . ."

There are at least four situations in which the failure to act may constitute breach of a legal duty. One can be held criminally liable: first, where a statute imposes a duty to care for another; second, where one stands in a certain status relationship to another;[9] third, where one has assumed a contractual duty to care for another; and fourth, where one has voluntarily assumed the care of another and so secluded the helpless person as to prevent others from rendering aid.

It is the contention of the Government that either the third or the fourth ground is applicable here. However, it is obvious that in any of the four situations, there are critical issues of fact which must be passed on by the jury — specifically in this case, whether appellant had entered into a contract with the mother for the care of Anthony Lee or, alternatively, whether she assumed the care of the child and secluded him from the care of his mother, his natural protector. On both of these issues, the evidence is in direct conflict, appellant insisting that the mother was actually living with appellant and Anthony Lee, and hence should have been taking care of the child herself, while Shirley Green testified she was living with her parents and was paying appellant to care for both children.

In spite of this conflict, the instructions given in the case failed even to suggest the necessity for finding a legal duty of care. The only reference to duty in the instructions was the reading of the indictment which charged, inter alia, that the defendants "failed to perform their legal duty." A finding of legal duty is the critical element of the crime charged and failure to instruct the jury concerning it was plain error. . . .

Reversed and remanded.

---

9. 10 A.L.R. 1137 (1921) (parent to child); Territory v. Manton, 8 Mont. 95, 19 P. 387 (husband to wife); Regina v. Smith, 8 Carr. & P. 153 (Eng. 1837) (master to apprentice); United States v. Knowles, 26 Fed. Cas. 800 (No. 15,540) (ship's master to crew and passengers); cf. State v. Reitze, 86 N.J.L. 407, 92 A. 576 (innkeeper to inebriated customers).

NOTES AND QUESTIONS

1. Specific statutory duties to act. The problem in the *Jones* case and in much of the material that follows raises one kind of omission problem: Where the crime charged is directed generally and ambiguously to conduct that produces defined consequences (such as the homicidal offenses), may a failure to act that results in those consequences be included within the conduct proscribed? This question should be distinguished from situations in which the conduct defined as criminal expressly includes a failure to act; for example, failure to register for the draft (50 U.S.C. App. §462(a)); failure to render assistance in putting out fire when called upon by firefighters (Wis. Stat. §941.12); misprision of felony (18 U.S.C. §4: "Whoever, having knowledge of the actual commission of a felony cognizable by a court of the United States, conceals and does not as soon as possible make known the same to some judge or other person in civil or military authority under the United States, shall be fined . . . or imprisoned . . . or both.").

2. Other sources of duties to act. Consider the Model Penal Code provisions specifying the extent of criminal liability for omissions (§2.01(3), Appendix to this casebook). How would the *Jones* case have been decided under the Model Penal Code? Note that §2.01(3) permits liability for an omission when "a duty to perform the omitted act is otherwise imposed by law." This states the usual rule governing omissions to act.

Query: Why should there be such a requirement? How can we explain the recourse to civil law to determine criminal liability? Moreover, what are the circumstances in which a duty to act has been held to exist, and on what criteria has the determination been made? Consider the following:

T. B. Macaulay, A Penal Code Prepared by the Indian Law Commissioners, Note M, 53-56 (1837):

> What we propose is this, that where acts are made punishable on the ground that they have caused, or have been intended to cause, or have been known to be likely to cause a certain evil effect, omissions which have caused, which have been intended to cause, or which have been known to be likely to cause the same effect shall be punishable in the same manner; provided that such omissions were, on other grounds, illegal. An omission is illegal . . . if it be an offence, if it be a breach of some direction of law, or if it be such a wrong as would be a good ground for a civil action.
>
> We cannot defend this rule better than by giving a few illustrations of the way in which it will operate. *A* omits to give *Z* food, and by that omission voluntarily causes *Z*'s death. Is this murder? Under our rule it is murder if *A* was *Z*'s gaoler, directed by the law to furnish *Z* with food. It is murder if *Z* was the infant child of *A*, and had therefore a legal right to sustenance, which right a Civil Court would enforce against *A*. . . . It is not murder if *Z* is a beggar who has no other claim on *A* than that of humanity. . . .
>
> We are sensible that in some of the cases which we have put our rule may appear too lenient. But we do not think that it can be made more severe, without disturbing the whole order of society. It is true that the man who, having abundance of wealth, suffers a fellow creature to die of hunger at his feet, is a bad man, — a worse man, probably, than many of those for whom we have provided very severe punishment. But we are unable to see where, if we make such a man legally punishable, we can draw the line. If the rich man who refuses to save a beggar's life at the cost of a little copper is a murderer, is the poor man just one degree above

beggary also to be a murderer if he omits to invite the beggar to partake his hard earned rice? Again: If the rich man is a murderer for refusing to save the beggar's life at the cost of a little copper, is he also to be a murderer if he refuses to save the beggar's life at the cost of a thousand rupees? . . .

It is, indeed, most highly desirable that men should not merely abstain from doing harm to their neighbours, but should render active services to their neighbours. In general however the penal law must content itself with keeping men from doing positive harm and must leave to public opinion, and to the teachers of morality and religion, the office of furnishing men with motives for doing positive good. It is evident that to attempt to punish men by law for not rendering to others all the service which it is their duty to render to others would be preposterous. We must grant impunity to the vast majority of those omissions which a benevolent morality would pronounce reprehensible, and must content ourselves with punishing such omissions only when they are distinguished from the rest by some circumstance which marks them out as peculiarly fit objects of penal legislation. Now, no circumstance appears to us so well fitted to be the mark as the circumstance which we have selected. It will generally be found in the most atrocious cases of omission: it will scarcely ever be found in a venial case of omission: and it is more clear and certain than any other mark that has occurred to us.[a]

Hughes, Criminal Omissions, 67 Yale L.J. 590, 599-600 (1958), discusses the categories of situations in which legal duties have been found:

The criminal law may impose a duty to act under a variety of circumstances. The duty to embark upon physical activity only arises when the particular surroundings envisaged by the notional pattern of conduct occur. Here may be found a useful way of classifying offenses of omission. The following categories are suggested.

In rare instances, a duty is geared by an event entirely unconnected with the activity of the defendant. In this category are the duty to aid anyone in peril, to be found in some European systems, the duty to report treasonable activities and the duty to register for military service. Such duties are imposed on the citizen solely by operation of law and because of his general participation in community life. Second, the duty may be imposed by virtue of a status relationship between

a. Michael & Wechsler, A Rationale of the Law of Homicide, 37 Colum. L. Rev. 701, 751 n. 175 (1937): "[T]he common law, like most legal systems, restricts criminal liability for omissions, regardless of the degree of obvious peril that action would avert, to cases where there is a legal duty to act specially created, as by statute or contract. The traditional justification of the rule does not carry the dogma of individualism to the point of denying the desirability of stimulating action on a wider scale. It rests upon the ground that no broader rule can be formulated which is not too indefinite as a measure of liability. See Macaulay. . . . It is worth observing, however, that an appeal to common decency is in essence no less specific than the standard of liability for negligent acts. Whereas the issue there is, as we have said, whether or not the act is a sufficiently necessary means to sufficiently desirable ends to compensate for the risk of death or injury which it creates, the issue here is whether or not freedom to remain inactive serves ends that are sufficiently desirable to compensate for the evil that inaction permits to befall. The extent of the burden imposed by the act is obviously a relevant factor in making such an evaluation. If the burden is negligible or very light, the case for liability is strong, and the difficulty of formulating a general rule no more insuperable an obstacle than in the case of acts."

While European statutes commonly use a criminal penalty to enforce a duty to rescue in emergency situations, such American statutes are very rare. An example is Vt. Stat. Ann. tit. 12, §519, which provides: "A person who knows that another is exposed to grave physical harm shall, to the extent that the same can be rendered without danger or peril to himself or without interference with important duties owed to others, give reasonable assistance to the exposed person unless that assistance or care is being provided by others." The penalty for a willful violation is a maximum $100 fine. See Weinrib, The Case for a Duty to Rescue, 90 Yale L.J. 247 (1980). — Eds.

individuals, as the duty of the husband to protect his wife or the parent to care for his child. Here, an element of voluntary assumption of the burden by the individual is apparent in his entrance into the relationship or his, possibly intentional, fathering of children. . . . As a third category, the duty may be imposed as a result of the defendant's exercise of a privilege to practice a calling or engage in a business or trade. Fourth, the duty may stem from the individual's decision to participate in some permitted sphere of public activity, such as the duty of those who have incomes to file tax returns or of those who drive automobiles to carry certain equipment. In this field, certain special duties may be imposed by the impingement of external events on the citizen in his chosen sphere of activity. The accident in which the motorist is involved, though none of his making, may place him under a duty to report to the authorities or to render aid to the injured. These third and fourth categories include the great bulk of offenses of omission, and they reflect the contemporary policy of approving the imposition of duties on those who elect certain activities. Last is the duty to discharge properly burdens which one has undertaken by contract or even gratuitously, where their neglect might and does lead to death. This category includes liability for homicide through neglect or reckless inactivity. Possibly, the proposition is true in other crimes as well. If *X* is requested by *Y* to copy *Y*'s will and deliberately omits a provision, thus altering the effect of the will, he may well be guilty of forgery.

This classification is probably neither exhaustive nor exclusive, but it does indicate the sphere in which most present offenses of omission are found and the policy which underlies their creation. To state that policy briefly, in the immense complexity and interdependency of modern life, those who elect to pursue certain activities or callings must, for the welfare of their fellow citizens, submit to a host of regulations, some of which will naturally and properly impose positive duties to act.

NOTES AND QUESTIONS: PROBLEM CASES

1. People v. Beardsley, 150 Mich. 206, 113 N.W. 1128 (1907). Beardsley spent a weekend at his home with a woman he was not married to. During this period, the woman took a fatal dose of morphine tablets. Beardsley failed to call a physician to help her. She died, and he was charged and convicted of manslaughter. The supreme court reversed the conviction on the ground that defendant owed deceased no legal duty, whatever his moral duty. The court stated:

> It is urged by the prosecutor that the respondent "stood towards this woman for the time being in the place of her natural guardian and protector, and as such owed her a clear legal duty which he completely failed to perform." The fact that this woman was in his house created no such legal duty as exists in law and is due from a husband towards his wife, as seems to be intimated by the prosecutor's brief. Such an inference would be very repugnant to our moral sense.

113 N.W. at 1131. Query: What if the relationship between defendant and deceased had been more permanent? Suppose she was his mistress of long standing instead of a weekend guest? Would it depend on whether a common law marriage could be made out and whether the common law marriage were recognized in the jurisdiction? Is there any sound reason why defendant should not have been held responsible?

2. Regina v. Instan, [1893] 1 Q.B. 450, 453-454. Defendant was a spinster who lived with and was maintained by deceased, her aged aunt. When deceased became ill and unable to care for herself, defendant continued to live with her and use her money to purchase food, but defendant failed to furnish deceased with food, provide medical assistance, or notify anyone of her illness. Defendant was convicted of manslaughter on her aunt's death. The court stated:

> It would not be correct to say that every moral obligation involves a legal duty: but every legal duty is founded upon a moral obligation. A legal common law duty is nothing else than the enforcing by law of that which is moral obligation without legal enforcement. There can be no question in this case that it was the clear duty of the prisoner to impart to the deceased so much as was necessary to sustain life of the food which she from time to time took in, and which was paid for by the deceased's own money for the purpose of maintenance of herself and the prisoner; it was only through the instrumentality of the prisoner that the deceased could get the food. There was, therefore, a common law duty imposed upon the prisoner which she did not discharge.

Would the result have been different if the defendant and her aunt had shared living expenses? If defendant was just visiting?

3. *Jones v. State, 220 Ind. 384, 43 N.E.2d 1017 (1942).* Defendant raped deceased, a child of 12, who, "distracted by pain and grief," fell or jumped into a creek where she drowned. Defendant intentionally abstained from rescuing her although able to do so without risk to himself. The supreme court affirmed a conviction of second-degree murder, stating: "Can it be doubted that one who by his own overpowering criminal act has put another in danger of drowning has the duty to preserve her life?" 220 Ind. at 387, 43 N.E.2d at 1018. Question: Is there criminal responsibility because there is a legal duty, or a legal duty because there is criminal responsibility? Suppose a person, altogether accidentally (for example, by tripping and falling) pushes a strange child into a creek and permits the child to drown without attempting rescue? Cf. King v. Commonwealth, 285 Ky. 654, 148 S.W.2d 1044 (1941).

4. *A, B, C,* and *D* watch a child drowning in a pool but take no steps to save her. *A* is her father. *B, C,* and *D* are all strangers. *B* had pushed the child into the pool deliberately by pushing *C* against her. The child drowns.

A presents a classic omission case in which liability would rest on a duty to the child. (Query: Would this be so even if *A* did not realize she was his own child?)

B would not be thought of as presenting an omission case at all; it would be said that *B* killed the child by his act of pushing her in. Query: Are Beardsley, Instan, and Jones, in the above problem cases, more like *A* or more like *B*? On what basis? Are *A* and *B* in wholly different kinds of situations, or is it possible to adduce a general principle sufficient to account for both *A*'s and *B*'s liability? May we do so by saying that *B*'s act in pushing the child into the pool creates a duty to rescue her, which duty is supplied in *A*'s case by his being her father? Or is it preferable to say that *A*'s being her father (or Instan's agreement to look after deceased in the above English case) are in the nature of acts making them responsible for the deceased's predicament to the same degree as *B*'s act of pushing her in?

How should the liability of *C* be analyzed?

D, of course, presents the classic omission case where at common law there is no duty and hence no liability.

These questions should be addressed again together with the materials on causation, particularly at page 531 infra.

PROBLEM

A comatose, terminal patient is being kept alive with a mechanical respirator, without which he would die in a matter of minutes. Even with the respirator his days are numbered. Assume a physician at the hospital switches off the respirator — perhaps because there are too few of them to go around and she wants to use it for another patient. Can a plausible argument be made that for purposes of analyzing the physician's liability her conduct should be treated as an omission? What difference would it make for determining the physician's liability? The issues are developed in Fletcher, Prolonging Life, 42 Wash. L. Rev. 999 (1967).

See Williams, Euthanasia, 41 Medico-Legal J. 14, 18-21 (1973):

A toehold for euthanasia principles is provided by the practice of letting die, or what is now called passive euthanasia. The Roman Catholic Church has for over twenty years accepted that whereas the physician may never kill his patient by positive act, there is a limit to the extent to which he is required to fight for the life of a dying patient. At some point he may refrain from what Pope Pius XII in his address to physicians in 1957 called "advanced techniques" as opposed to "conventional medical treatment." This is obviously a difficult distinction, because what is an advanced technique when it is first introduced speedily becomes conventional treatment. The more common phrases used to express the distinction are "extraordinary measures" as opposed to "ordinary measures.". . .

The propriety of passive euthanasia as now supported by dignitaries of the Church has not been tested in the English courts, but it is, to my mind, undoubted law. Passive euthanasia is acceptable legally because, although withholding the means of life (including medical treatment) for the purpose of causing death and in breach of duty is murder, the duty to supply the means of life is not coextensive with the duty not to kill. All that a doctor need positively do for his patient is to supply the service and care that are customarily to be expected of a doctor; and this does not involve him in an unlimited obligation to fight a hopeless battle. Now that medical science has made it possible to prolong the life of almost anyone for a few extra minutes or days, if sufficiently energetic steps are taken, it becomes more than ever necessary to deny any duty to take these steps when in human terms they are evidently useless. The doctor must conserve his own energy; he has other patients to consider; hospital resources are needed for many people; and the useless prolongation of life is no blessing to the patient. . . .

Giving up trying to keep a patient alive may involve something other than literal inaction. It may involve telling the sister in charge to discontinue certain treatment. It may involve moving the patient from one ward to another, or from hospital to home. It may involve disconnecting the mechanical respirator that is keeping the patient alive. If an "act" is defined as a willed movement (including a movement of the vocal organs), all these are acts; but they need not be regarded as acts for the purpose of the moral and legal rule, because in substance they merely put into effect a decision to take no further steps. The moral and legal rule, which distinguishes between acts and omissions, must be interpreted in accordance with the substance of the matter. . . .

The proposition that switching off the respirator should be regarded as an omission may be proved as follows. Suppose that the respirator worked only as long as the doctor turned a handle. Then, if he stopped turning, he would thereafter be regarded merely as omitting. Suppose, alternatively, that the respirator worked electrically but was made to shut itself off every 24 hours. Then the deliberate failure to restart it would again be an omission. It can make no moral difference that the respirator is constructed to run continuously and has to be stopped. Stopping the respirator is not a positive act of killing the patient, but a decision not to strive any longer to save him.

If this distinction between an act and an omission is thought to be artificial, its artificiality is imposed on us by our refusal to accord the same moral freedom for action as we do for inaction. Pending a change of thought, the concept of an omission is a useful way of freeing us from some of the consequences of overrigid moral attitudes.

For a different view, see Kennedy, Switching Off Life Support Machines: The Legal Implications, [1977] Crim. L. Rev. 443.

In In the Matter of Quinlan, 70 N.J. 10, 355 A.2d 647 (1976), the New Jersey Supreme Court was faced with a request from a father that he be appointed guardian of the person and property of his 21-year-old daughter, Karen, who was in a persistent vegetative state. The father also sought an explicit authorization to discontinue all extraordinary medical procedures for sustaining his daughter's vital processes. The court appointed the father guardian as requested. So far as discontinuing the life sustaining processes, the court concluded (355 A.2d at 671):

> Upon the concurrence of the guardian and family of Karen, should the responsible attending physicians conclude that there is no reasonable possibility of Karen's ever emerging from her present comatose condition to a cognitive, sapient state and that the life-support apparatus now being administered to Karen should be discontinued, they shall consult with the hospital "Ethics Committee" or like body of the institution in which Karen is then hospitalized. If that consultative body agrees that there is no reasonable possibility of Karen's ever emerging from her present comatose condition to a cognitive, sapient state, the present life-support system may be withdrawn and said action shall be without any civil or criminal liability therefor on the part of any participant whether guardian, physician, hospital or others.

Earlier in its opinion the court discussed the issue of criminal liability as follows (355 A.2d at 669-670):

> Having concluded that there is a right of privacy that might permit termination of treatment in the circumstances of this case, we turn to consider the relationship of the exercise of that right to the criminal law. We are aware that such termination of treatment would accelerate Karen's death. The County Prosecutor and the Attorney General maintain that there would be criminal liability for such acceleration. Under the statutes of this State, the unlawful killing of another human being is criminal homicide. . . . We conclude that there would be no criminal homicide in the circumstances of this case. We believe, first, that the ensuing death would

not be homicide but rather expiration from existing natural causes. Secondly, even if it were to be regarded as homicide, it would not be unlawful.

These conclusions rest upon definitional and constitutional bases. The termination of treatment pursuant to the right of privacy is, within the limitations of this case, ipso facto lawful. Thus, a death resulting from such an act would not come within the scope of the homicide statutes proscribing only the unlawful killing of another. There is a real and in this case determinative distinction between the unlawful taking of the life of another and the ending of artificial life-support systems as a matter of self-determination.

Furthermore, the exercise of a constitutional right such as we have here found is protected from criminal prosecution. . . . We do not question the State's undoubted power to punish the taking of human life, but that power does not encompass individuals terminating medical treatment pursuant to their right of privacy. . . . The constitutional protection extends to third parties whose action is necessary to effectuate the exercise of that right where the individuals themselves would not be subject to prosecution or the third parties are charged as accessories to an act which could not be a crime. . . .

And, under the circumstances of this case, these same principles would apply to and negate a valid prosecution for attempted suicide were there still such a crime in this State.

2. Mens Rea — Culpable Mental States

a. Basic Conceptions and Terminology

INTRODUCTORY NOTE

The criminal law constitutes a description of harms that society seeks to discourage with the threat of criminal punishment for those who commit those harms. At the same time, the criminal law comprises an elaborate body of qualifications to these prohibitions and threats. A common usage is to express all of these qualifications to liability in terms of the requirement of mens rea. This usage is the thought behind the classic maxim, *actus non facit reum, nisi mens sit rea.* Or in Blackstone's translation, "an unwarrantable act without a vicious will is no crime at all." The vicious will was the mens rea. And reduced to its essence, "vicious will" refers to the blameworthiness entailed in choosing to commit a criminal wrong. One way in which the requirement of mens rea may be rationalized is on the common sense view of justice that blame and punishment are inappropriate and unjust in the absence of choice.[1] So viewed, a great variety of defenses to criminal liability may be characterized as presenting mens rea defenses — involuntary act, duress, legal insanity, accident, mistake, etc.

This all-encompassing usage of mens rea may be referred to as mens rea in its general sense. For present purposes we propose to identify a narrower usage of mens rea, which may be referred to as mens rea in its special sense. In this special sense, mens rea refers only to the mental state required by the definition

---

1. This view, of course, is only one way of looking at the problem. H. L. A. Hart has given it its clearest expression. See his Punishment and Responsibility 28 (1968) and the Note on Hart on Excusing Conditions Generally, page 909 infra.

of the offense to accompany the act that produces or threatens the harm.[2] An attempt to commit a crime consists of an act that comes close to its commission done with the *purpose* that the acts constituting the crime be committed. Unlawful assembly is the act of joining with a group in a public place with *intent* to commit unlawful acts. Larceny consists of the appropriation of another's property, *knowing* that it is not your own, with *intent* to deprive the owner or possessor of it permanently. Receiving stolen goods is a crime when one receives stolen goods *knowing* they are stolen. Manslaughter is the killing of another by an act done with the *awareness* of a substantial and unjustifiable risk of doing so.

That the absence of the mens rea, in this special sense of the required mental state, precludes liability in all of these cases is of course the merest tautology. This is the way these crimes are defined. But it is important to see that they are so defined because the special mens rea element is crucial to the description of the conduct we want to make criminal. And description is crucial insofar as it is regarded as important to exclude from the definition of criminality what we do not want to punish as criminal. To revert to the examples just given, it would not be regarded as appropriate to make criminal the taking of another's property when the taker believed honestly that he or she was taking his or her own property. Neither would it make sense to make persons guilty of receiving stolen goods when they neither knew nor had occasion to know that the goods were stolen. And surely we should see nothing criminal in joining a group in a public place, apart from the intent to commit unlawful acts.

The mental element required by the definition of any crime, therefore, is of central concern. This subsection on basic conceptions and terminology is designed to help the student identify and distinguish the various kinds of mental states that may be used in the definition of crimes. In the subsections that follow, we explore the issue of mistake, which, though logically related to the definition of the mental element, has to some degree produced its own body of doctrine.

Of course, these subsections will not conclude our considerations of mens rea. The issue will be encountered at many points in this course — notably in the definition of specific crimes (for example, culpable homicides, attempt, conspiracy, rape, theft) and in some of the defenses to criminal liability, such as voluntary intoxication. It will be apparent as we encounter the issue of mens rea in these various contexts that legislatures have often left the mental element undefined or have treated it ambiguously, while courts have as often failed to analyze it with precision. This subsection on terminology should help provide a vocabulary and an analytic framework for understanding and assessing what Justice Jackson has called "the variety, disparity and confusion of [the courts'] definitions of the requisite but elusive mental element." Morissette v. United States, 342 U.S. 246, 252 (1952).

---

2. There is controversy over whether mens rea should properly be regarded as embracing all factors affecting blameworthiness (the general sense) as opposed to only the mental element required by the definition of a particular crime (the special sense). See H. Packer, The Limits of the Criminal Sanction 103-108 (1968); Griffiths, Book Review, 79 Yale L.J. 1388, 1439 (1970); Fletcher, The Theory of Criminal Negligence, 119 U. Pa. L. Rev. 401, 410-415 (1971); G. Williams, Criminal Law: The General Part 30-31 (2d ed. 1961).

REGINA v. CUNNINGHAM
Court of Criminal Appeal
41 Crim. App. 155 (1957)

BYRNE, J., read the following judgment. The appellant was convicted at Leeds Assizes upon an indictment framed under section 23 of the Offences against the Person Act, 1861, which charged that he unlawfully and maliciously caused to be taken by Sarah Wade a certain noxious thing, namely, coal gas, so as thereby to endanger the life of the said Sarah Wade.

The facts were that the appellant was engaged to be married and his prospective mother-in-law was the tenant of a house, No. 7A, Bakes Street, Bradford, which was unoccupied, but which was to be occupied by the appellant after his marriage. Mrs. Wade and her husband, an elderly couple, lived in the house next door. At one time the two houses had been one, but when the building was converted into two houses a wall had been erected to divide the cellars of the two houses, and that wall was composed of rubble loosely cemented.

On the evening of January 17, 1957, the appellant went to the cellar of No. 7A, Bakes Street, wrenched the gas meter from the gas pipes and stole it, together with its contents, and in a second indictment he was charged with the larceny of the gas meter and its contents. To that indictment he pleaded guilty and was sentenced to six months' imprisonment. In respect of that matter he does not appeal.

The facts were not really in dispute, and in a statement to a police officer the appellant said: "All right, I will tell you. I was short of money. I had been off work for three days, I got eight shillings from the gas meter. I tore it off the wall and threw it away." Although there was a stop tap within two feet of the meter the appellant did not turn off the gas, with the result that a very considerable volume of gas escaped, some of which seeped through the wall of the cellar and partially asphyxiated Mrs. Wade, who was asleep in her bedroom next door, with the result that her life was endangered.

At the close of the case for the prosecution, Mr. Brodie, who appeared for the appellant at the trial and who has appeared for him again in this court, submitted that there was no case to go to the jury, but the judge, quite rightly in our opinion, rejected this submission. The appellant did not give evidence.

The act of the appellant was clearly unlawful and therefore the real question for the jury was whether it was also malicious within the meaning of section 23 of the Offences against the Person Act, 1861.

Before this court Mr. Brodie has taken three points, all dependent upon the construction of that section. Section 23 provides:

> Whosoever shall unlawfully and maliciously administer to or cause to be administered to or taken by any other person any poison or other destructive or noxious thing, so as thereby to endanger the life of such person, or so as thereby to inflict upon such person any grievous bodily harm, shall be guilty of felony. . . .

Mr. Brodie argued, first, that mens rea of some kind is necessary. Secondly, that the nature of the mens rea required is that the appellant must intend to do the particular kind of harm that was done, or, alternatively, that he must foresee that that harm may occur yet nevertheless continue recklessly to do the act. Thirdly, that the judge misdirected the jury as to the meaning of the word "maliciously.". . .

. . . [T]he following principle was propounded by the late Professor C. S. Kenny in the first edition of his Outlines of Criminal Law published in 1902 and repeated at p. 186 of the 16th edition edited by Mr. J. W. Cecil Turner and published in 1952: "In any statutory definition of a crime, malice must be taken not in the old vague sense of wickedness in general but as requiring either (1) An actual intention to do the particular kind of harm that in fact was done; or (2) recklessness as to whether such harm should occur or not (i.e., the accused has foreseen that the particular kind of harm might be done and yet has gone on to take the risk of it). It is neither limited to nor does it indeed require any ill will towards the person injured." The same principle is repeated by Mr. Turner in his 10th edition of Russell on Crime at p. 1592.

We think that this is an accurate statement of the law. It derives some support from the judgments of Lord Coleridge, C.J., and Blackburn, J., in *Pembliton*'s case. In our opinion the word "maliciously" in a statutory crime postulates foresight of consequence.

In his summing-up Oliver, J., directed the jury as follows:

> You will observe that there is nothing there about "with intention that that person should take it." He has not got to intend that it should be taken; it is sufficient that by his unlawful and malicious act he causes it to be taken. What you have to decide here, then, is whether, when he loosed that frightful cloud of coal gas into the house which he shared with this old lady, he caused her to take it by his unlawful and malicious action. "Unlawful" does not need any definition. It is some-thing forbidden by law. What about "malicious"? "Malicious" for this purpose means wicked — something which he has no business to do and perfectly well knows it. "Wicked" is as good a definition as any other which you would get.
>
> "The facts which face you (and they are uncontradicted and undisputed; the prisoner has not gone into the box to seek to give any particular explanation) are these. Living in the house, which was now two houses but which had once been one and had been rather roughly divided, the prisoner quite deliberately, intending to steal the money that was in the meter . . . broke the gas meter away from the supply pipes and thus released the main supply of gas at large into that house. When he did that he knew that this old lady and her husband were living next door to him. The gas meter was in a cellar. The wall which divided his cellar from the cellar next door was a kind of honeycomb wall through which gas could very well go, so that when he loosed that cloud of gas into that place he must have known perfectly well that gas would percolate all over the house. If it were part of this offence — which it is not — that he intended to poison the old lady, I should have left it to you to decide, and I should have told you that there was evidence on which you could find that he intended that, since he did an action which he must have known would result in that. As I have already told you, it is not necessary to prove that he intended to do it; it is quite enough that what he did was done unlawfully and maliciously.

With the utmost respect to the judge, we think it is incorrect to say that the word "malicious" in a statutory offence merely means wicked. We think the judge was, in effect, telling the jury that if they were satisfied that the appellant acted wickedly — and he had clearly acted wickedly in stealing the gas meter and its contents — they ought to find that he had acted maliciously in causing the gas to be taken by Mrs. Wade so as thereby to endanger her life.

In our view, it should have been left to the jury to decide whether, even if the appellant did not intend the injury to Mrs. Wade, he foresaw that the removal of the gas meter might cause injury to someone but nevertheless removed it. We are unable to say that a reasonable jury, properly directed as to the meaning of the word "maliciously" in the context of section 23, would without doubt have convicted.

In these circumstances this court has no alternative but to allow the appeal and quash the conviction.

Conviction quashed.

REGINA v. FAULKNOR, 13 Cox Crim. Cas. 550, 555, 557 (1877): [Defendant was a sailor aboard the ship *Zemindar*. While on the high seas he went to the forecastle hold to steal some rum and lit a match in order to see better in the dark hold. Some of the rum caught fire and the fire spread, injuring him and completely destroying the ship. He was convicted by a jury of violating the Malicious Damage Act by maliciously setting fire to the ship (arson) upon an instruction by the judge that "although the prisoner had no actual intention of burning the vessel, still, if they found he was engaged in stealing the rum, and that the fire took place in the manner above stated, they ought to find him guilty." In stating the case for the Court for Crown Cases Reserved, the judge observed: "It was conceded that the prisoner had no actual intention of burning the vessel, and I was not asked to leave any question to the jury as to the prisoner's knowing the probable consequences of his act, or as to his reckless conduct." It was held that the conviction for arson of the ship should be quashed. Portions of the opinions of two of the judges follow.]

Barry, J. A very broad proposition has been contended for by the Crown, namely, that if, while a person is engaged in committing a felony, or, having committed it, is endeavoring to conceal his act, or prevent or spoil waste consequent on that act, he accidentally does some collateral act, which if done wilfully would be another felony either at common law or by statute, he is guilty of the latter felony. I am by no means anxious to throw any doubt upon, or limit in any way, the legal responsibility of those who engage in the commission of felony, or acts mala in se; but I am not prepared without more consideration to give my assent to so wide a proposition. I shall not pronounce any opinion, as I shall consider myself bound for the purpose of this case by the authority of Reg. v. Pembliton (12 Cox C.C. 607).[a] That case must be taken as deciding that to constitute an offence under the Malicious Injuries to Property Act, sect. 51, the act done must be in fact intentional and wilful, although the intention and will may (perhaps) be held to exist in, or be proved by, the fact that the accused knew that the injury would be the probable result of his unlawful act, and yet did the act reckless of such consequences. The present indictment

a. Defendant was convicted under §51 of the Malicious Damage Act for unlawfully and maliciously breaking a window. It appeared that defendant resumed a running fight with his opponents, after they had been thrown out of a public house, by throwing a stone at them from across the street. The stone missed and broke a window of the public house. The jury convicted despite a finding that he did not intend to break the window. Conviction was quashed by the Court for Crown Cases Reserved on the ground that intention or at least recklessness as to the window breaking had to be established. — Eds.

charges the offence to be under the 42nd section of the same Act, and it is not disputed that the same construction must be applied to both sections. The jury were, in fact, directed to give a verdict of guilty upon the simple ground that the firing of the ship, though accidental, was caused by an act done in the course of, or immediately consequent upon, a felonious operation, and no question of the prisoner's malice, constructive or otherwise, was left to the jury. I am of opinion that, according to Reg. v. Pembliton, that direction was erroneous, and that the conviction should be quashed.

Fitzgerald, J. I concur in opinion with my brother Barry, and for the reasons he has given, that the direction of the learned judge cannot be sustained in law, and that therefore the conviction should be quashed. Counsel for the prosecution in effect insisted that the defendant, being engaged in the commission of, or in an attempt to commit a felony, was criminally responsible for every result that was occasioned thereby, even though it was not a probable consequence of his act or such as he could have reasonably foreseen or intended. No authority has been cited for a proposition so extensive, and I am of opinion that it is not warranted by law.

MODEL PENAL CODE

SECTION 1.13(9)-(16). GENERAL DEFINITIONS

SECTION 2.02. GENERAL REQUIREMENTS OF CULPABILITY

[See Appendix for text of these sections.]

COMMENT TO §2.02 AT 123-129 [(TENT. DRAFT NO. 4, 1955)]

This section attempts the extremely difficult task of articulating the general mens rea requirements for the establishment of liability.

1. The approach is based upon the view that clear analysis requires that the question of the kind of culpability required to establish the commission of an offense be faced separately with respect to each material element of the crime; and that, as indicated in section 1.14, the concept of "material element" include the facts that negative defenses on the merits as well as the facts included in the definition of the crime.

The reason for this treatment is best stated by suggesting an example. Given a charge of murder, the prosecution normally must prove intent to kill (or at least to cause serious bodily injury) to establish the required culpability with respect to that element of the crime that involves the result of the defendant's conduct. But if self-defense is claimed as a defense, it is enough to show that the defendant's belief in the necessity of his conduct to save himself did not rest upon reasonable grounds. As to the first element, in short, purpose or knowledge is required; as to the second negligence appears to be sufficient. Failure to face the question separately with respect to each of these ingredients of the offense results in obvious confusion.

A second illustration is afforded by the law of rape. A purpose to effect the sexual relation is most certainly required. But other circumstances also are essential to establish the commission of the crime. The victim must not have been married to the defendant and her consent to sexual relations would, of course, preclude the crime. Must the defendant's purpose have encompassed the facts that he was not the husband of the victim and that she opposed his will? These are certainly entirely different questions. Recklessness, for example, on these points may be sufficient although purpose is required with respect to the sexual result which is an element of the offense.

Under the draft, therefore, the problem of the kind of culpability that is required for conviction must be faced separately with respect to each material element of the offense, although the answer may in many cases be the same with respect to each such element.

2. The draft acknowledges four different kinds of culpability: purpose, knowledge, recklessness and negligence. It also recognizes that the material elements of offenses vary in that they may involve (1) the nature of the forbidden conduct or (2) the attendant circumstances or (3) the result of conduct. With respect to each of these three types of elements, the draft attempts to define each of the kinds of culpability that may arise. The resulting distinctions are, we think, both necessary and sufficient for the general purposes of penal legislation.

The purpose of articulating these distinctions in detail is, of course, to promote the clarity of definitions of specific crimes and to dispel the obscurity with which the culpability requirement is often treated when such concepts as "general criminal intent," "mens rea," "presumed intent," "malice," "wilfulness," "scienter" and the like must be employed. . . .

3. In defining the kinds of culpability, a narrow distinction is drawn between acting purposely and knowingly, one of the elements of ambiguity in legal usage of "intent.". . . Knowledge that the requisite external circumstances exist is a common element in both conceptions. But action is not purposive with respect to the nature or the result of the actor's conduct unless it was his conscious object to perform an action of that nature or to cause such a result. The distinction is no doubt inconsequential for most purposes of liability; acting knowingly is ordinarily sufficient. But there are areas where the discrimination is required and is made under existing law, using the awkward concept of "specific intent." This is true in treason, for example, in so far as a purpose to aid the enemy is an ingredient of the offense (see Haupt v. United States, 330 U.S. 631, 641 [1947]) and in attempts and conspiracy, where a true purpose to effect the criminal result is requisite for liability. See e.g. Dennis v. United States, 341 U.S. 494, 499-500 (1951).

The distinction also has utility in differentiating among grades of an offense for purposes of sentence, e.g., in the case of homicide.

A broader discrimination is perceived between acting either purposely or knowingly and acting recklessly. As we use the term, recklessness involves conscious risk creation. It resembles acting knowingly in that a state of awareness is involved but the awareness is of risk, that is of probability rather than certainty; the matter is contingent from the actor's point of view. Whether the risk relates to the nature of the actor's conduct or to the existence of the requisite attendant circumstances or to the result that may ensue is immaterial; the concept is the same. The draft requires, however, that the risk thus consciously disregarded by the actor be "substantial" and "unjustifiable"; even substantial risks may be created without recklessness when the actor seeks to serve a proper purpose, as when a surgeon performs an operation which he knows is very likely to be fatal but reasonably thinks the patient has no other, safer chance. Accordingly, to aid the ultimate determination, the draft points expressly to the factors to be weighed in judgment: the nature and degree of the risk disregarded by the actor, the nature and purpose of his conduct and the circumstances known to him in acting.

Some principle must be articulated, however, to indicate what final judgment is demanded after everything is weighed. There is no way to state this value-judgment that does not beg the question in the last analysis; the point is that the jury must evaluate the conduct and determine whether it should be con-demned. The draft, therefore, proposes that this difficulty be accepted frankly and the jury asked if the defendant's conduct involved "culpability of high de-gree." The alternative suggested asks if it "involves a gross deviation from proper standards of conduct." This formulation is designed to avoid the difficulty inherent in defining culpability in terms of culpability, but the accomplishment seems hardly more than verbal; it does not really avoid the tautology or beg the question less. It may, however, be a better way to put the issue to a jury, especially as some of the conduct to which the section must apply may not involve great moral culpability, even when the defendant acted purposely or knowingly, as in the violation of some minor regulatory measure.

The fourth kind of culpability is negligence. It is distinguished from acting purposely, knowingly or recklessly in that it does not involve a state of awareness. It is the case where the actor creates inadvertently a risk of which he ought to be aware, considering its nature and degree, the nature and the purpose of his conduct and the care that would be exercised by a reasonable person in his situation. Again, however, it is quite impossible to avoid tautological articula-tion of the final question. The tribunal must evaluate the actor's failure of percep-tion and determine whether, under all the circumstances, it was serious enough to be condemned. Whether that finding is verbalized as "substantial culpability," as the draft proposes or as "substantial deviation from the standard of care that would be exercised by a reasonable man under the circumstances," as the alternative would put it, presents the same problem here as in the case of reck-lessness.[a] The jury must find fault and find it was substantial; that is all that either formulation says or, we believe, that can be said in legislative terms. . . .

4. Paragraph (3) provides that unless the kind of culpability sufficient to estab-lish a material element of an offense has been prescribed by law, it is established if a person acted purposely, knowingly or recklessly with respect thereto. This accepts as the basic norm what usually is regarded as the common law position. . . . More importantly, it represents the most convenient norm for drafting purposes, since when purpose or knowledge is to be required, it is normal to so state; and negligence ought to be viewed as an exceptional basis of lia-bility. . . .

6. Paragraph (4) seeks to assist in resolution of a common ambiguity in penal legislation, the statement of a particular culpability requirement in the definition of an offense in such a way that it is unclear whether the requirement applies to all the elements of the offense or only to the element that it immediately introduces. The draftsmen of the Wisconsin Code put the problem in these terms:

---

a. The alternative formulation of the tentative draft was adopted by the American Law Institute in the proposed official draft. — Eds.

When, for example, a statute says that it is unlawful to "wilfully, maliciously, or wantonly destroy, remove, throw down or injure any . . . [property] . . . upon the land of another," do the words denoting the requirement of intent apply only to the doing of the damage or do they also modify the phrase "upon the land of another," thus requiring knowledge or belief that the property is located upon land which belongs to another?

We agree with their view that these "problems can and should be taken care of in the definition of criminal intent.". . .

The draft proceeds in the view that if a particular kind of culpability has been articulated at all by the legislature, as sufficient with respect to any element of the offense, the normal probability is that it was designed to apply to all material elements. Hence this construction is required, unless a "contrary purpose plainly appears." When a distinction is intended, as it often is, proper drafting ought to make it clear. . . .

NOTES

1. The structure of the Code provisions. The Model Penal Code mens rea provisions represent a tightly drawn statutory scheme and as such do not make easy reading. Ease of comprehension is traded off for precision of meaning. They are worth reading and re-reading, with attention to the definition of each term.

There follow some non-Model Penal Code definitions of crimes. As an exercise, it is suggested that the student identify the material elements of each crime (nature of the conduct, attendant circumstances, and result), determine the mens rea required by the definition, and determine the mens rea that would be required if the Model Penal Code's general principles of interpretation were applicable.

Treason (U.S. Const. art. III §3):

Treason against the United States shall consist only in levying War against them, or in adhering to their Enemies, giving them Aid and Comfort.

Burglary (N.Y. Penal Law §140.25):

A person is guilty of burglary in the second degree when he knowingly enters or remains unlawfully in a building with intent to commit a crime therein, and when . . . [t]he building is a dwelling and the entering or remaining occurs at night.

Burglary (Cal. Penal Code §§459-60):

Every person who enters any house, room, apartment . . . or other building . . . with intent to commit grand or petit larceny or any felony is guilty of burglary.
. . . Every burglary of an inhabited dwelling house . . . committed in the night-time . . . is burglary of the first degree.
. . . All other kinds of burglary are burglary of the second degree.

Destruction of property (D.C. Code Ann. §22-3108):

Whoever maliciously cuts down or destroys by girding or otherwise, any standing or growing vine, bush, shrub, sapling, or tree on the land of another, . . . shall, if the value of the thing destroyed or the amount of the damage done . . . is fifty dollars or more, be imprisoned for not less than one year nor more than three years. . . .

Destruction of property (N.Y. Penal Law §145.10):

A person is guilty of criminal mischief in the second degree when with intent to damage property of another person, and having no right to do so nor any reasonable ground to believe that he has such right, he damages property of another person in an amount exceeding one thousand five hundred dollars.

Assault on an officer (Me. Rev. Stat. Ann. tit. 17-A, §752-A):

A person is guilty of assault on an officer if:
A. He intentionally, knowingly or recklessly causes bodily injury to a law enforcement officer while the officer is in the performance of his official duties; or
B. While in the custody in a penal institution or other facility pursuant to an arrest or pursuant to a court order, he commits an assault on a member of the staff of the institution or facility.[a]

2. *Influence of the Code.* The mens rea proposals of the Model Penal Code have had considerable influence on criminal law reform. Robinson, A Brief History of Distinctions in Criminal Culpability, 31 Hastings L. Rev. 815, 816 (1980), concludes:

Since the drafting of the Model Penal Code, nearly three-fourths of the states have revised their criminal codes. Recognizing the value of the Code's culpability structure, approximately seventy percent of those states . . . have adopted an essentially identical system.

Some of the variations enacted by states include (1) omitting the notion of acting purposely, as distinguished from knowingly, with respect to attendant circumstances (query: what can it mean to act purposely with regard to an attendant circumstance?) and (2) omitting the notion of acting recklessly or negligently with respect to the nature of the conduct (query: is this an improvement?).

3. *Purpose, intention, and "motive."* What is the significance of the actor's motive? Does it differ from the Code's concept of purpose? Consider G. Williams, The Mental Element in Crime 10, 14 (1965). The author defines intention in terms of desiring a consequence: "A consequence is intended when it is desired to follow as the result of the actor's conduct." He then cautions:

[T]he consequence need not be desired as an end in itself; it may be desired as a means to another end. . . . There may be a series of ends, each a link in a chain of purpose. Every link in the chain, when it happens, is an intended consequence of the original act. Suppose that a burglar is arrested when breaking into premises. It would obviously be no defence for him to say that his sole intention was to provide a nurse for his sick daughter, and for that purpose to take money from the premises, but that he had no desire or intention to deprive anyone of anything. Such an argument would be fatuous. He intended (1) to steal money (2) in order to help his daughter. These are two intentions, and the one does

a. See State v. Morey, 427 A.2d 479 (Me. 1981). — EDS.

not displace the other. English lawyers call the first an "intent" and the second a "motive"; this is because the first (the intent to steal) enters into the definition of burglary and is legally relevant, while the second (the motive of helping the daughter) is legally irrelevant, except perhaps in relation to sentence. Although the verbal distinction between "intention" and "motive" is convenient, it must be realized that the remoter intention called motive is still an intention.

4. Purpose, intention, and "wishing." Is there a difference between wishing and intending? Suppose a person makes a gift of an airplane ticket to someone he wants dead, in the hope that the plane will crash. Assume it does and the traveler is killed. Could it be said that defendant intentionally (or purposely) killed him?

Compare with this hypothetical the biblical story of Uriah the Hittite, a captain in King David's army, whom the good king ordered into the "forefront of the hottest battle," hoping Uriah would be killed so that the king could marry Uriah's wife, Bath-sheba. The plan succeeded. 2 Samuel 11:1-27.

Consider these hypotheticals again in connection with Chapter 7, Section A (Causation).

5. "Specific intent" and "general intent." Observe that the Model Penal Code does not find it necessary to make use of the concepts *specific intent* or *general intent* in identifying the mental states appropriate to defining crime. These concepts have been used extensively in non-Model Penal Code jurisdictions as well as in England. While their meaning varies, one common usage of the terms is to distinguish between purpose and recklessness (perhaps knowledge, as well) as the Model Penal Code defines these terms.

The term *specific intent* has been productive of untold confusion, partly because courts have not been consistent in their use of it and partly for the more fundamental reason that it is often quite difficult to determine whether a statute *should* be interpreted to require specific intent — that is, the Code concept of a true "purpose."[3] It will be instructive for students encountering the terms *general* or *specific intent* to consider precisely how those terms are being used, whether they are in effect equivalent to one of the mens rea concepts used in the Code, and whether the court has sound reasons for giving those terms whatever meaning it implicitly or explicitly chooses.

6. Knowledge versus recklessness. The Model Penal Code makes knowledge of a high probability of the existence of a fact equivalent to knowledge of the existence of that fact. Section 2.02(7), Appendix to this casebook. What is behind this move? Does it blur the distinction between recklessness and knowledge? Consider the case that follows.

---

3. Consider United States v. Bennie Stewart, 19 C.M.A. 58, 41 C.M.R. 58 (1969), where the Court of Military Appeals set aside a plea of guilty to desertion with intent to avoid hazardous duty. The court found the plea improvident on the ground that the defendant's statements to the court-martial suggested that while he knew he would miss hazardous duty by his unauthorized absence, he did not absent himself for that reason (at 59): "In our opinion, there is a fundamental difference between pleading guilty to such a desertion charge because one intends to avoid hazardous duty and pursuing the same course only because one believes that a consequence of his act was the avoidance of hazardous duty, regardless of intent." See also United States v. Bernard Warner Stewart, 19 C.M.A. 417, 42 C.M.R. 19 (1970) (willful destruction of an aircraft with intent to interfere with national defense not made out where the evidence showed that air-crew member's objective was to avoid another Mediterranean cruise).

UNITED STATES v. JEWELL
United States Court of Appeals, 9th Circuit
532 F.2d 697 (1976)

BROWNING, J. [Defendant was convicted of violating the Comprehensive Drug Abuse Prevention and Control Act of 1970 by knowingly transporting marijuana in his car from Mexico to the United States.]

It is undisputed that appellant entered the United States driving an automobile in which 110 pounds of marihuana worth $6,250 had been concealed in a secret compartment between the trunk and rear seat. Appellant testified that he did not know the marijuana was present. There was circumstantial evidence from which the jury could infer that appellant had positive knowledge of the presence of the marihuana, and that his contrary testimony was false. On the other hand there was evidence from which the jury could conclude that appellant spoke the truth — that although appellant knew of the presence of the secret compartment and had knowledge of facts indicating that it contained marijuana, he deliberately avoided positive knowledge of the presence of the contraband to avoid responsibility in the event of discovery. If the jury concluded the latter was indeed the situation, and if positive knowledge is required to convict, the jury would have no choice consistent with its oath but to find appellant not guilty even though he deliberately contrived his lack of positive knowledge. Appellant urges this view. . . .

Appellant tendered an instruction that to return a guilty verdict the jury must find that the defendant knew he was in possession of marihuana. The trial judge rejected the instruction because it suggested that "absolutely, positively, he has to know that it's there." The court said,

> I think, in this case, it's not too sound an instruction because we have evidence that if the jury believes it, they'd be justified in finding he actually didn't know what it was — he didn't because he didn't want to find it. . . .

. . . The court told the jury that the government must prove beyond a reasonable doubt that the defendant "knowingly" brought the marihuana into the United States (count 1: 21 U.S.C. §952(a)), and that he "knowingly" possessed the marihuana (count 2: 21 U.S.C. §841(a)(1)). The court continued:

> The Government can complete their burden of proof by proving, beyond a reasonable doubt, that if the defendant was not actually aware that there was marijuana in the vehicle he was driving when he entered the United States his ignorance in that regard was solely and entirely a result of his having made a conscious purpose to disregard the nature of that which was in the vehicle, with a conscious purpose to avoid learning the truth.

The legal premise of these instructions is firmly supported by leading commentators here and in England. . . .

The substantive justification for the rule is that deliberate ignorance and positive knowledge are equally culpable. The textual justification is that in common understanding one "knows" facts of which he is less than absolutely certain. To act "knowingly," therefore, is not necessarily to act only with positive knowledge, but also to act with an awareness of the high probability of the existence of the fact in question. When such awareness is present, "positive" knowledge is not required.

This is the analysis adopted in the Model Penal Code. Section 2.02(7) states:

> When knowledge of the existence of a particular fact is an element of an offense, such knowledge is established if a person is aware of a high probability of its existence, unless he actually believes that it does not exist.

As the Comment to this provision explains,

> Paragraph (7) deals with the situation British commentators have denominated "wilful blindness" or "connivance," the case of the actor who is aware of the probable existence of a material fact but does not satisfy himself that it does not in fact exist.

The Supreme Court in Leary v. United States, 395 U.S. 6, 46 n. 93 (1969), applied the Model Penal Code definition of knowledge in determining the meaning of "knowing" in former 21 U.S.C. §176a. In Turner v. United States, 396 U.S. 398, 416 & n. 29 (1970), the Court adopted the Model Penal Code definition in defining "knowingly" in 21 U.S.C. §174. The *Turner* opinion recognizes that this definition of "knowingly" makes actual knowledge unnecessary: "[T]hose who traffic in heroin will inevitably become aware that the product they deal in is smuggled, *unless they practice a studied ignorance to which they are not entitled.*" 396 U.S. at 417. . . .

Appellant's narrow interpretation of "knowingly" is inconsistent with the Drug Control Act's general purpose to deal more effectively "with the growing menace of drug abuse in the United States." Holding that this term introduces a requirement of positive knowledge would make deliberate ignorance a defense. It cannot be doubted that those who traffic in drugs would make the most of it. This is evident from the number of appellate decisions reflecting conscious avoidance of positive knowledge of the presence of contraband—in the car driven by the defendant or in which he is a passenger, in the suitcase or package he carries, in the parcel concealed in his clothing.

It is no answer to say that in such cases the fact finder may infer positive knowledge. It is probable that many who performed the transportation function, essential to the drug traffic, can truthfully testify that they have no *positive* knowledge of the load they carry. Under appellant's interpretation of the statute, such persons will be convicted only if the fact finder errs in evaluating the credibility of the witness or deliberately disregards the law. . . .

It is worth emphasizing that the required state of mind differs from positive knowledge only so far as necessary to encompass a calculated effort to avoid the sanctions of the statute while violating its substance. "A court can properly find wilful blindness only where it can almost be said that the defendant actually knew." In the language of the instruction in this case, the government must prove, "beyond a reasonable doubt, that if the defendant was not actually aware . . . his ignorance in that regard was *solely* and *entirely* a result of . . . a conscious purpose to avoid learning the truth."

No legitimate interest of an accused is prejudiced by such a standard, and society's interest in a system of criminal law that is enforceable and that imposes sanctions upon all who are equally culpable requires it.

The conviction is affirmed.

KENNEDY, J. The majority opinion justifies the conscious purpose jury instruction as an application of the wilful blindness doctrine recognized primarily by English authorities. . . .

The approach adopted in section 2.02(7) of the Model Penal Code clarifies, and, in important ways restricts, the English doctrine: . . . This provision requires an awareness of a high probability that a fact exists, not merely a reckless disregard, or a suspicion followed by a failure to make further inquiry. It also establishes knowledge as a matter of subjective belief, an important safeguard against diluting the guilty state of mind required for conviction. It is important to note that section 2.02(7) is a *definition* of knowledge, not a substitute for it; as such, it has been cited with approval by the Supreme Court.

In light of the Model Penal Code's definition, the "conscious purpose" jury instruction is defective in three respects. First, it fails to mention the requirement that Jewell have been aware of a high probability that a controlled substance was in the car. It is not culpable to form "a conscious purpose to avoid learning the truth" unless one is aware of facts indicating a high probability of that truth. To illustrate, a child given a gift-wrapped package by his mother while on vacation in Mexico may form a conscious purpose to take it home without learning what is inside; yet his state of mind is totally innocent unless he is aware of a high probability that the package contains a controlled substance. Thus, a conscious purpose instruction is only proper when coupled with a requirement that one be aware of a high probability of the truth.

The second defect in the instruction as given is that it did not alert the jury that Jewell could not be convicted if he "actually believed" there was no controlled substance in the car. The failure to emphasize, as does the Model Penal Code, that subjective belief is the determinative factor, may allow a jury to convict on an objective theory of knowledge — that a reasonable man should have inspected the car and would have discovered what was hidden inside. One recent decision reversed a jury instruction for this very deficiency — failure to balance a conscious purpose instruction with a warning that the defendant could not be convicted if he actually believed to the contrary.

Third, the jury instruction clearly states that Jewell could have been convicted even if found ignorant or "not actually aware" that the car contained a controlled substance. This is unacceptable because true ignorance, no matter how unreasonable, cannot provide a basis for criminal liability when the statute requires knowledge. A proper jury instruction based on the Model Penal Code would be presented as a way of defining knowledge, and not as an alternative to it. . . .

PROBLEM

In United States v. Neiswender, 590 F.2d 1269 (4th Cir. 1979), defendant was convicted of obstruction of justice under 18 U.S.C. §1503, which provided, "Whoever . . . endeavors to influence, obstruct, or impede the due administration of justice, shall be fined not more than $5,000 or imprisoned not more than five years or both." The prosecution established at the trial that defendant approached the lawyer defending former Maryland governor Marvin Mandel in a much publicized criminal prosecution and represented that he had contact with a juror sitting on the Mandel case through whom he could ensure that the trial "would come out the right way" for a fee of $2,000. The lawyer promptly informed the United States Attorney and the judge presiding over the Mandel trial. Government agents, posing as associates of Mandel's lawyer, sought to identify the supposedly corrupt juror, but to no avail: The prosecution was unable to establish the truth of defendant's representations to Mandel's counsel. On appeal defendant contended that the government thus failed to prove an essential element of the statutory crime — the "endeavor," or specific intent, to undermine judicial processes. All it established was a fraudulent attempt to obtain money by deception. Query: Should this contention be sustained?

The court summarized the opposing arguments of the parties as follows.

> The government concedes that the defendant's primary intent was one to defraud. It urges, however, that every man intends the natural consequences of his acts. Had Neiswender convinced Weiner that he had a juror under his control and induced Weiner to participate in the scheme, the natural consequence would have been to reduce Weiner's efforts in defending his client. This debilitating effect on defense counsel would have altered the normal course of trial and prejudiced the client. This "natural consequence," the government contends, would have obstructed the due administration of justice.

> Neiswender has a rejoinder to this argument. In his view, while operation of the time-honored "natural consequences" rule might normally suffice to establish specific intent, it should play no role in this case. Neiswender contends that whatever force a presumed intention has must give way to actual intent. Here Neiswender's motivation was directly at odds with any design to obstruct justice since a guilty verdict would have revealed Neiswender's fraud. It was in his best interest for Weiner to press hard in his efforts to obtain an acquittal. Indeed, the evidence suggests that Neiswender recognized this fact for, during negotiations with Weiner's "associate," he insisted that defense counsel were "not to slouch in their duties" and "were to give it the full effect."

The court upheld the conviction, stating:

> The state-of-mind requirement of §1503 has long confused the courts. Some cases require only that the defendant "intend to do some act which would tend to corruptly impede or influence the administration of justice.". . .

> Other cases, however, have imposed the ostensibly more demanding requirement of "a specific intent to obstruct justice.". . .

> None of these cases, however, has carefully considered how the specific intent requirement applies to a defendant whose hope is to avoid obstructing justice while the natural consequence of success in his endeavor would be to achieve precisely the opposite result. We see no need to undertake an extended excursion into the subtleties of specific intent. In our view, the defendant need only have had knowledge or notice that success in his fraud would have likely resulted in an obstruction of justice. Notice is provided by the reasonable foreseeability of the natural and probable consequences of one's acts.

The court recognized the "natural-consequences" rule to be a fiction but observed that this fiction is grounded upon sound policy, for, as outlined above, a rule focusing on foreseeable, rather than intended, consequences operates in sensible and fair fashion to deter the conduct sought to be avoided and to punish those whose actions are blameworthy, even though undertaken for purposes that may or may not be culpable.

b. Mistake of Fact

MODEL PENAL CODE

SECTION 2.04(1)-(2). IGNORANCE OR MISTAKE

SECTION 213.6(1). MISTAKE AS TO AGE

[See Appendix for text of these sections.]

COMMENTS TO §2.04 AT 135-137 [(TENT. DRAFT NO. 4, 1955)]

1. Paragraph (1) states the conventional position under which the significance of ignorance or mistake on the part of the defendant is determined by the mental state required for the commission of the offense involved. The ignorance or mistake is a defense when it negatives the existence of such an essential state of mind or establishes a state of mind which constitutes a defense under a rule of law establishing defenses. In other words, ignorance or mistake has only evidential import; it is significant whenever it is logically relevant and it may be relevant to negate the required mode of culpability or to establish a special defense. . . .

To put the matter in this way is not, of course, to say anything that would not otherwise be true, even if no provision on the subject should be made. As Glanville Williams summarized the matter, the rule relating to mistake "is not a new rule; and the law could be stated equally well without reference to mistake. . . . It is impossible to assert that a crime requiring intention or recklessness can be committed although the accused laboured under a mistake that negatived the requisite intention or recklessness. Such an assertion carries its own refutation." Criminal Law p. 137. . . .

It is true, of course, that whether recklessness or negligence suffices as a mode of culpability with respect to a given element of an offense is often raised for the first time in dealing with a question of mistake. . . . The fact that this may happen emphasizes the importance of perceiving that the question relates to the underlying rule as to the kind of culpability required with respect to the particular element of the offense involved.

NOTE

The Model Penal Code's mistake proposals have had a major influence on recent state penal code revisions. However, states have departed from the Model Penal Code in a number of ways. Consider, for example, the Pennsylvania provision (Pa. Cons. Stat. tit. 18, §304) that makes mistake of fact a defense when it negatives the "intent, knowledge, belief, recklessness, or negligence required" by the offense, but only if the mistake is one "for which there is a reasonable explanation or excuse." Query: What is the effect of the qualifying clause?

REGINA v. PRINCE
Court of Crown Cases Reserved
L.R. 2 Cr. Cas. Res. 154 (1875)

BRAMWELL, B. [Defendant was convicted of taking an unmarried girl under 16 years of age out of the possession and against the will of her father in violation of 24 & 25 Vict., c. 100, §55, providing:

> Whosoever shall unlawfully take or cause to be taken any unmarried girl, being under the age of sixteen years, out of the possession and against the will of her father or mother, or of any person having the lawful care or charge of her, shall be guilty of a misdemeanor. . . .

The jury found that though the girl, Annie Phillips, was 14 at the time, she had told the defendant that she was 18 before he took her away, that the defendant honestly believed that statement, and that his belief was reasonable. On a case stated by Denman, J., the Court for Crown Cases Reserved found that the prisoner was rightly convicted, Brett, J., dissenting.

[Bramwell, B., found that to sustain the defendant's position it was necessary to read into the statute language requiring that a person not believe the girl he takes is over the age of 16:]

These words are not there, and the question is, whether we are bound to construe the statute as though they were, on account of the rule that the mens rea is necessary to make an act a crime. I am of opinion that we are not, . . . and for the following reasons: The act forbidden is wrong in itself, if without lawful cause; I do not say illegal, but wrong. . . . [W]hat the statute contemplates, and what I say is wrong, is the taking of a female of such tender years that she is properly called a *girl,* can be said to be in another's *possession,* and in that other's *care or charge.* No argument is necessary to prove this; it is enough to state the case. The legislature has enacted that if anyone does this wrong act, he does it at the risk of her turning out to be under sixteen. This opinion gives full scope to the doctrine of the mens rea. If the taker believed he had the father's consent, though wrongly, he would have no mens rea; so if he did not know she was in anyone's possession, nor in the care or charge of anyone. In those cases he would not know he was doing the *act* forbidden by the statute — an act which, if he knew she was in possession and in care or charge of anyone, he would know was a crime or not, according as she was under sixteen or not. He would not know he was doing an act wrong in itself, whatever was his intention, if done without lawful cause. The same principle applies in other cases. A man was held liable for assaulting a police officer in the execution of his duty, though he did not know he was a police officer. Why? Because the act was wrong in itself. So, also, in the case of burglary, could a person charged claim an acquittal on the ground that he believed it was past six when he entered, or in housebreaking, that he did not know the place broken into was a house? It seems to me impossible to say that where a person takes a girl out of her father's possession, not knowing whether she is or is not under sixteen, that he is not guilty; and equally impossible when he believes, but erroneously, that she is old enough for him to do a wrong act with safety. I think the conviction should be affirmed.

BRETT, J., [dissenting.] . . . [I]f the facts had been as the prisoner, according to the findings of the jury, believed them to be, and had reasonable ground for believing them to be, he would have done no act which has ever been a criminal offence in England; he would have done no act in respect of which any civil action could have ever been maintained against him; he would have done no act for which, if done in the absence of the father, and done with the continuing consent of the girl, the father could have had any legal remedy. . . . Upon all the cases I think it is proved that there can be no conviction for crime in England in the absence of a criminal mind or mens rea. Then comes the question, what is the true meaning of the phrase. I do not doubt that it exists where the prisoner knowingly does acts which would constitute a crime if the result were as he anticipated, but in which the result may not improbably end by bringing the offence within a more serious class of crime. As if a man strikes with a dangerous weapon, with intent to do grievous bodily harm, and kills, the result makes the crime murder. The prisoner has run the risk. So, if a prisoner do the prohibited acts, without caring to consider what the truth is as to facts — as if a prisoner were to abduct a girl under sixteen without caring to consider whether she was in truth under sixteen — he runs the risk. So if he without abduction defiles a girl who is in fact under ten years old, with a belief that she is between ten and twelve. If the facts were as he believed he would be committing the lesser crime. Then he runs the risk of his crime resulting in the greater crime. It is clear that ignorance of the law does not excuse. It seems to me to follow that the maxim as to mens rea applies whenever the facts which are present in the prisoner's mind, and which he has reasonable ground to believe, and does believe to be the facts, would, if true, make his acts no criminal offence at all. I come to the conclusion that a mistake of facts, on reasonable grounds, to the extent that if the facts were as believed the acts of the prisoner would make him guilty of no criminal offence at all, is an excuse, and that such excuse is implied in every criminal charge and every criminal enactment in England.

NOTES AND QUESTIONS

1. In his book, An Inquiry into Criminal Guilt (1963), Professor Brett states at pages 148-149, in reference to the various opinions in the *Prince* case:

> Which of these minority views is the better? That of Bramwell, B., is to my mind clearly in accord with principle. It reflects the view that we learn our duties, not by studying the statute book, but by living in a community. A defense of mistake rests ultimately on the defendant's being able to say that he has observed the community ethic, and this Prince could not do.

For a critical response, see Hughes, Criminal Responsibility, 16 Stan. L. Rev. 470, 480 (1964). See the lecture delivered by Sir Rupert Cross on the centenary

year of the *Prince* case, entitled Centenary Reflections on *Prince*'s Case, 91 Law
Q. Rev. 540 (1975).

2. One finds approaches in American cases similar to that taken in *Prince*.
For example, in White v. State, 44 Ohio App. 331, 185 N.E. 64 (1933), defendant
was convicted of violating a statute providing that whoever, being the husband
of a pregnant woman, leaves with intent to abandon such pregnant woman
shall be imprisoned. The trial court had given an instruction to the effect that
the defendant was no less guilty because he did not know his wife was pregnant.
On appeal, held affirmed.

> The sound doctrine underlying the rule that guilty knowledge is not required to
> accomplish the crime of rape with consent is that the act of the accused is at
> best an immoral one, and that he cannot enter upon the accomplishment of an
> admittedly immoral act except at his peril, and if in law his act is in fact felony
> he must suffer the consequences thereof although so far as his actual knowledge
> was concerned he may not have known the enormity of the offense of which he
> is guilty. By like reasoning we take the view that a husband abandoning his wife
> is guilty of wrongdoing. It is a violation of his civil duty. He is charged with her
> support and protection. If he abandons her, he does so at his peril, and, if she
> be in fact at the time pregnant, though he may not have known it, he cannot
> plead that ignorance as a defense. He must make sure of his ground when he
> commits the simple wrong of leaving her at all.

3. *Questions.* What are the implications of the views in the *White* case and of
the opinions in the *Prince* case? Suppose a different situation obtained: Prince
had no interest in the girl but wanted only her father's horse and carriage.
He drove the horse and carriage away intending to steal them, totally unaware
that the girl was hidden inside the carriage. What result under these cases?

4. Compare with Regina v. Prince and White v. State the cases reprinted
earlier, Regina v. Cunningham, pages 269-271 supra, and Regina v. Faulknor,
page 271 supra. How would the latter be decided under the theory of the former?
How do you account for the differences? Are they reconcilable? If not, on what
basis is one or the other set of cases to be preferred?

NOTE ON STATUTORY RAPE

On the issue of when and whether a mistake about the age of the child in a
statutory rape case (consensual intercourse with a minor below a designated
age) is a defense, no jurisdictions allow a defense solely on the ground that
the defendant believed the minor to be over the designated age of consent.
Some recent decisions allow the defense, however, when the defendant's mistake
was reasonable; see e.g., People v. Hernandez, 61 Cal. 2d 529, 393 P.2d 673
(1964); State v. Guest, 583 P.2d 836 (Alaska 1978). Most courts adhere to the
older, contrary view that even a reasonable mistake is no defense, the defendant
acting at his peril in engaging in sex with a young person. See American Law
Institute, Model Penal Code and Commentaries, Pt. II, Comment to §213.6 at
413 (1980). As seen in §213.6(1), the Model Penal Code disallows the defense
where criminality turns on the child's being below the age of 10 but allows an
affirmative defense of reasonable belief when the critical age is higher (16 under

the Model Penal Code). A number of the newer codes adopt this distinction. Query: What is the theory behind it? See the Model Penal Code, Comments, supra, at 415-417. Note that sex with a child of 10 or under is the only instance of strict liability for crime in the Model Penal Code. Can one make a principled case for this exception?

REGINA v. MORGAN

House of Lords
[1976] A.C. 182

[The defendant Morgan and three other defendants were convicted of the forcible rape of Morgan's wife. Morgan's liability rested on his having aided and abetted the three others. The Court of Appeals affirmed all the convictions but certified the following question to the House of Lords:

Whether in rape the defendant can properly be convicted notwithstanding that he in fact believed that the woman consented, if such a belief was not based on reasonable grounds.

[A majority of the House of Lords answered this question in the negative. Selections from the addresses of several of their Lordships follow.]

LORD HAILSHAM of St. Marylebone. . . . The question arises in the following way. The appellant Morgan and his three co-appellants, who were all members of the RAF, spent the evening of 15th August 1973 in one another's company. The appellant Morgan was significantly older than the other three, and considerably senior to them in rank. He was . . . married to the alleged victim, but not, it seems, at the time habitually sleeping in the same bed. . . . [B]y the time the appellants arrived at Morgan's house, Mrs. Morgan was already in bed and asleep, until she was awoken by their presence.

According to the version of the facts which she gave in evidence, and which was evidently accepted by the jury, she was aroused from her sleep, . . . held by each of her limbs, . . . while each of the three young appellants in turn had intercourse with her in the presence of the others. . . .

According to Mrs. Morgan she consented to none of this and made her opposition to what was being done very plain indeed. . . .

All four appellants explained in the witness box that they had spent the evening together in Wolverhampton, and by the time of the alleged offences had had a good deal to drink. Their original intention had been to find some women in the town but, when this failed, Morgan made the surprising suggestion to the others that they should all return to his home and have sexual intercourse with his wife. According to the three younger appellants (but not according to Morgan who described this part of their story as "lying") Morgan told them that they must not be surprised if his wife struggled a bit, since she was "kinky" and this was the only way in which she could get "turned on." However this may be, it is clear that Morgan did invite his three companions home in order that they might have sexual intercourse with his wife and, no doubt, he may well have led them in one way or another to believe that she would consent to their doing so. This, however, would only be matter predisposing them to believe that Mrs. Morgan consented, and would not in any way establish that, at the time, they believed she did consent whilst they were having intercourse.

I need not enter into the details of what the appellants said happened after they had arrived at the house. As I have said they admitted that some degree of struggle took place in the wife's bedroom. But all asserted that after she got into the double bedroom she not merely consented to but actively co-operated with and enjoyed what was being done. . . .

The choice before the jury was thus between two stories each wholly incompatible with the other, and in my opinion it would have been quite sufficient for the judge, after suitable warnings about the burden of proof, corroboration, separate verdicts and the admissibility of the statements only against the makers, to tell the jury that they must really choose between the two versions. . . .

The certified question arises because counsel for the appellants raised the question whether, even if the victim [objected], the appellants may . . . have honestly believed that she did [not]. . . . [I]n the summing-up [to the jury] . . . [t]he learned judge said:

> . . . [T]he prosecution have to prove that each defendant intended to have sexual intercourse with this woman without her consent. Not merely that he intended to have intercourse with her but that he intended to have intercourse without her consent. Therefore if the defendant believed or may have believed that Mrs. Morgan consented to him having sexual intercourse with her, then there would be no such intent in his mind and he would be not guilty of the offence of rape, but such a belief must be honestly held by the defendant in the first place. He must really believe that. And, secondly, his belief must be a reasonable belief; such a belief as a reasonable man would entertain if he applied his mind and thought about the matter. It is not enough for a defendant to rely upon a belief, even though he honestly held it, if it was completely fanciful; contrary to every indication which could be given which would carry some weight with a reasonable man. . . .

It is on the second proposition about the mental element that the appellants concentrate their criticism. An honest belief in consent, they contend, is enough. It matters not whether it be also reasonable. No doubt a defendant will wish to raise argument or lead evidence to show that this belief was reasonable, since this will support its honesty. No doubt the prosecution will seek to cross-examine or raise arguments or adduce evidence to undermine the contention that the belief is reasonable, because, in the nature of the case, the fact that a belief cannot reasonably be held is a strong ground for saying that it was not in fact held honestly at all. Nonetheless, the appellants contend, the crux of the matter, the factum probandum, or rather the fact to be refuted by the prosecution, is honesty and not honesty plus reasonableness. . . .

The beginning of wisdom in all the "mens rea" cases to which our attention was called is, as was pointed out by Stephen, J., in R. v. Tolson, [23 Q.B.D. 168 (1889)], that "mens rea" means a number of quite different things in relation to different crimes. . . .

Once one has accepted, what seems to me abundantly clear, that the prohibited act in rape is non-consensual sexual intercourse, and that the guilty state of mind is an intention to commit it, it seems to me to follow as a matter of inexorable logic that there is no room either for a "defence" of honest belief or mistake, or of a defence of honest and reasonable belief and mistake. Either the prosecution proves that the accused had the requisite intent, or it does not. In the former case it succeeds, and in the latter it fails. Since honest belief clearly negatives intent, the reasonableness or otherwise of that belief can only be evidence for or against the view that the belief and therefore the intent was actually held. . . .

For the above reasons I would answer the question certified in the negative, but would apply the proviso to s. 2(1) of the Criminal Appeal Act 1968 on the ground that no miscarriage of justice has or conceivably could have occurred.[a] In my view, therefore these appeals should be dismissed.

LORD FRASER of Tulleybelton. . . . The argument for the Crown in support of an affirmative answer to the question in this case was not supported by any English decision on rape. It was supported by reference to English decisions in relation to other offences which are more or less analogous to rape. . . . The English case upon which most reliance was placed was Reg. v. Tolson, 23 Q.B.D. 168, which was concerned with bigamy, and which decided that a bona fide belief *on reasonable grounds* in the death of the husband at the time of the second marriage afforded a good defence to the indictment for bigamy. The main argument in the case was concerned with the question whether a mistaken belief could be a defence to a charge of bigamy at all, and comparatively little attention was given to the subsidiary point of whether the belief had to be based upon reasonable grounds. The case seems to me therefore of only limited assistance for the present purpose. . . . The difficulty of arguing by analogy from one offence to another is strikingly illustrated by reference to the case of Reg. v. Prince (1875) 13 Cox C.C. 138. That case dealt with abduction of a girl under the age of 16, an offence created by section 55 of the Act of 1861. Bramwell, B., with whom five other judges concurred, held that a mistaken and reasonable belief by the defendant that the abducted girl was aged 16 or more was no excuse, because abduction of a young girl was immoral as well as illegal, although a mistaken and reasonable belief by the defendant that he had the consent of the girl's father would have been an excuse. If such differences can exist about mistaken beliefs of different facts in one offence, it is surely dangerous to argue from one offence to another. No doubt a rapist, who mistakenly believes that the woman is consenting to intercourse, must be behaving immorally, by committing fornication or adultery. But those forms of immoral conduct are not intended to be struck at by the law against rape; indeed, they are not now considered appropriate to be visited with penalties of the criminal law at all. There seems therefore to be no reason why they should affect the consequences of the mistaken belief. . . .

For these reasons, I am of the opinion that there is no authority which compels me to answer the question in this case in what I would regard as an illogical way. I would therefore answer the question in the negative — that is in favour of the accused. But, for the reasons stated by . . . Lord Hailsham, . . . I would

---

a. Section 2(1) of the Criminal Appeal Act of 1968 provides that "the Court may, notwithstanding that they are of opinion that the point raised in the appeal might be decided in favour of the appellant, dismiss the appeal if they consider that no miscarriage of justice has actually occurred." The theory of the answer to the second question was that no reasonable jury could have failed to convict all four accused even had they been directed as counsel for the appellants urged they should. — EDS.

apply the proviso to the Criminal Appeal Act 1968, section 2 (1), and I would refuse the appeal.

Appeals dismissed.

LORD CROSS of Chelsea. . . . I would say something as to how far — if at all — the decision in Reg. v. Tolson, 23 Q.B.D. 168, which was, of course, a case of bigamy, has a bearing on this case. The statute there provided that "Whosoever, being married, shall marry any other person during the life of the former husband or wife, . . . shall be guilty of felony," with a proviso that

> nothing in this section contained shall extend . . . to any person marrying a second time whose husband or wife shall have been continually absent from such person for the space of seven years then last past, and shall not have been known by such person to be living within that time, . . .

The defendant who was found by the jury to have had reasonable grounds for believing that her husband was then dead — though in fact he was not — went through a ceremony of marriage with another man within seven years of the time when she last knew of his being alive. She therefore fell within the very words of the statute. Nevertheless, the majority of the Court of Crown Cases Reserved held that she was entitled to be acquitted because on general principles of criminal liability, having no particular relation to the crime of bigamy, a mistaken belief based on reasonable grounds in the existence of facts, which, if true, would have made the act charged against her innocent, afforded her a defence since it was not to be supposed that Parliament intended bigamy to be an "absolute" offence to the commission of which the state of mind of the defendant was wholly irrelevant. The minority of the judges, on the other hand, thought that the existence of the proviso which gave an express exemption from liability in certain circumstances made it impossible to imply an exemption from liability in other circumstances not covered by it. If the Sexual Offences Act 1956 had provided that it was an offence for a man to have sexual intercourse with a woman who did not consent to it then the case of Reg. v. Tolson, 23 Q.B.D. 168 would undoubtedly have been in point; but what the Act says is that it is an offence for a man to "rape" a woman and, as I see it, one cannot say that Reg. v. Tolson applies to rape unless one reads the words "rape a woman" as equivalent to "have intercourse with a woman who is not consenting to it." Counsel for the Director [of Public Prosecutions] says, of course, that they are equivalent but the question remains whether he is right.

Finally, I must refer to an alternative submission, made by counsel for the appellant — namely, that in Reg. v. Tolson the court was wrong in saying that to afford a defence to a charge of bigamy the mistaken belief of the defendant had to be based on reasonable grounds. . . .

[His Lordship then concluded that *Tolson* had been too long accepted to warrant overruling and continued:] So, even if I had been myself inclined to think that the inclusion of the element of reasonableness was wrong, I would not have thought it right for us to call it in question in this case. In fact, however, I can see no objection to the inclusion of the element of reasonableness in what I may call a "*Tolson*" case. If the words defining an offence provide either expressly or impliedly that a man is not to be guilty of it if he believes something to be true, then he cannot be found guilty if the jury think that he may have believed it to be true, however inadequate were his reasons for doing so. But, if the definition of the offence is on the face of it "absolute" and the defendant is seeking to escape his prima facie liability by a defence of mistaken belief, I can see no hardship to him in requiring the mistake — if it is to afford him a defence — to be based on reasonable grounds. As Lord Diplock said in Sweet v. Parsley [1970] A.C. 132, there is nothing unreasonable in the law requiring a citizen to take reasonable care to ascertain the facts relevant to his avoiding doing a prohibited act. To have intercourse with a woman who is not your wife is, even today, not generally considered to be a course of conduct which the law ought positively to encourage and it can be argued with force that it is only fair to the woman and not in the least unfair to the man that he should be under a duty to take reasonable care to ascertain that she is consenting to the intercourse and be at the risk of a prosecution if he fails to take such care. So if the Sexual Offences Act 1956 had made it an offence to have intercourse with a woman who was not consenting to it, so that the defendant could only escape liability by the application of the "*Tolson*" principle, I would not have thought the law unjust.

But, as I have said, section 1 of the Act of 1956 does not say that a man who has sexual intercourse with a woman who does not consent to it commits an offence; it says that a man who rapes a woman commits an offence. Rape is not a word in the use of which lawyers have a monopoly and the question to be answered in this case, as I see it, is whether according to the ordinary use of the English language a man can be said to have committed rape if he believed that the woman was consenting to the intercourse and would not have attempted to have it but for his belief, whatever his grounds for so believing. I do not think that he can. . . .

NOTE ON THE CONTROVERSY OVER THE MORGAN *DECISION*

The *Morgan* decision evoked a considerable reaction in the press. An editorial in The Times (London), May 5, 1975, at 15 stated that the decision "does not accord with common sense. Until this decision was given, it had been generally accepted that the belief in the woman's consent had to be reasonable. In ruling otherwise, the law lords have been unduly legalistic."

In a letter to The Times, May 7, 1975, Professor J. C. Smith responded:

> It is surprising that you think that the decision of the majority of the House of Lords in *Morgan,* namely that the crime of rape requires an intention to commit rape, "does not accord with common sense." A man who intends to have sexual intercourse with a consenting woman may have an immoral intention but it is scarcely the kind of criminal mind which should make him liable for an offence carrying a maximum sentence of life imprisonment.
>
> The fact that he *ought* to have known that the woman was not consenting is not a valid ground for imputing to him an intention which he did not possess. . . .
>
> *Morgan* is a victory for common sense so far as intention in the criminal law is concerned. For too long the courts have said, inconsistently, that while the prosecution must prove an intention to do the prohibited act, a mistake negativing the required intention in the accused is not a defence unless it is reasonable. If, as appears likely, *Morgan* authoritatively rejects this fallacy, it is a decision of the greatest importance to the basic principles of criminal liability. . . .

In another letter to The Times, May 8, 1975, Professor Glanville Williams stated:

There has been a good deal of misunderstanding of the recent decision of the law lords in the rape case, which merely applied established principles.

(1) With a few exceptions, which need not be considered (and ought not to exist), serious crimes require a mental element (an intention to do the act or to produce the result, and knowledge of the facts, or at least conscious recklessness).

(2) Rape is a serious crime, involving sexual intercourse with a woman without her consent.

(3) Therefore rape requires the mental element that the man must know that the woman does not consent.

This was the simple point decided by their lordships, and the decision is warmly to be welcomed. The opposing view was that a man could be convicted of rape although he honestly believed that the woman was consenting, if he was stupid (unreasonable) in forming that belief. To convict the stupid man would be to convict him for what lawyers call inadvertent negligence — honest conduct which may be the best that this man can do but that does not come up to the standard of the so-called reasonable man. People ought not to be punished for negligence except in some minor offences established by statute. Rape carries a possible sentence of imprisonment for life, and it would be wrong to have a law of negligent rape.

Further, it is unnecessary. Except perhaps in one situation to be mentioned in a moment it is virtually inconceivable that even a stupid man would fail to realise that a woman with whom he has sexual intercourse does not consent. Let me try to clear away some misconceptions.

(a) Many charges of rape fail because of a clash of evidence; if there is a doubt the jury have to give the man the benefit of it. This difficulty is inherent in the situation. It would make almost no difference even if rape were turned by statute into an offense of strict liability (not requiring a mental element or other fault on the man's part); there would still be conflicts of evidence on whether the man had intercourse with the woman or whether the woman consented. . . .

(b) What further difficulty does the prosecution face in proving that the man knew that the woman did not consent? Virtually none. . . . No one who uses threats against a woman will be heard to say that he thought she consented. If the man does not use threats, even by implication, the only way that anyone can tell whether the woman consents or not is by her words or behaviour. . . . If she protests, the man is bound to know it. There is nothing in the Lords' decision to prevent a judge directing the jury that if anyone would have realised from what the woman said and did that she was not consenting, then they are entitled to conclude that the defendant realised it, unless there are some other facts to raise a doubt in their minds. What the judge must not tell the jury, on a charge of rape or any other serious crime, is that they can convict the defendant although he did not know that the vital facts existed and was not reckless as to those facts, if he was stupid in not realising that they existed.

Critics of the recent decision should note not only that the jury convicted the defendants but that the House of Lords affirmed the conviction on the ground that any jury properly instructed would have convicted. The only type of case in which an insistence on the mental element in rape is likely to give any opening to the defence is where the defendant claims that he was so intoxicated that he did not realise that the woman was resisting, although any sober person would have realised it.

Two remarks may be made about this. First, there is no reported instance of the defence of intoxication having been set up in a rape case in this country, and before becoming alarmed about it we might wait to see if it ever succeeds. A sensible jury may take the view that a man who is sober enough to perform is sober enough to realise that the woman is resisting. Secondly, the question of intoxication in relation to the mental element in crime is a general one, and one that certainly needs legislative attention, though not particularly in relation to rape.

Mr. Jack Ashley, a Labor M.P., joined the debate, writing (May 12, 1975):

It is remarkable how sanguine some of your correspondents are about the law lords' judgment of law relating to rape. Professor Glanville Williams (May 8) is the latest of a number of eminent lawyers who share the Home Secretary's view that it will make little if any difference. But if they are wrong, as I am convinced they are, many women are going to suffer, and their rapists escape, as a consequence of this ruling.

I believe there will be three significant effects. First, it is utterly fallacious to assume that juries will be unaffected by the judgment. They now have to judge not only whether the woman was forced to submit but whether the man genuinely believed she consented — however irresponsible the grounds for that belief may be.

It is no answer to claim that as juries still have to be convinced the situation is unchanged. Juries are now forbidden to convict on the grounds that a man's belief is unreasonable.

Secondly, it will encourage potential rapists who are unlikely to be slow to take advantage of the new defence weapon in their hands. We must assume that rapists will lie in the witness box to escape the consequences of a vicious and degrading crime. It now depends on whether they tell the right lie. One of the law lords said that if the three men in that case had claimed that the woman was play acting when she struggled, instead of arguing that she did not struggle, they might have been acquitted. In other words, their mistake was to tell the wrong lie. Future rapists will learn from this error and lie accordingly.

Thirdly, a woman, who is in any case unwilling to report rape, will be even more reluctant to come forward. Why should she suffer the ordeal of hearing her rapist declaim his "belief" that she was willing to receive what she got — especially as this may be the overture to an orchestrated attack on her moral standards by enthusiastic defence lawyers? And if women do not report rapes, how are the rapists to be caught?

For discussion of a report of a committee set up, because of the decision in *Morgan,* to look into the law of rape, see J. C. Smith, The Heilbron Report, [1976] Crim. L. Rev. 97.

The culmination of the controversy over the *Morgan* decision was the enactment in 1976 of the Sexual Offences (Amendment) Act, which in §1(1) provided:

A man commits rape if (a) he has unlawful sexual intercourse with a woman who at the time of the intercourse does not consent to it; and (b) at that time he knows that she does not consent to the intercourse or he is reckless as to whether she consents to it.

Query: Does this enactment adopt the holding in the *Morgan* case? For further discussion, see Wells, Swatting the Subjectivist Bug, [1982] Crim. L. Rev. 209.

PEOPLE v. MAYBERRY

Supreme Court of California
15 Cal. 3d 143, 542 P.2d 1337 (1975)

RICHARDSON, J. An information was filed charging Franklin Mayberry . . . with various offenses against the prosecutrix (Miss Nancy B.). . . . Franklin was charged with kidnaping (Pen. Code, §207), rape by means of force and threat (Pen. Code, §261, subds. 2 & 3), assault by means of force likely to produce great bodily injury (Pen. Code, §245), and oral copulation (Pen. Code, §288a). Following a joint trial, a jury found defendant . . . guilty as charged on all counts. . . .

Defendant . . . appeal[s] from the judgments [of conviction]. . . .

Miss B., the prosecutrix, testified to the following effect:

About 4 P.M. on July 8, 1971, she left her apartment in Oakland to walk to a nearby grocery store. As she passed a liquor store, she heard "catcalls" from some men, and Franklin, whom she had never seen before, grabbed her arm. She dug her fingernails into his wrist, and he released her. After she turned to leave, he kicked her, threw a bottle which struck her, and shouted obscenities at her. She remonstrated and continued on her way.

After she entered the grocery store, Franklin suddenly appeared beside her and said something to the effect that she was going to go outside with him and if she did not cooperate she would "pay for it." She replied she did not want to accompany him and looked for a store security guard but saw none. The only store personnel she observed were busy with customers and were too far away for her to gain their attention. Because of her own confusion and fear of Franklin, she accompanied him outside the store, where they remained for approximately 20 minutes. During this time Miss B. observed no one available to assist her although two women left the store in her vicinity.

Franklin, in a threatening manner, mentioned to Miss B. having sex. She rejected this, but Franklin told her she "was going to have to go with him," and, when she refused, struck her in the chest with his fist, knocking her down. Franklin directed obscenities at her, held his fist up to her face, and told her "you are going to come with me" and added that if she did not do so he would "knock every tooth out of [her] mouth." She asked him to leave her alone, but Franklin seized her wrist and said "come on." In an attempt "to buy time," she told Franklin she wanted to purchase some cigarettes, and he agreed. Placing his hand beneath her elbow, he accompanied her to a store, approximately 100 feet away, where she purchased cigarettes for herself and Franklin. She did not explain to the clerk her predicament because she was feeling "completely beaten" and did not think the clerk would help her.

After completing the purchase, she sat on a curb, attempted to engage Franklin in conversation and smoked a cigarette. During this period, in her words, she "put on an act" and tried "to fool" Franklin, thinking that she might be able to escape. He eventually said, "we are leaving." She "tried to talk him out of it," and he became angry and, uttering an obscenity, ordered her to "get up." She complied, and he again seized her elbow and started to guide her. While walking several blocks, they passed some business establishments, but Miss B. noticed no one on the street. She did not want to accompany him but, because of fear, did not resist.

Franklin led her to an apartment house and entered ahead of her. After they entered his apartment, he barricaded the door behind them. She did not attempt to flee because, having a leg that was stiff from an arthritic condition, she could not run fast. Approximately 15 minutes of further conversation ensued during which she unsuccessfully attempted to persuade Franklin "to change his mind." Without her consent, he then engaged in several acts of sexual intercourse and oral copulation with her. During the sexual assault he struck her, and because of fear she did not physically resist his advances. . . .

. . . She immediately reported the incidents to her apartment manager, and the police were summoned.

At trial a police officer testified that around 10:40 P.M. on July 8, 1971, he went to Miss B.'s address in response to a kidnap-rape call and observed much bruising and swelling on her face, left arm and leg.

Franklin took the stand in his own behalf and testified as follows: he saw Miss B. about 4 P.M. on July 8, 1971, and engaged her in conversation, after which he accompanied her to the grocery and the store where she purchased cigarettes. They then walked to his home. He did not threaten her, nor did she protest but accompanied him willingly and agreed to, and did engage in, intercourse. . . .

In arguing that the prosecutrix' testimony is inherently improbable, [defendant points] to the facts that the prosecutrix did not report the assault in front of the liquor store to the police from a telephone that was available near the grocery store; that she did not physically resist Franklin after the initial encounter; that she failed to attempt to flee or obtain help even though there were opportunities for her to do so; that there was no evidence Franklin was armed; and that she had "a lighted cigarette just prior to the time that [she] left [defendant's apartment]," suggesting thereby, in some way, a friendly parting. . . .

. . . [I]t cannot be said that the prosecutrix' testimony is inherently improbable. . . . Her failure to elicit help from others (e.g., persons at the grocery store) might have been deemed suspicious, but it was also susceptible to a conclusion that she was too frightened to think clearly. Her testimony that "[she] did have a lighted cigarette just prior to the time that [she] left [defendant's apartment]," which testimony is not amplified, is not significant and discloses at most an unusual circumstance. . . .

The court refused to give requested instructions that directed the jury to acquit Franklin of the rape and kidnaping if the jury had a reasonable doubt as to whether Franklin reasonably and genuinely believed that Miss B. freely consented to her movement from the grocery store to his apartment and to sexual intercourse with him. Franklin contends that the court thereby erred. The Attorney General argues that the court properly refused to give the instructions because "mistake of fact instruction[s] as to consent should be rejected as against the law and public policy."

Penal Code section 207 provides,

> Every person who forcibly . . . takes . . . any person in this state, and carries him into . . . another part of the same county, . . . is guilty of kidnaping.

Penal Code section 261 provides,

Rape is an act of sexual intercourse, accomplished with a female not the wife of the perpetrator, under either of the following circumstances: . . . ; 2. Where she resists, but her resistance is overcome by force or violence; 3. Where she is prevented from resisting by threats of great and immediate bodily harm, accompanied by apparent power of execution. . . .

There is, of course, no kidnaping "when one, . . . with knowledge of what is taking place . . . , voluntarily . . . consents to accompany another . . ." . . . , and similarly there is no rape if a female of sufficient capacity consents to sexual intercourse. . . .

Penal Code section 26 recites, generally, that one is incapable of committing a crime who commits an act under a mistake of fact disproving any criminal intent. Penal Code section 20 provides, "In every crime . . . there must exist a union, or joint operation of act and intent, or criminal negligence." The word "intent" in section 20 means "wrongful intent." (See People v. Vogel, 46 Cal. 2d 798, 801, fn. 2.) . . .

In People v. Hernandez, 61 Cal. 2d 529, 393 P.2d 673, we considered the matter of intent within a context similar to that presented in the instant case. The defendant in *Hernandez* was convicted of statutory rape under former subdivision 1 of Penal Code section 261, which provided "Rape is an act of sexual intercourse, accomplished with a female not the wife of the perpetrator. . . . 1. Where the female is under the age of eighteen years." On appeal the defendant contended that the court erred in excluding evidence that he had in good faith a reasonable belief that the prosecutrix was 18 years or more in age, and in *Hernandez* we upheld the contention.

Hernandez emphasized that we gave recognition to the legislative declarations in Penal Code sections 20 and 26 when we held in People v. Vogel, supra, 46 Cal. 2d 798, that "a [reasonable and] good faith belief that a former wife had obtained a divorce was a valid defense to a charge of bigamy arising out of a second marriage when the first marriage had not in fact been terminated." *Hernandez* quoted from *Vogel*, " 'Nor would it be reasonable to hold that a person is guilty of bigamy who remarries in good faith in reliance on a judgment of divorce . . . that is subsequently found not to be the "judgment of a competent court.". . . Since it is often difficult for laymen to know when a judgment is not that of a competent court, we cannot reasonably expect them always to have such knowledge and make them criminals if their bona fide belief proves to be erroneous.' " *Hernandez* then declared, "Certainly it cannot be a greater wrong to entertain a bona fide but erroneous belief that a valid consent to an act of sexual intercourse has been obtained.". . .

Although *Hernandez* dealt solely with statutory rape its rationale applies equally to rape by means of force or threat and kidnaping. Those statutory provisions, like that involved in *Hernandez*, neither expressly nor by necessary implication negate the continuing requirement that there be a union of act and wrongful intent. The severe penalties imposed for those offenses and the serious loss of reputation following conviction make it extremely unlikely that the Legislature intended to exclude as to those offenses the element of wrongful intent. If a defendant entertains a reasonable and bona fide belief that a prosecutrix voluntarily consented to accompany him and to engage in sexual intercourse, it is apparent he does not possess the wrongful intent that is a prerequisite under

Penal Code section 20 to a conviction of either kidnaping or rape by means of force or threat. . . .

The Attorney General . . . argues that, even if instructions regarding mistake of fact as to consent are appropriate in some cases of kidnaping and rape, here the court properly determined that the evidence did not warrant such instructions. However, Franklin's testimony summarized above could be viewed as indicating that he reasonably and in good faith believed that Miss B. consented to accompany him to the apartment and to the subsequent sexual intercourse. In addition, part of Miss B.'s testimony furnishes support for the requested instructions. It appears from her testimony that her behavior was equivocal. . . . We by no means intimate that such is the *only* reasonable interpretation of her conduct, but we do conclude that there was some evidence "deserving of . . . consideration" which supported his contention that he acted under a mistake of fact as to her consent both to the movement and to intercourse. It follows accordingly, that the requested instructions, if correctly worded, should have been given. . . .

The convictions of rape and kidnaping are reversed. In all other respects, the judgments are affirmed.

c. Mistake of Law

INTRODUCTORY NOTE

The legal significance of defendant's mistake about a matter of law may vary depending on what law is mistaken. We may generally identify three kinds of mistakes.

(1) Mistake as to some matter of law, usually of the civil law, which is relevant because the criminal prohibition incorporates a legal element into its definition. For example, larceny requires the appropriation of property of another, knowing it *belongs* to another.

(2) Mistake as to the existence or meaning of the criminal prohibition itself.

(3) Mistake as to the law that justifies what would otherwise be a criminal act, for example, execution of a public duty.

These categories are not as analytically airtight as their statement may suggest at first blush, and part of the difficulty in the law is in determining in any given case what kind of mistake of law is involved. Nevertheless, these categories may be taken as a rough guide to the materials presented in this section: State v. Woods, pages 297-298 infra, opens consideration of the first category of mistake; United States v. International Minerals & Chemical Corporation, pages 303-304 infra, introduces consideration of the second category; United States v. Barker, pages 314-321 infra, introduces discussion of the third category.

STATE v. WOODS
Supreme Court of Vermont
107 Vt. 354, 179 A. 1 (1935)

BUTTLES, J. The respondent was convicted in Orleans county court of a violation of P.L. 8602, commonly known as the Blanket Act.[a]

A transcript of the evidence has not been furnished, but from the respondent's amended exceptions it appears:

> That the respondent, a single woman, with her three children, in company with one Leo Shufelt, of Lowell, Vermont, and of one John Ellis, motored in the summer of 1933 to Reno, Nevada, . . . where the said Leo Shufelt, who was a married man, instituted divorce proceedings against his wife, then living in Vermont; that process in said divorce proceedings was served upon the said wife; that she never accepted service of same, did not go to Nevada, and had no appearance entered in her behalf in said cause.

It further appears that after hearing, a decree was granted which purported to be a decree of divorce to the said Shufelt, and thereupon he and the respondent went through a marriage ceremony in Reno, which was performed by the same judge who granted the decree, and thereupon the respondent entered into marital relations with the said Shufelt, and after a week or so went with him to Connecticut, whence he subsequently went to Lowell, Vt., where the respondent later joined him and where the offense herein charged is alleged to have been committed.

The respondent does not challenge, by her exceptions, the submission to the jury of the questions of fact upon which the determination below of the invalidity of the attempted Nevada divorce for the purposes of this case was based. Neither does she challenge the manner in which those questions were submitted nor the determination by the court below that said attempted divorce is, for the purposes of this case, invalid. The verdict of the jury and the rulings of the trial court as to the invalidity of the attempted Nevada divorce are therefore conclusive upon the rights of the respondent in this case. . . .

The respondent has saved one exception to the charge as given, and four to the failure of the court to comply with requests to charge. The real question involved in all of these exceptions is the same, and we will consider them together, as the respondent has done in her brief.

The respondent contends, by these exceptions, that an honest belief in the validity of the Reno divorce and of her subsequent marriage to Shufelt would be a defense to this prosecution. There is much diversity of view as to whether a mistaken belief as to a fact, based upon reasonable grounds, may or may not constitute a defense in a criminal action of a nature similar to this one. In State v. Ackerly, 79 Vt. 69, 64 A. 450, this court held that an honest belief that his wife was dead was not a defense in a prosecution for bigamy, the respondent having attempted to remarry.

But in State v. Audette, 81 Vt. 400, 70 A. 833, it was held that, under the

---

a. "*Parties found in bed together.* A man with another man's wife, or a woman with another woman's husband, found in bed together, under circumstances affording presumption of an illicit intention, shall each be imprisoned in the state prison not more than three years or fined not more than $1,000.00." — EDS.

circumstances of the case, ignorance of the fact that the woman whom the respondent attempted to marry had a husband living was available as a defense in a prosecution for adultery, he having been misled by her false statements as to that fact.

Here the respondent relies upon a mistake of law rather than of fact. Her presence in Reno and her marriage to Shufelt immediately after the supposed divorce was granted by the judge who granted the decree indicate that she must have known all about the facts and circumstances of that proceeding. No claim is made that she did not know the facts. Her mistake, if one she made, was as to the legal effect in Vermont of the Nevada decree. The maxim *Ignorantia legis non excusat,* and the corresponding presumption that every one is conclusively presumed to know the law, are of unquestioned application in Vermont as elsewhere, both in civil and in criminal cases. . . .

This presumption applies as well in prosecutions for adultery as in other criminal prosecutions." It is no defense that the parties were mistaken as to the law and had no intention of committing the offense (adultery)." 2 Corpus Juris, 16. . . .

It remains to consider whether this presumption is applicable in this case in view of the phraseology of P.L. 8602, under which the respondent was prosecuted. Clearly it does apply if the words "under circumstances affording presumption of an illicit intention" mean that the act which the respondent intends to do is forbidden and not that the respondent must have acted with a guilty mind.

Obviously the real purpose of this section of the statute is to punish and prevent the commission of adultery. We perceive no reason why the rule regarding ignorance of the law should be any differently applied to a prosecution under this section than it would be if the prosecution were for adultery under one of the two preceding sections of the statute. Furthermore, the practical necessity for this rule if the criminal law is to be adequately enforced is as great with respect to this offense as any other. Our public policy as evidenced by our divorce statutes and our refusal to recognize the validity of attempted foreign divorces, under certain circumstances, would have little force if people could use such attempted foreign divorce coupled with a plea of ignorance of the law as a defense in prosecution for sexual offenses.

When it is proved that the parties were found in bed together under circumstances affording presumption of an intention to commit the act as charged in the indictment or information, then the requirement of the statute is met and ignorance of the law cannot be urged as a defense.

REGINA v. SMITH (DAVID)
Court of Appeal
[1974] 2 Q.B. 354, 58 Cr. App. 320

JAMES, L.J. . . . [T]he appellant, David Raymond Smith, was convicted of an offence of causing criminal damage contrary to section 1(1) of the Criminal Damage Act 1971. He appeals against that conviction on a question of law. . . .

The question of law in this appeal arises in this way. In 1970 the appellant became the tenant of a ground-floor flat at 209, Freemasons' Road, E.16. The letting included a conservatory. In the conservatory the appellant and his brother, who lived with him, installed some electric wiring for use with stereo equipment. Also, with the landlord's permission, they put up roofing material and asbestos wall panels and laid floor boards. There is no dispute that the roofing, wall panels and floor boards became part of the house and, in law, the property of the landlord. Then in 1972 the appellant gave notice to quit and asked the landlord to allow the appellant's brother to remain as tenant of the flat. On September 18, 1972, the landlord informed the appellant that his brother could not remain. On the next day the appellant damaged the roofing, wall panels and floorboards he had installed in order — according to the appellant and his brother — to gain access to and remove the wiring. The extent of the damage was £130. When interviewed by the police, the appellant said: "Look, how can I be done for smashing my own property. I put the flooring and that in, so if I want to pull it down it's a matter for me.". . .

The appellant's defence was that he honestly believed that the damage he did was to his own property, that he believed that he was entitled to damage his own property and therefore he had a lawful excuse for his actions causing the damage. In the course of his summing up the deputy judge directed the jury in these terms:

> Now, in order to make the offence complete, the person who is charged with it must destroy or damage that property belonging to another, "without lawful excuse," and that is something that one has got to look at a little more, members of the jury, because you have heard here that, so far as . ·. . defendant was concerned, it never occurred to [him] and, you may think, quite naturally never occurred to [him] that these various additions to the house were anything but [his] own property. . . . It is said that he had a lawful excuse by reason of his belief, his honest and genuinely held belief that he was destroying property which he had a right to destroy if he wanted to. But, members of the jury, I must direct you as a matter of law, and you must, therefore, accept it from me, that belief by the defendant David Smith that he had the right to do what he did is not lawful excuse within the meaning of the Act. Members of the jury, it is an excuse, it may even be a reasonable excuse, but it is not, members of the jury, a lawful excuse, because, in law, he had no right to do what he did. . . .

It is contended for the appellant that that is a misdirection in law, and that, as a result of the misdirection, the entire defence of the appellant was wrongly withdrawn from the jury.

Section 1 of the Criminal Damage Act 1971 reads:

> (1) A person who without lawful excuse destroys or damages any property belonging to another intending to destroy or damage any such property or being reckless as to whether any such property would be destroyed or damaged, shall be guilty of an offence.

The offence created includes the elements of intention or recklessness and the absence of lawful excuse. . . .

It is argued for the appellant that an honest, albeit erroneous, belief that the act causes damage or destruction was done to his own property provides a defence to a charge brought under section 1(1). The argument [is] that the offence charged includes the act causing the damage or destruction and the element of mens rea. The element of mens rea relates to all the circumstances of the criminal act. The criminal act in the offence is causing damage to or destruction of "property belonging to another" and the element of mens rea, therefore, must relate to "property belonging to another." Honest belief, whether justifiable or not, that the property is the defendant's own negatives the element of mens rea. . . .

It is conceded by Mr. Gerber [counsel for the Crown] that there is force in the argument that the element of mens rea extends to "property belonging to another." But, it is argued, the section creates a statutory offence and that it is open to the construction that the mental element in the offence relates only to causing damage to or destroying property. That if in fact the property damaged or destroyed is shown to be another's property the offence is committed although the defendant did not intend or foresee damage to another person's property. . . .

If the direction given by the deputy judge in the present case is correct, then the offence created by section 1(1) of the Act of 1971 involves a considerable extension of the law in a surprising direction. Whether or not this is so depends upon the construction of the section. Construing the language of section 1(1) we have no doubt that the actus reus is "destroying or damaging any property belonging to another." It is not possible to exclude the words "belonging to another" which describes the "property." Applying the ordinary principles of mens rea, the intention and recklessness and the absence of lawful excuse required to constitute the offence have reference to property belonging to another. It follows that in our judgment no offence is committed under this section if a person destroys or causes damage to property belonging to another if he does so in the honest though mistaken belief that the property is his own, and provided that the belief is honestly held it is irrelevant to consider whether or not it is a justifiable belief.

In our judgment, the direction given to the jury was a fundamental misdirection in law. The consequence was that the jury were precluded from considering facts capable of being a defence to the charge and were directed to convict.

For these reasons on November 5 at the conclusion of argument we allowed the appeal and ordered that the conviction be quashed.

NOTES

1. *The common law approach.* Considered in the light of the *Smith* (*David*) case, is the decision in the *Woods* case a proper application of the ignorance of the law maxim? Or is it an illustration of the following observation (Model Penal Code §2.02, Comment at 131 (Tent. Draft No. 4, 1955)):

> It should be noted that the general principle that ignorance or mistake of law is no excuse is usually greatly overstated; it has no application when the circumstances made material by the definition of the offense include a legal element. So, for example, it is immaterial in theft, when claim of right is adduced in defense, that the claim involves a legal judgment as to the right of property. It is a defense

because knowledge that the property belongs to someone else is a material element of the crime and such knowledge may involve matter of law as well as fact. . . . The law involved is not the law defining the offense; it is some other legal rule that characterizes the attendant circumstances that are material to the offense.

2. General and specific intent. What was the mens rea required by the English statute in the *Smith* (*David*) case? Was Smith's a specific- or a general-intent crime? Note that the court did not address this question. However, many courts would have regarded the answer to that question as dispositive of the issue whether the mistake constituted a defense. If the statute were held to designate a specific-intent crime — that is, that knowledge or purpose was required — then a mistake of law that negatived the existence of that purpose or knowledge would be a defense, just as would a mistake of fact having that effect. But if the statute were held to designate a general-intent crime — that is, that recklessness or negligence would suffice — then a mistake of law, even a reasonable one, would not be a defense, even though a reasonable mistake of fact would be. Thus, for example, larceny is generally held to be a specific-intent crime, in the sense that it requires that one have taken property with the purpose of permanantly depriving the owner of possession; a mistake of law about the ownership of the property taken could negative this intent. Therefore a defense of mistake of law traditionally has been allowed. In contrast, bigamy is thought of as a general-intent crime, in the sense that conviction can be based on recklessness or even negligence as to whether one party is still married; traditionally even a reasonable mistake of law about marital status, therefore, would not be allowed for these crimes as a defense, even though a reasonable mistake of fact would be. See, e.g., Long v. State, 44 Del. 262, 65 A.2d 489, 497 (1949); Perkins, Ignorance and Mistake in Criminal Law, 88 U. Pa. L. Rev. 35, 45 (1939).

How would the *Smith* (*David*) case have been decided under this analysis? Which approach seems the more defensible?

3. The Model Penal Code approach. The Code attempts to articulate the proper scope of the mistake of law principle by providing in §2.04(1): "Ignorance or mistake as to a matter of fact *or law* is a defense if . . . [it] negatives the purpose, knowledge, belief, recklessness or negligence required to establish a material element of the offense. . . ." (Emphasis added.) What, then, are the situations in which the traditional doctrine "ignorance of the law is no excuse" does apply? Section 2.02(9) identifies them as follows:

Neither knowledge nor recklessness or negligence as to whether conduct constitutes an offense or as to the existence meaning or application of the law determining the elements of an offense is an element of the offense, unless the definition of the offense or the Code so provides.

The interaction between §§2.04(1) and 2.02(9) needs to be traced with care. How would the *Woods* and *Smith* (*David*) cases be decided under the Code? In light of the reporter's Comment, set forth in Note 1 above, how do you think the drafters of the Code intended such cases to be treated?

PROBLEM

In People v. Weiss, 276 N.Y. 384, 12 N.E.2d 514 (1938), defendants were convicted of kidnapping a person suspected of the murder of the Lindbergh child. Kidnapping was defined as follows: "A person who wilfully: 1. Seizes, confines, inveigles, or kidnaps another, with intent to cause him, without authority of law, to be confined or imprisoned within this state, . . . against his will . . . is guilty of kidnapping." Defendants sought to introduce testimony showing that the defendants were led to believe that they had been authorized by a law enforcement officer to seize the victim. The testimony was excluded. Query: On appeal, what result?

UNITED STATES v. INTERNATIONAL MINERALS & CHEMICAL CORP.

Supreme Court of the United States
402 U.S. 558 (1971)

MR. JUSTICE DOUGLAS delivered the opinion of the Court.

The information charged that appellee shipped sulfuric acid and hydrofluosilicic acid in interstate commerce and "did knowingly fail to show on the shipping papers the required classification of said property, to wit, Corrosive Liquid, in violation of 49 C.F.R. 173.427."

Title 18 U.S.C. §834(a) gives the Interstate Commerce Commission power to "formulate regulations for the safe transportation" of "corrosive liquids" and 18 U.S.C. §834(f) states that whoever "knowingly violates any such regulation" shall be fined or imprisoned.

Pursuant to the power granted by §834(a) the regulatory agency promulgated the regulation already cited which reads in part:

> Each shipper offering for transportation any hazardous material subject to the regulations in this chapter, shall describe that article on the shipping paper by the shipping name prescribed in §172.5 of this chapter and by the classification prescribed in §172.4 of this chapter. . . .

The District Court, . . . ruled that the information did not charge a "knowing violation" of the regulation and accordingly dismissed the information. . . .

Here . . . strict or absolute liability is not imposed; knowledge of the shipment of the dangerous materials is required. The sole and narrow question is whether "knowledge" of the regulation is also required. It is in that narrow zone that the issue of "mens rea" is raised; and appellee bears down hard on the provision in 18 U.S.C. §834(f) that whoever "knowingly violates any such regulation" shall be fined, etc. . . .

. . . We . . . see no reason why the word "regulations" should not be construed as a shorthand designation for specific acts or omissions which violate the Act. The Act, so viewed, does not signal an exception to the rule that ignorance of the law is no excuse and is wholly consistent with the legislative history. [The Court's discussion of the legislative history is omitted.] . . .

The principle that ignorance of the law is no defense applies whether the law be a statute or a duly promulgated and published regulation. . . . [W]e decline to attribute to Congress the inaccurate view that that Act requires proof of knowledge of the law, as well as the facts, and that it intended to endorse that interpretation by retaining the word "knowingly." We conclude that the meager legislative history of the 1960 amendments makes unwarranted the conclusion that Congress abandoned the general rule and required knowledge of both the facts and the pertinent law before a criminal conviction could be sustained under this Act. . . .

[W]here as here, . . . dangerous or deleterious devices or products or obnoxious waste materials are involved, the probability of regulation is so great that anyone who is aware that he is in possession of them or dealing with them must be presumed to be aware of the regulation.

Reversed.

MR. JUSTICE STEWART, with whom MR. JUSTICE HARLAN and MR. JUSTICE BRENNAN join, dissenting.

This case stirs large questions — questions that go to the moral foundations of the criminal law. Whether postulated as a problem of "mens rea," of "willfulness," of "criminal responsibility," or of "scienter," the infliction of criminal punishment upon the unaware has long troubled the fair administration of justice. . . . But there is no occasion here for involvement with this root problem of criminal jurisprudence, for it is evident to me that Congress made punishable only knowing violations of the regulation in question. That is what the law quite clearly says, what the federal courts have held, and what the legislative history confirms. . . .

. . . Other federal courts, faced with the precise issue here presented, have held that the statute means exactly what it says — that the words "knowingly violates any such regulation" means no more and no less than "knowingly violates any such regulation." St. Johnsbury Trucking Co. v. United States, 220 F.2d 393 (C.A.1 1955), . . . Chief Judge Magruder filed a concurring opinion in the St. Johnsbury case, and he put the matter thus: . . . "If a statute provides that it shall be an offense "knowingly" to sell adulterated milk, the offense is complete if the defendant sells what he knows to be adulterated milk, even though he does not know of the existence of the criminal statute, on the time-honored principle of the criminal law that ignorance of the law is no excuse. But where a statute provides, as does 18 U.S.C. §835, that whoever knowingly violates a regulation of the Interstate Commerce Commission shall be guilty of an offense, it would seem that a person could not knowingly violate a regulation unless he knows of the terms of the regulation and knows that what he is doing is contrary to the regulation. . . ."

In 1960 these judicial decisions were brought to the attention of the appropriate committees of Congress by the Interstate Commerce Commission, which asked Congress to overcome their impact by amending the law, either by simply deleting the word "knowingly" or, alternatively, by substituting therefor the words "being aware that the Interstate Commerce Commission has formulated regulations for the safe transportation of explosives and other dangerous articles." The Senate passed a bill adopting the second alternative. . . .

The House, however, refused to accept the Senate's language and resubstituted the word "knowingly." . . . Three days later the Senate agreed to the resubstitution of the word "knowingly" by passing the House version of the bill. . . .

The Court today thus grants to the Executive Branch what Congress explicitly refused to grant in 1960. It effectively deletes the word "knowingly" from the law.[a] I cannot join the Court in this exercise, requiring as it does such a total disregard of plain statutory language, established judicial precedent, and explicit legislative history.

A final word is in order. Today's decision will have little practical impact upon the prosecution of interstate motor carriers or institutional shippers. . . . [P]rosecution of regular shippers for violations of the regulations could hardly be impeded by the "knowingly" requirement, for triers of fact would have no difficulty whatever in inferring knowledge on the part of those whose business it is to know, despite their protestations to the contrary. The only real impact of this decision will be upon the casual shipper, who might be any man, woman, or child in the Nation. A person who had never heard of the regulation might make a single shipment of an article covered by it in the course of a lifetime. It would be wholly natural for him to assume that he could deliver the article to the common carrier and depend upon the carrier to see that it was properly labeled and that the shipping papers were in order. Yet today's decision holds that a person who does just that is guilty of a criminal offense punishable by a year in prison. This seems to me a perversion of the purpose of criminal law.

I respectfully dissent from the opinion and judgment of the Court.

HOPKINS v. STATE
Maryland Court of Appeals
193 Md. 489, 69 A.2d 456 (1950)

DELAPLAINE, J. This appeal was taken by the Rev. William F. Hopkins, of Elkton, from the judgment of conviction entered upon the verdict of a jury in the Circuit Court for Cecil County for violation of the statute making it unlawful to erect or maintain any sign intended to aid in the solicitation or performance of marriages. Laws of 1943, ch. 532, Code Supp. 1947, art. 27, sec. 444A.

The State charged that on September 1, 1947, defendant maintained a sign at the entrance to his home at 148 East Main Street in Elkton, and also a sign along a highway leading into the town, to aid in the solicitation and performance of marriages. [The signs read, "Rev. W. F. Hopkins" and "W. F. Hopkins, Notary Public, Information."] . . .

Defendant contended that the judge erred in excluding testimony offered to show that the State's Attorney advised him in 1944 before he erected the signs, that they would not violate the law. It is generally held that the advice of counsel, even though followed in good faith, furnishes no excuse to a person for violating the law and cannot be relied upon as a defense in a criminal action. . . . Moreover, advice given by a public official, even a State's Attorney, that a contemplated act is not criminal will not excuse an offender if, as a matter of law, the act performed did amount to a violation of the law. . . . These rules are founded upon the maxim that ignorance of the law will not excuse

---

a. With respect to Justice Stewart's reading of the legislative history, the Court responded that "it is too much to conclude that in rejecting strict liability the House was also carving out an exception to the general rule that ignorance of the law is no excuse."— EDS.

its violation. If an accused could be exempted from punishment for crime by reason of the advice of counsel, such advice would become paramount to the law.

While ignorance of fact may sometimes be admitted as evidence of lack of criminal intent, ignorance of the law ordinarily does not give immunity from punishment for crime, for every man is presumed to intend the necessary and legitimate consequences of what he knowingly does. In the case at bar defendant did not claim that the State's Attorney misled him regarding any facts of the case, but only that the State's Attorney advised him as to the law based upon the facts. Defendant was aware of the penal statute enacted by the Legislature. He knew what he wanted to do, and he did the thing he intended to do. He claims merely that he was given advice regarding his legal rights. If there was any mistake, it was a mistake of law and not of fact. If the right of a person to erect a sign of a certain type and size depends upon the construction and application of a penal statute, and the right is somewhat doubtful, he erects the sign at his peril. In other words, a person who commits an act which the law declares to be criminal cannot be excused from punishment upon the theory that he misconstrued or misapplied the law. . . . For these reasons the exclusion of the testimony offered to show that defendant had sought and received advice from the State's Attorney was not prejudicial error. . . .

Judgment affirmed with costs.

COX v. LOUISIANA, 379 U.S. 559, 568, 571 (1965): [Defendant was convicted of violating a Louisiana statute prohibiting "pickets or parades in or near a building housing a court of the State of Louisiana" with intent to interfere with the administration of justice. The case arose out of defendant's leadership of a civil rights demonstration protesting the arrest and prosecution of a number of students the previous day. Defendant and a group of 2,000 persons paraded and demonstrated on the far side of the street from the courthouse, about 100 feet from the courthouse steps. The Supreme Court reversed the conviction on due process grounds, relying on the fact that the city officials present, the police chief and the sheriff, gave permission for the demonstration to take place across the street from the courthouse.

[The Court, noting the lack of specificity in the statutory term "near," stated: I]t is clear that the statute, with respect to the determination of how near the courthouse a particular demonstration can be, forsees a degree of on-the-spot administrative interpretation of how "near" the courthouse a particular demonstration might take place. . . . This administrative discretion to construe the term "near" concerns a limited control of the streets and other areas in the immediate vicinity of the courthouse and is the type of narrow discretion which this Court has recognized as the proper role of responsible officials in making determinations concerning the time, place, duration, and manner of demonstrations. . . . Nor does this limited administrative regulation of traffic, which the Court has consistently recognized as necessary and permissible, constitute a waiver of law which is beyond the power of the police. Obviously telling demonstrators how far from the courthouse steps is "near" the courthouse for purposes of a permissible peaceful demonstration is a far cry from allowing one to commit, for example, murder, or robbery. . . . [A]fter the public officials acted as they did, to sustain appellant's later conviction for demonstrating where they told him he could "would be to sanction an indefensible sort of entrapment by the State — convicting a citizen for exercising a privilege which the State had clearly told him was available to him." [Raley v. Ohio,] 360 U.S. at 426. The Due Process Clause does not permit convictions to be obtained under such circumstances.

[Justice Clark was one of the dissenters. He stated (379 U.S. at 586, 588):] One hardly needed an on-the-spot administrative decision that the demonstration was "near" the courthouse with the disturbance being conducted before the eyes and ringing in the ears of court officials, police officers and citizens throughout the courthouse. . . . Reading the facts in a way most favorable to the appellant would, in my opinion, establish only that the Chief of Police consented to the demonstration at that location. However, if the Chief's action be consent, I never knew until today that a law enforcement official — city, state or national — could forgive a breach of the criminal laws.

NOTE

Hopkins v. State and Cox v. Louisiana suggest one kind of circumstance that might warrant an exception to the general principle that ignorance of the law defining the offense is no defense. The Model Penal Code has attempted a general formulation of classes of exceptions of this character (§2.04(3), Appendix to this casebook).

Supporting this proposal the Commentary states ((Tent. Draft No. 4, 1955) at 138):

> All the categories dealt with in the formulation involve situations where the act charged is consistent with entire law-abidingness of the actor, where the possibility of collusion is minimal, and a judicial determination of the reasonableness of the belief in legality should not present substantial difficulty. It is difficult, therefore, to see how any purpose can be served by a conviction. It should be added that in the area of mala prohibita, where the defense would normally apply, the case that is appropriate for penal sanctions is that of deliberate evasion or defiance; when less than this is involved, lesser sanctions should suffice. For this typically is a situation where a single violation works no major public or private injury; it is persistent violation that must be brought to book. And obviously the defense afforded by this section would normally be available to a defendant only once; after a warning he can hardly have a reasonable basis for belief in the legality of his behavior.
>
> There is some statutory and decisional support for such defenses, though the principles have not been generalized to the extent presented here and there is, of course, much contrary authority. See Hall and Seligman, Mistake of Law and Mens Rea, 8 U. of Chi. L. Rev. 641 (1941).

The Model Penal Code, therefore, stayed close to traditional law, largely formulating a reliance theory that had already won fair support in the cases. Note also that the reliance standard is rather stringently defined. Would it apply, for example, to Hopkins v. State? To Cox v. Louisiana? For an attempt to develop the case for a more generous defense of official reliance, see Comment, Applying Estoppel Principles in Criminal Cases, 78 Yale L.J. 1046 (1969).

A number of states have followed the Model Penal code lead. See, e.g., N.Y. Penal Law §15.20(2); Conn. Gen. Stat. Ann. tit. 53A, §53a-6(b); Ill. Ann. Stat. tit. 38, §4-8(b); Kan. Stat. Ann. ch. 21, §3203(2); Utah Code Ann. §76-2-304(2). Does the Model Penal Code go far enough?

LAMBERT v. CALIFORNIA
Supreme Court of the United States
355 U.S. 225 (1957)

MR. JUSTICE DOUGLAS delivered the opinion of the Court.

Section 52.38(a) of the Los Angeles Municipal Code defines "convicted person" as follows:

> Any person who, subsequent to January 1, 1921, has been or hereafter is convicted of an offense punishable as a felony in the State of California, or who has been or who is hereafter convicted of any offense in any place other than the State of California, which offense, if committed in the State of California, would have been punishable as a felony.

Section 52.39 provides that it shall be unlawful for "any convicted person" to be or remain in Los Angeles for a period of more than five days without registering; it requires any person having a place of abode outside the city to register if he comes into the city on five occasions or more during a 30-day period; and it prescribes the information to be furnished the Chief of Police on registering.

Section 52.43(b) makes the failure to register a continuing offense, each day's failure constituting a separate offense.

Appellant, arrested on suspicion of another offense, was charged with a violation of this registration law. . . . The case was tried to a jury which found appellant guilty. The court fined her $250 and placed her on probation for three years. . . .

The registration provision, carrying criminal penalties, applies if a person has been convicted "of an offense punishable as a felony in the State of California" or, in case he has been convicted in another State if the offense "would have been punishable as a felony" had it been committed in California. No element of willfulness is by terms included in the ordinance nor read into it by the California court as a condition necessary for a conviction.

We must assume that appellant had no actual knowledge of the requirement that she register under this ordinance, as she offered proof of this defense which was refused. The question is whether a registration act of this character violates Due Process where it is applied to a person who has no actual knowledge of his duty to register, and where no showing is made of the probability of such knowledge.

. . . There is wide latitude on the lawmakers to declare an offense and to exclude elements of knowledge and diligence from its definition. . . . But we deal here with conduct that is wholly passive — mere failure to register. It is unlike the commission of acts, or the failure to act under circumstances that should alert the doer to the consequences of his deed. Cf. . . . United States

v. Balint, 258 U.S. 250; United States v. Dotterweich, 320 U.S. 277, 284. The rule that "ignorance of the law will not excuse" . . . is deep in our law, as is the principle that of all the powers of local government, the police power is "one of the least limitable." . . . On the other hand, Due Process places some limits on its exercise. Engrained in our concept of Due Process is the requirement of notice. Notice is sometimes essential so that the citizen has the chance to defend charges. Notice is required before property interests are disturbed, before assessments are made, before penalties are assessed. Notice is required in a myriad of situations where a penalty or forfeiture might be suffered for mere failure to act. Recent cases illustrating the point . . . involved only property interests in civil litigation. But the principle is equally appropriate where a person, wholly passive and unaware of any wrongdoing, is brought to the bar of justice for condemnation in a criminal case.

Registration laws are common and their range is wide. . . . Many such laws are akin to licensing statutes in that they pertain to the regulation of business activities. But the present ordinance is entirely different. Violation of its provisions is unaccompanied by any activity whatever, mere presence in the city being the test. Moreover, circumstances which might move one to inquire as to the necessity of registration are completely lacking. At most the ordinance is but a law enforcement technique designed for the convenience of law enforcement agencies through which a list of the names and addresses of felons then residing in a given community is compiled. The disclosure is merely a compilation of former convictions already publicly recorded in the jurisdiction where obtained. Nevertheless, this registrant on first becoming aware of her duty to register was given no opportunity to comply with the law and avoid its penalty, even though her default was entirely innocent. She could but suffer the consequences of the ordinance, namely, conviction with the imposition of heavy criminal penalties thereunder. We believe that actual knowledge of the duty to register or proof of the probability of such knowledge and subsequent failure to comply are necessary before a conviction under the ordinance can stand. As Holmes wrote in The Common Law, "A law which punished conduct which would not be blameworthy in the average member of the community would be too severe for that community to bear." Id., at 50. Its severity lies in the absence of an opportunity either to avoid the consequences of the law or to defend any prosecution brought under it. Where a person did not know of the duty to register and where there was no proof of the probability of such knowledge, he may not be convicted consistently with Due Process. Were it otherwise, the evil would be as great as it is when the law is written in print too fine to read or in a language foreign to the community.

Reversed. . . .[a]

a. After remand the municipal court ordered a new trial for Mrs. Lambert. The California Supreme Court granted a writ of prohibition on the grounds that the ordinance was in conflict with state legislation that already occupied the same field. Lambert v. Municipal Court, 53 Cal. 3d 690, 349 P.2d 834 (1960).

The Privy Council reached the same conclusion as the United States Supreme Court even without a due process clause. In Lim Chin Aik v. The Queen, [1963] A.C. 160, the Privy Council reversed the conviction of a person found in the colony of Singapore despite a Ministry of Labour order prohibiting his presence there, on the ground that there was no reasonable way the person could have been expected to know of the existence of the order. — EDS.

MR. JUSTICE FRANKFURTER, whom MR. JUSTICE HARLAN and MR. JUSTICE WHIT-
TAKER join, dissenting.

The present laws of the United States and of the forty-eight States are thick
with provisions that command that some things not be done and others be
done, although persons convicted under such provisions may have had no awareness of what the law required or that what they did was wrongdoing. The body
of decisions sustaining such legislation, including innumerable registration laws,
is almost as voluminous as the legislation itself. The matter is summarized in
United States v. Balint, 258 U.S. 250, 252: "Many instances of this are to be
found in regulatory measures in the exercise of what is called the police power
where the emphasis of the statute is evidently upon achievement of some social
betterment rather than the punishment of the crimes as in cases of mala in
se."

Surely there can hardly be a difference as a matter of fairness, of hardship,
or of justice, if one may invoke it, between the case of a person wholly innocent
of wrongdoing, in the sense that he was not remotely conscious of violating
any law, who is imprisoned for five years for conduct relating to narcotics, and
the case of another person who is placed on probation for three years on condition that she pay $250, for failure, as a local resident, convicted under local
law of a felony, to register under a law passed as an exercise of the State's
"police power." Considerations of hardship often lead courts, naturally enough,
to attribute to a statute the requirement of a certain mental element — some
consciousness of wrongdoing and knowledge of the law's command — as a matter
of statutory construction. Then, too, a cruelly disproportionate relation between
what the law requires and the sanction for its disobedience may constitute a
violation of the Eighth Amendment as a cruel and unusual punishment, and,
in respect to the States, even offend the Due Process Clause of the Fourteenth
Amendment.

But what the Court here does is to draw a constitutional line between a State's
requirement of doing and not-doing. What is this but a return to Year Book
distinctions between feasance and nonfeasance — a distinction that may have
significance in the evolution of common law notions of liability, but is inadmissible as a line between constitutionality and unconstitutionality. One can be confident that Mr. Justice Holmes would have been the last to draw such a line.
What he wrote about "blameworthiness" is worth quoting in its context:

"It is not intended to deny that criminal liability, as well as civil, is founded
on blameworthiness. Such a denial would shock the moral sense of any civilized
community; or, to put it another way, a law which punished conduct which
would not be blameworthy in the average in the average member of the community would be too severe for that community to bear." (This passage must be
read in the setting of the broader discussion of which it is an essential part.
Holmes, The Common Law, at 49-50.)

If the generalization that underlies, and alone can justify, this decision were
to be given its relevant scope, a whole volume of the United States Reports
would be required to document in detail the legislation in this country that
would fall or be impaired. I abstain from entering upon a consideration of
such legislation, and adjudications upon it, because I feel confident that the
present decision will turn out to be an isolated deviation from the strong current

of precedents — a derelict on the waters of the law. Accordingly, I content myself with dissenting.

NOTES

1. Consider the next-to-last sentence of the dissent. What precisely is the "generalization that underlies, and alone can justify" the decision in the case? That reasonable mistake of law is a defense to all crimes of omission? To some only? Only when the duty to act is triggered by mere presence in a community? Or is the relevant generalization wide enough to cover some cases of affirmative action? For example, suppose the ordinance prohibited "convicted persons" from hiring themselves out as baby-sitters in the city of Los Angeles.

What precisely is the legislation that would be imperiled by this generalization? All laws imposing absolute liability?

2. W. LaFave & A. Scott, Criminal Law 365 (1972), argue that *Lambert* does not create an exception to the general rule that ignorance of the criminal law is no excuse. They reason (at n. 73) that the opinion "was only concerned with 'knowledge of the duty to register,' not knowledge of the criminality of failure to register." They point out that Lambert would not have escaped a valid conviction merely because of ignorance that her conduct was punishable under the criminal law. "Rather, the important matter is ignorance of the legal duty — in *Lambert* the duty to register, . . . Awareness of that duty, just as with awareness of the immorality of the conduct for more traditional crimes, provides the element of blameworthiness which justifies even unexpected prosecution and conviction" (at 365). Query: Does this distinction really do its job in limiting the implications of *Lambert* for traditional mistake-of-law doctrine? Is the distinction significant where, as in *Lambert,* it is the criminal statute that imposes the duty?

3. Professor Graham Hughes has concluded (Criminal Omissions, 67 Yale L.J. 590, 600-603 (1958)) that, "The maxim, 'ignorance of the law is no excuse,' ought to have no application in the field of criminal omissions, for the mind of the offender has no relationship to the prescribed conduct if he has no knowledge of the relevant regulation." His argument has an obvious appeal in cases like *Lambert* where there is no fault to be found in the defendant's not knowing she had a duty to register. But would it have the same appeal in all omission cases? Vermont, for example, recently enacted a statute making it criminal for individuals to fail to come to the aid of a person in distress when they can do so without danger to themselves. See page 262 supra. Few other states, if any, impose criminal liability in such a situation. But what of an instance in which a New Yorker vacationing in Vermont fails to throw a life preserver to a drowning stranger? Should the maxim of no excuse for ignorance of the criminal law not be applicable to the New Yorker because his or her criminal conduct took the form of a failure to act?

CALIFORNIA JOINT LEGISLATIVE COMMITTEE FOR REVISION OF THE
PENAL CODE, PENAL CODE REVISION PROJECT

(Tent. Draft No. 2, 1968)

SECTION 500. IGNORANCE OR MISTAKE . . .

(2) A person's belief that his conduct does not constitute a crime is a defense
only if it is reasonable and,

(a) if the person's mistaken belief is due to his ignorance of the existence
of the law defining the crime, he exercised all the care which, in the circumstances, a law-abiding and prudent person would exercise to ascertain the
law; or

(b) if the person's mistaken belief is due to his misconception of the meaning
or application of the law defining the crime to his conduct,

(i) he acts in reasonable reliance upon an official statement of the law,
afterward determined to be invalid or erroneous, contained in a statute,
judical decision, administrative order or grant of permission, or an official
interpretation of the public officer or body charged by law with the responsibility for interpreting, administering or enforcing the law defining the crime;
or,

[(ii) he otherwise diligently pursues all means available to ascertain the
meaning and application of the crime to his conduct and honestly and in
good faith concludes his conduct is not a crime in circumstances in which
a law-abiding and prudent person would also so conclude.]

COMMENTS (64-67) . . .

Subsection (2)(a) is addressed to the situation where the defendant [reasonably]
failed to know of the existence of the criminal prohibition. Where this is so
and the jury finds on the preponderance of the evidence adduced by the defendant that he took all the care to ascertain the law which a law-abiding and
prudent person would take, the case for exculpation seems to us persuasive.
This provision states in general form the essence of the more particular provisions found in Section 2.04(2)(a) of the Model Penal Code and Section 4-8(b)(1)
of the Illinois Code to the effect that mistake is a defense where the criminal
prohibition was not published or otherwise reasonably made available. Certainly
in such cases the language we propose would exculpate. But we think exculpation
should be made out in all cases where a law-abiding and prudent person would
not have learned of the law's existence. One such case is Lambert v. California,
355 U.S. 225 (1957) where the nature of the offense (visiting Los Angeles and
failing to register as a previously convicted felon) itself gave such insufficient
notice of the criminal duty that a conviction was found unconstitutional in the
absence of circumstances showing probability of the knowledge of the offense
by the defendant. Certainly there would not be many cases of this kind. Where
the prohibition reaches plainly wrongful conduct, the conduct itself alerts the
law-abiding and prudent person to the need for inquiry if there is any doubt.
And even in the mala prohibita crimes the circumstances would normally suggest
inquiry — engaging in such closely regulated activities as liquor selling, food
merchandising, apartment renting, etc. But in the exceptional case, like *Lambert,*
where this is not the case only a blind and brutal law would insist on punishment.

Subsection (2)(b) is addressed to the situation where the defendant (still reasonably), although aware of the existence of the crime, was mistaken as to its meaning or its applicability to his conduct. Subsection (i), dealing with situations of reliance on official and responsible interpretations, we have already discussed. As stated, this imports no innovation in present law. Subsection (ii), however, does, insofar as it generalizes the essential quality of the unfairness in holding defendants who are misled by official reliance; i.e, they did all that could be done to learn the nature of the prohibition and in concluding that it was lawful reacted no differently than would any law-abiding and prudent person. The subsection is placed in brackets because some of the Reporters believe it may go too far for reasons that will be stated shortly. The case to be made in favor of this subsection is as follows:

The central point is that it is plainly unjust to hold a defendant criminally liable where a jury is prepared to conclude that the conditions of this subsection are met. A case which illustrates this is Long v. State, 44 Del. 262, 65 A.2d 489 (1949). The court reversed a conviction of bigamy because the court below excluded evidence offered by the defendant to show his reasonable belief that his Arkansas divorce legally severed his prior marriage relationship. The case may be strongly argued to be one where the mistake is not as to the meaning or applicability of the offense (bigamy) but rather as to an element of the offense (remarrying while having a spouse) and hence one where the mistake, though of a matter of law, negatived the necessary culpable mental state (negligence) with respect to that element. Be that as it may, the court dealt with the defense as though it were a defense of misconception of the law defining the offense and allowed the defense on the ground that the defendant "before engaging in the conduct made a bona fide, diligent effort, adopting a course and resorting to sources and means at least as appropriate as any afforded under our legal system, to ascertain and abide by the law, and . . . acted in good faith reliance upon the results of such effort." We agree with the Delaware court that in such circumstances the practical difficulties commonly invoked to deny the defense of mistake of law are inapposite. It cannot be said to "encourage ignorance" of the law where the defense requires a showing of diligent and exhaustive effort to comprehend the law. And difficulties of proof are not here substantial since the defendant is required to show affirmative acts of inquiry addressed to an objective standard. We also agree with the conclusion of the Delaware court that punishing in the circumstances would be "unjust and arbitrary. Most of the important reasons which support the prohibition of ex post facto legislation are opposed to such a holding. It is difficult to conceive what more could be reasonably expected of a 'model citizen' than that he guide his conduct by 'the law' ascertained in good faith, not merely by efforts which might seem adequate to a person in his situation, but by efforts as well designed to accomplish ascertainment as any available under our system."

In the Long case the steps taken by the defendant included centrally consulting a reputable Delaware lawyer, revealing to him all the relevant circumstances, and being without reason to believe his advice was ill-founded. However, under the proposed draft the defense is not available simply on the ground that an attorney advised the defendant of the noncriminality of the proposed conduct. Still such advice would normally figure in any defense made under this subdivision. But where the defendant's conduct constitutes a diligent pursuit of all means available to comprehend the law and his conclusion that his conduct is not criminal is one which he reaches honestly and in good faith, as opposed to a pretext, and that conclusion is found by the jury to be one which a law-abiding and prudent person would reach, the fact that the evidence leading to this conclusion rested in part on private legal advice should not dissolve the defense. The risk of disingenuous legal advice, which presumably is the main concern in this area, is substantially reduced by the additional requirements stated in the draft.

On the other hand some feel that this provision is subject to abuse. It opens up a new and potentially time-consuming defense in many cases. Further, the defense can be too easily fabricated out of disingenuous advice obtained from lawyers ready to lend themselves to a scheme of evasion through venality or partisanship in their client's cause. Finally, it is believed that the potential injustice is adequately guarded against by the use of the prosecutor's discretion not to prosecute in cases in which the accused acted in good faith, and his conduct was not harmful.

NOTES

1. The California proposal, §2(b)(ii), was adopted in New Jersey. See N.J. Stat. Ann. tit. 2C, §2C:2-4(c)(3).

2. Consider the observations of Professor Fuller concerning provisions sometimes found in complex economic regulation to the effect that the defendant must be shown to have knowledge of the law making his act criminal. Conceding that such provisions are designed to preclude punishing people for seemingly innocent acts he notes that the cure may be worse than the disease. (The Morality of Law 72-73 (1964):

> The required intent is so little susceptible of definite proof or disproof that the trier of fact is almost inevitably driven to asking, "Does he look like the kind who would stick by the rules or one who would cheat on them when he saw a chance?" This question unfortunately, leads easily into another, "Does he look like my kind?"

3. An alternative (or additional) strategy for avoiding the injustice of criminal conviction without fair notice (as a result of understandable ignorance of the law's meaning or validity) is the provision of declaratory relief. This would allow the person to obtain a judicial ruling of the legality of his contemplated conduct before the fact rather than after. The subject is explored in Note, Declaratory Relief in the Criminal Law, 80 Harv. L. Rev. 1490 (1967).

For further reflections on the problems of mistake of law, see Houlgate, Ignorantia Juris: A Plea for Justice, 78 Ethics 32 (1967); Brett, Mistake of Law as a Criminal Defense, 5 Melb. U.L. Rev. 179 (1966).

For a discussion of foreign experience see Bolgar, The Present Function of the Maxim *Ignorantia Juris Neminem Excusat* — A Comparative Study, 52 Iowa L. Rev. 626 (1967).

4. The German law treats the defense of mistake of law quite differently from English and American law.

The German Penal Code, 1969, Section 17 (effective 1975, Zweites Gesetz zur Reform des Strafrechts, [1969] Bundesgesetzblatt, Part 1, at 717, 720), provides:

> *Mistake as to the Prohibition.* If in the course of the act the actor lacks the perception that he is acting wrongfully, he acts without culpability if he could not avoid making the mistake. If he could avoid making it the punishment may be mitigated in accordance with §49, subsection 1.

This statutory formulation derives from a famous 1952 decision of the supreme court of West Germany in which the court, in response to long-standing academic criticism, overturned its past rulings and held that a mistake by the defendant about the criminality of his conduct, whether based on ignorance, on a mistaken interpretation of the statutory prohibition, or on a mistaken interpretation of justificatory privileges, could constitute a legal defense. The court reasoned that blameworthiness is a necessary condition for guilt; hence, where mistake of law is inconsistent with moral blameworthiness, guilt should not be attached. Moral blameworthiness does not exist, the court found, if the defendant was not aware that his conduct was unlawful or wrongful and if a proper application of his moral sensitivities would not have led him to such an awareness:

> As a free and moral agent and as a participant in the legal community, the individual is bound at all times to conform his behavior to law and to avoid doing the wrong thing. He does not fulfill this duty merely by avoiding that which seems to him clearly to be the wrong thing; rather he must attempt to determine whether that which he plans to do is compatible with the legal imperatives of the system. He must resolve his doubts by reflection or investigation. This requires that he apply his moral sensibility. . . . If despite the moral sensitivity that can fairly be demanded of him, the individual does not perceive the wrongfulness of his contemplated action, then his mistake is to be viewed as ineluctable; the act would be, for him, unavoidable. In a case of this sort, the individual cannot be blamed for his conduct.

The conscientious objector — one who is aware of the criminality of his conduct but rejects the moral judgment of the legislature — was excluded from the reach of this defense, because "The culpability of the morally committed violator consists in his knowing that he substitutes his own system of values for that of the legal community." For discussion of the German approach, see G. Fletcher, Rethinking Criminal Law 737-755 (1978).

UNITED STATES v. BARKER

United States Court of Appeals, District of Columbia Circuit,
546 F.2d 940(1976)

Per Curiam. The mandate of the court is that the Judgment of the District Court is reversed and the case is remanded for a new trial. Judges Wilkey and Merhige have filed separate opinions. Judge Leventhal dissents.

Wilkey, J. Two of the "footsoldiers" of the Watergate affair, Bernard Barker and Eugenio Martinez, . . . come before us this time to challenge their convictions under 18 U.S.C. §241,[a] for their parts in the 1971 burglary of the office of Dr. Louis J. Fielding.

During the summer of 1971, following the publication of the now famous "Pentagon Papers," a decision was made to establish a unit within the White House to investigate leaks of classified information. This "Room 16" unit, composed of Egil Krogh, David Young, G. Gordon Liddy, and E. Howard Hunt — and under the general supervision of John Ehrlichman — determined, or was instructed, to obtain all possible information on Daniel Ellsberg, the source of the Pentagon Papers leak. After Ellsberg's psychiatrist, Dr. Fielding, refused to be interviewed by FBI agents, the unit decided to obtain copies of Ellsberg's medical records through a covert operation.

Hunt had been a career agent in the CIA before his employment by the White House. One of his assignments was as a supervising agent for the CIA in connection with the Bay of Pigs invasion, and, as "Eduardo," he was well known and respected in Miami's Cuban-American community. A fact destined to be of considerable importance later, he had been Bernard Barker's immediate supervisor in that operation. When the "Room 16" unit determined that it would be best if the actual entry into Dr. Fielding's office were made by individuals not in the employ of the White House, Hunt recommended enlisting the assistance of some of his former associates in Miami.

Hunt had previously reestablished contact with Barker in Miami in late April 1971, and he met Martinez at the same time. He gave Barker an unlisted White House number where he could be reached by phone and wrote to Barker on White House stationery. On one occasion Barker met with Hunt in the Executive Office Building. By August 1971 Hunt returned to Miami and informed Barker that he was working for an organization at the White House level with greater jurisdiction than the FBI and the CIA. He asked Barker if he would become "operational" again and help conduct a surreptitious entry to obtain national security information on "a traitor to this country who was passing . . . classified information to the Soviet Embassy." He stated further that "the man in question . . . was being considered as a possible Soviet agent himself."

Barker agreed to take part in the operation and to recruit two additional people. He contacted Martinez and Felipe deDiego. Barker conveyed to Martinez the same information Hunt had given him, and Martinez agreed to participate. Like Barker, Martinez had begun working as a covert agent for the CIA after Castro came to power in Cuba. Although Barker's formal relationship with the CIA had ended in 1966, Martinez was still on CIA retainer when he was contacted.

Both testified at trial that they had no reason to question Hunt's credentials. He clearly worked for the White House and had a well known background with the CIA. During the entire time they worked for the CIA, neither Barker nor Martinez was ever shown any credentials by their superiors. Not once did

a. 18 U.S.C. §241. Conspiracy against rights of citizens: "If two or more persons conspire to injure, oppress, threaten, or intimidate any citizen in the free exercise or enjoyment of any right or privilege secured to him by the Constitution or laws of the United States, or because of his having so exercised the same; or

"If two or more persons go in disguise on the highway, or on the premises of another, with intent to prevent or hinder his free exercise or enjoyment of any right or privilege so secured —

"They shall be fined not more than $10,000 or imprisoned not more than ten years, or both; and if death results, they shall be subject to imprisonment for any term of years or for life."— Eds.

they receive written instructions to engage in the operations they were ordered to perform. Nevertheless, they testified, their understanding was always that those operations had been authorized by the Government of the United States. That they did not receive more detail on the purpose of the Fielding operation or its target was not surprising to them; Hunt's instructions and actions were in complete accord with what their previous experience had taught them to expect. They were trained agents, accustomed to rely on the discretion of their superiors and to operate entirely on a "need-to-know" basis.

On 2 September 1971 Hunt and Liddy met Barker, Martinez, and deDiego at a hotel in Beverly Hills, California. Hunt informed the defendants that they were to enter an office, search for a particular file, photograph it, and replace it. The following day the group met again. Hunt showed Barker and Martinez identification papers and disguises he had obtained from the CIA. That evening the defendants entered Dr. Fielding's office. Contrary to plan, it was necessary for them to use force to effect the break-in. As instructed in this event, the defendants spilled pills on the floor to make it appear the break-in had been a search for drugs. No file with the name Ellsberg was found.

The next day Barker and Martinez returned to Miami. The only funds they received from Hunt in connection with the entry of Dr. Fielding's office were reimbursement for their living expenses, the costs of travel, and $100.00 for lost income.

On 7 March 1974 the defendants were indicted under 18 U.S.C. §241, along with Ehrlichman, Liddy, and deDiego for conspiring to violate the Fourth Amendment rights of Dr. Fielding by unlawfully entering and searching his office. . . .[b]

On July 12 1974 the jury returned verdicts of guilty against both Barker and Martinez. . . .

[At the trial, the District Court rejected a proposed jury instruction allowing a defense for reasonable good faith reliance on Hunt's apparent legal authority to order the operation, and instructed instead that absent belief that a valid warrant had been obtained, any mistake as to the legality of the operation was no defense.[c]

[Judge Wilkey voted to reverse, stating that Appellants' possible good faith, reasonable, though mistaken reliance on Hunt's legal authority to authorize

---

b. Convictions of Ehrlichman and Liddy for the burglary of Dr. Fielding's office were upheld. United States v. Ehrlichman, 546 F.2d 910 (D.C. Cir. 1976). — Eds.

c. The instructions read: "In order to establish the requisite intent the Prosecutor must show that the object of the conspiracy and the purpose of each defendant was to carry out a warrantless entry into and search of Dr. Fielding's office without permission.

"In determining whether or not each defendant had the requisite intent, you should keep in mind that a mistake of fact may constitute a defense to the conspiracy charge but a mistake of law is not a defense.

"Thus, if one of the defendants honestly believed that a valid warrant had been obtained, such a mistake of fact would render him innocent of the alleged conspiracy because it cannot be said that he intended to conduct a warrantless search.

"On the other hand, if the defendant was fully aware of the relevant facts — that the search lacked both warrant and Dr. Fielding's permission, but erroneously believed that the search was still legal, that would constitute a mistake of law and a mistake of law is no excuse.

"In other words, an individual cannot escape the criminal law simply because he sincerely but incorrectly believes that his acts are justified in the name of patriotism, or national security, or a need to create an unfavorable press image, or that his superiors had the authority without a warrant to suspend the Constitutional protections of the Fourth Amendment."—Eds.

their warrantless search would negate the "intent" necessary for a conviction of conspiracy under §241, much as reasonable reliance on a judicial warrant subsequently held invalid would negate such "intent." He found that Appellants could establish the reasonableness of their reliance if they showed there was a believable — but not necessarily correct — legal theory on which such reliance could be based. The judge suggested that such a plausible theory was presented in the long-standing Justice Department contention that the President may authorize warrantless searches related to foreign espionage or intelligence.

[Judge Wilkey also reasoned that, on a "policy of encouraging citizens to respond ungrudgingly to the request of officials for help in the performance of their duties," the citizen's reasonable reliance on the officials' authority ought to be a defense to charges resulting from, for example, an unlawful search or arrest, even if the citizen had no legal duty to give assistance.

[Judge Merhige concurred in the reversal, but on different grounds. He found, pointing to Model Penal Code §2.04(3)(b) [see Appendix to this casebook], that Appellants might have a defense of reasonable reliance upon an authoritative interpretation of the law by an official charged with its enforcement. He stated that the jury could have concluded that Assistant to the President John Ehrlichman had expressed or implied that the break-in was legal under a national security rationale, and that this view was relayed to the Appellants by Hunt. Further, in view of the substantial power of the Executive Branch in the field of foreign affairs, a jury could further find that Appellants acted reasonably in relying on this interpretation of the law.]

LEVENTHAL, J., dissenting: . . . The defendants . . . urge that their error in believing that Hunt was a "duly authorized" agent was a factual error. Although defendants claim to maintain a distinction between mistake of fact and mistake of law, this contention entirely erodes the distinction. Defendants did not claim, or offer to prove a belief, that the President or Attorney General personally authorized the break-in; nor did they seek to advance any other specific factual basis for the belief that Hunt was "duly authorized." They certainly did not offer to prove that they believed John Ehrlichman "expressed or implied that the break-in of Dr. Fielding's office was legal under a national security rationale." (Merhige, J., concurring.) . . .

At bottom, the defendants' "mistake" was to rely on Hunt's White House and CIA connections as legally validating any activities undertaken in the name of national security. . . . Their mistake as to who or what the law authorized or required cannot be repackaged as a mistake of "fact" that Hunt had been duly authorized. . . . Even when the Executive acts to avert foreign security dangers, no Federal judge, indeed no Department of Justice submission, has ever suggested that action otherwise clearly prohibited by the Fourth Amendment would be valid in the absence of explicit authorization by the President or Attorney General. No generally delegable power to authorize such searches is reconcilable with the requirements of the Fourth Amendment. . . .

. . . The fact that defendants do not assert a belief that the President or Attorney General authorized their violation of Dr. Fielding's fundamental right to be free of warrantless government forays into his office takes this case outside the mistake of fact defense, for whatever defendants' other beliefs as to the facts, they would not, if true, establish exculpation. . . .

Viewed as a mistake of law, the defense raised by defendants requires us to confront a fundamental tension in our criminal law. The criminal law relies in general on the concept of culpability or blameworthiness as a prerequisite to guilt, expressed as a requirement of mens rea. . . . [However] as a society we have stopped short of requiring a subjective behavioral assessment of each offender's individual stock of knowledge about the law and its applicability. Instead, "the rule that 'ignorance of the law will not excuse' . . . is deep in our law." Lambert v. California, 355 U.S. 225, 228 (1957). . . . Similarly, the ALI's Model Penal Code §2.02(9) defines the requirements of culpability so that "neither knowledge nor recklessness or negligence as to whether conduct constitutes an offense or as to the existence, meaning or application of the law determining the elements of an offense is an element of such offense unless the definition of the offense or the Code so provides."

The general principle that rejects the defense of ignorance of the requirements of the criminal law, or of mistake as to those requirements . . . formed a part of English and canon law for centuries. . . . Its continuing vitality stems from preserving a community balance, put by Holmes as a recognition that "justice to the individual is rightly outweighed by the larger interests on the other side of the scales." Great minds like Holmes and Austin have struggled with the tension between individual injustice and society's need and have concluded that recognition of the mistake of law defense would encourage ignorance rather than a determination to know the law, and would interfere with the enforcement of law, because the claim would be so easy to assert and hard to disprove.

In some aspect the doctrine may be viewed as a doctrine of negligence, holding individuals to minimal conditions of responsibility and making acting without legal knowledge blameworthy for the failure to obtain that knowledge. Hall suggests in addition that the rationale can be expressed in terms of ethical policy — that the criminal law represents certain moral principles and that to recognize ignorance or mistake of law as a defense would contradict those values. Still, it must in the last analysis be recognized that at its core, the basic mistake of law doctrine imposes liability even though defendant acted in good faith and made a "reasonable" mistake. Otherwise, criminal statutes would be in suspense on any point not authoritatively settled.[30] In a particular case adherence to a generally formulated rule may seem to work injustice, but the jurists pondering the general doctrine have both deemed such individual hardships outweighed by the common good, and have taken into account that certain features of the overall system of criminal justice permit amelioration and relief. These flexible opportunities for mitigating the law's impact — through prosecutorial discretion, judicial sentencing, and executive clemency — avoid the necessity of bending and stretching the law, at the price of undermining its general applicability.

Every mature system of justice must cope with the tension between rule and discretion. Rules without exceptions may grind so harsh as to be intolerable, but exceptions and qualifications inflict a cost in administration and loss of control. The balance struck by the doctrine with which we are now concerned provides for certain rigorously limited exceptions (inapplicable to defendants' claim) but otherwise leaves amelioration of harsh results to other parts of the

---

30. It would fairly be argued that no liability attaches for e.g., action taken under a "reasonable," though erroneous, forecast of how far the courts might go in confining a statute through the doctrine of strict construction. Litigation could come to depend not on what the statute meant, but on the reasonableness of a legal view of its meaning.

system of justice. In my view, history has shaped a rule that works, and we should be slow to tinker. . . . To hold otherwise would be to ease the path of the minority of government officials who choose, without regard to the law's requirements, to do things their way, and to provide absolution at large for private adventurers recruited by them. . . .

Appellants invoke the acceptance of good faith reliance defenses in the Model Penal Code. However, the American Law Institute carefully limited the sections cited to persons responding to a call for aid from a police officer making an unlawful arrest,[34] and to obeying unlawful military orders,[35] and specifically rejected the defense for other mistake of law contexts.[36] In both instances, the ALI recognizes limited curtailment of the doctrine excluding a mistake of law defense on the ground that the actor is under a duty to act — to help a police officer in distress to make an arrest when called upon, or to obey military orders. . . . Punishing an individual for failure to inquire as to the lawful basis for the officer's request would frustrate the effective functioning of the duly constituted police (and military) force and in its operation on the individual would compel a choice between the whirlpool and the rock.[d]

Barker and Martinez were under no tension of conflicting duties comparable to that experienced by a soldier or citizen responding to orders. They had and claim no obligation to aid Hunt. . . .

. . . Judge Merhige votes to reverse on the ground that appellants could claim as a defense that a citizen has a right to take action in reliance on a government official's assurance that such action is permissible. . . . [Model Penal Code §2.04(3)] contemplates both accountability and responsible action on the part of the government official giving advice about the law. But defendants do not claim they received any advice, either express or implied, from [Assistant to the President, John] Ehrlichman, and Hunt had only an ad hoc, undefined position in the White House. He had no on-line enforcement or interpretative powers or responsibilities. His undifferentiated power stemmed solely from membership in a large White House bureaucracy. The potential for official abuse of power would be greatly magnified if such a government official can recruit assistance from the general public, constrained neither by accountability guidelines guiding agency action under statutorily mandated powers, nor by the recruited citizen who, under the defendants' formulation, would be under no duty to inquire about the legality of the official's request. . . . Certainly Hunt

---

34. See e.g., Model Penal Code §3.07(4) (P.O.D. 1962):
(4) Use of Force by Private Person Assisting an Unlawful Arrest. [See Appendix to this casebook.]
35. See Model Penal Code §2.10 (P.O.D. 1962). (See also Williams, Criminal Law §105, 296-301; United States v. Calley, 22 U.S.M.C.A. 534 (1973)).
36. When §3.07(4) does not specifically apply, §3.09(1) withdraws any justification defense to the use of improper force where the actor's "error is due to ignorance or mistake as to the provisions of the Code, any other provision of the criminal law or the law governing the legality of an arrest or search." The Commentary explained that provision as dealing with a "body of law [which] is not stated in the Code and may not appear in the form of penal law at all. It seems, clear, however, that the policy which holds mistake of penal law to be immaterial applies with no less force to the law of arrest or search." ALI Model Penal Code §3.09(1) comment referring to §3.04(1) comment (Tent. Draft. No. 8, 1958), at 18.
d. In an omitted footnote (31a), Judge Leventhal notes that a Justice Department decision not to prosecute CIA Director Richard Helms for his part in a similar break-in might be correct. The judge stated: "It should be noted that unlike the defendants in this case, Helms arguably acted in obedience to a duty imposed by statute, and this might have come within compass of a mistake of law defense grounded in the actor's being under a duty to act."—EDS.

cannot sensibly be described as having been charged by law with responsibility for interpreting or enforcing either §241, or the Constitution from which the violations of §241 in this case sprang. Nor can it be said in any meaningful sense that he had the power to provide an official interpretation of the law. . . .

While a mistake of law may negative a specific element of certain crimes, or may be accepted where the mistake pertains to a violation of purely civil law as contrasted with the requirements of the criminal law, none of these carefully wrought exceptions have application to the case at bar. Defendants' mistake of law did not pertain to some rule irrelevant to or remote from the criminal law. Nor does section 241 recognize a mistake of law defense or require a specific intent like the statute at issue in People v. Weiss, 276 N.Y. 384, 12 N.E.2d 514 (1938), punishing a "willful" seizure of a person with "intent to [act], without authority of law."

This brings me to the question whether the civil rights offenses involved here are of such a character, either in terms of required intent or affirmative defense, as to make available an extension of criminal defenses to include mistake of law. . . .

Conviction under Section 241 requires that the offender acted with a "specific intent" "to injure, oppress, threaten or intimidate any citizen in the free exercise or enjoyment of any right or privilege secured to him by the Constitution or laws of the United States. . . ." This does not mean that he must have acted with subjective awareness that his action was unlawful; nor need the defendant have thought in constitutional terms while acting. See, e.g., Screws v. United States, 325 U.S. 91, 104-07 (1945). It is enough that the constitutional right is clearly defined and that the conspirators intend to invade interests protected by the Constitution. . . .

. . . The price to society of tolerating reliance on the very official misconduct §241 was directed against, forces us to reject defendants' argument. . . . A private citizen must start with a beginning point in his understanding of what the law requires. Breaking and entering a home or office is malum in se — a gross and elementary crime when done for personal reasons, a gross and elementary violation of civil rights when done with the extra capability provided by a government position. Defendants were charged and convicted of violating a clearly defined constitutional right. They were not acting in an official law enforcement capacity. Their defense instead reduces to an arguable but untested speculation that their otherwise unlawful behavior would be vindicated by a foreign security exemption to the Fourth Amendment's protections. In regard to subjective "good faith," they are indistinguishable from any other criminal defendant who deliberately breaks the law in the mistaken expectation that he can assert a constitutional defense at trial or one who is civilly disobedient because his framework for moral action does not coincide with his society's legal framework. Such persons frequently act on a high plane of patriotism, as they view it, but that does not allow them to proceed in ignorance or disregard of the requirements of law. . . .

The ultimate point is that appellants' mistake of law, whether or not it is classified as reasonable, does not negative legal responsibility, but at best provides a reason for clemency on the ground that the strict rules of law bind too tight for the overall public good.[e] . . . We should refuse to cut away and

e. Barker and Martinez had been sentenced to three years' probation. — EDS.

weaken the core standards for behavior provided by the criminal law. Softening the standards of conduct rather than ameliorating their application serves only to undermine the behavioral incentives the law was enacted to provide. . . .

. . . I come back — again and again, in my mind — to the stark fact that we are dealing with a breaking and entering in the dead of night, both surreptitious and forcible, and a violation of civil rights statutes. This is simply light years away from the kinds of situations where the law has gingerly carved out exceptions permitting reasonable mistake of law as a defense — cases like entering a business transaction on the erroneous advice of a high responsible official or district attorney, or like responding to an urgent call for aid from a police officer. I dissent.

NOTES

1. United States v. Barker, 514 F.2d 208 (D.C. Cir. 1975), involved an earlier prosecution of Barker, Martinez, and others for the burglary of the Watergate premises of the Democratic headquarters. The defendants' motions to withdraw their guilty pleas were denied by the trial court, and the court of appeals sustained the trial court's action in a per curiam opinion. Chief Judge Bazelon wrote a separate opinion containing a critical assessment of the traditional doctrine, which assessment contrasted with the foregoing opinion of Judge Leventhal. A further exploration of these issues may well start with a reading of Chief Judge Bazelon's opinion. See also Note, Reliance on Apparent Authority as a Defense to Criminal Prosecutions, 77 Colum. L. Rev. 775 (1977); Comment, United States v. Barker: Misapplication of the Reliance on an Official Interpretation of the Law Defense, 66 Calif. L. Rev. 809 (1978); L. Schwartz, Reform of the Federal Criminal Laws: Issues, Tactics and Prospects, [1977] Duke L.J. 171, 213-217.

2. The administration-supported bill to revise the federal criminal code (Criminal Code Reform Act of 1973, S. 1400, 93d Cong., 1st Sess.) contained the following provisions:

SECTION 521. PUBLIC DUTY
(a) Defense. It is a defense to a prosecution under any federal statute that the defendant reasonably believed that the conduct charged was required or authorized by law: (1) to carry out his duty as a public servant, or as a person acting at the direction of a public servant. . . .[f]

---

f. An earlier version of this section provided:
"§1-3C3. EXECUTION OF PUBLIC DUTY
"(a) AUTHORIZED BY LAW. — It is a defense that conduct which would otherwise constitute an offense is engaged in by a public servant in the course of his official duties and that he reasonably believes under the circumstances as they appear to him that the conduct is required or authorized by law.
"(b) DIRECTED BY A PUBLIC SERVANT. — It is a defense that conduct which would otherwise constitute an offense is engaged in by a person who has been requested by a public servant to assist him and who is carrying out the specific request of such public servant, unless such person could reasonably know under the circumstances as they appear to him that the action was not required or authorized by law."
Criminal Justice Reform Act of 1972, S. 1, 93d Cong., 1st Sess.
Compare the approach of the Model Penal Code §3.03, Execution of Public Duty, Appendix to this casebook.

SECTION 532. OFFICIAL MISSTATEMENT OF LAW

It is an affirmative defense to a prosecution under any federal statue that the defendant's conduct in fact conformed with an official statement of the law, afterward determined to be invalid or erroneous:

(a) which is contained in: (1) a statute; or (2) a decision of the United States Supreme Court; or

(b) which is contained in: (1) a judicial decision entered in a proceeding to which the defendant was a party; (2) an administrative decision entered in a proceeding to which the defendant was a party, or an administrative grant of permission to the defendant; or (3) an official, written interpretation issued by the head of a government agency, or his delegate, charged by law with responsibility for administration of the law defining the offense

if the defendant acted in reasonable reliance on such statement of the law and with a good faith belief that his conduct did not constitute an offense.

Messrs. Korn and Craig, writing in the Washington Post, Jan. 20, 1974, at Cl, col. 1 (Making It All Perfectly Legal), attacked these proposals in the light of the Watergate experience. They objected to the "astonishing" breadth of exculpation it affords to governmental officials who simply have to convince a jury that their violation of law should be excused because they reasonably believed their acts were lawful or because a higher official who authorized those acts so believed. They observed:

Consider, for example, the criminal charges against former White House aides John D. Ehrlichman and Egil Krogh, charges stemming from the burglary of Daniel Ellsberg's psychiatrist's office. Before Krogh pleaded guilty, both he and Ehrlichman asked that their cases be dismissed, arguing that they were acting as "officers of the United States." Ehrlichman's lawyer carried the point further, stating: "The President . . . specifically directed Ehrlichman to make known to Krogh, [David] Young and Charles Colson that [the investigation of Ellsberg] was impressed with a national security characteristic."

Ehrlichman's attorney based his argument on the old principle that there can be no crime without a guilty mind, a mens rea. He stated: "The essence of the crime of conspiracy is . . . evil intent. The association of persons with honest intent is not a conspiracy, and the association of Ehrlichman with the others on a presidential assignment cannot be transformed into a criminal conspiracy."

Then consider Adolf Eichmann contending in an Israeli courtroom that he was not guilty of the mass slaughter of Jews because he did not have the requisite evil or criminal intent, that he had merely obeyed superior orders. Or consider the words of Lt. Calley, testifying Feb. 22, 1971, at his courtmartial for the Maylai [sic] massacre:

"Well, I was ordered to go in there and destroy the enemy. That was my job that day. That was the mission I was given . . . I felt then and I still do that I acted as I was directed and I carried out the orders that I was given, and I do not feel wrong in doing so, sir.". . .

Imagine what might have happened if S. 1400 had already been law when Ehrlichman and Krogh were contemplating a burglary. Ehrlichman need only seek an "administrative grant of permission" from, say a Justice Department confidante, and Krogh need only plan to persuade a jury that he "reasonably believed" the law not only authorized but required him to order the burglary.

Krogh's lawyers could submit a memorandum from the President describing the national security implications of the break-in. Ehrlichman could testify that he told Krogh national security made it all perfectly legal. And Ehrlichman's lawyers could introduce his "administrative grant of permission." Harry Truman's buck would be passed so rapidly from one person to another that, in the end, no criminal would have committed the crime, only public servants doing their duty. . . .

They quote Professor L. Hall's argument:

[T]he exact scope of public duty is so difficult to define that, in matters of criminal liability, the public servant should be given greater freedom of action and the benefit of the doubt. The law is so complex as to the duties and obligations of an official that . . . if an individual "reasonably believed" his duty required certain action, that individual should not be subjected to criminal punishment.

Messrs. Korn and Craig reply that law should not

give those who administer the law the special privilege of claiming ignorance when they break it. If anything, logic suggests that public officials should be held to a higher standard in understanding and obeying the law, not the lower one suggested by Prof. Hall.

In a subsequent piece, written in response to Assistant Attorney General Peterson's reply to them (Washington Post, Mar. 3, 1974, at B6, col. 1), they conclude:

To the extent that the "public duty" defense was originally intended to protect policemen from being prosecuted and convicted for honest mistakes made in the line of duty, the . . . law seems reasonable. The danger lies, however, in taking a principle from the military and applying it to all government officials. One of the lessons of Watergate surely is that a perceived insulation from criminal prosecution, whether it comes from a President or a statute, can lead to dangerous abuses of official power.

d. The Abandonment of Mens Rea

INTRODUCTORY NOTE

In the preceding sections we encountered criminal statutes that were interpreted so as to require no mens rea (not even negligence) with respect to one or more of the elements of the offense. This phenomenon of *strict* or *absolute liability* is sufficiently important to warrant consideration on its own, now that the meaning and implications of various alternative approaches to mens rea issues have been canvassed. In this section we consider the typical uses of strict liability legislation — how and why it came to be relied on by legislators as a regulatory device; the role of courts in affecting the extent of strict liability through their authority to interpret statutes; what the virtues and vices of strict liability are; how far it can be squared with the requirements of just punishment.

MORISSETTE v. UNITED STATES

Supreme Court of the United States
342 U.S. 246 (1952)

[Morissette, a junk dealer, openly entered an Air Force practice bombing range and appropriated spent bomb casings that had been lying about for years exposed to the weather and rusting away. He flattened them out and sold them at a city junk market at a profit of $84. He was indicted and convicted of violating 18 U.S.C. §641, which made it a crime to "knowingly convert" government property.[a] There was no question that defendant knew that what he took and sold were Air Force bomb casings. His defense was that he honestly believed that they had been abandoned by the Air Force and that he was therefore violating no one's rights in taking them. The trial court, which recognized that this claim of right would be a full defense to an ordinary theft charge, took the view that it was no defense to this statute because the statute contained no language requiring an intent to steal, the traditional mens rea of theft. The Supreme Court, in a lengthy opinion by Mr. Justice Jackson, reversed Morissette's conviction, declining to find that the absence of explicit language requiring an intent to steal revealed a congressional purpose to displace the traditional mens rea of theft in this case. Prior cases, like United States v. Balint, 258 U.S. 250 (1922), and United States v. Dotterweich, 320 U.S. 277 (1943), construing strict liability from the absence of statutory language requiring a mens rea, were distinguished on the ground that those cases involved new statutory crimes designed to deal with regulatory problems and were not, like 18 U.S.C. §641, a statutory formulation of a traditional theft offense. "Congressional silence as to mental elements in an Act merely adopting into federal statutory law a concept of crime already so well defined in common law and statutory interpretation by the states may warrant quite contrary inferences than the same silence in creating an offense new to general law, for whose definition the courts have no guidance except the Act."

[In the course of the opinion JUSTICE JACKSON explored the history and rationale of strict criminal liability.]

The contention that an injury can amount to a crime only when inflicted by intention is no provincial or transient notion. It is as universal and persistent in mature systems of law as belief in freedom of the human will and a consequent ability and duty of the normal individual to choose between good and evil. A relation between some mental element and punishment for a harmful act is almost as instinctive as the child's familiar exculpatory "But I didn't mean to," and has afforded the rational basis for a tardy and unfinished substitution of deterrence and reformation in place of retaliation and vengeance as the motivation for public prosecution. . . .

Crime, as a compound concept, generally constituted only from concurrence of an evil-meaning mind with an evil-doing hand, was congenial to an intense

---

a. "Whoever embezzles, steals, purloins, or knowingly converts to his use or the use of another, or without authority, sells, conveys or disposes of any record, voucher, money, or thing of value of the United States or of any department or agency thereof, or any property made or being made under contract for the United States or any department or agency thereof . . . shall be fined not more than $10,000 or imprisoned not more than ten years, or both; but if the value of such property does not exceed the sum of $100, he shall be fined not more than $1,000 or imprisoned not more than one year, or both."—EDS.

individualism and took deep and early root in American soil. As the states codified the common law of crimes, even if their enactments were silent on the subject, their courts assumed that the omission did not signify disapproval of the principle but merely recognized that intent was so inherent in the idea of the offense that it required no statutory affirmation. . . .

However, the *Balint* and *Behrman* [b] offenses belong to a category of another character, with very different antecedents and origins. The crimes there involved depend on no mental element but consist only of forbidden acts or omissions. This, while not expressed by the Court, is made clear from examination of a century-old but accelerating tendency, discernible both here and in England, to call into existence new duties and crimes which disregard any ingredient of intent. The industrial revolution multiplied the number of workmen exposed to injury from increasingly powerful and complex mechanisms, driven by freshly discovered sources of energy, requiring higher precautions by employers. Traffic of velocities, volumes and varieties unheard of, came to subject the wayfarer to intolerable casualty risks if owners and drivers were not to observe new cares and uniformities of conduct. Congestion of cities and crowding of quarters called for health and welfare regulations undreamed of in simpler times. Wide distribution of goods became an instrument of wide distribution of harm when those who dispersed food, drink, drugs, and even securities, did not comply with reasonable standards of quality, integrity, disclosure and care. Such dangers have engendered increasingly numerous and detailed regulations which heighten the duties of those in control of particular industries, trades, properties or activities that affect public health, safety or welfare.[20]

While many of these duties are sanctioned by a more strict civil liability, lawmakers, whether wisely or not, have sought to make such regulations more effective by invoking criminal sanctions to be applied by the familiar technique of criminal prosecutions and convictions. This has confronted the courts with a multitude of prosecutions, based on statutes or administrative regulations, for what have been aptly called "public welfare offenses." These cases do not fit neatly into any of such accepted classifications of common-law offenses, such as those against the state, the person, property, or public morals. Many of these offenses are not in the nature of positive aggressions or invasions, with which the common law so often dealt, but are in the nature of neglect where the law requires care, or inaction where it imposes a duty. Many violations of such regulations result in no direct or immediate injury to person or property but merely create the danger or probability of it which the law seeks to minimize.

b. United States v. Balint, 258 U.S. 250 (1922), and United States v. Behrman, 258 U.S. 280 (1922). The Supreme Court interpreted statutes prohibiting possession and traffic in defined narcotic substances as not requiring proof that the defendant knew that the substances he dealt with were narcotics. In *Balint,* the Court concluded: "Congress weighed the possible injustice of subjecting an innocent seller to a penalty against the evil of exposing innocent purchasers to danger from the drug, and concluded that the latter was the result preferably to be avoided. Doubtless considerations as to the opportunity of the seller to find out the fact and the difficulty of proof of knowledge contributed to this conclusion."—Eds.

20. Sayre, Public Welfare Offenses, 33 Col. L. Rev. 55, 73, 84, cites and classifies a large number of cases and concludes that they fall roughly into subdivisions of (1) illegal sales of intoxicating liquor, (2) sales of impure or adulterated food or drugs, (3) sales of misbranded articles, (4) violations of antinarcotic Acts, (5) criminal nuisances, (6) violations of traffic regulations, (7) violations of motor-vehicle laws, and (8) violations of general police regulations, passed for the safety, health or well-being of the community.

While such offenses do not threaten the security of the state in the manner of treason, they may be regarded as offenses against its authority, for their occurrence impairs the efficiency of controls deemed essential to the social order as presently constituted. In this respect, whatever the intent of the violator, the injury is the same, and the consequences are injurious or not according to fortuity. Hence, legislation applicable to such offenses, as a matter of policy, does not specify intent as a necessary element. The accused, if he does not will the violation, usually is in a position to prevent it with no more care than society might reasonably expect and no more exertion than it might reasonably exact from one who assumed his responsibilities. Also, penalties commonly are relatively small, and conviction does no grave damage to an offender's reputation. Under such considerations, courts have turned to construing statutes and regulations which make no mention of intent as dispensing with it and holding that the guilty act alone makes out the crime.[c] This has not, however, been without expressions of misgiving.

The pilot of the movement in this country appears to be a holding that a tavernkeeper could be convicted for selling liquor to an habitual drunkard even if he did not know the buyer to be such. Barnes v. State, 19 Conn. 398 (1849). Later came Massachusetts holdings that convictions for selling adulterated milk in violation of statutes forbidding such sales require no allegation of proof that defendant knew of the adulteration. . . .

After the turn of the Century, a new use for crimes without intent appeared when New York enacted numerous and novel regulations of tenement houses, sanctioned by money penalties. Landlords contended that a guilty intent was essential to establish a violation. Judge Cardozo wrote the answer:

"The defendant asks us to test the meaning of this statute by standards applicable to statutes that govern infamous crimes. The analogy, however, is deceptive. The element of conscious wrongdoing, the guilty mind accompanying the guilty act, is associated with a concept of crimes that are punished as infamous. Even there, it is not an invariable element. But in the prosecution of minor offenses there is a wider range of practice and of power. Prosecutions for petty penalties have always constituted in our law a class by themselves. That is true, though the prosecution is criminal in form." Tenement House Dept. v. McDevitt, 215 N.Y. 160, 168, 109 N.E. 88, 90, (1915). . . .

Thus, for diverse but reconcilable reasons, state courts converged on the same result, discontinuing inquiry into intent in a limited class of offenses against such statutory regulations. . . .

Before long, similar questions growing out of federal legislation reached this Court. Its judgments were in harmony with this consensus of state judicial opin-

---

c. But see Henry M. Hart, The Aims of the Criminal Law, 23 L. & Contemp. Prob. 401, 431 n. 70 (1958): "In relation to offenses of a traditional type, the Court's opinion seems to be saying, we must be much slower to dispense with a basis for genuine blameworthiness in criminal intent than in relation to modern regulatory offenses. But it is precisely in the area of traditional crimes that the nature of the act itself commonly gives some warning that there may be a problem about its propriety and so affords, without more, at least some slight basis of condemnation for doing it. Thus, Morissette knew perfectly well that he was taking property which, at least up to the moment of caption, did not belong to him.

"In the area of regulatory crimes, on the other hand, the moral quality of the act is often neutral; and on occasion, the offense may consist not of any act at all, but simply of an intrinsically innocent omission, so that there is no basis for moral condemnation whatever."—EDS.

ion, the existence of which may have led the Court to overlook the need for full exposition of their rationale in the context of federal law.

Neither this Court nor, so far as we are aware, any other has undertaken to delineate a precise line or set forth comprehensive criteria for distinguishing between crimes that require a mental element and crimes that do not. We attempt no closed definition, for the law on the subject is neither settled nor static. The conclusion reached in the *Balint* and *Behrman* Cases has our approval and adherence for the circumstances to which it was there applied. A quite different question here is whether we will expand the doctrine of crimes without intent to include those charged here.

Stealing, larceny, and its variants and equivalents, were among the earliest offenses known to the law that existed before legislation; they are invasions of rights of property which stir a sense of insecurity in the whole community and arouse public demand for retribution, the penalty is high and, when a sufficient amount is involved, the infamy is that of a felony, which, says Maitland, is ". . . as bad a word as you can give to man or thing." State courts of last resort, on whom fall the heaviest burden of interpreting criminal law in this country, have consistently retained the requirement of intent in larceny-type offenses. If any state has deviated, the exception has neither been called to our attention nor disclosed by our research.

Congress, therefore, omitted any express prescription of criminal intent from the enactment before us in the light of an unbroken course of judicial decision in all constituent states of the Union holding intent inherent in this class of offense, even when not expressed in a statute. Congressional silence as to mental elements in an Act merely adopting into federal statutory law a concept of crime already so well defined in common law and statutory interpretation by the states may warrant quite contrary inferences than the same silence in creating an offense new to general law, for whose definition the courts have no guidance except the Act. Because the offenses before this Court in the *Balint* and *Behrman* Cases were of this latter class, we cannot accept them as authority for eliminating intent from offenses incorporated from the common law. . . .

The Government asks us by a feat of construction radically to change the weights and balances in the scales of justice. The purpose and obvious effect of doing away with the requirement of a guilty intent is to ease the prosecution's path to conviction, to strip the defendant of such benefit as he derived at common law from innocence of evil purpose, and to circumscribe the freedom heretofore allowed juries. Such a manifest impairment of the immunities of the individual should not be extended to common-law crimes on judicial initiative. . . .

We hold that the mere omission from §641 of any mention of intent will not be construed as eliminating that element from the crimes denounced. . . .

Of course, the jury, considering Morissette's awareness that these casings were on government property, his failure to seek any permission for their removal and his self-interest as a witness, might have disbelieved his profession of innocent intent and concluded that his assertion of a belief that the casings were abandoned was an after-thought. Had the jury convicted on proper instructions it would be the end of the matter. But juries are not bound by what seems inescapable logic to judges. They might have concluded that the heaps of spent casings left in the hinterland to rust away presented an appearance of unwanted and abandoned junk, and that lack of any conscious deprivation of property or intentional injury was indicated by Morissette's good character, the openness of the taking, crushing and transporting of the casings, and the candor with which it was all admitted. They might have refused to brand Morissette as a thief. Had they done so, that too would have been the end of the matter.

Reversed.

UNITED STATES v. FREED, 401 U.S. 601, 607-609 (1971): [Appellees were indicted under the amended National Firearms Act for possessing and conspiring to possess unregistered hand grenades. The district court dismissed the indictment on the ground that it contravened due process by failing to allege scienter, that is, knowledge that the hand grenades were not registered. The Court reversed. Justice Douglas stated:] The Act requires no specific intent or knowledge that the hand grenades were unregistered. It makes it unlawful for any person "to receive or possess a firearm which is not registered to him." By the lower court decisions at the time that requirement was written into the Act the only knowledge required to be proved was knowledge that the instrument possessed was a firearm. . . .

The presence of a "vicious will" or mens rea (Morissette v. United States, 342 U.S. 246, 251) was long a requirement of criminal responsibility. But the list of exceptions grew, especially in the expanding regulatory area involving activities affecting public health, safety, and welfare. The statutory offense of embezzlement, borrowed from the common-law where scienter was historically required, was in a different category. . . .

At the other extreme is Lambert v. California, 355 U.S. 225, in which a municipal code made it a crime to remain in Los Angeles for more than five days without registering if a person had been convicted of a felony. Being in Los Angeles is not per se blameworthy. The mere failure to register, we held, was quite "unlike the commission of acts, or the failure to act under circumstances that should alert the doer to the consequences of his deed." . . .

In United States v. Dotterweich, 320 U.S. 277, 284, a case dealing with the imposition of a penalty on a corporate officer whose firm shipped adulterated and misbranded drugs in violation of the Food and Drug Act, we approved the penalty "though consciousness of wrong-doing be totally wanting."

The present case is in the category neither of *Lambert* nor *Morissette,* but is closer to *Dotterweich.* This is a regulatory measure in the interest of the public safety, which may well be premised on the theory that one would hardly be surprised to learn that possession of hand grenades is not an innocent act. They are highly dangerous offensive weapons, no less dangerous than the narcotics involved in United States v. Balint, 258 U.S. 250, 254.

NOTE ON STRICT LIABILITY IN TRADITIONAL OFFENSES

Despite the commitment of the traditional Anglo-American criminal law to the requirement of mens rea, described by Justice Jackson in *Morissette,* there have been departures from it in a number of instances. These departures have occurred mainly in the law of culpable homicide. Examples were the felony-murder and misdemeanor-manslaughter rules, according to which even a wholly accidental killing, otherwise not punishable, became murder if it occurred during the commission of a felony and manslaughter if it occurred during the commission of a misdemeanor. Another example was the treatment of a killing to defend another person, which act was justifiable if the person being defended had a right to kill but murder if, even despite all reasonable appearances, the person did not, as, for example, he or she would not if he or she were the aggressor. We will examine these doctrines in Chapter 6, Homicide, infra.

Two other notable instances of departures from the traditional mens rea requirement occurred in connection with the statutory crimes of sexual intercourse with minors and bigamy.

We have already seen (page 285 supra) that the prevailing view on sex offenses with minors was (and continues to be in most jurisdictions) that strict liability applies to the age of the minor: No mistake, even a wholly reasonable one, can be a defense.

Bigamy is generally defined by statute as occurring when a person having a living spouse marries another, except when the person's first spouse has been absent for a stated number of years (usually five or seven) and is not known by the person to be living or after a judgment of a court voiding, annulling, or dissolving the first marriage. In most jurisdictions even a reasonable mistake about the facts that, if existent, would render the second marriage nonbigamous is held to constitute no defense to a bigamy charge. In State v. Hendrickson, 67 Utah 15, 245 P. 375 (1926), for example, evidence of the defendant's good-faith belief that his first wife had obtained a divorce before his second marriage was held inadmissible. In Commonwealth v. Mash, 48 Mass. 472 (1844), a much relied on authority, defendant's marriage to a second husband within seven years of the disappearance of her first was held to constitute bigamy regardless of the reasonableness of her grounds for belief that he had in fact died before the time of the second marriage. English law is now to the contrary both when the reasonable mistake of the marrying spouse concerns the death of the first spouse (absent less than the statutory number of years) (Regina v. Tolson, [1889] 23 Q.B.D. 168) and when it concerns the existence of a decree of divorce (Regina v. Gould, [1966] 2 W.L.R. 643, overruling Rex v. Wheat, [1921] 2 K.B. 119). Some recent American cases have held to the same effect; e.g., People v. Vogel, 46 Cal. 2d 798, 299 P.2d 850 (1956).

PROBLEM

The Sherman Antitrust Act, 15 U.S.C. §1, provides:

> Every contract, combination . . . or conspiracy in restraint of trade or commerce among the United States, or with foreign nations, is declared to be illegal. Every person who shall make any contract or engage in any combination or conspiracy hereby declared to be illegal shall be deemed guilty of a felony.

Defendants — gypsum-board manufacturers and their officers — had participated in a practice of interstate price verification through which competitors would telephone one another to determine the price at which they were selling gypsum board to particular customers. In a criminal prosecution, the government charged that this practice facilitated price-fixing, in violation of the Sherman Act.

Defendants defended on the ground that the price-information exchanges were designed, not for the purpose of fixing prices, but to enable defendants to take advantage of §1(b) of the Robinson-Patman Act, which permits a seller to rebut a prima facie price-discrimination charge by showing that a lower price to a purchaser was made in good faith to meet an equally low price of a competitor. The jury convicted, on instructions that "if the effect of the exchanges of pricing information was to raise, fix, maintain, and stabilize prices, then the parties to them are presumed, as a matter of law, to have intended the result."

On appeal, defendants sought reversal on the ground that the above instruction permitted conviction without proof that the effect on prices was intended. What result? Is the Sherman Act similar to the statute involved in *Morissette* (where the Court insisted on proof of intent), or is it closer to the public welfare statutes (where, typically, the courts have construed the statutes as dispensing with such proof)? What criteria should be used to determine whether a statute is placed in the former category rather than the latter?

In United States v. United States Gypsum Co., 438 U.S. 422 (1978), the Supreme Court reversed the convictions, holding that the Sherman Act should not be construed to impose strict liability and that proof of an intent to fix prices was an essential element of the criminal offense. The Court particularly emphasized the severity of the sanctions specified by Congress for Sherman Act violations and the fact that "behavior proscribed by the Act is often difficult to distinguish from socially acceptable and economically justifiable business conduct."

Questions: Do the factors mentioned by the Court in United States v. Gypsum sufficiently differentiate the public welfare offense? In this connection, consider also United States v. Park, page 1027-1032 infra, where the Court reaffirmed strict liability under a federal regulatory statute in the food-and-drug area.

NOTE: SOME VIEWS ON STRICT LIABILITY

Sweet v. Parsley, [*1970*] *A.C. 132, 149-150 (H.L. 1968)*: [Defendant, who was obliged to live in town, rented her farm house to some people who, unknown to her, smoked cannabis on the premises. She was convicted of violating §5(b) of the Dangerous Drugs Act of 1965. Section 5 provided:

> If a person (a) being the occupier of any premises, permits those premises to be used for the purpose of smoking cannabis or cannabis resin or of dealing in cannabis or cannabis resin (whether by sale or otherwise); or (b) is concerned in the management of any premises used for any such purpose as aforesaid: he shall be guilty of an offence against this Act.

The House of Lords reversed, concluding that in the circumstances defendant could not be said to be concerned in the premises used for the purpose of smoking cannabis. Lord Reid approached the issue of whether the statute should be construed to impose absolute liability by trying to put himself in the position of the reasonable legislator. He observed:] When one comes to acts of a truly criminal character, it appears to me that there are at least two . . . factors which any reasonable legislator would have in mind. In the first place a stigma still attaches to any person convicted of a truly criminal offence, and the more serious or more disgraceful the offence the greater the stigma. So he would have to consider whether, in a case of this gravity, the public interest really requires that an innocent person should be prevented from proving his innocence in order that fewer guilty men may escape. And equally important is the fact that fortunately the Press in this country are vigilant to expose injustice and every manifestly unjust conviction made known to the public tends to injure the body politic by undermining public confidence in the justice of the law and of its administration. But I regret to observe that, in some recent cases where serious offences have been held to be absolute offences, the Court has taken into account no more than the wording of the Act and the character and seriousness of the mischief which constitutes the offence.

The choice would be much more difficult if there were no other way open than either mens rea in the full sense or an absolute offence; for there are many kinds of case where putting on the prosecutor the full burden of proving mens rea creates great difficulties and may lead to many unjust acquittals. But there are at least two other possibilities. Parliament has not infrequently transferred the onus as regards mens rea to the accused, so that, once the necessary facts are proved, he must convince the jury that on balance of probabilities he is innocent of any criminal intention. I find it a little surprising that more use has not been made of this method. . . . The other method would be in effect to substitute in appropriate classes of cases gross negligence for mens rea in the full sense as the mental element necessary to constitute the crime. It would often be much easier to infer that Parliament must have meant that gross negligence should be the necessary mental element than to infer that Parliament intended to create an absolute offence. . . . It may be that none of these methods is wholly satisfactory but at least the public scandal of convicting on a serious charge persons who are in no way blameworthy would be avoided.

If this section means what the Court of Appeal have held that it means, then hundreds of thousands of people who sublet part of their premises or take in lodgers or are concerned in the management of residential premises or institutions are daily incurring a risk of being convicted of a serious offence in circumstances where they are in no way to blame. For the greatest vigilance cannot prevent tenants, lodgers or inmates or guests whom they bring in from smoking cannabis cigarettes in their own rooms.

Goodhart, Possession of Drugs and Absolute Liability, 84 L.Q. Rev. 382, 385-386 (1968): The . . . function of absolute liability is in certain circumstances a procedural and not a penal one. Thus there are certain offences that have a serious effect on the public interest but which it is difficult to prove under the usual procedure. It is then necessary to take other and more stringent steps to wipe out the evil, even at a minimal risk that an innocent man may be convicted. Lord Reid cites, although he does not entirely agree with it, the long-established saying that "it is better that ten guilty men should escape than that one innocent man should be convicted." . . . On the other hand it may be necessary in certain circumstances to alter the strict rules where an act, such as tempting young persons to buy drugs, is peculiarly harmful, and where it may be difficult to prove the existence of mens rea, although it is almost certain that it does exist. . . . The point here is that the future harm that the ten guilty men who have been acquitted may do, either by repeating their own offences or by encouraging others by showing how easy it is to avoid conviction, far exceeds any injury that the innocent man can suffer by his conviction. The question then becomes: Is it better that ten young persons should be tempted to become drug addicts than that one innocent man should be convicted of being in possession of unauthorized drugs?[a]

NOTE

Few academic commentators write favorably about strict criminal liability. Three notable exceptions, who have made searching efforts to defend it as compatible, in certain forms and situations, with the basic principles of criminal liability, are Wasserstrom, Strict Liability in the Criminal Law, 12 Stan. L. Rev. 731 (1960); Brady, Strict Criminal Offenses: A Justification, 8 Crim. L. Bull. 217 (1973); Note, Criminal Liability without Fault: A Philosophical Perspective, 75 Colum. L. Rev. 1517 (1975).

STATE v. BAKER
Kansas Court of Appeal
571 P.2d 65 (1977)

SPENCER, J. Defendant has appealed his conviction of driving his motor vehicle at a speed of seventy-seven miles per hour in a fifty-five miles per hour zone in violation of K.S.A. 1976 Supp. 8-1336(a)(3).

Agreed upon facts are that prior to the trial of this matter to the court, the state moved to suppress evidence offered by the defendant that:

1. Defendant's cruise control stuck in the "accelerate" position causing the car to accelerate beyond the posted speed limit.
2. The defendant attempted to deactivate the cruise control by hitting the off button, and the coast button and tapping the brakes.
3. These actions were not immediately successful in deactivating the cruise control.
4. Subsequent to the date of this incident, the defendant had the defective cruise control repaired.

The trial court sustained the motion, thus precluding the defendant from pre-

a. Compare Model Penal Code, §2.05, Comment at 140 (Tent. Draft No. 4, 1955), which states: "The liabilities involved [for criminal punishment] are indefensible, unless reduced to terms that insulate conviction from the type of moral condemnation that is and ought to be implicit when a sentence of imprisonment may be imposed. In the absence of minimal culpability, the law has neither a deterrent nor corrective nor an incapacitative function to perform.

"It has been argued . . . that absolute liability is necessary for enforcement in a number of areas where it obtains. But if practical enforcement cannot undertake to litigate the culpability of alleged deviation from legal requirements, we do not see how the enforcers rightly can demand the use of penal sanctions for the purpose. Crime does and should mean condemnation and no court should have to pass that judgment unless it can declare that the defendant's act was wrong. This is too fundamental to be compromised. The law goes far enough if it permits the imposition of monetary penalty in cases where strict liability has been imposed." — EDS.

senting the proffered evidence as a defense. . . . The result was that the defendant was found guilty of driving in excess of the posted speed limit, and, also, that defendant was the "driver" of the car as defined by K.S.A. 8-1416. The sentence of $10 and costs was suspended pending this appeal. . . .

. . . [D]efendant readily concedes that a violation of the speeding statute (K.S.A. 1976 Supp. 8-1336) is an absolute liability offense when read in light of the absolute liability statute (K.S.A. 21-3204), which provides:

> A person may be guilty of an offense without having criminal intent if the crime is a misdemeanor and the statute defining the offense clearly indicates a legislative purpose to impose absolute liability for the conduct described. . . .

Defendant admits that this statute does away with the necessity of proving intent to commit the misdemeanor and, further, that any evidence of the defective cruise control would be inadmissible if introduced merely to negate an intent or culpable state of mind on the part of the motorist. His contention is that the evidence was offered to show that his speeding was not a voluntary act and, therefore, there was no criminal liability. He suggests that the evidence of a defective cruise control goes specifically to whether his speeding was a voluntary act on his part and has nothing to do "with the intent, or state of mind, of the defendant to do the crime to which his act amounted." In sum, the defendant suggests that even though the charge against him was an absolute liability offense per K.S.A. 21-3204, the state must prove that he acted voluntarily. . . .

We have no doubt that if defendant were able to establish that his act of speeding was the result of an unforeseen occurrence or circumstance, which was not caused by him and which he could not prevent, that such would constitute a valid defense to the charge. But, the evidence proffered suggests a malfunction of a device attached to the motor vehicle operated by the defendant over which he had or should have had absolute control. Defendant does not suggest that the operation of the motor vehicle on the day of his arrest was anything but a voluntary act on his part, nor that anyone other than himself activated the cruise control, which may have caused his excessive speed. . . .

In the New York case of People v. Shaughnessy, 66 Misc. 2d 19, 319 N.Y.S.2d 626 (1971), it was held that a defendant could not be found guilty of violating an ordinance prohibiting entry upon private property because the defendant was merely a passenger in the trespassing car and the state's evidence failed to show an overt voluntary act of omission by the defendant. In the case of State v. Kremer, 262 Minn. 190, 114 N.W.2d 88 (1962), the Minnesota Supreme Court held that a defendant could not be guilty of violating a city ordinance requiring all traffic to stop at a flashing red light when the evidence showed that defendant's brakes failed with no prior warning to the defendant. Again, the court found no overt voluntary act on the part of the defendant. . . .

. . . In [State v.] Weller, [230 A.2d 242 (1967),] the Connecticut court stated that the defendant had a valid defense to the speeding charge because the spring which closes the throttle plate broke due to no fault of the defendant. The court reasoned that because "[t]here is not one scintilla of evidence of any intent on the part of the defendant to do the prohibited act . . ." the defendant's conviction should be overturned. . . .

In our view, unexpected brake failure and unexpected malfunction of the throttle on an automobile, both being essential components to the operation of the vehicle, differ significantly from the malfunction of a cruise control device to which the driver has voluntarily delegated partial control of that automobile. We believe it must be said that defendant assumed the full operation of his motor vehicle and when he did so and activated the cruise control attached to that automobile, he clearly was the agent in causing the act of speeding. . . .

Judgment affirmed.

NOTE ON THE INVOLUNTARY-ACT DEFENSE TO ABSOLUTE-LIABILITY OFFENSES

In Hill v. Baxter, [1958] 1 Q.B. 277, defendant drove his truck at a fast speed through a halt sign, collided with a car, and overturned. He was charged with dangerous driving under Section 11(1) of the Road Traffic Act and with failing to conform to a traffic sign under Section 49(b). The trial justices dismissed the charges on the basis of some evidence that he had had a blackout. On appeal by the prosecutor, the divisional court reversed on the ground that the defendant had not proved he was in a state of automatism. Lord Goddard observed (at 282-283):

> The first thing to be remembered is that the Road Traffic Act, 1930, contains an absolute prohibition against driving dangerously or ignoring "Halt" signs. No question of mens rea enters into the offence; it is no answer to a charge under those sections to say: "I did not mean to drive dangerously" or "I did not notice the 'Halt' sign." The justices' finding that the respondent was not capable of forming any intention as to the manner of driving is really immaterial. What they evidently mean is that the respondent was in a state of automation. But he was driving and, as the case finds, exercising some skill, and undoubtedly the onus of proving that he was in a state of automation must be on him. . . .[a]
>
> The main contention before us on the part of the appellant was that there was no evidence on which the justices could find that the respondent was in a state of automatism or whatever term may be applied to someone performing acts in a state of unconsciousness. There was in fact no evidence except that of the respondent, and while the justices were entitled to believe him, his evidence shows nothing except that after the accident he cannot remember what took place after he left Preston Circus. This is quite consistent with being overcome with sleep or at least drowsiness. That drivers do fall asleep is a not uncommon cause of serious road accidents, and it would be impossible as well as disastrous to hold that falling asleep at the wheel was any defence to a charge of dangerous driving. If a driver finds that he is getting sleepy he must stop. . . .
>
> . . . I agree that there may be cases where the circumstances are such that the accused could not really be said to be driving at all. Suppose he had a stroke or an epileptic fit, both instances of what may properly be called acts of God; he might well be in the driver's seat even with his hands on the wheel, but in such a state of unconsciousness that he could not be said to be driving. A blow from a stone or an attack by a swarm of bees I think introduces some conception akin

---

a. Would this requirement be possible under American law? Consider Patterson v. New York, pages 67-75 supra. — EDS.

to novus actus interveniens. In this case, however, I am content to say that the evidence falls far short of what would justify a court holding that this man was in some automatous state.

For other discussion of the principle that absence of a voluntary act is a defense to even a strict liability offense, see Kilbride v. Lake, [1962] N.Z.L.R. 590, and comment thereon in Clark, Accident — or What Became of Kilbride and Lake, in Essays on Criminal Law in New Zealand 47 (1971).

Query: What is the justification in penal policy for this principle? Consider Budd & Lynch, Voluntariness, Causation and Strict Liability, [1978] Crim. L. Rev. 74, 75 n. 6:

> It is strange . . . that it is thought appropriate for the law to acquit those in a state of automatism of offences of strict liability but to convict those acting voluntarily. It seems to us that there is no sound basis for this difference in treatment. It must certainly be wrong for the law to treat differently those who are both equally free of moral blame and whose conviction would be equally relevant to advancing the purposes of strict liability. . . . Probably the principal argument in support of strict liability is that it is said to encourage research into measures which will prevent the social harm it prohibits. If this is so, its application to those in a state of automatism may act as a spur to improve knowledge of the causes, diagnoses and cures of automatism. The undoubted social harm which is caused by the "actions" of these people will be reduced either by curing them, or by permitting earlier diagnosis and earlier prohibition of their involvement in activities potentially productive of social harm, or by the establishment of measures effective in neutralising any risk of harm resulting from their diseases. There are at least two other, less significant reasons for strict liability. First, it is said that strict liability saves the court's time. But this applies equally strongly to the justification of the conviction of those in a state of automatism. Secondly, it is said that the imposition of strict liability prevents those who are morally guilty but may be able otherwise to take advantage of some false but successful plea of lack of fault from doing so and thereby escaping liability. The availability of the defence of automatism is, in fact, inconsistent with this reason for strict liability because it is just as possible for the morally guilty to plead falsely that they acted in a state of automatism as to maintain any other reason for lack of fault. . . . Since restricting the scope of strict liability in this way neither effectively distinguishes between the morally innocent and the morally guilty, nor can be justified in terms of the ends of strict liability, automatism should not be assigned special recognition as a defence.

On the other hand, see Murphy, Involuntary Acts and Criminal Liability, 81 Ethics 332, 340-342 (1971):

> Why do we feel a requirement to excuse the man whose actions are involuntary? Not merely for utilitarian reasons, surely. . . . A penal code so Draconian as to punish even epileptics might have high general deterrence and little disutility (as long as most of us could be fairly sure of not becoming epileptic). So another important reason against holding liable here is justice or fairness. And we always feel the pressure to take account of justice or fairness — even in strict liability cases. We may hold a man liable without fault in some areas and thus punish him even if he was not negligent — even if he took all reasonable care. But we would surely object to this on grounds of justice (no matter how high the general utility) if the man did not have fair warning that this was an area of conduct in

which he might have to expect this sort of thing. A drug manufacturer is under danger of strict liability prosecution for any faultless adulteration in his product. But we do not object to this as much as we otherwise might as long as he is given fair warning to choose to do something else with his life if he is not willing to assume this kind of risk. If he does many things to protect his product and fails, then we can always say that he could have done more. . . .

But compare strokes, seizures, and the like. We do not have any capacities to exercise when these are operative. And thus, by no stretch of the imagination can we regard their punishment as fair. When one is suffering a seizure, normal capacities just do not enter the picture. . . .

See also Wasserstrom, Strict Liability in the Criminal Law, 12 Stan. L. Rev. 731, 742-744 (1960).

NOTE ON THE ELIMINATION OF MENS REA FOR ALL CRIMES

The debate over strict criminal liability is usually cast in terms of the justification of eliminating mens rea requirements for particular categories of undesirable conduct. A more far-reaching debate has followed from proposals to extend the principle of strict liability throughout the substantive criminal law by eliminating the requirement of mens rea from the definition of all offenses. See, e.g., B. Wootton, Crime and the Criminal Law (1963); J. Marshall, Intention — in Law and Society (1968); Campbell, A Strict Accountability Approach to Criminal Responsibility, 29 Fed. Prob. 333 (1965).

Lady Wootton has been the most articulate exponent of these proposals. Her scheme is summarized as follows in Kadish, The Decline of Innocence, 26 Cambridge L.J. 273, 285-286 (1968):

[T]here would be two separate stages of determinations made in the case of a person accused of crime. At the first stage there would be decided only whether the defendant committed the act prohibited by the criminal law, without regard to whether he acted intentionally, knowingly, recklessly, and even negligently, or whether he had the capacity to conform to the law under the circumstances. His mental state would be altogether irrelevant. The second stage would arise if it were found that he committed the prohibited act. Now the issue would be to decide what ought to be done with the defendant considering all we know and can find out about him — from psychiatrists, from social workers or from any other source — including, but not limited to, his mental and emotional state at the time he acted. The choice of the disposition would be governed by whatever is desirable to protect the public from his further criminality, whether what is required be medical or psychiatric treatment, training, a permissive or a rigorous environment, punishment or incarceration. Presumably if the offender did not pose a danger he would be released immediately. If he did, he would be held whether he was a villain or a helpless victim of his own incapacities, and for as long as he continued to pose the danger. Thus, according to Lady Wootton, a forward looking approach would be substituted for a backward one we now use, a preventive system for a punitive one.

We should note at the outset what implications such a proposal would have for the whole body of substantive criminal law as we know it. Plainly it would not do to leave the criminal law as it is with only the mental element removed, because under our present law (the instances of strict liability apart) mens rea is crucial to the description of the behavior we want to prevent. Perjury without knowledge of the lie is simply making an incorrect statement under oath. An unlawful assembly without the intent to do unlawful acts is simply joining a group of people in a public place. An attempt to commit a crime without the intent to do so would be incoherent. It would follow under Lady Wootton's proposal that the substantive law of crimes would ultimately have to be rewritten to consist entirely in the specification of harms, somewhat on the order of following hypothetical provision dealing with crimes against the person:

"A person commits a crime" (or perhaps "subjects himself to the compulsory regime of social prevention and personal betterment") "who engages in conduct (in the sense only of bodily movements) as a factual consequence of which:

"(1) another person's life is lost; or,

"(2) another person is physically injured; or

"(3) another person's life or physical well-being is imperilled."

In the course of her argument, Lady Wootton observes (Crime and the Criminal Law 51-53 (1963)):

If . . . the primary function of the courts is conceived as the prevention of forbidden acts, there is little cause to be disturbed by the multiplication of offences of strict liability. If the law says that certain things are not to be done, it is illogical to confine this prohibition to occasions on which they are done from malice aforethought; for at least the material consequences of an action, and the reasons for prohibiting it, are the same whether it is the result of sinister malicious plotting, of negligence or of sheer accident. A man is equally dead and his relatives equally bereaved whether he was stabbed or run over by a drunken motorist or by an incompetent one; and the inconvenience caused by the loss of your bicycle is unaffected by the question whether or not the youth who removed it had the intention of putting it back, if in fact he had not done so at the time of his arrest. It is true, of course, as Professor Hart has argued, that the material consequences of an action by no means exhaust its effects. "If one person hits another, the person struck does not think of the other as just a cause of pain to him. . . . If the blow was light but deliberate, it has a significance for the person struck quite different from an accidental much heavier blow." To ignore this difference, he argues, is to outrage "distinctions which not only underlie morality, but pervade the whole of our social life." That these distinctions are widely appreciated and keenly felt no one would deny. Often perhaps they derive their force from a purely punitive or retributive attitude; but alternatively they may be held to be relevant to an assessment of the social damage that results from a criminal act. Just as a heavy blow does more damage than a light one, so also perhaps does a blow which involves psychological injury do more damage than one in which the hurt is purely physical.

The conclusion to which this argument leads is, I think, not that the presence or absence of the guilty mind is unimportant, but that mens rea has, so to speak — and this is the crux of the matter — got into the wrong place. Traditionally, the requirement of the guilty mind is written into the actual definition of a crime. No guilty intention, no crime, is the rule. Obviously this makes sense if the law's concern is with wickedness: where there is no guilty intention, there can be no wickedness. But it is equally obvious, on the other hand, that an action does not become innocuous merely because whoever performed it meant no harm. If the object of the criminal law is to prevent the occurrence of socially damaging actions, it would be absurd to turn a blind eye to those which were due to carelessness, negligence or even accident. The question of motivation is in the first instance irrelevant.

But only in the first instance. At a later stage, that is to say, after what is now known as a conviction, the presence or absence of guilty intention is all-important for its effect on the appropriate measures to be taken to prevent a recurrence of the forbidden act. The prevention of accidental deaths presents different problems from those involved in the prevention of wilful murders. The results of the actions of the careless, the mistaken, the wicked and the merely unfortunate may be indistinguishable from one another, but each case calls for a different treatment. Tradition, however, is very strong, and the notion that these differences are relevant only after the fact has been established that the accused committed the forbidden act seems still to be deeply abhorrent to the legal mind.

For critical assessments of Lady Wootton's proposals, see H. L. A. Hart, Punishment and Responsibility, chs. 7, 8 (1968); Hart, The Morality of the Criminal Law, ch. 1 (1965); Kadish, The Decline of Innocence, 26 Camb. L.J. 273 (1968). Consider the following comments on Lady Wootton's thesis in Professor Hart's book review of Wootton, Crime and the Criminal Law (1963) in 74 Yale L.J. 1325, 1328-1330 (1965):

[Lady Wootton argues] that if the aim of the criminal law is "the prevention of socially damaging actions" and not retribution for past wickedness, the doctrine of mens rea puts the investigation of the offender's mind "into the wrong place." Such investigation on a preventive theory of punishment can be relevant only after conviction as a guide to the measures to be taken to prevent a repetition of the crime. It is therefore "illogical" to make mens rea part of the definition of the crime and a necessary condition of the offender's liability to compulsory measures. The conventional doctrine of mens rea can only make sense or be "logical" within the framework of a retributive theory according to which punishment is used and justified as an "appropriate" return for past wickedness and not merely as a prevention of anti-social conduct.

This argument is I think mistaken though many writers besides Lady Wootton have used it, sometimes for purposes quite alien to hers. It rests I think on the illusory idea that our only interest in asking whether those whom we punish could at the time of their offence have conformed to the law is to determine whether they were "wicked" in doing what they did. This altogether ignores an outlook on punishment which is surely common, intelligible and, except perhaps for determinists (among whom Lady Wootton does not number herself) perfectly defensible. According to this outlook we should restrict even punishment designed as "preventive" to those who at the time of their offence had the capacity and a fair opportunity or chance to obey the law: and we should do this out of consideration of fairness or justice to those whom we punish. This is an intelligible ideal of justice to the individual and remains intelligible even when we punish to protect society from harm in the future and not to "pay back" the harm that those whom we punish have done. Viewed in this way as a restriction imposed on preventive punishment by considerations of fairness or justice to individuals the doctrine of mens rea presents an aspect neglect of which renders Lady Wootton's argument inconclusive. For such a restriction on punishment has a perfectly "logical" place even within a preventive theory. To show this we can usefully draw upon the ideas and terminology of economics. Let us consider the idea of maximising a certain variable subject to a restraint. In this case the variable will be the efficiency of the system in reducing harmful crime. Plainly, without any illogicality or inconsistency we might acknowledge this as our purpose in punishing but also wish it to be pursued only subject to certain restraints. Some of these restraints might be held absolute in the sense that no increase in the efficiency of the system would be allowed to compensate for the slightest infringement of the restraint. A veto on the use of torture might, for example, be such an absolute restraint; and it is conceivable (and perhaps desirable) that we should treat as an absolute restraint the principle of mens rea that no-one who lacked the capacity or a fair opportunity or chance to conform to law at the time of his offence should be punished. But of course we might have a less absolute system than this, and plainly, so far as we countenance strict liability for minor offences we have a mixed system which allows certain alleged increases in efficiency to counterbalance the injustice done to individuals by infringements of the restraint imposed by the principle of mens rea.

More persuasive than the mistaken identification of the doctrine of mens rea with a purely retributive theory of punishment are the practical considerations that Lady Wootton urges against the doctrine at least as it operates in England. It may well be that through the doctrine of mens rea we secure justice for those whom we punish at too great a cost in terms of social security and that this cost would be avoided if we abandoned the restraints imposed by the doctrine and made all offences into crimes of strict liability. It may well be as Lady Wootton says that too often "we turn a blind eye on socially damaging acts due to carelessness, negligence, or even accident." Yet important as these practical considerations are, there are equally practical objections to the wholesale elimination of mens rea from the criminal law and to these I think Lady Wootton pays insufficient attention. The first and most important concerns individual freedom. In a system in which proof of mens rea was no longer a necessary condition for conviction the occasions for official interferences in our lives would be vastly increased. If the doctrine of mens rea were abolished, every blow, even if it was apparent that it was accidental or merely careless, and therefore not under the present law a criminal assault, would in principle be a matter for investigation under the new scheme. This is so because the possibilities of a curable condition would have to be investigated and if possible treated. No doubt under the new regime prosecuting authorities would use their common-sense; but a very great discretion would have to be entrusted to them to sift from the mass the cases worth investigation for either penal or therapeutic treatment. This expansion of police powers would bring with it great uncertainty for the individual citizen and, though official interference with his life would be more frequent, he will be less able to predict their incidence if any accidental breach of the criminal law may be an occasion for them.

NOTE ON CULPABILITY AND EXCUSE

The principle of culpability, which we have thus far explored principally in the context of the mens rea elements of crimes, finds expression also in an important body of law having to do with excuses to criminal conduct — the defenses of intoxication and legal insanity; the defense of lack of legal responsibility more generally, such as the defense of alcoholism or narcotics addiction; the defense of duress or compulsion. These defenses are integrally related to the problems of actus reus and mens rea (in its special sense) with which we have so far been dealing; they all respond to fundamental principles in terms of which persons can be justly punished for their actions. We nonetheless defer their consideration for pedagogical reasons until we reach Chapter 9, Section B, infra.

C. PROPORTIONALITY

INTRODUCTORY NOTE

The requirement that punishment be proportional to the seriousness of the offense has traditionally been a salient principle of punishment. It is manifested explicitly today in the statement of purpose of various criminal codes. The Model Penal Code (§1.02) includes among the purposes of the definition of crimes the aim "to differentiate on reasonable grounds between serious and minor offenses," and it includes among the purposes of sentencing provisions the aim "to safeguard offenders against excessive, disproportionate or arbitrary punishment." The New York Penal Law includes among the purposes of its provisions (§1.05): "To differentiate on reasonable grounds between serious and minor offenses and to prescribe proportionate penalties therefor." The California Penal Code, as amended in 1976, declares in §1170 that punishment is the purpose of imprisonment for crimes, which purpose is "best served by terms proportionate to the seriousness of the offense."

What is the justification for this concern with proportionality? Is it part of the general principle that punishment must be just, on the view that excessive punishment of an offender is as unjust as punishing an innocent person? Can we hold to the latter view without necessarily holding to the former? Or is the injustice of excessive punishment rooted in other considerations?

If we believe excessive punishment, for whatever reason, is unjust, what constitutes excessive punishment? Is there a precise kind and degree of punishment appropriate to every criminal wrong, as Kant argued? How could it be determined? If this perspective is rejected, we may hold that some general proportion must be maintained between the crime and the amount of punishment in light of the seriousness of the crime. But if so, is the point that certain crimes cannot be punished with more than a given quantum of punishment or rather that whatever the scale of punishment meted out in a particular society, whether high or low, less serious crime must be punished less than more serious crimes?

Perhaps the aim is not justice and fairness, whatever they might mean, but strictly utilitarian goals. If we hold this view, must we accept that any amount of punishment, no matter how severe, can be justifiable if, in the circumstances, it yields a desirable balance of utilities?

These are some of the principal issues addressed in the material that follows.

BENTHAM, PRINCIPLES OF PENAL LAW
In 1 J. Bentham's Works, Pt. II, bk. 1 at 399-402 (J. Bowring ed. 1843)

Punishments may be too small or too great; and there are reasons for not making them too small, as well as not making them too great. The terms *minimum* and *maximum* may serve to mark the two extremes of this question, which require equal attention.

With a view of marking out the limits of punishment on the side of the first of these extremes, we may lay it down as a rule —

I. That the value of the punishment must not be less in any case than what is sufficient to outweigh that of the profit of the offence.

By the profit of the crime, must be understood not only pecuniary profit, but every advantage, real or apparent, which has operated as a motive to the commission of the crime.

The profit of the crime is the force which urges a man to delinquency — the pain of the punishment is the force employed to restrain him from it. If the first of these forces be the greater, the crime will be committed;[1] if the second, the crime will not be committed. If then a man, having reaped the profit of a crime, and undergone the punishment, finds the former more than equivalent to the latter, he will go on offending for ever; there is nothing to restrain him. If those, also, who behold him, reckon that the balance of gain is in favour of the delinquent, the punishment will be useless for the purposes of example. . . .

Rule III. *When two offences come in competition, the punishment for the greater offence must be sufficient to induce a man to prefer the less.*

Two offences may be said to be in competition, when it is in the power of an individual to commit both. When thieves break into a house, they may execute their purpose in different manners; by simply stealing, by theft accompanied with bodily injury, or murder, or incendiarism. If the punishment is the same for simple theft, as for theft and murder, you give the thieves a motive for committing murder, because this crime adds to the facility of committing the former, and the chance of impunity when it is committed.

The great inconvenience resulting from the infliction of great punishments for small offences, is, that the power of increasing them in proportion to the magnitude of the offence is thereby lost.

Rule IV. *The punishment should be adjusted in such manner to each particular offence, that for every part of the mischief there may be a motive to restrain the offender from giving birth to it.*

Thus, for example, in adjusting the punishment for stealing a sum of money, let the magnitude of the punishment be determined by the amount of the sum stolen. If for stealing ten shillings an offender is punished no more than for stealing five, the stealing of the remaining five of those ten shillings is an offence for which there is no punishment at all.

Rule V. *The punishment ought in no case to be more than what is necessary to bring it into conformity with the rules here given.* . . .

Of the above rules of proportion, the four first may serve to mark out the limits of the minimum side — the limits below which a punishment ought not to be diminished; the fifth will mark out the limits on the maximum side — the limits above which it ought not to be increased.

The minimum of punishment is more clearly marked than its maximum. What is *too little* is more clearly observed than what is *too much*. What is not sufficient is easily seen, but it is not possible so exactly to distinguish in excess: an approximation only can be attained. The irregularities in the force of temptations compel the legislator to increase his punishments, till they are not merely sufficient to restrain the ordinary desires of men, but also the violence of their desires when unusually excited.

The greatest danger lies in an error on the minimum side, because in this

---

1. That is to say, committed by those who are only restrained by the laws, and not by any other tutelary motives, such as benevolence, religion or honor.

case the punishment is inefficacious; but this error is least likely to occur, a slight degree of attention sufficing for its escape; and when it does exist, it is at the same time clear and manifest, and easy to be remedied. An error on the maximum side, on the contrary, is that to which legislators and men in general are naturally inclined: antipathy, or a want of compassion for individuals who are represented as dangerous and vile, pushes them onward to an undue severity. It is on this side, therefore, that we should take the most precautions, as on this side there has been shown the greatest disposition to err.

By way of supplement and explanation to the first rule, and to make sure of giving to the punishment the superiority over the offence, the . . . following rules may be laid down: —

Rule VII. *That the value of the punishment may outweigh the profit of the offence, it must be increased in point of magnitude, in proportion as it falls short in point of certainty.*

Rule VIII. *Punishment must be further increased in point of magnitude, in proportion as it falls short in points of proximity.*

The profit of a crime is commonly more certain than its punishment; or, what amounts to the same thing, appears so to the offender. It is generally more immediate: the temptation to offend is present; the punishment is at a distance. Hence there are two circumstances which weaken the effect of punishment, its *uncertainty* and its *distance.*

H. L. A. HART & A. HONORÉ, CAUSATION IN THE LAW 354 (1959): On a deterrent theory the rationale of the differential severity of punishments is complex. First, one crime if unchecked may cause greater harm than another, and hence on general utilitarian grounds greater severity may be used in its repression than in the repression of the less harmful crime. Secondly, the temptation to commit one sort of crime may be greater than another and hence a more severe penalty is needed to deter. Thirdly, the commission of one crime may be a sign of a more dangerous character in the criminal needing longer sentence for incapacitation or reform.

EWING, A STUDY OF PUNISHMENT II: PUNISHMENT AS VIEWED BY THE PHILOSOPHER, 21 Canadian B. Rev. 102, 115-116 (1943): We are now in a position also to give a satisfactory reason why a graver offence should be punished more than a lighter one. To punish a lesser crime more severely than a greater would be either to suggest to men's minds that the former was worse when it was not, or, if they could not accept this, to bring the penal law in some degree into discredit or ridicule. One of the requirements of a good moral code is that there should be a right proportion between values, and, in so far as penal laws affect popular morality, they ought to help and not hinder right judgment in this matter. This is not to fall back on the old retributive conception that a certain amount of pain intrinsically fits a certain degree of moral badness. Granted that a certain degree of punishment is inflicted in a given society, for, e.g., thefts, and that certain other acts, e.g., murders, are morally worse, moral condemnation of the latter can only be suitably expressed by inflicting a severer punishment for them than for the former; but this would not be an objection to lowering the penalty for both, because there is no necessarily fixed scale that we can see by which so much guilt deserves so much pain. There is another bad effect of disproportionate punishments in so far as they involve excessive severity. It is this: if a man is very severely punished for a comparatively slight offence, people will be liable to forget about his crime and think only of his sufferings, so that he appears a victim of cruel laws, and the whole process, instead of reaffirming the law and intensifying men's consciousness that the kind of act punished is wrong, will have the opposite effect of casting discredit on the law and making the action of the lawbreaker appear excusable or even almost heroic. These punishments are specially liable to produce an effect of this sort on their victim. He will be likely to think the penalty excessive in any case, and the great danger of punishment is that this will lead to self-pity and despair, or anger and bitterness, instead of repentence, but if he has really good grounds for complaint, this danger will be doubled. The primary object of punishment is to lead both the offender and others to realize the badness of the act punished; but, if great severity is shown, they are much more likely to realize instead the cruelty of the punishment.

We may then regard punishment as a kind of language intended to express moral disapproval.

J. F. STEPHEN, LAW, EQUALITY, FRATERNITY 152-154 (White ed. 1967): If vengeance affects, and ought to affect, the amount of punishment, every circumstance which aggravates or extenuates the wickedness of an act will operate in aggravation or diminution of punishment. If the object of legal punishment is simply the prevention of specific acts, this will not be the case. Circumstances which extenuate the wickedness of the crime will often operate in aggravation of punishment. If, as I maintain, both objects must be kept in view, such circumstances will operate in different ways according to the nature of the case.

A judge has before him two criminals, one of whom appears, from the circumstances of the case, to be ignorant and depraved, and to have given way to very strong temptation, under the influence of the other, who is a man of rank and education, and who committed the offence of which both are convicted under comparatively slight temptation. I will venture to say that if he made any difference between them at all every judge on the English bench would give the first man a lighter sentence than the second.

What should we think of such an address to the prisoners as this? You, *A*, are a most dangerous man. You are ignorant, you are depraved, and you are accordingly peculiarly liable to be led into crime by the solicitations or influence of people like your accomplice *B*. Such influences constitute to men like you a temptation practically all but irresistible. The class to which you belong is a large one, and is accessible only to the coarsest possible motives. For these reasons I must put into the opposite scale as heavy a weight as I can, and the sentence of the court upon you is that you be taken to the place from whence you came and from thence to a place of execution, and that there you be hanged by the neck till you are dead. As to you, *B*, you are undoubtedly an infamous wretch. Between you and your tool *A* there can, morally speaking, be no comparison at all. But I have nothing to do with that. You belong to a small and not a dangerous class. The temptation to which you gave way was slight, and the impression made upon me by your conduct is that you really did not care very much whether you committed this crime or not. From a moral point of view, this may perhaps increase your guilt; but it shows that the motive to be overcome is less powerful in your case than in *A*'s. You belong, moreover, to a class, and occupy a position in society, in which exposure and loss of character are much dreaded. This you will have to undergo. Your case is a very odd one, and it is not likely that you will wish to commit such a crime again, or that others will follow your example. Upon the whole, I think that what has passed will deter others from such conduct as much as actual punishment. It is, however, necessary to keep a hold over you. You will therefore be discharged on your own recognizances to come up and receive judgment when called upon, and unless you conduct yourself better for the future, you will assuredly be so called upon, and if you do not appear, your recognizances will be inexorably forfeited.

Caricature apart, the logic of such a view is surely unimpeachable. If all that you want of criminal law is the prevention of crime by the direct fear of punishment, the fact that a temptation is strong is a reason why punishment should be severe. In some instances this actually is the case. It shows the reason why political crimes and offences against military discipline are punished so severely. But in most cases the strength of the temptation operates in mitigation of punishment, and the reason of this is that criminal law operates not merely by producing fear, but also indirectly, but very powerfully, by giving distinct shape to the feeling of anger, and a distinct satisfaction to the desire of vengeance which crime excites in a healthy mind.

H. L. A. HART, LAW, LIBERTY AND MORALITY 36-37 (1963): [T]he questions "What sort of conduct may justifiably be punished?" and "How severely should we punish different offenses?" are distinct and independent questions. There are many reasons why we might wish the legal graduation of the seriousness of crimes, expressed in its scale of punishments, not to conflict with common estimates of their comparative wickedness. One reason is that such a conflict is undesirable on simple utilitarian grounds: it might either confuse moral judgments or bring the law into disrepute, or both.[a] Another reason is that principles of justice or fairness between different offenders require morally distinguishable offences to be treated differently and morally similar offences to be treated alike. These principles are still widely respected, although it is also true that there is a growing disinclination to insist on their application where this conflicts with the forward-looking aims of punishment, such as prevention or reform. But those who concede that we should attempt to adjust the severity of punishment to the moral gravity of offences are not thereby committed to the view that punishment merely for immorality is justified. For they can in perfect consistency insist on the one hand that the only justification for having a system of punishment is to prevent harm and only harmful conduct should be punished, and, on the other, agree that when the question of the quantum of punishment for such conduct is raised, we should defer to principles which make relative

a. See also H. L. A. Hart, Punishment and Responsibility 25 (1968): "The guiding principle is that of a proportion within a system of penalties between those imposed for different offences where these have a distinct place in a commonsense scale of gravity. This scale itself no doubt consists of very broad judgements both of relative moral iniquity and harmfulness of different types of offence: it draws rough distinctions like that between parking offences and homicide, or between "mercy killing" and murder for gain, but cannot cope with any precise assessment of an individual's wickedness in committing a crime (Who can?). Yet maintenance of proportion of this kind may be important: for where the legal gradation of crimes expressed in the relative severity of penalties diverges sharply from this rough scale, there is a risk of either confusing common morality or flouting it and bringing the law into contempt." — Eds.

moral wickedness of different offenders a partial determinant of the severity of punishment.

In re LYNCH
Supreme Court of California
8 Cal. 3d 410, 503 P.2d 921 (1972)

Mosk, J. One who commits an act of indecent exposure in California is guilty of a simple misdemeanor and can be punished by no more than a brief jail sentence or a small fine. If he commits the identical act a second time, however, the law declares him guilty of a felony and inflicts on him a punishment of imprisonment in the state prison for the indeterminate period of one year to life. We adjudicate here the question whether the aggravated penalty for second-offense indecent exposure provided by Penal Code section 314 violates the prohibition of the California Constitution against cruel or unusual punishments. (Cal. Const., art. I, §6.) We conclude that the penalty offends the Constitution in the respect charged, and petitioner is therefore entitled to relief.

[Defendant Lynch was convicted of indecent exposure in 1958 and again in 1967. The case was before the court on an original petition for a writ of habeas corpus.]

. . . We approach [the constitutional challenge] with full awareness of and respect for the distinct roles of the Legislature and the courts in such an undertaking. We recognize that in our tripartite system of government it is the function of the legislative branch to define crimes and prescribe punishments, and that such questions are in the first instance for the judgment of the Legislature alone. . . .

Yet legislative authority remains ultimately circumscribed by the constitutional provision forbidding the infliction of cruel or unusual punishment, adopted by the people of this state as an integral part of our Declaration of Rights. It is the difficult but imperative task of the judicial branch, as coequal guardian of the Constitution, to condemn any violation of that prohibition. . . .

[The court concluded that the sentence whose constitutionality was to be tested was the maximum term authorized by the statute rather than any lesser term the Adult Authority might use its discretion to set. It then concluded that the constitutional test was whether the length of the sentence "is so disproportionate to the crime for which it is inflicted that it shocks the conscience and offends fundamental notions of human dignity."] [a]

To aid in administering this rule, we point to certain techniques used in the decisions discussed herein. First, a number of courts have examined the nature

a. In support of its principle of proportionality the court cited cases that had held unconstitutionally disproportionate to the offense a sentence of life imprisonment without possibility of parole for rape committed by juvenile delinquents (Workman v. Commonwealth, 429 S.W.2d 374 (Ky. 1968)); life imprisonment for assault with intent to rape (Cannon v. Gladden, 203 Or. 629, 281 P.2d 233 (1955)) or for lewd and lascivious conduct upon a child (State v. Evans, 73 Idaho 50, 245 P.2d 788 (1952)); imprisonment for 30 years at hard labor as punishment for burglary (State v. Kembrough, 212 S.C. 348, 40 S.E.2d 273 (1948)) or for a mandatory minimum of 20 years for selling marijuana (People v. Lorentzen, 387 Mich. 167, 194 N.W.2d 827 (1972)). It also noted that disproportionality is not confined to long prison sentences, citing a case holding excessive a two-to-three-year imprisonment of a youthful first offender for marijuana possession (State v. Ward, 57 N.J. 75, 270 A.2d 1 (1970)). — Eds.

of the offense and/or the offender, with particular regard to the degree of danger both present to society. . . .

More specifically, in his dissenting opinion in *O'Neil* Justice Field [O'Neil v. Vermont, 144 U.S. 323 (1892)] relied on the facts of the crime in question to demonstrate its triviality: there, a New York liquor dealer was convicted in Vermont of selling liquor to residents of Vermont, a "dry" state. Justice Field stressed that such sales were legal under the law of New York (144 U.S. at p. 337) and that the defendant's sole connection with Vermont was to send individual jugs of liquor, one every three or four days, by common carrier, to persons in Vermont who had ordered them and would pay upon delivery. (337-341.) . . .

Also relevant to the question of proportionality is the nonviolent nature of the offense. Thus the court in *Lorentzen* took note of the fact that sale of marijuana is a nonviolent crime and that the defendant was 23 years old, living with his parents, employed at General Motors, and had no prior criminal convictions. . . .

Nor, finally, is nonviolence or absence of a victim a prerequisite to a finding of disproportionality. In appropriate cases the courts have nevertheless held the punishment excessive on the ground that no aggravating circumstances were shown. . . .

The second technique used by the courts is to compare the challenged penalty with the punishments prescribed in the *same jurisdiction* for *different offenses* which, by the same test, must be deemed more serious. The underlying but unstated assumption appears to be that although isolated excessive penalties may occasionally be enacted, e.g., through "honest zeal". . . generated in response to transitory public emotion, the Legislature may be depended upon to act with due and deliberate regard for constitutional restraints in prescribing the vast majority of punishments set forth in our statutes. The latter may therefore be deemed illustrative of constitutionally permissible degrees of severity; and if among them are found more serious crimes punished less severely than the offense in question, the challenged penalty is to that extent suspect.

The opinions are replete with examples of this technique. . . .[16]

Closely related to the foregoing is the third technique used in this inquiry, i.e., a comparison of the challenged penalty with the punishments prescribed for the *same offense* in *other jurisdictions* having an identical or similar constitutional provision. Here the assumption is that the vast majority of those jurisdictions will have prescribed punishments for this offense that are within the constitutional limit of severity; and if the challenged penalty is found to exceed the punishments decreed for the offense in a significant number of those jurisdictions, the disparity is a further measure of its excessiveness. . . .

16. In *Lorentzen* the court compared the penalty for sale of marijuana with the maximum punishments under Michigan law for five crimes similarly involving the "sale of harmful substances to others" (194 N.W.2d at p. 831), and to the maximum punishments for no less than 14 crimes involving "harm to people," including such offenses as manslaughter, aggravated assaults, rape, kidnaping, cruelty to children, and vehicle homicide (id. at pp. 831-832); in *Cannon* the court compared the penalty for assault with intent to commit rape to the lesser punishment for rape itself (281 P.2d at p. 235); in *Evans* the court noted that the punishment for lewd and lascivious acts upon a child was much greater than for forcible rape (245 P.2d at p. 793); in *Dembowski* the court measured the sentence for simple robbery against a lesser penalty for armed robbery (240 N.E.2d at pp. 816-818); and in *Driver* the court emphasized that a sentence of five years for wife-beating was cruel and unusual because it was "greater than has ever been prescribed or known or inflicted" (78 N.C. at p. 426).

There is ample authority, then, for applying the foregoing analyses to our inquiry into whether the life sentence prescribed by section 314 inflicts a penalty so disproportionate to the crime as to violate the cruel or unusual punishment clause of the California Constitution. We begin by examining the seriousness of the offense of indecent exposure.

At common law indecent exposure was deemed to be no more than a public nuisance, and was punished as a misdemeanor. . . .

In California a similar pattern prevailed until the present penalty was added in 1952. . . . Indeed, there was no statute whatever proscribing indecent exposure until the enactment of the Penal Code of 1872. At that time the offense was declared to be a misdemeanor, and there was no increased penalty for subsequent convictions. It was therefore punishable in all cases by a maximum of six months in jail and/or a fine of $500. . . . This was the law of our state for 80 years.

The low-key approach of the common law is also that adopted by modern psychiatric science. Clinical studies "support and confirm the traditional legal provisions which have treated this behaviour as a social nuisance, as disorderly conduct rather than an offence causing personal injury.". . . This is so because the commission of the offense invariably entails no physical aggression or even contact. . . .

Turning to the typical offender, we find a similar pattern of nonviolence. "The vast majority of exhibitionists are relatively harmless offenders; mostly they are public nuisances and sources of embarrassments.". . .

Finally, although indecent exposure is not a "victimless" crime, any harm it may cause appears to be minimal at most. As noted above, the nonviolence of the conduct ensures there is no danger of physical injury to the person who witnesses the exposure. Nor is there any convincing evidence that the person is likely to suffer either long-term or significant psychological damage. . . . Indeed, the statute itself defines the offense as exposure in public or in any place where there are persons present who may merely be "offended or annoyed" thereby. . . . Such an "annoyance" is not a sufficiently grave danger to society to warrant the heavy punishment of a life-maximum sentence.

These considerations make a persuasive case for a finding of unconstitutional disproportionality between the offense and the aggravated penalty prescribed by section 314. The case is further strengthened by a comparison of this penalty with the punishments for other crimes in California which are undeniably of far greater seriousness. For example, is it rational to believe that second-offense indecent exposure is a more dangerous crime than the unlawful *killing* of a human being without malice but in the heat of passion? Yet the punishment for manslaughter (up to 15 years) is far less than the life maximum inflicted by section 314. The same is true for such other violent crimes against the person as assault with intent to commit murder (1-14 years), kidnapping (1-25 years), mayhem (up to 14 years), assault with intent to commit mayhem or robbery (1-20 years), assault with caustic chemicals, with intent to injure or disfigure (1-14 years), and assault on a peace officer or fireman engaged in the performance of his duties (up to 2 years, or up to 1 year in jail).

Turning to crimes which, although somewhat more indirect, remain extremely dangerous to life and limb, we note that the penalty for second-offense indecent exposure is also far greater than that imposed for arson (2-20 years), burglary by torch or explosives (10-40 years), wrecking a vehicle of a common carrier, causing bodily harm (1-14 years), shooting at an inhabited dwelling (1-5 years, or up to 1 year in jail), poisoning food or drink with the intent to injure a human being (1-10 years), and drunk driving causing bodily injury (up to 5 years, or up to 1 year in jail). . . .

We recognize, of course, that an important additional element must be taken into account: section 314 prescribes a life-maximum sentence for indecent exposure only when the offender has previously been convicted of the same crime. . . . We further recognize that the potential for recidivism is here very real: "exhibitionists are more likely to repeat their offence than other kinds of sex offenders.". . . But this likelihood does not result in a pro tanto repeal of the cruel or unusual punishment clause. Petitioner does not challenge — nor do we consider — the validity of our general habitual criminal law (Pen. Code, §644) or of any other recidivist statute. He is entitled, however, to question whether in the particular context of indecent exposure the phenomenon of recidivism constitutionally justifies the greatly enhanced punishment of section 314. We hold that it does not.

At the outset we may put aside the Attorney General's suggestion that "in quite a number of such offenders the exhibitionism is only a facet of sexual problems which may manifest themselves in more aggressive acts." This risk appears to be mere fantasy. . . .

The last technique to be employed — a comparison of the challenged penalty with the punishments prescribed for the same offense in other jurisdictions — is no less revealing. A study of the indecent exposure statutes of each of our sister states and the District of Columbia reveals only two other states — Michigan and Oklahoma — which permit life-maximum sentences for second-offense exhibitionists. By contrast, 34 states and the District of Columbia do not enhance the punishment for any degree of recidivism; in each, indecent exposure remains a misdemeanor at all times. Of these 35 jurisdictions, the offense is punishable by no more than a fine in 2 states, by 3 years' imprisonment in one state, by a 1-year maximum in 10 states, by a 6-month maximum in 15 states, and by periods of 90 days or less in the remaining states. Seven other states do punish a second-offense indecent exposure more severely than the first; but none among these even approaches the life maximum decreed in California, and in 1 state the punishment for repeated exhibitionism is only 90 days. Three more states enhance the punishment only upon the third offense; of these none exceeds three years' imprisonment, and to reach even this penalty one requires that the three convictions occur within a five-year span. Finally, two states enhance punishment only if the second offense is committed on a minor.

Thus it is the virtually unanimous judgment of our sister states that indecent exposure, no matter how often it may recur, can be adequately and appropriately controlled by the imposition of a short jail sentence and/or a small fine. . . .

Viewing the total disparity between the life-maximum sentence currently inflicted by section 314 for second-offense indecent exposure and the far lighter penalties in force in California and elsewhere, we conclude with Justice McKenna in Weems [v. United States, 217 U.S. 349 (1910),] that "this contrast shows more than different exercises of legislative judgment. It is greater than that. It condemns the sentence in this case as cruel and unusual. It exhibits a difference between unrestrained power and that which is exercised under the spirit of constitutional limitations formed to establish justice." (217 U.S. at p. 381.) . . .

NOTE ON SUPREME COURT TREATMENT OF PROPORTIONALITY

The evolving jurisprudence of proportionality under state and federal constitutional provisions prohibiting "cruel and unusual punishment" is reviewed in Note, Disproportionality in Sentences of Imprisonment, 79 Colum. L. Rev. 1119 (1979).

Developments under the federal constitutional provision (the Eighth Amendment) were given an impetus by the Supreme Court's use of this provision in capital punishment cases. For example, in Ingraham v. Wright, 430 U.S. 651, 667 (1977), the Supreme Court declared that the Eighth Amendment "proscribes punishment grossly disproportionate to the severity of the crime." However, in Rummell v. Estelle, 445 U.S. 263, 281-284 (1980), the Court distinguished the capital punishment cases as "unique" and took a relatively restrictive view of the constitutional requirement of proportionality in all other punishments. In that case, the constitutionality of a Texas recidivist statute, which resulted in a mandatory life sentence for three crimes of fraud that netted the defendant a total sum of about $230, was at issue. The Court, in an opinion by Justice Rehnquist, upheld the punishment, emphasizing the highly subjective character of the judgment made in marking out constitutional limits on amounts of punishment, a judgment leaving much to the personal reactions of the justices or judges involved, and the desirability in a federal system of permitting a wide latitude of judgment to the states.

Responding to the attempt in the dissent to demonstrate the unconstitutionality of Rummell's sentence by comparing it to that for other crimes in Texas, Justice Rehnquist commented (id. at n. 27):

> Other crimes, of course, implicate other societal interests, making any such comparison inherently speculative. Embezzlement, dealing in "hard" drugs, and forgery, to name only three offenses, could be denominated "property related" offenses, and yet each can be viewed as an assault on a unique set of societal values as defined by the political process. The notions embodied in the dissent that if the crime involved "violence". . . a more severe penalty is warranted under objective standards simply will not wash, whether it be taken as a matter of morals, history or law. . . . The highly placed executive who embezzles huge sums from a state savings and loan association, causing many shareholders of limited means to lose substantial parts of their savings, has committed a crime very different from a man who takes a smaller amount of money from the same savings and loan at the point of a gun. Yet rational people could disagree as to which criminal merits harsher punishment. . . . Once the death penalty and other punishments different in kind from fine or imprisonment have been put to one side, there remains little in the way of objective standards for judging. . . .

Justice Rehnquist concluded:

> Even were we to assume that the statute employed against Rummel was the most stringent found in the 50 States, that severity hardly would render Rummel's

punishment "grossly disproportionate" to his offenses or to the punishment he would have received in the other States. As Mr. Justice Holmes noted in his dissenting opinion in Lochner v. New York, 198 U.S. 45, 76 (1905), our Constitution "is made for people of fundamentally differing views. . . ." Arizona punishes as a felony the theft of any "neat or horned animal," regardless of its value; California considers the theft of "avocados, citrus or deciduous fruits, nuts and artichokes" particularly reprehensible. In one State theft of $100 will earn the offender a fine or a short term in jail; in another State it could earn him a sentence of 10 years imprisonment. Absent a constitutionally imposed uniformity inimical to traditional notions of federalism, some State will always bear the distinction of treating particular offenders more severely than any other State.

Perhaps, as asserted in *Weems,* "time works changes" upon the Eighth Amendment, bringing into existence "new conditions and purposes." 217 U.S., at 373. We all, of course, would like to think that we are "moving down the road toward human decency[.]" Furman v. Georgia, 408 U.S. 238, 410 (1972) (Blackmun, J., dissenting). Within the confines of this judicial proceeding, however, we have no way of knowing in which direction that road lies. Penologists themselves have been unable to agree whether sentences should be light or heavy, discretionary or determinate. This uncertainty reinforces our conviction that any "nationwide trend" toward lighter, discretionary sentences must find its source and its sustaining force in the legislatures, not in the federal courts.

Continuing the trend of Rummell v. Estelle, in Hutto v. Davis, 102 S. Ct. 703 (1982), the Supreme Court upheld a 40-year term of imprisonment for conviction of two counts of possession and distribution of $200 worth of marijuana.

D. LEGALITY

SHAW v. DIRECTOR OF PUBLIC PROSECUTIONS
House of Lords
[1962] A. C. 220

[Appellant was convicted of an indictment containing three counts that alleged the following offenses: (1) conspiracy to corrupt public morals, (2) living on the earning of prostitution contrary to §30 of the Sexual Offences Act, 1956, and (3) publishing an obscene publication contrary to §2 of the Obscene Publications Act, 1959. The appeal on all three counts was dismissed, and the conviction upheld. Only discussion of the first count is included in the following extracts from several of the addresses.

[The essential facts, as stated by Viscount Simonds, are as follows: "When the Street Offences Act, 1959, came into operation it was no longer possible for prostitutes to ply their trade by soliciting in the streets, and it became necessary for them to find some other means of advertising the service that they were prepared to render. It occurred to the appellant that he could with advantage to himself assist them to this end. The device that he adopted was to publish on divers days between the dates mentioned in the particulars of offences a magazine or booklet which was called 'Ladies' Directory.' It contained the names, addresses and telephone numbers of prostitutes with photographs of nude female figures, and in some cases details which conveyed to initiates willingness to indulge not only in ordinary sexual intercourse but also in various perverse practices."

[The first count charged the appellant in the following terms:

> Statement of offense: Conspiracy to corrupt public morals. Particulars of offence: Frederick Charles Shaw on divers days between the 1st day of October, 1959, and 23rd July, 1960, within the jurisdiction of the Central Criminal Court conspired with certain persons, who inserted advertisements in issues of a magazine entitled "Ladies' Directory" numbered 7, 7 revised, 8, 9, 10 and a supplement thereto, and with certain other persons whose names are unknown, by means of the said magazine and the said advertisements to induce readers thereof to resort to the said advertisers for the purposes of fornication and of taking part in or witnessing other disgusting and immoral acts and exhibitions with intent thereby to debauch and corrupt the morals as well of youth as of divers other liege subjects of Our Lady the Queen and to raise and create in their minds inordinate and lustful desires.]

VISCOUNT SIMONDS. . . . I am concerned only to assert what was vigorously denied by counsel for the appellant, that such an offence is known to the common law, and that it was open to the jury to find on the facts of this case that the appellant was guilty of such an offence. I must say categorically that, if it were not so, Her Majesty's courts would strangely have failed in their duty as servants and guardians of the common law. Need I say, My Lords, that I am no advocate of the right of the judges to create new criminal offences? . . . But I am at a loss to understand how it can be said either that the law does not recognise a conspiracy to corrupt public morals or that, though there may not be an exact precedent for such a conspiracy as this case reveals, it does not fall fairly within the general words by which it is described. . . . In the sphere of criminal law I entertain no doubt that there remains in the courts of law a residual power to enforce the supreme and fundamental purpose of the law, to conserve not only the safety and order but also the moral welfare of the State, and that it is their duty to guard it against attacks which may be the more insidious because they are novel and unprepared for. . . . Such occasions will be rare, for Parliament has not been slow to legislate when attention has been sufficiently aroused. But gaps remain and will always remain since no one can foresee every way in which the wickedness of man may disrupt the order of society. Let me take a single instance. . . . Let it be supposed that at some future, perhaps early, date homosexual practices between adult consenting males are no longer a crime. Would it not be an offense if even without obscenity, such practices were publicly advocated and encouraged by pamphlet and advertisement? Or must we wait until Parliament finds time to deal with such conduct? I say, my Lords, that if the common law is powerless in such an event, then we should no longer do her reverence. . . .

The appeal on both counts should, in my opinion, be dismissed.

LORD MORRIS of Borth-y-Gest. . . . It is said that there is a measure of vagueness in a charge of conspiracy to corrupt public morals, and also that there might be peril of the launching of prosecutions in order to suppress unpopular or unorthodox views. My Lords, I entertain no anxiety on these lines. Even if accepted public standards may to some extent vary from generation to generation, current standards are in the keeping of juries, who can be trusted to maintain the corporate good sense of the community and to discern attacks upon values that must be preserved. If there were prosecutions which were not genuinely and fairly warranted juries would be quick to perceive this. There could be no conviction unless 12 jurors were unanimous in thinking that the accused person or persons had combined to do acts which were calculated to corrupt public morals. . . .

I would dismiss the appeal.

LORD REID. . . . In my opinion there is no such general offence known to the law as conspiracy to corrupt public morals. . . .

I agree with R. S. Wright, J., when he says . . ."There appear to be great theoretical objections to any general rule that agreement may make punishable that which ought not to be punished in the absence of agreement." And I think, or at least I hope, that it is now established, that the courts cannot create new offences by individuals. So far at least I have the authority of Lord Goddard, C.J., in delivering the opinion of the court in *Newland* [[1954] 1 Q.B. 158]: "The dictum in Rex v. Higgins was that all offences of a public nature, that is, all such acts or attempts as tend to the prejudice of the public are indictable, but no other member of the court stated the law in such wide terms. It is the breadth of that dictum that was so strongly criticised by Sir Fitzjames Stephen in the passage in his History of the Criminal Law (vol. 3., p. 359). . . . In effect it would leave it to the judges to declare new crimes and enable them to hold anything which they considered prejudicial to the community to be a misdemeanor. However beneficial that might have been in days when Parliament met seldom or at least only at long intervals it surely is now the province of the legislature and not of the judiciary to create new criminal offenses." Every argument against creating new offences by an individual appears to me to be equally valid against creating new offences by a combination of individuals. . . .

Even if there is still a vestigial power of this kind it ought not, in my view, to be used unless there appears to be general agreement that the offence to which it is applied ought to be criminal if committed by an individual. Notoriously, there are wide differences of opinion today as to how far the law ought to punish immoral acts which are not done in the face of the public. Some think that the law already goes too far, some that it does not go far enough. Parliament is the proper place, and I am firmly of opinion the only proper place, to settle that. When there is sufficient support from public opinion, Parliament does not hesitate to intervene. Where Parliament fears to tread it is not for the courts to rush in. . . .

In my judgment this House is in no way bound and ought not to sanction the extension of "public mischief" to any new field, and certainly not if such extension would be in any way controversial. . . .

Finally I must advert to the consequences of holding that this very general offence exists. It has always been thought to be of primary importance that our law, and particularly our criminal law, should be certain: that a man should be able to know what conduct is and what is not criminal, particularly when heavy penalties are involved. Some suggestion was made that it does not matter if this offence is very wide: no one would ever prosecute and if they did no jury would ever convict if the breach was venial. Indeed, the suggestion goes even further: that the meaning and application of the words "deprave" and "corrupt" (the traditional words in obscene libel now enacted in the 1959 Act) or the words "debauch" and "corrupt" in this indictment ought to be entirely for the jury, so that any conduct of this kind is criminal if in the end a jury think it so. In other words, you cannot tell what is criminal except by guessing what view a jury will take, and juries' views may vary and may change with the passing of time. Normally the meaning of words is a question of law for the court. For example, it is not left to a jury to determine the meaning of negligence: they have to consider on evidence and on their own knowledge a much more specific question — Would a reasonable man have done what this man did? . . . If the trial judge's charge in the present case was right, if a jury is entitled to water down the strong words "deprave," "corrupt" or "debauch" so as merely to mean lead astray morally, then it seems to me that the court has transferred to the jury the whole of its functions as censor morum, the law will be whatever any jury may happen to think it ought to be, and this branch of the law will have lost all the certainty which we rightly prize in other branches of our law.

NOTES

1. There have been a number of critical commentaries on the *Shaw* case. See W. Friedmann, Law in a Changing Society 54-62 (Pelican ed. 1964); H. L. A. Hart, Law, Liberty and Morality 7-12 (1963); Comment, 75 Harv. L. Rev. 1652 (1962); J. E. H. Williams, Note, 24 Mod. L. Rev. 626 (1961). For a favorable comment, see Goodhart, 77 Law Q. Rev. 560 (1961).

2. See A. T. Denning, Freedom under the Law 40-42 (1949):

[T]he doctrine that acts done to the public mischief are punishable by law . . . is a doctrine quite unknown to France and the other freedom-loving countries of Western Europe where the law is contained in a written code. They take their stand on the principle that no one shall be punished for anything that is not expressly forbidden by law. *Nullum crimen, nulla poena, sine lege.* They regard that principle as their charter of liberty. In this country, however, the common law has not limited itself in that way. It is not contained in a code but in the breasts of the judges, who enunciate and develop the principles needed to deal with any new situations which arise.

In recent years the judges have been faced with acts such as these: A man may call the fire brigade when there is no fire to attend to: or a woman may go to the police and tell them an invented story about being attacked: and thus these public servants may be diverted from their proper duties. In 1933 the judge declared such conduct to be criminal, even though it had not previously been expressly forbidden by law. No one will doubt that it was criminal, because it was a fraud affecting the public at large. But unfortunately the judges based their decision on a wider and much more questionable ground. They relied on an obiter dictum of a judge in 1801, who said that "all offences of a public nature, that is, such acts or attempts as tend to the prejudice of the community, are indictable."

Now that mode of reasoning is dangerously similar to the reasoning by which the Russian jurists justify the punishment of any acts which are socially dangerous. Starting from the point of view that the interests of the State are paramount, their jurists say that the judges ought to punish any act which is dangerous to the State, even though it is not expressly forbidden. Article 16 of the Soviet Code says that "if the Code has not made provision for any act which is socially dangerous, it is to be dealt with on the basis, and as carrying the same degree of responsibility, as the offences which it most nearly resembles." [a] So the only question for their judges is, Is the Act socially dangerous? That is precisely the same test as was stated by our judges in the public mischief case.

3. The doctrine of common law crimes, under which acts are made criminal if the court (or a court and a jury) regards them as directly tending to injure the public to such an extent as to require the state to punish the wrongdoer, even in the absence of an explicit statutory prohibition, was until recently recognized in many American jurisdictions. See Note, Common Law Crimes in the United States, 47 Colum. L. Rev. 1332 (1947). A recent example is Commonwealth v. Mochan, 177 Pa. Super. 454, 110 A.2d 788 (1955), in which this doctrine was successfully invoked to punish the maker of obscene telephone calls. While traces of this doctrine may still linger in a few states, the recent movement for penal code codification (as well as developing constitutional limitations under the due process clause) have now made the doctrine obsolete in the United States. The cognate doctrine that criminalizes a conspiracy to commit acts against the public interest (page 649 infra) has also been rejected in many jurisdictions. At all events, the *Shaw* case represents an extreme instance of the abandonment of the principle of legality. Scarcely any precept associated with that principle is absent — that judges should not create new crimes, that the criminal law may operate only prospectively, that crimes must be defined with sufficient precision to serve as a guide to lawful conduct and to confine the discretion of police and prosecutors. In the cases that follow we will be concerned with more problematic issues concerning the reach of the principle of legality.

KEELER v. SUPERIOR COURT
Supreme Court of California
2 Cal. 3d 619, 470 P.2d 617 (1970)

Mosk, J. In this proceeding for writ of prohibition we are called upon to decide whether an unborn but viable fetus is a "human being" within the meaning of the California statute defining murder (Pen. Code, §187). We conclude that the Legislature did not intend such a meaning, and that for us to construe the statute to the contrary and apply it to this petitioner would exceed our judicial power and deny petitioner due process of law.

[Five months after obtaining an interlocutory decree of divorce, a husband intercepted his wife on a mountain road. She was in an advanced state of pregnancy by another man; fetal movements had already been observed by her and by her obstetrician. Her husband said to her, "I hear you're pregnant," glanced at her body and added, "You sure are. I'm going to stomp it out of you." He

---

a. The 1958 revision of Soviet criminal law limits punishment for crime to acts specifically proscribed by law. See Fundamental Principles of Criminal Legislation of the USSR, Acts 3, 6, 7 (1958), and Criminal Code of the Russian Federated Socialist Republic, Acts 3, 6, 7 (1960), in H. Berman, Soviet Criminal Law and Procedure 47 (1966). However, the principle of analogy continues to exist in the Soviet statute regulating comrades' courts, which are paralegal bodies administering sanctions for minor offenses in residential and work units. See Berman, ibid. See generally Berman & Spindler, Soviet Comrades' Courts, 38 Wash. L. Rev. 843 (1963). For a harrowing account of the violations of the principle of legality in Stalinist Russia, see A. Solzhenitsyn, The Gulag Archipelago 60-65 (1978). — Eds.

shoved his knee into her abdomen and struck her. The fetus was delivered stillborn, its head fractured.]

An information was filed charging petitioner, in count I, with committing the crime of murder (Pen. Code, §187) in that he did "unlawfully kill a human being, to wit Baby Girl Vogt, with malice aforethought.". . . His motion to set aside the information for lack of probable cause (Pen. Code, §995) was denied, and he now seeks a writ of prohibition. . . .

Penal Code section 187 provides: "Murder is the unlawful killing of a human being, with malice aforethought." The dispositive question is whether the fetus which petitioner is accused of killing was, on February 23, 1969, a "human being" within the meaning of the statute. If it was not, petitioner cannot be charged with its "murder" and prohibition will lie.

Section 187 was enacted as part of the Penal Code of 1872. Inasmuch as the provision has not been amended since that date, we must determine the intent of the Legislature at the time of its enactment. But section 187 was, in turn, taken verbatim from the first California statute defining murder, part of the Crimes and Punishments Act of 1850. (Stats. 1850, ch. 99, §19, p. 231.) Penal Code section 5 (also enacted in 1872) declares: "The provisions of this code, so far as they are substantially the same as existing statutes, must be construed as continuations thereof, and not as new enactments." We begin, accordingly, by inquiring into the intent of the Legislature in 1850 when it first defined murder as the unlawful and malicious killing of a "human being."

It will be presumed, of course, that in enacting a statute the Legislature was familiar with the relevant rules of the common law, and, when it couches its enactment in common law language, that its intent was to continue those rules in statutory form. . . .

We therefore undertake a brief review of the origins and development of the common law of abortional homicide. [Discussion omitted.]

We conclude that in declaring murder to be the unlawful and malicious killing of a "human being" the Legislature of 1850 intended that term to have the settled common law meaning of a person who had been born alive, and did not intend the act of feticide — as distinguished from abortion — to be an offense under the laws of California.

Nothing occurred between the years 1850 and 1872 to suggest that in adopting the new Penal Code on the latter date the Legislature entertained any different intent. The case law of our sister states, for example, remained consonant with the common law. . . .

It is the policy of this state to construe a penal statute as favorably to the defendant as its language and the circumstances of its application may reasonably permit; just as in the case of a question of fact, the defendant is entitled to the benefit of every reasonable doubt as to the true interpretation of words or the construction of language used in a statute. . . . We hold that in adopting the definition of murder in Penal Code section 187 the Legislature intended to exclude from its reach the act of killing an unborn fetus.

The People urge, however, that the sciences of obstetrics and pediatrics have greatly progressed since 1872, to the point where with proper medical care a normally developed fetus prematurely born at 28 weeks or more has an excellent chance of survival, i.e., is "viable"; that the common law requirement of live birth to prove the fetus had become a "human being" who may be the victim of murder is no longer in accord with scientific fact, since an unborn but viable fetus is now fully capable of independent life; and that one who unlawfully and maliciously terminates such a life should therefore be liable to prosecution for murder under section 187. We may grant the premises of this argument. . . . But we cannot join in the conclusion sought to be deduced: we cannot hold this petitioner to answer for murder by reason of his alleged act of killing an unborn — even though viable — fetus. To such a charge there are two insuperable obstacles, one "jurisdictional" and the other constitutional.

Penal Code section 6 declares in relevant part that "No act or omission" accomplished after the code has taken effect "is criminal or punishable, except as prescribed or authorized by this code, or by some of the statutes which it specifies as continuing in force and as not affected by its provisions, or by some ordinance, municipal, county, or township regulation. . . ." This section embodies a fundamental principle of our tripartite form of government, i.e., that subject to the constitutional prohibition against cruel and unusual punishment, the power to define crimes and fix penalties is vested exclusively in the legislative branch. . . . Stated differently, there are no common law crimes in California. . . .

Settled rules of construction implement this principle. Although the Penal Code commands us to construe its provisions "according to the fair import of their terms, with a view to effect its objects and to promote justice" (Pen. Code, §4), it is clear the courts cannot go so far as to create an offense by enlarging a statute, by inserting or deleting words, or by giving the terms used false or unusual meanings. . . . Penal statutes will not be made to reach beyond their plain intent; they include only those offenses coming clearly within the import of their language. . . .

. . . We recognize that the killing of an unborn but viable fetus may be deemed by some to be an offense of similar nature and gravity; but as Chief Justice Marshall warned long ago, "It would be dangerous, indeed, to carry the principle, that a case which is within the reason or mischief of a statute, is within its provisions, so far as to punish a crime not enumerated in the statute, because it is of equal atrocity, or of kindred character, with those which are enumerated." (United States v. Wiltberger (1820) 18 U.S. (5 Wheat.) 76, 96.) Whether to thus extend liability for murder in California is a determination solely within the province of the Legislature. . . .

The second obstacle to the proposed judicial enlargement of section 187 is the guarantee of due process of law. Assuming arguendo that we have the power to adopt the new construction of this statute as the law of California, such a ruling, by constitutional command, could operate only prospectively, and thus could not in any event reach the conduct of petitioner on February 23, 1969.

The first essential of due process is fair warning of the act which is made punishable as a crime. "That the terms of a penal statute creating a new offense must be sufficiently explicit to inform those who are subject to it what conduct on their part will render them liable to its penalties, is a well-recognized requirement, consonant alike with ordinary notions of fair play and the settled rules of law." (Connally v. General Constr. Co. (1926) 269 U.S. 385, 391.) . . .

This requirement of fair warning is reflected in the constitutional prohibition against the enactment of ex post facto laws (U.S. Const., art. I, §§9, 10; Cal. Const., art. I, §16). When a new penal statute is applied retrospectively to make punishable an act which was not criminal at the time it was performed, the defendant has been given no advance notice consistent with due process. And precisely the same effect occurs when such an act is made punishable under a preexisting statute but by means of an unforeseeable *judicial* enlargement thereof. (Bouie v. City of Columbia (1964) 378 U.S. 347.)

In *Bouie* two Negroes took seats in the restaurant section of a South Carolina drugstore; no notices were posted restricting the area to whites only. When the defendants refused to leave upon demand, they were arrested and convicted of violating a criminal trespass statute which prohibited entry on the property of another "after notice" forbidding such conduct. Prior South Carolina decisions had emphasized the necessity of proving such notice to support a conviction under the statute. The South Carolina Supreme Court nevertheless affirmed the convictions, construing the statute to prohibit not only the act of entering after notice not to do so but also the wholly different act of remaining on the property after receiving notice to leave.

The United States Supreme Court reversed the convictions, holding that the South Carolina court's ruling was "unforeseeable" and when an "unforeseeable state-court construction of a criminal statute is applied retroactively to subject a person to criminal liability for past conduct, the effect is to deprive him of due process of law in the sense of fair warning that his contemplated conduct constitutes a crime." Analogizing to the prohibition against retrospective penal legislation, the high court reasoned "Indeed, an unforeseeable judicial enlargement of a criminal statute, applied retroactively, operates precisely like an ex post facto law, such as Art. I, §10, of the Constitution forbids. An ex post facto law has been defined by this Court as one 'that makes an action done before the passing of the law, and which was *innocent* when done, criminal; and punishes such action,' or 'that *aggravates* a *crime*, or makes it *greater* than it was, when committed.' Calder v. Bull, 3 Dall. 386, 390. If a state legislature is barred by the Ex Post Facto Clause from passing such a law, it must follow that a State Supreme Court is barred by the Due Process Clause from achieving precisely the same result by judicial construction. The fundamental principle that 'the required criminal law must have existed when the conduct in issue occurred,' Hall, General Principles of Criminal Law (2d ed. 1960), at 58-59, must apply to bar retroactive criminal prohibitions emanating from courts as well as from legislatures. If a judicial construction of a criminal statute is 'unexpected and indefensible by reference to the law which had been expressed prior to the conduct in issue,' it must not be given retroactive effect. Id., at 61." [a]

The court remarked in conclusion that "Application of this rule is particularly

a. The Supreme Court also observed: "By its terms, the statute prohibited only 'entry upon the lands of another . . . after notice from the owner . . . prohibiting such entry. . . .' There was nothing in the statute to indicate that it also prohibited the different act of remaining on the premises after being asked to leave. Petitioners did not violate the statute as it was written; they received no notice before entering either the drug store or the restaurant department. Indeed, they knew they would not receive any such notice before entering the store, for they were invited to purchase everything except food there. So far as the words of the statute were concerned, petitioners were given not only no 'fair warning' but no warning whatever, that their conduct in Eckerd's drug store would violate the statute. . . .

". . . If South Carolina had applied to this case its new statute prohibiting the act of remaining on the premises of another after being asked to leave, the constitutional proscription of ex post facto laws would clearly invalidate the convictions. The Due Process Clause compels the same result here, where the State has sought to achieve precisely the same effect by judicial construction of the statute. While such a construction is of course valid for the future, it may not be applied retroactively, any more than a legislative enactment may be, to impose criminal penalties for conduct committed at a time when it was not fairly stated to be criminal." — EDS.

compelling where, as here, the petitioners' conduct cannot be deemed improper or immoral." In the case at bar the conduct with which petitioner is charged is certainly "improper" and "immoral," and it is not contended he was exercising a constitutionally favored right. But the matter is simply one of degree, and it cannot be denied that the guarantee of due process extends to violent as well as peaceful men. The issue remains, would the judicial enlargement of section 187 now proposed have been foreseeable to this petitioner? . . .

forsee-able?

Turning to the case law, we find no reported decision of the California courts which should have given petitioner notice that the killing of an unborn but viable fetus was prohibited by section 187. . . .

Properly understood, the often cited case of People v. Chavez (1947) 77 Cal. App. 2d 621, 176 P.2d 92, does not derogate from this rule. . . .

Chavez . . . stands for the proposition — to which we adhere — that a viable fetus "in the process of being born" is a human being within the meaning of the homicide statutes. But it stands for no more; in particular it does not hold that a fetus, however viable, which is *not* "in the process of being born" is nevertheless a "human being" in the law of homicide. On the contrary, the opinion is replete with references to the common law requirement that the child be "born alive," however that term is defined, and must accordingly be deemed to reaffirm that requirement as part of the law of California. . . .

We conclude that the judicial enlargement of section 187 now urged upon us by the People would not have been foreseeable to this petitioner, and hence that its adoption at this time would deny him due process of law. . . .

BURKE, J. The majority hold that "Baby Girl" Vogt, who, according to medical testimony, had reached the 35th week of development, had a 96 percent chance of survival, and was "definitely" alive and viable at the time of her death, nevertheless was not a "human being" under California's homicide statutes. In my view, in so holding, the majority ignore significant common law precedents, frustrate the express intent of the Legislature, and defy reason, logic and common sense. . . .

The majority opinion suggests that we are confined to common law concepts, and to the common law definition of murder or manslaughter. However, the Legislature, in Penal Code sections 187 and 192, has defined those offenses for us: homicide is the unlawful killing of a "human being." Those words need not be frozen in place as of any particular time, but must be fairly and reasonably interpreted by this court to promote justice and to carry out the evident purposes of the Legislature in adopting a homicide statute. Thus, Penal Code section 4, which was enacted in 1872 along with sections 187 and 192, provides:

> The rule of the common law, that penal statutes are to be strictly construed, has no application to this code. All its provisions are to be construed according to the fair import of their terms, with a view to effect its objects and to promote justice. . . .

We commonly conceive of human existence as a spectrum stretching from birth to death. However, if this court properly might expand the definition of "human being" at one end of that spectrum, we may do so at the other end. Consider the following example: All would agree that "Shooting or otherwise damaging a corpse is not homicide. . . ." However, it is readily apparent that our concepts of what constitutes a "corpse" have been and are being continually modified by advances in the field of medicine, including new techniques for life revival, restoration and resuscitation such as artificial respiration, open heart massage, transfusions, transplants and a variety of life-restoring stimulants, drugs and new surgical methods. Would this court ignore these developments and exonerate the killer of an apparently "drowned" child merely because that child would have been pronounced dead in 1648 and 1850? Obviously not. Whether a homicide occurred in that case would be determined by medical testimony regarding the capability of the child to have survived prior to the defendant's act. And that is precisely the test which this court should adopt in the instant case.

The common law reluctance to characterize the killing of a quickened fetus as a homicide was based solely upon a presumption that the fetus would have been born dead. . . . Based upon the state of the medical art in the 17th, 18th and 19th centuries, that presumption may have been well-founded. However, as we approach the 21st century, it has become apparent that "This presumption is not only contrary to common experience and the ordinary course of nature, but it is contrary to the usual rule with respect to presumptions followed in this state." (People v. Chavez, supra, at p. 626. . . .)

The majority suggest that to do so would improperly create some new offense. However, the offense of murder is no new offense. Contrary to the majority opinion, the Legislature has not "defined the crime of murder in California to apply only to the unlawful and malicious killing of one who has been born alive." Instead, the Legislature simply used the broad term "human being" and directed the courts to construe that term according to its "fair import" with a view to effect the objects of the homicide statutes and promote justice. (Pen. Code, §4.) What justice will be promoted, what objects effectuated, by construing "human being" as excluding Baby Girl Vogt and her unfortunate successors? Was defendant's brutal act of stomping her to death any less an act of homicide than the murder of a newly born baby? No one doubts that the term "human being" would include the elderly or dying persons whose potential for life has nearly lapsed; their proximity to death is deemed immaterial. There is no sound reason for denying the viable fetus, with its unbounded potential for life, the same status.

The majority also suggest that such an interpretation of our homicide statutes would deny defendant "fair warning" that his act was punishable as a crime. Aside from the absurdity of the underlying premise that defendant consulted Coke, Blackstone or Hale before kicking Baby Girl Vogt to death, it is clear that defendant had adequate notice that his act could constitute homicide. Due process only precludes prosecution under a new statute insufficiently explicit regarding the specific conduct proscribed, or under a preexisting statute "by means of an unforeseeable *judicial* enlargement thereof."

Our homicide statutes have been in effect in this state since 1850. The fact that the California courts have not been called upon to determine the precise question before us does not render "unforeseeable" a decision which determines that a viable fetus is a "human being" under those statutes. Can defendant really claim surprise that a 5-pound, 18-inch, 34-week-old, living, viable child is considered to be a human being? . . .

NOTES

1. The Supreme Court's decision in Bouie v. City of Columbia has served in subsequent Supreme Court decisions mainly as a case to be distinguished. In Rose v. Locke, 423 U.S. 48 (1975), for example, defendant was convicted of violating a Tennessee statute that proscribed the "crime against nature." He was found to have engaged in the act of cunnilingus. While that act was not within the common law definition of crimes against nature and had never been applied to such acts in Tennessee, the state supreme court in this case, for the first time, construed its statute as extending to such acts. The United States Supreme Court distinguished *Bouie* on the ground that here defendant could not have been taken by surprise, stating:

> [R]espondent can make no claim that [the statute] afforded no notice that his conduct might be within its scope. Other jurisdictions had already reasonably construed identical statutory language to apply to such acts. And given the Tennessee court's clear pronouncements that its statute was intended to effect broad coverage,[a] there was nothing to indicate, clearly or otherwise, that respondent's acts were outside the scope of [the statute].

2. Do the decisions in the *Keeler* and *Bouie* cases seem to be required by the principle of legality? Was Keeler, when he "stomped" his pregnant wife, acting under the view that his conduct was not homicidal because the common law did not treat a developed fetus as a "human being"? Were the civil rights protestors in *Bouie* surprised to discover that they were acting in violation of South Carolina law? Or are these questions beside the point?

Consider the comments of Justice Stewart, dissenting, in Parker v. Levy, 417 U.S. 773, 774-775 (1974):

> As many decisions of this Court make clear, vague statutes suffer from at least two fatal constitutional defects. First, by failing to provide fair notice of precisely what acts are forbidden, a vague statute "violates the first essential of due process of law." Connally v. General Construction Co. 269 U.S. 385, 391. As the Court put the matter in Lanzetta v. New Jersey, 306 U.S. 451, 453, "No one may be required at peril of life, liberty or property to speculate as to the meaning of penal statutes. All are entitled to be informed as to what the State commands or forbids." "Words which are vague and fluid . . . may be as much of a trap for the innocent as the ancient laws of Caligula." United States v. Cardiff, 344 U.S. 174, 176.[3]
>
> Secondly, vague statutes offend due process by failing to provide explicit standards for those who enforce them, thus allowing discriminatory and arbitrary enforcement. Papachristou v. City of Jacksonville, 405 U.S. 156, 165-171. "A vague law impermissibly delegates basic policy matters to policemen, judges, and juries for resolution on an ad hoc and subjective basis. . . ." Grayned v. City of Rockford,

a. The Tennessee Supreme Court had earlier held that fellatio was included, repudiating jurisdictions that had taken a "narrow restrictive definition of the offense." — Eds.

3. See also United States v. Harriss, 347 U.S. 612, 617:
"The constitutional requirement of definiteness is violated by a criminal statute that fails to give a person of ordinary intelligence fair notice that his contemplated conduct is forbidden by the statute. The underlying principle is that no man shall be held criminally responsible for conduct which he could not reasonably understand to be proscribed."

408 U.S. 104, 108-109.[4] The absence of specificity in a criminal statute invites abuse on the part of prosecuting officials, who are left free to harass any individuals or groups who may be the object of official displeasure.

NASH v. UNITED STATES
Supreme Court of the United States
229 U.S. 373 (1912)

MR. JUSTICE HOLMES delivered the opinion of the Court.

This is an indictment in two counts, — the first for a conspiracy in restraint of trade, the second for a conspiracy to monopolize trade, contrary to the act of July 2, 1890, . . . commonly known as the Sherman act. . . .

The two counts before us were demurred to on the grounds that the statute was so vague as to be inoperative on its criminal side; that neither of the counts alleged any overt act; that the contemplated acts and things would not have constituted an offense if they had been done, and that the same acts, etc., were too vaguely charged. The demurrer was overruled and this action of the court raises the important questions of the case. We will deal with them before passing to matters of detail.

The objection to the criminal operation of the statute is thought to be warranted by Standard Oil Co. v. United States, 221 U.S. 1, and United States v. American Tobacco Co., 221 U.S. 106. Those cases may be taken to have established that only such contracts and combinations are within the act as, by reason of intent or the inherent nature of the contemplated acts, prejudice the public interests by unduly restricting competition or unduly obstructing the course of trade, 221 U.S. 179. And thereupon it is said that the crime thus defined by the statute contains in its definition an element of degree as to which estimates may differ, with the result that a man might find himself in prison because his honest judgment did not anticipate that of a jury of less competent men. The kindred proposition that "the criminality of an act cannot depend upon whether a jury may think it reasonable or unreasonable. There must be some definiteness and certainty," is cited from the late Mr. Justice Brewer, sitting in the circuit court. Tozer v. United States, 52 Fed. 917, 919.

But apart from the common law as to the restraint of trade thus taken up by the statute, the law is full of instances where a man's fate depends on his estimating rightly, that is, as the jury subsequently estimates it, some matter of degree. If his judgment is wrong, not only may he incur a fine or a short imprisonment, as here; he may incur the penalty of death. "An act causing death may be murder, manslaughter, or misadventure, according to the degree of danger attending it" by common experience in the circumstances known to the actor. "The very meaning of the fiction of implied malice in such cases at common law was, that a man might have to answer with his life for consequences which he neither intended nor foresaw." Com. v. Pierce, 138 Mass. 165, 178. . . ."The criterion in such cases is to examine whether common social duty would, under the circumstances, have suggested a more circumspect conduct."

---

4. See also Smith v. Goguen, 415 U.S. 566, 575:
"Statutory language of such a standard-less sweep allows policemen, prosecutors, and juries to pursue their personal predilections. Legislatures may not so abdicate their responsibilities for setting the standards of the criminal law."

1 East, P.C. 262. If a man should kill another by driving an automobile furiously into a crowd, he might be convicted of murder, however little he expected the result. . . . If he did no more than drive negligently through a street, he might get off with manslaughter or less. . . . And in the last case he might be held although he himself thought that he was acting as a prudent man should. . . . We are of opinion that there is no constitutional difficulty in the way of enforcing the criminal part of the act. . . .

NOTES

1. Mr. Justice Holmes's opinion in Nash v. United States has been widely invoked to justify criminal statutes defining criminal conduct in terms of degree. Statutes imposing criminal liability for negligent, reckless, or careless driving resulting in the death of another have commonly been upheld. E.g., People v. Garman, 411 Ill. 279, 103 N.E.2d 636 (1952); State v. Bolsinger, 221 Minn. 154, 21 N.W.2d 48 (1946); State v. Wojahn, 204 Or. 84, 282 P.2d 675 (1955). In United States v. Ragen, 314 U.S. 513, 523 (1941), the Court sustained a criminal conviction of a defendant for willfully taking a deduction of an unreasonable allowance for salaries on his income tax return, stating: "The mere fact that a penal statute is so framed as to require a jury upon occasion to determine a question of reasonableness is not sufficient to make it too vague to afford a practical guide to permissible conduct." See Freund, The Use of Indefinite Terms in Statutes, 30 Yale L.J. 437, 443-444 (1921).

In State v. Adams, 180 Neb. 542, 143 N.W.2d 920 (1966), defendant appealed a conviction for violating a statute providing: "Any person or persons who shall operate a vehicle upon any highway in such a manner as to (1) endanger the safety of others or (2) cause immoderate wear or damage to any highway, shall be deemed guilty of a misdemeanor. . . ." Neither in terms or by construction was a showing of negligence required. Query: Should the statute be held unconstitutionally vague?

2. Consider the following observations of Lord Simon on legal certainty (in Knuller v. Director of Public Prosecutions, [1973] A.C. 435):

> Certainty is a desirable feature of any system of law. But there are some types of conduct desirably the subject matter of legal rule which cannot be satisfactorily regulated by specific statutory enactment, but are better left to the practice of juries and other tribunals of fact. They depend finally for their juridical classification not upon proof of the existence of some particular fact, but upon proof of the attainment of some degree. The law cannot always say that if fact X and fact Y are proved (both of which will generally be known not only to the tribunal of adjudication, but also, in advance, to the persons involved) legal result Z will ensue. Often the law can only say that if conduct of a stipulated standard is attained (or more often, is not attained) legal result Z will ensue; and whether that standard has been attained cannot be with certainty known in advance by the persons involved, but has to await the evaluation of the tribunal of fact. This is, indeed, so characteristic a feature of English law that examples, even though drawn from many different spheres of jurisprudence, give an inadequate impression of how pervasive it is. Has an act been done, or a contract performed, or a duty discharged, within a reasonable time? Are goods reasonably fit for a particular purpose? Are

they of merchantable quality? Has the defendant so conducted himself that a reasonable person would assume that he was making a representation of fact meant to be acted on? What is a fair price in a quantum meruit? Has *A* exercised proper care for the safety of those to whom the law says he owes a duty of care (the standard varying according to the legal relationship of the persons in question)? Had *B* reasonable and probable cause for arresting *C,* or preferring a prosecution against him? . . . Has a husband wilfully neglected to provide reasonable maintenance for wife or child? Has one spouse behaved in such a way that the other cannot reasonably be expected to continue in cohabitation? . . . Has an employer complied with the manifold requirements of the Factories Acts so far as is reasonably practicable? What is reasonable overtime in industrial law? For the purpose of the Regulations for Preventing Collisions at Sea, was there in general due regard to the observance of good seamanship? Was the vessel proceeding at a moderate speed? Was a proper look-out being maintained? . . .

The law does not return an answer in advance to any of these questions, which arise both at common law and under statute: all must await the answer of the tribunal. They could be almost indefinitely multiplied.

Nor are such situations limited to the civil law. The breaches of duty under the Factories Acts give rise to criminal as well as civil liability. Whether conduct causing death falls so far short of a proper duty of care as to amount to manslaughter cannot be known until the jury returns its verdict. . . .

. . . The driver of a motor vehicle may be accompanied by leading and junior counsel and by his solicitor as well; but he will still not know whether or not he has committed the offence of driving in a manner dangerous to the public or without due care and attention or without reasonable consideration for others or at an excessive speed until jury or justices so find. Again, in criminal libel everyone must await the jury's adjudication before it can be ascertained whether the statement complained of was defamatory of the prosecutor; or, if justification is pleaded, whether publication was for the public benefit. Similarly with those many offences which depend on whether admitted conduct was perpetrated dishonestly. Again, did the accused convene an assembly in such a manner as to cause reasonable people to fear a breach of the peace? Did the alleged blackmailer have reasonable grounds for making the demand and was the use of menaces a proper means of reinforcing it? (Theft Act 1968, section 21.) Was it a public mischief that the accused conspired to effect? Did the accused publish an article or perform a theatrical play which had a tendency to deprave or corrupt? If so, was its publication or performance nevertheless on balance for the public good by reason of any of the matters set out in section 4 of the Obscene Publications Act 1959, or section 3 of the Theatres Act 1968? In none of these cases, which again could be greatly multiplied, can it in advance be said with certainty whether an offence has been committed: and those who choose, in such situations, to sail as close as possible to the wind inevitably run some risk.

3. In International Harvester Co. v. Kentucky, 234 U.S. 216 (1914), the Court invalidated a statute interpreted by the Kentucky Court of Appeals to prohibit certain combinations in restraint of trade, and which forbade the raising or lowering of the price above or below the "real value" of the article, taken to mean its market value under fair competition and under normal market conditions. Mr. Justice Holmes, speaking for the Court, stated (at 222-224):

Value is the effect in exchange of the relative social desire for compared objects expressed in terms of a common denominator. It is a fact, and generally is more or less easy to ascertain. But what it would be with such increase of a never extin-guished competition as it might be guessed would have existed had the combination not been made, with exclusion of the actual effect of other abnormal influences, and, it would seem, with exclusion also of any increased efficiency in the machines, but with inclusion of the effect of the combination so far as it was economically beneficial to itself and the community, is a problem that no human ingenuity could solve. The reason is not the general uncertainties of a jury trial, but that the elements necessary to determine the imaginary ideal are uncertain both in nature and degree of effect to the acutest commercial mind. . . . We regard this decision as consistent with Nash v. United States, . . . in which it was held that a criminal law is not unconstitutional merely because it throws upon men the risk of rightly estimating a matter of degree, — what is an undue restraint of trade. That deals with the actual, not with an imaginary condition other than the facts. It goes no further than to recognize that, as with negligence, between the two extremes of the obvi-ously illegal and the plainly lawful there is a gradual approach, and that the complex-ity of life makes it impossible to draw a line in advance without an artificial simplification that would be unjust. The conditions are as permanent as anything human, and a great body of precedents on the civil side, coupled with familiar practice, make it comparatively easy for common sense to keep to what is safe. But if business is to go on, men must unite to do it and must sell their wares. To compel them to guess, on peril of indictment, what the community would have given for them if the continually changing conditions were other than they are, to an uncertain extent; to divine prophetically what the reaction of only partially determinate facts would be upon the imaginations and desires of purchasers, is to exact gifts that mankind does not possess.

Cf. Mr. Justice Frankfurter, dissenting, in Winters v. New York, 333 U.S. 507, 539 (1948):

The teaching of the *Nash* and the *Harvester* Cases is that it is not violative of due process of law for a legislature in framing its criminal law to cast upon the public the duty of care and even of caution, provided that there is sufficient warning to one bent on obedience that he comes near the proscribed area.

PAPACHRISTOU v. CITY OF JACKSONVILLE
Supreme Court of the United States
405 U.S. 156 (1972)

MR. JUSTICE DOUGLAS delivered the opinion of the Court.
This case involves eight defendants who were convicted in a Florida municipal court of violating a Jacksonville, Florida, vagrancy ordinance.[1] . . . For reasons which will appear, we reverse. . . .

1. Jacksonville Ordinance Code §26-57 provided at the time of these arrests and convictions as follows: "Rogues and vagabonds, or dissolute persons who go about begging, common gamblers, persons who use juggling or unlawful games or plays, common drunkards, common night thieves, pilferers or pickpockets, traders in stolen property, lewd, wanton and lascivious persons, keepers of gambling places, common railers and brawlers, persons wandering or strolling around from place to place without any lawful purpose or object, habitual loafers, disorderly persons, persons neglecting all lawful business and habitually spending their time by frequenting houses of ill fame, gaming houses, or places where alcoholic beverages are sold or served, persons able to work but habitually living upon the earnings of their wives or minor children shall be deemed vagrants and, upon conviction in the Municipal Court shall be punished as provided for Class D offenses."
   Class D offenses at the time of these arrests and convictions were punishable by 90 days' imprison-ment, $500 fine, or both. . . .

Facts

The facts are stipulated. Papachristou and Calloway are white females. Melton and Johnson are black males. Papachristou was enrolled in a job-training program sponsored by the State Employment Service at Florida Junior College in Jacksonville. Calloway was a typing and shorthand teacher at a state mental institution located near Jacksonville. She was the owner of the automobile in which the four defendants were arrested. Melton was a Vietnam war veteran who had been released from the Navy after nine months in a veterans' hospital. On the date of his arrest he was a part-time computer helper while attending college as a full-time student in Jacksonville. Johnson was a tow-motor operator in a grocery chain warehouse and was a lifelong resident of Jacksonville.

At the time of their arrest the four of them were riding in Calloway's car on the main thoroughfare in Jacksonville. They had left a restaurant owned by Johnson's uncle where they had eaten and were on their way to a night club. The arresting officers denied that the racial mixture in the car played any part in the decision to make the arrest. The arrest, they said, was made because the defendants had stopped near a used-car lot which had been broken into several times. There was, however, no evidence of any breaking and entering on the night in question.

Of these four charged with "prowling by auto" none had been previously arrested except Papachristou who had once been convicted of a municipal offense.

Jimmy Lee Smith and Milton Henry (who is not a petitioner) were arrested between 9 and 10 A.M. on a weekday in downtown Jacksonville, while waiting for a friend who was to lend them a car so they could apply for a job at a produce company. Smith was a part-time produce worker and part-time organizer for a Negro political group. He had a common-law wife and three children supported by him and his wife. He had been arrested several times but convicted only once. Smith's companion, Henry, was an 18-year-old high school student with no previous record of arrest.

This morning it was cold, and Smith had no jacket, so they went briefly into a dry cleaning shop to wait, but left when requested to do so. They thereafter walked back and forth two or three times over a two-block stretch looking for their friend. The store owners, who apparently were wary of Smith and his companion, summoned two police officers who searched the men and found neither had a weapon. But they were arrested because the officers said they had no identification and because the officers did not believe their story.

Heath and codefendant were arrested for "loitering" and for "common thief." Both were residents of Jacksonville, Heath having lived there all his life and being employed at an automobile and body shop. Heath had previously been arrested but his codefendant had no arrest record. Heath and his companion were arrested when they drove up to a residence shared by Heath's girlfriend and some other girls. Some police officers were already there in the process of arresting another man. When Heath and his companion started backing out of the driveway, the officers signaled to them to stop and asked them to get out of the car, which they did. Thereupon they and the automobile were searched. Although no contraband or incriminating evidence was found, they were both arrested, Heath being charged with being a "common thief" because he was reputed to be a thief. The codefendant was charged with "loitering" because he was standing in the driveway, an act which the officers admitted was done only at their command.

Campbell was arrested as he reached his home very early one morning and was charged with "common thief." He was stopped by officers because he was traveling at a high rate of speed, yet no speeding charge was placed against him.

Brown was arrested when he was observed leaving a downtown Jacksonville hotel by a police officer seated in a cruiser. The police testified he was reputed to be a thief, narcotics pusher, and generally opprobrious character. The officer called Brown over to the car, intending at that time to arrest him unless he had a good explanation for being on the street. Brown walked over to the police cruiser, as commanded, and the officer began to search him, apparently preparatory to placing him in the car. In the process of the search he came on two small packets which were later found to contain heroin. When the officer touched the pocket where the packets were, Brown began to resist. He was charged with "disorderly loitering on the street" and "disorderly conduct — resisting arrest with violence." While he was also charged with a narcotics violation, that charge was *nolled.*

Jacksonville's ordinance and Florida's statute were "derived from early English law,". . . The history is an often-told tale. The breakup of feudal estates in England led to labor shortages which in turn resulted in the Statutes of Laborers, designed to stabilize the labor force by prohibiting increases in wages and prohibiting the movement of workers from their home areas in search of improved conditions. Later vagrancy laws became criminal aspects of the poor laws. The series of laws passed in England on the subject became increasingly severe. But "the theory of the Elizabethan poor laws no longer fits the facts," Edwards v. California, 314 U.S. 160, 174. The conditions which spawned these laws may be gone, but the archaic classifications remain.

This ordinance is void-for-vagueness, both in the sense that it "fails to give a person of ordinary intelligence fair notice that his contemplated conduct is forbidden by the statute," United States v. Harriss, 347 U.S. 612, 617, and because it encourages arbitrary and erratic arrests and convictions. Thornhill v. Alabama, 310 U.S. 88; Herndon v. Lowry, 301 U.S. 242.

Living under a rule of law entails various suppositions, one of which is that "[all persons] are entitled to be informed as to what the State commands or forbids." Lanzetta v. New Jersey, 306 U.S. 451, 453. . . .

The poor among us, the minorities, the average householder are not in business and not alerted to the regulatory schemes of vagrancy laws; and we assume they would have no understanding of their meaning and impact if they read them. Nor are they protected from being caught in the vagrancy net by the necessity of having a specific intent to commit an unlawful act.

The Jacksonville ordinance makes criminal activities which by modern standards are normally innocent. "Nightwalking" is one. Florida construes the ordinance not to make criminal one night's wandering, Johnson v. State, 202 So. 2d, at 855, only the "habitual" wanderer or, as the ordinance describes it, "common night walkers." We know, however, from experience that sleepless people often walk at night, perhaps hopeful that sleep-inducing relaxation will result.

Luis Munoz-Marin, former Governor of Puerto Rico, commented once that "loafing" was a national virtue in his Commonwealth and that it should be encouraged. It is, however, a crime in Jacksonville.

"[P]ersons able to work but habitually living upon the earnings of their wives or minor children"— like habitually living "without visible means of support"— might implicate unemployed pillars of the community who have married rich wives.

"[P]ersons able to work but habitually living upon the earnings of their wives or minor children" may also embrace unemployed people out of the labor market, by reason of a recession or disemployed by reason of technological or so-called structural displacements.

Persons "wandering or strolling" from place to place have been extolled by Walt Whitman and Vachel Lindsay. The qualification "without any lawful purpose or object" may be a trap for innocent acts. Persons "neglecting all lawful business and habitually spending their time by frequenting . . . places where alcoholic beverages are sold or served" would literally embrace many members of golf clubs and city clubs.

Walkers and strollers and wanderers may be going to or coming from a burglary. Loafers or loiterers may be "casing" a place for a holdup. Letting one's wife support him is an intra-family matter, and normally of no concern to the police. Yet it may, of course, be the setting for numerous crimes.

This aspect of the vagrancy ordinance before us is suggested by what this Court said in 1876 about a broad criminal statute enacted by Congress: "It would certainly be dangerous if the legislature could set a net large enough to catch all possible offenders, and leave it to the courts to step inside and say who could be rightfully detained, and who should be set at large." United States v. Reese, 92 U.S. 214, 221.

While that was a federal case, the due process implications are equally applicable to the States and to this vagrancy ordinance. Here the net cast is large, not to give the courts the power to pick and choose but to increase the arsenal of the police. . . .

Another aspect of the ordinance's vagueness appears when we focus, not on the lack of notice given a potential offender, but on the effect of the unfettered discretion it places in the hands of the Jacksonville police. Caleb Foote, an early student of this subject, has called the vagrancy-type law as offering "punishment by analogy." [Foote, Vagrancy Type Law and Its Administration, 104 U. Pa. L. Rev. 603,] 609. Such crimes, though long common in Russia, are not compatible with our constitutional system. We allow our police to make arrests only on "probable cause," a Fourth and Fourteenth Amendment standard applicable to the States as well as to the Federal Government. Arresting a person on suspicion, like arresting a person for investigation, is foreign to our system, even when the arrest is for past criminality. Future criminality, however, is the common justification for the presence of vagrancy statutes. . . .

A direction by a legislature to the police to arrest all "suspicious" persons would not pass constitutional muster. A vagrancy prosecution may be merely the cloak for a conviction which could not be obtained on the real but undisclosed grounds for the arrest. . . .

Those generally implicated by the imprecise terms of the ordinance — poor people, nonconformists, dissenters, idlers — may be required to comport themselves according to the life-style deemed appropriate by the Jacksonville police and the courts. Where, as here, there are no standards governing the exercise of the discretion granted by the ordinance, the scheme permits and encourages an arbitrary and discriminatory enforcement of the law. It furnishes a convenient tool for "harsh and discriminatory enforcement by prosecuting officials, against particular groups deemed to merit their displeasure." Thornhill v. Alabama, 310 U.S. 88, 97-98. It results in a regime in which the poor and the unpopular are permitted to "stand on a public sidewalk . . . only at the whim of any police officer." Shuttlesworth v. Birmingham, 382 U.S. 87, 90. . . .

A presumption that people who might walk or loaf or loiter or stroll or frequent houses where liquor is sold, or who are supported by their wives or who look suspicious to the police are to become future criminals is too precarious for a rule of law. The implicit presumption in these generalized vagrancy standards — that crime is being nipped in the bud — is too extravagant to deserve extended treatment. Of course, vagrancy statutes are useful to the police. Of course they are nets making easy the round-up of so-called undesirables. But the rule of law implies equality and justice in its application. Vagrancy laws of the Jacksonville type teach that the scales of justice are so tipped that even-handed administration of the law is not possible. The rule of law, evenly applied to minorities as well as majorities, to the poor as well as the rich, is the great mucilage that holds society together.

The Jacksonville ordinance cannot be squared with our constitutional standards and is plainly unconstitutional.

Reversed.

MODEL PENAL CODE

SECTION 250.6. LOITERING OR PROWLING

[See Appendix for text of this section.]

COMMENT TO §250.6 [AMERICAN LAW INSTITUTE, MODEL PENAL CODE AND COMMENTARIES, PT. II, AT 388-389 (1980)]

This provision differs from prior legislation in that it is narrowly designed to reach only alarming loitering. Typical situations covered would be the following: a known professional pickpocket is seen loitering in a crowded railroad station; a person not recognized as a local resident is seen lurking in a doorway and furtively looking up and down the street to see if he is being watched; an unknown man is seen standing for some time in a dark alley where he has no apparent business. Perhaps an even better example comes from the leading New York case of People v. Berck:

> [T]he police had been advised that certain residential premises would be temporarily unoccupied. On patrol, they observed defendant standing behind a tree, at 1:00 A.M., seeming to be examining the unoccupied premises. When questioned by the police, he refused to explain his presence, but more important, even to identify himself. No other person was present and there was, of course, no indication of a tryst.[19]

19. 32 N.Y.2d 567, 300 N.E.2d 411 (1973). [For another typical example see State v. Ecker, 311 So. 2d 104, 110 (Fla. 1975): The "record reflects that the defendant was hiding among bushes at a private dwelling at 1:20 A.M. When the officer came in response to a call, he saw the defendant jump from the fence surrounding the dwelling and start running. The officer apprehended the defendant and placed him under arrest."]

None of these situations would be covered by the law of attempt, even under the expanded definition of that offense in Section 5.01 of the Model Code. In no case has there been a "substantial step in a course of conduct planned to culminate in [the] commission of the crime." Also, none of these situations involves possession of burglar's tools or other instruments of crime that would sustain a conviction under Section 5.06.

The major issue of policy is what response to make to such situations. At least five courses are open:

    (i)   Loitering or wandering "at unusual hours" or "without lawful business" may be punished as a completed offense. This is the approach characteristic of prior law.

    (ii)   The situation giving rise to alarm for persons or property may be treated as an occasion for police inquiry. Failure to explain oneself satisfactorily would constitute an offense.

    (iii)   The situation giving rise to alarm may be deemed a proper basis for detention and interrogation but not for criminal prosecution.

    (iv)   The situation might be dealt with only as a basis for police orders to "move on" and thus to remove the immediate alarm.

    (v)   Finally, the kind of situation described above might be viewed as giving rise to no legal consequence. An officer, of course, could make inquiry of suspicious persons, most of whom would answer voluntarily. Where the responses do not dissipate suspicion, the officer could make such observations as would facilitate later identification of the suspect if a crime did take place.

None of these alternatives is entirely satisfactory. The first authorizes criminal conviction without proof of anti-social behavior or inclination. Additionally, . . . it is difficult to imagine a statute of this sort that could pass constitutional muster under current standards. The second option is no doubt better, but it still imposes liability for failure to identify oneself or to give a credible account of one's behavior without further proof of anti-social purpose. Another trouble with this approach is that the plausible lie about one's identity or purposes will in all probability avoid liability, while an implausible truth at least leaves one open to arrest. Finally, this kind of statute is also not free from constitutional doubt. The third approach involves a controversial and possibly unconstitutional change in the law of arrest rather than the definition of a substantive offense within the scope of the Model Code. The fourth solution, the police order to "move on," hardly solves the problem of the individual who is bent on crime and at the same time confers a disturbingly unbounded discretion on the police. The last option — authorizing no police action other than voluntary questioning and visual observation — is perhaps most consistent with the ideal of the role of police and with general normative principles governing the proper use of penal sanctions. Nonetheless, this total abandonment of the traditional vagrancy concept would lead to a significant loss in effective law enforcement and would encounter justifiably serious political resistance.

Section 250.6 of the Model seeks to provide the least objectionable form of the second alternative discussed above. . . .

As a matter of constitutional policy, abrogation of loitering statutes is arguably sound. There is irreducible indeterminancy in the definition of loitering, as there is necessarily discretion in the police to decide in the first instance what the "public safety demands" or whether the circumstances "justify suspicion" or "warrant alarm." It is worth pointing out, however, that the statutes discussed above are a far cry from the ordinance invalidated in *Papachristou.* If even the Model Code provision is unconstitutionally vague, . . . then it seems likely that no general provision against loitering can be drafted to survive constitutional review. Of course, narrower proscriptions of loitering with specific purpose — e.g., to solicit deviate sexual relations — may continue to be valid, but there would be no provision to deal with the person who is obviously up to no good but whose precise intention cannot be ascertained. Most courts are willing to consider in a void-for-vagueness analysis the need for some provision and the impossibility of achieving greater precision. This factor cuts strongly in favor of the constitutionality of the Model Code provision.

NOTE

Courts have divided on whether the Model Penal Code formulation of the crime of loitering meets the constitutional requirements of *Papachristou.* An Oregon court held a similar ordinance void for vagueness in City of Portland v. White, 9 Or. App. 239, 495 P.2d 778 (1972). However, substantially similar statutes were upheld in State v. Ecker, 311 So. 2d 104 (Fla. 1975); City of Seattle v. Drew, 70 Wash. 2d 405, 423 P.2d 522 (1967); State v. Sparks, 51 Wis. 2d 256, 186 N.W.2d 245 (1971).

CHAPTER
5

RAPE

One of the most violent and unsettling of all crimes, rape poses a difficult challenge for the administration of justice. The demand for effective enforcement is bound to be strong and insistent; the penalties imposed are and ought to be among the more stringent imposed by the criminal law. Correspondingly, the need for care in defining the behavior to be treated as rape and in identifying individuals responsible for that behavior will be felt with comparable force. Tensions among the needs for fairness to the public threatened by crime, fairness to the victim of a violent offense, and fairness to the individual charged with the offense come vividly into focus.

We take as our framework for the study of rape the principles of culpability and proof already examined in the preceding chapters of this book. We consider first the principal problems in defining the mens rea and the actus reus of rape and then take up the most important aspects of the law of evidence in rape prosecutions. Many of the doctrines we shall consider are not exclusively creatures of the law of rape; we have already encountered some of them in other contexts, such as the law relating to mistake of fact. Other doctrines explored in this chapter are truly peculiar to the law of rape. Rules of evidence governing cross-examination of the complaining witness are an important example. To some extent such rules may grow out of attitudes that do not play any comparable role in the definition or enforcement of other criminal laws. Even doctrines of this kind, however, reflect the tension between fairness and effectiveness that arises in every aspect of law enforcement. In previous chapters we examined the doctrinal responses to this tension that emerge as discrete principles in the law of procedure, evidence, and criminal culpability. We believe it is useful to draw together these diverse doctrinal strands for systematic examination in the context of a single crime. Rape merits study not only for its own sake but as an example of the way rules of substance, procedure, and evidence can reinforce or counteract one another in the setting of the actual trial process.

A. MENS REA

REGINA v. MORGAN
House of Lords
[1976] A.C. 182

[For the opinion in this case, see page 286 supra.]

PEOPLE v. MAYBERRY
California Supreme Court
15 Cal. 3d 143, 542 P.2d 1337 (1975)

[For the opinion in this case, see page 293 supra.]

NOTE

The above cases can usefully be read (or reviewed) at this point. Consider particularly the relationship between the mental element required by the courts and the degree of force necessary for conduct to constitute rape. Do the strict standards of proof applicable to the latter element in some measure explain (or justify) the rejection of a strictly "subjective" mental state on the issue of consent? Consider also whether changing attitudes about the amount of force and resistance required for conviction of rape (to be explored in detail in the next section) should affect the level of mens rea required with respect to the consent element, and if so, in what way.

B. ACTUS REUS

1. *Force, Nonconsent, and Resistance*

INTRODUCTORY NOTE

The materials in this section deal with the actus reus of *forcible* rape, the most serious of the sexual offenses. Most states punish certain other types of nonconsensual sexual intercourse, and they may also designate such behavior as rape. Consent may be absent or legally ineffective because the victim is below a given age ("statutory" rape), mentally incompetent, or unconscious. Consent may also be deemed ineffective when it results from certain particularly egregious forms of deception. Modern statutory codifications generally attempt to establish grades of rape that appropriately differentiate among these serious but behaviorally distinct forms of misconduct. Often they also attempt to distinguish explicitly between those forms of deception that do and do not warrant criminal condemnation. One of the most ambitious efforts to establish numerous, clearly delineated degrees of seriousness is Mich. Comp. Laws §§750.520b-750.520d. Its difficulties are explored in Note, Recent Statutory Developments in the Definition of Forcible Rape, 61 Va. L. Rev. 1500, 1523-1529 (1975). On the deception problem, see Puttkammer, Consent in Rape, 19 Ill. L. Rev. 410 (1925); Note, Towards a Consent Standard in the Law of Rape, 43 U. Chi. L. Rev. 613 (1976). See also Model Penal Code §§213.1-213.3, Appendix to this casebook.

STATE v. RUSK
Court of Appeals of Maryland
289 Md. 230, 424 A.2d 720 (1981)

MURPHY, C.J. Edward Rusk was found guilty by a jury . . . of second degree rape in violation of Maryland Code Art. 27, §463(a)(1), which provides in pertinent part:

A person is guilty of rape in the second degree if the person engages in vaginal intercourse with another person:

(1) By force or threat of force against the will and without the consent of the other person. . . .

On appeal, the Court of Special Appeals, sitting en banc, reversed the conviction; it concluded by an 8 – 5 majority that in view of the prevailing law as set forth in Hazel v. State, 221 Md. 464, 157 A.2d 922 (1960), insufficient evidence of Rusk's guilt had been adduced at the trial to permit the case to go to the jury. We granted certiorari to consider whether the Court of Special Appeals properly applied the principles of *Hazel*. . . .

At the trial, the 21-year-old prosecuting witness, Pat, testified that on the evening of September 21, 1977, she attended a high school alumnae meeting where she met a girl friend, Terry. After the meeting, Terry and Pat agreed to drive in their respective cars to Fells Point to have a few drinks. . . . They went to a bar where . . . Rusk approached and said "hello" to Terry. Terry, who was then conversing with another individual, momentarily interrupted her conversation and said "Hi, Eddie." Rusk then began talking with Pat and during their conversation both of them acknowledged being separated from their respective spouses and having a child. Pat told Rusk that she had to go home . . . [and] Rusk requested a ride to his apartment. Although Pat did not know Rusk, she thought that Terry knew him. She thereafter agreed to give him a ride. Pat cautioned Rusk on the way to the car that "I'm just giving a ride home, you know, as a friend, not anything to be, you know, thought of other than a ride." . . .

After a twenty-minute drive, they arrived at Rusk's apartment. . . . Pat testified that she was totally unfamiliar with the neighborhood. She parked the car at the curb . . . but left the engine running. Rusk asked Pat to come in, but she refused. . . . Pat said that Rusk was fully aware that she did not want to accompany him to his room. Notwithstanding her repeated refusals, Pat testified that Rusk reached over and turned off the ignition to her car and took her car keys. He got out of the car, walked over to her side, opened the door and said, "Now, will you come up?" Pat explained her subsequent actions:

> At that point, because I was scared, because he had my car keys. I didn't know what to do. I was someplace I didn't even know where I was. It was in the city. I didn't know whether to run. I really didn't think at that point, what to do.
>
> Now, I know that I should have blown the horn. I should have run. There were a million things I could have done. I was scared, at that point, and I didn't do any of them.

Pat testified that at this moment she feared that Rusk would rape her. She said: "[I]t was the way he looked at me, and said 'Come on up, come on up;' and when he took the keys, I knew that was wrong."

It was then about 1 A.M. Pat accompanied Rusk across the street into a totally dark house. . . . Rusk unlocked the door to his one-room apartment, and turned on the light. According to Pat, he told her to sit down. She sat in a chair beside the bed. Rusk sat on the bed. After Rusk talked for a few minutes, he left the room for about one to five minutes. Pat remained seated in the chair. She made no noise and did not attempt to leave. She said that she did not notice a telephone in the room. When Rusk returned, he turned off the light and sat down on the bed. Pat asked if she could leave; she told him that she wanted to go home and "didn't want to come up." She said, "Now, [that] I came up, can I go?" Rusk, who was still in possession of her car keys, said he wanted her to stay.

Rusk then asked Pat to get on the bed with him. He pulled her by the arms to the bed and began to undress her. . . . Pat removed the rest of her clothing, and then removed Rusk's pants because "he asked me to do it." After they were both undressed Rusk started kissing Pat as she was lying on her back. Pat explained what happened next:

> I was still begging him to please let, you know, let me leave. I said, "you can get a lot of other girls down there, for what you want," and he just kept saying, "no"; and then I was really scared, because I can't describe, you know, what was said. It was more the look in his eyes; and I said, at that point — I didn't know what to say; and I said, "If I do what you want, will you let me go without killing me?" Because I didn't know, at that point, what he was going to do; and I started to cry; and when I did, he put his hands on my throat, and started lightly to choke me; and I said, "If I do what you want, will you let me go?" And he said, yes, and at that time, I proceeded to do what he wanted me to.

Pat testified that Rusk made her perform oral sex and then vaginal intercourse.

Immediately after the intercourse, Pat asked if she could leave. She testified that Rusk said, "Yes," after which she got up and got dressed and Rusk returned her car keys. She said that Rusk then

> walked me to my car, and asked if he could see me again; and I said, "Yes"; and he asked me for my telephone number; and I said, "No, I'll see you down Fells Point sometime," just so I could leave.

Pat testified that she "had no intention of meeting him again." She asked him for directions out of the neighborhood and left.

. . . As she sat in her car reflecting on the incident, Pat said she began to

> wonder what would happen if I hadn't of done what he wanted me to do. So I thought the right thing to do was to go report it, and I went from there to Hillendale to find a police car.

She reported the incident to the police at about 3:15 A.M. . . .

Rusk and two of his friends, Michael Trimp and David Carroll, testified on his behalf. According to Trimp, they went in Carroll's car to Buggs' bar to dance, drink and "tr[y] to pick up some ladies." Rusk stayed at the bar, while the others went to get something to eat.

Trimp and Carroll next saw Rusk walking down the street arm-in-arm with a lady whom Trimp was unable to identify. . . .

Carroll's testimony corroborated Trimp's. He saw Rusk walking down the street arm-in-arm with a woman. He said "[s]he was kind of like, you know, snuggling up to him like. . . . She was hanging all over him then." Carroll was fairly certain that Pat was the woman who was with Rusk. . . .

According to Rusk, when they arrived in front of his apartment Pat parked the car and turned the engine off. They sat for several minutes "petting each other.". . . Rusk testified that Pat came willingly to his room and that at no time did he make threatening facial expressions. . . . Rusk explained that after the intercourse, Pat "got uptight."

> Well, she started to cry. She said that — she said, "You guys are all alike," she says, "just out for," you know, "one thing.". . . And she said, that she just wanted to leave; and I said, "Well, okay"; and she walked out to the car. I walked out to the car. She got in the car and left.

Rusk denied placing his hands on Pat's throat or attempting to strangle her. He also denied using force or threats of force to get Pat to have intercourse with him.

In reversing Rusk's second degree rape conviction, the Court of Special Appeals quoting from *Hazel*, noted that:

> Force is an essential element of the crime [of rape] and to justify a conviction, the evidence must warrant a conclusion either that the victim resisted and her resistance was overcome by force or that she was prevented from resisting by threats to her safety.

Writing for the majority, Judge Thompson said:

> In all of the victim's testimony we have been unable to see any resistance on her part to the sex acts and certainly can we see no fear as would overcome her attempt to resist or escape as required by *Hazel*. Possession of the keys by the accused may have deterred her vehicular escape but hardly a departure seeking help in the rooming house or in the street. We must say that "the way he looked" fails utterly to support the fear required by *Hazel*.

. . . Of course, due process requirements mandate that a criminal conviction not be obtained if the evidence does not reasonably support a finding of guilt beyond a reasonable doubt. However, as the Supreme Court made clear in Jackson v. Virginia, 443 U.S. 307 (1979), the reviewing court does not ask itself whether *it* believes that the evidence established guilt beyond a reasonable doubt; rather, the applicable standard is "whether, after viewing the evidence in the light most favorable to the prosecution, *any* rational trier of fact could have found the essential elements of the crime beyond a reasonable doubt." (emphasis in original). . . .

The Court [in *Hazel*] noted that lack of consent is generally established through proof of resistance or by proof that the victim failed to resist because of fear. The degree of fear necessary to obviate the need to prove resistance, and thereby establish lack of consent, was defined in the following manner: "The kind of fear which would render resistance by a woman unnecessary to support a conviction of rape includes, but is not necessarily limited to, a fear of death or serious bodily harm, or a fear so extreme as to preclude resistance, or a fear which would well nigh render her mind incapable of continuing to resist, or a fear that so overpowers her that she does not dare resist."

. . . While *Hazel* made it clear that the victim's fear had to be genuine, it did not pass upon whether a real but unreasonable fear of imminent death or serious bodily harm would suffice. The vast majority of jurisdictions have required that the victim's fear be reasonably grounded in order to obviate the need for either proof of actual force on the part of the assailant or physical resistance on the part of the victim. We think that, generally, this is the correct standard. . . .

We think the reversal of Rusk's conviction by the Court of Special Appeals was in error for the fundamental reason so well expressed in the dissenting opinion by Judge Wilner when he observed that the majority had "trampled upon the first principle of appellate restraint . . . [because it had] substituted [its] own view of the evidence (and the inferences that may fairly be drawn from it) for that of the judge and jury . . . [and had thereby] improperly invaded the province allotted to those tribunals." In view of the evidence adduced at the trial, the reasonableness of Pat's apprehension of fear was plainly a question of fact for the jury to determine.[a] . . . Quite obviously, the jury disbelieved Rusk and believed Pat's testimony. From her testimony, the jury could have reasonably concluded that the taking of her car keys was intended by Rusk to immobilize her alone, late at night, in a neighborhood with which she was not familiar; that after Pat had repeatedly refused to enter his apartment, Rusk commanded in firm tones that she do so; that Pat was badly frightened and feared that Rusk intended to rape her; . . . that Pat was afraid that Rusk would kill her unless she submitted; that she began to cry and Rusk then put his hands on her throat and began "lightly to choke" her; that Pat asked him if he would let her go without killing her if she complied with his demands; that Rusk gave an affirmative response, after which she finally submitted.

Just where persuasion ends and force begins in cases like the present is essentially a factual issue. . . . Considering all of the evidence in the case, with particular focus upon the actual force applied by Rusk to Pat's neck, we conclude that the jury could rationally find that the essential elements of second degree

a. In his opinion in support of this position in the court below, Judge Wilner added this comment: "As a result of the Battelle Study [prepared for the LEAA National Institute of Law Enforcement and Criminal Justice, and published in 1977 and 1978], we now know some things about this crime that we could only guess at before. . . . [A]s in this case, approximately one-third of rape victims had come into contact with their assailants voluntarily, under circumstances other than hitchhiking. *Physical force is absent in over half of reported cases and, in a third of the cases, no weapon is involved.* . . .

"Of particular significance is what was learned about *resistance.* The most common type of resistance offered by victims is *verbal.* Note: verbal resistance *is* resistance! In cases arising in the large cities, only 12.7% of the victims attempted flight, and only 12% offered physical resistance. The reason for this is apparent from the next thing learned: that '[r]*ape victims who resisted were more likely to be injured than ones who did not.*' (Emphasis supplied.) The statistics showed, for rapes in large cities, that, where physical resistance was offered, over 71% of the victims were physically injured in some way, 40% requiring medical treatment or hospitalization. . . .

"Law enforcement agencies throughout the country warn women not to resist an attack haphazardly, not to antagonize a potential attacker, but to protect themselves from more serious injury. The United States Department of Justice, for example, has published a pamphlet warning, among other things: 'If you are confronted by a rapist, stay calm and maximize your chances for escape. *Think* through what you will do. You should not *immediately* try to fight back. Chances are, your attacker has the advantage. Try to stay calm and take stock of the situation.' " — EDS.

rape had been established and that Rusk was guilty of that offense beyond a reasonable doubt.[b] . . .

COLE, J., dissenting. . . . The standard of appellate review in deciding a question of sufficiency, as the majority correctly notes, is "whether, after viewing the evidence in the light most favorable to the prosecution, *any* rational trier of fact could have found the essential elements of the crime beyond a reasonable doubt." Jackson v. Virginia, 443 U.S. 307, 319 (1979) (emphasis in original). However, it is equally well settled that when one of the essential elements of a crime is not sustained by the evidence, the conviction of the defendant cannot stand as a matter of law.

The majority, in applying this standard, concludes that "[i]n view of the evidence adduced at the trial, the reasonableness of Pat's apprehension of fear was plainly a question of fact for the jury to determine." In so concluding, the majority has skipped over the crucial issue. It seems to me that whether the prosecutrix's fear is reasonable becomes a question only after the court determines that the defendant's conduct under the circumstances was reasonably calculated to give rise to a fear on her part to the extent that she was unable to resist. . . .

While courts no longer require a female to resist to the utmost or to resist where resistance would be foolhardy, they do require her acquiescence in the act of intercourse to stem from fear generated by something of substance. She may not simply say, "I was really scared," and thereby transform consent or mere unwillingness into submission by force. These words do not transform a seducer into a rapist. She must follow the natural instinct of every proud female to resist, by more than mere words, the violation of her person by a stranger or an unwelcomed friend. She must make it plain that she regards such sexual acts as abhorrent and repugnant to her natural sense of pride. She must resist unless the defendant has objectively manifested his intent to use physical force to accomplish his purpose. The law regards rape as a crime of violence. The majority today attenuates this proposition. It declares the innocence of an at best distraught young woman. It does not demonstrate the defendant's guilt of the crime of rape.

. . . The majority suggests that "from her testimony the jury could have reasonably concluded that the taking of her keys was intended by Rusk to immobilize her alone, late at night, in a neighborhood with which she was unfamiliar. . . ." But on what facts does the majority so conclude? There is no evidence descriptive of the tone of his voice; her testimony indicates only the bare statement quoted above. . . .

She also testified that she was afraid of "the way he looked," and afraid of his statement, "come on up, come on up." But what can the majority conclude from this statement coupled with a "look" that remained undescribed? There is no evidence whatsoever to suggest that this was anything other than a pattern of conduct consistent with the ordinary seduction of a female acquaintance who at first suggests her disinclination. . . .

[Pat also] testified that she started to cry and he "started lightly to choke" her, whatever that means. Obviously, the choking was not of any . . . significance.

---

b. Four judges joined the opinion sustaining the conviction. Three judges joined the dissent. — EDS.

. . . [T]here are no acts or conduct on the part of the defendant to suggest that these fears were created by the defendant or that he made any objective, identifiable threats to her which would give rise to this woman's failure to flee, summon help, scream, or make physical resistance. . . .

In my judgment the State failed to prove the essential element of force beyond a reasonable doubt and, therefore, the judgment of conviction should be reversed. . . .

PEOPLE v. BAIN, 5 Ill. App. 3d 632, 283 N.E.2d 701 (1972): Defendant was convicted of rape.[a] . . . On this appeal defendant contends among other things, that he was not proved guilty beyond a reasonable doubt.

The act of sexual intercourse is not denied by defendant and most of the facts leading up to the incident are not in dispute. Defendant was twenty-one years of age and the prosecutrix nineteen. He met her on November 17, 1969 on a blind date prearranged the day before by Linda, a girl friend of prosecutrix. [D]efendant . . . came to the apartment of prosecutrix about 5:30 o'clock in the afternoon, picked her up, and with two other boys drove to Linda's house to join her and her date. . . . [Later] one of the boys asked defendant to take him home. Prosecutrix joined them for the ride. On the way back to Linda's defendant took a back way and finally stopped the car on a lonely country road where the incident occurred.

Prosecutrix testified that defendant wanted to stay there and park but that she protested that she wanted to go home. She stated that she reached for the door but he jerked her back. . . . [They] argued back and forth until finally he pushed her down on the seat. When she tried to get up he hit her in the mouth with his fist. She said she was scared and that he then removed her slacks and underpants and had intercourse with her. On cross-examination she admitted that after they had taken the boy home she had continued to sit close to defendant with her arm around him while he drove. She denied necking with defendant either at Linda's or after they parked on the country road, but she admitted that she had kissed him twice at Linda's. . . . She admitted that she did not kick, scream, hit or scratch.

In the case before us it is readily apparent that the girl made no serious physical effort to resist. The State argues that this was attributable to her fear of defendant, but such a conclusion is belied by the facts. She admitted kissing defendant at the party and riding close with her arm around him all the way to the country road. She did not remember whether he took off her clothes or whether she did herself. After her first effort to reach for the door she apparently made no further physical protest. Afterwards she said she put on her clothes and they sat and smoked a cigarette, and when he asked if she were ready to go she said that it was up to him. She did testify that defendant hit her on the mouth causing it to be bruised and cut inside and the State argues that the testimony of her mother and the officer corroborates this fact. Such argument is made, apparently, to come within the rule that where the testimony of prosecutrix is not otherwise clear and convincing it must be corroborated by other evidence. People v. Szybeko, 24 Ill. 2d 335, 181 N.E.2d 176. But

a. Ill. Rev. Stat. ch. 38, §11-1(a), defines rape as "sexual intercourse [by a male person] with a female, not his wife, by force and against her will."— EDS.

even this corroboration is weakened as it was in *Szybeko,* by failure to make a timely complaint. When they drove back to Linda's house it was the prosecutrix who did not want to stop because Linda's mother had just pulled into the driveway. When she was dropped off at her apartment she admitted that her roommate was home but there is no indication that she told her. It was not until later when she went to her mother's house that she made her first complaint. . . . In our opinion such failure to complain at both the first and second opportunity is more striking than the evidence of her bruised mouth which may or may not have been caused by an attempt of defendant to force her into submission.

From the above we cannot say that the State's evidence creates a clear and abiding conviction of defendant's guilt, and we conclude that a reasonable doubt of guilt exists which will not permit the judgment to stand.

PEOPLE v. EVANS

Supreme Court, New York County, Trial Term
85 Misc. 2d 1088, 379 N.Y.S.2d 912 (1975)

GREENFIELD, J. The question presented in this case is whether the sexual conquest by a predatory male of a resisting female constitutes rape or seduction. . . .

Since a jury has been waived, this Court is called upon to scrutinize the conduct involved and to draw the line between the legally permissible and the impermissible and to determine on which side of the line this conduct falls.

Rape is defined in our Penal Law, Section 130.35, subdivision 1, as follows: "A male is guilty of rape in the first degree when he engages in sexual intercourse with a female: 1. By forcible compulsion.". . .

Forcible compulsion is defined in Section 130.00 subdivision 8, of the Penal Law as

> physical force that overcomes earnest resistance; or a threat, express or implied, that places a person in fear of immediate death or serious physical injury to himself or another person, or in fear that he or another person will immediately be kidnapped.[a]

. . . [B]ased upon the testimony in this case, the Court first makes the following findings of fact:

The defendant, a bachelor of approximately thirty-seven years of age, aptly described in the testimony as "glib," on July 15, 1974, met an incoming plane at LaGuardia Airport, from which disembarked L. E. P., of Charlotte, North Carolina, a twenty-year-old petite, attractive second-year student at Wellesley College, an unworldly girl, evidently unacquainted with New York City and the sophisticated city ways, a girl who proved to be, as indicated by the testimony, incredibly gullible, trusting and naive.

The testimony indicates that the defendant struck up a conversation with her, posing as a psychologist doing a magazine article and using a name that was not his, inducing Miss P. to answer questions for an interview.

a. The language of §130.00(8) was modified in 1977. See page 382 footnote 2 infra. — EDS.

The evidence further shows that the defendant invited Miss P. to accompany him by automobile to Manhattan, her destination being Grand Central Station. . . . Then the evidence indicates that this defendant and a girl named Bridget took Miss P. to an establishment called Maxwell's Plum, which the defendant explained was for the purpose of conducting a sociological experiment in which he would observe her reactions and the reactions of males towards her in the setting of a singles bar. After several hours there, . . . she was induced to come up to an apartment . . . which the defendant explained was used as one of his five offices or apartments throughout the city. . . .

She had been there for one to two hours when the defendant made his move and pulled her on to the opened sofa-bed in the living room of that apartment and attempted to disrobe her. She resisted that, and she claims that as articles of clothing were attempted to be removed she would pull them back on and ultimately she was able to ward off these advances and to get herself dressed again. At that point, the defendant's tactics, according to her testimony, appeared to have changed.

First, he informed her of his disappointment that she had failed the test, that this was all part of his psychological experiment, that, in fact, this was a way in which he was trying to reach her innermost consciousness, one of the ways in which that could be done. Then, after expressing disappointment in the failure of this psychological experiment, he took steps to cause doubt and fear to arise in the mind of Miss P. He said, "Look where you are. You are in the apartment of a strange man. How do you know that I am really who I say I am? How do you know that I am really a psychologist?" Then, he went on and said, "I could kill you. I could rape you. I could hurt you physically."

Miss P. testified that at that point she became extremely frightened, that she realized, indeed, how vulnerable she was. The defendant did not strike her, did not beat her, he exhibited no weapons at the time, but he made the statement, "I could kill you; I could rape you."

Then there was . . . an abrupt switch in which the defendant attempted to play on the sympathy of Miss P. by telling her a story about his lost love, how Miss P. had reminded him of her, and the hurt that he had sustained when she had driven her car off a cliff. Obviously, Miss P.'s sympathy was engaged, and at that time acting instinctively, she took a step forward and reached out for him and put her hand on his shoulders, and then he grabbed her and said, "You're mine, you are mine." There thereupon followed an act of sexual intercourse, an act of oral-genital contact; a half-hour later a second act of sexual intercourse, and then, before she left, about seven o'clock that morning, an additional act. . . .

The testimony indicates that during these various sexual acts Miss P., in fact, offered little resistance. She said that she was pinned down by the defendant's body weight, but in some manner all her clothing was removed, all his clothing was removed, and the acts took place. There was no torn clothing, there were no scratches, there were no bruises. Finally, at approximately seven A.M. Miss P. dressed and left the apartment. . . .

The question is whether having had sexual intercourse by the . . . means described constitutes rape in the first degree. The essential element of rape in the first degree is forcible compulsion. The prevailing view in this country is that there can be no rape which is achieved by fraud, or trick, or stratagem.

Provided there is actual consent, the nature of the act being understood, it is not rape, absent a statute, no matter how despicable the fraud, even if a woman has intercourse with a man impersonating her husband or if a fraudulent ceremony leads her to believe she is legally married to a man (contra if an explicit statute to that effect exists) or even if a doctor persuades her that sexual intercourse is necessary for her treatment and return to good health. . . .

It should be noted that seduction, while not considered to be a criminal act at common law, has been made a criminal offense by statute in some jurisdictions. In seduction, unlike rape, the consent of the woman, implied or explicit, has been procured, by artifice, deception, flattery, fraud or promise. The declared public policy of this state looks with disfavor on actions for seduction since the civil action was abolished more than forty years ago. The statute did not repeal any Penal Law provisions, but there are no presently existing penal sanctions against seduction. The law recognizes that there are some crimes where trickery and deceit do constitute the basis for a criminal charge. Since the common law, we have recognized the existence of larceny by trick. But of course, for a larceny there has to be a taking of property of value. I do not mean to imply that a woman's right to her body is not a thing of value, but it is not property in the sense which is defined by the law.

It is clear from the evidence in this case that . . . P. was intimidated; that she was confused; that she had been drowned in a torrent of words and perhaps was terrified. But it is likewise clear from the evidence that the defendant did not resort to actual physical force. . . .

So the question here is not so much the use of force, but whether threats uttered by the defendant had paralyzed her capacity to resist and had, in fact, undermined her will. Now, what was it the defendant said? He said, ". . . I could kill you. I could rape you. I could hurt you physically." Those words, as uttered, are susceptible to two possible and diverse interpretations. The first would be in essence that — you had better do what I say, for you are helpless and I have the power to use ultimate force should you resist. That clearly would be a threat which would induce fear and overcome resistance. The second possible meaning of those words is, in effect, that — you are a foolish girl. You are in the apartment of a strange man. You put yourself in the hands of a stranger, and you are vulnerable and defenseless. The possibility would exist of physical harm to you were you being confronted by someone other than the person who uttered this statement.

Of course, it is entirely possible that Miss P., who heard the statements, construed that as a threat, even though it may not have been intended as such by the person who uttered those words. The question arises as to which is the controlling state of mind — that of a person who hears the words and interprets them as a threat, or the state of mind of the person who utters such words. It appears to the Court that the controlling state of mind must be that of the speaker.* She, the hearer, may, in fact, take the words as a threat and be terrified

* On the same date as this decision the press reported a decision by the British House of Lords, holding that there could be no conviction of rape if the accused really believed that there was consent, despite the vociferous protest of the woman, when he had been told beforehand that she preferred intercourse to be accomplished over her vehement protest. The principle, of course, is that the subjective state of mind of the defendant controls in determining criminal intent. [The court's footnote appears to be a reference to Regina v. Morgan, pages 286-290 supra.]

by them. . . . But this being a criminal trial, it is basic that the criminal intent of the defendant must be shown beyond a reasonable doubt. . . . And so, if he utters words which are taken as a threat by the person who hears them, but are not intended as a threat by the person who utters them, there would be no basis for finding the necessary criminal intent to establish culpability under the law.

So where a statement is ambiguous, where the words and the acts which purport to constitute force or threats are susceptible of diverse interpretations, which may be consistent with either guilt or innocence, the Court, as the trier of the facts, cannot say beyond a reasonable doubt that the guilt of the defendant has been established with respect to the crime of rape. . . . Since the Court, therefore, can find neither forcible compulsion nor threat beyond a reasonable doubt, the defendant is found not guilty on the charges of rape, sodomy and unlawful imprisonment.

Now, acquittal on these charges does not imply that the Court condones the conduct of the defendant. The testimony in the case reveals that the defendant was a predator, and that naive and gullible girls like . . . P. were his natural prey. He posed. He lied. He pretended and he deceived. He used confidences which were innocently bestowed as leverage to effect his will. He used psychological techniques to achieve vulnerability and sympathy, and the erosion of resistance. A young and inexperienced girl like . . . P. was then unable to withstand the practiced onslaught of the defendant. . . . The Court finds his conduct, if not criminal, to be reprehensible. It was conquest by con job. Truly, therefore, this defendant may be called "The Abominable Snowman.". . . [Nevertheless,] the Court must conclude that the defendant's conduct towards Miss P. cannot be adjudged criminal so as to subject him to the penalty of imprisonment for up to twenty-five years. . . .

NOTES

1. The "elements" of rape. Rape statutes typically specify that the prohibited conduct must involve sexual intercourse (1) "by force" and (2) "against the will" of the woman. See Note, Recent Statutory Developments in the Definition of Forcible Rape, 61 Va. L. Rev. 1500 (1975). Sometimes a third element —"without the consent"— is also mentioned, but the elements "against the will" and "without the consent" generally have been treated as synonymous.[1] What of the much-debated requirement of "resistance"? In some states, resistance is included among the formal statutory elements,[2] but more often resistance has

1. See generally R. Perkins, Criminal Law 160-161 (2d ed. 1969). One court has pointed out that in some contexts "without the consent" might not imply "against the will," since the latter may suggest a requirement of active resistance. State v. Studham, 572 P.2d 700, 702 (Utah 1977). Conversely, however, "against the will" presumably would imply "without the consent" in all cases.

2. People v. Evans, pages 379-382, supra, illustrates this type of statutory scheme. At the time of the decision, N.Y. Penal Law §130.35 defined rape to include sexual intercourse by "forcible compulsion," which in turn was defined in §130.00(8) to include "physical force that overcomes earnest resistance. . . ." Section 130.00(8) was amended in 1977 to read as follows: " 'Forcible compulsion' means physical force which is capable of overcoming earnest resistance; or a threat, express or implied, that places a person in fear of immediate death or serious physical injury to himself or another person, or in fear that he or another person will immediately be kidnapped. 'Earnest resistance' means resistance of a type reasonably to be expected from a person who genuinely refuses to participate in sexual intercourse, deviate sexual intercourse or sexual contact, under all the attendant circumstances. Earnest resistance does not mean utmost resistance."

been read into the statutes, as a requirement related in some way to the two principal elements of force and nonconsent.

What, precisely, is (or should be) the relationship between resistance and either force or nonconsent? With respect to force, are the courts assuming that it is permissible, as a substantive matter, for a man to use some force (beyond whatever force may be involved in the sexual act itself), so long as the woman does not physically resist? How could such an assumption be justified? Do the actual expectations and behavior of "typical" men and women have a bearing on this question, or should the answer turn on the kind of behavior that victims (women) or defendants (men) are entitled to expect?

With respect to nonconsent, is it the prevailing notion that resistance is required in order to insure that the woman's nonconsent is not feigned and is made sufficiently clear to the defendant? If so, does it make sense to require resistance when there is ample evidence that the defendant did know of the absence of consent? Are such concerns about nonconsent better dealt with through the mens rea requirements or through rules relating to the "objective" behavior of the parties?

2. *The scope of the resistance requirement.* The old requirement that the victim resist "to the utmost" now appears to have been abandoned by all American jurisdictions, but the courts still require what may be described as "reasonable" resistance. As one court puts it (State v. Dizon, 47 Hawaii 444, 452, 390 P.2d 759, 764 (1964)) [3]:

> The rule of "resistance to the uttermost," or "resistance to the utmost" has been repudiated or relaxed, but not to the extent of doing away with the need of showing some resistance or showing facts which fairly indicate some good reason for not resisting. Even where the term "utmost resistance" is still employed, it is held to be a relative term, which actually means the greatest effort of which the woman is capable to foil the assailant and preserve the sanctity of her person.

In many situations it may be "reasonable" for the victim to offer only verbal resistance or even no resistance at all. That might be the case, for example, if the victim is jumped from behind and thrown to the ground by a stranger pointing a gun at her head. In such a situation the fear aroused by the defendant's conduct could overpower the victim and prevent her from resisting. Thus, the question whether the victim offered "reasonable" resistance is in effect displaced by the question whether the victim "reasonably" feared serious bodily harm — so that the "reasonable" amount of resistance, under the circumstances, was no resistance at all.

3. *The requirement of a "reasonable" apprehension.* In *Rusk* all the judges appear to accept the rule that the fear must be reasonably grounded; they divide only over the question whether a jury could properly find that it was, on the facts. Most courts seem to agree with that principle, even in the context of cases involving overtones of violence far greater than in *Rusk*. Consider, for example, Gonzales v. State, 516 P.2d 592, 593-594 (Wyo. 1973). Defendant met the victim at a bar. She refused his request for a ride home, but when she got into her car, he got in on the other side. After at first refusing again, she became scared

---

3. Quoting 75 C.J.S. Rape §12, at 476-477. See also State v. Studham, 572 P.2d 700, 702 (Utah 1977): "The victim need do no more than her age and her strength of body and mind make it reasonable for her to do under the circumstances to resist."

and began driving without further protest. After she had driven for a while, defendant asked her to turn down a side road, and he then:

> asked her to stop "to go to the bathroom" and took her keys out of the ignition, telling her she would not drive off and leave him. She stayed in the car when he "went to the bathroom" and made no attempt to leave. When he returned he told her he was going to rape her and she kept trying to talk him out of it. He told her he was getting mad at her and then put his fist against her face and said, "I'm going to do it. You can have it one way or the other."

After this threat, the victim in *Gonzales* submitted. The trial judge, sitting without a jury, found defendant guilty of rape, stating that a woman "does not have to subject herself to a beating, knifing or anything of that nature. As long as she is convinced something of a more serious nature will happen she is then given by law the right to submit." The Wyoming Supreme Court reversed the conviction, holding that the standard applied by the judge was erroneous "because it would place the determination solely in the judgment of the prosecutrix and omit the necessary element of a reasonable apprehension and reasonable ground for such fear; and the reasonableness must rest with the fact finder." [4]

Is it sound to require that the absence of resistance be explained by fears that are objectively "reasonable"? If the victim's fear was genuine, shouldn't that alone be sufficient to establish nonconsent? One answer may be that the state must prove not only nonconsent but also some force or threat. If the victim's fear is unreasonable, it may be unfair to say that defendant realized that his conduct was threatening. (Similarly, it may be unfair to say that defendant was aware of the lack of consent). But then would it not make more sense to focus directly on defendant's state of mind rather than on the "reasonableness" of the victim's reactions?

Suppose, for example, that defendant *knows* that the victim is genuinely (though perhaps "unreasonably") afraid and that he subtly but deliberately reinforces those fears. (Reconsider the facts of *Rusk* and *Evans*). Shouldn't a conviction be proper here regardless of the "reasonableness" of the fears? Conversely, suppose that the victim's fears are reasonable but that defendant is totally unaware of them. Shouldn't a conviction be *improper* here, regardless of whether the fears are "reasonable"? Or is it appropriate to require defendants at their peril to know when their conduct reasonably arouses fear of bodily harm?

PROBLEM

Consider Salsman v. Commonwealth, 565 S.W.2d 638 (Ky. App. 1978). A salesman, finding the prosecutrix alone at home, asked her to have sexual relations, grabbed her by the hand to pull her up from a chair, and then performed several sex acts. She protested by saying "no, no" but did not otherwise resist. Evidence established that the prosecutrix was mentally retarded and partially deaf; a psychologist testified that she was "easily threatened and frightened."

---

4. The court added that "the evidence of the nature and sufficiency of the threat to justify nonresistance is far from overwhelming in this case. . . ." 516 P.2d at 594.

Kentucky statutes define third-degree rape to include the situation in which a "mentally defective" woman is incapable of consent. However, the court held that defendant was properly charged with first-degree rape based on "forcible compulsion" (defined to include "a threat, express or implied, that overcomes earnest resistance by placing a person in fear of immediate death or physical injury. . . ."). Relying on legislative history stating that "the victim's fear need not be 'reasonable,' " the court held that a subjective standard should be used and that the jury could properly find that the victim was terror-stricken at the time she submitted.

The report of the case does not indicate whether defendant knew (or should have known) of the victim's mental condition. Should that matter?

NOTES AND QUESTIONS ON STATUTORY REFORM

Consider the following efforts to cope with the force-resistance-consent dilemma by changes in statutory wording. The first approach, exemplified by a recent Pennsylvania statute, completely abolishes the requirement of resistance. Is this abolition going too far? Or will its language produce little change in practice? The second approach, exemplified by the Model Penal Code, seeks to shift the focus of attention from the victim's behavior to that of the defendant. Is the language chosen adequate for this purpose? How much difference will the Model Penal Code approach really make? Consider how the *Rusk, Bain,* and *Evans* cases would have been decided under the Model Penal Code and Pennsylvania formulations.

Pennsylvania Statutes Annotated ch. 18 (Purdon's 1973; 1980-81 Cum. Supp.): Section 3121. Rape. A person commits a felony of the first degree when he engages in sexual intercourse with another person not his spouse:
  (1) by forcible compulsion
  (2) by threat of forcible compulsion that would prevent resistance by a person of reasonable resolution. . . .
  Section 3107. Resistance not required [effective 1976]. The alleged victim need not resist the actor in prosecutions under this chapter. Provided, however, That nothing in this section shall be construed to prohibit a defendant from introducing evidence that the alleged victim consented to the conduct in question.

MODEL PENAL CODE

SECTION 213.1. RAPE AND RELATED OFFENSES

[See Appendix for text of this section.]

COMMENTS TO §213.1 [AMERICAN LAW INSTITUTE, MODEL PENAL CODE AND COMMENTARIES, PT. II, AT 304-307 (1980)]

(a) *Forcible Rape.* Subsection (1)(a) of Section 213.1 punishes forcible rape. The definition of the offense is stated not in terms of the victim's lack of consent but of the actor's use of force that "compels her to submit" to intercourse.

Similar language has been used in a number of recently drafted statutes and proposals.

Under traditional rape statutes, many courts demanded proof of "utmost resistance" by the victim to demonstrate her non-consent. At its flood tide, the notion of "utmost resistance" stated two distinct requirements: first, that the intensity of the struggle must reflect the victim's physical capacity to oppose sexual aggression; and second, that her efforts must not have abated during the encounter. "Utmost resistance" was not required where precluded by fear of grave harm, and many modern decisions have further moderated the rigor of the doctrine. . . .

To some degree, these variations of the resistance inquiry share common faults. First, resistance may prove an invitation to danger of death or serious bodily harm. Second, it is wrong to excuse the male assailant on the ground that his victim failed to protect herself with the dedication and intensity that a court might expect of a reasonable person in her situation. As a practical matter, juries may require resistance to show that the male compelled her to submit, but there is little reason to encase this generalization in a rule of law. Where the proof establishes that the actor did compel submission to intercourse by force, the failure of a weak or fearful victim to display "utmost" or even "earnest" resistance should not be exculpatory.

The new Michigan statute follows the Model Code on this point, but takes the matter to the opposite extreme by adding the provision that the "victim need not resist." [92] There are contexts, to be sure, where the law should not require resistance, but the Michigan provision seems to imply that the failure to resist is always irrelevant and thus seems to make an overbroad response to the problem. . . . While the Michigan statute seems correct, therefore, in shifting the emphasis away from the preoccupation of much prior law on the victim's resistance, it seems similarly unsound to adopt as a rule of law the judgment that resistance need never be made.

By focusing upon the actor who "compels" the victim "to submit by force" and by omitting express language of consent and resistance, the Model Code casts away encrusted precedents and strikes a fresh approach. This is not to say that consent by the victim is irrelevant or that inquiry into the level of resistance by the victim cannot or should not be made. Compulsion plainly implies non-consent, just as resistance is evidence of non-consent. By the same token, the lack of resistance on a particuar occasion will not preclude a conviction of rape if the jury can be convinced by the context and the degree of force employed by the actor that the submission was by compulsion.

92. Mich. §750.520i. Cf. Iowa §709.5; Ohio §2907.02(c); Pa. tit. 18, §3107; Vt. tit. 13, §3254(1). The recently enacted New Jersey statute contains an interesting variation of the Michigan provision: "The prosecutor shall not be required to offer proof that the victim resisted, or resisted to the utmost, or reasonably resisted the sexual assault in any offense proscribed by this chapter." N.J. §2C:14-5(a). This language offers the advantages of discarding ancient doctrine on the resistance issue, of avoiding judicial dismissal of the charges for failure of evidence regarding resistance, and of responding to the legitimate concerns of those who regard the traditional offense of rape as imbalanced. By the same token, it avoids the difficulties posed by the Michigan formulation by permitting the defendant to rely on lack of resistance to negate the claim that he forced the victim to submit. Resistance is not made irrelevant, in other words — as surely it cannot be as an analytical matter — but the rigors of ancient doctrine are effectively mitigated.

2. *The Marital Exemption*

STATE v. SMITH

Essex County Court, New Jersey
148 N.J. Super. 219, 372 A.2d 386 (1977)

SCALERA, J. . . . Albert Smith stands accused of raping his wife in violation of N.J.S.A. 2A: 138-1, and of having committed an atrocious assault and battery upon her.

Defendant moves to dismiss the rape charge, asserting that "a husband cannot rape his wife as a matter of law." No court in New Jersey has had occasion to rule directly upon this issue in any reported decision. . . .

The pertinent part of N.J.S.A. 2A:138-1 provides that

> Any person who has carnal knowledge of a woman forcibly against her will . . . is guilty of a high misdemeanor and shall be punished by a fine of not more than $5,000, or by imprisonment for not more than 30 years, or both. . . .

The principle that a husband as prime actor cannot be guilty of rape committed upon his lawful wife appears to have been accepted without exception by courts and authorities that have treated the subject in this country. . . .

This common law principle appears to have its genesis in a statement in Sir Matthew Hale's Pleas of the Crown wherein it is stated, "But the husband cannot be guilty of a rape committed by himself upon his lawful wife, for by their mutual matrimonial consent and contract, the wife hath given up herself in this kind unto her husband, which she cannot retract." [1 Hale, Pleas of the Crown 629 (1847)] . . .

The State urges that our rape statute does brand as criminal a forcible sexual attack by a husband upon his wife because the language of the statute does not specifically *exclude* from its proscription a wife-victim.

Critics have argued that the creation of such an interdiction would increase the risk of fabricated accusations, unduly invade the sanctity of the marriage relationship, increase the wife's ability to gain an advantage over an estranged husband with respect to property settlements, become a weapon of vengeance for the spurned wife and lessen the likelihood of reconciliation. These are not totally persuasive arguments when one considers that the law already furnishes an arsenal of such weapons to a woman bent on revenge. Charges of assault and battery, larceny, fraud and other offenses may just as readily be the subject of such false accusations between spouses. Also, reconciliation hardly seems an expected or likely consequence of a relationship that has deteriorated to the point of forcible sexual advances by a husband.

Moreover, it is hardly uncommon for our criminal justice system to deal with false and fabricated criminal charges. Indeed, our jurisprudence is designed to test the very truth or falsity of accusations in all criminal proceedings. We see no basis for the supposition that it will completely and utterly fail to operate in the circumstances here presented, notwithstanding Hale's naked assertion that "It is an accusation easily to be made and hard to be proved and harder to be defended by the party accused, tho never so innocent."

Rape is necessarily and essentially an act of male self-aggrandizement, while sexual communion mutually entered into connotes and communicates love, respect and a gift of physical pleasure. Rape subjugates and humiliates the woman, leaving her with little retaliatory capability save that provided by law — to charge her attacker so that a civilized society may lawfully exact a just penalty or punishment for the trespass committed. . . .

Hale's rationale, in our judgment, if acceptable in a 17th Century setting, simply has lost touch with the reality of the 20th Century. . . . It is small comfort to a married woman whose husband has forcibly ravished her against her will to know that she may resort to the matrimonial courts to recapture or retrieve her right to sexual privacy. If she chooses not to seek such formal (and sometimes, formidable) judicial relief, how can one logically defend the result — that a husband has an unbridled right, *protected by law,* to force himself sexually upon her at any time he chooses, no matter how far the marriage relationship has deteriorated between them? . . .

For the reasons stated above, this court agrees with neither the rationale nor the policy arguments advanced in support of the principle that a husband cannot be guilty of a rape upon his wife. . . . The question here, however, is whether this court has the authority, power, or indeed the right to denounce and depart from existing law and, by mandate, change it. . . . We are dealing here with a penal statute whose genesis is rooted in common law. Hence, in construing statutes merely declaratory of a common law offense the elements of the common law offense will be recognized. . . . More particularly, a penal statute must be strictly construed lest it be applied to persons or conduct beyond the Legislature's contemplation. . . .

The State here urges that this court *construe* that portion of the rape statute which interdicts "carnal knowledge of a woman forcibly against her will" to include a husband's forcible sexual attacks upon a non-consenting wife. Recognizing that sensitive evaluations will arise in such prosecutions, the State proposes that the rape statute, when applied in prosecuting a husband-defendant, be judicially limited in scope. It suggests that in such instances this court rule that there does exist a rebuttable presumption of consent by the wife-victim because of the relationship, and further, that the element of "forcible" carnal knowledge encompass only those instances where more than minimal physical violence accompanies the sexual assault. Both qualifications are not now elements of rape as against a non-husband defendant.

Worthy of note is the recent proposal of the New Jersey Criminal Law Revision Commission in this area. In reconsidering and redefining the crime of rape in the proposed New Jersey Penal Code, the Commission suggests that such offense not include sexual invasion of a wife of the aggressor *except* when it occurs between spouses "living apart in a state of separation." (This provision represents a departure from the position taken by the American Law Institute's Model Penal Code, where the privilege is removed only upon a judgment of divorce or a "decree of judicial separation" following the common law approach. Sec. 213.6(2) (Proposed Official Draft 1962). See also, §207.4(4), Comment (Tent. Draft No. 4, 1955).

Additionally, it is noteworthy that after public hearing on the proposed New Jersey Penal Code, [the provision] was specifically amended to require that the privilege not become inoperative until spouses are "living apart in a state of legal separation or for a period of more than 18 months." One may conclude that the Assembly's addition of a specific time requirement for the separation period reflects that body's concern for the policy considerations in this area. . . .

This court has sought to note rather forcibly its disagreement and lack of confidence in the continued perpetuation of the common law rule here applicable. However, we feel that we lack the authority to simply ignore the settled principles of law that bind us and depart from the common law rule because, in our judgment, it is unfair and discriminatory, and thus create, with a sweep of the pen, criminal responsibility where none has heretofore existed. . . .

Accordingly, defendant's motion to dismiss that count of the indictment charging him with rape is hereby granted.

NOTES

1. Judicial reform and fair warning. In connection with the discussion of strict construction and problems of fair warning, reconsider the legality principle and the decision in Keeler v. Superior Court, pages 354-359 supra.

On appeal from the trial court's decision in *Smith,* the appellate division affirmed the dismissal of the rape indictment, 169 N.J. Super. 98, 404 A.2d 331, 332-333 (1979), but added this caveat:

> We have no doubt that the "common law," imported into our jurisprudence by [state] constitutional edict, is not in any sense immutable. As Justice Jacobs said so succinctly and yet so eloquently in Collopy v. Newark Eye and Ear Infirmary, 27 N.J. 29, 43-44, 141 A.2d 276, 284-285 (1958), "The common law has always had the inherent capacity to develop and adapt itself to current needs; indeed, if this were not true it would have withered and died long ago rather than have grown and flowered so gloriously." While these changes almost invariably are left to legislative action or appellate court pronouncement, we see no reason why the trial court, in situations such as this one where neither legislative fiat nor superior precedent constrains, should not contribute to this growth process on the rarely appropriate occasion. . . . [Judge Scalera's] refusal to "depart from the common law rule because [such a departure] is unfair and discriminatory" to this defendant in the creation of "criminal responsibility where none has heretofore existed," — wholly laudable and entirely correct with respect to this defendant and the principles of fair play which we sometimes call due process — must not be mistaken for an absence of authority where there is no other legislative or judicial constraint.
> . . . But even were we to . . . declare that in this more enlightened age there is no longer room for such parochial thinking [as is reflected in the common law rule], we could not apply the effect of such a determination retrospectively. Dismissal of [the rape] count of the indictment by Judge Scalera was eminently correct. . . .

The New Jersey Supreme Court disagreed with the two lower courts and reinstated the indictment:

State v. Smith, 85 N.J. 193, 426 A.2d 38 (1981): The common law which was adopted as the law of this State in 1776 consisted of the underlying reasons and policies that justified particular rules of law as well as the legal rules themselves. . . . We believe that Hale's statements concerning the common law of spousal rape derived from the nature of marriage at a particular time in history. . . . In the years since Hale's formulation of the rule, attitudes towards the permanency of marriage have changed and divorce has become far easier to obtain. The rule may simply not have been applicable to revocable marriages, which exist today as a result of changes in divorce laws.

Since the common law exemption supposedly operated by negating an essential element of the crime — lack of consent — it could not be applied where marital consent to sexual intercourse could be legally revoked. By 1975 our matrimonial laws recognized the right of a wife to withdraw consent prior to the dissolution of a marriage and even prior to a formal judicial order of separation.

. . . [In some states a wife cannot] rely on her unilateral decision outside the legal process to mark the end of the marriage, for unless she could allege and prove proper grounds, a court would probably decline to terminate the marriage. The legal setting in this State is different. Since the advent of the no-fault ground for divorce, see N.J.S.A. 2A:34-2(d), any spouse may make a unilateral decision to end the marriage. By separating from her husband and living apart for 18 months, a wife is entitled to a divorce without further proof of proper grounds. The corollary of this right is that a wife can refuse sexual intercourse with her husband during the period of separation. . . .

[Here the husband and wife had been living apart for approximately one year.[a] Therefore, defendant] cannot claim that in 1975 his wife consented to have sexual intercourse with him although they were living separately. Whether or not any other husband could have based a defense on such implied consent — a proposition that we doubt seriously but do not decide — this husband could not.

This due process argument [accepted by the courts below] assumes that at the time of defendant's acts the law of this State would have exempted him from prosecution for rape. We have held, however, that no rule of law would have exempted this defendant from the charge of raping his estranged wife. . . .

Although no court in this State prior to 1975 had held that a husband could be liable for the rape of his wife under N.J.S.A. 2A:138-1, our holding does not present a due process problem because our interpretation of the statute is not unexpected. Rose v. Locke, 423 U.S. 48 (1975) [page 360 supra].

The Supreme Court's decision in Bouie v. Columbia, [378 U.S. 347 (1964)], is distinguishable on another ground. In *Bouie*, the Court held that "an unforeseeable judicial enlargement of a criminal statute, applied retroactively," violates due process. The judicial construction in that case had "unexpectedly broaden[ed] a statute which on its face had been definite and precise," and had not

---

a. Neither of the lower courts had adverted to the details of the alleged offense. (Were the details relevant?) The New Jersey Supreme Court, at another point in its opinion, described the facts as follows (426 A.2d at 40): "At the time of the alleged incident on October 1, 1975, defendant and his wife lived in different cities. The State accuses defendant of arriving at his wife's apartment at about 2:30 A.M., breaking through two doors to get inside, and once there threatening, choking and striking her. According to the State, over a period of a few hours he repeatedly beat her, forced her to have sexual intercourse and committed various other atrocities against her person. As a result of these alleged attacks, Alfreda Smith required medical care at a hospital."—EDS.

previously covered defendants' conduct. The rape statute under consideration in this case, . . . unlike the statute in *Bouie,* seemed to cover defendant's acts against his wife. There was no surprise or absence of fair warning to defendant because a criminal statute seemingly inapplicable had suddenly been expanded to encompass his conduct. . . .

Finally, in a more general sense, defendant had ample notice and fair warning that the people of this State would no longer tolerate a husband's violent sexual assault of his wife. . . . No person in this State in 1975 could justifiably claim that a man had a legal right to impose his sexual will forcefully and violently on a woman, even if it was his wife, over her unmistakable objection.

The judgment of the Appellate Division is reversed and the rape count of the indictment against defendant is reinstated.

2. Legislative developments. As finally enacted, the New Jersey Penal Code rejected the various limitations on interspousal rape prosecution discussed in the trial court's opinion in *Smith* and instead abolished the marital exemption entirely. See N.J. Stat. Ann. §2C:14-5(b). Several other jurisdictions have also abolished the marital exemption in recent years. See, e.g., Cal. Penal Code §262; Del. Code Ann. tit. 11 §763-64; Neb. Rev. Stat. §28-320; Or. Rev. Stat. §163.375. For discussion of developments in other countries, see Geis, Rape-in-Marriage: Law and Law Reform in England, the United States, and Sweden, 6 Adel. L. Rev. 284 (1978).

Most of the recently revised penal codes preserve the spousal exemption. See American Law Institute, Model Penal Code and Commentaries, Pt. II, Comment to §213.1 at 341 (1980). Consider the following defense of the traditional position (id. at 344-346):

> First, marriage or equivalent relationship, while not amounting to a legal waiver of the woman's right to say "no," does imply a kind of generalized consent that distinguishes some versions of the crime of rape from parallel behavior by a husband. . . . At a minimum, therefore, husbands must be exempt from those categories of liability based not on force or coercion but on a presumed incapacity of the woman to consent. For example, a man who has intercourse with his unconscious wife should scarcely be condemned to felony liability on the ground that the woman in such circumstances is incapable of consenting to sex with her own husband, at least unless there are aggravating circumstances. . . . Plainly there must also be some form of spousal exclusion applicable to the crime of statutory rape. . . .
>
> The major context of which those who would abandon the spousal exclusion are thinking, however, is the situation of rape by force or threat. . . . Here the law already authorizes a penalty for assault. If the actor causes serious bodily injury, the punishment is quite severe. The issue is whether the still more drastic sanctions of rape should apply. . . . The gravity of the crime of forcible rape derives not merely from its violent character but also from its achievement of a particularly degrading kind of unwanted intimacy. Where the attacker stands in an ongoing relation of sexual intimacy, that evil, as distinct from the force used to compel submission, may well be thought qualitatively different. The character of the voluntary association of husband and wife, in other words, may be thought to affect the nature of the harm involved in unwanted intercourse. That, in any event, is the conclusion long endorsed by the law of rape and carried forward in the Model Code provision. . . .

C. PROBLEMS OF PROOF

The preceding sections suggest some of the ways in which concerns about unfounded accusations of rape may have influenced the law relating to the required
actus reus and mens rea. The same concerns have also influenced, in a much
more direct way, the law of evidence. Their influence has been felt in three
important areas: requirements of corroboration, jury instructions relating to
the complainant's credibility, and rules relating to cross-examination. The present section examines these three areas, the first two briefly (their interest is
now largely historical) and the third, which presents problems of continuing
difficulty and importance, in some detail.

1. History and Policies

UNITED STATES v. WILEY
United States Court of Appeals, D.C. Circuit
492 F.2d 547 (1974)

[The court held that a complainant's testimony had not been adequately corroborated by independent evidence, as the District of Columbia cases then required. Judge Bazelon's concurring opinion, excerpted here, gives voice to the
basic dilemma presented not only by the corroboration issue but by all of the
problems of proof examined in this section.]

BAZELON, J. (concurring). The notion that the testimony of a single witness
is inadequate to prove a crime is an ancient one. The Code of the Emperor
Justinian provided that on any important issue the testimony of one witness
was insufficient. Ecclesiastical law refined this approach by requiring, for example, that against the word of a Cardinal, forty-four witnesses were required.
But the common law gradually moved toward other modes of inquiry into the
truth. Ultimately the common law rejected the requirement of corroboration
for all crimes except perjury. Thus there was no common law requirement of
corroboration for any sex offense.

Today thirty-five states have similarly rejected the corroboration requirement
for rape. Of those jurisdictions that retain the requirement, about half, including
the District of Columbia, do so in the absence of legislation. The substance of
corroboration requirements varies enormously from state to state, ranging from
a requirement of corroboration for force, penetration and identity, to minimal
corroboration of any part of the complainant's testimony.

Numerous justifications have been advanced for the requirement of corroboration in sex cases. An examination of these rationales reveals a tangled web of
legitimate concerns, out-dated beliefs, and deep-seated prejudices.

The most common basis advanced for the requirement is that false charges
of rape are more prevalent than false charges of other crimes. A statement
such as this is extremely difficult to prove, and little or no evidence has been
adduced to support it. Two reasons are generally given for the belief that unfounded rape charges are common. It is argued, first, that women often have

a motive to fabricate rape accusations and second, that women may fantasize rapes.

It is contended that a woman may fabricate a rape accusation because, having consented to intercourse she is ashamed and bitter, or because she is pregnant and feels pressured to create a false explanation, or because she hates the man she accuses or wishes to blackmail him. It is said to be relatively easy to create a false description of rape in convincing detail.

There are, however, countervailing reasons not to report a rape. One said to be a victim of rape may be stigmatized by society, there may be humiliating publicity, and the necessity of facing the insinuations of defense counsel may be a deterrent. Moreover, those claiming to have been raped may be treated harshly by the police and by hospitals. One result of all of these obstacles is that rape is one of the most under-reported of all crimes. . . .

In addition to the problem of false charges, the corroboration requirement is justified on the theory that rape is a charge unusually difficult to defend against. In 1680 Lord Chief Justice Hale wrote, in one of the most oft-quoted passages in our jurisprudence, that rape "is an accusation easily to be made and hard to be proved, and harder to be defended by the party accused, tho never so innocent." The same theme has been echoed by modern commentators and courts. The usual absence of eyewitnesses damages the defendant as well as the complainant. Juries are said to be unusually sympathetic to a woman wronged, thus weakening the presumption of innocence.

Again, there is little hard evidence with which to test this theory. What studies are available suggest that a defendant is unlikely to be convicted of rape on the uncorroborated testimony of the complainant in those jurisdictions that do not require corroboration. Thus juries may be more skeptical of rape accusations than is often supposed.

Another justification for the corroboration requirement is the prevalence of severe penalties for rape. . . . Proposals that the corroboration requirement be abandoned are at times coupled with proposals that the penalties for rape be reduced. Reformers are subject to certain tensions on this issue. On the one hand, they seek to bring standards of proof and punishment for rape in line with those for other crimes of violence. . . . On the other hand, reformers note that rape is an unusually traumatic experience. . . . In light of this there may well be resistance to lowering the penalties.

Still another basis for the corroboration requirement lies in "the sorry history of racism in America." There has been an enormous danger of injustice when a black man accused of raping a white woman is tried before a white jury. Of the 455 men executed for rape since 1930, 405 (89 percent) were black. In the vast majority of these cases the complainant was white.

All of the safeguards that developed in this context should not be automatically applied today. Juries are more integrated than in the past and racial prejudice may be at a somewhat lower level. Numerous rape victims are black and their interests, as well as those of white women, may have been slighted by the concern for black defendants.

A final theory of the corroboration requirement is that it stems from discrimination against women. It is said that traditional sex stereotypes have resulted in rape laws that protect men rather than women. Penalties are high because a "good" woman is a valued possession of a man. Corroboration is required because to a "good" woman rape is "a fate worse than death" and she should fight to the death to resist it. If no such fight is put up, the woman must have consented or at least enticed the rapist, who is therefore blameless. In sum it is said to be the "male desire to 'protect' his 'possession' which results in laws designed to protect the male — both the 'owner' and the assailant — rather than protecting the physical well-being and freedom of movement of women."

This point of view, which has been expressed by men as well as women, may well have some validity. It would be surprising if entrenched notions of sexuality did not play a role in the law of crimes dealing with sexual violations. . . .

Ultimately modern notions of sexual equality may help break down those aspects of rape law which stem from unjust discrimination against women.

Analyzing all of these justifications in order to separate the valid from the invalid is no easy task. As I have said in another context, we are in that terrible period known as "meanwhile." We know enough to be troubled but not enough to know how to resolve our troubles. . . . But at least for the immediate present, I find that the flexible corroboration rule developed by this Court provides the best accommodation of numerous conflicting considerations. . . . To guard against [the] possible dangers [of fabrication] we retain a corroboration rule which provides that "independent corroborative evidence will be regarded as sufficient when it would permit the jury to conclude beyond a reasonable doubt that the victim's account of the crime was not a fabrication.". . . In cases such as this one where that evidence is lacking the dangers to the defendant outweigh the difficulties created for the prosecution.

The net effect of our current approach does not appear to make convictions for rape unusually difficult in this jurisdiction. Available statistics indicate that the conviction rate for rape in the District of Columbia is actually higher than it is for the United States as a whole, and most states do not require corroboration.[44]

Thus I concur in the court's opinion reversing defendant's conviction.

NOTES ON CURRENT LAW

1. The corroboration requirement. By the time of the *Wiley* decision, most American jurisdictions had already abandoned a specific corroboration requirement for rape prosecutions. See Note, The Rape Corroboration Requirement: Repeal Not Reform, 81 Yale L.J. 1365, 1367-1370 (1972). Since then, most of the remaining jurisdictions have moved in the same direction. See Note, Recent Statutory Developments in the Definition of Forcible Rape, 61 Va. L. Rev. 1500, 1530-1533 (1975); State v. Byers, 627 P.2d 788 (Idaho 1981). New York, which once had one of the nation's strictest corroboration rules, now requires corroboration only in statutory rape prosecutions. See N.Y. Penal Law §130.16; People

---

44. The latest estimate for the District of Columbia is that about 45% of those charged with rape are convicted of rape. (120 convictions of 269 tried). The comparable figure for the United States as a whole is 36.1%. Statistics generally indicate that only states with a very strict corroboration requirement, such as the old New York requirement, have a markedly low percentage of rape convictions.

v. Fuller, 50 N.Y.2d 628, 409 N.E.2d 834 (1980). Nebraska may now be the only American state that requires corroboration in all rape cases.[5]

Three years after the *Wiley* decision, the United States Court of Appeals for the District of Columbia Circuit also decided to abandon the corroboration requirement in rape cases. In United States v. Sheppard, 569 F.2d 114, 118-119 (D.C. Cir. 1977), Judge J. Skelley Wright wrote for the court: [6]

> The corroboration requirement poses a potentially severe obstacle to legitimate convictions for sex offenses. Operation of the rule serves to foreclose jury consideration of cases in which a highly credible complainant prosecutes charges, on the basis of her testimony alone, against a defendant whose account of the events is clearly less credible. And the mere existence of the rule may encourage victims never to report, and prosecutors never to bring charges for, rapes in which independent corroboration is absent or marginal. Elimination of the corroboration requirement, however, hardly leaves defendants unprotected against unjust convictions. The defendant is entitled to all of the established constitutional safeguards of our criminal justice system. Moreover, it is the trial judge's responsibility to charge the jury as to the Government's burden of proving all elements of the offense beyond a reasonable doubt. Where the motivation of the complainant in bringing the charge is an issue, as in a case where the defendant contends that she consented to the intercourse, the defense attorney is free to emphasize to the jury the dangers of falsification, and the judge should instruct the jury as to those dangers and the difficulty of establishing consent. Finally, protection against unjust convictions on a case-by-case basis is afforded by the general rule that judgments of acquittal or reversals of convictions must be granted where substantial evidence does not exist to support a guilty verdict, whether or not independent corroboration is technically present.[a]

2. Special jury instructions. Many American jurisdictions have long required that in a rape prosecution the jury must be given an instruction like the following (from Cal. Jury Instructions — Criminal No. 10.22 (3d ed. 1970)):

> A charge such as that made against the defendant in this case is one which is easily made and, once made, difficult to defend against, even if the person accused is innocent. Therefore, the law requires that you examine the testimony of the female person named in the information with caution.

The instruction, based on the remarks of Sir Matthew Hale previously quoted (page 393 supra), has fallen into disfavor for essentially the same reasons that have brought the corroboration requirement under attack. In recent years several jurisdictions have barred the instruction, either by statute (e.g., Pa. Stat. Ann. tit. 18 §3106, as amended 1976) or by judicial decision (e.g., People v. Rincon-Pineda, 14 Cal. 3d 864, 538 P.2d 247 (1975).

5. The recent authorities are reviewed in State v. Byers, 627 P.2d 788 (Idaho 1981). For an account of the weakening of corroboration requirements in other common law countries, see Clarke, Corroboration in Sexual Cases, [1980] Crim. L. Rev. 362.

6. Judge Bazelon, who was also a member of the three-judge panel, joined in the opinion and did not write separately. The other judges of the District of Columbia Circuit declined to rehear the case en banc.

a. Does Judge Wright's emphasis on the "substantial evidence" requirement suggest that appellate courts should not defer heavily to the trier of fact? Or that they should not do so when corroboration is absent? How would Judge Wright have decided the *Rusk* case (pages 372-378 supra)? — EDS.

2. Cross-examination and shield laws

STATE ex rel. POPE v. SUPERIOR COURT
Supreme Court of Arizona
113 Ariz. 22, 545 P.2d 946 (1976)

GORDON, J. The County Attorney of Mohave County acting on behalf of the State of Arizona brings this special action requesting that this Court reconsider existing law on the admissibility of evidence concerning the unchaste character of a complaining witness in a prosecution for first degree rape. . . .

[The court first reviewed the rules relating to character evidence in criminal prosecutions generally. The major problems fall into two broad categories — use of character evidence to impeach the credibility of a witness and "substantive use" of character evidence. The latter involves use of the evidence as direct support for the existence of some material fact. With respect to both uses of character evidence, further distinctions are sometimes drawn between two *kinds* of character evidence — general reputation in the community and specific instances of bad conduct (such as commission of a crime). The relevant principles of evidence law, as they apply in criminal prosecutions generally, are examined in Chapter 2, pages 36-44 supra. The Arizona court, summarizing the general rules, said that there, as in virtually all jurisdictions, a poor reputation for veracity may be used to impeach the credibility of a witness. Arizona is in the minority, however, in holding that specific prior bad acts may not be used for impeachment, unless the witness was actually convicted of a felony. With respect to "substantive use," Arizona, like most states, holds that neither general reputation nor specific prior bad acts may be used. The court then turned to consideration of the ways these general rules had been modified in the context of rape prosecutions.]

Almost every jurisdiction permits as an exception to one or more of the general rules of exclusion discussed above the substantive use of evidence concerning the unchastity of a prosecutrix where the defense of consent is raised in a forcible rape prosecution. A majority of states limit the scope of this character evidence to a showing of the general reputation of the complaining witness for unchastity, while a minority in addition allow the presentation to extend to specific prior acts of unchastity. The leading case in Arizona is State v. Wood, 59 Ariz. 48, 122 P.2d 416 (1942), where we adopted the existing rule in California which admitted both types of evidence on the theory that it "best conforms to logic and the common experience of mankind": "If consent be a defense to the charge, then certainly any evidence which reasonably tends to show consent is relevant and material, and common experience teaches us that the woman who has once departed from the paths of virtue is far more apt to consent to another lapse than is the one who has never stepped aside from that path." The reasoning in *Wood* has been consistently followed.

The admissibility in Arizona of character evidence concerning unchastity to attack the credibility of the complaining witness in a forcible rape prosecution is less clear.[a] . . . We find the cases rejecting such evidence far more compelling.

---

a. An attack on credibility could differ from an attack on the testimony about nonconsent, in that in the former situation the defendant might be seeking to show that intercourse never took place or that the victim had falsely identified him as the assailant. — EDS.

The law does not and should not recognize any necessary connection between a witness' veracity and her sexual immorality.

A more difficult question is posed when one balances the probative value of evidence concerning the prosecutrix' unchastity against its prejudicial effect when the defense of consent is raised. Where a defense other than consent is raised, the substantive use of such evidence is obviously improper because it is irrelevant and serves only to inflame the minds of jurors. Opponents of the use of evidence concerning unchastity in rape prosecutions argue that where consent is alleged the complaining witness is subjected to embarrassing questions about the most private aspects of her life, leaving her and possibly the jury with the feeling that her moral background rather than the defendant is on trial.

The "logic" and "common experience of mankind" upon which we rested our holding in State v. Wood, supra, now clearly dictate that the case be overturned. It is no longer satisfactory to argue that we should "more readily infer assent in the practised [sic] Messalina, in loose attire, than in the reserved and virtuous Lucretia." People v. Abbot, 19 Wend. 192 (N.Y. 1838). The reasoning consistently advanced by this Court to bar most prior bad acts of a witness applies with even greater force in a rape prosecution. Reference to prior unchaste acts of the complaining witness "injects collateral issues into the case which . . . divert the jury's attention from the real issue, the guilt or innocence of the accused." A prosecutrix in a forcible rape prosecution "should not be expected to come prepared to defend every incident of [her] past life.". . .

We recognize there are certain limited situations where evidence of prior unchaste acts has sufficient probative value to outweigh its inflammatory effect and require admission. These would include evidence of prior consensual sexual intercourse with the defendant or testimony which directly refutes physical or scientific evidence, such as the victim's alleged loss of virginity, the origin of semen, disease or pregnancy.

The presentation of reputation evidence to demonstrate the unchastity of the prosecutrix where the defense of consent is raised should also be barred for reasons similar to those which render substantive evidence of prior acts inadmissible. . . . As with evidence concerning prior acts, this rule of exclusion must be subject to certain exceptions, such as where the prosecution offers evidence of the complaining witness' chastity. Reputation evidence concerning unchastity may also be relevant in an attempted rape prosecution, where the subjective intent of the assailant is an element of the crime.

We envision that there may be exceptions other than those noted above to the inadmissibility of evidence concerning the complaining witness' unchastity. Where, for instance, the defendant alleges the prosecutrix actually consented to an act of prostitution, the accused should be permitted to present evidence of her reputation as a prostitute and her prior acts of prostitution to support such a defense. In addition, evidence concerning unchastity would be admissible in conjunction with an effort by the defense to show that the complaining witness has made unsubstantiated charges of rape in the past.

In these and other instances in which the evidence concerning unchastity is alleged to be sufficiently probative to compel its admission despite its inflammatory effect, a hearing should be held by the court outside the presence of the jury prior to the presentation of the evidence. . . . If the defendant alleges that profferred evidence falls into one of the above exceptions, the trial court should allow its admission if it is not too remote and appears credible. . . .

HAYS, J. (specially concurring). I concur with the result reached by the majority opinion, but I cannot approve a procedure which permits evidence of the prosecutrix' reputation as a prostitute even on the limited issue of consent. In advancing to a more reasonable and logical position by overruling State v. Wood, 59 Ariz. 48, 122 P.2d 416 (1942), we should take a full step rather than mincing toward the final goal. Reputation evidence is questionable evidence at best and should not be given a special standing in the limited field of rape. If it has no place in other offenses, it should not be singled out for this one offense.

I am also unable to concur with the majority's position which rather vaguely states that the defense may show that "the complaining witness has made unsubstantiated charges of rape in the past." The reason or logic in carving out such an exception to the rule excluding evidence of the unchastity of the complaining witness in a rape case escapes me. . . .

NOTES

1. Did the court go far enough in *Pope?* If the court's assumptions about sexual mores are sound, how can one justify its willingness to admit evidence of prior acts of prostitution? On what basis can one justify an exception even for evidence of prior consensual intercourse with defendant? See Berger, Man's Trial, Woman's Tribulation: Rape Cases in the Courtroom, 77 Colum. L. Rev. 1, 58-59 (1977).

2. Did the court go too far in *Pope?* Recall that the general test for the probative value of evidence requires not that the evidence by itself make some fact in issue likely to be true; rather probative value requires only that the fact be somewhat more likely to be true given the evidence than it would be without the evidence. See pages 35-36 supra. Can it be said that evidence of prior sexual activity has no probative value, even by this minimal standard? For example, if a complaining witness has often consented to sexual intercourse with men shortly after meeting them in a bar, wouldn't that fact make it somewhat more likely that the witness consented to intercourse with defendant shortly after meeting him in a bar? Shortly after meeting him elsewhere? If the evidence has some probative value in these situations, can its exclusion nevertheless be justified on the ground that probative value is outweighed by prejudicial effect (overestimated value, confusion of issues) or by harmful impact on the victim?

3. In response to the problems in *Pope,* 46 American jurisdictions have in recent years enacted "victim shield laws" that limit the admissibility in rape prosecutions of evidence bearing on the complainant's past behavior. Some of these laws are extremely restrictive, admitting evidence of sexual history only when it involves prior incidents with defendant. Other statutes include a somewhat more extensive list of exceptions to the general rule of inadmissibility. For analysis of these statutes, see Tanford & Bocchino, Rape Victim Shield Laws and the Sixth Amendment, 128 U. Pa. L. Rev. 544 (1980); Berger, Man's Trial, Woman's Tribulation: Rape Cases in the Courtroom, 77 Colum. L. Rev. 1 (1977).

<u>STATE v. DeLAWDER</u>
Maryland Court of Special Appeals
28 Md. App. 212, 344 A.2d 446 (1975)

ORTH, C.J. On June 1972 Lee Franklin DeLawder was found guilty by a jury in the Circuit Court for Montgomery County of carnal knowledge of a female under the age of 14 years. A 15 year sentence was imposed. The judgment was affirmed on direct appeal. [DeLawder then sought postconviction relief.] . . .

In affirming the judgment on direct appeal, we held that the trial court did not err in sustaining objections made to questions attempting to show that the prosecuting witness had sexual intercourse with other men on other occasions. The general rule is that because consent is not an issue in a carnal knowledge prosecution, evidence that the prosecutrix had prior intercourse with men other than the accused, or that her reputation for chastity was bad is immaterial when offered as an excuse or justification, and so is inadmissible for that reason. . . .

The trial judge correctly applied these rules. . . .

As Davis [v. Alaska, 415 U.S. 308 (1974)] was decided subsequent to our decision, we must determine whether it affects the validity of DeLawder's conviction. In *Davis,* the Supreme Court of the United States reviewed the reach of the Confrontation Clause of the Sixth Amendment to the federal Constitution. "The Sixth Amendment to the Constitution guarantees the right of an accused in a criminal prosecution 'to be confronted with the witnesses against him.' This right is secured for defendants in state as well as federal criminal proceedings under Pointer v. Texas, 380 U.S. 400 (1965). Confrontation means more than being allowed to confront the witness physically. 'Our cases construing the [confrontation] clause hold that a primary interest secured by it is the right of cross-examination.' Douglas v. Alabama, 380 U.S. 415, 418 (1965)." "Cross-examination," the Court observed, "is the principal means by which the believability of a witness and the truth of his testimony are tested. Subject always to the broad discretion of a trial judge to preclude repetitive and unduly harassing interrogation, the cross-examiner is not only permitted to delve into the witness' story to test the witness's perceptions and memory, but the cross-examiner has traditionally been allowed to impeach, i.e., discredit, the witness." A witness may be discredited by a general attack on his credibility by introducing evidence of a prior criminal conviction of that witness. "By so doing the cross-examiner intends to afford the jury a basis to infer that the witness' character is such that he would be less likely than the average trustworthy citizen to be truthful in his testimony." A witness may also be discredited by a more particularized attack. This is done by means of cross-examination directed toward revealing possible biases, prejudices, or ulterior motives of the witness as they may relate directly to issues or personalities in the case at hand. "The partiality of a witness is subject to exploration at trial, and is 'always relevant as discrediting the witness and affecting the weight of his testimony.' 3A J. Wigmore, Evidence §940, p. 775 (Chadbourn rev. 1970)." The Supreme Court has recognized "that the exposure of a witness' motivation in testifying is a proper and important function of the constitutionally protected right of cross-examination." The denial of effective cross-examination " 'would be constitutional error of the first magnitude and no amount of showing of want of prejudice would cure it.' "

We look to see how these rules were applied in *Davis.*

Davis was convicted of burglary and grand larceny in a state court at a trial in which the court on motion of the prosecution issued a protective order prohibiting the questioning of Richard Green, a key prosecution witness, concerning Green's adjudication as a juvenile delinquent relating to a burglary and his probation status at the time of the events as to which he was to testify. The motion was granted in reliance on a state rule and statute which preserved the confidentiality of juvenile adjudications of delinquency. The evidence against Davis was entirely circumstantial. . . . The defense made clear that it did not intend to use Green's juvenile record to impeach his credibility generally, but only as necessary to examine him for any possible bias and prejudice. "Not only might Green have made a hasty and faulty identification of [Davis] to shift suspicion away from himself as one who robbed the Polar Bar, but Green might have been subject to undue pressure from the police and made his identification under fear of possible probation revocation." The trial court rejected even this limited use of Green's adjudication, but defense counsel did his best to expose Green's state of mind at the time he discovered the safe. Green, however, made a flat denial to questions whether he was upset by the fact that the [stolen] safe was found on his property, whether he felt the authorities might suspect him, and whether he felt uncomfortable about it. . . . It was elicited that Green was questioned about the incident by the investigating officers. He was then asked, "Had you ever been questioned like that before by any law enforcement officers?" and answered, "No." The prosecution objected and the court sustained the objection. Thus "[w]hile counsel was permitted to ask Green *whether* he was biased, counsel was unable to make a record from which to argue *why* Green might have been biased or otherwise lacked that degree of impartiality expected of a witness at trial."

The Alaska Supreme Court refused to reach the issue of whether the State's policy of preserving the anonymity of a juvenile offender denied Davis his Sixth Amendment right of confrontation. It affirmed the conviction on the grounds that the scope of cross-examination allowed was adequate to develop the issue of bias and convey it to the jury. The Supreme Court did not accept this. It said: "On the basis of the limited cross-examination that was permitted, the jury might well have thought that defense counsel was engaged in a speculative and baseless line of attack on the credibility of an apparently blameless witness or, as the prosecutor's objection put it, a 'rehash' of prior cross-examination. On these facts it seems clear to us that to make any such inquiry effective, defense counsel should have been permitted to expose to the jury the facts from which jurors, as the sole triers of fact and credibility, could appropriately draw inferences relating to the reliability of the witness." It held that disallowance of the defense's attempt to show bias of the prosecution's crucial witness by cross-examination concerning the witness' juvenile record violated Davis's Sixth and Fourteenth Amendment rights.[2] . . .

2. The Court did not challenge the State's interest as a matter of its own policy in the administration of criminal justice to seek to preserve the anonymity of a juvenile offender. "Here, however, petitioner sought to introduce evidence of Green's probation for the purpose of suggesting that Green was

DeLawder's counsel made clear from the onset of the case that the defense strategy would be to discredit the prosecuting witness by revealing her possible biases, prejudices, or ulterior motives in alleging that DeLawder carnally knew her in the early morning of 20 January 1972. This strategy would be pursued by the tactic of proving that at the time of the alleged incident, she thought she was pregnant by someone else and claimed that DeLawder raped her because she was afraid to tell her mother she voluntarily had sexual intercourse with others. To show that she thought she was pregnant at the time of the alleged encounter with DeLawder, it would be necessary to establish that she had engaged in prior acts of sexual intercourse. . . .

We cannot speculate, more than the Court could in *Davis,* as to whether the jury, as the sole judge of the credibility of a witness, would have accepted this line of reasoning had counsel been permitted to present it fully. But we do conclude, as the Court concluded in *Davis,* that the jurors were entitled to have the benefit of the defense theory before them so they could make an informed judgment as to the weight to place on the prosecutrix's testimony which provided "a crucial link in the proof . . . of [the accused's] act." The accuracy and truthfulness of the prosecutrix's testimony, perhaps even more so than was the case with the witness in *Davis,* were key elements in the State's case against DeLawder. In fact, its case depended entirely on her veracity. The claim of bias, prejudice or ulterior motive which the defense sought to develop was admissible to afford a basis for an inference of undue pressure because of the prosecutrix's possible fear of her mother. The defense was unable to make a record from which to argue to the jury *why* the prosecutrix might have been biased or otherwise lacked that degree of impartiality expected of a witness at trial. It seems clear to us, in the light of *Davis,* that defense counsel should have been permitted to expose to the jury the facts from which jurors, as the sole triers of fact and credibility, could appropriately draw inferences relating to the reliability of the witness. By being prevented from so doing DeLawder was denied the right of effective cross-examination, a constitutional error of the first magnitude which no amount of showing of want of prejudice would cure. . . . We conclude, as the Court concluded in *Davis,* that the desirability that the prosecutrix fulfill her public duty to testify free from embarrassment and with her reputation unblemished must fall before the right of an accused to seek out the truth in the process of defending himself. . . .

MILENOVIC v. STATE, 86 Wis. 2d 272, 272 N.W.2d 320 (1978): [In a prosecution for forcible rape, defendant did not claim consent but instead denied having had intercourse with the complainant. To establish a motive for the allegedly false accusation, defendant sought to introduce evidence that the complainant had been promiscuous, that she had contracted a venereal disease, and that

---

-biased and, therefore, that his testimony was either not to be believed in his identification of petitioner or at least very carefully considered in that light. Serious damage to the strength of the State's case would have been a real possibility had petitioner been allowed to pursue this line of inquiry. In this setting we conclude that the right of confrontation is paramount to the State's policy of protecting a juvenile offender. Whatever temporary embarrassment might result to Green or his family by disclosure of his juvenile record — if the prosecution insisted on using him to make its case — is outweighed by petitioner's right to probe into the influence of possible bias in the testimony of a crucial identification witness. . . ."

she feared she had infected her boyfriend. The defense theory was that the complainant feared her boyfriend's anger and had sought to establish a more acceptable explanation for the source of the venereal disease by accusing defendant of rape. The Wisconsin Supreme Court held the proffered evidence inadmissible: T]he offer of proof was fatally defective because what was offered to be proved does not support and establish the evidentiary hypothesis. Essential to the hypothesis was the offer to prove that the boyfriend did not know prior to the alleged rape that the prosecutrix had contracted gonorrhea or that the prosecutrix did not know whether the boyfriend knew she had contracted gonorrhea. If the boyfriend knew of the venereal disease and the prosecutrix was aware that he knew of the disease, the entire inference of intent, plan, or motive to falsely accuse fails and the offered evidence becomes irrelevant.

It is in that respect that the instant case differs from State v. DeLawder. . . . [I]mplicit in the Maryland Court of Appeals decision is the assumption that the mother was at the time in question unaware of the pregnancy. Having made that assumption, the Maryland court applied Davis v. Alaska, and found a violation of DeLawder's confrontation right in the denial of cross-examination of the prosecutrix with respect to prior sexual intercourse and other evidence offered in support of the offer of proof. We believe the assumption of the lack of knowledge of the mother was unwarranted. The defendant did not offer to prove that fact. . . . An offer of proof need not be syllogistically perfect but it ought to enable a reviewing court to act with reasonable confidence that the evidentiary hypothesis can be sustained and is not merely an enthusiastic advocate's overstated assumption. We hold that the offer of proof was inadequate to establish the relevance of the information sought to be elicited from the complainant or offered through other witnesses.

NOTE

Is the result in *Milenovic* sound? Why should the boyfriend's knowledge be relevant at all, if the complainant *thought* he did not yet know about the venereal disease? Why should defendant be required to establish *either* of these points before the other evidence suggestive of motive can be considered at all?

On the other hand, consider the dangers implicit in the *DeLawder* approach. If the victim's prior behavior provides a sufficient motive for false accusation in cases like *DeLawder* and *Milenovic,* will imaginative defense counsel very often be able to suggest similarly plausible grounds for opening up the matter of the complainant's sexual history?

GOVERNMENT OF THE VIRGIN ISLANDS v. SCUITO
United States Court of Appeals, 3d Circuit
623 F.2d 869 (1980)

ADAMS, J. In this appeal from a conviction for forcible rape, the defendant Louis Scuito asserts . . . [that the] trial judge abused or failed to exercise his discretion in denying the defendant's motion for a psychiatric examination of the complainant. . . .

The complainant worked as a waitress at the Drunken Shrimp restaurant, where the defendant was a frequent patron. When the complainant worked late on the night of July 9, 1978, the owner of the restaurant arranged for Scuito to give the complainant a ride to her apartment. It is undisputed that Scuito took a detour down a beach road, where the two had sexual intercourse, after which he took the complainant home. The crucial issue at trial was solely whether she consented.

According to the complainant, Scuito turned down the beach road to relieve himself, and then continued to a turnaround, stopped the jeep, and began kissing her. She expressed lack of interest, but the defendant then told her he had a knife and would throw her into the ocean if she did not cooperate. She testified that she did not actually see the knife in the dark, but felt "something metal" cut into her neck, after which she ceased resistance and attempted to calm him and avoid harm by cooperating. At trial there was medical and other testimony of a cut on the side of the complainant's neck where she said the knife was held. After taking off her clothes, the defendant raped and sodomized her. During the course of the assault she prayed and recited her "mantra." [2] Upon being dropped off at home, she kissed the defendant on the forehead because, she testified, "I was praying for him" and "it was just kind of like an end to the prayer."

Scuito testified that he casually knew the complainant and her sister and had previously driven them home from the restaurant. He said that on the night of July 9, when he gave the complainant a ride to her apartment, she seemed "a little spaced, not all there." While riding home, she offered him marijuana and he drove off the main road to smoke it with her. He later "came on to her," he said. Although initially she protested, he eventually changed her mind without using or threatening any physical force.

Prior to the first trial there had been a discussion between counsel and the court regarding the admissibility of evidence that Scuito previously had raped another young woman after threatening to shoot her with a flare gun. Defense counsel contended that such evidence would be relevant only if the defendant put his character in issue, which he did not at that time intend to do. The prosecutor agreed not to mention the other alleged rape in the opening statement to the jury, but reserved the right to seek admission of the evidence under Fed. R. Evid. 404(b),[3] if the testimony that was adduced created the opportunity. . . .

[The first trial ended in a mistrial after the prosecutor indirectly referred to the previous flare-gun rape by the defendant.]

. . . Scuito moved before the second trial for a psychiatric examination of the complainant. In a supporting affidavit, his attorney made the following specific representations:

> [1] I have been informed by any number of persons in the community that the said complainant appears to be often, if not almost constantly, in a "spaced out"

---

2. A mantra has been defined as "[a] sound aid used while meditating. Each meditator has his own personal mantra which is never to be revealed to any other person." Malnak v. Yogi, 592 F.2d 197, 198 (3d Cir. 1979). . . .

3. That rule states: "1. Evidence of other crimes, wrongs, or acts, is not admissible to prove the character of a person in order to show that he acted in conformity therewith. It may, however, be admissible for other purposes, such as proof of motive, opportunity, intent, preparation, plan, knowledge, identity, or absence of mistake or accident."

or trancelike state; I have personally observed this; I have been further informed
by persons in the community that the said complainant is addicted to, and does
continually use, controlled substances, and that she is frequently in altered states
of consciousness therefrom; and I have further observed and been told of the
said complainant's habit of dressing and being seen publicly in see-through top
garments which seem indicative of socially aberrant behavior;

[2] Further, my observation of the said complainant at the first trial herein showed,
in my opinion, a rather strange and mysterious countenance on her part, and
her testimony appeared strange, not only from the standpoint of her account of
not reporting the alleged crimes until the next day, but particularly from her admitted interest and devotion to a certain book, written by a guru devotee of Timothy
Leary which contains passages of religious-like worship of LSD and other mind-
altering drugs; [and]

[3] That the foregoing observations are highly indicative of a personality which
fantasizes to extremes and which indulges in and seeks altered states of consciousness. . . .

Defendant does not press the extreme position, espoused by Wigmore, that
a psychiatric examination of a complainant should be required in all sexual
offense prosecutions.[14] Rather, defendant agrees with the Government that the
decision to order an examination is "entrusted to the sound discretion of the
trial judge in light of the particular facts." United States v. Benn, 476 F.2d
1127, 1131 (D.C. Cir. 1972) (Bazelon, C.J.). . . .

This discretion is not, of course, unbounded, for there are countervailing
considerations weighing heavily against ordering a psychiatric examination of
a complainant. As set out by the Court of Appeals for the District of Columbia
Circuit, they are that "a psychiatric examination may seriously impinge on a
witness' right to privacy; the trauma that attends the role of complainant to
sex offense charges is sharply increased by the indignity of a psychiatric examination; the examination itself could serve as a tool of harassment; and the impact
of all these considerations may well deter the victim of such a crime from lodging
any complaint at all." United States v. Benn, 476 F.2d at 1131. *Benn*, it should
be noted, held that the trial judge did not abuse his discretion in declining to
order the examination of an admittedly mentally defective complainant.[15]

Fed. R. Evid. 412 is specifically addressed to evidence of a rape victim's prior
sexual conduct,[16] whereas defendant's motion was not an attempt to introduce

14. See 3A Wigmore on Evidence §924a, at 737 (Chadbourne rev. 1970) ("No judge should
let a sex offense charge go to the jury unless the female complainant's social history and mental
makeup have been examined and testified to by a qualified physician.") (italics deleted). The Wigmore
position does not seem to be accepted in any jurisdiction. See Tanford & Bocchino, Rape Victim
Shield Laws and the Sixth Amendment, 128 U. Pa. L. Rev. 544, 547 n. 11 (1980) (describing
Wigmore's position as "untenable as a general rule").

15. . . . The Supreme Court of California has stated that a necessity authorizing the court to
order the complainant to undergo such an examination "would generally arise only if little or no
corroboration supported the charge and if the defense raised the issue of the effect of the complaining
witness' mental or emotional condition on her veracity." Ballard v. Superior Court, 64 Cal. 2d
159, 410 P.2d 838, 849 (1966). In the case sub judice, a key element of the complainant's testimony
was corroborated. She testified that the defendant held a knife to her throat, and the medical
examiner reported a cut on the side of her throat where the weapon was held. . . .

16. The principle portion of the Rule qualified in subsections (b)-(d), states: "Notwithstanding
any other provision of law, in a criminal case in which a person is accused of rape or of assault
with intent to commit rape, reputation or opinion evidence of the past sexual behavior of an alleged
victim of such rape or assault is not admissible."

such evidence, but an effort to obtain an expert opinion regarding the complainant's general ability to perceive reality and separate fact from fantasy. Because the rule does not directly apply to his motion, the defendant argues that the court either abused or did not exercise its discretion in denying the motion. The judge's ruling, however, was not based on the letter but on the spirit of Rule 412. The principal purpose of that rule is, as its legislative history demonstrates, quite similar to the countervailing considerations quoted above: "to protect rape victims from the degrading and embarrassing disclosure of intimate details about their private lives." The rationale, according to one commentator, "is to prevent the victim, rather than the defendant, from being put on trial." [19]

We hold that in relying on the *spirit* of Rule 412 the trial judge exercised discretion, and that nothing alleged in defense counsel's affidavit indicates that he abused his discretion. To the extent admissible, and we express no opinion on that matter, evidence that the complainant was thought by members of the community to indulge in drugs leading to "altered states of consciousness" or to dress in a manner "indicative of socially aberrant behavior" could be introduced by direct rather than expert testimony. If, however, such matters are not relevant or otherwise admissible, there is no justification for letting them into the trial by allowing an expert to give his opinion regarding them. . . .

The judgment of the trial court will be affirmed.

PROBLEM

Suppose that defendant had sought to present the evidence about the complainant's state of mind through ordinary witnesses rather than through expert testimony. Should such evidence have been admissible under the circumstances? If so, is it really preferable for the matter to be explored through testimony about haphazard observations and "general reputation," rather than through the testimony of experts? Can the disfavoring of expert testimony be justified in terms of the truth-seeking function of the trial or only in terms of the desire to protect the complainant from degrading psychological tests? If the latter explanation is the more satisfactory, is the result in *Scuito* consistent with Davis v. Alaska?

---

19. 2 J. Weinstein & M. Berger, Weinstein's Evidence §412[01], at 412-9 (1979). The rule may also be seen as part of a movement toward making rape prosecutions less special and treating the rape complainant like complainants in other crimes. See Berger, [page 398 supra, Note 3,] at 97.

CHAPTER
6

HOMICIDE

A. INTRODUCTION

INTRODUCTORY NOTE

There are two principal questions one may ask in considering a particular category of crime. The first is a question of criminality: What distinguishes criminal behavior from noncriminal behavior? The second is a question of punishment grading: What factors warrant greater or lesser punishment within the area of behavior defined as criminal? In the preceding chapter on rape we dealt with questions of the first kind. In this chapter we will deal primarily with questions of the latter kind.

The distinction between criminal and noncriminal homicide usually raises such basic issues as causation, necessity, self-defense, defense of another, insanity, duress, etc. We will deal separately with such general issues later, though there is one problem of criminality that we will deal with here — the basis for distinguishing between criminal and noncriminal unintended killings. See Section C1 of this chapter infra.

The questions of the second kind — those of grading — will constitute the principal focus of the materials in this section. Following the introductory historical and statutory materials, which themselves should be mainly examined in the framework of the grading problem, we deal in Section B with the factors that influence the categorization of intended killings into homicidal crimes of greater or lesser punishment — murder in the several degrees and voluntary manslaughter. In Section C a similar inquiry is pursued with respect to killings that are unintentional. It will be helpful to bear in mind that virtually all the varieties of behavior dealt with are without question crimes of some sort, the only question being the determination of what crime is involved, which is to say, what punishment is authorized.

REPORT OF THE ROYAL COMMISSION
ON CAPITAL PUNISHMENT, 1949-1953
25-28 (1953)

BASIC PRINCIPLES OF THE LAW OF MURDER IN ENGLAND

72. Homicide is the killing of a human being by a human being. Unlawful homicide may be murder, manslaughter, suicide or infanticide. Murder and manslaughter are felonies at common law and are not defined by statute. The traditional definition or description of murder derives from that given in the seventeenth century by Coke. "When a man of sound memory and of the age of discretion unlawfully kills any reasonable creature in being, and under the King's peace, with malice aforethought, either express or implied by the law, the death taking place within a year and a day." [a] It is in common practice often more briefly defined as "unlawful killing with 'malice aforethought' "; while manslaughter is defined as "unlawful killing without 'malice aforethought.' " . . .

74. The meaning of "malice aforethought," which is the distinguishing criterion of murder, is certainly not beyond the range of controversy. The first thing that must be said about it is that neither of the two words is used in its ordinary sense: the phrase "malice aforethought" is now a highly technical term of art. "It is now only an arbitrary symbol. For the 'malice' may have in it nothing really malicious; and need never be really 'aforethought,' except in the sense that every desire must necessarily come before — though perhaps only an instant before — the act which is desired. The word 'aforethought;' in the definition, has thus become either false or else superfluous. The word 'malice' is neither; but it is apt to be misleading, for it is not employed in its original (and its popular) meaning." "Malice aforethought" is simply a comprehensive name for a number of different mental attitudes which have been variously defined at different stages in the development of the law, the presence of any one of which in the accused has been held by the courts to render a homicide particularly heinous and therefore to make it murder. These states of mind have been variously expressed by various authorities, but the statement of the modern law most commonly cited as authoritative is that given in 1877 by Sir James Stephen in his Digest of the Criminal Law:

> Malice aforethought means any one or more of the following states of mind preceding or co-existing with the act or omission by which death is caused, and it may exist where that act is unpremeditated.
> (a) An intention to cause the death of, or grievous bodily harm to, any person, whether such person is the person actually killed or not;
> (b) knowledge that the act which causes death will probably cause the death of, or grievous bodily harm to, some person, whether such person is the person actually killed or not, although such knowledge is accompanied by indifference whether death or grievous bodily harm is caused or not, or by a wish that it may not be caused;

---

a. For a historical and critical analysis of the year-and-a-day requirement, see Commonwealth v. Ladd, 402 Pa. 164, 166 A.2d 501 (1960), and Commonwealth v. Lewis, 409 N.E.2d 771 (Mass. 1980). The requirement has been abandoned by many statutes but continues in a number of states. See Annot., 60 A.L.R.3d 1323 (1974). — EDS.

(c) an intent to commit any felony whatever;

(d) an intent to oppose by force any officer of justice on his way to, in, or returning from the execution of the duty of arresting, keeping in custody, or imprisoning any person whom he is lawfully entitled to arrest, keep in custody, or imprison, or the duty of keeping the peace or dispersing an unlawful assembly, provided that the offender has notice that the person killed is such an officer so employed. . . .

75. We must now consider how "malice aforethought" came to be the distinctive element of murder and to bear such a meaning as is given to it at the present time. . . . It is sufficient to say here that "murder" originally meant a "secret killing" and only gradually, from the fourteenth century onwards, came to be the name of the worst form of homicide characterised by "malice prepense" or "malice aforethought." The next stage is marked by a series of statutes in the reigns of Henry VII and VIII which largely took away the benefit of clergy from murders "of malice prepensed." It seems clear that at this period and for sometime afterwards "malice prepense" or "malice aforethought" was understood to mean a deliberate, premeditated intent to kill formed some time beforehand, and that no killing "on a sudden," even without provocation or on slight provocation, was considered to be murder. In effect the law regarded unlawful killings as being of only two kinds — killing with malice aforethought and killing on a sudden quarrel. Experience showed, however, that this view was much too simple and the definitions founded upon it inadequate. There were many kinds of killing which should clearly be considered unlawful but which did not fall into either of these categories, and many such cases seemed to deserve the extreme penalty although the offender had no premeditated desire to kill his victim. During the last four centuries the meaning to be given to the term "malice aforethought" has been affected by the changes in the conception of mens rea as a necessary ingredient in criminal liability at common law for all crimes. The courts and the writers of legal textbooks have responded to this change by giving to "malice aforethought" a wider and more technical meaning. As Stephen put it, "the loose term 'malice' was used, and then when a particular state of mind came under their notice the Judges called it 'malice' or not, according to their view of the propriety of hanging particular people. That is, in two words, the history of the definition of murder." There can be no doubt that the term now covers, and has for long covered, all the most heinous forms of homicide, as well as some cases — those of "constructive murder" — whose inclusion in the category of murder has often been criticised.

76. Thus the following propositions are commonly accepted:

(i) It is murder if one person kills another with intent to do so, without provocation or on slight provocation, although there is no premeditation in the ordinary sense of the word.

(ii) It is murder if one person is killed by an act intended to kill another.

(iii) It is murder if a person is killed by an act intended to kill, although not intended to kill any particular individual, as if a man throws a bomb into a crowd of people.

(iv) It is murder if death results from an act which is intended to do no more than cause grievous bodily harm. An early example may be found in the case of Grey, where a blacksmith, who had had words with an apprentice, struck him on the head with an iron bar and killed him. It was held that it "is all one as if he had run him through with a sword" and he was found guilty of murder.

(v) It is murder if one person kills another by an intentional act which he knows to be likely to kill or to cause grievous bodily harm, although he may not intend to kill or to cause grievous bodily harm and may either be recklessly indifferent as to the results of his act or may even desire that no harm should be caused by it. Two examples may be given. A woman may be guilty of murder if she exposes a helpless infant in circumstances where there is not a reasonable expectation that it will be found and preserved by someone else. A man was convicted of murder when he had killed a number of persons in the street by exploding a barrel of gunpowder against the wall of a prison, although his purpose was only to enable a prisoner to escape. Lord Dockburn, L.C.J., told the jury that such an act was murder, quite apart from the fact that it was committed in the prosecution of a felony.

CALIFORNIA PENAL CODE

Section 187. Murder Defined

(a) Murder is the unlawful killing of a human being, or a fetus,[a] with malice aforethought. . . .

Section 188. Malice Defined: Express and Implied Malice

Such malice may be express or implied. It is express when there is manifested a deliberate intention unlawfully to take away the life of a fellow-creature. It is implied, when no considerable provocation appears, or when the circumstances attending the killing show an abandoned and malignant heart.

When it is shown that the killing resulted from the intentional doing of an act with express or implied malice as defined above, no other mental state need be shown to establish the mental state of malice aforethought. An awareness of the obligation to act within the general body of laws regulating society is not included within the definition of malice.

Section 189. Degrees of Murder

All murder which is perpetrated by means of a bomb, poison, or lying in wait, torture, or by any other kind of willful, deliberate, and premeditated killing, or which is committed in the perpetration or attempt to perpetrate arson, rape, robbery, burglary, mayhem, or any act punishable under Section 288 [sexual perversion], is murder of the first degree [punishable by death or imprisonment for life without possibility of parole, where special enumerated circumstances

a. Except where done in the course of a legal abortion or by a physician pursuant to a medical judgment or where consented to by the mother. Section 187(b). The language was added following Keeler v. Superior Court, page 354 supra. 1970 Cal. Laws ch. 1311 §1. — Eds.

exist, or life imprisonment]; and all other kinds of murders are of the second degree [punishable by imprisonment for 15 years to life]. . . .

To prove the killing was "deliberate and premeditated," it shall not be necessary to prove the defendant maturely and meaningfully reflected upon the gravity of his or her act.

SECTION 192. MANSLAUGHTER DEFINED: KINDS

Manslaughter is the unlawful killing of a human being without malice. It is of three kinds:

1. VOLUNTARY — upon a sudden quarrel or heat of passion. [Punishable by imprisonment for two, four, or six years.]

2. INVOLUNTARY — in the commission of an unlawful act, not amounting to felony; or in the commission of a lawful act which might produce death, in an unlawful manner, or without due caution and circumspection; provided that this subdivision shall not apply to acts committed in the driving of a vehicle. [Punishable by imprisonment for two, three, or four years.]

3. IN THE DRIVING OF A VEHICLE —

(a) In the commission of an unlawful act, not amounting to felony, with gross negligence; or in the commission of a lawful act which might produce death, in an unlawful manner, and with gross negligence. [Punishable by maximum imprisonment of one year.]

(b) In the commission of an unlawful act, not amounting to felony, without gross negligence; or in the commission of a lawful act which might produce death, in an unlawful manner, but without gross negligence. [Punishable by maximum imprisonment of one year.]

This section shall not be construed as making any homicide in the driving of a vehicle punishable which is not a proximate result of the commission of an unlawful act, not amounting to felony, or of the commission of a lawful act which might produce death in an unlawful manner.

PENNSYLVANIA CONSOLIDATED STATUTES TITLE 18

SECTION 2501. CRIMINAL HOMICIDE

(a) OFFENSE DEFINED. — A person is guilty of criminal homicide if he intentionally, knowingly, recklessly or negligently causes the death of another human being.

(b) CLASSIFICATION. — Criminal homicide shall be classified as murder, voluntary manslaughter, or involuntary manslaughter.

SECTION 2502. MURDER

(a) MURDER OF THE FIRST DEGREE. — A criminal homicide constitutes murder of the first degree when it is committed by an intentional killing. [Punishable by death or life imprisonment.]

(b) MURDER OF THE SECOND DEGREE. — A criminal homicide constitutes murder of the second degree when it is committed while defendant was engaged as a principal or an accomplice in the perpetration of a felony. [Punishable by life imprisonment.]

(c) MURDER OF THE THIRD DEGREE. — All other kinds of murder shall be murder of the third degree. Murder of the third degree is a felony of the first degree. [Punishable by maximum of 20 years.]

(d) DEFINITIONS. — As used in this section the following words and phrases shall have the meanings given to them in this subsection: . . .

"Intentional killing." Killing by means of poison, or by lying in wait, or by any other kind of willful, deliberate and premeditated killing.

"Perpetration of a felony." The act of the defendant in engaging in or being an accomplice in the commission of, or an attempt to commit, or flight after committing, or attempting to commit robbery, rape, or deviate sexual intercourse by force or threat of force, arson, burglary or kidnapping. . . .

SECTION 2503. VOLUNTARY MANSLAUGHTER

(a) GENERAL RULE. — A person who kills an individual without lawful justification commits voluntary manslaughter if at the time of the killing he is acting under a sudden and intense passion resulting from serious provocation by:

(1) the individual killed; or

(2) another whom the actor endeavors to kill, but he negligently or accidentally causes the death of the individual killed.

(b) UNREASONABLE BELIEF KILLING JUSTIFIABLE. — A person who intentionally or knowingly kills an individual commits voluntary manslaughter if at the time of the killing he believes the circumstances to be such that, if they existed, would justify the killing under Chapter 5 of this title, but his belief is unreasonable.

(c) GRADING. — Voluntary manslaughter is a felony of the second degree. [Ten-year maximum.]

SECTION 2504. INVOLUNTARY MANSLAUGHTER

(a) GENERAL RULE. — A person is guilty of involuntary manslaughter when as a direct result of the doing of an unlawful act in a reckless or grossly negligent manner, or the doing of a lawful act in a reckless or grossly negligent manner, he causes the death of another person.

(b) GRADING. — Involuntary manslaughter is a misdemeanor of the first degree. [Five-year maximum.]

SECTION 2505. CAUSING OR AIDING SUICIDE

(a) CAUSING SUICIDE AS CRIMINAL HOMICIDE. — A person may be convicted of criminal homicide for causing another to commit suicide only if he intentionally causes such suicide by force, duress or deception.

(b) Aiding or Soliciting Suicide as an Independent Offense. — A person who intentionally aids or solicits another to commit suicide is guilty of a felony of the second degree if his conduct causes such suicide or an attempted suicide, and otherwise of a misdemeanor of the second degree. [Two-year maximum.]

NEW YORK PENAL LAW

Section 125.00. Homicide Defined

Homicide means conduct which causes the death of a person . . . under circumstances constituting murder, manslaughter in the first degree, manslaughter in the second degree, criminally negligent homicide. . . .

Section 125.10. Criminally Negligent Homicide

A person is guilty of criminally negligent homicide when, with criminal negligence,[a] he causes the death of another person.

Criminally negligent homicide is a class E felony. [One to four years.]

Section 125.15 Manslaughter in the Second Degree

A person is guilty of manslaughter in the second degree when:

1. He recklessly[b] causes the death of another person; or . . .
3. He intentionally[c] causes or aids another person to commit suicide.

Manslaughter in the second degree is a class C felony. [One to 15 years.]

Section 125.20. Manslaughter in the First Degree

A person is guilty of manslaughter in the first degree when:

1. With intent to cause serious physical injury to another person, he causes the death of such person or of a third person; or

2. With intent to cause the death of another person, he causes the death of such person or of a third person under circumstances which do not constitute murder because he acts under the influence of extreme emotional disturbance, as defined in paragraph (a) of subdivision one of section 125.25. The fact that homicide was committed under the influence of extreme emotional disturbance constitutes a mitigating circumstance reducing murder to manslaughter in the first degree and need not be proved in any prosecution initiated under this subdivision. . . .

Manslaughter in the first degree is a class B felony. [One to 25 years.]

a. Defined similarly to Model Penal Code §2.02(2)(d), Appendix to this casebook. See N.Y. Penal Law §15.05(4). — Eds.

b. Defined similarly to Model Penal Code §2.02(2)(c), Appendix to this casebook. See N.Y. Penal Law §15.05(3). — Eds.

c. Defined similarly to "purposely" in Model Penal Code §2.02(2)(a), Appendix to this casebook. See N.Y. Penal Law §15.05(1). — Eds.

SECTION 125.25. MURDER IN THE SECOND DEGREE

A person is guilty of murder in the second degree when:

1. With intent to cause the death of another person, he causes the death of such person or of a third person; except that in any prosecution under this subdivison, it is an affirmative defense that:

(a) The defendant acted under the influence of extreme emotional disturbance for which there was a reasonable explanation or excuse, the reasonableness of which is to be determined from the viewpoint of a person in the defendant's situation under the circumstances as the defendant believed them to be. Nothing contained in this paragraph shall constitute a defense to a prosecution for, or preclude a conviction of, manslaughter in the first degree or any other crime; or

(b) The defendant's conduct consisted of causing or aiding, without the use of duress or deception, another person to commit suicide. Nothing contained in this paragraph shall constitute a defense to a prosecution for, or preclude a conviction of, manslaughter in the second degree or any other crime; or

2. Under circumstances evincing a depraved indifference to human life, he recklessly engages in conduct which creates a grave risk of death to another person, and thereby causes the death of another person; or

3. Acting either alone or with one or more other persons, he commits or attempts to commit robbery, burglary, kidnapping, arson, rape in the first degree, sodomy in the first degree, sexual abuse in the first degree, escape in the first degree, or escape in the second degree, and, in the course of and in furtherance of such crime or of immediate flight therefrom, he, or another participant, if there be any, causes the death of a person other than one of the participants; except that in any prosecution under this subdivision, in which the defendant was not the only participant in the underlying crime, it is an affirmative defense that the defendant:

(a) Did not commit the homicidal act or in any way solicit, request, command, importune, cause or aid the commission thereof; and

(b) Was not armed with a deadly weapon, or any instrument, article or substance readily capable of causing death or serious physical injury and of a sort not ordinarily carried in public places by law-abiding persons; and

(c) Had no reasonable ground to believe that any other participant was armed with such a weapon, instrument, article or substance; and

(d) Had no reasonable ground to believe that any other participant intended to engage in conduct likely to result in death or serious physical injury.

Murder in the second degree is a class A-I felony. [Punishable by from 15 years to life imprisonment.]

SECTION 125.27. MURDER IN THE FIRST DEGREE

A person is guilty of murder in the first degree when:

1. With intent to cause the death of another person, he causes the death of such person; and

(a) Either:

(i) the victim was a police officer . . . who was killed in the course of performing his official duties, and the defendant knew or reasonably should have known that the victim was a police officer; or

(ii) the victim was an employee of a state correctional institution or was an employee of a local correctional facility . . . who was killed in the course of performing his official duties, and the defendant knew or reasonably should have known that the victim was an employee of a state correctional institution or a local correctional facility; or

(iii) at the time of the commission of the crime, the defendant was confined in a state correctional institution, or was otherwise in custody upon a sentence for the term of his natural life, or upon a sentence commuted to one of natural life, or upon a sentence for an indeterminate term the minimum of which was at least fifteen years and the maximum of which was natural life, or at the time of the commission of the crime, the defendant had escaped from such confinement or custody and had not yet been returned to such confinement or custody; and

(b) The defendant was more than eighteen years old at the time of the commission of the crime.

2. In any prosecution under subdivision one, it is an affirmative defense that:

(a) The defendant acted under the influence of extreme emotional disturbance for which there was a reasonable explanation or excuse, the reasonableness of which is to be determined from the viewpoint of a person in the defendant's situation under the circumstances as the defendant believed them to be. Nothing contained in this paragraph shall constitute a defense to a prosecution for, or preclude a conviction of, manslaughter in the first degree or any other crime except murder in the second degree; or

(b) The defendant's conduct consisted of causing or aiding, without the use of duress or deception, another person to commit suicide. Nothing contained in this paragraph shall constitute a defense to a prosecution for, or preclude a conviction of, manslaughter in the second degree or any other crime except murder in the second degree.

MODEL PENAL CODE

SECTION 210.1 to 210.4

[See Appendix for text of this section.]

THE PENAL CODE OF SWEDEN[1]

SECTION 1

A person, who takes the life of another, shall be sentenced for murder to imprisonment for ten years or life.

1. 17 The American Series of Foreign Penal Codes (1972).

SECTION 2

If, in view of the circumstances that led to the act or for other reasons, the crime mentioned in Section 1 is considered to be less grave, imprisonment for manslaughter shall be imposed for at least six and at most ten years. . . .

SECTION 7

A person, who through carelessness causes the death of another, shall be sentenced for causing another's death to imprisonment for at most two years, or, if the crime is petty, to pay a fine.

B.   LEGISLATIVE GRADING OF INTENDED KILLINGS

1.   *The Premeditation-Deliberation Formula*

COMMONWEALTH v. CARROL
Supreme Court of Pennsylvania
412 Pa. 525, 194 A.2d 911 (1963)

BELL, C.J. The defendant, Carrol, pleaded guilty generally to an indictment charging him with the murder of his wife, and was tried by a Judge without a jury in the Court of Oyer and Terminer of Allegheny County. The Court found him guilty of first degree murder and sentenced him to life imprisonment. Following argument and denial of motions in arrest of judgment and for a new trial, defendant took this appeal. The only questions involved are thus stated by the appellant:

> [1] Does not the evidence sustain a conviction no higher than murder in the second degree?
> [2] Does not the evidence of defendant's good character, together with the testimony of medical experts, including the psychiatrist for the Behavior Clinic of Allegheny County, that the homicide was not premeditated or intentional, *require* the Court below to fix the degree of guilt of defendant no higher than murder in the second degree?

The defendant married the deceased in 1955, when he was serving in the Army in California. Subsequently he was stationed in Alabama, and later in Greenland. During the latter tour of duty, defendant's wife and two children lived with his parents in New Jersey. Because this arrangement proved incompatible, defendant returned to the United States on emergency leave in order to move his family to their own quarters. On his wife's insistence, defendant was forced first to secure a "compassionate transfer" back to the States, and subsequently to resign from the Army in July of 1960, by which time he had attained the rank of Chief Warrant Officer. Defendant was a hard worker, earned a substantial salary and bore a very good reputation among his neighbors.

In 1958, decedent-wife suffered a fractured skull while attempting to leave defendant's car in the course of an argument. Allegedly this contributed to her mental disorder which was later diagnosed as a schizoid personality type. In 1959 she underwent psychiatric treatment at the Mental Hygiene Clinic in Aberdeen, Maryland. She complained of nervousness and told the examining doctor "I feel like hurting my children." This sentiment sometimes took the form of sadistic "discipline" toward their very young children. Nevertheless, upon her discharge from the Clinic, the doctors considered her much improved. With this background we come to the immediate events of the crime.

In January, 1962, defendant was selected to attend an electronics school in Winston-Salem, North Carolina, for nine days. His wife greeted this news with violent argument. Immediately prior to his departure for Winston-Salem, at the suggestion and request of his wife, he put a *loaded* .22 calibre pistol on the window sill at the head of their common bed, so that she would feel safe. On the evening of January 16, 1962, defendant returned home and told his wife that he had been temporarily assigned to teach at a school in Chambersburg, which would necessitate his absence from home four nights out of seven for a ten week period. A violent and protracted argument ensued at the dinner table and continued until four o'clock in the morning.

Defendant's own statement after his arrest details the final moments before the crime:

> We went into the bedroom a little before 3 o'clock on Wednesday morning where we continued to argue in short bursts. Generally she laid with her back to me facing the wall in bed and would just talk over her shoulder to me. I became angry and more angry especially what she was saying about my kids and myself, and sometime between 3 and 4 o'clock in the morning I remembered the gun on the window sill over my head. I think she had dozed off. *I reached up and grabbed the pistol and brought it down and shot her twice in the back of the head.*[2]

Defendant's testimony at the trial elaborated this theme. He started to think about the children,

> seeing my older son's feet what happened to them. I could see the bruises on him and Michael's chin was split open, four stitches. I didn't know what to do. I wanted to help my boys. Sometime in there she said something in there, she called me some kind of name. I kept thinking of this. *During this time I either thought or felt — I thought of the gun, just thought of the gun.* I am not sure whether I felt my hand move toward the gun — I saw my hand move, the next thing — the only thing I can recollect after that is right after the shots or right during the shots I saw the gun in my hand just pointed at my wife's head. She was still lying on her back — I mean her side. I could smell the gunpowder and I could hear something — it sounded like running water. I didn't know what it was at first, didn't realize what I'd done at first. Then I smelled it. I smelled blood before. . . .
>
> Q. At the time you shot her, Donald, were you fully aware and intend to do what you did?
> A. I don't know positively. All I remember hearing was two shots and feeling myself go cold all of a sudden.

2. When pressed on cross-examination defendant approximated that five minutes elapsed between his wife's last remark and the shooting.

Shortly thereafter defendant wrapped his wife's body in a blanket, spread and sheets, tied them on with a piece of plastic clothesline and took her down to the cellar. He tried to clean up as well as he could. That night he took his wife's body, wrapped in a blanket with a rug over it to a desolate place near a trash dump. He then took the children to his parents' home in Magnolia, New Jersey. He was arrested the next Monday in Chambersburg where he had gone to his teaching assignment.

Although defendant's brief is voluminous, the narrow and only questions which he raises on this appeal are as hereinbefore quoted. Both are embodied in his contention that the crime amounted only to second degree murder and that his conviction should therefore be reduced to second degree or that a new trial should be granted. . . .

[The court then reviewed the Pennsylvania murder statute, which, then as now, made first-degree murder killings by poison, lying in wait "or any other kind of willful, deliberate and premeditated killing."]

The specific intent to kill which is necessary to constitute in a nonfelony murder, murder in the first degree, may be found from a defendant's words or conduct or from the attendant circumstances together with all reasonable inferences therefrom, and may be inferred from the intentional use of a deadly weapon on a vital part of the body of another human being. . . .

If we consider only the evidence which is favorable to the Commonwealth, it is without the slightest doubt sufficient in law to prove first degree. However, even if we believe all of defendant's statements and testimony, there is no doubt that this killing constituted murder in the first degree. Defendant first urges that there was insufficient time for premeditation in the light of his good reputation. This is based on an isolated and oft repeated statement in Commonwealth v. Drum, 58 Pa. 9, 16, that " 'no time is too short for a wicked man to frame in his mind the scheme of murder.' " Defendant argues that, conversely, a long time is necessary to find premeditation in a "good man." We find no merit in defendant's analogy or contention. As Chief Justice Maxey appropriately and correctly said in Commonwealth v. Earnest, 342 Pa. 544, 549-550, 21 A.2d 38, 40: "Whether the intention to kill and the killing, that is, the premeditation and the fatal act, were within a brief space of time or a long space of time is immaterial if the killing was in fact intentional, wilful, deliberate and premeditated." . . .

Defendant further contends that the time and place of the crime, the enormous difficulty of removing and concealing the body, and the obvious lack of an escape plan, militate against and make a finding of premeditation legally impossible. This is a "jury argument"; it is clear as crystal that such circumstances do not negate premeditation. This contention of defendant is likewise clearly devoid of merit.

Defendant's most earnestly pressed contention is that the *psychiatrist's opinion of what defendant's state of mine must have been and was at the time of the crime,* clearly establishes not only the lack but also the legal impossibility of premeditation. Dr. Davis, a psychiatrist of the Allegheny County Behavior Clinic, testified that defendant was

for a number of years . . . passively going along with a situation which he . . . [was] not controlling and he . . . [was] not making any decisions, and finally a decision . . . [was] forced on him. . . . He had left the military to take this assignment, and he was averaging about nine thousand a year; he had a good job. He knew that if he didn't accept this teaching assignment in all probability he would be dismissed from the Government service, and at his age and his special training he didn't know whether he would be able to find employment. More critical to that was the fact that at this point, as we understand it, his wife issued an ultimatum that if he went and gave this training course she would leave him. . . . He was so dependent upon her he didn't want her to leave. He couldn't make up his mind what to do. He was trapped. . . .

The doctor then gave *his opinion* that "rage," "desperation," and "panic" produced

an impulsive automatic reflex type of homicide . . . as opposed to an intentional premeditated type of homicide. . . . Our feeling was that if this gun had fallen to the floor he wouldn't have been able to pick it up and consummate that homicide. And I think if he had to load the gun he wouldn't have done it. This is a matter of opinion, but this is our opinion about it.

There are three answers to this contention. First, as we have hereinbefore stated, neither a Judge nor a jury has to believe all or any part of the testimony of the defendant or of any witness. Secondly, the opinion of the psychiatrists was based to a large extent upon statements made to them by the defendant, which need not be believed and which are in some instances opposed by the facts themselves. Thirdly, a psychiatrist's opinion of a defendant's impulse or lack of intent or state of mind is, in this class of case, entitled to very little weight, and this is especially so when defendant's own actions, or his testimony or confession, or the facts themselves, belie the opinion. . . .

Defendant's *own statement* after his arrest, upon which his counsel so strongly relies, *as well as his testimony at his trial,* clearly convict him of first degree murder and justify the finding and sentence of the Court below. Defendant himself described his actions at the time he killed his wife. From his own statements and from his own testimony, it is clear that, terribly provoked by his allegedly nagging, belligerent and sadistic wife, *defendant remembered the gun, deliberately took it down, and deliberately fired two shots into the head of his sleeping wife.* There is no doubt that this was a wilful, deliberate and premeditated murder.

While defendant makes no contention that he was insane at the commission of the murder or at any time, what this Court said in Commonwealth v. Tyrrell, 405 Pa. 210 pages 220-221, 174 A.2d 852, 856-857 is equally appropriate here:

"Defendant's psychiatrist did not testify that the defendant was insane. What he did say was that because defendant's wife frequently picked on him and just before the killing insulted or goaded him, defendant had an emotional impulse to kill her which he could not resist.

". . . *society would be almost completely unprotected from criminals if the law permitted a blind or irresistible impulse or inability to control one's self, to excuse or justify a murder or to reduce it from first degree to second degree.* In the times in which we are living, nearly every normal adult human being has moments or hours or days or longer periods when he or she is depressed and disturbed with resultant emotional upset feelings and so-called blind impulses; and the young especially have many uncontrolled emotions every day which are euphemistically called irresistible impulses. *The Courts of Justice should not abdicate their function and duty of determining criminal responsibility to the psychiatrist.* In such event, the test will differ not only with each psychiatrist but also with the prevailing psychiatric winds of the moment." . . .

Just as the Courts cannot abdicate to the psychiatrists the task of determining criminal responsibility in law, so also they cannot remit to psychiatrists the right to determine the intent or the state of mind of an accused at the time of the commission of a homicide. . . .

Judgment and sentence affirmed.

PEOPLE v. ANDERSON

Supreme Court of California
70 Cal. 2d 15, 447 P.2d 942 (1968)

TOBRINER, J. . . . Defendant was indicted for the murder of Victoria Hammond, a 10-year-old girl, in 1962. . . . [T]he jury . . . found defendant guilty of first degree murder, found that he was sane, and fixed the penalty at death. This appeal is automatic. . . .

. . . [W]e conclude that the evidence is insufficient to support a verdict of first degree murder on the theory of either (a) premeditated and deliberate murder, or (b) murder committed during the perpetration or attempted perpetration of a violation of Penal Code section 288. [Discussion of latter issue omitted.]

[The defendant had been living for about eight months with Mrs. Hammond and her three children. On the morning of the murder, the defendant did not go to work, and when Mrs. Hammond left for work at 7:30 A.M., she left him at home with one of her children, Victoria, aged 10. He had been home from work the previous two days, during which time he had been drinking heavily. Witnesses to the defendant's whereabouts on the day of the murder were the owner of a nearby liquor store, who testified that the defendant purchased a quart of whisky between 1 and 2 P.M. that day, and Victoria's 13-year-old brother, Kenneth.

[Kenneth returned home from school at 3:30 P.M. and found the front door locked, which was not unusual. He went around to the back of the house and down into the basement, where, while working on his microscope, he heard noises coming from upstairs that sounded like objects being moved around "like someone was cleaning up." He also heard shower water running. When Kenneth went upstairs to change clothes, the back-door screen was locked, which also was not unusual, so he jerked on the screen to force the hook to pop out. When he went to the kitchen, he found that door locked also. The defendant answered Kenneth's knock dressed only in slacks. He gave Kenneth $1.00 for a teen dance he was going to attend that night, and when Kenneth noticed blood on the kitchen floor, the defendant told him that he had cut himself. Kenneth then left the house sometime before 4 P.M.

[Mrs. Hammond returned home at 4:45 P.M. and noticed blood on the living-room couch. The defendant told her that Kenneth had cut himself. She then went to the grocery store and returned at about 5:30 P.M. Meanwhile, Kenneth discovered at 6:30 P.M. that he had forgotten his wallet and returned home. When his mother found that he had not cut himself, she again asked the defendant about the blood, and defendant told her that Victoria had cut herself, but that the cut was not serious. He also told Mrs. Hammond that Victoria was at a friend's house for dinner, and Mrs. Hammond then desired to take Kenneth with her to get Victoria. When Kenneth went back to his room to get a jacket, he looked into Victoria's room and found her nude, bloody body under some boxes and blankets on the floor. The last person to see Victoria alive was a classmate, who had left her in front of the Hammond house at about 3:45 P.M.

[Several witnesses testified that the defendant did not appear intoxicated that night. But Mrs. Hammond testified that he had been drinking when she returned home both times; the officers who talked to defendant smelled alcohol on his breath; a blood test taken at 7:45 P.M. indicated that defendant's blood alcohol content was higher than that necessary to classify an automobile driver as "under the influence."

[Officers found the shades down on all the windows and the doors locked when they came to arrest the defendant, who finally opened the door for them. They also found the defendant's blood-spotted shorts, a knife, and defendant's socks, with blood encrusted on the soles. Additional evidence included Victoria's bloodstained clothes, which were found throughout the house, bloody footprints that matched the size of Victoria's feet, and blood in almost every room except the kitchen, which appeared to have been mopped. Over 60 wounds, extending over Victoria's entire body, were found. Several of the wounds, including vaginal lacerations, were post mortem. No evidence of spermatozoa was found in the victim, on her panties, or on the bed next to which she was found.]

We must, in the absence of substantial evidence to support the verdict of first degree murder, reduce the conviction to second degree murder. . . .

Recognizing the need to clarify the difference between the two degrees of murder and the bases upon which a reviewing court may find that the evidence is sufficient to support a verdict of first degree murder, we set forth standards, derived from the nature of premeditation and deliberation as employed by the Legislature and interpreted by this court, for the kind of evidence which is sufficient to sustain a finding of premeditation and deliberation. . . .

As we noted in People v. Bender, 27 Cal. 2d 164, 183, we find no indication that the Legislature intended to give the words "deliberate" and "premeditated" other than their ordinary dictionary meanings. Moreover, we have repeatedly pointed out that the legislative classification of murder into two degrees would be meaningless if "deliberation" and "premeditation" were construed as requiring no more reflection than may be involved in the mere formation of a specific intent to kill.[a] . . .

a. See Cardozo, What Medicine Can Do for Law, in B. Cardozo, Law and Literature and Other Essays and Addresses 99-100 (1931): "There can be no intent unless there is choice, yet by the hypothesis, the choice without more is enough to justify the inference that the intent was deliberate and premeditated. The presence of a sudden impulse is said to mark the dividing line, but how can an impulse be anything but sudden when the time for its formation is measured by the lapse of seconds? Yet the decisions are to the effect that seconds may be enough. . . . If intent is deliberate and premeditated whenever there is choice, then in truth it is always deliberate and premeditated, since choice is involved in the hypothesis of the intent. What we have is merely a privilege offered to the jury to find the lesser degree when the suddenness of the intent, the vehemence of the passion, seems to call irresistibly for the exercise of mercy. I have no objection to giving them this dispensing power, but it should be given to them directly and not in a mystifying cloud of words. —EDS.

Thus we have held that in order for a killing with malice aforethought to be first rather than second degree murder, " '[t]he intent to kill must be . . . formed upon a *pre-existing* reflection,' . . . [and have] been the subject of actual deliberation or *forethought*. . . ." (People v. Thomas, 25 Cal. 2d at pp. 900-901.) (Italics added.) We have therefore held that "[a] verdict of murder in the first degree . . . [on a theory of a wilful, deliberate, and premeditated killing] is proper only if the slayer killed 'as a result of careful thought and weighing of considerations; as a *deliberate* judgment or plan; carried on coolly and steadily, [especially] according to a *preconceived design*.' " . . . (People v. Caldwell, 43 Cal. 2d 864, at p. 869.)

The type of evidence which this court has found sufficient to sustain a finding of premeditation and deliberation falls into three basic categories: (1) facts about how and what defendant did *prior* to the actual killing which show that the defendant was engaged in activity directed toward, and explicable as intended to result in, the killing — what may be characterized as "planning" activity; (2) facts about the defendant's *prior* relationship and/or conduct with the victim from which the jury could reasonably infer a "motive" to kill the victim, which inference of motive, together with facts of type (1) or (3), would in turn support an inference that the killing was the result of "a pre-existing reflection" and "careful thought and weighing of considerations" rather than "mere unconsidered or rash impulse hastily executed" . . . ; (3) facts about the nature of the killing from which the jury could infer that the *manner* of killing was so particular and exacting that the defendant must have intentionally killed according to a "preconceived design" to take his victim's life in a particular way for a "reason" which the jury can reasonably infer from facts of type (1) or (2).

Analysis of the cases will show that this court sustains verdicts of first degree murder typically when there is evidence of all three types and otherwise requires at least extremely strong evidence of (1) or evidence of (2) in conjunction with either (1) or (3). . . .

In People v. Hillery, 62 Cal. 2d 692, the jury could reasonably infer that the defendant engaged in the following "extended course of conduct": defendant parked his car near the victim's (a 15-year-old girl's) house, entered the house surreptitiously, seized the victim while she was sewing and covered her head with a towel and slip to prevent outcry or identification, cut a length of cord in another room to secure her hands behind her, took the victim's scissors, dragged her to a nearby irrigation ditch where her body was subsequently found, engaged in a struggle with the victim, and then plunged the scissors directly into her chest.

Hillery represents a case of very strong type (1) evidence: the defendant's surreptitious conduct, subjection of his victim to his complete control, and carrying off of his victim to a place where others were unlikely to intrude, can be described as "planning" activity directly related to the killing. Moreover, there is also strong evidence of type (3): directly plunging a lethal weapon into the chest evidences a deliberate intention to kill as opposed to the type of "indiscriminate" multiple attack of both severe and superficial wounds which defendant engaged in in the instant case. . . .

In People v. Kemp (1961) 55 Cal. 2d 458, the defendant entered his victim's apartment through a window after removing the screen, found the victim alone in bed, tied stockings around her neck and hands, gagged her with a washcloth, and then raped and strangled her. In *Kemp,* as in *Hillery,* defendant's surreptitious coming upon the victim and calculated efforts to prevent her from identifying her assailant or crying out for help, together with the deliberate manner of killing — evidence of types (1) and (3) — point to a killing which is the result of "preconceived design" as opposed to "an explosion of violence." (People v. Anderson, supra. 63 Cal. 2d at p. 360.) . . .

People v. Cole (1956) 47 Cal. 2d 99, involved a defendant living with an impecunious woman (his victim) and desirous of marrying a well-to-do woman. The evidence established that the defendant secretly took the latter's gun from her dresser the week before the killing, that he was carrying it on the evening of the killing, and that he used it to kill his victim. Moreover, the evidence also tended to show that defendant planned to implicate the wealthier woman so as to secure her assistance in concealing his guilt and that he killed the victim to remove her as an obstacle to his marital plans. As the court pointed out, "a showing of motive indicating that the killing was planned" tends to support an inference of premeditation and deliberation. *Cole* thus represents a case of primarily type (2) evidence supported by type (1) evidence. . . .

The present case is strikingly similar to People v. Granados, 49 Cal. 2d 490, in which this court reduced a verdict of first degree murder to second degree murder on the ground that the evidence was insufficient to show either premeditation or deliberation. . . . The evidence of premeditation and deliberation in *Granados,* while clearly insufficient to sustain the verdict of first degree murder on that theory, was stronger than in the present case in which we find no evidence from which the jury could *reasonably* infer that defendant acted *"with a deliberate and clear intent to take life."* . . .

In *Granados,* defendant lived in a common law relationship with the mother of his victim, a 13-year-old girl. After taking the deceased and her brother to a real estate office, defendant gave the brother a note requesting money to take to his mother who worked nearby. When the brother returned home with the requested money he saw defendant at the rear of the house. As he started to enter the house, defendant came running to him and asked him to get some alcohol for his sister (decedent) who had fainted. The brother noticed blood on one of defendant's hands and that defendant had the other hand behind his back.

The brother unsuccessfully looked for some alcohol. Defendant then suggested they get a doctor and an ambulance. The brother then noticed that defendant's hand had been washed. Defendant then drove the brother to a drugstore, gave him 50 cents for some alcohol, and told him he would wait for him. The defendant drove away and did not return for the brother.

Defendant then called the mother and told her the victim had poisoned herself. The mother returned to the house with a friend who found the victim's body in the bedroom lying on the floor. Her skirt was pulled up exposing her private parts, there were bloodstains on the wall, floor, and decedent's head, and a machete covered with blood was lying in a corner of the living room behind a small heater.

Defendant testified that on the day of the killing the girl was helping him clean the house and that he asked her if she was a virgin, to which she replied that it was none of his business. Defendant said that she had never answered him in that way and that he therefore struck her with his hand, but did not remember striking her with the machete.

Decedent's mother testified that she had warned defendant that the next time he bothered her daugher, she would tell the police, and that defendant in reply threatened to kill her and both her children if she did.

The prosecution argued that the murder was sexually motivated. This court, per justice McComb, held that the evidence was insufficient as a matter of law to support a verdict of first degree murder.

Applying the standards developed above to *Granados,* we find that the only evidence of (1) defendant's behavior prior to the killing which could be described as "planning" activity related to a killing purpose was defendant's sending the victim's brother on an errand and apparently returning home alone with the decedent. Such evidence is highly ambiguous in terms of the various inferences it could support as to defendant's purpose in so behaving. The evidence of (2) defendant's prior behavior with the victim (alleged sexual molestation and his question as to her virginity) is insufficient to support a reasonable inference that defendant had a "motive" to kill the girl, which could in turn support an inference that the striking with the machete was the result of a "preconceived design" and "forethought." Finally, the evidence of (3) the manner of killing (brutal hacking) does not support a reasonable inference of deliberately placed blows, which could in turn support an inference that the act of killing was premeditated rather than "hasty and impetuous." . . .

We conclude that a finding of premeditation and deliberation cannot be sustained in the absence of any evidence of (1) defendant's actions prior to the killing, (2) a "motive" or "reason" from which the jury could reasonably infer that defendant intended to kill Victoria, or (3) a manner of killing from which the jury could reasonably infer that the wounds were deliberately calculated to result in death. . . .

The judgment is modified by reducing the degree of the crime to murder of the second degree and, as so modified, is affirmed. . . .[b]

NOTES

1. How would Commonwealth v. Carrol have been decided under the approach of People v. Anderson? Which approach is the better one?

2. The California Supreme Court developed a novel interpretation of premeditation and deliberation, which required not only prior reflection and planning but also prior reflection of a sufficiently mature quality. In People v. Wolff, 61 Cal. 2d 795, 394 P.2d 959 (1964), defendant, a 15-year-old boy, murdered his mother with an axe after very considerable advance planning. Evidence presented by psychiatrists revealed a highly disturbed youngster with a bizarre history, whose ability to behave rationally was substantially impaired even though he could not be found legally insane under the test of legal insanity then prevailing.

b. In portions of the opinion omitted, the court held that first-degree felony murder could not stand because the evidence did not show a specific intent to commit the felony (sexual molestation of a minor) before or during the homicidal assault. Felony murder is considered in this chapter, Section C2 infra. — EDS.

The court reversed a first-degree murder conviction, holding that "the true test must include consideration of the somewhat limited extent to which this defendant could maturely and meaningfully reflect upon the gravity of his contemplated act" and concluding that, in view of the psychiatric evidence, the defendant could not be found to have met this test.

In 1981 the California legislature rejected this construction of premeditation and deliberation by adding a paragraph to California Penal Code §189 (see page 411 supra), stating that to prove a killing deliberate and premeditated, "it shall not be necessary to prove the defendant maturely and meaningfully reflected upon the gravity of his or her act." Cal. Senate Bill No. 54 (1981). This bill was part of a general legislative revolt against the use of psychiatric evidence to support interpretations of mens rea concepts at odds with traditional concepts. See the material on diminished capacity at pages 863-878 infra.

3. Use of the premeditation-deliberation formula as a basis for identifying murders deserving of the greatest punishment has been rejected by many of the recent criminal-law revisions (see, e.g., the New York provisions, page 413 supra), which followed the lead of the Model Penal Code in this respect. The Comment to §210.6 of the Model Penal Code criticized this formula as follows (American Law Institute, Model Penal Code and Commentaries, Pt. II, at 127-128 (1980)):

> [T]his distinction . . . probably rests on the premise that there exists some dependable relation between the duration of reflection and the gravity of the offense. Crudely put, the judgment is that the person who plans ahead is worse than the person who kills on sudden impulse. This generalization does not, however, survive analysis. . . .
>
> . . . [T]he case for a mitigated sentence on conviction of murder does not depend on a distinction between impulse and deliberation. Prior reflection may reveal the uncertainties of a tortured conscience rather than exceptional depravity. The very fact of a long internal struggle may be evidence that the homicidal impulse was deeply aberrational and far more the product of extraordinary circumstances than a true reflection of the actor's normal character. Thus, for example, one suspects that most mercy killings are the consequence of long and careful deliberation, but they are not especially appropriate cases for imposition of capital punishment. The same is likely to be true with respect to suicide pacts, many infanticides, and cases where a provocation gains in its explosive power as the actor broods about his injury.
>
> It also seems clear, moreover, that some purely impulsive murders will present no extenuating circumstance. The suddenness of the killing may simply reveal callousness so complete and depravity so extreme that no hesitation is required.
>
> . . . [T]he argument was advanced by the Home Office in testimony submitted to the Royal Commission on Capital Punishment:
>
> > Among the worst murders are some which are not premeditated, such as murders committed in connection with rape, or murders committed by criminals who are interrupted in some felonious enterprise and use violence without premeditation, but with a reckless disregard of the consequences to human life. . . . There are also many murders where the killing is clearly intentional, unlawful and unaccompanied by any mitigating circumstances, but where there is no evidence to show whether there was or was not premeditation.
>
> In short, the notion that prior reflection should distinguish capital from non-capital murder is fundamentally unsound.

2. The Provocation Formula

MAHER v. PEOPLE
Supreme Court of Michigan
10 Mich. 212, 81 Am. Dec. 781 (1862)

CHRISTIANCY, J. The prisoner was charged with an assault with intent to kill and murder one Patrick Hunt. The evidence on the part of the prosecution was, that the prisoner entered the saloon of one Michael Foley, in the village of Houghton, where said Hunt was standing with several other persons; that prisoner entered through a back door and by a back way leading to it, in his shirt sleeves, in a state of great perspiration, and appearing to be excited; and on being asked if he had been at work, said he had been across the lake; that on entering the saloon, he immediately passed nearly through it to where said Hunt was standing, and, on his way towards Hunt, said something, but it did not appear what, or to whom; that as soon as the prisoner came up to where Hunt was standing, he fired a pistol at Hunt, the charge of which took effect upon the head of Hunt, in and through the left ear, causing a severe wound thereon; by reason of which Hunt in a few moments fell to the floor, was partially deprived of his sense of hearing in that ear, and received a severe shock to his system which caused him to be confined to his bed for about a week, under the care of a physician; that immediately after the firing of the pistol prisoner left the saloon, nothing being said by Hunt or the prisoner. It did not appear how, or with what, the pistol was loaded. The prisoner offered evidence tending to show an adulterous intercourse between his wife and Hunt on the morning of the assault, and within less than half an hour previous; that the prisoner saw them going into the woods together about half an hour before the assault; that on their way out of the woods the prisoner followed them immediately (evidence having already been given that the prisoner had followed them to the woods); that, on their coming out of the woods, the prisoner followed them and went after said Hunt into the saloon, where, on his arrival, the assault was committed; that the prisoner on his way to the saloon, a few minutes before entering it, was met by a friend who informed him that Hunt and the prisoner's wife had had sexual intercourse the day before in the woods. This evidence was rejected by the court, and the prisoner excepted. Was the evidence properly rejected? This is the main question in the case, and its decision must depend upon the question whether the proposed evidence would have tended to reduce the killing — had death ensued — from murder to manslaughter, or rather, to have given it the character of manslaughter instead of murder? If the homicide — in case death had ensued — would have been but manslaughter, then defendant could not be guilty of the assault *with intent to murder,* but only of a simple assault and battery. The question therefore involves essentially the same principles as where evidence is offered for a similar purpose in a prosecution for murder; except that, in some cases of murder, an actual intention to kill need not exist; but in a prosecution for an assault *with intent* to murder, the actual intention to kill must be found, and that under circumstances which would make the killing murder. . . .

To give the homicide the legal character of murder, all the authorities agree that it must have been perpetrated with malice prepense or aforethought. . . .

It is not necessary here to enumerate all the elements which enter into the legal definition of malice aforethought. It is sufficient to say that, within the principle of all the recognized definitions, the homicide must, in all ordinary cases, have been committed with some degree of coolness and deliberation, or, at least, under circumstances in which ordinary men, or the average of men recognized as peaceable citizens, would not be liable to have their reason clouded or obscured by passion; and the act must be prompted by, or the circumstances indicate that it sprung from, a wicked, depraved or malignant mind — a mind which, even in its habitual condition, and when excited by no provocation which would be liable to give undue control to passion in ordinary men, is cruel, wanton or malignant, reckless of human life, or regardless of social duty.

But if the act of killing, though intentional, be committed under the influence of passion or in heat of blood, produced by an adequate or reasonable provocation, and before a reasonable time has elapsed for the blood to cool and reason to resume its habitual control, and is the result of the temporary excitement, by which the control of reason was disturbed, rather than of any wickedness of heart or cruelty or recklessness of disposition: then the law, out of indulgence to the frailty of human nature, or rather, in recognition of the laws upon which human nature is constituted, very properly regards the offense as of a less heinous character than murder, and gives it the designation of manslaughter.

To what extent the passions must be aroused and the dominion of reason disturbed to reduce the offense from murder to manslaughter, the cases are by no means agreed. . . .

The principle involved in the question, and which I think clearly deducible from the majority of well considered cases, would seem to suggest as the true general rule, that reason should, at the time of the act, be disturbed or obscured by passion to an extent which *might render* ordinary men, of fair average disposition, *liable* to act rashly or without due deliberation or reflection, and from passion, rather than judgment.

To the question, what shall be considered in law a reasonable or adequate provocation for such state of mind, so as to give to a homicide, committed under its influence, the character of manslaughter? on principle, the answer, as a general rule, must be, anything the natural tendency of which would be to produce such a state of mind in ordinary men, and which the jury are satisfied did produce it in the case before them — not such a provocation as must, by the laws of the human mind, produce such an effect with the *certainty that physical effects follow from physical causes;* for then the individual could hardly be held morally accountable. Nor, on the other hand, must the provocation, in every case, be held sufficient or reasonable, because such a state of excitement has followed from it; for then, by habitual and long continued indulgence of evil passions, a bad man might acquire a claim to mitigation which would not be available to better men, and on account of that very wickedness of heart which, in itself, constitutes an aggravation both in morals and in law.

In determining whether the provocation is sufficient or reasonable, *ordinary human nature,* or the average of men recognized as men of fair average mind and disposition, should be taken as the standard — unless, indeed, the person whose guilt is in question be shown to have some peculiar weakness of mind or infirmity of temper, not arising from wickedness of heart or cruelty of disposition.

It is doubtless, in one sense, the province of the court to define what, in law, will constitute a reasonable or adequate provocation, but not, I think, in ordinary cases, to determine whether the provocation proved in the particular case is sufficient or reasonable. This is essentially a question of fact, and to be decided with reference to the peculiar facts of each particular case. As a general rule, the court, after informing the jury to what extent the passions must be aroused and reason obscured to render the homicide manslaughter, should inform them that the provocation must be one, the *tendency* of which would be to produce such a degree of excitement and disturbance in the minds of ordinary men; and if they should find that it did produce that effect in the particular instance, and that the homicide was the result of such provocation, it would give it the character of manslaughter. Besides the consideration that the question is essentially one of fact, jurors from the mode of their selection, coming from the various classes and occupations of society, and conversant with the practical affairs of life, are, in my opinion, much better qualified to judge of the sufficiency and tendency of a given provocation and much more likely to fix, with some degree of accuracy, the standard of what constitutes the average of ordinary human nature, than the judge whose habits and course of life give him much less experience of the workings of passion in the actual conflicts of life.

The judge, it is true, must, to some extent, assume to decide upon the sufficiency of the alleged provocation, when the question arises upon the admission of testimony, and when it is so clear as to admit of no reasonable doubt upon any theory, that the alleged provocation could not have had any tendency to produce such state of mind, in ordinary men, he may properly exclude the evidence; but, if the alleged provocation be such as to admit of any reasonable doubt, whether it might not have had such tendency, it is much safer, I think, and more in accordance with principle, to let the evidence go to the jury under the proper instructions. As already intimated, the question of the reasonableness or adequacy of the provocation must depend upon the facts of each particular case. That can, with no propriety, be called a rule (or a question) of law which must vary with, and depend upon the almost infinite variety of facts presented by the various cases as they arise. The law can not with justice assume by the light of past decision, to catalogue all the various facts and combinations of facts which shall be held to constitute reasonable or adequate provocation. Scarcely two past cases can be found which are identical in all their circumstances; and there is no reason to hope for greater uniformity in future. Provocations will be given without reference to any previous model, and the passions they excite will not consult the precedents.

The same principles which govern, as to the extent to which the passions must be excited and reason disturbed, apply with equal force to the time during which its continuance may be recognized as a ground for mitigating the homicide to the degree of manslaughter, or, in other words, to the question of cooling time. This, like the provocation itself, must depend upon the nature of man and the laws of the human mind, as well as upon the nature and circumstances of the provocation, the extent to which the passions have been aroused, and the fact, whether the injury inflicted by the provocation is more or less permanent or irreparable. The passion excited by a blow received in a sudden quarrel, though perhaps equally violent for the moment, would be likely much sooner to subside than if aroused by rape committed upon a sister or a daughter, or the discovery of an adulterous intercourse with a wife; and no two cases of the latter kind would be likely to be identical in their circumstances of provocation. . . . I am aware there are many cases in which it has been held a question of law, but I can see no principle on which such a rule can rest. The court should, I think, define to the jury the principles upon which the question is to be decided, and leave them to determine whether the time was reasonable under all the circumstances of the particular case. I do not mean to say that the time may not be so great as to enable the court to determine that it is sufficient for the passion to have cooled, or so to instruct the jury, without error; but the case should be very clear. And in cases of applications for a new trial, depending upon the discretion of the court, the question may very properly be considered by the court.

It remains only to apply these principles to the present case. The proposed evidence, in connection with what had already been given, would have tended strongly to show the commission of adultery by Hunt with the prisoner's wife, within half an hour before the assault; that the prisoner saw them going to the woods together, under circumstances calculated strongly to impress upon his mind the belief of the adulterous purpose; that he followed after them to the woods; that Hunt and the prisoner's wife were, not long after, seen coming from the woods, and that the prisoner followed them, and went in hot pursuit after Hunt to the saloon, and was informed by a friend on the way that they had committed adultery the day before in the woods. I can not resist the conviction that this would have been sufficient evidence of provocation to go to the jury, and from which, when taken in connection with the excitement and "great perspiration" exhibited on entering the saloon, the hasty manner in which he approached and fired the pistol at Hunt, it would have been competent for the jury to find that the act was committed in consequence of the passion excited by the provocation, and in a state of mind which, within the principle already explained, would have given to the homicide had death ensued, the character of manslaughter only. In holding otherwise the court below was doubtless guided by those cases in which courts have arbitrarily assumed to take the question from the jury, and to decide upon the facts or some particular fact of the case, whether a sufficient provocation had been shown, and what was a reasonable time for cooling. . . .[a]

The judgment should be reversed and a new trial granted.

MANNING, J. I differ from my brethren in this case. I think the evidence was properly excluded. To make that manslaughter which would otherwise be murder, the provocation — I am not speaking of its sufficiency, but of the provocation itself — must be given in the presence of the person committing the homicide. The cause of the provocation must occur in his presence. . . . Any other rule in an offense so grave as taking the life of a fellow-being, in the heat of passion, I fear would be more humane to the perpetrator than wise in its effects on society. More especially since the abolition of the death penalty for murder, and the division of the crime into murder in the first and second degree there is not now the same reason, namely, the severity of the punishment, for relaxing

a. On allocating the burden of proving provocation, see Patterson v. New York, pages 67-75 supra. — EDS.

the rules of law in favor of a party committing homicide as before. It would, it seems to me, be extremely mischievous to let passion engendered by suspicion, or by something one has heard, enter into and determine the nature of a crime committed while under its influence. The innocent as well as the guilty, or those who had not as well as those who had given provocation, might be the sufferers. If it be said that in such cases the giving of the provocation must be proved or it would go for nothing; the answer is, that the law will not, and should not permit the lives of the innocent to be exposed with the guilty in this way, as it would do did it not require the cause of the provocation to occur in the presence of the person committing the homicide.

NOTES ON LEGALLY SUFFICIENT PROVOCATION

1. The provoking circumstances. The *Maher* case was ahead of its time. The traditional common law view, followed in most states until recently, did not permit a jury to return a verdict of manslaughter in any and all situations which the jury might find reasonably provocative. In only certain narrowly defined provoking circumstances, cases of "legally sufficient" provocation, would a jury be authorized to return a manslaughter verdict. The principal "legally sufficient" provocation was an actual physical battery (although there were others, such as personally witnessing a wife having sexual relations with another). Insulting words never sufficed except in the context of a threatened attack.

The justification for this restrictive view was stated as follows in Starr v. Starr, 38 Mo. 270, 277 (1886):

> To have the effect to reduce the guilt of killing to the lower grade, the provocation must consist of personal violence. This rule is well established, and we imagine it would not be the part of wisdom to substitute in its place one fluctuating or less rigid, which would require the accused to be judged in each case according to the excitement incident to his natural temperament when aroused by real or fancied insult given by words alone. There must be an assault upon the person, as where the provocation was by pulling the nose, purposely jostling the slayer aside in the highway, . . . or other direct and actual battery.

Bearing in mind that the choice is not guilt or innocence but guilt of murder (with a possible maximum punishment of death) or guilt of manslaughter (with a possible maximum punishment of life imprisonment), is the argument in *Starr* convincing? See generally Note, Provocation: The Reasonableness of the Reasonable Man, 106 U. Pa. L. Rev. 1021 (1958).

In the Homicide Act, 1957, England abandoned the requirement of legally sufficient provocation. Section 3 provides:

> Where on a charge of murder there is evidence on which the jury can find that the person charged was provoked (whether by things done or by things said or by both together) to lose his self-control, the question whether the provocation was enough to make a reasonable man do as he did shall be left to be determined by the jury; and in determining that question the jury shall take into account everything both done and said according to the effect which, in their opinion, it would have on a reasonable man.

The revised New York law (N.Y. Penal Law §125.25(1)(a), page 413 supra) reduces murder to voluntary manslaughter when the defendant

> acted under the influence of extreme emotional disturbance for which there was a reasonable explanation or excuse, the reasonableness of which is to be determined from the viewpoint of a person in the defendant's situation under the circumstances as the defendant believed them to be.

This adaptation of the Model Penal Code formulation (§210.3, Appendix to this casebook) has been followed in a number of states. See, e.g., Del. Code Ann., tit. II, §§632, 641; Or. Rev. Stat. §163.125; Utah Code Ann. §76-5-205.

Some states have used other formulas for departing from the rigid common law definition of legally adequate provocation. See, e.g., Ill. Ann. Stat. tit. 38, §9-2 ("sudden and intense passion resulting from serious provocation," defined as "conduct sufficient to excite an intense passion in a reasonable person"); Minn. Stat. Ann. §609.20 ("heat of passion provoked by such words or acts of another as would provoke a person of ordinary self-control under like circumstances"); Tex. Pen. Code §19.04 ("sudden passion arising from an adequate cause," defined as that which "would commonly produce a degree of anger, rage, resentment, or terror in a person of ordinary temper, sufficient to render the mind incapable of cool reflection"); Ohio Rev. Code tit. 29, §2903.03 ("extreme emotional stress brought on by serious provocation reasonably sufficient to incite him into using deadly force").

Other states have departed from the common law by judicial decisions. See, e.g., People v. Valentine, 28 Cal. 2d 121, 169 P.2d 1 (1946); Commonwealth v. McCusker, 448 Pa. 382, 292 A.2d 286 (1972).

2. Cooling time. Contrary also to the decision in the *Maher* case, the common law view was that too long a lapse of time between the provocation and the act would render the provocation inadequate "as a matter of law" and therefore deprive defendant of the benefit of a jury instruction on manslaughter. People v. Ashland, 20 Cal. App. 168, 128 P. 798 (1912), affords an example. Defendant searched for some 17 hours before finding and killing the man he believed to have raped his wife. On appeal from a conviction of murder, the appellate court upheld the trial court's refusal to give the jury a manslaughter instruction, stating:

> While the taking of life in the heat of passion will make the crime manslaughter, it will be conclusively inferred that the homicide was not committed in the heat of passion from the fact of the intervention of a long period of time between the provocation and the act of killing. In other words . . . the law will not permit the defendant to deliberate upon his wrong and, avenging it by killing the wrong-doer, set up the plea that his act was committed in the heat of passion.

This approach attributes substantive significance to the lapse of time between the provocation and the act: If it is too long, in the view of the court, provocation may not be found. The competing view, now more generally accepted, is exemplified in a later decision of the California Supreme Court, People v. Berry, 18 Cal. 3d 509, 556 P.2d 777 (1976). Here defendant waited for his victim in her apartment for 20 hours before killing her. The court held that the defendant was nevertheless entitled to a manslaughter instruction, since the jury could find that defendant's heat of passion resulted from a long-smoldering prior course of provocative conduct by the victim, the wait serving to aggravate rather than cool defendant's agitation. On this view, cooling time is treated as an evidentiary consideration to be evaluated by the jury under all the circumstances. This treatment of cooling time is made explicit in the following Georgia provision (Ga. Code Ann. §26-1102):

> If there should have been an interval between the provocation and the killing sufficient for the voice of reason and humanity to be heard, of which the jury in all cases shall be the judge, the killing shall be attributed to deliberate revenge and be punished as murder.

PROBLEM

Even under the modern view, which makes the reasonableness of the provocation a jury issue, should there be an exception when the defendant is at fault in creating the circumstances that led the victim to provoke him? See, e.g., Edwards v. Regina, [1973] 1 All E.R. 152 (P.C. 1972), where defendant killed in response to a violent assault by deceased, which in turn had been produced by defendant's attempts to blackmail deceased. The trial judge directed the jury:

> in my view the defence of provocation cannot be of any avail to the accused in this case. Provocation . . . is undoubtedly a valid legal defence in certain circumstances, but you may well think that it ill befits the accused in this case, having gone there with the deliberate purpose of blackmailing this man — you may well think that it ill befits him to say out of his own mouth that he was provoked by any attack. In my view the defence of provocation is not one which you need consider in this case.

Was this error? Some recent statutory formulations take a stand on this issue. Oregon, for example, permits reduction of the charge to manslaughter only when the extreme emotional disturbance "is not the result of the person's own intentional, knowing, reckless or criminally neligent act." Or. Rev. Stat. ch. 166, §163.115(2).

DIRECTOR OF PUBLIC PROSECUTIONS v. CAMPLIN
House of Lords
[1978] 2 All E.R. 168

LORD DIPLOCK. My Lords, for the purpose of answering the question of law on which this appeal will turn only a brief account is needed of the facts that have given rise to it. The respondent, Camplin, who was 15 years of age, killed a middle-aged Pakistani, Mohammed Lal Khan, by splitting his skull with a chapati pan, a heavy kitchen utensil like a rimless frying pan. At the time the two of them were alone together in Khan's flat. At Camplin's trial for murder before Boreham, J., his only defence was that of provocation so as to reduce the offence to manslaughter. According to the story that he told in the witness box but which differed materially from that which he had told to the police, Khan had buggered him in spite of his resistance and had then laughed at him, whereupon Camplin had lost his self-control and attacked Khan fatally with the chapati pan.

In his address to the jury on the defence of provocation, counsel for Camplin had suggested to them that when they addressed their minds to the question whether the provocation relied on was enough to make a reasonable man do as Camplin had done, what they ought to consider was not the reaction of a reasonable adult but the reaction of a reasonable boy of Camplin's age. The judge thought that this was wrong in law. So in this summing-up he took pains to instruct the jury that they must consider whether —

> the provocation was sufficient to make a reasonable man in like circumstances act as the defendant did. Not a reasonable boy, as [counsel for Camplin] would have it, or a reasonable lad; it is an objective test — a reasonable man.

The jury found Camplin guilty of murder. On appeal the Court of Appeal, Criminal Division, allowed the appeal and substituted a conviction for manslaughter on the ground that the passage I have cited from the summing-up was a misdirection. The court held that —

> the proper direction to the jury is to invite the jury to consider whether the provocation was enough to have made a reasonable person of the same age as the appellant in the same circumstances do as he did.

The point of law of general public importance involved in the case has been certified as being:

> Whether, on the prosecution for murder of a boy of 15, where the issue of provocation arises, the jury should be directed to consider the question, under S. 3 of the Homicide Act 1957, whether the provocation was enough to make a reasonable man do as he did by reference to a "reasonable adult" or by reference to a "reasonable boy of 15."

/Maturity

My Lords, the doctrine of provocation in crimes of homicide has always represented an anomaly in English law. In crimes of violence which result in injury short of death, the fact that the act of violence was committed under provocation, which has caused the accused to lose his self-control, does not affect the nature of the offence of which he is guilty; it is merely a matter to be taken into consideration in determining the penalty which it is appropriate to impose: whereas in homicide provocation effects a change in the offence itself from murder, for which the penalty is fixed by law (formerly death and now imprisonment for life), to the lesser offence of manslaughter, for which the penalty is in the discretion of the judge. . . .

[Lord Diplock then surveyed the development of the doctrine of provocation at common law and concluded that a question in this appeal was the extent to which propositions of law laid down in several leading cases — in particular,

Bedder v. Director of Public Prosecutions, [1954] All E.R. 801 — were affected by §3 of the Homicide Act of 1957.[a] Turning to *Bedder,* he continued:]

. . . The accused had killed a prostitute. He was sexually impotent. According to his evidence he had tried to have sexual intercourse with her and failed. She taunted him with his failure and tried to get away from his grasp. In the course of her attempts to do so she slapped him in the face, punched him in the stomach and kicked him in the groin, whereupon he took a knife out of his pocket and stabbed her twice and caused her death. The struggle that led to her death thus started because the deceased taunted the accused with his physicial infirmity; but in the state of the law as it then was, taunts unaccompanied by any physicial violence did not constitute provocation. The taunts were followed by violence on the part of the deceased in the course of her attempt to get away from the accused [she kicked him in the genitals], and it may be that this subsequent violence would have a greater effect on the self-control of an impotent man already enraged by the taunts than it would have had on a person conscious of possessing normal physical attributes. So there might be some justification for the judge to instruct the jury to ignore the fact that the accused was impotent when they were considering whether the deceased's conduct amounted to such provocation as would cause a reasonable or ordinary person to lose his self-control. This indeed appears to have been the ground on which the Court of Criminal Appeal had approved the summing-up when they said:

> . . . no distinction is to be made in the case of a person who, though it may not be a matter of temperament, is physically impotent, is conscious of that impotence, *and therefore mentally liable to be more excited unduly* if he is "twitted" or attacked on the subject of that particular infirmity.

This statement, for which I have myself supplied the emphasis, was approved by Lord Simonds, L.C., speaking on behalf of all the members of this House who sat on the appeal; but he also went on to lay down the broader proposition that:

> It would be plainly illogical not to recognise an unusually excitable or pugnacious temperament in the accused as a matter to be taken into account but yet to recognise for that purpose some unusual physical characteristic, be it impotence or another. . . .

My Lords, [Section 3 of the 1957 Act] was intended to mitigate in some degree the harshness of the common law of provocation as it had been developed by recent decisions in this House. It recognizes and retains the dual test: the provocation must not only have caused the accused to lose his self-control but also be such as' might cause a reasonable man to react to it as the accused did. Nevertheless it brings about two important changes in the law. The first is it abolishes all previous rules of law as to what can or cannot amount to provocation and in particular the rule of law that, save in the two exceptional cases I have mentioned, words unaccompanied by violence could not do so. Secondly it makes it clear that if there was any evidence that the accused himself at the time of the act which caused the death in fact lost his self-control in

a. Reprinted at page 430 supra.—Eds.

consequence of some provocation however slight it might appear to the judge, he was bound to leave to the jury the question, which is one of opinion not of law, whether a reasonable man might have reacted to that provocation as the accused did. . . .

The public policy that underlay the adoption of the "reasonable man" test in the common law doctrine of provocation was to reduce the incidence of fatal violence by preventing a person relying on his own exceptional pugnacity or excitability as an excuse for loss of self-control. The rationale of the test may not be easy to reconcile in logic with more universal propositions as to the mental element in crime. Nevertheless it has been preserved by the 1957 Act but falls to be applied now in the context of a law of provocation that is significantly different from what it was before the Act was passed.

Although it is now for the jury to apply the "reasonable man" test, it still remains for the judge to direct them what, in the new context of the section, is the meaning of this apparently inapt expression, since powers of ratiocination bear no obvious relationships to powers of self-control. Apart from this the judge is entitled, if he thinks it helpful, to suggest considerations which may influence the jury in forming their own opinions as to whether the test is satisfied; but he should make it clear that these are not instructions which they are required to follow: it is for them and no one else to decide what weight, if any, ought to be given to them.

As I have already pointed out, for the purposes of the law of provocation the "reasonable man" has never been confined to the adult male. It means an ordinary person of either sex, not exceptionally excitable or pugnacious, but possessed of such powers of self-control as everyone is entitled to expect that his fellow citizens will exercise in society as it is today. A crucial factor in the defence of provocation from earliest times has been the relationship between the gravity of provocation and the way in which the accused retaliated, both being judged by the social standards of the day. When Hale was writing in the 17th century pulling a man's nose was thought to justify retaliation with a sword: when *Mancini* [[1942] A. C. 1] was decided by this House, a blow with a fist would not justify retaliation with a deadly weapon. But so long as words unaccompanied by violence could not in common law amount to provocation the relevant proportionality between provocation and retaliation was primarily one of degrees of violence. Words spoken to the accused before the violence started were not normally to be included in the proportion sum. But now that the law has been changed so as to permit of words being treated as provocation, even though unaccompanied by any other acts, the gravity of verbal provocation may well depend on the particular characteristics or circumstances of the person to whom a taunt or insult is addressed. To taunt a person because of his race, his physical infirmities or some shameful incident in his past may well be considered by the jury to be more offensive to the person addressed, however equable his temperament, if the facts on which the taunt is founded are true than it would be if they were not. It would stultify much of the mitigation of the previous harshness of the common law in ruling out verbal provocation as capable of reducing murder to manslaughter if the jury could not take into consideration all those factors which in their opinion would affect the gravity of taunts and insults when applied to the person to whom they are addressed. So to this extent at any rate the unqualified proposition accepted by this House in *Bedder*

[[1954] All E.R. 801] that for the purposes of the "reasonable man" test any unusual physical characteristics of the accused must be ignored requires revision as a result of the passing of the 1957 Act.

That he was only 15 years of age at the time of the killing is the relevant characteristic of the accused in the instant case. It is a characteristic which may have its effects on temperament as well as physique. If the jury think that the same power of self-control is not to be expected in an ordinary, average or normal boy of 15 as in an older person, are they to treat the lesser powers of self-control possessed by an ordinary, average or normal boy of 15 as the standard of self-control with which the conduct of the accused is to be compared?

It may be conceded that in strict logic there is a transition between treating age as a characteristic that may be taken into account in assessing the gravity of the provocation addressed to the accused and treating it as a characteristic to be taken into account in determining what is the degree of self-control to be expected of the ordinary person with whom the accused's conduct is to be compared. But to require old heads on young shoulders is inconsistent with the law's compassion of human infirmity to which Sir Michael Foster ascribed the doctrine of provocation more than two centuries ago. The distinction as to the purpose for which it is legitimate to take the age of the accused into account involves considerations of too great nicety to warrant a place in deciding a matter of opinion, which is no longer one to be decided by a judge trained in logical reasoning but by a jury drawing on their experience of how ordinary human beings behave in real life. . . .

In my opinion a proper direction to a jury on the question left to their exclusive determination by S. 3 of the 1957 Act would be on the following lines. The judge should state what the question is, using the very terms of the section. He should then explain to them that the reasonable man referred to in the question is a person having the power of self-control to be expected of an ordinary person of the sex and age of the accused, but in other respects sharing such of the accused's characteristics as they think would affect the gravity of the provocation to him, and that the question is not merely whether such a person would in like circumstances be provoked to lose his self-control but also would react to the provocation as the accused did. . . .

LORD SIMON OF GLAISDALE. . . . The original reasons in this branch of the law were largely reasons of the heart and of common sense, not the reasons of pure juristic logic. . . . But justice and common sense then demanded some limitation: it would be unjust that the drunk man or one exceptionally pugnacious or bad-tempered or over-sensitive should be able to claim that these matters rendered him peculiarly susceptible to the provocation offered, where the sober and even-tempered man would hang for his homicide. Hence . . . the development of the concept of the reaction of a reasonable man to the provocation offered. . . .

The provision that words alone can constitute provocation accentuates the anomalies, inconveniences and injustices liable to follow from the *Bedder* decision. The effect of an insult will often depend entirely on a characteristic of a person to whom the insult is directed. "Dirty nigger" would probably mean little if said to a white man or even if said by one coloured man to another, but is obviously more insulting when said by a white man to a coloured man. Similarly, such an expression as "Your character is as crooked as your back" would have a different connotation to a hunchback on the one hand and to a man with a back like a ramrod on the other. . . .

. . . In my judgment the reference to "a reasonable man" at the end of the section means "a man of ordinary self-control." If this is so the meaning satisfies what I have ventured to suggest as the reasons for importing into this branch of the law the concept of the reasonable man, namely to avoid the injustice of a man being entitled to rely on his exceptional excitability (whether idiosyncratic or by cultural environment or ethnic origin) or pugnacity or ill-temper or on his drunkenness (I do not purport to be exhaustive in this enumeration).

I think that the standard of self-control which the law requires before provocation is held to reduce murder to manslaughter is still that of the reasonable person (hence his invocation in S. 3 of the 1957 Act), but that, in determining whether a person of reasonable self-control would lose it in the circumstances, the entire factual situation which includes the characteristics of the accused, must be considered. . . .[b]

PROBLEM

In Regina v. Newell, 71 Crim. App. 331 (1981), defendant, a long-time alcoholic, was convicted of the murder of a friend. During a drinking session, after both had become drunk, the friend insulted defendant's mistress and then made homosexual advances to defendant. Defendant became enraged and battered his friend to death with an ashtray. The trial judge instructed the jurors that, in applying the objective element of the provocation test, they should apply the standard of the reasonable, sober man. The Court of Appeal upheld the conviction, holding that even if the alcoholism of defendant was a factor to be taken into account under the *Camplin* case, there had to be some reference to that fact in the provoking circumstances, such, for example, as a reference to his drinking habits.

Query: Can this decision be reconciled with the *Camplin* case? The case is commented on in Note, The Provok'd Drunk, 44 Mod. L. Rev. 567 (1981).

NOTES

1. Should there be an objective element of provocation at all? See Williams, Provocation and the Reasonable Man, [1954] Crim. L. Rev. 740, 741-742, 751-752:

It is . . . an easy transition from saying that the law makes reasonable allowance for provocation to saying that the test of provocation is the behaviour of the reasonable or ordinary man. . . .

b. Compare §169 of the New Zealand Crimes Act of 1961: "(1) Culpable homicide that would otherwise be murder may be reduced to manslaughter if the person who caused the death did so under provocation. (2) Anything done or said may be provocation if — (a) In the circumstances of the case it was sufficient to deprive a person having the power of self-control of an ordinary person, but otherwise having the characteristics of the offender, of the power of self-control; and (b) It did in fact deprive the offender of the power of self-control and thereby induced him to commit the act of homicide." For a discussion of this provision see F. B. Adams, Criminal Law and Practice in New Zealand 343-346 (1971). — EDS.

Plausible as this formulation may appear, it creates a serious problem. In the law of contract and tort, and elsewhere in the criminal law, the test of the reasonable man indicates an ethical standard; but it seems absurd to say that the reasonable man will commit a felony the possible punishment for which is imprisonment for life. To say that the "ordinary" man will commit this felony is hardly less absurd. The reason why provoked homicide is punished is to deter people from committing the offence; and it is curious confession of failure on the part of the law to suppose that, notwithstanding the possibility of heavy punishment, an ordinary person will commit it. If the assertion were correct, it would raise serious doubts whether the offence should continue to be punished.

Surely the true view of provocation is that it is a concession to "the frailty of human nature" in those exceptional cases where the legal prohibition fails of effect. It is a compromise, neither conceding the propriety of the act nor exacting the full penalty for it. This being so, how can it be admitted that that paragon of virtue, the reasonable man, gives way to provocation? . . .

A curious error of reasoning seems to have been committed by some judges in supporting the reasonable-man test. In *Lesbini* [1914] 3 K.B. 1116, Avory, J., in support of the rule that mental unbalance was irrelevant, said that if the law were otherwise a bad-tempered man would be entitled to a verdict of manslaughter where a good-tempered one would be liable to be convicted of murder. Other judges supported the reasonable-man test before the Royal Commission on Capital Punishment for the same reason, and with some hesitation the Commission accepted the argument (Cmd. 8932, paras. 139-45).[a] However, reflection will perhaps show that the argument is mistaken. Even under the law as it stands, a bad-tempered man may be entitled to be acquitted of murder where a good-tempered one may be liable to be convicted. . . . Ever since the time of East the legal requirement has been that the accused should have acted in the heat of passion or in blind rage; and the question whether he acted in this way or with cool calculation is one of fact. This rule, which has never been questioned, does, therefore, discriminate between good-tempered and bad-tempered men, to the advantage of the latter. The only way of removing from the law the privilege given by bad temper would be by abolishing the law of provocation; for good-tempered men are never provoked to kill. The good-tempered man may, of course, kill from a motive of gain or other profit, but by definition he does not kill from bad temper, which is the only sort of killing with which provocation deals.

Consider the following defense of the objective element in Michael & Wechsler, A Rationale of the Law of Homicide, 37 Colum. L. Rev. 1261, 1281-1282 (1937):

Provocation may be greater or less, but it cannot be measured by the intensity of the passions aroused in the actor by the provocative circumstances. It must be

a. Paragraph 143: "It is a fundamental principle of the criminal law that it should be based on a generally accepted standard of conduct applicable to all citizens alike, and it is important that this principle should not be infringed. Any departure from it might introduce a dangerous latitude into the law. Those idiosyncrasies of individual temperament or mentality that make a man more easily provoked, or more violent in his response to provocation, ought not, therefore, to affect his liability to conviction, although they may justify mitigation of sentence." Cf. Model Penal Code §201.3, Comment at 48 n. 13 (Tent. Draft No. 9, 1959): "The Royal Commission on Capital Punishment found 'serious objections of principle' to the abrogation of the 'reasonable man' test, namely, that the criminal law 'should be based on a generally accepted standard of conduct applicable to all citizens alike,' but nevertheless expressed 'sympathy with the view which prompted the proposal that provocation should be judged by the standard of the accused.' This is to treat the issue, however, as if the definition of criminality were involved rather than a mitigation for the purposes of sentence."— EDS.

estimated by the probability that such circumstances would affect most men in like fashion; although the passions stirred up in the actor were violent, the provocation can be said to be great only if the provocative circumstances would have aroused in most men similar desires of comparable intensity. Other things being equal, the greater the provocation, measured in that way, the more ground there is for attributing the intensity of the actor's passions and his lack of self-control on the homicidal occasion to the extraordinary character of the situation in which he was placed rather than to any extraordinary deficiency in his own character. While it is true, it is also beside the point, that most men do not kill on even the gravest provocation; the point is that the more strongly they would be moved to kill by circumstances of the sort which provoked the actor to the homicidal act, and the more difficulty they would experience in resisting the impulse to which he yielded, the less does his succumbing serve to differentiate his character from theirs. But the slighter the provocation, the more basis there is for ascribing the actor's act to an extraordinary susceptibility to intense passion, to an unusual deficiency in those other desires which counteract in most men the desires which impel them to homicidal acts, or to an extraordinary weakness of reason and consequent inability to bring such desires into play.

Cf. J. W. Salmond, Jurisprudence 440 (8th ed. 1930).

2. *Statutory reform.* The argument for eliminating the objective element of provocation has made very small headway. One rare example is the new New Hampshire code which, omitting any requirement of reasonableness, reduces murder to manslaughter where a person kills another "under the influence of extreme mental or emotional disturbance." N.H. Rev. Stat. Ann. §630:2.

The Model Penal Code retains the objective element but qualifies it in a way consonant with the *Camplin* case. Section 210.3 provides:

> (1) Criminal homicide constitutes manslaughter when: . . .
> (b) a homicide which would otherwise be murder is committed under the influence of extreme mental or emotional disturbance for which there is a reasonable explanation or excuse. The reasonableness of such explanation or excuse shall be determined from the viewpoint of a person in the actor's situation under the circumstances as he believes them to be.

In defense of this formulation, the reporters state as follows (American Law Institute, Model Penal Code and Commentaries, Pt. II, Comment to §210.3 at 62-63 (1980)):

> The critical element in the Model Code formulation is the clause requiring that reasonableness be assessed "from the viewpoint of a person in the actor's situation." The word "situation" is designedly ambiguous. On the one hand, it is clear that personal handicaps and some external circumstances must be taken into account. Thus, blindness, shock from traumatic injury, and extreme grief are all easily read into the term "situation." This result is sound, for it would be morally obtuse to appraise a crime for mitigation of punishment without reference to these factors. On the other hand, it is equally plain that idiosyncratic moral values are not part of the actor's situation. An assassin who kills a political leader because he believes it is right to do so cannot ask that he be judged by the standard of a reasonable extremist. Any other result would undermine the normative message of the criminal law. In between these two extremes, however, there are matters neither as clearly distinct from individual blameworthiness as blindness or handicap nor as integral

a part of moral depravity as a belief in the rightness of killing. Perhaps the classic illustration is the unusual sensitivity to the epithet "bastard" of a person born illegitimate. An exceptionally punctilious sense of personal honor or an abnormally fearful temperament may also serve to differentiate an individual actor from the hypothetical reasonable man, yet none of these factors is wholly irrelevant to the ultimate issue of culpability. The proper role of such factors cannot be resolved satisfactorily by abstract definition of what may constitute adequate provocation. The Model Code endorses a formulation that affords sufficient flexibility to differentiate in particular cases between those special aspects of the actor's situation that should be deemed material for purpose of grading and those that should be ignored. There thus will be room for interpretation of the word "situation," and that is precisely the flexibility desired. There will be opportunity for argument about the reasonableness of explanation or excuse, and that too is a ground on which argument is required. In the end, the question is whether the actor's loss of self-control can be understood in terms that arouse sympathy in the ordinary citizen. Section 210.3 faces this issue squarely and leaves the ultimate judgment to the ordinary citizen in the function of a juror assigned to resolve the specific case.

3. The California Supreme Court found in the statutory requirement of malice a basis for imparting a subjective test into the voluntary manslaughter charge. People v. Conley, 64 Cal. 2d 310, 411 P.2d 911 (1966). After defendant's lover told him that she was ending their affair in order to return to her husband, defendant bought a rifle, practiced shooting with it, and announced to friends that he intended to kill the couple. One evening he drank a great deal with friends and rejected their efforts to dissuade him from his plan. He took the rifle, went to the couple's home, and fired four shots, killing both husband and wife. A defense psychologist testified that defendant was in a dissociative state of mind and, because of personality fragmentation, did not function with his normal personality. On appeal of a first-degree murder conviction, the defendant charged error in the failure of the trial court to give a voluntary-manslaughter instruction. The court agreed and reversed the conviction. It interpreted "malice," whose presence was necessary for murder, to require that the defendant have an ability "to comprehend his duty to govern his actions in accordance with the duty imposed by law." In view of the evidence of defendant's intoxication and of its effect on him, therefore, the court held that the jury should have been permitted to return a verdict of voluntary manslaughter.

The approach of the California Supreme Court was not influential with other courts (but see State v. Santiago, 55 Hawaii 162, 516 P.2d 1256 (1973)), and the application of *Conley* to a notorious case involving the assassination of San Francisco Mayor George Moscone and Supervisor Harvey Milk eventuated in legislation to overrule it. An amendment to §188 of the Cal. Penal Code (see page 410 supra) now reads:

> When it is shown that the killing resulted from the intentional doing of an act with express or implied malice as defined above, no other mental state need be shown to establish the mental state of malice aforethought. An awareness of the obligation to act within the general body of laws regulating society is not included within the definition of malice.

Cal. Senate Bill No. 54 (1981). This amendment was part of the same bill that overruled People v. Wolff, discussed at page 424 supra.

The doctrine of People v. Conley was no more popular with academic commentators than with the public. See Johnson, Foreword: The Accidental Decision and How It Happens, 65 Calif. L. Rev. 231, 239-243 (1977); Morse, Diminished Capacity: A Moral and Legal Conundrum, 2 Intl. J.L. & Psych. 271, 281-283. Consider the observations in American Law Institute, Model Penal Code and Commentaries, Pt. II, Comment to §210.3 at 70-71 (1980):

> Very few jurisdictions allow mental disease or defect to reduce intentional homicide to manslaughter. Traditionally, such mitigation arises only from the rule of provocation. As the earlier discussion makes clear, provocation has been a predominantly objective determination. . . . It seeks to identify cases of intentional homicide where the situation is as much to blame as the actor. Recognizing diminished responsibility as an alternative ground for reducing murder to manslaughter undermines this scheme. Unlike provocation, diminished responsibility is entirely subjective in character. . . . It recognizes the defendant's own mental disorder or emotional instability as a basis for partially excusing his conduct. This position undoubtedly achieves a closer relation between criminal liability and moral guilt. . . . But this approach has its costs. By evaluating the abnormal individual on his own terms, it decreases the incentives for him to behave as if he were normal. . . . And the factors that call for mitigation under this doctrine are the very aspects of an individual's personality that make us most fearful of his future conduct. In short, diminished responsibility brings formal guilt more closely into line with moral blameworthiness, but only at the cost of driving a wedge between dangerousness and social control.

C. LEGISLATIVE GRADING OF UNINTENDED KILLINGS

1. The Creation of Homicidal Risk

The material in this section is organized around the following issues:

Section C1a deals with the criteria for establishing criminal, as opposed to solely civil, liability for unintended homicide.

Section C1b raises the issue whether criminal liability for unintended homicide should rest on a subjective or objective standard.

Section C1c considers the special circumstances that may make an unintended killing murder.

Section C1d considers the case for treating the criminality or punishment of reckless conduct differently depending on whether or not death actually results.

a. Distinguishing Civil and Criminal Liability

STATE v. BARNETT
Supreme Court of South Carolina
218 S.C. 415, 63 S.E.2d 57 (1951)

Oxner, J. Appellant was convicted of involuntary manslaughter. It was alleged in the indictment that the homicide resulted from criminal negligence in the operation of an automobile. The exceptions on this appeal relate solely to the charge. . . .

Error is assigned in the instructions relating to the degree of negligence necessary to sustain a conviction of involuntary manslaughter. It is said that the Court erred in charging that ordinary negligence is sufficient and that the jury should have been instructed that it was incumbent upon the State to show gross negligence or recklessness.

After defining involuntary manslaughter and distinguishing that offense from voluntary manslaughter, the Court stated that involuntary manslaughter may consist in the "killing of another without malice and unintentionally, but while one is engaged in the commission of some unlawful act not amounting to a felony and not naturally tending to cause death or great bodily harm," or in "the killing of another without malice and unintentionally but while one is negligently engaged in doing a lawful act." The jury was given the usual definition of negligence but was not instructed as to gross negligence, recklessness or wantonness. . . .

The degree of negligence necessary to establish criminal liability has perplexed the courts of England and America for centuries. The subject has at times been the source of much confusion. In the early development of the criminal law in England it was held that ordinary negligence, that is, the failure to exercise due care, was sufficient. Later it was found that this rule was too harsh. A noted English authority observed that an accident brought about by an act of ordinary negligence "may be the lot of even the wisest and the best of mankind." The English courts finally concluded that more carelessness was required to create criminal liability than civil but they found it difficult to determine "how much more." They use such words as "gross," "reckless" and "culpable," and hold that it is for the jury to decide, in view of all the circumstances, whether the act was of such character as to be worthy of punishment. . . . There was a tendency in the early American decisions to follow the rule first adopted in England to the effect that ordinary negligence was sufficient. That standard was soon repudiated, however, by the great majority of the courts in this country and it is now generally held that the negligence of the accused must be "culpable," "gross," or "reckless," that is, the conduct of the accused must be such a departure from what would be the conduct of an ordinarily prudent or careful man under the same circumstances as to be incompatible with a proper regard for human life, or conduct amounting to an indifference to consequences. Of course, under all the authorities the conduct of the accused must be judged in the light of the potential danger involved in the lawful act being performed. In perhaps a majority of the states, the offense of involuntary manslaughter is now defined by statute. Although variously worded, these statutes, with a few exceptions, have been construed as requiring gross negligence or recklessness.

Adverting now to homicides resulting from the operation of automobiles, in almost all jurisdictions, either by statute or by application of the rule governing involuntary manslaughter at common law, the rule is that the negligence necessary to convict a motorist of involuntary manslaughter must be of a higher degree than is required to establish negligent default on a mere civil issue and that the proof must show recklessness or such carelessness as is incompatible with proper regard for human life. . . . Most courts have refused to consider an automobile as an inherently dangerous instrumentality so as to warrant the application of the "deadly weapon" rule. [The court then reviewed the South Carolina authorities.]

It seems to be thoroughly settled by the foregoing decisions that where the instrument involved is not inherently dangerous, we follow the general rule requiring more than ordinary negligence to support a conviction for involuntary manslaughter, but hold that simple negligence causing the death of another is sufficient if the instrumentality is of such character that its negligent use under the surrounding circumstances is necessarily dangerous to human life or limb. This Court is also committed to the view that firearms and motor vehicles fall within the latter category. . . . [T]he rationale of this distinction . . . may perhaps be explained upon the theory that want of ordinary care in the handling of a dangerous instrumentality is the equivalent of culpable or gross negligence. . . .

We have reviewed at great length . . . the decisions in this State, as well as the authorities elsewhere, relating to involuntary manslaughter. This has been deemed necessary in deciding whether we should adhere to the rule that an automobile is an instrumentality of such character that simple negligence in its operation is sufficient to support the common law offense of involuntary manslaughter. It must be conceded that only scant support can be found for this rule in other jurisdictions. But public policy requires that due consideration should be given to the principle of stare decisis. . . . If a change or modification is desirable, it should come from the law-making body.

TAYLOR J., and the writer desire to say that they regard the simple negligence rule in automobile homicide cases as too harsh and if the question were one of original impression, they would not be in favor of adopting it.

NOTE ON CONTRIBUTORY NEGLIGENCE

In civil cases the effect of the deceased's contributory negligence has traditionally been to preclude imposing liability on the defendant. (Recent adoption of comparative negligence in some jurisdictions is an exception to this general approach.) In criminal cases, however, the deceased's negligence or other misconduct does not have this consequence: It does not bear on the defendant's liability except as an evidentiary consideration relevant to a finding of causation. See State v. Williams, 238 Iowa 838, 844, 28 N.W.2d 514, 518 (1947):

> The defendant, under the statute, had the right to assume that others were not violating the law, but this right gave him no excuse heedlessly and recklessly to endanger the safety of others, whether violating the law or not. As we have said, it might be urged as a defense in a civil action that the plaintiff was guilty of contributory negligence, but the law was not designed merely for the protection of those innocent of negligence, but of all persons. The court . . . correctly instructed that if the proximate cause of the collision and death of June LaVelle Davy was her own negligence and conduct then the defendant must be acquitted, but that on the other hand if she, by her own negligence and conduct, contributed to her own death, that would not relieve the defendant of criminal responsibility if the jury found that her death was naturally and proximately caused by the doing by the defendant of an unlawful act or acts as defined, in such a manner as to

show a wanton and reckless disregard of and indifference to the safety of other persons who might be reasonably expected to be injured thereby.

What suffices to establish legally sufficient cause also is not necessarily the same in civil and criminal cases. See Chapter 7, Section A, Causation, infra.

NOTE ON DEFINING UNINTENDED CRIMINAL HOMICIDE

A persistent problem faced by the courts and legislatures has been the formulation of the "extra" or "plus" qualities that differentiate unintended homicides that give rise to criminal liability from those that, at most, produce civil liability for negligence. Consider the following formulations:

Andrews v. Director of Public Prosecutions, [1937] A.C. 576, 581-583: My Lords, of all crimes manslaughter appears to afford more difficulties of definition, for it concerns homicide in so many and so varying conditions. From the early days when any homicide involved penalty the law has gradually evolved "through successive differentiations and integrations" until it recognizes murder on the one hand, based mainly, though not exclusively, on an intention to kill, and manslaughter on the other hand, based mainly, though not exclusively, on the absence of intention to kill but with the presence of an element of "unlawfulness" which is the elusive factor. In the present case it is only necessary to consider manslaughter from the point of view of an unintentional killing caused by negligence, that is, the omission of a duty to take care. . . .

Expressions will be found which indicate that to cause death by any lack of due care will amount to manslaughter; but as manners softened and the law became more humane a narrower criterion appeared. After all, manslaughter is a felony, and was capital, and men shrank from attaching the serious consequences of a conviction for felony to results produced by mere inadvertence. The stricter view became apparent in prosecutions of medical men or men who professed medical or surgical skill for manslaughter by reason of negligence. . . . So . . . in Rex v. Bateman [19 Crim. App. 8] a charge of manslaughter was made against a qualified medical practitioner in similar circumstances to those of *Williamson*'s case. In a considered judgment of the Court the Lord Chief Justice, after pointing out that in a civil case once negligence is proved the degree of negligence is irrelevant, said, "In a criminal Court, on the contrary, the amount and degree of negligence are the determining question. There must be mens rea." After citing Cashill v. Wright [[1856] 6 E. & B. 891], a civil case, the Lord Chief Justice proceeds: "In explaining to juries the test which they should apply to determine whether the negligence, in the particular case, amounted or did not amount to a crime, judges have used many epithets such as 'culpable,' 'criminal,' 'gross,' 'wicked,' 'clear,' 'complete.' But whatever epithet be used and whether an epithet be used or not, in order to establish criminal liability the facts must be such that, in the opinion of the jury, the negligence of the accused went beyond a mere matter of compensation between subjects and showed such disregard for the life and safety of others as to amount to a crime against the State and conduct deserving punishment." . . .

I think with respect that the expressions used are not, indeed they probably were not intended to be, a precise definition of the crime. I do not myself find the connotations of mens rea helpful in distinguishing between degrees of negligence, nor do the ideas of crime and punishment in themselves carry a jury much further in deciding whether in a particular case the degree of negligence shown is a crime and deserves punishment. But the substance of the judgment is most valuable, and in my opinion is correct. In practice it has generally been adopted by judges in charging juries in all cases of manslaughter by negligence, whether in driving vehicles or otherwise.

The principle to be observed is that cases of manslaughter in driving motor cars are but instances of a general rule applicable to all charges of homicide by negligence. Simple lack of care such as will constitute civil liability is not enough: for purposes of the criminal law there are degrees of negligence: and a very high degree of negligence is required to be proved before the felony is established. Probably of all the epithets that can be applied "reckless" most nearly covers the case. It is difficult to visualize a case of death caused by reckless driving in the connotation of that term in ordinary speech which would not justify a conviction for manslaughter: but it is probably not all-embracing, for "reckless" suggests an indifference to risk whereas the accused may have appreciated the risk and intended to avoid it and yet shown such a high degree of negligence in the means adopted to avoid the risk as would justify a conviction. If the principle of *Bateman's* case is observed it will appear that the law of manslaughter has not changed by the introduction of motor vehicles on the road. Death caused by their negligent driving, though unhappily much more frequent, is to be treated in law as death caused by any other form of negligence: and juries should be directed accordingly.

Commonwealth v. Welansky, 316 Mass. 383, 55 N.E.2d 902, 902-912 (1944): [Defendants were convicted of manslaughter arising out of a fire in their nightclub in Boston in which a great number of patrons lost their lives. The evidence revealed a variety of respects in which the premises constituted a hopeless fire trap, which the defendants permitted to be jammed with people apparently without regard for the consequences of a fire outbreak. In the course of the decision affirming the conviction the court made the following observations concerning the governing principles of liability:] The Commonwealth disclaimed any contention that the defendant intentionally killed or injured the persons named in the indictments as victims. It based its case on involuntary manslaughter through wanton or reckless conduct. The judge instructed the jury correctly with respect to the nature of such conduct.

Usually wanton or reckless conduct consists of an affirmative act, like driving an automobile or discharging a firearm, in disregard of probable harmful consequences to another. But where as in the present case there is a duty of care for the safety of business visitors invited to premises which the defendant controls, wanton or reckless conduct may consist of intentional failure to take such care in disregard of the probable harmful consequences to them or of their right to care.

To define wanton or reckless conduct so as to distinguish it clearly from negligence and gross negligence is not easy. Sometimes the word "wilful" is prefaced to the words "wanton" and "reckless" in expressing the concept. That only blurs it. Wilful means intentional. In the phrase "wilful, wanton or reckless conduct," if "wilful" modifies "conduct" it introduces something different from wanton or reckless conduct, even though the legal result is the same. Wilfully causing harm is a wrong, but a different wrong from wantonly or recklessly causing harm. If "wilful" modifies "wanton or reckless conduct" its use is accurate. What must be intended is the conduct, not the resulting harm. The words "wanton" and "reckless" are practically synonymous in this connection, although the word "wanton" may contain a suggestion of arrogance or insolence or heartlessness that is lacking in the word "reckless." But intentional conduct to which either word applies is followed by the same legal consequences as though both words applied.

The standard of wanton or reckless conduct is at once subjective and objective, as has been recognized ever since Commonwealth v. Pierce, 138 Mass. 165, 52 Am. Rep. 264. Knowing facts that would cause a reasonable man to know the danger is equivalent to knowing the danger. . . . The judge charged the jury correctly when he said, "To constitute wanton or reckless conduct, as distinguished from mere negligence, grave danger to others must have been apparent and the defendant must have chosen to run the risk rather than alter his conduct so as to avoid the act or omission which caused the harm. If the grave danger was in fact realized by the defendant, his subsequent voluntary act or omission which caused the harm amounts to wanton or reckless conduct, no matter whether the ordinary man would have realized the gravity of the danger or not. But even if a particular defendant is so stupid (or) so heedless . . . that in fact he did not realize the grave danger, he cannot escape the imputation of wanton or reckless conduct in his dangerous act or omission, if an ordinary normal man under the same circumstances would have realized the gravity of the danger. A man may be reckless within the meaning of the law although he himself thought he was careful.

The essence of wanton or reckless conduct is intentional conduct, by way either of commission or of omission where there is a duty to act, which conduct involves a high degree of likelihood[a] that substantial harm will result to another. Wanton or reckless conduct amounts to what has been variously described as indifference to or disregard of probable consequences to that other.

The words "wanton" and "reckless" are thus not merely rhetorical, vituperative expressions used instead of negligent or grossly negligent. They express a difference in the degree of risk and in the voluntary taking of risk so marked, as compared with negligence, as to amount substantially and in the eyes of the law to a difference in kind.

Notwithstanding language used commonly in earlier cases, and occasionally in later ones, it is now clear in this Commonwealth that at common law conduct does not become criminal until it passes the borders of negligence and gross negligence and enters into the domain of wanton or reckless conduct. There is in Massachusetts at common law no such thing as "criminal negligence."

To convict the defendant of manslaughter, the Commonwealth was not required to prove that he caused the fire by some wanton or reckless conduct. Fire in a place of public resort is an ever present danger. It was enough to

---

a. Was there a "high degree of likelihood" that a raging fire would break out in this restaurant at a time when it was filled to capacity? On a statistical basis, is it not improbable that a fire will break out in any particular restaurant? — Eds.

prove that death resulted from his wanton or reckless disregard of the safety of patrons in the event of fire from any cause.

Model Penal Code §2.02, Comment at 128 (Tent. Draft No. 4, 1955): Under statutes, as at common law, the concept of criminal negligence has been left to judicial definition and the definitions vary greatly in their terms. As Jerome Hall has put it, the judicial essays run in terms of " 'wanton and wilful negligence,' 'gross negligence,' and more illuminating yet, 'that degree of negligence that is more than the negligence required to impose tort liability.' The apex of ambiguity is 'wilful, wanton negligence' which suggests triple contradiction —'negligence' implying inadvertence; 'wilful,' intention; and 'wanton,' recklessness." Principles of Criminal Law 227-228. Much of this confusion is disspelled, in our view, by a clear-cut distinction between recklessness and negligence, in terms of the actor's awareness of the risk involved.

[The Model Penal Code makes homicide manslaughter when it is committed recklessly. Section 210.3, Appendix to this casebook. "Recklessly" is defined in §2.02(2)(c), Appendix to this casebook.

[When homicide is committed negligently, the Model Penal Code denominates it "negligent homicide" and provides for a lesser punishment than for manslaughter. Section 210.4, Appendix to this casebook. "Negligently" is defined in §2.02(2)(d).

[The Model Penal Code's formulations on criminal negligence have had a substantial influence on the many new penal codes in the United States. See Fischer, Criminal Liability for Negligent Conduct in the United States, in Law in the United States of America in Social and Technological Revolution 569 (J. N. Hazard & W. J. Wagner eds. 1974).]

PROBLEM

In Parrish v. State, 97 So. 2d 356 (Fla. Dist. App. 1957), defendant, in a car with companions, pursued his ex-wife through the city streets of Jacksonville in the early hours of the morning. He was armed with a bayonet and was apparently endeavoring to carry out his threat to kill her. He caught up with her at one point and broke her car window with his bayonet, but she maneuvered her car and eluded him. Continuing her escape she disregarded a stop sign and drove at a high rate of speed into a through street. In so doing she struck another car and subsequently died of the injuries. Defendant was convicted of second-degree murder, on the basis of having killed deceased by an act "imminently dangerous to another, and evidencing a depraved mind regardless of human life."

Questions: Suppose the deceased had survived but the driver of the car she struck had been killed. Could *she* be held for manslaughter? Was the magnitude of the risk she created any less or the violation of the traffic laws excused because she was fleeing from an attacker? If not, on what basis could her conduct be distinguished from a driver who was simply in a hurry? Is the concept of justification the distinguishing factor? If so, can the creation of risk of death or injury to other innocent persons be justified where it is employed as a means to save oneself from like injury? Would her conduct be noncriminal if she drove through a group of people blocking the street and killed several?

These kinds of issues arise when a person, acting in lawful self-defense against an aggressor, accidentally kills an innocent bystander. See Annot., Unintentional killing of or injury to third person during attempted self-defense, 55 A.L.R.3d 620 (1974). The courts commonly require that the defendant have acted "prudently" in self-defense. But at what point does the risk to innocent persons become so great that the action is not prudent, even though taken in lawful self-defense?

Consider the tort liability of a police officer for damage caused by a vehicle operated by a fleeing suspect who is being pursued by the officer in the performance of his or her duty. In Roll v. Timberman, 94 N.J. Super. 530, 229 A.2d 281, 284-285 (Super. Ct. App. Div. 1967), the court held against liability, stating that the officer was doing his duty in chasing the suspect and he was explicitly exempt from speed regulations. "To argue that the officer's pursuit caused [the suspect] to speed may be factually true, but it does not follow that the officer is liable for the results of [the suspect's] speed." Query: Is this analysis convincing? Why? Are there any situations in which a contrary result might be appropriate?

See J. W. Salmond, Jurisprudence 416 (8th ed. 1930):

> What amounts to reasonable care depends entirely on the circumstances of the particular case as known to the person whose conduct is the subject of inquiry. Whether in those circumstances, as so known to him, he used due care — whether he acted as a reasonably prudent man — is in general a mere question of fact as to which no legal rules can be laid down. It would seem clear, however, that for the proper determination of this question of fact there are two chief matters of consideration. The first is the magnitude of the risk to which other persons are exposed, while the second is the importance of the object to be attained by the dangerous form of activity. The reasonableness of any conduct will depend upon the proportion between these two elements. To expose others to danger for a disproportionate object is unreasonable, whereas an equal risk for a better cause may lawfully be run without negligence. By driving trains at the rate of fifty miles an hour, railway companies have caused many fatal accidents which could quite easily have been avoided by reducing the speed to ten miles, but this additional safety would be attained at too great a cost of public convenience, and therefore in neglecting this precaution the companies do not fall below the standard of reasonable care and are not guilty of negligence.

b. Objective versus Subjective Standards of Liability

STATE v. WILLIAMS
Washington Court of Appeals
4 Wash. App. 908, 484 P.2d 1167 (1971)

HOROWITZ C.J. Defendants, husband and wife, were charged by information filed October 3, 1968, with the crime of manslaughter for negligently failing to supply their 17-month child with necessary medical attention, as a result of which he died on September 12, 1968. Upon entry of findings, conclusions and judgment of guilty, sentences were imposed on April 22, 1969. Defendants appeal.

The defendant husband, Walter Williams, is a 24-year-old full-blooded She-shone Indian with a sixth-grade education. His sole occupation is that of laborer. The defendant wife, Bernice Williams, is a 20-year-old part Indian with an 11th grade education. At the time of the marriage, the wife had two children, the younger of whom was a 14-month-old son. Both parents worked and the children were cared for by the 85-year-old mother of the defendant husband. The defendant husband assumed parental responsibility with the defendant wife to provide clothing, care and medical attention for the child. Both defendants possessed a great deal of love and affection for the defendant wife's young son.

The court expressly found:

> That both defendants were aware that William Joseph Tabafunda was ill during the period September 1, 1968 to September 12, 1968. The defendants were ignorant. They did not realize how sick the baby was. They thought that the baby had a toothache and no layman regards a toothache as dangerous to life. They loved the baby and gave it aspirin in hopes of improving its condition. They did not take the baby to a doctor because of fear that the Welfare Department would take the baby away from them. They knew that medical help was available because of previous experience. They had no excuse that the law will recognize for not taking the baby to a doctor.
>
> The defendants Walter L. Williams and Bernice J. Williams were negligent in not seeking medical attention for William Joseph Tabafunda.
>
> That as a proximate result of this negligence, William Joseph Tabafunda died.

Findings 5, 6, and 7. From these and other findings, the court concluded that the defendants were each guilty of the crime of manslaughter as charged. . . . [The court then found that both defendants were under a legal duty to obtain medical assistance for the child.[a]] On the question of the quality or seriousness of breach of the duty, at common law, in the case of involuntary manslaughter, the breach had to amount to more than mere ordinary or simple negligence — gross negligence was essential. . . . In Washington, however, R.C.W. 9.48.060[2] (since amended by Laws of 1970, ch. 49, §2) and R.C.W. 9.48.150[3] supersede both voluntary and involuntary manslaughter as those crimes were defined at common law. Under these statutes the crime is deemed committed even though the death of the victim is the proximate result of only simple or ordinary negligence. . . . *in Wash.*

a. In footnote 1, the court observed that the information, in charging the violation of the duty owed, alleged:

"[T]hey, the said defendants, then and there being the father, mother, guardian and custodian of one William Joseph Tabafunda, and being then and there under the legal duty of providing necessary food, clothing, care and medical attention to said William Joseph Tabafunds [sic], a minor child under the age of sixteen years, to-wit: of the age of seventeen (17) months, did then and there unlawfully and feloniously fail and neglect, without lawful excuse, to provide said . . . child . . . with necessary food, clothing, care and medical attention. . . ."— Eds.

2. R.C.W. 9.48.060 provided in part:

"In any case other than those specified in R.C.W. 9.48.030, 9.48.040, and 9.48.050, homicide, not being excusable or justifiable, is manslaughter."

3. R.C.W. 9.48.150 provides:

"Homicide is excusable when committed by accident or misfortune in doing any lawful act by lawful means, with ordinary caution and without any unlawful intent."

The concept of simple or ordinary negligence describes a failure to exercise the "ordinary caution" necessary to make out the defense of excusable homicide. R.C.W. 9.48.150. Ordinary caution is the kind of caution that a man of reasonable prudence would exercise under the same or similar conditions. If, therefore, the conduct of a defendant, regardless of his ignorance, good intentions and good faith, fails to measure up to the conduct required of a man of reasonable prudence, he is guilty of ordinary negligence because of his failure to use "ordinary caution." . . . If such negligence proximately causes the death of the victim, the defendant, as pointed out above, is guilty of statutory manslaughter. . . .

The remaining issue of proximate cause requires consideration of the question of when the duty to furnish medical care became activated. If the duty to furnish such care was not activated until after it was too late to save the life of the child, failure to furnish medical care could not be said to have proximately caused the child's death. Timeliness in the furnishing of medical care also must be considered in terms of "ordinary caution." . . . In our opinion, the duty as formulated in People v. Pierson, 176 N.Y. 201, 68 N.E. 243 (1903) . . . properly defines the duty contemplated by our manslaughter statutes. . . . The court there said: "We quite agree that the Code does not contemplate the necessity of calling a physician for every trifling complaint with which the child may be afflicted, which in most instances may be overcome by the ordinary household nursing by members of the family; that a reasonable amount of discretion is vested in parents, charged with the duty of maintaining and bringing up infant children; and that the standard is at what time would an ordinarily prudent person, solicitous for the welfare of his child and anxious to promote its recovery, deem it necessary to call in the services of a physician."

It remains to apply the law discussed to the facts of the instant case.

Defendants have not assigned error to the findings either on the ground that the evidence is insufficient to prove negligence or proximate cause, or that the state has failed to prove the facts found by failing to apply the required standard of proof beyond a reasonable doubt. . . . They contended below and on appeal that they are not guilty of the crime charged. Because of the serious nature of the charge against the parent and step-parent of a well-loved child, and out of our concern for the protection of the constitutional rights of the defendants, we have made an independent examination of the evidence to determine whether it substantially supports the court's express finding on proximate cause and its implied finding that the duty to furnish medical care became activated in time to prevent death of the child. . . .

Dr. Gale Wilson, the autopsy surgeon and chief pathologist for the King County Coroner, testified that the child died because an abscessed tooth had been allowed to develop into an infection of the mouth and cheeks, eventually becoming gangrenous. This condition, accompanied by the child's inability to eat, brought about malnutrition, lowering the child's resistance and eventually producing pneumonia, causing the death. Dr. Wilson testified that in his opinion the infection had lasted for approximately 2 weeks, and that the odor generally associated with gangrene would have been present for approximately 10 days before death. He also expressed the opinion that had medical care been first obtained in the last week before the baby's death, such care would have been obtained too late to have saved the baby's life. Accordingly, the baby's apparent condition between September 1 and September 5, 1968 became the critical period for the purpose of determining whether in the exercise of ordinary caution defendants should have provided medical care for the minor child.

The testimony concerning the child's apparent condition during the critical period is not crystal clear, but is sufficient to warrant the following statement of the matter. The defendant husband testified that he noticed the baby was sick about 2 weeks before the baby died. The defendant wife testified that she noticed the baby was ill about a week and a half or 2 weeks before the baby died. The evidence showed that in the critical period the baby was fussy; that he could not keep his food down; and that a cheek started swelling up. The swelling went up and down, but did not disappear. In that same period, the cheek turned "a bluish color like." The defendants, not realizing that the baby was as ill as it was or that the baby was in danger of dying, attempted to provide some relief to the baby by giving the baby aspirin during the critical period and continued to do so until the night before the baby died. The defendants thought the swelling would go down and were waiting for it to do so; and defendant husband testified, that from what he had heard, neither doctors nor dentists pull out a tooth "when it's all swollen up like that." There was an additional explanation for not calling a doctor given by each defendant. Defendant husband testified that "the way the cheek looked, . . . and that stuff on his hair, they would think we were neglecting him and take him away from us and not give him back." Defendant wife testified that the defendants were "waiting for the swelling to go down," and also that they were afraid to take the child to a doctor for fear that the doctor would report them to the welfare department, who, in turn, would take the child away. "It's just that I was so scared of losing him." They testified that they had heard that the defendant husband's cousin lost a child that way. The evidence showed that the defendants did not understand the significance or seriousness of the baby's symptoms. However, there is no evidence that the defendants were physically or financially unable to obtain a doctor, or that they did not know an available doctor, or that the symptoms did not continue to be a matter of concern during the critical period. Indeed, the evidence shows that in April 1968 defendant husband had taken the child to a doctor for medical attention.

In our opinion, there is sufficient evidence from which the court could find, as it necessarily did, that applying the standard of ordinary caution, i.e., the caution exercisable by a man of reasonable prudence under the same or similar conditions, defendants were sufficiently put on notice concerning the symptoms of the baby's illness and lack of improvement in the baby's apparent condition in the period from September 1 to September 5, 1968 to have required them to have obtained medical care for the child. The failure so to do in this case is ordinary or simple negligence, and such negligence is sufficient to support a conviction of statutory manslaughter.

The judgment is affirmed.

QUESTIONS

Many will find the conviction of the Williams couple unjust and, perhaps, pointless. What were defendants punished for in this case? Was it only for their ignorance? If it is thought that their conviction was unjust, is this because they were unaware of the danger to their child? If so, does it follow that punishment for negligence (where there is no awareness of the risk) is always unjust? Consider the materials in the following Note in thinking about these questions.

NOTES ON THE CONTROVERSY OVER STANDARDS OF LIABILITY

1. Objective and subjective liability defined. The concepts of objective and subjective standards are subject to a variety of interpretations. See G. Fletcher, Rethinking Criminal Law 504 et seq. (1978). In general, objective or external standards determine liability on the basis of general norms of proper and reasonable behavior. Thus, the provocation standard imports an objective standard insofar as the law requires that what provoked the defendant to kill would have severely tested the self-control of a reasonable person. Recklessness and negligence are objective standards insofar as liability turns on whether the action of defendant created a risk of a kind and degree which, in the circumstances, a reasonable person would not have taken. Subjective, individualized, or internal standards of liability, on the other hand, look to the personal characteristics of the actor, and, insofar as they are thoroughgoing in their subjectivity, take "account of the infinite varieties of temperament, intellect and education which make the internal character of a given act so different." O. W. Holmes, The Common Law 108 (1881). Premeditation and deliberation are subjective standards, since they look to what the particular defendant experienced. The same is true of the diminished-capacity defense. Tension between these two kinds of standards runs through the whole of our substantive criminal law.

A standard of negligence is, as we have indicated, substantially objective. Should its objectivity be qualified by requiring that defendant have been aware of the risk his or her action entailed (or, in the Model Penal Code's terminology, by requiring recklessness rather than negligence) before criminal liability may be imposed?

2. In defense of an objective standard. Justice Holmes believed that the direction of legal development was toward objective standards. Consistent with that view, he explained the criminal law's lack of concern with whether the defendant was aware of the risk as follows (The Criminal Law 53-55, 59 (1881)):

> . . . If the known present state of things is such that the act done will very certainly cause death, and the probability is a matter of common knowledge, one who does the act, knowing the present state of things, is guilty of murder, and the law will not inquire whether he did actually foresee the consequences or not. The test of foresight is not what this very criminal foresaw, but what a man of reasonable prudence would have foreseen.
>
> On the other hand, there must be actual present knowledge of the present facts which make an act dangerous. The act is not enough by itself. . . . A fear of punishment for causing harm cannot work as a motive, unless the possibility of harm may be foreseen. So far, then, as criminal liability is founded upon wrongdoing in any sense, and so far as the threats and punishments of the law are intended to deter men from bringing about various harmful results, they must be confined to cases where circumstances making the conduct dangerous were known.
>
> Still, in a more limited way, the same principle applies to knowledge that applies to foresight. It is enough that such circumstances were actually known as would

have led a man of common understanding to infer from them the rest of the group making up the present state of things. For instance, if a workman on a housetop at mid-day knows that the space below him is a street in a great city, he knows facts from which a man of common understanding would infer that there were people passing below. He is therefore bound to draw that inference, or, in other words, is chargeable with knowledge of that fact also, whether he draws the inference or not. If, then, he throws down a heavy beam into the street, he does an act which a person of ordinary prudence would foresee is likely to cause death, or grievous bodily harm, and he is dealt with as if he foresaw it, whether he does so in fact or not. If a death is caused by the act, he is guilty of murder. . . .

[I]t is to be remembered that the object of the law is to prevent human life being endangered or taken; and that, although it so far considers blameworthiness in punishing as not to hold a man responsible for consequences which no one, or only some exceptional specialist, could have foreseen, still the reason for this limitation is simply to make a rule which is not too hard for the average member of the community. As the purpose is to compel men to abstain from dangerous conduct, and not merely to restrain them from evil inclinations, the law requires them at their peril to know the teachings of common experience, just as it requires them to know the law. Subject to these explanations, it may be said that the test of murder is the degree of danger to life attending the act under the known circumstances of the case. [The difference between murder and manslaughter Holmes saw] in the degree of danger attaching to the act in the given state of facts.

A few years after writing the foregoing, Holmes had occasion to apply his views in Commonwealth v. Pierce, 138 Mass. 165, 171-176 (1884). In this case defendant was convicted of manslaughter

on evidence that he publicly practised as a physician, and, being called to attend a sick woman, caused her, with her consent, to be kept in flannels saturated with kerosene for three days, more or less, by reason of which she died. There was evidence that he had made similar applications with favorable results in other cases, but that in one the effect had been to blister and burn the flesh as in the present case.

The alleged errors in the trial court's instructions to the jury turned on its refusal to charge in terms of recklessness. Holmes formulated the issue as follows (id. at 175-176):

But recklessness in a moral sense means a certain state of consciousness with reference to the consequences of one's acts. No matter whether defined as indifference to what those consequences may be, or as a failure to consider their nature or probability as fully as the party might and ought to have done, it is understood to depend on the actual condition of the individual's mind with regard to consequences, as distinguished from mere knowledge of present or past facts or circumstances from which some one or everybody else might be led to anticipate or apprehend them if the supposed act were done. We have to determine whether recklessness in this sense was necessary to make the defendant guilty of felonious homicide, or whether his acts are to be judged by the external standard of what would be morally reckless, under the circumstances known to him, in a man of reasonable prudence.

More specifically, the questions raised by the foregoing requests and rulings are whether an actual good intent and the expectation of good results are an absolute justification of acts, however foolhardy they may be if judged by the external standard supposed, and whether the defendant's ignorance of the tendencies of kerosene administered as it was will excuse the administration of it.

After reviewing the objective standards applicable in civil cases, Holmes concluded:

If this is the rule adopted in regard to the redistribution of losses, which sound policy allows to rest where they fall in the absence of a clear reason to the contrary, there would seem to be at least equal reason for adopting it in the criminal law, which has for its immediate object and task to establish a general standard, or at least general negative limits, of conduct for the community, in the interest of the safety of all.

3. Criticism of the objective standard. Summarizing the arguments against negligent liability, Professor Glanville Williams wrote (Criminal Law: The General Part 122-123 (2d ed. 1961)):

The use of the criminal law to punish negligence has been challenged. An American writer expressed the objection as follows:

"If the defendant, being mistaken as to material facts, is to be punished because his mistake is one which an average man would not make, punishment will sometimes be inflicted when the criminal mind does not exist. Such a result is contrary to fundamental principles, and is plainly unjust, for a man should not be held criminal because of lack of intelligence."

The retributive theory of punishment is open to many objections, which are of even greater force when applied to inadvertent negligence than in crimes requiring mens rea. Some people are born feckless, clumsy, thoughtless, inattentive, irresponsible, with a bad memory and a slow "reaction time." With the best will in the world, we all of us at some times in our lives make negligent mistakes. It is hard to see how justice (as distinct from some utilitarian reason) requires mistakes to be punished.

Again, the deterrent theory, which is normally accepted as a justification for criminal punishment, finds itself in some difficulty when applied to negligence. At best the deterrent effect of the legal sanction is a matter of faith rather than of proved scientific fact; but there is no department in which this faith is less firmly grounded than that of negligence. Hardly any motorist but does not firmly believe that if he is involved in an accident it will be the other fellow's fault. It may seem, therefore, that the threat of punishment for negligence must pass him by, because he does not realize that it is addressed to him. Even if a person admits that he occasionally makes a negligent mistake, how, in the nature of things, can punishment for inadvertence serve to deter?

4. The Model Penal Code approach. The Model Penal Code takes the position, as we saw, that while awareness of the risk (recklessness) is required for the greater offense of manslaughter, a person who is unaware of the risk may be punished for the lesser crime of negligent homicide. Compare §§210.3(1)(a) and 210.4, Appendix to this casebook. In support of retaining negligence as a basis of criminal liability, the Comment to §2.02 states ((Tent. Draft No. 4, 1955) at 126-127):

Knowledge that conviction and sentence, not to speak of punishment, may follow conduct that inadvertently creates improper risk supplies men with an additional motive to take care before acting, to use their faculties and draw on their experience in gauging the potentialities of contemplated conduct. To some extent, at least, this motive may promote awareness and thus be effective as a measure of control. Certainly legislators act on this assumption in a host of situations and it seems to us dogmatic to assert that they are wholly wrong. Accordingly, we think that negligence, as here defined, cannot be wholly rejected as a ground of culpability which may suffice for purposes of penal law, though we agree that it should not be generally deemed sufficient in the definition of specific crimes. . . .

5. *The issue of the defendant's ability to conform. (a) The argument for individual-ized liability.* Professor Hart has argued that the difficulty with punishing for negligence does not arise from punishing a person who is unaware of the risk he or she is creating but from punishing the person for departing from an external or invariant standard without inquiring into the person's ability to have acted otherwise. (H. L. A. Hart, Punishment and Responsibility 152-154 (1968)):

> Excessive distrust of negligence and excessive confidence in the respectability of "foresight of harm" or "having the thought of harm in the mind" as a ground of responsibility have their roots in a common misunderstanding. Both oversimplify the character of the subjective element required in those whom we punish, if it is to be morally tolerable, according to common notions of justice, to punish them. The reason why, according to modern ideas, strict liability is odious, and appears as a sacrifice of a valued principle which we should make, if at all, only for some overriding social good, is not merely because it amounts, as it does, to punishing those who did not at the time of acting "have in their minds" the elements of foresight or desire for muscular movement. These psychological elements are not in themselves crucial though they are important as aspects of responsibility. What is crucial is that those whom we punish should have had, when they acted, the normal capacities, physical and mental, for doing what the law requires and abstaining from what it forbids, and a fair opportunity to exercise these capacities. Where these capacities and opportunities are absent, as they are in different ways in the varied cases of accident, mistake, paralysis, reflex action, coercion, insanity, etc., the moral protest is that it is morally wrong to punish because "he could not have helped it" or "he could not have done otherwise" or "he had no real choice." But, as we have seen, there is no reason (unless we are to reject the whole business of responsibility and punishment) *always* to make this protest when someone who "just didn't think" is punished for carelessness. For in some cases at least we may say "he could have thought about what he was doing" with just as much rational confidence as one can say of any intentional wrongdoing "he could have done otherwise." . . .[a]

---

a. Professor Hart in a subsequent passage (id. at 156-157) responds as follows to Professor Williams's criticism of punishing for negligence:

"Equally obscure to me are the reasons given by Dr. Williams for doubting the efficacy of punishment for negligence. He asks, 'Even if a person admits that he occasionally makes a negligent mistake, how, in the nature of things, can punishment for inadvertence serve to deter?' But if this question is meant as an argument, it rests on the old, mistaken identification of the 'subjective element' involved in negligence with 'a blank mind,' whereas it is in fact a failure to exercise the capacity to advert to, and to think about and control, conduct and its risks. Surely we have plenty of empirical evidence to show that, as Professor Wechsler has said, 'punishment supplies men with an additional motive to take care before acting, to use their facilities, and to draw upon their experience.' Again there is no difficulty here peculiar to negligence, though of course we can doubt the efficacy of any punishment to deter any kind of offence."— EDS.

The most important compromise which legal systems make over the subjective element consists in its adoption of what has been unhappily termed the "objective standard." This may lead to an individual being treated for the purposes of conviction and punishment as if he possessed capacities for control of his conduct which he did not possess, but which an ordinary or reasonable man possesses and would have exercised. The expression "objective" and its partner "subjective" are unhappy because, as far as negligence is concerned, they obscure the real issue. We may be tempted to say with Dr. Turner that just because the negligent man does not have "the thought of harm in his mind," to hold him responsible for negligence is necessarily to adopt an objective standard and to abandon the "subjective" element in responsibility. It then becomes vital to distinguish this (mistaken) thesis from the position brought about by the use of objective standards in the application of laws which make negligence criminally punishable. For, when negligence is made criminally punishable, this itself leaves open the question: whether, before we punish, both or only the first of the following two questions must be answered affirmatively:

> (i) Did the accused fail to take those precautions which any reasonable man with normal capacities would in the circumstances have taken?
> (ii) Could the accused, given his mental and physical capacities, have taken those precautions?

Modify it →

One use of the dangerous expressions "objective" and "subjective" is to make the distinction between these two questions; given the ambiguities of those expressions, this distinction would have been more happily expressed by the expressions "invariant" standard of care, and "individualized conditions of liability." It may well be that, even if the "standard of care" is pitched very low so that individuals are held liable only if they fail to take very elementary precautions against harm, there will still be some unfortunate individuals who, through lack of intelligence, powers of concentration or memory, or through clumsiness, could not attain even this low standard. If our conditions of liability are invariant and not flexible, i.e. if they are not adjusted to the capacities of the accused, then some individuals will be held liable for negligence though they could not have helped their failure to comply with the standard. In *such* cases, indeed, criminal responsibility will be made independent of any "subjective element," since the accused could not have conformed to the required standard. But this result is nothing to do with negligence being taken as a basis for criminal liability; precisely the same result will be reached if, in considering whether a person acted intentionally, we were to attribute to him foresight of consequences which a reasonable man would have foreseen but which he did not. "Absolute liability" results, not from the admission of the principle that one who has been grossly negligent is criminally responsible for the consequent harm even if "he had no idea in his mind of harm to anyone," but from the refusal in the application of this principle to consider the capacities of an individual who has fallen below the standard of care.

(*b*) *Questions.* The power of Hart's argument is that the kind of individualization he defends would result in legal guilt and moral blameworthiness being made more nearly the same. What are the costs of this approach? Consider the arguments against the use of diminished responsibility to reduce murder to manslaughter made in the Model Penal Code Comment at page 441 supra.

Are there other costs as well? Consider the observation of Professor Fuller that to ask whether the defendant "with all his individual limitations and quirks, fell short of what he ought to have achieved" invites the kind of potentially discriminatory judgments that would destroy the possibility of evenhandedness in the law. (L. Fuller, The Morality of Law 71-72 (1964).)

It is helpful to observe that the German law defines negligence consonantly with Hart's analysis. The settled view as announced in a leading 1922 case was as follows:

> A harm caused by defendants can be said to be caused by negligence only when it is established that they disregarded the care which they were obliged to exercise and of which they were capable under the circumstances and according to their personal knowledge and abilities. . . .

(The Case of the Gable-Wall (Giebelmauer), 56 RGSt 343, 349 (1922). See H. H. Jescheck, Lehrbuch des Strafrechts 379 (1969).)

(c) *The Model Penal Code on individualization.* The contrast between the Model Penal Code's definition of negligence (see §2.02(2)(c), Appendix to this casebook) and that of German law above highlights the former's rejection of a fully individualized standard. However, some elements of an individualized standard are invited by its reference to "the care that would be exercised by a reasonable person in his [the actor's] situation." The Comment to this provision ((Tent. Draft No. 4, 1955) at 126) states:

> There is an inevitable ambiguity in "situation." If the actor were blind or if he had just suffered a blow or experienced a heart attack, these would certainly be facts to be considered, as they would be under present law. But the heredity, intelligence or temperament of the actor would not now be held material in judging negligence; and could not be without depriving the criterion of all its objectivity. . . . The draft is not intended to displace discriminations of this kind; it is designed to leave the issue to the courts.

Recall that the Model Penal Code took a similar approach in its formulation of provocation, where the objectivity of the standard is qualified by the sentence (§210.3):

> The reasonableness of such explanation or excuse shall be determined from the viewpoint of a person *in the actor's situation* under the circumstances as he believes them to be. [Italics added]

See page 439 supra.

Query: How would the *Williams* case be decided under the Code?

c. The Line between Murder and Manslaughter

COMMONWEALTH v. MALONE
Supreme Court of Pennsylvania
354 Pa. 180, 47 A.2d 445 (1946)

MAXEY, C.J. This is an appeal from the judgment and sentence under a conviction of murder in the second degree. William H. Long, age 13 years, was killed by a shot from a 32-caliber revolver held against his right side by the defendant, then aged 17 years. These youths were on friendly terms at the time of the homicide. The defendant and his mother while his father and brother were in the U.S. Armed Forces, were residing in Lancaster, Pa., with the family of William H. Long, whose son was the victim of the shooting.

On the evening of February 26th, 1945, when the defendant went to a moving picture theater, he carried in the pocket of his raincoat a revolver which he had obtained at the home of his uncle on the preceding day. In the afternoon preceding the shooting, the decedent procured a cartridge from his father's room and he and the defendant placed it in the revolver.

After leaving the theater, the defendant went to a dairy store and there met the decedent. Both youths sat in the rear of the store ten minutes, during which period the defendant took the gun out of his pocket and loaded the chamber to the right of the firing pin and then closed the gun. A few minutes later, both youths sat on stools in front of the lunch counter and ate some food. The defendant suggested to the decedent that they play "Russian Poker."[1] Long replied: "I don't care; go ahead." The defendant then placed the revolver against the right side of Long and pulled the trigger three times. The third pull resulted in a fatal wound to Long. The latter jumped off the stool and cried: "Oh! Oh! Oh!" and Malone said: "Did I hit you, Billy? Gee, Kid, I'm sorry." Long died from the wounds two days later.

The defendant testified that the gun chamber he loaded was the first one to the right of the firing chamber and that when he pulled the trigger he did not "expect to have the gun go off." He declared he had no intention of harming Long, who was his friend and companion. The defendant was indicted for murder, tried and found guilty of murder in the second degree and sentenced to a term in the penitentiary for a period not less than five years and not exceeding ten years. A new trial was refused and after sentence was imposed, an appeal was taken.

Appellant alleges certain errors in the charge of the court and also contends that the facts did not justify a conviction for any form of homicide except involuntary manslaughter. This contention we overrule. A specific intent to take life is, under our law, an essential ingredient of murder in the first degree. At common law, the "grand criterion" which "distinguished murder from other killing" was malice on the part of the killer and this malice was not necessarily "malevolent to the deceased particularly" but "any evil design in general; the dictate of a wicked, depraved and malignant heart"; 4 Blackstone 199. . . .

. . . When an individual commits an act of gross recklessness for which he must reasonably anticipate that death to another is likely to result, he exhibits that "wickedness of disposition, hardness of heart, cruelty, recklessness of consequences, and a mind regardless of social duty" which proved that there was at that time in him "the state or frame of mind termed malice." This court has declared that if a driver "wantonly, recklessly, and in disregard of consequences" hurls "his car against another, or into a crowd" and death results from that act "he ought . . . to face the same consequences that would be meted out to him if he had accomplished death by wantonly and wickedly firing a gun": Com. v. Mayberry, 290 Pa. 195, 199, 138 A. 686, 688, citing cases from four jurisdictions. . . .

1. It has been explained that "Russian Poker" is a game in which the participants, in turn, place a single cartridge in one of the five chambers of a revolver cylinder, give the latter a quick twirl, place the muzzle of the gun against the temple and pull the trigger, leaving it to chance whether or not death results to the trigger puller.

The killing of William H. Long by this defendant resulted from an act intentionally done by the latter, in reckless and wanton disregard of the consequences which were at least sixty percent certain from his thrice attempted discharge of a gun known to contain one bullet and aimed at a vital part of Long's body. This killing was, therefore, murder, for malice in the sense of a wicked disposition is evidenced by the intentional doing of an uncalled-for act in callous disregard of its likely harmful effects on others. The fact that there was no motive for this homicide does not exculpate the accused. In a trial for murder proof of motive is always relevant but never necessary.

All the assignments of error are overruled and the judgment is affirmed. The record is remitted to the court below so that the sentence imposed may be carried out.

NOTES

1. The facts in Malone. In concluding that there was a 60 percent chance of the gun's discharging, the court apparently assumed that defendant twirled the revolver cylinder before beginning to pull the trigger (see footnote 1 of the opinion), contrary to the implication of defendant's testimony that he loaded the chamber to the right of the firing pin before pulling the trigger. On the court's assumption, pulling the trigger of a five-chambered gun three consecutive times creates, as the court said, a three-out-of-five chance of the gun's discharging. Some, however, might want to argue that the relevant risk is that of the gun's discharging on the third pull, which is one out of three. Which is the appropriate way to characterize the defendant's course of conduct? Would it make any difference to the defendant's liability? Suppose the gun discharged at the very first pull, when the chance of that happening would have been one out of five? Would that have made a difference?

If, in fact, defendant did just what he testified he did — loaded the chamber to the right of the firing pin and then fired without twirling the chamber — how is it that the gun discharged? There are several possibilities. Conceivably the gun misfired in some fashion. Or conceivably there was *more than one* bullet in the gun. (Recall the testimony about how the gun was handled during the afternoon preceding the shooting.) If the court had accepted defendant's version of the facts, would the result have been different? If a defendant pulls the trigger of a gun believed to be empty, forgetting that it had been loaded the previous day, and death results, should he or she be guilty of murder rather than manslaughter?

2. Definitions of unintentional murder. The common law formulations of the circumstances under which an unintentional killing constituted murder rather than manslaughter have been incorporated into many American statutes either directly or by reference to such common law terms as *malice.* The formulas have tended to carry more flavor than meaning —"the dictate of a wicked, depraved and malignant heart"; when the circumstances show "an abandoned and malignant heart"; where the circumstances show "a depraved heart regardless of human life." The *Malone* case is an example of circumstances in which the criteria have been held to have been met. Many states continue to adhere to these formulations, although many have altered them in ways more or less suggested by the Model Penal Code's proposals. See American Law Institute, Model Penal Code and Commentaries, Pt. II, Comment to §210.2 at 22-27 (1980).

The Model Penal Code treats an unintended killing as murder when it is committed recklessly (as defined in §2.02(2)(c)) and "under circumstances manifesting extreme indifference to the value of human life." (§210.2, Appendix to this casebook.)

The Comment supporting §210.2 states as follows (American Law Institute, Model Penal Code and Commentaries, Pt. II, Comment to §210.2 at 21-22 (1980)):

> Recklessness, as defined in Section 2.02(2)(c), presupposes an awareness of the creation of substantial homicidal risk, a risk too great to be deemed justifiable by any valid purpose that the actor's conduct serves. Since risk, however, is a matter of degree and the motives for risk creation may be infinite in variation, some formula is needed to identify the case where recklessness may be found and where it should be assimilated to purpose or knowledge for purposes of grading. Under the Model Code, this judgment must be made in terms of whether the actor's conscious disregard of the risk, given the circumstances of the case, so far departs from acceptable behavior that it constitutes a "gross deviation from the standard of conduct that a law-abiding person would observe in the actor's situation." Ordinary recklessness in this sense is made sufficient for a conviction of manslaughter under Section 210.3(1)(a). In a prosecution for murder, however, the Code calls for the further judgment whether the actor's conscious disregard of the risk, under the circumstances, manifests extreme indifference to the value of human life. The significance of purpose or knowledge as a standard of culpability is that, cases of provocation or other mitigation apart, purposeful or knowing homicide demonstrates precisely such indifference to the value of human life. Whether recklessness is so extreme that it demonstrates similar indifference is not a question, it is submitted, that can be further clarified. It must be left directly to the trier of fact under instructions which make it clear that recklessness that can fairly be assimilated to purpose or knowledge should be treated as murder and that less extreme recklessness should be punished as manslaughter.
>
> Insofar as Subsection (1)(b) includes within the murder category cases of homicide caused by extreme recklessness, though without purpose to kill, it reflects both the common law and much pre-existing statutory treatment usually cast in terms of conduct evidencing a "depraved heart regardless of human life" or some similar words.

3. *Murder by omission.* We have seen that the death of an infant through its parents' neglect may constitute manslaughter. State v. Williams, pages 449-451 supra. May such neglect constitute murder? A California court upheld a second-degree murder conviction of a father for his conscious and callous failure to feed his child resulting in its death through malnutrition and dehydration. The evidence showed that the father was aware during the last two weeks of the baby's life that it was starving to death, that he did not remember anyone's having fed the baby in that period, and that he did nothing himself to feed the baby, although he could have if he had really wanted to, since he "just didn't care." The court stated: "The omission of a duty is in law the equivalent of an act and when death results, the standard for determination of the degree of homicide is identical." People v. Burden, 72 Cal. App. 3d 603, 616 (Dist.

App. 1977). In accord see Biddle v. Commonwealth, 206 Va. 14, 141 S.E.2d 710 (1965); Albright v. State, 291 Ala. 801, 280 So. 2d 186 (1973).

4. Awareness of the risk. Holmes was of the view, as we saw at page 452 supra, that an unintended killing could be murder, even in the absence of advertence to the risk, if the danger to life was great enough. There is some authority to support this view at common law (see, e.g., Regina v. Ward, [1956] 1 Q.B. 351), but it would rarely be thought that the traditional formulations would be satisfied ("depraved heart," etc.) when the defendant was not in fact aware of the danger he or she was creating.

The Model Penal Code clearly rejected the possibility of inadvertent murder by requiring that defendant have acted recklessly. The Comment states (American Law Institute, Model Penal Code and Commentaries, Pt. II, Comment to §210.2 at 28 (1980)):

> This result is consistent with the general conception of the Model Code that serious felony sanctions should be grounded securely in the subjective culpability of the actor. To the extent that inadvertent risk creation, or negligence, should be recognized as a form of criminal homicide, that question should be faced separately from the offense of murder. . . . At the least it seems clear that negligent homicide should not be assimilated to the most serious forms of criminal homicide catalogued under the offense of murder.

These issues may be usefully considered in the context of Hamilton v. Commonwealth, 560 S.W.2d 539 (Ky. 1978). Defendant was convicted of murder under a statute based on the Model Penal Code provision but different to the extent that "wantonly" was substituted for "recklessly." Ky. Rev. Stat. §507.020(1)(b). That statute provided:

> A person is guilty of murder when . . . under circumstances manifesting extreme indifference to human life, he wantonly engages in conduct which creates a grave risk of death to another person and thereby causes the death of another person.

The record showed that while in a heavily intoxicated condition defendant drove his truck substantially over the speed limit through an intersection where another car was crossing. Defendant ignored the stop sign in the intersection. Defendant's truck collided with the other car and killed its driver.

A majority of the Kentucky Supreme Court affirmed, stating (560 S.W.2d at 543-544):

> Hamilton's conduct surpasses the usual vehicle manslaughter case and demonstrates "wanton" conduct and extreme indifference to human life. The jury was instructed on murder, second degree manslaughter and reckless homicide. It found that Hamilton should have known of the plain and obvious likelihood that death or great bodily injury could have resulted from operating his truck, while in a drunken condition, through an intersection where a red light demanded that he stop.
>
> This is a "hurry-up" world of people on the go, with heavy traffic by high-powered vehicles on all types of roads and at all times of the day or night. Such a situation coupled with a driver's inclination to take "one or more [drinks] for the road," increases the vehicular death rate on the highways of this Commonwealth. A major-

ity of the members of this court is of the opinion that the legislature enacted K.R.S. 507.020(1)(b) to deter such conduct. The legislature is commended for taking a giant step forward. Its action in enacting this statute will do much to decrease vehicular highway deaths by persons operating an automobile while under the influence of intoxicants.

The dissent stated (id. at 544):

I do not believe that either the drafters of the Kentucky Penal Code or the members of the General Assembly that enacted it had any intention of placing the reckless act of an automobile driver, whether drunk or sober, in the same category as that of a deliberate murderer. I concede that fatal carelessness in the operation of a motor vehicle calls for stern punishment, but murder is something else. There simply is a difference in culpability between committing an act that endangers people whose presence is known and an act that endangers people whose presence *should be* anticipated but *in fact* is not known.

5. *Intent to inflict great bodily harm.* In a case of unintended killing, what legal effect should be given to the fact that defendant intended to injure the deceased seriously? Obviously, this fact has evidentiary significance on the issue of recklessness or negligence. The common law went further, however, by giving it independent substantive significance: The malice required for murder was established by the intent of defendant to do great bodily harm to the victim. See G. Williams, Textbook of Criminal Law 210 (1978).

The following case and Notes provide a basis for considering this doctrine.

DIRECTOR OF PUBLIC PROSECUTIONS v. SMITH (JIM)

House of Lords
[1961] A.C. 290

[Respondent was driving a car; in the trunk and back of the car were sacks of scaffolding clips that were, to respondent's knowledge, stolen. A police constable, with whom respondent was acquainted, noticed the sacks and directed him to pull over to the curb. Respondent began to do so, with the constable walking alongside. Suddenly the respondent accelerated, and the constable, in order to prevent his escape, clung to the car, although it had no running board. He held on for some 130 yards while respondent, in panic, pursued an erratic course at a fairly high speed, in a desperate effort to get free of the policeman. He finally succeeded. The constable was thrown in the path of an oncoming vehicle, which struck him, causing injuries from which he died. Respondent drove on for another 200 yards but returned after dumping the stolen property from his car.]

Viscount Kilmuir, L.C. My Lords, the respondent, Jim Smith, was convicted on April 7, 1960, of the wilful murder on March 2, 1960, of Leslie Edward Vincent Meehan, a police officer acting in the execution of his duty. Such a crime constitutes capital murder under section 5 of the Homicide Act, 1957, and, accordingly, the respondent was sentenced to death. There was never any suggestion that the respondent meant to kill the police officer, but it was contended by the prosecution that he intended to do the officer grievous bodily harm, as a result of which the officer died.

In his final direction to the jury the trial judge, Donovan, J., said:

> If you are satisfied that . . . he must as a reasonable man have contemplated that grievous bodily harm was likely to result to that officer . . . and that such harm did happen and the officer died in consequence, then the accused is guilty of capital murder. On the other hand, if you are not satisfied that he intended to inflict grievous bodily harm upon the officer — in other words, if you think he could not as a reasonable man have contemplated that grievous bodily harm would result to the officer in consequence of his actions — well, then, the verdict would be guilty of manslaughter.

The respondent appealed to the Court of Criminal Appeal alleging misdirection by the trial judge, the main ground being that the direction cited above was wrong in that the question for the jury was what he, the respondent, in fact contemplated. The appeal was heard by the Court of Criminal Appeal on May 9 and 10, 1960, when the court allowed the appeal, substituted a verdict of guilty of manslaughter and imposed a sentence of 10 years' imprisonment. The court gave its reasons on May 18, 1960. They upheld the respondent's contention, holding [[1960] 2 All E.R. 451] that "there always remained the question whether the appellant" (the present respondent) "really did . . . realise what was the degree of likelihood of serious injury." . . .

My Lords, the proposition has only to be stated thus to make one realise what a departure it is from that upon which the courts have always acted. The jury must, of course, in such a case as the present make up their minds on the evidence whether the accused was unlawfully and voluntarily doing something to someone. The unlawful and voluntary act must clearly be aimed at someone in order to eliminate cases of negligence or of careless or dangerous driving. Once, however, the jury are satisfied as to that, it matters not what the accused in fact contemplated as the probable result or whether he ever contemplated at all, provided he was in law responsible and accountable for his actions, that is, was a man capable of forming an intent, not insane within the *M'Naughten* Rules and not suffering from diminished responsibility. On the assumption that he is so accountable for his actions, the sole question is whether the unlawful and voluntary act was of such a kind that grievous bodily harm was the natural and probable result. The only test available for this is what the ordinary responsible man would, in all the circumstances of the case, have contemplated as the natural and probable result. . . .

The last criticism of the summing-up which was raised before your Lordships was in regard to the meaning which the learned judge directed the jury was to be given to the words "grievous bodily harm." The passages of which complaint is made are the following:

> When one speaks of an intent to inflict grievous bodily harm upon a person, the expression grievous bodily harm does not mean for that purpose some harm which is permanent or even dangerous. It simply means some harm which is sufficient seriously to interfere with the victim's health or comfort.
>
>   In murder the killer intends to kill, or to inflict some harm which will seriously interfere for a time with health or comfort.

If the accused intended to do the officer some harm which would seriously interfere at least for a time with his health and comfort, and thus perhaps enable the accused to make good his escape for the time being at least, but that unfortunately the officer died instead, that would be murder too. . . .

. . . I can find no warrant for giving the words "grievous bodily harm" a meaning other than that which the words convey in their ordinary and natural meaning. "Bodily harm" needs no explanation and "grievous" means no more and no less than "really serious." . . .

It was, however, contended before your Lordships on behalf of the respondent that the words ought to be given a more restricted meaning in considering the intent necessary to establish malice in a murder case. It was said that the intent must be to do an act "obviously dangerous to life" or "likely to kill." It is true that in many of the cases the likelihood of death resulting has been incorporated into the definition of grievous bodily harm, but this was done, no doubt, merely to emphasise that the bodily harm must be really serious, and it is unnecessary, and I would add inadvisable, to add anything to the expression "grievous bodily harm" in its ordinary and natural meaning. . . .

In the result the appeal should, in my opinion, be allowed and the conviction of capital murder restored.

NOTES

1. Later English developments. The Criminal Justice Act, 1967, overruled the first portion of the foregoing decision by providing in §8 as follows (Eliz. II pt. II, ch. 80):

A court or jury, in determining whether a person has committed an offence, (a) shall not be bound in law to infer that he intended or foresaw a result of his actions by reason only of its being a natural and probable consequence of those actions; but (b) shall decide whether he did intend or foresee that result by reference to all the evidence, drawing such inferences from the evidence as appear proper in the circumstances.

The House of Lords further considered the intent-to-inflict-grievous-harm formula in Hyam v. Director of Public Prosecutions, [1974] 2 All E.R. 41. The case involved a woman who set fire to the home of a woman rival by igniting gasoline-soaked newspapers stuffed in the letter box, in order, she testified, to frighten the woman and get her to leave the neighborhood. Two of the woman's children died of suffocation from the fumes. The House of Lords upheld a conviction of murder under an instruction that it sufficed that, when she acted, defendant knew that it was highly probable her action would result in serious bodily harm. It was not necessary that she "intend" the injury — only that she knew it was highly probable. See Hogan, The Killing Ground, [1974] Crim. L. Rev. 387, 388; Commentary, [1974] Crim. L. Rev. 366.

2. Critique of the intent-to-inflict-grievous-harm formula. Devlin, Criminal Responsibility and Punishment: Functions of Judge and Jury, [1954] Crim. L. Rev. 661, 668-670, writes:

The Report [of the Royal Commission on Capital Punishment] (para. 94) says: "A Person may therefore properly be convicted of murder if he has caused death either by an act intended to kill or do grievous bodily harm, or by an act likely to cause death or grievous bodily harm, and committed with reckless disregard of the consequences." The Commission takes the view that there is nothing constructive about a rule in this form. I respectfully differ from them. A rule in that form mixes intent with recklessness, and assumes that because a man does an act that is likely to cause grievous bodily harm, he intends murder. . . . [T]hey state (para. 472): "We believe that few people would dispute the propriety of making the definition of murder wide enough to include cases where death is caused by an act intended to cause serious bodily injury." I think that the number of disputants would be greater than the Commission supposes. Most cases of murder which come before the courts are cases of death by sudden violence manifestly done by the accused: in many of them the only really debatable point is whether he intended death to result. Under the existing law the jury is properly directed to ignore that question, and that it need only be satisfied that there was an intent to cause grievous bodily harm. On that, the facts generally speak for themselves, and if considered dispassionately would lead almost automatically to a verdict of murder; in an attempt to avert this the defence resorts to suggestions of accident, provocation, or mental blackout. Thus, what many people would take to be the fundamental question, and the one which ought to be answered by the jury if the nature of the crime and the degree of gravity is to be determined by the appropriate tribunal, is not put to the jury at all. . . .

The other side of the argument is that a man ought to know that if he deliberately commits an act of grievous bodily harm, he runs the risk that death may result. If he chooses to run the risk of endangering life, ought he not to be held liable for the consequences? The answer, I think, is that he is in any event held liable for the consequences, that is to say, he may be found guilty either of manslaughter or causing grievous bodily harm with intent, and for either offence may be sentenced to imprisonment for life. The question is not whether he should be exempt from the consequences, but whether his degree of guilt should be equated with that of a man who deliberately intended the consequences.

3. American law. The intent-to-inflict-grievous-harm formula is followed in many American jurisdictions. See Collings, Negligent Murder — Some Stateside Footnotes to D.P.P. v. Smith, 49 Calif. L. Rev. 254 (1961); W. LaFave & A. Scott, Criminal Law 540-541 (1972). On the issue of the meaning of "grievous bodily harm," American courts have taken different views. The view that an injury that "seriously interferes with the victim's health and comfort" suffices has been accepted in some jurisdictions. See, e.g., State v. Bowers, 178 Minn. 589, 228 N.W. 164 (1929); Commonwealth v. Dorazio, 365 Pa. 291, 301, 74 A.2d 125, 130 (1950) (a case in which a former professional fighter beat up the deceased, the court saying, "it is not necessary that the injury be intended to be permanent or dangerous to life, it is malicious to intend injury such as to seriously interfere with health and comfort"). Many courts have required more. See, e.g., People v. Crenshaw, 298 Ill. 412, 416, 131 N.E. 576, 577 (1921) (injury "likely to be attended with dangerous or fatal consequences"); Wellar v. People, 30 Mich. 16, 20 (1874) ("such an injury as may be expected to involve serious consequences, either periling life or leading to great bodily harm"). The issue in the *Smith* case of whether a "specific" intent to inflict the injury is required was squarely faced in People v. Drumheller, 15 Ill. App. 3d 418,

304 N.E.2d 455 (1973), decided in accord with *Smith*. While disciplining a 14-month-old child for whom he was caring, defendant struck the child in the stomach. The child died from acute diffused peritonitis, which resulted from an external trauma. Defendant's conviction for murder was upheld (id. at 457):

> It is not necessary to directly prove that he had an intent to kill, only that he voluntarily and wilfully committed an act, the natural tendency of which was to destroy another's life. In such instances the intent can be implied or inferred from the character of the act.

The Model Penal Code did not include the doctrine on the ground that the "reckless indifference to human life" formula for murder made it unnecessary to have a special rule for cases in which that indifference is shown by the intent to inflict great bodily harm. See American Law Institute, Model Penal Code and Commentaries, Pt. II, Comment to §210.2 at 28-29 (1980).

Recent codes have taken several approaches. Those that retain the common law definition of murder (malice aforethought) apparently carry over the doctrine intact. Others specifically articulate the doctrine. Ill. Ann. Stat. ch. 38 §9-1[2]; La. Rev. Stat. §14.30. Some states, like New York, have made intention "to cause serious physical injury"[3] a basis for manslaughter. See N.Y. Penal Law §125.20 at page 413 supra. Minnesota is among these states, but Minnesota explicitly adopts the *Smith* doctrine making it sufficient that great bodily harm was "reasonably foreseeable." Minn. Stat. Ann. §609.20. Other states, such as Oregon, have followed the Model Penal Code and abandoned the doctrine. Or. Rev. Stat. §163.115.

d. The Requirement of a Resulting Death

NOTES AND QUESTIONS

1. The issue. It may at this point be profitable to pursue a digression from the main theme of the criminality and punishment of unintended homicide. Suppose the behavior of the actor, although sufficient to make him or her criminally liable under murder or manslaughter statutes if death results (we will call this culpable negligence, for purposes of convenience), does not, fortunately, result in death. Should this difference in the result of the actor's conduct exculpate him or her from criminal liability or even reduce the punishment? This question is at the bottom of much of the material in Chapter 7, The Significance of Resulting Harm, infra. An analysis of these problems appears in Schulhofer,

---

2. "A person who kills an individual without lawful justification commits murder if, in performing the acts which cause death: (1) He either intends to kill or do great bodily harm to that individual or another, or knows that such acts will cause death to that individual or another; or (2) He knows that such acts create a strong probability of death or great bodily harm to that individual or another. . . ."

3. This is defined in §10(9) as "physical injury which creates a substantial risk of death, or which causes serious and protracted disfigurement, protracted impairment of health or protracted loss or impairment of the function of any bodily organ."

Harm and Punishment: A Critique of Emphasis on the Results of Conduct in the Criminal Law, 122 U. Pa. L. Rev. 1497 (1974).

See Wechsler, The Challenge of a Model Penal Code, 65 Harv. L. Rev. 1097, 1106-1107 (1952):

> From the preventive point of view, the harmfulness of conduct rests upon its tendency to cause the injuries to be prevented far more than on its actual results; results, indeed, have meaning only insofar as they may indicate or dramatize the tendencies involved. Reckless driving is no more than reckless driving if there is a casualty and no less if by good fortune nothing should occur. Actual consequences may, of course, arouse resentments that have bearing on the proper sanction. But if the criminality of conduct is to turn on the result, it rests upon fortuitous considerations unrelated to the major purpose to be served by declaration that behavior is a crime.
>
> This point is reflected broadly in existing law when criminality involves intentional misconduct; if the act is of the kind that tends to cause the injury forbidden it will normally be criminal as an assault or an attempt if it has failed of its object in the concrete case. Moreover, many substantive offenses, such as burglary, blackmail, perjury and forgery, for example, are defined without regard to whether the ultimate evil sought to be avoided has occurred. So too, much conduct is made criminal because it tends to promote or facilitate the criminality of other persons — as in receiving stolen goods, incitement and some of the forms of accessorial responsibility. There are many situations, nonetheless, especially involving recklessness or negligence, where the criminality of highly dangerous behavior turns on whether it has actually caused the untoward consequence that it portends. A major issue to be faced, therefore, is whether penal law ought to be shaped to deal more comprehensively with risk creation, without reference to actual results.

To make our inquiry more concrete, suppose, for example, in Commonwealth v. Malone, pages 457-459 supra, that the bullet only injured the boy or that the loaded chamber was not fired at all; or suppose in State v. Barnett, pages 441-443 supra, that the person struck by defendant's car recovered or came out unscathed; or in Commonwealth v. Welansky, pages 445-446 supra, that no one was killed, although some received burns, or that all escaped without injury or, indeed, that the fire violations were discovered before any fire occurred; or in Commonwealth v. Pierce, pages 453-454 supra, that the kerosene-soaked patient recovered or was sufficiently tough-skinned not to have been injured at all. In each case, of what crimes would defendant be punishable under present law? Consider the following possibilities and whether they are adequate:

In *Malone* there might be a special statute against playing Russian roulette or discharging firearms; in *Barnett* there probably could be a careless driving prosecution; in *Welansky* the violation of the fire safety code would provide a basis for prosecution; in *Pierce* it is doubtful there could be any prosecution at all. In general, under the common law and under traditional American codes, the only possible prosecution in cases of these kinds is for that based on ad hoc statutory crimes, which, apart from reckless driving, are narrowly focused on limited classes of conduct of little general consequence. And, of course, punishments are substantially less for these crimes than when a death results. See American Law Institute, Model Penal Code and Commentaries, Pt. II, Comment to §211.1 at 195-197 (1980).

Is there any good reason for the law to attribute such great significance to the fortuity of a homicidal result?

2. Some views on the issue.

3 J. F. Stephen, A History of the Criminal Law 311 (1883): If two persons are guilty of the very same act of negligence, and if one of them causes thereby a railway accident, involving the death and mutilation of many persons, whereas the other does no injury to anyone, it seems to me that it would be rather pedantic than rational to say that each had committed the same offence, and should be subjected to the same punishment. In one sense, each has committed an offence, but the one has had the *bad luck* to cause a horrible misfortune, and to attract public attention to it, and the other the good *fortune* to do no harm. Both certainly deserve punishment, but it gratifies a natural public feeling to choose out for punishment the one who actually has caused great harm, and the effect in the way of preventing a repetition of the offence is much the same as if both were punished.

Smith, The Element of Chance in Criminal Liability, [1971] Crim. L. Rev. 63, 74-75: Something certainly depends on the public sentiment to which Stephen attached so much importance. If the law runs directly counter to public sentiment there is a danger that it will not be enforced. This might provide a case against extending the criminal law to cases of culpable conduct where no harm is caused. We already have some such offences in our law and there is some evidence that they are rarely used unless harm has in fact been caused. Lady Wootton, a magistrate of great experience, has written that it is exceptional for a driving charge to be made unless an accident actually occurs and that the nature of the charge is apt to be determined by the severity of the accident. Although the offences of careless and dangerous driving require no harm, those administering the law still look for it. Lady Wootton recalls a case of a man who was charged with careless driving after knocking an elderly man down on a pedestrian crossing. When the victim died a month later, the offence was upgraded to causing death by dangerous driving. The death was entirely irrelevant to the question whether the proper charge was careless or dangerous driving; but the harm caused was evidently the main consideration in the eyes of the police. It is wrong to enact criminal laws which will not be enforced. . . .

A final argument, and perhaps a decisive one, is the question whether the deterrent effect of the criminal law is lessened by the immunity of those who act in a culpable way but who do not cause harm. Stephen, you will recall, argued that the deterrent effect of the criminal law is not materially reduced by excusing the *negligent* who do not cause harm. . . . Is society any less secure because a reckless wrongdoer escapes liability because he does not do harm? The principle should be that we have the minimum criminal law necessary. The law should not be extended merely because to introduce logic and consistency, but only if the extension is shown to be necessary for the proper protection of society.

H. L. A. Hart, The Morality of the Criminal Law 52-53 (1965): [Professor Hart, after quoting the above extract from Stephen, observes:]

This doctrine allocating to "public feeling" so important a place in the determination of punishment reflects the element of populism which, as we have seen, is often prominent in English judicial conceptions of the morality of punishment. But it conflicts with important principles of justice as between different offenders which would prima facie preclude treating two persons, guilty of "the very same act" of negligence, differently because of a fortuitous difference in the outcome of these acts. No doubt there is often an inclination to treat punishment like compensation and measure it by the outcome alone. There may even be at times a public demand that this should be done. And no doubt if the machinery of justice were nullified or could not proceed unless the demand were gratified we might have to gratify it and hope to educate people out of this misassimilation of the principles of punishment to those of compensation. But there seems no good reason for adopting this misassimilation as a principle or to stigmatise as pedantic the refusal to recognise that the difference made by "bad fortune" and "good luck" to the outcome of the very same acts justifies punishing the one and not the other.

3. Statutory reforms. The Model Penal Code led the way to a change in the law with its reckless-endangerment provision. Section 211.2 provides: "A person commits a misdemeanor if he recklessly engages in conduct which places or may place another person in danger of death or serious bodily injury."

Most states which have undertaken revisions of their criminal codes in recent years have adopted comparable provisions. Many of these states have found the penalty inadequate. An example of a more stringent treatment is the New York statute, which has been followed in a number of jurisdictions. The New York Penal Law provides:

SECTION 120.20
A person is guilty of reckless endangerment in the second degree when he recklessly engages in conduct which creates a substantial risk of serious physical injury to another person. [Maximum one-year imprisonment.]

SECTION 120.25
A person is guilty of reckless endangerment in the first degree when, under circumstances evincing a depraved indifference to human life, he recklessly engages in conduct which creates a grave risk of death to another person. [Maximum seven-years imprisonment.]

Do such reforms eliminate the disparities in grading that were associated with fortuitous results? Under the Model Penal Code and New York provisions, to what extent will the punishment authorized for reckless endangerment depend on the actual result of the defendant's conduct?

4. A recent version of the proposed federal Criminal Code Reform Act (Senate Judiciary Committee Bill No. S. 1722, December 1979) provides in §1617:

A person is guilty of an offense if he engages in conduct that he knows places another person in imminent danger of death or serious bodily injury, and (1) his conduct in the circumstances manifests an extreme indifference to human life [five-year maximum term]; or (2) his conduct in the circumstances manifests an unjustified disregard for human life [two-year maximum term].

The section also provides that there is federal jurisdiction if the offense is committed within the special jurisdiction of the United States and also where the imminent danger is created by conduct constituting an offense under several federal statutes — that is, the Environmental Pollution Act, the Federal Mine Safety and Health Act, the Occupational Safety and Health Act, the Federal Hazardous Substances Act, the Public Health Service Act, or the Federal Food, Drug and Cosmetic Act.

2. The Commission of Crime

a. The Unlawful-Act Doctrine

STATE v. HUPF

Supreme Court of Delaware

48 Del. 254, 101 A.2d 355 (1953)

SOUTHERLAND, C.J. The Superior Court of New Castle County has certified to us for answer, pursuant to Art. IV, §11(9) of the Constitution questions of law growing out of a prosecution for manslaughter.

The essential question is whether the crime of involuntary manslaughter is established by proof of death resulting proximately from the commission of an unlawful act, or whether there must also be proof of conduct evidencing reckless disregard for the lives or safety of others.

Defendant was involved in an automobile accident when the car that he was driving collided with another car. As a result of the collision a passenger in his car was killed.

Defendant was indicted for manslaughter. The indictment was in six counts. Four of these counts charged violations of four sections of the Delaware Motor Vehicle Laws embodying rules of the road. The other two counts charged "common law manslaughter" and failure to keep a proper lookout. The case was tried by the court without a jury. The State established, and the defendant admitted, the violation of the four sections of the motor vehicle laws as charged in the indictment. The court found, however, that the State had failed to establish a reckless disregard for the life and safety of others so as to make the defendant guilty of "common law manslaughter," i.e., criminal negligence. . . .

[The question submitted to the Supreme Court of Delaware was whether, if death results proximately from any of a series of motor-vehicle violations, a finding of manslaughter is justified in the absence of any showing of a reckless disregard for life and safety of others. The Delaware Motor Vehicle Laws provisions violated included: (a) failure to stop at a stop sign, (b) failure to observe right of way at intersection, (c) failure to slow down at intersection, (d) driving faster than reasonable and proper.]

To answer these questions we must determine the elements of the species of the crime of manslaughter that involves an unintentional killing and hence is called "involuntary manslaughter." Since our statute, 11 Del. C. §575, contains no definition, we must look to common law principles. The classic definition is that of Blackstone, "the unlawful killing of another . . . involuntarily, but in the commission of some unlawful act." Com. Vol. 4, p. 191. It is clear from the illustrations in Blackstone's text that by the phrase "unlawful act" the learned author meant either an act unlawful in itself or a lawful act done "in an unlawful manner, and without due caution and circumspection." Id. p. 192.

The textbooks have followed generally this division of involuntary manslaughter, into two classes, one characterized by the commission of an unlawful act, and the other by the doing of a lawful act in a negligent (or grossly negligent) manner. . . .

. . . [T]he Delaware cases have accepted this classification, although the two concepts — disobedience to law and negligence — have sometimes been confused.

In the instant case counts, 2, 3, 4 and 5 of the indictment charge offenses falling within the first class; counts 1 and 6 charge offenses falling within the second class. The questions certified by the lower court concern the four counts based on violations of law. These questions will be considered together since they present a single point for determination: Does a homicide resulting proximately from violation of a penal law, not amounting to a felony, constitute involuntary manslaughter without proof of rash or reckless conduct amounting to gross negligence?

If the definitions above quoted correctly state the law the answer to this question must be in the affirmative. And a review of the Delaware cases leaves no doubt that our courts, in dealing with the first class of cases involving violations of law, have followed the common-law rule. . . .

Defendant argues that the common-law rule is too harsh. When applied to the operation of the motor vehicle it results, he says, in stamping as a felon any automobile operator who may, without conscious wrongdoing, have violated one of the many statutory regulations governing the use of the automobile, if he is involved in an accident resulting in death. Thus, defendant says that the driver of an automobile taking a seriously injured person to the hospital is, under the common-law rule, equally guilty of manslaughter if he violates the speed limit and a child is killed by darting out in front of him, as is the driver who consciously attempts to pass another car upon a twisting hill and as a result is involved in a fatal collision.

The answer to this argument is that if, in such a case, the excessive speed was the proximate cause of the accident, the driver is indeed guilty, but the circumstances would go in mitigation of punishment; and that if the excessive speed was not the proximate cause of death (as might be inferred from the use of the phrase "darting out"), the driver is not guilty. The doctrine of proximate cause is an important limitation on the common-law rule that a homicide occurring in the commission of an unlawful act is manslaughter. The mere violation of the statute is not enough; the violation must be the proximate cause of the death, and that causal connection must affirmatively appear. The unlawful act must be "something more than a factor which might be denominated more properly as an attendant condition than a cause of the death." So said the Superior Court of Pennsylvania in Commonwealth v. Williams, 133 Pa. Super. 104, 1 A.2d 812, 814, in reversing a conviction for manslaughter by motor vehicle where the unlawful act charged was a failure to renew an operator's license.

We agree that by no means all the American authorities are in accord with the common-law rule. Some courts have imported into the law of involuntary manslaughter a distinction, in respect of unlawful acts, between one malum prohibitum and one malum in se. Such a distinction has never been recognized in our cases, and we see no reason to adopt it. To do so would be to introduce confusion and uncertainty into a rule of law now plain and understandable.

There are no doubt many regulations applicable to motor vehicles the violation of which does not evince moral turpitude; but it does not seem too much to ask that the automobile driver be held to strict accountability for violation of regulations prescribed by the law-making power in the interest of public order and safety, if that violation is the cause of the death of another. A careful application by the courts of the doctrine of proximate cause, and the common sense of the jury, should prevent any undue hardship in the enforcement of the common-law rule.

We hold that death resulting proximately from the commission of an unlawful act not a felony or tending to great bodily harm constitutes manslaughter, and that it is unnecessary for the State to prove conscious or reckless disregard of the lives or safety of others. [Questions certified answered in affirmative.]

NOTES

1. The "proximate-cause" limitation. As indicated in the *Hupf* case, the unlawful-act doctrine (sometimes called the misdemeanor-manslaughter rule) comes into play only when the unlawful act is the proximate cause of death. The proximate-cause concept is explored in depth in Chapter 7, The Significance of Resulting Harm, infra, but at a minimum it means, in this context, that the death must be related to the illegal aspects of the defendant's conduct. Thus, in Commonwealth v. Williams, discussed in *Hupf,* the court reversed a manslaughter conviction because the expiration of the driver's license was unrelated to the accident, which was caused by the carelessness of another driver.

Although virtually all courts accept the proximate-cause limitation, at least one jurisdiction has rejected it. The Florida "driving-when-intoxicated" statute has been interpreted to make a death manslaughter when it results from the defendant's operation of a vehicle if the defendant was intoxicated at the time, regardless of whether the intoxication was the cause of the death. Upholding the constitutionality of the statute so interpreted, the Florida Supreme Court, in Baker v. State, 377 So. 2d 17, 20 (Fla. 1979), indicated that the arguments used to justify the elimination of mens rea can be extended to justify eliminating proximate-cause requirements as well:

> Given . . . that the operation of a motor vehicle while intoxicated is a reckless (and therefore culpable) act, is it rational for the legislature to impose criminal sanctions for any death which occurs without regard to the tort law concept of proximate causation between operation of the automobile and the death? If the legislature can reasonably conclude that such a measure operates as a deterrent to those who create a recognized and serious social problem, then certainly it is. Although . . . legal scholars have questioned the efficacy of the deterrent effect of strict liability statutes, an argument can be made that the presence of strict liability sanctions for a particular activity has the effect not only of inducing persons to engage in that activity with greater caution, but may also have the effect of keeping a relatively large class of persons from engaging in the conduct at all. This thesis cannot be proved empirically, but neither can the position of the opponents of strict criminal liability. Consequently, it cannot be asserted that the legislature has acted irrationally in enacting section 860.01(2) where it is just as plausible

as not that it does have the desired deterrent effect. . . . Accordingly, we hold
that neither negligence nor proximate causation is an element of the crime embodied in section 860.01(2), Florida Statutes (1977), and the failure to include them
as elements of proof does not deprive appellant of due process of law.

In a dissenting opinion, Judge Boyd responded (id. at 22):

The way to deter such anti-social conduct is to impose severe penalties upon all
those who are apprehended engaging in it. To reserve an especially harsh penalty
for the relatively few offenders whose conduct happens to coincide with a collision
causing death does not serve the purpose of deterrence, nor is it supported by
any other rational basis. . . . Since the conduct of one who drives while intoxicated
is of the same degree of culpability regardless of whether such a collision and
death occur, the provision for a possible maximum sentence of fifteen years' imprisonment [when death occurs, compared to a maximum penalty of six months in
jail or a $500 fine in the absence of death,] constitutes excessive punishment in
violation of the Eighth and Fourteenth Amendments to the United States Constitution. A punishment is excessive if it "makes no measurable contribution to acceptable goals of punishment and hence is nothing more than the purposeless and
needless imposition of pain and suffering; or . . . is grossly out of proportion to
the severity of the crime." Coker v. Georgia, 433 U.S. 584, 592 (1977).

2. *Other limitations on the unlawful-act doctrine.* A variety of other rules is sometimes invoked to limit the operation of the unlawful-act doctrine, but there is
little consensus about which limitations are proper. Some courts restrict the
doctrine to malum in se as opposed to malum prohibitum misdemeanors, e.g.,
Mills v. State, 13 Md. App. 196, 282 A.2d 147 (1971), but many courts have
explicitly rejected this approach. (See, for example, the *Hupf* case, supra.) Other
approaches include requiring that the act, apart from its unlawfulness, amount
to criminal negligence, State v. Strobel, 130 Mont. 442, 304 P.2d 606 (1950),
or "evince a marked disregard for the safety of others," State v. Lingman, 97
Utah 180, 91 P.2d 457 (1939). See generally W. LaFave & A. Scott, Criminal
Law 597-601 (1972).

3. *The justifications for the unlawful-act doctrine.* Even as limited by the proximate-
cause requirement or in the various other ways just mentioned, is the unlawful-
act doctrine a sound and useful doctrine for achieving the purposes of a penal
code? The Model Penal Code drafters did not think so, regarding it as a species
of strict liability:

It dispenses with proof of culpability and imposes liability for serious crime without
reference to the actor's state of mind. This result is not only morally unjustified,
but it also operates quite inequitably among individuals.

American Law Institute, Model Penal Code and Commentaries, Pt. II, Comment
to §210.3 at 77 (1980). Does this argument apply to the *Hupf* case? Does the
requirement of culpability for the misdemeanor meet the criticism? Is the inequity
among individuals greater than that in any case where the fortuity of a resulting
death substantially enhances the punishment?

4. *Statutory reform.* Under the influence of the Model Penal Code, many statutory
revisions have abolished the unlawful-act doctrine, but a fair number have pre-

served it, and of course the doctrine continues in force in most jurisdictions that have not recodified their law. See American Law Institute, Model Penal Code and Commentaries, Pt. II, Comment to §210.3 at 77 (1980).

PROBLEMS

Suppose that the underlying misdemeanor is a strict-liability offense itself and therefore requires no culpability. Is this a reason for holding the unlawful-act doctrine inapplicable? Consider the following situations.

(a) Defendant drives through an intersection marked by a stop sign that defendant should but does not see. A pedestrian is killed because of the failure to stop.

(b) Defendant drives through an intersection without stopping for a stop sign that defendant does not see. Because the sign is largely obscured by a hedge, most careful drivers would not have noticed it either. Nevertheless the traffic law would treat the failure to stop as an offense under these circumstances. A pedestrian is killed because of the failure to stop.

(c) Defendant, a pharmacist, sells a contaminated drug, in violation of state law making this a strict-liability offense. No reasonable amount of care on his part would have alerted him to the contamination. The purchaser is killed because of the contamination. Compare People v. Stuart, 47 Cal. 2d 167, 302 P.2d 5 (1956) (unlawful-act doctrine inapplicable), with People v. Nelson, 309 N.Y. 231, 128 N.E.2d 391 (1955) (to the contrary).

b. The Felony-Murder Doctrine

(i)   The Basic Doctrine

REGINA v. SERNÉ
Central Criminal Court
16 Cox Crim. Cas. 311 (1887)

The prisoners Leon Serné and John Henry Goldfinch were indicted for the murder of a boy, Sjaak Serné, the son of the prisoner Leon Serné, it being alleged that they wilfully set on fire a house and shop, No. 274 Strand, London, by which act the death of the boy had been caused.

It appeared that the prisoner Serné with his wife, two daughters, and two sons were living at the house in question; and that Serné, at the time he was living there, in Midsummer, 1887, was in a state of pecuniary embarrassment, and had put into the premises furniture and other goods of but very little value, which at the time of the fire were not of greater value than £30. It also appeared that previously to the fire the prisoner Serné had insured the life of the boy Sjaak Serné, who was imbecile, and on the first day of September, 1887, had insured his stock at 274 Strand, for £500, his furniture for £100, and his rent for another £100; and that on the 17th of the same month the premises were burnt down.

Evidence was given on behalf of the prosecution that fires were seen breaking out in several parts of the premises at the same time, soon after the prisoners had been seen in the shop together, two fires being in the lower part of the house and two above, on the floor whence escape could be made on the roof of the adjoining house, and in which part were the prisoners, and the wife, and two daughters of Serné, who escaped. That on the premises were a quantity of tissue transparencies for advertising purposes, which were of a most inflammable character; and that on the site of one of the fires was found a great quantity of these transparencies close to other inflammable materials. That the prisoner Serné, his wife and daughters, were rescued from the roof of the adjoining house, the other prisoner being rescued from a window in the front of the house, but that the boys were burnt to death, the body of the one being found on the floor near the window from which the prisoner Serné, his wife, and daughters had escaped, the body of the other being found at the basement of the premises.

STEPHEN, J. Gentlemen, it is now my duty to direct your attention to the law and the facts into which you have to inquire. The two prisoners are indicted for the wilful murder of the boy Sjaak Serné, a lad of about fourteen years of age; and it is necessary that I should explain to you, to a certain extent, the law of England with regard to the crime of wilful murder, inasmuch as you have heard something said about constructive murder. Now that phrase, gentlemen, has no legal meaning whatever. There was wilful murder according to the plain meaning of the term, or there was no murder at all in the present case. The definition of murder is unlawful homicide with malice aforethought, and the words malice aforethought are technical. You must not, therefore, construe them or suppose that they can be construed by ordinary rules of language. The words have to be construed according to a long series of decided cases, which have given them meanings different from those which might be supposed. One of those meanings is, the killing of another person by an act done with an intent to commit a felony. Another meaning is, an act done with the knowledge that the act will probably cause the death of some person. Now it is such an act as the last which is alleged to have been done in this case; and if you think that either or both of these men in the dock killed this boy, either by an act done with intent to commit a felony, that is to say, the setting of the house on fire in order to cheat the insurance company, or by conduct which to their knowledge was likely to cause death and was therefore eminently dangerous in itself — in either of these cases the prisoners are guilty of wilful murder in the plain meaning of the word. I will say a word or two upon one part of this definition, because it is capable of being applied very harshly in certain cases, and also because, though I take the law as I find it, I very much doubt whether the definition which I have given, although it is the common definition, is not somewhat too wide. Now when it is said that murder means killing a man by an act done in the commission of a felony, the mere words cover a case like this, that is to say, a case where a man gives another a push with an intention of stealing his watch, and the person so pushed, having a weak heart or some other internal disorder, dies. To take another very old illustration, it was said that if a man shot a fowl with intent to steal it and accidentally killed a man, he was to be accounted guilty of murder, because the act was done in the commission of a felony.[a] I very much doubt, however, whether that is really the law, or whether the Court for the Consideration of Crown Cases Reserved would hold it to be so. The present case, however, is not such as I have cited, nor anything like them. In my opinion the definition of the law which makes it murder to kill by an act done in the commission of a felony might and ought to be narrowed, while that part of the law under which the Crown in this case claim to have proved a case of murder is maintained. I think that, instead of saying that any act done with intent to commit a felony and which causes death amounts to murder, it would be reasonable to say that any act known to be dangerous to life and likely in itself to cause death, done for the purpose of committing a felony which causes death, should be murder. As an illustration of this, suppose that a man, intending to commit a rape upon a woman, but without the least wish to kill her, squeezed her by the throat to overpower her, and in so doing killed her, that would be murder.[b] I think that every one would say in a case like that, that when a person began doing wicked acts for his own base purposes, he risked his own life as well as that of others. That kind of crime does not differ in any serious degree from one committed by using a deadly weapon, such as a bludgeon, a pistol, or a knife. If a man once begins attacking the human body in such a way, he must take the consequences if he goes further than he intended when he began. That I take to be the true meaning of the law in the subject. In the present case, gentlemen, you have a man sleeping in a house with his wife, his two daughters, his two sons, and a servant, and you are asked to believe that this man, with all these people under

a. Coke, 3d Institute 56 (1644): "If the act be unlawful it is murder. As if *A* meaning to steale a deer in the park of *B*, shooteth at the deer, and by the glance of the arrow killeth a boy that is hidden in a bush; this is murder, for that the act was unlawful, although *A* had no intent to hurt the boy, nor knew not of him. But if *B* the owner of the park had shot at his own deer, and without any ill intent had killed the boy by the glance of his arrow, this had been homicide by misadventure, and no felony.

"So if one shoot at any wild fowle upon a tree, and the arrow killeth any reasonable creature afar off, without any evill intent in him, this is per infortunium: for it was not unlawful to shoot at the wilde fowle: but if he had shot at a cock or hen, or any tame fowle of another mans, and the arrow by mischance had killed a man, this had been murder, for the act was unlawfull."

Foster's Crown Law 258-259 (1762): "Accidental Homicide: In order to bring the case within this description, the act upon which death ensueth must be lawful: for if the act be unlawful, I mean if it be malum in se, the case will amount to felony, either murder or manslaughter, as circumstances may vary the nature of it. If it be done in prosecution of a felonious intention it will be murder, but if the intent went no farther than to commit a bare trespass, manslaughter: though, I confess, Lord Coke seemeth to think otherwise. . . .

"[For example,] *A* shooteth at the poultry of *B*, and by accident killeth a man; if his intention was to steal the poultry, which must be collected from circumstances, it will be murder by reason of that felonious intent; but if it was done wantonly and without that intention it will be barely manslaughter."—EDS.

b. Cf. D.P.P. v. Beard, [1920] A.C. 479. Beard was convicted of the murder of a 13-year-old girl whom he raped. The evidence indicated that "when she struggled to escape from him, he placed his hand over her mouth, and his thumb on her throat, thereby causing her death by suffocation." On appeal to the court of criminal appeal the point was taken that the judge committed error in instructing the jury by failing to tell them that if they thought that the violent act which was the immediate cause of death, that is, the pressure of the defendant's thumb on the child's throat, was not intentional on his part but was an accidental consequence of his placing his hand over her mouth to stop her screams, they should, or could, return a verdict of manslaughter. The court rejected this contention holding that the defendant killed the child by "an act of violence done in the course of or in furtherance of a felony involving violence; and beyond all questions and beyond the range of controversy that is murder." The House of Lords upheld the court of appeal stating: "No attempt has been made in Their Lordships' House to displace this view of the law, and there can be no doubt as to its soundness." (Id. at 493.) — EDS.

his protection, deliberately set fire to the house in three or four different places and thereby burnt two of them to death. It is alleged that he arranged matters in such a way that any person of the most common intelligence must have known perfectly well that he was placing all those people in deadly risk. It appears to me that if that were really done, it matters very little indeed whether the prisoners hoped the people would escape or whether they did not. If a person chose, for some wicked purpose of his own to sink a boat at sea, and thereby caused the deaths of the occupants, it matters nothing whether at the time of committing the act he hoped that the people would be picked up by a passing vessel. He is as much guilty of murder if the people are drowned, as if he had flung every person into the water with his own hand. Therefore, gentlemen, if Serné and Goldfinch set fire to this house when the family were in it, and if the boys were by that act stifled or burnt to death, then the prisoners are as much guilty of murder as if they had stabbed the children. I will also add, for my own part, that I think, in so saying, the law of England lays down a rule of broad, plain common-sense. Treat a murderer how you will, award him what punishment you choose, it is your duty, gentlemen, if you think him really guilty of murder, to say so. That is the law of the land, and I have no doubt in my mind with regard to it. There was a case tried in this court which you will no doubt remember, and which will illustrate my meaning. It was the Clerkenwell explosion case in 1868, when a man named Barrett was charged with causing the death of several persons by an explosion which was intended to release one or two men from custody; and I am sure that no one can say truly that Barrett was not justly hanged. With regard to the facts in the present case, the very horror of the crime, if crime it was, the abomination of it, is a reason for your taking the most extreme care in the case, and for not imputing to the prisoners anything which is not clearly proved. God forbid that I should, by what I say, produce on your minds, even in the smallest degree any feeling against the prisoners. You must see, gentlemen, that the evidence leaves no reasonable doubt upon your minds; but you will fail in the performance of your duty if, being satisfied with the evidence, you do not convict one or both the prisoners of wilful murder, and it is wilful murder of which they are accused.

[Verdict, not guilty.]

PEOPLE v. STAMP, 2 Cal. App. 2d 203, 82 Cal. Rptr. 598 (1969): [Defendant burglarized the business premises of the deceased and robbed him at the point of a gun. Deceased, who suffered from acute heart disease, died shortly thereafter of a heart attack partly brought on by the fright and rough handling he experienced during the robbery. Defendant's conviction of first-degree murder was upheld. The court stated:] The [felony-murder] doctrine is not limited to those deaths which are forseeable. Rather a felon is held strictly liable for *all* killings committed by him or his accomplices in the course of the felony. As long as the homicide is the direct causal result of the robbery the felony-murder rule applies whether or not the death was a natural or probable consequence of the robbery. So long as a victim's predisposing physical condition, regardless of its cause, is not the *only* substantial factor bringing about his death, that condition and the robber's ignorance of it, in no way destroys the robber's criminal responsibility for the death. So long as life is shortened as a result of the felonious act it does not matter that the victim might have died soon anyway. In this respect, the robber takes his victim as he finds him.

NOTE ON THE RATIONALE OF THE FELONY-MURDER RULE

We have previously examined the proposition sometimes asserted that the mens rea of a lesser offense may substitute for the mens rea of a greater offense. Reconsider Regina v. Cunningham, pages 269-271 supra, and Regina v. Faulknor, pages 271-272 supra, where that proposition was rejected. As we saw in connection with the misdemeanor-manslaughter doctrine and now again in connection with felony-murder, precisely that proposition serves as the basis of liability. Does the proposition have any greater justification in homicidal crimes than in other crimes? If the law is sound in requiring a particular mens rea to establish murder, is it, by definition, unsound to require less solely because the actor is guilty of another crime? The offense accompanying the killing has its own punishment. In what sense does the offense also add to the criminality of the killing (as by making an otherwise noncriminal killing criminal) or to the grade of the criminal killing (as by making murder what otherwise would be manslaughter)?

Consider the following arguments against the felony-murder rule:

T. B. Macaulay, A Penal Code Prepared by the Indian Law Commissioners, Note M, 64-65 (1837): It will be admitted that, when an act is in itself innocent, to punish the person who does it because bad consequences which no human wisdom could have foreseen have followed from it would be in the highest degree barbarous and absurd.

A Pilot is navigating the Hooghly with the utmost care and skill; he directs the vessel against a sand bank which has been recently formed, and of which the existence was altogether unknown till this disaster. Several of his passengers are consequently drowned. To hang the Pilot as a murderer on account of this misfortune would be universally allowed to be an act of atrocious injustice. But if the voyage of the Pilot be itself a high offence, ought that circumstance alone to turn his misfortune into a murder? Suppose that he is engaged in conveying an offender beyond the reach of justice, that he has kidnapped some natives, and is carrying them to a ship which is to convey them to some foreign slave-colony, that he is violating the laws of quarantine at a time when it is of the highest importance that those laws should be strictly observed, that he is carrying supplies, deserters, and intelligence to the enemies of the State. The offence of such a Pilot ought undoubtedly to be severely punished. But to pronounce him guilty of one offence because a misfortune befell him while he was committing another offence, — to pronounce him the murderer of people whose lives he never meant to endanger, whom he was doing his best to carry safe to their destination, and whose death has been purely accidental, — is surely to confound all the boundaries of crime. . . .

To punish as a murderer every man who, while committing a heinous offence, causes death by pure misadventure, is a course which evidently adds nothing to the security of human life. No man can so conduct himself as to make it absolutely certain that he shall not be so unfortunate as to cause the death of a fellow creature. The utmost that he can do is to abstain from every thing which is at all likely to cause death. No fear of punishment can make him do more than this: and therefore to punish a man who has done this can add nothing to the security of human life. The only good effect which such punishment can produce will be to deter people from committing any of those offences which turn into murders what are in themselves mere accidents. It is in fact an addition to the punishment of those offences, and it is an addition in the very worst way. For example, hundreds of persons in some great cities are in the habit of picking pockets. They know that they are guilty of a great offence. But it has never occurred to one of them, nor would it occur to any rational man, that they are guilty of an offence which endangers life. Unhappily one of these hundreds attempts to take the purse of a gentleman who has a loaded pistol in his pocket. The thief touches the trigger: the pistol goes off: the gentleman is shot dead. To treat the case of this pick-pocket differently from that of the numerous pick-pockets who steal under exactly the same circumstances, with exactly the same intentions, with no less risk of causing death, with no greater care to avoid causing death, — to send them to the house of correction as thieves, and him to the gallows as a murderer, — appears to us an unreasonable course. If the punishment for stealing from a person be too light, let it be increased, and let the increase fall alike on all the offenders. Surely the worst mode of increasing the punishment of an offence is to provide that, besides the ordinary punishment, every offender shall run an exceedingly small risk of being hanged. The more nearly the amount of punishment can be reduced to a certainty the better. But if chance is to be admitted there are better ways of admitting it. It would be a less capricious, and therefore a more salutary course, to provide that every fiftieth or every hundredth thief selected by lot should be hanged, than to provide that every thief should be hanged who, while engaged in stealing, should meet with an unforeseen misfortune such as might have befallen the most virtuous man while performing the most virtuous action.

Model Penal Code, Comment to §210.2, American Law Institute, Model Penal Code and Commentaries, Pt. II, at 37-39 (1980): [The American Law Institute recommended eliminating the felony-murder rule except to the extent that for the purpose of establishing murder by an act "committed recklessly under circumstances manifesting extreme indifference to the value of human life," the fact that the actor is "engaged, or is an accomplice in the commission of, or an attempt to commit, or flight after committing or attempting to commit robbery, rape or deviate sexual intercourse by force or threat of force, arson, burglary, kidnapping or felonious escape" creates a rebuttable presumption (defined in §1.12(5)) that the required indifference and recklessness existed.

[In support of this proposal, the Comment states:] Principled argument in favor of the felony-murder doctrine is hard to find. The defense reduces to the explanation that Holmes gave for finding the law "intelligible as it stands":

[I]f experience shows, or is deemed by the law-maker to show, that somehow or other deaths which the evidence makes accidental happen disproportionately often in connection with other felonies, or with resistance to officers, or if on any other ground of policy it is deemed desirable to make special efforts for the prevention of such deaths, the law-maker may consistently treat acts which, under the known

circumstances, are felonious, or constitute resistance to officers, as having a sufficiently dangerous tendency to be put under a special ban. The law may, therefore,
throw on the actor the peril, not only of the consequences foreseen by him, but
also of consequences which, although not predicted by common experience, the
legislator apprehends.[95]

The answer to such argument is twofold. First, there is no basis in experience
for thinking that homicides *which the evidence makes accidental* occur with disproportionate frequency in connection with specified felonies.[96] Second, it remains
indefensible in principle to use the sanctions that the law employs to deal with
murder unless there is at least a finding that the actor's conduct manifested
an extreme indifference to the value of human life. The fact that the actor
was engaged in a crime of the kind that is included in the usual first-degree
felony-murder enumeration or was an accomplice in such crime, as has been
observed, will frequently justify such a finding. Indeed, the probability that such
a finding will be justified seems high enough to warrant the presumption of
extreme indifference that Subsection (1)(b) creates.[a] But liability depends, as
plainly it should, upon the crucial finding. The result may not differ often under
such a formulation from that which would be reached under some form of
the felony-murder rule. But what is more important is that a conviction on
this basis rests solidly upon principle.

NOTE ON STATUTORY RESPONSES

England, whose judges created the felony-murder rule through the common
law process, abolished it by statute with the enactment of §1 of the Homicide
Act of 1957, 5 & 6 Eliz. 2, ch. 11, which provided:

95. O. Holmes, The Common Law 49 (1881). [See also Justice Traynor in People v. Washington,
62 Cal. 2d 777, 402 P.2d 130, 133 (1965): "The purpose of the felony-murder rule is to deter
felons from killing negligently or accidentally by holding them strictly responsible for killings they
commit."]

96. In fact, the number of all homicides which occur in the commission of such crimes as robbery,
burglary, or rape is lower than might be expected. For example, comparison of the figures for
solved and unsolved homicides from M. Wolfgang, Criminal Homicide (1958), with statistics on
basic felonies taken from the FBI Uniform Crime Reports reveals the following for Philadelphia
from 1948-1952:

Relation of Total Felonies to Homicides Occurring
during the Felony
Philadelphia 1948-1952

Offense	No. of Crimes Reported	No. Accompanied by Homicide	%	No. per 1000
Robbery	6,432	38	0.59	5.9
Rape	1,133	4	0.35	3.5
Burglary	27,669	1	0.0036	[.036]
Auto Theft	10,315	2	0.019	[.19]

Similar figures are found in Cook County, Illinois, robbery statistics from 1926-1930. . . . More
recent statistics derived from N.J. State Police, Crime in New Jersey: Uniform Crime Reports 42-
45 (1975) reveal strikingly similar percentages. In 1975, 16,273 robberies were committed in New
Jersey, and 66 homicides resulted from these robberies, only .41 per cent, a figure even lower
than the earlier statistics from Cook County and Philadelphia. When other violent felonies are
taken into account, this percentage drops even lower. . . .
a. Does this sentence square with the point made at the beginning of the same paragraph and
with the evidence offered in footnote 96? — Eds.

> Where a person kills another in the course or furtherance of some other offence, the killing shall not amount to murder unless done with the same malice aforethought (express or implied) as is required for a killing to amount to murder when not done in the course or furtherance of another offence.

In this country the felony-murder rule has proven of greater durability. Despite the substantial influence of the Model Penal Code in other areas, it has had a smaller measure of success here: Only New Hampshire adopted the Model Penal Code's formulation (N.H. Rev. Stat. Ann. tit. 62 §630:1-b); two states went further and followed the English example of abolishing the doctrine (Ky. Rev. Stat. Ann. tit. 50, §507.020; Haw. Rev. Stat. tit. 37, §§707-701).

However, statutes over the years have qualified the severity of the common law rule in a variety of ways. Many states have designated what are regarded as particularly dangerous felonies — such as rape, arson, burglary, kidnapping, robbery — as the only felonies on which a first-degree felony-murder conviction may be obtained, other felonies serving as the possible basis only of a second-degree felony-murder conviction (see Cal. Pen. Code §189; Pa. Cons. Stat. tit. 18, §2502) or a manslaughter conviction (La. Rev. Stat. tit. 14, §31; Ind. Code §35-13-4-2) or not serving at all as the basis for a culpable homicide (N.Y. Pen. Law §125.25(3)). Another approach is to require that a killing in the course of the felony be otherwise culpable before it may constitute murder — for example, that defendant have "recklessly" caused the death of another (Del. Code Ann. tit. 11, §636) or that defendant have caused it by "an act clearly dangerous to human life" (Tex. Pen. Code §19.02).

Query: Consider to what extent these various qualifications meet the criticisms of the felony-murder rule made by Macaulay and the Model Penal Code.

The remaining materials in this chapter involve judicial responses to a variety of problems confronted in administering the felony-murder rule as well as some statutory treatments of these responses.

But before proceeding to these cases, we should mention the most remarkable judicial response of all to the felony-murder rule — the singular decision of the Michigan Supreme Court in People v. Aaron, 409 Mich. 672, 299 N.W.2d 304 (1980) to abrogate the rule without benefit of statutory change. The Michigan statute, an old one going back to 1837 (Mich. Stat. Ann. §28.548), provided:

> Murder which is perpetrated by . . . wilful, deliberate and premeditated killing, or which is committed in the perpetration, or attempt to perpetrate arson [and other designated felonies] is murder in the first degree.

The court regarded this provision as serving only to grade murder, which, being undefined statutorily, had to be determined according to the common law's treatment. The court accepted that the presence of malice made a killing murder at common law and that a killing in the course of a felony was a killing with malice at common law. Apparently, however, on the grounds that the definition of *malice* is a judicial matter and that it was proper for the court to alter the common law definition, the court restricted malice to an intent to kill, an intent to do great bodily harm, and wanton disregard of the likelihood of death or great bodily harm. It held, therefore, that when murders so defined occur, they become murder in the first degree if committed in the perpetration of a named felony under §28.548, but that simply because a killing occurs in the perpetration of these felonies does not make it a killing with malice and hence murder.

The possibilities for other courts to follow the lead of the Michigan Supreme Court have been drastically reduced by the recent criminal-code revisions in most states supplanting the common law of murder with exclusively statutory formulations, virtually all of which include versions of the felony-murder rule.

The Michigan Supreme Court thought that abrogation of the felony-murder rule was not so drastic a move in light of the significant restrictions courts had already imposed. We now turn to these.

(ii) The "Inherently-Dangerous-Felony" Limitation

PEOPLE v. PHILLIPS
Supreme Court of California
64 Cal. 2d 574, 414 P.2d 353 (1966)

TOBRINER, J. Defendant, a doctor of chiropractic, appeals from a judgment of the Superior Court of Los Angeles County convicting him of second degree murder in connection with the death from cancer of one of his patients. We reverse solely on the ground that the trial court erred in giving a felony-murder instruction. . . .

[Deceased was an eight-year-old child with a fast-growing cancer of the eye. Her parents were advised at a medical center to consent to immediate removal of the eye as the only means of saving or prolonging her life. However, defendant induced them not to do so by representing that he could cure her without surgery by treatment designed "to build up her resistance." Defendant charged the parents $700 for his treatment and medicine. The child died in about six months.]

As we have noted, the trial court gave an instruction on felony murder; we point out, although defendant could, of course, be prosecuted for grand theft, such a crime, not an inherently dangerous felony, does not support an instruction on felony murder. The giving of that instruction caused defendant prejudice and compels reversal. . . .

Defendant challenges the propriety of the trial court's instructions to the jury. The court gave the following tripartite instruction on murder in the second degree:[4]

> [T]he unlawful killing of a human being with malice aforethought, but without a deliberately formed and premeditated intent to kill, is murder of the second degree:

---

4. The record suggests that the evidence would have supported a finding of involuntary manslaughter. The jury might, for example, have found that defendant sincerely, though *unreasonably*, believed that the removal of Linda from the hospital and treatment according to the principles of chiropractic would be in her best interests. Having so found, the jury could have concluded that in causing Linda's removal from the hospital and so endangering her life defendant acted "without due caution and circumspection." (Pen. Code, §192, subd. 2.) Accordingly, the trial court should have given a manslaughter instruction. The record reveals, however, that defendant's counsel strongly opposed the manslaughter instruction and indicated to the trial court that he considered it "tactically" to defendant's advantage to confront the jury with the limited choice between murder and acquittal. Thus the failure of the trial court to instruct on manslaughter, though erroneous, was invited error; defendant may not properly complain of such error on appeal.

(1) If the killing proximately results from an unlawful act, the natural consequences of which are dangerous to life, which act is deliberately performed by a person who knows that his conduct endangers the life of another, or

(2) If the circumstances proximately causing the killing show an abandoned and malignant heart, or

(3) If the killing is done in the perpetration or attempt to perpetrate a felony such as Grand Theft. If a death occurs in the perpetration of a course of conduct amounting to Grand Theft, which course of conduct is a proximate cause of the unlawful killing of a human being, such course of conduct constitutes murder in the second degree, even though the death was not intended.

The third part of this instruction rests upon the felony-murder rule and reflects the prosecution's theory that defendant's conduct amounted to grand theft by false pretenses in violation of Penal Code secton 484. . . .

Despite defendant's contention that the Penal Code does not expressly set forth any provision for second degree felony murder and that, therefore, we should not follow any such doctrine here, the concept lies imbedded in our law. We have stated in People v. Williams (1965) 63 Cal. 2d 452, 406 P.2d 647, that the cases hold that the perpetration of some felonies, exclusive of those enumerated in Penal Code section 189, may provide the basis for a murder conviction under the felony-murder rule.[a]

We have held, however, that only such felonies as are in themselves "inherently dangerous to human life" can support the application of the felony-murder rule. We have ruled that in assessing such peril to human life inherent in any given felony "we look to the elements of the felony in the abstract, not the particular 'facts' of the case." (People v. Williams, 63 Cal. 2d 452, 458, fn. 5.)[b]

We have thus recognized that the felony-murder doctrine expresses a highly artificial concept that deserves no extension beyond its required application. Indeed, the rule itself has been abandoned by the courts of England, where it had its inception. It has been subjected to severe and sweeping criticism. No case to our knowledge in any jurisdiction has held that because death results from a course of conduct involving a felonious perpetration of a fraud, the felony-murder doctrine can be invoked.

Admitting that grand theft is not inherently dangerous to life, the prosecution asks us to encompass the entire course of defendant's conduct so that we may incorporate such elements as would make his crime inherently dangerous. In so framing the definition of a given felony for the purpose of assessing its inherent peril to life the prosecution would abandon the statutory definition of the felony as such and substitute the factual elements of defendant's actual conduct. In the present case the Attorney General would characterize that conduct as "grand theft medical fraud," and this newly created "felony," he urges, clearly involves danger to human life and supports an application of the felony-murder rule.

To fragmentize the "course of conduct" of defendant so that the felony-murder

a. Query: On what basis is this statement justifiable? Cf. the relevant provisions of the Cal. Penal Code, page 410 supra. — EDS.

b. This case held it was error to instruct the jury to find defendant guilty of second-degree murder if the killing occurred during a conspiracy to obtain methedrine. — EDS.

rule applies if any segment of that conduct may be considered dangerous to life would widen the rule beyond calculation. It would then apply not only to the commission of specific felonies, which are themselves dangerous to life, but to the perpetration of *any* felony during which defendant may have acted in such a manner as to endanger life.

The proposed approach would entail the rejection of our holding in *Williams.* That case limited the felony-murder doctrine to such felonies as were themselves inherently dangerous to life. That decision eschews the prosecution's present sweeping concept because, once the Legislature's own definition is discarded, the number or nature of the contextual elements which could be incorporated into an expanded felony terminology would be limitless. We have been, and remain, unwilling to embark on such an uncharted sea of felony murder.

The felony-murder instruction should not, then, have been given; its rendition, further, worked prejudice upon defendant. It withdrew from the jury the issue of malice, permitting a conviction upon the bare showing that Linda's death proximately resulted from conduct of defendant amounting to grand theft. The instruction as rendered did not require the jury to find either express malice or the implied malice which is manifested in an "intent with conscious disregard for life to commit acts likely to kill." (People v. Washington, 62 Cal. 2d 777, 780. . . .

The prosecution does not deny that the giving of a felony-murder instruction engendered the possibility of a conviction of murder in the absence of a finding of malice. It contends, however, that even if the jury acted on the erroneous instruction it must necessarily have found facts which establish, as a matter of law, that defendant acted with conscious disregard for life and hence with malice. The prosecution thus asks us to dissect the jury's verdict, setting the facts of the case against the instructions in an attempt to isolate the facts which the jury necessarily found in reaching its verdict. From these facts it further asks us to infer the existence of others which the jury was never asked to find.

Examination of the record suggests that even this doubtful enterprise would not enable us to overcome the effect of the erroneous instruction. The prosecution urges that the jury could not have convicted defendant under the felony-murder instruction without having found that he made representations to the Eppings which he knew to be false or which he recklessly rendered without information which would justify a reasonable belief in their truth. Such a finding does not, however, establish as a matter of law the existence of an "intent with conscious disregard for life to commit acts likely to kill." (People v. Washington, supra.) In the absence of a finding that defendant subjectively appreciated the peril to which his conduct exposed the girl, we cannot determine that he acted with conscious disregard for life. The record contains evidence from which a trier of fact could reasonably have concluded that although defendant made false representations concerning his ability to cure, he nevertheless believed that the treatment which he proposed to give would be as efficacious in relieving pain and prolonging life as the scheduled surgery.

Of course the jury could have concluded from some of the evidence that defendant did *not* entertain any such belief in the relative efficacy of his proposed treatment. We cannot, however, undertake to resolve this evidentiary conflict without invading the province of the trier of fact. We cannot predicate a finding of conscious disregard of life upon a record that would as conclusively afford a basis for the opposite conclusion. . . .

The judgment is reversed.[c]

PEOPLE v. SATCHELL, 6 Cal. 3d 28, 33-34, 39-43, 489 P.2d 1361, 1365, 1369-1372 (1972): [Defendant, an ex-felon with four prior felony convictions, was convicted of second-degree murder arising out of a street fight. Defendant shot and killed the deceased with a sawed-off shotgun he obtained from his car. Section 12021 of the Penal Code made it a felony for an ex-felon to possess such a weapon. The trial judge gave the following second-degree felony-murder instruction:

> The unlawful killing of a human being, whether intentional, unintentional or accidental, which occurs as a direct causal result of the commission of or attempt to commit a felony inherently dangerous to human life, namely, the crime of possession of a concealable firearm by a felon, and where there was in the mind of the perpetrator the specific intent to commit such crime, is murder of the second degree.

The supreme court held this instruction erroneous and reversed the conviction, concluding that the felony of possession of a concealable weapon by an ex-felon was not a "felóny inherently dangerous to human life," within the meaning of this California qualification to the felony-murder rule.

[The court started by recalling the approach to felony murder established by several recent California decisions; to wit, that, "Although it is the law in this state, it should not be extended beyond any rational function that it is designed to serve," and that the "highly artificial concept of strict criminal liability incorporated in the felony-murder doctrine be given the narrowest possible application consistent with its ostensible purpose — which is to deter those engaged in felonies from killing negligently or accidentally."

[The court then reasoned as follows:]

It bears emphasis that, in determining whether a felony is inherently dangerous for purposes of the felony-murder rule we assess that felony *in the abstract.* The felony here in question is possession of a concealable firearm by one who has previously been convicted of a (i.e., another) felony. We do *not* look to the specific facts of the case before us in order to determine whether, in light of the nature of the particular felony of which defendant was previously convicted, his possession of a concealable firearm was inherently dangerous. Rather, we direct our attention to the genus of crimes known as felonies and determine whether the possession of a concealable firearm by one who has been convicted of *any crime within that genus* is an act inherently dangerous to human life which, as such, justifies the extreme consequence (i.e., imputed malice) which the felony-murder doctrine demands.

It is manifest that the range of antisocial activities which are criminally punishable as felonies in this state is very wide indeed. Some of these felonies, such as certain well-known crimes against the person of another, distinctly manifest

---

c. On retrial Phillips was convicted of second-degree murder. The theory of the prosecution this time was that defendant had maliciously caused the deceased to terminate a surgical treatment that would have prolonged her life. The court of appeal affirmed the conviction. People v. Phillips, 270 Cal. App. 2d 381, 75 Cal. Rptr. 720 (1969). — Eds.

a propensity for acts dangerous to human life on the part of the perpetrator. Others, of which a random sampling is set forth in the margin,[19] just as distinctly fail to manifest such a propensity. Surely it cannot be said that a person who has committed a crime in this latter category, when he arms himself with a concealable weapon, presents a danger to human life so significantly more extreme than that presented by a nonfelon similarly armed as to justify the imputation of malice to him if a homicide should result. Accordingly, because we can conceive of such a vast number of situations wherein it would be grossly illogical to impute malice, we must conclude that the violation of section 12021 by one previously convicted of a felony is not itself a felony *inherently* dangerous to human life which will support a second-degree felony-murder instruction.

NOTES AND QUESTIONS

1. *Query.* Suppose §12021 had made it a felony for a person who had been convicted of a felony of violence to the person to possess a concealable firearm.

2. In a comparable case, the Kansas Supreme Court reached a conclusion contrary to that reached in the *Satchell* case. State v. Goodseal, 220 Kan. 487, 553 P.2d 279 (1977). The court stated:

> Where doubt may exist, we see nothing wrong in considering both the nature of the offense in the abstract and the circumstances of its commission in determining whether a particular felony was inherently dangerous to human life. Some felonies, such as aggravated robbery, viewed in the abstract alone, are of such nature as to be inherently dangerous to human life, while another which seems of itself not to involve any element of human risk may be committed in such a dangerous manner as to be of the same character. Hence we hold that the nature of the felony and, where necessary for determination, the circumstances of its commission are relevant factors in considering whether the particular felony was inherently and foreseeably dangerous to human life so as to support a conviction of felony murder. These are questions for the trial court and jury to decide in appropriate cases.

However, in State v. Underwood, 615 P.2d 153 (Kan. 1980), which also involved firearm possession by an ex-felon, the Kansas Supreme Court overruled the *Goodseal* case and brought the Kansas law into line with the California law as announced in *Satchell.*

3. Was the Kansas Supreme Court right the first time or the second? Or neither time? What is the justification for the inherently-dangerous-felony limitation developed by the courts? What considerations favor interpreting that limitation in terms of the definition of the felony in the abstract, apart from the circumstances of its actual commission?

Note that in *Satchell* dangerousness must be found solely in the definition of the felony in the abstract; in *Goodseal* it may be found either in the felony

___

19. See, for example, Corporations Code (fraudulent and deceptive acts relating to corporations); Elections Code, (elections offenses); Financial Code, (unauthorized sale of investment certificates); Government Code, (interference with the legislative process); Insurance Code, (false or fraudulent insurance claim). . . .

The Penal Code, of course, renders felonious many activities which do not indicate a propensity for dangerous acts.

in the abstract or in the circumstances of its actual commission. What might be said for a third alternative which would look solely to the circumstances of the commission of the felony, so that the inquiry would seek in every case, regardless of how the felony might be viewed in the abstract, to determine whether the crime were committed in a manner creating a forseeable danger to human life?

4. For holdings in other jurisdictions on the inherently-dangerous-felony rule, see Annot., 50 A.L.R.3d 397 (1973).

5. In People v. Henderson, 19 Cal. 3d 86, 560 P.2d 1180 (1977), the California Supreme Court reversed a second-degree felony-murder conviction based on the felony of "false imprisonment . . . effected by violence, menace, fraud or deceit." Defendant held the victim hostage by holding a gun to his head. When the victim ducked and attempted to deflect the barrel of the gun from his head, the gun went off and killed a bystander. The court found that unlawful restraint of another does not necessarily involve the requisite danger to human life for a felony-murder conviction and that the factors elevating the offense to a felony — violence, menace, fraud, or deceit — do not all involve conduct that is life endangering. While the factors of violence or menace may involve such danger, the others do not. Therefore, viewing the offense as a whole and in the abstract, it is not an offense inherently dangerous to human life. The prosecution argued that the matter would not differ in substance if the legislature had created two separate false imprisonment felonies, one by violence or menace, the other by fraud or deceit. The court disagreed, finding this formal difference to be crucial (19 Cal. 3d at 95):

> The Legislature has not evinced a particular concern for violent as opposed to nonviolent acts of false imprisonment by separate statutory treatment, proscription, or punishment. Accordingly, we cannot conclude that the cause of deterring homicide during the commission of false imprisonment is better served by imputing malice to one who kills in the course of committing false imprisonment rather than allowing the jury to determine directly the question of the presence of malice aforethought.

Is there anything to be said for the court's reasoning, besides the result? Is that enough?

(*iii*) *The Limitation to Felonies "Independent" of the Homicide*

PEOPLE v. BURTON
Supreme Court of California
6 Cal. 3d 375, 491 P.2d 793 (1971)

SULLIVAN, J. [Defendant was convicted of murdering two persons during the course of an armed robbery. The California Supreme Court reversed because of the erroneous introduction of a confession. It then addressed the felony-murder instructions of the trial court.]

We now turn to defendant's contention that it was error, in the circumstances of this case, to instruct the jury on first degree felony murder, because the

underlying felony was armed robbery. He claims that armed robbery is an offense
included *in fact* within the offense of murder and, therefore, under the rule
announced in People v. Ireland [1969] 70 Cal. 2d 522, 538-540 as applied in
People v. Wilson (1969) 1 Cal. 3d 431, such offense cannot support a felony-
murder instruction.

"Murder," as defined in Penal Code section 187, "is the unlawful killing of
a human being . . . with malice aforethought." In *Ireland,* we said: "The felony-
murder rule operates (1) to posit the existence of malice aforethought in
homicides which are the direct causal result of the perpetration or attempted
perpetration of *all* felonies inherently dangerous to human life, and (2) to posit
the existence of malice aforethought *and* to classify the offense as murder of
the first degree in homicides which are the direct causal result of those six
felonies specifically enumerated in section 189 of the Penal Code."

The net effect of this imputation of malice by means of the felony-murder
rule is to eliminate the possibility of finding unlawful killings resulting from
the commission of a felony to be manslaughter, rather than murder. Even intentional killings can be mitigated to voluntary manslaughter if the killing occurred
with sufficient provocation to arouse the reasonable man to a fit of passion or
sudden quarrel or if the defendant did not attain the mental state of malice
due to mental illness, mental defect or intoxication. Unintentional killings in
the appropriate circumstances may well be mitigated to involuntary manslaughter, or even not be subject to criminal penalty.

In *Ireland* the "defense . . . rested its entire case upon a contention that
defendant's mental state at the time of his act — as affected by cumulative emotional pressure and the ingestion of alcohol and prescribed medications was
not that required for murder." The defendant in that case shot his wife with
a gun. The judge instructed the jury on the felony-murder rule, utilizing assault
with a deadly weapon as the supporting felony. The effect of such instruction,
as *Ireland* pointed out, was, therefore, to substantially eviscerate the defense
of diminished capacity to negative malice, since malice was imputed. The net
effect of this imputation would be to hold that all intentional killings accomplished by means of a deadly weapon were murder regardless of the circumstances and could never be mitigated to manslaughter, since all such killings
included in fact an assault with a deadly weapon. We held that such effect was
impermissible: "This kind of bootstrapping finds support neither in logic nor
in law. We therefore hold that a second degree felony-murder instruction may
not properly be given when it is based upon a felony which is an integral part
of the homicide and which the evidence produced by the prosecution shows
to be an offense included *in fact* within the offense charged."

In *Wilson* the underlying felony which supported the felony-murder instruction
was burglary — specifically entry coupled with the intent to commit assault with
a deadly weapon.[a] Since in *Ireland* we had held that assault with a deadly weapon
could not support an instruction on second degree felony murder, in *Wilson*
we were faced with the question whether it could support first degree felony
murder because coupled with an entry. We concluded there was no meaningful

a. Section 459 of the Cal. Penal Code provides that "Every person who enters any house, room,
apartment [and other defined structures] . . . with intent to commit . . . any felony is guilty of
burglary."— Eds.

distinction between assaults with deadly weapons indoors and outdoors, saying: "Where the intended felony of the burglar is an assault with a deadly weapon, the likelihood of homicide from the lethal weapon is not significantly increased by the site of the assault. Furthermore, the burglary statute in this state includes within its definition numerous structures other than dwellings as to which there can be no conceivable basis for distinguishing between an assault with a deadly weapon outdoors and a burglary in which the felonious intent is solely to assault with a deadly weapon." Thus, even though burglary is one of the felonies specifically enumerated in Penal Code section 189, we excluded burglary from the operation of the felony-murder rule in those cases where the intended felony was assault with a deadly weapon for the reasons stated in *Ireland.*

Defendant contends that the language and reasoning of *Ireland* and *Wilson* compel us to hold that armed robbery is included in fact within murder and, therefore, cannot support a felony-murder instruction. He argues that armed robbery includes as a necessary element assault with a deadly weapon by the following chain of reasoning: robbery "is the felonious taking of personal property in the possession of another, from his person or immediate presence, and against his will, accomplished by means of force or fear" (Pen. Code, §211); thus robbery is assault (force or fear directed against a person) coupled with larceny, which when accomplished by means of a deadly weapon necessarily includes in fact assault with a deadly weapon; any charge of murder with respect to a killing arising out of armed robbery then necessarily includes in fact assault with a deadly weapon and cannot support a felony-murder instruction.

The net effect of defendant's argument would be to eliminate the application of the felony-murder rule to all unlawful killings which were committed by means of a deadly weapon, since in each case the homicide would include *in fact* assault with a deadly weapon, even if the homicide resulted from the commission of one of the six felonies (arson, rape, mayhem, robbery, burglary or lewd and lascivious acts upon the body of a child) enumerated in section 189 of the Penal Code. It is, of course, possible to interpret our language in *Ireland*[5] and *Wilson* to mean merely that if the facts proven by the prosecution demonstrate that the felony offense is included in fact within the facts of the homicide and integral thereto, then that felony cannot support a felony-murder instruction. However, we reject this interpretation of that language and its consequent assertion that the felony-murder rule has been abolished in all homicides accomplished by means of a deadly weapon as unwarranted both in logic and in principle.

We conclude that there is a very significant difference between deaths resulting from assaults with a deadly weapon, where the purpose of the conduct was the very assault which resulted in death, and deaths resulting from conduct for an independent felonious purpose, such as robbery or rape, which happened to be accomplished by a deadly weapon and therefore technically includes assault with a deadly weapon. Our inquiry cannot stop with the fact that death resulted from the use of a deadly weapon and, therefore, technically included an assault

---

5. "We therefore hold that a second degree felony-murder instruction may not properly be given when it is based upon a felony which is an integral part of the homicide and which the evidence produced by the prosecution shows to be an offense included *in fact* within the offense charged." (People v. Ireland, supra, 70 Cal. 2d 522, 539.)

with a deadly weapon, but must extend to an investigation of the purpose of the conduct. In both *Ireland* and *Wilson* the purpose of the conduct which eventually resulted in a homicide was assault with a deadly weapon, namely the infliction of bodily injury upon the person of another. The desired infliction of bodily injury was in each case[6] not satisfied short of death. Thus, there was a single course of conduct with a single purpose.

However, in the case of armed robbery, as well as the other felonies enumerated in section 189 of the Penal Code, there is an independent felonious purpose, namely in the case of robbery to acquire money or property belonging to another. Once a person has embarked upon a course of conduct for one of the enumerated felonious purposes, he comes directly within a clear legislative warning — if a death results from his commission of that felony it will be first degree murder, regardless of the circumstances. This court has reiterated numerous times that "The purpose of the felony-murder rule is to deter felons from killing negligently or accidentally by holding them strictly responsible for killings they commit." (People v. Washington (1965), 62 Cal. 2d 777, 781.) The Legislature has said in effect that this deterrent purpose outweighs the normal legislative policy of examining the individual state of mind of each person causing an unlawful killing to determine whether the killing was with or without malice, deliberate or accidental, and calibrating our treatment of the person accordingly. Once a person perpetrates or attempts to perpetrate one of the enumerated felonies, then in the judgment of the Legislature, he is no longer entitled to such fine judicial calibration, but will be deemed guilty of first degree murder for any homicide committed in the course thereof.

Wilson, when properly understood, does not eliminate this rule as urged by defendant, but merely excludes from its effect one small area of conduct, which would be irrationally included, due to the unusual nature of burglary. The key factor as indicated earlier in the enumerated felonies is that they are undertaken for a felonious purpose independent of the homicide. In the normal case, burglary is also undertaken with an independent felonious purpose, namely to acquire the property of another. In such instances the felony-murder rule would apply to burglary as well, even if the burglary were accomplished with a deadly weapon. However, in *Wilson* the entry was coupled with the intent to commit assault with a deadly weapon, the defendant in that case bursting through the bathroom door intending to do violent injury upon the body of his wife. We were there presented with the exact situation we faced in *Ireland,* namely a single purpose, a single course of conduct, except that in *Wilson* the single course of conduct happened to include an entry, and thus technically became burglary all of which brought the incident within the ambit of section 189 of the Penal Code. We merely excluded from the first degree felony-murder rule the special circumstances of *Wilson* where the entry was with the intent to commit assault with a deadly weapon because we found them indistinguishable from those in *Ireland.* We regard the holding in *Wilson* as specifically limited to those

---

6. *Wilson* involved two separate entries, one into the apartment through the front door and one into the bathroom. Each was coupled with the intent to commit assault with a deadly weapon. However, the crucial entry for the purpose of the first degree felony-murder instruction, was the entry into the bathroom by defendant bearing a shotgun for the purpose of inflicting violent injury upon the body of his wife.

situations where the entry is coupled with the intent to commit assault with a deadly weapon.

Defendant in this case by embarking upon the venture of armed robbery brought himself within the class of persons who the Legislature has concluded must avoid causing death or bear the consequences of first degree murder. The trial judge quite correctly instructed on felony murder based on homicides directly resulting from the commission of armed robbery.

NOTES

1. In People v. Miller, 32 N.Y.2d 157, 297 N.E.2d 85, 344 N.Y.S.2d 342 (1973), the New York Court of Appeals rejected the position of the California Supreme Court in People v. Wilson, discussed in the foregoing case. Defendant entered the apartment of another, Fennell, intending to assault him with a deadly weapon. When another occupant, Aleem, attempted to help Fennell, defendant killed Aleem. The court held that since defendant committed the crime of burglary by knowingly and unlawfully entering Fennell's apartment with intent to assault him, and since the defendant killed Aleem in the course of and in furtherance of his commission of that burglary, the requirements of the felony-murder statute were satisfied. The court stated (344 N.Y.S.2d at 345):

> Defendant would have us extend the merger doctrine to the facts of this case with the result that neither the assault on Fennell, nor the assault on Aleem, could, for the purposes of the felony-murder statute, be used as the intended crime element of burglary. The considerations which prompted our court to announce the merger doctrine do not justify its extension here. We developed this doctrine to remedy a fundamental defect in the old felony-murder statute (Penal Law of 1909, §1044). Under that statute, any felony, including assault, could be the predicate for a felony murder. Since, a fortiori, every homicide, not excusable or justifiable, occurs during the commission of assault, every homicide would constitute a felony murder.
>
> This defect was remedied by the Legislature in 1965 by including in the revised Penal Law a list of specified felonies — all involving violence or substantial risk of physical injury — as the only felonies forming a basis for felony murder. The legislative purpose for this limitation was "to exclude from felony murder, cases of accidental or not reasonably foreseeable fatality occurring in an unlikely manner in the course of a non-violent felony." (Denzer and McQuillan, Practice Commentary, McKinney's Cons. Laws of N.Y., vol. 39, p. 236.)
>
> It should be apparent that the Legislature, in including burglary as one of the enumerated felonies as a basis for felony murder, recognized that persons within domiciles are in greater peril from those entering the domicile with criminal intent, than persons on the street who are being subjected to the same criminal intent. Thus, the burglary statutes prescribe greater punishment for a criminal act committed within the domicile than for the same act committed on the street. Where, as here, the criminal act underlying the burglary is an assault with a dangerous weapon, the likelihood that the assault will culminate in a homicide is significantly increased by the situs of the assault. When the assault takes place within the domicile, the victim may be more likely to resist the assault; the victim is also less likely to be able to avoid the consequences of the assault, since his paths of retreat and escape may be barred or severely restricted by furniture, walls and other obstructions incidental to buildings. Further, it is also more likely that when the assault

occurs in the victim's domicile, there will be present family or close friends who
will come to the victim's aid and be killed. Since the purpose of the felony-murder
statute is to reduce the disproportionate number of accidental homicides which
occur during the commission of the enumerated predicate felonies by punishing
the party responsible for the homicide not merely for manslaughter, but for murder
(see Model Penal Code, Tent. Draft No. 9, pp. 37, 38), the Legislature, in enacting
the burglary and felony-murder statutes, did not exclude from the definition of
burglary, a burglary based upon the intent to assault, but intended that the definition
be "satisfied if the intruder's intent, existing at the time of the unlawful entry or
remaining, is to commit any crime." (Denzer and McQuillan, Practice Commentary,
McKinney's Cons. Laws of N.Y., vol. 39, p. 355; emphasis supplied.)

2. Most jurisdictions adopt some version of the merger doctrine. But see
State v. Wanrow, 91 Wash. 2d 301, 588 P.2d 1320 (1978). For a general review
of the cases see Annot., 40 A.L.R.3d 1341 (1971). For critical analysis of the
doctrine, see Note, Merger and the California Felony-Murder Rule, 20
U.C.L.A.L. Rev. 250 (1972); Note, The California Supreme Court Assaults the
Felony-Murder Rule, 22 Stan. L. Rev. 1059 (1970).

(*iv*)   *Killings by Persons Other Than the Felons*

STATE v. CANOLA
Supreme Court of New Jersey
73 N.J. 206, 374 A.2d 20 (1977)

CONFORD, J. Defendant, along with three confederates, was in the process
of robbing a store when a victim of the robbery, attempting to resist the perpetration of the crime, fatally shot one of the co-felons. The sole issue for our resolution is whether, under N.J.S.A. 2A:113-1, defendant may be held liable for felony
murder. . . .

The facts of this case . . . may be summarized as follows. The owner of a
jewelry store and his employee, in an attempt to resist an armed robbery, engaged
in a physical skirmish with one of the four robbers. A second conspirator, called
upon for assistance, began shooting, and the store owner returned the gunfire.
Both the owner and the felon, one Lloredo, were fatally shot in the exchange,
the latter by the firearm of the owner.

Defendant and two others were indicted on two counts of murder, one count
of robbery and one count of having been armed during the robbery. The murder
counts were based on the deaths, respectively, of the robbery victim and the
co-felon. After trial on the murder counts defendant was found guilty on both
and was sentenced to concurrent terms of life imprisonment. The Appellate
Division unanimously affirmed the conviction for the murder of the robbery
victim, and this court denied a petition for certification addressed thereto. However, when the Appellate Division majority upheld the trial court's denial of a
motion to dismiss the count addressed to the homicide of the co-felon, Judge
Handler dissented, [and we granted a petition for certification addressed to
this count.]

Conventional formulations of the felony murder rule would not seem to encompass liability in this case. . . . [T]he early formulations of the felony murder

rule by such authorities as Lord Coke, Foster and Blackstone and of later ones by Judge Stephen and Justice Holmes . . . were concerned solely with situations where the felon or a confederate did the actual killing. . . . [T]he English courts never applied the felony murder rule to hold a felon guilty of the death of his co-felon at the hands of the intended victim. . . .

The precise issue in the present case is whether a broader concept than the foregoing — specifically, liability of a felon for the death of a co-felon effected by one resisting the felony — is required by the language of our statute applicable to the general area of felony murder. N.J.S.A. 2A:113-1. This reads:

> If any person, in committing or attempting to commit arson, burglary, kidnapping, rape, robbery, sodomy or any unlawful act against the peace of this state, of which the probable consequences may be bloodshed, kills another, *or if the death of anyone ensues from the committing or attempting to commit any such crime or act; . . . then such person so killing is guilty of murder.* (emphasis added). . . .

Before attempting, through analysis of the statutory language itself, a resolution of the contrasting views of the statute entertained below, it will be helpful to survey the progress of the pertinent law in the other American jurisdictions. . . .

It is clearly the majority view throughout the country that, at least in theory, the doctrine of felony murder does not extend to a killing, although growing out of the commission of the felony, if directly attributable to the act of one other than the defendant or those associated with him in the unlawful enterprise. . . . See Annot. 56 A.L.R.3d 239 (1974). This rule is sometimes rationalized on the "agency" theory of felony murder.[2]

A contrary view, which would attach liability under the felony murder rule for *any* death proximately resulting from the unlawful activity — even the death of a co-felon — notwithstanding the killing was by one resisting the crime, does not seem to have the present allegiance of any court. See Johnson v. State, 386 P.2d 336 (Okl. Cr. App. 1963); Miers v. State, 157 Tex. Cr. R. 572, 251 S.W.2d 404 (Cr. App. 1952); and Hornbeck v. State, 77 So. 2d 876 (Fla. 1955), in all of which either an officer or other innocent person was killed. . . .

At one time the proximate cause theory was espoused by the Pennsylvania Supreme Court. . . . Commonwealth v. Almeida, 362 Pa. 596, 68 A.2d 595 (1949). The reasoning of the *Almeida* decision, involving the killing of a policeman shot by other police attempting to apprehend robbers, was distinctly circumvented when the question later arose whether it should be applied to an effort to inculpate a defendant for the killing of his co-felon at the hands of the victim of the crime. Commonwealth v. Redline, 391 Pa. 486, 137 A.2d 472 (1958). The court there held against liability. Examining the common-law authorities relied upon by the *Almeida* majority, the *Redline* court concluded: "As already indicated, *Almeida* was, itself, an extension of the felony-murder doctrine by judicial decision and is not to be extended in its application beyond facts such

---

2. The classic statement of the theory is found in an early case applying it in a context pertinent to the case at bar, Commonwealth v. Campbell, 89 Mass. (7 Allen) 541, 544 (Sup. Jud. Ct. 1863), as follows: "No person can be held guilty of homicide unless the act is either actually or constructively his, and it cannot be his act in either sense unless committed by his own hand or by someone acting in concert with him or in furtherance of a common object or purpose."

as those to which it was applied." 137 A.2d at 482. The court then held that "in order to convict for felony-murder, *the killing must have been done by the defendant or by an accomplice or confederate or by one acting in furtherance of the felonious undertaking.*" The court refused, however, actually to overrule the *Almeida* decision, thereby creating a distinction . . . between the situation in which the victim was an innocent party and the killing therefore merely "excusable" and that in which the deceased was a felon and the killing thus "justifiable." [4] Twelve years later the Pennsylvania court did overrule *Almeida* in a case involving Almeida's companion, Smith. (Commonwealth ex rel. Smith v. Myers, 438 Pa. 218, 261 A.2d 550 (1970)). The court noted, inter alia, the harsh criticism leveled against the common-law felony rule, its doubtful deterrent effect, the failure of the cases cited in *Almeida* to support the conclusions reached therein, the inappropriateness of tort proximate-cause principles to homicide prosecution, and the "will-of-the-wisp" distinction drawn by the *Almeida* court between justifiable and excusable homicides. . . .

The course of the decisions in Michigan illustrates the influence of the Pennsylvania cases in the development of the felony murder rule in other jurisdictions. In People v. Podolski, 332 Mich. 508, 52 N.W.2d 201 (1952), the bullet killing the deceased officer came from the revolver of a fellow officer attempting to stop defendant's armed robbery of a bank. In affirming the murder conviction, the court adopted both the language and reasoning of the Pennsylvania court . . . , to the effect that if a robber sets in motion a chain of events which should have been within his contemplation, he is liable for any death which results.

After the Pennsylvania court changed course in *Redline,* supra, the Michigan court followed suit in People v. Austin, 370 Mich. 12, 120 N.W.2d 766 (1963), where defendants' indictments for the slaying of their accomplice by the robbery victim were quashed. Relying heavily on Pennsylvania's curtailment of the expansion of the felony murder rule, the court, while not overruling *Podolski,* nonetheless refused to extend liability to instances where the deceased was a co-felon. . . .

The Pennsylvania developments were also influential in Illinois. Prior to any of the Pennsylvania cases cited above, Illinois had adopted a rule of proximate causation in People v. Payne, 359 Ill. 246, 194 N.E. 539 (1935), where a felon's conviction of murder for the death of a bystander was affirmed despite the absence of any proof of who fired the fatal shot. The court found this fact immaterial: "It reasonably might be anticipated that an attempted robbery would meet with resistance, during which the victim might be shot either by himself or some one else in attempting to prevent the robbery, and those attempting to perpetrate the robbery would be guilty of murder."

Nevertheless, following the Pennsylvania *Redline* decision, the Illinois courts refused to apply the proximate causation test where the decedent was an accomplice of the defendant killed by a victim of the felony. People v. Morris, 1 Ill. App. 3d 566, 274 N.E.2d 898 (Ct. App. 1971). The rationale, quite inconsistent

---

4. Although, as will be seen, this distinction survives in a few jurisdictions, it has been criticized in principle, since, inter alia, the criminal immunity or liability of the third person killer is irrelevant to the criminal culpability of the accused felon. See Comment, 71 Harv. L. Rev. 1565, 1566 (1958). . . .

with that applied in *Payne,* supra, was that the lethal act was not done in further-ance of the common design to commit a felony.

In the most recent Illinois case, People v. Hickman, 12 Ill. App. 3d 412, 297 N.E.2d 582 (Ct. App. 1973), *aff'd* 59 Ill. 2d 89, 319 N.E.2d 511 (Sup. Ct. 1974), where an officer chasing burglars mistakenly shot and killed a fellow officer, and liability was imposed pursuant to *Payne,* supra, yet another theory of differentiation of the co-felon killing cases was advanced — the dubious as-sumption-of-risk concept that the co-felon "assisted in setting in motion a chain of events which was the proximate cause of his death and therefore in the criminal law as in the civil law there is no redress for the victim." 297 N.E.2d at 586. . . .

To be distinguished from the situation before us here, and from the generality of the cases discussed above, are the so-called "shield" cases. The first of these were the companion cases of Taylor v. State, 41 Tex. Cr. R. 564, 55 S.W. 961 (Cr. App. 1900), and Keaton v. State, 41 Tex. Cr. R. 621, 57 S.W. 1125 (Cr. App. 1900). In attempting to escape after robbing a train, defendants thrust the brakeman in front of them as a shield, as a result of which he was fatally shot by law officers. The court had no difficulty in finding defendants guilty of murder. The court in *Taylor* noted the correctness of the *Campbell* case doctrine that a person could not be held liable for homicide unless the act is either actually or constructively committed by him, but indicated it was inapplicable to a case where defendants forced deceased to occupy a place of danger in order that they might carry out the crime. In *Keaton,* the court said defendant would be responsible for the "reasonable, natural and probable result of his act" of placing deceased in danger of his life. The conduct of the defendants in cases such as these is said to reflect "express malice," justifying a murder conviction. Commonwealth v. Redline, supra (137 A.2d at 482).

This review of the development in this country of the felony murder rule in relation to culpability for lethal acts of non-felons shows that, despite its early limitation to deadly acts of the felons themselves or their accomplices, the rule has undergone several transformations and can no longer be stated in terms of universal application. As one commentator noted, it appears from the reported cases that up until 1922 all cases in the general field denied liability; the period from 1922 to 1935 was one of vacillation; and cases from 1935 . . . to 1956 tended to impose liability on the grounds of proximate causation where the defendant knew that forceful resistance could be expected. But when the Pennsyl-vania court in *Redline,* supra, overruled its prior holding of liability, in apparent return to the original position of the common law, a number of other jurisdictions followed suit, and the trend since has been towards nonliability; see Annot., 56 A.L.R.3d 237.

Reverting to our immediate task here, it is to determine whether our own statute necessarily mandates the proximate cause concept of felony murder, as thought by the Appellate Division majority. . . . [T]he view of the Appellate Division was that the "ensues clause" of N.J.S.A. 2A:113-1 must be deemed to have expanded the culpability of the felon to killings by others not confeder-ated with him, if proximately related to the felonious enterprise, else the clause would be meaningless surplusage in the act. However, other plausible motiva-tions for the ensues clause can be postulated consistent with a legislative intent to adhere to the traditional limitations of the felony murder doctrine.

Judge Handler, dissenting below, suggested that the purpose of the clause might have been to expand the class of victims of the felon's acts to cover all killings within the res gestae of the felony, even if they formerly would have been considered too distant to be connected therewith, so long as in furtherance of the felony. It seems to us, moreover, that the ensues clause could well have been intended to ensure effectuation of either or both of the following concomitants of the traditional felony murder rule: (a) that accidental or fortuitous homicides "ensuing" from the felony were contemplated for inclusion, the purpose of the statutory language being to repel the inference of a requisite of intent to kill, normally associated with the unqualified word "kill" as used in the initial clause of the section; and (b) that liability extend to acts of or participation by the accomplice of the killer-felon, as well as those of the killer himself. . . .

. . . [A]ssuming the statute is facially susceptible of the interpretation here advocated by the State, it is appropriate to consider the public policy implications of the proposed doctrine as an extension of prior assumptions in this State as to the proper limitations of the felony murder rule.

Most modern progressive thought in criminal jurisprudence favors restriction rather than expansion of the felony murder rule. A leading text states: "The felony murder rule is somewhat in disfavor at the present time. The courts apply it when the law requires, but they do so grudgingly and tend to restrict its application where the circumstances permit." Perkins on Criminal Law (2d ed. 1969) 44. It has frequently been observed that although the rule was logical at its inception, when all felonies were punishable by death, its survival to modern times when other felonies are not thought to be as blameworthy as premeditated killings is discordant with rational and enlightened views of criminal culpability and liability. . . .

The final report of the New Jersey Criminal Law Revision Commission was, however, unwilling totally to reject the felony murder rule. . . .

The proposed New Jersey Penal Code does nevertheless offer limited defenses not hitherto available under the felony murder rule, and it confines the rule to deaths caused by the felon or his co-felons "in the course of and in furtherance of [the felony]." New Jersey Penal Code §2C:11-3 (Final Report 1971). This is standard "agency theory" formulation and would seem intended to exclude liability for acts of persons other than felons or co-felons though generally arising out of the criminal episode.

In view of all of the foregoing, it appears to us regressive to extend the application of the felony murder rule beyond its classic common-law limitation to acts by the felon and his accomplices, to lethal acts of third persons not in furtherance of the felonies scheme. The language of the statute does not compel it, and, as indicated above, is entirely compatible with the traditional limitations of the rule. Tort concepts of foreseeability and proximate cause have shallow relevance to culpability for murder in the first degree. Gradations of criminal liability should accord with degree of moral culpability for the actor's conduct. . . .

The judgment of the Appellate Division is modified so as to strike the conviction and sentencing of defendant for murder of the co-felon Lloredo.

SULLIVAN, J. (concurring in result only).

The practical result of the majority holding is that even though some innocent person or a police officer be killed during the commission of an armed robbery, the felon would bear no criminal responsibility of any kind for that killing as long as it was not at the hand of the felon or a confederate. The legislative intent, as I see it, is otherwise.

The thrust of our felony murder statute, N.J.S.A. 2A:113-1, is to hold the criminal liable for any killing which ensues during the commission of a felony, even though the felon, or a confederate, did not commit the actual killing. The only exception I would recognize would be the death of a co-felon, which could be classified as a justifiable homicide and not within the purview of the statute. . . .

NOTES

As we can observe in the discussion in the *Canola* case, the situations vary depending on who does the killing and who is killed. Consider what legal differences should depend on the identity of the actual killer or victim.

1. Who does the killing? The distinction based on the identity of the killer, whether one of the felons or someone else, is central to the agency theory as a limitation on felony murder. Only a cofelon or one acting in concert with a cofelon can be said to be the agent of the felon; a policeman, the victim, or any other innocent person cannot be. On the other hand, under the proximate-cause theory, the central issue is whether the killing, no matter by whose hand, was within the foreseeable risk of the commission of the felony.

Some of the recent statutory revisions appear to adopt the agency theory. For example, the New York provision (N.Y. Penal Law §125.25) (see page 414 supra) provides that a person is guilty of murder if such individual commits one of the designated felonies and "in the course of and in furtherance of such crime . . . he, or another participant . . . causes the death of a person other than one of the participants." Several other states follow the New York model. See, e.g., Conn. Gen. Stat. §53A-54(c); Or. Rev. Stat. §163.115.

Other statutory formulations leave even more room for argument. Consider a situation in which the killing is the act of a police officer or of the victim in resisting the felony. (To keep the issue focused, we shall assume that a bystander is accidentally killed during the course of a felony.) Under the following statutes could the felon be held for felony murder?

N.J. Stat. Ann. tit. 2C, §2C:11-3:[4]

[A] criminal homicide constitutes murder when: . . . It is committed when the actor . . . is engaged in the commission of, or an attempt to commit, or flight after committing or attempting to commit [designated felonies], and in the course of and in furtherance of such crime or of immediate flight therefrom, any person causes the death of a person other than one of the participants. . . .

Colo. Rev. Stat. tit. 18, §18-3-102:

A person commits the crime of murder in the first degree if: . . . he commits or attempts to commit [designated felonies] and, in the course of or in furtherance

---

4. The felony-murder provision quoted in the *Canola* case was repealed in 1978, as part of an enactment of a comprehensive new criminal code. The above formulation now states the New Jersey law.

of the crime that he is committing or attempting to commit, or of immediate flight therefrom, the death of a person, other than one of the participants, is caused by anyone. . . .

Utah Code Ann. §76-5-203:

Criminal homicide constitutes murder in the second degree if the actor: . . . While in the commission, attempted commission, or immediate flight from the commission or attempted commission of [designated felonies] causes the death of another person other than a party.

We have been considering killings committed by persons other than the felons. But suppose one of the felons does the killing. Under what circumstances is a cofelon also guilty of felony murder? In United States v. Heinlein, 490 F.2d 725 (D.C. Cir. 1973), three defendants committed a rape upon a woman, who was held down by two defendants as Heinlein had intercourse with her. In defending herself, the woman slapped Heinlein, who, enraged at the blow, stabbed and killed her. On these facts Heinlein could, of course, be held for felony murder. But what of the other two? Is it enough that Heinlein killed in the course of a felony they were helping him commit? Or is the killing by Heinlein outside their common purpose, unplanned and unexpected by them, and therefore not attributable to them? Insofar as a jurisdiction adopts an agency theory in dealing with the liability of a felon for killings committed by another, as the court did in *Canola*, it would appear that the unanticipated actions of a felon not in furtherance of the common purpose could no more be attributed to other felons than the actions of a policeman or victim could be attributed to them. The court so held in the *Heinlein* case.

Some statutes now deal explicitly with this problem. See, for example, N.Y. Penal Code §125.25(3)(a)-(d), page 414 supra. How would the *Heinlein* situation be dealt with under such provisions?

2. Who is killed? The *Canola* case discusses a number of decisions which exclude the death of one of the felons as a basis for felony murder regardless of who actually does the killing. The same pattern is revealed in recent statutes (including those quoted above). What is the appeal of this distinction?

If the agency theory is followed, it is, of course, essential that one of the felons do the killing, but as long as that requirement is met and the killing is committed in furtherance of the felony, on what rationale can it matter who the victim is? A case in which a felon kills another felon in furtherance of the felony is readily conceivable. Suppose, for example, one robber accidentally shoots and kills a cofelon while firing at a policeman. Is the act of killing not done by him in furtherance of the felony regardless of whom the bullet strikes?

If, on the other hand, the proximate-cause theory is adopted, so that the central issue is the foreseeable risk of death, on what ground can such a death be excluded simply because the victim happens to be another felon? Consider the situation in State v. Chambers, 373 N.E.2d 393 (Ohio App. 1977). Ohio has long been one of the rare states without a felony-murder rule. However, under the Ohio Revised Code §2903.04, it is involuntary manslaughter for a person "to cause the death of another as a proximate result of the offender's committing or attempting to commit" a felony or misdemeanor. In *Chambers,* defendant and his partner, apparently unarmed, were surprised by the return of the owner of the home they were burglarizing. While the owner was holding them at gunpoint, the partner knocked the owner aside, and both he and defendant ran to make an escape. The owner shot and killed the retreating partner. The court read the statute as squarely adopting the proximate-cause theory rather than the agency theory. It upheld a conviction of defendant, concluding that the end result in this case was a foreseeable consequence of the burglary: "The risk of actual serious physical harm to a victim or wrongdoer, the threat of surprise of one by the other, the natural inclination of the victim, if present, to defend his abode and his family are all factors too clear to discuss further." Was the court in error in failing to accord any significance to the fact that it was one of the felons who was killed?

One argument for special treatment of cases in which a felon is killed was advanced in the *Redline* case, discussed in *Canola*:

> The victim of the homicide was one of the robbers who, while resisting apprehension in his effort to escape was shot and killed by a policeman in the performance of his duty. Thus, the homicide was justifiable and, obviously, could not be availed of, on any rational legal theory, to support a charge of murder. How can anyone, no matter how much of an outlaw he may be, have a criminal charge lodged against him for the consequences of the lawful conduct of another person?

How cogent is the reasoning?

Suppose two felons are holed up in a house and engaged in a gun battle with police officers surrounding the house. Felon *A* tells felon *B* to run out the back door where, he says, the coast is clear. He says this because he wants felon *B* dead and he knows that the police have the back door well covered. As felon *B* dashes out, gun in hand, he is shot dead by police. Is it self-evident that felon *A* is not criminally liable for the police officer's killing of felon *B*?

Another argument for the exemption of the death of felons was stated as follows in State v. Williams, 254 So. 2d 548, 550-551 (Fla. Dist. App. 1971):

> The test we suggest is predicated upon the obvious ultimate purpose of the felony-murder statute itself which is, we think, to prevent the death of innocent persons likely to occur during the commission of certain inherently dangerous and particularly grievous felonies. . . . [T]he statute is primarily designed to protect the *innocent public;* and it would be incongruous to reach a conclusion having the effect of placing the perpetrators themselves beneath its mantle. . . .
>
> We hold, therefore, that the felony-murder statute is applicable only when an innocent person is killed as a sequential result of events or circumstances set in motion by one or more persons acting in furtherance of an intent or attempt to commit one of the felonies specified in such statute. . . .
>
> This does not mean to say however, that co-conspirators acting in furtherance of their conspiracy, even to commit the high crimes contemplated by the felony-murder statute, can kill or murder each other with impunity. . . . Certainly, one conspirator may be guilty of the murder of a co-conspirator if the facts support premeditated murder or a lesser degree of unlawful homicide. But this is quite apart from the felony-murder concept with which we are here concerned.

Similarly, in Jackson v. State, 92 N.M. 461, 589 P.2d 1052 (1979), the court held that under New Mexico law, the felony-murder rule applies when an innocent person is killed by the action of one trying to thwart the felony but does not apply when a cofelon is killed by the same action. A dissenting judge commented (589 P.2d at 1053-1054):

> The present rule in New Mexico . . . is that if an innocent third party's aim is true and one of two robbers is killed, the surviving felon is not guilty of felony-murder. If the third party's aim is not accurate and an innocent person is killed, the surviving felon may be convicted of felony-murder. Thus, responsibility and accountability for the loss of life resulting from the commission of a crime rests not upon any well-reasoned principle of law, but rather upon the accuracy of the aim of a party resisting a criminal act. Public respect for the law is not enhanced by courts engaging in distinctions based on such fortuitous circumstances as the marksmanship of victims.

TAYLOR v. SUPERIOR COURT
Supreme Court of California
3 Cal. 3d 578, 477 P.2d 131 (1970)

BURKE, J. Petitioner and his codefendant Daniels were charged by information with the murder of John H. Smith, robbery, assault with a deadly weapon against Linda West, and assault with a deadly weapon against Jack West. The superior court denied petitioner's motion to set aside the information as to the murder count (Pen. Code, §995), and we issued an alternative writ of prohibition.

At the preliminary hearing, the following facts were adduced regarding the murder count: On the evening of January 12, 1969, two men attempted to rob Jax Liquor Store which was operated by Mrs. Linda Lee West and her husband Jack. Mrs. West testified that James Daniels entered the store first and asked Mr. West, who was behind the counter, for a package of cigarettes. While Mr. West was getting the cigarettes, John Smith entered the store and approached the counter. Mrs. West, who was on a ladder at the time the two men entered the store, then heard her husband say something about money. Turning her attention to the counter, she heard Daniels repeatedly saying, "Put the money in the bag," and observed her husband complying with the order.

While Mr. West was putting the money from the register in the bag, Daniels repeatedly referred to the fact that he and Smith were armed. According to Mrs. West, Daniels "chattered insanely" during this time, telling Mr. West "Put the money in the bag. Put the money in the bag. Put the money in the bag. Don't move or I'll blow your head off. He's got a gun. He's got a gun. Don't move or we'll have an execution right here. Get down on the floor. I said on your stomach, on your stomach." Throughout this period, Smith's gun was pointed at Mr. West. Mrs. West testified that Smith looked "intent" and "apprehensive" as if "waiting for something big to happen." She indicated that Smith's apparent apprehension and nervousness was manifested by the way he was staring at Mr. West.

While Daniels was forcing Mr. West to the floor, Mrs. West drew a pistol from under her clothing and fired at Smith, who was standing closest to her. Smith was struck on the right side of the chest. Mrs. West fired four more shots in rapid succession, and observed "sparks" coming from Smith's gun, which was pointed in her direction. A bullet hole was subsequently discovered in the wall behind the place Mrs. West had been standing, approximately eight or nine feet above the floor. During this period, Mr. West had seized a pistol and fired two shots at Smith. Mrs. West's last shot was fired at Daniels as he was going out of the door. He "lurched violently and almost went down, [but] picked himself up and kept going." Smith died as the result of multiple gunshot wounds.

The evidence at the preliminary examination indicated that petitioner was waiting outside the liquor store in a getaway car. He was apprehended later and connected with the crime through bills in his possession and through the automobile which was seen by a witness leaving the scene of the robbery.

Under Penal Code section 995, an information must be set aside if the defendant has been committed without "reasonable or probable cause." Of course, the probable cause test is not identical with the test which controls a jury in a murder case. The jury must be convinced to a moral certainty and beyond a reasonable doubt of the existence of the crime charged in the information and of every essential element of that crime. But a magistrate conducting a preliminary examination must be convinced of only such a state of facts as would lead a man of ordinary caution or prudence to believe, and conscientiously entertain a strong suspicion of the guilt of the accused. . . .

The information herein charged petitioner with the crime of murder. "Murder is the unlawful killing of a human being, with malice aforethought." (Pen. Code, §187.) "Except when the common-law-felony-murder doctrine is applicable, an essential element of murder is an intent to kill or an intent with conscious disregard for life to commit acts likely to kill." (People v. Washington, 62 Cal. 2d 777, 780, 402 P.2d 130, 133.) Petitioner correctly contends that he cannot be convicted under the felony-murder doctrine, since

> When a killing is not committed by a robber or by his accomplice but by his victim, malice aforethought is not attributable to the robber, for the killing is not committed by him in the perpetration or attempt to perpetrate robbery.

(People v. Washington, supra). However, apart from the felony-murder doctrine, petitioner could be found guilty of murder on a theory of vicarious liability.

As stated in People v. Gilbert, 63 Cal. 2d 690, 408 P.2d 365, *rev. on other grounds*, 388 U.S. 263, "When the defendant or his accomplice, with a conscious disregard for life, intentionally commits an act that is likely to cause death, and his victim or a police officer kills in reasonable response to such act, the defendant is guilty of murder. In such a case, the killing is attributable, not merely to the commission of a felony, but to the intentional act of the defendant or his accomplice committed with conscious disregard for life. Thus, the victim's self-defensive killing or the police officer's killing in the performance of his duty cannot be considered an independent intervening cause for which the defendant is not liable, for it is a reasonable response to the dilemma thrust upon the victim or the policeman by the intentional act of the defendant or his accomplice."

Therefore, if petitioner were an accomplice to the robbery, he would be vicariously responsible[1] for any killing attributable to the intentional acts of his associates committed with conscious disregard for life, and likely to result in death. We must determine whether the committing magistrate had any rational ground for believing that Smith's death was attributable to intentional acts of Smith and Daniels meeting those criteria.

Petitioner relies upon the following language in *Washington*, wherein defendant's accomplice merely pointed a gun at the robbery victim who, without further provocation, shot and killed him: "In every robbery there is a possibility that the victim will resist and kill. The robber has little control over such a killing once the robbery is undertaken as this case demonstrates. To impose an additional penalty for the killing would discriminate between robbers, *not on the basis of any difference in their own conduct,* but solely on the basis of the response by others that the robber's conduct happened to induce."

As indicated by the italicized words in the foregoing quotation, the central inquiry in determining criminal liability for a killing committed by a resisting victim or police officer is whether the *conduct* of a defendant or his accomplices was sufficiently provocative of lethal resistance to support a finding of implied malice. If the trier of fact concludes that under the particular circumstances of the instant case Smith's death proximately resulted from acts of petitioner's accomplices done with conscious disregard for human life, the natural consequences of which were dangerous to life, then petitioner may be convicted of first degree murder.[2]

For example, we pointed out in *Washington* that "Defendants who initiate gun battles may also be found guilty of murder if their victims resist and kill. Under such circumstances, 'the defendant for a base, anti-social motive and with wanton disregard for human life, does an act that involves a high degree of probability that it will result in death,' and it is unnecessary to imply malice by invoking the felony-murder doctrine."

Petitioner contends that since neither Daniels nor Smith fired the first shot, they did not "initiate" the gun battle which led to Smith's death. However, depending upon the circumstances, a gun battle can be initiated by acts of provocation falling short of firing the first shot. Thus, in People v. Reed, 270 Cal. App. 2d 37, defendant resisted the officers' commands to "put up your hands," and pointed his gun toward the officers and toward the kidnap-robbery victim. The officers commenced firing, wounding defendant and killing the victim. Although defendant did not fire a single shot, his murder conviction was upheld on the theory that his "aggressive actions" were sufficient evidence of implied malice, and that "under these circumstances it may be said that defendant initiated the gunplay. . . ."

Similarly, in Brooks v. Superior Court, 239 Cal. App. 2d 538, petitioner had directed "opprobrious language" to the arresting officer and had grasped the officer's shotgun. The officer, being startled and thinking that petitioner was

1. "Under the rules defining principals and criminal conspiracies, the defendant may be guilty of murder for a killing attributable to the act of his accomplice. To be so guilty, however, the accomplice must cause the death of another human being by an act committed in furtherance of the common design." (People v. Gilbert, supra). Petitioner does not dispute that the conduct of his confederates set forth above was in furtherance of the robbery.

2. . . . When murder has been established pursuant to the foregoing principles. Penal Code section 189 may be invoked to determine its degree. (People v. Gilbert, supra.)

trying to disarm him, yanked backwards and fired the gun, mortally wounding a fellow officer. In upholding an indictment for murder, the court concluded that under the circumstances, the petitioner's act of reaching for and grasping the officer's shotgun was "fraught with grave and inherent danger to human life," and therefore sufficient to raise an inference of malice.

In the instant case, the evidence at the preliminary hearing set forth above discloses acts of provocation on the part of Daniels and Smith from which the trier of fact could infer malice, including Daniels' coercive conduct toward Mr. West and his repeated threats of "execution," and Smith's intent and nervous apprehension as he held Mr. West at gunpoint. The foregoing conduct was sufficiently provocative of lethal resistance to lead a man of ordinary caution and prudence to conclude that Daniels and Smith "initiated" the gun battle, or that such conduct was done with conscious disregard for human life and with natural consequences dangerous to life.[3] Accordingly, we conclude that the evidence supported the magistrate's finding that reasonable and probable cause existed to charge petitioner with first degree murder.

The alternative writ heretofore issued is discharged and the peremptory writ is denied.

PETERS, J. (dissenting). I dissent. In holding that petitioner can be convicted of murder of John H. Smith, the majority repudiate this court's holdings in People v. Washington, and People v. Gilbert, that robbers cannot be convicted of murder for a killing by a victim unless the robbers commit malicious acts, in addition to the acts constituting the underlying felony, which demonstrate culpability beyond that of other robbers. . . .

In *Washington*, two robbers held up a service station. The owner, Carpenter, was in the office totaling up the receipts and disbursements while an employee was depositing the money in a vault in an adjoining room. Upon hearing someone yell "robbery," Carpenter opened his desk and took out a revolver. A few moments later one of the robbers, Ball, entered the office and pointed a revolver at Carpenter. Carpenter fired immediately, mortally wounding Ball. Washington, the accomplice, was convicted of the murder of Ball. We reversed the murder conviction. We held that the felony-murder doctrine could not be invoked to convict Washington of murder because the killing was not committed by Washington or his accomplice: "When a killing is not committed by a robber or by his accomplice but by his victim, malice aforethought is not attributable to the robber, for the killing is not committed by him in the perpetration or attempt to perpetrate robbery." . . .

We further stated that, apart from the felony-murder rule, a defendant may be guilty of murder on a vicarious liability theory for a killing committed by the victim: "Defendants who initiate gun battles may also be found guilty of

---

3. Petitioner contends that we should ignore evidence regarding Smith's conduct, on the theory that Smith could not have been held responsible for his own death. We rejected a similar contention in *Washington*, stating that "A distinction based on the person killed, however, would make the defendant's criminal liability turn upon the marksmanship of victims and policemen. A rule of law cannot reasonably be based on such a fortuitous circumstance. The basic issue therefore is whether a robber can be convicted of murder for the killing of *any* person by another who is resisting the robbery." Therefore, the trier of fact may find that Smith set into motion, through the intentional commission of acts constituting implied malice and in furtherance of the robbery, a gun battle resulting in his own death. Since petitioner may be held vicariously responsible for *any* killing legally attributable to his accomplices, he may be charged with Smith's death. . . .

murder if their victims resist and kill. Under such circumstances, 'the defendant for a base, antisocial motive and with wanton disregard for human life, does an act that involves a high degree of probability that it will result in death' (People v. Thomas, 41 Cal. 2d 470, 480, 261 P.2d 1, 7. . . . [concurring opinion]), and it is unnecessary to imply malice by invoking the felony-murder doctrine. To invoke the felony-murder doctrine to imply malice in such a case is unnecessary and overlooks the principles of criminal liability that should govern the responsibility of one person for a killing committed by another." . . .

In *Washington* the decedent-accomplice pointed a gun directly at the victim. If this court was of the opinion that a defendant in such a situation could properly be convicted of murder for the killing committed by the victim, it would have so stated and would have held that Washington could be so convicted of murder. Instead, it held that Washington could not be convicted of murder and mentioned only one case where defendants could properly be convicted of murder for a killing committed by the victim: the case where the defendants initiate the gun battle. Therefore, *Washington* stands for the proposition that the act of pointing a gun at the victim, unlike the act of initiating a gun battle, is *not* an act done " 'with wanton disregard for human life,' " involving " 'a high degree of probability that it will result in death' " from which malice can be implied. . . .

The majority do not contest the *Washington* holding that the defendant in that case could not be convicted of murder on a vicarious liability theory. However, they purport to distinguish that case simply by characterizing it as a case "wherein defendant's accomplice *merely* pointed a gun at the robbery victim who, *without further provocation,* shot and killed him." . . . (Italics added.)

In *Washington,* a gun was pointed at the victim by a robber appearing suddenly in the victim's office; in the instant case, a gun was pointed at one of the victims and threatening language was used. The majority are making the incredible statement that because the robber in *Washington* did not articulate his obvious threat — because, in the majority's words, he "merely" pointed a gun at the victim — it cannot be said that he committed an act with conscious disregard for life and likely to result in death, whereas if he articulated his threat — as did the robbers in the instant case — his act could be found to have met such criteria.

To me, it is too obvious to dispute that inherent in the brandishing of a gun in a robbery is the conditional threat of the robber that he will use the gun if his demands are not complied with. The fact that the robber makes his threat express does not serve to distinguish *Washington.* It is unreasonable to assume that, just because the robber in *Washington* did not articulate his threat, the victim in that case had less reason to fear for his safety or, as the majority assert, less "provocation" for shooting the robber than did the victims in the instant case. It is absurd to suggest that the robber's acts in *Washington* were, as a matter of law, not "sufficiently provocative of lethal resistance to support a finding of implied malice," whereas the robbers' acts in the instant case could be so considered.

In sum, the articulation of threats does not without more show that the robber's acts were done " 'with wanton disregard for human life,' " involving " 'a high degree of probability that it will result in death' " from which malice can be implied. . . . The difference between an implied and an express threat furnishes no significant basis for discrimination between robbers. . . .

In conclusion, the majority have rejected the *Washington* holding that robbers can be convicted of murder for a killing by a victim only if the robbers commit malicious acts, in addition to the acts which constitute the underlying felony, which demonstrate culpability beyond that of other robbers. By purporting to distinguish *Washington* from the instant case, the majority have set forth a new, wholly irrational, rule: if robbers point guns at their victims without articulating the obvious threat inherent in such action they cannot be convicted of murder for a killing committed by the victims, whereas if they articulate their threat they can be convicted of murder in the same situation. As we have seen, the majority's purported distinction of *Washington* makes absolutely no sense. In my opinion, it simply demonstrates a desire on the part of the majority to overrule *Washington* sub silento. . . .

NOTES

1. Developments in other jurisdictions. Courts in at least two other states have expressed agreement with the principle adopted in *Taylor* — namely that, apart from the felony-murder rule, the doctrine of malice based on recklessness can be invoked to hold a felon responsible for a killing committed by a victim in response to provocative behavior by one of the felons. See Blansett v. Texas, 556 S.W.2d 322 (Tex. Crim. App. 1977); People v. Guraj, 431 N.Y.S.2d 925 (Sup. Ct. 1980).

Of course, as the *Canola* case indicates, all jurisdictions will hold a felon for murder, under a theory of malice based on recklessness, in a "shield" situation — that is, where a hostage is shot by someone acting in opposition to the felony. Is there some reason why this result should be less controversial than the result in *Taylor*? On what basis can the two situations be distinguished?

2. Recklessness of the person killed. In *Taylor* the finding of recklessness was based on the behavior of cofelons Smith and Daniels. This presented a potential problem since it was Smith himself who was killed, but the court rejected the argument that Taylor should not be held liable for Smith's recklessness in provoking his own death. See supra page 503 footnote 3.

That aspect of the *Taylor* holding was subsequently modified by People v. Antick, 15 Cal. 3d 79, 539 P.2d 43 (1975). Following a residential burglary, during which a variety of household goods was stolen, police observed a moving car, packed with household goods, occupied by a driver and one passenger. Shortly, they came upon the car, parked beside the road. Only the driver, Bose, was in it. As Bose was being frisked, he pulled a gun from his waist and fired at one of the officers, who returned the fire. Bose then broke away and sought to escape, but another officer brought him down with gunfire. Bose died from the wounds. Subsequently, the police uncovered evidence that defendant was the other man in the car when it was first spotted and that he had participated with Bose in the burglary. Defendant was charged with murder under both the felony-murder and vicarious-liability theories, and the jury convicted. The court ruled that the conviction could not be upheld under either theory. The felony-murder theory was inapplicable inasmuch as the killing was not committed by a felon or a confederate acting in furtherance of the felony. Turning to the vicarious-liability theory, the court said:

In order to predicate defendant's guilt upon this theory [of vicarious liability], it is necessary to prove that Bose committed a murder, in other words, that he caused the death of another human being and that he acted with malice.

It is well settled that Bose's conduct in initiating a shootout with police officers may establish the requisite malice. . . . However, Bose's malicious conduct did not result in the unlawful killing of *another* human being, but rather in Bose's own death. The only homicide which occurred was the justifiable killing of Bose by the police officer. Defendant's criminal liability certainly cannot be predicated upon the actions of the officer. As Bose could not be found guilty of murder in connection with his own death, it is impossible to base defendant's liability for this offense upon his vicarious responsibility for the crime of his accomplice. . . .

. . . [D]efendant in the instant case may not be held vicariously liable for a crime which his accomplice did not commit.

Question: Suppose a case with identical facts except that the police officer's bullet struck and killed someone other than the confederate who initiated the gun battle — another confederate, say, or a bystander. Presumably, in this event, defendant could have been held for murder. But would there be any difference whatsoever in defendant's culpability?

3. What degree of murder? Note the *Taylor* court's holding that when robbers recklessly provoke a killing, they are liable for murder in the *first degree*. Does this holding make sense? The California Supreme Court reaffirmed this aspect of *Taylor* in Pizzano v. Superior Court, 21 Cal. 3d 128, 577 P.2d 659 (1978). Writing for the majority, Justice Clark said:

Section 189 of the Penal Code provides in pertinent part: "All murder . . . which is committed in the perpetration of, or attempt to perpetrate . . . robbery . . . is murder of the first degree. . . ."

In People v. Washington, 62 Cal. 2d 777, 781, this court held that "[w]hen a killing is not committed by a robber or by his accomplice but by his victim, malice aforethought is not attributable to the robber [under the felony-murder rule], for the killing is not committed by him in the perpetration or attempt to perpetrate robbery."

Reading section 189 in light of the quoted passage from *Washington,* the dissent concludes that the *Gilbert* court [63 Cal. 2d 690 (1965)] erred insofar as it held that section 189 may be invoked to determine the degree of a murder established under the implied malice/vicarious liability doctrine. . . .

. . . The killing itself, having been committed by the policeman to thwart the robbery, cannot be said to have been committed in perpetration of it. *But the act which made the killing a murder attributable to the robber — initiating the gun battle — was committed in the perpetration of the robbery.* Therefore, as *Gilbert* held, section 189 may properly be invoked to determine that the murder is of the first degree.

Chief Justice Bird, in dissent, wrote:

While conceding that the *killing* of Vaca was *not* "committed in the perpetration of . . . robbery . . . ," the majority assert that the *murder* of Vaca was, because Esquivel's *act* of using Vaca as a shield was committed in the perpetration of robbery. . . .

Assuming, arguendo, the conceptual possibility of the majority's analysis, their goal can be achieved only by writing into section 189 a third "kind" of first degree murder not provided for by the Legislature, i.e., a murder in which "the act which made the killing a murder attributable to the robber . . . was committed in the perpetration of the robbery." To do so, however, expressly contradicts the Legislature's provision that "all other [nonenumerated] kinds of murder are of the second degree."

D. THE DEATH PENALTY

The preceding materials suggest the variety of homicidal behavior and the importance of classifying such behavior in degrees of seriousness, by reference to the dangerousness of the conduct and the moral turpitude of the offender. What penalty should be authorized for the most serious homicidal offenses? Are there situations in which capital punishment is an appropriate or even a necessary response to a criminal offense? In this section we explore the case for and against the death penalty, in terms of principles applicable to criminal punishments generally and in terms of the special requirements of constitutional law flowing from the Eighth Amendment prohibition of "cruel and unusual punishments." Of course, the two perspectives are closely intertwined. We believe it preferable to put constitutional problems to one side, for a moment, and to consider first the factors that might motivate a state legislator or a concerned citizen in supporting or opposing capital punishment as a policy matter.

1. Policy Considerations

Suppose that a bill pending in the legislature of your state proposes to abolish the death penalty. Would you support or oppose such a bill? Or would you support it only with certain amendments or exceptions? (Which ones?) What reasons would you advance in support of your position? Consider the following materials as they bear on these questions.

a. Deterrence

J. T. SELLIN, THE DEATH PENALTY
A Report for the Model Penal Code Project of the American Law Institute
21-22, 34, 63 (1959)

It seems reasonable to assume that if the death penalty exercises a deterrent or preventive effect on prospective murderers, the following propositions would be true:

(a) Murders should be less frequent in states that have the death penalty than in those that have abolished it, other factors being equal. Comparisons of this nature must be made among states that are as alike as possible in all other respects — character of population, social and economic condition, etc. — in order not to introduce factors known to influence murder rates in a serious manner but present in only one of these states.

(b) Murders should increase when the death penalty is abolished and should decline when it is restored.

(c) The deterrent effect should be greatest and should therefore affect murder rates most powerfully in those communities where the crime occurred and its consequences are most strongly brought home to the population.

(d) Law enforcement officers would be safer from murderous attacks in states that have the death penalty than in those without it.

Prior to any analysis of available data we are compelled to make certain assumptions. . . . We do not know with any great degree of accuracy how many murders *punishable by death* occur. In the United States, for instance, where only murders in the first degree or similar murders are subject to the death penalty, no accurate statistics of such offenses exist, yet this is the only type of murder which people are presumably to be deterred from committing. . . .

. . . Students of criminal statistics . . . have arrived at the conclusion that the homicide death rate is adequate for an estimate of the trend of murder. This conclusion is based on the assumption that the *proportion* of capital murders in the total of such deaths remains reasonably constant. . . . One may challenge the assumption, but the fact remains that there are no better statistical data on which to base arguments about deterrence. Other statistics, such as conviction statistics, have greater defects.

The data examined reveal that

1. The *level* of the homicide death rates varies in different groups of states. It is lowest in the New England areas and in the northern states of the middle west and lies somewhat higher in Michigan, Indiana and Ohio.

2. Within each group of states having similar social and economic conditions and populations, it is impossible to distinguish the abolition state from the others.

3. The *trends* of the homicide death rates of comparable states with or without the death penalty are similar. . . .

Any one who carefully examines the above data is bound to arrive at the conclusion that the death penalty, as we use it, exercises no influence on the extent or fluctuating rates of capital crimes. It has failed as a deterrent. If it has utilitarian value, it must rest in some other attribute than its power to influence the future conduct of people.

VAN DEN HAAG, ON DETERRENCE AND THE DEATH PENALTY, 60 J. Crim. L.C. & P.S. 141, 145-146 (1969): In some fairly infrequent but important circumstances the death penalty is the only possible deterrent. Thus, in case of acute coups d'état, or of acute substantial attempts to overthrow the government, prospective rebels would altogether discount the threat of any prison sentence. . . . Execution would be the only deterrent because, unlike prison sentences, it cannot be revoked by victorious rebels. The same reasoning applies to deterring spies or traitors in wartime. Finally, men who, by virtue of past acts, are already serving, or are threatened, by a life sentence, could be deterred from further offenses only by the threat of the death penalty.

What about criminals who do not fall into any of these (often ignored) classes? Prof. Thorsten Sellin has made a careful study of the available statistics: he concluded that they do not yield evidence for the deterring effect of the death penalty. Somewhat surprisingly, Prof. Sellin seems to think that this lack of evidence for deterrence is evidence for the lack of deterrence. It is not. It means that deterrence has not been demonstrated statistically — not that non-deterrence has been.

It is entirely possible, indeed likely (as Prof. Sellin appears willing to concede), that the statistics used, though the best available, are nonetheless too slender a reed to rest conclusions on. They indicate that the homicide rate does not vary greatly between similar areas with or without the death penalty, and in the same area before and after abolition. However, the similar areas are not similar enough; the periods are not long enough; many social differences and changes, other than the abolition of the death penalty, may account for the variation (or lack of) in homicide rates with and without, before and after abolition; some of these social differences and changes are likely to have affected homicide rates. . . .

Homicide rates do not depend exclusively on penalties any more than do other crime rates. A number of conditions which influence the propensity to crime, demographic, economic or generally social, changes or differences — even such matters as changes of the divorce laws or of the cotton price — may influence the homicide rate. Therefore variation or constancy cannot be attributed to variations or constancy of the penalties, unless we know that no other factor influencing the homicide rate has changed. Usually we don't. . . .

Contrary to what Prof. Sellin et al. seem to presume, I doubt that offenders are aware of the absence or presence of the death penalty state by state or period by period. Such unawareness argues against the assumption of a calculating murderer. However, unawareness does not argue against the death penalty if by deterrence we mean a preconscious, general response to a severe, but not necessarily specifically and explicitly apprehended, or calculated threat . . . : people remain deterred for a lengthy interval by the severity of the penalty in the past, or by the severity of penalties used in similar circumstances nearby.

I do not argue for a version of deterrence which would require me to believe that an individual shuns murder while in North Dakota, because of the death penalty, and merrily goes to it in South Dakota since it has been abolished there; or that he will start the murderous career from which he had hitherto refrained, after abolition. I hold that the generalized threat of the death penalty may be a deterrent, and the more so, the more generally applied. Deterrence will not cease in the particular areas of abolition or at the particular times of abolition. Rather, general deterrence will be somewhat weakened, through local (partial) abolition. Even such weakening will be hard to detect owing to changes in many offsetting, or reinforcing, factors.

H. BEDAU, THE COURTS, THE CONSTITUTION, AND CAPITAL PUNISHMENT 55-57 (1977): Van den Haag rests considerable weight on the claims that "the added severity of the death penalty adds to deterrence, or may do so"; and that "the generalized threat of the death penalty may be a deterrent, and the more so, the more generally applied.". . . [T]he abolitionist . . . of course, can play the same game. He has his own equally plausible first principle: *the greater the severity of punishment the greater the brutality provoked throughout society.* When at last, frustrated and exhausted by mere plausibilities, we once again turn to study the evidence, we will find that the current literature on deterrence in criminology does not encourage us to believe in van den Haag's principle.

. . . Van den Haag has not given any reason why, in the quest for deterrent efficacy, one should fasten (as he does) on the severity of the punishments in question, rather than, as Bentham long ago counseled, on all the relevant factors, notably the facility, celerity, and reliability with which the punishment can be inflicted. Van den Haag cannot hope to convince anyone who has studied the matter that the death penalty and "life" imprisonment differ only in their severity, and that in all other respects affecting deterrent efficacy they are equivalent. . . .

NOTES

1. Subsequent empirical studies. Whatever the weaknesses of studies suggesting the absence of a deterrent effect, those who would abolish the death penalty long drew comfort from the fact that no empirical study had ever succeeded in detecting the *presence* of a deterrent effect. The abolitionist position was dealt a significant blow, therefore, when University of Chicago economist Isaac Ehrlich, using complex techniques pioneered in econometric analysis, did find a significant correlation between capital punishment and the deterrence of homicide. See Ehrlich, The Deterrent Effect of Capital Punishment: A Question of Life and Death, 65 Am. Econ. Rev. 397 (1975). The nature of Ehrlich's research and the principal criticisms of it were summarized by Justice Marshall, dissenting in Gregg v. Georgia, 428 U.S. 153, 234-236 (1976):

> The Ehrlich study focused on the relationship in the Nation as a whole between the homicide rate and "execution risk"— the fraction of persons convicted of murder who were actually executed. Comparing the differences in homicide rate and execution risk for the years 1933 to 1969, Ehrlich found that increases in execution risk were associated with increases in the homicide rate. But when he employed the statistical technique of multiple regression analysis to control for the influence of other variables posited to have an impact on the homicide rate, Ehrlich found a negative correlation between changes in the homicide rate and changes in execution risk. His tentative conclusion was that for the period from 1933 to 1967 each additional execution in the United States might have saved eight lives.
>
> The methods and conclusions of the Ehrlich study have been severely criticized on a number of grounds.[8] It has been suggested, for example, that the study is defective because it compares execution and homicide rates on a nationwide, rather than a state-by-state, basis. . . . Under Ehrlich's methodology, a decrease in the execution risk in one State combined with an increase in the murder rate in another

8. See . . . Passell, The Deterrent Effect of the Death Penalty: A Statistical Test, 28 Stan. L. Rev. 61 (1975); Baldus & Cole, A Comparison of the Work of Thorsten Sellin & Isaac Ehrlich on the Deterrent Effect of Capital Punishment, 85 Yale L.J. 170 (1975); Bowers & Pierce, The Illusion of Deterrence in Isaac Ehrlich's Research on Capital Punishment, 85 Yale L.J. 187 (1975); Peck, The Deterrent Effect of Capital Punishment: Ehrlich and His Critics, 85 Yale L.J. 359 (1976). See also Ehrlich, Deterrence: Evidence and Inference, 85 Yale L.J. 209 (1975); Ehrlich, Rejoinder, 85 Yale L.J. 368 (1976). . . .

State would, all other things being equal, suggest a deterrent effect that quite obviously would not exist. . . .

The most compelling criticism of the Ehrlich study is that its conclusions are extremely sensitive to the choice of the time period included in the regression analysis. Analysis of Ehrlich's data reveals that all empirical support for the deterrent effect of capital punishment disappears when the five most recent years are removed from his time series — that is to say, whether a decrease in the execution risk corresponds to an increase or a decrease in the murder rate depends on the ending point of the sample period. This finding has cast severe doubts on the reliability of Ehrlich's tentative conclusions. Indeed, a recent regression study, based on Ehrlich's theoretical model but using cross-section state data for the years 1950 and 1960, found no support for the conclusion that executions act as a deterrent.[12]

The Ehrlich study, in short, is of little, if any, assistance in assessing the deterrent impact of the death penalty. . . .[a]

2. The burden of proof. If neither retentionists nor abolitionists can make a definitive case on the deterrence question, which side offers the more persuasive evidence? The more plausible intuitive arguments? If the debate simply seems inconclusive, which side should bear the burden of proof? Compare van den Haag, On Deterrence and the Death Penalty, 60 J. Crim. L.C. & P.S. 141, 146-147 (1969), with Bedau, The Courts, the Constitution, and Capital Punishment 57-58 (1977).

b. Error and Irrevocability

BEDAU, MURDER, ERRORS OF JUSTICE, AND CAPITAL PUNISHMENT
in The Death Penalty in America 434-440 (H. Bedau ed. 1964)

. . . [R]etentionists are skeptical when they are told that one of the most important arguments against the death penalty is the risk of executing an innocent man; even if the possibility is there, the risk cannot be very great when there are no documented cases of its occurrence, especially in recent years.

It must be acknowledged that on this question, abolitionists tend to argue as inconclusively as do retentionists on the question of deterrence. . . . Jerome Frank has stated, "No one knows how many innocent men, erroneously convicted of murder, have been put to death by American governments."[3] This is, of course, true, but as a forensic tactic it is deceptive. Were a retentionist to say, "No one knows how many persons have been deterred from crimes by the threat of capital punishment," either he would be stating a platitude or he would be making a fallacious appeal to ignorance, i.e., begging the question by assuming from the start that the death penalty is known to be a superior deterrent and that the only thing not known is the exact number of persons deterred. Judge Frank's remark suffers from precisely the same defect. . . .

In this essay, I have abstracted seventy-four cases occurring in the United States since 1893, in which a wrongful conviction of criminal homicide has been

---

12. Passell, supra, n. 8.

a. For a thorough discussion of the various empirical studies completed to date, see Lempert, Desert and Deterrence: An Assessment of the Moral Bases of the Case for Capital Punishment, 79 Mich. L. Rev. 1177 (1981). — EDS.

3. Jerome and Barbara Frank, Not Guilty (1957), p. 248.

alleged and, in most cases, proved beyond doubt. . . . For purposes of classification by the original sentence of the trial court, the seventy-four cases abstracted here may be broken down as follows:

Death sentence executed	8
Death sentence not executed	23
Life sentence	30
Less than life sentence	10
Conviction averted	3
Total	74 . . .

The wonder is, with more than 7,000 persons executed in this century, that only eight probably erroneous executions and an additional twenty-three erroneous death sentences have been discovered. Is this nearly all, or merely a few, of the wrongful executions and death sentences in recent decades? How is it that nearly ninety percent of the cases reported here did not result in a death sentence and execution? There are several reasons. . . . Discovery of error in such cases, not to mention success in persuading those with the power of life and death to admit that a mistake had been made, almost always rests on tireless persistence and luck. It seems very probable that there have been other cases in which poverty, faint-heartedness or lack of ingenuity allowed judicial error in homicide convictions to go unchallenged, unproved, or uncorrected. . . . No doubt, however, attaches to the fact that nearly two dozen men have been sentenced to death for crimes they demonstrably did not commit.

E. VAN DEN HAAG, PUNISHING CRIMINALS 219-220 (1975): Errors would not justify the abolition of the death penalty for retributionists. Many social policies have unintended effects that are statistically certain, irrevocable, unjust, and deadly. Automobile traffic unintentionally kills innocent victims; so does surgery (and most medicines); so does the death penalty. These activities are justified, nevertheless, because benefits (including justice) are felt to outweigh the statistical certainty of unintentionally killing innocents. The certain death of innocents argues for abolishing the death penalty no more than for abolishing surgery or automobiles. Injustice justifies abolition only if the losses to justice outweigh the gains — if more innocents are lost than saved by imposing the penalty compared to whatever net result alternatives (such as no punishment or life imprisonment) would produce. If innocent victims of future murderers are saved by virtue of the death penalty imposed on convicted murderers, it must be retained, just as surgery is, even though some innocents will be lost through miscarriages of justice—as long as more innocent lives are saved than lost. More justice is done with than without the death penalty. . . .

c. Discriminatory Administration

C. BLACK, CAPITAL PUNISHMENT: THE INEVITABILITY
OF CAPRICE AND MISTAKE
29, 96-101 (2d ed. augmented, 1981)

. . . [I]n one way or another, the official choices — by prosecutors, judges, juries, and governors — that divide those who are to die from those who are to live are on the whole not made, and cannot be made, under standards that are consistently meaningful and clear . . . [;] they are often made, and in the foreseeable future will continue often to be made, under no standards at all or under pseudo-standards without discoverable meaning. . . .

. . . [I]f a defense cannot be presented in the best possible manner, the chances of even a valid defense's being rejected are obviously increased. . . . But we are not ready to furnish poor defendants with really adequate resources for the development of a defense, by investigation at early stages while the trail is still warm. . . . This is, of course, just another way of saying that both conviction and conviction by mistake are from the beginning made much more likely for the poor. . . .

Now what about blackness? Why are more than half of the people on death row black in a country with about eleven percent blacks?

A great deal of the explanation is contained in what has already been written in this chapter. There is a high correlation between blackness and poverty. But I must, to be candid, open up another possibility — . . . where standardless "discretion" plays a part, or where close decisions of fact must be made on disputed evidence, or where vague and ambiguous concepts ("premeditation," "insanity") must be applied to concrete facts, we are one and all susceptible to the tendency to see things in a better or worse light depending on our general sympathies; we fight against this, but in the end only the self-deluding think they can wholly avoid it. If this idea is right, then there is the ever-present danger that anyone against whom, for any reason, conscious or unconscious prejudice exists will come off worse than a person against whom such feeling does not exist. And of course the *unconscious* prejudice, the prejudice one thinks one has wholly overcome, is the more dangerous.

In any case, most people on death row are black, and almost all are poor. What is *your* explanation? And can you go on living with such a system?

E. VAN DEN HAAG, PUNISHING CRIMINALS 220-221 (1975): Now, since abolitionists remain opposed to capital punishment even where it is distributed without discrimination, e.g., where populations are nearly racially homogeneous, as in England or Sweden, it appears that the discrimination argument is used to screen objections to the death penalty that do not depend on that argument. At any rate, objections to unwarranted discrimination are relevant to the discriminatory distribution of penalties, not to the penalties distributed. . . . Unjust distribution — either through unjust convictions or through unjust (unequal and biased) penalization of equally guilty convicts — can occur with respect to any penalty. The vice must be corrected by correcting the distributive process that produces it. There is no reason to limit such a correction to any specific penalty. Nor can much be accomplished by abolishing any penalty, since all penalties can be meted out discriminatorily. The defect to be corrected is in the courts.[a]

H. BEDAU, THE CASE AGAINST THE DEATH PENALTY 12-14 (ACLU 1977): More than thirty years ago, Gunnar Myrdal, in his classic An American

---

a. Van den Haag adds (at 219 n.*): "[T]o insist that only the total elimination of 'capriciousness' — which [Professor Black] knows to be impossible in the prosecution of any crime and generally in human affairs — would make the death penalty legally or morally justifiable is a counsel of perfection meant to exclude a disliked policy, and not a serious argument."— EDS.

Dilemma (1944), reported that "the South makes the widest application of the death penalty, and Negro criminals come in for much more than their share of the executions." Statistics confirm this discrimination, only it is not confined to the South. Since 1930, 3,859 persons have been executed in the United States. Of these, 2,066, or 54 percent, were black. For the crime of murder, 3,334 have been executed; 1,630, or 49 percent, were black. During these years blacks were about 9 percent of the population. For rape, punishable by death in 1972 in only sixteen states and by the federal government, 455 have been executed, all but two in the South; 405, or 90 percent, were black. . . .

More exact statistical studies show that the higher rate of executions of blacks for rape and homicide cannot be explained by any factor except the race of the defendant. . . . Despite a whole new set of capital statutes enacted since 1972, bias in death sentencing has not abated. An examination of 800 condemned prisoners in 28 states before and after *Furman*[b] showed that the new post-*Furman* death statutes did little or nothing to reduce the preponderance of blacks on death row. The evidence shows that "nationwide and especially in the West, the proportion of non-whites who received the death penalty is significantly higher than it was before the 1972 decision." [20]

The race of the victim, as well as the offender, is a significant factor. Crimes against whites are disproportionately more likely to receive a death sentence. Though blacks constitute 54% of murder victims, only 13% of the people on death row had black victims, while 87% had white victims.[21] . . .

Such evidence of racial discrimination at both the trial and commutation phases of death penalty proceedings has not been shown in every state. In some states, e.g., California, studies have revealed no evidence of race discrimination.[23] The California study did, however, show discrimination against the poor. . . .

A study of post-*Furman* death row inmates confirms the trend: 62% were unskilled, service, or domestic workers, while only 3% were professional or technical workers. Fully 60% of those on death row were unemployed at the time of their crimes.[24] In North Carolina, the vast majority was represented by appointed counsel; most of these lawyers had less than five years' experience. . . .

d. The Sanctity of Human Life

RAMSEY CLARK, STATEMENT, Hearings on S. 1760 ("To Abolish the Death Penalty") before the Subcommittee on Criminal Laws and Procedures, Senate Judiciary Committee, 90th Cong., 2d Sess. (July 2, 1968): In the midst of anxiety

b. In Furman v. Georgia, 408 U.S. 238 (1972), the Supreme Court held unconstitutional the procedures then used for deciding whether to impose the death penalty. Laws enacted since *Furman* have established a more elaborately structured process. See page 520 infra. — Eds.

20. The New York Times, April 4, 1976, p. 42; see also Reidel, [Discrimination in the Imposition of the Death Penalty: A Comparison of the Characteristics of Offenders Sentenced Pre-*Furman* and Post-*Furman*, 49 Temp. L.Q. 261 (1976).]

21. Reidel, [supra footnote 20, at 282. See also Zeisel, Race Bias in the Administration of the Death Penalty: The Florida Experience, 95 Harv. L. Rev. 456 (1981).]

23. [Judson et al., A Study of the California Penalty Jury in First-Degree-Murder Cases, 21 Stan. L. Rev. 1297 (1969).]

24. Reidel, [supra footnote 20, at 284.]

and fear, complexity and doubt, perhaps our greatest need is reverence for life — mere life: our lives, the lives of others, all life. Life is an end in itself. A humane and generous concern for every individual, for his safety, his health and his fulfillment, will do more to soothe the savage heart than the fear of state-inflicted death which chiefly serves to remind us how close we remain to the jungle.

"Murder and capital punishment are not opposites that cancel one another, but similars that breed their kind," Shaw advises. When the state itself kills, the mandate "thou shalt not kill" loses the force of the absolute.

Surely the abolition of the death penalty is a major milestone in the long road up from barbarism. There was a time when self preservation necessitated its imposition. . . . Our civilization has no such excuse. . . .

Our emotions may cry vengeance in the wake of a horrible crime. But reason and experience tell us that killing the criminal will not undo the crime, prevent other crimes, or bring justice to the victim, the criminal, or society. Executions cheapen life. We must cherish life. . . .

E. VAN DEN HAAG, PUNISHING CRIMINALS 213 (1975): No matter what can be said for abolition of the death penalty, it will be perceived symbolically as a loss of nerve: social authority no longer is willing to pass an irrevocable judgment on anyone. Murder is no longer thought grave enough to take the murderer's life, no longer horrendous enough to deserve so fearfully irrevocable a punishment. When murder no longer forfeits the murderer's life (though it will interfere with his freedom), respect for life itself is diminished, as the price for taking it is. Life becomes cheaper as we become kinder to those who wantonly take it. The responsibility we avoid is indeed hard to bear. Can we sit in judgment and find that anyone is so irredeemably wicked that he does not deserve to live? Many of us no longer believe in evil, only in error or accident. How can one execute a murderer if one believes that he became one only by error or accident and is not to blame? Yet if life is to be valued and secured, it must be known that anyone who takes the life of another forfeits his own.

NOTE

For further development of the argument that respect for the sanctity of life *requires* the death penalty, see W. Berns, For Capital Punishment 153-176 (1979).

Ethical arguments based on the sanctity of life are closely related to concepts derived from specifically religious sources. Although we cannot present here an adequate sampling of arguments advanced from the viewpoint of the principal religious faiths, that perspective is of considerable importance for this aspect of the capital punishment debate. In Punishing Criminals, Professor van den Haag comments (id. at 225):

[I]t is not easy to see what "sanctity" [of life] could mean outside of its religious context other than the assertion, disguised as proof, that it is wrong to put criminals to death. . . . Unless one resorts to a religiously or, in some other way, revealed source, one cannot show that society, unlike the murderer, must hold life unconditionally inviolate; and the fact that the nonreligious urge it so religiously cannot commend this precept to believers. The death penalty has been part of all major religious traditions: Graeco-Roman, Judaic, Islamic, and Christian.

Note, however, that many American religious denominations have officially condemned capital punishment on religious grounds. For discussion of the religious issues by several leading theologians, see The Death Penalty in America 123-130, 171-182 (H. Bedau ed. 1964).

BARZUN, IN FAVOR OF CAPITAL PUNISHMENT
31 Am. Scholar 181 (Spring 1962)

. . . The propaganda for abolition speaks in hushed tones of the sanctity of human life, as if the mere statement of it should silence all opponents who have any moral sense. . . . [I]s the movement then campaigning also against the principle of self-defense? Absolute sanctity means letting the cutthroat have his sweet will of you, even if you have a poker handy to bash him with, for you might kill. And again, do we hear any protest against the police firing at criminals on the street — mere bank robbers usually — and doing this, often enough, with an excited marksmanship that misses the artist and hits the bystander? The absolute sanctity of human life is, for the abolitionist, a slogan rather than a considered proposition.

. . . [T]here are hundreds and indeed thousands whom, in our concern with the horrors of execution, we forget: on the one hand, the victims of violence; on the other, the prisoners in our jails.

The victims are easy to forget. Social science tends steadily to mark a preference for the troubled, the abnormal, the problem case. Whether it is poverty, mental disorder, delinquency or crime, the "patient material" monopolizes the interest of increasing groups of people among the most generous and learned. . . . [W]ho are the victims? Only dull ordinary people going about their business. We are sorry, of course, but they do not interest science on its march. . . .

It is all very well to say that many of these killers are themselves "children," that is, minors. Doubtless a nine-year-old mind is housed in that 150 pounds of unguided muscle. Grant, for argument's sake, that the misdeed is "the fault of society," trot out the broken home and the slum environment. The question then is, What shall we do, not in the Utopian city of tomorrow, but here and now? The "scientific" means of cure are more than uncertain. The apparatus of detention only increases the killer's antisocial animus. Reformatories and mental hospitals are full and have an understandable bias toward discharging their inmates. . . .

As in all great questions, the moralist must choose, and choosing has a price. I happen to think that if a person of adult body has not been endowed with adequate controls against irrationally taking the life of another, that person must be judicially, painlessly, regretfully killed before that mindless body's horrible automation repeats.

. . . [T]here is one form of barbarity in our law that I want to see mitigated before any other. I mean imprisonment. The enemies of capital punishment — and liberals generally — seem to be satisfied with any legal outcome so long as they themselves avoid the vicarious guilt of shedding blood. They speak of the sanctity of life, but have no concern with its quality. . . . They do not see and suffer the cell, the drill, the clothes, the stench, the food; they do not feel the sexual racking of young and old bodies, the hateful promiscuity, the insane monotony, the mass degradation, the impotent hatred. . . .

Nothing is revocable here below, imprisonment least of all. . . . A writer on Death and the Supreme Court is at pains to point out that when that tribunal reviews a capital case, the judges are particularly anxious and careful. What a lefthanded compliment to the highest judicial conscience of the country! . . .

What we accept, and what the abolitionist will clamp upon us all the more firmly if he succeeds, is an incoherence which is not remedied by the belief that second-degree murder merits a kind of second-degree death; that a doubt as to the identity of a killer is resolved by commuting real death into intolerable life. . . .

BEDAU, DEATH AS A PUNISHMENT, in The Death Penalty in America 216-219 (H. Bedau ed. 1964): [O]ne distinction of importance, neglected by Professor Barzun, is between a man's killing someone else when there is a clear and present danger that he will otherwise be the victim of some violent act, and the state's killing a man as a punishment, i.e., between a man's right to defend himself and society's right to punish criminals. . . . So far as law and the prevailing morality of Western civilization have been concerned, respect for human life has never been an obstacle to the use of force in self-defense; indeed, it has always been thought to be its justification. It has, however, obligated anyone who pleads self-defense in justification of a killing to satisfy society that the force he used really was necessary in the circumstances and was motivated solely by a desire to ward off imminent harm to himself. . . . Were it to be shown that there is a threat to society, or to any of its members, in allowing a criminal in prison to remain there, comparable to the danger a man invites in a dark alley if he turns his back on a thug who has a weapon in his hand and violence on his mind, then — but *only* then — would it be inconsistent for the abolitionist to tolerate force sufficient to kill the thug in the alley but to refuse to kill the prisoner. . . .

On the issue of whether abolition of the death penalty would improve the lot of persons unjustly convicted, I think . . . Professor Barzun [is] misled and confusing. Barzun is unquestionably right when he points to cases where men have been exonerated after years in prison, only to find that their lives have been destroyed. Of course, abolishing the death penalty is no remedy for the injustice of convicting and punishing an innocent man. It is obviously as *wrong* to imprison an innocent man as it is to kill him. But I should have thought it is just as obviously *worse* for him to be killed than for him to be imprisoned. This point must not be blurred by speculating whether it is worse from the convict's point of view to be dead than to be imprisoned and perhaps never vindicated or released. If an innocent convict thinks he is better off dead than alive, this is for *him* to determine, not us. . . .

. . . [W]e ought to consider allowing our penal authorities, under proper judicial and medical supervision, to cooperate with any long-term prisoner who is too dangerous to be released and who would honestly and soberly prefer to be dead rather than endure further imprisonment. That there are such convicts I am willing to concede. The question here is this: is it wisest for the state to allow a convict to take his own life if he decides that it would be better for him to be dead than to suffer any more imprisonment? Can a person in good physical health, in a tolerable prison environment, and who professes to want to die be of sound mind? (or isn't that important?) Does not civilized society always have a fundamental interest, if not an obligation, to try to provide even for its most incompetent members in that most oppressive of environments, a prison, some opportunity to make their lives worth living? Wouldn't a policy that amounts to euthanasia for certain convicts run counter to this interest and sap the motive to satisfy it?

These questions are not new, for they arise whenever "mercy killing" as a social policy is advocated. . . . [W]e are asking whether we ought to allow a convict, if he so wishes, to be painlessly put to death for no other reason than so that his imprisonment and his despair may come to an end — as if there were no better alternatives! . . .

2. Constitutional Limitations

INTRODUCTORY NOTE

Until the 1950s, opponents of the death penalty had largely devoted their efforts to legislative reform, but thereafter abolitionists began a concentrated assault on the constitutionality of capital punishment.[5] Recall that at common law all murder had been punishable by death. Gradually, the scope of capital punishment had been narrowed, first by the division of murder into two degrees, so that only the more serious was subject to mandatory capital punishment, and then by the introduction of discretion in sentencing even for the highest category of criminal homicides. By the beginning of the twentieth century, 23 American jurisdictions made capital punishment discretionary in first-degree murder cases, and by 1962 all the remaining jurisdictions had adopted this approach.[6]

Litigation challenging this punishment scheme focused principally on three constitutional requirements:

(1) Equal protection. Evidence relating to the disproportionate numbers of blacks executed (see pages 513-514 supra) was marshalled in an effort to establish that the death penalty, as administered, violated the equal protection requirements of the Fourteenth Amendment. In Maxwell v. Bishop, 398 F.2d 138 (8th Cir. 1968), rev'd on other grounds, 398 U.S. 262 (1970), the Court of Appeals, in an opinion by then-Judge Blackmun, found the statistical evidence insufficient to establish discriminatory enforcement. Subsequent developments made it unnecessary for the Supreme Court to confront the problem of discrimination under the statutory schemes of the 1960s, and the Court has not yet faced a fully developed claim of discrimination in the administration of more recently enacted statutes.

---

5. The development of a detailed strategy for litigation against the death penalty is recounted in M. Meltsner, Cruel and Unusual: The Supreme Court and Capital Punishment (1973).

6. The history is detailed in American Law Institute, Model Penal Code and Commentaries, Pt. II, Comment to §210.6 at 120-132 (1980).

(2) *Procedural due process.* All the states committed the death penalty decision to the discretion of judge or jury, but none provided any standards to guide the exercise of that discretion. The reliance on unguided discretion was of course prevalent in sentencing decisions generally, but many thought that when a choice between life and death was to be made, due process required some explicit criteria of decision. The Court rejected that view in McGautha v. California, 402 U.S. 183, 207-208 (1971), holding instead that "committing to the untrammelled discretion of the jury the power to pronounce life or death is [not] offensive to anything in the Constitution." The Court reasoned that

> [an] attempt to catalog the appropriate factors in this elusive area could inhibit rather than expand the scope of consideration. . . . The infinite variety of cases . . . would make general standards either meaningless "boiler plate" or a statement of the obvious that no jury would need.

McGautha proved to be less significant than it seemed, however, because the same concerns about unguided discretion soon surfaced in attacks based on the cruel-and-unusual-punishment clause.

(3) *Cruel and unusual punishment.* Only a year after *McGautha*, a 5 – 4 majority of the Court held in Furman v. Georgia, 408 U.S. 238 (1972), that capital punishment, as then administered, violated the Eighth Amendment's prohibition of "cruel and unusual punishments." The Court's holding was stated in a brief per curiam opinion that made no attempt to set forth the majority's reasoning. Each of the justices filed a separate concurring or dissenting opinion explaining his own approach to the Eighth Amendment issue.

Justices Brennan and Marshall concluded that all capital punishment was unconstitutional. Justice Brennan's test was (id. at 222):

> If a punishment is unusually severe, if there is a strong probability that it is inflicted arbitrarily, if it is substantially rejected by contemporary society, and if there is no reason to believe that it serves any penal purpose more effectively than some less severe punishment, then the continued infliction of that punishment, violates the command of the Clause that the State may not inflict inhuman and uncivilized punishments upon those convicted of crimes.

Justice Brennan found these conditions met with respect to capital punishment. Justice Marshall focused on the last two tests. He concluded that capital punishment does not serve the various purposes offered to justify it, and hence is "excessive and unnecessary." Id. at 358. He further concluded that even if it were not excessive, "it nonetheless violates the Eighth Amendment because it is morally unacceptable to the people of the United States at this time in their history." Id. at 360. His test of popular unacceptability did not rest on prevailing opinion "but on whether people who were fully informed as to the purposes of the penalty and its liabilities would find the penalty shocking, unjust, and unacceptable." Id. at 361.

The other three concurring justices appeared to rest their objections to capital punishment on much narrower grounds. Justice Douglas stressed the potential for discriminatory administration of the death penalty and indications of its disproportionate impact on blacks and the poor. Justices White and Stewart also focused on the administration of the penalty, but their emphasis differed from that of Justice Douglas. Justice Stewart said (id. at 309-310), in a passage that reflects Justice White's position as well:

> These death sentences are cruel and unusual in the same way that being struck by lightning is cruel and unusual. . . . [I]f any basis can be discerned for the selection of these few to be sentenced to die, it is the constitutionally impermissible basis of race. But racial discrimination has not been proved, and I put it to one side. I simply conclude that the Eighth and Fourteenth Amendments cannot tolerate the infliction of a sentence of death under legal systems that permit this unique penalty to be so wantonly and so freakishly imposed.

The Chief Justice and Justices Blackmun, Powell and Rehnquist dissented. The dissenters stressed the long tradition and continued acceptance of capital punishment and argued that the majority's position involved an unwarranted intrusion into the legislative process.

Because a clear majority of the justices had neither rejected capital punishment outright nor indicated under what conditions it might be preserved, *Furman* created considerable confusion for states that desired to retain the death penalty. Two alternatives appeared viable: (1) enacting legislation to make capital punishment mandatory in certain cases and (2) establishing guidelines to determine who would be subjected to capital punishment. By 1976, at least 35 states and the United States Congress had enacted new capital punishment legislation; half of these jurisdictions had adopted provisions for a mandatory death penalty, while the remainder opted for schemes under which the sentencing authority would be required to consider specified aggravating and mitigating circumstances.[7] The Court soon confronted challenges to the new legislation.

GREGG v. GEORGIA
Supreme Court of the United States
428 U.S. 153 (1976)

[Gregg was convicted by a jury on two counts of armed robbery and two counts of murder. After the guilty verdicts, a penalty hearing was held before the same jury, under guidelines enacted in response to the *Furman* decision. The jury imposed the death sentence on each count. The Georgia Supreme Court set aside the death sentences for armed robbery, on the ground that capital punishment had rarely been imposed for that crime, but the court affirmed the convictions on all counts and upheld the death sentences on the murder counts. The United States Supreme Court granted certiorari.]

MR. JUSTICE STEWART, MR. JUSTICE POWELL, and MR. JUSTICE STEVENS announced the judgment of the Court and filed an opinion delivered by MR. JUSTICE STEWART. . . .

We address initially the basic contention that the punishment of death for the crime of murder is, under all circumstances, "cruel and unusual" in violation of the Eighth and Fourteenth Amendments of the Constitution. . . . We now

---

7. For details concerning these enactments, see American Law Institute, Model Penal Code and Commentaries, Pt. II, Comment to §210.6 at 156-157 & nn. 144-148 (1980).

hold that the punishment of death does not invariably violate the Constitution. . . .

It is clear from the . . . precedents that the Eighth Amendment has not been regarded as a static concept. As Chief Justice Warren said, in an oft-quoted phrase, "[t]he Amendment must draw its meaning from the evolving standards of decency that mark the progress of a maturing society." Trop v. Dulles, 356 U.S. 86, 101 (1958). Thus, an assessment of contemporary values concerning the infliction of a challenged sanction is relevant to the application of the Eighth Amendment. . . .

But our cases also make clear that public perceptions of standards of decency with respect to criminal sanctions are not conclusive. A penalty also must accord with "the dignity of man," which is the "basic concept underlying the Eighth Amendment." Trop v. Dulles, supra, 356 U.S., at 100. This means, at least, that the punishment not be "excessive." . . . [T]he inquiry into "excessiveness" has two aspects. First, the punishment must not involve the unnecessary and wanton infliction of pain. Second, the punishment must not be grossly out of proportion to the severity of the crime.

Of course, the requirements of the Eighth Amendment must be applied with an awareness of the limited role to be played by the courts. . . . [W]hile we have an obligation to insure that constitutional bounds are not overreached, we may not act as judges as we might as legislators. . . .

Therefore, in assessing a punishment selected by a democratically elected legislature against the constitutional measure, we presume its validity. We may not require the legislature to select the least severe penalty possible so long as the penalty selected is not cruelly inhumane or disproportionate to the crime involved. And a heavy burden rests on those who would attack the judgment of the representatives of the people.

. . . We now consider specifically whether the sentence of death for the crime of murder is a per se violation of the Eighth and Fourteenth Amendments to the Constitution. We note first that history and precedent strongly support a negative answer to this question. It is apparent from the text of the Constitution itself that the existence of capital punishment was accepted by the Framers. . . . For nearly two centuries, this Court, repeatedly and often expressly, has recognized that capital punishment is not invalid per se. . . .

Four years ago, the petitioners in *Furman* and its companion cases predicated their argument primarily upon the asserted proposition that standards of decency had evolved to the point where capital punishment no longer could be tolerated. . . . The petitioners in the capital cases before the Court today renew the "standards of decency" argument, but developments during the four years since *Furman* have undercut substantially the assumptions upon which their argument rested. Despite the continuing debate, dating back to the 19th century, over the morality and utility of capital punishment, it is now evident that a large proportion of American society continues to regard it as an appropriate and necessary criminal sanction.

The most marked indication of society's endorsement of the death penalty for murder is the legislative response to *Furman*. The legislatures of at least 35 States have enacted new statutes that provide for the death penalty for at least some crimes that result in the death of another person. And the Congress of the United States, in 1974, enacted a statute providing the death penalty for aircraft piracy that results in death. . . .

The jury also is a significant and reliable objective index of contemporary values because it is so directly involved. . . . [T]he relative infrequency of jury verdicts imposing the death sentence does not indicate rejection of capital punishment per se. Rather, the reluctance of juries in many cases to impose the sentence may well reflect the humane feeling that this most irrevocable of sanctions should be reserved for a small number of extreme cases. . . .

As we have seen, however, the Eighth Amendment demands more than that a challenged punishment be acceptable to contemporary society. The Court also must ask whether it comports with the basic concept of human dignity at the core of the Amendment. Although we cannot "invalidate a category of penalties because we deem less severe penalties adequate to serve the ends of penology," the sanction imposed cannot be so totally without penological justification that it results in the gratuitous infliction of suffering.

The death penalty is said to serve two principal social purposes: retribution and deterrence of capital crimes by prospective offenders.

In part, capital punishment is an expression of society's moral outrage at particularly offensive conduct. This function may be unappealing to many, but it is essential in an ordered society that asks its citizens to rely on legal processes rather than self-help to vindicate their wrongs. "The instinct for retribution is part of the nature of man, and channeling that instinct in the administration of criminal justice serves an important purpose in promoting the stability of a society governed by law. When people begin to believe that organized society is unwilling or unable to impose upon criminal offenders the punishment they 'deserve,' then there are sown the seeds of anarchy — of self-help, vigilante justice, and lynch law." Furman v. Georgia, 408 U.S., at 308 (Stewart, J., concurring). "Retribution is no longer the dominant objective of the criminal law," Williams v. New York, 337 U.S. 241, 248 (1949), but neither is it a forbidden objective nor one inconsistent with our respect for the dignity of men. Indeed, the decision that capital punishment may be the appropriate sanction in extreme cases is an expression of the community's belief that certain crimes are themselves so grievous an affront to humanity that the only adequate response may be the penalty of death.

Statistical attempts to evaluate the worth of the death penalty as a deterrent to crimes by potential offenders have occasioned a great deal of debate. The results simply have been inconclusive. . . .

The value of capital punishment as a deterrent of crime is a complex factual issue the resolution of which properly rests with the legislatures, which can evaluate the results of statistical studies in terms of their own local conditions and with a flexibility of approach that is not available to the courts. . . .

Finally, we must consider whether the punishment of death is disproportionate in relation to the crime for which it is imposed. There is no question that death as a punishment is unique in its severity and irrevocability. . . . But we are concerned here only with the imposition of capital punishment for the crime of murder, and when a life has been taken deliberately by the offender,[35] we

---

35. We do not address here the question whether the taking of the criminal's life is a proportionate sanction where no victim has been deprived of life — for example, when capital punishment is imposed for rape, kidnapping, or armed robbery that does not result in the death of any human being.

cannot say that the punishment is invariably disproportionate to the crime. It is an extreme sanction, suitable to the most extreme of crimes.

We hold that the death penalty is not a form of punishment that may never be imposed, regardless of the circumstances of the offense, regardless of the character of the offender, and regardless of the procedure followed in reaching the decision to impose it.

We now consider whether Georgia may impose the death penalty on the petitioner in this case.

While *Furman* did not hold that the infliction of the death penalty per se violates the Constitution's ban on cruel and unusual punishments, it did recognize that the penalty of death is different in kind from any other punishment imposed under our system of criminal justice. Because of the uniqueness of the death penalty, *Furman* held that it could not be imposed under sentencing procedures that created a substantial risk that it would be inflicted in an arbitrary and capricious manner. . . .

Jury sentencing has been considered desirable in capital cases in order "to maintain a link between contemporary community values and the penal system — a link without which the determination of punishment could hardly reflect 'the evolving standards of decency that mark the progress of a maturing society.' " But it creates special problems. Much of the information that is relevant to the sentencing decision may have no relevance to the question of guilt, or may even be extremely prejudicial to a fair determination of that question. This problem, however, is scarcely insurmountable. Those who have studied the question suggest that a bifurcated procedure — one in which the question of sentence is not considered until the determination of guilt has been made — is the best answer. . . . When a human life is at stake and when the jury must have information prejudicial to the question of guilt but relevant to the question of penalty in order to impose a rational sentence, a bifurcated system is more likely to ensure elimination of the constitutional deficiencies identified in *Furman.*

But the provision of relevant information under fair procedural rules is not alone sufficient to guarantee that the information will be properly used in the imposition of punishment, especially if sentencing is performed by a jury. Since the members of a jury will have had little, if any, previous experience in sentencing, they are unlikely to be skilled in dealing with the information they are given. . . . It seems clear, however, that the problem will be alleviated if the jury is given guidance regarding the factors about the crime and the defendant that the State, representing organized society, deems particularly relevant to the sentencing decision. . . .

While some have suggested that standards to guide a capital jury's sentencing deliberations are impossible to formulate, the fact is that such standards have been developed. . . . [The Court here referred to the Model Penal Code proposals. See §210.6, Appendix to this casebook.] While such standards are by necessity somewhat general, they do provide guidance to the sentencing authority and thereby reduce the likelihood that it will impose a sentence that fairly can be called capricious or arbitrary. . . .

In summary, the concerns expressed in *Furman* that the penalty of death not be imposed in an arbitrary or capricious manner can be met by a carefully drafted statute that ensures that the sentencing authority is given adequate information and guidance. As a general proposition these concerns are best met

by a system that provides for a bifurcated proceeding at which the sentencing
authority is apprised of the information relevant to the imposition of sentence
and provided with standards to guide its use of the information. . . .

We now turn to consideration of the constitutionality of Georgia's capital-
sentencing procedures. In the wake of *Furman*, Georgia amended its capital
punishment statute, but chose not to narrow the scope of its murder provisions.
Thus, now as before *Furman*, in Georgia "[a] person commits murder when
he unlawfully and with malice aforethought, either express or implied, causes
the death of another human being." Ga. Code Ann., §26-1101(a) (1972). All
persons convicted of murder "shall be punished by death or by imprisonment
for life." §26-1101(c) (1972).

Georgia did act, however, to narrow the class of murderers subject to capital
punishment by specifying 10 statutory aggravating circumstances, one of which
must be found by the jury to exist beyond a reasonable doubt before a death
sentence can ever be imposed.[48] In addition, the jury is authorized to consider
any other appropriate aggravating or mitigating circumstances. §27-2534.1(b)
(Supp. 1975). The jury is not required to find any mitigating circumstance in
order to make a recommendation of mercy that is binding on the trial court,
see §27-2302 (Supp. 1975), but it must find a *statutory* aggravating circumstance
before recommending a sentence of death. . . .

As an important additional safeguard against arbitrariness and caprice, the
Georgia statutory scheme provides for automatic appeal of all death sentences
to the State's supreme court. That court is required by statute to review each
sentence of death and determine whether it was imposed under the influence
of passion or prejudice, whether the evidence supports the jury's finding of a
statutory aggravating circumstance, and whether the sentence is disproportionate
compared to those sentences imposed in similar cases. §27-2537(c) (Supp. 1975).

. . . On their face these procedures seem to satisfy the concerns of *Furman*.
No longer should there be "no meaningful basis for distinguishing the few
cases in which [the death penalty] is imposed from the many cases in which it
is not."

The petitioner contends, however, that the changes in the Georgia sentencing
procedures are only cosmetic, that the arbitrariness and capriciousness condemned by *Furman* continue to exist in Georgia — both in traditional practices
that still remain and in the new sentencing procedures adopted in response
to *Furman*.

---

48. The text of the statute enumerating the various aggravating circumstances is [as follows:

"(a) The death penalty may be imposed for the offenses of aircraft hijacking or treason, in any
case.

"(b) In all cases of other offenses for which the death penalty may be authorized, the judge
shall consider, or he shall include in his instructions to the jury for it to consider, any mitigating
circumstances or aggravating circumstances otherwise authorized by law and any of the following
statutory aggravating circumstances which may be supported by the evidence:

"(1) The offense of murder, rape, armed robbery, or kidnapping was committed by a person
with a prior record of conviction for a capital felony, or the offense of murder was committed
by a person who has a substantial history of serious assaultive criminal convictions.

"(2) The offense of murder, rape, armed robbery, or kidnapping was committed while the
offender was engaged in the commission of another capital felony, or aggravated battery, or
the offense of murder was committed while the offender was engaged in the commission of
burglary or arson in the first degree.

"(3) The offender by his act of murder, armed robbery, or kidnapping knowingly created a

First, the petitioner focuses on the opportunities for discretionary action that are inherent in the processing of any murder case under Georgia law. He notes that the state prosecutor has unfettered authority to select those persons whom he wishes to prosecute for a capital offense and to plea bargain with them. Further, at the trial the jury may choose to convict a defendant of a lesser included offense rather than find him guilty of a crime punishable by death, even if the evidence would support a capital verdict. And finally, a defendant who is convicted and sentenced to die may have his sentence commuted by the Governor of the State and the Georgia Board of Pardons and Paroles.

The existence of these discretionary stages is not determinative of the issues before us. At each of these stages an actor in the criminal justice system makes a decision which may remove a defendant from consideration as a candidate for the death penalty. *Furman*, in contrast, dealt with the decision to impose the death sentence on a specific individual who had been convicted of a capital offense. Nothing in any of our cases suggests that the decision to afford an individual defendant mercy violates the Constitution. *Furman* held only that, in order to minimize the risk that the death penalty would be imposed on a capriciously selected group of offenders, the decision to impose it had to be guided by standards so that the sentencing authority would focus on the particularized circumstances of the crime and the defendant.

The petitioner further contends that . . . the statute is so broad and vague as to leave juries free to act as arbitrarily and capriciously as they wish in deciding whether to impose the death penalty. . . . In light of the decisions of the Supreme Court of Georgia we must disagree. . . . [That court held §1 of the statute] to be impermissibly vague in Arnold v. State, 236 Ga. 534, 540, 224 S.E.2d 386, 391 (1976), because it did not provide the jury with "sufficiently 'clear and objective standards.' " Second, the petitioner points to §3 which speaks of creating a "great risk of death to more than one person." While such a phrase might be susceptible to an overly broad interpretation, the Supreme Court of Georgia has not so construed it. . . .

---

great risk of death to more than one person in a public place by means of a weapon or device which would normally be hazardous to the lives of more than one person.

"(4) The offender committed the offense of murder for himself or another, for the purpose of receiving money or any other thing of monetary value.

"(5) The murder of a judicial officer, former judicial officer, district attorney or solicitor or former district attorney or solicitor during or because of the exercise of his official duty.

"(6) The offender caused or directed another to commit murder or committed murder as an agent or employee of another person.

"(7) The offense of murder, rape, armed robbery, or kidnapping was outrageously or wantonly vile, horrible or inhuman in that it involved torture, depravity of mind, or an aggravated battery to the victim.

"(8) The offense of murder was committed against any peace officer, corrections employee or fireman while engaged in the performance of his official duties.

"(9) The offense of murder was committed by a person in, or who has escaped from, the lawful custody of a peace officer or place of lawful confinement.

"(10) The murder was committed for the purpose of avoiding, interfering with, or preventing a lawful arrest or custody in a place of lawful confinement, of himself or another.

"(c) The statutory instructions as determined by the trial judge to be warranted by the evidence shall be given in charge and in writing to the jury for its deliberation. The jury, if its verdict be a recommendation of death, shall designate in writing, signed by the foreman of the jury, the aggravating circumstance or circumstances which it found beyond a reasonable doubt. In non-jury cases the judge shall make such designation. Except in cases of treason or aircraft hijacking, unless at least one of the statutory aggravating circumstances enumerated in section 27-2534.1(b) is so found, the death penalty shall not be imposed." §27-2534.1 (Supp. 1975).]

The petitioner objects, finally, to the wide scope of evidence and argument allowed at presentence hearings. We think that the Georgia court wisely has chosen not to impose unnecessary restrictions on the evidence that can be offered at such a hearing and to approve open and far-ranging argument. So long as the evidence introduced and the arguments made at the presentence hearing do not prejudice a defendant, it is preferable not to impose restrictions. We think it desirable for the jury to have as much information before it as possible when it makes the sentencing decision.

For the reasons expressed in this opinion, we hold that the statutory system under which Gregg was sentenced to death does not violate the Constitution. Accordingly, the judgment of the Georgia Supreme Court is affirmed. . . .

[The concurring opinion of JUSTICE WHITE, joined by the CHIEF JUSTICE and JUSTICE REHNQUIST, the concurring opinion of JUSTICE BLACKMUN, and the dissenting opinion of JUSTICE BRENNAN are omitted.]

MR. JUSTICE MARSHALL, dissenting. . . .

I would be less than candid if I did not acknowledge that [legislative] developments [since *Furman*] have a significant bearing on a realistic assessment of the moral acceptability of the death penalty to the American people. But if the constitutionality of the death penalty turns, as I have urged, on the opinion of an *informed* citizenry, then even the enactment of new death statutes cannot be viewed as conclusive. In *Furman,* I observed that the American people are largely unaware of the information critical to a judgment on the morality of the death penalty, and concluded that if they were better informed they would consider it shocking, unjust, and unacceptable. . . .

The two purposes that sustain the death penalty as nonexcessive in the Court's view are general deterrence and retribution. . . . The evidence I reviewed in *Furman* remains convincing, in my view, that "capital punishment is not necessary as a deterrent to crime in our society." . . .

The other principal purpose said to be served by the death penalty is retribution. The notion that retribution can serve as a moral justification for the sanction of death finds credence in the opinion of my Brothers Stewart, Powell, and Stevens, . . . [but their] statement is wholly inadequate to justify the death penalty. As my Brother Brennan stated in *Furman,* "[t]here is no evidence whatever that utilization of imprisonment rather than death encourages private blood feuds and other disorders." It simply defies belief to suggest that the death penalty is necessary to prevent the American people from taking the law into their own hands. . . .

NOTES

1. Mandatory death penalty statutes. (a) In Woodson v. North Carolina, 428 U.S. 280 (1976), the Court held that a mandatory death sentence for any first-degree murder violates the Eighth Amendment. Justice Stewart, joined by Justices Powell and Stevens, enunciated three reasons for this conclusion:

(i) Mandatory capital punishment is inconsistent with contemporary standards of decency. He noted that the recent enactment of mandatory-sentence statutes was not a reversal of the historical trend of popular rejection of mandatory sentences but was only an effort to retain the death penalty in light of *Furman.*

(ii) Mandatory sentences fail to provide standards that will effectively guide the jury. Justice Stewart noted experience with earlier mandatory schemes, under which "[j]uries continued to find the death penalty inappropriate in a significant number of first-degree murder cases and refused to return guilty verdicts for that crime." Id. at 291. He therefore concluded that "mandatory statutes enacted in response to *Furman* have simply papered over the problem of unguided and unchecked jury discretion." Id. at 302. (Do you find this point convincing? If so, does it not apply with virtually equal force to the statute upheld in *Gregg*?)

(iii) Most important, Justice Stewart reasoned that the fundamental respect for individual dignity underlying the Eighth Amendment requires (id. at 303-304)

> the particularized consideration of relevant aspects of the character and record of each convicted defendant [and the circumstances of the offense] before the imposition upon him of a sentence of death. . . . A process that [fails to provide such consideration] . . . treats all persons convicted of a designated offense not as uniquely individual human beings, but as members of a faceless, undifferentiated mass to be subjected to the blind infliction of the penalty of death.

Justice Stewart mentioned in a footnote, however, that he was not considering the constitutionality of "a mandatory death penalty statute limited to an extremely narrow category of homicide, such as murder by a prisoner serving a life sentence, defined in large part in terms of the character or record of the offender."

Justices Brennan and Marshall concurred in the result, on the basis of their view that any death penalty violates the Eighth Amendment. The Chief Justice and Justices White, Blackmun, and Rehnquist dissented.

(b) In Roberts v. Louisiana, 431 U.S. 633 (1977), the Court relied on *Woodson* in striking down a Louisiana statute that imposed a mandatory death sentence for the murder of a police officer. Again, the Court left open the possibility of a mandatory death sentence for murder by a prisoner serving a life sentence.

2. Other guided-discretion statutes. (a) In Proffitt v. Florida, 428 U.S. 242 (1976), the Court considered a post-*Furman* statute under which the jury is instructed to determine sentence by balancing eight specified aggravating factors and seven specified mitigating factors, all closely patterned on Model Penal Code §210.6(3)-(4). See Appendix. Unlike the Code, however, the Florida statute provides that the jury's decision may be made by majority vote and that its determination is not binding on the trial judge. The judge may impose the death sentence, whether or not the jury recommends it, provided that he or she balances the same criteria and enters written findings concerning factors in mitigation and aggravation. The Court sustained this approach, in a plurality opinion (by Justices Stewart, Powell, and Stevens) finding that the Florida scheme afforded an adequately focused inquiry.

(b) In Jurek v. Texas, 428 U.S. 262 (1976), the Court considered a post-*Furman* statute that limits capital punishment to five categories of intentional homicide[8] and then provides the following procedure for determining whether

---

8. The categories are: murder of a peace officer or firefighter, intentional murder in the course of specified felonies, murder committed for remuneration, murder committed while escaping from prison, or murder of a prison employee by an inmate.

to impose the death penalty in any such case. The jury is directed to answer three questions: (1) whether the conduct was done deliberately and with a reasonable expectation of causing death; (2) whether "there is a probability that the defendant would commit criminal acts of violence that would constitute a continuing threat to society" (id. at 269); and (3) if raised by the evidence, whether the defendant's conduct was an unreasonable response to provocation by the deceased. If the jury gives a negative answer to any question, life imprisonment is imposed, but if the jury finds beyond a reasonable doubt that the answer to all three questions is affirmative, then the death sentence must be imposed. Although this approach is quasi-mandatory in directing capital punishment under specified conditions, the Court treated the case as closer to *Gregg* than to *Woodson* and sustained the statutory scheme. The plurality opinion (by Justices Stewart, Powell, and Stevens) reasoned that the five categories of capital murder were equivalent to aggravating circumstances and noted that Texas courts had read the second question put to the jury, the probability of future violence, as permitting the defense to place before the jury whatever mitigating circumstances might exist. The plurality did not, however, clarify how a jury, unaided by further guidelines, could make a rational response to the broad and ambiguously worded second question. The plurality simply concluded that "[b]ecause this system serves to assure that sentences of death will not be 'wantonly' or 'freakishly' imposed, it does not violate the Constitution." Id. at 276.

(c) Lockett v. Ohio, 438 U.S. 586 (1978), involved a post-*Furman* statute which specified that once any of seven aggravating circumstances was found, the death penalty must be imposed unless it is found that (1) the victim had induced or facilitated the offense, (2) it was unlikely that the defendant would have committed the offense but for the fact that he or she was under duress, coercion, or strong provocation, or (3) the offense was primarily the product of the defendant's psychosis or mental deficiency. With only eight Justices participating, the Court struck down this statute by a 7 – 1 vote, but once again the Court was widely split in its reasoning. Chief Justice Burger, writing for himself and Justices Stewart, Powell, and Stevens, found the narrow range of permissible mitigating circumstances to be a fatal flaw. "[T]he sentencer, in all but the rarest kind of capital case, [must] not be precluded from considering *as a mitigating factor,* any aspect of a defendant's character or record and any of the circumstances of the offense that the defendant proffers as a basis for a sentence less than death." Id. at 604. In separate opinions Justices White, Marshall, and Blackmun concurred in the result. Justice Rehnquist dissented.

Query: The Chief Justice's view seems to flow naturally from *Woodson,* but is it compatible with the goals of confining and structuring the jury's decision? Is it consistent with the principles implicit in *Furman* and *Gregg?*

3. Crimes other than intentional murder. (a) In Coker v. Georgia, 433 U.S. 584, 592 (1977), the Court held that the death penalty "is grossly disproportionate and excessive punishment for the crime of rape and is therefore forbidden by the Eighth Amendment. . . ." Justice White, in an opinion joined by Justices Stewart, Blackmun, and Stevens, said (id. at 597-598):

> We do not discount the seriousness of rape as a crime. It is highly reprehensible, both in a moral sense and in its almost total contempt for the personal integrity and autonomy of the female victim. . . . Short of homicide, it is "the ultimate violation of self."

Rape is without doubt deserving of serious punishment; but in terms of moral depravity and of the injury to the person and to the public, it does not compare with murder. . . . Although it may be accompanied by another crime, rape by definition does not include the death of or even the serious injury to another person. . . . We have the abiding conviction that the death penalty, which "is unique in its severity and revocability," . . . is an excessive penalty for the rapist who, as such, does not take human life.

Justices Brennan, Marshall, and Powell concurred in the result. The Chief Justice and Justice Rehnquist dissented.

(b) The Court has not yet considered the constitutionality of capital punishment for such crimes as espionage or aircraft hijacking. Of course, these crimes may create a risk of death, perhaps to many persons. But given *Coker,* should the death penalty be permissible when death does not actually occur? For that matter, given *Coker,* should death be an impermissible penalty for such a crime even if death does occur? The hijacker, like the rapist, may simultaneously commit another crime, but the hijacker, "as such, does not take human life."

(c) The Court also has not considered the constitutionality of capital punishment for someone guilty of first-degree murder who did not actually intend to take life.[9] Consider the situations of this kind that have been explored in previous sections of this chapter: an offender who causes death accidentally or even recklessly in the course of committing rape; an accomplice, not intending to kill, who is held for a homicide perpetrated accidentally, recklessly, or even intentionally by his cofelon. Given *Coker,* should capital punishment be permissible in such cases? For Eighth Amendment purposes, should the proportionality analysis focus on the injury caused or on the injury intended?

---

9. The issue is presented in Enmund v. Florida, 399 So. 2d 1362 (Fla. 1981), *cert. granted,* 102 S. Ct. 473 (1981).

CHAPTER

7

THE SIGNIFICANCE OF RESULTING HARM

A. CAUSATION

INTRODUCTORY NOTE

Where a crime is defined without regard to any consequence of the defendant's conduct (for example, attempt, conspiracy, burglary), there is no occasion to face the issue of causation. But where a particular result of a defendant's conduct is a necessary element of the crime charged, a perplexing problem sometimes arises as to whether the act of the actor caused the result. The homicidal crimes, which by definition involve a defendant who has killed another, are the most fertile source of causation problems. Where the actor kills the very person he meant to kill (or knew he would kill) in the manner he had in mind, no causation difficulty arises. Nor is there difficulty in the case of unintended killings where the death as it occurred was the very risk that rendered the defendant's conduct culpable. But where the intended death occurs in a way not intended or the unintended death occurs in a way that there was no reason to apprehend, the law is faced with the problem of distinguishing variations (between the actual result and the result intended or risked) that preclude liability from variations that do not preclude liability. The following hypotheticals will suggest the scope of the problem.

(1) Accused places poison by the bedside of his sick wife intending that she drink it. During the night she dies of a heart attack without having consumed the drink.

(2) Same as above, except that the wife sips the poison, is repelled by the taste; she goes to the bathroom for water, slips and injures herself fatally.

(3) Accused attempts to shoot her husband, but she misses. He thereupon boards a train for his mother's home and is killed in a train wreck.

(4) Accused shoots at deceased intending to kill him. The bullet misses but deceased dies of fright.

(5) While thoroughly intoxicated, accused No. 1 drives his car containing sleeping children at a speed greatly in excess of the speed limit. He crashes into the rear of a truck stalled in the middle of the road around a bend, the

truck's driver, accused No. 2 having failed to leave his lights on or otherwise give warning to approaching cars. The children of accused No. 1 are killed in the crash.

(6) Accused administers a vicious blow to victim's head with a blackjack. The victim is taken to a hospital for treatment where (a) due to negligent medical treatment of the wound he dies of meningitis, (b) he dies of scarlet fever communicated by a nurse, (c) he is mortally wounded by a knife-wielding maniac, (d) he is decapitated by a maniac, (e) he deliberately takes a fatal dose of sleeping pills to end his misery, or (f) he is seized with an attack of appendicitis from which he dies.

(7) Accused No. 1 throws a live hand grenade into the room of accused No. 2 intending to kill him. The latter seizes it and throws it out his window where it falls to the crowded street below, exploding and killing several persons.

(8) Accused and deceased engage in an armed robbery. Deceased is killed in an exchange of bullets with the police.

PEOPLE v. ARZON
Supreme Court, New York County
92 Misc. 2d 739, 401 N.Y.S.2d 156 (1978)

MILONAS, J. The defendant was indicted on September 28, 1977 for two counts of murder in the second degree and arson in the third degree after he allegedly intentionally set fire to a couch, thus causing a serious fire on the fifth floor of an abandoned building at 358 East 8th Street in New York County. The New York City Fire Department, in responding to the conflagration, arrived to find the rear portion of the fifth and sixth floors burning. The firemen attempted to bring the situation under control, but making no progress and there being no additional assistance available, they decided to withdraw from the building. At that point, they were suddenly enveloped by a dense smoke, which was later discovered to have arisen from another independent fire that had broken out on the second floor.

Although this fire was also determined to have originated in arson, there is virtually no evidence implicating the defendant in its responsibility. However, the combination of the thick smoke and the fifth floor fire made evacuation from the premises extremely hazardous, and, in the process, Fireman Martin Celic sustained injuries from which he subsequently died. Accordingly, the defendant was accused of murder in the second degree for having, "Under circumstances evincing a depraved indifference to human life, recklessly engaged in conduct which created a grave risk of death to another person," thereby causing the death of Martin Celic, and with felony murder. The third charge of the indictment, arson, is not at issue for purposes of the instant application.

It is the defendant's contention that the evidence before the grand jury is insufficient to support the first two counts. He argues that . . . murder requires a causal link between the underlying crime and the death, a connection which, in the defendant's view, is here lacking.

There is remarkably little authority on precisely what sort of behavior constitutes "depraved indifference to human life." In the leading case on the subject, People v. Kibbe, 35 N.Y.2d 407, 321 N.E.2d 773 (1974), the Court of Appeals affirmed the conviction of defendants who had abandoned their helplessly intoxicated robbery victim by the side of a dark road in subfreezing temperature, one-half mile from the nearest structure, without shoes or eyeglasses, with his trousers at his ankles, his shirt pulled up and his outer clothing removed. The court held that while the deceased was actually killed by a passing truck, the defendants' conduct was a sufficiently direct cause of the ensuing death to warrant criminal liability and that "it is not necessary that the ultimate harm be intended by the actor. It will suffice if it can be said beyond a reasonable doubt, as indeed it can here be said, that the ultimate harm is something which should have been foreseen as being reasonably related to the acts of the accused."

Clearly, an obscure or merely probable connection between the defendant's conduct and another person's death is not enough to support a charge of homicide. People v. Stewart, [40 N.Y.2d 692, 358 N.E.2d 487 (1976)]. In *Stewart*, the victim had been operated upon for a stab wound in the stomach inflicted by the defendant. Afterwards, the surgeon performed an entirely unrelated hernia procedure on him, and he died. According to the court, "the prosecutor must, at least, prove that the defendant's conduct was an actual cause of death, in the sense that it forged a link in the chain of causes which actually brought about the death. . . ." In this instance, the possibility that death resulted from a factor not attributable to the defendant could not be ruled out beyond a reasonable doubt, since the patient would, in all likelihood, have survived except for the hernia operation. . . .

[T]he defendant's conduct need not be the sole and exclusive factor in the victim's death. In the standard established by People v. Kibbe, supra, and People v. Stewart, supra, an individual is criminally liable if his conduct was a sufficiently direct cause of the death, and the ultimate harm is something which should have been foreseen as being reasonably related to his acts. It is irrelevant that, in this instance the fire which had erupted on the second floor intervened, thus contributing to the conditions that culminated in the death of Fireman Celic. In *Kibbe*, the victim was killed when he was struck by a truck. This did not relieve the defendants in that case from criminal responsibility for his murder, as it does not absolve the defendant here. Certainly, it was foreseeable that firemen would respond to the situation, thus exposing them, along with the persons already present in the vicinity, to a life-threatening danger. The fire set by the defendant was an indispensable link in the chain of events that resulted in the death. It continued to burn out of control, greatly adding to the problem of evacuating the building by blocking off one of the access routes. At the very least, the defendant's act, as was the case in *Kibbe*, placed the deceased in a position where he was particularly vulnerable to the separate and independent force, in this instance, the fire on the second floor.

Consequently, the defendant's motion to dismiss the first count of the indictment is denied.

The defendant's claim that there is no evidence showing a causal connection between the arson and the concomitant death sufficient to sustain the second count is also rejected for the reasons already set forth. Thus, the motion to dismiss the felony-murder charge is denied as well.

PEOPLE v. WARNER-LAMBERT CO., 51 N.Y.2d 295, 414 N.E.2d 660 (1980): [Defendant corporation and several of its officers and employees were indicted for second-degree manslaughter (N.Y. Penal Law §125.15, page 413 supra) and criminally negligent homicide (N.Y. Penal Law §125.10, page 413 supra). Several of the corporation's employees were killed (and many more injured) in a massive explosion at one of its chewing-gum factories. Evidence before the grand jury showed that the corporation used two potentially explosive substances in its manufacturing process, magnesium stearate (MS) and liquid nitrogen; that defendants had earlier been warned by their insurance carrier that the high concentrations of MS dust, combined with other conditions, created an explosion hazard; and that these hazards were not eliminated by the time of the accident. On the issue of what triggered the explosion there was apparently no hard proof, only speculations by experts that it could have been caused by mechanical sparking in the machines or by the liquid nitrogen dripping onto a concentration of MS and igniting under the impact of a moving metal part. The court held that the evidence before the grand jury was not legally sufficient to establish the forseeability of the actual, immediate, triggering cause of the explosion and therefore dismissed the indictment.

[The court stated:] It has been the position of the People that but-for causation is all that is required for the imposition of criminal liability. Thus, it is their submission, reduced to its simplest form, that there was evidence of a foreseeable and indeed foreseen risk of explosion of MS dust and that in consequence of defendants' failure to remove the dust a fatal explosion occurred. The chain of physical events by which the explosion was set off, i.e., its particular cause, is to them a matter of total indifference. On oral argument the People contended that liability could be imposed if the cause of the explosion were the lighting of a match by an uninvited intruder or the striking of a bolt of lightning. In effect they would hold defendants to the status of guarantors until the ambient dust was removed. It thus appears that the People would invoke an expanded application of proximate cause principles lifted from the civil law of torts.

We have rejected the application of any such sweeping theory of culpability under our criminal law, however. . . . [In People v. Kibbe (discussed in the *Arzon* case, supra)] the critical issue was whether the defendants should be held criminally liable for murder when the particular cause of death was vehicular impact rather than freezing. Under the theory now advanced by the People it would have been irrelevant that death had been the consequence of one particular chain of causation rather than another; it would have been enough that the defendants exposed their victim to the risk of death and that he died. That, of course, was not the analysis of culpability that we adopted. . . . [W]e held that . . . "We subscribe to the requirement that the defendants' actions must be a *sufficiently direct cause* of the ensuing death before there can be any imposition of criminal liability, and recognize, of course, that this standard is greater than that required to serve as a basis for tort liability." Thus, we were concerned for the nature of the chain of particularized events which in fact led to the victim's death; it was not enough that death had occurred as the result of the defendants' abandonment of their helpless victim. To analogize the factual situation in the case now before us to that in *Kibbe* it might be hypothesized that the abandoned victim in *Kibbe* instead of being either frozen to death or killed when struck by a passing motor vehicle was killed when struck by an airplane making an emergency landing on the highway or when hit by a stray bullet from a hunter's rifle — occasions of death not reasonably to have been foreseen when the defendants abandoned their victim.

STEPHENSON v. STATE
Supreme Court of Indiana
205 Ind. 141, 179 N.E. 633 (1932)

[Defendant, with the aid of several of his associates, abducted the deceased, a woman he had known socially for several months, and in the ensuing days subjected her to various forms of sexual perversion, including the infliction of extensive and severe bite wounds. Deceased seized an opportunity secretly to buy and take six tablets of bichloride of mercury in an effort to commit suicide. She became violently ill. Defendant had her drink a bottle of milk and suggested that he take her to a hospital; she refused. Defendant thereupon proceeded to drive her to her home. On the way deceased's pain grew worse, and she screamed for a doctor. Defendant, however, did not stop until he reached his home. Soon thereafter she was taken to her parents. They summoned a doctor who treated her for poisoning. In the ensuing 10 days, all her wounds healed normally except one which became infected. She grew worse and died, although the infected wound had healed at the time of her death. The medical cause of death was apparently a combination of shock, loss of food and rest, action of the poison and the infection, and lack of early treatment, probably none of which, taken singly, would have been sufficient to result in death.

[The indictment against defendant was in four counts.

[The first count charged him with murder arising from the following: that on March 16 he kidnapped the deceased from his home in Indianapolis, where she had been visiting, detained her on a railroad train en route to Chicago, struck, beat, bit, and grievously wounded her with intent to rape in a drawing room on the train, and forced her to get off at Hammond and to occupy a hotel bed with him; that on March 17 deceased, "distracted with the pain and shame so inflicted upon her," swallowed poison; that defendant neither administered an antidote nor called for medical help although able to do so; that the same day he forced her into a car and drove her back to Indianapolis where he kept her in his garage without administering an antidote or calling for medical help until March 18; and that finally she died on April 14 "from the effects of her wounds inflicted as aforesaid and said poison taken as aforesaid."

[The jury found defendant guilty of second-degree murder under this first count of the indictment,[a] and the supreme court affirmed.]

Per Curiam. . . . Appellant very earnestly argues that the evidence does not show appellant guilty of murder. He points out in his brief that, after they

---

a. The relevant statutes provided: "*Murder, first degree.* Whoever, purposely and with premeditated malice, or in the perpetration of, or attempt to perpetrate, a rape, arson, robbery or burglary, or by administering poison, or causing the same to be administered, kills any human being, is guilty of murder in the first degree, and, on conviction, shall suffer death or be imprisoned in the state prison during life.

"*Murder, second degree.* Whoever purposely and maliciously but without premeditation, kills any human being, is guilty of murder in the second degree, and, on conviction, shall be imprisoned in the state prison during life." — Eds.

reached the hotel, Madge Oberholtzer left the hotel and purchased a hat and the poison, and voluntarily returned to his room, and at the time she took the poison she was in an adjoining room to him, and that she swallowed the poison without his knowledge, and at a time when he was not present. From these facts he contends that she took her life by committing suicide; that her own act in taking the poison was an intervening responsible agent which broke the causal connection between his acts and the death; that his acts were not the proximate cause of her death, but the taking of the poison was the proximate cause of death. In support of his contention, he cites State v. Preslar (1856) 48 N.C. 421; . . . Bush v. Com. (1880) 78 Ky. 268 . . . and other cases from other jurisdictions.

In the case of State v. Preslar, supra, the defendant in the nighttime fought with his wife, and she left to go to the home of her father. When she reached a point about two hundred yards from her father's home, she, for some reason, did not want to go in the house till morning, laid down on a bed cover, which she had wrapped around her, till daylight. The weather was cold and the next morning she could not walk, but made herself known. She afterwards died. The court held that the wife without necessity exposed herself, and the defendant was not guilty. In Bush v. Com., 78 Ky. 268, defendant wounded one V. who was taken to the hospital and treated by a physician who communicated to her scarlet fever from which disease she died. The court held in that case, that if the wound is not dangerous, and when in the natural course of events a new and intervening cause appears and causes the death, there is no guilt. If death was not connected with the wound in the regular chain of cause and consequence, there ought not to be any responsibility. If a new and wholly independent instrumentality interposed and produced death, the wound is not the proximate cause. The principle laid down in the last case is well supported by decided cases and text-book writers, and we agree that the reasoning is sound and that it was properly applied in those cases. It is quite clear that in the *Bush* Case there was no causal connection between the wound inflicted and the death. But we do not believe that the rule stated in the above case is controlling here. . . .

In the case of Rex. v. Beech [23 Cox Crim. Cas. 181 (1912)] the prosecutrix was the village nurse and lived alone. At 11:45 P.M. on an evening in November, the appellant came to her house when she was in bed. He entered the house by breaking a window and went upstairs to the bedroom occupied by the prosecutrix. The door was locked, and the appellant threatened to break it open if the prosecutrix would not let him in. She refused, and the appellant then tried to burst open the door. The prosecutrix called out that if he got in he would not find her in the room, and, as the appellant continued his attack upon the door, the prosecutrix jumped out of the window sustaining injuries. The prosecutrix also testified that the appellant had attempted to interfere with her on a previous occasion when she had threatened to take poison if he touched her. The court approved the proposition as stated by the lower court as follows: "Whether the conduct of the prisoner amounted to a threat of causing injury to the young woman; was the act of jumping the natural consequence of the conduct of the prisoner and was the grievous bodily harm the result of the conduct of the prisoner." The court held that, if these questions were answered in the affirmative, he would be guilty. In Rex v. Valade (Que.) 22 Rev. de Jur.

524, 26 Can. Cr. Cas. 233, where the accused induced a young girl under the age of consent to go along with him to a secluded apartment, and there had criminal sexual intercourse with her, following which she jumped from a window to the street to get away from him, and was killed by the fall, the accused was held guilty of murder. Bishop in his work on Criminal Law, vol. 2 (9th Ed.), page 484, says: "When suicide follows a wound inflicted by the defendant his act is homicidal, if deceased was rendered irresponsible by the wound and as a natural result of it."

We do not understand that by the rule laid down by Bishop, supra, that the wound which renders the deceased mentally irresponsible is necessarily limited to a physical wound. We should think the same rule would apply if a defendant engaged in the commission of a felony such as rape or attempted rape, and inflicts upon his victim both physical and mental injuries the natural and probable result of which would render the deceased mentally irresponsible and suicide followed, we think he would be guilty of murder. In the case at bar, appellant is charged with having caused the death of Madge Oberholtzer while engaged in the crime of attempted rape. The evidence shows that appellant, together with Earl Gentry and the deceased, left their compartment on the train and went to a hotel about a block from the depot, and there appellant registered as husband and wife, and immediately went to the room assigned to them. This change from their room on the train to a room in the hotel is of no consequence, for appellant's control and dominion over the deceased was absolute and complete in both cases. The evidence further shows that the deceased asked for money with which to purchase a hat, and it was supplied her by "Shorty," at the direction of appellant, and that she did leave the room and was taken by Shorty to a shop and purchased a hat and then, at her request, to a drug store where she purchased the bichloride of mercury tablets, and then she was taken back to the room in the hotel, where about 10 o'clock A.M. she swallowed the poison. Appellant argues that the deceased was a free agent on this trip to purchase a hat, etc., and that she voluntarily returned to the room in the hotel. This was a question for the jury, and the evidence would justify them in reaching a contrary conclusion. Appellant's chauffeur accompanied her on this trip, and the deceased had, before she left appellant's home in Indianapolis, attempted to get away, and also made two unsuccessful attempts to use the telephone to call help. She was justified in concluding that any attempt she might make, while purchasing a hat or while in the drug store to escape or secure assistance, would be no more successful in Hammond than it was in Indianapolis. We think the evidence shows that the deceased was at all times from the time she was entrapped by the appellant at his home on the evening of March 15th till she returned to her home two days later, in the custody and absolute control of appellant. Neither do we think the fact that the deceased took the poison some four hours after they left the drawing-room on the train or after the crime of attempted rape had been committed necessarily prevents it from being a part of the attempted rape. . . . At the very moment Madge Oberholtzer swallowed the poison she was subject to the passion, desire, and will of appellant. She knew not what moment she would be subjected to the same demands that she was while in the drawing-room on the train. What would have prevented appellant from compelling her to submit to him at any moment? The same forces, the same impulses, that would impel her to shoot herself during the actual attack or throw herself out of the car window after the attack had ceased, was pressing and overwhelming her at the time she swallowed the poison. The evidence shows that she was so weak that she staggered as she left the elevator to go to the room in the hotel, and was assisted by appellant and Gentry; that she was very ill, so much that she could not eat, all of which was the direct and proximate result of the treatment accorded to her by appellant.

We think the situation no different here than we find in the *Beech* Case or the *Valade* Case, supra. To say that there is no causal connection between the acts of appellant and the death of Madge Oberholtzer, and that the treatment accorded her by appellant had no causal connection with the death of Madge Oberholtzer would be a travesty on justice. The whole criminal program was so closely connected that we think it should be treated as one transaction, and should be governed by the same principles of law as was applied in the case of Rex v. Beech and Rex v. Valade, supra. We therefore conclude that the evidence was sufficient and justified the jury in finding that appellant by his acts and conduct rendered the deceased distracted and mentally irresponsible, and that such was the natural and probable consequence of such unlawful and criminal treatment, and that the appellant was guilty of murder in the second degree as charged in the first count of the indictment. . . .

Instruction No. 43, given by the court of his own motion, told the jury that one who inflicts an injury on another is deemed by the law to be guilty of homicide, if the injury contributes mediately or immediately to the death of such other. The fact that other causes contribute to the death does not relieve the actor from responsibility. While it is true that a person cannot be killed twice, yet it is equally true that two persons can contribute to cause the death of another, in which case each will be responsible for such death.

We think the evidence justified the court in submitting the question to the jury, as there was evidence that the deceased died from the joint effect of the injuries inflicted on her, which, through natural cause and effect, contributed mediately to the death. We think the proposition of law stated in this instruction is well supported by authority. "The general rule, both of law and reason, is, that whenever a man contributes to a particular result, brought about, either by sole volition of another, or by such volition added to his own, he is to be held responsible for the result, the same as if his own unaided hand had produced it. The contribution, however, must be of such magnitude and so near the result that sustaining to it the relation of cause and effect, the law takes it within its cognizance. Now, these propositions conduct us to the doctrine, that whenever a blow is inflicted under circumstances to render the party inflicting it criminally responsible, if death follows, he will be holden for murder or manslaughter, though the person beaten would have died from other causes, or would not have died from this one, had not others operated with it; provided, that the blow really contributed mediately or immediately to the death as it actually took place in a degree sufficient for the law's notice." Bishop on Criminal Law, §653. . . .

COMMENT ON *STEPHENSON*
31 Mich. L. Rev. 659, 668-674 (1933)

At the outset it is clear that homicide cannot be committed by the defendant unless the intervening actor who strikes the fatal blow has been rendered irresponsible by defendant's unlawful act. This act may provide another with the opportunity, the instrument, or the motive for striking, but if it leaves him sane, the courts will not look behind the last responsible, self-determining actor. . . . Suppose a man commits suicide after losing all his money to a criminal swindler; is the swindler guilty of homicide? Suppose a man kills himself or kills his wife after she has been seduced, or perhaps merely slandered, as Desdemona was slandered by Iago; is the seducer or slanderer guilty of homicide? . . . Our common law, whatever may be said of divine law, does not hold him responsible for the death.

A new element enters the situation when the intervening actor is insane. . . . Where a policeman was grappling with a lunatic to arrest him, and defendant by freeing his hand enabled the lunatic to shoot the policeman, defendant was held guilty of homicide. From this case we may derive the principle that an insane intervening actor will not break the causal connection between defendant's act and the death.

We have been assuming, however, that the intervening actor is already insane at the time of defendant's act. The facts of Stephenson v. State put a further strain on the causal connection. To convict of homicide there, it was necessary to prove, not only that deceased was irresponsible when she took the poison, but also that defendant's unlawful acts caused her irresponsibility. For such a conviction no square precedent is to be found. Indeed the cases reveal, if anything, a marked reluctance to permit proof of any purely mental link in the causal chain.[27] . . .

It is true that certain psychological phenomena have been admitted to proof when they have been induced by physical violence. The mentally paralyzing effect of fear and the mentally unbalancing effect of pain and fever are sufficiently familiar to the average man so that he can pass a sound judgment upon their causal relation. . . . Where a dangerous wound has been inflicted, which unseats the mind of deceased through pain or fever and so causes him to kill himself, the courts are . . . ready to hold defendant for homicide.

These last cases come nearest to supporting the majority opinion in Stephenson v. State, but they are not squarely in point. The prosecution did not seriously contend, nor did the court think, that deceased was rendered irresponsible by the physical injuries, the bruises and bites, inflicted by defendant. It was rather the shame and humiliation of having been raped. "We do not understand,"

---

27. . . . In Germany also the point seems to be mooted. The following hypothetical case is borrowed from F. von Liszt, Strafrechtsfälle zum akademischen Gebrauch, 12th ed., tit. Kausalzusammenhang (1920). In a certain district of Oldenburg there reigns the superstition that a man whose shoes are thrown into the grave with a corpse must himself die within a short time. When an old peasant died, L secretly put the shoes of M, a young girl, in the coffin, and they were buried with it. (a) Through C, to whom L had confided nothing but who had observed the foregoing, the superstitious M learned of it, fell into a nervous fever, and died. Can L, who acted in fun, be punished? (b) How, then, if he shared the superstition and desired to bring about the death of M, who had spurned him as a lover? (c) How would it be decided if he, though convinced of the foolishness of the superstition, nevertheless reckoned that the girl would fall ill of anxiety and die, and with this in view told the girl himself of what he had done? (d) Is C punishable?

wrote the majority, ". . . that the wound which renders the deceased mentally irresponsible is necessarily limited to a physical wound." These words hint at new developments in the field we have been canvassing, and it would be rash to pronounce them prima facie unsound in view of the scientific researches which are steadily increasing our knowledge of the human mind and its working. It may be ventured, however, that Stephenson v. State will not be followed to its full length on this point except to punish defendants of exceptional depravity. . . .

We have noted above that all prior unlawful actors in the causal chain are insulated from liability if the person who strikes the fatal blow is a responsible, self-determining actor. The law recognizes a number of situations, however, in which a man who takes his own life or another's is not responsible. Insanity destroys his responsibility, as we have seen, and criminal liability for the death may then be cast on the next previous actor. So also the actual killer's responsibility will be destroyed if he acts innocently in ignorance of fact, or in necessary self-defense, or instinctively as a result of fear, or in pursuance of public duty. Here, human nature being what it is, the law excuses the homicidal act because it represents the average man's natural and instinctive reaction to a situation in which he finds himself; and conversely because the reaction is natural and instinctive, the law holds for homicide the previous actor who unlawfully created the situation. . . .

Such liability of an antecedent actor is best illustrated where he has created a situation in which another's mortal blow is motivated by the powerful instinct of self-preservation. At the point of a gun A commands B to jump from a moving train, and B is killed in the jump; by violence and threats of death A drives his wife poorly-clad from the house, and she dies of exposure; A shoots at a boat to frighten its occupants, B jumps overboard upsetting the boat, and C is drowned. In these cases desperate measures of escape are warranted; the imminence of deadly peril prompts B to act first and think afterwards. . . .

When a situation arises in which the law makes the performance of a homicidal act a duty, and prescribes penalties for disobedience, we feel without hesitation that the unlawful creator of that situation is criminally guilty of the death. Where A obtains C's conviction of a capital offense by perjured testimony, and executioner B hangs C, the proximity of causation between A's unlawful act and the death seems amply clear. So the master of a vessel is guilty of homicide if he sends a sailor into the rigging, knowing or chargeable with knowledge that he is not fit to go aloft, and the sailor falls to his death. . . .

It is difficult to fit Stephenson v. State into this picture of liability. True, the law justifies the taking of life when necessary to prevent the commission of rape. And had deceased been helpless in the manual grasp of defendant at the time of her suicidal act, or had a third-party defender, bursting upon the scene, shot her to death through faulty aim, then defendant might have been liable for her death within the principles developed above. But one can scarcely overlook the fact that deceased was alone and unmolested, and in a position to summon help, at the time she took the poison. The predominant motive for her suicide, clearly, was not to escape further assault but to escape the shame of what had already been done to her. The case represents a new and doubtful departure in so far as it suggests that the unlawful infliction of shame and disgrace may lead so naturally to suicide as to amount to a killing by him who inflicted it.

PROBLEM

An article in the N.Y. Times, Feb. 7, 1968, stated:

PHOENIX, Ariz., Feb. 6 (AP) — Linda Marie Ault killed herself, policemen said today, rather than make her dog Beauty pay for her night with a married man.

"I killed her. I killed her. It's just like I killed her myself," a detective quoted her grief-stricken father as saying.

"I handed her the gun. I didn't think she would do anything like that."

The 21-year-old Arizona State University coed died in a hospital yesterday of a gunshot wound in the head.

The police quoted her parents, Mr. and Mrs. Joseph Ault, as giving this account:

Linda failed to return home from a dance in Tempe Friday night. On Saturday she admitted she had spent the night with an Air Force lieutenant.

The Aults decided on a punishment that would "wake Linda up." They ordered her to shoot the dog she had owned about two years.

On Sunday, the Aults and Linda took the dog into the desert near their home. They had the girl dig a shallow grave. Then Mrs. Ault grasped the dog between her hands, and Mr. Ault gave his daughter a .22-caliber pistol and told her to shoot the dog.

Instead, the girl put the pistol to her right temple and shot herself.

The police said there were no charges that could be filed against the parents except possibly cruelty to animals.

NOTES ON RELATED CAUSATION PROBLEMS

Courts have been called upon to pass on the issue of causation in a great variety of situations. The situation exemplified in the main portion of the *Stephenson* case and the comment that follows is that in which a sufficient relationship is sought to be found between the conduct of the defendant and the consequential self-destructive acts of the deceased. Several other typical situations are as follows.

1. Neglect or maltreatment of the injury. Consider the following responses to the causation problem in this situation:

1 M. Hale, Pleas of the Crown 428: If a man give another a stroke, which it may be, is not in itself so mortal, but that with good care he might be cured, yet if he die of this wound within the year and day, it is homicide or murder, as the case is, and so it hath been always ruled. 3 Inst. 47.

But if the wound or hurt be not mortal, but with ill applications by the party, or those about him, of unwholesome salves or medicines the party dies, if it can clearly appear, that this medicine, and not the wound, was the cause of his death, it seems it is not homicide, but then that must appear clearly and certainly to be so.

But if a man receives a wound, which is not in itself mortal, but either for want of helpful applications, or neglect thereof, it turns to a gangrene, or a fever, and that gangrene or fever be the immediate cause of his death, yet, this is murder or manslaughter in him that gave the stroke or wound, for that wound, tho it were not the immediate cause of his death, yet, if it were the mediate cause thereof, and the fever or gangrene was the immediate cause of his death, yet the wound was the cause of the gangrene or fever, and so consequently is causa causati.

If a man be sick of some such disease, which possibly by course of nature would end his life in half a year, and another gives him a wound or hurt, which hastens his end by irritating and provoking the disease to operate more violently or speedily, this hastening of his death sooner than it would have been is homicide or murder, as the case happens, in him, that gives the wound or hurt, for he doth not die simply ex visitatione Dei, but the hurt that he receives hastens it, and an offender of such a nature shall not apportion his own wrong, and thus I have often heard that learned and wise judge Justice Rolle frequently direct.

Hall v. State, 199 Ind. 592, 159 N.E. 420 (1927): [During the course of a robbery, defendant struck several blows to the head of deceased, using an instrument and fracturing deceased's skull. Deceased died some 10 days later. The cause of death was given by the state's witnesses as blood poisoning following a fractured skull (meningitis). Defendant appealed from a conviction of first-degree murder alleging error in the trial court's sustaining objections to the questions asked on cross-examination of the coroner designed to show that the deceased's "wound in the head received improper or incompetent medical treatment and that the cause of his death was the doctor's treatment, or a disease brought on by the wound or by the treatment, and not the act of the appellant." The court sustained the conviction finding that even entirely favorable answers to the questions put would not have authorized the jury to return a different verdict, in view of the principles stated in Hale's Pleas of the Crown, supra. Citing many cases, the court asserted the following propositions (159 N.E. at 425-426):] (A) It is not indispensable to a conviction that a wound be necessarily fatal and the direct cause of death. If the wound caused death indirectly through a chain of natural effects and causes unchanged by human action, such as the consequential development of septicaemia or blood poisoning, he who inflicted the wound or injury is responsible.[a] (B) A person who inflicts a serious wound upon another, calculated to destroy or endanger his life, will not be relieved of responsibility, even though unskilled or improper medical treatment aggravates the wound and contributes to the death. Every person is held to contemplate and be responsible for the natural consequences of his own acts, and the criminality of an act is not altered or diminished by the fact that other causes co-operated in producing the fatal result.

Regina v. Jordan, 40 Crim. App. 152 (1956): [Defendant, an American serviceman, was convicted by an English court of the murder of deceased by stabbing.

a. In a footnote the court observed: "Where, however, the wound is not in its nature mortal, and death results solely from an entirely independent cause not traceable in any way to the wound, the person inflicting the wound cannot be held responsible for the death. Bush v. Com. (1880) 78 Ky. 268; Livingston v. Com. (1857) 14 Grat. (Va.) 601; note 8 A.L.R. 520."— EDS.

At the trial no issue was made as to whether the stabbing was the cause of death. On appeal to the Court of Criminal Appeal leave was sought and granted to defendant to submit further evidence, not available at the time of the trial. Two medical witnesses testified that two things other than the wound were the cause of the death. (1) The stab wound had penetrated the intestine in two places but was mainly healed at the time of death. In order to prevent infection an antibiotic, Terramycin, was administered. This was proper. However, subsequently the deceased manifested symptoms indicating he was intolerant to Terramycin. In recognition of this fact the administration of the drug was stopped, but the next day its resumption was ordered by another doctor. The witnesses agreed that to introduce a poisonous substance after the intolerance of the patient was shown was palpably wrong. (2) The other aspect of the medical treatment that in their view caused the death was the intravenous introduction of wholly abnormal quantities of liquid far exceeding the output. This caused waterlogging of the lungs, pulmonary edema, and finally bronchopneumonia, from which the deceased died. The court quashed the conviction, stating (id. at 157-158):] We are disposed to accept it as the law that death resulting from any normal treatment employed to deal with a felonious injury may be regarded as caused by the felonious injury, but we do not think it necessary to examine the cases in detail. . . . It is sufficient to point out here that this was not normal treatment. Not only one feature, but two separate and independent features, of treatment were, in the opinion of the doctors, palpably wrong and these produced the symptoms discovered at the post-mortem examination which were the direct and immediate cause of death. The question then is whether it can be said that, if that evidence had been before the jury, it ought not to have, and in all probability would not have, affected their decision. We feel no uncertainty at all that, whatever direction had been given to the jury and however correct it had been, the jury would have felt precluded from saying that they were satisfied that death was caused by the stab wound.

2. *Subsequent injury inflicted by another.* Consider the following:

Payne v. Commonwealth, 255 Ky. 533, 75 S.W.2d 14 (1935): [Effie Payne was convicted of the murder of her husband by striking him on the head two times with a blunt instrument. The evidence disclosed that after defendant had struck deceased another person struck him on the head several times with a car tool. The court affirmed the conviction, stating (75 S.W.2d at 19):] If one willfully and with malice aforethought mortally wounds another with a deadly weapon, the fact that another immediately thereafter unlawfully, willfully, and maliciously inflicts a distinct wound, whether of itself mortal or not, on the wounded person, and thereby accelerates or hastens his death, both are guilty of murder. The terms "mortally wounded" and "mortal wound," as here used, mean "deadly," "death-producing," and is defined by Webster as "destructive to life, causing or occasioning death." State v. Baker, 122 Kan. 552, 253 P. 221. The acts of Effie Payne as described by Ruby Nell Mathis, corroborated by the wounds on the head of Joe Payne, and his profusely bleeding before he was jerked or pulled from the car and struck with a "car tool," leave no doubt the wounds inflicted by her were mortal and were sufficient to warrant the submission of the case to the jury on the question of her killing him with a blunt instrument.

State v. Scates, 50 N.C. 420, 423-424 (1858): [W]e are satisfied that a broader proposition was laid down, to-wit, that if the prisoner inflicted a mortal wound, of which the deceased must surely die, and then another person, having no connection with him, struck the child a blow, which merely hastened its death, the prisoner would still be guilty. The testimony presented a view of the case to which this proposition was applicable, and it becomes our duty to decide whether it can be sustained upon any recognized principles of law. An attempt, only, to kill, with the most diabolical intent, may be moral, but cannot be legal, murder. If one man inflicts a mortal wound, of which the victim is languishing, and then a second kills the deceased by an independent act, we cannot imagine how the first can be said to have killed him, without involving the absurdity of saying that the deceased was killed twice. In such a case the two persons could not be indicted as joint murderers, because there was no understanding or connection between them. It is certain that the second person could be convicted of murder, if he killed with malice aforethought, and to convict the first would be assuming that he had also killed the same person at another time. Such a proposition cannot be sustained.

[Accord: Walker v. State, 116 Ga. 537, 42 S.E. 787 (1902); State v. Wood, 53 Vt. 560, 565 (1881).][a]

People v. Lewis, 124 Cal. 551, 57 P. 470 (1889): [The deceased himself inflicted the subsequent injury in this case, but — in the view the court took of the case — the decision has relevance for the situation in which the injury is inflicted by another. Defendant shot deceased in the abdomen inflicting a mortal wound — a severing of the mesenteric artery, which would produce death in an hour. Deceased was put to bed in defendant's house and, upon procuring a knife, cut his own throat, inflicting a wound from which he would necessarily have died in five minutes. Defendant appealed his conviction of manslaughter alleging that the facts showed a case where one languishing from a mortal wound is killed by an intervening cause taken in the sense of an act which shortens the life of deceased for any period whatever. The court conceded that if the knife wound was an intervening cause the conviction could not stand unless it were established that the knife wound itself could be attributed to defendant, either by his wielding the knife or because of the causal connection between the gunshot and the knife wound, that is, self-inflicted because of grief and pain or through desire to shield the first actor. After considering the matter in light of the principles articulated by Hale, the court held that the conviction should stand in any event, since (57 P. at 473):] when the throat was cut, Farrell was not merely languishing from a mortal wound. He was actually dying; and after the throat was cut he continued to languish from both wounds. Drop by drop the life current went out from both wounds, and at the very instant of death the gunshot wound was contributing to the event.

Query: In light of these principles and the fact that the bites were plainly nonmortal wounds, was the court in Stephenson v. State in error in upholding the trial court's Instruction No. 43, which did not depend on the irresponsibility of Oberholtzer's action in taking the poison?

a. See criticism in Williams, Causation in Homicide, [1957] Crim. L. Rev. 429, 435-437.

See Comment, 31 Mich. L. Rev. 659, 667-668 (1933):

In Stephenson v. State, had the defendant bitten the deceased after the taking of poison had induced acute nephritis, and so hastened her death, the bite would clearly have been regarded as a punishable cause of death. Since the bite came first, however, and "was not in itself a dangerous wound," the dissenting judges sought to bring the case within the doctrine . . . that a minor assault should not be punished as a homicide. The majority opinion glided over this point of argument with the general observation that "there was evidence that the deceased died from the joint effect of the injuries inflicted upon her, which, through natural cause and effect, contributed mediately to her death." We may criticize this observation as a questionable statement of the law, but there is no quarrel with the result it aimed to reach. It seems that the majority really distinguished Livingston v. Commonwealth, albeit subconsciously, on the quite adequate ground that in the instant case the wound, though not in itself dangerous, was inflicted in pursuance of a peculiarly heinous intent, the intent to rape.

Compare H. L. A. Hart & A. Honoré, Causation in the Law 294 (1958):

The actual reasoning adopted by the court is . . . open to the criticism that the voluntary act of taking poison happened after the breast wound and would be regarded, on ordinary causal principles which the court itself appears to recognize, as negativing causal connexion between wound and death. Of course it is natural to sympathize with the attempts of a court to find a way to convict a brutal criminal on a capital charge and not merely for a lesser offence. The doctrine that a person whose conduct excites moral disapproval may be punished for doing what he has not done is, however, a dangerous one and it was this doctrine that, in effect, the Indiana court was applying.

PROBLEM

In the Matter of J. N., Jr., 406 F.2d 1275 (D.C. App. 1979), defendant struck an 85-year-old woman to the ground in the course of an attempted robbery. The woman was taken to a hospital where her condition degenerated so much that she exhibited only primitive reflexes to stimuli. Six days later, on the basis of patient's condition and age, after consultation with other physicians involved in the case and on agreement by the victim's son, the neurosurgeon discontinued all "heroic measures," [1] and the woman died. At the time the measures were discontinued, she was alive within any accepted definition of death, even under modern "brain-death" statutes.[2] Query: On these facts, could defendant be convicted of killing the woman, or was the action of the physician an "intervening cause" insulating defendant from homicidal liability? How would the doctrines presented in the foregoing notes apply to this situation?

1. "Heroic measures" were defined at trial as "[m]easures that are other than normal supportive care. For example normal supportive care would be assuring that the patient has food to eat, that they have clothing to keep them warm, to prevent pneumonia. What I consider heroic in this case was infusions of drugs in order to reduce the pressure in the head, maintenance of the patient on a machine, where there was no obvious response to those measures of therapy in the sense of improvement in the patient's condition."
2. See Guthrie, Brain Death and Criminal Liability, 15 Crim. L. Bull. 40 (1979).

COMMONWEALTH v. ROOT

Supreme Court of Pennsylvania
403 Pa. 571, 170 A.2d 310 (1961)

JONES, C.J. The appellant was found guilty of involuntary manslaughter for the death of his competitor in the course of an automobile race between them on a highway. The trial court overruled the defendant's demurrer to the Commonwealth's evidence and, after verdict, denied his motion in arrest of judgment. On appeal from the judgment of sentence entered on the jury's verdict, the Superior Court affirmed. We granted allocatur because of the important question present as to whether the defendant's unlawful and reckless conduct was a sufficiently direct cause of the death to warrant his being charged with criminal homicide.

The testimony, which is uncontradicted in material part, discloses that, on the night of the fatal accident, the defendant accepted the deceased's challenge to engage in an automobile race; that the racing took place on a rural 3-lane highway; that the night was clear and dry, and traffic light; that the speed limit on the highway was 50 miles per hour; that, immediately prior to the accident, the two automobiles were being operated at varying speeds of from 70 to 90 miles per hour; that the accident occurred in a no-passing zone on the approach to a bridge where the highway narrowed to two directionally-opposite lanes; that, at the time of the accident, the defendant was in the lead and was proceeding in his right hand lane of travel; that the deceased, in an attempt to pass the defendant's automobile, when a truck was closely approaching from the opposite direction, swerved his car to the left, crossed the highway's white dividing line and drove his automobile on the wrong side of the highway head-on into the oncoming truck with resultant fatal effect to himself.

This evidence would of course amply support a conviction of the defendant for speeding, reckless driving and, perhaps, other violations of The Vehicle Code. . . . In any event, unlawful or reckless conduct is only one ingredient of the crime of involuntary manslaughter. Another essential and distinctly separate element of the crime is that the unlawful or reckless conduct charged to the defendant was the *direct* cause of the death in issue. The first ingredient is obviously present in this case but, just as plainly, the second is not.

While precedent is to be found for application of the tort law concept of "proximate cause" in fixing responsibility for criminal homicide, the want of any rational basis for its use in determining criminal liability can no longer be properly disregarded. When proximate cause was first borrowed from the field of tort law and applied to homicide prosecutions in Pennsylvania, the concept connoted a much more direct causal relation in producing the alleged culpable result than it does today. Proximate cause, as an essential element of a tort founded in negligence, has undergone in recent times, and is still undergoing, a marked extension. More specifically, this area of civil law has been progressively liberalized in favor of claims for damages for personal injuries to which careless conduct of others can in some way be associated. To persist in applying the tort liability concept of proximate cause to prosecutions for criminal homicide after the marked expansion of *civil* liability of defendants in tort actions for negligence would be to extend possible *criminal* liability to persons chargeable with unlawful or reckless conduct in circumstances not generally considered to present the likelihood of a resultant death. . . .

. . . [The] accused is not guilty unless his conduct was a cause of death sufficiently direct as to meet the requirements of the *criminal,* and not the *tort,* law. . . .

. . . Here, the action of the deceased driver in recklessly and suicidally swerving his car to the left lane of a 2-lane highway into the path of an oncoming truck was not forced upon him by any act of the defendant; it was done by the deceased and by him alone, who thus directly brought about his own demise. . . .

Legal theory which makes guilt or innocence of criminal homicide depend upon such accidental and fortuitous circumstances as are now embraced by modern tort law's encompassing concept of proximate cause is too harsh to be just. A few illustrations should suffice to so demonstrate.

In Mautino v. Piercedale Supply Co., 1940, 338 Pa. 435, 12 A.2d 51, — a civil action for damages — we held that where a man sold a cartridge to a person under 16 years of age in violation of a State statute and the recipient subsequently procured a gun from which he fired the cartridge injuring someone, the injury was proximately caused by the act of the man who sold the cartridge to the underage person. If proximate cause were the test for criminal liability and the injury to the plaintiff in the *Mautino* case had been fatal, the man who sold the bullet to the underage person (even though the boy had the appearance of an adult) would have been guilty of involuntary manslaughter, for his unlawful act would, according to the tort law standard, have been the proximate cause of the death.

In Schelin v. Goldberg, 1958, 188 Pa. Super. 341, 146 A.2d 648, it was held that the plaintiff, who was injured in a fight, could recover in tort against the defendants, the owners of a taproom who prior to the fight had unlawfully served the plantiff drinks while he was in a visibly intoxicated condition, the unlawful action of the defendants being held to be the proximate cause of the plaintiff's injuries. Here, again, if proximate cause were the test for criminal liability and the plaintiff had been fatally injured in the fight, the taproom owners would have been guilty of involuntary manslaughter, for their unlawful act would have been no less the proximate cause of death.[a] . . .

Even if the tort liability concept of proximate cause were to be deemed applicable, the defendant's conviction of involuntary manslaughter in the instant case, could not be sustained under the evidence. The operative effect of a supervening cause would have to be taken into consideration. Commonwealth v. Redline, supra, 391 Pa. at page 505. But, the trial judge refused the defendant's point for charge to such effect and erroneously instructed the jury that "negligence or want of care on the part of [the deceased] is no defense to the criminal responsibility of the defendant. . . ." . . .

a. In tort cases it is also widely held that the action of a motorist in fleeing from police in an attempt to escape is the legal cause of death resulting from collision of the pursuing police vehicle with another vehicle or stationary object. See Annot., Automobiles: liability of one fleeing police for injury resulting from collision of police vehicle with another vehicle, person, or object, 51 A.L.R.3d 1226 (1973). — EDS.

If the tort liability concept of proximate cause were to be applied in a criminal homicide prosecution, then the conduct of the person whose death is the basis of the indictment would have to be considered, not to prove that it was merely an *additional* proximate cause of the death, but to determine, under fundamental and long recognized law applicable to proximate cause, whether the subsequent wrongful act *superseded* the original conduct chargeable to the defendant. If it did in fact supervene, then the original act is so insulated from the ensuing death as not to be its proximate cause.

Under the uncontradicted evidence in this case, the conduct of the defendant was not the proximate cause of the decedent's death as a matter of law. In Kline v. Moyer and Albert, 1937, 325 Pa. 357, 364, 191 A. 43, 46, the rule is stated as follows: "Where a second actor has become aware of the existence of a potential danger created by the negligence of an original tort-feasor, and thereafter, by an independent act of negligence, brings about an accident, the first tort-feasor is relieved of liability, because the condition created by him was merely a circumstance of the accident and not its proximate cause."

In [Johnson v. Angretti, 361 Pa. 602, 73 A.2d 666 (1950)], while Angretti was driving his truck eastward along a highway, a bus, traveling in the same direction in front of him, stopped to take on a passenger. Angretti swerved his truck to the left into the lane of oncoming traffic in an attempt to pass the bus but collided with a tractor-trailer driven by the plaintiff's decedent, who was killed as a result of the collision. In affirming the entry of judgment n.o.v. in favor of the defendant bus company, we held that any negligence on the part of the bus driver, in suddenly bringing his bus to a halt in order to pick up a passenger, was not a proximate cause of the death of the plaintiff's decedent since the accident "was due entirely to the intervening and superseding negligence of Angretti in allowing his truck to pass over into the pathway of the westbound tractor-trailer. . . ."

In the case now before us, the deceased was aware of the dangerous condition created by the defendant's reckless conduct in driving his automobile at an excessive rate of speed along the highway but, despite such knowledge, he recklessly chose to swerve his car to the left and into the path of an oncoming truck, thereby bringing about the head-on collision which caused his own death. . . .

. . . In the instant case, the defendant's reckless conduct was not a sufficiently direct cause of the competing driver's death to make him criminally liable therefor.

The judgment of sentence is reversed and the defendant's motion in arrest of judgment granted.[b]

EAGEN, J., dissenting. . . .

If the defendant did not engage in the unlawful race and so operate his automobile in such a reckless manner, this accident would never have occurred. He helped create the dangerous event. He was a vital part of it. The victim's acts were a natural reaction to the stimulus of the situation. The race, the attempt to pass the other car and forge ahead, the reckless speed, all of these factors the defendant himself helped create. He was part and parcel of them. That

b. See the Note on Contributory Negligence page 443 supra. — EDS.

the victim's response was normal under the circumstances, that his reaction should have been expected and was clearly foreseeable, is to me beyond argument. That the defendant's recklessness was a substantial factor is obvious. All of this, in my opinion, makes his unlawful conduct a direct cause of the resulting collision. . . .

JACOBS v. STATE, 184 So. 2d 711, 716, 717 (Fla. 1966): [This was another drag race homicide, comparable on its facts to the *Root* case, with the exception that an innocent victim was killed as well as one of the race participants. The court reached the opposite result, concluding:] The race entailed the operation of three motor vehicles traveling in the same direction at excessive and unlawful rates of speed contrary to the laws of this state. While engaged in such unlawful activity one of the three vehicles actively participating in the race was negligently operated in such manner as to cause the death of the person who drove that vehicle, as well as another innocent party who had no connection with the race. The deaths which proximately resulted from the activities of the three persons engaged in the unlawful activity of drag racing made each of the active participants equally guilty of the criminal act which caused the death of the innocent party.

[A dissenting opinion observed:]

If the appellant is to be held criminally liable for manslaughter because he participated in a race during which an act of manslaughter occurred during the race, I would think that by the extension of such reasoning the spectators lined up along the road to watch the race might be legally tried and convicted as aiders and abettors to the manslaughter, simply because the collision might not have occurred if they had not congregated and encouraged the racing. By like reasoning, also, I would think that, if the starter in a foot race at a track meet had with culpable negligence loaded his pistol with live cartridges instead of the usual blanks and shot and killed someone in the grand stand, the sprinters might be held criminally liable as aiders and abettors. . . . [T]here was no proof of a causal connection between the acts of the appellant and the culpable negligence of Willie Kinchen that caused the death in question. . . . There is, in my opinion, not a word of testimony in the transcript from which reasonable men could conclude that the defendant knew that Kinchen was planning to try to pass the racing cars, nor knew that Kinchen had even left the starting point for this or any other purpose, and certainly not a word that the defendant knew or had the slightest notion that Kinchen would be so reckless as to try to pass Carter's car by turning into the east lane in the face of oncoming traffic.

COMMONWEALTH v. ATENCIO
Supreme Judicial Court of Massachusetts
345 Mass. 627, 189 N.E.2d 223 (1963)

WILKINS, C.J. Each defendant has been convicted upon an indictment for manslaughter in the death of Stewart E. Britch. . . . The defendants argue assignments of error in the denial of motions for directed verdicts. . . .

Facts which the jury could have found are these. On Sunday, October 22, 1961, the deceased, his brother Ronald, and the defendants spent the day drinking wine in the deceased's room in a rooming house in Boston. At some time in the afternoon, with reference to nothing specific so far as the record discloses, Marshall said, "I will settle this," went out, and in a few minutes returned clicking a gun, from which he removed one bullet. Early in the evening Ronald left, and the conversation turned to "Russian roulette.". . .

. . . The "game" was played. The deceased and Atencio were seated on a bed, and Marshall was seated on a couch. First, Marshall examined the gun, saw that it contained one cartridge, and after spinning it on his arm, pointed it at his head, and pulled the trigger. Nothing happened. He handed the gun to Atencio, who repeated the process, again without result. Atencio passed the gun to the deceased, who spun it, put it to his head, then pulled the trigger. The cartridge exploded, and he fell over dead. . . .

We are of opinion that the defendants could properly have been found guilty of manslaughter. This is not a civil action against the defendants by the personal representatives of Stewart Britch. In such a case his voluntary act, we assume, would be a bar. Here the Commonwealth had an interest that the deceased should not be killed by the wanton or reckless conduct of himself and others. . . . Such conduct could be found in the concerted action and cooperation of the defendants in helping to bring about the deceased's foolish act. . . .

The defendants argue as if it should have been ruled, as matter of law, that there were three "games" of solitaire and not one "game" of "Russian roulette." That the defendants participated could be found to be a cause and not a mere condition of Stewart Britch's death. It is not correct to say that his act could not be found to have been caused by anything which Marshall and Atencio did, nor that he would have died when the gun went off in his hand no matter whether they had done the same. The testimony does not require a ruling that when the deceased took the gun from Atencio it was an independent or intervening act not standing in any relation to the defendants' acts which would render what he did imputable to them. It is an oversimplification to contend that each participated in something that only one could do at a time. There could be found to be mutual encouragement in a joint enterprise. In the abstract, there may have been no duty on the defendants to prevent the deceased from playing. But there was a duty on their part not to cooperate or join with him in the "game." Nor, if the facts presented such a case, would we have to agree that if the deceased, and not the defendants, had played first that they could not have been found guilty of manslaughter. The defendants were much more than merely present at a crime. It would not be necessary that the defendants force the deceased to play or suggest that he play.

We are referred in both briefs to cases of manslaughter arising out of automobiles racing upon the public highway. . . .

Whatever may be thought of those . . . decisions, there is a very real distinction between drag racing and "Russian roulette." In the former much is left to the skill, or lack of it, of the competitor. In "Russian roulette" it is a matter of luck as to the location of the one bullet, and except for a misfire (of which there was evidence in the case at bar) the outcome is a certainty if the chamber under the hammer happens to be the one containing the bullet. . . .

The judgments on the indictments for manslaughter are affirmed. . . .

NOTES AND QUESTIONS

1. Compare the *Atencio* case with another Russian roulette case examined earlier, Commonwealth v. Malone, pages 457-459 supra. In *Atencio,* the deceased was held guilty of manslaughter; in the *Malone* case, defendant was held guilty of murder. Yet it would appear that the only difference between the facts in these cases is the way in which the game was played, that is, in *Atencio* each participant directed the gun at himself, and in *Malone* each participant directed it at another player. Does this difference justify the difference in degree of legal culpability of the defendants?

2. The issues posed in the three preceding cases — *Root, Jacobs,* and *Atencio* — should be considered again in connection with the material on accessorial liability. In each of those cases an alternative theory of liability could be that the defendant was guilty as an aider and abettor of the person who proximately caused the death. Compare Regina v. Creamer, pages 624-625 infra, and People v. Marshall, page 626 infra.

3. In Commonwealth v. Feinberg, 433 Pa. 558, 253 A.2d 636 (1969), defendant was a proprietor of a cigar store in the skid-row area of Philadelphia. One of the items he had regularly stocked and sold was sterno, a canned heat containing methanol. Late in 1963 he received a single shipment of a new kind of sterno called "industrial" sterno which contained a much higher percentage of methanol. This made it far more dangerous for persons to consume internally. Imprinted on the lids of the new sterno was the legend: "Institutional sterno. Danger. Poison. For use only as a fuel. Not for consumer use. For industrial and commercial use." Defendant sold approximately 400 cans of the new industrial sterno before returning the remainder of the shipment to the manufacturer. About 32 persons in the skid-row area died as a result of methanol poisoning caused by drinking the cans of industrial sterno sold by defendant. Defendant was subsequently tried and convicted of manslaughter. The record showed that defendant was aware of the proclivity of some of his customers to consume the sterno for its intoxicating effect. There was also sufficient evidence to warrant the conclusion that defendant was aware or should have been aware that the sterno he was selling was toxic if consumed. On appeal the Supreme Court of Pennsylvania affirmed the conviction.

Defendant argued the absence of legal causation, relying on the *Root* decision, supra. In response the court stated that *Root* was no help to defendant since it involved a drag race in which the court found no direct causal relation between defendant's act in engaging in the race and the deceased's death. It then quoted from Thiede v. State, 106 Neb. 48, 58, 182 N.W. 570, 574, (1921), which upheld a manslaughter conviction of a defendant who gave deceased moonshine containing methanol, the drinking of which resulted in his death:

> Defendant contends that the drinking of liquor by deceased was his voluntary act and served as an intervening cause, breaking the causal connection between the giving of the liquor by defendant and the resulting death. The drinking of the liquor, in consequence of defendant's act, was, however, what the defendant contemplated. Deceased, it is true, may have been negligent in drinking, but, where the defendant was negligent, then the contributory negligence of the deceased will be no defense in a criminal action.

PROBLEM

If *D* gives *V* a gun with which to kill himself and *V* kills himself with it, can *D* be held for causing *V*'s death? Could he be held for manslaughter or even murder, depending on what his mens rea was? According to the principles that have been presented above, the answer is probably no, since the voluntary action of *V* (assuming, of course, he was not irresponsible) would be regarded as an intervening action and the cause of *V*'s death would be attributed to his own action rather than to that of *D*. Cf. Lanham, Murder by Instigating Suicide, [1980] Crim. L. Rev. 213. This, of course, is not to say that *D* could not be held for the death, only that he would have to be held on some basis other than that of causing the death. For example, he might be held for being an accessory to the crime of suicide (that is, on the conventional basis of intentionally having helped another to commit a crime; see pages 611-643 infra), provided that suicide is itself a crime. Where suicide is not a crime (as it no longer is in most jurisdictions), some special statutory provision is generally thought necessary. See Model Penal Code §210.5, Appendix to this casebook.

But suppose *D* gives *V* phenobarbital tablets at *V*'s request and *V* takes a fatal dosage and dies. And assume phenobarbital is classified as a "dangerous drug," which the law makes it a felony to give to another except under the prescription of a physician. Now if *D* knew that *V* wanted the drug in order to kill himself, the case is close to the previous hypothetical. Query: Could it be said, consistently with the answer offered to the first hypothetical, that *D* caused the death of *V* so that he is guilty of murder under the felony-murder doctrine? If the answer is no, consider the much weaker case for the prosecution in which *D* gives *V* phenobarbital tablets to satisfy *V*'s desire to experience its intoxicating effect and *V* takes a mortal overdose by accident. In this situation a number of courts have found *D* guilty of felony-murder, on the ground that *D*'s act of furnishing the drug was the cause of *V*'s death, notwithstanding that it was *V*'s own volitional act of consuming the pills that caused the death.[3] Can these results be justified?

MODEL PENAL CODE

SECTION 2.03. CAUSAL RELATIONSHIP BETWEEN CONDUCT AND RESULT; DIVERGENCE BETWEEN RESULT DESIGNED OR CONTEMPLATED AND ACTUAL RESULT OR BETWEEN PROBABLE AND ACTUAL RESULT

[See Appendix for text of this section.]

---

3. Martin v. State, 377 So. 2d 706 (Fla. 1979); United States v. Moglia, 3 M.J. 216 (C.M.A. 1977); People v. Taylor, 11 Cal. App. 3d 57, 89 Cal. Rptr. 697 (1970); People v. Cline, 270 Cal. App. 2d 328, 75 Cal. Rptr. 459 (1969). For contrary cases, see People v. Pinchney, 38 A.D.2d 217, 328 N.Y.S.2d 550 (1972), aff'd, 32 N.Y.2d 749, 297 N.E.2d 523 (1973); State v. Dixon, 109 Ariz. 441, 511 P.2d 623 (1973); State v. Mauldin, 215 Kan. 956, 529 P.2d 124 (1974).

NOTES AND QUESTIONS

1. The supporting commentary appears in Comment to §2.03 at 132-135 (Tent. Draft No. 4, 1955). In the course of the Comment, the reporter states (id. at 132):

> When concepts of "proximate causation," disassociate the actor's conduct and a result of which it was a but-for cause, the reason always inheres in the judgment that the actor's culpability with reference to the result, i.e., his purpose, knowledge, recklessness or negligence, was such that it would be unjust to permit the result to influence his liability or the gravity of the offense of which he is convicted. Since this is so, the draft proceeds upon the view that problems of this kind ought to be faced as problems of the culpability required for conviction, and not as problems of "causation."

For a critical evaluation of the Model Penal Code's proposals see Hart & Honoré, Causation in the Law 353-361 (1959). Pennsylvania has substantially adopted the Model Penal Code proposal. Pa. Cons. Stat. Ann. tit. 18, §303. Delaware's new code also closely parallels it. Del. Code Ann. tit. 11, §§261-264. Hawaii has adopted only the provisions on reckless or negligent causation. Hawaii Rev. Stat. tit. 37, §702-216.

2. Consider the relevance of the answers to the following two questions in the formulation of a causation provision: First, what difference does it make in terms of whether the actor's conduct is criminal or of how severely it is punishable that the actor is found to have caused the result? One may instructively put this question to each of the hypotheticals and cases in these materials. Second, on what basis or theory does the law recognize such differences in liability or punishment? That is, why should the result of conduct ever make a difference?

The Model Penal Code offers the following observations on these questions (§2.03, Comment at 133-134 (Tent. Draft No. 4, 1955)):

> What will usually turn on the determination [of whether the defendant caused the result] will not be the criminality of a defendant's conduct but rather the gravity of his offense. Since the actor, by hypothesis, has sought to cause a criminal result, or has been reckless or negligent with respect to such a result, he will be guilty of some crime under a well-considered penal code even if he is not held for the actual result; i.e., he will be guilty of attempt, assault, or some offense involving risk creation, such as reckless driving. Thus the issue in penal law is very different than in torts. Only in form is it, in penal law, a question of the actor's liability. In substance, it is a question of the severity of sentence which the Court is authorized or obliged to impose. Its practical importance thus depends on the disparity in sentences for the various offenses that may be involved; e.g., the sentences for an attempted and completed crime.
>
> How far a Model Code ought to attribute importance in the grading of offenses to the actual result of conduct, as distinguished from results attempted or threatened, presents an issue of some difficulty, which is of general importance in the Code. It may be said, however, the distinctions of this order are to some extent essential, at least when the severest sanctions are involved. For juries will not lightly find convictions that will lead to the severest types of sentences unless the

resentments caused by the infliction of important injuries have been aroused. Whatever abstract logic may suggest, a prudent legislator cannot disregard these facts of life in the enactment of a penal code.

It may be added that attributing importance to the actual result does not substantially detract from the deterrent efficacy of the law, at least in dealing with cases of purposeful misconduct. One who attempts to kill, and thus expects to bring about the result punishable by the gravest penalty, is unlikely to be influenced in his behavior by the treatment that the law provides for those who fail in such attempts; his expectation is that he is going to succeed. See Michael & Wechsler, A Rationale of the Law of Homicide, 37 Colum. L. Rev. 1261, 1294-1298.

In this connection reconsider the issues raised in the Note, pages 466-470 supra. See generally Smith, The Element of Chance in Criminal Liability, [1971] Crim. L. Rev. 63.

In Note, Causation in the Model Penal Code, 78 Colum. L. Rev. 1249, 1252 (1978), the author finds that imposing more severe punishment when harm occurs cannot be justified on the basis of the conventional grounds of punishment. He concludes (at 1254):

More satisfactory justifications for such differentiation may be found, however, through analysis of the advantages gained by coordinating the level of punishment to the degree of resentment aroused by the offender. These advantages include the avoidance of nullification by jurors and others, the satisfaction of the desire for retaliation against the offender, and the increased efficacy of the law as a means of expressing societal condemnation.

For a contrasting view, see Schulhofer, Harm and Punishment: A Critique of Emphasis on the Results of Conduct in the Criminal Law, 122 U. Pa. L. Rev. 1497, 1508-1514, 1522-1557 (1974).

CALIFORNIA JOINT LEGISLATIVE COMMITTEE FOR REVISION OF THE PENAL CODE, PENAL CODE REVISION PROJECT
(Tent. Draft No. 2, 1968)

Section 408. Causation: Responsibility for Causing a Result

(1) An element of an offense which requires that the defendant have caused a particular result is established when his conduct is an antecedent but for which the result would not have occurred, and,

(a) if the offense requires that the defendant intentionally or knowingly cause the result, that the actual result, as it occurred,

(i) is within the purpose or contemplation of the defendant, whether the purpose or contemplation extends to natural events or to the conduct of another, or, if not,

(ii) involves the same kind of injury or harm as that designed or contemplated and is not too remote, accidental in its occurrence or dependent on another's volitional act to have a just bearing on the defendant's liability or on the gravity of his offense;

(b) if the offense requires that the defendant recklessly or negligently cause the result, that the actual result, as it occurred,

(i) is within the risk of which the defendant was or should have been aware, whether that risk extends to natural events or to the conduct of another, or, if not,

(ii) involves the same kind of injury or harm as that recklessly or negligently risked and is not too remote, accidental in its occurrence or dependent on another's volitional act to have a just bearing on the defendant's liability or on the gravity of his offense;

(c) if the offense imposes strict liability, that the actual result, as it occurred, is a probable consequence of the actor's conduct.

QUESTIONS

The foregoing California draft builds upon the Model Penal Code's formulation but makes several changes in substance as well as arrangement. What are those changes, and how significant are they?

Consider the comments of H. L. A. Hart & A. Honoré, Causation in the Law 357 (1959). Referring to the Model Penal Code formulation, they observe that it does not provide specifically for

> those cases where causal problems arise because . . . another human action besides accused's is involved in the production of the proscribed harm. These are treated merely as one kind of case where harm may or may not be "too accidental" in its manner or occurrence. . . . This is surely a weakness in a scheme which is designed to reproduce, and to allow the jury to express, the convictions of common sense that, even if harm would not have occurred without the act of accused, it is still necessary to distinguish, for purposes of punishment, one manner of upshot from another. For whatever else may be vague or disputable about common sense in regard to causation and responsibility, it is surely clear that the primary case where it is reluctant to treat a person as having caused harm which would not have occurred without his act is that where another voluntary human action has intervened.

Elsewhere they observe (id. at 292):

> Because the common law has never developed the notion of criminal negligence to the extent that continental codes have done, the risk theory, by which an actor is held responsible for occasioning harm by giving others the opportunity to do mischief, has not become as prominent in crime as in tort.

Are these appropriate suggestions in drafting a causation provision? Does the California draft meet them? For example, do you agree with the drafters that the formulation in paragraphs (a)(ii) and (b)(ii) ("too . . . dependent on another's volitional act," etc.) [4] provides the right framework for dealing with intentional acts whose result is affected by intervening acts of another? In the Comment, the drafters state (at 58):

---

4. Some states have adopted this formulation. See N.J. Code of Criminal Justice, N.J. Stat. Ann. tit. 2C, §2C:2-3; Del. Code Ann. tit. 11, §702-216; Hawaii Rev. Stat. §§702-215(2) & 702-216(2).

While it furnishes no easy formula it does, we believe, direct attention to the governing consideration in deciding a large number of the kinds of cases which have troubled courts in the past. For example, the death caused by another driving a car over the deceased who had been struck by defendant and left lying on the road (People v. Fowler, 178 Cal. 657, 174 Pac. 892 (1918)); that caused by the deceased himself who cut his throat while in the hospital after having been grievously wounded by defendant (People v. Lewis, 124 Cal. 551, 57 Pac. 470 (1889)); the medical maltreatment cases following a deadly assault by the defendant (Hall v. State, 199 Ind. 592, 159 N.E. 420 (1927)); the death inflicted by another while the deceased lies languishing from a serious wound inflicted by defendant (Payne v. Comm., 255 Ky. 533, 75 S.W.2d 14 (1935)).

Does the formulation in paragraphs (a)(i) and (b)(i) ("whether that risk extends to natural events or to the conduct of another") suitably handle the cases of negligent or reckless conduct in which another person's negligent or reckless conduct plays a part in producing the result? The Comment states (at 59):

A typical example is the Russian Roulette game in which defendant and deceased take turns spinning the cylinder and clicking the revolver at themselves and the deceased shoots himself. (Comm. v. Atencio, 345 Mass. 627, 189 N.E.2d 223 (1963).) Another example is drag-race in which one of the participants crashes to his death or kills another. (Comm. v. Root, 403 Pa. 571, 170 A.2d 310 (1961).) Another is the case of a defendant who lends his car keys to a person who he knows has no driver's license or is too drunk to drive. (People v. Marshall, 362 Mich. 170, 106 N.W.2d 842 (1961).) There should be no difficulty in holding the defendant [liable] in any of these cases for an offense requiring recklessness or negligence as to the resultant death so long as it is found that the recklessly disregarded or negligently overlooked risk included the risk that the deceased would in the process cause his own or another's death.

Consider also the extent to which the proposed California formulation provides a better means than the felony-murder doctrine for dealing with the liability of a felon for the fatal acts of his confederate or of a victim or police officer in resisting the felony. Would it provide the right framework for dealing with the homicidal liability of the defendants in cases like People v. Canola, pages 492-497 supra, and Taylor v. Superior Court, pages 500-505 supra?

PALMER v. STATE
Maryland Court of Appeals
223 Md. 341, 164 A.2d 467 (1960)

PRESCOTT, J. [Defendant lived with her paramour, McCue, and her 20-month-old baby, Terry. McCue subjected the child to continued and merciless beatings from which it died. McCue had previously been convicted of manslaughter. In this proceeding, defendant was prosecuted for the same offense. The basis for the case against her was that she clearly had a duty to the child that she breached by failing to take steps, available to her, to protect the child, whether by seeking help, moving away, or physically protecting it. The court affirmed the conviction. On the issue of whether defendant could be said to have caused the death the court stated as follows:]

This Court has stated that the question of proximate cause is usually a question of fact for the determination of the jury, or other trier of the facts. The question of proximate cause here turns largely upon the foreseeability of the consequence of the defendant's permitting McCue to "discipline" the child by repeated and violent beatings. The trial judge, as the trier of the facts in this case, found that there was a causal connection between the mother's negligence and the death. We think the evidence sufficient to sustain his conclusion.

There seems to be no doubt that the direct and immediate cause of Terry's death was the violent blow or blows inflicted upon her by McCue on September 3rd. But we do not deem this action upon his part to amount to an "intervening efficient cause" (as distinguished from one that is concurrent or contributing), as that term is used in the statement of the doctrine of proximate cause. McCue's brutal striking of the child so as to cause her death would constitute a ground of defense for the appellant's gross negligence only if it were the sole cause of the injury. . . .

. . . We pointed out above that McCue's violent and unrestrained actions were of such a nature as to put any ordinary, reasonable person on notice that the child's life was truly and realistically in immediate peril. The appellant easily could, and should, have removed Terry from this danger. Her failure to do so, under the circumstances previously described, is sufficient, as indicated before, to support a finding by the trial judge that her gross and criminal negligence was a contributing cause of Terry's unfortunate death. . . .

NOTE

How can a failure to act ever be said to cause anything? Reconsider at this point the material on omissions presented earlier, particularly Jones v. United States, pages 259-260 supra and Problem Case 4, page 264 supra, to all of which the problem of causation is central. In connection with Problem Case 4 consider the following argument in Mack, Bad Samaritanism and the Causation of Harm, 9 Philosophy & Pub. Aff. 230, 240 (1980):

[I]f A has a positive duty to B to do X, it will be because of A's causal role in B's being in a position such that harm will ensue for B unless A does X. A would have played such a causal role if, for example, he threw B into the dangerous waters (against B's wishes), if he coerced B into the waters at gunpoint, if he contracted with B to save him should the waters turn out to be dangerous. Such a prior causal role account of the emergence of positive duties helps explain why one might want to say . . . that it is specifically when A's inactivity involves a violation of B's rights that A's omission causes injury to B. For, on such prior causal role account of positive duties, when A violates a positive duty to B there has been some (prior) act of A which does eventually result in B's loss. When A has violated some positive duty to B we can say that A's inaction completes the causation of B's harm, set in motion by A's prior affirmative actions. This, perhaps, is the fact behind [the] claim that in violating positive duties (through inaction) one causes harm. But if we do not want misleadingly to shift attention away from this A's prior actions, it would be better to say that this A's subsequent *inaction allows the completion of* A*'s causation* of injury to B. A current "duty to care" simply is the form which the duty not to do harm takes within a context such that harm will ensue from *A*'s past act unless *A* intervenes now. When the duty is violated, it is the prior endangering act which causes the harm.

PROBLEM

Can the actor ever be an intervening and superseding cause of a result initiated by the actor's original conduct? For example, in Thabo Meli v. Regina, [1954] 1 All E.R. 373 (P.C.), defendants attacked deceased with the intent to kill him. Believing he was dead, when in fact he was alive, they rolled him over a cliff where he subsequently died from exposure rather than from the original attack. Presumably defendants might be found guilty of manslaughter in their reckless treatment of a body that might have been alive. But could they have been found guilty of murder on the basis of their initial assault? Another example is Regina v. Church, [1965] 49 Crim. App. 206, where defendant, after assaulting and injuring deceased, threw her body into the Thames in panic, believing he had killed her. In fact, she was then alive and died rather from drowning. Murder? See also Regina v. Ramsay, [1967] N.Z.L.R. 1005. See discussion in Elliot, Australian Letter, [1969] Crim. L. Rev. 511-514; Marston, Contemporaneity of Act and Intention in Crimes, 86 Law Q. Rev. 208 (1970).

B. ATTEMPT

1. Introduction

INTRODUCTORY NOTE

Statutory definitions of the crime of attempt are usually minimal. Consider some representative examples: "A person is guilty of an attempt to commit a crime when, with the intent to commit a crime, he engages in conduct which tends to effect the commission of such crime" (N.Y. Penal Law §110.00); "Every person who attempts to commit any crime, but fails, or is prevented or intercepted in the perpetration thereof is punishable . . ." (Cal. Penal Code §664); "A person commits an attempt when, with intent to commit a specific offense, he does any act which constitutes a substantial step toward the commission of that offense" (Ill. Ann. Stat. ch. 38, §8-4).

At common law attempts were misdemeanors. Today the usual punishment grading system for attempt involves making it punishable by a reduced factor of the punishment for the completed crime. In California (Cal. Penal Code §664) attempt carries a maximum term of not more than one-half of the highest maximum term authorized for the completed offense. Under the New York Penal Law, which uses punishment classification of offenses, the sentence for an attempt is one classification below that for the completed crime (§110.05), except for certain offenses, notably drug offenses, where the punishment is the same. Since the Model Penal Code proposals, however, a substantial minority of states have departed from the predominant scheme by making the punishment the same for the attempt as for the crime attempted, except for crimes punishable by death or life imprisonment. See, e.g., Conn. Gen. Stat. Ann. §53a-51; Del. Code Ann. tit. 11, §531; Ill. Ann. Stat. ch. 38, §8-4(c); Pa. Stat. Ann. tit. 18, §905.

What is the justification for the traditional approach to the punishment grading of attempt? This question raises once again the issue of the significance of harm in the criminal law. See page 466 supra (nonhomicidal recklessness) and page 553 supra (causation). Consider the following comments:

J. WAITE, THE PREVENTION OF REPEATED CRIME 8-9 (1943): Obviously this apportionment of punishment [for attempt] can be explained only by an assumption that to some extent it is designed for retribution. If the law's purpose were merely preventive, it would apply to the act done the same consequence, regardless of whether the act were successful or unsuccessful, since its objective would be the prevention of acts likely to result in harm. The fact that the punishment for success is twice as severe as the punishment for an unsuccessful attempt must mean that the additional suffering consequent upon success is a matter of expiation of retribution because of that success.

MODEL PENAL CODE: *Section 5.05(1)*. Except as otherwise provided in this Section, attempt, solicitation and conspiracy are crimes of the same grade and degree as the most serious offense which is attempted or solicited or is an object of the conspiracy. An attempt, solicitation or conspiracy to commit a [capital crime or a] felony of the first degree is a felony of the second degree. [Under §6.06, a felony of the first degree is punishable by imprisonment for a term whose minimum is between 1 and 10 years and whose maximum is life. A felony of the second degree is punishable by imprisonment for a term whose minimum is between one and three years and whose maximum is 10 years.]

Comment to §5.05 at 178-179 [(Tent. Draft No. 10, 1960)]. The theory of this grading system may be stated simply. To the extent that sentencing depends upon the anti-social disposition of the actor and the demonstrated need for a corrective sanction, there is likely to be little difference in the gravity of the required measures depending on the consummation or the failure of the plan. It is only and insofar as the severity of sentence is designed for general deterrent purposes that a distinction on this ground is likely to have reasonable force. It is, however, doubtful, that the threat of punishment for the inchoate crime can add significantly to the net deterrent efficacy of the sanction threatened for the substantive offense that is the actor's object — and which he, by hypothesis, ignores. Hence, there is basis for economizing in use of the heaviest and most afflictive sanctions by removing them from the inchoate crimes.

H. L. A. HART, PUNISHMENT AND RESPONSIBILITY 129 (1968): It is perfectly true that those who commit crimes intend to succeed, but this does not show that punishing a man for an unsuccessful attempt will not increase the efficacy of the law's threats, or that failure to punish him would not often diminish their efficacy. This is so for two reasons: first, there must be many who are not completely confident that they will succeed in their criminal objective, but will be prepared to run the risk of punishment if they can be assured that they have to pay nothing for attempts which fail; whereas if unsuccessful attempts were also punished the price might appear to them to be too high. Again, there must be many cases where men might with good or bad reason believe that if they succeed in committing some crime they will escape, but if they fail they may be caught. Treason is only the most obvious of such cases, and unless attempts were punished, there would, in such cases, be no deterrent force in the law's threat attached to the main crime.

H. L. A. HART, INTENTION AND PUNISHMENT, Oxford Rev. No. 4 at 17-19 (Hilary 1967)[5]: A . . . difficult question concerns the almost universal practice of legal systems of fixing a more severe punishment for the completed crime than for the mere attempt. How is this to be justified? Here a retributive theory in which severity of punishment is proportioned to the allegedly evil intentions of the criminal is in grave difficulty; for there seems to be no difference in wickedness, though there may be in skill, between the successful and the unsuccessful attempt in this respect. Very often an unsuccessful attempt is merely the accidental failure to commit the crime because somebody unexpectedly intervenes and frustrates the attempt. As far as I can see a deterrent theory, except in relation to a very specialized class of crimes, is in similar difficulties. The exceptions, which have been mooted since Beccaria first discussed them, are those crimes whose consummation occupies a considerable space of time so that the criminal may have time between the attempt and its consummation to think again. He may have what is called a locus poententiae, and he might desist, but if he is already involved in the full penalty by virtue of merely having attempted to commit the crime, he may have no motive for desisting. Similar reasoning is presented when it is pointed out that if a man shoots and misses there is no reason why he should not shoot again if he is already liable to the full penalty for his unsuccessful attempt. Such cases are, of course, realities; but they are surely very rare, if only because in the law of most systems in order to be guilty of an attempt one has to get very near to the completion of the full offence, and the question of a second shot may arise only seldom. Yet apart from this, there seems no reason on any form of deterrent theory, whether we consider the general deterrent or the individual deterrent, for punishing the unsuccessful attempt less severely than the completed crime. The individual who has tried but failed to carry out the planned crime may need just as much punishment to keep him straight in the future as the successful criminal. He may be as much disposed to repeat his crime.

The almost universal tendency in punishing to discriminate between attempts and completed crimes rests, I think, on a version of the retributive theory which has permeated certain branches of English law, and yet has on occasion been stigmatized even by English judges as illogical. This is the simple theory that it is a perfectly legitimate ground to grade punishments according to the amount of harm actually done, whether this was intended or not; "if he has done the harm he must pay for it, but if he has not done it he should pay less." To many people such a theory of punishment seems to confuse punishment with compensation, the amount of which should indeed be fixed in relation to harm done. Even if punishment and compensation were not distinguished in primitive law, many think that this is no excuse for confusing them now. Why should the accidental fact that an intended harmful outcome has not occurred be a ground for punishing less a criminal who may be equally dangerous and equally

5. Republished in Punishment and Responsibility 129-131 (1968).

wicked? I may be wrong in thinking that there is so little to be said for this form of retributive theory. It is certainly popular, and the nearest to a rational defence that I know of it is the following. It is pointed out that in some cases the successful completion of a crime may be a source of gratification, and, in the case of theft, of actual gain, and in such cases to punish the successful criminal more severely may be one way of depriving him of these illicit satisfactions which the unsuccessful have never had. This argument, which certainly has some attraction where the successful criminal has hidden loot to enjoy on emerging from prison, would be an interesting addition to theories of punishment of the principle that the wicked should not be allowed to profit by their crimes.

My own belief is that this form of retributive theory appeals to something with deeper instinctive roots than the last mentioned principle. Certainly the resentment felt by a victim actually injured is normally much greater than that felt by the intended victim who has escaped harm because an attempted crime has failed. Bishop Butler, in his sermon on resentment explains on this ground the distinction men draw between 'an injury done' and one 'which, though designed, was prevented, in cases where the guilt is perhaps the same.' But again the question arises, if this form of retributive theory depends on the connexion between blame and resentment, whether the law should give effect to such a theory. Can we not control resentment, however natural, in the interests of some deliberate forward-looking policy, much as we control our natural fears in the interest of forward-looking prudential aims? And if we can do this, should we not do so? And might not this require us in some cases to punish attempts as severely as the completed offence?

These issues are canvassed in Schulhofer, Harm and Punishment: A Critique of Emphasis on the Results of Conduct in the Criminal Law, 122 U. Pa. L. Rev. 1497 (1974).

2. Mens Rea

REGINA v. MOHAN
Court of Appeal, Criminal Division
[1975] 2 All E.R. 193

JAMES, L.J. . . . The appellant was convicted on 30th August 1974, at the Central Criminal Court, of driving a motor vehicle in a manner dangerous to the public (count 3) and of, having charge of a vehicle, attempting by wanton driving to cause bodily harm to be done to Harry James Sales (count 2). He was acquitted by the jury on count 1 of the indictment of attempting to cause grievous bodily harm to Pc. Sales with intent to cause him grievous bodily harm.

In the afternoon of 22nd April 1974 Pc. Sales, in uniform, saw a motor car being driven towards him along Hillbury Road, Whyteleafe. The road conditions were good, visibility unimpaired and it was of course daylight. The officer estimated the speed of the vehicle to be in excess of the permitted limit of 30

M.P.H. He stepped into the road and, by holding up his hand, signalled the driver to stop. The car slowed down. The driver appeared to be looking menacingly at the officer. When the car reached a point some ten yards from the officer the driver suddenly increased the speed and drove straight at him. Pc. Sales leapt out of the way and so avoided being struck. The car was driven on without stopping. Within half an hour, at the home of the appellant, he and the car were identified by Pc. Sales as the driver and vehicle involved in the incident. The appellant denied that he was the driver and denied that his car was the one seen by the officer. At his trial these denials were maintained. The only issues for the jury were (1) the identification of the driver, and (2) if the appellant was proved to be the driver, did the evidence establish the offences charged or any of them? . . .

The directions of the learned judge as to "wanton" driving are not challenged. Indeed no criticism is made as to any of the directions given except those relating to the requirement of intention as an ingredient in the offence in count 2. The first direction as to this followed immediately after that relating to the attempt to cause grievous bodily harm with intent, in respect of which the judge directed that it must be proved that —

> he deliberately drove his car at an accelerating speed, having slowed down in response to the signal, close to the officer, in the position which the officer described in his evidence; and that by such conduct he was intending to do grievous bodily harm. . . .

The judge continued, omitting the words not relevant for present purposes:

> The second count is less grave. It is alternative to the first. . . . Looking therefore at the second charge observe the different language. . . . There the offence is an attempt to cause bodily harm by wanton driving. According to our law any person who causes bodily harm to another by wanton driving is guilty of a criminal offence. . . . Observe there is no allegation in the second charge, and it is not necessary to prove that he intended to cause bodily harm. And that is why the second charge is much less grave than the first. . . . Observe again here the offence is charged as an attempt . . . and an attempt again merely means action, doing acts, on the way to the offence. An offence which would have been completed but for something which intervened, namely, the officer stepping out of the way. . . . In order therefore to prove the second charge it has to be proved, of course, that the [appellant] was the person in question, that he deliberately drove, drove in a manner wholly unjustified, and recklessly, and that the driving was likely to cause bodily harm. . . .

[Later, in response to a question from the jury, the trial judge further instructed:]

> It is not necessary to prove an intention actually to cause bodily harm. That is the count on which you have acquitted him. It has to be proved that he deliberately drove wantonly, realising that such wanton driving would be likely to cause, unless interrupted for some reason, bodily harm to Sales, or that he was reckless as to whether such bodily harm would be caused by his wanton driving. Have I made that quite clear?

The foreman answered, "Yes."

Whether, after that final direction, the jury focussed their attention on the terms of that direction alone, or whether they sought to apply it together with the earlier directions cannot be known. It is unfortunate that, owing to some momentary confusion or infelicitous choice of words, in the final direction the judge told the jury that they had acquitted the appellant of an intention actually to cause bodily harm. That was not so. The striking features, however, of the final direction are that, whereas the judge repeats that there is no requirement of proof of "intention," he departs from the earlier directions in two ways. First, by incorporating the requirement that the person charged with attempt must be proved to have realised that his act or acts were likely, unless interrupted, to result in the commission of the completed offence. Secondly, by incorporating, as an alternative to realisation that the acts are likely to result in the commission of the completed offence, the concept of recklessness in the mind of the accused.

Counsel's argument for the Crown was that the judge was right in his direction that the Crown did not have to prove, in relation to count 2, any intention in the mind of the appellant. His argument was that where the attempt charged is an attempt to commit a crime which itself involves a specific state of mind, then to prove the attempt the Crown must prove that the accused had that specific state of mind, but where the attempt relates to a crime which does not involve a specific state of mind, the offence of attempt is proved by evidence that the accused committed an act or acts proximate to the commission of the complete offence and which unequivocally point to the completed offence being the result of the act or acts committed. Thus to prove a charge of attempting to cause grievous bodily harm with intent there must be proof that the accused intended to cause grievous bodily harm at the time of the act relied on as the attempt. But, because the offence of causing bodily harm by wanton or furious driving . . . does not require proof of any intention or other state of mind of the accused, proof of attempt to commit that crime does not involve proof of the accused's state of mind, but only that he drove wantonly and that the wanton driving was proximate to, and pointed unequivocally to, bodily harm being caused thereby.

The attraction of this argument is that it presents a situation in relation to attempts to commit crime which is simple and logical, for it requires in proof of the attempt no greater burden in respect of mens rea than is required in proof of the completed offence. The argument in its extreme form is that an attempt to commit a crime of strict liability is itself a strict liability offence. It is argued that the contrary view involves the proposition that the offence of attempt includes mens rea when the offence which is attempted does not and in that respect the attempt takes on a graver aspect than, and requires an additional burden of proof beyond that which relates to, the completed offence.

Counsel for appellant does not shrink from this anomalous situation. . . . In support of his argument he cited the words of Lord Goddard, C.J., in R. v. Whybrow [(1951) 35 Cr. App. Rep. 141, 146]:

Therefore, if one person attacks another, inflicting a wound in such a way that an ordinary, reasonable person must know that at least grievous bodily harm will result, and death results, there is the malice aforethought sufficient to support the charge of murder. But, if the charge is one of attempted murder, the intent becomes the principal ingredient of the crime. It may be said that the law, which

is not always logical, is somewhat illogical in saying that, if one attacks a person intending to do grievous bodily harm and death results, that is murder, but that if one attacks a person and only intends to do grievous bodily harm, and death does not result, it is not attempted murder, but wounding with intent to do grievous bodily harm. It is not really illogical because, in that particular case, the intent is the essence of the crime while, where the death of another is caused, the necessity is to prove malice aforethought, which is supplied in law by proving intent to do grievous bodily harm. . . .

In our judgment it is well established law that intent (mens rea) is an essential ingredient of the offence of attempt. . . . Insofar as the learned judge directed the jury that it was not necessary to prove any intent in relation to count 2 he fell into error.

That does not, however, dispose of this appeal. As has been pointed out, the judge varied the terms of the direction in his answer to the jury's question. It has been necessary, therefore, to consider whether taken as a whole the directions did, by the words "he must have realised . . . that such driving, unless it were to stop . . . was likely to cause bodily harm if he went on, or he was reckless as to whether bodily harm was caused" include the need for proof of the element of mens rea. The first question we have to answer is: what is the meaning of "intention" when that word is used to describe the mens rea in attempt? It is to be distinguished from "motive" in the sense of an emotion leading to action; it has never been suggested that such a meaning is appropriate to "intention" in this context. It is equally clear that the word means what is often referred to as "specific intent" and can be defined as "a decision to bring about a certain consequence," or as the "aim." . . .

. . . In our judgment, evidence of knowledge of likely consequences, or from which knowledge of likely consequences can be inferred, is evidence by which intent may be established but it is not, in relation to the offense of attempt, to be equated with intent.[a] If the jury find such knowledge established they may and, using common sense, they probably will find intent proved, but it is not the case that they must do so.

An attempt to commit crime is itself an offence. Often it is a grave offence. Often it is as morally culpable as the completed offence which is attempted but not in fact committed. Nevertheless it falls within the class of conduct which is preparatory to the commission of a crime and is one step removed from the offence which is attempted. The court must not strain to bring within the offence of attempt conduct which does not fall within the well-established bounds of the offence. On the contrary, the court must safeguard against extension of those bounds save by the authority of Parliament. The bounds are presently set requiring proof of specific intent, a decision to bring about, insofar as it lies within the accused's power, the commission of the offence which it is alleged the accused attempted to commit, no matter whether the accused desired that consequence of this act or not.

a. The court derived this proposition from The Criminal Justice Act, 1967, §8, which provides: "A court or jury, in determining whether a person has committed an offence. — (a) shall not be bound in law to infer that he intended or foresaw a result of his actions by reason only of its being a natural and probable consequence of those actions but (b) shall decide whether he did intend or foresee that result by reference to all the evidence, drawing such inferences from the evidence as appear proper in the circumstances." — Eds.

In the present case the final direction was bad in law. Not only did the judge maintain the exclusion of "intent" as an ingredient of the offence in count 2, but he introduced an alternative basis for a conviction which did not and could not constitute the necessary mens rea. . . .

It is for the above reasons that we allowed the appeal against conviction on count 2. Fortunately, in the interests of justice, the jury convicted of dangerous driving and that conviction stands, as does the richly deserved sentence of 12 months imprisonment.

NOTES AND QUESTIONS

1. Illinois Revised Statutes, ch. 38, §8-4(a), defines an attempt as an act done with intent to commit a specific offense (if the act is a substantial step toward the commission of the intended offense). Section 9-1(a) defines murder as an act that causes death, which act is done either with intent to kill or do great bodily harm or with knowledge of the strong probability that it will cause death or great bodily harm or while the actor is committing a forcible felony.

In People v. Harris, 72 Ill. 2d 16, 377 N.E.2d 28 (1978), defendant was convicted of attempted murder under an instruction which stated:

To sustain the charge of attempt, the State must prove the following propositions: First: That the defendant performed an act which constituted a substantial step toward the commission of the crime of murder; and Second: That the defendant did so with intent to commit the crime of murder. . . . A person commits the crime of murder who kills an individual if, in performing the acts which cause the death, he intends to kill or do great bodily harm to that individual.

Defendant appealed on the ground that this instruction told the jury that it could find him guilty of attempted murder if the jury found that he had acted only with the intent to do great bodily harm and did not have the intent to cause death.

How should this case be decided? Suppose the indictment for attempted murder charged that defendant's acts were committed while he was engaged in a forcible felony and the trial judge instructed the jury as the judge did in the *Harris* case, except that he added, "or he intends to commit a forcible felony." See People v. Viser, 62 Ill. 2d 568, 343 N.E.2d 903 (1975).

2. Assume a defendant who, in order to destroy his competitor's experimental aircraft, plants a bomb on it set to explode in midair, knowing that the test pilot will be killed. The bomb fails to explode. May defendant be convicted of attempted murder? (Cf. C. Howard, Australian Criminal Law 292 (2d ed. 1970).

See Model Penal Code §5.01(1), Appendix to this casebook. How should this hypothetical be decided under this provision?

3. What reasons underlie the common requirement of a "specific intent" or "purpose" in the law of attempt? Would it ever be justifiable to hold a person for an attempted crime where the person does not intend the consequences, which would constitute a substantive crime if they occurred? Cf. O. W. Holmes, The Common Law 68 (1881): "The importance of the intent is not to show that the act was wicked, but to show that it was likely to be followed by hurtful consequences." Consider Thacker v. Commonwealth, 134 Va. 767, 114 S.E. 504 (1922), where a drunk, aggrieved by the refusal of a woman in a tent to admit him, walked down the road a way, turned, and shot at the light shining through the canvas. If the bullet accidentally kills the woman, he could, as we have seen, be held for murder, or at least the lesser homicidal offense of manslaughter. But if the bullet fortunately does not strike the woman, that case holds he cannot be convicted of attempted murder. Is this logic sound?

Consider another observation of Justice Holmes in The Common Law at 66:

> It may be true in the region of attempts, as elsewhere, the law began with cases of actual intent, as those cases are the most obvious ones. But it cannot stop with them, unless it attaches more importance to the etymological meaning of the word *attempt* than to the general principles of punishment. Accordingly there is at least color of authority for the proposition that an act is punishable as an attempt, if, supposing it to have produced its natural and probable effect, it would have amounted to a substantive crime.

Compare Smith, The Element of Chance in Criminal Liability, [1971] Crim. L. Rev. 63, 72-73:

> You will recall my example of the man who threw the stone through the window, being reckless whether it injured anyone. He could not be convicted of attempted wounding because he was not trying to wound anyone. I had assumed that it was impossible to deal with this sort of case as an attempt until I found that this is exactly what has been done in South Africa.[9a] What I have called recklessness is there regarded simply as a variety of intention; the thrower of the stone is regarded as having intended injury to the person and, therefore, he may be convicted of an attempt. He was not, of course, "attempting" to cause injury within the ordinary natural meaning of the word "attempt" but it is perfectly possible for the law to use words in a different sense from that which they bear in ordinary usage. I would say, however, that I think this course is to be avoided as far as possible in the criminal law, where it is particularly important that the layman should understand what the lawyer is talking about. It did moreover occur to me that the South African rule about intention if generally applied would lead to some rather odd results. Suppose that a driver, X, overtakes on the brow of a hill when he cannot see whether anything is coming in the opposite direction. If anything were coming, there would certainly be a crash and, obviously, someone might be killed. But nothing is coming and no harm is done. Certainly X ought to be convicted of dangerous driving; but to convict him of attempted murder would be rather startling. Yet there is evidence that he was reckless whether he caused death and if recklessness is indistinguishable in law from intention, there is equally evidence that he was guilty of attempted murder.

See Enker, Mens Rea and Criminal Attempt, [1977] Am. B. Foundation Research J. 845.

4. Intention to achieve a particular result (that is, a purpose or, perhaps, knowledge) is required to convict a defendant for an attempt to achieve that result. Does it follow that no lesser mens rea as to other elements of the crime

9a. Huebsch, 1953 (2) S.A. 561 (A.D.) at 567-568. Burchell and Hunt, South African Criminal Law and Procedure, I, 378-379.

(attendant circumstances, for example) will suffice for an attempt conviction, even though a lesser mens rea as to those elements would suffice for the completed crime? See generally Enker, Mens Rea and Criminal Attempt, [1977] Am. B. Foundation Research J. 845, 866; Smith, Two Problems in Criminal Attempts, 70 Harv. L. Rev. 422, 434 (1957); Stuart, Mens Rea, Negligence and Attempts, [1968] Crim. L. Rev. 647, 659.

Consider the following:

(a) G. Williams, Criminal Law: The General Part 619-620 (2d ed. 1961), observes:

> *D* posts a letter to *P* asking for money on a representation which so far as *D* knows may be true or false. If *P* receives the letter and, relying on the representation, gives *D* the money, and if the representation turns out to be false, *D* will be guilty of obtaining money by false pretences, his deceit being of the reckless variety. Now suppose that the letter is never received by *P*. It may be thought that *D* is guilty of an attempt to obtain money by false pretences. His state of mind as to the falsity of the pretence is reckless, not intentional; but does this negative an attempt? Common sense suggests that it is legally possible to attempt a crime of recklessness.
>
> In a sense it is possible to attempt a crime of negligence. A crime of negligence is one that can be committed negligently; but some crimes of this class are sometimes committed intentionally or recklessly. There is no reason why a person should not be convicted of attempting to commit an intentional violation of a law prohibiting negligence. Suppose that *D*, knowing that his car has no brakes, attempts to start it in order to drive it; he is stopped by a policeman. He has, in fact, intentionally attempted to do an act that when done would be negligent and dangerous. There is no logical reason why he should not be convicted of attempt to drive dangerously. If *D* had not known that his car had no brakes, his actual driving might be a statutory offence of dangerous driving, but his attempt to drive could not be a punishable attempt at common law, since attempt requires mens rea.

(b) In Gardner v. Akeroyd, [1952] 2 Q.B. 743, defendant Akeroyd was a butcher carrying on business at Morecambe, England. He employed defendant Mugliston as an assistant. On November 1, 1951, two Ministry of Food inspectors visited the shop and found 33 parcels of meat made up ready for delivery bearing price and name tickets. The price tickets on each of these parcels disclosed overcharges contrary to a meat-pricing order made under the Defence Regulations. The parcels and tickets had been prepared by Mugliston in the absence of Akeroyd. Both defendants were charged under regulation 90(1) of the Defence Regulations, which provided: "[A]ny person who attempts to commit, or does any act preparatory to the commission of, an offence against any of these regulations shall be guilty of an offence against that regulation." The courts had previously interpreted the meat-pricing order as imposing an absolute and vicarious liability; if the meat parcels in question had been delivered to customers there was no question that both Mugliston and Akeroyd could be successfully prosecuted, despite the latter's lack of knowledge or participation. Nonetheless, while Mugliston was convicted, the informations against Akeroyd were dismissed, and the prosecutor appealed. What result?

(c) Assume a burglary statute that makes it a higher offense to commit burglary in the nighttime than in the daytime and assume that the statute has been interpreted to impose absolute liability as to the time of day. A person who burglarized in the nighttime would be guilty of the higher offense regardless of his or her belief, even if well-founded, that it was still day time. But suppose the burglar had been stopped before completing the offense of burglary: Could he or she be convicted for attempted burglary in the nighttime?

Consider the approach of the Model Penal Code to these issues (§5.01, Comment at 27-28 (Tent. Draft No. 10, 1960)):

> [Section 5.01(1)] adopts the view that the actor must have for his purpose to engage in the criminal conduct or accomplish the criminal result which is an element of the substantive crime but that his purpose need not encompass all the surrounding circumstances included in the formal definition of the substantive offense. As to them, it is sufficient that he acts with the culpability that is required for commission of the crime. Suppose, for example, that it is a federal offense to kill or injure an FBI agent and that recklessness or even negligence with respect to the identity of the victim as an agent suffices for commission of the crime. There would be an attempt to kill or injure such an agent under the present formulation if the actor with recklessness or negligence as to the official position of the victim attempts to kill or injure him. Under paragraph (b) the killing or injuring would be the required purpose; the fact that the victim is an agent would be only a circumstance as to which the actor had "the kind of culpability otherwise required for the commission of the crime."
>
> It is difficult to say what the result would be in this kind of case under prevailing principles of attempt liability. However, the proposed formulation imposes attempt liability in a group of cases where the normal basis of such liability is present — purposive conduct manifesting dangerousness — and allows the policy of the substantive crime, respecting recklessness or negligence as to surrounding circumstances, to be applied to the attempt to commit that crime.

Query: Is it clear why the results described in this Commentary necessarily follow from the formulations of §5.01(1)? Examine the text in the Appendix to this casebook carefully. If the draft is inadequate, how would you amend it?

3. Preparation

THE KING v. BARKER
New Zealand Court of Appeal
[1924] N.Z.L.R. 865

SALMOND, J. . . . . That the common law has recognized the distinction between acts of attempt and acts of preparation — between acts which are, and acts which are not, too remote to constitute a criminal attempt — is undoubted. Thus, in R. v. Eagleton [169 E.R. 826 (1855)] it is said by Parke, B.: "The mere intention to commit a misdemeanor is not criminal; some act is required; and we do not think that all acts towards committing a misdemeanor are indictable. Acts remotely leading towards the commission of the offence are not to be considered as attempts to commit it, but acts immediately connected with it are."

If, however, we proceed to inquire as to the precise nature of the distinction thus recognised and indicated, we find that the common law authorities are almost as silent as the Crimes Act itself. Indeed, the lacuna in this codifying Statute is merely the reflection of a similar defect in the common law expressed by the Statute. An endeavour was indeed made in the case which I have cited — R. v. Eagleton — to formulate a definite test of the distinction in question but the test so suggested has been repudiated and departed from by subsequent authorities, though without the provision of any definite substitute. The rule so suggested in R. v. Eagleton was that in order to constitute a criminal attempt, as opposed to mere preparation, the accused must have taken the last step which he was able to take along the road of his criminal intent. He must have done all that he intended to do and was able to do for the purpose of effectuating his criminal purpose. When he has stopped short of this, whether because he has repented, or because he has been prevented, or because the time or occasion for going further has not arrived, or for any other reason, he still has a locus penitentiae and still remains within the region of innocent preparation. Until he has done his best to complete his guilty purpose, he has not attempted to complete it. On this principle the act of firing a pistol at a man would be attempted murder, although the bullet missed him. So would the act of pulling the trigger, although the pistol missed fire. But the prior and preliminary acts of procuring and loading the pistol, and of going with it to look for his enemy, and of lying in wait for him, and even of presenting the pistol at him, would not constitute criminal attempts, none of these being the proximate and final step towards the fulfilment of his criminal purpose. . . .

Subsequent authorities make it clear that the test so suggested and adopted is not the true one. It is now settled law that to constitute an attempt, it is not necessary that the accused should have done his best or taken the last or proximate step towards the completed offence. The suggested rule was definitely rejected by the Court of Criminal Appeal in R. v. White, [1910] 2 K.B. 124; 4 Cr. App. R. 257. It was held that the first administration of poison in a case of intended slow poisoning by repeated doses amounted in itself to attempted murder. It is said by the Court: "The completion [or attempted completion] of one of a series of acts intended by a man to result in killing is an attempt to murder, even though the completed act would not, unless followed by other acts, result in killing. It might be the beginning of an attempt but would none the less be an attempt."

Although the test adopted by Parke, B., has been rejected, no definite substitute for it has been formulated. All that can be definitely gathered from the authorities is that to constitute a criminal attempt, the first step along the way of criminal intent is not necessarily sufficient and the final step is not necessarily required. The dividing line between preparation and attempt is to be found somewhere between these two extremes; but as to the method by which it is to be determined the authorities give no clear guidance.[a] . . .

a. Cf. Model Penal Code, §5.01, Comment at 26 (Tent. Draft No. 10, 1960): "Needless to say, we are in full agreement that the law must be concerned with conduct, not with evil thoughts alone. The question is what conduct, when engaged in with a purpose to commit a crime or to advance towards the attainment of a criminal objective, should suffice to constitute a criminal attempt?"

Reconsider the Note material, page 257 supra, on the reasons why the law declines to punish for bare intentions. For a fuller discussion, see Morris, Punishment for Thoughts, 49 Monist 342 (1965); Dworkin & Blumenfeld, Punishment for Intentions, 75 Mind 396 (1966). — Eds.

COMMONWEALTH v. PEASLEE

Supreme Judicial Court of Massachusetts
177 Mass. 267, 59 N.E. 55 (1901)

HOLMES, C.J. This is an indictment for an attempt to burn a building and certain goods therein, with intent to injure the insurers of the same. The defense is that the overt acts alleged and proved do not amount to an offense. It was raised by a motion to quash, and also by a request to the judge to direct a verdict for the defendant. We will consider the case in the first place upon the evidence, apart from any question of pleading, and afterwards will take it up in connection with the indictment as actually drawn.

The evidence was that the defendant had constructed and arranged combustibles in the building in such a way that they were ready to be lighted, and if lighted would have set fire to the building and its contents. To be exact, the plan would have required a candle which was standing on a shelf six feet away to be placed on a piece of wood in a pan of turpentine and lighted. The defendant offered to pay a younger man in his employment if he would go to the building, seemingly some miles from the place of the dialogue, and carry out the plan. This was refused. Later the defendant and the young man drove towards the building, but when within a quarter of a mile the defendant said that he had changed his mind, and drove away. This is as near as he ever came to accomplishing what he had in contemplation.

The question on the evidence, more precisely stated, is whether the defendant's acts come near enough to the accomplishment of the substantive offense to be punishable. The statute does not punish every act done towards the commission of a crime, but only such acts done in an attempt to commit it. The most common types of an attempt are either an act which is intended to bring about the substantive crime, and which sets in motion natural forces that would bring it about in the expected course of events, but for the unforeseen interruption, as, in this case, if the candle had been put out by the police, or an act which is intended to bring about the substantive crime, and would bring it about but for a mistake of judgment in a matter of nice estimate or experiment, as when a pistol is fired at a man, but misses him, or when one tries to pick a pocket which turns out to be empty. In either case the would-be criminal has done his last act.

Obviously new considerations come in when further acts on the part of the person who has taken the first steps are necessary before the substantive crime can come to pass. In this class of cases there is still a chance that the would-be criminal may change his mind. In strictness, such first steps cannot be described as an attempt, because that word suggests an act seemingly sufficient to accomplish the end, and has been supposed to have no other meaning. That an overt act, although coupled with an intent to commit the crime, commonly is not punishable if further acts are contemplated as needful, is expressed in the familiar rule that preparation is not an attempt. But some preparations may amount to an attempt. It is a question of degree. If the preparation comes very near to the accomplishment of the act, the intent to complete it renders the crime so probable that the act will be a misdemeanor, although there is still a locus poenitentiae, in the need of a further exertion of the will to complete the crime.[b] As was observed in a recent case, the degree of proximity held sufficient may vary with circumstances, including, among other things, the apprehension which the particular crime is calculated to excite. Com. v. Kennedy, 170 Mass. 18, 22, 48 N.E. 770.[c]

[The court suggested, but declined to decide, that on the evidence a conviction of attempt was proper. The conviction was reversed on the procedural ground that the indictment failed to allege the solicitation of the employee to set the fire as one of the overt acts.]

PROBLEMS

1. In Rex v. Robinson, [1915] 2 K.B. 342, 348-349, defendant staged a fake holdup of his jewelry store and reported it to the police as part of a plan to defraud the insurance carrier. His scheme was revealed before he made any claim on the insurance company. The court reversed a conviction of attempt to obtain money by false pretenses from the underwriters, stating:

> In the present case the real difficulty lies in the fact that there is no evidence of any act done by the appellant in the nature of a false pretence which ever reached the minds of the underwriters, though they were the persons who were to be induced to part with the money. The evidence falls short of any communication of such a pretence to the underwriters or to any agent of theirs. The police were not acting on behalf of the underwriters. In truth what the appellant did was preparation for the commission of a crime, not a step in the commission of it. It consisted in the preparation of evidence which might indirectly induce the underwriters to pay; for if the police had made a report that a burglary had taken place, — and that was presumably what the appellant intended, — it may very well be that the underwriters would have paid without further inquiry. But there must be some act beyond mere preparation if a person is to be charged with an attempt. Applying the rule laid down by Parke, B., we think that the appellant's act was only remotely connected with the commission of the full offence, and not immediately connected with it. If we were to hold otherwise we should be going further than any case has ever yet gone, and should be opening the door to convictions for acts which are not at present criminal offences. We think the conviction must be quashed, not on the technical ground that no information or evidence as to the property lost was given to the underwriters as required by the policy, but upon the broad ground that no communication of any kind of the false pretence was made to them.

Suppose Robinson had taken the further step of addressing a letter to his insurance carrier stating he had been robbed and asking for particulars on whether and how he could make a claim? This was the situation in Comer v.

---

b. "Combination, intent and overt act may all be present without amounting to a criminal attempt — as if all that were done should be an agreement to murder a man fifty miles away and the purchase of a pistol for the purpose. There must be a dangerous proximity to success." Holmes, J., dissenting in Hyde v. United States, 225 U.S. 347, 387 (1912). — EDS.

c. Justice Holmes observed in that case: "As the aim of the law is not to punish sins, but is to prevent certain external results, the act done must come pretty near to accomplishing that result before the law will notice it." 48 N.E. at 770. — EDS.

Bloomfield, [1970] 55 Crim. App. 305, where defendant crashed his car, hid it, reported to the police that it had been stolen, and wrote a letter of inquiry of the kind just described to his insurance carrier. The divisional court found that the letter, being an inquiry rather than a claim, was not sufficiently proximate to the offense of obtaining money by deception to amount to an attempt — the defendant might still (id. at 309) "have desisted from the course on which he had embarked and proceeded no further." The court stated the general test to be as follows (id. at 308-309):

> The actus reus necessary to constitute an attempt is complete if the prisoner does an act which is a step towards the commission of the specific crime, which is immediately and not merely remotely connected with the commission of it, and the doing of which cannot reasonably be regarded as having any other purpose than the commission of the specific crime.

2. In People v. Rizzo, 246 N.Y. 334, 335, 338-339, 158 N.E. 888, 889-890 (1927), defendant and his confederates, all armed, were driving through the streets of an area in New York searching for Rao, a payroll clerk, whom they planned to rob of about $1,200. Their futile efforts to find their victim attracted the attention of the police, who apprehended them after a period of surveillance. The court of appeals reversed a conviction of attempted robbery on the ground that defendants' acts constituted mere preparation, stating:

> To constitute the crime of robbery, the money must have been taken from Rao by means of force or violence, or through fear. The crime of attempt to commit robbery was committed, if these defendants did an act tending to the commission of this robbery. Did the acts above described come dangerously near to the taking of Rao's property? Did the acts come so near the commission of robbery that there was reasonable likelihood of its accomplishment but for the interference? Rao was not found; the defendants were still looking for him; no attempt to rob him could be made, at least until he came in sight; he was not in the building [where he was expected to be]. There was no man there with the pay roll for the United Lathing Company whom these defendants could rob. Apparently no money had been drawn from the bank for the pay roll by anybody at the time of the arrest. In a word, these defendants had planned to commit a crime, and were looking around the city for an opportunity to commit it, but the opportunity fortunately never came. Men would not be guilty of an attempt at burglary if they had planned to break into a building and were arrested while they were hunting about the streets for the building not knowing where it was. Neither would a man be guilty of an attempt to commit murder if he armed himself and started out to find the person whom he had planned to kill but could not find him. So here these defendants were not guilty of an attempt to commit robbery in the first degree when they had not found or reached the presence of the person they intended to rob.

However, the court commented that,

> The police of the city of New York did excellent work in this case by preventing the commission of a serious crime. It is a great satisfaction to realize that we have such wide-awake guardians of our peace.

3. Is it necessarily the case that a defendant is guilty of an attempt if the person does the last act she thought necessary to commit the completed offense? Consider Hope v. Brown, [1954] 1 All E.R. 330, 332. A storekeeper prepared price tags showing prices in excess of those permitted by law. He placed them in a drawer, expecting that in due course a sales clerk would affix them to the meat packages in place of the lawful price tags. The court held that the defendant could not be convicted of an attempt to sell meat in excess of the maximum price. Lord Goddard stated:

> [W]hat remained to be done before there would be an attempt was the affixing to the meat of the false tickets. Until that was done, in my opinion the matter remained simply in embryo and in intention. The girl would have affixed the ticket, no doubt, because she was delivering the meat on behalf of the respondent on his instructions, and what she was doing was the act of the respondent, but, until she had done that, one cannot say that an offence had been committed. The preparation of the false tickets and putting them in the drawer is too remote from the actual transaction which would be necessary to constitute the attempt. There might be a sudden change of heart, or an intervention by the master, which would have prevented any attempt being made to sell this meat to the customers. In all these cases where it has been held that there has been an attempt the court has always found that the crime would have been committed but for the intervention of someone. The crime here would not have been committed until, at any rate, the meat had got the false ticket on it and it had been sold with that false ticket on it to the customer. Therefore, the mere fact that the respondent prepared a false ticket is not enough.

Compare Director of Public Prosecutions v. Stonehouse, [1977] 2 All E.R. 909. Defendant, a well-known politician, found himself in financial and other difficulties. Seeking to make a fresh start for himself and provision for his wife, he insured his life, naming his wife as beneficiary, feigned his own death in a staged drowning incident in Miami, and secretly traveled to Australia under a false passport and a new identity. He was later discovered in Australia and his plot revealed — before his wife, who was not a party to his scheme, had applied for the insurance benefits. The House of Lords upheld a conviction of attempting dishonestly to obtain money from the insurance company by deception under §15 of the Theft Act, specifically its extended definition of "obtain" as including "enabling another to obtain." Query: Was the conviction inconsistent with Hope v. Brown?

NOTE

Bearing the foregoing cases in mind, consider the following observations of Professor Glanville Williams:

> In a rational system of justice the police would be given every encouragement to intervene early where a suspect is clearly bent on crime. Yet in England, if the police come on the scene too early they may find that they can do nothing with the intending offender except admonish him. This is largely because of the rule that an attempt, to be indictable, must be sufficiently "proximate" to the crime

intended. . . . One is led to ask whether there is any real need for the requirement of proximity in the law of attempt. Quite apart from this requirement, it must be proved beyond reasonable doubt that the accused intended to commit the crime . . . and that he did some act towards committing it. If only a remote act of preparation is alleged against him, that will weigh with the court in deciding whether he had the firm criminal intention alleged against him. If, however, the court finds that this intention existed, is there any reason why the would-be criminal should not be dealt with by the police and by the criminal courts?

Police Control of Intending Criminals, [1955] Crim. L. Rev. 66, 69.

Another way of supporting the proximity rule is to say that it results from the notion of crime as a punishable wrong. Society has not thought it desirable to extend the scope of punishment too widely. So long as the law was purely deterrent or retributive in its aim, this circumscription of the offence of attempt was perhaps justified. At the present day, when courts have wide powers of probation, there is much to be said for a broader measure of responsibility. Any act done with the fixed intention of committing a crime, and by way of preparation for it, however remote it may be from the crime, might well be treated as criminal. The rational course would be to catch intending offenders as soon as possible, and set about curing them of their evil tendencies: not leave them alone on the ground that their acts are mere preparation. It must be said, however, that this opinion is not generally held in the legal profession.

Criminal Law: The General Part 632 (2d ed. 1961).

STATE v. YOUNG
Supreme Court of New Jersey
57 N.J. 240, 271 A.2d 569 (1970)

WEINTRAUB, C.J. A jury found defendant guilty on an indictment charging that he entered Trenton High School with the intent to disrupt classes therein and otherwise to interfere with the peace and good order of that school. He was fined $500. We certified his appeal before the Appellate Division acted upon it.

The statute, N.J.S.A. 2A:149A-2, reads:

Any person, other than a bona fide student therein or parent or legal guardian of such student or a teacher, administrator, or other school employee while in the performance of his duties, who enters any building structure or place used for any educational purpose with the intent of disrupting classes or of otherwise interfering with the peace and good order of the place shall be guilty of a misdemeanor.

Defendant advances several constitutional issues. In one of his points, defendant argues that his entry into the school building was "innocent." We are not sure whether the thrust is only that the State is powerless to punish an "innocent" act notwithstanding the intent or purpose with which the act is done, or whether defendant contends also that there was no evidence that he entered the school with the purpose the statute forbids. We will deem both questions to be before us and deal first with the sufficiency of the proof. . . .

[There was evidence that the defendant, a lay minister, was active in organizing student protests initially over suspension of a student for refusing to stand for a flag salute. On the day in question he was present at the school and took a leadership role in a student sit-in, although he had been asked to leave by the superintendent of schools.]

. . . [T]he question is whether the evidence could fairly support a finding by a jury that guilt was established beyond a reasonable doubt. . . . The issue was whether defendant, when he entered the school building, did so "with the intent of disrupting classes or of otherwise interfering with the peace and good order of the place." On the basis of the circumstances antedating his entry and the facts relating to his behavior after the entry, the jury could reasonably find that defendant came to the school with the intent to support the sit-in and thereby to disrupt classes and to interfere with the peace and good order of the place. . . .

Next, defendant contends that the act of entering a public school is in itself "blameless" and that it is beyond the power of the State to punish an innocent act merely because of a forbidden purpose. We think the police power of the State is not thus restricted. . . .

There are a host of statutes, federal and State, which condemn acts, themselves innocent, if done with a forbidden intent. We will summarize them in approximate terms, sufficient for our immediate purpose.

The possession of certain counterfeit obligations is made criminal but only if the obligation is possessed "with intent to defraud," 18 U.S.C.A. §480. There is nothing necessarily wrong in teaching or demonstrating the use, application or making of a firearm or explosive or incendiary device or a technique capable of causing injury or death, but 18 U.S.C.A. §231(a)(1) makes it a crime to do so "intending that the same will be unlawfully employed for use in, or in further-ance of, a civil disorder which may in any way or degree obstruct, delay, or adversely affect commerce" or the performance of any federally protected func-tion. . . .

There are a number of statutes which make possession criminal if there is an intent to do some hostile act. See N.J.S.A. 2A:94-3 relating to possession of burglar tools; and see N.J.S.A. 2A:109-2 subds. a and b, relating to possession of counterfeits. As to weapons and explosives, see N.J.S.A. 2A:151-56, 59 and 60. It is a disorderly persons offense to possess certain implements if the intent is to break and enter, or to have on one's person an offensive or dangerous weapon with intent to assault another, or to be in any place of public resort or assemblage for business, travel, worship, amusement of other lawful place, with intent to steal, N.J.S.A. 2A:170-3.

We refer to this array of statutes solely to evidence the widely held legislative view that such measures are within the legislative power, and to reveal the impact upon public safety and order if it should be held that government, in seeking to anticipate and prevent criminal events, may punish only if a step taken in pursuit of a criminal objective itself bespeaks criminality.

The common law concept of crime called for both an act and a wrongful intent. Intent alone would not suffice; the right, or more accurately the power, to think evil was absolute. Nor was innocuous conduct punished. But in combina-tion, an evil purpose and an innocuous step could be explosive. And as between the two, the evil purpose is the more dangerous for it harbors the ultimate threat. For that reason, it ultimately evolved at common law that an "attempt" to commit a crime was itself punishable as a crime. The evil purpose being shown, the common law punished an act in pursuit of the purpose even though the act fell short of actual harm or injury. Nor need the act in isolation bespeak criminality. "Hence the assertion that 'an act which is in itself and on the face of it innocent, is not a criminal attempt' is untenable. It has long been held that an act might be quite innocent in itself, but found to express a criminal intention on knowledge of surrounding circumstances." Hall, "Criminal Attempt — A Study of the Foundation of Criminal Liability," 49 Yale L.J. 789, 825 (1940).

Generally a line is sought to be drawn between an "attempt" and mere "preparation," preparation itself not being punishable as an attempt. Nonetheless some conduct short of an attempt was punishable at common law. So a solicitation to commit a crime, though not equalling an attempt, was dealt with as a crime. The most conspicuous proscription of the common law in anticipation of actual injury or an attempt thereat was the crime of conspiracy, for that crime required no more than an agreement for an unlawful end. The conspiracy was itself punished, realistically, not because the act of agreeing to seek an unlawful end was itself hurtful, but rather because the combination of the wills of several was "much more likely to result in evil consequences than the mere intent of only one person." 3 Burdick, Law of Crime (1946) §984. p. 435. . . .

To meet the added dangers of a complex and congested society, legislatures have gone beyond the common law in punishing conduct which by common law standards might fall short of an attempt. Professor Perkins observes that "it is becoming increasingly common for legislative enactment to provide a penalty (often a severe one) for what the common law regarded as an unpunishable act of preparation." Perkins, Criminal Law (1957), p. 486. . . . [T]he many statutes we recounted above have the common feature of punishing an act only because of the evil purpose it pursues, without regard to whether the act would constitute an attempt to commit the offense the statutes seek to head off, and even though the act, absent such purpose, may be one protected by the Constitution.

We see no serious challenge to the power of a legislature to make it an offense to take a step, otherwise lawful, in furtherance of a hostile end. . . .

Affirmed.

NOTE ON SUBSTANTIVE CRIMES OF PREPARATION

As the *Young* case makes clear, the kinds of concerns expressed by Professor Williams, page 573 supra, inadequately met as they were by the traditional limitations of the law of attempt, were met by the formulation of substantive crimes, common law and statutory, that are satisfied by preparatory behavior. There are important instances of this, other than those discussed in the *Young* decision.

One such instance is represented by prophylactic measures to deal with suspicious actions of suspicious persons in circumstances that create grounds for fearing the person may soon try to commit a crime. In light of the invalidation of the traditional vagrancy-type statutes (see Papachristou v. City of Jacksonville, page 364 supra), two principal approaches have been used. One is procedural, allowing police to stop and detain a suspect in circumstances short of those justifying an arrest on probable cause under the Fourth Amendment. See Terry v. Ohio, 392 U.S. 1 (1968). The other approach is substantive, making it a crime, in effect, to loiter or prowl in circumstances giving rise to alarm that a crime will be attempted. See Model Penal Code §250.6, Appendix to this casebook, and the supporting commentary reprinted at pages 368-370 supra.

Two traditional instances of making preparatory behavior criminal as substantive crimes are the crimes of burglary and assault.

(1) Burglary. Common law burglary consisted of breaking and entering a dwelling of another at night with the intent to commit a felony inside. Cases and statutes gradually enlarged the offense: Under some statutes an entry is all that is required, in day as well as at night, into any structure, with intent to commit any crime. The relationship between burglary and the general crime of attempt is developed in the following excerpt from the Comments to the Model Penal Code (American Law Institute, Model Penal Code and Commentaries, Pt. II, Comment to §221.1 at 62-63 (1980)):

> The initial development of the offense of burglary, as well as much of the later expansion of the offense, probably resulted from an effort to compensate for defects of the traditional law of attempt. The common law of attempt ordinarily did not reach a person who embarked on a course of criminal behavior unless he came very close to his goal. Sometimes it was stated that to be guilty of attempt one had to engage in the final act which would have accomplished his object but for the intervention of circumstances beyond his control. Under that view of the law of attempt, a person apprehended while breaking into a dwelling with intent to commit a felony therein would not have committed an attempt, for he would not have arrived at the scene of his projected theft, rape, or murder. Moreover, even when the actor's conduct reached the stage where an attempt was committed, penalties for attempt were disproportionately low as compared to the penalties for the completed offense.
>
> The development and expansion of the offense of burglary provided a partial solution to these problems. Making entry with criminal intent an independent substantive offense carrying serious sanctions moved back the moment when the law could intervene in a criminal design and authorized penalties more nearly in accord with the seriousness of the actor's conduct.

A further difficulty with the law of attempt that is overcome with the crime of burglary is pointed out in the above comments (id. at 67-68):

> It is not uncommon for surreptitious entry to occur under circumstances where law enforcement officials are hard pressed to establish precisely what crime the actor contemplated within the premises. A serious penalty may be justified whether it is assault or theft that is the object of the entry, though the facts of the case may make it difficult to establish beyond a reasonable doubt that it was the one rather than the other. An attempt prosecution would require just such specific proof, whereas prosecution under a burglary statute requires only that it be established that the intrusion was made as a conscious step toward the accomplishment of one of a number of possible criminal objectives.

The line separating innocence from criminality in the steps leading up to the commission of a substantive offense has been pushed back along the stages of preparation even further than the definition of burglary itself pushes it. First, courts have often upheld convictions of attempted burglary. Typical instances are as follows: Police officers discovered from the external signs that someone had tried to open a shop door, and defendant was identified as the person seen leaving the front of the shop shortly before the police made the discovery, Taylor v. State, 233 S.W.2d 306 (Tex. Crim. App. 1950); defendant was proven to have entered a store yard at night carrying a ladder and bag of tools and wearing gloves, People v. Gibson, 94 Cal. App. 2d 468, 210 P.2d 747 (1949); defendant was apprehended in the early morning hours climbing the stairs to a second-floor cigar store and carrying a bolt cutter, State v. Kleier, 69 Idaho 491, 210 P.2d 388 (1949). Second, many legislatures have enacted statutes making criminal the manufacture, repair, or possession of burglars' tools, most requiring proof of intent to commit a felony, most often burglary. See, e.g., Cal. Penal Code §466.

(2) *Assault.* Assault is another substantive crime that is essentially a kind of attempt. It is generally defined as an attempt to commit a battery on another. May the point of criminality be pushed back by convicting a person of an attempt to commit an assault? Some courts have held not. See Wilson v. State, 53 Ga. 205, 206 (1874):

> As an assault is itself an attempt to commit a crime, and attempt to make an assault can only be an attempt to attempt to do it, or to state the matter still more definitely, it is to do any act towards doing an act towards the commission of the offense. This is simply absurd. As soon as any act is done towards committing a violent injury on the person of another, the party doing the act is guilty of an assault, and he is not guilty until he has done the act. Yet it is claimed that [defendant] may be guilty of an attempt to make an assault, when, under the law, he must do an act before the attempt is complete. The refinement and metaphysical acumen that can see a tangible idea in the words an attempt to attempt to act is too great for practical use. It is like conceiving of the beginning of eternity or the starting place of infinity.

Other courts have held to the contrary. See, e.g., State v. Wilson, 218 Or. 575, 346 P.2d 115 (1959) (defendant came looking for his wife at her place of work carrying a shotgun and intending to shoot her, but her fellow workers hid her and he was unable to find her). See Perkins, An Analysis of Assault and Attempts to Assault, 47 Minn. L. Rev. 71 (1962); Annot., Attempt to commit assault as criminal offense, 79 A.L.R.2d 597 (1961). Compare Arnold, Criminal Attempts — The Rise and Fall of an Abstraction, 40 Yale L.J. 53, 65 (1930):

> [It is said that] there can be no attempt at a direct attempt. But the query immediately arises. Why not? We do not punish attempts at ordinary assaults which carry light penalties. But suppose the accused is guilty of conduct tending toward an aggravated assault but which does not seem to require the heavier penalty. The court is confronted with the alternative of either discharging the accused or modifying the penalty to make it more nearly fit his conduct. An easy way to accomplish this is by making attempts at aggravated assaults punishable, and this is frequently done. It is academic to call such cases "wrong" because assault is in the nature of an attempt and hence cannot be attempted, particularly when a common sense result is reached. In short the generalization that there can be no attempt tells us nothing and tends merely to divert the court's mind from the real issue.

McQUIRTER v. STATE

Alabama Court of Appeals
36 Ala. App. 707, 63 So. 2d 388 (1953)

PRICE, J. Appellant, a Negro man, was found guilty of an attempt to commit an assault with intent to rape, under an indictment charging an assault with intent to rape. The jury assessed a fine of $500.

About 8:00 o'clock on the night of June 29, 1951, Mrs. Ted Allen, a white woman, with her two children and a neighbor's little girl, were drinking Coca-Cola at the "Tiny Diner" in Atmore. When they started in the direction of Mrs. Allen's home she noticed appellant sitting in the cab of a parked truck. As she passed the truck appellant said something unintelligible, opened the truck door and placed his foot on the running board.

Mrs. Allen testified appellant followed her down the street and when she reached Suell Lufkin's house she stopped. As she turned into the Lufkin house appellant was within two or three feet of her. She waited ten minutes for appellant to pass. When she proceeded on her way, appellant came toward her from behind a telephone pole. She told the children to run to Mr. Simmons' house and tell him to come and meet her. When appellant saw Mr. Simmons he turned and went back down the street to the intersection and leaned on a stop sign just across the street from Mrs. Allen's home. Mrs. Allen watched him at the sign from Mr. Simmons' porch for about thirty minutes, after which time he came back down the street and appellant went on home. . . .

Mr. W. E. Strickland, Chief of Police of Atmore, testified that appellant stated in the Atmore jail he didn't know what was the matter with him; that he was drinking a little; that he and his partner had been to Pensacola; that his partner went to the "Front" to see a colored woman; that he didn't have any money and he sat in the truck and made up his mind he was going to get the first woman that came by and that this was the first woman that came by. He said he got out of the truck, came around the gas tank and watched the lady and when she started off he started off behind her; that he was going to carry her in the cotton patch and if she hollered he was going to kill her. He testified appellant made the same statement in the Brewton jail. . . .

Appellant, as a witness in his own behalf, testified he and Bill Page, another Negro, carried a load of junk-iron from Monroeville to Pensacola; on their way back to Monroeville they stopped in Atmore. They parked the truck near the "Tiny Diner" and rode to the "Front," the colored section, in a cab. Appellant came back to the truck around 8:00 o'clock and sat in the truck cab for about thirty minutes. He decided to go back to the "Front" to look for Bill Page. As he started up the street he saw prosecutrix and her children. He turned around and waited until he decided they had gone, then he walked up the street toward the "Front." When he reached the intersection at the street telegraph pole he decided he didn't want to go to the "Front" and sat around there a few minutes, then went on the "Front" and stayed about 25 to 30 minutes, and came back to the truck.

He denied that he followed Mrs. Allen or made any gesture toward molesting her or the children. He denied making the statements testified to by the officers. . . .

Appellant insists the trial court erred in refusing the general affirmative charge and in denying the motion for a new trial on the ground the verdict was contrary to the evidence.

" 'An attempt to commit an assault with intent to rape,' . . . means an attempt to rape which has not proceeded far enough to amount to an assault." Burton v. State, 8 Ala. App. 295, 62 So. 394, 396.

Under the authorities in this state, to justify a conviction for an attempt to commit an assault with intent to rape the jury must be satisfied beyond a reasonable doubt that defendant intended to have sexual intercourse with prosecutrix against her will, by force or by putting her in fear.

Intent is a question to be determined by the jury from the facts and circumstances adduced on the trial, and if there is evidence from which it may be inferred that at the time of the attempt defendant intended to gratify his lustful desires against the resistance of the female a jury question is presented.

In determining the question of intention the jury may consider social conditions and customs founded upon racial differences, such as that the prosecutrix was a white woman and defendant was a Negro man.

After considering the evidence in this case we are of the opinion it was sufficient to warrant the submission of the question of defendant's guilt to the jury, and was ample to sustain the judgment of conviction. . . .

Affirmed.[a]

QUESTIONS

What is bothersome about this case? The racial context certainly is, as well as the evidence of intent, coming as it did from only the sheriff's testimony of what defendant said in jail. But suppose these factors were removed: Assume a similar case in a northern town in which defendant was white and in which the evidence of intent was less suspect. Would the decision still be troubling?

<hr>

PEOPLE v. BERGER
California District Court of Appeal
131 Cal. App. 2d 127, 280 P.2d 136 (1955)

DOOLING, J. Defendant appeals from a judgment convicting him of an attempt to commit an abortion and from the order of the trial court denying his motion for a new trial. Appellant was indicted jointly with Inez L. Burns. The indictment contained several counts but it was agreed that the prosecution would proceed on count 2 charging an attempt to commit abortion, appellant and his counsel waived a jury trial and stipulated to submit the charge to the trial judge on the testimony given before the grand jury.

The evidence may be summarized as follows: Adrienne Scheuplein, an investigator for the district attorney, went to the office of appellant, a licensed physician. She introduced herself as Kathryn Phillips and told appellant that she was pregnant and that she had come to him for the same reason as the young woman

<hr>

a. See Annot., Indecent proposal to woman as assault, 12 A.L.R.2d 971 (1950); Decision, 29 N.Y.U.L. Rev. 219 (1954). — EDS.

who had referred her to him. He directed her to go to a laboratory for a test to establish pregnancy. She was later informed by telephone that the test was positive and requested to call again at appellant's office. When she went to his office the second time the co-defendant Burns was there. Appellant told Mrs. Scheuplein that it was difficult to do anything about her problem and asked if the operation could be performed at the place where she was staying. It was subsequently arranged that the operation should be performed at Mrs. Scheuplein's home. Appellant told Mrs. Scheuplein that a suitcase would be delivered at her home and that the person who would perform the operation would get in touch with her and he gave her specific instructions on preparing herself for surgery. The suitcase was delivered that night and the following morning Inez Burns arrived.

Mrs. Burns went to the kitchen and began making arrangements for the operation. The suitcase containing the surgical instruments was brought into the kitchen, the instruments were wrapped in towels and placed on the stove in pans of water to boil. A sheet was placed over the window to conceal it from the view of any person outside. Mrs. Burns placed cotton, jars of pitocin, ergotrate, metsol and ammonia and a large roll of gauze on a side table. Mrs. Scheuplein paid Mrs. Burns $525 in marked money. These activities occupied about 45 minutes during which Mrs. Burns talked of her past activities and reassured Mrs. Scheuplein about the pending operation. When the water in the pans containing the instruments was starting to boil Mrs. Scheuplein went upstairs, supposedly to disrobe, and the police arrived and arrested Mrs. Burns. Mrs. Burns admitted that she was there for the purpose of performing an abortion. Other details of evidence connecting appellant with these activities need not be stated since no claim is made that if Mrs. Burns was guilty of the crime charged the appellant could not under the evidence be found guilty also.

Appellant makes two arguments on appeal: 1, that under our statutory law there can be no such crime as an attempt to commit abortion; 2, that the evidence in any event is not sufficient to support the conviction.

Penal Code, §274 defines the crime of abortion as follows:

Every person who provides, supplies, or administers to any woman, or procures any woman to take any medicine, drug, or substance, or uses or employs any instrument or other means whatever, with intent thereby to procure the miscarriage of such woman, unless the same is necessary to preserve her life, is punishable by imprisonment in the state prison not less than two nor more than five years.

It is appellant's position that this section itself makes an attempt to procure a miscarriage the substantive offense and hence Pen. Code, §664, which only applies "where no provision is made by law for the punishment of such attempts," is not applicable. Tersely, appellant argues that there can be no such crime as an attempt to attempt. The argument is one of semantics rather than logic. . . . No good reason appears why any person who attempts "to use or employ any instrument" with the same intent is not guilty of an attempt under Pen. Code, §664. . . .

The more serious question is whether the acts performed by Mrs. Burns amounted to no more than mere preparation. The cases make clear that mere preparation to commit a crime does not constitute an attempt to commit it, but the drawing of the line between mere preparation and attempt in close cases is not an easy task. It may be drawn from the cases that where the intent to commit the substantive offense is as clearly established as it is here acts done toward the commission of the crime may constitute an attempt, where the same acts would be held insufficient to constitute an attempt if the intent with which they were done is equivocal and not clearly proved. Thus in People v. Miller, 2 Cal. 2d 527, 531-532, 42 P.2d 308 (1935) [defendant, who had earlier in the day threatened to kill Jeans, entered a field, where Jeans and the local constable were planting hops. Defendant was carrying a rifle, and he walked toward them. Walking in a straight line, he had to pass the constable to reach Jeans. At one point he stopped, apparently to load his rifle, but at no time did he lift it to take aim. Jeans fled, and the constable took the gun, which was loaded, from defendant when he came by. A conviction of attempted murder was reversed.] Mr. Justice Shenk, writing for the court, said: "The reason for requiring evidence of a direct act, however slight, toward consummation of the intended crime, is . . . that in the majority of cases up to that time the conduct of the defendant, consisting merely of acts of preparation, has never ceased to be equivocal; and this is necessarily so, irrespective of his declared intent. It is that quality of being equivocal that must be lacking before the act becomes one which may be said to be a commencement of the commission of the crime, or an overt act, or before any fragment of the crime itself has been committed, and this is so for the reason that, so long as the equivocal quality remains, no one can say with certainty what the intent of the defendant is. [In the present case, up to the moment the gun was taken from defendant, no one could say with certainty whether defendant had come into the field to carry out his threat to kill Jeans or merely to demand his arrest by the constable.]"

After reviewing certain [contrary] cases Justice Shenk commented: "These cases illustrate the small class of cases where the acts of preparation themselves clearly indicate the certain unambiguous intent and suffice to constitute the attempt."

More concisely the court said in People v. Anderson, 1 Cal. 2d 687, 690, 37 P.2d 67, 68: "Whenever the design of a person to commit crime is clearly shown, slight acts in furtherance of the design will constitute an attempt." . . .

In People v. Gibson, 94 Cal. App. 2d 468, 210 P.2d 747, defendant took a ladder in the nighttime with intent to burglarize some building in the locality. He had not yet selected the building to be burglarized when he was apprehended. The court affirmed a conviction of attempt to commit burglary since the intent was clearly proved by defendant's admissions. The court said "It is not necessary that the overt act proved should have been the ultimate step toward the consummation of the design. It is sufficient if it was 'the first or some subsequent step in a direct movement towards the commission of the offense after the preparations are made.'"

It is a matter of common knowledge that the sterilization of the instruments to be used in a surgical operation is the first step taken in the performance of the operation in modern surgical procedure. In a case where the intent was not clearly established the boiling of surgical instruments might be too equivocal an act to be held to constitute an attempt, but we have concluded that, since the intent with which this act was done in this case is established beyond any doubt, the boiling of the surgical instruments under the reasoning of the authorities cited was an act done toward the commission of the crime and hence sufficient to support the judgment.

Judgment and order affirmed.

NOTE ON THE EQUIVOCALITY TEST

Worth comparing with the approach in the *Berger* case is the so-called equivocality test, which had some influence on doctrinal developments in various jurisdictions and was the law in New Zealand until it was eliminated by statute.

The equivocality test was formulated by Justice Salmond in The King v. Barker, [1924] N.Z.L.R. 865, 874-876, in the following terms:

> A criminal attempt is an act which shows criminal intent on the face of it. The case must be one in which Res ipsa loquitur. An act, on the other hand, which is in its own nature and on the face of it innocent is not a criminal attempt. It cannot be brought within the scope of criminal attempt by evidence aliunde as to the criminal purpose with which it is done. A criminal attempt is criminal intent made manifest by the very nature and circumstances of some act done in pursuance of that intent. The law does not punish men for their guilty intentions or resolutions in themselves. Nor does it commonly punish them even for the expression, declaration, or confession of such intentions or resolutions. That a man's unfulfilled criminal purposes should be punishable they must be manifested not by his words merely, or by acts which are in themselves of innocent or ambiguous signficance, but by overt acts which are sufficient in themselves to declare and proclaim the guilty purpose with which they are done. Until he has so far committed himself to his criminal design as to have manifested and declared it by his acts he has not passed beyond the line of innocent preparation into the region of criminal attempt, and he still preserves for himself a locus poenitentiae. . . .
>
> . . . To buy a box of matches with intent to use them in burning a haystack is not an attempt to commit arson, for it is in itself and in appearance an innocent act, there being many other reasons than arson for buying matches. The act does not speak for itself of any guilty design. . . . But he who takes matches to a haystack and there lights one of them and blows it out on finding that he is observed, has done an act which speaks for itself, and he is guilty of a criminal attempt accordingly.
>
> As already indicated, an act which is on the face of it innocent or ambiguous cannot be transformed into a criminal attempt by evidence aliunde as to the criminal intent with which it is done. The purchaser of matches would not be guilty of attempted arson even if he declared to the vendor or to any other person the guilty purpose with which he bought them. Such evidence is relevant for the purpose of satisfying the jury that the requisite criminal intent existed, but it is not relevant in determining the prior question of law whether the act charged amounts in law to an attempt or is too remote for that purpose. For this purpose the only evidence of criminal intent is to be found in the nature and circumstances of the act itself. . . .

Questions: What considerations underlie this approach? Why should it have been rejected by statute? What are the differences between this test and that used in the *Berger* case?

UNITED STATES v. STALLWORTH
United States Court of Appeals, 2d Circuit
543 F.2d 1038 (1976)

KAUFMAN C.J. . . . Since an understanding of the facts is critical to any consideration of inchoate crimes, we summarize the pertinent events culminating in the arrest. Rodney Campbell, a convicted bank robber, agreed to cooperate with the FBI on January 12, 1976 in return for a grant of immunity from prosecution for four armed bank robberies in which he admittedly participated between June and September, 1975. Arrangements were made for Campbell to use an undercover Government vehicle, provided with a tape recorder and monitoring equipment, to assist the authorities in apprehending some of his former accomplices. Campbell consented to the tape recording of all conversations taking place in his car.

After reestablishing contact with individuals named Larry Peterson, Willie Young, and appellant Johnny Sellers, Campbell transported the men in his specially equipped vehicle as they reconnoitered several banks in Queens, New York. The group began actual preparations for a robbery on Wednesday, January 21, by stealing ski masks from a department store. Later that day Peterson and Young appropriated surgical gloves from a hospital while Sellers, a recent patient, engaged several nurses in conversation. Finally, Peterson purchased a hacksaw and roofing nails which, he told Campbell, he needed to "fix" a shotgun.

On January 22, Sellers, Peterson, Young and Campbell perfected their plan to rob a branch of the First National City Bank in Whitestone, Queens. Peterson, formerly a factory worker in the neighborhood, advised the group that on Fridays (in this instance, January 23) large amounts of money would be on hand to accommodate industrial employees in cashing their salary checks. Young entered the bank on Thursday afternoon to examine its internal physical structure and reported to his colleagues that the tellers' counters were of average height and security was thin. The participants agreed to recruit appellant Clarence Stallworth to drive the getaway car.

On Friday morning Stallworth joined Young and Sellers, to whom he handed a .38 calibre revolver, and assumed the role of driver. Peterson met his comrades, gave them a sawed-off shotgun and distributed other paraphernalia required for the crime. En route to the bank in Whitestone the occupants of the Government-owned automobile covered their fingers with band-aids, their hands with surgical gloves and donned the ski masks. They prepared to destroy the vehicle after the robbery by stuffing gasoline-soaked newspapers under the seats.

The target bank was located in a small shopping center. As the car entered the parking lot, Sellers alighted and strolled past the bank several times, peering inside at each opportunity, as his accomplices circled the shopping center. At approximately 11 A.M., Stallworth stopped the vehicle directly in front of the bank. Sellers, who had stationed himself at an adjacent liquor store, started to approach the bank. Simultaneously, Campbell said, "let's go," and the occupants of the car reached for the doors. At this point, FBI agents and New York City policemen, who had saturated the area as a result of intelligence acquired through the would-be robbers' monitored conversations, arrested the men without incident.

Appellants contend that their conduct, while admittedly sufficient to sustain a conspiracy conviction, punishable by a maximum of five years incarceration, will not support a judgment of attempted bank robbery, carrying a potential twenty-year prison term.[a] They argue that their activities did not transcend a hypothetical fixed point on a spectrum of conduct culminating in the substantive offense of bank robbery. Thus, appellants assert they cannot be convicted of attempted bank robbery because they neither entered the bank nor brandished weapons. . . .

. . . The Fifth Circuit in United States v. Mandujano, 499 F.2d 370 (5th Cir. 1974), has properly derived from the writings of many distinguished jurists a two-tiered inquiry to determine whether given conduct constitutes an attempt. Initially, the defendant must have been acting with the kind of culpability otherwise required for the commission of the crime he is charged with attempting. Then, the defendant must have engaged in conduct which constitutes a substantial step toward commission of the crime, conduct strongly corroborative of the firmness of the defendant's criminal intent. We note that the Fifth Circuit's analysis conforms closely to the sensible definition of an attempt proffered by the American Law Institute's Model Penal Code. . . .

Application of the foregoing to the instant case emphasizes the importance of a rule encouraging early police intervention where a suspect is clearly bent on the commission of crime. The undisputed testimony of Campbell and Young established that appellants intended to execute a successful bank robbery. Moreover, Stallworth and Sellers, in furtherance of their plan, took substantial steps that strongly corroborated their criminal intent. . . . A jury could properly find that preparation was long since complete. All that stood between appellants and success was a group of FBI agents and police officers. Their timely intervention probably prevented not only a robbery but possible bloodshed in an area crowded with noontime shoppers.

. . . Because the conduct of Stallworth and Sellers constituted an attempted bank robbery, the convictions must be affirmed.

PROBLEM

In United States v. Mandujano, 499 F.2d 370 (5th Cir. 1974), defendant was convicted of attempting to distribute heroin on the following facts:

> Alfonso H. Cavalier, Jr., [was] a San Antonio police officer assigned to the Office of Drug Abuse Law Enforcement. Agent Cavalier testified that, at the time the case arose, he was working in an undercover capacity and represented himself as a narcotics trafficker. . . . [P]ursuant to information Cavalier had received, he and a government informer went to the Tally-Ho Lounge. . . . Once inside the bar, the informant introduced Cavalier to Roy Mandujano. After some general conversation, Mandujano asked the informant if he was looking for "stuff." Cavalier said,

a. In footnote 4, the court noted: "The federal criminal code, unlike some state counterparts, see New York Penal Law §110.00, does not contain a general provision for the crime of attempt. . . . Attempted bank robbery is, however, an offense under federal law: 'Whoever, by force and violence, or by intimidation, takes, or attempts to take, from the person or presence of another any property or money or any other thing of value belonging to, or in the care, custody, control, management, or possession of, any bank . . . Shall be fined not more than $5,000 or imprisoned not more than twenty years, or both.' 18 U.S.C. §2113(a)."— EDS.

"Yes" . . . and told Mandujano he was looking for an ounce sample of heroin to
determine the quality of the material. Mandujano replied that he had good brown
Mexican heroin for $650.00 an ounce, but that if Cavalier wanted any of it he
would have to wait until later in the afternoon when the regular man made his
deliveries. Cavalier said that he was from out of town and did not want to wait
that long. Mandujano offered to locate another source, and made four telephone
calls in an apparent effort to do so. The phone calls appeared to be unsuccessful,
for Mandujano told Cavalier he wasn't having any luck contacting anybody. Cavalier
stated that he could not wait any longer. Then Mandujano said he had a good
contact, a man who kept narcotics around his home, but that if he went to see
this man, he would need the money "out front.". . . Cavalier counted out $650.00
to Mandujano, and Mandujano left the premises of the Tally-Ho Lounge at about
3:30 P.M. About an hour later, he returned and explained that he had been unable
to locate his contact. He gave back the $650.00 and told Cavalier he could still
wait until the regular man came around. Cavalier left, but arranged to call back
at 6:00 P.M. When Cavalier called at 6:00 and again at 6:30, he was told that
Mandujano was not available. Cavalier testified that he did not later attempt to
contact Mandujano, because, "based on the information that I had received, it
would be unsafe for either my informant or myself to return to this area."

If the so-called two-tiered test formulated in *Mandujano* and adopted in *Stallworth* is applied, should the conviction be affirmed?

MODEL PENAL CODE

Section 5.01. Criminal Attempt

[See Appendix for text of this section.]

NOTE

The eclectic approach of the Model Penal Code requires that conduct be
both a "substantial" step and itself corroborative of the actor's criminal purpose.
This approach has influenced courts in some jurisdictions that have not revised
their statutes, as may be seen in the *Stallworth* and *Mandujano* cases. Though
none of the recent codes appear to have adopted the Model Penal Code's use
of examples of substantial steps (but see La. Rev. Stat. Ann. tit. 14, 27(B)), a
fair number have adopted both the substantial-step formulation and the requirement that the act corroborate the intent. See, e.g., Conn. Gen. Stat. §53a-49;
Ill. Ann. Stat. ch. 38, 8-4; N.J. Stat. Ann. tit. 2C, §2C:5-1; Utah Code Ann.
§76-4-101. Others have adopted the substantial-step formulation without the
corroboration element. See, e.g., Ga. Code Ann. §26-1001; Minn. Stat. Ann.
§609.17; Pa. Stat. Ann. tit. 18, §901.

Worth special consideration are those states that have adopted approaches
different from that of the Model Penal Code:

(1) Some states adopt the substantial-step formulation but define it as an
"act or omission which leaves no reasonable doubt as to the defendant's intention
to commit the crime he is charged with attempting." See Del. Code Ann. tit.

11, §§531, 532; Ky. Rev. Stat. Ann. §500.010. Query: How does this alter the effect of the Model Penal Code formulation? Colorado defines a "substantial step" as one "which is strongly corroborative of the firmness of the actor's purpose" to commit the crime. Colo. Rev. Stat. ch. 40, §18-2-101. Query: What intention is behind the variation from the Model Penal Code's proposal?

(2) The Wisconsin provision states:

> An attempt to commit a crime requires that the actor have an intent to perform acts and attain a result which, if accomplished, would constitute such crime and that he does acts toward the commission of the crime which demonstrate unequivocally, under all the circumstances, that he formed that intent and would commit the crime except for the intervention of another person or some other extraneous factor.

Wis. Stat. Ann. tit. 45, §939.32(2). Supporting this provision, its drafter stated: "Emphasis upon the dangerous propensities of the actor as shown by his conduct, rather than upon how close he came to succeeding, is more appropriate to the purposes of the criminal law to protect society and reform offenders or render them temporarily harmless." Quoted in State v. Adams, 9 Wis. 2d 183, 188, 100 N.W.2d 592, 595 (1959). Query: Is the Wisconsin provision a formulation of Justice Salmond's equivocality test? How does it differ?

(3) Ohio provides: "No person, purposely or knowingly, and when purpose or knowledge is sufficient culpability for the commission of an offense, shall engage in conduct which, if successful, would constitute or result in the offense." Ohio Rev. Code tit. 29, §2923.0. In State v. Woods, 357 N.E.2d 1059 (1976), the Ohio Supreme Court interpreted this language as leaving it to the courts to determine what conduct suffices for an attempt and thereupon adopted the Model Penal Code formulation. Query: Is this a defensible interpretation? Would it be possible under the Montana statute, which states: "A person commits the offense of attempt when, with the purpose to commit a specific offense, he does any act toward commission of such offense"? Mont. Rev. Code Ann. tit. 94, §45-4-103.

STATE v. DAVIS

Supreme Court of Missouri
319 Mo. 1222, 6 S.W.2d 609 (1928)

Davis, C. [Defendant was convicted of attempted murder in the first degree on the following facts. He and Alberdina Lourie planned to have the latter's husband, Edmon Lourie, killed in order to collect the insurance and live together. He sought the help of Earl Leverton in obtaining an ex-convict to do the job, but Leverton disclosed the plot to Dill, a police officer, who decided to pose as the ex-convict. Defendant paid Dill $600 to carry out plans he had devised for killing Lourie. After several conferences and one aborted plan (the victim telegraphed that he would not be present at the planned site of the crime), a scheme was arranged whereby Dill was to appear at the Lourie home, kill Edmon, and feign a robbery by "mussing up" Alberdina and taking her jewels. At the appointed hour Dill appeared at the Lourie home but at this point revealed his identity. He then proceeded to defendant's home where he made an arrest.]

The sufficiency of the evidence to sustain the conviction is raised. The defining of an attempt to commit a crime and the ascertaining of its essential elements is necessary in the consideration of the question. . . .

The elements of an attempt are stated in 16 Corpus Juris, p. 113, thus: "An attempt to commit a crime consists of three elements: (1) The intention to commit the crime; (2) performance of some act toward the commission of the crime; and (3) the failure to consummate its commission."

The proof adduced advises us that the only debatable question is the presence of sufficient facts to demonstrate the second element. . . .

The physical overt act, which with intent and failure to consummate brings the crime of attempt into existence, is distinguishable from solicitation and preparation. An attempt to commit a crime involves an act on the part of the defendant moving directly toward the commission of the offense. With these concepts in mind we proceed to review the solicitations and preparations by defendant to murder Lourie as constituting an overt act.

In State v. Hayes, 78 Mo. 307, this court, through Phillips, C., said: "It is the recognized law of this country that the solicitation of another to commit a crime is an act toward the commission."

However, the proof in the above case developed, in addition to solicitations, an act on the part of the accused extending beyond solicitation or preparation, that of saturating a portion of the floor with coal oil, as well as the furnishing of plans and an oil can. Conceding that the court reached the proper result in that case, concerning which it is unnecessary to express an opinion, the basic facts there shown extend far beyond the facts here developed. While a few of the courts have treated solicitation to commit a crime as an attempt, the great weight of authority warrants the assertion that mere solicitation, unaccompanied by an act moving directly toward the commission of the intended crime, is not an overt act constituting an element of the crime of attempt. Solicitation of itself is a distinct offense when declared so by law. Therefore, in conformity with the weight of authority, we hold that merely soliciting one to commit a crime does not constitute an attempt.

The state contends that the arrangement of a plan for the accomplishment of the murder of Lourie and the selecting and hiring of the means or instrumentality by which the murder was to be consummated were demonstrated. We take it that the state means by the foregoing declarations that overt acts were shown. To that we do not agree. The evidence goes no further than developing a verbal arrangement with Dill, the selection of Dill as the one to kill Lourie, the delivery of a certain drawing and two photographs of Lourie to Dill, and the payment of a portion of the agreed consideration. These things were mere acts of preparation, failing to lead directly or proximately to the consummation of the intended crime. In this regard we have found no authority which holds that preparations constitute an overt act. . . .

The plans or arrangements amounted to nothing more than mere preparations. The contract of hiring entered into between defendant and Dill also fails to extend beyond mere preparation. In regard to the hiring, the trial court instructed the jury that the payment of money by defendant to Dill to commit the intended crime did not constitute such an overt act as was tantamount to an attempt. The ruling of the court we think was right, for the payment of money, was not an act moving directly toward the consummation of the intended crime. . . .

The employment of Dill as agent to murder Lourie was not tantamount to an attempt. Dill not only had no intention of carrying out the expressed purpose of defendant, but was guilty of no act directly or indirectly moving toward the consummation of the intended crime. He did nothing more than listen to the plans and solicitations of defendant without intending to act upon them. It was not shown that Dill committed an act that could be construed as an attempt. The arrest of Lourie, his wife, and defendant as detailed in the evidence could not be said to be an act involving the consummation of the crime. . . .

Whether it is necessary to make an actual assault before the crime of attempt can be said to come into existence, we need not decide, for the solicitations and preparations upon the part of defendant were not equivalent to an overt act which must take place before the crime of attempt comes into existence. . . .

It follows from what we have said that the judgment must be reversed, and the defendant discharged. It is so ordered.

NOTE ON THE CRIME OF SOLICITATION

At the common law, inciting or soliciting another to commit a crime was a crime itself, independent of any other act either of the person soliciting or the person solicited. For a long time, American codes did not, by and large, contain provisions incorporating this offense but rather made criminal the solicitation of particular crimes. However, as a result of the many criminal law revisions in recent years, a substantial number of states by now have general solicitation statutes. They are usually patterned after §5.02 of the Model Penal Code:

> A person is guilty of solicitation to commit a crime if with the purpose of promoting or facilitating its commission he commands, encourages or requests another person to engage in specific conduct which would constitute such crime or an attempt to commit such crime or which would establish his complicity in its commission or attempted commission.

See §5.02, Comment at 82, 88 (Tent. Draft No. 10, 1960), where this formulation of the crime of solicitation is defended as follows:

> There has been difference of opinion as to whether a genuine social danger is presented by solicitation to commit a crime. It has been argued, on the one hand, that the conduct of the solicitor is not dangerous since between it and the commision of the crime that is his object is the resisting will of an independent moral agent. By the same token it is urged that the solicitor, manifesting his reluctance to commit the crime himself, is not a menace of significance. Against this is the view that a solicitation is, if anything, more dangerous than a direct attempt, since it may give rise to the cooperation among criminals that is a special hazard. Solicitation may, indeed, be thought of as an attempt to conspire. Moreover, the solicitor, working his will through one or more agents, manifests an approach to crime more intelligent and masterful than the efforts of his hireling. Indeed, examples drawn from the controversial fields of political agitation and labor unrest suggest as a noncontroversial lesson that the imposition of liability for criminal solicitation

may be an important means by which the leadership of a movement deemed criminal may be suppressed.

We have no doubt ourselves upon the issue posed, which arises — it is well to note — not only in relation to inchoate crime but also (though less controversially) in dealing with complicity. Purposeful solicitation presents dangers calling for preventive intervention and is sufficiently indicative of a disposition towards criminal activity to call for liability. Moreover, the fortuity that the person solicited does not agree to commit or attempt to commit the incited crime plainly should not relieve the solicitor of liability, when otherwise he would be a conspirator or an accomplice. . . .

. . . [I]t remains a . . . question whether the punishment of solicitations should be curtailed in order to protect free speech. It cannot be seriously contended that one who uses words as a means to crime, who intends that his words should cause a criminal result, makes a contribution to community discussion which is worthy of protection. The problem is not in guarding him. The problem is in preventing legitimate agitation of an extreme or inflammatory nature from being misinterpreted as solicitation to crime. It would not be difficult to convince a jury that inflammatory rhetoric in behalf of an unpopular cause is in reality an invitation to violate the law rather than an effort to seek its change through legitimate criticism. Minority criticism has to be extreme in order to be politically audible and if it employs the typical device of lauding a martyr, who is likely to be a lawbreaker, the eulogy runs the risk of being characterized as a request for emulation.[26]

No solution to this problem has been found which is entirely satisfactory. The present section makes an effort to protect legitimate agitation by requiring that the criminal conduct allegedly solicited by the speaker must be "specific." It is, of course, unnecessary for the actor to go into great detail as to the manner in which the crime solicited is to be committed. But it is necessary under this formulation that, in the context of the knowledge and the position of the intended recipient, the solicitation carry meaning in terms of some concrete course of conduct that it is the actor's object to incite.

For a revealing examination of the issues created by the crime of solicitation to commit crime, see Greenawalt, Speech and Crime, [1980] Am. B. Foundation Research J. 645, 655-670.

NOTES AND QUESTIONS

1. Near the end of its opinion in the *Davis* case, the court states: "It was not shown that Dill committed an act that could be construed as an attempt." What difference would it have made if Dill *had* gone further than he had? Would the prosecution's difficulties have been resolved if Dill had been instructed by the district attorney to play the scene to the hilt, as, for example, by leveling his pistol at the husband's chest? Could this feigned overt act of attempt be

26. [Masses Pub. Co. v. Patten, 246 Fed. 24 (2d Cir. 1917)], involving a statutory incitement, brings home this point with great forcefulness. There was a scathing criticism of the United States' role in World War I and of the draft then existent, but the words used were equivocal and could be interpreted as mere agitation without advocacy to crime. Judge Hand, in the district court, found they did not constitute an incitement to crime, but the Court of Appeals reversed, holding that if the natural and reasonable result of what was said was to encourage resistance to a law, and the words were used in an endeavor to persuade such resistance, the words constituted an incitement to crime.

attributed to defendant as his, defendant's, genuine overt act of attempt? Since Dill was only a feigned participant, can defendant's guilt be made to rest at all on any of Dill's acts? See State v. Hayes, pages 634-635 infra.

The Commentary to the Model Penal Code, §5.02, Comment at 85-86 (Tent. Draft No. 10, 1960), reviews the judicial treatment of the question whether solicitation constitutes an attempt as follows:

> Whether the solicitation of another to commit a crime constitutes an attempt by the solicitor is a question which has been answered in several ways. One approach to the problem treats every solicitation as a specific type of attempt to be governed by ordinary attempt principles, the solicitation being an overt act which alone or together with other overt acts may surpass preparation and result in liability. A second position is that a naked solicitation is not an attempt, but a solicitation accompanied by other overt acts — for example, the offer of a reward or the furnishing of materials — does constitute an attempt. The third view is similar to the second except that in order to find the solicitor guilty of an attempt the other overt acts must proceed beyond what would be called preparation if the solicitor himself planned to commit the crime. Finally, there is the view that no matter what acts the solicitor does he cannot be guilty of an attempt because it is not his purpose personally to commit the offense.

2. In the normal solicitation situation, *D* solicits *E* to commit the crime. But in the *Davis* case, defendants solicited Leverton to solicit another person to kill Edmon Lourie, that is, *D* solicits *E* to solicit *F* to commit the crime. Although the court makes nothing of this difference and suggests that defendants would be guilty of the crime of solicitation, can it be argued to the contrary? In Regina v. Bodin and Bodin (Lincoln Crown Court, 1978), reported in [1979] Crim. L.R. 176, the trial court dismissed an incitement prosecution in this situation. There would obviously be serious objections to making it criminal to attempt to attempt. Should there be the same objections to making it criminal to incite to incite? Examine §5.02 of the Model Penal Code, Appendix to this casebook. Would this conduct be made criminal under that provision?

3. In considering the issues posed in the *Davis* case, compare G. Williams, Criminal Law: The General Part 616-617 (2d ed. 1961):

> The difference between incitement and attempt is that in the former the inciter will, if successful in his incitement, become a secondary party (an accessory or principal before the fact or in the second degree), whereas the attempter intends to be the principal in the first degree. (There may, of course, be a principal in the second degree to an attempt.)
>
> It follows from this distinction that one who "incites" an innocent agent, such as a dog or a young child, to commit a crime is guilty of attempt, not incitement. Again suppose that *D* unlawfully tells *E* to set a fire to a haystack, and gives him a match to do it with. (1) If, as *D* knows, *E* (mistakenly) believes that it is *D*'s stack and that the act is lawful, *E* is an innocent agent, and *D* is guilty of attempted arson; *D*, in instructing *E*, does the last thing that he intends in order to effect his criminal purpose. (It would be the same if he only used words and did not give *E* a match.) (2) If, as *D* knows, *E* is to be a conscious party to the crime, *D* is guilty of incitement. He is not guilty of attempt, because he does not intend to commit the crime as principal in the first degree.
>
> Two points may be noticed upon this example.

(1) The distinction is not precisely whether *E* is innocent or not, but whether *D* thinks *E* will be innocent.

(2) The distinction does not rest on the theory of proximity . . . for *D*'s words are just as proximate to the crime (if it comes to be committed) in the one case as in the other.

In the second of Professor Williams's hypotheticals, it is clear that *D* would be guilty of arson (as an accomplice) if *E* succeeded in setting fire to the haystack. But if *E* tries but fails, is there any reason why *D* should not be held as an accomplice in the crime of attempt committed by *E*? (Note that Professor Williams does not suggest that there is.) Is there any difficulty with the concept of aiding and abetting an attempt? See People v. Berger, pages 580-584 supra, where this was precisely the basis of defendant's liability.

Suppose, however, that *E* was apprehended before his acts had gone far enough to constitute an attempt, or that *E*, unknown to *D*, was actually a police agent who had no intention of committing the crime, as in the *Davis* case. Since *E* committed no crime of attempt, it would seem plain enough that *D* could not be successfully held as *E*'s accomplice. But why could he not be held for his own acts, that is, as guilty of attempting to be an accomplice in the crime of arson? But would such an approach not make every person guilty of attempt who solicits another to commit a crime? Is such a result not unnecessary so long as solicitation is itself a crime? Even where it is, however, is the doctrine of attempt to be an accomplice necessary in other situations, that is, where a person *aids* another (in contrast to *solicits* another) to commit a crime where the crime is neither committed nor attempted by the other person? Suppose, for example, a police officer, desiring to assist an illegal gambling operation, telephones the persons in charge to warn them that the police are on their way (Commonwealth v. Haines, 147 Pa. Super. 165, 24 A.2d 85 (1942)), or a driver brings a truck loaded with supplies of yeast and sugar to within yards of a still, which, unknown to him, is then in the hands of the police (West v. Commonwealth, 156 Va. 975, 157 S.E. 538 (1931)).

Consider the proposal of the Model Penal Code for dealing with these situations. Section 5.01(3) states:

> A person who engages in conduct designed to aid [a] another to commit a crime which would establish his complicity under Section 2.06 if the crime were committed by such other person is guilty of an attempt to commit the crime, although the crime is not committed or attempted by such other person.[b]

Consider how the *Davis* case would be decided under this provision.

PROBLEM

A hypothetical put by Professor Greenawalt, Speech and Crime, [1980] Am. B. Foundation Research J. 645, 662, is as follows:

---

a. Note that the provision does not say "aid *or solicit,*" the latter being the other way in which complicity may be established under §2.06. — Eds.

b. A number of recent statutes have adopted this approach. See, e.g., Colo. Rev. Stat. Ann. tit. 18, 18-2-101(2); Del. Code Ann. tit. 11, §533; Hawaii Rev. Stat. Ann. tit. 37, §705-501; Ky. Rev. Stat. Ann. ch. 500, §506.010(4); N.J. Stat. Ann. tit. 2C, §2C:5-1. — Eds.

A knows that his neighbor *B* is an important figure in organized crime, but *A* conceals his knowledge of this fact from *B*. Wishing that *C*, one of *B*'s employees, might be killed, *A* lets the fact that *C* is a police informer "slip out" in a conversation with *B*.

Query: Is *A* guilty of solicitation under traditional formulations? Under the Model Penal Code formulation in §5.02? Would *A* be criminally liable under any other section of the Model Penal Code, for example §2.06(3)(a)(ii) (attempting to aid)? If *B* kills *C*, can *A* be held for murder as an accomplice under §2.06? Under the causation provisions of §2.03 for having purposely caused the killing?

NOTE ON ABANDONMENT

Once the defendant has gone far enough toward the commission of an intended crime, so that under the prevailing tests the acts cease being mere preparation and constitute an attempt, can he or she escape punishment by abandoning the criminal purpose? If inchoate crimes are to be treated as consummated substantive crimes, the answer, of course, is negative, since remorse after the crime, whatever its effect on sentence, cannot affect criminality. But should the rule be otherwise when dealing with the inchoate crimes, like attempt, where the evil against which the crime is directed is the injury that is anticipated but that has not yet occurred? Should the answer depend on the reason for the defendant's change of heart? Defendant *A* voluntarily blows out a match he had lit for the purpose of committing arson because he hears a police siren. Defendant *B* does so because of last-minute promptings of conscience or perhaps because of a final failure of courage. In the first instance, there is little to be said for permitting defendant *A* to escape punishment; the cases clearly deny the defense. See People v. Corkery, 134 Cal. App. 294, 297, 25 P.2d 257, 258 (1933). But in the case of defendant *B*, if the requirement that a defendant's acts go beyond mere preparation is designed to insure that the danger of the defendant's committing the substantive crime (on this or another occasion) is real and substantial, can it be said that *B*'s voluntary abandonment at the last minute rebuts the inference that otherwise might properly be drawn from his prior acts? Does this depend on whether timidity or conscience is the motivating cause? Moreover, would the threat of punishment even after abandonment and retreat tend to undermine the promptings of the will to desist for whatever internal reason and therefore increase the chances of the crime's being committed? Might it matter whether defendant has committed his or her last act, as, for example, would be the case with defendant *B* if he had already lit a fuse, but then blew it out for the reasons given?

In Le Barron v. State, 32 Wis. 2d 294, 145 N.W.2d 79, 80 (1966), defendant assaulted a woman with intent to rape her. He forced her into a shack and up against the wall.

As she struggled for her breath he said, "You know what else I want," unzipped his pants and started pulling up her skirt. She finally succeeded in removing his hand from her mouth, and after reassuring him that she would not scream, told him she was pregnant and pleaded with him to desist or he would hurt her baby.

He then felt of her stomach and took her over to the door of the shack, where in the better light he was able to ascertain that, under her coat, she was wearing maternity clothes. He thereafter let her alone and left after warning her not to scream or call the police or he would kill her.

Query: Should a defense of abandonment be upheld on these facts?

The Model Penal Code formulates a defense of "renunciation of criminal purpose" in §5.01(4). Its text should be carefully examined. See Appendix to this casebook.

Compare the provision in N.Y. Penal Code §40.10:

> 3. In any prosecution pursuant to Section 110.00 for an attempt to commit a crime, it is an affirmative defense that, under circumstances manifesting a voluntary and complete renunciation of his criminal purpose, the defendant avoided the commission of the crime attempted by abandoning his criminal effort and, if mere abandonment was insufficient to accomplish such avoidance, by taking further and affirmative steps which prevented the commission thereof.

Similar provisions have been enacted in a number of jurisdictions that have revised their criminal codes in recent years.

4. Impossibility

PEOPLE v. JAFFE
New York Court of Appeals
185 N.Y. 497, 78 N.E. 169 (1906)

BARTLETT, J. The indictment charged that the defendant on the 6th day of October, 1902, in the county of New York, feloniously received 20 yards of cloth, of the value of 25 cents a yard, belonging to the copartnership of J. W. Goddard & Son, knowing that the said property had been feloniously stolen, taken, and carried away from the owners. It was found under section 550 of the Penal Code, which provides that a person who buys or receives any stolen property knowing the same to have been stolen is guilty of criminally receiving such property. The defendant was convicted of an attempt to commit the crime charged in the indictment. The proof clearly showed, and the district attorney conceded upon the trial, that the goods which the defendant attempted to purchase on October 6, 1902, had lost their character as stolen goods at the time when they were offered to the defendant and when he sought to buy them. In fact the property had been restored to the owners and was wholly within their control and was offered to the defendant by their authority and through their agency. The question presented by this appeal, therefore, is whether upon an indictment for receiving goods, knowing them to have been stolen, the defendant may be convicted of an attempt to commit the crime where it appears without dispute that the property which he sought to receive was not in fact stolen property.

The conviction was sustained by the Appellate Division chiefly upon the authority of the numerous cases in which it has been held that one may be convicted of an attempt to commit a crime notwithstanding the existence of facts unknown to him which would have rendered the complete perpetration of the crime itself impossible. Notably among these are what may be called the "Pickpocket Cases," where, in prosecutions for attempts to commit larceny from the person by pocket-picking, it is held not to be necessary to allege or prove that there was anything in the pocket which could be the subject of larceny. Much reliance was also placed in the opinion of the learned Appellate Division upon the case of People v. Gardner, 144 N.Y. 119, 38 N.E. 1003, where a conviction of an attempt to commit the crime of extortion was upheld, although the woman from whom the defendant sought to obtain money by a threat to accuse her of a crime was not induced to pay the money by fear, but was acting at the time as a decoy for the police, and hence could not have been subjected to the influence of fear. In passing upon the question here presented for our determination, it is important to bear in mind precisely what it was that the defendant attempted to do. He simply made an effort to purchase certain specific pieces of cloth. He believed the cloth to be stolen property, but it was not such in fact. The purchase, therefore, if it had been completely effected, could not constitute the crime of receiving stolen property, knowing it to be stolen, since there could be no such thing as knowledge on the part of the defendant of a nonexistent fact, although there might be a belief on his part that the fact existed. As Mr. Bishop well says, it is a mere truism *that there can be no receiving of stolen goods which have not been stolen.* 2. Bishop's New Crim. Law, §1140. It is equally difficult to perceive how there can be an attempt to receive stolen goods, knowing them to have been stolen, when they have not been stolen in fact.

The crucial distinction between the case before us and the pickpocket cases, and others involving the same principle, lies not in the possibility or impossibility of the commission of the crime, but in the fact that, in the present case, the act, which it was doubtless the intent of the defendant to commit would not have been a crime if it had been consummated. If he had actually paid for the goods which he desired to buy and received them into his possession, he would have committed no offense under section 550 of the Penal Code, because the very definition in that section of the offense of criminally receiving property makes it an essential element of the crime that the accused shall have known the property to have been stolen or wrongfully appropriated in such a manner as to constitute larceny. This knowledge being a material ingredient of the offense it is manifest that it cannot exist unless the property has in fact been stolen or larcenously appropriated. No man can know that to be so which is not so in truth and in fact. He may believe it to be so but belief is not enough under this statute. In the present case it appeared, not only by the proof, but by the express concession of the prosecuting officer, that the goods which the defendant intended to purchase had lost their character as stolen goods at the time of the proposed transaction. Hence, no matter what was the motive of the defendant, and no matter what he supposed, he could do no act which was intrinsically adapted to the then present successful perpetration of the crime denounced by this section of the Penal Code, because neither he nor any one in the world could know that the property was stolen property inasmuch as it was not, in fact, stolen property. In the pickpocket cases the immediate act which the defendant had in contemplation was an act which, if it could have been carried out, would have been criminal, whereas in the present case the immediate act which the defendant had in contemplation (to wit, the purchase of the goods which were brought to his place for sale) could not have been criminal under the statute even if the purchase had been completed, because the goods had not, in fact, been stolen, but were, at the time when they were offered to him, in the custody and under the control of the true owners.

If all which an accused person intends to do would, if done, constitute no crime, it cannot be a crime to attempt to do with the same purpose a part of the thing intended. The crime of which the defendant was convicted necessarily consists of three elements: First, the act; second, the intent; and third, the knowledge of an existing condition. There was proof tending to establish two of these elements, the first and second, but none to establish the existence of the third. This was knowledge of the stolen character of the property sought to be acquired. There could be no such knowledge. The defendant could not know that the property possessed the character of stolen property when it had not in fact been acquired by theft. The language used by Ruger, Ch. J., in People v. Moran, 123 N.Y. 254, 25 N.E. 412, to the effect that "the question whether an attempt to commit a crime has been made is determinable solely by the condition of the actor's mind and his conduct in the attempted consummation of his design," although accurate in those cases, has no application to a case like this, where, if the accused had completed the act which he attempted to do, he would not be guilty of a criminal offense. A particular belief cannot make that a crime which is not so in the absence of such belief. Take, for example, the case of a young man who attempts to vote, and succeeds in casting his vote under the belief that he is but 20 years of age, when he is in fact over 21 and a qualified voter. His intent to commit a crime, and his belief that he was committing a crime, would not make him guilty of any offense under these circumstances, although the moral turpitude of the transaction, on his part, would be just as great as it would if he were in fact under age. So also, in the case of a prosecution under the statute of this state, which makes it rape in the second degree for a man to perpetrate an act of sexual intercourse with a female not his wife under the age of 18 years. There could be no conviction if it was established upon the trial that the female was in fact over the age of 18 years, although the defendant believed her to be younger and intended to commit the crime. No matter how reprehensible would be his act in morals, it would not be the act forbidden by this particular statute. "If what a man contemplates doing would not be in law a crime, he could not be said, in point of law, to intend to commit the crime. If he thinks his act will be a crime, this is a mere mistake of his understanding where the law holds it not to be such, his real intent being to do a particular thing. If the thing is not a crime, he does not intend to commit one whatever he may erroneously suppose." 1 Bishop's Crim. Law (7th Ed.) §742.

The judgment of the Appellate Division and of the Court of General Sessions must be reversed, and the defendant discharged upon this indictment, as it is manifest that no conviction can be had thereunder. This discharge, however, in no wise affects the right to prosecute the defendant for other offenses of a like character concerning which there is some proof in the record, but which were not charged in the present indictment.

PEOPLE v. DLUGASH

New York Court of Appeals
41 N.Y.2d 725, 363 N.E.2d 1155 (1977)

JASEN, J. . . . For years, serious studies have been made on the subject in an effort to resolve the continuing controversy when, if at all, the impossibility of successfully completing the criminal act should preclude liability for even making the futile attempt. The 1967 revision of the Penal Law approached the impossibility defense to the inchoate crime of attempt in a novel fashion. The statute provides that, if a person engages in conduct which would otherwise constitute an attempt to commit a crime,

> it is no defense to a prosecution for such attempt that the crime charged to have been attempted was, under the attendant circumstances, factually or legally impossible of commission, if such crime could have been committed had the attendant circumstances been as such person believed them to be.

(Penal Law, §110.10.) This appeal presents to us, for the first time, a case involving the application of the modern statute. We hold that, under the proof presented by the People at trial, defendant Melvin Dlugash may be held for attempted murder, though the target of the attempt may have already been slain, by the hand of another [Bush], when Dlugash made his felonious attempt.

On December 22, 1973, Michael Geller, 25 years old, was found shot to death in the bedroom of his Brooklyn apartment. The body, which had literally been riddled by bullets, was found lying face up on the floor. An autopsy revealed that the victim had been shot in the face and head no less than seven times. Powder burns on the face indicated that the shots had been fired from within one foot of the victim. Four small caliber bullets were recovered from the victim's skull. The victim had also been critically wounded in the chest. . . . Subsequent ballistics examination established that the four bullets recovered from the victim's head were .25 caliber bullets and that the heart-piercing bullet was of .38 caliber. . . .

. . . Defendant stated [to police] that, on the night of December 21, 1973, he, Bush and Geller had been out drinking. Bush had been staying at Geller's apartment and, during the course of the evening, Geller several times demanded that Bush pay $100 towards the rent on the apartment. According to defendant, Bush rejected these demands, telling Geller that "you better shut up or you're going to get a bullet." All three returned to Geller's apartment at approximately midnight, took seats in the bedroom, and continued to drink until sometime between 3:00 and 3:30 in the morning. When Geller again pressed his demand for rent money, Bush drew his .38 caliber pistol, aimed it at Geller and fired three times. Geller fell to the floor. After the passage of a few minutes, perhaps two, perhaps as much as five, defendant walked over to the fallen Geller, drew his .25 caliber pistol, and fired approximately five shots in the victim's head and face. Defendant contended that, by the time he fired the shots, "it looked like Mike Geller was already dead.". . .

After [Officer] Carrasquillo had taken the bulk of the statement, he asked the defendant why he would do such a thing. According to Carrasquillo, the defendant said, "gee, I really don't know." Carrasquillo repeated the question

10 minutes later, but received the same response. After a while, Carrasquillo asked the question for a third time and defendant replied, "well, gee, I guess it must have been because I was afraid of Joe Bush."

. . . At the trial . . . the prosecution sought to establish that Geller was still alive at the time defendant shot at him. Both physicians testified that each of the two chest wounds, for which defendant alleged Bush to be responsible, would have caused death without prompt medical attention. Moreover, the victim would have remained alive until such time as his chest cavity became fully filled with blood. Depending on the circumstances, it might take 5 to 10 minutes for the chest cavity to fill. Neither prosecution witness could state, with medical certainty, that the victim was still alive when, perhaps five minutes after the initial chest wounds were inflicted, the defendant fired at the victim's head.

The defense produced but a single witness, the former Chief Medical Examiner of New York City. This expert stated that, in his view, Geller might have died of the chest wounds "very rapidly" since, in addition to the bleeding, a large bullet going through a lung and the heart would have other adverse medical effects. . . .

The trial court declined to charge the jury, as requested by the prosecution, that defendant could be guilty of murder on the theory that he had aided and abetted the killing of Geller by Bush. Instead, the court submitted only two theories to the jury: that defendant had either intentionally murdered Geller or had attempted to murder Geller.

The jury found the defendant guilty of murder. . . .

On appeal, the Appellate Division reversed the judgment of conviction on the law and dismissed the indictment. The court ruled that "the People failed to prove beyond a reasonable doubt that Geller had been alive at the time he was shot by defendant; defendant's conviction of murder thus cannot stand.". . . Further, the court held that the judgment could not be modified to reflect a conviction for attempted murder because "the uncontradicted evidence is that the defendant, at the time that he fired the five shots into the body of the decedent, believed him to be dead, and . . . there is not a scintilla of evidence to contradict his assertion in that regard.". . .

Preliminarily, we state our agreement with the Appellate Division that the evidence did not establish, beyond a reasonable doubt, that Geller was alive at the time defendant fired into his body. To sustain a homicide conviction, it must be established, beyond a reasonable doubt, that the defendant caused the death of another person. (Penal Law, §125.00; C.P.L. 70.20.). . . While the defendant admitted firing five shots at the victim approximately two to five minutes after Bush had fired three times, all three medical expert witnesses testified that they could not, with any degree of medical certainty, state whether the victim had been alive at the time the latter shots were fired by the defendant. Thus, the People failed to prove beyond a reasonable doubt that the victim had been alive at the time he was shot by the defendant. Whatever else it may be, it is not murder to shoot a dead body. . . .

[W]e must now decide whether, under the evidence presented, the defendant may be held for attempted murder, though someone else perhaps succeeded in killing the victim. . . .

The most intriguing attempt cases are those where the attempt to commit a crime was unsuccessful due to mistakes of fact or law on the part of the would-be criminal. A general rule developed in most American jurisdictions that legal impossibility is a good defense but factual impossibility is not. . . . Thus, for example, it was held that defendants who shot at a stuffed deer did not attempt to take a deer out of season, even though they believed the dummy to be a live animal. The court stated that there was no criminal attempt because it was no crime to "take" a stuffed deer, and it is no crime to attempt to do that which is legal. (State v. Guffey, 262 S.W.2d 152 [Mo. App.]; see, also, State v. Taylor, 345 Mo. 325, 133 S.W.2d 336 [no liability for attempt to bribe a juror where person bribed was not, in fact, a juror].) These cases are illustrative of legal impossibility. . . .

On the other hand, factual impossibility was no defense. For example, a man was held liable for attempted murder when he shot into the room in which his target usually slept and, fortuitously, the target was sleeping elsewhere in the house that night. (State v. Mitchell, 170 Mo. 633, 71 S.W. 175.) Although one bullet struck the target's customary pillow, attainment of the criminal objective was factually impossible. . . . On the same view, it was held that men who had sexual intercourse with a woman, with the belief that she was alive and did not consent to the intercourse, could be charged for attempted rape when the woman had, in fact, died from an unrelated ailment prior to the acts of intercourse. (United States v. Thomas, 13 U.S.C.M.A. 278.)

The New York cases can be parsed out along similar lines. One of the leading cases on legal impossibility is People v. Jaffe, 185 N.Y. 497, 78 N.E. 169, in which we held that there was no liability for the attempted receipt of stolen property when the property received by the defendant in the belief that it was stolen was, in fact under the control of the true owner. . . . Similarly, in People v. Teal, 196 N.Y. 372, 89 N.E. 1086, a conviction for attempted subornation of perjury was overturned on the theory that the testimony attempted to be suborned was irrelevant to the merits of the case. Since it was not subornation of perjury to solicit false, but irrelevant, testimony, "the person through whose procuration the testimony is given cannot be guilty of subornation of perjury and, by the same rule, an unsuccessful attempt to that which is not a crime when effectuated, cannot be held to be an attempt to commit the crime specified." Factual impossibility, however, was no defense. Thus, a man could be held for attempted grand larceny when he picked an empty pocket. (People v. Moran, 123 N.Y. 254, 25 N.E. 412.). . .

As can be seen from even this abbreviated discussion, the distinction between "factual" and "legal" impossibility was a nice one indeed and the courts tended to place a greater value on legal form than on any substantive danger the defendant's actions posed for society. The approach of the draftsmen of the Model Penal Code was to eliminate the defense of impossibility in virtually all situations. [See §5.01(1), Appendix to this casebook.] Under the code provision, to constitute an attempt, it is still necessary that the result intended or desired by the actor constitute a crime. However, the code suggested a fundamental change to shift the locus of analysis to the actor's mental frame of reference and away from undue dependence upon external considerations. The basic premise of the code provision is that what was in the actor's own mind should be the standard for determining his dangerousness to society and, hence, his liability for attempted criminal conduct. . . . In the belief that neither of the two branches of the traditional impossibility arguments detracts from the offender's moral culpability . . . the Legislature substantially carried the [Model Penal] code's treatment of impossibility into the 1967 revision of the Penal Law. . . . Thus, a person is guilty of an attempt when, with intent to commit a crime, he engages in conduct which tends to effect the commission of such crime. (Penal Law, §110.00.) It is no defense that, under the attendant circumstances, the crime was factually or legally impossible of commission, "if such crime could have been commited had the attendant circumstances been as such person believed them to be." (Penal Law, §110.10.) Thus, if defendant believed the victim to be alive at the time of the shooting, it is no defense to the charge of attempted murder that the victim may have been dead.

Turning to the facts of the case before us, we believe that there is sufficient evidence in the record from which the jury could conclude that the defendant believed Geller to be alive at the time defendant fired shots into Geller's head. . . .

The jury convicted the defendant of murder. Necessarily, they found that defendant intended to kill a live human being. Subsumed within this finding is the conclusion that defendant acted in the belief that Geller was alive. Thus, there is no need for additional fact findings by a jury. Although it was not established beyond a reasonable doubt that Geller was, in fact, alive, such is no defense to attempted murder since a murder would have been committed "had the attendant circumstances been as [defendant] believed them to be." (Penal Law, §110.10.) The jury necessarily found that defendant believed Geller to be alive when defendant shot at him.

The Appellate Division erred in not modifying the judgment to reflect a conviction for the lesser included offense of attempted murder. . . .

NOTE ON THE IMPOSSIBILITY DEFENSE

Prior to the enactment of statutes addressed to the issue of impossibility, courts had taken a variety of positions on the defense of impossibility in attempt prosecutions. All courts agreed that legal impossibility is a defense where what the actor actually had in mind to do was not made criminal, even if he or she thought it was. But there was a great dispute over whether legal impossibility as a defense had any other applications and, if it did, what distinguished it from factual impossibility, which was not a defense.

For example, the California Supreme Court, without any statute on the subject, reached the opposite conclusion from that reached in *Jaffe* on a case virtually on all fours with it. People v. Rojas, 55 Cal. 2d 252, 358 P.2d 921, 924 (1961). As in New York at the time *Jaffe* was decided, the California court had approved convictions of attempted larceny where a pickpocket picked an empty pocket and of attempted extortion where the "victim" was not acting under defendant's threat, but rather in league with the police. It had also upheld a conviction of attempted theft by false pretenses where, for the same reason, the "victim" was not deceived. However, the California court failed to see the distinction the *Jaffe* court saw between these cases and the case before it of attempted receipt of stolen property. Each of those cases, it concluded, was decided

on a hypothesis that the defendants had the specific intent to commit the substantive offense and that under the circumstances as the defendants reasonably saw them they did the acts necessary to consummate the substantive offense; but because of circumstances unknown to defendants, essential elements of the substantive crime were lacking.

The court saw the case before it as falling under the same principle and invoked the reasoning of the false pretenses case, People v. Camodeca, 52 Cal. 2d 142, 338 P.2d 903, 906 (1959),[6] in which the court stated:

> One of the purposes of the criminal law is to protect society from those who intend to injure it. When it is established that the defendant intended to commit a specific crime and that in carrying out this intention he committed an act that caused harm or sufficient danger of harm, it is immaterial that for some collateral reason he could not complete the intended crime. Although the law does not impose punishment for guilty intent alone, it does impose punishment when guilty intent is coupled with action that would result in a crime but for the intervention of some fact or circumstance unknown to the defendant. . . . In the present case there was not a legal but only a factual impossibility of consummating the intended offense, i.e., the intended victim was not deceived.

The extensive rewriting of American criminal codes stimulated by the Model Penal Code has had a decisive influence on the result, if not the merits, of the debate. About two-thirds of the states have completed new codes. All of them, except for a few with no provisions on the subject,[7] have rejected the impossibility defense entirely. Most have adopted provisions, modeled on the New York provision discussed in the *Dlugash* case, that explicitly deny the defense.[8] The rest adopted the Model Penal Code provision, which excludes the defense by defining an attempt as purposely engaging in conduct "which would constitute the crime if the attendant circumstances were as [the actor] believes them to be." Section 5.01.[9]

The debate continues, however, where the legislature has not resolved it, with some courts continuing to adhere to the *Jaffe* view or variations of it. The legislative rejection of the defense has been matched by a striking judicial acceptance of it,[10] and it will help illuminate some basic issues of the criminal law to reflect on why this has been so. Consider the following cases:

---

6. In this case, defendant tried to exact money from a bar owner on the false representation that he needed it to bribe a state official to clear up some difficulty with the bar owner's license. The bar owner learned that defendant was lying and arranged for police to overhear and record a meeting at which these representations were renewed. The court upheld a conviction of attempted grand larceny by false pretenses.

7. E.g., N.M. Stat. Ann. ch. 30, §30-28-1; Tex. Pen. Code Ann. §15.01.

8. E.g., Colo. Rev. Stat. Ann. tit. 18, §18-2-101; Ill. Ann. Stat. ch. 28, §8-4; La. Rev. Stat. Ann. tit. 14, §27; Pa. Cons. Stat. Ann. tit. 18, §901.

9. E.g., Hawaii Rev. Stat. tit. 17, §705.500; N.J. Stat. Ann. tit. 2C, §2C-5-1.

10. On facts substantially the same as those presented in People v. Jaffe and People v. Rojas, both the House of Lords (Haughton v. Roger Smith, [1975] A.C. 476) and the Supreme Court of New Zealand (Regina v. Donnelly, [1970] N.Z.L.R. 980) reached conclusions in accord with *Jaffe*. The position of the House of Lords in the *Roger Smith* case was later rejected by Parliament in §1(2) of The Criminal Attempts Act of 1981: "A person may be guilty of attempting to commit an offence . . . even though the facts are such that the commission of the offence is impossible." Professor Glanville Williams, in his Textbook of Criminal Law 392 (1978), introduces his searching examination of the *Roger Smith* case with a piece from the Daily Telegraph headlined Equine to Asinine: "A man who bought an ounce of horse manure from a hippie in the West End, thinking it was cannabis, was fined £5 at North London court yesterday for attempting to procure cannabis."

UNITED STATES v. BERRIGAN, 482 F.2d 171 (3d Cir. 1973): [Father Berrigan, an imprisoned Vietnam War resister, was convicted of an attempt to violate a federal statute making it criminal to take anything into or out of a federal prison contrary to regulations of the Attorney General. The latter had promulgated a regulation prohibiting such traffic "without the knowledge and consent" of the prison warden. The conviction was based on evidence that Berrigan had smuggled letters into and out of a prison through a courier, believing that the warden was ignorant of what was going on, though in fact the warden had prior knowledge of the arrangement and had agreed to let the courier pretend cooperation in the plan. The court reversed a conviction on the following reasoning:] Generally speaking factual impossibility is said to occur when extraneous circumstances unknown to the actor or beyond his control prevent consummation of the intended crime. The classic example is the man who puts his hand in the coat pocket of another with the intent to steal his wallet and finds the pocket empty. . . . Legal impossibility is said to occur where the intended acts, even if completed, would not amount to a crime. Thus, legal impossibility would apply to those circumstances where (1) the motive, desire and expectation is to perform an act in violation of the law; (2) there is intention to perform a physical act; (3) there is a performance of the intended physical act; and (4) the consequence resulting from the intended act does not amount to a crime.[35]

Were intent to break the law the sole criterion to be considered in determining criminal responsibility . . . we could sustain the conviction. . . . Clearly, it can be said that Father Berrigan intended to send letters to Sister McAlister. . . . Normally, of course, the exchange of letters is not a federal offense. Where one of the senders is in prison, however, the sending may or may not be a criminal offense. If the letter is sent within normal channels with the consent and knowledge of the warden it is not a criminal offense. Therefore, an attempt to send a letter through normal channels cannot be considered an attempt to violate the law because none of the intended consequences is in fact criminal. If the letter is sent without the knowledge and consent of the warden, it is a criminal offense and so is the attempt because both the intended consequence and the actual consequence are in fact criminal. Here, we are faced with a third situation where there is a motivation, desire and expectation of sending a letter without the knowledge and consent, and the intended act is performed, but unknown to the sender, the transmittal is accomplished with the knowledge and consent of the warden.

Applying the principles of the law of attempt to the instant case, the writing of the letters, and their copying and transmittal by the courier . . . constituted the *Act.* This much the government proved. What the government did not prove — and could not prove because it was a legal impossibility — was the "external, objective situation which the substantive law may require to be present," to-wit, absence of knowledge and consent of the warden. Thus, the govern-

---

35. Intent as used in this connection must be distinguished from motive, desire and expectation. If C by reason of his hatred of A plans to kill him, but mistaking B for A shoots B, his motive desire and expectation are to kill A but his intent is to kill B. . . . If A takes an umbrella which he believes to belong to B, but which in fact is his own, he does not have the intent to steal, his intent being to take the umbrella he grasps in his hand, which is his own umbrella. . . . If a man mistakes a stump for his enemy and shoots at it, notwithstanding his desire and expectation to shoot his enemy, his intent is to shoot the object aimed at, which is the stump. Keedy, Criminal Attempts at Common Law, 102 U. of Pa. L. Rev. 464, 466-467 (1954). . . .

ment failed to prove the *"Circumstances or attendant circumstances"* vital to the offense. Without such proof, the *Consequence* or *Result* did not constitute an offense that violated the federal statute. . . . Simply stated, attempting to do that which is not a crime is not attempting to commit a crime.

UNITED STATES v. OVIEDO, 525 F.2d 881 (5th Cir. 1976): [An undercover agent contacted defendant and asked to buy heroin. Defendant agreed and appeared at an arranged time and place with what he claimed was heroin. The agent then performed a field test with positive result and arrested defendant. However, a later laboratory test of the substance revealed it was not in fact heroin but procaine hydrochloride (not a controlled substance), which happens to give a positive reaction to the usual field test. The prosecution therefore charged defendant with attempted distribution of heroin, and a jury convicted, apparently rejecting defendant's testimony that he knew the substance was not heroin and was only trying to "rip off" the agent. On appeal, the Fifth Circuit reversed the conviction.

[The court rejected the traditional distinction between legal and factual impossibility, saying:] These definitions are not particularly helpful here, for they do nothing more than provide a different focus for the analysis. In one sense, the impossibility involved here might be deemed legal, for those *acts* which Oviedo set in motion, the transfer of the substance in his possession, were not a crime. In another sense, the impossibility is factual, for the *objective* of Oviedo, the sale of heroin, was proscribed by law, and failed only because of a circumstance unknown to Oviedo.

[However, the court also rejected an approach that would find an attempt because the objective of defendant was criminal, since "It would allow us to punish one's thoughts, desires, or motives, through indirect evidence, without reference to any objective fact." The court concluded:] We reject the notion . . . , adopted by the district court, that the conviction in the present case can be sustained since there is sufficient proof of intent, not because of any doubt as to the sufficiency of the evidence in that regard, but because of the inherent dangers such a precedent would pose in the future. . . .

When the defendant sells a substance which is actually heroin, it is reasonable to infer that he knew the physical nature of the substance, and to place on him the burden of dispelling that inference. . . . However, if we convict the defendant of attempting to sell heroin for the sale of a non-narcotic substance, we eliminate an objective element that has major evidentiary significance and we increase the risk of mistaken conclusions that the defendant believed the goods were narcotics.

Thus, we demand that in order for a defendant to be guilty of a criminal attempt, the objective acts performed, without any reliance on the accompanying mens rea, mark the defendant's conduct as criminal in nature. . . .

. . . We cannot conclude that the objective acts of Oviedo apart from any indirect evidence of intent mark his conduct as criminal in nature. Rather, those acts are consistent with a noncriminal enterprise. Therefore, we will not allow the jury's determination of Oviedo's intent to form the sole basis of a criminal offense.

THE CASE OF LADY ELDON'S FRENCH LACE
A hypothetical decision on a hypothetical state of facts, by the editors

A perennial in the crop of attempt hypotheticals was suggested by Dr. Wharton.[1] "Lady Eldon, when traveling with her husband on the Continent, bought what she supposed to be a quantity of French lace, which she hid, concealing it from Lord Eldon in one of the pockets of the coach. The package was brought to light by a customs officer at Dover. The lace turned out to be an English manufactured article, of little value, and of course, not subject to duty. Lady Eldon had bought it at a price vastly above its value, believing it to be genuine, intending to smuggle it into England." Dr. Wharton, supra, and Professor Sayre[2] conclude that she could be found guilty of an attempt since she intended to smuggle dutiable lace into England. Professor Keedy disagrees, finding the fallacy of the argument in the failure to recognize "that the particular lace which Lady Eldon intended to bring into England was not subject to duty and therefore, although there was the wish to smuggle, there was not the intent to do so."[3]

Keedy, of course, was employing the distinction he has advanced between intent, on the one hand, and motive, desire, and expectation, on the other,[4] a distinction that served as the linchpin of the decision in People v. Jaffe, supra, and United States v. Berrigan, supra. As he sees it, what people intend to do on a particular occasion is to be determined by what they do in fact, rather than by what they thought they were doing. The lace was in fact not dutiable; thus, there was no intent on the part of Lady Eldon to smuggle dutiable French lace into the country, and there could be no conviction of the crime of attempt to do so, since what she intended to do on this view was not a crime — a straightforward case of legal impossibility. Professor Perkins has not, so far as we can tell, addressed himself to this particular case. But from what he has written it is clear that he would concur with Keedy. Presumably his analysis would rest on his distinction between primary and secondary intent.[5] Only the former may be considered in determining the existence of the necessary intent to establish an attempt. It, like Keedy's term *intent,* is determined by what the actor objectively and in fact did. What the actor believed he was doing, on the level of the facts as the actor took them to be, constitutes secondary intent. Apparently the latter is basically the same in description and function as what Keedy refers to as the motive, desire, or expectation.

We concur with Wharton and Sayre.

We submit, with respect, that Keedy and Perkins, and the courts that follow their reasoning, have been guilty of some plain silliness in supporting their position. Their conclusion that Lady Eldon must be acquitted rests on the premise that what a person intends to do is what he actually does, even if that was the furthest thing from the person's mind:

"You're eating my salad."

"Sorry, I didn't mean to; I thought it was mine."

1. 1 Criminal Law 304 n. 9 (12th ed. 1932).
2. Criminal Attempts, 41 Harv. L. Rev. 821, 852 (1928).
3. Criminal Attempts at Common Law, 102 U. Pa. L. Rev. 464, 477 n. 85 (1954).
4. Id. at 466-468.
5. Perkins, Criminal Attempt and Related Problems, 2 U.C.L.A.L. Rev. 319, 330-332 (1955).

"You might have *thought* it was yours. But in fact it was mine. Therefore you intended to eat mine. You should be ashamed!"

Surely this is an extraordinary way of regarding what a person intended, quite at odds with common sense and common language. Where a circumstance is not known to the actor, in no way consistent with straight thought can his act be regarded as intentional as to that circumstance.[6]

But, of course, it is hardly unknown for courts to adopt strained and artificial reasoning in support of a sound result otherwise thought beyond their reach. Is that the case here? Is it sound to conclude that the type of conduct engaged in by Lady Eldon should not be made criminal? Let us consider if it is.

Suppose Lady Eldon believed she had purchased an inexpensive English lace but in fact had purchased an expensive French lace. Certainly she could not be found guilty of smuggling if she got past the customs inspector or of an attempt if she failed. The reason is that the intent to smuggle French lace, necessary to establish either offense, does not exist. (We are assuming this is not a crime of absolute liability). And it does not exist because her intent is judged by what she believed she was doing and not by what she in fact did. Now why should it make any more difference in Wharton's hypothetical that her act was objectively lawful than it does in our variation that her act was objectively unlawful? Why in both cases should not the intent be judged by the same standard, what she believed she was doing, rather than what she did in fact?

It may be answered that while an innocent mind can exculpate, a criminal mind simpliciter cannot implicate. The reasoning might be as follows: There is no legitimate purpose to be served by punishing those who mean to act blamelessly; and while a purpose could be served by punishing a person who decides to commit a crime (to the extent that all must first decide to commit an intentional crime before actually committing it, some will thereby be prevented from committing it, at this or another occasion) other considerations make it inexpedient and undesirable to do so. What are those considerations? They are those, presumably, which underlie the principle which forbids punishing a man for his thoughts alone; i.e., that thinking evil is not a reliable indication that a man will do evil and the criminal law may properly concern itself only with acts. See pages 257-259 supra.

But can this be said of Lady Eldon? Has she merely *thought* to smuggle French lace? Or rather has she *done* everything in her power and all she thought necessary to smuggle French lace? Has she shown herself to be less eligible for the imposition of criminal sanctions because, through no fault of her own, she failed? Surely not.

From the basic postulate that the law concerns itself with acts and not thoughts, it may be argued that the law is concerned not with what a person *may* do but with what he in fact *does*. This, however, is quite erroneous. There are many crimes that may be established without proof that acts have occurred that have invaded the interest sought to be protected. The law of attempts and conspiracy are prime examples. It is what is apprehended that the actor would subsequently do and not what he has done that constitutes the basis of

---

6. G. Williams, Criminal Law: The General Part 113 (1953).

criminality. As Holmes has pointed out, even larceny may be viewed in this way, since there is no requirement that the possessor be permanently deprived of his property, only that the actor intend so to deprive him.[7] Looked at objectively, apart from intent, the acts done may be wholly innocuous — like striking a match or having a quiet conversation. The innocuous acts are made criminal because, combined with the requisite intent of the actor, they demonstrate him to be sufficiently likely to commit the injury that the law seeks to prevent, to justify the application of criminal sanctions.

Perhaps it may be argued that there is a different policy consideration supporting exculpation in cases like Lady Eldon's — namely, that in real cases, as opposed to hypotheticals, intention must be proved rather than supposed, and it is too dangerous to the innocent to permit juries to speculate on a defendant's intent in the absence of actions that strongly evidence that intent. One may fully agree with this, however, without concluding that Lady Eldon should be acquitted. Of course it would be evidentiary of Lady Eldon's intent to smuggle if she had been found with dutiable French lace at the border. (But only evidentiary — after all, she might have thought it was English lace, or it might have been put with her things by her maid without her knowledge.) But why should it be held, as it was in United States v. Oviedo, supra, that, since the lace was nondutiable in fact, a finding of intent will necessarily be suspect, regardless of the strength of the evidence? Is it not perfectly possible that a reasonable jury could find this intent beyond a reasonable doubt even if the lace was nondutiable? Suppose, for example, that the lace were carefully secreted in a specially tailored, concealed pocket of the coach; that the coachman testified to incriminating statements Lady Eldon made to Lord Eldon; that a letter from her to her sister, which described her newly bought "French lace" in exquisite and appreciative detail, had been introduced; that her receipt showed she paid a price appropriate for French lace rather than for the vastly less expensive English lace. There would seem little danger to the innocent in allowing a jury to find an attempt to smuggle French lace on these facts. Indeed, in cases like *Jaffe* and *Berrigan*, "attempt" is charged only because of the involvement of an undercover agent, whose participation prevents completion of the intended crime. Whatever else one may say about such investigatory tactics, they do not necessarily render suspect the evidence of the defendant's intent; indeed, in practice, they usually render that evidence far *less* speculative than it otherwise would be. The proper remedy for speculative and unreliable jury findings of intent is a court alert to preclude such findings in particular cases where the evidence is insufficient.

In the end, then, the arguments in favor of Lady Eldon (and those which have been used to reverse conviction in cases like *Jaffe*, *Oviedo*, and *Berrigan*) are founded on unpersuasive policy considerations rationalized by a peculiar and Pickwickian interpretation of what it means to intend to do an act, one

---

7. The Common Law 72 (1881). Cf. Model Penal Code, Tent. Draft No. 10 (1960), Comments to Art. 5 at 24: "[Attempt, solicitation and conspiracy] are not the only crimes which are so defined that their commission does not rest on proof of the occurrence of the evil that is the object of the law to prevent; many specific, substantive offenses also have a large inchoate aspect. This is true not only with respect to crimes of risk-creation, such as reckless driving, or specific crimes of preparation, like those of possession with unlawful purpose. It is also true, at least in part, of crimes like larceny, forgery, kidnaping and even arson, not to speak of burglary, where a purpose to cause greater harm than that which is implicit in the actor's conduct is an element of the offense."

that is utterly at odds both with the common usage of our language and its usage elsewhere in the criminal law.[8] *We conclude that the innocuous character of the action actually done (innocuous in the sense that it could not constitute a crime under the actual circumstances) will not save her from an attempt conviction if she did the act believing that the circumstances were otherwise than what they were, and, had her belief been correct, what she set out to do would constitute a crime.* This is the principle that has found favor in virtually every serious statutory effort to deal with the problem,[9] and in the decisions of numerous cases without benefit of a specific statute to tell the court that a person intends to do what he thinks he intends to do.

We must say a few words more about the final qualification to the principle just asserted; namely, that "had her belief (in the circumstances) been correct, what she set out to do would constitute a crime." The point can best be made by altering the hypothetical. Suppose the lace that Lady Eldon had purchased was in fact the expensive French lace she meant to buy. The customs officer at Dover brings it to light. He then says to Lady Eldon: "Lucky for you you returned to England today rather than yesterday. I just received word this morning that the government has removed French lace from the duty list." Could Lady Eldon be held for attempt to smuggle in these circumstances?[10] Certainly what she did and what she intended to do were not different simply because she acted one day later, when French lace was removed from the duty list. But there is this important difference: that at the time she acted, *what* she intended to do (always judged, of course, from her own perspective) was not a violation of the criminal law, even though she thought it was. Of course, in doing what she did she showed that she was a person who would break a law. But what law? The law against smuggling French lace? There no longer was such a law. The criminal laws generally, on the ground that if she is ready to break what she thinks is a criminal law, she is ready to break what are in fact criminal laws? Fortunately our law has not gone so far in accepting the social-defense theories of the criminal positivists. At least for purposes of criminal liability (as opposed to sentencing) we are not prepared to generalize proclivities beyond the proclivity to commit the specific crime charged. And, as Professor Williams has pointed out, "if the legislature has not seen fit to prohibit the consummated act, a mere approach to consummation should a fortiori be guilt-

---

8. Consider the Missouri court's justification for reversing the conviction of a hunter for attempting to take a deer out of season where the evidence showed that he shot a stuffed deer, placed in the woods by a game warden, believing it to be alive: "If the state's evidence showed an attempt to take the dummy, it fell far short of proving an attempt to take a deer." State v. Guffey, 262 S.W.2d 152 (Mo. App. 1953).

9. From the English Criminal Code Bill Commission's Draft Code §74 (1879) ("Every one who, believing that a certain state of facts exists, does or omits an act the doing or omitting of which would, if that state of facts existed, be an attempt to commit the offence, attempts to commit that offence, although its commission in the manner proposed was by reason of the non-existence of that state of facts at the time of the act or omission impossible") to the proposal of the Model Penal Code and the New York statute.

10. Consider the following news story during the 1974 sugar shortage in England: "Travellers trying to beat Britian's sugar shortage are smuggling more and more of it into this country. They do not know that importing sugar is legal. A woman filled a shoebox with sugar and wrapped it like a gift, with fancy ribbons and bright paper. Another woman had sugar in a can marked 'face powder.' Customs officials chuckled at the reaction of sugar smugglers when they found out there was nothing wrong in what they were doing." N.Y. Herald Tribune, Oct. 22, 1974, reprinted in G. Williams, Textbook of Criminal Law 398 (1978).

less. Any other view would offend against the principle of legality; in effect the law of attempt would be used to manufacture a new crime, when the legislature has left the situation outside the ambit of the law." G. Williams, Criminal Law: The General Part 633-634 (2d ed. 1961). Had the criminal law been changed as supposed in our variation of the Lady Eldon hypothetical, therefore, it would be no more justified to convict her than to convict an abortionist of attempted abortion where the abortion was committed, unknown to the defendant, after the abortion law was repealed or held invalid. These are the true cases of legal impossibility.

But, it should be noted, these situations are totally different from cases like *Jaffe* and *Berrigan,* even though the courts in each case, by asserting that what the defendants intended to do could not have constituted a crime, made it seem otherwise. What the abortionist intended to do (and did) could not constitute a crime because there was no such crime. What Jaffe and Berrigan intended to do (and thought they did) was indeed a crime. It is only through a perverse use of intent that we can say that Jaffe intended to receive honestly obtained property or that Berrigan intended to send out a letter the warden knew about, and that therefore they intended to do what was no crime at all.

Lady Eldon, in the actual hypothetical, in contrast to the hypothetical hypothetical, represents no more a case of genuine legal impossibility than *Jaffe* and *Berrigan.* She will be convicted of attempt to smuggle French lace.

COMMENT, 4 Hypothetical L. Rev. 1, 3-4 (1962-1982): The hypothetical *Lady Eldon* decision is a good effort, but it doesn't quite work.

First: Consider the case of a voodoo practitioner who practices his art upon a doll firmly intending to kill his victim and believing he will succeed. Or consider a safecracker who tries to open a safe with magic incantations. Under the formulation of *Lady Eldon,* each of these defendants, more pathetic than dangerous, would be guilty of attempt. Conviction of the defendants in these cases would be no less absurd than their own actions.

The Model Penal Code, in recognition of this problem, gives a court the power to dismiss a prosecution or decrease the penalty if "the particular conduct charged to constitute a criminal attempt . . . is so inherently unlikely to result or culminate in the commission of a crime that neither such conduct nor the actor presents a public danger." Section 5.05(2). But this is to commend the matter to the discretion of the judge; it is not a statement of a rule of law. A better approach is that taken by the revised Minnesota Criminal Code which states an exception to its rule that impossibility is no defense where the "impossibility would have been clearly evident to a person of normal understanding." Minn. Stat. Ann. §609.17, subd. 2. New Jersey takes a similar approach. N.J. Stat. Ann. tit. 2C, §2C:5-1.

Second: The effort to deal with the so-called "true legal impossibility" problem comes off more smoothly than convincingly. Consider the following case. Two friends, Mr. Fact and Mr. Law, go hunting in the morning of October 15 in the fields of the state of Dakota, whose law makes it a misdemeanor to hunt any time other than from October 1 to November 30. Both kill deer on the first day out, October 15. Mr. Fact, however, was under the erroneous belief that the date was September 15, and Mr. Law was under the erroneous belief that the hunting season was confined to the month of November, as it was the previous year. Under the *Lady Eldon* formulation, Mr. Fact could be convicted of an attempt to hunt out of season, but Mr. Law could not be. We fail to see how any rational system of criminal law could justify convicting one and acquitting the other on so fragile and unpersuasive a distinction that one was suffering under a mistake of fact, and the other under a mistake of law. Certainly if the ultimate test is the dangerousness of the actor (i.e., readiness to violate the law), as *Lady Eldon* would have it, no distinction is warranted — Mr. Law has indicated himself to be no less "dangerous" than Mr. Fact." [a]

Third: In formulating a rule that would eliminate the defense of factual impossibility in all cases the opinion overlooks the strong case for retaining the defense in one class of cases. These are the cases in which the acts done by the defendant are as consistent with an innocent as with a culpable state of mind. Take for example the old saw about the professor who takes his own umbrella thinking it belongs to his colleague. The act is utterly neutral. A man taking his own umbrella conveys no evidence of guilt. Now of course the matter changes if it can be *proven* that he believed it was his colleague's umbrella. But proof of state of mind where there are only ambiguous acts to support the inference is inherently unreliable.

Consider how the Model Penal Code deals with this very concern when it addresses itself to a different problem, i.e., drawing the line between preparation and attempt. This is typically the situation in which the actor has not yet completed all he set out to do. In Section 5.01, the Model Penal Code not only reflects existing law in requiring some substantial step toward commission of the crime. It also requires that the step at the same time be "strongly corroborative of the actor's criminal purpose." Why is this required? It may be supposed that the primary function of this requirement is to avoid the risk of false convictions; the animating idea is that where the evidence of intent falls below a certain level we are not willing to allow the jury to speculate.

Now both the *Lady Eldon* opinion and the Model Penal Code are shortsighted for not seeing that the same concern may exist in the class of impossibility cases under discussion. If apprehension of false convictions calls for the requirement that the acts strongly corroborate the intent in those cases where the acts fall short of what was intended by the actor, then the same concern calls for the same requirement where the actor has done all he meant to do. If it is answered that in the latter cases the completed pattern of conduct carries the

---

a. For analyses of the problems posed by this hypothetical, see Hughes, One Further Footnote on Attempting the Impossible, 42 N.Y.U.L. Rev. 1005, 1012-1013, 1033 (1967), and Dutile & Moore, Mistake and Impossibility: Arranging a Marriage Between Two Difficult Partners, 74 Nw. U.L. Rev. 166, 166-167 (1979). The latter article disagrees with the reasoning of the Hypothetical Law Review comment on this point: "[We argue] that Mr. Law in the Kadish and Paulsen example would be acquitted, since the transaction, even as he contemplated it, was not within the statute, while Mr. Fact would not. From the standpoint of symmetry, or the dangerous propensities of the defendant, there is no way to justify the result. From a 'moral' standpoint they are equally culpable.

"The key to finding the result anomalous, however, is the tacit assumption that there are no other relevant concerns. From the standpoint of the criminal law, no *socially protected* value is violated by the 'attempt' in a 'Mr. Law' case of genuine legal impossibility. In such a case, it need not be claimed that the actor is harmless. He may be extremely dangerous, yet what precisely is he guilty of? What penalty should he receive? . . . It is totally unclear how any system based on liability for intending to violate the law, as opposed to intending *conduct* that *is* in violation of the law, could function as a properly justified system of criminal law. Such a system provides neither appropriate deterrence to crime nor proper retribution for crime."— EDS.

criminal intent on its face, the response must be that while this is generally so, it need not be so. The professor taking his own umbrella surely is such a case.

To put the suggestion in statutory form, we suggest the following amendment to the Model Penal Code's Section 5.01:

"A person is guilty of an attempt to commit a crime if, acting with the kind of culpability otherwise required for commission of the crime, he: (a) purposely engages in conduct that *strongly corroborates the required culpability and* would constitute the crime if the attendant circumstances were as he believes them to be. . . ." [b]

b. On the issues raised in this third point of the Hypothetical Law Review comment, see the Hughes article again. See also Weigend, Why Lady Eldon Should Be Acquitted: The Social Harm in Attempting the Impossible, 27 De Paul L. Rev. 231 (1979). — EDS.

CHAPTER
8

GROUP CRIMINALITY

A. ACCOUNTABILITY FOR THE ACTS OF OTHERS

At the common law there were distinct categories of circumstances that rendered a person a participant in a course of criminal conduct. These distinctions had consequences for both procedure and punishment. The following excerpts from 4 Blackstone, Commentaries, ch. 3, *34-39, broadly describe those categories:

> A man may be *principal* in an offence in two degrees. A principal, in the first degree, is he that is the actor, or absolute perpetrator of the crime; and, in the second degree, he is who is present, aiding, and abetting the fact to be done. Which presence need not always be an actual immediate standing by, within sight or hearing of the fact; but there may be also a constructive presence, as when one commits a robbery or murder, and another keeps watch or guard at some convenient distance. . . .
>
> An *accessory* is he who is not the chief actor in the offence, nor present at its performance, but is some way concerned therein, either before or after the fact committed. . . .
>
> As to . . . who may be an accessory *before* the fact, Sir Matthew Hale defines him to be one, who being absent at the time of the crime committed, doth yet procure, counsel, or command another to commit a crime. Herein absence is necessary to make him an accessory; for if such procurer, or the like, be present, he is guilty of the crime as principal. . . .
>
> An accessory *after* the fact may be, where a person, knowing a felony to have been committed, receives, relieves, comforts, or assists the felon. . . .

Modern statutes have largely obliterated the significance of these discrete modes of criminal participation: (1) Apart from the accessory after the fact, who is still generally subject to a lesser punishment, the punishment is the same for the three main modes of complicity. (2) It is no longer the case that accessories to crime cannot be convicted until their principal is convicted (although, of course, it must be proved that a crime was committed). (3) It is no longer necessary in most states for a defendant to be charged with and convicted of a particular form of complicity.

These changes are the result of statutes antedating the wave of legislative reform initiated by the Model Penal Code. These older statutes abolish all distinctions between principals and accessories before the fact, requiring that all be treated as principals. For example, the federal statute, 18 U.S.C. §2, provides:

(a) Whoever commits an offense against the United States or aids, abets, counsels, commands, induces or procures its commission, is punishable as a principal. (b) Whoever willfully causes an act to be done which if directly performed by him or another would be an offense against the United States, is punishable as a principal.

Many statutory schemes are more detailed. The California Penal Code is representative:

Section 31
All persons concerned in the commission of a crime, whether it be felony or misdemeanor, and whether they directly commit the act constituting the offense, or aid and abet in its commission, or, not being present, have advised and encouraged its commission, and all persons counseling, advising or encouraging children under the age of fourteen years, lunatics or idiots to commit any crime, or who, by fraud, contrivance, or force, occasion the drunkenness of another for the purpose of causing him to commit any crime, or who, by threats, menaces, command, or coercion, compel another to commit any crime, are principals in any crime so committed.

Section 32
Every person who, after a felony has been committed, harbors, conceals or aids a principal in such felony, with the intent that said principal may avoid or escape from arrest, trial, conviction or punishment, having knowledge that said principal has committed such felony or has been charged with such felony or convicted thereof, is an accessory to such felony.

Section 33
Except in cases where a different punishment is prescribed, an accessory is punishable by imprisonment in the state prison not exceeding five years, or in a county jail not exceeding two years, or by fine not exceeding five thousand dollars.

Section 971
The distinction between an accessory before the fact and a principal, and between principals in the first and second degree is abrogated; and all persons concerned in the commission of a crime, who by the operation of other provisions of this code are principals therein, shall hereafter be prosecuted, tried, and punished as principals, and no other facts need be alleged in any accusatory pleading against any such person than are required in an accusatory pleading against a principal.

Section 972
An accessory to the commission of a felony may be prosecuted, tried, and punished, though the principal may be neither prosecuted nor tried, and though the principal may have been acquitted.

The statutes of more recent vintage, influenced by the Model Penal Code proposals (see §2.06, Appendix to this casebook), typically make people who are accomplices of another person accountable for that person's conduct and define people as accomplices in the other person's offense if they solicit him or her to commit such an offense or aid him or her in planning or committing it. See, e.g., N.J. Stat. Ann. tit. 2C, §2C:2-6.

An additional and independent basis of complicity in the crimes of another derives from the doctrine of conspiracy. In general terms, a criminal conspiracy is an agreement or combination by two or more persons to commit a crime. Conspiracy is a substantive crime in itself, but it has the further consequence of making each of the coconspirators criminally responsible for the criminal acts of fellow conspirators committed in furtherance of the planned criminal enterprise, whether or not those particular criminal acts were planned, so long as they were reasonably foreseeable. A coconspirator, therefore, may be liable for the criminal acts of fellow conspirators even though strictly under the law of principals and accessories (requiring aiding, abetting, encouraging, etc.) the person might not be liable. This problem is explored in the conspiracy section, in connection with Pinkerton v. United States, pages 654-656 infra and the materials following.

1. Mens Rea

HICKS v. UNITED STATES
Supreme Court of the United States
150 U.S. 442 (1893)

MR. JUSTICE SHIRAS delivered the opinion of the court.

In the Circuit Court of the United States for the Western District of Arkansas, John Hicks, an Indian, was jointly indicted with Stand Rowe, also an Indian, for the murder of Andrew J. Colvard, a white man, by shooting him with a gun on the 13th of February, 1892. Rowe was killed by the officers in the attempt to arrest him, and Hicks was tried separately and found guilty in March, 1893. We adopt the statement of the facts in the case made in the brief for the government as correct and as sufficient for our purposes:

> It appears that on the night of the 12th of February, 1892, there was a dance at the house of Jim Rowe, in the Cherokee Nation; that Jim Rowe was a brother to Stand Rowe, who was indicted jointly with the defendant; . . . that Stand Rowe and the defendant were engaged in what was called "scouting," viz., eluding the United States marshals who were in search of them with warrants for their arrest, and were armed for the purpose of resisting arrest; they appeared at the dance, each armed with a Winchester rifle; they were both Cherokee Indians. The deceased, Andrew J. Colvard, was a white man who had married a Cherokee woman; he [was also at] the dance on . . . on the evening of the 12th. A good deal of whiskey was drank [sic] during the night by the persons present, and Colvard appears to have been drunk at some time during the night. Colvard spoke Cherokee fluently, and appears to have been very friendly with Stand Rowe and the defendant Hicks. . . .
> Some time after sunrise on the morning of the 13th, about 7 o'clock, [four witnesses] saw Stand Rowe, coming on horseback in a moderate walk, with his Winchester rifle lying down in front of him. . . . Stand Rowe halted within five or six feet of the main road, and the men on the porch saw Mr. Colvard and the defendant Hicks riding together down the main road from the direction of Jim Rowe's house.
> As Colvard and Hicks approached the point where Stand Rowe was sitting on his horse, Stand Rowe rode out into the road and halted. Colvard then rode up

to him in a lope or canter, leaving Hicks, the defendant, some 30 or 40 feet in his rear. The point where the three men were together on their horses was about 100 yards from where the four witnesses stood on the porch. The conversation between the three men on horseback was not fully heard by the four men on the porch, and all that was heard was not understood, because part of it was carried on in the Cherokee tongue; but some part of this conversation was distinctly heard and clearly understood by these witnesses; they saw Stand Rowe twice raise his rifle and aim it at Colvard, and twice he lowered it; they heard Colvard say, "I am a friend to both of you"; they saw and heard the defendant Hicks laugh aloud when Rowe directed his rifle toward Colvard; they saw Hicks take off his hat and hit his horse on the neck or shoulder with it; they heard Hicks say to Colvard, "Take off your hat and die like a man"; they saw Stand Rowe raise his rifle for the third time, point it at Colvard, fire it; . . . they saw Colvard fall from his horse; they went to where he was lying in the road and found him dead; they saw Stand Rowe and John Hicks ride off together after the shooting.

Hicks testified in his own behalf, denying that he had encouraged Rowe to shoot Colvard, and alleging that he had endeavored to persuade Rowe not to shoot. . . .

The language attributed to Hicks, and which he denied having used, cannot be said to have been entirely free from ambiguity. It was addressed not to Rowe, but to Colvard. Hicks testified that Rowe was in a dangerous mood, and that he did not know whether he would shoot Colvard or Hicks. The remark made — if made — accompanied with the gesture of taking off his own hat, may have been an utterance of desperation, occasioned by his belief that Rowe would shoot one or both of them. That Hicks and Rowe rode off together after seeing Colvard fall was used as a fact against Hicks, pointing to a conspiracy between them. Hicks testified that he did it in fear of his life; that Rowe had demanded that he should show him the road which he wished to travel. Hicks further testified, and in this he was not contradicted, that he separated from Rowe a few minutes afterwards, on the first opportunity, and that he never afterwards had any intercourse with him, nor had he been in the company of Rowe for several weeks before the night of the fatal occurrence.

Two of the assignments of error are especially relied on by the counsel of the accused. One arises out of that portion of the charge wherein the judge sought to instruct the jury as to the evidence relied on as showing that Hicks aided and abetted Rowe in the commission of the crime. . . .

We agree with the counsel for the plaintiff in error in thinking that this instruction was erroneous in two particulars. It omitted to instruct the jury that the acts or words of encouragement and abetting must have been used by the accused with the intention of encouraging and abetting Rowe. So far as the instruction goes, the words may have been used for a different purpose, and yet have had the actual effect of inciting Rowe to commit the murderous act. Hicks, indeed, testified that the expressions used by him were intended to dissuade Rowe from shooting. But the jury were left to find Hicks guilty as a principal because the effect of his words may have had the result of encouraging Rowe to shoot, regardless of Hicks' intention. In another part of the charge the learned judge did make an observation as to the question of intention in the use of the words, saying:

If the deliberate and intentional use of words has the effect to encourage one man to kill another, he who uttered these words is presumed by the law to have intended that effect, and is responsible therefor.

This statement is itself defective in confounding the intentional use of the words with the intention as respects the effect to be produced. Hicks no doubt, *intended* to use the words he did use, but did he thereby *intend* that they were to be understood by Rowe as an encouragment to act? However this may be, we do not think this expression of the learned judge availed to cure the defect already noticed in his charge, that the mere use of certain words would suffice to warrant the jury in finding Hicks guilty, regardless of the intention with which they were used.

Another error is contained in that portion of the charge now under review, and that is the statement:

> that if Hicks was actually present at that place at the time of the firing by Stand Rowe, and he was there for the purpose of either aiding, abetting, advising, or encouraging the shooting of Andrew J. Colvard by Stand Rowe, and that, as a matter of fact, he did not do it, but was present for the purpose of aiding or abetting or advising or encouraging his shooting, but he did not do it because it was not necessary, it was done without his assistance, the law says there is a third condition where guilt is fastened to his act in that regard.

We understand this language to mean that where an accomplice is present for the purpose of aiding and abetting in a murder, but refrains from so aiding and abetting because it turned out not to be necessary for the accomplishment of the common purpose, he is equally guilty as if he had actively participated by words or acts of encouragement. Thus understood, the statement might, in some instances, be a correct instruction. Thus, if there had been evidence sufficient to show that there had been a previous conspiracy between Rowe and Hicks to waylay and kill Colvard, Hicks, if present at the time of the killing, would be guilty, even if it was found unnecessary for him to act. But the error of such an instruction, in the present case, is in the fact that there was no evidence on which to base it. The evidence, so far as we are permitted to notice it, as contained in the bills of exception, and set forth in the charge, shows no facts from which the jury could have properly found that the encounter was the result of any previous conspiracy or arrangement. The jury might well, therefore, have thought that they were following the court's instructions, in finding the accused guilty because he was present at the time and place of the murder, although he contributed neither by word or action to the crime, and although there was no substantial evidence of any conspiracy or prior arrangement between him and Rowe. . . .

The judgment of the court below is reversed and the cause remanded, with directions to set aside the verdict and award a new trial.

NOTES

1. Variations on Hicks. Consider the responsibility of Hicks for the killing by Rowe in the following hypothetical situations.

(a) Hicks hears that Rowe has set out to kill his old enemy, Colvard, and goes along to enjoy the spectacle.

(b) Same situation as in (a), except that while watching Rowe's assault on Colvard with satisfaction, Hicks shouts such words of encouragement to Rowe as "Go get him!" and "Attaboy!"

(c) Same situation as in (a), except that Hicks resolves to make certain Rowe succeeds — by helping him if necessary. (Would it make a difference if Hicks were a sheriff? See Model Penal Code §2.06(3)(a)(iii), Appendix to this case-book.)

(d) Same situation as in (c), except that Hicks tells Rowe on the way that he will help him if it seems necessary.

2. *Strict liability offenses.* In Johnson v. Youden, [1950] 1 K.B. 544, 546, defendant solicitors were charged with aiding and abetting a builder in his sale to a customer of a house at a price in excess of that permitted by law, in violation of a criminal statute. On appeal from a dismissal of the information, the prosecutor argued that the lack of knowledge by the solicitors that their client was charging an unlawful price was no defense, since the crime they were charged with aiding and abetting was a crime of absolute liability. He argued:

> The justices formed the view that the offence of aiding and abetting involved mens rea, and that the burden of proving mens rea was on the prosecution. They were clearly wrong: mens rea is irrelevant. Mens rea is not an essential ingredient of the offence of aiding and abetting the commission of a substantive offence of which mens rea is not an essential ingredient.

The court affirmed the dismissal of the informations, stating:

> Before a person can be convicted of aiding and abetting the commission of an offence, he must at least know the essential matters which constitute that offence. He need not actually know that an offence has been committed, because he may not know that the facts constitute an offence and ignorance of the law is not a defence. If a person knows all the facts and is assisting another person to do certain things, and it turns out that the doing of those things constitutes an offence, the person who is assisting is guilty of aiding and abetting that offence, because to allow him to say, "I knew of all those facts but I did not know that an offence was committed," would be allowing him to set up ignorance of the law as a defence. The reason why, in our opinion, the justices were right in dismissing the informations against the first two defendants is that they found, and found on good grounds, that they did not know of the matters which in fact constituted the offence; and, as they did not know of those matters, it follows that they cannot be guilty of aiding and abetting the commission of the offence.

See also Ferguson v. Weaving, [1951] 1 K.B. 814. Compare Commonwealth v. Koczwara, 397 Pa. 575, 155 A.2d 825 (1979).

3. *Aiding law enforcement.* (a) In Wilson v. People, 103 Colo. 441, 87 P.2d 5, (1939), defendant Wilson was convicted on the following facts of feloniously aiding and abetting one Pierce in the commission of a burglary and larceny: Wilson and Pierce spent the evening drinking together. At one point Wilson discovered his watch missing and accused Pierce of stealing it. Pierce adamantly denied the accusation. The subject of their conversation turned to feats of crime.

They decided to burglarize the Hecker Brothers' drugstore that evening. This they accomplished by Wilson boosting Pierce through a transom. While Pierce was inside, Wilson telephoned the police and returned to receive bottles of whiskey that Pierce handed to him through the transom. When the police arrived Wilson told them that Pierce was inside the store. Pierce escaped through the back door, and Wilson led police to Pierce's hotel room, where he identified Pierce as the burglar. Shortly after Pierce's arrest Wilson told the police that his connection with the burglary was for the purpose of getting even with Pierce for taking his watch, which he hoped in this way to recover. On appeal, defendant contended the trial court committed error in charging:

> One may not participate in the commission of a felony and then obtain immunity from punishment on the ground that he was a mere detective or spy. One who attempts to detect the commission of crime in others must himself stop short of lending assistance, or participation in the commission of the crime.

The Colorado Supreme Court reversed, agreeing that the instruction was erroneous and quoting 1 F. Wharton, Criminal Law §271 (12th ed. 1932):

> A detective entering apparently into a criminal conspiracy already formed for the purpose of exploding it is not an accessory before the fact. For it should be remembered that while detectives, when acting as decoys, may apparently provoke the crime, the essential element of dolus, or malicious determination to violate the law, is wanting in their case. And it is only the formal, and not the substantive, part of the crime that they provoke. They provoke, for instance, in larceny, the asportation of the goods, but not the ultimate loss by the owner. They may be actuated by the most unworthy of motives, but the animus furandi in larceny is not imputable to them; and it is in larcenous cases or cheats that they are chiefly employed.

(b) Questions. Since Wilson was not a law enforcement official, how can the principle quoted from Wharton apply to him? Does this case stand for the proposition that a secondary party must have a true purpose to achieve the object sought by the primary party? Suppose Wilson, with the same purpose of trapping Pierce, assisted him in the malicious destruction of property or handed him a loaded revolver to be used to kill one against whom Wilson had no personal animus? How could these cases be distinguished?

(c) Consider the following prosecution, as reported in the S.F. Chronicle, Sept. 7, 1974, at 2, col. 1.

> Millionaire soap heir George Gamble was found guilty in U.S. District Court here last night of transporting into California an elk killed illegally on the Crow Indian Reservation in Montana and a big horn sheep killed illegally in Yellowstone National Park. . . .
>
> But at the same time, U.S. District Judge Robert F. Peckham, who presided over the non-jury trial, expressed strong displeasure at government undercover agents who he said had intentionally and illegally killed seven elk, sheep, and polar bears in order to make a case against Gamble and other suspect hunting violators. . . .
>
> Addressing the court . . . Peckham said:

"The fascinating aspect of this case is that the agents go out and kill these same animals that the defendant is charged with killing.

"They (the government) brought a road contractor all the way from Vermont to illegally kill animals. No matter what happens here, I am going to pursue this."

Assistant U.S. Attorney Janet Aiken, who represented the government, responded:

"This was legitimate undercover work. If the undercover agents (posing as hunters) missed every shot, the guides would get suspicious."

Consider also the case of two reporters for the Indianapolis Star as reported in Time, Sept. 30, 1974, at 76. In the course of their year-long investigation into police corruption, the reporters encountered an informant who offered to demonstrate how easy it was to bribe the police — he would bribe a police lieutenant before their very eyes. The informant made good his promise. At a local restaurant, he handed an envelope containing money to a police lieutenant while the reporters observed from their car. The reporters recounted this incident as part of their anticorruption series, giving the names of the informant and the police officer. Several months later the reporters were indicted for conspiring to bribe the lieutenant, ostensibly to halt investigation of a burglary. Do they have a defense? (Since we have not yet discussed conspiracy, for present purposes assume they were indicted for being accomplices to the informant's bribery of the lieutenant.)

(d) Statutory solutions. Note the approach of the New York statute to cases in which the defendant is a law enforcement official. Section 35.05 of the N.Y. Penal Code provides,

> Unless otherwise limited by the ensuing provisions of this article defining justifiable use of physical force, conduct which would otherwise constitute an offense is justifiable and not criminal when . . . [the] conduct is required or authorized by law or by a judicial decree, or is performed by a public servant in the reasonable exercise of his official powers, duties or functions. . . .

See also Utah Code Ann. §76-2-401:

> The defense of justification may be claimed . . . when the actor's conduct is reasonable and in fulfillment of his duties as a governmental officer or employee.

Query: Do you perceive any difficulties with these provisions? Would you make them wider or narrower? Compare the materials on Choice of the Lesser Evil, pages 769-788 infra.

(e) Entrapment. Some of the foregoing situations may suggest the possibility of a defense of entrapment. That defense has a number of requirements: For example, the individual leading the defendant on must be a law officer. For one formulation of the entrapment defense, see Model Penal Code §2.13, Appendix to this casebook. A helpful review of the law of entrapment may be found in the Commentary to that provision at 14 (Tent. Draft No. 9, 1959).

STATE v. GLADSTONE

Supreme Court of Washington
78 Wash. 2d 306, 474 P.2d 274 (1980)

HALE, J. A jury found defendant Bruce Gladstone guilty of aiding and abetting one Robert Kent in the unlawful sale of marijuana. . . .

Gladstone's guilt as an aider and abettor in this case rests solely on evidence of a conversation between him and one Douglas MacArthur Thompson concerning the possible purchase of marijuana from one Robert Kent. There is no other evidence to connect the accused with Kent who ultimately sold some marijuana to Thompson. . . .

[Thompson, Kent, and defendant, Gladstone, were all students at the University of Puget Sound. Thompson was hired by the Tacoma Police Department to attempt a purchase of marijuana from Gladstone. Thompson visited defendant at his home and asked to buy marijuana. Defendant replied that he did not have enough to sell him any but volunteered the name of Kent as someone who did have enough and who was willing to sell. He then gave Thompson Kent's address and, at Thompson's request, drew a map to direct him to Kent's residence. Thompson went there and bought marijuana from Kent. There was no evidence of any communication between defendant and Kent concerning marijuana, but only, the court said, of "a possible accommodation to someone who said he wanted to buy marijuana."]

If all reasonable inferences favorable to the state are accorded the evidence, it does not, in our opinion, establish the commission of the crime charged. That vital element — a nexus between the accused and the party whom he is charged with aiding and abetting in the commission of a crime — is missing. The record contains no evidence whatever that Gladstone had any communication by word, gesture or sign, before or after he drew the map, from which it could be inferred that he counseled, encouraged, hired, commanded, induced or procured Kent to sell marijuana to Douglas Thompson as charged, or took any steps to further the commission of the crime charged. He was not charged with aiding and abetting Thompson in the purchase of marijuana, but with Kent's sale of it. . . .

. . . [E]ven without prior agreement, arrangement or understanding, a bystander to a robbery could be guilty of aiding and abetting its commission if he came to the aid of a robber and knowingly assisted him in perpetrating the crime. But . . . there is no aiding and abetting unless one " 'in some sort associate himself with the venture, that he participate in it as in something that he wishes to bring about, that he seek by his action to make it succeed.' " Nye & Nissen v. United States, 336 U.S. 613, 619 (1949).

Gladstone's culpability, if at all, must be brought within R.C.W. 9.01.030, which makes a principal of one who aids and abets another in the commission of the crime. Although an aider and abettor need not be physically present at the commission of the crime to be held guilty as a principal, his conviction depends on proof that he did something in association or connection with the principal to accomplish the crime. Learned Hand, J., we think, hit the nail squarely when, in United States v. Peoni, 100 F.2d 401, 402 (2d Cir. 1938), he wrote that, in order to aid and abet another to commit a crime, it is necessary that a defendant "in some sort associate himself with the venture, that he participate in it as in something that he wishes to bring about, that he seek by his action to make it succeed. All the words used — even the most colorless, "abet"— carry an implication of purposive attitude towards it.". . .

It would be a dangerous precedent indeed to hold that mere communications to the effect that another might or probably would commit a criminal offense amount to an aiding and abetting of the offense should it ultimately be committed.

There being no evidence whatever that the defendant ever communicated to Kent the idea that he would in any way aid him in the sale of any marijuana, or said anything to Kent to encourage or induce him or direct him to do so, or counseled Kent in the sale of marijuana, or did anything more than describe Kent to another person as an individual who might sell some marijuana, or would derive any benefit, consideration or reward from such a sale, there was no proof of an aiding and abetting, and the conviction should, therefore, be reversed as a matter of law. Remanded with directions to dismiss.

HAMILTON, J. (dissenting). . . . I am satisfied that the jury was fully warranted in concluding that appellant, when he affirmatively recommended Kent as a source and purveyor of marijuana, entertained the requisite conscious design and intent that his action would instigate, induce, procure or encourage perpetration of Kent's subsequent crime of selling marijuana to Thompson. . . .

NOTES AND QUESTIONS

1. *Questions on* Gladstone. The court emphasizes that defendant was "not charged with aiding and abetting Thompson in the purchase of marijuana, but with Kent's sale of it." Could he have been charged and convicted of aiding and abetting Thompson's purchase? What difficulties would be presented? Cf. Model Penal Code §§2.06(3) and 5.01(3). Would the reasoning of the majority, finding defendant not liable as an aider and abettor of Kent's sale, be equally applicable to preclude his liability as an aider and abettor (or an attempted aider and abettor) of Thompson's purchase? Why should it not? Why should it matter that Thompson asked for and received the aid? Would defendant's state of mind as to the purchase by Thompson be any different than it was as to the sale by Kent?

2. Model Penal Code §2.04(3), Comment at 27-28 (Tent. Draft No. 1, 1953) states:

> The issue is whether knowingly facilitating the commission of a crime ought to be sufficient for complicity, absent a true purpose to advance the criminal end. The problem, to be sure, is narrow in its focus: often, if not usually, aid rendered with guilty knowledge implies purpose since it has no other motivation. But there are many and important cases where this is the central question in determining liability. A lessor rents with knowledge that the premises will be used to establish a bordello. A vendor sells with knowledge that the subject of the sale will be used in commission of a crime. A doctor counsels against an abortion but, at the patient's insistence refers her to a competent abortionist. A utility provides telephone or telegraph service, knowing it is used for book-making. An employee puts through a shipment in the course of his employment though he knows the shipment is illegal. A farm boy clears the ground for setting up a still, knowing that the venture is illicit.

Consider whether the following cases present the same or a distinguishable set of problems.

(a) In People v. Roberts, 211 Mich. 187, 178 N.W. 690, 693 (1920), defendant's wife was incurably ill with multiple sclerosis. Yielding to her urging, he mixed a poison and placed it in a glass by her bedside, let us assume (the case does not clearly say) deeply hoping that she would decide not to drink it. She subsequently did drink it, and she died. Defendant's conviction of murdering his wife by poison was affirmed. The court concluded:

> We are of the opinion that, when defendant mixed the paris green with water and placed it within the reach of his wife to enable her to put an end to her suffering by putting an end to her life, he was guilty of murder by means of poison within the meaning of the statute, even though she requested him to do so. By this act he deliberately placed within her reach the means of taking her own life, which she could have obtained in no other way by reason of her helpless condition.[a]

(b) Regina v. Fretwell, 169 Eng. Rep. 1345, 1346 (1862):

> The deceased, Elizabeth Bradley, was pregnant, and, for the purpose of producing abortion, took a dose of corrosive sublimate, which had been procured for her by the prisoner with a full knowledge of the purpose to which it was to be applied. In procuring the poison, the prisoner had acted at the instigation of the deceased, and under the influence of threats by her of self-destruction if the means of procuring abortion were not supplied to her. . . . In the present case, the prisoner was unwilling that the woman should take the poison. He procured it for her at her instigation, and under a threat by her of self-destruction. He did not administer it to her, or cause her to take it, and the facts of the case are quite consistent with the supposition that he hoped and expected that she would change her mind and would not resort to it.

Accordingly, the court concluded that the prisoner could not be convicted of murder, either as a principal or as an accessory before the fact.

3. The merits considered. Consider the following proposal of an early draft of the Model Penal Code (§2.04(3)(b) (Tent. Draft No. 1, 1953)).

> A person is an accomplice of another person in the commission of a crime if . . . acting with knowledge that such other person was committing or had the purpose of committing the crime, he knowingly, substantially facilitated its commission.

Commenting on that proposal, the following observations were made (id., Comment at 27-32):

> The issue is whether knowingly facilitating the commission of a crime ought to be sufficient for complicity, absent a true purpose to advance the criminal end. . . .
> The problem has had most attention in the federal courts where there is division of opinion as to the criterion that measures liability. The Second Circuit, speaking

---

a. Contrary to the *Roberts* case, which treats aiding another to commit suicide as plain murder, such conduct was sometimes held not criminal at all because suicide was itself not a crime. Some modern statutes, following the Model Penal Code (§210.5, Appendix to this casebook), resolve the dilemma by making aiding or soliciting another to commit suicide an independent crime. See N.H. Rev. Stat. Ann. tit. 62, §630.4; N.J. Stat. Ann. tit. 2C, §2C:11-6. — Eds.

through Judge Learned Hand, has taken the position that the traditional definitions of complicity (aiding, abetting, counseling, procuring, etc.) "have nothing whatever to do with the probability that the forbidden result would follow upon the accessory's conduct; and that they all demand that he in some sort associate himself with the venture, that he participate in it as in something that he wishes to bring about, that he seek by his action to make it succeed. All the words used — even the most colorless, 'abet'— carry an implication of purposive attitude towards it." [United States v. Peoni, 100 F.2d 401, 402 (1938).] . . .

Strong disagreement has, however, been expressed. Judge Parker, for example, has declared that guilt "as an accessory depends, not on 'having a stake' in the outcome of the crime . . . but on aiding and assisting the perpetrators. . . . The seller may not ignore the purpose for which the purchase is made if he is advised of that purpose, or wash his hands of the aid that he has given the perpetrator of a felony by the plea than he has merely made a sale of merchandise. One who sells a gun to another knowing that he is buying it to commit a murder, would hardly escape conviction as an accessory to the murder by showing that he received full price for the gun." [Backun v. United States, 112 F.2d 635, 637 (4th Cir. 1940)]. . .

The draft, it is submitted, should not embrace the *Peoni* limitation. Conduct which knowingly facilitates the commission of crimes is by hypothesis a proper object of preventive effort by the penal law, unless, of course, it is affirmatively justifiable. It is important in that effort to safeguard the innocent but the requirement of guilty knowledge adequately serves this end — knowledge both that there is a purpose to commit a crime and that one's own behavior renders aid. There are, however, infinite degrees of aid to be considered. This is the point, we think, at which distinctions should be drawn. Accordingly, when a true purpose to further the crime is lacking, the draft requires that the accessorial behavior substantially facilitate commission of the crime and that it do so to the knowledge of the actor. This qualification provides a basis for discrimination that should satisfy the common sense of justice. A vendor who supplies materials readily available upon the market arguably does not make substantial contribution to commission of the crime since the materials could have as easily been gotten elsewhere. The minor employee may win exemption on this ground, though he minded his own business to preserve his job. What is required is to give the courts and juries a criterion for drawing lines that must be drawn. The formula proposed accomplishes this purpose by a standard that is relevant, it is submitted, to all the legal ends involved. There will, of course, be arguable cases; they should, we think, be argued in these terms. . . .

We also agree that a problem of conflicting interests is presented but submit that, absent special grounds that constitute legal justification, it ought to be resolved in favor of a principle that regards crime prevention as the prior value to be served. . . . [W]hen the only interest of the actor is his wish for freedom to forego concern about the criminal purposes of others, though he knowingly facilitates in a substantial measure the achievement of such purposes, it is an interest that, we think, is properly subordinated generally to the larger interest of preventing crime. It should be added that the issue here is that of liability, not that of treatment on conviction; discriminations among parties with respect to punishment or treatment is, of course, in order; the basis for them will be furnished by the draft.

The Model Penal Code's tentative formulations on this issue were rejected by the American Law Institute. The Code now requires that the actor have "the purpose of promoting or facilitating" the commission of the crime. Section 2.06(3)(a), Appendix to this casebook.

Question: What are the inadequacies, if any, in the reporter's arguments that led to its rejection? Consider G. Williams, Criminal Law: The General Part 369-370 (2d ed. 1961):

> From the point of view of policy the question is one of some complexity. On the one side are the policy of repressing crime, and the difficulty of distinguishing between the merchant who knowingly assists a crime and the ordinary accessory before the fact. On the other side stand the undesirability of giving too great an extension to the criminal law, and the inconvenience to legitimate trade of requiring a merchant to concern himself with the affairs of his customers. The difficulty is increased by the number of different modes in which the question may arise. The merchant may desire the crime, or he may foresee it as certain if he sells the commodity, or he may foresee it as belonging to one of many degrees of probability. The sale may be completely in the ordinary course of business, or the order may in some way be a special one — as when a tailor makes a suit with secret pockets for poaching or smuggling. The merchant may charge the usual price or an extra price on account of the legal risk. The commodity may be appropriate only to a single crime (as with poison that is consumed only once), or may enable the purchaser to engage in a life of crime. The crime in contemplation may be a serious or a trivial one.

See also G. Fletcher, Rethinking Criminal Law 676 (1978):

> From the standpoint of the supplier, the problem of refusing services to known criminals closely resembles the problem of intervening to prevent impending harm. The grocery store, the gas station, the physician, the answering service all provide routine services. Does the business-person have a duty to make an exception just because he or she knows that the purchaser is engaged in illegal activity? That question of duty corresponds to the problem of the motorist who must decide whether to stop his car and render aid to an accident victim. The assumption underlying both fields is that people are entitled to carry on their lives without deviating every time doing so might help a person in distress or hamper the execution of a criminal plan.

4. *Criminal facilitation.* One response to these contending considerations is to make giving less than purposeful aid a separate crime with a lesser penalty than the crime aided. New York has pioneered this approach with a new crime called "criminal facilitation."[1] N.Y. Penal Code §115 provides:

> A person is guilty of criminal facilitation in the second degree when, believing it probable that he is rendering aid to a person who intends to commit a crime, he engages in conduct which provides such person with means or opportunity for the commission thereof and which in fact aids such person to commit a felony. Criminal facilitation in the second degree is a class A misdemeanor.[a]

Note that the formula of liability is wider than that originally proposed by the Model Penal Code, which would have required "knowing" aid as a basis of

---

1. Very few jurisdictions have followed the lead. Arizona is one state that has. Ariz. Rev. Stat. Ann. tit. 13, §13-1004.

a. Section 115.05 makes such conduct first-degree criminal facilitation when the crime committed is a class A felony (such crimes as murder, for example) and subjects it to punishment as a class C felony (maximum 15 years of imprisonment). — EDS.

accomplice liability. It is enough under the New York formulation that the aider believes it "probable" that the person aided will commit a crime.

Query: Would the defendant in the *Gladstone* case be guilty of criminal facilitation under the New York statute? See People v. Gordon, 32 N.Y.2d 62, 295 N.E.2d 777 (1973), holding in the negative. Do you agree?

5. *Conspiracy.* A closely related problem is whether assistance given another with knowledge, but not a true purpose, constitutes a conspiracy between the person giving and the person receiving the aid. See People v. Lauria, pages 675-681 infra, and the cases discussed therein. Judge Learned Hand took the position that the requisite intent in aiding and abetting and in conspiracy are the same. See United States v. Falcone, 109 F.2d 579, 581 (2d Cir. 1940). For a contrary view, see People v. Samarjian, 240 Cal. App. 2d 13, 49 Cal. Rptr. 180 (1966). The court there held that the supplier of forged parimutuel betting tickets to a person who uses them for fraudulent purposes cannot, on those facts alone, be convicted of conspiring with the user. But those facts were held sufficient to sustain a conviction for aiding and abetting.

REGINA v. CREAMER
Court of Criminal Appeal
[1965] 3 All E.R. 257

LORD PARKER, C.J., delivered the following judgment of the court: In March, 1965, at the Central Criminal Court the appellant, together with a Mrs. Harris, were jointly indicted with unlawfully killing one Angela Price, and both were convicted of manslaughter. Mrs. Harris was sentenced to three years' imprisonment and the appellant was fined £150, and in default six months' imprisonment. The appellant now appeals by certificate of the learned common serjeant, the ground of appeal being whether being an accessory before the fact to manslaughter, i.e., involuntary manslaughter resulting from criminal abortion, is an offence known to the law. It was the case for the prosecution that the deceased died in the course of an abortion performed solely by Mrs. Harris, and that the appellant, who was not present at the time, had arranged for the abortion to be performed, and indeed had introduced the parties, and was, accordingly, an accessory before the fact. . . .

. . . [Counsel for appellant] takes a number of points. In the first instance, he points out that it is of the essence of counselling and procuring that you intend the result which you counsel or procure. A man cannot procure what he cannot intend, and he cannot intend an accidental killing. . . . He secondly invokes the principle . . . that a man cannot be guilty of being an accessory before the fact to a felony different from that which he counselled and procured. Here counsel for the appellant contends that the appellant only counselled and procured the felony of abortion, whereas manslaughter is a separate felony. Thirdly, he contends that, in any event, the death is too remote to constitute the appellant an accessory to the causing of that death. He points out that the principal himself who commits the act from which death results is anyhow one stage removed from the death. Accordingly, a person who counsels and procures the act is two stages removed from the death. Bearing in mind that the appellant in the present case could have been charged as accessory before the fact to the abortion, he invites the court to say that the consequences here are too remote.

In the opinion of this court, the conclusion reached by Edmund Davies, J. [in R. v. Buck, 44 Cr. App. 213 (1960)], is correct. A man is guilty of involuntary manslaughter when he intends an unlawful act and one likely to do harm to the person and death results which was neither foreseen nor intended. It is the accident of death resulting which makes him guilty of manslaughter as opposed to some lesser offence, such as assault or, in the present case, abortion. This can no doubt be said to be illogical, since the culpability is the same, but, nevertheless, it is an illogicality which runs throughout the whole of our law, both the common law and the statute law. A comparatively recent example is clearly that of dangerous driving and causing death by dangerous driving. Bearing that in mind, it is quite consistent that a man who has counselled and procured such an illegal and dangerous act from which death, unintended, results should be guilty of being accessory before the fact to manslaughter. Nor can it be validly said that, when death results, a different felony has been committed. . . . The act intended is the same whether or not death results, and it is merely the accident of death which gives that act a different label. This court is quite satisfied that the law is as stated in 4 Blackstone's Commentaries (23rd Edn.), p. 38 . . . :

"It is likewise a rule, that he who in any wise commands or counsels another to commit an unlawful act, is accessory to all that ensues upon that unlawful act; but is not accessory to any act distinct from the other."

For these reasons, this court is of opinion that this appeal fails and must be dismissed.[a]

COMMONWEALTH v. ROOT
Supreme Court of Pennsylvania
403 Pa. 571, 170 A.2d 310 (1961)

[For the opinion in this case, see page 546 supra.]

JACOBS v. STATE, 184 So. 2d 711 (Fla. 1966): [For excerpts from this case, see page 549 supra.[b]]

COMMONWEALTH v. ATENCIO
Supreme Judicial Court of Massachusetts
345 Mass. 627, 189 N.E.2d 223 (1963)

[For the opinion of this case, see page 549 supra.]

a. See Annot., Who other than actor is liable for manslaughter, 95 A.L.R.2d 175, 191 (1964). — Eds.

b. For a drag race case in which participants in another car were held as aiders and abettors of the reckless driver of the car that caused the killing, see Stallard v. State, 209 Tenn. 13, 348 S.W.2d 489 (1961). — Eds.

PROBLEMS

1. Reexamine Model Penal Code §2.06, Appendix to this casebook. Subsection 3 provides that one who aids or solicits another person to commit an offense is an accomplice of that person only if he or she acts "with the purpose of promoting or facilitating the commission of the offense." Subsection 4, however, provides:

> When causing a particular result is an element of an offense, an accomplice in the conduct causing such result is an accomplice in the commission of that offense, if he acts with the kind of culpability, if any, with respect to that result that is sufficient for the commission of the offense.

Query: What does this section mean? Would it yield the same result as that reached in the *Creamer* case? Would it help in dealing with the cases that immediately follow it — the drag race and Russian roulette cases? On what basis can these cases be distinguished from *Creamer?*

2. In People v. Marshall, 362 Mich. 170, 106 N.W.2d 842 (1961), defendant lent his car keys to McCleary with knowledge that the latter was drunk; this act was a misdemeanor under Michigan law because defendant acted with knowledge that McCleary was intoxicated. McCleary drove the car into a head-on collision, killing both himself and the driver of the other car. On defendant's appeal from a conviction of involuntary manslaughter, the state relied on Story v. United States, 16 F.2d 342, 344 (D.C. Cir. 1926), in which an owner, driving with a drunk, permitted him to take the wheel and was held liable for aiding and abetting him in his criminal negligence. The owner, said that court, sat by his side and permitted him "without protest so recklessly and negligently to operate the car as to cause the death of another." Question: Should defendant's conviction be affirmed on the principle of the *Story* case? On any other principle?

3. The accused surreptitiously laced a friend's drink with a double measure of alcohol, knowing that his friend would shortly be driving his car home. His friend then drove home and was found with alcohol concentration in his blood over the statutory limit. He was convicted of the offense of driving under the influence, an absolute-liability offense. The accused was then charged with aiding, abetting, counseling, or procuring the statutory offense of his friend. The judge acquitted the accused. The attorney-general referred the ruling to the Court of Appeal as authorized by statute. The court held that the trial court was in error on the ground that shared intention was not needed for accessorial liability and that "procuring" was satisfied by the causal link between the act of the accused and the offense by the driver. Attorney-General's Reference (No. 1 of 1975), [1975] W.L.R. 11.

Consider the following situations:

(a) Suppose the crime of driving under the influence was not an absolute-liability offense and the driver was acquitted (or not charged). What then would have been the liability of the accused?

(b) Suppose that the driver had become so far intoxicated by the drink that his action of driving the car was not volitional at all.

(c) Suppose, finally, the situation put by counsel for the accused in the above case:

> . . . if [the Court] held that there may be a procuring on the facts of the present case, it would be but a short step to a similar finding for the generous host, with somewhat bibulous friends, when at the end of the day his friends leave him to go to their houses in circumstances in which they are not fit to drive and in circumstances in which an offense under the Road Traffic Act is committed. The suggestion has been made that the host may in those circumstances be guilty with his guests on the basis that he has either aided, abetted, counselled or procured the offense.

REGINA v. ANDERSON AND MORRIS
Court of Criminal Appeal
[1966] 2 W.L.R. 1195

LORD PARKER, C.J. [When Anderson learned that Welch had attacked his wife, he obtained a knife and, in the company of his friend Morris, sought out Welch. A fight ensued in which Anderson used his knife to kill Welch. Morris was convicted of manslaughter. Only that portion of the opinion that deals with his appeal is included here.]

What is complained of is a passage of the summing-up. It is unnecessary to read the direction on law in full. The material direction is:

> If you think there was a common design to attack Welch but it is not proved, in the case of Morris, that he had any intention to kill or cause grievous bodily harm, but that Anderson, without the knowledge of Morris, had a knife, took it from the flat and at some time formed the intention to kill or cause grievous bodily harm to Welch and did kill him — an act outside the common design to which Morris is proved to have been a party — then you would or could on the evidence find it proved that Anderson committed murder and Morris would be liable to be convicted of manslaughter provided you are satisfied that he took part in the attack or fight with Welch. . . .

Mr. Lane [for the defense] submits that that was a clear misdirection. He would put the principle of law to be invoked in this form: that where two persons embark on a joint enterprise, each is liable for the acts done in pursuance of that joint enterprise, that that includes liability for unusual consequences if they arise from the execution of the agreed joint enterprise but (and this is the crux of the matter) that, if one of the adventurers goes beyond what has been tacitly agreed as part of the common enterprise, his co-adventurer is not liable for the consequences of that unauthorised act. . . .

In support of that, he refers to a number of authorities to which this court finds it unnecessary to refer in detail, which in the opinion of this court shows that at any rate for the last 130 or 140 years that has been the true position. . . .

Mr. Caulfield [for the prosecution], on the other hand, while recognising that he cannot go beyond this long string of decided cases, has said really that they are all part and parcel of a much wider principle which he would put in this form, that if two or more persons engaged in an unlawful act and one suddenly develops an intention to kill whereby death results, not only is he guilty of murder, but all those who have engaged in the unlawful act are guilty of manslaughter. He recognises that the present trend of authority is against that proposition, but he goes back to Salisbury's case in 1553. In that case a master had laid in wait to attack a man, and his servants, who had no idea of what his, the master's, idea was, joined in the attack, whereby the man was killed. It was held there that those servants were themselves guilty of man-slaughter.

The court is . . . quite clear that the principle is wholly out of touch with the position today. It seems to this court that to say that adventurers are guilty of manslaughter when one of them has departed completely from the concerted action of the common design and has suddenly formed an intent to kill and has used a weapon and acted in a way which no party to that common design could suspect is something which would revolt the conscience of people today.

Mr. Caulfield, in his attractive argument, points to the fact that it would seem to be illogical that, if two people had formed a common design to do an unlawful act and death resulted by an unforeseen consequence, they should be held, as they would undoubtedly be held, guilty of manslaughter; whereas if one of them in those circumstances had in a moment of passion decided to kill, they would be acquitted altogether. The law, of course, is not completely logical, but there is nothing really illogical in such a result, in that it could well be said as a matter of common sense that in the latter circumstances the death resulted or was caused by the sudden action of the adventurer who decided to kill and killed. Considered as a matter of causation there may well be an overwhelming supervening event which is of such a character that it will relegate into history matters which would otherwise be looked upon as causative factors. Looked at in that way, there is really nothing illogical in the result to which Mr. Caulfield points. . . .

. . . In the case of Morris, the court will allow the appeal and quash the conviction.

NOTES

1. Consider the following commentary on the *Anderson and Morris* case in [1966] Crim. L. Rev. 385, 386:

> If *A.* knows *B.* is carrying a knife and expects him, in the course of a common enterprise, to use it to kill or to cause grievous bodily harm, *A.* will clearly be liable for murder if *B.* does use the knife to kill. If *A.* knows that *B.* has a knife and expects him to use the knife merely to threaten, he will be liable for man-slaughter if *B.* kills with the knife — even, apparently, if *B.* does so deliberately. If *A.* does not know that *B.* is carrying a knife but expects *B.* to fight with his fists and, in the course of that fight, *B.* uses the knife to kill, *A.* will, so the present case decides, be guilty of neither murder nor manslaughter though he would have been liable for manslaughter had *B.* killed by a blow of the fist. If *A.*, a passenger

in *B*.'s car, expects *B*. to drive the car near to *C*. so as to terrify him and *B*. deliberately drives the car over *C*. and kills him, *A*. will be liable for manslaughter: Murtagh and Kennedy [1955] Crim. L.R. 315. But if *B*. unknown to *A*. is carrying a revolver and shoots *C*. as the car goes by, *A*. will be liable for neither murder nor manslaughter.

See Sayre, Criminal Responsibility for the Acts of Another, 43 Harv. L. Rev. 689, 702-706 (1930):

> Apart from exceptional groups of cases . . . the law may be summarized as follows:
>
> (1) If the defendant can be shown himself to have counseled, procured, commanded, incited, authorized, or encouraged the commission of the particular act which forms the subject of the prosecution, all courts agree in holding him criminally liable, even though the agent committed the act through a different instrumentality, or at a different time, or in a different place from that ordered or authorized.
>
> (2) Where the defendant has neither authorized nor consented to the particular criminal act, even though he has authorized the general business in the course of which the act was committed, the defendant may be civilly, but is not, except as under (3), criminally liable.
>
> (3) On the other hand, even if the particular criminal act has not been authorized or consented to, if it grows out of and is the proximate consequence of one that has been authorized or procured, the defendant is criminally liable, whether or not the agent is acting in the course of the defendant's business.
>
> Whether or not the crime committed is a "proximate consequence" of the crime ordered or procured is often an exceedingly nice question. Such a problem is closely analogous to that arising in the case where one of several accomplices acting in pursuance of a joint plan commits some crime not specifically planned but growing out of the joint enterprise. In such a case, the other accomplices will be liable for the crime thus committed only if it grew out of and was the proximate consequence of the one planned. For instance, where *A* and *B* join in a robbery, if *A* in the commission of the robbery kills the victim, *B* will be separately liable not only for the robbery, but also for the murder. The same is true where *A* and *B* join in a concerted burglary. For death is not an improbable consequence of robbery or burglary, and proximate causation can in most such cases be established. On the other hand, if *A* and *B* set out to commit larceny, and *A* while in the commission of the larceny robs a night watchman, *B* is not guilty of the robbery. So, confederates who combine to commit an assault merely, are not liable for a robbery of the victim by one of their number; nor are confederates who plan to kill *A* ordinarily liable if one of their number intentionally kills *B*.

2. See Model Penal Code §2.04 [now §2.06], Comment at 26 (Tent. Draft No. 1, 1953):

> Whatever may be law upon the point, it is submitted that the liability of an accomplice ought not to extend beyond the criminal purposes that he shares or knows. Probabilities have an important evidential bearing on these issues; to make them independently sufficient is to predicate the liability on negligence when, for good reason, more is normally required before liability is found.

Accordingly, §2.06 requires that for a person to be "an accomplice of another person in the commission of an offense," he must act with the purpose of promoting or facilitating "the commission of the offense."

A contrasting approach is taken in several recent criminal code revisions.

Kan. Stat. Ann. §21-3205(2), for example, provides that where one is criminally liable for a crime of another he "is also liable for any other crime committed in pursuance of the intended crime if reasonably foreseeable by him as a probable consequence of committing or attempting to commit the crime intended." See also Minn. Stat. Ann. §609.05(2); Wis. Stat. Ann. §929.05. See the discussion of this issue in LaFave & Scott, Criminal Law 515-517 (1972).

3. In judging the various approaches to the problem of variation between the crime the defendant thought he or she was assisting or encouraging and the crime actually committed, consider the following:

(a) In Regina v. Bainbridge, [1960] 1 Q.B. 129, defendant procured oxyacety-lene equipment for another, believing it was to be used for cutting up stolen property. Contrary to his expectation it was used to break into a bank. Query: Did defendant have the mens rea to be considered an accomplice to the bank robbery? The court held that he did because he knew that a crime of the same type as that actually committed was intended by the principal.

(b) In Director of Public Prosecutions for Northern Ireland v. Maxwell, [1978] 3 All E.R. 1140, defendant, a member of a terrorist organization, used his car to lead another car containing a group of his fellow members to a designated place. After he left, the others exploded a bomb in a public place. He knew the others intended a military operation of some sort but did not know they had in mind exploding a bomb or that they had a bomb with them. Query: Did he have the mens rea to be considered an accomplice to this bombing? The House of Lords held yes, on the ground that it sufficed that the crime actually committed was one that defendant had in contemplation as an obvious possibility among those crimes likely to be committed by the people he helped.

For a discussion of these cases, see Buxton, Note, 42 Mod. L. Rev. 315 (1979).

2.   Actus Reus

WILCOX v. JEFFERY
King's Bench Division
[1951] 1 All E.R. 464

LORD GODDARD, C.J. This is a Case stated by the metropolitan magistrate at Bow Street Magistrate's Court before whom the appellant, Herbert William Wilcox, the proprietor of a periodical called "Jazz Illustrated," was charged on an information that

> on Dec. 11, 1949, he did unlawfully aid and abet one Coleman Hawkins in contraven-ing art. 1(4) of the Aliens Order, 1920, by failing to comply with a condition attached to a grant of leave to land, to wit, that the said Coleman Hawkins should take no employment paid or unpaid while in the United Kingdom, contrary to art. 18(2) of the Aliens Order, 1920. . . .

The case is concerned with the visit of a celebrated professor of the saxophone, a gentleman by the name of Hawkins who was a citizen of the United States. He came here at the invitation of two gentlemen of the name of Curtis and Hughes, connected with a jazz club which enlivens the neighbourhood of Willes-

den. . . . Mr. Hawkins . . . arrived with four French musicians. When they
came to the airport, among the people who were there to greet them was the
appellant. He had not arranged their visit, but he knew they were coming and
he was there to report the arrival of these important musicians for his magazine.
So, evidently, he was regarding the visit of Mr. Hawkins as a matter which
would be of interest to himself and the magazine which he was editing and
selling for profit. Messrs. Curtis and Hughes arranged a concert at the Princes
Theatre, London. The appellant attended that concert as a spectator. He paid
for his ticket. Mr. Hawkins went on the stage and delighted the audience by
playing the saxophone. The appellant did not get up and protest in the name
of the musicians of England that Mr. Hawkins ought not to be here competing
with them and taking the bread out of their mouths or the wind out of their
instruments. It is not found that he actually applauded, but he was there having
paid to go in, and, no doubt, enjoying the performance, and then, lo and behold
out comes his magazine with a most laudatory description, fully illustrated, of
this concert. On those facts the magistrate has found that he aided and abetted.

Reliance is placed by the prosecution on R. v. Coney ((1882), 8 Q.B.D. 534)
which dealt with a prize fight. This case relates to a jazz band concert, but the
particular nature of the entertainment provided, whether by fighting with bare
fists or playing on saxophones, does not seem to me to make any difference
to the question which we have to decide. The fact is that a man is charged
with aiding and abetting an illegal act, and I can find no authority for saying
that it matters what that illegal act is, provided that the aider and abettor knows
the facts sufficiently well to know that they would constitute an offence in the
principal. In R. v. Coney the prize fight took place in the neighbourhood of
Ascot, and four or five men were convicted or aiding and abetting the fight.
The conviction was quashed on the ground that the chairman had not given a
correct direction to the jury when he told them that, as the prisoners were
physically present at the fight, they must be held to have aided and abetted.
That direction, the court held, was wrong, it being too wide. The matter was
very concisely put by Cave, J., whose judgment was fully concurred in by that
great master of the criminal law, Stephen, J. Cave, J., said (8 Q.B.D. 540):
"Where presence may be entirely accidental, it is not even evidence of aiding
and abetting. Where presence is prima facie not accidental it is evidence, but
no more than evidence, for the jury."

There was not accidental presence in this case. The appellant paid to go to
the concert and he went there because he wanted to report it. He must, therefore,
be held to have been present, taking part, concurring, or encouraging, whichever
word you like to use for expressing this conception. It was an illegal act on
the part of Hawkins to play the saxophone or any other instrument at this
concert. The appellant clearly knew that it was an unlawful act for him to play.
He had gone there to hear him, and his presence and his payment to go there
was an encouragement. He went there to make use of the performance, because
he went there, as the magistrate finds and was justified in finding, to get "copy"
for his newspaper. It might have been entirely different, as I say, if he had
gone there and protested, saying: "The musicians' union do not like you foreign-
ers coming here and playing and you ought to get off the stage." If he had
booed, it might have been some evidence that he was not aiding and abetting.
If he had gone as a member of a claque to try to drown the noise of the saxophone,

he might very likely be found not guilty of aiding and abetting. In this case it seems clear that he was there, not only to approve and encourage what was done, but to take advantage of it by getting "copy" for his paper. In those circumstances there was evidence on which the magistrate could find that the appellant aided and abetted, and for these reasons I am of opinion that the appeal fails. . . .

Appeal dismissed with costs.

STATE ex rel. ATTORNEY GENERAL v. TALLY, JUDGE, 102 Ala. 25, 69, 15 So. 722, 739 (1894): [On an impeachment proceeding against Judge Tally, it was shown as follows: that deceased had seduced the judge's sister-in-law and that her brothers, seeking retribution, followed him to the nearby town of Stevenson in order to kill him; that the judge went to the local telegraph office; that while there one of deceased's relatives sent deceased a telegram warning him that the brothers were after him; that the judge thereupon sent his own telegram to the Stevenson telegraph operator, whom he knew, telling him not to deliver the warning telegram; that the operator received both telegrams and failed to deliver the message to the deceased; and that the brothers caught up with deceased and killed him. On these facts the court found that the judge was an accomplice of the brothers in the killing, saying:]

We are therefore clear to the conclusion that before Judge Tally can be found guilty of aiding and abetting the Skeltons to kill Ross, it must appear that his vigil at Scottsboro to prevent Ross from being warned of his danger was by preconcert with them, or at least known to them, whereby they would naturally be incited, encouraged and emboldened, 'given confidence' to the deed, or that he aided them to kill Ross, contributed to Ross's death in point of physical fact by means of the telegram he sent to Huddleston [the telegraph operator]. . . .

The assistance given, however, need not contribute to the criminal result in the sense that but for it the result would not have ensued. It is quite sufficient if it facilitated a result that would have transpired without it. It is quite enough if the aid merely renders it easier for the principal actor to accomplish the end intended by him and the aider and abetter, though in all human probability the end would have been attained without it. If the aid in homicide can be shown to have put the deceased at a disadvantage, to have deprived him of a single chance of life, which but for it he would have had, he who furnished such aid is guilty though it can not be known or shown that the dead man, in the absence thereof, would have availed himself of that chance. As where one counsels murder he is guilty as an accessory before the fact, though it appears to be probable that murder would have been done without his counsel. . . .

PROBLEMS ON THE MATERIALITY OF AID OR ENCOURAGEMENT GIVEN

1. Consider the contrast between causation and accessorial liability. In both kinds of liability, the issue is whether the defendant is liable for an event that takes place through intermediate occurrences. For the defendant to be held to have caused the event, the prosecution must establish — as a minimum — that, but for the defendant's action, the event would not have occurred. On the other hand, for the defendant to be held accessorially liable for an event through the intermediate action of another person, as the *Tally* case and Wilcox v. Jeffery make clear, it is not necessary to establish a but-for relation between the defendant's action and the criminal conduct of another. Even if the same result would have occurred without the defendant's contribution, he will be liable as an accomplice if he or she acted with the required mens rea (for example, in the *Hicks* case, pages 613-615 supra, if Hicks was only one of a hundred people in a crowd all shouting words of encouragement and all intending to spur Rowe on. See Wilcox v. Jeffery).

How should we account for this difference between causation and accessorial liability? What difficulties would a prosecution face in proving beyond a reasonable doubt that the help or encouragement of the accessory was a but-for cause of the action of the primary party? See G. Williams, Criminal Law, The General Part 381-383 (2d ed. 1961).

2. We just noted that even a minimal possibility of actual aid or encouragement suffices for accessorial liability. Question: Need there be any actual aid or encouragement at all? Consider these variations on cases we have just read:

In *Hicks,* suppose defendant deliberately shouted encouragement to Rowe to spur him on to kill Colvard, but it is shown at the trial that Rowe was completely deaf and was, moreover, totally unaware of Hicks's presence.

In *Tally,* what would have been the result:

(a) if the telegraph operator had disregarded the judge's instructions and had tried, though in vain, to deliver the warning telegram;

(b) if the pursuers never succeeded in catching up with their intended victim;

(c) if the pursuers did catch up, but were effectively resisted by their victim?

In the *Hicks* and the first *Tally* hypothetical, there is attempted encouragement or aid to the person who commits the crime, but none in fact rendered. What should be the liability of the defendants? Under the Model Penal Code, §2.06(3), and the states that follow its lead,[2] the defendants would be accomplices since under that provision a person acting with the required mens rea is an accomplice of another in the commission of an offense whether he or she aids or "attempts to aid such other person in planning or committing it." Is this view sound? The drafters' comment states (§2.04 [now §2.06], Comment at 27 (Tent. Draft No. 1, 1956)): "The inclusion of attempts to aid may go in part beyond the present law, but attempted complicity ought to be criminal and to distinguish it from effective complicity appears unnecessary when the crime has been committed." Some state statutes follow the Model Penal Code.

Consider again the second *Tally* hypothetical. Here the situation is the same except that the crime defendant tried to aid is not committed. Does §2.06(3) cover the situation? How should it be dealt with? As an attempt to be an accomplice by attempting to aid in the commission of a crime? See the Model Penal Code solution to this problem in §5.01(3), Appendix to this casebook.

---

2. See, e.g., Haw. Rev. Stat. tit. 17, §705-202; Ky. Rev. Stat. Ann. ch. 500, §502.020; N.J. Stat. Ann. tit. 2C, §2C:2-6(c); Or. Rev. Stat. tit. 16, §161.155; Pa. Cons. Stat. Ann. tit. 18, §306(c); Tex. Pen. Code Ann. §7.02.

3. The Relationship between the Liability of the Parties

INTRODUCTORY NOTE

A recent decision, citing numerous cases, observes that "It is hornbook law
that a defendant charged with aiding and abetting the commission of a crime
by another cannot be convicted in the absence of proof that the crime was
actually committed." United States v. Ruffin, 613 F.2d 408, 412 (2d Cir. 1979).
The cases in this section explore the meaning and implications of that proposition.

STATE v. HAYES
Supreme Court of Missouri
105 Mo. 76, 16 S.W. 514 (1891)

THOMAS, J. The defendant appeals from a sentence of five years' imprisonment
in the penitentiary for burglary and larceny. . . . [Defendant proposed to one
Hill that he join him in the burglary of a general store. Hill, actually a relative
of the store owners, feigned acquiescence in order to obtain the arrest of defendant and advised the store owners of the plan. On the night of the planned
burglary, defendant and Hill arrived at the store together. Defendant raised
the window and assisted Hill in climbing through into the building. Hill handed
out a side of bacon. Shortly thereafter they were apprehended.] It will be seen
the trial court told the jury in [its] instruction that defendant was guilty of
burglary if he, with a felonious intent, assisted and aided Hill to enter the building, notwithstanding Hill himself may have had no such intent. In this we think
the court erred. One cannot read this record without being convinced beyond
a reasonable doubt that Hill did not enter the warehouse with intent to steal.
. . . We may assume, then, for the sake of the argument, that Hill committed
no crime in entering the wareroom. The act of Hill, however, was by the instruction of the court imputed to defendant. This act, according to the theory of
the instructions, so far as Hill was concerned, was not a criminal act, but when
it was imputed to defendant it became criminal because of the latter's felonious
intent. This would probably be true if Hill had acted under the control and
compulsion of defendant, and as his passive and submissive agent. But he was
not a passive agent in this transaction. He was an active one. He acted of his
own volition. He did not raise the window and enter the building with intent
to commit crime, but simply to entrap defendant in the commission of crime,
and have him captured.

Judge Brewer sets this idea in a very clear light in State v. Jansen, 22 Kan.
498. He says: "The act of a detective may perhaps be not imputable to the
defendant, as there is a want of community of motive. The one has a criminal
intent, while the other is seeking the discovery and punishment of crime." Where
the owner learns that his property is to be stolen, he may employ detectives
and decoys to catch the thief. And we can do no better than to quote again
from Judge Brewer in the case above cited, as to the relation of the acts of
detectives and the thief when a crime is alleged to have been committed by

the two. He says: "Where each of the overt acts going to make up the crime charged is personally done by the defendant, and with criminal intent, his guilt is complete, no matter what motives may prompt or what acts be done by the party who is with him, and apparently assisting him. Counsel have cited and commented upon several cases in which detectives figured, and in which defendants were adjudged guiltless of the crimes charged. But this feature distinguishes them: that some act essential to the crime charged was in fact done by the detective, and not by the defendant, and, this act not being imputable to the defendant, the latter's guilt was not made out. The intent and act must combine, and all the elements of the act must exist and be imputable to the defendant." Applying the principle here announced to the case at bar, we find that defendant did not commit every overt act that went to make up the crime. He did not enter the warehouse, either actually or constructively, and hence he did not commit the crime of burglary, no matter what his intent was, it clearly appearing that Hill was guilty of no crime. To make defendant responsible for the acts of Hill, they must have had a common motive and common design. The design and the motives of the two men were not only distinct, but dissimilar, even antagonistic. . . . The court should instruct the jury that if Hill broke into and entered the wareroom with a felonious intent, and defendant was present, aiding him with the same intent, then he is guilty; but if Hill entered the room with no design to steal, but simply to entrap defendant, and capture him in the commission of crime, and defendant did not enter the room himself, then he is not guilty of burglary and larceny as charged. He may be found guilty, however, of petit larceny, in taking and removing the bacon after it was handed to him. This overt act he did in fact commit. . . . The judgment is reversed, and the cause remanded for new trial.

All concur.

NOTES

1. The feigned accomplice. Apparently if the participation of Hill and defendant had been the other way around, Hill opening the window and defendant climbing through, defendant could have been readily convicted of burglary.[3] But is defendant more or less a proper subject for penal sanction depending on whether he climbed through the window or helped his supposed confrere do so? Does this fortuitous aspect of the incident have a proper bearing on the criminality of defendant's acts? Could a contrary conclusion have been reached without doing injustice to the concept of accessorial liability? Could defendant have been convicted of an attempt to aid and abet Hill? Consider Model Penal Code §2.06(3).

2. The innocent or irresponsible accomplice. (a) Suppose that the absence of a "common motive and common design" on the part of Hill was not due to his motive to catch Hayes but to the fact that he was being coerced at gunpoint by Hayes. Would Hayes here also not be guilty of burglary?

See Model Penal Code §2.06(2)(a): "A person is legally accountable for the conduct of another person when . . . acting with the kind of culpability that

3. This outcome would obtain unless Hill was a police officer and a defense of entrapment had been made out. See Model Penal Code §2.13, Appendix to this casebook.

is sufficient for the commission of the offense, he causes an innocent or irresponsible person to engage in such conduct." The drafter's comment states (§2.04 [now §2.06], comment at 15 (Tent. Draft No. 1, 1953)):

> This paragraph is based upon the universally acknowledged principle that one is no less guilty of the commission of a crime because he uses the overt behavior of an innocent or irresponsible agent. He is accountable in such cases as if the behavior were his own; at common law he was a principal.

(b) Compare Regina v. Cogan, [1975] 2 All E.R. 1059. In this case, Leak forced his wife, against her will, to have intercourse with Cogan, after leading an intoxicated Cogan falsely to believe that his wife really desired intercourse with him despite her seeming distress and protestation. Both men were convicted of rape, Cogan as principal and Leak as aider and abettor. Under a House of Lords decision following the conviction, Regina v. Morgan, [1976] A.C. 182, page 286 supra, Cogan's actual, albeit unreasonable, belief that Mrs. Leak was consenting precluded his conviction. Since the trial court had instructed the jury to the contrary, and the jury stated, in response to the judge's questions, that Cogan did believe she was consenting, Cogan's conviction was quashed. Leak argued that since Cogan was not guilty of rape, Leak could not be found guilty of aiding and abetting Cogan to rape Mrs. Leak. The Court of Appeal rejected this contention and upheld Leak's conviction, concluding that, while he could not technically be held as an aider and abettor as charged, his guilt as a principal offender was clear.

Note, however, that England, like most American jurisdictions, still recognizes the common law immunity of a husband for the rape of his own wife. See page 387 supra. This rule would present no barrier to holding Leak as an aider or abettor, if Cogan had been guilty of rape,[4] but how can Leak be convicted as a principal? The English court reasoned,

> [A] man cannot by his own physical act rape his wife during cohabitation . . . because the law presumes consent from the marriage ceremony. . . . There is no such presumption when a man procures a drunken friend to do the physical act for him.

Questions: Is the result sound? Could it be reached under the Model Penal Code (consider especially §2.06(5), Appendix to this casebook) or under the New York statute quoted in footnote 4. For analysis of this general problem under the federal accomplice statute, see United States v. Ruffin, 613 F.2d 408 (2d Cir. 1979).

3. *The culpable-but-unconvictable accomplice.* In the situations described in the two preceding notes, courts can avoid conflict with the general principle that "there must be a guilty principal before there can be an aider and abettor." (United States v. Jones, 425 F.2d 1048, 1056 (9th Cir. 1970).) Courts can treat

---

4. The English, as well as the generally accepted American, position is represented by the New York Penal Code, which declares in §20.05(3): "In any prosecution for a offense in which the criminal liability of the defendant is based upon the conduct of another person, it is no defense that . . . the offense in question, as defined, can be committed only by a particular class or classes of persons, and the defendant, not belonging to such class or classes, is for that reason legally incapable of committing the offense in an individual capacity."

the liability of defendant as resting solely on his or her own actions (as principal) rather than derivatively on the actions of another (as aider and abettor). But if defendant's cohort is a fully responsible actor, that strategy will not work. In that event, where the principal actor cannot, for some legal reason, be held liable, does it necessarily mean that the person helping him cannot possibly be held liable as an accomplice?

(a) Defendant conspired with and aided another in the commission of espionage, but the latter could not be convicted because of diplomatic immunity. See Farnsworth v. Zerbst, 98 F.2d 541 (5th Cir. 1938).

(b) Defendant aided a principal who has been acquitted on grounds of entrapment. See United States v. Azadian, 436 F.2d 81 (9th Cir. 1971).

(c) In Cole v. United States, 329 F.2d 437, 443 (9th Cir. 1964), defendant knew he was under investigation by a grand jury for possible perjury and feared that the testimony of his former employee would reveal his perjury. Being aware that the employee had himself previously filed a false affidavit, he succeeded in persuading the employee to decline to answer the grand jury's questions on the basis of the employee's constitutional privilege against self-incrimination. Later the employee turned informer, and Cole was charged and convicted of violating §1503 of the United States Code, Title 18, which made it criminal for a person to "corruptly influence, intimidate, or impede any witness" or to "endeavor to influence, obstruct or impede, the due administration of justice." The basis of the conviction was his influencing the employee to invoke the latter's constitutional privilege. The court of appeals upheld the conviction, holding that the evidence was sufficient if defendant had simply advised the witness, with a corrupt motive, to invoke the privilege, even if the witness' invocation of the privilege was constitutionally protected in the circumstances. The court said:

> We hold the constitutional privilege against self-incrimination is an integral part of the due administration of justice, designed to do and further justice, and to the exercise of which there is an absolute right in every witness. A witness violates no duty to claim it, but one who bribes, coerces, forces or threatens a witness to claim it, or advises with corrupt motive the witness to take it, can and does himself obstruct or influence the due administration of justice.

(d) In United States v. Standefer, 447 U.S. 10 (1980), defendant, the head of Gulf Oil Company's tax department, was prosecuted for providing five separate vacations, at company expense, to one Niederberger, an Internal Revenue Service agent in charge of the audit of Gulf's tax returns. In an indictment involving separate counts for each of the various vacations, defendant and Gulf Oil were charged both with violating 18 U.S.C. §201(f) (making gifts to a public official) and with aiding and abetting Niederberger in violating 26 U.S.C. §7214(a)(2) (acceptance of unauthorized compensation by a government employee). Another multicount indictment charged Niederberger with violations of related statutory provisions in connection with each of the various vacations. Prior to defendant's trial, Gulf Oil pled guilty to all counts. Niederberger was tried and convicted on some counts but acquitted on counts relating to certain of the vacations. Defendant moved for dismissal of the charges corresponding to those on which Niederberger had been acquitted, but the motion was denied, and defendant was convicted on all counts.

The Supreme Court upheld defendant's convictions for aiding and abetting Niederberger in the commission of the very crimes for which Niederberger had been acquitted. The Court noted that, under the doctrine of "nonmutual collateral estoppel," a party who has had a fair opportunity to litigate a question of fact in a civil suit sometimes can be precluded from relitigating that fact in a subsequent civil suit. But the Court reasoned that the special rules of procedure and evidence applicable in criminal cases sometimes deny the prosecution a fair opportunity to litigate and prevent correction of an erroneous acquittal. Accordingly, the Court held that the acquittal of Niederberger at his trial should not be given preclusive effect (447 U.S. at 25-26):

> In denying preclusive effect to Niederberger's acquittal, we do not deviate from the sound teaching that "justice must satisfy the appearance of justice." Offutt v. United States, 348 U.S. 11, 14 (1954). This case does no more than manifest the simple, if discomforting, reality that "different juries may reach different results under any criminal statute. That is one of the consequences we accept under our jury system." Roth v. United States, 354 U.S. 476, 492 (1957). While symmetry of results may be intellectually satisfying, it is not required.
>
> Here, [defendant] received a fair trial at which the Government bore the burden of proving beyond reasonable doubt that Niederberger violated 26 U.S.C. §7214(a)(2) and that petitioner aided and abetted him in that venture. He was entitled to no less — and to no more.

4. Discrepancies in the degree of culpability. Given the principle that the secondary actor cannot be guilty as such if the primary actor has committed no crime, does it follow that the secondary actor can be guilty of no lesser or higher grade of crime than that which the primary actor has committed? Consider the following case.

REGINA v. RICHARDS
Court of Appeal
[1974] Q.B. 776

JAMES, L.J. This is an appeal by the defendant, Isabelle Christina Richards, by leave of the single judge against a conviction that she sustained on May 8, 1973, at the Bournemouth Crown Court, the conviction being for an offence of wounding her husband with intent under section 18 of the Offences against the Person Act 1861. . . .

What happened at the trial was that the defendant was charged with two co-accused, Bryant and Squires, both male. There were two counts in the indictment. The first count charged the offence under section 18 of the Offences against the Person Act 1861,[a] the second charge, based on the same facts, being the alternative charge under section 20 not involving the specific intent.[b] . . .

a. Section 18 provides: "Whosoever shall unlawfully and maliciously . . . wound or cause any grievous bodily harm to any person . . . with intent . . . to do some . . . grievous bodily harm to any person . . . shall be guilty of felony. . . ."— EDS.
b. Section 20 provides: "Whosoever shall unlawfully and maliciously wound or inflict any grievous bodily harm upon any other person . . . shall be guilty of a misdemeanor. . . ."— EDS.

. . . [A]t the end of the trial the defendant was convicted of the offence under count 1; Bryant was acquitted on count 1 and was sentenced to 12 months' imprisonment suspended for two years on count 2; Squires was convicted on count 2 and acquitted on count 1. He received a fine of £50 with three months' imprisonment in default of payment. In respect of the defendant she was sentenced to six months' imprisonment to take immediate effect. The defendant appeals not only against conviction but also against sentence.

The facts of the matter can be stated quite shortly. On the evening of February 25, 1973, the defendant's husband, Mr. Richards, left his home in Weymouth in order to go to work. Shortly afterwards in a lane not far away he was attacked by two men, who were wearing black balaclavas over their heads. He was struck on the back of his head. He tried to escape but was grabbed by the coat sleeves. Eventually he struggled free from his assailants. The medical evidence was that he sustained a laceration on the top of his scalp which required two stitches. There was no need for him to be detained in hospital; it was not a serious injury in fact.

On February 26 the defendant was arrested and at the police station she explained that, according to her, her marriage had been deteriorating, she had become very depressed and started drinking. She was asked if it was at her suggestion that her co-accused Bryant (known as Alan) and Squires (known as Paul) attacked her husband, and to that she replied that she had made the suggestion but in fact she did not want them to hurt him. She said: "All I wanted was for us to get together again. I thought if he was hurt, he would turn to me for affection." But in her statement she admitted in these words: "I told them that I wanted them to beat him up bad enough to put him in hospital for a month." She agreed that she had told them that she would give them £5 if they would beat up her husband. She also admitted that she had suggested the appropriate time that her husband might be attacked, namely, when he went out to work, and that she would give a signal by putting on the kitchen light in the house where they lived so that those lying in wait would know when he was setting off for work. As it turned out, there was a power cut at the time so she could not put the light on; she had to hold a candle up to the window, but she played her part as she had promised.

None of the accused gave evidence at the trial and they were content to rest upon the basis that the jury might find them guilty of the second less serious offence. Thus in the upshot the two persons who committed the acts which were the foundation of the offence alleged in count 2 were guilty of an offence under section 20; the defendant, who committed no physical act upon the victim herself at all, was convicted of the more serious offence.

Mr. Aplin's submissions [for appellant] are brief. He says that looking at the facts of this case the defendant is in the position of one who aided and abetted, or counselled and procured, to use the old language, the other two to commit the offence, and that she cannot be guilty of a graver crime than the crime of which the two co-accused were guilty. There was only one offence that was committed, committed by the co-accused, an offence under section 20, and therefore there is no offence under section 18 of the Act of which his client can properly be found guilty on the facts of this case.

Mr. Purvis [for the prosecution] has referred us to a number of authorities in support of his submissions and argument that it is possible, and it should be on the facts of this case, that a person who did no physical act herself by way of assault should nevertheless be guilty of the graver crime of wounding with intent if it is established that she had that specific intent, although persons who were acting at her counselling and command did not have the specific intent that she had and therefore are not themselves guilty of the graver offence. . . .

. . . Mr. Purvis invites our attention to Smith and Hogan, Criminal Law, 2nd ed. (1969): . . . ". . . if there were malice in the abettor, and none in the person who struck the party, it will be murder as to the abettor, and manslaughter only as to the other.". . . It is convenient to cite again from p. 93 of Smith and Hogan, Criminal Law because this puts in a very short compass an essential part of Mr. Purvis's argument: "The true principle, it is suggested,"— Mr. Purvis says this is right — "is that where the principal has caused an actus reus, the liability of each of the secondary parties should be assessed according to his own mens rea. If there is no actus reus, then certainly no one can be convicted.". . .

Mr. Purvis says that here one can properly look at the actus reus, that is the physical blows struck upon Mr. Richards, and separately the intention with which the blows were struck. The defendant, he says, is responsible for the blows being struck, the actus reus, because they were struck at her request by the co-accused. If, as Mr. Purvis says is the case, the specific intention of the defendant was different from the specific intention if any proved to be entertained on the part of the co-accused, then it is proper that the defendant should be convicted of the section 18 offence if that specific intention goes so far as to amount to intent to cause grievous bodily harm, although that intention was never in the minds of the persons who committed the acts at her request.

We do not take that view. Looking at the facts of this case the acts were perpetrated at some distance from where the defendant was. She was not truly in a position which would earlier have been described as an abettor of those who did the acts. There is proved on the evidence in this case one offence and one offence only, namely, the offence of unlawful wounding without the element of specific intent. We do not think it right that one could say that that which was done can be said to be done with the intention of the defendant who was not present at the time and whose intention did not go to the offence which was in fact committed. That is the short point in the case as we see it. If there is only one offence committed, and that is the offence of unlawful wounding, then the person who has requested that offence to be committed, or advised that that offence be committed, cannot be guilty of a graver offence than that in fact which was committed.

For those reasons we think that this conviction cannot stand. On the other hand it is quite clear that the defendant was guilty of the offence which was in fact committed, namely, an offence of unlawful wounding, and Mr. Aplin does not seek to suggest otherwise. . . . [S]o what this court will do is to quash the conviction that was sustained and substitute a conviction for unlawful wounding.

There remains the question of sentence. [His Lordship considered the facts and varied the sentence from one of six months' imprisonment to six months' imprisonment suspended for two years.]

PROBLEM

Compare Moore v. Lowe, 116 W. Va. 165, 168, 180 S.E. 1, 2 (1935), quoting
1 Wharton, Criminal Law 363-364 (12th ed. 1932):

> Under the old law, the defendant was first convicted, and then the accessory was
> charged with being accessory to the offense which the conviction covered. But
> now that instigation is a substantive offense, it must be remembered that the offense
> of the instigator is not necessarily of the same grade as that of the perpetrator.
> The instigator may act in hot blood, in which case he will be guilty only of man-
> slaughter, while the perpetrator may act coolly, and thus be guilty of murder.
> The converse, also, may be true; the instigation may be cool and deliberate, the
> execution in hot blood by a person whom the instigator finds in a condition of
> unreasoning frenzy. A person desiring cooly to get rid of an enemy, for instance,
> may employ as a tool someone whom that enemy has aggrieved, and who is infuri-
> ated by his grievance.[a] Hence an accessory before the fact (or, to adopt the terms
> of recent codes, an instigator) may be guilty of murder, while the principal (or
> perpetrator) may be guilty of manslaughter; or the accessory before the fact (instiga-
> tor), acting in hot blood, may be guilty of manslaughter, while the perpetrator
> (principal), acting with deliberate malice, may be guilty of murder.

Compare also G. Williams, Criminal Law: The General Part 211 (1953):

> To put the matter generally, a secondary party can be convicted of a crime of a
> higher degree than the principal. In effect the primary party is an innocent agent
> in respect of part of the responsibility of the secondary party.

Questions: Do these propositions show the decision in Regina v. Richards
to be incorrect? What, if anything, distinguishes the cases contemplated by the
above writers from *Richards*? Is it that in the former a homicidal crime was
mutually intended, the variation being only in the emotional state of the parties,
which the law recognizes as an aggravating or mitigating factor? If so, why
should the factor of the degree of harm intended not be regarded in *Richards*
as a comparable factor?

NOTE: MUST THE SECONDARY PARTY BE GUILTY IF THE
PRIMARY PARTY IS?

We have been examining cases in which the principal party for various reasons
is not guilty of the crime which the secondary party is charged with helping
or encouraging the principal party to commit. We have seen that the secondary
party can sometimes be liable in this situation. Consider now cases in which
the principal party has committed the crime which the secondary party, acting
with the required mens rea, helped or encouraged the principal party to commit.
Should the secondary party always be liable where this is so?

(a) In The Queen v. Tyrell, [1894] 1 Q.B. 710, a conviction of a minor for
aiding, abetting and encouraging statutory rape upon her by an adult was re-

---

a. A commonly used example is Othello's hot blooded killing of Desdemona engineered by Iago's
cool and deliberate plotting. — EDS.

versed on the ground that the statutory rape law was designed for the protection and not for the prosecution of young girls. The court stated:

> [I]t is impossible to say that the Act, which is absolutely silent about aiding or abetting, or soliciting or inciting, can have intended that the girls for whose protection it was passed should be punishable under it for the offences committed upon themselves.

The same reasoning has been applied to victims charged with conspiracy to commit an offense. See Gebardi v. United States, pages 714-715 infra. See generally Hogan, Victims as Parties to Crime, [1962] Crim. L. Rev. 683.

(b) The Model Penal Code contains a provision, followed in many states,[5] holding that a person is not an accomplice in an offense committed by another either if he is a victim of that offense or if the defense is so defined that his conduct is inevitably incident to its commission. Section 2.06(6)(a), (b). The Comment on this provision states (Tent. Draft No. 1, 1953, at 35-36):

> Exclusion of the victim does not wholly meet the problems that arise. Should a woman be deemed an accomplice when an abortion is performed upon her? Should the man who has intercourse with a prostitute be viewed as an accomplice in the act of prostitution, the purchaser an accomplice in the unlawful sale, the unmarried party to a bigamous marriage an accomplice of the bigamist, the bribe-giver an accomplice of the taker? . . . What is common to these cases is . . . that the question is before the legislature when it defines the individual offense involved. No one can draft a prohibition of adultery without awareness that two parties to the conduct necessarily will be involved. It is proposed, therefore, that in such cases the general section on complicity be made inapplicable, leaving to the definition of the crime itself the selective judgment that must be made. If legislators know that buyers will not be viewed as accomplices in sales unless the statute indicates that this behavior is included in the prohibition, they will focus on the problem as they frame the definition of the crime. And since the exception is confined to behavior "inevitably incident to" the commission of the crime, the problem, we repeat, inescapably presents itself in defining the crime.

Query: Note the reference to the case of the bribe-giver, where the statute makes criminal only receiving the bribe, as a typical case for the defense described. Reconsider in this regard United States v. Standefer, page 637 supra, in which Standefer, the Gulf Oil Company's tax department head, authorized company payment for golf trips for the IRS agent auditing the company's tax returns and was convicted of being an accomplice to the agent's crime of receiving compensation for services unauthorized by law. Is there any reason why Standefer could not have successfully invoked the defense described in the Model Penal Code? Is there a significant distinction between the participation of Standefer, acting, as he was, for the corporation, and the typical situation of the bribe-giver contemplated in the Model Penal Code comment? Was Standefer's conduct "inevitably incident" to the agent's commission of the crime?

(c) Suppose that the complicity of the secondary party ends before the offense is committed. The law prior to the Model Penal Code proposals was unclear

---

5. See, e.g., Del. Code Ann. tit. 11, §273; Hawaii Rev. Stat. tit. 37, §702-224; Ill. Ann. Stat. ch. 38, §5-2(c); Ky. Rev. Stat. Ann. ch. 500, §502.040(1); N.J. Stat. Ann. tit. 2C, §2C:2-6(c); Pa. Cons. Stat. Ann. tit. 18, §306(f).

about what circumstances, if any, sufficed to insulate the secondary party from liability. Section 2.06 of the Model Penal Code, followed more or less closely in many states,[6] requires that the defendant "terminate his complicity prior to the commission of the offense" and either (1) wholly deprive it of effectiveness or (2) give timely warning to law enforcement authorities or otherwise make proper effort to prevent the crime.

Compare N.Y. Penal Code §40.10(1), which requires (in addition to acts of withdrawal and substantial efforts to prevent the crime) that the defendant have acted under circumstances manifesting a "voluntary and complete renunciation" of his or her criminal purpose. The provision states that the renunciation is not of the required character if it is motivated (1) by a belief that circumstances exist to increase the probability of detection of the defendant or another participant or to make it more difficult to accomplish the criminal purpose or (2) by a decision to postpone the criminal conduct to another time. These requirements are substantially those proposed by the Model Penal Code for the defense of abandonment of an attempt. See §5.01(4). Query: Are they equally apposite for terminating liability as an accomplice? What situations would be treated differently under the Model Penal Code and New York provisions?

B. CONSPIRACY

1. General View

KRULEWITCH v. UNITED STATES
Supreme Court of the United States
336 U.S. 440 (1949)

MR. JUSTICE BLACK delivered the opinion of the court.

A federal district court indictment charged in three counts that petitioner and a woman defendant had (1) induced and persuaded another woman to go on October 20, 1941, from New York City to Miami, Florida for the purpose of prostitution, in violation of 18 U.S.C.A. §399 [now §2422]; (2) transported or caused her to be transported from New York to Miami for that purpose, in violation of 18 U.S.C.A. §398 [now §2421]; and (3) conspired to commit those offenses in violation of 18 U.S.C.A. §88 [now §371]. Tried alone, the petitioner was convicted on all three counts of the indictment. The Court of Appeals affirmed. We granted certiorari limiting our review to consideration of alleged error in admission of certain hearsay testimony against petitioner over his timely and repeated objections.

The challenged testimony was elicited by the Goverment from its complaining witness, the person whom petitioner and the woman defendant allegedly induced to go from New York to Florida for the purpose of prostitution. The testimony narrated the following purported conversation between the complaining witness and petitioner's alleged co-conspirator, the woman defendant.

6. See, e.g., Conn. Gen. Stat. tit. 53a, §53a-10; Ky. Rev. Stat. Ann. ch. 500, §502.040(2); Minn. Rev. Stat. Ann. tit. 609, §609.05(3); N.J. Stat. Ann. tit. 2C, §2C:2-6e(3); Pa. Cons. Stat. Ann. tit. 18, §306(f)(3).

She asked me, she says, "You didn't talk yet?" And I says, "No." And she says, "Well, don't," she says, "until we get you a lawyer." And then she says, "Be very careful what you say." And I can't put it in exact words. But she said, "It would be better for us two girls to take the blame than Kay (the defendant) because he couldn't stand it, he couldn't stand to take it."

The time of the alleged conversation was more than a month and a half after October 20, 1941, the date the complaining witness had gone to Miami. Whatever original conspiracy may have existed between petitioner and his alleged co-conspirator to cause the complaining witness to go to Florida in October, 1941, no longer existed when the reported conversation took place in December, 1941. For on this latter date the trip to Florida had not only been made — the complaining witness had left Florida, had returned to New York, and had resumed her residence there. Furthermore, at the time the conversation took place, the complaining witness, the alleged co-conspirator, and the petitioner had been arrested. They apparently were charged in a United States District Court of Florida with the offense of which petitioner was here convicted.

It is beyond doubt that the central aim of the alleged conspiracy — transportation of the complaining witness to Florida for prostitution — had either never existed or had long since ended in success or failure when and if the alleged co-conspirator made the statement attributed to her. The statement plainly implied that petitioner was guilty of the crime for which he was on trial. It was made in petitioner's absence and the Government made no effort whatever to show that it was made with his authority. The testimony thus stands as an unsworn, out-of-court declaration of petitioner's guilt. This hearsay declaration, attributed to a co-conspirator, was not made pursuant to and in furtherance of objectives of the conspiracy charged in the indictment, because if made, it was after those objectives either had failed or had been achieved. Under these circumstances, the hearsay declaration attributed to the alleged co-conspirator was not admissible on the theory that it was made in furtherance of the alleged criminal transportation undertaking. . . .

Although the Government recognizes that the chief objective of the conspiracy — transportation for prostitution purposes — had ended in success or failure before the reported conversation took place, it nevertheless argues for admissibility of the hearsay declaration as one in furtherance of a continuing subsidiary objective of the conspiracy. Its argument runs this way. Conspirators about to commit crimes always expressly or implicitly agree to collaborate with each other to conceal facts in order to prevent detection, conviction and punishment. Thus the argument is that even after the central criminal objectives of a conspiracy have succeeded or failed, an implicit subsidiary phase of the conspiracy always survives, the phase which has concealment as its sole objective. The Court of Appeals adopted this view. It viewed the alleged hearsay declaration as one in furtherance of this continuing subsidiary phase of the conspiracy, as part of "the implied agreement to conceal." It consequently held the declaration properly admitted.

We cannot accept the Government's contention. There are many logical and practical reasons that could be advanced against a special evidentiary rule that permits out-of-court statements of one conspirator to be used against another. But however cogent these reasons, it is firmly established that where made in furtherance of the objectives of a going conspiracy, such statements are admissible as exceptions to the hearsay rule.[a] This prerequisite to admissibility, that hearsay statements by some conspirators to be admissible against others must be made in furtherance of the conspiracy charged, has been scrupulously observed by federal courts. The Government now asks us to expand this narrow exception to the hearsay rule and hold admissible a declaration, not made in furtherance of the alleged criminal transportation conspiracy charged, but made in furtherance of an alleged implied but uncharged conspiracy aimed at preventing detection and punishment. The rule contended for by the Government could have far-reaching results. For under this rule plausible arguments could generally be made in conspiracy cases that most out-of-court statements offered in evidence tended to shield co-conspirators. We are not persuaded to adopt the Government's implicit conspiracy theory which in all criminal conspiracy cases would create automatically a further breach of the general rule against the admission of hearsay evidence. . . .

Reversed.

MR. JUSTICE JACKSON, concurring in the judgment and opinion of the Court.

This case illustrates a present drift in the federal law of conspiracy which warrants some further comment because it is characteristic of the long evolution of that elastic, sprawling and pervasive offense. Its history exemplifies the "tendency of a principle to expand itself to the limit of its logic." [1] The unavailing protest of courts against the growing habit to indict for conspiracy in lieu of prosecuting for the substantive offense itself, or in addition thereto, suggests that loose practice as to this offense constitutes a serious threat to fairness in our administration of justice.

The modern crime of conspiracy is so vague that it almost defies definition. Despite certain elementary and essential elements,[4] it also, chameleon-like, takes on a special coloration from each of the many independent offenses on which it may be overlaid. It is always "predominantly mental in composition" because it consists primarily of a meeting of minds and an intent.[6]

. . . It is not intended to question that the basic conspiracy principle has some place in modern criminal law, because to unite, back of a criminal purpose, the strength, opportunities and resources of many is obviously more dangerous and more difficult to police than the efforts of a lone wrongdoer. It also may be trivialized, as here, where the conspiracy consists of the concert of a loathsome panderer and a prostitute to go from New York to Florida to ply their trade and it would appear that a simple Mann Act prosecution would vindicate the majesty of federal law. However, even when appropriately invoked, the looseness

---

a. This aspect of the conspiracy doctrine will be examined further shortly. See page 652 infra. — EDS.

1. The phrase is Judge Cardozo's — Nature of Judicial Process, p. 51. [See Justice Holmes in Hudson County Water Co. v. McCarter, 209 U.S. 349, 355 (1908): "All rights tend to declare themselves absolute to their logical extreme. Yet all in fact are limited by the neighborhood of principles of policy which are other than those on which the particular right is founded, and which become strong enough to hold their own when a certain point is reached."]

4. Justice Holmes supplied an oversimplified working definition in United States v. Kissel, 218 U.S. 601, 608: "A conspiracy is a partnership in criminal purposes." This was recently restated "A conspiracy is a partnership in crime." Pinkerton v. United States, 328 U.S. 640, 644. The latter is inaccurate, since concert in criminal purposes, rather than concert in crime, establishes the conspiracy. . . .

6. Harno, Intent in Criminal Conspiracy, 89 U. of Pa. L. Rev. 624, 632.

and pliability of the doctrine present inherent dangers which should be in the background of judicial thought wherever it is sought to extend the doctrine to meet the exigencies of a particular case.

Conspiracy in federal law aggravates the degree of crime over that of unconcerted offending. The act of confederating to commit a misdemeanor, followed by even an innocent overt act in its execution, is a felony and is such even if the misdemeanor is never consummated. The more radical proposition also is well-established that at common law and under some statutes a combination may be a criminal conspiracy even if it contemplates only acts which are not crimes at all when perpetrated by an individual or by many acting severally.

Thus, the conspiracy doctrine will incriminate persons on the fringe of offending who would not be guilty of aiding and abetting or of becoming an accessory, for those charges only lie when an act which is a crime has actually been committed.

Attribution of criminality to a confederation which contemplates no act that would be criminal if carried out by any one of the conspirators is a practice peculiar to Anglo-American law. "There can be little doubt that this wide definition of the crime of conspiracy originates in the criminal equity administered in the Star Chamber." In fact, we are advised that "The modern crime of conspiracy is almost entirely the result of the manner in which conspiracy was treated by the Court of the Star Chamber." The doctrine does not commend itself to jurists of civil law countries, despite universal recognition that an organized society must have legal weapons for combatting organized criminality. Most other countries have devised what they consider more discriminating principles upon which to prosecute criminal gangs, secret associations, and subversive syndicates. . . .

Doctrines of conspiracy are not only invoked for criminal prosecution, but also in civil proceedings for damages or for injunction, and in administrative proceedings to apply regulatory statutes. . . .

The interchangeable use of conspiracy doctrine in civil as well as penal proceedings opens it to the danger, absent in the case of many crimes, that a court having in mind only the civil sanctions will approve lax practices which later are imported into criminal proceedings. In civil proceedings this Court frankly has made the end a test of the means, saying, "To require a greater showing would cripple the Act," United States v. Griffith, 334 U.S. 100, in dispensing with the necessity for specific intent to produce a result violative of the statute. Further, the Court has dispensed with even the necessity to infer any definite agreement, although that is the gist of the offense. "It is elementary that an unlawful conspiracy may be and often is formed without simultaneous action or agreement on the part of the conspirators." United States v. Masonite Corp., 316 U.S. 265, 275. One might go on from the reports of this and lower courts and put together their decisions condoning absence of proof to demonstrate that the minimum of proof required to establish conspiracy is extremely low, and we may expect our pronouncements in civil cases to be followed in criminal ones also.

Of course, it is for prosecutors rather than courts to determine when to use a scatter gun to bring down the defendant, but there are procedural advantages from using it which add to the danger of unguarded extension of the concept.

An accused, under the Sixth Amendment, has the right to trial "by an impartial jury of the state and district wherein the crime shall have been committed." The leverage of a conspiracy charge lifts this limitation from the prosecution and reduces its protection to a phantom, for the crime is considered so vagrant as to have been committed in any district where any one of the conspirators did any one of the acts, however innocent, intended to accomplish its object. The Government may, and often does, compel one to defend at a great distance from any place he ever did any act because some accused confederate did some trivial and by itself innocent act in the chosen district.

When the trial starts, the accused feels the full impact of the conspiracy strategy. Strictly, the prosecution should first establish prima facie the conspiracy and identify the conspirators, after which evidence of acts and declarations of each in the course of its execution are admissible against all. But the order of proof of so sprawling a charge is difficult for a judge to control. As a practical matter, the accused often is confronted with a hodgepodge of acts and statements by others which he may never have authorized or intended or even known about, but which help to persuade the jury of existence of the conspiracy itself. In other words, a conspiracy often is proved by evidence that is admissible only upon assumption that conspiracy existed. The naive assumption that prejudicial effects can be overcome by instructions to the jury, cf. Blumenthal v. United States, 332 U.S. 539, 559, all practicing lawyers know to be unmitigated fiction.

The trial of a conspiracy charge doubtless imposes a heavy burden on the prosecution, but it is an especially difficult situation for the defendant. The hazard from loose application of rules of evidence is aggravated where the Government institutes mass trials. Moreover, in federal practice there is no rule preventing conviction on uncorroborated testimony of accomplices, as there are in many jurisdictions, and the most comfort a defendant can expect is that the court can be induced to follow the "better practice" and caution the jury against "too much reliance upon the testimony of accomplices." Caminetti v. United States, 242 U.S. 470, 495.

A co-defendant in a conspiracy trial occupies an uneasy seat. There generally will be evidence of wrongdoing by somebody. It is difficult for the individual to make his own case stand on its own merits in the minds of jurors who are ready to believe that birds of a feather are flocked together. If he is silent, he is taken to admit it and if, as often happens, co-defendants can be prodded into accusing or contradicting each other, they convict each other. There are many practical difficulties in defending against a charge of conspiracy which I will not enumerate.

Against this inadequately sketched background, I think the decision of this case in the court below introduced an ominous expansion of the accepted law of conspiracy.[b]

b. The Supreme Court has since reaffirmed the holding of *Krulewitch* in a case involving the issue of when the crime ends for purposes of determining when the statute of limitations begins to run. Grunewald v. United States, 353 U.S. 391 (1957). Some jurisdictions have taken a different view. See cases in 2 F. Wharton, Criminal Evidence §420; Dutton v. Evans, 400 U.S. 74, 83 (1970). — EDS.

NOTES

1. Compare the observations of Professor Johnson in The Unnecessary Crime of Conspiracy, 61 Calif. L. Rev. 1137, 1139-1140 (1973):

> The law of criminal conspiracy is not basically sound. It should be abolished, not reformed.
>
> The central fault of conspiracy law and the reason why any limited reform is bound to be inadequate can be briefly stated. What conspiracy adds to the law is simply confusion, and the confusion is inherent in the nature of the doctrine. The confusion stems from the fact that conspiracy is not only a substantive inchoate crime in itself, but the touchstone for invoking several independent procedural and substantive doctrines. We ask whether a defendant agreed with another person to commit a crime initially for the purpose of determining whether he may be convicted of the offense of conspiracy even when the crime itself has not yet been committed. If the answer to that question is in the affirmative, however, we find that we have also answered a number of other questions that would otherwise have to be considered independently. Where there is evidence of conspiracy, the defendant may be tried jointly with his criminal partners and possibly with many other persons whom he has never met or seen, the joint trial may be held in a place he may never have visited, and hearsay statements of other alleged members of the conspiracy may be used to prove his guilt. Furthermore, a defendant who is found guilty of conspiracy is subject to enhanced punishment and may also be found guilty of any crime committed in furtherance of the conspiracy, whether or not he knew about the crime or aided in its commission.
>
> Each of these issues involves a separate substantive or procedural area of the criminal law of considerable importance and complexity. The essential vice of conspiracy is that it inevitably distracts the courts from the policy questions or balancing of interests that ought to govern the decision of specific legal issues and leads them instead to decide those issues by reference to the conceptual framework of conspiracy. Instead of asking whether public policy or the interests of the parties requires a particular holding, the courts are led instead to consider whether the theory of conspiracy is broad enough to permit it. What is wrong with conspiracy, in other words, is much more basic than the overbreadth of a few rules. The problem is not with particular results, but with the use of a single abstract concept to decide numerous questions that deserve separate consideration in light of the various interests and policies they involve.

2. The common law doctrine punishing conspiracy to commit a misdemeanor as a felony is no longer as widely accepted as it was when Justice Jackson wrote. The revised federal criminal statute has eliminated it. 18 U.S.C. §371 now provides:

> If two or more persons conspire either to commit any offense against the United States, or to defraud the United States, or any agency thereof in any manner or for any purpose, and one or more of such persons do any act to effect the object of the conspiracy, each shall be fined not more than $10,000 or imprisoned not more than five years, or both. If, however, the offense, the commission of which is the object of the conspiracy, is a misdemeanor only, the punishment for such conspiracy shall not exceed the maximum punishment provided for such misdemeanor.

Many states have made comparable changes in their law.

However, remnants of the old doctrine persist. Even under the revised California conspiracy provision, Cal. Penal Code §182, a conspiracy to commit any crime against designated federal or state officials is a felony punishable by imprisonment for five, seven, or nine years. Presumably an agreement to throw an egg at such an official would be so punishable, though the actual throwing of the egg without any agreement to do so would only be a minor assault.

The cognate common law doctrine of conspiracy, what Justice Jackson termed the "more radical proposition" that an agreement to commit noncriminal acts may be treated as a criminal conspiracy, we had occasion to examine earlier in Director of Public Prosecutions v. Shaw, page 350 supra. Recent codifications tend to confine criminal conspiracies to actions whose objectives are otherwise criminal. See Note, Conspiracy: Statutory Reform since the Model Penal Code, 75 Colum. L. Rev. 1122, 1129 (1975). However, there still remain jurisdictions that designate agreements to commit noncriminal actions as criminal[7] and others that retain the traditional looseness in the specification of the objectives of criminal conspiracies. See Commonwealth v. Bessette, 351 Mass. 148, 217 N.E.2d 893 (1966). For example, Cal. Penal Code §182 provides:

If two or more persons conspire:
1. To commit any crime.
2. Falsely and maliciously to indict another for any crime, or to procure another to be charged or arrested for any crime.
3. Falsely to move or maintain any suit, action or proceeding.
4. To cheat and defraud any person of any property, by any means which are in themselves criminal, or to obtain money or property by false pretenses or by false promises with fraudulent intent not to perform such promises.
5. To commit any act injurious to the public health, to public morals, or to pervert or obstruct justice, or the due administration of the laws. . . .
   They are punishable as follows. . . .

It is doubtful that applications of some of these provisions, particularly the traditional common law formulation of subsection 5, would today survive constitutional attack under the expanded vagueness criteria of the Supreme Court. See Musser v. Utah, 333 U.S. 95 (1948), and State v. Musser, 118 Utah 537, 223 P.2d 193 (1950) (litigation resulting in an invalidation of a comparable Utah provision when it was sought to be applied to preaching and practicing plural marriage). See also Papachristou v. City of Jacksonville, pages 364-368 supra; State v. Bowling, 5 Ariz. App. 436, 427 P.2d 928 (1967).

The other consequences of the conspiracy doctrine mentioned in Justice Jackson's concurring opinion continue to have considerable significance. Some of them are explored further in the cases and notes that follow.

---

7. Recall the federal conspiracy statute (18 U.S.C. §371), discussed in this Note, making it criminal to commit any offense against or defraud the United States. In United States v. Hutto, 256 U.S. 524 (1921), it was held that a conspiracy to commit any act that by federal statute is prohibited in the interest of the United States, although not made punishable by criminal prosecution but only by suit for civil penalty, is a conspiracy to commit an offense against the United States. For an account of the kinds of noncriminal conduct reached through wide interpretations of the term "defraud the United States" see Goldstein, Conspiracy to Defraud the United States, 68 Yale L.J. 405 (1959).

UNITED STATES v. VINSON
United States Court of Appeals, 6th Circuit
606 F.2d 149 (1979)

MERRITT, J. After a jury trial . . . Vinson, Sheriff of Lawrence County, and
Thompson, a county magistrate, were convicted of extorting money from a
coal company and of conspiring to do so. 18 U.S.C. Section 1951 (1976). We
affirm the defendants' convictions. . . .

During the government's case-in-chief, the District Court admitted testimony
describing out-of-court statements of Sheriff Vinson which tended to incriminate
Magistrate Thompson in both the conspiracy and the substantive offenses. An
officer of the coal company who was the target of the extortion plan testified
that the Sheriff told him that the Magistrate was his agent in the extortion
scheme and would pick up the extortion payments. Upon timely objection, the
District Judge instructed the jury as follows:

> That [hearsay] will not be considered by you, ladies and gentlemen, as any evidence
> against [the Magistrate] until you are satisfied or the Court makes a ruling of a
> prima facie case of conspiracy.

Further along in the government's case, the District Judge made a preliminary
finding that the government had proved a conspiracy involving the Sheriff and
Magistrate by a preponderance of the evidence. He then ruled that the out-
of-court statements of the Sheriff, made in the course of and in furtherance of
the conspiracy, could be used as evidence against the Magistrate. He instructed
the jury:

> Ladies and gentlemen . . . let me advise you that the admonition that I have
> given you earlier in the case about not considering certain testimony as to [the
> Magistrate] is now withdrawn.

Both defendants objected to the judge's second statement on the ground
that it amounted to an improper comment on the sufficiency of the evidence.
Although we believe that the judge should have made neither statement, we
find that no prejudice resulted to defendants. The government's proof of the
conspiracy as well as of the substantive offense rested on strong non-hearsay
evidence which showed that the Sheriff, the Magistrate and an unindicted third
person conspired to and, in fact, did extort money from the coal company.
Sheriff Vinson was the principal in the scheme, and the Magistrate and the
third person were his agents. The three threatened to harass the coal company's
trucks which operated on county roads unless extortion payments were made.
Two such payments were made before authorities apprehended the defendants.
There was relatively little co-conspirator hearsay admitted both before and after
the District Judge made his preliminary finding, and the jury had abundant,
non-hearsay evidence on which to base its verdict. Moreover, any confusion
which might have been caused by the trial judge's comments to the jury was
cured by his final conspiracy instruction in which the elements of a criminal
conspiracy and the government's burden of proof were clearly and correctly
stated.

In [United States v. Enright, 579 F.2d 980 (6th Cir. 1978),] we held that before the government can take advantage of the co-conspirator exception to the hearsay rule, it must show by a preponderance of the evidence (1) that a conspiracy existed, (2) that the defendant against whom the hearsay is offered was a member of the conspiracy, and (3) that the hearsay statement was made in the course and in furtherance of the conspiracy. We also held that this preliminary finding is the sole province of the trial judge. Fed. R. Evid. 104(a). In *Enright,* however, we did not decide whether, before the judge has made his finding on the preliminary question, he may admit the hearsay subject to connection later in the trial, as did the trial judge here. We also did not decide whether the trial judge may consider the hearsay itself in making his preliminary finding.

A trial judge must have considerable discretion in controlling the mode and order of proof at trial and his rulings should not cause reversal of a criminal conviction unless they "affect substantial rights." Thus, we do not believe that it is appropriate to set forth hard and fast procedures. Rather, we set forth alternative means for District Judges to structure conspiracy trials, that will allow the government to present its proof while at the same time protecting defendants from inadmissible hearsay evidence.

One acceptable method is the so-called "mini-hearing" in which the court, without a jury, hears the government's proof of conspiracy and makes the preliminary *Enright* finding. If the hearsay is found admissible, the case, including co-conspirator hearsay, is presented to the jury. Although this procedure has been criticized as burdensome, time-consuming and uneconomic,[4] a trial judge, in the exercise of his discretion, may choose to order the proof in this manner if the circumstances warrant.

The judge may also require the government to meet its initial burden by producing the non-hearsay evidence of conspiracy first prior to making the *Enright* finding concerning the hearsay's admissibility. This procedure clearly avoids "the danger . . . of injecting the record with inadmissible hearsay in anticipation of proof of a conspiracy which never materializes."[5]

The judge may also, as was done here, admit the hearsay statements subject to later demonstration of their admissibility by a preponderance of the evidence. If this practice is followed, the court should stress to counsel that the statements are admitted subject to defendant's continuing objection and that the prosecution will be required to show by a preponderance of the evidence that a conspiracy existed, that the defendant against whom the statements are hearsay was a participant and that the statement was made in the course and in furtherance thereof. At the conclusion of the government's case-in-chief, the court should rule on the defendant's hearsay objection. If the court finds that the government has met the burden of proof described in *Enright,* it should overrule the objection and let all the evidence, hearsay included, go to the jury, subject, of course, to instructions regarding the government's ultimate burden of proof beyond a reasonable doubt and the weight and credibility to be given to co-conspirators' statements. If, on the other hand, the court finds that the government has failed to carry its burden, it should, on defendant's motion, declare a mistrial unless convinced that a cautionary jury instruction would shield the defendant from prejudice.

4. See the majority and concurring opinions in the Fifth Circuit's en banc decision in United States v. James, 590 F.2d 575 (1979).

5. United States v. Macklin, 573 F.2d 1046, 1049 n. 3 (8th Cir. 1978).

If the trial judge does choose to admit the hearsay (a) after the government has established the conspiracy by a preponderance at the trial, or (b) at a "mini-hearing," or (c) conditionally subject to connection, he should refrain from advising the jury of his findings that the government has satisfactorily proved the conspiracy. The judge should not describe to the jury the government's burden of proof on the preliminary question. Such an instruction can serve only to alert the jury that the judge has determined that a conspiracy involving the defendant has been proven by a preponderance of the evidence.[7] This may adversely affect the defendant's right to trial by jury. The judge's opinion is likely to influence strongly the opinion of individual jurors when they come to consider their verdict and judge the credibility of witnesses.

Finally, we believe that, whatever procedure a District Judge uses, the hearsay statements themselves may be considered by the judge in deciding the preliminary question of admissibility. The preliminary finding of conspiracy for purposes of the co-conspirator exception to the hearsay rule is a "question concerning . . . the admissibility of evidence" governed by Fed. R. Evid. 104(a), and we believe that the final sentence of Rule 104(a) — stating that the judge "is not bound by the rules of evidence"— modifies prior law to the contrary.[8] The fact that the judge may consider under Rule 104(a) hearsay evidence which the jury could not consider is an added reason the judge should refrain from advising the jury of his findings. . . .

NOTES

1. What is hearsay? The law of hearsay is a complex chapter in the law of evidence which cannot be explored here at any length. Federal Rules of Evidence, Rule 801 defines hearsay as "a statement, other than one made by the declarant [the person who makes the statement] while testifying at the trial or hearing, offered in evidence to prove the truth of the matter asserted." Thus in the *Vinson* case, testimony of the coal company executive that the sheriff told him that the magistrate was his agent in the extortion scheme and would pick up the extortion payments was hearsay under traditional evidence law. Such evidence is normally inadmissable. Its admissibility under the coconspirator exception to the hearsay rule is a significant advantage for the prosecution.

2. Rationale of the exception. See United States v. Gil, 604 F.2d 546, 549 (7th Cir. 1979). Defendant argued that hearsay testimony by a witness should not have been admitted because the witness had been found not guilty of conspiracy with him on grounds of police entrapment. The court responded:

> The logical structure of this argument falls . . . because . . . it equates "conspiracy"
> as a concept of substantive criminal law, governing who may be punished for which
> acts, with "conspiracy" as part of an evidentiary principle, and burdens the latter

7. Herein lies the error that defendants claim was committed in the instant case. In fact, the District Judge did not state to the jury his opinion nor findings on the conspiracy, but perhaps his finding could be inferred from his ruling.

8. See United States v. Enright, 579 F.2d at 985 n. 4. There is a split of authority on this question. Compare United States v. James, 590 F.2d at 592 (Tjoflat, J., concurring) and United States v. Martorano, 557 F.2d 1, 12 (1st Cir. 1977), with United States v. James, 590 F.2d at 581 and United States v. Bell, 573 F.2d at 1044.

with all of the theoretical limitations and formal requirements of the former. The two are not the same, though it is likely that any provable criminal conspiracy will satisfy the requirements of the evidentiary rule. . . . As the Third Circuit pointed out in United States v. Trowery, 542 F.2d 623 (3d Cir. 1976):

> The distinction should be noted between "conspiracy" as a crime and the co-conspirator exception to the hearsay rule. Conspiracy as a crime comprehends more than mere joint enterprise. It also includes other elements, such as a meeting of the minds, criminal intent and, where required by statute, an overt act. When these elements are established, the crime of conspiracy is proved.
>
> The co-conspirator exception to the hearsay rule, on the other hand, is merely a rule of evidence founded, to some extent, on concepts of agency law. It may be applied in both civil and criminal cases. . . . Its rationale is the common sense appreciation that a person who has authorized another to speak or to act to some joint end will be held responsible for what is later said or done by his agent, whether in his presence or not.

Thus, it is well established that the crime of conspiracy need not be charged (as it was not in this case) in order to invoke the coconspirator exception to the hearsay rule to admit out-of-court statements. . . . Furthermore, the difference between what must be proved to invoke the hearsay exception and what must be proved in order to convict a person of the crime of conspiracy, as well as the difference in burden of proof, means that neither collateral estoppel nor res judicata automatically bars the use of statements by a person who has been acquitted of the crime of conspiracy, . . . though an acquittal might be relevant and persuasive in the determination of whether the Government has demonstrated the requisite criminal joint venture.

The evidentiary principle . . . is a limited application of agency principles, viewing a conspiracy as a "partnership in crime." It is justified in part because of the assurances of accuracy traditionally associated with statements against interest and the community of interest among the conspirators. It has also been candidly proposed by commentators . . . that the exception is largely a result of necessity, since it is most often invoked in conspiracy cases in which the proof would otherwise be very difficult and the evidence largely circumstantial. Levie, "Hearsay and Conspiracy," 52 Mich. L. Rev. 920, 989 (1959).

Compare Johnson, The Unnecessary Crime of Conspiracy, 61 Calif. L. Rev. 1137, 1183 (1973):

This exception to the hearsay rule is a particular application of the more general principle that statements of an agent concerning matters within the scope of the agency relationship and made during the existence of that relationship are admissible against the principal.

The justification for admitting these "vicarious admissions" is not altogether easy to grasp. Some authorities have found the analogy to the substantive liability of the principal for his agent's acts compelling. Because the employer is liable for the torts of his servant committed within the scope of the employment, and the conspirator for the crimes of his co-conspirator committed in furtherance of the common objective, these authorities have reasoned that the principal should bear the risk of what his agents say as well as the risk of what they do. It does not seem that hearsay statements of agents are admitted because they are regarded as carrying some particular guarantee of trustworthiness. Although there are some suggestions in the literature that an agent is not likely to make statements against his principal's interest unless they are true, the authorities agree that admissions of the agent, like those of the principal himself, are admissible whether or not he thought the statements to be against his or his principal's interest at the time he made them.

3. *Bootstrapping.* Consider the holding of the court in *Vinson* that the hearsay statement may itself be considered by the trial judge in deciding whether there is enough evidence of a conspiracy between the defendant and the declarant to allow the jury to consider it. Does this allow hearsay to "lift itself by its own bootstraps to the level of competent evidence"? United States v. Glasser, 315 U.S. 60, 75 (1942).

4. *Standard of proof.* The federal courts are generally in agreement that under the new Federal Rules of Evidence, wherein the trial judge, rather than the jury, decides on admissibility, the judge must find the existence of the conspiracy and defendant's participation in it on a "preponderance of the evidence." This requirement is usually interpreted to mean that the judge must find these facts more probable than not. A lesser standard would be that the judge must find that a prima facie case has been made for these facts — in other words, that a jury's finding that the facts existed could not be set aside as unreasonable. A higher standard would be that the judge must find these facts "beyond a reasonable doubt." Query: Is either the lesser or the higher standard to be preferred? See Judge Friendly's opinion in United States v. Geaney, 417 F.2d 1116 (2d Cir. 1969).

5. See generally Note, Developments in the Law — Criminal Conspiracy, 72 Harv. L. Rev. 920, 984-989 (1959); Comment, The Hearsay Exception for Co-Conspirator's Declaration, 25 U. Chi. L. Rev. 530 (1958). On treatment of the issue under the Federal Rules of Evidence, see Comment, The Co-Conspirator's Exception to the Hearsay Rule: Bootstrapping in the New Procedure from the First Circuit, 50 Colo. L. Rev. 93 (1978); Comment, Reconstructing the Independent Evidence Requirement of the Co-Conspirator Hearsay Exception, 127 U. Pa. L. Rev. 143 (1979); Marcus, Co-Conspirators' Declarations: The Federal Rules of Evidence and Other Recent Developments, From a Criminal Law Perspective, 7 Am. J. Crim. L. 287 (1979).

PINKERTON v. UNITED STATES

Supreme Court of United States
328 U.S. 640 (1946)

MR. JUSTICE DOUGLAS delivered the opinion of the Court.

Walter and Daniel Pinkerton are brothers who live a short distance from each other on Daniel's farm. They were indicted for violations of the Internal Revenue Code. The indictment contained ten substantive counts and one conspiracy count. The jury found Walter guilty of nine of the substantive counts and on the conspiracy count. It found Daniel guilty on six of the substantive counts and on the conspiracy count. Walter was fined $500 and sentenced generally on the substantive counts to imprisonment for thirty months. On the conspiracy count he was given a two year sentence to run concurrently with the other sentence. Daniel was fined $1,000 and sentenced generally on the substantive counts to imprisonment for thirty months. On the conspiracy count he was fined $500 and given a two year sentence to run concurrently with the other sentence. The judgments of conviction were affirmed by the Circuit Court of Appeals. . . .

It is contended that there was insufficient evidence to implicate Daniel in the conspiracy. But we think there was enough evidence for submission of the issue to the jury.

There is, however, no evidence to show that Daniel participated directly in the commission of the substantive offenses on which his conviction has been sustained, although there was evidence to show that these substantive offenses were in fact committed by Walter in furtherance of the unlawful agreement or conspiracy existing between the brothers. The question was submitted to the jury on the theory that each petitioner could be found guilty of the substantive offenses, if it was found at the time those offenses were committed petitioners were parties to an unlawful conspiracy and the substantive offenses charged were in fact committed in furtherance of it.[6]

Daniel relies on United States v. Sall (C.C.A. 3d) 116 F.2d 745. That case held that participation in the conspiracy was not itself enough to sustain a conviction for the substantive offense even though it was committed in furtherance of the conspiracy. The court held that, in addition to evidence that the offense was in fact committed in furtherance of the conspiracy, evidence of direct participation in the commission of the substantive offense or other evidence from which participation might fairly be inferred was necessary.

We take a different view. We have here a continuous conspiracy. There is here no evidence of the affirmative action on the part of Daniel which is necessary to establish his withdrawal from it. Hyde v. United States, 225 U.S. 347, 369. As stated in that case, "Having joined in an unlawful scheme, having constituted agents for its performance, scheme and agency to be continuous until full fruition be secured, until he does some act to disavow or defeat the purpose he is in no situation to claim the delay of the law. As the offense has not been terminated or accomplished, he is still offending. And we think, consciously offending, offending as certainly, as we have said, as at the first moment of his confederation, and consciously through every moment of its existence." And so long as the partnership in crime continues the partners act for each other in carrying it forward. It is settled that "an overt act of one partner may be the act of all without any new agreement specifically directed to that act." United States v. Kissell, 218 U.S. 601, 608. Motive or intent may be proved by the acts or declarations of some of the conspirators in furtherance of the common objective. The governing principle is the same when the substantive offense is committed by one of the conspirators in furtherance of the unlawful project. The criminal intent to do the act is established by the formation of the conspiracy. Each conspirator instigated the commission of the crime. The unlawful agreement contemplated precisely what was done. It was formed for the purpose. The act done was in execution of the enterprise. The rule which holds responsible one who counsels, procures, or commands another to commit a crime is founded on the same principle. That principle is recognized in the law of conspiracy when the overt act of one partner in crime is attributable to all. An overt act

---

6. . . . Daniel was not indicted as an aider or abetter (see Criminal Code, §332, 18 U.S.C.A. 550), nor was his case submitted to the jury on that theory.

is an essential ingredient of the crime of conspiracy under §37 of the Criminal Code, 18 U.S.C.A. §88 [now §371]. If that can be supplied by the act of one conspirator, we fail to see why the same or other acts in furtherance of the conspiracy are likewise not attributable to the others for the purpose of holding them responsible for the substantive offense.

A different case would arise if the substantive offense committed by one of the conspirators was not in fact done in furtherance of the conspiracy, did not fall within the scope of the unlawful project, or was merely a part of the ramifications of the plan which could not be reasonably foreseen as a necessary or natural consequence of the unlawful agreement. But as we read this record, that is not this case.

Affirmed.

MR. JUSTICE RUTLEDGE, dissenting in part.

The judgment concerning Daniel Pinkerton should be reversed. In my opinion it is without precedent here and is a dangerous precedent to establish.

Daniel and Walter, who were brothers living near each other, were charged in several counts with substantive offenses, and then a conspiracy count was added naming those offenses as overt acts. The proof showed that Walter alone committed the substantive crimes. There was none to establish that Daniel participated in them, aided and abetted Walter in committing them, or knew that he had done so. Daniel in fact was in the penitentiary, under sentence for other crimes, when some of Walter's crimes were done.

There was evidence, however, to show that over several years Daniel and Walter had confederated to commit similar crimes concerned with unlawful possession, transportation, and dealing in whiskey, in fraud of the federal revenues. On this evidence both were convicted of conspiracy. Walter also was convicted on the substantive counts on the proof of his committing the crimes charged. Then, on that evidence without more than the proof of Daniel's criminal agreement with Walter and the latter's overt acts, which were also the substantive offenses charged, the court told the jury they could find Daniel guilty of those substantive offenses. They did so. . . .

. . . Daniel has been held guilty of the substantive crimes committed only by Walter on proof that he did no more than conspire with him to commit offenses of the same general character. There was no evidence that he counseled, advised or had knowledge of those particular acts or offenses. There was therefore, none that he aided, abetted or took part in them. There was only evidence sufficient to show that he had agreed with Walter at some past time to engage in such transactions generally. As to Daniel this was only evidence of conspiracy, not of substantive crime.

The court's theory seems to be that Daniel and Walter became general partners in crime by virtue of their agreement and because of that agreement without more on his part Daniel became criminally responsible as a principal for everything Walter did thereafter in the nature of a criminal offense of the general sort the agreement contemplated, so long as there was not clear evidence that Daniel had withdrawn from or revoked the agreement. Whether or not his commitment to the penitentiary had that effect, the result is a vicarious criminal responsibility as broad as, or broader than, the vicarious civil liability of a partner for acts done by a co-partner in the course of the firm's business. . . .

PEOPLE v. McGEE, 49 N.Y.2d 48, 399 N.E.2d 1177, 1181-1182 (1979): [The New York Court of Appeals rejected the doctrine that membership in a conspiracy itself suffices to establish liability for the crime that was the objective of the conspiracy. In reversing a conviction of defendant McGee for bribing a police officer, the Court stated:] McGee argues that the Trial Judge erred in charging the jury that he could be found guilty of the substantive offense of bribery by virtue of his status as a conspirator. . . . As there was no evidence of McGee's complicity in the bribery counts submitted to the jury, and thus no basis for accomplice liability, there must be a reversal of the conviction of bribery and a dismissal of the indictment as to those counts. . . .

The crime of conspiracy is an offense separate from the crime that is the object of the conspiracy. Once an illicit agreement is shown, the overt act of any conspirator may be attributed to other conspirators to establish the offense of conspiracy . . . and that act may be the object crime. But the overt act itself is not the crime in a conspiracy prosecution; it is merely an element of the crime that has as its basis the agreement. . . . It is not offensive to permit a conviction of conspiracy to stand on the overt act committed by another, for the act merely provides corroboration of the existence of the agreement and indicates that the agreement has reached a point where it poses a sufficient threat to society to impose sanctions. . . . But it is repugnant to our system of jurisprudence, where guilt is generally personal to the defendant, . . . to impose punishment, not for the socially harmful agreement to which the defendant is a party, but for substantive offenses in which he did not participate. . . .

We refuse to sanction such a result and thus decline to follow the rule adopted for Federal prosecutions in Pinkerton v. United States (328 U.S. 640). Accessorial conduct may not be equated with mere membership in a conspiracy and the State may not rely solely on the latter to prove guilt of the substantive offense.

PROBLEM

In the following hypothetical case, consider the liability of each of the parties for the crimes committed by the others under (1) the normal doctrines of complicity and (2) the doctrine of conspiratorial accessorial liability (Note, Developments in the Law — Criminal Conspiracy, 72 Harv. L. Rev. 920, 926 (1959)):

> *A* is the organizer and ringleader of a conspiracy to rob banks. He hires *B* and *C* to rob banks *1* and *2* respectively. Although *B* and *C* do not meet face-to-face, both know that they are members of a large conspiracy and each knows of the other's assignment. At *A*'s instigation, *D*, knowing of the conspiracy, steals a car for use in the robberies. *B* and *C* perform their robberies, the former using *D*'s car.

NOTES

1. The Model Penal Code, as well as most (though not all) of the reformed state codes, have rejected the *Pinkerton* doctrine. See Note, 75 Colum. L. Rev.

1122, 1151 (1975). Supporting that position, the drafters of the Model Penal Code stated as follows (§2.04(3) [now §2.06(3)], Comment at 20-23 (Tent. Draft No. 1, 1953)):

> The most important point at which the draft diverges from the language of the courts is that it does not make "conspiracy," as such, a basis of complicity in substantive offenses committed in furtherance of its aims. It asks, instead, as do the present statutes, more specific questions about the behavior charged to constitute complicity, such as whether the defendant commanded, encouraged, aided or agreed to aid in the commission of the crime.
>
> The reason for this treatment is that there appears to be no other or no better way to confine within reasonable limits the scope of liability to which conspiracy may theoretically give rise. In People v. Luciano, 277 N.Y. 348, 14 N.E.2d 433 (1938), for example, Luciano and others were convicted of sixty-two counts of compulsory prostitution, each count involving a specific instance of placing a girl in a house of prostitution, receiving money for so doing or receiving money from the earnings of a prostitute, acts proved to have been done pursuant to a combination to control commercialized vice in New York City. The liability was properly imposed with respect to these defendants, who directed and controlled the combination; they commanded, encouraged and aided the commission of numberless specific crimes. But would so extensive a liability be just for each of the prostitutes or runners involved in the plan? They have, of course, committed their own crimes; they may actually have assisted others; but they exerted no substantial influence on the behavior of a hundred other girls or runners, each pursuing his or her own ends within the shelter of the combination. A court would and should hold that they all are parties to a single, large, conspiracy; this is itself, and ought to be, a crime. But it is one crime. Law would lose all sense of just proportion if in virtue of that one crime, each were held accountable for thousands of offenses that he did not influence at all. . . .
>
> No decision has been found in which the liability of co-conspirators for acts of one another has been pressed to limits such as these, though the limits have been approached. The cases that declare the doctrine normally involve defendants who have had a hand in planning or directing or in executing the crimes charged. When that is so, the other principles of accessorial responsibility establish liability; under the present draft the defendant has "commanded," "aided" or "agreed to aid" in planning or committing the crime. Indeed, when that is not so, courts may be expected to seek ways to avoid the conclusion of complicity, though current doctrine hardly points the way. The right way, it is submitted, is to measure liability by the criteria proposed. Conspiracy may prove command, encouragement, assistance or agreement to assist, etc.; it is evidentially important and may be sufficient for that purpose. But whether it suffices ought to be decided by the jury; they should not be told that it establishes complicity as a matter of law.

But compare Johnson, The Unnecessary Crime of Conspiracy, 61 Calif. L. Rev. 1137, 1148 (1973):

> Once it is established that all participants conspired generally to further all the crimes of the organization, it is not surprising that they each should be held responsible for all of the crimes actually committed in furtherance of that agreement. Reforms which would abolish the conspiracy-complicity rule without also abandoning the principle that all participants in a conspiracy are guilty of the same crime of conspiracy are basically inconsistent. The discussion of People v. Luciano in the

Model Penal Code commentary exemplifies this inconsistency. . . . If each prostitute and runner is a party to a "single, large conspiracy," why should each not also be liable for the individual crimes which that conspiracy existed to further? Extended liability of this sort flows from the basic absurdity of considering each of the pawns to be conspiring with the king to play the chess game.

2. In support of the *Pinkerton* rule, see the statement of Deputy Assistant Attorney General Kenney to a Senate subcommittee considering this issue in the context of a revision of the federal criminal law (quoted in Note, 75 Colum. L. Rev. 1122, 1152 (1975)):

The ever-increasing sophistication of organized crime presents a compelling reason against abandonment of *Pinkerton.* Complicated and highly refined stock frauds . . . and narcotics conspiracies represent a substantial and ever-increasing threat to society justifying retention of the *Pinkerton* doctrine. Empirical evidence has repeatedly demonstrated that those who form and control illegal enterprises are generally well insulated from prosecutions, with the exception of prosecutions predicated upon the theory of conspiracy. To preclude uniformly their exposure to additional sanctions, regardless of the circumstances, for the very crimes which sustain their illegal ventures, would have the most unfortunate and inequitable consequences.

See also Note, Developments in the Law — Criminal Conspiracy, 72 Harv. L. Rev. 920, 998-999 (1959):

Criminal acts done in furtherance of a conspiracy may be sufficiently dependent upon the encouragement and material support of the group as a whole to warrant treating each member as a causal agent to each act. Under this view, which of the conspirators committed the substantive offense would be less significant in determining the defendant's liability than the fact that the crime was performed as part of a larger division of labor to which the defendant had also contributed his efforts. . . . If a defendant can be convicted as an accomplice for advising or counseling the perpetrator, it likewise seems fair to impose vicarious liability upon one who, in alliance with others, has declared his allegiance to a particular common object, has implicitly assented to the commission of foreseeable crimes in furtherance of this object, and has himself collaborated or agreed to collaborate with his associates, since these acts necessarily give support to the other members of the conspiracy. Perhaps the underlying theme of this argument is that the strict concepts of causality and intent embodied in the traditional doctrine of complicity are inadequate to cope with the phenomenon of modern-day organized crime.

NOTES ON THE RATIONALE OF THE CRIME OF CONSPIRACY

Model Penal Code §5.03, Comment at 96-97 (Tent. Draft No. 10, 1960) states:

Conspiracy as an offense has two different aspects, reflecting different functions it serves in the legal system. In the first place, it is an inchoate crime, complementing the provisions dealing with attempt and solicitation in reaching preparatory conduct before it has matured into commission of a substantive offense. Secondly it is a means of striking against the special danger incident to group activity, facilitating prosecution of the group and yielding a basis for imposing added penalties when combination is involved.

The following notes are designed to allow further thought on these two aspects of conspiracy.

1. Conspiracy as "inchoate crime." Both at common law and under statutory formulations, conspiracy establishes the beginning of criminality at a point much further back than that provided for by the crime of attempt.[8]

(a) *The overt-act limitation.* At common law, no overt act beyond the agreement itself was required. What is the basis for this position? Consider Mulcahy v. The Queen, L.R. 3 E. & I. App. 306, 316-317 (H.L. Ire. 1868). Defendants were indicted for conspiracy to foment the Irish rebellion. They argued that the indictment was defective for failing to charge some overt act, such as publishing writings or procuring arms. The court rejected the argument, stating:

> A conspiracy consists not merely in the intention of two or more, but in the agreement of two or more to do an unlawful act, or to do a lawful act by unlawful means. So long as such a design rests in intention only, it is not indictable. When two agree to carry it into effect, the very plot is an act in itself, and the act of each of the parties, promise against promise, actus contra actum, capable of being enforced, if lawful, punishable if for a criminal object or for the use of criminal means. And so far as proof goes, conspiracy . . . is generally a matter of inference deduced from certain criminal acts of the parties accused, done in pursuance of an apparent criminal purpose in common between them. The number and the compact give weight and cause danger, and this is more especially the case in a conspiracy like those charged in this indictment. Indeed, it seems a reduction to absurdity, that procuring a single stand of arms should be a sufficient overt act to make the disloyal design indictable, and that conspiring with a thousand men to enlist should not.

American statutes came to add an overt-act requirement, sometimes with an exception for conspiracies to commit the most serious offenses, and continue to do so in recent code revisions, along with §5.03 of the Model Penal Code, supra. But the requirement may be satisfied by acts which, under the law of attempts, would be merely preparatory or equivocal. See Holmes, J., dissenting in Hyde v. United States, 225 U.S. 347, 387-388 (1912):

> An attempt, in the strictest sense, is an act expected to bring about a substantive wrong by the forces of nature. With it is classed the kindred offence where the act and the natural conditions present or supposed to be present are not enough to do the harm without a further act, but where it is so near to the result that if coupled with an intent to produce that result, the danger is very great. But combination, intention and overt act may all be present without amounting to a criminal attempt — as if all that were done should be an agreement to murder a man fifty miles away and the purchase of a pistol for the purpose. There must be dangerous proximity to success. But when that exists the overt act is the essence of the offence. On the other hand, the essence of the conspiracy is being combined for an unlawful purpose — and if an overt act is required, it does not matter how remote the act

---

8. Cf. Note, 14 U. Toronto Faculty L. Rev. 56, 61-62 (1956): "Since we are fettered by an unrealistic law of criminal attempts, overbalanced in favour of external acts, awaiting the lit match or the cocked and aimed pistol, the law of criminal conspiracy has been employed to fill the gap. If there are two persons involved, legal sanctions can be applied to the actor's intentions; this can seldom be done if only one person is involved and if he is wise in the ways of the law but acts unsuccessfully alone."

may be from accomplishing the purpose, if done to effect it; that is, I suppose, in furtherance of it in any degree.

See Yates v. United States, 354 U.S. 298, 334 (1957): "The function of the overt act in a conspiracy prosecution is simply to manifest 'that the conspiracy is at work' . . . and is neither a project still resting solely in the minds of the conspirators nor a fully completed operation no longer in existence."

By contrast, a handful of states in recent years have enlarged the requirement of an overt act and thereby have undercut the significance of conspiracy as an inchoate crime. Ohio, for example, requires that there be a "substantial overt act in furtherance of the conspiracy" and states that an overt act is substantial "when it is of such character as to manifest a purpose on the part of the actor that the object of the conspiracy should be completed." Ohio Rev. Code Ann. tit. 29, §2923.01(B). The Washington statute requires that there be a "substantial step" in furtherance of the conspiracy, parallel to the requirement for attempt. Wash. Rev. Code Ann. tit. 9A, §28.040(1). Maine goes further toward bringing together the points at which liability for attempt and conspiracy begins: The statute requires a "substantial step," which it defines as "conduct which, under the circumstances in which it occurs is strongly corroborative of the firmness of the actor's intent to complete commission of the crime"; it further provides that "speech alone is not a substantial step." Maine Rev. Stat. Ann. tit. 17, §151.4.

(b) *Justifications for the traditional approach.* Under the statutes just mentioned, conspiracy is not punishable until substantial preparatory conduct has occurred. Is this approach preferable to the traditional view that any "overt act" (or sometimes just the act of agreement) suffices? What is there about an agreement to commit a crime that justifies dispensing with the normal requirement for preparatory conduct to be made criminal? If it were not for the historical development of the crime of conspiracy, unique to Anglo-American law, would we likely treat any agreement to commit an offense as an attempt to commit it?

In support of the traditional position consider Model Penal Code, §5.03, Comment at 97 (Tent. Draft No. 10, 1960):

> The act of agreeing with another to commit a crime, like the act of soliciting, is concrete and unambiguous; it does not present the infinite degrees and variations possible in the general category of attempts. The danger that truly equivocal behavior may be misinterpreted as preparation to commit a crime is minimized; purpose must be relatively firm before the commitment involved in agreement is assumed. . . .
>
> In the course of preparation to commit a crime, the act of combining with another is significant both psychologically and practically, the former since it crosses a clear threshold in arousing expectations, the latter since it increases the likelihood that the offense will be committed. Sharing lends fortitude to purpose. The actor knows, moreover, that the future is no longer governed by his will alone; others may complete what he has had a hand in starting, even if he has a change of heart.

(c) *Problem.* In United States v. Alvarez, 610 F.2d 1250 (5th Cir. 1980) (other aspects of which are excerpted at page 683 infra) defendant was convicted of conspiracy to import marijuana into the United States. The evidence showed

that several other individuals made an arrangement with an undercover agent
for a marijuana shipment to be made by air from Colombia to the United States.
In the presence of defendant, one of the others told the agent that defendant would unload the shipment in the United States and, when the agent
asked defendant if that were so, defendant nodded his head affirmatively.
Since all the alleged conspirators were arrested at this moment, no further actions occurred.

Query: Apart from the conspiracy doctrine, would defendant's actions have
constituted an attempt? Were they "substantial steps" that strongly corroborated
his purpose? They seem to be hardly so if he were acting alone, since he would
have done no more than to indicate his intention to participate in a criminal
act at a future time. What does the fact of conspiracy add to his actions? In
light of the policies against treating preparatory behavior as criminal, did his
expressed willingness to help unload the shipment when it arrived render it
justifiable to treat his conduct as criminal?

2. *Conspiracy as sanction against group activity.* The Model Penal Code Commentary observes (§5.03, Comment at 98 (Tent. Draft No. 10, 1960)):

> Group prosecution is undoubtedly made easier by the procedural advantages
> enjoyed by the prosecution when conspiracy is charged.[a] . . . Acts and declarations
> of participants may be admissible against each other, under an exception to the
> hearsay rule, and ordinarily will be received, subject to later ruling, even before
> the required basis has been laid. Vicarious responsibility may relax venue rules
> and the conception of conspiracy as a continuous offense extends the period of
> limitations. The presentation in one case of a full picture of the workings of a
> large and complex network of related criminal activities will often help the jury
> to grasp the part played by individuals who otherwise might be forgotten; a strong
> case against some defendants may unduly blacken all; the need to work a root
> and branch extermination of the organized activity may overcome doubts that would
> otherwise prevail.

In Callanan v. United States, 364 U.S. 587 (1961), the Supreme Court found
support in the rationale of conspiracy for the doctrine permitting punishment
for the completed offense as well as for the conspiracy to commit it. In that
case, defendant was convicted of an actual obstruction of interstate commerce
by extortion and of a conspiracy to obstruct commerce by that same extortion.
The maximum punishment provided for obstructing commerce by any means,
including extortion, was 20 years. The trial court imposed a sentence of 12
years on the extortion count and another 12 years to run consecutively on the
conspiracy count (subsequently suspended and replaced with a five-year probation to commence at the expiration of the sentence on the first count). Defendant
sought a correction of the sentence under Rule 35 of the Federal Rules of
Criminal Procedure on the ground that the sentence was illegal on the face of
the indictment, contending that the maximum punishment for obstructing commerce by any of the proscribed means was 20 years and Congress did not intend

a. But, as observed in a subsequent paragraph (id. at 98), not all these advantages "are intrinsic
to conspiracy as an offense, however much it is believed by prosecutors that it is by virtue of
indictment for conspiracy that the advantages are gained. The same rule as to joinder and venue,
the same rules of evidence, will normally apply although the prosecution is for substantive offenses,
in which joint complicity is charged." — EDS.

to subject individuals to two penalties. Mr. Justice Frankfurter, for the Court, rejected the claim, stating (id. at 593-594):

> The distinctiveness between a substantive offense and a conspiracy to commit it is a postulate of our law. "It has been long and consistently recognized by the Court that the commission of the substantive offense and a conspiracy to commit it are separate and distinct offenses." Pinkerton v. United States, 328 U.S. 640, 643. Over the years this distinction has been applied in various situations. For example, in Clune v. United States, 159 U.S. 590, the Court upheld a two-year sentence for conspiracy over the objection that the crime which was the object of the unlawful agreement could only be punished by a $100 fine. The same result was reached when, as in the present case, both offenses were described within the same statute. In Carter v. McClaughry, 183 U.S. 365, cumulative sentences for conspiracy to defraud and fraud were upheld. "Cumulative sentences," the Court pronounced, "are not cumulative punishments, and a single sentence for several offences, in excess of that prescribed for one offence, may be authorized by statute."
>
> This settled principle derives from the reason of things in dealing with socially reprehensible conduct: collective criminal agreement — partnership in crime — presents a greater potential threat to the public than individual delicts. Concerted action both increases the likelihood that the criminal object will be successfully attained and decreases the probability that the individuals involved will depart from their path of criminality. Group association for criminal purposes often, if not normally, makes possible the attainment of ends more complex than those which one criminal could accomplish. Nor is the danger of a conspiratorial group limited to the particular end toward which it has embarked. Combination in crime makes more likely the commission of crimes unrelated to the original purpose for which the group was formed. In sum, the danger which a conspiracy generates is not confined to the substantive offense which is the immediate aim of the enterprise.

But compare Model Penal Code §5.03, Comment at 99 (Tent. Draft No. 10, 1960):

> When a conspiracy is declared criminal because its object is a crime, we think it is entirely meaningless to say that the preliminary combination is more dangerous than the forbidden consummation; the measure of its danger is the risk of such a culmination. On the other hand, the combination may and often does have criminal objectives that transcend any particular offenses that have been committed in pursuance of its goals. In the latter case, we think that cumulative sentences for conspiracy and substantive offenses ought to be permissible. . . . . In the former case, when the preliminary agreement does not go beyond the consummation, double conviction and sentence are barred.

See Model Penal Code §1.07(1)(b). Compare also Wis. Stat. Ann. tit. 45, §939.72, which precludes convicting defendant of the conspiracy and the crime which was its object. However, simultaneous prosecutions are authorized by §939.65. See Remington & Joseph, Charging, Convicting, and Sentencing the Multiple Criminal Offender, [1961] Wis. L. Rev. 528, 546-547.

For more on the use of conspiracy doctrine to reach concerted group activity, in the context of organized crime, see United States v. Elliott, pages 705-707 infra.

NOTE ON LEGISLATIVE GRADING OF PUNISHMENT FOR CONSPIRACY

It once was common for conspiracies to be made punishable at a set number of years of imprisonment regardless of the punishment for the offense that was its object.[9] Today this practice is rare. The great majority of states now are split much as they are on the issue of punishment for attempt:[10] Almost a third follow the lead of the Model Penal Code by making punishment for conspiracy the same as that for the object crime, providing the same kind of exceptions for the most afflictive punishments as are made for attempt.[11] Most jurisdictions fix the punishment for conspiracy at some term less than that provided for the object crime.

The choice between these two alternatives turns on what impact the fact that the harm sought by the actor did not happen should have on the grading of crime. This issue is part of the larger problem of the significance of a resulting harm, which we have examined previously. See especially page 466 supra.

Query: If one is persuaded generally by the Model Penal Code approach, are there reasons special to the definition of the crime of conspiracy for reducing the punishment to less than that for the completed offense? As we saw earlier, §5.05(2) of the Model Penal Code authorizes a court to reduce the punishment in all inchoate crimes where success is "inherently unlikely." New Jersey has added to this an authorization for reduction where "The conspiracy, as to the particular defendant charged, is . . . peripherally related to the main unlawful enterprise." N.J. Stat. Ann. tit. 2C, §2C:5-4(b)(2). Is the point well taken?

A different approach to the same problem is contained in the North Dakota provision (N.D. Cent. Code tit. 12.2, §12.1-06-05(6)), which is modeled after a proposed federal provision (National Commission on Reform of Federal Criminal Laws, Final Report §§1104(6), 1001(3) (1971)), according to which punishment for conspiracy must be dropped to a lower punishment classification whenever it is established by a preponderance of the evidence that the conduct constituting the conspiracy did not come "dangerously close" to the commission of the crime.

NOTE ON RENUNCIATION AND WITHDRAWAL

Once the crime of conspiracy has been committed by the making of an agreement and the performance of whatever overt act may be required, under what circumstances may a conspirator avoid the consequences of his or her action by a change of heart? The answer may depend on the particular consequence at issue.

May the conspirator escape liability for the crime of conspiracy? The traditional common law answer was no, as it was in the case of attempt. See page 593

---

9. See Model Penal Code, Appendix to Tent. Draft No. 10 at 162 (1960).

10. Note, 75 Colum. L. Rev. 1122, 1183-1188 (1975), surveys state law on conspiracy grading.

11. Two exceptions are Cal. Penal Code §182 and Mont. Code Ann. tit. 45, §§45-4-102(3), which appear to make the punishment the same as for the substantive offense regardless of how severely the latter is punished. This provision results in a curious anomaly in California, where punishment for attempt is set at one-half that for the crime attempted. Section 665.

supra. Once a crime is committed, no action of the defendant can undo it. See Model Penal Code §5.03, Comment at 142 (Tent. Draft No. 10, 1962). Query: Aside from the fact that this conclusion follows logically as a consequence of the definition of the crime, are there reasons of policy to support the traditional rule? Most states today have followed the lead of the Model Penal Code and allow the defense. See Note, 75 Colum. L. Rev. 1122, 1169 (1975). The Model Penal Code based its position on the same considerations that persuaded it to propose a defense of abandonment to a charge of attempt: "[R]enunciation manifests a lack of firmness of purpose that evidences individual dangerousness, and . . . the law should provide a means for encouraging persons to desist from pressing forward with their criminal designs." Model Penal Code §5.03, Comment at 144 (Tent. Draft No. 10, 1962). The Code therefore allows a defense when the circumstances manifest renunciation of the actor's criminal purpose *and* when the actor succeeds in preventing commission of the criminal objectives. Model Penal Code §5.03(6). Some states have found this latter requirement too severe and have required only that the actor have made a substantial effort to prevent the crime, on the view that no more can be expected than that a person do all that is possible. See, e.g., Ark. Stat. Ann. tit. 41, §710; Hawaii Rev. Stat. tit. 37, §530(3). Query: Is this position an improvement over that of the Model Penal Code?

Another consequence of a conspirator's change of heart may be the start of the running of the statute of limitations as to this conspirator. Courts traditionally have held that change of heart may have this effect, provided the conspirator takes "affirmative action" to make known his or her withdrawal to the coconspirators. Hyde v. United States, 225 U.S. 347, 369 (1912). Query: Why should it not be enough that the conspirator's withdrawal is manifested in any way that gives credence to the claim? Some courts have required more: not only that the conspirator notify the coconspirators of his or her withdrawal but that the conspirator thwart the criminal objectives. See Eldridge v. United States, 62 F.2d 449 (10th Cir. 1932). Query: Does this holding confuse renunciation for the purpose of relieving the defendant of liability for the crime of conspiracy with withdrawal for the purpose of starting the running of the statute of limitations as to a particular defendant? See the solution of the Model Penal Code §5.03(7)(c), Appendix to this casebook. For a review of current case and statute law, see Note, 75 Colum. L. Rev. 1122, 1174-1176 (1975).

There are other legal purposes for which change of heart may be relevant — for example, to limit the admissibility against the defendant of subsequent acts and declarations of the other conspirators or as a defense to substantive crimes subsequently committed by other conspirators. Query: What actions should the law require of a defendant before either of these legal effects is achieved? As to the first effect, see Model Penal Code §5.03(7), Comment at 145 (Tent. Draft No. 10, 1962); as to the second, see Model Penal Code §2.06(5)(c), Comment at 37 (Tent. Draft No. 1, 1953).

2. Mens Rea

UNITED STATES v. FEOLA
Supreme Court of the United States
420 U.S. 672 (1975)

MR. JUSTICE BLACKMUN delivered the opinion of the Court.

This case presents the issue whether knowledge that the intended victim is a federal officer is a requisite for the crime of conspiracy, under 18 U.S.C §371, to commit an offense violative of 18 U.S.C. §111,[1] that is, an assault upon a federal officer while engaged in the performance of his official duties.

Respondent Feola and three others (Alsondo, Rosa, and Farr) were indicted for violations of §371 and §111. A jury found all four defendants guilty of both charges. Feola received a sentence of four years for the conspiracy and one to three years, plus a $3,000 fine, for the assault. The three-year sentence, however, was suspended and he was given three years' probation "to commence at the expiration of confinement" for the conspiracy. The . . . United States Court of Appeals for the Second Circuit . . . affirmed the judgment of conviction on the substantive charges, but reversed the conspiracy convictions. Because of a conflict among the federal circuits on the scienter issue with respect to a conspiracy charge, we granted the Government's petition for a writ of certiorari in Feola's case.

The facts reveal a classic narcotics "rip-off." The details are not particularly important for our present purposes. We need note only that the evidence shows that Feola and his confederates arranged for a sale of heroin to buyers who turned out to be undercover agents for the Bureau of Narcotics and Dangerous Drugs. The group planned to palm off on the purchasers, for a substantial sum, a form of sugar in place of heroin and, should that ruse fail, simply to surprise their unwitting buyers and relieve them of the cash they had brought along for payment. The plan failed when one agent, his suspicions being aroused,[6] drew his revolver in time to counter an assault upon another agent from the rear. Instead of enjoying the rich benefits of a successful swindle, Feola and his associates found themselves charged, to their undoubted surprise, with conspiring to assault, and with assaulting, federal officers.

At the trial, the District Court, without objection from the defense, charged the jurors that, in order to find any of the defendants guilty on either the conspiracy count or the substantive one, they were not required to conclude that the defendants were aware that their quarry were federal officers.

The Court of Appeals reversed the conspiracy convictions on a ground not

---

1. "**§111. ASSAULTING, RESISTING, OR IMPEDING CERTAIN OFFICERS OR EMPLOYEES**

"Whoever forcibly assaults, resists, opposes, impedes, intimidates, or interferes with any person designated in section 1114 of this title while engaged in or on account of the performance of his official duties, shall be fined not more than $5,000 or imprisoned not more than three years, or both.

"Whoever, in the commission of any such acts uses a deadly or dangerous weapon, shall be fined not more than $10,000 or imprisoned not more than ten years, or both."

Among the persons "designated in section 1114" of 18 U.S.C. is "any officer or employee . . . of the Bureau of Narcotics and Dangerous Drugs."

6. The agent opened a closet door in the Manhattan apartment where the sale was to have taken place and observed a man on the floor, bound and gagged.

advanced by any of the defendants. Although it approved the trial court's instructions to the jury on the substantive charge of assaulting a federal officer, it nonetheless concluded that the failure to charge that knowledge of the victim's official identity must be proved in order to convict on the conspiracy charge amounted to plain error. The court perceived itself bound by a line of cases, commencing with Judge Learned Hand's opinion in United States v. Crimmins, 123 F.2d 271 (C.A.2 1941), all holding that scienter of a factual element that confers federal jurisdiction, while unnecessary for conviction of the substantive offense, is required in order to sustain a conviction for conspiracy to commit the substantive offense.

The Government's plea is for symmetry. It urges that since criminal liability for the offense described in 18 U.S.C. §111 does not depend on whether the assailant harbored the specific intent to assault a federal officer, no greater scienter requirement can be engrafted upon the conspiracy offense, which is merely an agreement to commit the act proscribed by §111. Consideration of the Government's contention requires us preliminarily to pass upon its premise, the proposition that responsibility for assault upon a federal officer does not depend upon whether the assailant was aware of the official identity of his victim at the time he acted.

That the "federal officer" requirement is anything other than jurisdictional[9] is not seriously urged upon us. . . . Nevertheless, we are not always guided by concessions of the parties, and the very considerations of symmetry urged by the Government suggest that we first turn our attention to the substantive offense. . . .

In the present case, we see again the possible consequences of an interpretation of §111 that focuses on only one of the statute's apparent aims. If the primary purpose is to protect federal law enforcement personnel, that purpose could well be frustrated by the impositions of a strict scienter requirement. On the other hand, if §111 is seen primarily as an anti-obstruction statute [i.e., to prevent hinderance to the execution of official duty], it is likely that Congress intended criminal liability to be imposed only when a person acted with the specific intent to impede enforcement activities. Otherwise, it has been said: "Were knowledge not required in obstruction of justice offenses described by these terms, wholly innocent (or even socially desirable) behavior could be transformed into a felony by the wholly fortuitous circumstance of the concealed identity of the person resisted." Although we adhere to the conclusion . . . that either view of legislative intent is "plausible," we think it plain that Congress intended to protect *both* federal officers and federal functions, and that, indeed, furtherance of the

9. We are content to state the issue this way despite its potential to mislead. Labeling a requirement "jurisdictional" does not necessarily mean, of course, that the requirement is not an element of the offense Congress intended to describe and to punish. Indeed, a requirement is sufficient to confer jurisdiction on the federal courts for what otherwise are state crimes precisely because it implicates factors that are an appropriate subject for federal concern. With respect to the present case, for example, a mere general policy of deterring assaults would probably prove to be an undesirable or insufficient basis for federal jurisdiction; but where Congress seeks to protect the integrity of federal functions and the safety of federal officers, the interest is sufficient to warrant federal involvement. The significance of labeling a statutory requirement as "jurisdictional" is not that the requirement is viewed as outside the scope of the evil Congress intended to forestall, but merely that the existence of the fact that confers federal jurisdiction need not be one in the mind of the actor at the time he perpetrates the act made criminal by the federal statute. The question, then, is not whether the requirement is jurisdictional, but whether it is jurisdictional only.

one policy advances the other. The rejection of a strict scienter requirement is consistent with both purposes. . . .

[The Court then reviewed the legislative history of §111 and its antecedents.]

We conclude, from all this, that in order to effectuate the congressional purpose of according maximum protection to federal officers by making prosecution for assaults upon them cognizable in the federal courts, §111 cannot be construed as embodying an unexpressed requirement that an assailant be aware that his victim is a federal officer. All the statute requires is an intent to assault, not an intent to assault a federal officer. A contrary conclusion would give insufficient protection to the agent enforcing an unpopular law, and none to the agent acting under cover.

This interpretation poses no risk of unfairness to defendants. It is no snare for the unsuspecting. Although the perpetrator of a narcotics "rip-off," such as the one involved here, may be surprised to find that his intended victim is a federal officer in civilian apparel, he nonetheless knows from the very outset that his planned course of conduct is wrongful. . . . The concept of criminal intent does not extend so far as to require that the actor understand not only the nature of his act but also its consequence for the choice of a judicial forum. . . .

We hold, therefore, that in order to incur criminal liability under §111 an actor must entertain merely the criminal intent to do the acts therein specified. We now consider whether the rule should be different where persons conspire to commit those acts.

Our decisions establish that in order to sustain a judgment of conviction on a charge of conspiracy to violate a federal statute, the Government must prove at least the degree of criminal intent necessary for the substantive offense itself. Respondent Feola urges upon us the proposition that the Government must show a degree of criminal intent in the conspiracy count greater than is necessary to convict for the substantive offense; he urges that even though it is not necessary to show that he was aware of the official identity of his assaulted victims in order to find him guilty of assaulting federal officers, in violation of 18 U.S.C. §111, the Government nonetheless must show that he was aware that his intended victims were undercover agents, if it is successfully to prosecute him for conspiring to assault federal agents. . . .

The general conspiracy statute, 18 U.S.C. §371, offers no textual support for the proposition that to be guilty of conspiracy a defendant in effect must have known that his conduct violated federal law. The statute makes it unlawful simply to "conspire . . . to commit any offense against the United States." A natural reading of these words would be that since one can violate a criminal statute simply by engaging in the forbidden conduct, a conspiracy to commit that offense is nothing more than an agreement to engage in the prohibited conduct. Then where, as here, the substantive statute does not require that an assailant know the official status of his victim, there is nothing on the face of the conspiracy statute that would seem to require that those agreeing to the assault have a greater degree of knowledge. . . .

With no support on the face of the general conspiracy statute or in this Court's decisions, respondent relies solely on the line of cases commencing with United States v. Crimmins, 123 F.2d 271 (C.A.2 1941), for the principle that the Government must prove "anti-federal" intent in order to establish liability under §371.

In *Crimmins,* the defendant had been found guilty of conspiring to receive stolen bonds that had been transported in interstate commerce.[a] Upon review, the Court of Appeals pointed out that the evidence failed to establish that Crimmins actually knew the stolen bonds had moved into the State. Accepting for the sake of argument the assumption that such knowledge was not necessary to sustain a conviction on the substantive offense, Judge Learned Hand nevertheless concluded that to permit conspiratorial liability where the conspirators were ignorant of the federal implications of their acts would be to enlarge their agreement beyond its terms as they understood them. He capsulized the distinction in what has become well known as his "traffic light" analogy: "While one may, for instance, be guilty of running past a traffic light of whose existence one is ignorant, one cannot be guilty of conspiring to run past such a light, for one cannot agree to run past a light unless one supposes that there is a light to run past." Id., at 273.[b]

Judge Hand's attractive, but perhaps seductive, analogy has received a mixed reception in the courts of appeals. . . . We conclude that the analogy, though effective prose, is, as applied to the facts before us, bad law.[24]

The question posed by the traffic light analogy is not before us, just as it was not before the Second Circuit in *Crimmins.* Criminal liability, of course, may be imposed on one who runs a traffic light regardless of whether he harbored the "evil intent" of disobeying the light's command. . . . Traffic violations generally fall into that category of offenses that dispense with a mens rea requirement. These laws embody the social judgment that it is fair to punish one who intentionally engages in conduct that creates a risk to others, even though no risk is intended or the actor, through no fault of his own, is completely unaware of the existence of any risk. The traffic light analogy poses the question whether it is fair to punish parties to an agreement to engage intentionally in apparently innocent conduct where the unintended result of engaging in that conduct is the violation of a criminal statute.

But this case does not call upon us to answer this question, and we decline to do so, just as we have once before. United States v. Freed, 401 U.S., at 609 n. 14. We note in passing, however, that the analogy comes close to stating what has been known as the *"Powell* doctrine," originating in People v. Powell, 63 N.Y. 88 (1875), to the effect that a conspiracy, to be criminal, must be animated by a corrupt motive or a motive to do wrong. Under this principle, such a motive could be easily demonstrated if the underlying offense involved an act clearly wrongful in itself; but it had to be independently demonstrated if the acts agreed to were wrongful solely because of statutory proscription. Interest-

---

a. This statement is not quite accurate. Crimmins was convicted of a conspiracy to transport stolen securities in interstate commerce, in violation of 18 U.S.C. §415, which made it criminal for a person to "transport or cause to be transported in interstate . . . commerce any . . . securities . . . knowing the same to have been stolen."— EDS.

b. Judge Hand concluded: "[T]here can be no conspiracy to 'cause' stolen securities 'to be transported in interstate . . . commerce' unless it is understood to be part of the project that they shall cross state lines."— EDS.

24. The Government rather effectively exposes the fallacy of the *Crimmins* traffic light analogy by recasting it in terms of a jurisdictional element. The suggested example is a traffic light on an Indian reservation. Surely, one may conspire with others to disobey the light but be ignorant of the fact that it is on the reservation. As applied to a jurisdictional element of this kind the formulation makes little sense.

ingly, Judge Hand himself was one of the more severe critics of the *Powell* doctrine.[25]

That Judge Hand should reject the *Powell* doctrine and then create the *Crimmins* doctrine seems curious enough. . . . [But] the traffic light analogy, even if it were a correct statement of the law, is inapt, for the conduct proscribed by the substantive offense, here assault, is not of the type outlawed without regard to the intent of the actor to accomplish the result that is made criminal. If the analogy has any vitality at all, it is to conduct of the latter variety; that, however, is a question we save for another day. We hold here only that where a substantive offense embodies only a requirement of mens rea as to each of its elements, the general federal conspiracy statute requires no more.

The *Crimmins* rule rests upon another foundation: that it is improper to find conspiratorial liability where the parties to the illicit agreement were not aware of the fact giving rise to federal jurisdiction, because the essence of conspiracy is agreement and persons cannot be punished for acts beyond the scope of their agreement. This "reason" states little more than a conclusion, for it is clear that one may be guilty as a conspirator for acts the precise details of which one does not know at the time of the agreement. See Blumenthal v. United States, 332 U.S. 539, 557 (1947). The question is not merely whether the official status of an assaulted victim was known to the parties at the time of their agreement, but whether the acts contemplated by the conspirators are to be deemed legally different from those actually performed solely because of the official identity of the victim. Put another way, does the identity of the proposed victim alter the legal character of the acts agreed to, or is it no more germane to the nature of those acts than the color of the victim's hair?

Our analysis of the substantive offense . . . supra, is sufficient to convince us that for the purpose of individual guilt or innocence, awareness of the official identity of the assault victim is irrelevant. We would expect the same to obtain with respect to the conspiracy offense unless one of the policies behind the imposition of conspiratorial liability is not served where the parties to the agreement are unaware that the intended target is a federal law enforcement official.

It is well settled that the law of conspiracy serves ends different from, and complementary to, those served by criminal prohibitions of the substantive offense. Because of this, consecutive sentences may be imposed for the conspiracy and for the underlying crime. . . . Our decisions have identified two independent values served by the law of conspiracy. The first is protection of society from the dangers of concerted criminal activity. . . . That individuals know that their planned joint venture violates federal as well as state law seems totally irrelevant to that purpose of conspiracy law which seeks to protect society from the dangers of concerted criminal activity. . . .

The second aspect is that conspiracy is an inchoate crime. This is to say, that, although the law generally makes criminal only antisocial conduct, at some point in the continuum between preparation and consummation, the likelihood of a commission of an act is sufficiently great and the criminal intent sufficiently well formed to justify the intervention of the criminal law. . . .

---

25. "Starting with People v. Powell . . . the anomalous doctrine has indeed gained some footing in the circuit courts of appeals that for conspiracy there must be a 'corrupt motive. . . .' Yet it is hard to see any reason for this, or why more proof should be necessary than that the parties had in contemplation all the elements of the crime they are charged with conspiracy to commit." United States v. Mack, 112 F.2d 290, 292 (C.A.2 1940).

Again, we do not see how imposition of a strict "anti-federal" scienter requirement would relate to this purpose of conspiracy law. Given the level of intent needed to carry out the substantive offense, we fail to see how the agreement is any less blameworthy or constitutes less of a danger to society solely because the participants are unaware which body of law they intend to violate. Therefore, we again conclude that imposition of a requirement of knowledge of those facts that serve only to establish federal jurisdiction would render it more difficult to serve the policy behind the law of conspiracy without serving any other apparent social policy. . . .

Again we point out, however, that the state of knowledge of the parties to an agreement is not always irrelevant in a proceeding charging a violation of conspiracy law. First, the knowledge of the parties is relevant to the same issues and to the same extent as it may be for conviction of the substantive offense. Second, whether conspirators knew the official identity of their quarry may be important, in some cases, in establishing the existence of federal jurisdiction. The jurisdictional requirement is satisfied by the existence of facts tying the proscribed conduct to the area of federal concern delineated by the statute. Federal jurisdiction always exists where the substantive offense is committed in the manner therein described, that is, when a federal officer is attacked. Where, however, there is an unfulfilled agreement to assault, it must be established whether the agreement, standing alone, constituted a sufficient threat to the safety of a federal officer so as to give rise to federal jurisdiction. . . . Where the object of the intended attack is not identified with sufficient specificity so as to give rise to the conclusion that had the attack been carried out the victim would have been a federal officer, it is impossible to assert that the mere act of agreement to assault poses a sufficient threat to federal personnel and functions so as to give rise to federal jurisdiction.

To summarize, with the exception of the infrequent situation in which reference to the knowledge of the parties to an illegal agreement is necessary to establish the existence of federal jurisdiction, we hold that where knowledge of the facts giving rise to federal jurisdiction is not necessary for conviction of a substantive offense embodying a mens rea requirement, such knowledge is equally irrelevant to questions of responsibility for conspiracy to commit that offense.

The judgment of the Court of Appeals with respect to the respondent's conspiracy conviction is reversed.

MR. JUSTICE STEWART, with whom MR. JUSTICE DOUGLAS joins, dissenting.

Does an assault on a federal officer violate 18 U.S.C. §111 even when the assailant is unaware, and has no reason to know, that the victim is other than a private citizen or, indeed, a confederate in crime? . . .

The Court recognizes that "[t]he question . . . is not whether the ['federal officer'] requirement is jurisdictional, but whether it is jurisdictional only." . . . Put otherwise, the question is whether Congress intended to write an aggravated assault statute, analogous to the many state statutes which protect the persons and functions of state officers against assault, or whether Congress intended merely to federalize every assault which happens to have a federal officer as its victim. The Court chooses the latter interpretation, reading the federal-officer requirement to be jurisdictional only. This conclusion is inconsistent with the pertinent legislative history, the verbal structure of §111, accepted canons of statutory construction, and the dictates of common sense.

Many States provide an aggravated penalty for assaults upon state law enforcement officers; typically the victim-status element transforms the assault from a misdemeanor to a felony. These statutes have a twofold purpose: to reflect the societal gravity associated with assaulting a public officer and, by providing an enhanced deterrent against such assault, to accord to public officers and their functions a protection greater than that which the law of assault otherwise provides to private citizens and their private activities. Consonant with these purposes, the accused's knowledge that his victim had an official status or function is invariably recognized by the States as an essential element of the aggravated offense. Where an assailant had no such knowledge, he could not of course be deterred by the statutory threat of enhanced punishment, and it makes no sense to regard the unknowing assault as being any more reprehensible, in a moral or retributive sense, than if the victim had been, as the assailant supposed, a private citizen.

The state statutes protect only state officers. I would read §111 as filling the gap and supplying analogous protection for federal officers and their functions. An aggravated penalty should apply only where an assailant knew, or had reason to know, that his victim had some official status or function. It is immaterial whether the assailant knew the victim was employed by the federal, as opposed to a state or local, government. That *is* a matter of "jurisdiction only," for it does not affect the moral gravity of the act. If the victim was a federal officer, §111 applies, if he was a state or local officer, an analogous state statute or local ordinance will generally apply. But where the assailant reasonably thought his victim a common citizen or, indeed, a confederate in crime, aggravation is simply out of place, and the case should be tried in the appropriate forum under the general law of assault, as are unknowing assaults on state officers.

The history of §111 permits no doubt that this is an aggravated assault statute, requiring proof of scienter. [Discussion omitted.]

Turning from the history of the statute to its structure, the propriety of implying a scienter requirement becomes manifest. The statute proscribes not only assault but also a whole series of related acts. It applies to any person who "forcibly assaults, *resists, opposes, impedes, intimidates,* or *interferes* with [a federal officer] . . . while engaged in or on account of the performance of his official duties." (Emphasis added.) It can hardly be denied that the emphasized words imply a scienter requirement. Generally speaking, these acts are legal and moral wrongs only if the actor knows that his "victim" enjoys a moral or legal privilege to detain him or order him about. These are terms of art, arising out of the common and statutory law proscribing obstruction of justice. . . .

If the words grouped in the statute with "assaults" require scienter, it follows that scienter is also required for an assault conviction. One need hardly rely on such Latin phrases as ejusdem generis and noscitur a sociis to reach this obvious conclusion. The Court suggests that assault may be treated differently, "with no risk of unfairness," because an assailant — unlike one who merely "opposes" or "resists"—"knows from the very outset that his planned course of conduct is wrongful" even though he "may be surprised to find that his intended victim is a federal officer in civilian apparel." This argument will not do, either as a matter of statutory construction or as a matter of elementary justice.

The Court is saying that because all assaults are wrong, it is "fair" to regard them all as *equally* wrong. This is a strange theory of justice. As the States recognize, an unknowing assault on an officer is less reprehensible than a knowing assault; to provide that the former may be punished as harshly as the latter is to create a very real "risk of unfairness." It is not unprecedented for Congress to enact stringent legislation, but today it is the Court that rewrites a statute so as to create an inequity which Congress itself had no intention of inflicting.

For the reasons stated, I believe that before there can be a violation of 18 U.S.C. §111, an assailant must know or have reason to know that the person he assaults is an officer. It follows a fortiori that there can be no criminal conspiracy to violate the statute in the absence of at least equivalent knowledge. Accordingly, I respectfully dissent from the opinion and judgment of the Court.

NOTES AND QUESTIONS

1. The *Powell* doctrine referred to in *Feola* (sometimes called the "corrupt motive" doctrine) is illustrated in Commonwealth v. Gormley, 77 Pa. Super. 298, 301-303 (1921). Defendant, an election officer, was indicted for conspiracy to violate the election law by entering the votes cast in the official tally sheets before the time set by law and for the substantive offense of entering false figures on the sheets. The jury acquitted him on the substantive charge but found him guilty of the conspiracy. The court reversed on appeal finding error in the trial judge's refusal to allow testimony of defendant's good faith (there was apparently no opposition candidate) and ignorance of the criminality of his act. The court said:

> The reason for the court's refusal . . . was that a defendant having violated the plain provisions of a statute, he cannot give his reasons why he did so. That a violation of the act subjects the defendant to the penalties prescribed whether he is conscious that he is violating the law or not. This view is no doubt correct as applied to the second count of the indictment charging a violation of the election laws. The legislature can declare an act a crime regardless of intent. As to the charge of conspiracy, we think the testimony was admissible. This is the pivotal question in the case. May a defendant when charged with conspiracy show that he had no intention to violate the law; that there was no corrupt motive? . . .
>
> [In] People v. Powell, 63 N.Y. 88, . . . it was said, "To make an agreement between two or more persons to do an act innocent in itself a criminal conspiracy, it is not enough that it appears that the act which was the object of the agreement was prohibited. The confederation must be corrupt. The agreement must have been entered into with an evil purpose, as distinguished from a purpose simply to do the act prohibited, in ignorance of the prohibition. This is implied in the meaning of the word conspiracy." And later on it was said: "It was open to the jury to find upon the evidence that no criminal intention existed; and if this had been found to have acquitted the defendants." . . .
>
> It follows that if a material part of the crime is the intention, the defendant may introduce any testimony that throws light on it. On the charge of making fraudulent entries on the tally sheet, the defendants had no right to show their intention and ignorance of the law was no answer to the charge, but the trial being had upon two counts, one charging conspiracy, the testimony should not

have been excluded and defendants should have been allowed to explain their action and their motives.[a]

The doctrine has been much criticized. It has been rejected in England (see Churchill v. Walton, [1967] 2 A.C. 224) and in the Model Penal Code (see §5.03, Comment at 115-116 (Tent. Draft No. 10, 1960)):

> The *Powell* rule, and many of the decisions that rely upon it, may be viewed as a judicial endeavor to import fair mens rea requirements into statutes creating regulatory offenses that do not rest upon traditional concepts of personal fault and culpability. We believe, however, that this should be the function of the statutes defining such offenses. Section 2.04(3) specifies the limited situations where ignorance of the criminality of one's conduct is a defense in general. . . . We see no reason why the fortuity of concert should be used as the device for limiting criminality in this area, just as we see no reason for using it as a device for expanding liability through imprecise formulations of objectives that include activity not otherwise criminal.

Most of the state statutory codifications follow the Model Penal Code in rejecting the *Powell* doctrine. See Note, Conspiracy: Statutory Reform Since the Model Penal Code, 75 Colum. L. Rev. 1122, 1131 n. 48 (1975).

2. The Court in *Feola* charges Judge Hand with inconsistency in rejecting the *Powell* doctrine while holding as he did in the *Crimmins* case. Is this point well taken? In his holding in *Crimmins* that defendant cannot be said to have agreed to cause stolen securities to be transported in interstate commerce unless he understood that the securities were to cross state lines, in what sense was Judge Hand implying any acceptance of the *Powell* doctrine?

3. In cases like Commonwealth v. Gormley and People v. Powell (see Note 1 supra), the "corrupt motive" defense amounts to a claim of ignorance of the law, and in this context the current trend is toward parity between the requirements for conspiracy and the substantive offense: If such ignorance is no defense with respect to the substantive offense, it is likewise no defense to a conspiracy charge. Should the result be different where the defendant claims a mistake of *fact;* that is, should mistake of fact be a defense to a conspiracy charge even if it would not be a defense in a prosecution for the substantive offense?

(a) In United States v. Freed, 401 U.S. 601 (1971), the Supreme Court upheld an indictment both for possession and conspiracy to possess unregistered hand grenades, despite its failure to allege that defendant knew the grenades were unregistered. The Court treated the substantive offense of possessing unregistered hand grenades as imposing strict liability so far as the fact of registration was concerned. The Court disposed of the conspiracy charge as follows (id. at n. 14):

---

a. Accord, Commonwealth v. Benesch, 290 Mass. 125, 194 N.E. 905 (1935). But see Commonwealth v. Kirk, 141 Pa. Super. 123 (1941), *aff'd,* 340 Pa. 346, 17 A.2d 195 (1941), and Commonwealth v. O'Rourke, 311 Mass. 213, 40 N.E.2d 883 (1942). See also the review of authorities in People v. Bowman, 156 Cal. App. 2d 784, 320 P.2d 70 (1958) and in Judge Bazelon's concurring opinion in United States v. Barker, 514 F.2d 208, 227, 234 n. 34 (D.C. Cir. 1975). — Eds.

We need not decide whether a criminal conspiracy to do an act "innocent in itself" and not known by the alleged conspirators to be prohibited must be actuated by some corrupt motive other than the intention to do the act which is prohibited and which is the object of the conspiracy. An agreement to acquire hand grenades is hardly an agreement innocent in itself. Therefore what we have said of the substantive offense satisfies on these special facts the requirements for a conspiracy. Cf. United States v. Mack, 2 Cir., 112 F.2d 290.

Query: Is this holding sound? So far as the conspiracy count was concerned, was defendant's argument simply that he did not know it was possibly a crime to possess grenades or that he did not agree to possess unregistered hand grenades? Did the Court confuse two separate mens rea defenses, namely, the defense of ignorance of the criminality or immorality of the agreement and the defense of lack of agreement to do the act that was criminal?

(b) Suppose that the conspiracy charged does involve an act "innocent in itself." For example, suppose that two men, *A* and *B*, agree to drive a young woman to a hotel, where *A* will have sexual relations with her. The group is stopped by police at the hotel entrance, and though neither *A* nor *B* could have known it, the "woman" proves to be 16 years old. Can *A* and *B* be convicted of conspiracy to commit statutory rape? (Incidentally, can *A* be convicted of attempted statutory rape? Should different principles govern with respect to conspiracy?) [12]

PEOPLE v. LAURIA

California District Court of Appeal
251 Cal. App. 2d 471, 59 Cal. Rptr. 628 (1967)

FLEMING, J. In an investigation of call-girl activity the police focused their attention on three prostitutes actively plying their trade on call, each of whom was using Lauria's telephone answering service, presumably for business purposes.

On January 8, 1965, Stella Weeks, a policewoman, signed up for telephone service with Lauria's answering service. Mrs. Weeks, in the course of her conversation with Lauria's officer manager, hinted broadly that she was a prostitute concerned with the secrecy of her activities and their concealment from the police. She was assured that the operation of the service was discreet and "about as safe as you can get." It was arranged that Mrs. Weeks need not leave her address with the answering service, but could pick up her calls and pay her bills in person.

On February 11, Mrs. Weeks talked to Lauria on the telephone and told him her business was modeling and she had been referred to the answering service by Terry, one of the three prostitutes under investigation. She complained

12. These problems are dealt with explicitly in the English Criminal Law Act, 1977, ch. 45, §1(2): "Where liability for any offence may be incurred without knowledge on the part of the person committing it of any particular fact or circumstance necessary for the commission of the offence, a person shall nevertheless not be guilty of conspiracy to commit that offence by virtue of subsection (1) above unless he and at least one other party to the agreement intend or know that that fact or circumstance shall or will exist at the time when the conduct constituting the offence is to take place."

that because of the operation of the service she had lost two valuable customers, referred to as tricks. Lauria defended his service and said that her friends had probably lied to her about having left calls for her. But he did not respond to Mrs. Weeks' hints that she needed customers in order to make money, other than to invite her to his house for a personal visit in order to get better acquainted. In the course of his talk he said "his business was taking messages."

On February 15, Mrs. Weeks talked on the telephone to Lauria's office manager and again complained of two lost calls, which she described as a $50 and a $100 trick. On investigation the office manager could find nothing wrong, but she said she would alert the switchboard operators about slip-ups on calls.

On April 1 Lauria and the three prostitutes were arrested. Lauria complained to the police that this attention was undeserved, stating that Hollywood Call Board had 60 to 70 prostitutes on its board while his own service had only 9 or 10, that he kept separate records for known or suspected prostitutes for the convenience of himself and the police. When asked if his records were available to police who might come to the office to investigate call girls, Lauria replied that they were whenever the police had a specific name. However, his service didn't "arbitrarily tell the police about prostitutes on our board. As long as they pay their bills we tolerate them." In a subsequent voluntary appearance before the Grand Jury Lauria testified he had always cooperated with the police. But he admitted he knew some of his customers were prostitutes, and he knew Terry was a prostitute because he had personally used her services, and he knew she was paying for 500 calls a month.

Lauria and the three prostitutes were indicted for conspiracy to commit prostitution, and nine overt acts were specified. Subsequently the trial court set aside the indictment as having been brought without reasonable or probable cause. (Pen. Code, §995). The People have appealed, claiming that a sufficient showing of an unlawful agreement to further prostitution was made.

To establish agreement, the People need show no more than a tacit, mutual understanding between co-conspirators to accomplish an unlawful act. . . . Here the People attempted to establish a conspiracy by showing that Lauria, well aware that his codefendants were prostitutes who received business calls from customers through his telephone answering service, continued to furnish them with such service. This approach attempts to equate knowledge of another's criminal activity with conspiracy to further such criminal activity, and poses the question of the criminal responsibility of a furnisher of goods or services who knows his product is being used to assist the operation of an illegal business. Under what circumstances does a supplier become a part of a conspiracy to further an illegal enterprise by furnishing goods or services which he knows are to be used by the buyer for criminal purposes?

The two leading cases on this point face in opposite directions. In United States v. Falcone, 311 U.S. 205, the sellers of large quantities of sugar, yeast, and cans were absolved from participation in a moonshining conspiracy among distillers who bought from them, while in Direct Sales Co. v. United States, 319 U.S. 703, a wholesaler of drugs was convicted of conspiracy to violate the federal narcotic laws by selling drugs in quantity to a codefendant physician who was supplying them to addicts. The distinction between these two cases appears primarily based on the proposition that distributors of such dangerous products as drugs are required to exercise greater discrimination in the conduct of their business than are distributors of innocuous substances like sugar and yeast.

In the earlier case, *Falcone,* the sellers' knowledge of the illegal use of the goods was insufficient by itself to make the sellers participants in a conspiracy with the distillers who bought from them. Such knowledge fell short of proof of a conspiracy, and evidence on the volume of sales was too vague to support a jury finding that respondents knew of the conspiracy [with others] from the size of the sales alone.

In the later case of *Direct Sales,* the conviction of a drug wholesaler for conspiracy to violate federal narcotic laws was affirmed on a showing that it had actively promoted the sale of morphine sulphate in quantity and had sold codefendant physician, who practiced in a small town in South Carolina, more than 300 times his normal requirements of the drug, even though it had been repeatedly warned of the dangers of unrestricted sales of the drug. The court contrasted the restricted goods involved in *Direct Sales* with the articles of free commerce involved in *Falcone:* "All articles of commerce may be put to illegal ends," said the court. "But all do not have inherently the same susceptibility to harmful and illegal use. . . . This difference is important for two purposes. One is for making certain that the seller knows the buyer's intended illegal use. The other is to show that by the sale he intends to further, promote and cooperate in it. This intent, when given effect by overt act, is the gist of conspiracy. While it is not identical with mere knowledge that another purposes unlawful action, it is not unrelated to such knowledge. . . . The step from knowledge to intent and agreement may be taken. There is more than suspicion, more than knowledge, acquiescence, carelessness, indifference, lack of concern. There is informed and interested cooperation, stimulation, instigation. And there is also a 'stake in the venture' which, even if it may not be essential, is not irrelevant to the question of conspiracy." (319 U.S. at 710-713.)

While *Falcone* and *Direct Sales* may not be entirely consistent with each other in their full implications, they do provide us with a framework for the criminal liability of a supplier of lawful goods or services put to unlawful use. Both the element of *knowledge* of the illegal use of the goods or services and the element of *intent* to further that use must be present in order to make the supplier a participant in a criminal conspiracy.

Proof of *knowledge* is ordinarily a question of fact and requires no extended discussion in the present case. The knowledge of the supplier was sufficiently established when Lauria admitted he knew some of his customers were prostitutes and admitted he knew that Terry, an active subscriber to his service, was a prostitute. In the face of these admissions he could scarcely claim to have relied on the normal assumption an operator of a business or service is entitled to make, that his customers are behaving themselves in the eyes of the law. Because Lauria knew in fact that some of his customers were prostitutes, it is a legitimate inference he knew they were subscribing to his answering service for illegal business purposes and were using his service to make assignations for prostitution. On this record we think the prosecution is entitled to claim positive knowledge by Lauria of the use of his service to facilitate the business of prostitution.

The more perplexing issue in the case is the sufficiency of proof of *intent* to further the criminal enterprise. The element of intent may be proved either by direct evidence, or by evidence of circumstances from which an intent to further a criminal enterprise by supplying lawful goods or services may be inferred. Direct evidence of participation, such as advice from the supplier of legal goods or services to the user of those goods or services on their use for illegal purpose, such evidence as appeared in a companion case we decide today, People v. Roy, 59 Cal. Rptr. 636 provides the simplest case.[a] . . . But in cases where direct proof of complicity is lacking, intent to further the conspiracy must be derived from the sale itself and its surrounding circumstances in order to establish the supplier's express or tacit agreement to join the conspiracy.

In the case at bench the prosecution argues that since Lauria knew his customers were using his service for illegal purposes but nevertheless continued to furnish it to them, he must have intended to assist them in carrying out their illegal activities. Thus through a union of knowledge and intent he became a participant in a criminal conspiracy. Essentially, the People argue that knowledge alone of the continuing use of his telephone facilities for criminal purposes provided a sufficient basis from which his intent to participate in those criminal activities could be inferred.

1. Intent may be inferred from knowledge, when the purveyor of legal goods for illegal use has acquired a stake in the venture. (United States v. Falcone, 2 Cir. 109 F.2d 579, 581.) [b] For example, in Regina v. Thomas, (1957), 2 All E.R. 181, 342, a prosecution for living off the earnings of prostitution, the evidence showed that the accused, knowing the woman to be a convicted prostitute, agreed to let her have the use of his room between the hours of 9 P.M. and 2 A.M. for a charge of £3 a night. The Court of Criminal Appeal refused an appeal from the conviction, holding that when the accused rented a room at a grossly inflated rent to a prostitute for the purpose of carrying on her trade, a jury could find he was living on the earnings of prostitution.

In the present case, no proof was offered of inflated charges for the telephone answering services furnished the codefendants.

2. Intent may be inferred from knowledge, when no legitimate use for the goods or services exists. The leading California case is People v. McLaughlin, 111 Cal. App. 2d 781, 245 P.2d 1076, in which the court upheld a conviction of the suppliers of horse-racing information by wire for conspiracy to promote bookmaking, when it had been established that wire service information had

a. In this case the court reached an opposite conclusion on a closely parallel set of facts on the evidence that the answering service operator actively participated in the business of prostitution by making arrangements for the sharing of customers between two supposed prostitutes who used the service. The court said, speaking of the operator, "Perhaps she was motivated solely by a desire to further the welfare and serve the interests of her customers and acted without thought of added profit for herself. But disinterested loyalty and devotion to the patrons of her service provide no excuse for the promotion of a criminal enterprise." 59 Cal. Rptr. at 641. — EDS.

b. In United States v. Falcone, Judge Learned Hand wrote the opinion of the Second Circuit Court of Appeals. He stated: "Civilly, a man's liability extends to any injuries which he should have apprehended to be likely to follow from his acts. . . . There are indeed instances of criminal liability of the same kind, where the law imposes punishment merely because the accused did not forbear to do that from which the wrong was likely to follow; but in prosecutions for conspiracy or abetting, his attitude towards the forbidden undertaking must be more positive. It is not enough that he does not forego a normally lawful activity, of the fruits of which he knows that others will make an unlawful use; he must in some sense promote their venture himself, make it his own, have a stake in its outcome. The distinction is especially important today when so many prosecutors seek to sweep within the drag-net of conspiracy all those who have been associated in any degree whatever with the main offenders. We may agree that morally the defendants at bar should have refused to sell to illicit distillers; but, both morally and legally, to do so was toto coelo different from joining with them in running the stills." — EDS.

no other use than to supply information needed by bookmakers to conduct illegal gambling operations. . . .

In Shaw v. Director of Public Prosecutions, [1962] A.C. 220, the defendant was convicted of conspiracy to corrupt public morals and of living on the earnings of prostitution, when he published a directory consisting almost entirely of advertisements of the names, addresses, and specialized talents of prostitutes. Publication of such a directory, said the court, could have no legitimate use and serve no other purpose than to advertise the professional services of the prostitutes whose advertisements appeared in the directory. The publisher could be deemed a participant in the profits from the business activities of his principal advertisers. . . .

However, there is nothing in the furnishing of telephone answering service which would necessarily imply assistance in the performance of illegal activities. Nor is any inference to be derived from the use of an answering service by women, either in any particular volume of calls, or outside normal working hours. Nightclub entertainers, registered nurses, faith healers, public stenographers, photographic models, and free lance substitute employees, provide examples of women in legitimate occupations whose employment might cause them to receive a volume of telephone calls at irregular hours.

3. Intent may be inferred from knowledge, when the volume of business with the buyer is grossly disproportionate to any legitimate demand, or when sales for illegal use amount to a high proportion of the seller's total business. In such cases an intent to participate in the illegal enterprise may be inferred from the quantity of the business done. For example, in *Direct Sales*, supra, the sale of narcotics to a rural physician in quantities 300 times greater than he would have normal use for provided potent evidence of an intent to further the illegal activity. In the same case the court also found significant the fact that the wholesaler had attracted as customers a disproportionately large group of physicians who had been convicted of violating the Harrison Act. In Shaw v. Director of Public Prosecutions, [1962] A.C. 220, almost the entire business of the directory came from prostitutes.

No evidence of any unusual volume of business with prostitutes was presented by the prosecution against Lauria.

Inflated charges, the sale of goods with no legitimate use, sales in inflated amounts, each may provide a fact of sufficient moment from which the intent of the seller to participate in the criminal enterprise may be inferred. In such instances participation by the supplier of legal goods to the illegal enterprise may be inferred because in one way or another the supplier has acquired a special interest in the operation of the illegal enterprise. His intent to participate in the crime of which he has knowledge may be inferred from the existence of his special interest.

Yet there are cases in which it cannot reasonably be said that the supplier has a stake in the venture or has acquired a special interest in the enterprise, but in which he has been held liable as a participant on the basis of knowledge alone. Some suggestion of this appears in *Direct Sales*, supra, where both the knowlege of the illegal use of the drugs and the intent of the supplier to aid' that use were inferred. In Regina v. Bainbridge (1959), 3 W.L.R. 656 (CCA 6), a supplier of oxygen-cutting equipment to one known to intend to use it to break into a bank was convicted as an accessory to the crime. . . . It seems apparent from these cases that a supplier who furnishes equipment which he *knows* will be used to commit a serious crime may be deemed from that knowledge alone to have intended to produce the result. Such proof may justify an inference that the furnisher intended to aid the execution of the crime and that he thereby became a participant. For instance, we think the operator of a telephone answering service with positive knowledge that his service was being used to facilitate the extortion of ransom, the distribution of heroin, or the passing of counterfeit money who continued to furnish the service with knowledge of its use, might be chargeable on knowledge alone with participation in a scheme to extort money, to distribute narcotics, or to pass counterfeit money. The same result would follow the seller of gasoline who knew the buyer was using his product to make Molotov cocktails for terroristic use.

Logically, the same reasoning could be extended to crimes of every description. Yet we do not believe an inference of intent drawn from knowledge of criminal use properly applies to the less serious crimes classified as misdemeanors. The duty to take positive action to dissociate oneself from activities helpful to violations of the criminal law is far stronger and more compelling for felonies than it is for misdemeanors or petty offenses. In this respect, as in others, the distinction between felonies and misdemeanors, between more serious and less serious crimes, retains continuing vitality. In historically the most serious felony, treason, an individual with knowledge of the treason can be prosecuted for concealing and failing to disclose it. (Pen. Code, §38; 18 U.S. Code, §2382.) In other felonies, both at common law and under the criminal laws of the United States, an individual knowing of the commission of a felony is criminally liable for concealing it and failing to make it known to proper authority. (4 Blackstone 121; Sykes v. Director of Public Prosecutions [1962] A.C. 528; 18 U.S. Code, §4.) But this crime known as misprision of felony, has always been limited to knowledge and concealment of felony and has never extended to misdemeanor. A similar limitation is found in the criminal liability of an accessory, which is restricted to aid in the escape of a principal who has committed or been charged with a *felony*. (Pen. Code, §32.) We believe the distinction between the obligations arising from knowledge of a felony and those arising from knowledge of a misdemeanor continues to reflect basic human feelings about the duties owed by individuals to society. Heinous crime must be stamped out, and its suppression is the responsibility of all. Venial crime and crime not evil in itself present less of a danger to society, and perhaps the benefits of their suppression through the modern equivalent of the posse, the hue and cry, the informant, and the citizen's arrest, are outweighed by the disruption to everyday life brought about by amateur law enforcement and private officiousness in relatively inconsequential delicts which do not threaten our basic security. . . .

With respect to misdemeanors, we conclude that positive knowledge of the supplier that his products or services are being used for criminal purposes does not, without more, establish an intent of the supplier to participate in the misdemeanors. With respect to felonies, we do not decide the converse, viz. that in all cases of felony knowledge of criminal use alone may justify an inference of the supplier's intent to participate in the crime. The implications of *Falcone* make the matter uncertain with respect to those felonies which are merely prohibited wrongs. . . . But decision on this point is not compelled, and we leave the matter open.

From this analysis of precedent we deduce the following rule: the intent of a supplier who knows of the criminal use to which his supplies are put to participate in the criminal activity connected with the use of his supplies may be established by (1) direct evidence that he intends to participate, or (2) through an inference that he intends to participate based on, (a) his special interest in the activity, or (b) the aggravated nature of the crime itself.

When we review Lauria's activities in the light of this analysis, we find no proof that Lauria took any direct action to further, encourage, or direct the call-girl activities of his codefendants and we find an absence of circumstances from which his special interest in their activities could be inferred. Neither excessive charges for standardized services, nor the furnishing of services without a legitimate use, nor an unusual quantity of business with call girls, are present. The offense which he is charged with furthering is a misdemeanor, a category of crime which has never been made a required subject of positive disclosure to public authority. Under these circumstances, although proof of Lauria's knowledge of the criminal activities of his patrons was sufficient to charge him with that fact, there was insufficient evidence that he intended to further their criminal activities, and hence insufficient proof of his participation in a criminal conspiracy with his codefendants to further prostitution. Since the conspiracy centered around the activities of Lauria's telephone answering service, the charges against his codefendants likewise fail for want of proof.

In absolving Lauria of complicity in a criminal conspiracy we do not wish to imply that the public authorities are without remedies to combat modern manifestations of the world's oldest profession. Licensing of telephone answering services under the police power, together with the revocation of licenses for the toleration of prostitution, is a possible civil remedy. The furnishing of telephone answering service in aid of prostitution could be made a crime. (Cf. Pen. Code, §316, which makes it a misdemeanor to let an apartment with knowledge of its use for prostitution.) Other solutions will doubtless occur to vigilant public authorities if the problem of call-girl activity needs further suppression.

The order is affirmed.

NOTES

1. How defensible is the distinction drawn by the court in *Lauria* between conspiracies to commit misdemeanors and conspiracies to commit felonies? On what policy grounds can it be justified? Can it be defended analytically? If a true purpose is needed to constitute an agreement, what bearing can the grading of the object of the agreement as a felony or as a misdemeanor have?

2. The solution of the Model Penal Code to these problems, now adopted in many jurisdictions (see Note, 75 Colum. L. Rev. 1122, 1145 (1975)), is the same for conspiracy as it is for accomplice liability. See page 620 supra. Its position is stated as follows (§5.03, Comment at 107 (Tent. Draft No. 10, 1960)):

> [Section 5.03 of the Code] requires in all cases a "purpose to promote or facilitate" commission of the crime. . . . The purpose requirement is crucial to the resolution of the difficult problems presented when a charge of conspiracy is leveled against a person whose relationship to a criminal plan is essentially peripheral. Typical

is the case of the person who sells sugar to the producers of illicit whiskey. He may have little interest in the success of the distilling operation and be motivated mainly by the desire to make the normal profit of an otherwise lawful sale. To be criminally liable, of course, he must at least have knowledge of the use to which the materials are being put, but the difficult issue presented is whether knowingly facilitating the commission of a crime ought to be sufficient, absent a true purpose to advance the criminal end. In the case of vendors conflicting interests are also involved: that of the vendors in freedom to engage in gainful and otherwise lawful activities without policing their vendees, and that of the community in preventing behavior that facilitates the commission of crimes. The decisions are in conflict, although many of those requiring purpose properly emphasize that it can be inferred from such circumstances as, for example, quantity sales, the seller's initiative or encouragement, continuity of the relationship, and the contraband nature of the materials sold. The considerations are the same whether the charge be conspiracy or complicity in the substantive crime, and the Institute has resolved them, in the complicity provisions of the Code, in favor of requiring a purpose to advance the criminal end. Under the [Code], the same purpose requirement that governs complicity is essential for conspiracy: the actor must have "the purpose of promoting or facilitating" the commission of the crime.

PROBLEM

Suppose that two brothers, *A* and *B,* are drinking in a bar with *C,* who taunts them with stories of promiscuous behavior by *A*'s wife, *W. A* and *B* agree that if *C* opens his mouth again, they will silence him once and for all. When *C* resumes taunting them, *A* and *B* pull knives and attack, inflicting several stab wounds before onlookers separate the three men. *C* is seriously wounded but survives. Of what offenses can *A* and *B* be convicted?

Note that if *C* had been killed, *A* and *B* might be charged with first-degree murder, but *A* would surely be entitled to have the jury consider whether *C*'s behavior constituted reasonable provocation reducing the offense to voluntary manslaughter. *B* likewise might be entitled to a voluntary manslaughter instruction (though his case for reasonable provocation would be weaker). But since *C* has survived, what criminal charges are appropriate? Could *A* and *B* be convicted of conspiracy to murder *C?* Does the provocation in some sense affect the intent required for such a conspiracy charge? And what would be the appropriate punishment in such a case?

In People v. Horn, 12 Cal. 3d 290, 524 P.2d 1300 (1974), the California Supreme Court held that conspirators must intend to bring about all the elements of the object offense, and, therefore, in a case like that above, the trial court must instruct the jury on the elements of voluntary manslaughter. If such elements would have been established in the event of the victim's death, then the offense is "conspiracy to commit voluntary manslaughter," and under California law the appropriate penalty would be the same as that authorized for voluntary manslaughter.[13]

13. The California Supreme Court was aided by a relatively specific statute governing the punishment for conspiracies to commit different object offenses. Cal. Penal Code §182 provides:
"When [persons] conspire to commit any other felony, they shall be punishable in the same manner and to the same extent as is provided for the punishment of the said felony. If the felony is one for which different punishments are prescribed for different degrees, the jury or court which

Queries: (1) Suppose, in the example previously mentioned, that the jury is persuaded that *A* (the husband ridiculed by *C*) was subjected to reasonable provocation but that a reasonable man in *B*'s position (a brother-in-law) would not have been provoked to kill under the circumstances. Plainly, if *C* had died, *A* could be convicted of voluntary manslaughter and *B* of first-degree murder. But since *C* has survived, what are the proper verdicts? Is it proper to convict *A* and *B* of conspiracy to murder? Of conspiracy to commit manslaughter? Is there a conspiracy between *A* and *B* at all?

(2) Suppose that instead of agreeing to kill *C, A* and *B* agree to frighten *C* by shooting at his feet and *B* then does so. Can *A* and *B* be charged with a conspiracy recklessly to endanger *C*? If *C* is killed, can *A* and *B* be charged with conspiracy to commit involuntary manslaughter?

For consideration of analogous problems in connection with accessorial liability and attempts, see Regina v. Creamer, pages 624-625 supra; People v. Marshall, page 626 supra; Regina v. Anderson and Morris, pages 627-628 supra.

3. The Concert-of-Action Requirement

a. The Agreement

UNITED STATES v. ALVAREZ

United States Court of Appeals, 5th Circuit
610 F.2d 1250 (1980)

RUBIN, J. Manuel Juan Alvarez was convicted of joining with three other persons in a conspiracy to import 110,000 pounds of marijuana from Colombia by air. The evidence against Alvarez, viewed in the light most favorable to the government, portrays him as an underling who loaded electrical appliances aboard a plane that was to fly from the United States to Colombia, and who had stated he would unload a cargo of marijuana upon its return. His attack on the sufficiency of the evidence to prove that a conspiracy existed or that he knowingly joined in it requires us to consider how much of the conspiratorial darkness must be illuminated to warrant a jury's determination that a specific defendant joined in a plot. We conclude that, while the evidence sufficed to show that Alvarez planned to assist others in one of the acts involved in consummating a criminal venture, it failed to show that he had joined in an agreement to violate the law, and we, therefore, reverse his conviction.

At the outset, we sum up the entirety of the evidence against Alvarez. The indictment named John Cifarelli, Genaro Mercia Cruz and Edward John Peterson as co-conspirators in a plan to import marijuana into the United States. Except for his joinder in the indictment, Alvarez is mentioned in only one other place in the indictment; it is charged as one of the overt acts that he together with

---

finds the defendant guilty thereof shall determine the degree of the felony defendant conspired to commit. If the degree is not so determined, the punishment for conspiracy to commit such felony shall be that prescribed for the lesser degree, except in the case of conspiracy to commit murder, in which case the punishment shall be that prescribed for murder in the first degree."

Cifarelli and Cruz met two DEA agents at the Opa-Locka, Florida, airport. The indictment against Peterson was dismissed, Cifarelli pleaded guilty and Cruz was found guilty when tried jointly with Alvarez. There was ample evidence of a conspiracy between Cruz and Cifarelli to import marijuana into the United States.

Pursuant to arrangements with an undercover DEA agent, Cifarelli came to meet the agent at the Opa-Locka airport. Alvarez drove a pickup truck in which Cruz and Cifarelli were riding. The truck was loaded with some household appliances, including a washer and dryer; the DEA agent asked Cifarelli who Alvarez was and Cifarelli said Alvarez "would be at the off-loading side in the United States." The agent then spoke to Alvarez in Spanish and asked him if he planned to be at the unloading site. Alvarez nodded his head, signifying "yes," smiled, and asked the DEA agent if he was going on the plane. The agent said he was. After the conversation, Alvarez unloaded the household appliances from the truck. The agent then spoke with Cruz, and, after Cruz outlined his plans for arrival of the plane and its unloading, all were arrested. . . .

The use of conspiracy as a device for prosecuting minor actors in criminal dramas is limited by the fact that conspiracy itself is not primarily a means of assessing the culpability of criminal accessories; it is a separate substantive offense.[4] Its prohibition is directed not at its unlawful object, but at the process of agreeing to pursue that object. . . . A defendant does not join a conspiracy merely by participating in a substantive offense, or by associating with persons who are members of a conspiracy. It is hornbook law that the criminalization of conspiracy does not proscribe purely a mental state; the agreement itself is the criminal act, an act "in advancement of the intention which each of [the conspirators] has conceived in his mind." The conspirator must knowingly agree to join others in a concerted effort to bring about a common end. These elements of the conspiratorial offense may of course be shown by circumstantial evidence.

In conspiracy, as in most criminal acts, intent is an element of the offense. Conspiracy is, however, more complex because it involves two elements of intent that shade into each other: each party must have intended to enter into the agreement and the schemers must have had a common intent to commit an unlawful act. There often may be no practical purpose in distinguishing these two intentions, but, for the crime to be proved, there must be evidence sufficient to warrant belief beyond reasonable doubt that the defendant intentionally entered into an agreement to do an illegal act with the intention of consummating that act.

It is not enough that a defendant may have wittingly aided a criminal act or that he may have intended to do so in the future; to convict a defendant of conspiracy the government must demonstrate that the defendant agreed with others that together they would accomplish the unlawful object of the conspiracy.

---

4. Civil-law countries have not developed a comparably broad doctrine of conspiracy. "European criminal codes frequently make concerted action a basis for aggravating the penalties for completed substantive crimes, but when no substantive offense has been completed, only certain types of conspiracies are proscribed — notably those directed against the security of the state, those involving many participants organized for the purpose of committing numerous crimes and those contemplating particularly serious offenses." Comment, Developments in the Law — Criminal Conspiracy, 72 Harv. L. Rev. 920 (1959).

The indictment against Alvarez identifies the agreement as a plan to import marijuana. The intent to do an illegal act is embraced in the charge to violate the law by *importing marijuana,* but both the knowing agreement and the intent to import marijuana must be proved. We turn our attention first to the alleged agreement.

What people do is logical, albeit, circumstantial, evidence of what lies in their mind. Extending this somewhat, courts have also considered that a person's acts might create an inference concerning what he has agreed to do. Therefore, whether or not an overt act is a component of the offense as defined by statute, an agreement to join a criminal conspiracy may be inferred from the performance of acts that further its purpose. This evidentiary rule should not be permitted to obscure what it is admitted to prove, an agreement, for sans agreement there can be no conspiracy. Therefore, even if a conspiracy between two parties is established, not every act of a third person that assists in the accomplishment of the objective of the conspiracy is a sufficient basis to demonstrate his concurrence in that agreement. . . .

[The opinion then reviewed the decisions of the Supreme Court in United States v. Falcone and Direct Sales v. United States, both discussed in the opinion of the California court in People v. Lauria, pages 675-681 supra, from which it concluded that an intent to promote and cooperate in the illegal activity must be shown. It then continued:] A mere promise, however, to do some act that might assist an embryonic conspiracy in achieving its yet unconsummated criminal end does not of itself demonstrate beyond reasonable doubt that the promisor knows of the conspiracy and has agreed to join it.

While "a conspiracy is seldom born of 'open covenants openly arrived at,' . . . there must be proof of a common purpose and plan." . . . It is essential . . . that the prosecution show beyond reasonable doubt that the defendant had "the deliberate, knowing, specific intent to join the conspiracy." . . .

The evidence against Alvarez is insufficient to prove that he joined in an agreement to import marijuana. Obviously, there is no direct proof of his consent. Neither is there any proof of his performance of an act directly in furtherance of the scheme. What was proved, construed most favorably to the prosecution and thus most strongly against Alvarez, is his statement that he planned to perform an act subsequent to importation, unloading the plane. That this would have been a criminal act, if done, is indisputable, but it is insufficient to prove beyond reasonable doubt that he had joined in a conspiracy to import a prohibited substance.

To justify a conviction for conspiracy, there must be evidence that Alvarez agreed to join in the unlawful plan. The evidence presented to the jury in this case permits that conclusion only by a long chain of compounded inferences: that Alvarez knew illegal activity was afoot; that Alvarez intended to unload illegal cargo upon the plane's return; that Alvarez, therefore, knew of an agreement between others to import the illegal cargo; and that, consequently, Alvarez must have joined that illegal agreement. There is direct proof only of Alvarez's intentions. That he knew the activity was criminal is a reasonable inference. The other two conclusions are logical non-sequiturs.

What Alvarez intended to do is culpable. But without more his statements are not punishable as conspiracy. It requires no imagination to construct a reasonable hypothesis of Alvarez's innocence of the charge against him. He may demonstrably have striven to aid an uncompleted crime; he was not proved to be a conspirator. . . .

There is one other route, seldom used, by which to implicate an accessory in a conspiracy: it is to charge that he aided and abetted the conspiracy. See Comment, Complicity in a Conspiracy as an Approach to Conspiratorial Liability, 16 U.C.L.A.L. Rev. 155 (1968). That charge is not made here and patently could not be, for Alvarez actually did nothing to further the conspiracy whatever he may have planned to do in the future.[6]

When we consider all the evidence in the case, we find that, at most, the government proved that Alvarez was a menial who intended to lend his pickup truck and his strong back to a plot confected by the mind of others. The crime they planned was still-born and Alvarez's criminal disposition was never employed. Whatever his subjective transgressions, he was not shown to have been a conspirator or to have adopted or joined in the scheme contrived by others.

For these reasons, the judgment of conviction is reversed.

NOTE

As shown in *Alvarez*, a strict adherence by courts to the requirement of an agreement by demanding that the prosecution show a shared purpose by the defendant to achieve the object crime serves to confine the reach of the conspiracy doctrine. In many cases, however, proof of the essential agreement rests on inference and circumstantial evidence. As a result, the requirement of an agreement becomes less of a safeguard for defendants.

The court in United States v. James, 528 F.2d 999, 1011 (5th Cir. 1976), gives a fairly representative formulation of the legal standards governing the finding of the necessary element of an agreement in a conspiracy prosecution:

> To establish the common plan element of a conspiracy, it is not necessary for the government to prove an express agreement between the alleged conspirators to go forth and violate law. The "common purpose and plan may be inferred from a development and collocation of circumstances." Glasser v. United States, 315 U.S. 60, 90 (1942). "A conspiracy is seldom born of open covenants openly arrived at. The proof, by the very nature of the crime, must be circumstantial and therefore inferential to an extent varying with the conditions under which the crime may be consummated." Direct Sales Co. v. United States, 319 U.S. 703, 714. Knowledge by a defendant of all details or phases of a conspiracy is not required. It is enough that he knows the essential nature of it. Blumenthal v. United States, 332 U.S. 539 (1947). "And, it is black letter law that all participants in a conspiracy need not know each other; all that is necessary is that each know that it has a scope and that for its success it requires an organization wider than may be disclosed by his personal participation."

How do these general and open formulas work in the context of proof in particular situations? What kinds of evidence will support finding an agreement and what kinds will not?

---

6. For a discussion of the question whether to be guilty of aiding and abetting a conspiracy one must assist the conspirators in reaching an agreement or whether it suffices to do some act to help them attain its goals, see W. LaFave & A. Scott, Criminal Law §61 at 463.

WENIGER v. UNITED STATES, 47 F.2d 692 (9th Cir. 1931): Appellants were charged by the indictment in the District Court with having engaged in a conspiracy to violate the National Prohibition Act. Conviction of the Offense was followed by judgments of imprisonment. During all of the time that the alleged conspiracy continued, appellant Weniger was the sheriff of the county of Shoshone, in the state of Idaho, and appellant Bloom was a deputy sheriff in the same county. The alleged conspiracy had to do with the selling and dealing in intoxicating liquor in the village of Mullan, which village contained a population of about 3,000 inhabitants and is located seven miles from Wallace, the county seat of Shoshone county, where the sheriff had his office. The deputy Bloom lived in the village of Mullan.

A number of other persons were included as defendants and convicted of the offense charged. Among the latter were persons who had served as members of the board of trustees and police officers of the village. None of the latter appealed from the judgments.

It was the contention of the prosecution, and the evidence shown in the record seems to establish the truth of the charge in that respect, that the city officials of the village of Mullan purposely encouraged and connived at the unlawful sale of liquor within the town by collecting monthly license charges and contributions of money from persons dealing in liquor, in order that the revenue for village upkeep and improvements might be augmented. It was shown, without question, that the city officials did agree that in consideration of the payment of license fees and contributions from liquor sellers, the business of the latter would not be interfered with. It matters not that the ordinances imposing a license tax, as adopted by the board of trustees, might have been within the power of the board to enact. Where the underlying purpose was to use the same in promoting the business of liquor selling in violation of the National Prohibition Act, such purpose, and the conduct of the officers pursuant thereto, would establish the truth of the charge made by the indictment as against the persons so involved. . . .

. . . The law requires proof of the common and unlawful design and the knowing participation therein of the persons charged as conspirators before a conviction is justified.

The United States attorney relies largely upon a showing of inaction on the part of the sheriff of the county and his deputy in enforcing the liquor laws as establishing connection of these appellants with the conspiracy charged.

There existed at the time a law in the state of Idaho prohibiting the sale of intoxicating liquor, and no doubt it was the duty of the sheriff to enforce that law. Apparently he was not disposed to do this and apparently, too, this action on his part applied to all parts of his county, and not in particular to the village of Mullan. . . . The summary now given is not an abstract of all of the evidence offered by the government, but it fairly represents the class of proof relied upon, taken in a light most damaging to appellants.

It was shown that appellant Bloom drank whiskey at a place kept by one of the witnesses at Mullan on several occasions; that Bloom did not interfere with the selling of liquor; that in 1928 at Christmas time, the federal officers were reported to be making raids in the village and appellant Bloom said to the witness referred to, "You got your car here, get your stuff in the car and get it out of here, get it out of the way." . . .

Another witness named Barron, a miner, testifed that he gave information to two federal prohibition agents respecting the liquor traffic in Mullan; that on a certain day thereafter he was in Wallace, the county seat, and saw appellant Weniger; that he (the witness) had an altercation with a woman on the street and that Weniger and Bloom arrested him. . . . At the time he was arrested by Weniger, the witness stated that a notebook was found on his person and that Weniger remarked to him: "You should not do anything like that, go ahead and stool on these people. I will deport you into Canada if you come up here from Canada and try to get smart." . . .

The case as made here by the evidence of the prosecution can be said to go no further than to establish that the sheriff of Shoshone county felt no interest in, but was opposed to, the enforcement of the National Prohibition Act. The evidence, in our opinion, falls short of showing that the particular conspiracy which was organized by the city officials of the village of Mullan was joined in by these appellants.

The judgments are reversed.

WILLIAMS v. UNITED STATES, 218 F.2d 276 (4th Cir. 1954), Dobie, J.: The appellants, Julian T. Williams, Charles G. Croft, Milton W. Johns, Albert D. Roth, William H. Overstreet, Thomas Pierson, Wilbur L. Dyches, and Henry Chassereau, were tried in the United States District Court for the Eastern District of South Carolina upon an indictment alleging a violation of Section 371, Title 18, of the United States Code, of conspiracy to violate a number of sections of the Internal Revenue laws relating to liquor. These appellants, with William J. Koster and Julius D. Zerbst, Jr., were convicted under Count One alleging conspiracy. . . .

Sentence was duly imposed upon all of the appellants and upon William J. Koster and Julius D. Zerbst. William J. Koster and Julius D. Zerbst have not appealed. With the exception of Harry Chassereau, all of the appellants were members of the Police Force of Charleston County, South Carolina. Harry Chassereau operated a filling station, which was one of the distribution points maintained for whiskey, on which the federal tax had not been paid. . . .

We proceed to dispose of the contention that the record fails to disclose sufficient evidence to take to the jury the question of a general conspiracy among appellants but that the record shows only numerous unrelated and separate violations of the federal internal revenue laws with the only nexus between these acts and these appellants lying in the fact that the appellants (with the exception of Harry Chassereau) were members of the same police department.

This evidence, which was quite voluminous and given by many witnesses, may be likened to the web of the spider. No single strand, or even several strands, would be sufficient. Yet when all these strands are considered together, and their interrelations and connections are considered, they form, we think, a complete web, which was more than sufficient to take to the jury the question of a general conspiracy among the appellants. On all this evidence, the jury might well have found (as we think they did find) that all those acts just could not have happened save on the theory of a consistent pattern of agreement between these appellants.

This evidence is far too voluminous to be discussed here in detail. Even a compact summary of the most important parts of it covers a dozen pages of the Government's brief. We content ourselves with mentioning only a few high spots of this evidence.

There was, for example, evidence that Harvey Grooms went into the illicit liquor business with Harry Chassereau upon the latter's assurance that the Charleston County Police Force had been "bought off" and would not interfere and, further, that if Grooms should be stopped by the police while hauling illicit liquor, Grooms was to tell the police that the liquor belonged to Harry Chassereau. A like assurance was made to Jordan Schofield who helped Grooms to haul this liquor.

Ample proof was offered of the cover-up activities of Sergeants Overstreet and Roth as to illicit liquor and of an extensive escort service for bootleggers operated by Overstreet and Police Officers Croft and Zerbst. Elaborate instructions seem to have been issued to members of the Charleston County Police Force by Lieutenant Welch and Sergeant Johns as to the proper method of handling bootleg cases, to the economic profit of policemen and the corresponding detriment of law enforcement. James Chassereau testified that in one instance, when a bribe was taken from a bootlegger named Moore, twenty-five dollars was to be paid to Chief of Police Williams; and James Chassereau further testified that Sergeant Johns and Officer Koster each took a case of the bootlegger's whiskey.

Sergeants Roth, Limehouse and McCormack took whiskey from a bootlegger in part payment for his release. Solomon Ford, a bootlegger, stated that he had paid money to Chief Williams, Sergeants Johns and Croft and Officer Zerbst. Levinia Washington paid a weekly stipend to Officer Pierson for protection, and when she stopped these payments, Chief Williams raided her establishment. Chief Williams seems to have sold whiskey to Solomon Ford, Sergeant Croft collecting the money.

Particularly damaging to these appellants was the testimony of James Chassereau, who for some time was a member of the Charleston County Police Force, as to the sinister operating relationship between Chief Williams, Sergeant Johns, Sergeant Roth and Officer Koster. The testimony of West and Ford indicated the close cooperation with this group on the part of Officers Croft and Pierson. Agent Connell's evidence indicated an extensive and well organized system of police escorts for bootleggers operating in Charleston County, upon adequate compensation to the police, in which Officers Overstreet, Dyches and Zerbst were involved. On one occasion, Overstreet complained that he was not being paid enough money by Harry Chassereau for the protection of Chassereau's bootleg runners.

Further evidence of the sordid activities of appellants, as individuals and in various combinations, was given by witnesses Burroughs, Investigator Gwynne, distillery operator Causey, Barker, Schofield and Jones. The record here disclosed a police department honeycombed with graft, under the leadership of Chief Williams. There was more than ample evidence to support the jury's finding that the appellants were engaged in a well organized conspiracy to violate the federal internal revenue laws as to illicit whiskey. . . .

Since, as we have held, there was sufficient evidence to take to the jury the question of a general conspiracy to violate the federal internal revenue laws, there was no reversible error committed in trying the appellants together instead of granting separate trials. . . .

INTERSTATE CIRCUIT v. UNITED STATES, 306 U.S. 208 (1939), Stone, J.: . . . This case is here on appeal . . . from a final decree of the District Court for northern Texas restraining appellants from continuing in a combination and conspiracy condemned by the court as a violation of Section 1 of the Sherman Anti-Trust Act . . . and from enforcing or renewing certain contracts found by the court to have been entered into in pursuance of the conspiracy. . . . The case is now before us on findings of the District Court specifically stating that appellants did in fact agree with each other to enter into and carry out the contracts, which the court found to result in unreasonable and therefore unlawful restraints of interstate commerce. . . .

[There were two groups of appellants — motion picture distributors and motion picture exhibitors. The former consisted of eight corporations which distributed about 75% of all first class films exhibited in the United States. The latter included mainly Interstate Circuit, Inc. and Texas Consolidated Theatres, which dominated the motion picture business in the cities where their theatres were located.]

On July 11, 1934, following a previous communication on the subject to the eight branch managers of the distributor appellants, O'Donnell, the manager of Interstate and Consolidated, sent to each of them a letter on the letterhead of Interstate, each letter naming all of them as addressees, in which he asked compliance with two demands as a condition of Interstate's continued exhibition of the distributors' films in its "A" or first-run theatres at a night admission of 40 cents or more. One demand was that the distributors "agree that in selling their product to subsequent runs, that this 'A' product will never be exhibited at any time or in any theatre at a smaller admission price than 25¢ for adults in the evening." The other was that "on 'A' pictures which are exhibited at a night admission of 40¢ or more — they shall never be exhibited in conjunction with another feature picture under the so-called policy of double features." . . .

The admission price customarily charged for preferred seats at night in independently operated subsequent-run theatres in Texas at the time of these letters was less than 25 cents. . . . It was also the general practice in those theatres to provide double bills either on certain days of the week or with any feature picture which was weak in drawing power. The distributor appellants had generally provided in their license contracts for a minimum admission price of 10 or 15 cents, and three of them had included provisions restricting double-billing. But none was at any time previously subject to contractual compulsion to continue the restrictions. The trial court found that the proposed restrictions constituted an important departure from prior practice.

[Subsequently each distributor agreed with Interstate for the 1934-1935 season to accept the proposed restrictions in some of the cities in which they operated. The trial court found, therefore, that the distributor appellants agreed and conspired among themselves to take uniform action upon the proposals made by Interstate, and that they agreed and conspired with each other and with Interstate to impose the demanded restrictions, all in violation of the Sherman Act.]

. . . As is usual in cases of alleged unlawful agreements to restrain commerce, the Government is without the aid of direct testimony that the distributors entered into any agreement with each other to impose the restrictions upon subsequent-run exhibitors. In order to establish agreement it is compelled to rely on inferences drawn from the course of conduct of the alleged conspirators.

The trial court drew the inference of agreement from the nature of the proposals made on behalf of Interstate and Consolidated; from the manner in which they were made; from the substantial unanimity of action taken upon them by the distributors; and from the fact that appellants did not call as witnesses any of the superior officials who negotiated the contracts with Interstate or any official who, in the normal course of business, would have had knowledge of the existence or non-existence of such an agreement among the distributors. This conclusion is challenged by appellants because not supported by subsidiary findings or by the evidence. We think this inference of the trial court was rightly drawn from the evidence. In the view we take of the legal effect of the cooperative action of the distributor appellants in carrying into effect the restrictions imposed upon subsequent-run theatres in the four Texas cities and of the legal effect of the separate agreements for the imposition of those restrictions entered into between Interstate and each of the distributors, it is unnecessary to discuss in great detail the evidence concerning this aspect of the case.

The O'Donnell letter named on its face as addressees the eight local representatives of the distributors, and so from the beginning each of the distributors knew that the proposals were under consideration by the others. Each was aware that all were in active competition and that without substantially unanimous action with respect to the restrictions for any given territory there was risk of a substantial loss of the business and good will of the subsequent-run and independent exhibitors, but that with it there was the prospect of increased profits. There was, therefore, strong motive for concerted action, full advantage of which was taken by Interstate and Consolidated in presenting their demands to all in a single document.

There was risk, too, that without agreement diversity of action would follow. Compliance with the proposals involved a radical departure from the previous business practices of the industry and a drastic increase in admission prices of most of the subsequent-run threatres. . . .

. . . Numerous variations in the form of the provisions in the distributors' license agreements and the fact that in later years two of them extended the restrictions into all six cities, do not weaken the significance or force of the nature of the response to the proposals made by all the distributor appellants. It taxes credulity to believe that the several distributors would, in the circumstances, have accepted and put into operation with substantial unanimity such far-reaching changes in their business methods without some understanding that all were to join, and we reject as beyond the range of probability that it was the result of mere chance. . . .

While the District Court's finding of an agreement of the distributors among themselves is supported by the evidence, we think that in the circumstances of this case such agreement for the imposition of the restrictions upon subsequent-run exhibitors was not a prerequisite to an unlawful conspiracy. It was enough that, knowing that concerted action was contemplated and invited, the distributors gave their adherence to the scheme and participated in it. Each distributor was advised that the others were asked to participate; each knew that cooperation was essential to successful operation of the plan. They knew that the plan, if carried out, would result in a restraint of commerce, which, we will presently point out, was unreasonable within the meaning of the Sherman Act, and knowing it, all participated in the plan. The evidence is persuasive that each distributor early became aware that the others had joined. With that knowledge they renewed the arrangement and carried it into effect for the two successive years.

It is elementary that an unlawful conspiracy may be and often is formed without simultaneous action or agreement on the part of the conspirators. . . .

We think the conclusion is unavoidable that the conspiracy and each contract between Interstate and the distributors by which those consequences were effected are violations of the Sherman Act and that the District Court rightly enjoined enforcement and renewal of these agreements, as well as of the conspiracy among the distributors. Affirmed.[a]

NOTES

1. In Rex v. Murphy, 173 Eng. Rep. 502, 508 (1837), Coleridge, J., directed the jury as follows:

> You have been properly told that this being a charge of conspiracy, if you are of opinion that the acts, though done, were done without common concert and design between these two parties, the present charge cannot be supported. On the other hand, I am bound to tell you, that although the common design is the root of the charge, it is not necessary to prove that these two parties came together and actually agreed in terms to have this common design, and to pursue it by common means, and so to carry it into excecution. This is not necessary, because in many cases of the most clearly-established conspiracies there are no means of proving any such thing, and neither law nor common sense requires that it should be proved. If you find that these two persons pursued by their acts the same object, often by the same means, one performing one part of an act and the other another part of the same act, so as to complete it, with a view to the attainment of the object which they were pursuing, you will be at liberty to draw the conclusion that they have been engaged in a conspiracy to effect that object. The question you have to ask yourselves is, "Had they this common design, and did they pursue it by these common means — the design being unlawful."

Commenting on this instruction, Professor Williams observed (Criminal Law: The General Part 667 (2d ed. 1961)):

> Properly read, this direction is a valuable statement of a principle of the law of evidence; but it is capable of dangerous misinterpretation. . . . A conspiracy is not merely a concurrence of wills but a concurrence resulting from agreement. Of course, if . . . two burglars actually executed their respective plans and were both caught in the house, they would be under a heavy suspicion of having acted in concert, and would be fortunate to convince a jury that they had not. . . . Nevertheless, if the jury are satisfied that the concurrence of the defendants' acts was accidental, the conspiracy charge must fail, for the concurrence of acts is only evidence of conspiracy, not equivalent to conspiracy. It is submitted that Coleridge, J., did not mean anything other than this; his direction meant only that agreement

a. See generally, Turner, The Defintion of Agreement Under the Sherman Act: Conscious Parallelism and Refusals to Deal, 75 Harv. L. Rev. 655 (1962); Rahl, Conspiracy and the Anti-Trust Laws, 44 Ill. L. Rev. 743 (1950). — EDS.

could be implied from acts in the absence of evidence that the concurrence was accidental.

See also Cousens, Agreement as an Element of Conspiracy, 23 Va. L. Rev. 898 (1937), describing the importation of the Coleridge instruction into the United States through Greenleaf (3 Evidence §93 (1st ed. 1853)) and its subsequent widespread acceptance by American courts. Its interpretation in the sense criticized by Professor Williams occurred originally in cases involving conspiracy charges arising out of labor disputes. Cousens, id. at 909-911, writes:

> Spontaneous non-concerted action and even continued association after such action by others, perhaps far distant, is under certain circumstances described as "agreement" on the part of labor organizations. . . . The tendency in these labor cases may almost be said to be toward converting the question from one of agreement to a plan to one of urging or desiring a result.

2. Note, Developments in the Law — Criminal Conspiracy, 72 Harv. L. Rev. 920, 933-935 (1959):

> The basic principle that a conspiracy is not established without proof of an agreement has been weakened, or at least obscured, by three factors. The first is the courts' unfortunate tendency to overemphasize a rule of evidence at the expense of a rule of law. Conspiracy is by nature a clandestine offense. It is improbable that the parties will enter into their illegal agreement openly; it is not necessary, in fact, that all the parties ever have direct contact with one another, or know one another's identity, or even communicate verbally their intention to agree. It is therefore unlikely that the prosecution will be able to prove the formation of the agreement by direct evidence, and the jury must usually infer its existence from the clear co-operation among the parties. But in their zeal to emphasize that the agreement need not be proved directly, the courts sometimes neglect to say that it need be proved at all. The second factor tending to undermine the strict rule that agreement must be proved is the existence of what are perhaps more liberal requirements in antitrust cases, which, although they may be justified in that area, are ever likely to be extended to the general law of conspiracy.
>
> The third, and perhaps the most important, factor is another result of the verbal ambiguity which leads courts to deal with the crime of conspiracy as though it were a group rather than an act. If a "conspiracy" consists of the people who are working towards a proscribed object, and if one who aids and abets a substantive offense becomes liable as a principal thereto, then it follows that one who aids and abets these men in the attainment of their object becomes liable as a conspirator. It is this reasoning from a faulty premise — a premise difficult to discover since it is assumed rather than articulated — which leads an appellate court to say: "The (lower) court clearly instructed the jury that, if defendant had knowledge that Jensen and Clark were in a conspiracy . . . and . . . assisted and aided Jensen and Clark by selling and delivering the materials to be used, thus making it possible to carry out the unlawful object of the conspiracy, defendant was a coconspirator. This is a correct statement of the law." But to aid and abet a crime it is necessary not merely to help the criminal, but to help him in the commission of the particular criminal offense. A person does not aid and abet a conspiracy by helping the "conspiracy" to commit a substantive offense, for the crime of conspiracy is separate from the offense which is its object. It is necessary to help the "conspiracy" in the commission of the crime of conspiracy, that is in the commission of the act

of agreement. Only then is it justifiable to dispense with the necessity of proving commission of the act of agreement by the defendant himself. In all other cases, to convict the defendant of conspiracy it is necessary to prove not only knowledge on his part that he was helping a wrongful enterprise, but also knowledge on another's part that he intended to do so, and at least a tacit agreement to give and accept such help.

3. Model Penal Code §5.03, Comment at 117 (Tent. Draft No. 10, 1960) states:

> We think it clear that neither combination as distinguished from agreement nor the analogy of partnership should be included in the formal definition [of conspiracy]. If a consensus is demanded, it is clearly indicated by demanding an "agreement," which need not, of course, be formal or, indeed, explicit in the sense that it is put in words. The only other question, and we deem it one of substance, is whether aid without consensus should suffice for a conspiracy between the aider and the beneficiary of his aid. A testing case upon the issue is State v. Tally [102 Ala. 25, 15 So. 722 (1894)] where the defendant sought to aid two murderers to kill their victim by stopping the delivery of a telegram of warning, but acted without knowledge or preconcert on their part.
>
> The major argument for treating aid as a basis of conspiratorial liability is that such conduct should be criminal, whether or not it is accompanied by a consensus and whether or not the ultimate offense is consummated so that liability as an accomplice can be found. Moreover, if aid were made an independent ground for conviction of conspiracy, the impetus to derive a fictional consensus to support the liability would be diminished. In many far-flung syndicates of crime, with countless persons playing relatively minor roles, purposeful aid would be a realistic description of their parts; agreement frequently is not.
>
> For the reasons stated, the Draft put before the Council treated aid with purpose as sufficient for conviction of conspiracy, without reference to finding an agreement. The Council, after full consideration, voted 12 to 10 against this feature of the formulation the majority considering that aid of this kind is made criminal as an attempt by Section 5.01(3) and that this is the proper view of liability for such conduct. To treat it as conspiracy, either alternatively or cumulatively, draws the aider into the vicarious features of the conspiratorial relationship, a consequence which it was thought should only follow from a true consensus.

b. Scope of the Agreement — Single or Multiple Conspiracies

MODEL PENAL CODE §5.03, Comment at 117-118 (Tent. Draft No. 10, 1960): Much of the most perplexing litigation in conspiracy has been concerned less with the essential elements of the offense than with the scope to be accorded to a combination, i.e., the singleness or multiplicity of the conspiratorial relationships typical in a large, complex and sprawling network of crime. The question differs from that discussed . . . [in the immediately preceding subsection of this casebook] in that in most of these cases it is clear that each defendant has committed or conspired to commit one or more crimes; the question now is, to what extent is he a conspirator with each of the persons involved in the larger criminal network to commit the crimes that are its objects — i.e., what is the scope of the conspiracy in which he is involved.

A narcotics operation may involve smugglers, distributors and many retail sellers and result in numerous instances of the commission of different types of crimes, e.g., importing, possessing and selling the narcotics. A vice ring may involve an overlord, lesser officers, and numerous runners and prostitutes; it may comprehend countless instances of the commission of such crimes as prostitution, placing a female in a house of prostitution, and receiving money from her earnings. Has a retailer conspired with the smugglers to import the narcotics? Has a prostitute conspired with the leaders of the vice ring to commit the acts of prostitution of each other girl who is controlled by that ring?

The inquiry may be crucial for a number of purposes. These include not only defining each defendant's liability but also the propriety of joint prosecution, admissibility against a defendant of the hearsay acts and declarations of others, questions of multiple prosecution or conviction and double jeopardy, satisfaction of the overt act requirement or statutes of limitation or rules of jurisdiction and venue, and possibly also liability for substantive crimes executed pursuant to the conspiracy. The scope problem is thus central to the present concern of courts and commentators about the use of conspiracy — the conflict between the need for effective means of prosecuting large criminal organizations, and the dangers of prejudice to individual defendants.

NOTE

While the cases that follow are distinguishable from those in the foregoing subsection (for the reasons stated in the foregoing extract from the Model Penal Code), it will be apparent that the cases following also involve the definition and application of the concept of agreement in the law of conspiracy. For whether the issue is, "Did *A* agree with *B*, thereby establishing a conspiracy between them?" or "Are the conspiracies between *A* and *B* and between *C* and *D* two separate conspiracies or one single conspiracy?," a central issue in each case is the meaning of the requirement of an agreement in the law of conspiracy.

KOTTEAKOS v. UNITED STATES
Supreme Court of the United States
328 U.S. 750 (1946)

MR. JUSTICE RUTLEDGE delivered the opinion of the Court.

The only question is whether petitioners have suffered substantial prejudice from being convicted of a single general conspiracy by evidence which the Government admits proved not one conspiracy but some eight or more different ones of the same sort executed through a common key figure, Simon Brown. Petitioners were convicted under the general conspiracy section of the Criminal Code, 18 U.S.C.A. §88 [now §371], of conspiring to violate the provisions of the National Housing Act. The judgments were affirmed by the Circuit Court of Appeals. 151 F.2d 170. We granted certiorari because of the importance of the question for the administration of criminal justice in the federal courts.

The indictment named thirty-two defendants, including the petitioners. The gist of the conspiracy, as alleged, was that the defendants had sought to induce various financial institutions to grant credit, with the intent that the loans for advances would then be offered to the Federal Housing Administration for insurance upon applications containing false and fraudulent information.

Of the thirty-two persons named in the indictment nineteen were brought to trial and the names of thirteen were submitted to the jury. Two were acquitted; the jury disagreed as to four; and the remaining seven, including petitioners, were found guilty.

The government's evidence may be summarized briefly, for the petitioners have not contended that it was insufficient, if considered apart from the alleged errors relating to the proof and the instructions at the trial.

Simon Brown, who pleaded guilty, was the common and key figure in all of the transactions proven. He was president of the Brownie Lumber Company. Having had experience in obtaining loans under the National Housing Act, he undertook to act as broker in placing for others loans for modernization and renovation, charging a five per cent commission for his services. Brown knew, when he obtained the loans, that the proceeds were not to be used for the purposes stated in the applications. [The Court then summarized the evidence against several defendants.]

The evidence against the other defendants whose cases were submitted to the jury was similar in character. They too had transacted business with Brown relating to National Housing Act loans. But no connection was shown between them and petitioners, other than that Brown had been the instrument in each instance for obtaining the loans. In many cases the other defendants did not have any relationship with one another, other than Brown's connection with each transaction. As the Circuit Court of Appeals said, there were "at least eight, and perhaps more, separate and independent groups, none of which had any connection with any other, though all dealt independently with Brown as their agent." 151 F.2d at 172. As the Government puts it, the pattern was "that of separate spokes meeting at a common center," though we may add without the rim of the wheel to enclose the spokes.

The proof therefore admittedly made out a case, not of a single conspiracy, but of several, notwithstanding only one was charged in the indictment. The Court of Appeals aptly drew analogy in the comment, "Thieves who dispose of their loot to a single receiver — a single 'fence' — do not by that fact alone become confederates; they may, but it takes more than knowledge that he is a 'fence' to make them such." 151 F.2d at 173. It stated that the trial judge "was plainly wrong in supposing that upon the evidence there could be a single conspiracy; and in the view which he took of the law, he should have dismissed the indictment." 151 F.2d at 172.[a] Nevertheless the appellate court held the

a. Judge Learned Hand wrote the opinion for the court of appeals. The sentences quoted are part of the following paragraph in which he stated, in reference to the view of the trial judge: "He was apparently misled by an erroneous understanding of the rule that, when anyone joins an existing conspiracy, he takes it over as it is, and becomes a party to it in its earlier phases, and that the declarations of other conspirators, even though made before he has entered, are competent against him. What he failed to remember was that to bring this rule into operation it is not enough that, when one joins with another in a criminal venture, he knows that his confederate is engaged in other criminal undertakings with other persons, even though they may be of the same general nature. The acts and declarations of confederates, past or future, are never competent against a party except in so far as they are steps in furtherance of a purpose common to him and them. Declarations are no different from other acts; they become competent only when they are uttered in order to accomplish the common purpose. In the case at bar, we assume that Lekacos and

error not prejudicial, saying among other things that "especially since guilt was so manifest, it was 'proper' to join the conspiracies," and "to reverse the conviction would be a miscarriage of justice." This is indeed the Government's entire position. . . .

. . . [T]he trial court itself was confused in the charge which it gave to guide the jury in deliberation. The court instructed:

> The indictment charges but one conspiracy, and to convict each of the defendants of a conspiracy the Government would have to prove, and you would have to find, that each of the defendants was a member of that conspiracy. You cannot divide it up. It is one conspiracy, and the question is whether or not each of the defendants or which of the defendants, are members of that conspiracy.

On its face, as the Court of Appeals said, this portion of the charge was plainly wrong in application to the proof made; and the error pervaded the entire charge, not merely the portion quoted. The jury could not possibly have found, upon the evidence, that there was only one conspiracy. The trial court was of the view that one conspiracy was made out by showing that each defendant was linked to Brown in one or more transactions, and that it was possible on the evidence for the jury to conclude that all were in a common adventure because of this fact and the similarity of purpose presented in the various applications for loans.

The view, specifically embodied throughout the instructions, obviously confuses the common purpose of a single enterprise with the several, though similar purposes of numerous separate adventures of like character. It may be that, notwithstanding the misdirection, the jury actually understood correctly the purport of the evidence, as the Government now concedes it to have been; and came to the conclusion that the petitioners were guilty only of the separate conspiracies in which the proof shows they respectively participated. But, in the fact of the misdirection and in the circumstances of this case, we cannot assume that the lay triers of fact were so well informed upon the law or that they disregarded the permission expressly given to ignore that vital difference.

As we have said, the error permeated the entire charge, indeed the entire trial. Not only did it permit the jury to find each defendant guilty of conspiring with thirty-five other potential co-conspirators, or any less number as the proof might turn out for acquittal of some, when none of the evidence would support such a conviction, as the proof did turn out in fact. It had other effects. One was to prevent the court from giving a precautionary instruction such as would be appropriate, perhaps required, in cases where related but separate conspiracies are tried together under §557 of the Code, namely, that the jury should

---

Kotteakos and Regenbogen knew that Brown was for the time being acting as a broker for a number of other persons, who were getting loans in fraud of the Act, and who were making false representations to the bank like those which they themselves were making. But that was not enough to make them confederates with the other applicants; it did not give them any interest in the success of any loans but their own; there was no interest, no venture, common to them and anyone else but Brown himself. Thieves who dispose of their loot to a single receiver — a single 'fence' — do not by that fact alone become confederates: they may, but it takes more than knowledge that he is a 'fence' to make them such. United States v. Falcone, 311 U.S. 205; United States v. Peoni, 2 Cir., 10 F.2d 401." — Eds.

take care to consider the evidence relating to each conspiracy separately from that relating to each other conspiracy charged. . . .

Moreover, the effect of the court's misconception extended also to the proof of overt acts. Carrying forward his premise that the jury could find one conspiracy on the evidence, the trial judge further charged that, if the jury found a conspiracy,

> then the acts or the statements of *any* of those whom you so find to be conspirators between the two dates that I have mentioned, may be considered by you in evidence as against *all* of the defendants whom you so find to be members of *the* conspiracy.

(Emphasis added.) The instructions in this phase also declared:

> It is not necessary, as a matter of law, that an overt act be charged against each defendant. It is sufficient if the conspiracy be established and the defendant be found to be a member of the conspiracy — it is sufficient to allege overt acts on the part of any others who may have been members of the conspiracy, if those acts were done in furtherance of, and for the purpose of accomplishing the conspiracy.

On those instructions it was competent not only for the jury to find that all of the defendants were parties to a single common plan, design and scheme, where none was shown by the proof, but also for them to impute to each defendant the acts and statements of the others without reference to whether they related to one of the schemes proven or another, and to find an overt act affecting all in conduct which admittedly could only have affected some. . . .

Here toleration went too far. . . .

Reversed.

BLUMENTHAL v. UNITED STATES, 332 U.S. 539, 557-559 (1947): [Defendants Weiss and Goldsmith were, respectively, owner and sales manager of the Francisco Distributing Company, a licensed wholesale liquor dealing agency; defendants Feigenbaum and Blumenthal were local businesspeople with no connection with the company except as hereafter stated. Francisco received shipment of two carloads of whiskey from an unidentified person or persons and, through Weiss and Goldsmith, arranged with Feigenbaum and Blumenthal for the latter two to handle sales and deliveries of portions of the shipment to various taverns. The sales were made at prices above the maximum prices prescribed by law to the knowledge of all defendants. The identity of the owner was unknown to Feigenbaum and Blumenthal; however, each knew of the fact that Weiss and Goldsmith were not the real owners but were acting for an unidentified person in handling the shipments in Francisco's name to give the transaction the guise of legality. Defendants were charged and convicted of a single conspiracy in a single count holding they had conspired together and with the unidentified owner to sell the shipment of whiskey at prices over the ceiling set by regulations of the Office of Price Administration in violation of the Emergency Price Control Act. On appeal it was contended that there was not one but two conspiracies — one between the unidentified owner and Weiss and Goldsmith; the other between Weiss and Goldsmith, on the one hand, and Feigenbaum and Blumenthal, on the other. The Supreme Court affirmed, holding the finding of one large conspiracy proper, stating:] We think that in the special circumstances of this case the two agreements were merely steps in the formation of the larger and ultimately more general conspiracy. In that view it would be perversion of justice to regard the salesmen's ignorance of the unknown owner's participation as furnishing adequate ground for reversal of their convictions. Nor does anything in the *Kotteakos* decision require this. The scheme was in fact the same scheme; the salesmen knew or must have known that others unknown to them were sharing in so large a project; and it hardly can be sufficient to relieve them that they did not know, when they joined the scheme, who those people were or exactly the parts they were playing in carrying out the common design and object of all. By their separate agreements, if such they were, they became parties to the larger common plan, joined together by their knowledge of its essential features and broad scope, though not of its exact limits, and by their common single goal.

The case therefore is very different from the facts admitted to exist in the *Kotteakos* case. Apart from the much larger number of agreements there involved, no two of those agreements were tied together as stages in the formation of a larger all-inclusive combination, all directed to achieving a single unlawful end or result. On the contrary each separate agreement had its own distinct, illegal end. Each loan was an end in itself, separate from all others, although all were alike in having similar illegal objects. Except for Brown, the common figure, no conspirator was interested in whether any loan except his own went through. And none aided in any way, by agreement or otherwise, in procuring another's loan. The conspiracies therefore were distinct and disconnected, not parts of a larger general scheme, both in the phase of agreement with Brown and also in the absence of any aid given to others as well as in specific object and result. There was no drawing of all together in a single, over-all, comprehensive plan.

Here the contrary is true. All knew of and joined in the overriding scheme. All intended to aid the owner, whether Francisco or another, to sell the whiskey unlawfully, though the two groups of defendants differed on the proof in knowledge and belief concerning the owner's identity. All by reason of their knowledge of the plan's general scope, if not its exact limits, sought a common end, to aid in disposing of the whiskey. True, each salesman aided in selling only his part. But he knew the lot to be sold was larger and thus that he was aiding in a larger plan. He thus became a party to it and not merely to the integrating agreement with Weiss and Goldsmith.

We think therefore that in every practical sense the unique facts of this case reveal a single conspiracy of which the several agreements were essential and integral steps, and accordingly that the judgments should be affirmed.

ANDERSON v. SUPERIOR COURT, 78 Cal. App. 2d 22, 24-25, 177 P.2d 315, 317 (1947): [Petitioner sought a writ of prohibition to prevent her prosecution under an indictment returned by the grand jury. Evidence before the grand jury revealed that one Stern was engaged in the commission of abortions as a regular business. He had made arrangements with many persons for them to refer to him women desiring abortions. Such persons were paid a fee for this service. Petitioner was one of these people. She had referred several women to Stern. She was indicted for conspiring to commit abortions, the conspiracy embracing not only Stern and herself but the greater enterprise among Stern and the others who referred women to him. She was also indicted for the substantive offenses of several abortions performed on women she had referred to Stern and abortions committed by Stern upon women who had been referred by others. Denying the writ, the court stated:] The inference is almost compelled, if the evidence is believed, that this petitioner knew that Stern was engaged in the commission of abortions not casually but as a regular business and that others, like herself, had conspired with him to further his operations. If the grand jury concluded that, with this knowledge, she saw fit to join with him and those others, even though unknown to her, in furthering the unlawful activities of the group we cannot say that the grand jury did not have substantial evidence upon which to find the indictment.

If she did join the conspiracy she is responsible for the substantive offenses later committed as a part of the conspiracy.

UNITED STATES v. BRUNO

United States Court of Appeals, 2d Circuit
105 F.2d 921, rev'd on other grounds, 308 U.S. 287 (1939)

PER CURIAM. Bruno and Iacono were indicted along with 86 others for a conspiracy to import, sell and possess narcotics; some were acquitted; others, besides these two, were convicted, but they alone appealed, They complain, (1), that if the evidence proved anything, it proved a series of separate conspiracies, and not a single one, as alleged in the indictment; (2) that unlawful telephone "taps" were allowed in evidence against them; (3) that the judge refused to charge the jury properly as to the effect of their failure to take the stand; and (4) that there was not enough evidence to support the verdict.

The first point was made at the conclusion of the prosecution's case: the defendants then moved to dismiss the indictment on the ground that several conspiracies had been proved, and not the one alleged. The evidence allowed the jury to find that there had existed over a substantial period of time a conspiracy embracing a great number of persons, whose object was to smuggle narcotics into the Port of New York and distribute them to addicts both in this city and in Texas and Louisiana. This required the cooperation of four groups of persons: the smugglers who imported the drugs; the middlemen who paid the smugglers and distributed to retailers; and two groups of retailers — one in New York and one in Texas and Louisiana — who supplied the addicts. The defendants assert that there were, therefore, at least three separate conspiracies: one between the smugglers and the middlemen, and one between the middlemen and each group of retailers. The evidence did not disclose any cooperation or communication between the smugglers and either group of retailers, or between the two groups of retailers themselves; however, the smugglers knew that the middlemen must sell to retailers, and the retailers knew that the middlemen must buy of importers of one sort or another. Thus the conspirators at one end of the chain knew that the unlawful business would not, and could not, stop with their buyers; and those at the other end knew that it had not begun with their sellers. That being true, a jury might have found that all the accused were embarked upon a venture, in all parts of which each was a participant, and an abettor in the sense that the success of that part with which he was immediately concerned, was dependent upon the success of the whole. That distinguishes the situation from that in United States v. Peoni, 2 Cir., 100 F.2d 401, where Peoni, the accused, did not know that Regno, his buyer, was to sell the counterfeit bills to Dorsey, and had no interest in whether he did, since Regno might equally well have passed them to innocent persons himself. It might still be argued that there were two conspiracies; one including the smugglers, the middlemen and the New York group, and the other, the smugglers, the middlemen and the Texas & Louisiana group, for there was apparently no privity between the two groups of retailers. That too would be fallacious. Clearly, quoad the smugglers, there was but one conspiracy, for it was of no moment to them whether the middlemen sold to one or more groups of retailers, provided they had a market somewhere. So too of any retailer; he knew that he was a necessary link in a scheme of distribution, and the others, whom he knew to be convenient to its execution, were as much parts of a single undertaking or enterprise as two salesmen in the same shop. We think therefore that there was only one conspiracy.

UNITED STATES v. BORELLI, 336 F.2d 376 (2d Cir. 1964): [In this case, dealing with an elaborate heroin importing and distributing operation extending over a long period of time and involving numerous participants, Judge Friendly wrote:] As applied to the long term operation of an illegal business, the common pictorial distinction between "chain" and "spoke" conspiracies can obscure as much as it clarifies. The chain metaphor is indeed apt in that the links of a narcotics conspiracy are inextricably related to one another, from grower, through exporter and importer, to wholesaler, middleman, and retailer, each depending for his own success on the performance of all the others. But this simple picture tends to obscure that the links at either end are likely to consist of a number of persons who may have no reason to know that others are performing a role similar to theirs — in other words the extreme links of a chain conspiracy may have elements of the spoke conspiracy.[2] Moreover, whatever the value of the chain concept where the problem is to trace a single operation from the start through its various phases to its successful conclusion, it becomes confusing when, over a long period of time, certain links continue to play the same role but with new counterparts, as where importers who regard their partnership as a single continuing one, having successfully distributed one cargo through *X* distributing organization, turn, years later, to moving another cargo obtained from a different source through *Y*. . . .

The basic difficulty arises in applying the seventeenth century notion of conspiracy, where the gravamen of the offense was the making of an *agreement* to commit a readily identifiable crime or series of crimes, such as murder or robbery, to what in substance is the conduct of an illegal business over a period of years. . . . Although it is usual and often necessary in conspiracy cases for

---

2. Thus, in the oft-cited *Bruno* case, although it is clear enough that "quoad the smugglers, there was but one conspiracy, for it was of no moment to them whether the middlemen sold to one or more groups of retailers, provided they had a market somewhere," 105 F.2d at 923, it is not so clear why the New York and Texas groups of retailers were not in a "spoke" relation with the smugglers and the middleman, so that there would be two conspiracies unless the evidence permitted the inference that each group of retailers must have known the operation to be so large as to require the other as an outlet.

the agreement to be proved by inference from acts, the gist of the offense remains the agreement, and it is therefore essential to determine what kind of agreement or understanding existed as to each defendant. It is a great deal harder to tell just *what* agreement can reasonably be inferred from the purchase, even the repeated purchase, of contraband, than from the furnishing of dynamite to prospective bank robbers or the exchange of worthless property for securities to be subsequently distributed. Purchase or sale of contraband may, of course, warrant the inference of an agreement going well beyond the particular transaction. A seller of narcotics in bulk surely knows that the purchasers will undertake to resell the goods over an uncertain period of time, and the circumstances may also warrant the inference that a supplier or a purchaser indicated a willingness to repeat. But a sale or a purchase scarcely constitutes a sufficient basis for inferring agreement to cooperate with the opposite parties for whatever period they continue to deal in this type of contraband, unless some such understanding is evidenced by other conduct which accompanies or supplements the transaction.

The view that if the evidence warrants the finding that some defendants were parties to a single agreement to sell contraband for a nine-year period, it necessarily does so as to every defendant who has conspired with them at any time for any purpose, is thus a considerable over-simplification.

BRAVERMAN v. UNITED STATES
Supreme Court of the United States
317 U.S. 49 (1942)

Mr. Chief Justice Stone delivered the opinion of the Court.

The [question] for decision [is]: Whether a conviction upon the several counts of an indictment, each charging conspiracy to violate a different provision of the Internal Revenue laws, where the jury's verdict is supported by evidence of but a single conspiracy, will sustain a sentence of more than two years' imprisonment, the maximum penalty for a single violation of the conspiracy statute. . . .

Petitioners were indicted, with others, on seven counts, each charging a conspiracy to violate a separate and distinct internal revenue law of the United States.[1] On the trial there was evidence from which the jury could have found that, for a considerable period of time, petitioners, with others, collaborated in the illicit manufacture, transportation, and distribution of distilled spirits, involving the violations of statute mentioned in the several counts of the indictment. At the close of the trial, petitioners renewed a motion which they had

---

1. The seven counts respectively charged them with conspiracy, in violation of §37 of the Criminal Code, unlawfully (1) to carry on the business of wholesale and retail liquor dealers without having the special occupational tax stamps required by statute, 26 U.S.C. §3253; (2) to possess distilled spirits, the immediate containers of which did not have stamps affixed denoting the quantity of the distilled spirits which they contained and evidencing payment of all Internal Revenue taxes imposed on such spirits, 26 U.S.C. §2803; (3) to transport quantities of distilled spirits, the immediate containers of which did not have affixed the required stamps, 26 U.S.C. §2803; (4) to carry on the business of distillers without having given bond as required by law, 26 U.S.C. §2833; (5) to remove, deposit and conceal distilled spirits in respect whereof a tax is imposed by law, with intent to defraud the United States of such tax, 26 U.S.C. §3321; (6) to possess unregistered stills and distilling apparatus, 26 U.S.C. §2810; and (7) to make and ferment mash, fit for distillation, on unauthorized premises, 26 U.S.C. §2834.

made at its beginning to require the Government to elect one of the seven counts of the indictment upon which to proceed, contending that the proof could not and did not establish more than one agreement. In response the Government's attorney took the position that the seven counts of the indictment charged as distinct offenses the several illegal objects of one continuing conspiracy, that if the jury found such a conspiracy it might find the defendants guilty of as many offenses as it had illegal objects and that for each such offense the two-year statutory penalty could be imposed.

The trial judge submitted the case to the jury on that theory. The jury returned a general verdict finding petitioners "guilty as charged," and the court sentenced each to eight years' imprisonment. On appeal the Court of Appeals for the Sixth Circuit affirmed. . . . The Government, in its argument here, submitted the case for our decision with the suggestion that the decision below is erroneous.

Both courts below recognized that a single agreement to commit an offense does not become several conspiracies because it continues over a period of time, see United States v. Kissel, 218 U.S. 601, 607; cf. In re Snow, 120 U.S. 274, 281-3, and that there may be such a single continuing agreement to commit several offenses. But they thought that, in the latter case, each contemplated offense renders the agreement punishable as a separate conspiracy. . . .

The gist of the crime of conspiracy as defined by the statute is the agreement or confederation of the conspirators to commit one or more unlawful acts "where one or more of such parties do any act to effect the object of the conspiracy."

. . . [W]hen a single agreement to commit one or more substantive crimes is evidenced by an overt act, as the statute requires, the precise nature and extent of the conspiracy must be determined by reference to the agreement which embraces and defines its objects. Whether the object of a single agreement is to commit one or many crimes, it is in either case that agreement which constitutes the conspiracy which the statute punishes. The one agreement cannot be taken to be several agreements and hence several conspiracies because it envisages the violation of several statutes rather than one.

The allegation in a single count of a conspiracy to commit several crimes is not duplicitous, for "The conspiracy is the crime, and that is one, however diverse its objects." Frohwerk v. United States, 249 U.S. 204, 210. A conspiracy is not the commission of the crime which it contemplates, and neither violates nor "arises under" the statute whose violation is its object. Since the single continuing agreement, which is the conspiracy here, thus embraces its criminal objects, it differs from successive acts which violate a single penal statute and from a single act which violates two statutes. See Blockburger v. United States, 284 U.S. 299, 301-4; Albrecht v. United States, 273 U.S. 1, 11-12. The single agreement is the prohibited conspiracy, and however diverse its objects it violates but a single statute, §37 of the Criminal Code. For such a violation, only the single penalty prescribed by the statute can be imposed. . . . Reversed.

NOTE

See Model Penal Code §5.03, Comment at 128 (Tent. Draft No. 10, 1960):

This rule [of the *Braverman* decision] may seem somewhat at odds with a view of conspiracy as strictly an inchoate crime; for it might be expected that criminal preparation to commit a number of substantive crimes would be treated as a number of inchoate crimes, as would be the case if the preparation amounted to attempt. Further, it is arguable that, insofar as this rule avoids a serious cumulation of penalties problem under federal law and in other jurisdictions, there is less need for it in a penal code which treats cumulation problems directly in the sentencing provisions. See §7.06. It is submitted, however, that the rule is desirable not only as a logical consequence of the definition of conspiracy in terms of an agreement — upon which the *Braverman* decision relies primarily — but also because of the extremely inchoate form of preparation that may be involved in conspiracy. A rule treating the agreement as several crimes, equivalent in number and grade to the substantive crimes contemplated, might be unduly harsh in cases — uncommon though they may be — where the conspirators are apprehended in the very early stages of preparation.

The significance of the *Braverman* rule of course extends beyond the question of cumulation of penalties. By holding that a single conspiracy may embrace a multiplicity of criminal objectives the rule affects the determination of the conspiracy's scope for all purposes. Consequently, it operates to the defendant's disadvantage insofar as these purposes involve a conspirator's accountability for all the activities of all the persons embraced in the conspiracy — e.g., with respect to his liability under present law for substantive crimes, the admissibility against him of hearsay acts and declarations, and satisfaction of the overt act requirements or statutes of limitation or rules of venue and jurisdiction.

PROBLEM

The provisions of the Model Penal Code relevant to the problems presented by the foregoing cases (§5.03) are set forth in the Appendix to this casebook.

The Comment to these proposals states ((Tent. Draft No. 10, 1960) at 119-120):

> The Draft relies upon the combined operation of Subsections (1), (2) and (3) to delineate the identity and scope of a conspiracy. All three provisions focus upon the culpability of the individual actor. Subsections (1) and (2) limit the scope of his conspiracy (a) in terms of its criminal objects, to those crimes which he had the purpose of promoting or facilitating and (b) in terms of parties, to those with whom he agreed, except where the same crime that he conspired to commit is, to his knowledge, also the object of a conspiracy between one of his co-conspirators and another person or persons. Subsection (3) provides that his conspiracy is a single one despite a multiplicity of criminal objectives so long as such crimes are the object of the same agreement or continuous conspiratorial relationship.

Consider how the *Kotteakos, Blumenthal, Anderson,* and *Bruno* cases would be decided under this formulation. For a discussion see Model Penal Code §5.03, Comment at 120-126 (Tent. Draft No. 10, 1960). The *Bruno* case is discussed, in part, as follows:

> The Draft would require a different approach to a case such as *Bruno* and might produce different results.
>
> Since the overall operation involved separate crimes of importing by the smugglers and possession and sale by each group — smugglers, distributors and retailers — the question as to each defendant would be whether and with whom he conspired to commit each of these crimes, under the criteria set forth in Subsections

(1) and (2). The conspiratorial objective for the purpose of this inquiry could not be characterized in the manner of the *Bruno* court, as "to smuggle narcotics into the Port of New York and distribute them to addicts both in [New York] and in Texas and Louisiana." This is indeed the overall objective of the entire operation. It might also be true of some of the participants that they conspired to commit all of the crimes involved in the operation: under Subsection (3) of the Draft as under prevailing law they would be guilty of only one conspiracy if all these crimes were the object of the same agreement or continuing conspiratorial relationship . . . and the objective of that conspiracy or relationship could fairly be phrased in terms of the overall operation. But this multiplicity of criminal objectives affords a poor referent for testing the culpability of each individual who is in any manner involved in the operation.

With the conspiratorial objectives characterized as the particular crimes and the culpability of each participant tested separately, it would be possible to find in a case such as *Bruno* — considering for the moment only each separate chain of distribution — that the smugglers conspired to commit the illegal sales of the retailers but that the retailers did not conspire to commit the importing of the smugglers. Factual situations warranting such a finding may easily be conceived: the smugglers might depend upon and seek to foster their retail markets while the retailers might have many suppliers and be indifferent to the success of any single source. The court's approach in *Bruno* does not admit of such a finding, for in treating the conspiratorial objective as the entire series of crimes involved in smuggling, distributing and retailing it requires either a finding of no conspiracy or a single conspiracy in which all three links in the chain conspired to commit all of each other's crimes.

It would also be possible to find, with the inquiry focused upon each individual's culpability as to each criminal objective, that some of the parties in a chain conspired to commit the entire series of crimes while others conspired only to commit some of these crimes. Thus the smugglers and the middlemen in *Bruno* may have conspired to commit, promote or facilitate the importing and the possession and sales of all of the parties down to the final retail sale; the retailers might have conspired with them as to their own possession and sales but might be indifferent to all the steps prior to their receipt of the narcotics. In this situation, a smuggler or a middleman might have conspired with all three groups to commit the entire series of crimes, while a retailer might have conspired with the same parties but to commit fewer criminal objectives. Such results are conceptually difficult to reach under existing doctrine not only because of the frequent failure to focus separately upon the different criminal objectives, but because of the traditional view of the agreement as a bilateral relationship between each of the parties, congruent in scope both as to its party and its objective dimensions.

For a fuller explication of the Model Penal Code's approach to these problems, see Wechsler, Jones & Korn, The Treatment of Inchoate Crimes in the Model Penal Code of the American Law Institute: Attempt, Solicitation and Conspiracy, 61 Colum. L. Rev. 957, 983-985 (1968).

UNITED STATES v. ELLIOTT

United States Court of Appeals, 5th Circuit
571 F.2d 880 (1978)

SIMPSON, J. In this case we deal with the question of whether and, if so, how a free society can protect itself when groups of people, through division of labor, specialization, diversification, complexity of organization, and the accumulation of capital, turn crime into an ongoing business. Congress fired a telling shot at organized crime when it passed the Racketeer Influenced and Corrupt Organizations Act of 1970, popularly known as RICO. 18 U.S.C. §§1961 et seq. (1970). Since the enactment of RICO, the federal courts, guided by constitutional and legislative dictates, have been responsible for perfecting the weapons in society's arsenal against criminal confederacies.

Today we review the convictions of six persons accused of conspiring to violate the RICO statute, two of whom were also accused and convicted of substantive RICO violations. The government admits that in this prosecution it has attempted to achieve a broader application of RICO than has heretofore been sanctioned. Predictably, the government and the defendants differ as to what this case is about. According to the defendants, what we are dealing with is a leg, a tail, a trunk, an ear — separate entities unaffected by RICO proscriptions. The government, on the other hand, asserts that we have come eyeball to eyeball with a single creature of behemoth proportions, securely within RICO's grasp. After a careful, if laborious study of the facts and the law, we accept, with minor exceptions, the government's view. . . .

[All six defendants were indicted and convicted of conspiracy to violate a substantive provision of the RICO statute, 18 U.S.C. §1962(c),[a] in violation of 18 U.S.C. §1962(d).[b] The essence of the conspiracy charge was that the defendants agreed to participate, directly and indirectly, in the conduct of the affairs of an enterprise whose purposes were to commit thefts, fence stolen property, illegally traffic in narcotics, obstruct justice, and engage in other criminal activi-

---

a. "(c) It shall be unlawful for any person employed by or associated with any enterprise engaged in, or the activities of which affect, interstate or foreign commerce, to conduct or participate, directly or indirectly, in the conduct of such enterprise's affairs through a pattern of racketeering activity or collection of unlawful debt."

The crucial terms are defined in 18 U.S.C. §1961:

"(1) 'racketeering activity' means (A) any act or threat involving murder, kidnapping, gambling, arson, robbery, bribery, extortion, or dealing in narcotic or other dangerous drugs, which is chargeable under State law and punishable by imprisonment for more than one year; (B) any act which is indictable under any of the following provisions of title 18, United States Code: [References are to sections relating to bribery, counterfeiting, theft from interstate shipment, embezzlement from pension and welfare funds, extortionate credit transactions, the transmission of gambling information, mail fraud, wire fraud, obstruction of justice, obstruction of criminal investigations, obstruction of State or local law enforcement, interference with commerce, robbery, or extortion, racketeering, interstate transportation of wagering paraphernalia, unlawful welfare fund payments, prohibition of illegal gambling businesses, interstate transportation of stolen property, white slave traffic.] (C) any act which is indictable under title 29, United States Code, section 186 (dealing with restrictions on payments and loans to labor organizations) or section 501(c) (relating to embezzlement from union funds), or (D) any offense involving bankruptcy fraud, fraud in the sale of securities, or the felonious manufacture, importation, receiving, concealment, buying, selling, or otherwise dealing in narcotic or other dangerous drugs, punishable under any law of the United States. . . .

"(4) 'enterprise' includes any individual, partnership, corporation, association, or other legal entity, and any union or group of individuals associated in fact although not a legal entity.

"(5) 'pattern of racketeering activity' requires at least two acts of racketeering activity, one of which occurred after the effective date of this chapter [Oct. 15, 1970] and the last of which occurred within ten years (excluding any period of imprisonment) after the commission of a prior act of racketeering activity."— EDS.

b. "(d) It shall be unlawful for any person to conspire to violate any of the provisions of subsections (a), (b), or (c) of this section." This is a special conspiracy provision for RICO offenses whose maximum penalty is more severe than that of the general conspiracy statute, 18 U.S.C. §371. — EDS.

ties. Thirty-seven unindicted co-conspirators were named, and 25 overt acts were listed. The acts took place between 1970 and 1976.

[The Court of Appeals described the facts as falling into ten specific episodes. Each defendant was involved in one or several of these episodes, but never in concert with more than two other defendants. Only J. C. Hawkins was involved in every episode.

[In 1970 defendant Foster defrauded a group of investors in a nursing home, built by his construction company and leased to the investor group by a corporation set up by Foster. The day before the nursing home was to open Foster paid J. C. Hawkins and Recea Hawkins to burn it down.

[Between 1971 and 1974 defendants J. C. Hawkins, Delph, and Taylor furnished counterfeit titles to and sold cars stolen by a major car theft ring.

[In 1972 and 1973 defendant J. C. Hawkins masterminded several thefts. In 1972 he and defendants Elliott and Recea Hawkins stole and fenced a truckload of Hormel meat. When a friend of J. C. Hawkins who had stored the stolen meat in his grocery store was indicted for possession of stolen goods, J. C. attempted to, and did, influence the outcome of the trial by tampering with a juror.

[In 1973 J. C. Hawkins stole two trucks and attempted to sell them to another man, Jimmy Reeves. Suspecting that Reeves was informing to the police, J. C. had Reeves killed by Recea Hawkins.

[Later in 1973, defendants J. C. Hawkins and Foster were involved in two thefts, J. C. committing the thefts and Foster providing storage for the stolen goods. A third theft in late 1973 involved defendant Recea Hawkins as well. Defendants Delph and Taylor were not involved in any of the thefts committed in 1972 and 1973.

[Between 1971 and 1976 a number of either attempted or successful drug transactions took place. One involved defendant Taylor alone, another defendant Elliott alone, and another, defendant J. C. Hawkins alone. Another transaction involved defendants Delph and Taylor together, and another J. C. Hawkins and Recea Hawkins.

[Finally, in 1976, defendant J. C. Hawkins planned to steal fungicide from a chemical company. None of the other defendants was involved.

[Following conviction, the trial court imposed these sentences: J. C. Hawkins, 80 years' imprisonment; Recea Hawkins, 50 years' imprisonment; Delph and Taylor, each 10 years' imprisonment; Foster, one year in prison and five years of probation; Elliott, five years' probation.]

All six defendants were convicted under 18 U.S.C. §1962(d) of having conspired to violate a substantive RICO provision, §1962(c). In this appeal, all defendants, with the exception of Foster, argue that while the indictment alleged but one conspiracy, the government's evidence at trial proved the existence of several conspiracies, resulting in a variance which substantially prejudiced their rights and requires reversal, citing Kotteakos v. United States, 328 U.S. 750 (1946). Prior to the enactment of the RICO statute, this argument would have been more persuasive. However, as we explain below, RICO has displaced many of the legal precepts traditionally applied to concerted criminal activity. Its effects in this case is to free the government from the strictures of the multiple conspiracy doctrine and to allow the joint trial of many persons accused of diversified crimes.

A. Prior Law: Wheels and Chains

1. *Kotteakos* and the Wheel Conspiracy Rationale: The Court in *Kotteakos* held
that proof of multiple conspiracies under an indictment alleging a single conspiracy constituted a material variance requiring reversal where a defendant's substantial rights had been affected. At issue was "the right not to be tried en
masse for the conglomeration of distinct and separate offenses committed by
others." 328 U.S. at 775. *Kotteakos* thus protects against the "spill-over effect,"
the transference of guilt from members of one conspiracy to members of another. . . .

[The] facts in *Kotteakos* led the Court to speak in terms of a "wheel conspiracy,"
in which one person, the "hub" of the wheel, was accused of conspiring with
several others, the "spokes" of the wheel. As we explained in United States v.
Levine, 546 F.2d 658, 663 (5th Cir. 1977): "For a [single] wheel conspiracy
to exist those people who form the wheel's spokes must have been aware of
each other and must do something in furtherance of some single, illegal enterprise. Otherwise the conspiracy lacks 'the rim of the wheel to enclose the spokes.'
If there is not some interaction between those conspirators who form the spokes
of the wheel as to at least one common illegal object, the 'wheel' is incomplete,
and two conspiracies rather than one are charged."

2. *Blumenthal* and the Chain Conspiracy Rationale: The impact of *Kotteakos*
was soon limited by the Court in Blumenthal v. United States, 332 U.S. 539
(1947), where the indictment charged a single conspiracy to sell whiskey at
prices above the ceiling set by the Office of Price Administration. The owner
of the whiskey, through a series of middlemen, had devised an intricate scheme
to conceal the true amount he was charging for the whiskey. Although some
of the middlemen had no contact with each other and did not know the identity
of the owner, they had to have realized that they were indispensible cogs in
the machinery through which this illegal scheme was effectuated. The Court
concluded that "in every practical sense the unique facts of this case reveal a
single conspiracy of which the several agreements were essential and integral
steps." Thus the "chain conspiracy" rationale evolved.

The essential element of a chain conspiracy — allowing persons unknown to
each other and never before in contact to be jointly prosecuted as co-conspirators — is interdependence. The scheme which is the object of the conspiracy
must depend on the successful operation of each link in the chain. "An individual
associating himself with a 'chain' conspiracy knows that it has a 'scope' and
that for its success it requires an organization wider than may be disclosed by
his personal participation." United States v. Agueci, 310 F.2d 817, 827 (2d
Cir. 1962). "Thus, in a 'chain' conspiracy prosecution, the requisite element —
knowledge of the existence of remote links — may be inferred solely from the
nature of the enterprise." United States v. Perez, 489 F.2d at 59 n. 10.[24]

---

24. Although *Perez* was a hybrid case, involving a wheel conspiracy in which each spoke was
itself a chain conspiracy, we applied the interdependence rationale to find a single, overall conspiracy.
Perez involved a series of fraudulent insurance claims based on several staged car accidents involving
different groups of people, with minimal overlap among the groups. The scheme could not be
described as a "chain" in the ordinary sense, but we noted that each participant had to realize
that the single fraudulent claim in which he or she was involved could not be profitable unless it
was one of multiple claims and that, in turn, multiple claims could not be successfully made unless
they involved many different people and accidents in different locations across the state.

3. Limits of the Chain Conspiracy Rationale: The rationale of *Blumenthal* applies only insofar as the alleged agreement has "a common end or single unified purpose." . . . Generally, where the government has shown that a number of otherwise diverse activities were performed to achieve a simple goal, courts have been willing to find a single conspiracy. This "common objective" test has most often been used to connect the many facets of drug importation and distribution schemes. The rationale falls apart, however, where the remote members of the alleged conspiracy are not truly interdependent or where the various activities sought to be tied together cannot reasonably be said to constitute a unified scheme. In United States v. Miley, 513 F.2d 1191, 1207 (2d Cir. 1975), for example, the Second Circuit held that the value and quantity of drugs sold by the defendant-suppliers was insufficient to justify the inference that each knew his supplies were only a small part of the drugs handled by a larger operation. . . .

Applying pre-RICO conspiracy concepts to the facts of this case, we doubt that a single conspiracy could be demonstrated. Foster had no contact with Delph and Taylor during the life of the alleged conspiracy. Delph and Taylor, so far as the evidence revealed, had no contact with Recea Hawkins. The activities allegedly embraced by the illegal agreement in this case are simply too diverse to be tied together on the theory that participation in one activity necessarily implied awareness of others. Even viewing the "common objective" of the conspiracy as the raising of revenue through criminal activity, we could not say, for example, that Foster, when he helped to conceal stolen meat, had to know that J. C. was selling drugs to persons unknown to Foster, or that Delph and Taylor, when they furnished counterfeit titles to a car theft ring, had to know that the man supplying the titles was also stealing goods out of interstate commerce. The enterprise involved in this case probably could not have been successfully prosecuted as a single conspiracy under the general federal conspiracy statute, 18 U.S.C. §371.

B. RICO TO THE RESCUE: THE ENTERPRISE CONSPIRACY

In enacting RICO, Congress found that "organized crime continues to grow" in part "because the sanctions and remedies available to the Government are unnecessarily limited in scope and impact." Thus, one of the express purposes of the Act was "to seek the eradication of organized crime . . . by establishing new penal prohibitions, and by providing enhanced sanctions and new remedies to deal with the unlawful activities of those engaged in organized crime." Pub. L. 91-452, §1, 84 Stat. 922 (1970). Against this background, we are convinced that, through RICO, Congress intended to authorize the single prosecution of a multi-faceted, diversified conspiracy by replacing the inadequate "wheel" and "chain" rationales with a new statutory concept: the enterprise.

To achieve this result, Congress acted against the backdrop of hornbook conspiracy law. Under the general federal conspiracy statute, "the precise nature and extent of the conspiracy must be determined by reference to the agreement which embraces and defines its objects. Whether the object of a single agreement is to commit one or many crimes, it is in either case that agreement which constitutes the conspiracy which the statute punishes." Braverman v. United

States, 317 U.S. 49, 53. In the context of organized crime, this principle inhibited mass prosecutions because a single agreement or "common objective" cannot be inferred from the commission of highly diverse crimes by apparently unrelated individuals. RICO helps to eliminate this problem by creating a substantive offense which ties together these diverse parties and crimes. Thus, the object of a RICO conspiracy is to violate a substantive RICO provision — here, to conduct or participate in the affairs of an enterprise through a pattern of racketeering activity — and not merely to commit each of the predicate crimes necessary to demonstrate a pattern of racketeering activity. The gravamen of the conspiracy charge in this case is not that each defendant agreed to commit arson, to steal goods from interstate commerce, to obstruct justice, and to sell narcotics; rather, it is that each agreed to participate, directly and indirectly, in the affairs of the enterprise by committing two or more predicate crimes. Under the statute, it is irrelevant that each defendant participated in the enterprise's affairs through different, even unrelated crimes, so long as we may reasonably infer that each crime was intended to further the enterprise's affairs. To find a single conspiracy, we still must look for agreement on an overall objective. What Congress did was to define that objective through the substantive provisions of the Act.

C. Constitutional Considerations

The "enterprise conspiracy" is a legislative innovation in the realm of individual liability for group crime. We need to consider whether this innovation comports with the fundamental demand of due process that guilt remain "individual and personal." *Kotteakos, supra,* 328 U.S. at 772.

The substantive proscriptions of the RICO statute apply to insiders *and outsiders* — those merely "associated with" an enterprise — who participate directly *and indirectly* in the enterprise's affairs through a pattern of racketeering activity. 18 U.S.C. §1962(c). Thus, the RICO net is woven tightly to trap even the smallest fish, those peripherally involved with the enterprise. This effect is enhanced by principles of conspiracy law also developed to facilitate prosecution of conspirators at all levels. Direct evidence of agreement is unnecessary: "proof of such an agreement may rest upon inferences drawn from relevant and competent circumstantial evidence — ordinarily the acts and conduct of the alleged conspirators themselves." United States v. Morado, 454 F.2d at 174. Additionally, once the conspiracy has been established, the government need show only "slight evidence" that a particular person was a member of the conspiracy. Id. at 175. Of course, "a party to a conspiracy need not know the identity, or even the number, of his confederates." United States v. Andolschek, 142 F.2d 503, 507 (2d Cir. 1944).

Undeniably, then, under the RICO conspiracy provision, remote associates of an enterprise may be convicted as conspirators on the basis of purely circumstantial evidence. We cannot say, however, that this section of the statute demands inferences that cannot reasonably be drawn from circumstantial evidence or that it otherwise offends the rule that guilt be individual and personal. The Act does not authorize that individuals "be tried en masse for the conglomeration of distinct and separate offenses committed by others." *Kotteakos, supra.* Nor does it punish mere association with conspirators or knowledge of illegal activity;

its proscriptions are directed against conduct, not status. To be convicted as a member of an enterprise conspiracy, an individual, by his words or actions, must have objectively manifested an agreement to participate, directly or indirectly, in the affairs of an enterprise *through the commission of two or more predicate crimes.* One whose agreement with the members of an enterprise did not include this vital element cannot be convicted under the Act. Where, as here, the evidence establishes that each defendant, over a period of years, committed several acts of racketeering activity in furtherance of the enterprise's affairs, the inference of an agreement to do so is unmistakable.

It is well established that "[t]he government is not required to prove that a conspirator had full knowledge of all the details of the conspiracy; knowledge of the essential nature of the plan is sufficient." United States v. Brasseaux, 509 F.2d 157, 160 n. 3 (5th Cir. 1975). The Supreme Court explained the policy behind this rule in Blumenthal v. United States, supra, 332 U.S. at 556-57.

"For it is most often true, especially in broad schemes calling for the aid of many persons, that after discovery of enough to show clearly the essence of the scheme and the identity of a number participating, the identity and the fact of participation of others remain undiscovered and undiscoverable. Secrecy and concealment are essential features of successful conspiracy. The more completely they are achieved, the more successful the crime. Hence the law rightly gives room for allowing the conviction of those discovered upon showing sufficiently the essential nature of the plan and their connections with it, without requiring evidence of knowledge of all its details or of the participation of others. Otherwise the difficulties, not only of discovery, but of certainty in proof and of correlating proof with pleading would become insuperable, and conspirators would go free by their very ingenuity."

In the instant case, it is clear that "the essential nature of the plan" was to associate for the purpose of making money from repeated criminal activity. Defendant Foster, for example, hired J. C. Hawkins to commit arson, helped him to conceal large quantities of meat and shirts stolen from interstate commerce, and bought a stolen forklift from him. It would be "a perversion of natural thought and of natural language" to deny that these facts give rise to the inference that Foster knew he was directly involved in an enterprise whose purpose was to profit from crime. As we noted in United States v. Gonzalez, 491 F.2d 1202, 1206 (5th Cir. 1974), "persons so associating and forming organizations for furthering such illicit purposes do not normally conceive of the association as engaging in one unlawful transaction and then disbanding. Rather the nature of such organizations seems to be an ongoing operation. . . ." Foster also had to know that the enterprise was bigger than his role in it, and that others unknown to him were participating in its affairs. He may have been unaware that others who had agreed to participate in the enterprise's affairs did so by selling drugs and murdering a key witness. That, however, is irrelevant to his own liability, for he is charged with agreeing *to participate* in the enterprise through his own crimes, not with agreeing *to commit* each of the crimes through which the overall affairs of the enterprise were conducted. We perceive in this no significant extension of a co-conspirator's liability. When a person "embarks upon a criminal venture of indefinite outline, he takes his chances as to its content and membership, so be it that they fall within the common purposes as he understands them." United States v. Andolschek, supra, 142 F.2d at 507.[31]

Our society disdains mass prosecutions because we abhor the totalitarian doctrine of mass guilt. We nevertheless punish conspiracy as a distinct offense because we recognize that collective action toward an illegal end involves a greater risk to society than individual action toward the same end. That risk is greatly compounded when the conspirators contemplate not a single crime but a career of crime. "There are times when of necessity, because of the nature and scope of the particular federation, large numbers of persons taking part must be tried together or perhaps not at all. . . . When many conspire, they invite mass trial by their conduct." *Kotteakos,* supra, 328 U.S. at 773.

We do not lightly dismiss the fact that under this statute four defendants who did not commit murder have been forced to stand trial jointly with, and as confederates of, two others who did. Prejudice inheres in such a trial; great Neptune's ocean could not purge its taint.[33] But the Constitution does not guarantee a trial free from the prejudice that inevitably accompanies any charge of heinous group crime; it demands only that the potential for transference of guilt be minimized to the extent possible under the circumstances in order "to individualize each defendant in his relation to the mass." *Kotteakos,* supra, 328 U.S. at 773. The RICO statute does not offend this principle. Congress, in a proper exercise of its legislative power, has decided that murder, like thefts from interstate commerce and the counterfeiting of securities, qualifies as racketeering activity. This, of course, ups the ante for RICO violators who personally would not contemplate taking a human life. Whether there is a moral imbalance

---

31. Although the evidence here supports the inference that each remote member of this enterprise knew he was a part of a much larger criminal venture, we do not wish to imply that each "department" of the enterprise was wholly independent of the others. A close look at the modus operandi of the enterprise reveals a pattern of interdependence which bolsters our conclusion that the functions of each "department" directly contributed to the success of the overall operation. Many of the enterprise's practices were analogous to those common in legitimate businesses:

— *Investment Capital:* Most of the enterprise's activities depended upon the ready availability of investment capital, or "front money," to finance the purchase of stolen goods and narcotics for eventual resale at a profit. In this sense, money brought in from one project could be used to purchase goods in another unrelated project.

— *"Good Will":* Part of the value of a business is the reputation it has established in the community, its "good will." The enterprise here benefited from a negative form of "good will." For example, Foster and J. C. exploited their cooperation in the Sparta nursing home arson to gain the confidence of James Gunnells when they needed his help in concealing stolen meat; that earlier endeavor furnished proof that Foster and J. C. could be trusted in criminal pursuits. Similarly, J. C.'s threats of physical harm to many of those involved with the enterprise helped to build a fear in the community which deterred potential witnesses from going to the police. In this way, each successful criminal act and each threat contributed to the success of the enterprise as a whole.

— *Arrangements to Limit Liability:* Like most large business organizations, this enterprise conducted its affairs in a manner calculated to limit its liability for the acts of its agents. J. C. erroneously believed that he could limit each person's liability by keeping him as isolated from the others as possible — in other words, that it would be safer to have the affairs of the enterprise conducted through chains composed of many persons playing limited roles than through a small circle of individuals performing many functions. Where overlap was unavoidable, the enterprise's ongoing operations depended upon each member's confidence that the others would remain silent. When J. C. spoke to Joe Fuchs in January, 1976, for example, he expressed confidence that the government could never make a case against his enterprise. He was certain that James Elliott would not talk because "James is scared." He also assured Fuchs that he, J. C., and Scooter Herring would say nothing; as for Recea, "that's plum out of the question, you can eliminate that." Thus, he concluded, the only other persons who might implicate Fuchs could provide only uncorroborated accounts which would "mean nothing" in court.

33. Cf. Shakespeare, Macbeth, Act III, Scene I.

in the equation of thieves and counterfeiters with murderers is a question whose answer lies in the halls of Congress, not in the judicial conscience. . . .

[The court affirmed all the conspiracy convictions except Elliott's, the evidence of whose involvement the court found insufficient to support a reasonable inference of guilt. The court's discussion is instructive:]

Viewed in a light most favorable to the government, the evidence against Elliott proved the following:

(1) Early in the spring of 1971, Joe Fuchs gave Elliott a bottle of 500 amphetamine capsules without a prescription.

(2) Shortly thereafter, Elliott negotiated a deal with Fuchs for Joe Breland to build an enclosed porch and for Fuchs to repay Elliott and Breland with amphetamine pills. During the next year, Fuchs delivered the pills in installments of 400.

(3) In April, 1972, Elliott, apparently as a favor for J. C., either sold or gave to Fuchs a 50 pound piece of stolen Hormel meat.

(4) In May, 1973, Elliott, serving as a juror in the trial of Rudolph Flanders for possession of meat from the same stolen shipment, held out for acquittal, causing a mistrial. No evidence was presented that Elliott had been contacted in advance about how he would vote in the Flanders case, although J. C. had told others that he felt Elliott would cooperate.

(5) In January, 1976, Elliott encouraged Fuchs to lie to a federal grand jury about how he acquired the stolen meat given to him by Elliott in 1972.

This evidence could not be taken to support, to the exclusion of all other reasonable hypotheses, a conclusion by the jury that Elliott agreed to participate, directly or indirectly, in the affairs of an enterprise through a pattern of racketeering activity. At best, this evidence discloses that Elliott used a close friend, Joe Fuchs, as a personal source of amphetamines and that he became peripherally involved in a stolen meat deal, an involvement he later attempted to conceal. The government failed to prove that Elliott's amphetamine transactions with Fuchs were in any way connected with the affairs of the enterprise. The Hormel meat, on the other hand, undeniably was acquired as a result of enterprise activity, but Elliott's cooperation with J. C. Hawkins in disposing of a small portion of the meat is insufficient to prove beyond a reasonable doubt that Elliott knowingly and intentionally joined the broad conspiracy to violate RICO. Elliott's acts are equally consistent with the hypothesis that he conspired with J. C. and Fuchs for the limited purpose of aiding in the distribution of stolen meat, an offense with which he was not charged in this case. Under this hypothesis, Elliott agreed to participate in the affairs of the enterprise, but not through a *pattern* of racketeering activity, hence, not in violation of the Act. Similarly, Elliott's two subsequent attempts to cover up the facts in the Hormel meat case are subject to two interpretations: (1) as possible overt acts in furtherance of an agreement to participate in the enterprise's affairs through a pattern of racketeering activity, or (2) as efforts at concealment undertaken after the object of his more limited conspiracy with J. C. and Fuchs had been accomplished, on the theory that "every conspiracy will inevitably be followed by actions taken to cover the conspirators' traces." Grunewald v. United States, 353 U.S. 391 (1957). To allow these predictable acts of concealment to be construed as independent evidence that Elliott agreed to conduct a pattern of racketeering activity would unjustifiably broaden the already pervasive scope of the RICO statute.

We hold, then, that the more reasonable conclusion dictated by these facts is that, while Elliott may have conspired to distribute stolen meat, the jury could not reasonably conclude that he conspired to violate RICO.

NOTE

A critique of the *Elliott* case appears in Note, Elliott v. United States: Conspiracy Law and the Judicial Pursuit of Organized Crime through RICO, 65 Va. L. Rev. 109 (1978). It is there denied that RICO provides a new definition of conspiratorial action or that it authorizes federal courts to establish a new conspiracy theory.

The case law interpreting RICO is reviewed in Blakey & Goldstock, "On the Waterfront": RICO and Labor Racketeering, 17 Am. Crim. L. Rev. 341, 350 et seq. (1980).

4. Parties

INTRODUCTORY NOTE

Since conspiracy liability shares with accomplice liability the necessary participation of another party, it is to be expected that very similar issues arise when the required relationship is put into question in special circumstances. We considered in the chapter on accomplices whether the secondary party is ever not liable where he or she satisfies the required participation with the first party — for example, where the secondary party is a victim or where the definition of the substantive offense evinces a policy inconsistent with holding the secondary party. We also considered whether a secondary party may be liable even when the other party is for various reasons not liable — for example, where the principal party was a feigned participant or had a personal immunity or was acquitted or otherwise dealt with in ways inconsistent with his or her guilt. Here we consider similar issues in connection with the crime of conspiracy. Attention should be given to the parallels and differences in the legal treatment of these issues in the two kinds of liability.

GEBARDI v. UNITED STATES
Supreme Court of the United States
287 U.S. 112 (1932)

MR. JUSTICE STONE delivered the opinion of the Court.

This case is here on certiorari to review a judgment of conviction for conspiracy to violate the Mann Act. Petitioners, a man and a woman, not then husband and wife, were indicted in the District Court for Northern Illinois, for conspiring together, and with others not named, to transport the woman from one state to another for the purpose of engaging in sexual intercourse with the man. At the trial without a jury there was evidence from which the court could have found that the petitioners had engaged in illicit sexual relations in the course of each of the journeys alleged; that the man purchased the railway tickets for both petitioners for at least one journey, and that in each instance the woman, in advance of the purchase of the tickets, consented to go on the journey and did go on it voluntarily for the specified immoral purpose. There was no evidence supporting the allegation that any other person had conspired. The trial court overruled motions for a finding for the defendants, and in arrest of judgment, and gave judgment of conviction, which the Court of Appeals . . . affirmed.

Congress set out in the Mann Act to deal with cases which frequently, if not normally, involve consent and agreement on the part of the woman to the forbidden transportation. In every case in which she is not intimidated or forced into the transportation, the statute necessarily contemplates her acquiescence. Yet this acquiescence, though an incident of a type of transportation specifically dealt with by the statute, was not made a crime under the Mann Act itself. Of this class of cases we say that the substantive offense contemplated by the statute itself involves the same combination or community of purpose of two persons only which is prosecuted here as conspiracy. If this were the only case covered by the Act, it would be within those decisions which hold, consistently with the theory upon which conspiracies are punished, that where it is impossible under any circumstances to commit the substantive offense without cooperative action, the preliminary agreement between the same parties to commit the offense is not an indictable conspiracy either at common law [citing cases], or under the federal statute. . . . But criminal transportation under the Mann Act may be effected without the woman's consent as in cases of intimidation or force (with which we are not now concerned). We assume, therefore, . . . that the decisions last mentioned do not in all strictness apply. We do not rest our decision upon the theory of those cases. . . . We place it rather upon the ground that we perceive in the failure of the Mann Act to condemn the woman's participation in those transportations which are effected with her mere consent, evidence of an affirmative legislative policy to leave her acquiescence unpunished. . . . It would contravene that policy to hold that the very passage of the Mann Act effected a withdrawal by the conspiracy statute of that immunity which the Mann Act itself confers.

It is not to be supposed that the consent of an unmarried person to adultery with a married person, where the latter alone is guilty of the substantive offense, would render the former an abettor or a conspirator, or that the acquiescence of a woman under the age of consent would make her a co-conspirator with the man to commit statutory rape upon herself. Compare Reg. v. Tyrell [1894] 1 Q.B. 710. The principle, determinative of this case, is the same.[a]

On the evidence before us the woman petitioner has not violated the Mann Act and, we hold, is not guilty of a conspiracy to do so. . . .

a. Cf. G. Williams, Criminal Law: The General Part 673 (2d ed. 1961): "One may submit with some confidence that a person cannot be convicted of conspiracy when there is a recognized rule of justice or policy exempting him from prosecution for the substantive crime." See also Ill. Ann. Stat. tit. 38, §8-3: "It is a defense to a charge of solicitation or conspiracy that if the criminal object were achieved the accused would not be guilty of an offense." Cf. Model Penal Code §5.04(2), Appendix to this casebook. — EDS.

NOTE

The foregoing opinion distinguishes those decisions holding that "where it is impossible under any circumstances to commit the substantive offense without cooperative action, the preliminary agreement between the same parties to commit the offense is not an indictable conspiracy." Those decisions exemplify what has become known as the "Wharton rule." It was explained by its eponym as follows (2 F. Wharton, Criminal Law §1604 at 1862 (12th ed. 1932)):

> When to the idea of an offense plurality of agents is logically necessary, conspiracy, which assumes the voluntary accession of a person to a crime of such a character that it is aggravated by a plurality of agents, cannot be maintained. . . . In other words, when the law says, "a combination between two persons to effect a particular end shall be called, if the end be effected, by a certain name," it is not lawful for the prosecution to call it by some other name; and when the law says, such an offense — e.g., adultery — shall have a certain punishment, it is not lawful for the prosecution to evade this limitation by indicting the offense as conspiracy.

The Comment to the Model Penal Code contains the following observations on the Rule (§5.04, Comment at 173 (Tent. Draft No. 10, 1960)):

> The classic Wharton rule cases involve crimes such as dueling, bigamy, adultery, and incest, but it has also been said to apply to gambling, the giving and receiving of bribes, and the buying and selling of contraband goods. The rule is unevenly applied and is subject to a number of exceptions and limitations.
>
> It seems clear that Wharton's rule as generally stated and the rationale that conspiracy "assumes . . . a crime of such a nature that it is aggravated by plurality of agents" completely overlook the functions of conspiracy as an inchoate crime. That an offense inevitably requires concert is no reason to immunize criminal preparation to commit it. Further, the rule operates to immunize from a conspiracy prosecution both parties to any offense that inevitably requires concert, thus disregarding the legislative judgment that at least one should be punishable and taking no account of the varying policies that ought to determine whether the other should be. The rule is supportable only insofar as it avoids cumulative punishment for conspiracy and the completed substantive crime, for it is clear that the legislature would have taken the factor of concert into account in grading a crime which inevitably requires concert.

In Iannelli v. United States, 420 U.S. 770 (1975), a number of defendants were convicted and punished for violating the federal gambling act, making it a crime for five or more persons to conduct a gambling business in violation of state law, and for conspiracy to violate the gambling act by conducting the same gambling business. The Supreme Court treated the Wharton rule as functioning only to create a judicial presumption to be applied in the absence of legislative intent to the contrary. It sustained the conviction and punishment of both offenses, finding evidence of congressional intent to permit conviction and punishment of the substantive offense and the conspiracy to commit it, even though the only way the substantive offense could be committed was by the concerted action of defendants. For comment, see Note, An Analysis of Wharton's Rule, 71 Nw. U.L. Rev. 547 (1976).

GARCIA v. STATE

Supreme Court of Indiana
71 Ind. 366, 394 N.E.2d 106 (1979)

PRENTICE, J. Defendant was convicted in a trial by jury of conspiracy to commit murder, a class A felony, . . . and sentenced to twenty years imprisonment. Her sentence was suspended and she was placed on five years probation. On appeal she raises the . . . issue . . . whether the defendant can be convicted of conspiracy when the only person with whom the defendant conspired was a police informant who only feigned his acquiescence in the scheme. . . .

The evidence introduced at trial consisted of the following: On September 30, 1977, State's witness, Allen Young, was first contacted by the defendant with regard to certain marital problems that she was having. She stated that her husband constantly beat her and her children and that she "couldn't take it any longer"— that she wanted her husband killed. Young suggested that she go to the police or see an attorney, but she refused, stating that to do so would only make matters worse. Young then mentioned the sum of $5000.00 in an attempt to discourage her. She responded that the amount was out of the question and ended the conversation. Young testified that he had not taken the defendant seriously at that point, because he thought that she was simply upset and needed to "blow off steam." He received a second call from the defendant on October 4, 1977. During this conversation, the defendant said that she had $200 in cash and wanted to know whether he had found anyone to kill her husband. Young responded that he did not think he could help her since he did not know anyone who was in that line of "business." She asked him to look around anyway. Young testified that, although he did not directly promise to find someone for her, he probably left her with the impression that he would do so. Shortly after talking with the defendant, Young went to the Whiting Police Department and discussed the matter with two detectives. He offered to call the defendant and let them listen and record the conversation, which they did. During the conversation, Young again asked the defendant if she wanted him to help her find someone to kill her husband, and she responded affirmatively. Young replied that he would try to find someone. Several more conversations took place between the defendant and Young. On each occasion the defendant reaffirmed her desire to have her husband killed, and she rejected the idea of going to the police instead. At their final meeting, Young, accompanied by a plain-clothed detective, introduced the defendant to the detective, stating that here was a man who might be willing to do the job. The defendant then produced $200, a picture of her husband, and a record of his daily habits and gave them to the detective. She agreed to pay the balance of the contract price when the "job" was completed. Defendant was subsequently arrested.

At trial, Young testified that he only feigned his acquiescence in the plan and at no time did he intend to actually carry it out.

The issue is whether the conspiracy section of our new penal code adopts the Model Penal Code's "unilateral" concept or whether it retains the traditional "bilateral" concept.

The bilateral concept is the traditional view of conspiracy as derived from common law. It is formulated in terms of two or more persons agreeing to commit a crime, each with intent to do so. In cases where the person or persons with whom the defendant conspired only feigned his acquiescence in the plan, the courts have generally held that neither person could be convicted of conspiracy because there was no "conspiratorial agreement." . . .

Reacting to criticism of this viewpoint, the drafters of the Model Penal Code, though not without internal disagreement, adopted a "unilateral" concept, as follows: [The court then quoted Model Penal Code §§5.03(1) and 5.04(1). See Appendix to this casebook.]

In explanation of their new approach, the Drafters of the Model Penal Code commented:

> Unilateral Approach of the Draft. The definition of the Draft departs from the traditional view of conspiracy as an entirely bilateral or multilateral relationship, the view inherent in the standard formulation cast in terms of "two or more persons" agreeing or combining to commit a crime. Attention is directed instead to each individual's culpability by framing the definition in terms of the conduct which suffices to establish the liability of any given actor, rather than the conduct of a group of which he is charged to be a part — an approach which in this comment we have designated "unilateral."
>
> One consequence of this approach is to make it immaterial to the guilt of a conspirator whose culpability has been established that the person or all of the persons with whom he conspired have not been or cannot be convicted. Present law frequently holds otherwise, reasoning from the definition of conspiracy as an agreement between two or more persons that there must be at least two guilty conspirators or none. The problem arises in a number of contexts. . . .
>
> Second: Where the person with whom the defendant conspired secretly intends not to go through with the plan. In these cases it is generally held that neither party can be convicted because there was no "agreement" between two persons. Under the unilateral approach of the Draft, the culpable party's guilt would not be affected by the fact that the other party's agreement was feigned. He has conspired, within the meaning of the definition, in the belief that the other party was with him; apart from the issue of entrapment often presented in such cases, his culpability is not decreased by the other's secret intention. True enough, the project's chances of success have not been increased by the agreement; indeed, its doom may have been sealed by this turn of events. *But the major basis of conspiratorial liability — the unequivocal evidence of a firm purpose to commit a crime — remains the same.* The result would be the same under the Draft if the only co-conspirator established a defense of renunciation under Section 5.03(6). While both the Advisory Committee and the Council support the Draft upon this point, it should be noted that the Council vote was 14–11, the dissenting members deeming mutual agreement on the part of two or more essential to the concept of conspiracy. (Our emphasis)

M.P.C. §5.03, [Tent. Draft No. 10,] Comments at pp. 104-105. . . .

This concept has been adopted, in whole or in part, in at least 26 states and is under consideration in most of the remaining states. See Note, Conspiracy: Statutory Reform Since the Model Penal Code, 75 Col. L. R. 1122, 1125 (1975).

In 1976, our Indiana Legislature repealed the existing conspiracy statute[2] and adopted Ind. Code §35-41-5-2 . . . which reads as follows:

2. The repealed conspiracy statute read as follows: "35-1-111-1 [10-1101]. Conspiracy to commit a felony. — Any person or persons who shall unite or combine with any other person or persons

Section 35-41-5-2. CONSPIRACY

[Sec. 2.] (a) A person conspires to commit a felony when, with intent to commit the felony, he agrees with another person to commit the felony. . . .

(c) It is no defense that the person with whom the accused person is alleged to have conspired:

(1) has not been prosecuted; (2) has not been convicted; (3) has been acquitted; (4) has been convicted of a different crime; (5) cannot be prosecuted for any reason; or (6) lacked the capacity to commit the crime.

The adopted statute is similar in all respects relevant herein to the final draft proposed by the Criminal Law Study Commission. The comments accompanying that draft state that the present law is *not* sought to be changed, and defendant's position is that the Legislature did not adopt the unilateral concept in the act under which she was tried and convicted.

We are unable to determine with certainty what the commission intended by this comment, i.e. whether the enactment would merely restate the definition, without changing the result, or whether the law relative to the offense, except for the elimination of enumerated defenses, would remain unchanged. If the former was intended by the commenter, it can only be viewed as a mental lapse and proofreading oversight; as it is clear upon the face of the act that defenses available under the multilateral concept were to be eliminated. The inclusion of the "catch-all" sub-proviso (5) can leave no doubt. Clearly "any reason," as recited therein, includes the absence of criminal culpability on the part of a co-conspirator — including a sole co-conspirator. The words "agrees" and "agreement" have not been used as words of art denoting a "meeting of the minds" and "contract." Rather, the former is descriptive of the defendant's state of mind at the time he communicated with another in furtherance of the felony; and the latter refers to the defendant's understanding.

Defendant has cited us to numerous cases supporting the bilateral concept requiring "concurrence of sentiment and cooperative conduct in the unlawful and criminal enterprise"; however, those cases were not decided under statutes remotely similar to our own. She has distinguished those cases upholding the unilateral concept upon the basis of better articulated legislative commentary or differences in the wording of the statute under attack which we do not perceive to be material. For example, the Minnesota statute (Minn. St. 609.175, subd. 2) reads "Whoever conspires with another" whereas our own refers to *agreeing* with another. Her argument that, by definition, an agreement requires the concurrence of sentiment of at least two individuals could be applied with even greater logic to the Minnesota statute and its use of the word "conspires."[a] It is not persuasive in the light of the express wording of the entire enactment. . . .

The judgment of the trial court is affirmed.

---

for the purpose of committing a felony, within or without this state; or any person or persons who shall knowingly unite with any other person or persons, body, association or combination of persons, whose object is the commission of a felony or felonies, within or without this state, shall, on conviction, be [punished.]"

a. However, the Minnesota Supreme Court reached the same conclusion as that reached in this case. State v. St. Christopher, 305 Minn. 226, 232 N.W. 2d 798 (1975). — EDS.

NOTES

1. The unilateral approach to conspiracy taken in Indiana and in many other states that have followed the Model Penal Code extends liability not only in the feigned-conspirator and other such cases where the only other participant is not liable but also, as the Model Penal Code intended, in cases where "the person with whom the defendant conspired has not been apprehended or tried, or his case has been disposed of in a manner that would raise questions of consistency about a conviction of the defendant" (§5.03, Comment at 105-106 (Tent. Draft No. 10, 1960)). Compare United States v. Standefer, pages 637-638 supra.

2. For criticisms of the unilateral definition of conspiracy, see Burgman, Unilateral Conspiracy: Three Critical Perspectives, 29 De Paul L. Rev. 75 (1979); Marcus, Conspiracy: The Criminal Agreement in Theory and Practice, 65 Geo. L.J. 925, 927 (1977). The latter argues that the group-danger rationale of conspiracy is not applicable in the absence of a multiparty agreement.

CHAPTER

9

EXCULPATION

A. PRINCIPLES OF JUSTIFICATION

1. Protection of Life and Person

UNITED STATES v. PETERSON

United States Court of Appeals, District of Columbia Circuit
483 F.2d 1222 (1973)

ROBINSON, J. More than two centuries ago, Blackstone, best known of the expositors of the English common law, taught that "all homicide is malicious, and of course, amounts to murder, unless . . . *justified* by the command or permission of the law; *excused* on the account of accident or self-preservation; or *alleviated* into manslaughter, by being either the involuntary consequence of some act not strictly lawful, or (if voluntary) occasioned by some sudden and sufficiently violent provocation." . . .

Self-defense, as a doctrine legally exonerating the taking of human life, is as viable now as it was in Blackstone's time, and in the case before us the doctrine is invoked in its purest form. But "[t]he law of self-defense is a law of necessity"; the right of self-defense arises only when the necessity begins, and equally ends with the necessity; and never must the necessity be greater than when the force employed defensively is deadly. The "necessity must bear all semblance of reality, and appear to admit of no other alternative, before taking life will be justifiable as excusable." Hinged on the exigencies of self-preservation, the doctrine of homicidal self-defense emerges from the body of the criminal law as a limited though important exception to legal outlawry of the arena of self-help in the settlement of potentially fatal personal conflicts.

So it is that necessity is the pervasive theme of the well defined conditions which the law imposes on the right to kill or maim in self-defense. There must have been a threat, actual or apparent, of the use of deadly force against the defender. The threat must have been unlawful and immediate. The defender must have believed that he was in imminent peril of death or serious bodily harm, and that his response was necessary to save himself therefrom. These beliefs must not only have been honestly entertained, but also objectively reasonable in light of the surrounding circumstances. It is clear that no less than a concurrence of these elements will suffice.

<u>STATE v. WANROW</u>
Supreme Court of Washington
88 Wash. 2d 221, 559 P.2d 548 (1977)

UTTER, J. Yvonne Wanrow was convicted by a jury of second-degree murder and first-degree assault. She appealed her conviction to the Court of Appeals. The Court of Appeals reversed and remanded the case. . . . We granted review and affirm the Court of Appeals.

We order a reversal of the conviction on two grounds. [Discussion of first ground omitted.] The second ground is error committed by the trial court in improperly instructing the jury on the law of self-defense as it related to the defendant.

On the afternoon of August 11, 1972, defendant's (respondent's) two children were staying at the home of Ms. Hooper, a friend of defendant. Defendant's son was playing in the neighborhood and came back to Ms. Hooper's house and told her that a man tried to pull him off his bicycle and drag him into a house. Some months earlier, Ms. Hooper's 7-year-old daughter had developed a rash on her body which was diagnosed as venereal disease. Ms. Hooper had been unable to persuade her daughter to tell her who had molested her. It was not until the night of the shooting that Ms. Hooper discovered it was William Wesler (decedent) who allegedly had violated her daughter. A few minutes after the defendant's son related his story to Ms. Hooper about the man who tried to detain him, Mr. Wesler appeared on the porch of the Hooper house and stated through the door, "I didn't touch the kid, I didn't touch the kid." . . . Joseph Fah, Ms. Hooper's landlord, saw Wesler as he was leaving and informed Shirley Hooper that Wesler had tried to molest a young boy who had earlier lived in the same house, and that Wesler had previously been committed to the Eastern State Hospital for the mentally ill. Immediately after this revelation from Mr. Fah, Ms. Hooper called the police. . . . Ms. Hooper requested that Wesler be arrested then and there, but the police stated, "We can't, until Monday morning." Ms. Hooper was urged by the police officer to go to the police station Monday morning and "swear out a warrant." . . . (A week before this incident Shirley Hooper had noticed someone prowling around her house at night. Two days before the shooting someone had attempted to get into Ms. Hooper's bedroom and had slashed the window screen. She suspected that such person was Wesler.)

That evening, Ms. Hooper called the defendant and asked her to spend the night with her in the Hooper house. At that time she related to Ms. Wanrow the facts we have previously set forth. The defendant arrived sometime after 6 P.M. with a pistol in her handbag. The two women ultimately determined that they were too afraid to stay alone and decided to ask some friends to come over for added protection. The two women then called the defendant's sister and brother-in-law, Angie and Chuck Michel. The four adults did not go to bed that evening, but remained awake talking and watching for any possible prowlers. There were eight young children in the house with them. At around 5 A.M., Chuck Michel, without the knowledge of the women in the house, went to Wesler's house, carrying a baseball bat. Upon arriving at the Wesler residence, Mr. Michel accused Wesler of molesting little children. Mr. Wesler then suggested that they go over to the Hooper residence and get the whole thing straightened out. . . . Mr. Michel . . . remained outside while Wesler entered the residence.

The testimony as to what next took place is considerably less precise. It appears that Wesler, a large man who was visibly intoxicated, entered the home and when told to leave declined to do so. A good deal of shouting and confusion then arose. . . . Ms. Wanrow, a 5'4" woman who at the time had a broken leg and was using a crutch, testified that she then went to the front door to enlist the aid of Chuck Michel. She stated that she shouted for him and, upon turning around to reenter the living room, found Wesler standing directly behind her. She testified to being gravely startled by this situation and to having then shot Wesler in what amounted to a reflex action.

After Wesler was shot, Ms. Hooper called the police via a Spokane crime check emergency phone number, stating, "There's a guy broke in, and my girl-friend shot him." . . .

Reversal of respondent's conviction is . . . required by a . . . serious error committed by the trial court. Instruction No. 10, setting forth the law of self-defense, incorrectly limited the jury's consideration of acts and circumstances pertinent to respondent's perception of the alleged threat to her person. . . .

In the opening paragraph of instruction No. 10, the jury, in evaluating the gravity of the danger to the respondent, was directed to consider only those acts and circumstances occurring "at or immediately before the killing. . . ."[7] This is not now, and never has been, the law of self-defense in Washington. On the contrary, the justification of self-defense is to be evaluated in light of *all* the facts and circumstances known to the defendant, including those known substantially before the killing.

In State v. Ellis, 30 Wash. 369, 70 P. 963 (1902), this court reversed a first-degree murder conviction obtained under self-defense instructions quite similar to that in the present case. The defendant sought to show that the deceased had a reputation and habit of carrying and using deadly weapons when engaged in quarrels. The trial court instructed that threats were insufficient justification unless " 'at the time of the alleged killing the deceased was making or immediately preceding the killing had committed some overt act. . . .' " This court found the instruction "defective and misleading," stating "the apparent facts should all be taken together to illustrate the motives and good faith of the defendant. . . ." "[I]t is apparent that a man who habitually carries and uses such weapons in quarrels must cause greater apprehension of danger than one who does not bear such reputation. . . . The vital question is the reasonableness of the defendant's apprehension of danger. . . . The jury are [sic] entitled to stand as nearly as practicable in the shoes of defendant, and from this point of view determine the character of the act." Thus, circumstances predating the killing by weeks and months were deemed entirely proper, and in fact essential, to a proper disposition of the claim of self-defense. . . .

. . . By limiting the jury's consideration of the surrounding acts and circum-

---

7. Instruction No. 10 reads:

"To justify killing in self-defense, there need be no actual or real danger to the life or person of the party killing, but there must be or reasonably appear to be, at or immediately before the killing, some overt act, or some circumstances which would reasonably indicate to the party killing that the person slain, is, at the time, endeavoring to kill him or inflict upon him great bodily harm. . . ."

stances to those occurring "at or immediately before the killing," instruction No. 10 in the present case was an erroneous statement of the applicable law on the critical focal point of the defendant's case. . . .

. . . Respondent's knowledge of the victim's reputation for aggressive acts was gained many hours before the killing and was based upon events which occurred over a period of years. Under the law of this state, the jury should have been allowed to consider this information in making the critical determination of the " 'degree of force which . . . a reasonable person in the same situation . . . seeing what [s]he sees and knowing what [s]he knows, then would believe to be necessary.' " State v. Dunning, 8 Wash. App. 340, 342, 506 P.2d 321, 322 (1973). . . .

The second paragraph of instruction No. 10 contains an equally erroneous and prejudicial statement of the law. That portion of the instruction reads:

> However, when there is no reasonable ground for the person attacked to believe that *his* person is in imminent danger of death or great bodily harm, and it appears to *him* that only an ordinary battery is all that is intended, and all that he has reasonable grounds to fear from *his* assailant, *he* has a right to stand *his* ground and repel such threatened assault, yet *he* has no right to repel a threatened assault with naked hands, by the use of a deadly weapon in a deadly manner, unless *he* believes, and has reasonable grounds to believe, that *he* is in imminent danger of death or great bodily harm.

(Italics ours.) In our society women suffer from a conspicuous lack of access to training in and the means of developing those skills necessary to effectively repel a male assailant without resorting to the use of deadly weapons.[8] Instruction No. 12 does indicate that the "relative size and strength of the persons involved" may be considered; however, it does not make clear that the defendant's actions are to be judged against her own subjective impressions and not those which a detached jury might determine to be objectively reasonable. . . . The applicable rule of law is clearly stated in *Miller* [141 Wash. 104, 250 P.2d 645]: "If the appellants, at the time of the alleged assault upon them, as reasonably and ordinarily cautious and prudent men, honestly believed that they were in danger of great bodily harm, they would have the right to resort to self-defense, and their conduct is to be judged by the condition appearing to them at the time, not by the condition as it might appear to the jury in the light of testimony before it."

The second paragraph of instruction No. 10 not only establishes an objective standard, but through the persistent use of the masculine gender leaves the jury with the impression the objective standard to be applied is that applicable to an altercation between two men. The impression created — that a 5' 4" woman with a cast on her leg and using a crutch must, under the law, somehow repel an assault by a 6' 2" intoxicated man without employing weapons in her defense, unless the jury finds her determination of the degree of danger to be objectively reasonable — constitutes a separate and distinct misstatement of the law and,

---

8. See B. Babcock, A. Freedman, E. Norton and S. Ross, Sex Discrimination and the Law: Causes and Remedies 943-1070 (1975); S. Brownmiller, Against our Will: Men, Women and Rape (1975).

in the context of this case, violates the respondent's right to equal protection of the law. The respondent was entitled to have the jury consider her actions in the light of her own perceptions of the situation, including those perceptions which were the product of our nation's "long and unfortunate history of sex discrimination." Frontiero v. Richardson, 411 U.S. 677, 684 (1973). Until such time as the effects of that history are eradicated, care must be taken to assure that our self-defense instructions afford women the right to have their conduct judged in light of the individual physical handicaps which are the product of sex discrimination. To fail to do so is to deny the right of the individual woman involved to trial by the same rules which are applicable to male defendants. . . . The portion of the instruction above quoted misstates our law in creating an objective standard of "reasonableness." It then compounds that error by utilizing language suggesting that the respondent's conduct must be measured against that of a reasonable male individual finding himself in the same circumstances.

We conclude that the instruction here in question contains an improper statement of the law on a vital issue in the case, is inconsistent, misleading and prejudicial when read in conjunction with other instructions pertaining to the same issue, and therefore is a proper basis for a finding of reversible error. . . .

NOTES

1. The objective test. The requirement that defendant's belief (in the need to use the defensive force she used) be reasonable is the generally prevailing view, both traditionally and under modern statutes. As we saw, however, in other instances in which the law employs an objective standard, there is always the further question of determining just how objective the standard is to be — that is, how far should features of defendant's particular situation be taken into account in determining whether the choice of defensive force was reasonable? Compare the treatment of this problem with discussion of the reasonable-provocation standard, pages 437-440 supra, and with the definitions of negligence and recklessness, pages 452-457 supra. The holding in the *Wanrow* case favors a degree of subjectivism that is not always followed.

Recall the Model Penal Code standards (§2.02), calling for a judgment (in the case of recklessness) whether the risk is of a nature and degree that "its disregard involves a gross deviation from the standard of conduct that a law-abiding person would observe in the actor's situation" and (in the case of negligence) whether that risk "involves a gross deviation from the standard of care that a reasonable person would observe in the actor's situation." Query: What analysis and conclusion would be indicated by these provisions in the circumstances of *Wanrow?*

2. The battered-woman syndrome. The problem of how far particular aspects of defendant's situation should be considered in characterizing the meaning of "reasonable" self-defensive action has been sharply raised in cases in which women charged with spouse killings have sought to introduce evidence of what has come to be called the "battered-woman syndrome." The following is such a case.

IBN-TAMAS v. UNITED STATES
District of Columbia Court of Appeals
407 A.2d 626 (1979)

FERREN, J. [Defendant was charged with the murder of her husband. She claimed self-defense, testifying to a two-year history of violent assaults she suffered at his hands and to the immediate circumstances leading to her shooting him, circumstances which instilled a fear in her that her husband was about to kill her. The testimony of a prosecution witness cast doubt on her account of the killing and tended to support the theory of the prosecution that, feeling she had endured enough of her husband's abuse, she ambushed him and shot him in cold blood. In cross-examining defendant, the prosecution suggested through its questions that her account of her husband's physical abuse over the years was overdrawn and that her testimony about perceiving herself in immediate danger was implausible. Supporting its view of the facts, the prosecution implied to the jury that the logical reaction of a woman who was truly frightened of her husband (let alone regularly brutalized by him) would have been to call the police from time to time or to leave him. To rebut this line of attack, the defense proferred the testimony of Dr. Lenore Walker, a clinical psychologist, for three purposes: (1) to inform the jury that there is an identifiable class of persons who can be characterized as "battered women," (2) to explain why the mentality and behavior of such women are at variance with the ordinary lay perception of how someone would be likely to react to a spouse who is a batterer, and (3) to provide a basis from which the jury could understand why Mrs. Ibn-Tamas perceived herself in imminent danger at the time of the shooting.

[The trial judge excluded this expert testimony on the ground, inter alia, that it would invade the province of the jury by preempting judgment on the ultimate issue of guilt and that its limited probative value was outweighed by its prejudicial impact. The jury convicted the defendant of second-degree murder, and defendant appealed.]

. . . Dr. Walker told the trial court, out of the presence of the jury, that she had studied 110 women who had been beaten by their husbands. Her studies revealed three consecutive phases in the relationships: "tension building," when there are small incidents of battering; "acute battering incident," when beatings are severe; and "loving-contrite," when the husband becomes very sorry and caring. Dr. Walker then testified that women in this situation typically are low in self-esteem, feel powerless, and have few close friends, since their husbands commonly "accuse them of all kinds of things with friends, and they are embarrassed. They don't want to cause their friends problems, too." Because there are periods of harmony, battered women tend to believe their husbands are basically loving, caring men; the women assume that they, themselves, are somehow responsible for their husbands' violent behavior. They also believe, however, that their husbands are capable of killing them, and they feel there is no escape. Unless a shelter is available, these women stay with their husbands, not only because they typically lack a means of self-support but also because they fear that if they leave they will be found and hurt even more. Dr. Walker stressed that wife batterers come from all racial, social and economic groups (including professionals), and that batterers commonly "escalate their abusiveness" when their wives are pregnant. She added that battered women are very reluctant

[handwritten margin notes: "what 'reasonable' std?" and "WTF!"]

to tell anyone that their husbands beat them. Of those studied, 60% had never done so before (Dr. Walker typically found them in hospitals), 40% had told a friend, and only 10% had called the police.

When asked about appellant, whom she had interviewed, Dr. Walker replied that Mrs. Ibn-Tamas was a "classic case" of the battered wife. Dr. Walker added her belief that on the day of the killing, when Dr. Ibn-Tamas had been beating his wife despite protests that she was pregnant, Mrs. Ibn-Tamas' pregnancy had had a "major impact on the situation. . . . [T]hat is a particularly crucial time."

Dr. Walker's testimony, therefore, arguably would have served at least two basic functions: (1) it would have enhanced Mrs. Ibn-Tamas' general credibility in responding to cross-examination designed to show that her testimony about the relationship with her husband was implausible; and (2) it would have supported her testimony that on the day of the shooting her husband's actions had provoked a state of fear which led her to believe she was in imminent danger ("I just knew he was going to kill me"), and thus responded in self-defense. . . . Dr. Walker's testimony would have supplied an interpretation of the facts which differed from the ordinary lay perception ("she could have gotten out, you know") advocated by the government. The substantive element of the . . . test [of the admissibility of expert testimony — that it be] "beyond the ken of the average layman"— is accordingly met here.

We conclude, therefore, that as to either substantive basis for ruling that Dr. Walker's testimony would "invade the province of the jury"— either the "ultimate issue" or the "beyond the ken" basis — the trial court erred as a matter of law.

[The court then considered two additional considerations governing the admissibility of expert evidence: The witness must have sufficient skill, knowledge or experience in the field; the state of scientific knowledge must be sufficient for an expert opinion. It concluded that the record was not adequate to warrant a judgment on these issues and remanded for the trial judge to make a determination, on the basis of an expanded record, if necessary.

[The court then turned to the issue of the prejudicial impact of the evidence.]

Because "admissibility" remains an open question, we turn to the second level of inquiry: probative value versus prejudicial impact. . . . [T]he court stated that the evidence would "go beyond those [prior violent] acts" which a jury should consider and that, in effect, the testimony put the decedent on trial as "a batterer, [a]nd that is not being tried in this case."

We have stated, apropos of this first ground, that prior acts of violence are admissible in "homicide cases where the defendant raises the claim of self-defense against the decedent as the alleged first aggressor." United States v. Akers, D.C. App., 374 A.2d 874, 877 (1977). The trial court, in fact, admitted a substantial amount of evidence relating to the decedent's earlier attacks on the appellant and other persons. In light of the admission of this evidence, it is apparent that the incremental, prejudicial impact of Dr. Walker's testimony on battered wives, including the labeling of Dr. Ibn-Tamas as a batterer, would have been minimal.

In contrast, as we have previously observed, the testimony on battered wives was highly probative. Because Mrs. Ibn-Tamas' identity as a "battered wife," if established, may have had a substantial bearing on her perceptions and behavior at the time of the killing, it was central to her claim of self-defense. We conclude, accordingly, as a matter of law, that the probative value of this expert testimony would out-weigh the risk of "engender[ing] vindictive passions within the jury or . . . confus[ing] the issues."

NOTES

1. In accord with *Ibn-Tamas,* see Smith v. State, 247 Ga. 612, 277 S.E.2d 678 (1981); State v. Baker, 120 N.H. 773, 424 A.2d 171 (1980). Other courts have rejected the evidence. Buhrle v. State, 627 P.2d 1374 (Wyo. 1981); State v. Thomas, 66 Ohio St. 2d 518, 423 N.E.2d 137 (1981). In an unusual case of a battered husband, the court excluded the testimony of defendant's psychologist designed to explain the apparent overreaction of the husband. Commonwealth v. Battle, 433 A.2d 496 (Super. Ct. Pa. 1981). Commentators also are divided. Compare Mitchell, Does Wife Abuse Justify Homicide?, 24 Wayne L. Rev. 1705 (1978) (critical) with Vandenbraak, Limits on the Use of Defensive Force to Prevent Intramarital Assaults, 10 Rutgers-Camden L.J. 643 (1979) (favorable). For a practically oriented approach, see E. Bochnak, Women's Self-Defense Cases (1981).

When the evidence is rejected, it is usually a case in which the evidence of self-defense is thin. In the *Buhrle* case (627 P.2d at 1376-1377), for example:

Appellant testified that her husband returned to the family home in the late afternoon of October 2, 1979, and requested that appellant drive out to the motel where he was staying so they could talk. When appellant arrived at the motel she had a hunting rifle and a pair of rubber gloves in her possession. Mr. Buhrle kept the night chain on the door of his motel room the entire time that the two talked. After standing outside her husband's motel room for an hour and forty-five minutes while they argued over money and the divorce, appellant shot her husband.

After appellant shot her husband she pushed open the motel room door and was kneeling over Mr. Buhrle when the people from the adjoining rooms arrived at the scene. Appellant then began shouting that someone had shot her husband. In addition, while appellant asserts that she made no effort to flee, she did attempt to conceal the pair of rubber gloves she was seen wearing shortly after the shooting and she hid the rifle underneath a nearby trailer-house. At the time that appellant was arrested she had her husband's wallet in her possession.

At trial appellant relied upon the theory of self-defense. Edith Buhrle took the stand and told of a history of violence on the part of the deceased towards her, her children and the household furnishings. She further testified that when she shot her husband she had thought that he was reaching for the gun that he customarily kept under his bed so that he could kill her. No gun, however, was found in Mr. Buhrle's motel room. . . .

Appellant's offer of proof indicated that Dr. Walker would testify that:
    1) Mrs. Buhrle was a battered woman and a battered woman's behavior differs from that of other women.
    2) Mrs. Buhrle was in a state of learned helplessness resulting in loss of free will.

3) Because of learned helplessness, Mrs. Buhrle's ability to walk away from a situation or escape was impaired.

4) Mrs. Buhrle perceived herself to be acting in self-defense.

Query: Is there good ground for excluding Dr. Walker's evidence in this case while admitting it in *Ibn-Tamas?*

2. *Problem.* Consider the following newspaper account of a jury acquittal of a woman who killed her husband (S.F. Chronicle, July 3, 1980, at 5):

LYNDON, Kan. A jury returned a not-guilty verdict yesterday in the murder trial of a young woman who said she killed her husband on Christmas Day rather than suffer more sexual torture and possible imprisonment in a coffin. . . .

Prosecutor Michael Hines said he was shocked by the decision. "When you kill someone in cold blood you expect the jury to come back with something other than not guilty," he said.

Davis was tried for shooting her husband of six months, James Curnutt, 38, in the back of the head as he lay sleeping on their waterbed on Dec. 25, 1979.

She did not deny killing him. But she told jurors that after years of sexual abuse — including torture with pins, rubber balls and an electric cattle prod and imprisonment underground — she began to fear for her life.

Davis said the decision to kill her husband came after he told her he was planning to build a coffin, wrap her in adhesive tape like a mummy and keep her alive but imprisoned beneath their bed.

But the prosecutor said Davis — who left her Vermont home at 16 to serve as live-in babysitter for Curnutt's children at his Kansas farm — knew about his sexual habits for years and had participated willingly with Curnutt's first wife.

Query: Should "battered women" evidence be admissible in a case like this? How does it bear on the legal requirements of the claim of self-defense?

3. *A subjective test.* The foregoing discussion naturally raises the question whether a wholly subjective test should be applied to defensive killings; that is, so long as defendant honestly believed that she needed to kill in order to thwart an imminent threat to her life, the defense would be made out. Such a proposal has been advocated by English commentators (see, e.g., G. Williams, Textbook on Criminal Law 451-455 (1978); J. C. Smith & B. Hogan, Criminal Law 328-329, 364-365 (4th ed. 1978)) and has been proposed as a legislative change by the Criminal Law Revision Committee (Criminal Law Revision Committee, 14th Report, Offences against the Person ¶72(a) (Cmnd. 7844, 1980)). Professor Glanville Williams has advanced the following argument in behalf of a subjective view (Model Penal Code §3.09, Comment at 79 (Tent. Draft No. 8, 1958)):

The criminal law of negligence works best when it gives effect to the large number of rules of prudence which are commonly observed though not directly incorporated into the law. Such rules include the rule against pulling out on a blind corner, the rule against carrying a gun in such a way that it is pointing at another person, the rule against deliberately pointing a gun at another person, even in play, and so on. These rules are not part either of enacted or of common law, but as customary standards of behavior they become binding via the law of negligence. Are there any similar rules of behavior applicable when a person acts in self-defense or in making an arrest? It must be recollected that the injury he inflicts on the other is in itself intentional, so that the usual rules of prudence in respect to the handling of weapons are not in question. The only question is whether the defendant was negligent in arriving at the conclusion that the use of the force in question was called for. It is hard to imagine what rules of prudence could normally serve in this situation.

4. A grading problem. Note that the objective test renders defendant's motive in self-defense legally irrelevant, and, if defendant acts unreasonably, she becomes liable for an intentional homicide, making the killing legally indistinguishable from a killing for revenge or gain. This, indeed, is the law in England (see Palmer v. Regina, [1971] 1 All E.R. 1077 (P.C. 1971)), which explains why many commentators (and courts as well, see Albert v. Lavin, [1981] 1 All E.R. 628, *leave to appeal to the House of Lords granted*) have advocated abandoning the objective test altogether. In the United States, however, this logical consequence of the objective test has been avoided through two doctrinal approaches: (a) *Imperfect self-defense.* When a person has killed another in honest but unreasonable apprehension of the need to kill to save her own life or when she uses more force than is reasonably necessary, many courts have treated this as an instance of "imperfect self-defense" and classify the crime as voluntary manslaughter. In Commonwealth v. Colandro, 231 Pa. 343, 80 A. 571, 574 (1911), the court held, reversing a conviction for murder:

> The dividing line between self-defense and this character of manslaugher seems to be the existence, as the moving force, of a reasonably founded belief of imminent peril to life or great bodily harm, as distinguished from the influence of an uncontrollable fear or terror, conceivable as existing, but not reasonably justified by the immediate circumstances. If the circumstances are both adequate to raise, and sufficient to justify, a belief in the necessity to take life in order to save oneself from such a danger, where the belief exists and is acted upon, the homicide is excusable upon the theory of self-defense. . . . [W]hile, if the act is committed under the influence of an uncontrollable fear of death or great bodily harm, caused by the circumstances, but without the presence of all the ingredients necessary to excuse the act on the ground of self-defense, the killing is manslaughter.

This approach to the problem is common in the United States. See, e.g., Commonwealth v. Beverley, 237 Ky. 35, 34 S.W. 941 (1931); People v. Flannel, 25 Cal. 3d 668, 603 P.2d 1 (1979). A number of statutes adopt a similar ad hoc approach to unreasonable self-defensive killings. See Pa. Cons. Stat. tit. 18, §2503(b), page 412 supra; Ill. Ann. Stat. ch. 38, §9-2(b).

Query: Where does this approach leave a defendant whose victim does not die? Consider People v. Bramlett, 194 Colo. 205, 573 P.2d 94 (1977). While the Colorado statute formulated an objective definition of self-defense, the homicide provisions reduced what would be murder to criminally negligent homicide (with a maximum of two years' imprisonment) if defendant killed another in the good-faith-but-unreasonable belief that one or more of the statutory grounds of justification existed. However, in this case, the victim survived the attack, and defendant was convicted of first-degree assault (assault intended to cause and causing serious injury with a deadly weapon) carrying a penalty of 4 to

40 years' imprisonment. The court found the statutory scheme to violate equal protection, stating (573 P.2d at 97-98):

> In the present case, the intent and conduct proscribed by the first-degree assault statute and subsection (b) of the criminally-negligent homicide statute are not sufficiently distinguishable to justify a greater penalty when that conduct results in serious bodily injury rather than in death. . . .
>
> Accordingly, the judgment is reversed, and cause is remanded to the district court for a new trial. . . . If the affirmative defense is raised, and if the jury determines that the defendant acted with the good faith, but unreasonable belief, that his actions were justified, the sentence imposed can be no greater than that which could be imposed upon a defendant under the criminally-negligent homicide statute.

(*b*) *The Model Penal Code approach.* The Code takes an original approach to these problems. Section 2.02(10) provides:

> When the grade or degree of an offense depends on whether the offense is committed purposely, knowingly, recklessly or negligently, its grade or degree shall be the lowest for which the determinative kind of culpability is established with respect to any material element of the offense.

Section 2.02, Comment at 131-132 (Tent. Draft No. 4, 1955) states:

> Paragraph (10) is addressed to the case where the grade or degree of an offense is made to turn on whether it was committed purposely, knowingly, recklessly or negligently, a common basis of discrimination for the purposes of sentence. The position taken is that when distinctions of this kind are made, the degree of a conviction ought to be the lowest for which the determinative kind of culpability is established with respect to any material element of the offense. The theory is, of course, that when the kinds of culpability involved vary with respect to different material elements, it is the lowest common denominator that indicates the quality of the defendant's conduct.
>
> The best illustration is afforded by the case of homicide where an intentional killing is normally treated as an offense of higher degree than a homicide by negligence. But even though the actor meant to kill, he may have acted only negligently with respect to another material element of the offense, e.g., he may have deemed the homicide to be in necessary self-defense or necessary to prevent a felony or to effect arrest, without sufficient ground for such belief. For purposes of sentence, such a homicide ought to be viewed as reckless or as negligent, since recklessness or negligence is all that is established with respect to justifying elements as integral to the offense as the killing itself. A person who believes that justifying facts exist but has been reckless or negligent in so concluding presents from the point of view of sentence the same type of problem as a person who acts recklessly or negligently with respect to the creation of a risk of death. . . .

The drafting device through which the Model Penal Code achieves this result is to specify in the various justification provisions the circumstances that the actor must believe to exist in order for his or her action to be justified [1] and

---

1. Section 3.04(2) explicitly provides that "a person employing protective force may estimate the necessity thereof under the circumstances as he believes them to be when the force is used."

to employ the following general provision (§3.09(2)) to deal with mistaken belief in those circumstances:

> When the actor believes that the use of force upon or toward the person of another is necessary for any of the purposes for which such belief would establish a justification under §§3.03 to 3.08 but the actor is reckless or negligent in having such belief or in acquiring or failing to acquire any knowledge or belief which is material to the justifiability of his use of force, the justification afforded by those Sections is unavailable in a prosecution for an offense for which recklessness or negligence, as the case may be, suffices to establish culpability.

The approach has not been influential in state statutory reform. See Note, Justification: The Impact of the Model Penal Code on State Law Reform, 75 Colum. L. Rev. 914, 920 (1975).

NOTES AND QUESTIONS ON SELF-DEFENSE

There are a variety of other issues of self-defense that bear consideration at this point.

1. *Defense of another.* Though the universal view in this country makes justification turn on the reasonableness of the judgment of defendant in appraising the need to use the defensive force he used, a special problem has arisen when the actor acted in the defense of another person. The problem is often put in terms of whether defendant should be regarded as "standing in his own shoes," or "in the shoes" of the person in whose defense he acted. Is defendant exculpated if defendant reasonably believed he had to attack in order to save the person he reasonably took to be the victim? Or is defendant exculpated only if that other person in fact had a right to use defensive force?

The issue was clearly presented in People v. Young, 12 A.D.2d 262, 210 N.Y.S.2d 358 (1st Dept. 1961), *rev'd,* 11 N.Y.2d 274, 183 N.E.2d 319 (1962). In this case a 40-year-old Western Union messenger came upon two middle-aged men beating and struggling with a youth of 18. Believing the youth was being unlawfully assaulted, he entered the affray, in the course of which his leg locked with that of one of the older men, who suffered a broken leg. It turned out the older men were detectives in plain clothes making a lawful arrest. The Appellate Division reversed an assault conviction and, in reliance on Model Penal Code §3.05, rejected the "other person's shoes" doctrine, stating (210 N.Y.S.2d at 365):

> It is a sterile and desolate legal system that would exact punishment for an intentional assault from one like this defendant, who acted [reasonably] from the most commendable motives and without excessive force. Had the facts been as he thought them, he would have been a hero and not condemned as a criminal actor.

The New York Court of Appeals reversed, stating (183 N.E.2d at 319-320):

> [O]ne who goes to the aid of a third person does so at his own peril. While the doctrine espoused by the . . . court below may have support in some States, we feel that such a policy would not be conducive to an orderly society. . . . [T]he

right of a person to defend another ordinarily should not be greater than such person's right to defend himself.

The New York legislature had the last word. N.Y. Penal Law §35.15 now provides:

A person may . . . use physical force upon another person when and to the extent he reasonably believes such to be necessary to defend himself or a third person from what he reasonably believes to be the use or imminent use of unlawful physical force by such other person.

States are divided on the issue raised by the *Young* case. In some jurisdictions the law is in accord with that of the Appellate Division and the New York statute. See, e.g., United States v. Ochoa, 526 F.2d 1278 (5th Cir. 1976); Coleman v. State, 320 A.2d 740 (Del. 1974); Commonwealth v. Martin, 369 Mass. 640, 341 N.E.2d 885 (1976); Ky. Rev. Stat. §503.070. Other jurisdictions hold in accord with the New York Court of Appeals. See, e.g., State v. Gelinas, 417 A.2d 1381 (R.I. 1980); State v. Weniger, 55 Ohio St. 2d 336, 390 N.E.2d 801 (1979).

2. The imminence of the danger. (a) In State v. Huett, 340 Mo. 934, 950, 104 S.W.2d 252, 262 (1937), the court stated the generally prevailing requirement with respect to the timing of the feared danger. Upholding an instruction on self-defense requiring the jury to find a reasonable belief by defendant that his defensive action was necessary to prevent an "imminent" danger, the court stated:

The word "imminent" means, according to Webster's New International Dictionary, "threatening to occur immediately; near at hand, impending." The idea that the danger, in order to justify homicide on the ground of self-defense, must be, or must reasonably appear to the person claiming that defense to be, "imminent," "impending" or "about to fall" runs through all our decisions on that subject. It would be a work of supererogation to cite cases.

In place of the prevailing requirement that the danger reasonably apprehended be immediate or imminent, the Model Penal Code proposes that the actor believe the defensive force to be "immediately necessary . . . on the present occasion." Section 3.04(1). See §3.04(1), Comment at 17 (Tent. Draft No. 8, 1958).

(*b*) *Problem.* In an English motion picture, a cuckolded husband imprisons and chains his wife's latest lover in an abandoned cellar with the announced intention of killing him after the passage of sufficient time for the stir over his disappearance to quiet down, probably several months. Must the intended victim wait until the final moment when the husband is about to commit the fatal act, or may he kill the husband in self-defense at any time during the period of imprisonment that he can succeed in laying hands on him?

In State v. Schroeder, 199 Neb. 822, 261 N.W.2d 759 (1978), a 19-year-old inmate stabbed his older cell-mate at 1 A.M. while the latter was asleep and was convicted of assault with intent to inflict great bodily harm. The evidence was that the deceased had a reputation for sex and violence, that defendant had incurred a large gambling debt to deceased who threatened to make a "punk" out of him by selling his debt to another prisoner, that before going to bed the morning of the incident deceased said he might walk in his sleep and "collect" some of the money owed.

The majority found no error in the trial court's failure to give any instruction on self-defense. While Nebraska had adopted the Model Penal Code formulation, the court read it as making no change in the former Nebraska requirement of imminent danger. The court said (261 N.W.2d at 761):

> The problem in this case is that there was no evidence to sustain a finding that the defendant could believe an assault was imminent except the threat that Riggs had made before he went to bed. The general rule is that words alone are not sufficient justification for an assault. . . . There is a very real danger in a rule which would legalize preventive assaults involving the use of deadly force where there has been nothing more than threats. We conclude that the trial court did not err in refusing to instruct the jury as requested.

The dissent stated (id. at 761, 762):

> In this case the defendant was faced with a threat by Riggs that he would "collect some of this money I got owed to me tonight." The defendant could not be expected to remain awake all night, every night, waiting for the attack that Riggs had threatened to make. The defendant's evidence here was such that the jury could have found the defendant was justified in believing the use of force was necessary to protect himself against an attack by Riggs "on the present occasion."

3. Deadly force. Against what kinds of threats may deadly force be used? The recent tendency has been to confine its use to narrow bounds. See, e.g., State v. Clay, 297 N.C. 555, 256 S.E.2d 176, 182 (1979):

> [B]oth *Anderson* and *Fletcher* [two prior decisions of the North Carolina Supreme Court] may leave the impression that a defendant may assault another with a deadly weapon if it reasonably appears that such assault is necessary to protect the defendant from bodily injury or offensive physical contact. Notwithstanding the language in *Anderson* and *Fletcher,* we hold that a defendant may employ deadly force in self-defense *only* if it reasonably appears to be necessary to protect against death or great bodily harm. We define deadly force as force likely to cause death or great bodily harm. . . . In so holding, we expressly reject defendant's contention, and any implication in our cases in support thereof, that a defendant would be justified by the principles of self-defense in employing deadly force to protect against bodily injury or offensive physical contact. Our decision says, in effect, that where the assault being made upon defendant is insufficient to give rise to a reasonable apprehension of death or great bodily harm, then the use of deadly force by defendant to protect himself from bodily injury or offensive physical contact is excessive force as a matter of law. Although we may hear protestations to the contrary, this decision will not compel anyone "to submit in meekness to indignities or violence to his person merely because such indignities or violence stop short of threatening him with death or great bodily harm." In such cases, a person so accosted may use such force, short of deadly force, as reasonably appears to him to be necessary under the circumstances to prevent bodily injury or offensive physical contact. This decision precludes the use of deadly force to prevent bodily injury or offensive physical contact and in so doing recognizes the premium we place on human life. However, it does not preclude the use of deadly force where such force reasonably appears to be necessary to prevent death or great bodily harm.

The reasonableness of defendant's apprehension of death or great bodily harm must be determined by the jury on the basis of all the facts and circumstances as they appeared to defendant at the time. Among the circumstances to be considered by the jury are the size, age and strength of defendant's assailant in relation to that of defendant; the fierceness or persistence of the assault upon defendant; whether the assailant had or appeared to have a weapon in his possession; and the reputation of the assailant for danger and violence.

The Model Penal Code §3.04(2)(b) limits the use of deadly force to cases where the threatened danger is "death, serious bodily harm, kidnapping or sexual intercourse compelled by force or threat." Query: On what theory were the latter two dangers included?

The pattern of state statutes is described in Note, Justification: The Impact of the Model Penal Code on Statutory Reform, 75 Colum. L. Rev. 914, 933-934 (1975).

4. *The risk of injury to others.* In People v. Adams, 9 Ill. App. 3d 61, 291 N.E.2d 54, 55-56 (1972), defendant, acting in self-defense, shot and killed his assailant, Robinson, who was threatening his life. Deceased, Mary Davis, was at the time sitting in a car with some friends. One of defendant's bullets passed through Robinson's body and struck and killed Mary Davis, who was sitting next to him. Defendant was convicted of manslaughter of the woman. On appeal, the prosecution contended that:

[S]elf-defense does not necessarily protect an individual from criminal responsibility for all his acts performed in defending his life against a felonious assault, and that even though defendant's conduct here may have been justified as to Robinson nonetheless it constituted a reckless disregard for the consequences towards Mary Davis, and, as such, supported his conviction for involuntary manslaughter.

The court rejected these arguments and reversed the conviction, stating:

[I]f the circumstances are such that they would excuse the killing of an assailant in self-defense, the emergency will be held to excuse the person assailed from culpability, if in attempting to defend himself he unintentionally kills or injures a third person. . . .

We are aware that the above rule is not absolute and that . . . , it may be subject to modification depending on the circumstances involved. But we do not believe such circumstances present themselves in the case before us. There were other persons present in the car with defendant's assailant, but it was dark and defendant was being fired on at close range. He had very little time to think or assess the situation. He had to act immediately to protect himself from a man who had been drinking all day and who was not just threatening him but was shooting at him. Even under such circumstances defendant did not shoot wildly or carelessly. From the record it can be inferred that he hit his assailant with every shot and that the innocent victim was killed only as a result of a bullet passing through the body of the assailant. We conclude that under the circumstances of this case the killing of Mary Davis constituted no crime.

Suppose that defendant knew or should have known that there was a substantial possibility that in shooting at his assailant in self-defense one of the innocent persons in the car would be killed. For example, suppose he were armed only with a shotgun. Would the decision then have been otherwise? Or consider a more extreme situation in which defendant knew there was a high probability or a virtual certainty that in killing his assailant one or more of the others would also be killed. See the material on choice of evils, pages 769-788 infra and Kadish, Respect for Life and Regard for Rights in the Criminal Law, 64 Calif. L. Rev. 871, 888-894 (1976).

Compare §3.09(3) of the Model Penal Code:

> When the actor is justified under Sections 3.03 to 3.08 in using force upon or toward the person of another but he recklessly or negligently injures or creates a risk of injury to innocent persons, the justification afforded by these Sections is unavailable in a prosecution for such recklessness or negligence towards innocent persons.

5. *The innocent aggressor.* What difference does it make to the right to use force in self-defense that the source of the threat is not the usual wrongdoer, but a person who is not legally culpable? It is clear enough that a person may not employ an innocent person as a shield against an attack by an aggressor. But consider these cases in which the innocent person himself is the aggressor.

(a) A known psychotic inmate of a mental institution attacks a hospital physician with a kitchen knife. May the physician kill him if necessary to save her own life? On what theory?

(b) A five-year-old child picks up a loaded pistol and starts running toward a police officer. The child shouts that she is a robber who will shoot the police officer dead, then giggles, and pulls the trigger. The first shot misses, but she laughs, keeps approaching, and says she will shoot again. There is no cover or help available to the officer. Can the officer shoot at the child to stop her advance? On what theory?

(c) Consider the following hypotheticals and comments on them in R. Nozick, Anarchy, State and Utopia 34-35 (1974):

> [A] principle that prohibits physical aggression . . . does not prohibit use of force in defense against another party who is a threat, even though he is innocent and deserves no retribution. An *innocent threat* is someone who innocently is a causal agent in a process such that he would be an aggressor had he chosen to become such an agent. If someone picks up a third party and throws him at you down at the bottom of a deep well, the third party is innocent and a threat; had he chosen to launch himself at you in that trajectory he would be an aggressor. Even though the falling person would survive his fall onto you, may you use your ray gun to disintegrate the falling body before it crushes and kills you? Libertarian prohibitions are usually formulated so as to forbid using violence on innocent persons. But innocent threats, I think, are another matter to which different principles must apply. Thus, a full theory in this area also must formulate the *different* constraints on response to innocent threats. Further complications concern *innocent shields of threats,* those innocent persons who themselves are nonthreats but who are so situated that they will be damaged by the only means available for stopping the threat. Innocent persons strapped onto the front of the tanks of aggressors so that the tanks cannot be hit without also hitting them are innocent shields of threats. (Some uses of force on people to get at an aggressor do not act upon innocent shields of threats; for example, an aggressor's innocent child who is tortured in order to get the aggressor to stop wasn't *shielding* the parent.) May one

knowingly injure innocent shields? *If* one may attack an aggressor and injure an innocent shield, may the innocent shield fight back in self-defense (supposing that he cannot move against or fight the aggressor)? Do we get two persons battling each other in self-defense? Similarly, if you use force against an innocent threat to you, do you thereby become an innocent threat to him, so that he may now justifiably use additional force against you (supposing that he can do this, yet cannot prevent his original threateningness)? I tiptoe around these incredibly difficult issues here, merely noting that a view that says it makes nonaggression central must resolve them explicitly at some point.

The Model Penal Code deals with some of these issues through the definition of "unlawful force," the necessity to prevent which is the basis for justifying defensive force. See §3.11(1), Appendix to this casebook.

The Commentary states ((Tent. Draft No. 8, 1958) at 29):

> The reason for legitimizing protective force extends to cases where the force it is employed against is neither criminal nor actionable — so long as it is not affirmatively privileged. It must, for example, be permissible to defend against attacks by lunatics or children and defenses to liability such as duress, family relationship or diplomatic status are plainly immaterial. . . . Whatever may be thought in tort, it cannot be regarded as a crime to safeguard an innocent person, whether the actor or another, against threatened death or injury which is unprivileged, even though the source of the threat is free from fault. The definition assimilates such conduct, therefore, to unlawful force.

Query: Why can it "not be regarded as a crime to safeguard an innocent person . . . even though the source of the threat is free from fault?" Do the reasons have to do with the workability or the morality of the matter? Is there a moral basis for one innocent person's killing another innocent person, or perhaps even several others, because they have the misfortune to be a threat to his life? See Kadish, Respect for Life and Regard for Rights in the Criminal Law, 64 Calif. L. Rev. 871 (1976); Fletcher, Proportionality and the Psychotic Aggressor: A Vignette in Comparative Criminal Theory, 8 Israel L. Rev. 367 (1973).

6. *Burden of proof.* The majority of jurisdictions imposes the burden on the prosecution of disproving self-defense beyond a reasonable doubt once the issue is presented by the evidence. See Annot., 43 A.L.R.3d 221 (1972). Whether this rule is now constitutionally required turns on a reading of several recent Supreme Court decisions, which we explored at pages 67-82 supra.

7. *Exceptions to the right of self-defense.* In a number of situations, the law disallows the use of defensive force, even though defendant faces an imminent threat of injury or death from the unlawful action of another. These situations are explored in the cases that follow.

STATE v. ABBOTT

Supreme Court of New Jersey
36 N.J. 63, 174 A.2d 881 (1961)

WEINTRAUB, C.J. Frank Abbott was convicted of atrocious assault and battery. The Appellate Division affirmed . . . and we granted certification. . . .

Abbott shared a common driveway with his neighbors, Michael and Mary
Scarano. The Scaranos engaged a contractor to pave their portion. Abbott obtained some asphalt from the contractor and made a doorstop to keep his garage
door from swinging onto the Scaranos' property. Nicholas Scarano, who was
visiting with the Scaranos, his parents, objected to Abbott's innovation. After
some words between them a fist fight ensued.

Although Abbott managed to land the first punch, with which he sent Nicholas
to the ground, a jury could find Nicholas was the aggressor. At this point Michael
Scarano came at Abbott with a hatchet. Michael said the tool had just been
returned to him by the contractor, and denied he meant to use it as a weapon.
According to Abbott, Mary Scarano followed, armed with a carving knife and
large fork. The actors gave varying versions of what happened, but the end
result was that all of the Scaranos were hit by the hatchet. Nicholas received
severe head injuries. Abbott claimed he too suffered a laceration.

Abbott admitted he finally wrested the hatchet from Michael but denied he
wielded it at all. Rather he insisted that the Scaranos were injured during a
common struggle for the instrument. A jury could, however, find Abbott intentionally inflicted the blows.

Abbott was separately indicted for atrocious assault and battery upon each
of the Scaranos. There was a common trial of these indictments. The jury acquitted Abbott of the charges relating to Michael and Mary, but found him guilty
as to Nicholas.

The principal question is whether the trial court properly instructed the jury
upon the issue of self-defense. The trial court charged upon the subject of
excessive force as to which Abbott does not complain. It charged also upon
the subject of retreat, and it is here that error is alleged. Although the jury
could have found Abbott used excessive force, we cannot know whether the
jury found for him on that subject and convicted because he had failed to retreat
in accordance with the trial court's instruction.

As to retreat, the trial court charged upon two hypotheses. One was that
the critical events occurred upon Abbott's property. Upon that basis, the court
said Abbott could stand his ground, and, of course, of this Abbott does not
complain. The second hypothesis was that the alleged offense occurred upon
the common driveway. Presumably on the authority of State v. Pontery, 19 N.J.
457, 475, 117 A.2d 473 (1955), the trial court held that since all the principals
were equally entitled to be on the driveway, Abbott could not claim immunity
from the ordinary retreat rule. Abbott does not question that thesis, but disputes
the court's statement of the conditions under which an obligation to retreat
would arise. . . .

The subject of retreat usually arises in homicide matters. We will first discuss
it in that context, and then consider whether the principles apply to a charge
of atrocious assault and battery, and if they do, whether the trial court correctly
guided the jury in this difficult area.

We should make it clear that we are discussing the doctrine of retreat and
not the subject of the use of excessive force. If the force used was unnecessary
in its intensity, the claim of self-defense may fall for that reason. In the discussion
which follows we assume a defendant used no more force than he believed
necessary to protect himself in the circumstances as they reasonably appeared
to him, and consider only whether the claim of self-defense should be denied
because he could have avoided the use of that force by retreating.

The question whether one who is neither the aggressor nor a party to a mutual combat must retreat has divided the authorities. Self-defense is measured against necessity. . . . From that premise one could readily say there was no necessity to kill in self-defense if the use of deadly force could have been avoided by retreat. The critics of the retreat rule do not quarrel with the theoretical validity of this conclusion, but rather condemn it as unrealistic. The law of course should not denounce conduct as criminal when it accords with the behavior of reasonable men. Upon this level, the advocates of no-retreat say the manly thing is to hold one's ground and hence society should not demand what smacks of cowardice. Adherents of the retreat rule reply it is better that the assailed shall retreat than that the life of another be needlessly spent. They add that not only do right-thinking men agree, but further a rule so requiring may well induce others to adhere to that worthy standard of behavior. There is much dispute as to which view commands the support of ancient precedents, a question we think it would be profitless to explore.

Other jurisdictions are closely divided upon the retreat doctrine. It is said the preponderant view rejects it.[a] . . . Our Court of Errors and Appeals deliberately adopted the retreat rule with an awareness of the contending views. . . . The Model Penal Code embraces the retreat rule while acknowledging that on numerical balance a majority of the precedents oppose it. Model Penal Code §3.04, Comment 3, at p. 24 (Tent. Draft No. 8, 1958).

We are not persuaded to depart from the principle of retreat. We think it salutary if reasonably limited. Much of the criticism goes not to its inherent validity but rather to unwarranted applications of the rule. For example, it is correctly observed that one can hardly retreat from a rifle shot at close range. But if the weapon were a knife, a lead of a city block might well be enough. Again, the rule cannot be stated baldly, with indifference to the excitement of the occasion. As Mr. Justice Holmes cryptically put it, "Detached reflection cannot be demanded in the presence of an uplifted knife." Brown v. United States, 256 U.S. 335, 343 (1921). Such considerations, however, do not demand that a man should have the absolute right to stand his ground and kill in any and all situations. Rather they call for a fair and guarded statement of appropriate principles. . . .

We believe the following principles are sound:

1. The issue of retreat arises only if the defendant resorted to a deadly force. It is a deadly force which is not justifiable when an opportunity to retreat is at hand. Model Penal Code §3.04(2)(b)(iii). As defined in §3.11(2) a deadly force means "force which the actor uses with the purpose of causing or which he knows to create a substantial risk of causing death or serious bodily harm."

Hence it is not the nature of the force defended against which raises the

---

a. But a number of states have adopted the retreat rule in the course of recent statutory revisions. See, e.g., Conn. Gen. Stat. §53a-19(b); Del. Code Ann., tit. 11, §464(e); N.H. Rev. Stat. tit. 62, §627:4(III); N.Y. Penal Law §3515(2)(a). They all tend to build upon the Model Penal Code's formulation. The New York provision is typical: "(2) A person may not use deadly physical force upon another person under circumstances specified in subdivision one unless: (a) He reasonably believes that such other person is using or about to use deadly physical force. Even in such case, however, the actor may not use deadly physical force if he knows that he can with complete safety as to himself and others avoid the necessity of so doing by retreating; except that he is under no duty to retreat if he is: (i) in his dwelling and not the initial aggressor; or (ii) a peace officer or a person assisting a peace officer at the latter's direction, acting pursuant to section 35.30 [governing the use of physical force in making an arrest or in preventing an escape]."— EDS.

issue of retreat, but rather the nature of the force which the accused employed in his defense. If he does not resort to a deadly force, one who is assailed may hold his ground whether the attack upon him be of a deadly or some lesser character. Although it might be argued that a safe retreat should be taken if thereby the use of *any* force could be avoided, yet, as the comment in the Model Penal Code observes (at p. 23), "The logic of this position never has been accepted when moderate force is used in self-defense; here all agree that the actor may stand his ground and estimate necessity upon that basis." Hence, in a case like the present one, the jury should be instructed that Abbott could hold his ground when Nicholas came at him with his fists, and also when Michael and Mary came at him with the several instruments mentioned, and that the question of retreat could arise only if Abbott intended to use a deadly force.

2. What constitutes an opportunity to retreat which will defeat the right of self-defense? As §3.04(2)(b)(iii) of the Model Penal Code states, deadly force is not justifiable "if the actor *knows* that he can avoid the necessity of using such force *with complete safety* by retreating. . . ." We emphasize "knows" and "with complete safety." One who is wrongfully attacked need not risk injury by retreating, even though he could escape with something less than serious bodily injury. It would be unreal to require nice calculations as to the amount of hurt, or to ask him to endure any at all. And the issue is not whether in retrospect it can be found the defendant could have retreated unharmed. Rather the question is whether he knew the opportunity was there, and of course in that inquiry the total circumstances including the attendant excitement must be considered. We add that upon a retrial the facts as developed in the light of this principle may be such that Abbott would be entitled to an instruction that if his version of the approach by Michael and Mary is accepted, the issue of retreat must be resolved in Abbott's favor. . . .

As we have said, the subject of retreat arises most often in homicide cases. It is equally pertinent if the charge is assault with intent to kill. . . . Here the charge is atrocious assault and battery, a crime which involves vicious or brutal conduct. . . . An intent to kill is not an ingredient of that offense, but an intent to do serious bodily harm would seem to be implicit. The doctrine of retreat reflects a policy with respect to the use of deadly force, and the same policy considerations equally obtain if the end result is something less than murder. The Appellate Division held the doctrine applicable to atrocious assault and battery. The comment to Article 3 of the Model Penal Code (at p. 3) expresses the same view, saying, "If the particular force, for example, would be unjustifiable in a prosecution for homicide it should be equally unjustifiable if the victim survives and what is charged is an assault." This seems sound, and hence an instruction upon the subject is appropriate in a trial for atrocious assault and battery, but the instruction should be expressly centered about the use of deadly force.

We turn to the instruction of the trial court. It reads:

> . . . If you find the charges involved or either of them happened on the joint or common driveway and that the defendant had an available opportunity to retreat and you also find that he was or appeared to be threatened by assault and battery with imminent danger of life or serious bodily harm, again there is no duty to retreat. On the other hand, under the latter circumstances, if you find that he did not appear to be threatened by assault and battery with imminent danger of

life or great bodily harm, he had a duty to retreat and if he failed to retreat the defense of self-defense would not avail him and would not constitute a defense if you find that he had a duty to retreat.

It is at once apparent that the charge consists of abstract propositions, unanchored to the factual setting. It will be recalled the encounter had two phases, although one quickly followed the other. The first phase was an unarmed attack by Nicholas which Abbott met in kind; the second involved, as the jury could find, an attack or apparent attack by hatchet in the hands of Michael and by kitchen utensils allegedly wielded by Mary, both aided by Nicholas who had arisen from the initial punch. We have no way of knowing whether the jury understood Abbott was required to retreat when first assailed by Nicholas alone. The jury may well have so gathered since the instruction excluded self-defense "if you find that he [Abbott] did *not* appear to be threatened by assault and battery with imminent danger of life or great bodily harm," and of course Nicholas's attack with his fists readily fitted within those terms.

The State asks us to assume the jury understood an unarticulated premise, i.e., that the court was referring solely to the hatchet affair. If we could so assume, still under the instruction the obligation to retreat would depend upon the nature of the attack upon Abbott rather than the amount of force Abbott intended to employ. In short, there was no reference to the use of a deadly force by Abbott. And if we should read the charge in still another way, to wit, that the court was merely defining its prior reference to "an available opportunity" to retreat and hence meant that the opportunity was not "available" if retreat would have subjected Abbott to imminent danger to his life or great bodily harm but was "available" if he could get away with a hurt of lesser character, still the charge would be incorrect. This is so because there is no obligation to retreat unless retreat can be effected "with complete safety," and indeed with knowledge that retreat can be so effected. Further, upon that interpretation, the instruction would be devoid of any statement of the facts prerequisite for consideration of the subject, i.e., an intent by the defendant to use a deadly force.

We have said enough to indicate the insufficiency of the charge. Even upon study and restudy we are not sure we can extract the thesis the trial court held. A jury which listens to a single reading of an instruction cannot be expected to debate its meaning and reach a correct view of it. A charge should be a clear, unambiguous guide related to the evidence in the case. The conviction must be reversed. . . .

PROBLEMS

1. In jurisdictions adhering to the duty of retreat before deadly force may be used, an exception is commonly made when the defendant is attacked in his own home. Thus, in People v. Tomlins, 213 N.Y. 240, 243, 107 N.E. 496, 497 (1914), Judge Cardozo, in reversing a conviction of a father for killing his son in his own home, stated:

It is not now and never has been the law that a man assailed in his own dwelling is bound to retreat. If assailed there, he may stand his ground and resist the attack.

He is under no duty to take to the fields and the highways, a fugitive from his own home. More than 200 years ago it was said by Lord Chief Justice Hale (1 Hale's Pleas of the Crown, 486): In case a man "is assailed in his own house, he need not flee as far as he can, as in other cases of se defendendo, for he hath the protection of his house to excuse him from flying, as that would be to give up the protection of his house to his adversary by flight." Flight is for sanctuary and shelter, and shelter, if not sanctuary, is in the home. That there is, in such a situation, no duty to retreat is, we think, the settled law in the United States as in England. It was so held by the United States Supreme Court in Beard v. United States, 158 U.S. 550.

Questions: What basis is there for this exception? Does it apply when the defendant is attacked: In his place of work or business? State v. Bartta, 242 Iowa 1308, 49 N.W.2d 866 (1951) (yes); State v. Turner, 95 Utah 129, 79 P.2d 46 (1938) (yes); Wilson v. State, 69 Ga. 224 (1882) (no). See Annots., 52 A.L.R.2d 1458 (1957) and 41 A.L.R.3d 584 (1972). In his automobile? Weaver v. State, 35 Ala. App. 158, 44 So. 2d 773 (1950) (no). In another's home as a guest? Kelley v. State, 226 Ala. 80, 145 So. 816 (1933) (yes). In his private club? State v. Marlowe, 120 S.C. 205, 112 S.E. 921 (1922) (yes).

Is the exception when one is attacked in his own home, or in any of the extensions thereof, a defensible exception to the retreat rule?

In evaluating the rationale of this exception, consider further whether it should matter that the deceased-aggressor is another occupant or an intruder. Some cases decline to make a distinction, holding one need not retreat in one's home even as against another occupant. See People v. Tomlins, supra. Other courts have disagreed. See Oney v. Commonwealth, 225 Ky. 590, 9 S.W.2d 723 (1928); State v. Pontery, 19 N.J. 457, 117 A.2d 473 (1955). The Restatement of Torts §62(2)(a) makes the distinction so far as civil liability is concerned.

2. In jurisdictions following the retreat rule, when does the duty to retreat arise? (1) Suppose a friend warns D, who is on duty picketing a struck supermarket, that V has just set out with a knife to kill D. D remains where he is. (2) Ten minutes later D sees V a block away hobbling in his direction with the aid of a crutch. D still remains where he is. (3) D watches V carefully and as V gets within 20 feet of D, he pulls out a knife and screams he is going to kill D. D still remains where he is. (4) As V gets within reach, he raises his knife to strike, and D shoots him dead. Query: At what point was D obliged to retreat in order to maintain his right to kill in self-defense? Cf. Regina v. Field, [1972] Crim. L. Rev. 435, where a comparable case is briefly noted. The report indicates that the court reversed a conviction because the instruction could have led the jury to believe that if defendant could, without difficulty and reasonably, have left the place where he was before his attackers arrived, as the result of the notice others had given him, he had a duty to do so and it was not reasonable for him to stay and defend himself. The report summarizes the court's reasoning as follows ([1972] Crim. L. Rev. 435-436):

It was not the law that a man could be driven off the streets and compelled not to go to a place where he might lawfully be because he had reason to believe that he would be confronted by people intending to attack him. No duty to retreat could arise until the parties were at any rate within sight of each other and the threat to the person relying on self-defence so imminent that he was able to demonstrate that he did not mean to fight. Although it was a matter of degree, no one was obliged to get out of the way of possible attackers. The relevance of *F*'s conduct was that it was a factor for the jury to consider when deciding whether it was reasonable for him to use force, and to use a knife.

Is this the right approach to the question? Or is it rather that the duty to retreat arises only at the point where killing in self-defense is otherwise justified?

<hr>

UNITED STATES v. PETERSON [2]

United States Court of Appeals, District of Columbia Circuit
483 F.2d 1222 (1973)

ROBINSON, J. Indicted for second-degree murder, and convicted by a jury of manslaughter as a lesser included offense, Bennie L. Peterson urges . . . reversal. . . . He complains . . . that the judge . . . erred in the instructions given the jury in relation to his claim that the homicide was committed in self-defense. [The] error alleged was an instruction that the jury might consider whether Peterson was the aggressor in the altercation that immediately foreran the homicide. . . . After careful study of these arguments in light of the trial record, we affirm Peterson's conviction.

The events immediately preceding the homicide are not seriously in dispute. The version presented by the Government's evidence follows. Charles Keitt, the deceased, and two friends drove in Keitt's car to the alley in the rear of Peterson's house to remove the windshield wipers from the latter's wrecked car. While Keitt was doing so, Peterson came out of the house into the back yard to protest. After a verbal exchange, Peterson went back into the house, obtained a pistol, and returned to the yard. In the meantime, Keitt had reseated himself in his car, and he and his companions were about to leave.

Upon his reappearance in the yard, Peterson paused briefly to load the pistol. "If you move," he shouted to Keitt, "I will shoot." He walked to a point in the yard slightly inside a gate in the rear fence and, pistol in hand, said, "If you come in here I will kill you." Keitt alighted from his car, took a few steps toward Peterson and exclaimed, "What the hell do you think you are going to do with that?" Keitt then made an about-face, walked back to his car and got a lug wrench. With the wrench in a raised position, Keitt advanced toward Peterson, who stood with the pistol pointed toward him. Peterson warned Keitt not to "take another step" and, when Keitt continued onward shot him in the face from a distance of about ten feet. Death was apparently instantaneous . . .

. . . Peterson's complaints centers upon an instruction that the right to use deadly force in self-defense is not ordinarily available to one who provokes a conflict or is the aggressor in it. Mere words, the judge explained, do not constitute provocation or aggression; and if Peterson precipitated the altercation but thereafter withdrew from it in good faith and so informed Keitt by words or acts, he was justified in using deadly force to save himself from imminent danger or death or grave bodily harm. And, the judge added, even if Keitt was the aggressor and Peterson was justified in defending himself, he was not entitled

<hr>

2. Portions of this opinion were reproduced at the beginning of this chapter. See page 721.

to use any greater force than he had reasonable ground to believe and actually believed to be necessary for that purpose. Peterson contends that there was no evidence that he either caused or contributed to the conflict, and that the instructions on the topic could only [have] misled the jury.

It has long been accepted that one cannot support a claim of self-defense by a self-generated necessity to kill. The right of homicidal self-defense is granted only to those free from fault in the difficulty; it is denied to slayers who incite the fatal attack, encourage the fatal quarrel or otherwise promote the necessitous occasion for taking life. The fact that the deceased struck the first blow, fired the first shot or made the first menacing gesture does not legalize the self-defense claim if in fact the claimant was the actual provoker. In sum, one who is the aggressor in a conflict culminating in death cannot invoke the necessities of self-preservation. Only in the event that he communicates to his adversary his intent to withdraw and in good faith attempts to do so is he restored to his right of self-defense.

This body of doctrine traces its origin to the fundamental principle that a killing in self-defense is excusable only as a matter of genuine necessity. Quite obviously, a defensive killing is unnecessary if the occasion for it could have been averted, and the roots of that consideration run deep with us. . . .

In the case at bar, the trial judge's charge fully comported with these governing principles. The remaining question, then, is whether there was evidence to make them applicable to the case. A recapitulation of the proofs shows beyond peradventure that there was. . . .

The evidence is uncontradicted that when Peterson reappeared in the yard with his pistol, Keitt was about to depart the scene. . . . The uncontroverted fact that Keitt was leaving shows plainly that so far as he was concerned the confrontation was ended. It demonstrates just as plainly that even if he had previously been the aggressor, he no longer was.

Not so with Peterson, however, as the undisputed evidence made clear. Emerging from the house with the pistol, he paused in the yard to load it, and to command Keitt not to move. He then walked through the yard to the rear gate and, displaying his pistol, dared Keitt to come in, and threatened to kill him if he did. While there appears to be no fixed rule on the subject, the cases hold, and we agree, that an affirmative unlawful act reasonably calculated to produce an affray foreboding injurious or fatal consequences is an aggression which, unless renounced, nullifies the right of homicidal self-defense. We cannot escape the abiding conviction that the jury could readily find Peterson's challenge to be a transgression of that character.

The situation at bar is not unlike that presented in *Laney*.[66] There the accused, chased along the street by a mob threatening his life, managed to escape through an areaway between two houses. In the back yard of one of the houses, he checked a gun he was carrying and then returned to the areaway. The mob beset him again, and during an exchange of shots one of its members was killed by a bullet from the accused's gun. In affirming a conviction of manslaughter, the court reasoned: "It is clearly apparent . . . that, when defendant escaped from the mob into the back yard . . . he was in a place of comparative safety, from which, if he desired to go home, he could have gone by the back way, as he subsequently did. The mob had turned its attention to a house on

---

66. Laney v. United States, 294 Fed. 412 (1923).

the opposite side of the street. According to Laney's testimony, there was shooting going on in the street. His appearance on the street at that juncture could
mean nothing but trouble for him. Hence, when he adjusted his gun and stepped
out into the areaway, he had every reason to believe that his presence there
would provoke trouble. We think his conduct in adjusting his revolver and going
into the areaway was such as to deprive him of any right to invoke the plea of
self-defense."

Similarly, in Rowe v. United States,[68] the accused was in the home of friends
when an argument, to which the friends became participants, developed in the
street in front. He left, went to his nearby apartment for a loaded pistol and
returned. There was testimony that he then made an insulting comment, drew
the pistol and fired a shot into the ground. In any event, when a group of
five men began to move toward him, he began to shoot at them, killing two,
and wounding a third. We observed that the accused "left an apparently safe
haven to arm himself and return to the scene," and that "he inflamed the situation
with his words to the men gathered there, even though he could have returned
silently to the safety of the [friends'] porch." We held that "[t]hese facts could
have led the jury to conclude that [the accused] returned to the scene to stir
up further trouble, if not actually to kill anyone, and that his actions instigated
the men into rushing him. Self-defense may not be claimed by one who deliberately places himself in a position where he has reason to believe "his presence
. . . would provoke trouble." We noted the argument "that a defendant may
claim self-defense if he arms himself in order to proceed upon his normal activities, even if he realizes that danger may await him"; we responded by pointing
out "that the jury could have found that the course of action defendant here
followed was for an unlawful purpose." We accordingly affirmed his conviction
of manslaughter over his objection that an acquittal should have been directed.

We are brought much the readier to the same conclusion here. We think
the evidence plainly presented an issue of fact as to whether Peterson's conduct
was an invitation to and provocation of the encounter which ended in the fatal
shot. We sustain the trial judge's action in remitting that issue for the jury's
determination.

NOTES AND QUESTIONS

1. How should the problem of the initial aggressor be treated when the aggression has proceeded to the point of a physical attack on defendant? See Model
Penal Code §3.04, Comment at 21 (Tent. Draft No. 8, 1958):

> The typical case to be imagined in this: *A* attacks with his fists; *B* defends himself
> and knocks *A* down, then starts to batter *A*'s head savagely against the floor. *A*
> manages to rise and, since *B* is still attacking him and *A* now reasonably fears
> that if he is thrown again he will be killed, he uses a knife. *B* is killed or seriously
> wounded.
>
> If no special rule is devised for the case, the solution under the Code provisions
> is as follows:
>
> *B* is entitled to defend himself against *A*'s attack but only to the extent of using
> moderate, non-deadly force. He exceeds the bounds of necessary force, however,

68. Rowe v. United States, 370 F.2d 240 (D.C. Cir. 1966).

when, reducing *A* to helplessness he batters his head on the floor. Since this excessive force is, in its turn, unlawful, *A* is entitled to defend himself against it and, if he believes that he is then in danger of death or serious bodily harm without apparent opportunity for safe retreat, to use his knife in self-protection. Thus *A* is criminally liable for his initial battery on *B* but not for the ultimate homicide or wounding.

Query: What would have been the result in the *Peterson* case if the Model Penal Code's approach had been followed?

Note that, in view of its approach to the problem of the initial aggressor, the Code has no general provision whereby the right of such a person to self-defense is lost, with one exception — the case, in which the actor provoked the victim's use of force purposely in order to kill the victim in "self-defense." Section 3.04(b)(i).

Compare N.Y. Penal Law §35.15:

> 1. A person may, subject to the provisions of subdivision two [governing deadly force],[a] use physical force upon another person when and to the extent he reasonably believes such to be necessary to defend himself or a third person from what he reasonably believes to be the use or imminent use of unlawful physical force by such other person, unless: . . .
>
>   (a) The latter's conduct was provoked by the actor himself with intent to cause physical injury to another person; or
>   (b) The actor was the initial aggressor; except that in such case his use of physical force is nevertheless justifiable if he had withdrawn from the encounter and effectively communicated such withdrawal to such other person but the latter persists in continuing the incident by the use or threatened imminent use of unlawful physical force. . . .

Query: What are the differences between the Model Penal Code and New York approaches? How would the *Peterson* case have been decided under the New York statute?

2. How far should the doctrine of fault-forfeiting self-defense be extended? Suppose defendant is discovered in flagrante delicto by the woman's husband, who, enraged by the discovery, attacks defendant. Has defendant lost his right of self-defense, having become, in a way, the aggressor, by offering this provocation to the husband? Some courts have held affirmatively. See Barger v. State, 235 Md. 556, 202 A.2d 344 (1964); Annot., Relationship with assailant's wife as provocation depriving defendant of right of self-defense, 9 A.L.R.3d 926 (1966).

<hr>

PEOPLE v. CURTIS

Supreme Court of California
70 Cal. 2d 347, 450 P.2d 33 (1969)

Mosk, J. Defendant Albert Allen Curtis appeals from a conviction of battery upon a peace officer, a felony. . . .

<hr>

a. Subdivision 2 generally precludes use of deadly physical force unless the actor reasonably believes that the other person is himself using or about to use deadly force. — Eds.

Defendant was arrested on the night of July 9, 1966, by Lt. Riley of the Stockton Police Department. Riley was investigating a report of a prowler and had received a cursory description of the suspect as a male Negro, about six feet tall, wearing a white shirt and tan trousers. While cruising the neighborhood in his patrol car, the officer observed defendant, who matched the foregoing general description, walking along the street. Riley pulled up next to defendant and called to him to stop; defendant complied. The officer then emerged from his patrol car in full uniform and told defendant he was under arrest and would have to come along with him. Riley reached for the arm of defendant, and the latter attempted to back away. A violent struggle ensued, during which both men were injured, and defendant was finally subdued and taken into custody by several officers.

Defendant was subsequently acquitted of a charge of burglary, but was convicted of battery upon a peace officer. . . .

Defendant initially contends that his arrest was unlawful due to a lack of probable cause and that it was accomplished by the use of excessive force, and therefore his resistance was justified. Under the general common law rule prevailing in most states, an unlawful arrest may be resisted reasonably, and excessive force used by an officer in effecting an arrest may be countered lawfully. Until 1957, this rule prevailed in California. However, as we shall first discuss, Penal Code section 834a, enacted in 1957, revised the first aspect of that rule.

Section 834a provides:

> If a person has knowledge, or by the exercise of reasonable care, should have knowledge, that he is being arrested by a peace officer, it is the duty of such person to refrain from using force or any weapon to resist such arrest. . . .

We hold . . . that section 834a prohibits forceful resistance to unlawful as well as lawful arrests. Immediately, however, we are met with a challenge to the constitutionality of that construction; it is said to violate the Fourth Amendment's prohibition against unreasonable seizures and the due process clause of the Fourteenth Amendment.

An arrest is a "seizure" and an arrest without a warrant or probable cause is "unreasonable" within the purview of the Fourth Amendment. . . . If section 834a, by eliminating the remedy of self-help, facilitates or sanctions arrests which are by definition unlawful, it could be urged with considerable persuasion that defendant's constitutional rights would be violated by the statute.

While defendant's rights are no doubt violated when he is arrested and detained a matter of days or hours without probable cause, we conclude the state in removing the right to resist does not contribute to or effectuate this deprivation of liberty. In a day when police are armed with lethal and chemical weapons, and possess scientific communication and detection devices readily available for use, it has become highly unlikely that a suspect, using *reasonable* force, can escape from or effectively deter an arrest, whether lawful or unlawful. His accomplishment is generally limited to temporary evasion, merely rendering the officer's task more difficult or prolonged. Thus self-help as a practical remedy is anachronistic, whatever may have been its original justification or efficacy in an era when the common law doctrine permitting resistance evolved. . . . Indeed, self-help not infrequently causes far graver consequences for both the officer and the suspect than does the unlawful arrest itself. Accordingly, the state, in deleting the right to resist, has not actually altered or diminished the remedies available against the illegality of an arrest without probable cause, it has merely required a person to submit peacefully to the inevitable and to pursue his available remedies through the orderly judicial process.

We are not unmindful that under present conditions the available remedies for unlawful arrest — release followed by civil or criminal action against the offending officer — may be deemed inadequate. . . . However, this circumstance does not elevate physical resistance to anything other than the least effective and desirable of all possible remedies; as such its rejection, particularly when balanced against the state's interest in discouraging violence, cannot realistically be considered an affirmative "seizure" or deprivation of liberty. . . .

Our task, however, is by no means completed with the foregoing construction of section 834a. Defendant was charged not with simply battery, a misdemeanor, but with battery upon a peace officer "engaged in the performance of his duties," a felony under Penal Code, section 243.[a] Unlike section 834a, which had no predecessor when enacted in 1957, the language of section 243, speaking in terms of the officer's "duty," has been incorporated in section 148 of the Penal Code since 1872. The latter section makes it a misdemeanor to resist, delay or obstruct an officer in the discharge of "any duty of his office." Section 148 has long been construed by the courts as applying only to lawful arrests, because "An officer is under no duty to make an unlawful arrest." . . . Even if section 834a now makes it a *citizen's* duty not to resist an unlawful arrest, this change in the law in no way purports to include an unlawful arrest within the performance of an *officer's* duty.

Moreover, simply as a matter of statutory construction, it is clear that section 834a was meant at most to eliminate the common law defense of resistance to unlawful arrest, and not to make such resistance a new substantive crime. . . . Therefore we must construe section 243, like section 148, as excluding unlawful arrests from its definition of "duty." This in no way thwarts the legislative purpose to consign to the courtroom all controversies over legality. . . . We confirm that a resisting defendant commits a public offense; but if the arrest is ultimately determined factually to be unlawful, the defendant can be validly convicted only of simple assault or battery. Cases holding or implying the contrary are disapproved.

Defendant contends that his arrest was not only lacking in probable cause and thus unlawful, but also was accomplished with excessive force and hence he was justified in employing counterforce in self-defense. Some courts appear to have incorrectly treated these two problems unitarily . . . as if a technically unlawful arrest were identical with an overly forceful arrest.

There are, however, two distinct and separate rights at stake. The common law rule allowing resistance to technically unlawful arrests protects a person's freedom from unreasonable seizure and confinement; the rule allowing resistance to excessive force, which applies during a technically lawful *or* unlawful arrest,

---

a. "When [a battery] is committed against the person of a peace officer . . . , and the person committing the offense knows or reasonably should know that such victim is a peace officer . . . engaged in the performance of his duties, and such peace officer . . . is engaged in the performance of his duties, the offense shall be punished by imprisonment in the county jail not exceeding one year or by imprisonment in the state prison for not less than 1 or more than 10 years."— EDs.

protects a person's right to bodily integrity and permits resort to self-defense. Liberty can be restored through legal processes, but life and limb cannot be repaired in a courtroom. Therefore any rationale, pragmatic or constitutional, for outlawing resistance to unlawful arrests and resolving the dispute over legality in the courts has no determinative application to the right to resist excessive force. The commentators are unanimous on this point . . . , and the Model Penal Code states it explicitly.[7] . . .

To summarize, then, construing sections 834a and 243, it is now the law of California that a person may not use force to resist any arrest, lawful or unlawful, except that he may use reasonable force to defend life and limb against excessive force; but if it should be determined that resistance was not thus justified, the felony provisions of section 243 apply when the arrest is lawful, and if the arrest is determined to be unlawful the defendant may be convicted only of a misdemeanor.

We now apply the foregoing principles to the facts before us. First, as to the lawfulness of the arrest, it appears that the officer lacked probable cause when he arrested defendant. . . .

The question of the exercise of reasonable force and the right to self-defense, which we emphasize is distinct from that of the lawfulness of the arrest, is for the trier of fact to determine. Here the jury had before it evidence which could justify a finding either way, depending upon the credibility of witnesses and the weight of the evidence. The court's instructions merely quoted or paraphrased the Penal Code sections regarding the privilege of self-defense, the duty not to resist an arrest, and an officer's privilege to use reasonable force in effecting an arrest. In view of our conclusions on the law, we must hold that the jury was not adequately instructed as to the rights and duties of the respective parties. . . .

The judgment is reversed.

NOTES

1. The rule in many jurisdictions, contrary to that in California, is that a person is privileged to use such force as is necessary, short of deadly force, to prevent the effectuation of an unlawful arrest. See Annot., 44 A.L.R.3d 1078 (1972). Where a person employs deadly force for this purpose, such jurisdictions follow one of two lines of reasoning (Davis v. State, 204 Md. 44, 53-54, 102 A.2d 816, 820-821 (1954)):

> One says that once the illegality of the arrest is established, the degree of homicide cannot be greater than manslaughter unless malice is shown. The second major line of cases recognizes the wisdom and necessity of the social policy but refuses to permit a reduction of the grade of the homicide to come about automatically.

7. Model Penal Code (Tent. Draft No. 8, 1958) section 3.04. The comments thereto state, at page 19: "The paragraph, it should be noted, forbids the use of force for the purpose of preventing an arrest; it has *no application when the actor apprehends bodily injury,* as when the arresting officer unlawfully employs or threatens deadly force, unless the actor knows that he is in no peril greater than arrest if he submits to the assertion of authority." (Italics added.) . . . [For a recent case upholding the right of self-defense against excessive police force, see State v. Mulvihill, 105 N.J. Super. 458, 253 A.2d 175 (1970).]

These cases apply a subjective standard and hold that the accused must in fact have been filled with passion aroused by the illegal arrest sufficient to meet the usual provocation tests, if murder is to be reduced to manslaughter.

2. Defending the view that resistance is allowable, the New York Court of Appeals stated (People v. Cherry, 307 N.Y. 308, 310-311, 121 N.E.2d 238, 240 (1954)):

> Whether or not the police officers exhibited their badges to defendant is completely beside the point. A badge may not substitute for a warrant of arrest, nor excuse its absence, when one is required. Lacking the essential warrant, having abused the authority which was their trust, the officers stood bereft of their usual prerogatives and whether or not defendant believed that they were police officers he had a right to resist, and that quite apart from any fear or threat of physical harm and injury. For most people, an illegal arrest is an outrageous affront and intrusion — the more offensive because under the color of law — to be resisted as energetically as a violent assault.

See also Chevigny, The Right to Resist an Unlawful Arrest, 78 Yale L.J. 1128 (1969). New York law is now in accord with that of California; see N.Y. Penal Law §35.27. A number of states have made a similar change by statute (see, e.g., Del. Code Ann. tit. 11, §464(d); Conn. Gen. Stat. Ann. §53a-23) or by common law development. See Miller v. State, 462 P.2d 421 (Alaska 1969); State v. Koonce, 89 N.J. Super. 169, 214 A.2d 428 (1965). The Model Penal Code reached the same conclusion (§3.04, Comment at 19 (Tent. Draft No. 8, 1958)):

> [T]here ought not be a privilege to employ force against a public officer who, to the actor's knowledge, is attempting only to arrest him and subject him to the processes of law. It should be possible to provide adequate remedies against illegal arrest, without permitting the arrested person to resort to force — a course of action highly likely to result in greater injury even to himself than the detention.

2. Protection of Property and Law Enforcement

PEOPLE v. CEBALLOS
Supreme Court of California
12 Cal. 3d 470, 526 P.2d 241 (1974)

BURKE, J. Don Ceballos was found guilty by a jury of assault with a deadly weapon (Pen. Code, §245). Imposition of sentence was suspended and he was placed on probation. . . .

Defendant lived alone in a home in San Anselmo. The regular living quarters were above the garage, but defendant sometimes slept in the garage and had about $2,000 worth of property there.

In March 1970 some tools were stolen from defendant's home. On May 12, 1970, he noticed the lock on his garage doors was bent and pry marks were on one of the doors. The next day he mounted a loaded .22 caliber pistol in the garage. The pistol was aimed at the center of the garage doors and was connected by a wire to one of the doors so that the pistol would discharge if the door was opened several inches.

The damage to defendant's lock had been done by a 16-year-old boy named Stephen and a 15-year-old boy named Robert. On the afternoon of May 15, 1970, the boys returned to defendant's house while he was away. Neither boy was armed with a gun or knife. After looking in the windows and seeing no one, Stephen succeeded in removing the lock on the garage doors with a crowbar, and, as he pulled the door outward, he was hit in the face with a bullet from the pistol.

Stephen testified: He intended to go into the garage "[f]or musical equipment" because he had a debt to pay to a friend. His "way of paying that debt would be to take [defendant's] property and sell it" and use the proceeds to pay the debt. He "wasn't going to do it [i.e., steal] for sure, necessarily." He was there "to look around," and "getting in, I don't know if I would have actually stolen."

Defendant, testifying in his own behalf, admitted having set up the trap gun. He stated that after noticing the pry marks on his garage door on May 12, he felt he should "set up some kind of a trap, something to keep the burglar out of my home." When asked why he was trying to keep the burglar out, he replied, ". . . Because somebody was trying to steal my property . . . and I don't want to come home some night and have the thief in there . . . usually a thief is pretty desperate . . . and . . . they just pick up a weapon . . . if they don't have one . . . and do the best they can."

When asked by the police shortly after the shooting why he assembled the trap gun, defendant stated that "he didn't have much and he wanted to protect what he did have."

. . . [T]he jury found defendant guilty of assault with a deadly weapon. An assault is "an unlawful attempt, coupled with a present ability, to commit a violent injury on the person of another." (Pen. Code, §240.)

Defendant contends that had he been present he would have been justified in shooting Stephen since Stephen was attempting to commit burglary, that under cases such as United States v. Gilliam, 25 Fed. Cas. p. 1319, No. 15, 205a, defendant had a right to do indirectly what he could have done directly, and that therefore any attempt by him to commit a violent injury upon Stephen was not "unlawful" and hence not an assault. The People argue that the rule in *Gilliam* is unsound, that as a matter of law a trap gun constitutes excessive force, and that in any event the circumstances were not in fact such as to warrant the use of deadly force. . . .

In the United States, courts have concluded that a person may be held criminally liable under statutes proscribing homicides and shooting with intent to injure, or civilly liable, if he sets upon his premises a deadly mechanical device and that device kills or injures another. . . . However, an exception to the rule that there may be criminal and civil liability for death or injuries caused by such a device has been recognized where the intrusion is, in fact, such that the person, were he present, would be justified in taking the life or inflicting the bodily harm with his own hands. . . .

Allowing persons, at their own risk, to employ deadly mechanical devices imperils the lives of children, firemen and policemen acting within the scope of their employment, and others. Where the actor is present, there is always the possibility he will realize that deadly force is not necessary, but deadly mechanical devices are without mercy or discretion. Such devices "are silent instrumentalities of death. They deal death and destruction to the innocent as well as the criminal intruder without the slightest warning. The taking of human life [or infliction of great bodily injury] by such means is brutally savage and inhuman." (See State v. Plumlee, . . . 149 So. 425, 430).

It seems clear that the use of such devices should not be encouraged. Moreover, whatever may be thought in torts, the foregoing rule setting forth an exception to liability for death or injuries inflicted by such devices "is inappropriate in penal law for it is obvious that it does not prescribe a workable standard of conduct; liability depends upon fortuitous results." (See Model Penal Code (Tent. Draft No. 8), §3.06, com. 15.) We therefore decline to adopt that rule in criminal cases.

Furthermore, even if that rule were applied here, as we shall see, defendant was not justified in shooting Stephen. Penal Code section 197 provides:

> Homicide is . . . justifiable . . . 1. When resisting any attempt to murder any person, or to commit a felony, or to do some great bodily injury upon any person; or, 2. When committed in defense of habitation, property, or person, against one who manifestly intends or endeavors, by violence or surprise, to commit a felony. . . .

Since a homicide is justifiable under the circumstances specified in section 197, a fortiori an attempt to commit a violent injury upon another under those circumstances is justifiable.

By its terms subdivision 1 of Penal Code section 197 appears to permit killing to prevent any "felony," but in view of the large number of felonies today and the inclusion of many that do not involve a danger of serious bodily harm, a literal reading of the section is undesirable. People v. Jones, 191 Cal. App. 2d 478, 481, in rejecting the defendant's theory that her husband was about to commit the felony of beating her (Pen. Code §273d) [a] and that therefore her killing him to prevent him from doing so was justifiable, stated that Penal Code section 197 "does no more than codify the common law and should be read in light of it." *Jones* read into section 197, subdivision 1, the limitation that the felony be "some atrocious crime attempted to be committed by force." *Jones* further stated, "the punishment provided by a statute is not necessarily an adequate test as to whether life may be taken for in some situations it is too artificial and unrealistic. We must look further into the character of the crime and the manner of its perpetration. . . . *When these do not reasonably create a fear of great bodily harm,* as they could not if defendant apprehended only a misdemeanor assault, *there is no cause for the exaction of a human life.*" (Italics added. . . .)

Jones involved subdivision 1 of Penal Code section 197, but subdivision 2 of that section is likewise so limited. The term "violence or surprise" in subdivision 2 is found in common law authorities . . . and, whatever may have been the very early common law . . . the rule developed at common law that killing or use of deadly force to prevent a felony was justified only if the offense was a forcible and atrocious crime. . . . "Surprise" means an unexpected attack —

---

a. She relied on a statutory amendment that raised a simple assault from a misdemeanor to a felony where committed by a husband upon his wife. — EDS.

which includes force and violence . . . and the word thus appears redundant.

Examples of forcible and atrocious crimes are murder, mayhem, rape and robbery. . . . In such crimes "from their atrocity and violence human life [or personal safety from great harm] either is, or is presumed to be, in peril" (see United States v. Gilliam, supra, 25 Fed. Cas. pp. 1319, 1320 . . .).

Burglary has been included in the list of such crimes. . . . However, in view of the wide scope of burglary under Penal Code section 459, as compared with the common law definition of that offense, in our opinion it cannot be said that under all circumstances burglary under section 459 constitutes a forcible and atrocious crime.[2]

Where the character and manner of the burglary do not reasonably create a fear of great bodily harm, there is no cause for exaction of human life . . . or for the use of deadly force. The character and manner of the burglary could not reasonably create such a fear unless the burglary threatened, or was reasonably believed to threaten, death or serious bodily harm.

In the instant case the asserted burglary did not threaten death or serious bodily harm, since no one but Stephen and Robert was then on the premises. A defendant is not protected from liability merely by the fact that the intruder's conduct is such as would justify the defendant, were he present, in believing that the intrusion threatened death or serious bodily injury. . . .

We thus conclude that defendant was not justified under Penal Code section 197, subdivisions 1 or 2, in shooting Stephen to prevent him from committing burglary. . . .

We recognize that our position regarding justification for killing under Penal Code section 197, subdivisions 1 and 2, differs from the position of section 143, subdivision (2), of the Restatement Second of Torts, regarding the use of deadly force to prevent a "felony . . . of a type . . . involving the breaking and entry of a dwelling place" . . . but in view of the supreme value of human life, we do not believe deadly force can be justified to prevent all felonies of the foregoing type, including ones in which no person is, or is reasonably believed to be, on the premises except the would-be burglar.

Defendant also argues that had he been present he would have been justified in shooting Stephen under subdivision 4 of Penal Code section 197, which provides, "Homicide is . . . justifiable . . . 4. When necessarily committed in *attempting*, by lawful ways and means, to *apprehend* any person for any felony committed. . . ." (Italics added.) The argument cannot be upheld. The words "attempting . . . to apprehend" contain the idea of acting for the purpose of apprehending. . . . Here no showing was made that defendant's intent in shooting was to apprehend a felon. Rather it appears from his testimony and extrajudicial statement heretofore recited that his intent was to prevent a burglary, to protect his property, and to avoid the possibility that a thief might get into defendant's house and injure him upon his return. . . .

Defendant also does not, and could not properly, contend that the intru-

---

2. At common law burglary was the breaking and entering of a mansion house in the night with the intent to commit a felony. . . . Burglary under Penal Code section 459 differs from common law burglary in that the entry may be in the daytime and of numerous places other than a mansion house . . . and breaking is not required. . . . For example, under section 459 a person who enters a store with the intent of committing theft is guilty of burglary. . . . It would seem absurd to hold that a store detective could kill that person if necessary to prevent him from committing that offense. . . .

sion was in fact such that, were he present, he would be justified under Civil Code section 50 in using deadly force. That section provides, "Any necessary force may be used to protect from wrongful injury the person or property of oneself. . . ." This section also should be read in the light of the common law, and at common law in general deadly force could not be used solely for the protection of property. . . . "The preservation of human life and limb from grievous harm is of more importance to society than the protection of property." (Commonwealth v. Emmons, 157 Pa. Super. 495, 43 A.2d 568, 569.) Thus defendant was not warranted under Civil Code section 50 in using deadly force to protect his personal property. . . .

At common law an exception to the foregoing principle that deadly force could not be used solely for the protection of property was recognized where the property was a dwelling house in some circumstances. "According to the older interpretation of the common law, even extreme force may be used to prevent dispossession [of the dwelling house]." (Model Penal Code, Tent. Draft No. 8 (1958), Comment at pp. 48-51.) Also at common law if another attempted to burn a dwelling the owner was privileged to use deadly force if this seemed necessary to defend his "castle" against the threatened harm. Further, deadly force was privileged if it was, or reasonably seemed, necessary to protect the dwelling against a burglar.

Here we are not concerned with dispossession or burning of a dwelling, and, as heretofore concluded, the asserted burglary in this case was not of such a character as to warrant the use of deadly force.

We conclude that as a matter of law the exception to the rule of liability for injuries inflicted by a deadly mechanical device does not apply under the circumstances here appearing. . . .

The judgment is affirmed.

NOTE: TWO STATUTORY SCHEMES

Compare the following Model Penal Code and New York provisions governing the use of deadly force in the protection of property and habitation and the prevention of crime.

Model Penal Code: Section 3.04(2)(b). Use of Force in Self-Protection [see Appendix for text of this section].

Section 3.05(1). Use of Force for the Protection of Other Persons [see Appendix for text of this section].

Section 3.06(3)(d). Use of Force for the Protection of Property [see Appendix for text of this section].

Section 3.07(5). Use of Force in Law Enforcement [see Appendix for text of this section].

New York Penal Law [3]: *Section 35.15.* Justification; Use of Physical Force in Defense of a Person. 1. A person may, subject to the provisions of subdivision two, use physical force upon another person when and to the extent he reasonably

---

3. See Note, Justifiable Use of Force under Article 35 of the Penal Law of New York, 18 **Buff.** L. Rev. 285 (1969).

believes such to be necessary to defend himself or a third person from what he reasonably believes to be the use or imminent use of unlawful physical force by such other person, unless: . . .

2. A person may not use deadly physical force upon another person under circumstances specified in subdivision one unless:

(a) He reasonably believes that such other person is using or about to use deadly physical force. . . .

(b) He reasonably believes that such other person is committing or attempting to commit a kidnapping, forcible rape, forcible sodomy [a] or robbery; or

(c) He reasonably believes that such other person is committing or attempting to commit a burglary, and the circumstances are such that the use of deadly physical force is authorized by subdivision three of section 35.20.

Section 35.20. Justification; Use of Physical Force in Defense of Premises and in Defense of a Person in the Course of Burglary. 1. Any person may use physical force upon another person when he reasonably believes such to be necessary to prevent or terminate what he reasonably believes to be the commission or attempted commission by such other person of a crime involving damage to premises. He may use any degree of physical force, other than deadly physical force, which he reasonably believes to be necessary for such purpose, and he may use deadly physical force if he reasonably believes such to be necessary to prevent or terminate the commission or attempted commission of arson.

2. A person in possession or control of any premises, or a person licensed or privileged to be thereon or therein, may use physical force upon another person when he reasonably believes such to be necessary to prevent or terminate what he reasonably believes to be the commission or attempted commission by such other person of a criminal trespass upon such premises. He may use any degree of physical force, other than deadly physical force, which he reasonably believes to be necessary for such purpose, and he may use deadly physical force in order to prevent or terminate the commission or attempted commission of arson, as prescribed in subdivision one, or in the course of a burglary or attempted burglary, as prescribed in subdivision three.

3. A person in possession or control of, or licensed or privileged to be in, a dwelling or an occupied building, who reasonably believes that another person is committing or attempting to commit a burglary of such dwelling or building, may use deadly physical force upon such other person when he reasonably believes such to be necessary to prevent or terminate the commission or attempted commission of such burglary.[b]

a. A similar Maine statute uses the term *forcible sex offense.* In State v. Philbrick, 402 A.2d 59 (1979), the Maine Supreme Court held that this statute justified defendant in killing in order to prevent a person who forcibly fondled defendant's crotch from doing so again, so long as defendant reasonably believed his action was necessary to prevent a repetition of that offense. Query: Who was at fault — the legislature or the court? — Eds.

b. This provision changed an earlier formulation, which required a reasonable belief by the burglary victim that the burglar is "using or about to use physical force" against such victim. The drafters point out that by contrast "the amended provision dispenses with any requirement of fear on the part of the victim and authorizes him to use deadly force merely upon a reasonable belief that such is 'necessary to prevent or terminate the commission or attempted commission of such burglary.' Whether this amendment really works any change in the law from a practical standpoint is debatable. It would seem that anyone seeking to check a burglar from committing his crime, and having reasonable cause to believe deadly force necessary for that purpose, would also have reasonable cause to fear some physical force by the burglar." Supplementary Practice Commentary, R. G. Denzer & P. McQuillan (McKinney's Consol. Laws N.Y., bk. 39 §35.20, Cum. Ann. Pkt. Part, 1973-1974). — Eds.

Section 35.25. Justification; Use of Physical Force to Prevent or Terminate Larceny or Criminal Mischief. A person may use physical force, other than deadly physical force, upon another person when and to the extent that he reasonably believes such to be necessary to prevent or terminate what he reasonably believes to be the commission or attempted commission by such other person of larceny or of criminal mischief with respect to property other than premises.

DURHAM v. STATE
Supreme Court of Indiana
199 Ind. 567, 159 N.E. 145 (1927)

[Defendant, a deputy game warden, arrested one Long for illegal fishing. Long jumped into his boat in an attempt to escape. Defendant pursued him, grabbing first the gunwale and then the anchor chain. While Long was beating defendant about the head with an oar, defendant shot him in the arm. Defendant was convicted of assault and battery and appealed.]

MARTIN, J. . . . Instruction 12 was to the effect that, if Long resisted arrest, appellant would not be authorized to use such force and instrumentalities as would imperil the life of Long in order to overcome his resistance; that human life is too precious to be imperiled by the arrest of one who is only guilty of a misdemeanor; that, if appellant, in order to overcome Long's resistance, used a dangerous and deadly weapon, and in such manner as to endanger his life, and thereby inflict serious wounds, then the appellant would be guilty of assault and battery, at least. This instruction, standing alone, or considered in conjunction with instruction 15 and the other instructions, did not correctly state the law, and the court erred in giving it.

Our general statutes concerning arrests, and applicable to all classes of criminal cases, provide that:

"The defendant shall not be subject to any more restraint than is necessary for his arrest and detention." Section 2157, Burns' 1926.

"If, after notice of the intention to arrest the defendant, he either flees or forcibly resists, the officer may use all necessary means to effect the arrest." Section 2159, Burns' 1926.

In Plummer v. State (1893) 135 Ind. 308, 34 N.E. 968, the court said:

"The law does not allow a peace officer to use more force than is necessary to effect an arrest. And if he does use such unnecessary force, he . . . may be lawfully resisted. If the officer is resisted before he has used needless force and violence, he may then press forward and overcome such resistance, even to the taking of the life of the person arrested, if absolutely necessary."

The degree or limit of force that lawfully may be employed by an officer in arresting one charged with a misdemeanor (as distinguished from a felony) has been considered in a large number of cases in other jurisdictions. . . .

The general rules deduced therefrom may be stated to be: (a) That an officer having the right to arrest a misdemeanant may use all the force that is reasonably necessary to accomplish the arrest, except (b) that he may not, merely for the purpose of effecting the arrest, kill or inflict great bodily harm, endangering the life of the misdemeanant. Thus an officer may not kill or shed blood in attempting to arrest a misdemeanant who is fleeing, but not resisting.[2] (c) That, if the defendant physically resists, the officer need not retreat but may press forward and repel the resistance with such force, short of taking life, as is necessary to effect the arrest; and, if in so doing the officer is absolutely obliged to seriously wound or take the life of the accused, in order to prevent the accused from seriously wounding, or killing him, he will be justified.[3] . . .

To adopt the rule contended for by the prosecution in the trial below, and stated by the court in instruction 12, would be to paralyze the strong arm of the law, and render the state powerless to use extreme force when extreme resistance is offered, and would permit misdemeanants to stay the power of the state by unlawful resistance.

"To say to a defendant, 'You may measure strength with the arresting officer, and avoid being taken if you are the stronger or after your arrest you may break away unless he can prevail over you in a wrestle,' is to elevate mere brute force to a position of command over the wheels of justice." 1 Bishop's Cr. Proc. (2d Ed.) §16. . . .

The judgment is reversed, with directions to sustain appellant's motion for a new trial, and for further proceedings not inconsistent herewith.

MATTIS v. SCHNARR

United States Court of Appeals, 8th Circuit
547 F.2d 1007 (1967)

HEANEY, J. This appeal concerns the constitutionality of Missouri statutes [1] which permit law enforcement officers to use deadly force to effect the arrest of a person who has committed a felony if the person has been notified that he or she is under arrest and if the force used is restricted to that reasonably necessary to effect the arrest. We hold the statutes unconstitutional as applied to arrests in which an officer uses deadly force against a fleeing felon who has not used deadly force in the commission of the felony and whom the officer does not reasonably believe will use deadly force against the officer or others if not immediately apprehended.

The challenge to the constitutionality of the Missouri statutes arose out of the killing of Michael Mattis by Robert Marek, a police officer.

---

2. The most common examples of this class of cases are those where officers shoot at misdemeanants, their mounts, or their automobile tires, and wound or kill the misdemeanants. "To permit the life of one charged with a mere misdemeanor to be taken when fleeing from the officer would, aside from its inhumanity, be productive of more abuse than good. The law need not go unenforced. The officer can summon his posse, and take the offender." Head v. Martin (1887) 85 Ky. 480, 3 S.W. 622.

3. . . . [T]he protection which an officer is entitled to receive in making an arrest is a different thing from self-defense, for it is his duty to push forward and make the arrest and to secure and retain custody of the prisoner. . . .

1. "*Justifiable Homicide*

"Homicide shall be deemed justifiable when committed by any person in either of the following cases: . . .

"(3) When necessarily committed in attempting by lawful ways and means to apprehend any person for any felony committed, or in lawfully . . . keeping or preserving the peace." V.A.M.S. §559.040.

"*Rights of officer in making arrests*

"If, after notice of the intention to arrest the defendant, he either flee or forcibly resist, the officer may use all necessary means to effect the arrest." V.A.M.S. §544.190.

Michael Mattis, age eighteen, and Thomas Rolf, age seventeen, were discovered in the office of a golf driving range at approximately 1:20 A.M. by police officer, Richard Schnarr. Shortly thereafter, the two boys left the office by climbing out through the back window. Schnarr shouted at the boys to halt. They ran in different directions. Schnarr then shouted, "Halt or I'll shoot" two times. When the boys failed to stop, he fired one shot into the air and one shot at Rolf. Meanwhile, Officer Robert Marek, who had arrived on the scene, ran to intercept the boys. He collided with Mattis as he came around the corner of the building. Both fell to the pavement. Marek grabbed Mattis by the leg. Mattis broke away. Marek ran after him. Marek was losing ground. He shouted, "Stop or I'll shoot." Mattis did not stop. Marek, believing it was necessary to take further action to prevent Mattis's escape, fired one shot in the direction of Mattis and killed him. Both officers believed that the use of their guns was reasonably necessary to effect an arrest and was authorized by valid Missouri statutes.

Robert Dean Mattis, the father of Michael, brought an action against the officers and the City of Olivette under 42 U.S.C. §§1983 and 1988, and the Constitution of the United States, Amendments XIV, VIII and IX. It is alleged in the complaint that the officers, acting under color of law, deprived Michael Mattis of his life without due process of law, deprived him of the equal protection of the laws in violation of the Fourteenth Amendment to the Constitution, and inflicted a cruel and unusual punishment on him in violation of the Fourteenth, Eighth and Ninth Amendments of the Constitution. The court was asked to declare V.A.M.S. §§559.040 and 544.190 unconstitutional and to award damages of $100,000. . . .

At common law, deadly force could be used by a law enforcement officer if necessary to effect the arrest of a felony suspect but not of a suspected misdemeanant. While the rule has been severely criticized by legal scholars, most jurisdictions governed by common law have continued to adhere to the distinction. . . .

At least twenty-four states, including five in this Circuit — Arkansas, Iowa, Minnesota, Missouri, South Dakota — codify the common law and provide that deadly force may be used to arrest any felony suspect. Seven states depart from the common law by specifying the felonies for which deadly force may be used to arrest or by stating that only "forcible felonies" justify the use of deadly force. . . . Another seven states, including Nebraska of this Circuit, have adopted the Model Penal Code approach, which permits the use of deadly force only when the crime for which the arrest is made involves conduct including use or threatened use of deadly force or when there is a substantial risk that the person to be arrested will cause death or serious bodily harm if his apprehension is delayed.

The President's Commission on Law Enforcement and Administration of Justice, the National Commission on Reform of Federal Criminal Laws, and legal scholars whose writings span the last five decades generally support a rule which would limit the use of deadly force by police officers to those circumstances where the use of force is essential to the protection of human life and bodily security, or where violence was used in committing the felony.

The reasons advanced by the President's Commission are particularly important. The Commission found, through its studies, that "[p]olice use of firearms to apprehend suspects often strains community relations or even results in serious disturbances. . . . When studied objectively and unemotionally, particular uses of firearms by police officers are often unwarranted." . . .

More recent studies indicate that an important factor in increasing community tensions is that there is often a disproportionate use of deadly force against non-white suspects.[15]

Professor Michael Mikell has challenged the legal basis for permitting deadly force to be used against fleeing nonviolent felons since neither their original offense or their flight is ever punishable by death. His statement at the American Law Institute Proceeding in 1931 puts the matter aptly:

"It has been said, 'Why should not this man be shot down, the man who is running away with an automobile? Why not kill him if you cannot arrest him?' We answer: because, assuming that the man is making no resistance to the officer, he does not deserve death. . . . May I ask what we are killing him for when he steals an automobile and runs off with it? Are we killing him for stealing the automobile? If we catch him and try him, we throw every protection around him. We say he cannot be tried until 12 men of the grand jury indict him, and then he cannot be convicted until 12 men of the petit jury have proved him guilty beyond a reasonable doubt, and then when we have done all that, what do we do to him? Put him before a policeman and have a policeman shoot him? Of course not. We give him three years in a penitentiary. It cannot be then that we allow the officer to kill him because he stole the automobile, because the statute provides only three years in a penitentiary for that. Is it then for fleeing? . . . Fleeing from arrest is also a common law offense and is punishable by a light penalty, a penalty much less than that for stealing the automobile. If we are not killing him for stealing the automobile and are not killing him for fleeing, what are we killing him for?" 9 ALI Proceedings 186-187 (1931). . . .

A number of local law enforcement agencies [as well as the FBI and the Bureau of Narcotics] have adopted policies similar to those recommended by the Model Penal Code.

The foregoing review clearly establishes that the historical basis for permitting the use of deadly force by law enforcement officers against nonviolent fleeing felons has been substantially eroded, that federal and many state and local law enforcement agencies prohibit the use of deadly force against such felons except where human life is threatened, and the policy of permitting deadly force to be used against all fleeing felons contributes little or nothing to public safety or the deterrence of crime. Instead, the use of deadly force often tends to increase hostility towards law enforcement and to exacerbate community tensions. In short, there is little or no informed contemporary support for statutes

---

15. The Metropolitan Applied Research Center, Inc., conducted a study, in 1974, which showed that of 248 persons killed by the New York City Police from 1970 through 1973, seventy-three percent were black or Puerto Rican and under thirty years of age.

A similar study conducted of the Chicago Police Department, entitled The Police and Their Use of Fatal Force, concluded:

"Blacks were more than six times as likely to die at the hands of police as were whites during the period surveyed. . . ."

From 1950 through 1960, the death rate for blacks at the hands of police was nine times higher than that for whites in Akron, Chicago, Kansas City, Miami, Buffalo, Philadelphia, Boston and Milwaukee. . . .

as broad as these are. Moreover, no evidence was introduced below, either by the defendants or the intervening State of Missouri, indicating that a societal purpose is served by statutes as broad as these two.

However, it is not for this Court to decide whether the Missouri statutes are wise or not. The sole question before this Court is whether the statutes are unconstitutional. We hold they are.

We are concerned with the right of an individual to life, expressly recognized in the due process clauses of the Fifth and Fourteenth Amendments to the United States Constitution. . . .

Clearly, the right to life is "fundamental," and has often been so recognized in the equal protection and due process contexts. . . .

Even though the right to life is fundamental, the recent Supreme Court death penalty cases establish that when an offender has feloniously taken the life of another, capital punishment is not invariably disproportionate to the crime. It may be imposed without violating his Eighth or Fourteenth Amendment rights under "a carefully drafted statute that ensures that the sentencing authority is given adequate information and guidance." Gregg v. Georgia, 428 U.S. 153 (1976).

If we were to read the due process clause literally, we would have to conclude that life could never be taken without a trial. Such a literal reading would fail to recognize the interests of the state in protecting the lives and safety of its citizens.

The District Court properly recognized that the situations in which the state can take a life, without according a trial to the individual whose life is taken, are to be determined by balancing the interests of society in guaranteeing the right to life of an individual against the interest of society in insuring public safety. It went on to hold that the task of determining how the balance should be struck was exclusively within the province of the legislature. It is with the latter statement that we disagree. The legislature has an important role to play in the balancing process, but the court has the ultimate responsibility to determine whether the balance struck is a constitutional one.

Because we deal with a fundamental right, the Missouri statutes can be sustained only if they protect a compelling state interest and are "narrowly drawn to express only the legitimate state interests at stake." Roe v. Wade, 410 U.S. at 155. The state, in this case, must demonstrate the existence of an interest equivalent to, or greater than, the right to life to justify the use of deadly force against fleeing felons. No such demonstration has been made here. Rather, the statute creates a conclusive presumption that all fleeing felons pose a danger to the bodily security of the arresting officers and of the general public. The presumption is incorrect in its application to the facts of this case and has not otherwise been shown to be factually based.[30] We find nothing in this record,

---

30. The Public Interest Law Center, of Philadelphia, completed a study of the use of firearms by Philadelphia policemen for the period 1970 through 1974. Among the conclusions that they reached were the following: approximately forty-five percent of the victims shot were unarmed; approximately forty-five percent of the victims were shot while fleeing from the police; in approximately one of four incidents, an unarmed victim was shot while fleeing; approximately fourteen percent of the victims shot were juveniles; and the police department consistently failed to discipline policemen who misused their firearms.

A study conducted by the Planning and Research Division of the Boston Police Department reveals police officers discharged their firearms in 210 cases between 1970 and 1973, 102 of the

in the briefs of the parties or of the Attorney General, in scholarly literature, in the reports of distinguished study commissions, or in the experience of the nation's law enforcement agencies, to support the contention of the state that statutes as broad as these deter crime, insure public safety or protect life. Felonies are infinite in their complexity, ranging from the violent to the victimless. The police officer cannot be constitutionally vested with the power and authority to kill any and all escaping felons, including the thief who steals an ear of corn, as well as one who kills and ravishes at will. For the reasons we have outlined, the officer is required to use a reasonable and informed professional judgment, remaining constantly aware that death is the ultimate weapon of last resort, to be employed only in situations presenting the gravest threat to either the officer or the public at large. Thus, we have no alternative but to find V.A.M.S. §§559.040 and 544.190 unconstitutional in that they permit police officers to use deadly force to apprehend a fleeing felon who has used no violence in the commission of the felony and who does not threaten the lives of either the arresting officers or others.

It is not for this Court to write new statutes for the State of Missouri. We can only say that the statutes would be constitutional if carefully drawn to limit the use of deadly force by law enforcement officers in the apprehension of fleeing felons to situations where the officer has a warrant or probable cause to arrest the felon where the felon could not be otherwise apprehended and where the felon had used deadly force in the commission of the felony, or the officer reasonably believed the felon would use deadly force against the officer or others if not immediately apprehended.

GIBSON, C.J., dissenting. . . . The majority's decision fails to recognize that Mo. Rev. Stat. Sec. 544.190 (1969) only permits such force as may be reasonably necessary to apprehend a fleeing felon. The statute requires (1) that the arresting officer give a suspect notice of his intention to arrest, (2) that the suspect must either flee or forcibly resist, and (3) that whatever force the officer uses must be necessary. Furthermore, the officer must have probable cause to believe that the suspect has committed a crime. Thus, any unreasonable and unnecessary application of force would be arbitrary and an abuse of authority entailing proper sanctions against the officer. . . .

In the present case, the need for judicial restraint is particularly compelling in light of recent consideration of the problem by the Missouri legislature. In 1975 the Missouri legislature had before it a bill providing modifications of the common law based upon the Model Penal Code. The very fact that the Missouri legislature has so recently considered amending the statute now struck down by the majority indicates that Missouri is not oblivious to this area of public policy, which is in fact a sensitive one.

Indeed, the sensitivity of this issue is easily blurred by a single-minded focus on the seemingly absolute right of an individual to life. An individual's right to life is, however, beset with many obstacles, limitations and contradictions. Life is not permanent; it is subject to obliteration by accidents, inadvertence and by the hazards of everyday living. There is no constitutional right to commit felonious offenses and to escape the consequences of those offenses. There is

---

shots were in response to a fleeing suspect. In none of the 102 instances was there an assault on a police officer. In 80 of the cases, the fleeing suspect was unarmed.

no constitutional right to flee from officers lawfully exercising their authority in apprehending fleeing felons.

To measure the constitutionality of the Missouri statutes here, the individual's right must be weighed aganst the interests of the state. Rather than identifying the state interests involved here, however, the majority simply concludes that the state has failed to show an interest equivalent to the right to life. Thus, the majority balances a specific individual right to life against amorphous, unidentified state interests and, not surprisingly, finds the right to life to be weightier. I believe that the state's interests must be identified before a proper constitutional balancing can be made. These interests include effective law enforcement, the apprehension of criminals, the prevention of crime and the protection of members of the general populace, who, like fleeing felons, also possess a right to life.

Furthermore, I consider the majority's proposed modification of the common law rule a remarkably impractical means of balancing the interests and rights at stake. The majority states . . . that:

"[S]tatutes would be constitutional if carefully drawn to limit the use of deadly force by law enforcement officers in the apprehension of fleeing felons to situations where the office has a warrant or probable cause to arrest the felon where the felon could not be otherwise apprehended and where the felon had used deadly force in the commission of the felony, or the officer reasonably believed the felon would use deadly force against the officer or others if not immediately apprehended."

This standard presupposes that law enforcement officers are endowed not only with foresight, but also with that most characteristic judicial vision, hindsight. The majority does not suggest how law enforcement officers are to make the on-the-spot constitutional analysis called for by its proposal and still react quickly enough to meet the exigencies of an emergency situation. How can a police officer ever know, reasonably or otherwise, whether the felon will use force against others if not immediately apprehended? It is clearly the prerogative of the state legislature to decide whether such restrictions on the use of force are consonant with public policy. . . .

The state is not required to adopt a policy which might encourage the fleet of foot and the foolhardy felon or reject a policy of apprehending suspects by use of all reasonable force. . . .

NOTE

The Mattis v. Schnarr decision was vacated by the United States Supreme Court (*sub. nom.* Ashcroft v. Mattis, 431 U.S. 171 (1977)) on the ground that the district court's denial of the damage claim (because of the officer's good faith), which was not appealed, eliminated any present case or controversy. For comments on this litigation, see 21 St. Louis L.J. 513 (1977); 42 Mo. L. Rev. 452 (1977).

UNITED STATES v. HILLSMAN
United States Court of Appeals, 7th Circuit
522 F.2d 454 (1975)

PELL, J. The defendants James Hillsman and Clinton Bush were convicted by a jury of assaulting a federal officer, in violation of 18 U.S.C. §111. On appeal, the defendants contend that . . . the district court erred in refusing to instruct the jury that if the defendants reasonably believed the federal officer to be a fleeing felon, the defendants should be acquitted. . . .

On February 8, 1974, the defendants, along with two to three hundred other persons, attended a funeral in Gary, Indiana. Several agents of the Drug Enforcement Administration were conducting undercover surveillance at the funeral home for the purpose of observing and identifying suspected narcotics dealers. All of the agents involved in the surveillance wore ordinary "street" clothes and drove unmarked cars.

Agent David Munson, who was equipped with a video tape camera, stationed himself outside the funeral home alongside photographers from a Gary newspaper and began filming the mourners as they left the funeral home. Most of the several hundred mourners at the funeral home (including the defendants) were black and a group of the black mourners demanded that Munson, who is white, cease taking pictures and leave the area. One member of the crowd, William Hanyard, began shoving and hitting Munson when he continued to film the mourners. The defendants Hillsman and Bush were not identified as being in any way involved in the verbal or physical exchange with Munson.

Agent Kenneth Rhodes, the acting agent in charge of the DEA in the area, was approximately six feet from Munson at this time and observed Hanyard's attack on the agent. Intending to shoot Hanyard, Rhodes, who is black, drew his revolver and began to assume the "combat position." However, before he was able to get into this position, Rhodes either stepped back or was pushed from the rear and his gun discharged prematurely. The bullet merely grazed Hanyard but struck and killed Albert Griffin, an innocent bystander.

Immediately after the shot was fired, Rhodes announced that he was a federal agent and told Munson, "Let's get out of here." Although Munson heard the later statement, he did not hear Rhodes announce that he was a federal officer. Rhodes and Munson then moved to their cars. . . .

As Rhodes was moving toward his car, a woman in the crowd pointed at him and said, "He is the one; there he goes." A group of the mourners then began running after Rhodes. As Rhodes drove away, shots were fired at his car. One bullet struck the car but Rhodes himself was not injured.

Hillsman and Bush were identified as being members of the group that chased Rhodes and were observed firing weapons at Rhodes' car. . . .

With respect to the defendants' claim that they were only seeking to stop a person they believed to be a fleeing felon, the district court gave a lengthy instruction concerning the right of a private citizen to make an arrest. The court however, refused to give a defense instruction which provided: . . .

> If you find from the evidence that the Defendants, James Hillsman and Clinton Bush, acted out of reasonable belief that Kenneth Rhodes was not a Federal Agent but instead was a private citizen who the Defendants, James Hillsman and Clinton

Bush, had reasonable cause to believe had committed a felony and was fleeing the scene in order to avoid apprehension, and that the Defendants, James Hillsman and Clinton Bush, chased Kenneth Rhodes in order to stop his flight and detain him then you must find the Defendants, James Hillsman and Clinton Bush not guilty. . . .

The Supreme Court has recently held, in a decision rendered after the trial in the present case, that a person may be criminally liable under §111 for assaulting a federal officer, even though he did not know that his victim was a federal officer. United States v. Feola, 420 U.S. 671 (1975). [See pages 666-673 supra.] . . .

In short, then, where a defendant charged with violating §111 claims that he was unaware that the victim was a federal officer, the question becomes: would the defendant have been justified, because of the agent's actions, in using force against the agent had the latter, in fact, been a "civilian." . . .

. . . Since the incident would have been governed by Indiana law if Rhodes had been a private citizen, we look to the law of that state in making this determination.

Indiana follows the general common law rule that "a private citizen has the right to arrest one who has committed a felony in his presence, and may even arrest one he reasonably believes to have committed a felony, so long as the felony was in fact committed." Surratt v. Petrol, Inc., Ind. App., 312 N.E.2d 487, 495 (1974). . . .

The private citizen's right to make an arrest . . . is limited by the fact that he, unlike a police officer, acts at his own peril. . . . Hillsman and Bush would have been justified in making a citizen's arrest only if they reasonably believed that Rhodes had committed a felony *and* a felony had in fact been committed.

The instructions actually given to the jury . . . did adequately inform the jury of the requirements of a valid defense. . . . The trial court . . . accurately stated that although deadly force could be used to effect such an arrest in an appropriate case, no citizen's arrest would be valid unless a felony had in fact been committed. . . .

In addition, the district court instructed the jury with respect to the question of whether a felony had occurred when Rhodes shot Hanyard and Griffin. The jury was expressly told that if they found that a felony had occurred, then they could apply the law of citizen's arrest. The court admittedly instructed the jury with respect to only one type of felony, voluntary manslaughter.[7] This, however, was the only felony for which the defense requested an instruction and the defense does not contend on appeal that instructions on other felonies were necessary. Although it may be argued that a jury could have found that Rhodes committed a felony other than voluntary manslaughter, we cannot say that the

---

7. The instruction stated: "The crime of voluntary manslaughter is defined by statute in the State of Indiana as follows:

'Whoever voluntarily kills any human being without malice, express or implied, in a sudden heat, is guilty of voluntary manslaughter.'

"If, from the evidence, in this case you find that Kenneth Rhodes committed the crime of manslaughter in the presence of the defendants and was fleeing from the scene of the commission of said crime in order to avoid arrest and apprehension, then you may apply the law that a private individual may make a citizen's arrest of the fleeing felon."

district court's failure to instruct on other felonies, in the absence of any request by the defendant, was plain error requiring reversal. . . .

TONE J. (concurring). . . . I am uncomfortable in holding a defendant criminally accountable for conduct which, we hypothesize for present purposes, he thought was not only lawful but socially desirable. . . . The defendants here were each sentenced to nine years' imprisonment. The severity of the sentences indicates that the judge did not believe that they were merely trying to apprehend a felon, but the jury might have found otherwise. . . . I concur . . . only because I believe *Feola* requires that result. If I were free to do so, I would hold otherwise.

MODEL PENAL CODE

SECTION 3.07. USE OF FORCE IN LAW ENFORCEMENT[a]

[See Appendix for text of this section.]

COMMENT TO §3.07 AT 55-63 [(TENT. DRAFT NO. 8, 1958)]

3. Use of Deadly Force. Paragraph (2)(b) is addressed to the crucial problem of the extent to which it should be justifiable to use deadly force to effect an arrest.

The problem, it should be noted, is much narrower than the question when an officer or other person making an arrest is justified in using deadly force. As Section 3.04(2)(b)(iii)(2) recognizes, one justified in making an arrest is not obliged to desist because resistance is encountered. He may not only stand his ground but may press forward to achieve his object, meeting force with force, and if he believes that deadly force is necessary to protect himself, he may, of course, employ such force. The issue here is when he should be justified in using deadly force when there is no belief in its necessity for self-protection or for the protection of another but only to effect arrest. The problem arises in this form primarily in cases where the person sought to be arrested flees and the actor believes it necessary that he shoot to prevent the escape.

The common law approach to a solution of the problem — which underlies much, though not all of the existing law — is based on the distinction between felony and misdemeanor; deadly force is authorized where necessary to prevent the escape of one fleeing from arrest for felony, but not for misdemeanor. . . .

This distinction, whatever its virtues for the period in which the rules of justification were formulated, seems manifestly inadequate for modern law. Such rational justification for the common law rule as can be adduced rests largely on the fact that virtually all felonies in the common law period were punishable

a. For a review of the considerable extent to which the Model Penal Code formulation has been influential in statutory reform, see Note, 75 Colum. L. Rev. 914, 949-953 (1975). In Commonwealth v. Klein, 372 Mass. 823, 363 N.E.2d 1313 (1977), the court adopted §3.07 by judicial ruling.

For two informative recent opinions discussing the sharply controversial issue of the privilege of an officer to use deadly force to apprehend a fleeing felon, with particular attention to the American Law Institute's proposals, see Jones v. Marshall, 528 F.2d 132 (2d Cir. 1975), and Schumann v. McGinn, 307 Minn. 446, 240 N.W.2d 525 (1976). See also Day, Shooting the Fleeing Felon: State of the Law, 14 Crim. L. Bull. 285 (1978). — EDS.

by death. Though effected without the protections and formalities of an orderly trial and conviction, the killing of a resisting or fleeing felon resulted in no greater consequences than those authorized for punishment of the felony of which the individual was charged or suspected.

Today, the significance of the distinction between felony and misdemeanor has wholly altered. Relatively few crimes are punishable by death. . . . Moreover, under modern legislation, many statutory misdemeanors involve conduct more dangerous to life and limb than some felonies. Compare, for example, such felonies as the distillation of alcohol in violation of the revenue laws, on the one hand, and such misdemeanors as reckless and drunken driving, on the other. Even a felony which often is committed in such a way as to endanger life, may in many particular cases be committed in a fashion which creates no such peril. Accordingly the felony-misdemeanor distinction is inherently incapable of separating out those persons of such dangerousness that the perils arising from failure to accomplish immediate apprehension justify resort to extreme force to accomplish it.

In some jurisdictions, the existing law is unsatisfactory, also, in its defintion of the mental element required to justify the use of deadly force in these cases. The extreme breadth of the privilege has apparently induced some courts and legislatures to limit its application in the very worst way — by imposing a rule of absolute liability. Thus, the privilege is at times said to attach only when the deceased has in fact committed a felony, apart from all considerations of good faith and reasonable belief on the part of the arresting officer. . . . In other jurisdictions the rule appears to require that a felony must have in fact been committed, though the deceased need not have committed it, if the officer reasonably believed he did. . . . Such a rule also creates the possibility of an absolute liability. Still other jurisdictions appear to adhere to a rule of reasonable belief, but the law is in a state of considerable ambiguity and uncertainty on this vital point. . . .

The approach of the draft differs in many particulars from earlier attempts at reform. Like the common law rule, the use of extreme force is restricted to arrests for felonies. But unlike the common law rule, certain additional qualifications are imposed on the privilege. First, the use of deadly force is restricted to those who, under the law of the jurisdiction, are authorized to act as peace officers. It has seemed important in an age of firearms to restrict the use of deadly force to official personnel, where the purpose to be served is the apprehension of persons to answer to criminal charges.[b] Second, the draft recognizes that the public interest is poorly served if the use of deadly force creates a substantial risk of injury to innocent bystanders; and, accordingly, the privilege is withheld unless the actor believes that there is no such risk. Beyond this, the draft proceeds upon the principle that use of deadly force should only be justifiable in those situations where the *immediate* apprehension of the person to be arrested overrides all competing considerations. When the issue is stated in this way, it seems clear that the only case that fits the principle is one where the arresting officer believes that there is a substantial risk that the person to

---

b. As finally formulated this restriction is modified and the privilege is extended to those assisting a peace officer. See Model Penal Code §3.07(2)(b)(ii) (1962). — Eds.

be arrested will cause death or serious bodily harm if his apprehension is delayed. . . .

NEW YORK PENAL LAW

SECTION 35.30. JUSTIFICATION; USE OF PHYSICAL FORCE IN MAKING AN ARREST OR IN PREVENTING AN ESCAPE

1. A peace officer, in the course of effecting or attempting to effect an arrest, or of preventing or attempting to prevent the escape from custody, of a person whom he reasonably believes to have committed an offense, may use physical force when and to the extent he reasonably believes such to be necessary to effect the arrest, or to prevent the escape from custody, or to defend himself or a third person from what he reasonably believes to be the use or imminent use of physical force; except that he may use deadly physical force for such purposes only when he reasonably believes that:

(a) The offense committed by such person was:

(i) a felony or an attempt to commit a felony involving the use or attempted use or threatened imminent use of physical force against a person; or

(ii) kidnapping, arson, escape in the first degree, burglary in the first degree or any attempt to commit such a crime; or

(b) The offense committed or attempted by such person was a felony and that, in the course of resisting arrest therefor or attempting to escape from custody, such person is armed with a firearm or deadly weapon; or

(c) Regardless of the particular offense which is the subject of the arrest or attempted escape, the use of deadly physical force is necessary to defend the peace officer or another person from what the officer reasonably believes to be the use or imminent use of deadly physical force.

2. The fact that a peace officer is justified in using deadly physical force under circumstances prescribed in paragraphs (a) and (b) of subdivision one does not constitute justification for reckless conduct by such peace officer amounting to an offense against or with respect to innocent persons whom he is not seeking to arrest or retain in custody.

3. A person who has been directed by a peace officer to assist such peace officer to effect an arrest or to prevent an escape from custody may use physical force, other than deadly physical force, when and to the extent that he reasonably believes such to be necessary to carry out such peace officer's direction, unless he knows that the arrest or prospective arrest is not or was not authorized and he may use deadly physical force under such circumstances when:

(a) He reasonably believes such to be necessary to defend himself or a third person from what he reasonably believes to be the use or imminent use of deadly physical force; or

(b) He is directed or authorized by such peace officer to use deadly physical force unless he knows that the peace officer himself is not authorized to use deadly physical force under the circumstances.

4. A private person acting on his own account may use physical force, other than deadly physical force, upon another person and to the extent that he reason-

ably believes such to be necessary to effect an arrest or to prevent the escape from custody of a person whom he reasonably believes to have committed an offense and who in fact has committed such offense; and he may use deadly physical force for such purpose when he reasonably believes such to be necessary to:

(a) Defend himself or a third person from what he reasonably believes to be the use or imminent use of deadly physical force; or

(b) Effect the arrest of a person who has committed murder, manslaughter in the first degree, robbery, forcible rape or forcible sodomy and who is in immediate flight therefrom. . . .

PRACTICE COMMENTARY, R. G. Denzer & P. McQuillan (McKinney's Consol. Laws N.Y., Bk. 39, §35.30, Cum. Ann. P. Part, 1973-1974): The greatest difficulties arise in situations where there may be no danger to the officer or anyone else but the officer simply cannot catch the arrestee without using deadly force (ordinarily his revolver). Here, the deadly force authorization is made to rest upon the kind of offense which is, or is reasonably believed to be, the subject of the arrest. The old Penal Law required merely that it be a felony. The original Revised Penal Law section required that it be "a felony involving the use or threatened use of deadly physical force."

The latter provision was intended to exclude non-violent felonies (e.g., forgery, car theft) but to preserve the officer's right to use his revolver for apprehension of persons reasonably believed to have committed felonies of a violent and physically dangerous nature, such as homicide, robbery and forcible rape. It was criticized, however, as being too narrow and imprecise for the purpose. One contention advanced was that some robberies (e.g., muggings) and some forcible rapes may not involve either the use or threatened use of "deadly physical force," and that in any event it is unfair to saddle the police with the difficult burden of determining when the force used in any given case was of a "deadly" nature.

Out of these considerations, the amending bill changes the provision in question to authorize deadly force by the officer in apprehending for any felony or felony attempt involving the actual, attempted or threatened use of any physical force, whether of a deadly nature or otherwise (amended §35.30[lai]). This clearly covers, inter alia, every conceivable robbery and forcible rape. In addition, moreover, four specific felonies — kidnapping, arson, first degree escape and first degree burglary — are explicitly placed in the same category (id. [laii]). The reason for this is that those crimes, which do not necessarily involve the use of any physical force at all, and, hence, are not necessarily covered by the previous clause, are nevertheless of such a serious and dangerous character as to merit the use of deadly force by the police in their efforts to apprehend the perpetrators.

Another situation justifying deadly force by peace officers for arrest purposes involves the armed fleeing felon. The original section permitted deadly force by the officer to arrest any felon, regardless of the kind of felony committed, "attempting to escape by *the use of* a deadly weapon. . . . What was not covered was the situation in which the pursuing officer knows or has good reason to believe that the fleeing felon, though not brandishing or using a deadly weapon at the moment, has a gun or knife in his pocket which he may well use on the verge of capture. With this in mind the amended provision (subd. lb) expands the original one by authorizing deadly force by the officer where necessary upon a reasonable belief merely that the felon "is armed with a firearm or deadly weapon," regardless of whether he is presently using it.

Another significant change in §35.30 appears in the provision addressed to the use of physical force by a private person making or attempting an arrest on his own account. . . . Under both the old Penal Law and the original Revised Penal Law (§35.30[6]), the private citizen or non-peace officer was never authorized to use deadly force to effect an arrest for any previously committed offense except upon him or another. That rule was grounded in an aversion to the picture of an ordinary citizen stalking an alleged criminal in bounty hunting style with the intention of capturing him dead or alive. Though logical and sound from that viewpoint, the doctrine has frequently been criticized in its application to arrests made or attempted immediately after the commission of particularly heinous crimes. The criticism may be illustrated by considering the case of a man who, immediately after burglary of his home during which he was robbed and his wife raped, seizes a gun, looks out the window and sees the culprit fleeing down the street. Under the indicated doctrine, he would not be justified in using the gun for apprehension purposes.

With cases of that nature in mind, the provision has been amended to authorize the use of deadly force by a private person to "effect the arrest of a person who has committed murder, manslaughter in the first degree, robbery, forcible rape or forcible sodomy and who is in immediate flight therefrom."

3. Choice of the Lesser Evil — The Residual Principle of Justification

PEOPLE v. UNGER

Supreme Court of Illinois
66 Ill. 2d 333, 362 N.E.2d 319 (1977)

RYAN, J. Defendant, Francis Unger, was charged with the crime of escape and was convicted following a jury trial before the circuit court of Will County. Defendant was sentenced to a term of three to nine years to be served consecutively to the remainder of the sentence for which he was imprisoned at the time of the escape. The conviction was reversed upon appeal and the cause was remanded for a new trial. . . . We granted leave to appeal and now affirm the judgment of the appellate court.

At the time of the present offense, the defendant was confined at the Illinois State Penitentiary in Joliet, Illinois. Defendant was serving a one- to three-year term as a consequence of a conviction for auto theft. . . . On February 23, 1972, the defendant was transferred to the prison's minimum security, honor farm. It is undisputed that on March 7, 1972, the defendant walked off the honor farm. Defendant was apprehended two days later in a motel room in St. Charles, Illinois.

At trial, defendant testified that prior to his transfer to the honor farm he had been threatened by a fellow inmate. This inmate allegedly brandished a six-inch knife in an attempt to force defendant to engage in homosexual activities. Defendant was 22 years old and weighed approximately 155 pounds. He testified that he did not report the incident to the proper authorities due to fear of retaliation. Defendant also testified that he is not a particularly good fighter.

Defendant stated that after his transfer to the honor farm he was assaulted and sexually molested by three inmates, and he named the assailants at trial. The attack allegedly occurred on March 2, 1972, and from that date until his escape defendant received additional threats from inmates he did not know. On March 7, 1972, the date of the escape, defendant testified that he received a call on an institution telephone. Defendant testified that the caller, whose voice he did not recognize, threatened him with death because the caller had heard that defendant had reported the assault to prison authorities. Defendant said that he left the honor farm to save his life and that he planned to return once he found someone who could help him. None of these incidents were reported to the prison officials. As mentioned, defendant was apprehended two days later still dressed in his prison clothes. . . .

Defendant's first trial for escape resulted in a hung jury. The jury in the second trial returned its verdict after a five-hour deliberation. The following instruction (People's Instruction No. 9) was given by the trial court over defendant's objection. "The reasons, if any, given for the alleged escape are immaterial and not to be considered by you as in any way justifying or excusing, if there were in fact such reasons." The appellate court majority found that the giving of People's Instruction No. 9 was reversible error. . . . Two instructions which were tendered by defendant but refused by the trial court are also germane to this appeal. Defendant's instructions Nos. 1 and 3 were predicated upon the affirmative defenses of compulsion and necessity. (Ill. Rev. Stat. 1971, ch. 38, pars 7-11 (compulsion), 7-13 (necessity.) Defendant's instructions Nos. 1 and 3 read as follows:

> It is a defense to the charge made against the Defendant that he left the Honor Farm of the Illinois State Penitentiary by reason of necessity if the accused was without blame in occasioning or developing the situation and reasonably believed such conduct was necessary to avoid a public or private injury greater than the injury which might reasonably result from his own *conduct.*
>
> It is a defense to the charge made against the Defendant that he acted under the compulsion of threat or menace of the imminent infliction of death or great bodily harm, if he reasonably believed death or great bodily harm would be inflicted upon him if he did not perform the conduct with which he is charged.

The principal issue in the present appeal is whether it was error for the court to instruct the jury that it must disregard the reasons given for defendant's escape and to conversely refuse to instruct the jury on the statutory defenses of compulsion and necessity. . . . The State contends that, under the facts and circumstances of this case, the defenses of compulsion and necessity are, as a matter of law, unavailable to defendant. . . .

. . . Traditionally, the courts have been reluctant to permit the defenses of compulsion and necessity to be relied upon by escapees. This reluctance appears to have been primarily grounded upon considerations of public policy. Several recent decisions, however, have recognized the applicability of the compulsion and necessity defenses to prison escapes. In People v. Harmon (1974), 53 Mich. App. 482, 220 N.W.2d 212, the defense of duress was held to apply in a case where the defendant alleged that he escaped in order to avoid repeated homosexual attacks from fellow inmates. In People v. Lovercamp (1974), 43 Cal. App.

3d 823, 118 Cal. Rptr. 110, a limited defense of necessity was held to be available to two defendants whose escapes were allegedly motivated by fear of homosexual attacks.

As illustrated by *Harmon* and *Lovercamp,* different courts have reached similar results in escape cases involving sexual abuse, though the question was analyzed under different defense theories. A certain degree of confusion has resulted from the recurring practice on the part of the courts to use the terms "compulsion" (duress) and "necessity" interchangeably, though the defenses are theoretically distinct. . . .

In our view, the defense of necessity, as defined by our statute (Ill. Rev. Stat. 1971, ch. 38, par. 7-13), is the appropriate defense in the present case. In a very real sense, the defendant here was not deprived of his free will by the threat of imminent physical harm which, according to the Committee Comments, appears to be the intended interpretation of the defense of compulsion as set out in section 7-11 of the Criminal Code. . . . Rather, if defendant's testimony is believed, he was forced to choose between two admitted evils by the situation which arose from actual and threatened homosexual assaults and fears of reprisal. Though the defense of compulsion would be applicable in the unlikely event that a prisoner was coerced by the threat of imminent physical harm to perform the specific act of escape, no such situation is involved in the present appeal. . . .

The defendant's testimony was clearly sufficient to raise the affirmative defense of necessity. That defense is defined by statute (Ill. Rev. Stat. 1971, ch. 38, par. 7-13):

> Conduct which would otherwise be an offense is justifiable by reason of necessity if the accused was without blame in occasioning or developing the situation and reasonably believed such conduct was necessary to avoid a public or private injury greater than the injury which might reasonably result from his own conduct.

Defendant testified that he was subjected to threats of forced homosexual activity and that, on one occasion, the threatened abuse was carried out. He also testified that he was physically incapable of defending himself and that he feared greater harm would result from a report to the authorities. Defendant further testified that just prior to his escape he was told that he was going to be killed, and that he therefore fled the honor farm in order to save his life. Though the State's evidence cast a doubt upon the defendant's motives for escape and upon the reasonableness of defendant's assertion that such conduct was necessary, the defendant was entitled to have the jury consider the defense on the basis of his testimony. . . .

The State, however, would have us apply a more stringent test to prison escape situations. The State refers to the *Lovercamp* decision, where only a limited necessity defense was recognized. In *Lovercamp,* it was held that the defense of necessity need be submitted to the jury only where five conditions had been met. Those conditions are: "(1) The prisoner is faced with a specific threat of death, forcible sexual attack or substantial bodily injury in the immediate future; (2) There is no time for a complaint to the authorities or there exists a history of futile complaints which make any result from such complaints illusory; (3) There is no time or opportunity to resort to the courts; (4) There is no evidence of force or violence used towards prison personnel or other 'innocent' persons in the escape; and (5) The prisoner immediately reports to the proper authorities when he has attained a position of safety from the immediate threat."

The State correctly points out that the defendant never informed the authorities of his situation and failed to report immediately after securing a position of safety. Therefore, it is contended that, under the authority of *Lovercamp*, defendant is not entitled to a necessity instruction. We agree with the State and with the court in *Lovercamp* that the above conditions are relevant factors to be used in assessing claims of necessity. We cannot say, however, that the existence of each condition is, as a matter of law, necessary to establish a meritorious necessity defense.

The preconditions set forth in *Lovercamp* are, in our view, matters which go to the weight and credibility of the defendant's testimony. . . . The absence of one or more of the elements listed in *Lovercamp* would not necessarily mandate a finding that the defendant could not assert the defense of necessity.

By way of example, in the present case defendant did not report to the authorities immediately after securing his safety. In fact, defendant never voluntarily turned himself in to the proper officials. However, defendant testified that he intended to return to the prison upon obtaining legal advice from an attorney and claimed that he was attempting to get money from friends to pay for such counsel. Regardless of our opinion as to the believability of defendant's tale, this testimony, if accepted by the jury, would have negated any negative inference which would arise from defendant's failure to report to proper authorities after the escape. The absence of one of the *Lovercamp* preconditions does not alone disprove the claim of necessity and should not, therefore, automatically preclude an instruction on the defense. We therefore reject the contention that the availability of the necessity defense be expressly conditioned upon the elements set forth in *Lovercamp*.

In conclusion, we hold that under the facts and circumstances of the present case the defendant was entitled to submit his defense of necessity to the jury. It was, therefore, reversible error to give People's Instruction No. 9 to the jury and to refuse to give an appropriate instruction defining the defense of necessity, such as the instruction tendered by the defendant. . . .

Affirmed and remanded.

UNDERWOOD, J., dissenting: My disagreement with my colleagues stems from an uneasy feeling that their unconditional recognition of necessity as a defense to the charge of escape carries with it the seeds of future troubles. Unless narrowly circumscribed, the availability of that defense could encourage potential escapes, disrupt prison discipline, and could even result in injury to prison guards, police or private citizens. For these reasons courts have been quite reluctant to honor the defenses of duress, necessity or compulsion in prison escapes, and, until recent years, they were uniformly held insufficient to justify escapes. . . .

I am not totally insensitive to the sometimes brutal and unwholesome problems faced by prison inmates, and the frequency of sexually motivated assaults. Prisoner complaints to unconcerned or understaffed prison administrations may produce little real help to a prisoner or may actually increase the hazard from fellow inmates of whose conduct complaint has been made. Consequently, and until adequate prison personnel and facilities are realities, I agree that a necessity defense should be recognized. The interests of society are better served, however, if the use of that defense in prison-escape cases is confined within well-defined boundaries such as those in *Lovercamp*. In that form it will be available, but with limitations precluding its wholesale use.

It is undisputed that defendant here did not meet those conditions. . . . Rather, he stole a truck some nine hours after his escape, drove to Chicago, and later drove to St. Charles, using the telephone to call friends in Canada. This conduct, coupled with his admitted intent to leave in order to gain publicity for what he considered an unfair sentence, severely strain the credibility of his testimony regarding his intention to return to the prison.

[handwritten marginalia: bad behavior]

NOTES

1. In United States v. Bailey, 444 U.S. 394 (1980), the court of appeals had interpreted the federal escape statute as requiring "an intent to avoid confinement." It held that this intent was not established where defendant's purpose was to avoid intolerable conditions that were not a proper or necessary part of confinement; rather, the prosecution had to establish an intent to avoid confinement in the sense of the "normal aspects of punishment." The Supreme Court held this interpretation "insupportable," finding nothing in the statutory language or its legislative history to support it, and held that knowledge by defendant that his actions would result in leaving prison without permission was all the prosecution had to prove to establish the mens rea of escape.

On the issue of duress or necessity the Court held, contrary to the *Unger* case, that a prerequisite to an instruction on these theories is evidence that defendant made a bona fide effort to surrender or return "as soon as the duress or necessity had lost its coercive force." The Court found no such evidence where the various defendants who escaped had remained at large from one month to three and one-half months before they were recaptured.

2. For commentary on the prison-escape problem, see Fletcher, Should Intolerable Conditions Generate a Justification or an Excuse for Escape?, 26 U.C.L.A.L. Rev. 1355 (1979); Comment, Intolerable Conditions as a Defense to Prison Escapes, 26 U.C.L.A.L. Rev. 1126 (1979); Note, The Necessity Defense to Prison Escape after United States v. Bailey, 65 Va. L. Rev. 359 (1979); Comment, From Duress to Intent: Shifting the Burden in Prison-Escape Prosecutions, 127 U. Pa. L. Rev. 1142 (1979); Gardner, The Defense of Necessity and the Right to Escape from Prison, 49 S. Cal. L. Rev. 110 (1975).

MODEL PENAL CODE

SECTION 3.02. JUSTIFICATION GENERALLY: CHOICE OF EVILS

[See Appendix for text of this section.]

COMMENTS TO §3.02 AT 5-9 [(TENT. DRAFT NO. 8, 1958)]

1. This Section accepts the view that a principle of necessity, properly conceived, affords a general justification for conduct that otherwise would constitute an

offense; and that such a qualification, like the requirements of culpability, is essential to the rationality and justice of all penal prohibitions.

The principle is subject to three vital limitations:

(a) The necessity must be avoidance of an evil greater than the evil sought to be avoided by the law defining the offense charged. The balancing of evils cannot, of course, be committed merely to the private judgment of the actor; it is an issue for determination in the trial. What is involved may be described as an interpretation of the law of the offense, in light of the submission that the special situation calls for an exception to the prohibition that the legislature could not reasonably have intended to exclude, given the competing values to be weighed.

(b) The issue of competing values must not have been foreclosed by a deliberate legislative choice, as when the law has dealt explicitly with the specific situation that presents the choice of evils or a legislative purpose to exclude the justification claimed otherwise appears . . .

(c) When the actor has made a proper choice of values, his belief in the necessity of his conduct to serve the higher value exculpates — unless the crime involved can be committed recklessly or negligently. But when the latter is the case, recklessness or negligence in bringing about this situation requiring the choice of evils or in appraising the necessity for his conduct may be the basis of conviction. . . .

NEW YORK PENAL LAW

SECTION 35.05 JUSTIFICATION; GENERALLY

Unless otherwise limited by the ensuing provisions of this article defining justifiable use of physical force, or with some other provision of law, conduct which would otherwise constitute an offense is justifiable and not criminal when: . . .

2. Such conduct is necessary as an emergency measure to avoid an imminent public or private injury which is about to occur by reason of a situation occasioned or developed through no fault of the actor, and which is of such gravity that, according to ordinary standards of intelligence and morality, the desirability and urgency of avoiding such injury clearly outweigh the desirability of avoiding the injury sought to be prevented by the statute defining the offense in issue. The necessity and justifiability of such conduct may not rest upon considerations pertaining only to the morality and advisability of the statute, either in its general application or with respect to its application to a particular class of cases arising thereunder.[a] Whenever evidence relating to the defense of justification under this subdivision is offered by the defendant, the court shall rule as a matter of law whether the claimed facts and circumstances would, if established, constitute a defense.

---

a. "The prohibition against violation of a statute because of doubts concerning its 'morality' or 'advisability' renders the provision in question unavailable to the mercy killer, the crusader who considers a penal statute unsalutary because it tends to obstruct his cause, and the like." Practice Commentary, McKinney's Consol. Laws N.Y., Bk. 39, §35.05, Penal Law 57 (1967). — EDS.

STATUTORY NOTE

The necessity proposals of the Model Penal Code influenced a number of states to codify this defense. Many of them preferred the New York formulation.[4] What are the principal differences? Cf. Note, Justification: The Impact of the Model Penal Code on Statutory Reform, 75 Colum. L. Rev. 914, 925-928 (1975).

Codifications of the necessity defense are also common in foreign law. For example, §34 of the new German Penal Code of 1969 provides (StGB, Law of July 4, 1969 (Zweites Gesetz zur Reform des Strafrechts) [1969] Bundesgesetzblatt, Pt. 1, at 717, 721):

> One who commits an act in order to save himself or another from an imminent and otherwise unavoidable danger to life, person, freedom, honor, property or other legally protected interest, does not act unlawfully if, in weighing the conflicting interests, particularly the legally protected interest which is threatened and the degree of the threat, the interest he protects significantly outweighs the interest he harms. However the foregoing applies only insofar as the act committed is an appropriate measure for avoiding the danger.

Article 14 of the Criminal Code of the R.S.F.S.R. (largest of the 15 union republics of the USSR) provides (from H. Berman, Soviet Criminal Law and Procedure 149 (1966)):

> Extreme necessity. Although falling within the category of an act provided for in the Special Part of the present Code, an action shall not constitute a crime if it is committed in extreme necessity, that is, in order to eliminate a danger which threatens the interests of the Soviet state, social interests, or the person or rights of the given person or of other citizens, if in the given circumstances such danger cannot be eliminated by other means and if the harm caused is less significant than the harm prevented.

NOTES

1. Consider the defense of necessity in the following situations: (a) Defendant was convicted of the statutory offense of killing moose out of season and without a license. He admitted these facts, but it was stipulated that it was necessary for him to do so to protect his ranch property, prior efforts to use fences and airplanes and to enlist the aid of the authorities having proved futile. The statutory offense made no exception for such or other situations, and there was no statutory necessity provision. The court upheld the defense. Cross v. State, 370 P.2d 371 (Wyo. 1962). Other courts have held likewise in comparable situations, some holding that failure to grant a defense would deprive the person of property without due process of law. See State v. Ward, 170 Iowa 185, 152 N.W. 501 (1915); Annot., 93 A.L.R.2d 1366 (1964).

(b) Earlier in this casebook, in connection with the liability of accomplices,

---

4. See, e.g., Colo. Rev. Stat. Ann. tit. 18, §18-1-702; Del. Code Ann. tit. 11, §463; N.H. Rev. Stat. Ann. tit. 62, §627:3; Or. Rev. Stat. tit. 16, §161.200. Pennsylvania followed the Model Penal Code: Pa. Cons. Stat. Ann. tit. 18, §503.

we presented the cases of the undercover agents hunting illegally, pages 617-618 supra, and of the reporters investigating police bribery, page 618 supra. Consider the applicability of the necessity defense to those cases.

(c) In Regina v. Kitsun, 39 Crim. App. 66, 67, 71 (1955), defendant fell asleep drunk in a car that his brother had parked and from which he had removed the ignition key. On awakening he found the car moving down the hill. He immediately grabbed the steering wheel and steered the car harmlessly to the shoulder of the road. He was convicted of driving the car under the influence of drink. On appeal, his counsel argued:

> The appellant was not in law driving the car at the material time. There must be some line drawn with regard to what constitutes "driving"; for example, a person who jumped on a runaway vehicle and tried to stop it would not be "driving" it for the purposes of the Road Traffic Acts. He would be doing a highly commendable action, and would not involve himself in criminal liability in respect of his attempt to control the vehicle.

The Court of Criminal Appeal upheld the conviction, stating:

> [I]t is quite impossible to say that on the evidence of the appellant himself he was not in fact driving this car. The car was subject to his control. It was subject to his direction and he steered it in some way so as to bring it on to the grass verge at the bottom of the hill.

Did the court miss the point? Did counsel for appellant put his cause felicitously?

(d) Should it be a good defense to a charge of possession of marijuana that defendant suffered from glaucoma, the symptoms of which are alleviated by inhalation of marijuana? Suppose other, lawful medication were equally effective? If not, suppose surgery offers a complete cure but entails a high risk of immediate blindness? Does it matter whether possession of marijuana is a strict-liability offense? See Note, Medical Necessity as a Defense to Criminal Liability: United States v. Randall, 46 Geo. Wash. L. Rev. 273 (1978).

2. Tiffany & Anderson, Legislating the Necessity Defense in Criminal Law, 52 Den. L.J. 839, 861-862 (1975), write:

> A question which needs to be clarified is posed by LaFave and Scott: "*A*, driving a car, suddenly finds himself in a predicament where he must either run down *B* or hit *C*'s house and he reasonably chooses the latter, unfortunately killing two people in the house who by bad luck happened to be just at that place inside the house where *A*'s car struck. . . ." [106]
>
> Of course, the defendant in this case is guilty of no crime to begin with. Were defendant charged with manslaughter (reckless homicide), the difficulty would be that recklessness means a conscious disregard of a risk that is "substantial and unjustifiable." [109] The same is true of crimes defined in terms of negligence. Defendant needs no general justification defense when charged with a crime based on recklessness or negligence since it is implicit in the charge itself that the defendant's conduct was not justified; unjustifiability of conduct becomes an element of the charge itself and must be proved by the state.

Cf. Problem, pages 447-448 supra.

106. LaFave and Scott, Criminal Law 386 (1972).
109. Model Penal Code Section 2.02(2)(c).

3. What perils are created by the inevitable uncertainty and elasticity of the defense of necessity? We saw earlier, in the section on the principle of legality, pages 350-370 supra, that these characteristics are regarded as vices in the criminal law. Are these characteristics less offensive when they characterize defenses to, rather than definitions of, criminal conduct? Consider the views of James Fitzjames Stephen on this question. Defending the position of his Draft Code of 1879, which contained one provision eliminating judicial authority to create new crimes while retaining another authorizing judges to develop new defenses, he stated (quoted in Williams, (2) Necessity, [1978] Crim. L. Rev. 128, 130):

> . . . [T]he reason why the common law definitions of offences should be taken away, whilst the common law principles as to justification and excuse are kept alive, is like the reason why the benefit of a doubt should be given to a prisoner. The worst result that could arise from the abolition of the common law offences would be the occasional escape of a person morally guilty. The only result which can follow from preserving the common law as to justification and excuse is, that a man morally innocent, not otherwise protected, may avoid punishment. In the one case you remove rusty spring-guns and man-traps from unfrequented plantations, in the other you decline to issue an order for the destruction of every old-fashioned drag or life-buoy which may be found on the banks of a dangerous river, but is not in the inventory of the Royal Humane Society.
>
> This indeed does not put the matter strongly enough. The continued existence of the undefined common law offences is not only dangerous to individuals, but may be dangerous to the administration of justice itself. By allowing them to remain, we run the risk of tempting the judges to express their disapproval of conduct which, upon political, moral, or social grounds, they consider deserving of punishment, by declaring upon slender authority that it constitutes an offence at common law; nothing, I think, could place the bench in a more invidious position, or go further to shake its authority.[a]

Does Stephen's analysis satisfactorily respond to the argument that since what a person may and may not do is determined both by the definition of the crime and by the definition of justifying circumstances, so long as either the former or the later is vague and uncertain, he must guess at what is prohibited and what is permitted and be equally subject to the extralegal predilections of judges? Cf. M. Kadish & S. Kadish, Discretion to Disobey 123-126 (1973).

Compare Schwartz, Reform of the Federal Criminal Laws, [1977] Duke L.J. 171, 217. Criticizing the so-called Left for opposing the proposed revision of the federal criminal law ("S. 1") because it granted a defense to public officials

---

a. A modern-day version of the formulations offered by Stephen is represented in the New Jersey Code of Criminal Justice. N.J. Stat. Ann. tit. 2C, §1-5 provides: "Common law crimes are abolished and no conduct constitutes an offense unless the offense is defined by this code or another statute of this State." But §3-2 provides: "a. *Necessity.* Conduct which would otherwise be an offense is justifiable by reason of necessity to the extent permitted by law and as to which neither the code nor other statutory law defining the offense provides exceptions or defenses dealing with the specific situation involved and a legislative purpose to exclude the justification claimed does not otherwise plainly appear." The drafters' commentary states: "The Commission believes it more appropriate to leave the issue to the Judiciary. The rarity of the defense and the imponderables of the particulars of specific cases convince us that the Courts can better define and apply this defense than can be done through legislation." 2 N.J. Crim. Law Rev. Commn., Final Report, The New Jersey Penal Code, Commentary 80 (1971). — Eds.

acting in reasonable performance of their duty (see the material on this issue at pages 321-323 supra), he states:

> But of course S. 1 was amendable, and the Left eventually acknowledged that by sponsoring H.R. 10850, its own amended version of S. 1. In that bill, section 501 provided that the defenses specified "are not exclusive. . . . Additional bars and defenses may be developed by the Courts of the U.S. in the light of reason and experience." This departure from the Commission Code is both vague and counterintuitive. Quite plainly, for example, the public duty defense just discussed has not been "abolished" as the draftsmen seem to have intended. The courts are left free to adopt whatever rule they like. The open-ended invitation to judges to *add* to the listed defenses is a civil liberties monster. It was earlier urged on the Brown Commission by the Right in order to retain all sorts of bad things — for example, the right of police to kill in suppressing riots and the right of a householder to shoot to kill a supposedly burglarious intruder whether or not he is perceived as a threat to life (as where the burglar is shot leaving the house). To leave the judges free to define defenses is virtually to abandon the effort to define crimes, since an offense is defined by the combination of what it prohibits and what is declared to be justified.

UNITED STATES v. KRONCKE
United States Court of Appeals, 8th Circuit
459 F.2d 697 (1972)

HEANEY, J. . . . . This prosecution for willfully attempting to interfere with the administration of the draft law arose out of a demonstration against the Vietnam War in 1970. Defendants forcibly entered a local draft office in Little Falls, Minnesota, equipped with various tools and with the admitted intent to interfere with the administration of the draft law by taking and destroying draftee registration cards and destroying the draft files for the county. Their defense was justification based on the need to bring to the attention of Congress and the public the evils of the Vietnam War, which was immoral and illegal and to end which there was no effective political or legal recourse.

[At the trial, defendants called many witnesses who testified to the evils and injustices of the war and its destructive impact, internationally and domestically, all subject to the government's standing objection on which the trial court reserved decision.]

The defendants requested the court to instruct the jury as follows: (1) that if the jury found that the evils sought to be avoided by the defendants were far greater than those sought to be prevented by the law defining the offense and that the defendants acted to avoid those evils upon the belief that their acts were necessary and such belief in the necessity of their acts was reasonable, then the defendants' acts were justified and a verdict of not guilty should be entered; and (2) if the jury found that the evils sought to be avoided and exorcised by the defendants were far greater than those sought to be prevented by the law defining the offense and that the defendants acted to avoid those evils upon the belief that their acts were necessary religious acts, and that such belief in the necessity of their acts was reasonable, then the defendants' acts were justified and protected by the First Amendment of the United States Constitution. . . .

The court . . . instructed the jury as follows:

. . . [The attempted justification is] based on the theory as to both defendants that the Vietnam war is an evil and the evil sought to be avoided by defendants is greater than the evil sought to be prevented by the law defining the offense; that they believed their acts to be necessary, that their belief was reasonable and therefore they were justified in their actions. . . . In addition, both defendants . . . claim that they were compelled or moved by religious and theological motives and that what they did is characterized in some way as a religious act. . . . [A]ll of what has been received along this line is immaterial. . . . I now . . . strike all of the testimony offered by both defendants except for their own personal testimony, and I strike that part which attempts to rely on a justification on account of the Vietnam war or religious oriented reasons. Consequently, all that you have before you for consideration are the facts concerning what occurred at Little Falls, Minnesota on the late evening of July 10, 1970. . . .

The defendants contend on appeal that the trial court erred in refusing to submit the defense of justification to the jury. . . . We reject [the] contention. . . .

The defendants cite a number of cases and a tentative draft of Section 3.02 of the Model Penal Code to support their view that the jury should have been permitted to determine whether their acts were justified. We do not believe that the code or the cases support the defendants' view that the requested instructions should have been given. Two of the cases, U.S. v. Nye, 27 F. Cas. 210 (No. 15,906) (C.C.D. Mass 1855), and U.S. v. Ashton, 24 F. Cas. 873 (No. 14,470) (C.C.D. Mass 1834), involved revolts by seamen because they believed that their ships were unseaworthy and their lives endangered. U.S. v. Holmes involved a case in which a sailor threw passengers out of a lifeboat and sought to justify his action on the grounds that it was necessary to save other lives. Commonwealth v. Wheeler, 53 N.E.2d 4 (Mass. 1944) and Rex v. Borne, 1 K.B. 687, 3 All E.R. 615 (1939) involved abortions by doctors who sought to justify their acts on the grounds that the abortions were necessary to protect the health or life of the mother. State v. Jackson, 53 Atl. 1021 (N.H. 1902), involved a case in which a father kept his child out of school to protect her health. In Chesapeake & O.R. Co. v. Commonwealth, 84 S.W. 506 (Ky. 1905), a railway company charged with violating a criminal statute requiring it to maintain separate railway cars for blacks and whites, defended against the charge on the grounds that an unavoidable accident had prevented it from complying on this one occasion. And in State v. Johnson, 183 N.W.2d 541, the court denied the defendant the right to assert the defense of justification to a charge of operating a snowmobile on a trunk highway, on the grounds that the defense of necessity applied only in emergency situations where the peril is instant and overwhelming, and leaves no alternative but the conduct in question.

The common thread running through most of these cases in which the defense of necessity was asserted is that there was a reasonable belief on the part of the defendant that it was necessary for him to act to protect his life or health, or the life or health of others, from a direct and immediate peril. None of the cases even suggests that the defense of necessity would be permitted where the actor's purpose is to effect a change in governmental policies which, according to the actor, may in turn result in a future saving of lives.

The Model Penal Code is broader than the cited cases in that it extends the defense beyond those cases in which the evil to be avoided is death or bodily harm. Nevertheless, the Code does not, in our view, extend the defense to cases in which the relationship between the defendant's act and the "good" to be accomplished is as tenuous and uncertain as here. Furthermore, the Code specifically limits the defense to those situations in which "a legislature purpose to exclude the justification claimed does not otherwise plainly appear." We hesitate to say that Congress did not intend the statute to be applied to those who violated it for the express purpose of challenging our nation's foreign policies.

We turn, then, to the broader contentions on which we believe the defendants truly rely to justify their acts: (1) that the war in Indochina is invalid because it has not been formally declared by Congress; (2) that the Selective Service system is being operated in an unconstitutional manner in that it is used to draft men for the Indochina war; (3) that the war is immoral and unjust, and the defendants were justified in committing the acts they did in order to protest the war and help bring it to an end; and (4) that Kroncke's acts were religious and were protected by the First Amendment to the Constitution.

To the extent that the defendants acted as they did to test the constitutionality of the war and the draft, they rely in part on the precedent of the early 1960 "sit-ins," used by civil rights workers to test the constitutionality of state and local laws and customs requiring segregation of public eating facilities.[6] As legitimate as this technique may be, those who use it must risk the possibility that their tactics will be found inappropriate or the governmental action valid. The latter is the case here. . . .

[The court then referred to cases rejecting constitutional challenges to the Vietnam War.]

The defendants rely most heavily on the third and fourth arguments. We turn to their contention that they were legally justified in violating the provisions of the Selective Service Act as a protest to the "immoral" war in Indochina and as a means of bringing that war to an end.

This issue was dealt with in United States v. Moylan, 417 F.2d 1002 (4th Cir. 1969), wherein several defendants, including the Berrigan brothers, were convicted of seizing and mutilating draft records. They had attempted to raise a similar defense which the trial court rejected. The Fourth Circuit, in affirming the convictions, stated:

"From the earliest times when man chose to guide his relations with fellow men by allegiance to the rule of law rather than force, he has been faced with the problem how best to deal with the individual in society who through moral conviction concluded that a law with which he was confronted was unjust and therefore must not be followed. Faced with the stark reality of injustice, men of sensitive conscience and great intellect have sometimes found only one morally justified path, and that path led them inevitably into conflict with established authority and its laws. Among philosophers and religionists throughout the ages there has been an incessant stream of discussion as to when, if at all, civil disobedience, whether by passive refusal to obey a law or by its active breach, is morally justified. However, they have been in general agreement that while

---

6. Bell v. Maryland, 378 U.S. 226 (1964); Peterson v. City of Greenville, 373 U.S. 244 (1963); Garner v. Louisiana, 368 U.S. 157 (1961).

in restricted circumstances a morally motivated act contrary to law may be ethically justified, the action must be nonviolent and the actor must accept the penalty for his action. In other words, it is commonly conceded that the exercise of a moral judgment based upon individual standards does not carry with it legal justification or immunity from punishment for breach of the law."

It follows that the defendants' motivation in this case cannot be accepted as a legal defense or justification. We do not question their sincerity, but we also recognize that society cannot tolerate the means they chose to register their opposition to the war.

. . . We make no moral judgment on the defendants' acts. We counsel only that the fabric of our democratic society is fragile, that there are broad opportunities for peaceful and legal dissent, and that the power of the ballot, if used, is great. Peaceful and constant progress under the Constitution remains, in our view, the best hope for a just society. . . .

Affirmed.[a]

PROBLEMS

1. Some abortion opponents in recent years have protested by disrupting abortion clinics through such tactics as chaining themselves to equipment and blocking passageways. Charged with criminal trespass, the protestors in a number of cases have raised the defense of necessity, claiming that their actions were justified by the desire to save the lives of the fetuses that otherwise would be killed. The various incidents and the general problem are reviewed in Note, Necessity as a Defense to a Charge of Criminal Trespass in an Abortion Clinic, 48 Cin. L. Rev. 501, 516 (1979). The author concludes:

> The principles underlying the doctrine of necessity do not support expansion of the defense into this new context. If American women are to be denied their constitutional right to safe abortions, the right can only be denied by a change in the Court's position or by a constitutional amendment; it cannot be denied by those who seek to violate the laws in order to enforce their own ideas.

2. Consider the applicability of the choice-of-evils defense to the facts of the Bisbee Deportation case (State v. Wooton), a famous prosecution rising out of developments in Arizona during World War I. The following summary of the facts is taken from Comment, The Law of Necessity as Applied in the Bisbee Deportation Case, 13 Ariz. L. Rev. 264 (1961):

> On April 26, 1917, hard on the heels of our declaration of war against Germany, a strike of copper miners in the Warren District of Cochise County, Arizona, was

a. Reaching a comparable conclusion in a similar situation, the 7th Circuit concluded: "One who elects to serve mankind by taking the law into his own hands thereby demonstrates his conviction that his own ability to determine policy is superior to democratic decision making. [Defendant's] professed unselfish motivation, rather than a justification, actually identifies a form of arrogance which organized society cannot tolerate." United States v. Cullen, 454 F.2d 386 (7th Cir. 1971). See also State v. Dorsey, 118 N.H. 844, 395 A.2d 855 (N.H. 1978), where a similar defense to a protest trespass upon a nuclear power plant was rejected. — EDS.

ordered by the Industrial Workers of the World — the I.W.W. On July 12th an armed posse, organized by the sheriff and numbering more than 1000, rounded up some 1100 to 1200 of the strikers and their associates, including practically every member of the I.W.W. in the district, put them aboard a special freight train, and transported them under guard to Hermanas, near Columbus, New Mexico, where they were left to be cared for by federal troops. Eventually, about 200 of the possemen were charged with kidnaping, and one of them, H. E. Wootton, was selected to be brought to trial.

At the close of the state's case in chief, the defendant offered to prove that the I.W.W. had been organized about 1908 as an anarchistic conspiracy to overthrow the government and the capitalistic system by force; that these strikes in the Warren District and elsewhere were designed to obstruct the successful prosecution of the war; that at the time of the alleged kidnaping the conspirators were present in the Warren District in great numbers, to destroy the lives and property of its inhabitants; that they had assaulted and threatened its citizens and had accumulated quantities of dynamite, firearms, and ammunition to be used for their purposes; that the day before the deportation a leader of the conspirators had told the sheriff that he would no longer be responsible for the acts of his men; that the sheriff and possemen reasonably believed that the conspirators intended to commit many felonies in the district, including riot, treason, assault, murder, and the destruction of property; and that protection by the state and federal troops had been sought without avail; that the jails of the county were inadequate to confine the conspirators, and that as prudent men the defendant and his associates had reasonably believed that the deportation was imminently necessary for the preservation of life and property in the district.

The judge instructed the jury as follows (id. at 277):

Laying aside for the moment the offer of proof with respect to a conspiracy existing long prior to the acts complained of, the offer of proof as to conditions existing in the Warren District at the time of the so-called deportation, the purpose and intent of the persons deported, the contemplated destruction of lives and property within that district, the preparations to carry out that intent and the acts and conduct as well as the statements of the persons deported, present a situation where it cannot be said as a matter of law that the rule of necessity cannot be applicable, but rather leaves the question of the existence of such necessity to be determined by the jury as a question of fact under proper instructions. If such were the conditions and the citizens of Bisbee had called in vain upon state and federal authorities for protection against a threatened calamity such as is set forth in the offer of proof, it cannot be said as a matter of law that they must sit supinely by and await the destruction of their lives and property without having the right to take steps to protect themselves.

The jury deliberated for 15 minutes and reached a verdict of "not guilty" on the first ballot.

REGINA v. DUDLEY AND STEPHENS
Queen's Bench Division
14 Q.B.D. 273 (1884)

[For the opinion in this case, see page 182 supra.]

NOTES

1. J. F. Stephen, Digest of the Criminal Law 25 n. 1 (5th ed. 1894):

I can discover no principle in the judgment in R. v. Dudley. It depends entirely on its peculiar facts. The boy was deliberately put to death with a knife in order that his body might be used for food. This is quite different from any of the following cases — (1) The two men on a plank. Here the successful man does no direct bodily harm to the other. He leaves him the chance of getting another plank. (2) Several men are roped together on the Alps. They slip, and the weight of the whole party is thrown on one, who cuts the rope in order to save himself. Here the question is not whether some shall die, but whether one shall live. (3) The choice of evils. The captain of a ship runs down a boat, as the only means of avoiding shiprwreck. A surgeon kills a child in the act of birth, as the only way to save the mother. A boat being too full of passengers to float, some are thrown overboard. Such cases are best decided as they arise.

Compare Glazebrook, The Necessity Plea in English Criminal Law, 30 Camb. L.J. 87, 113-114 (1972):

The Court simply held that the facts did not disclose a situation of necessity which would justify the killing of the lad. The defendants, it was said, had not chosen the lesser of two evils, for when they killed the lad they did not, and could not, know that killing him would probably save their lives, or that the lad would probably have died anyway. They had no idea when, or whether, they might be rescued by a passing ship. The lad would not have died if a vessel had rescued them on their twenty-first day in the boat; they would not have survived if a ship had not appeared within four days. Granted that in such cases a person can only be expected to act on the probable balance of advantage from action or inaction, there was no probable balance of advantage likely to accrue from killing the lad. . . . The defendants could, therefore, on this view of the facts, only escape conviction if it was the law that "a man may save his life by killing, if necessary an innocent and unoffending neighbour," and this certainly was not the law.

The facts were, however, open to another, and better, interpretation: namely, that the choice which had to be made, given that the defendants could not know when, if at all, they might be rescued, was between, on the one side, the lad's very slight chance of survival and, on the other, the increase in the already greater chances of survival of the men (who were not in so weak a state) which would accrue from their killing and eating the lad. On this analysis, the choice was not between a certainty and a chance (as Lord Coleridge supposed), but between two chances, and had the Court realised this, it might have been recognized a necessity situation. But it did not, and, therefore, Dudley and Stephens is not, as is sometimes supposed, an authority against the recognition of a necessity plea on a charge of murder. It was decided in the aftermath of the debate as to whether or not the projected Criminal Code of 1878-79 should provide for a defence of necessity, and Lord Coleridge's wide ranging judgment reiterates many of the arguments that had then been employed. But Stephen was right to point out that the decision (in which, he said, he would have concurred) still leaves a court free to hold that it is not murder to kill another when this is the lesser of two evils, as it would be where to kill one would save the lives of several.

Professor Glanville Williams offers a critical analysis of *Dudley and Stephens* in Williams, A Commentary on R. v. Dudley and Stephens, 8 Cambrian L. Rev. 94 (1977).

2. The American case referred to in Lord Coleridge's opinion was United States v. Holmes, 26 F. Cas. 360, 1 Wall Jr. 1 (C.C.E.D. Pa. 1842). The first mate, 8 seamen and 32 passengers were cast adrift on a life boat following a shipwreck on the high seas. The boat was grossly overcrowded and sprang a leak making it necessary to bail constantly in order to stay afloat. After a day and a half bailing became difficult because of the rough seas and the overcrowding, and the passengers panicked. The first mate ordered all male passengers whose wives were not in the boat to be thrown overboard. Eighteen passengers were jettisoned before a rescue ship arrived. Subsequently Holmes, one of the crew who assisted in ejecting the passengers, was charged with manslaughter, after the grand jury declined to return an indictment for murder. In charging the jury the judge made these points: that generally if two persons face a situation in which only one can survive "neither is bound to save the other's life by sacrificing his own, nor would either commit a crime in saving his own life for the only means of safety"; that while this principle prevailed between sailor and sailor it did not prevail between sailor and passenger because of the special duty owed the latter by the former; that absent this special relationship the choice of who should be sacrificed must be made by lot, since, "In no other way than this or some like way are those having equal rights put on an equal footing, and in no other way is it possible to guard against partiality and oppression, violence and conflict. . . ." Holmes was convicted and sentenced to six months' imprisonment and a fine of $20. Shortly thereafter the penalty was remitted.

For accounts of this case see F. Hicks, Human Jettison (1927); B. Cardozo, Law and Literature 110-114 (1930). The latter observes (at 113):

> Where two or more are overtaken by a common disaster, there is no right on the part of one to save the lives of some by the killing of another. There is no rule of human jettison. Men there will often be who, when told that their going will be the salvation of the remnant, will choose the nobler part and make the plunge into the waters. In that supreme moment the darkness for them will be illumined by the thought that those behind will ride to safety. If none of such mold are found aboard the boat, or too few to save the others, the human freight must be left to meet the chances of the waters. Who shall choose in such an hour between the victims and the saved? Who shall know when masts and sails of rescue may emerge out of the fog?

3. For an illuminating treatment of these issues, see the remarkable tour de force by Professor Lon Fuller, The Case of the Spelunkean Explorers, 62 Harv. L. Rev. 616 (1949).

NOTE ON TAKING LIFE TO SAVE LIFE

May the choice-of-evils principle ever justify the intentional killing of an innocent person who is not an aggressor? The Model Penal Code plainly anticipates an affirmative answer. In the Commentary on the necessity proposal, the drafters state (§3.02, Comment at 8 (Tent. Draft No. 8, 1958)):

> We see no reason why the scope of the defense ought to be limited to cases where the evil sought to be avoided is death or bodily injury or any other specified harm; nor do we see a reason for excluding cases where the actor's conduct portends a particular evil, such as homicide. . . .
>
> It would be particularly unfortunate to exclude homicidal conduct from the scope of the defense, as the new Wisconsin formulation does. For recognizing that the sanctity of life has a supreme place in the hierarchy of values, it is nonetheless true that conduct which results in taking life may promote the very value sought to be protected by the law of homicide. Suppose, for example, that the actor has made a breach in a dike, knowing that this will inundate a farm, but taking the only course available to save a whole town. If he is charged with homicide of the inhabitants of the farm house, he can rightly point out that the object of the law of homicide is to save life, and that by his conduct he has effected a net saving of innocent lives. The life of every individual must be assumed in such a case to be of equal value and the numerical preponderance in the lives saved compared to those sacrificed surely establishes an ethical and legal justification for the act. See Wechsler and Michael, A Rationale of the Law of Homicide, 37 Columbia L. Rev. 701, 783-39 (1937). So too a mountaineer, roped to a companion who has fallen over a precipice, who holds on as long as possible but eventually cuts the rope, must certainly be granted the defense that he accelerated one death slightly but avoided the only alternative, the certain death of both. . . .

How sound is the use of a numerical calculus to justify the intentional killing of an innocent, nonthreatening person? Resistance to such a position is evident in its explicit rejection by statutes [5] and commentators. Professor Andenaes, for example, has observed (J. Andenaes, The General Part of the Criminal Law of Norway 169 (1965)): "Even though many lives could be saved by the sacrifice of one, this would hardly be justifiable. It would conflict with the general attitude toward the inviolability of human life to interfere in this way with the course of events." [6] But if it is better, when accidents happen, that fewer lives be lost, why is it wrong for a person to bring this about by his action? How can it be wrong to make things better?

KADISH, RESPECT FOR LIFE AND REGARD FOR RIGHTS IN THE CRIMINAL LAW, 64 Calif. L. Rev. 871, 888-890 (1976): . . . The one circumstance in which the law arguably justifies killing [an innocent, nonthreatening] person is that in which killing him is necessary to avoid the death of several. This represents the lesser-evil principle . . . in which killing one person is deemed a lesser evil than the death of more than one.

It is apparent that the right to resist aggression cannot account for the justifica-

5. See, e.g., Ky. Rev. Stat. Ann. ch. 500, §500.410, which states, "No justification can exist under this section [providing for the defense of choice of evils] for an intentional homicide." See also Wis. Stat. Ann. tit. 45, §939; Mo. Ann. Stat. tit. 38, §563.026.

6. See also Note, Justification: The Impact of the Model Penal Code on Statutory Reform, 75 Colum. L. Rev. 914, 923 (1975), concluding that "where homicidal conduct is the subject of the defense, the innocent lives in the balance cannot be 'compared' by any standard" and arguing that excuse rather than justification is the appropriate approach to these situations. And see Taurek, Should the Numbers Count?, 6 Phil. & Pub. Aff. 293 (1977); Murphy, The Killing of the Innocent, 57 Monist 527 (1973).

tion of this type of intentional killing. Neither the actor nor those on whose behalf he acts are threatened in their rights by the one whose life is taken. To use the example of the Model Penal Code itself, the families whose lives are imperiled by the deflection of flood waters to their homes to avoid the death of a great number who live in the normal path of the waters are totally uninvolved in the threat to the latter persons. Moreover, the deflection of the waters to their homes is itself an aggressive act against them, which violates their rights not to be used as a means for the benefit of others. When the law justifies this action it therefore violates the right we earlier posited to the state's protection against aggression. That this category of killings is usually explained in terms of the choice of the lesser evil suggests its theory of justification: on a judgment of end results it is better that the fewer number of lives is lost. In the case of the non-threatening bystanders, therefore, a balance of utilities becomes determinative, in which the preservation of several lives justifies the intentional taking of a lesser number, even at the cost of violating a fundamental right the law otherwise recognizes they possess. That is to say, within this category of killings a force is at work manifesting a very different notion of right: rightness in the sense of the desirable social consequence of an action — whether it will produce a net loss or savings of lives.

But stories tell more than propositions. Suppose a terrorist and her insane husband and 8-year old son are operating a machine gun emplacement from a flat in an apartment building. They are about to shoot down a member of the diplomatic corps, whose headquarters the terrorist band is attacking. His only chance is to throw a hand grenade (which he earlier picked up from a fallen terrorist) through his assailants' window. Probably under Anglo-American law he will be legally justified in doing so. His right to resist the aggressors' threat is determinative. The value of preserving even the lives of the terrorist, her legally insane husband and their infant son carry no weight on the scale of rights.

Add to the facts that the victim knows there is one person in an adjoining flat who will surely be killed by the blast. Now he would *not* be legally justified in throwing the grenade (though he might be excused), for his action will not result in a net saving of lives. The right of the person in the adjoining flat (who is no part of the threat against him) not to be subjected to his agression is, therefore, determinative.

Finally, assume in addition that the machine gun is being directed against a companion as well as himself. Under the lesser-evil doctrine the victim will be legally justified in throwing the grenade. The right of the person in the adjoining flat is the same, but that person's claim of right yields to the social valuation that the two other lives are to be preferred over his one life.

This last case reveals the anomaly in the law: that rights prevail over lives in the aggression cases, even multiple or innocent lives, but that lives prevail over rights in the bystander cases like this one or the flood deflection case. As suggested above, we must conclude that, to the extent this is the law, a bystander's right against aggression yields to a utilitarian assessment in terms of net saving of lives. Yet, it should be added, this is not always so, for there are some killings fairly within the net-saving-of-lives, lesser-evil doctrine that it is very doubtful courts would sanction — for example, killing a person to obtain his organs to save the lives of several other people, or even removing them for that purpose against his will without killing him. The unreadiness of the law to justify such aggression against non-threatening bystanders reflects a moral uneasiness with reliance on a utilitarian calculus for assessing the justification of intended killings, even when a net savings of lives is achieved.[32]

PROBLEM

How far may the innocent victim of a lesser-evil choice be justified in using force to protect himself? For example, *A*'s house stands just outside the main village. A storm of unusual intensity threatens to break the levee protecting the village from flooding by a nearby river. *B*, seeking to avert the danger to the village and its occupants, prepares to explode a hole in the levee at a point calculated to cause the flood to miss the town but to inundate *A*'s house, which has been evacuated. *A* holds *B* off with a loaded gun, preventing *B* from setting the explosion. The village is flooded, with loss of life and property. Is *A* guilty of assault with a deadly weapon? Of murder or manslaughter of the dead villagers? See Glazebrook, The Necessity Plea in English Criminal Law, 30 Camb. L.J. 87, 93 (1972); G. Williams, Criminal Law: The General Part 745 (2d ed. 1961).

Professor Andenaes puts the following problem:

An immediate blood transfusion must be made in order to save an injured person: the only one who has the same blood type as the injured refuses to give blood. Can he be overpowered and the blood taken from him?

The General Part of the Criminal Law of Norway 169 (1965).

Consider 2 J. F. Stephen, History of the Criminal Law of England 108-109 (1883):

In an American case in which sailors threw passengers overboard to lighten a boat it was held that the sailors ought to have been thrown overboard first unless they were required to work the boat, and that at all events the particular persons to be sacrificed ought to have been decided on by ballot. (Comm. v. Holmes, 1 Wall. Jr. 1). Such a view appears to me to be over refined. Self-sacrifice may or may not be a moral duty, but it seems hard to make it a legal duty, and it is impossible to state its limits or the principle on which they can be determined.

---

32. It is worth observing that some instances of the net-saving-of-lives principle do not produce this conflict . . . [I]n the often-discussed hostage cases, . . . a band threatens to kill two persons in their power in order to obtain the death of one person in the custody of another group. Consistent with a rights approach, the group may desist from protecting the wanted person and permit the band to enter and kill him, for in doing so they will effect a net saving of lives and violate no one's rights. Contrariwise, it would be inconsistent with the rights approach were they themselves to kill the one person in their custody.

An instance of a quite different kind is suggested in the commentary to the Model Penal Code itself: "A mountaineer, roped to a companion who has fallen over a precipice, who holds on as long as possible but eventually cuts the rope, must certainly be granted the defense," of the net-savings-of-lives principle "because the only alternative was the certain death of both." Model Penal Code §3.02, Comment 3, at 8 (Tent. Draft No. 8, 1958). Here, however, the dangling mountaineer is no bystander. He constitutes a threat, although an innocent one, so that the right to resist aggression suffices to justify cutting the rope. [Query: If this is so, should the excess people in an overcrowded lifeboat be regarded as "aggressors," thereby privileging some to throw others overboard? See R. Nozick, Anarchy, State and Utopia 34-35 (1974), page 736 supra.]

Suppose one of the party in the boat had a revolver and was able to use it, and refused either to draw lots or to allow himself or his wife or daughter to be made to do so or to be thrown overboard, could any one deny that he was acting in self-defence and the defence of his nearest relations, and would he violate any legal duty in so doing?

B. PRINCIPLES OF EXCUSE

1. *Introduction*

INTRODUCTORY NOTE

We pointed out earlier (Note on Culpability and Excuse, page 339 supra), the close relation between the mens rea doctrines there explored (mens rea in its special sense) and the general principles of excuse (mens rea in its general sense). The materials that follow in this introductory section are designed further to explicate that relationship.

AUSTIN, A PLEA FOR EXCUSES
57 Proceedings Aristotelian Socy. 1, 1 (1956-1957)

I am here using the word "excuses" *for a title,* but it would be unwise to freeze too fast to this one noun and its partner verb: indeed for some time I used to use "extenuation" instead. Still, on the whole "excuses" is probably the most central and embracing term in the field, although this includes others of importance —"plea," "defence," "justification" and so on. When, then, do we "excuse"˙ conduct, our own or somebody else's? When are "excuses" proffered?

In general, the situation is one where someone is *accused* of having done something, or (if that will keep it any cleaner) where someone is *said* to have done something which is bad, wrong, inept, unwelcome, or in some other of the numerous possible ways untoward. Thereupon he, or someone on his behalf, will try to defend his conduct or to get him out of it.

One way of going about this is to admit flatly that he, X, did do that very thing, A, but to argue that it was a good thing, or the right or sensible thing, or a permissible thing to do, either in general or at least in the special circumstances of the occasion. To take this line is to *justify* the action, to give reasons for doing it: not to say, to brazen it out, to glory in it, or the like.

A different way of going about it is to admit that it wasn't a good thing to have done, but to argue that it is not quite fair or correct to say *baldly* "X did A.)." We may say it isn't fair just to say X did it; perhaps he was under somebody's influence, or was nudged. Or, it isn't fair to say baldly he *did A;* it may have been partly accidental or an unintentional slip. Or, it isn't fair to say he did simply *A* — he was really doing something quite different and *A* was only incidental, or he was looking at the whole thing quite differently. Naturally these arguments can be combined or overlap or run into each other.

In the one defence, briefly, we accept responsibility but deny that it was bad: in the other, we admit that it was bad but don't accept full, or even any, responsibility.

By and large, justifications can be kept distinct from excuses, and I shall not be so anxious to talk about them because they have enjoyed more than their fair share of philosophical attention. But the two certainly can be confused, and can *seem* to go very near to each other, even if they do not perhaps actually do so. You dropped the tea-tray: Certainly, but an emotional storm was about to break out: or, Yes, but there was a wasp. In each case the defence, very soundly, insists on a fuller description of the event in its context; but the first is a justification, the second an excuse. . . . [W]hen we plead, say, provocation, there is genuine uncertainty or ambiguity as to what we mean — is *he* partly responsible, because he roused a violent impulse or passion in me, so that it wasn't truly or merely me acting "of my own accord" (excuse)? Or is it rather that, he having done me such injury, I was entitled to retaliate (justification)? Such doubts merely make it the more urgent to clear up the usage of these various terms. But that the defences I have for convenience labelled "justification" and "excuse" are in principle distinct can scarcely be doubted.

HART, LEGAL RESPONSIBILITY AND EXCUSES
in Determinism and Freedom in the Age of Modern Science 81-87 (S. Hook ed. 1958) [7]

It is characteristic of our own and all advanced legal systems that the individual's liability to punishment, at any rate for serious crimes carrying severe penalties, is made by law to depend, among other things, on certain mental conditions. These conditions can best be expressed in negative form as *excusing* conditions: the individual is not liable to punishment if at the time of his doing what would otherwise be a punishable act he was unconscious, mistaken about the physical consequences of his bodily movements or the nature or qualities of the thing or persons affected by them, or, in some cases, if he was subjected to threats or other gross forms of coercion or was the victim of certain types of mental disease. This is a list, not meant to be complete, giving broad descriptions of the principal excusing conditions; the exact definition of these and their precise character and scope must be sought in the detailed exposition of our criminal law. . . .

In the criminal law of every modern state responsibility for serious crimes is excluded or "diminished" by some of the conditions we have referred to as "excusing conditions." In Anglo-American criminal law this is the doctrine that a "subjective element," or "mens rea," is required for criminal responsibility, and it is because of this doctrine that a criminal trial may involve investigations into the sanity of the accused; into what he knew, believed, or foresaw; or into the questions whether or not he was subject to coercion by threats or provoked into passion, or was prevented by disease or transitory loss of consciousness from controlling the movements of his body or muscles. These matters come

---

7. Reprinted in H. L. A. Hart, Punishment and Responsibility, ch. 2, at 28 (1968).

up under the heads known to lawyers as Mistake, Accident, Provocation, Duress, and Insanity, and are most clearly and dramatically exemplified when the charge is one of murder or manslaughter.

Though this general doctrine underlies the criminal law, no legal system in practice admits without qualification the principle that *all* criminal responsibility is excluded by *any* of the excusing conditions. In Anglo-American law this principle is qualified in two ways. First, our law admits crimes of "strict liability." These are crimes where it is no defence to show that the accused, in spite of the exercise of proper care, was ignorant of the facts that made his act illegal. Here he is liable to punishment even though he did not intend to commit an act answering the definition of the crime. . . . Secondly, even in regard to crimes where liability is not "strict," so that mistake or accident rendering the accused's action *unintentional* would provide an excuse, many legal systems do not accept some of the other conditions we have listed as excluding liability to punishment. This is so for a variety of reasons.

For one thing, it is clear that not only lawyers but scientists and plain men differ as to the relevance of some excusing conditions, and this lack of agreement is usually expressed as a difference of view regarding what kind of factor limits the human *capacity* to control behaviour. Views so expressed have indeed changed with the advance of knowledge about the human mind. Perhaps most people are now persuaded that it is possible for a man to have volitional control of his muscles and also to know the physical character of his movements and their consequences for himself and others, and yet be *unable* to resist the urge or temptation to perform a certain act; yet many think this incapacity exists only if it is associated with well-marked physiological or neurological symptoms or independently definable psychological disturbances. . . .

Another reason limiting the scope of the excusing conditions is difficulty of *proof.* Some of the mental elements involved are much easier to prove than others. It is relatively simple to show that an agent lacked, either generally or on a particular occasion, volitional muscular control; it is somewhat more difficult to show that he did not know certain facts about either present circumstance (e.g., that a gun was loaded) or the future (that a man would step into the line of fire); it is much more difficult to establish whether or not a person was deprived of "self-control" by passion provoked by others, or by partial mental disease. As we consider these different cases not only do we reach much vaguer concepts, but we become progressively more dependent on the agent's own statements about himself, buttressed by inferences from "common-sense" generalizations about human nature, such as that men are capable of self-control when confronted with an open till but not when confronted with a wife in adultery. The law is accordingly much more cautious in admitting "defects of the will" than "defect in knowledge" as qualifying or excluding criminal responsibility. Further difficulties of proof may cause a legal system to limit its inquiry into the agent's "subjunctive condition" by asking what a "reasonable man" would in the circumstances have known or foreseen, or by asking whether "a reasonable man" in the circumstances would have been deprived (say, by provocation) of self-control; and the system may then impute to the agent such knowledge or foresight or control.

For these practical reasons, no simple identification of the necessary mental subjective elements in responsibility with the full list of excusing conditions can be made; and in all systems far greater prominence is given to the more easily provable elements of volitional control of muscular movement and knowledge of circumstances or consequences than to the other more elusive elements.

2. Duress

STATE v. TOSCANO

Supreme Court of New Jersey
74 N.J. 421, 378 A.2d 755 (1977)

PASHMAN, J. Defendant Joseph Toscano was convicted of conspiring to obtain money by false pretenses in violation of N.J.S.A. 2A:98-1. Although admitting that he had aided in the preparation of a fraudulent insurance claim by making out a false medical report, he argued that he had acted under duress. The trial judge ruled that the threatened harm was not sufficiently imminent to justify charging the jury on the defense of duress. After the jury returned a verdict of guilty, the defendant was fined $500.

The Appellate Division affirmed the conviction. . . .

We granted certification to consider the status of duress as an affirmative defense to a crime. . . .

On April 20, 1972, the Essex County Grand Jury returned a 48-count indictment alleging that eleven named defendants and two unindicted co-conspirators had defrauded various insurance companies by staging accidents in public places and obtaining payments in settlement of fictitious injuries. . . .

Dr. Joseph Toscano, a chiropractor, was named as a defendant in the First Count and in two counts alleging a conspiracy to defraud the Kemper Insurance Company (Kemper). Prior to trial, seven of the eleven defendants pleaded guilty to various charges, leaving defendant as the sole remaining defendant charged with the conspiracy to defraud Kemper. Among those who pleaded guilty was William Leonardo, the architect of the alleged general conspiracy and the organizer of each of the separate incidents. . . .

The State attempted to show that Toscano agreed to fill out the false medical report because he owed money to Richard Leonardo [William's brother] for gambling debts. It also suggested that Toscano subsequently sought to cover up the crime by fabricating office records of non-existent office visits by Hanaway.[a] Defendant sharply disputed these assertions and maintained that he capitulated to William Leonardo's demands only because he was fearful for his wife's and his own bodily safety. Since it is not our function here to assess these conflicting versions, we shall summarize only those facts which, if believed by the jury, would support defendant's claim of duress. . . .

[The court recited a number of overtures made by William Leonardo to defendant, which defendant refused, to prepare a false medical report for submission to a claims adjuster.]

The third and final call occurred on Friday evening. Leonardo was "boisterous and loud" repeating, "You're going to make this bill out for me." Then he

---

a. Hanaway was an unindicted coconspirator who acted as the victim in a number of staged accidents. — EDS.

said: "Remember, you just moved into a place that has a very dark entrance and you leave there with your wife. . . . You and your wife are going to jump at shadows when you leave that dark entrance." Leonardo sounded "vicious" and "desperate" and defendant felt that he "just had to do it" to protect himself and his wife. He thought about calling the police, but failed to do so in the hope that "it would go away and wouldn't bother me any more."

In accordance with Leonardo's instructions, defendant left a form in his mailbox on Saturday morning for Leonardo to fill in with the necessary information about the fictitious injuries. It was returned that evening and defendant completed it. On Sunday morning he met Hanaway at a prearranged spot and delivered a medical bill and the completed medical report. He received no compensation for his services, either in the form of cash from Willian Leonardo or forgiven gambling debts from Richard Leonardo. He heard nothing more from Leonardo after that Sunday.

Shortly thereafter, still frightened by the entire episode, defendant moved to a new address and had his telephone number changed to an unlisted number in an effort to avoid future contacts with Leonardo. He also applied for a gun permit but was unsuccessful. His superior at his daytime job with the Newark Housing Authority confirmed that the quality of defendant's work dropped so markedly that he was forced to question defendant about his attitude. After some conversation, defendant explained that he had been upset by threats against him and his wife. He also revealed the threats to a co-worker at the Newark Housing Authority.

After defendant testified, the trial judge granted the State's motion to exclude any further testimony in connection with defendant's claim of duress, and announced his decision not to charge the jury on that defense. . . .

After stating that the defense of duress is applicable only where there is an allegation that an act was committed in response to a threat of present, imminent and impending death or serious bodily harm, the trial judge charged the jury:

> Now, one who is standing and receiving instructions from someone at the point of a gun is, of course, in such peril. . . .
>
> Now, where the peril is not imminent, present and pending to the extent that the defendant has the opportunity to seek police assistance for himself and his wife as well, the law places upon such a person the duty not to acquiesce in the unlawful demand and any criminal conduct in which he may thereafter engage may not be excused. Now, this principle prevails regardless of the subjective estimate he may have made as to the degree of danger with which he or his wife may have been confronted. Under the facts of this case, I instruct you, as members of the jury, that the circumstances described by Dr. Toscano leading to his implication in whatever criminal activities in which you may find he participated are not sufficient to constitute the defense of duress.

The trial judge's formulation of the law of duress appears in harmony with recent decisions of this Court. [The court then considered these cases but concluded that they were not controlling on their facts.] Thus, we approach this case as the first instance in which a defendant charged with a crime other than murder allegedly committed under the threat of serious bodily injury to himself and a near relative has raised the issue of whether such harm must be "present, imminent and impending.". . . .

Since New Jersey has no applicable statute defining the defense of duress,[b] we are guided only by common law principles which conform to the purposes of our criminal justice system and reflect contemporary notions of justice and fairness.

At common law the defense of duress was recognized only when the alleged coercion involved a use or threat of harm which is "present, imminent and pending" and "of such a nature as to induce a well grounded apprehension of death or serious bodily harm if the act is not done." Nall v. Commonwealth, 208 Ky. 700, 271 S.W. 1059 (1925).

It was commonly said that duress does not excuse the killing of an innocent person even if the accused acted in response to immediate threats. Aside from this exception, however, duress was permitted as a defense to prosecution for a range of serious offenses. . . .

To excuse a crime, the threatened injury must induce "such a fear as a man of ordinary fortitude and courage might justly yield to." United States v. Haskell, 26 Fed. Cas. 207 (Pa. Cir. Ct. 1823). Although there are scattered suggestions in early cases that only a fear of death meets this test, . . .[8] an apprehension of immediate serious bodily harm has been considered sufficient to excuse capitulation to threats. Thus, the courts have assumed as a matter of law that neither threats of slight injury nor threats of destruction to property are coercive enough to overcome the will of a person of ordinary courage. [The court then referred to cases in which threats of loss of job, denial of food rations, economic need, and prospect of financial ruin were held inadequate.] A "generalized fear of retaliation" by an accomplice, unrelated to any specific threat, is also insufficient. See People v. Robinson, 41 Ill. App. 3d 526, 354 N.E.2d 117 (1976). When the alleged source of coercion is a threat of "future" harm, courts have generally found that the defendant had a duty to escape from the control of the threatening person or to seek assistance from law enforcement authorities.

Assuming a "present, imminent and impending" danger, however, there is no requirement that the threatened person be the accused. . . . [C]oncern for the well-being of another, particularly a near relative, can support a defense of duress if the other requirements are satisfied. . . .

A less rigorous standard has been imposed in a few cases involving relatively minor, non-violent crimes. . . .

For the most part, however, the same test has been utilized to assess the sufficiency of the defendant's allegations for the purpose of charging the jury, regardless of the nature of the crime. . . .

The insistence under the common law on a danger of immediate force causing death or serious bodily injury may be ascribed to its origins in early cases dealing with treason, to the proclivities of a "tougher-minded age," R. I. Recreation Center v. Aetna Casualty & Surety Co., 177 F.2d at 605, or simply to judicial fears of perjury and fabrication of baseless defenses. We do not discount the latter concern as a reason for caution in modifying this accepted rule, but we are concerned by its obvious shortcomings and potential for injustice. Under

---

b. New Jersey does have such a statute at the present time, the legislature having enacted in the meantime the draft proposal referred to subsequently in the court's opinion. — EDS.

8. Several states, by statute, continue to require that the actor have reasonable cause to believe that his life was in danger. . . . . Minnesota limits the defense to situations in which "instant death" is threatened. Minn. Stat. 609.08 (1965).

some circumstances, the commission of a minor criminal offense should be excusable even if the coercive agent does not use or threaten force which is likely to result in death or "serious" bodily injury.[10] Similarly, it is possible that authorities might not be able to prevent a threat of future harm from eventually being carried out. . . . [T]he courts have not wholly disregarded the predicament of an individual who reasonably believes that appeals for assistance from law enforcement officials will be unavailing, but there has been no widespread acknowledgment of such an exception. . . .

Commentators have expressed dissatisfaction with the common law standard of duress. Stephen viewed the defense as a threat to the deterrent function of the criminal law, and argued that "it is at the moment when temptation is strongest that the law should speak most clearly and emphatically to the contrary." Stephen, 2 History of the Criminal Law in England 107 (1883). . . .

Others have been more skeptical about the deterrent effects of a strict rule. As the Alabama Supreme Court observed in an early case: "That persons have exposed themselves to imminent peril and death for their fellow man, and that there are instances where innocent persons have submitted to murderous assaults, and suffered death, rather than take life, is well established; but such self-sacrifice emanated from other motives than the fear of legal punishment." [Arp v. State, 97 Ala. at 12, 12 So. at 303].

Building on this premise, some commentators have advocated a flexible rule which would allow a jury to consider whether the accused actually lost his capacity to act in accordance with "his own desire, or motivation, or will" under the pressure of real or imagined forces. See Newman & Weitzer, "Duress, Free Will and the Criminal Law," 30 S. Cal. L. Rev. 313, 331 (1957); Fletcher, "The Individualization of Excusing Conditions," 47 S. Cal. L. Rev. 1269, 1288-93 (1974). The inquiry here would focus on the weaknesses and strengths of a particular defendant, and his subjective reaction to unlawful demands. Thus, the "standard of heroism" of the common law would give way, not to a "reasonable person" standard, but to a set of expectations based on the defendant's character and situation.

The drafters of the Model Penal Code and the New Jersey Penal Code sought to steer a middle course between these two positions by focusing on whether the standard imposed upon the accused was one with which "normal members of the community will be able to comply. . . .

Thus, they proposed that a court limit its consideration of an accused's "situation" to "stark, tangible factors which differentiate the actor from another, like his size or strength or age or health," excluding matters of temperament. They substantially departed from the existing statutory and common law limitations requiring that the result be death or serious bodily harm, that the threat be immediate and aimed at the accused, or that the crime committed be a noncapital offense. While these factors would be given evidential weight, the failure

---

10. If the only consideration were the maximization of social benefits in a single instance, there would undoubtedly be situations in which even the destruction of property or of a person's reputation would constitute a greater evil than the commission of an act proscribed by the criminal law. Both the Model Penal Code and the proposed New Jersey Penal Code established a general principle of justification as a defense, which would encompass many of those cases. See Model Penal Code §3.02, Comment (Tent. Draft No. 8, 1958); New Jersey Penal Code §2C:3-1 (1971). . . .

to satisfy one or more of these conditions would not justify the trial judge's withholding the defense from the jury. . . .

Although they are not entirely identical, under both model codes defendant would have had his claim of duress submitted to the jury.[12] Defendant's testimony provided a factual basis for a finding that Leonardo threatened him and his wife with physical violence if he refused to assist in the fraudulent scheme. Moreover, a jury might have found from other testimony adduced at trial that Leonardo's threats induced a reasonable fear in the defendant. Since he asserted that he agreed to complete the false documents only because of this apprehension, the requisite elements of the defense were established. Under the model code provisions, it would have been solely for the jury to determine whether a "person of reasonable firmness in his situation" would have failed to seek police assistance or refused to cooperate, or whether such a person would have been, unlike defendant, able to resist.

Exercising our authority to revise the common law, we have decided to adopt this approach as the law of New Jersey. Henceforth, duress shall be a defense to a crime other than murder if the defendant engaged in conduct because he was coerced to do so by the use of, or threat to use, unlawful force against his person or the person of another, which a person of reasonable firmness in his situation would have been unable to resist. . . .

Defendant's conviction of conspiracy to obtain money by false pretenses is hereby reversed and remanded for a new trial.

MODEL PENAL CODE

SECTION 2.09. DURESS

[See Appendix for text of this section.]

COMMENT TO §2.09 AT 6-7 [TENT. DRAFT NO. 10, 1960]

The problem of this Section then reduces to the question whether there are cases where the actor cannot justify his conduct under Section 3.02, as when his choice involves an equal or a greater evil than that threatened, but where he nonetheless should be excused because he was subjected to coercion. If he is so far overwhelmed by force that his behavior is involuntary, as when his

---

12. The most significant difference between the two provisions is the treatment of duress as a defense to murder. The Model Penal Code permits it as an affirmative defense, while the New Jersey Penal Code allows it only to reduce a crime from murder to manslaughter. [See Model Penal Code §2.09, Appendix to this casebook.]

New Jersey Penal Code §2C:2-9:

"a. Subject to Subsection b of this Section, it is an affirmative defense that the actor engaged in the conduct charged to constitute an offense because he was coerced to do so by the use of, or a threat to use, unlawful force against his person or the person of another, which a person of reasonable firmness in his situation would have been unable to resist.

"b. The defense provided by this Section is unavailable if the actor recklessly placed himself in a situation in which it was probable that he would be subject to duress. The defense is also unavailable if he was criminally negligent in placing himself in such a situation, whenever criminal negligence suffices to establish culpability for the offense charged. In a prosecution for murder, the defense is only available to reduce the degree of the crime to manslaughter."

arm is physically moved by someone else, Section 2.01(1) . . . stands as a barrier to liability, following in this respect the long tradition of the penal law. The case that here is our concern is that in which the actor makes a choice but claims in his defense that he was so intimidated that he was unable to choose otherwise than as he did. Should such psychical incapacity be given the same exculpative force as the physical incapacity that may afford a defense under Section 2.01? . . .

In favor of allowing the defense, it may be argued that the legal sanction cannot be effective in the case supposed and that the actor may not properly be blamed for doing what he had to choose to do. It seems clear, however, that the argument must be rejected. The crucial reason is the same as that which elsewhere leads to an unwillingness to vary legal norms with the individual's capacity to meet the standards they prescribe, absent a disability that is both gross and verifiable, such as the mental disease or defect that may establish irresponsibility. The most that it is feasible to do with lesser disabilities is to accord them proper weight in sentencing. To make liability depend upon the fortitude of any given actor would be no less impractical or otherwise impolitic than to permit it to depend upon such other variables as intelligence or clarity of judgment, suggestibility or moral insight.

We may not lightly grant, moreover, that the legal standard does not gain in its effectiveness by being unconditional in this respect. We do not and we cannot know what choices may be different if the actor thinks he has a chance of exculpation on the ground of his peculiar disabilities than if he knows that he does not. No less important, legal norms and sanctions operate not only at the moment of climatic choice but also in the fashioning of values and of character.[a]

Though we believe, for the foregoing reasons, that the submission that the actor lacked the fortitude to make the moral choice should not be entertained as a defense, we think a different situation is presented if the claimed excuse is based upon the incapacity of men in general to resist the coercive pressures to which the individual succumbed. . . . [L]aw is ineffective in the deepest sense, indeed . . . it is hypocritical, if it imposes on the actor who has the misfortune to confront a dilemmatic choice, a standard that his judges are not prepared to affirm that they should and could comply with if their turn to face the problem should arise. Condemnation in such case is bound to be an ineffective threat; what is, however, more significant is that it is divorced from any moral base and is unjust. . . .

The draft accordingly provides for the defense in cases where the actor was coerced by force or threats of force "which a person of reasonable firmness in his situation would have been unable to resist." The standard, however, is not wholly external in its reference; account is taken of the actor's "situation," a term which we should think would here be given the same scope it is accorded in appraising negligence. See Section 2.02(2)(d), Tentative Draft No. 4 (1955) and Comments, id. p. 126. Stark, tangible factors that differentiate the actor from another, like his size or strength or age or health, would be considered. Matters of temperament would not.

a. For an argument to the contrary see Fletcher, The Individualization of Excusing Conditions, 47 S. Cal. L. Rev. 1269 (1974). — Eds.

PROBLEMS

1. In those jurisdictions in which duress may not be a defense to murder or other extremely serious crime, how might it be argued that duress may still be a defense where the compelled participation of the defendant is relatively minor? Consider the observations of Bray, C.J., dissenting in Regina v. Brown, [1968] S.A.S.R. 467, 494:

> The reasoning generally used to support the proposition that duress is no defence to a charge of murder is, to use the words of Blackstone cited above, that "he ought rather to die himself, than escape by the murder of an innocent." Generally speaking I am prepared to accept this position. Its force is obviously considerably less where the act of the threatened man is not the direct act of killing but only the rendering of some minor form of assistance, particularly when it is by no means certain that if he refuses the death of the victim will be averted, or conversely when it is by no means certain that if he complies the death will be a necessary consequence. It would seem hard, for example, if an innocent passer-by seized in the street by a gang of criminals visibly engaged in robbery and murder in a shop and compelled at the point of a gun to issue misleading comments to the public, or an innocent driver compelled at the point of a gun to convey the murderer to the victim, were to have no defence. . . .

See generally O'Regan, Duress and Murder, 35 Mod. L. Rev. 596 (1972).

In Lynch v. Director of Public Prosecutions, [1975] 1 All E.R. 913, the appellant, Lynch, was charged as a principal in the second degree (that is, accomplice) in the murder of a police constable in Northern Ireland. Lynch had driven three armed members of the I.R.A. to a place near where the policeman was stationed and, after the shooting, had driven the three men away again. At his trial Lynch alleged that he had been ordered by one of the three, Meehan, who was well known as a ruthless gunman, to participate in the events which led to the crime. There was evidence that Lynch was in peril of being shot if he disobeyed Meehan. The trial judge refused to instruct the jury on duress, taking the view that, as a matter of law, the defense of duress was not available on a charge of murder.

The House of Lords majority, following generally the reasoning of Bray, C.J., ordered a new trial and held that on a charge of murder the defense of duress is open at least to a person who is accused as an accomplice.

Query: Does the line between first- and second-degree principals serve as a secure basis for determining when duress is potentially available? May there not be circumstances where action of the second-degree principal is at least as heinous as that of the first-degree principal — for example, planning the murder, hiring the actual killer, and providing the means? Contrariwise, may there not be circumstances where the action of the first-degree principal is at least as extenuating as that of the second-degree principal?

2. The Model Penal Code takes the position that its defense of general justification (the §3.02 principle of choice of the lesser evil) is applicable where the external circumstance compelling the choice has its source in the threatened action of another, and also where its source is some force of the physical world. See §2.09(4). At the same time, however, its defense of duress is so formulated that it applies only where the external circumstance creating the predicament has its source in the threatened action of another person, and not where its source is some force of the physical world. Is the latter position defensible? If an individual acted under such coercive pressure that people in general would lack the capacity to act otherwise, on what ground can a formulation be defended that would excuse such individual if the coercive pressure came from the threats of another but not if the identical pressure arose from a natural predicament?

Consider the following cases:

(a) *X* is unwillingly driving a car along a narrow and precipitous mountain road which drops off sharply on both sides, under the command of *Y*, an armed escaping felon. The headlights pick out two drunken persons lying across the road in such a position as to make passage impossible without running them over. *X* is prevented from stopping by the threat of *Y* to shoot him dead if he declines to drive straight on. If *X* does go on and kills the drunks in order to save himself, he will be excused under §2.09 if the jury should find that "a person of reasonable firmness in his situation would have been unable to resist," although he would not be justified under the lesser evil principle of §3.02.

(b) The same situation as above except that *X* is prevented from stopping by suddenly inoperative brakes. His alternatives are either to run down the drunks or to run off the road and down the mountainside. If *X* chooses the first alternative to save his own life and kills the drunks, he will not be excused under §2.09 even if a jury should find that a person of reasonable firmness would have been unable to do otherwise.

Can the difference between these two cases be defended? If so, on what grounds? If not, how might the Model Penal Code be amended to reach the desired result? Does the logic of the matter necessarily push to a formulation that would excuse an actor whenever he or she commits a criminal act in such circumstances that people in general would lack the fortitude to do otherwise? If so, it would be open in every criminal case for the accused to present evidence to try to show that reasonable people in defendant's situation would lack the will to act otherwise than as defendant acted. Would this be unacceptable for some reason? If so, how could the "person of reasonable firmness" formula be narrowed other than the way the Model Penal Code chose to narrow it, that is, by restricting it to cases of physical duress by another?

Consider the following models:

Criminal Codes of Queensland and Western Australia:

> Subject to the express provisions of this Code relating to acts done upon compulsion or provocation or in self-defence, a person is not criminally responsible for an act or omission done or made under such circumstances of sudden or extraordinary emergency that an ordinary person possessing ordinary power of self-control could not reasonably be expected to act otherwise.

California Joint Legislative Committee for Revision of the Penal Code, Penal Code Revision Project §520 (Tent. Draft No. 1, 1967):

> In a prosecution for any offense: (1) it is an affirmative defense that the defendant engaged in the conduct otherwise constituting the offense because he was coerced into doing so by the threatened use of unlawful force against his person or the person of another in circumstances where a person of reasonable firmness in his

situation would not have done otherwise; (2) it is an affirmative defense that the defendant engaged in the conduct otherwise constituting the offense in order to avoid death or great bodily harm to himself or another in circumstances where a person of reasonable firmness in his situation would not have done otherwise.

3. The prosecution of Patty Hearst for bank robbery generated considerable discussion of the possible defense of "brainwashing" as an extension of the traditional exculpatory defenses, including duress. Ms. Hearst, it will be recalled, was kidnapped and held in confinement for months by members of the Symbionese Liberation Army. During that period, she participated with her abductors in a bank robbery, with apparent enthusiasm, to judge by the testimony and the bank's television tapes. On her subsequent apprehension, she was charged with the crime of bank robbery. An issue in the case was not only whether she was forced to participate by threats of death, principally a factual question, but also whether, even if that were not the case, her actions should be regarded as excusable because they resulted from the inculcation of beliefs by her captors through pressures of psychological indoctrination while she was held in captivity and complete subservience. As one article put it, "The jury in the Hearst case was faced with the question of when coerced behavior ends and truly voluntary action begins for persons who appear to have changed their loyalties and values while held in captivity." Lunde & Wilson, Brainwashing as a Defense to Criminal Liability: Patty Hearst Revisited, 13 Crim. L. Bull. 341, 342 (1977).

Consider what possible defenses might be plausibly argued for Ms. Hearst, what changes in existing doctrine, if any, would be needed to cover the case, and whether it would be sound to make those changes.

See, in addition to the article by Lunde & Wilson, Delgado, Ascription of Criminal States of Mind: Toward a Defense Theory for the Coercively Persuaded ("Brainwashed") Defendant, 63 Minn. L. Rev. 1 (1978), as well as an exchange generated by this article between Professors Dressler and Delgado in 63 Minn L. Rev. 335 & 361 (1979).

PROBLEM OF THE MILGRAM EXPERIMENTS

Consider the tests of "person of reasonable firmness" or "person of ordinary power of self control" in the light of the experiments and findings of Professor Milgram, Obedience to Authority (1974).

In 1960, Milgram began a series of experiments to study obedience to authority. The subjects of his study, selected from newspaper advertisements promising $4.50 for an hour of participation, represented a cross-section of people from diverse walks of life. When a subject arrived at the laboratory, the subject met two other individuals: one was the "experimenter" and the other was, ostensibly, another subject. In reality, both were play-acting their respective roles.

Through a manipulated series of "chance" drawings, the real subject was given the role of teacher, and the pseudo-subject became the learner. The learner, who was then strapped to a chair and fitted with electrodes, was to be taught a series of word associations by the teacher-subject. Whenever the learner made a mistake, the subject was to administer a shock from a control apparatus equipped with 30 switches, running from 15 volts to 450 volts in

15-volt steps. These gradations were further divided on the control panel into 7 zones, ranging from "slight shock" to "danger: severe shock." As the experimenter explained, the subject was to increase the voltage one step each time the learner made a mistake.

Actually, the learner did not receive a shock. The learner answered according to a predetermined schedule of responses. In the basic "Remote" experiment, the subject was in one room and the learner in another. There was no communication between them until the shock level reached 330 volts, at which point the learner pounded the walls in protest. At a higher voltage, the pounding ceased and no further answers were registered. In the "Voice-Feedback" variation, the subject was able to hear the learner's protests. The learner went through a prearranged series of reactions to the shock: At low levels of voltage the learner grunted; at 120 volts, the learner cried out in pain and demanded to be released; from 330 volts to 450 volts, the learner made no more sounds and refused to answer.

From Milgram's description of the procedures employed, it appears that the subjects were convinced that they were inflicting painful shocks on the learner. Nearly all of the subjects demonstrated discomfort and internal conflict. Yet the overall result was that in the basic "Remote" experiment, 65 percent of the subjects inflicted shocks all the way to the highest possible range; and in the "Voice-Feedback" variation, 62.5 percent participated to the conclusion. Although the subjects frequently expressed reluctance to continue, they responded to the authority of the experimenter by continuing to increase the voltage. Hesitant subjects were coerced by the statement, "The experiment requires that you continue." Balky subjects were given sterner commands, such as, "You have no other choice, you must go on."

In addition to the above results, Milgram obtained results indicating that physical proximity of the experimenter to the subject determined the degree of obedience. When the learner was placed in a room only a few feet away from the subject, the percentage of obedient subjects dropped to 40 percent. And when the subject was required to force the learner's hand to the shock plate, the percentage of obedience fell to 30 percent. But when the subject was relieved of the responsibility for shocking the learner and only participated to the extent of recording the shock durations while another person administered the shock, 68.75 percent of the subjects participated to the conclusion. In Milgram's view, even though subjects were accessories to the act of administering the shock, the fact that they no longer actively produced the shock themselves meant that they were no longer implicated psychologically to the degree that the strain led to disobedience.

Milgram explains the results of his experiments with the notion that human beings function within hierarchical structures, a characteristic developed through evolution. In his view, human beings are born with the potential to obey, which then interacts with societal influences to produce obedient persons. Conscience (or superego) is seen as the inhibitory system used to guard against the unregulated expression of impulse, but the inhibitory mechanism may fail when the individual becomes secondary to the need to allow a higher authority to control. Milgram describes the phenomenological expression of this shift (id. at 133):

> The critical shift in functioning is reflected in an alteration of attitude. Specifically, the person entering an authority system no longer sees himself as acting out of

his own purposes but rather comes to see himself as an agent for executing the wishes of another person.

Indeed, the most far-reaching result of this shift, in Milgram's view, is that one comes to feel responsible for the authority but feels no responsibility for the content of the action the authority directs.

Significantly, the results Milgram achieved were not as predicted. He described the experiment to psychiatrists, college students, and middle-class adults, and asked them to predict their own performances. None of the respondents predicted participation beyond 300 volts, and most saw themselves as disobeying the experimenter at a lower shock level (id. at 30):

> These subjects see their reactions flowing from empathy, compassion, and a sense of justice. They enunciate a conception of what is desirable and assume that action follows accordingly. But they show little insight into the web of forces that operate in a real social situation.

When asked to predict how others would perform, the groups predicted that all subjects, with the exception of a "pathological fringe" (not exceeding 2 percent), would refuse to obey the experimenter at some point. The psychiatrists predicted that most subjects would not go beyond 150 volts, the point at which the learner first explicitly demands to be released; that only 4 percent would reach 300 volts; and that only one subject in 1,000 would administer the highest shock.

3. Intoxication

ROBERTS v. PEOPLE

Supreme Court of Michigan
19 Mich. 401 (1870)

CHRISTIANCY, J. The defendant was tried in the Circuit Court for the County of Calhoun, upon an information charging him with assaulting, with intent to murder, one Charles E. Greble, by shooting at him with a loaded pistol.

The first question presented by the record is, whether, under this information, the jury could properly find the defendant guilty of the assault with the intent charged, without finding, as matter of fact, that the defendant entertained that particular intent?

We think the general rule is well settled, to which there are few, if any exceptions, that when a statute makes an offense to consist of an act combined with a particular intent, that intent is just as necessary to be proved as the act itself, and must be found by the jury, as matter of fact, before a conviction can be had. . . .

This case, so far as regards the intention to kill, is not identical with that of murder. To find the defendant guilty of the whole charge, it is true, the jury must find the intent to kill under circumstances which would have made the killing murder — and it is not denied that had death ensued in the present case, it would have been murder. But the converse of the proposition does not necessarily follow; that, because the killing would have been murder, therefore there must have been an intention to kill. Murder may be and often is committed without any specific or actual intention to kill. . . .

The second question raised by the exceptions, is whether the voluntary drunkenness of the defendant, immediately prior to and at the time of the assault, to a degree that would render him incapable of entertaining, in fact, the intent charged, would constitute a valid defense, so far as related to the intent, and leave the defendant liable only for what he actually did — the assault, without the aggravation of the intent. . . .

In determining the question whether the assault was committed with the intent charged, it was therefore material to inquire whether the defendant's mental faculties were so far overcome by the effect of intoxication, as to render him incapable of entertaining the intent. And for this purpose, it was the right and duty of the jury — as upon the question of intent of which this forms a part — to take into consideration the nature and circumstances of the assault, the actions, conduct and demeanor of the defendant, and his declaration before, at the time, and after the assault; and especially to consider the nature of the intent and what degree of mental capacity was necessary to enable him to entertain the simple intent to kill, under circumstances of this case. . . . And as a matter of law, I think the jury should have been instructed, that if his mental faculties were so far overcome by intoxication, that he was not conscious of what he was doing, or if he did know what he was doing, but did not know why he was doing it, or that his actions and the means he was using were naturally adapted or calculated to endanger life or produce death; that he had not sufficient capacity to entertain the intent, and in that event they could not infer that intent from his acts. But if he knew what he was doing, why he was doing it, and that his actions with the means he was using were naturally adapted or likely to kill, then the intent to kill should be inferred from his acts in the same manner and to the same extent as if he was sober. But that on the other hand, to be capable of entertaining the intent, it was not necessary that he should so far have the possession of his mental faculties as to be capable of appreciating the moral qualities of his actions, or of any intended results, as being right or wrong. He must have presumed to have intended the obscuration and perversion of his faculties which followed from his voluntary intoxication. He must be held to have purposely blinded his moral perceptions, and set his will free from the control of reason — to have suppressed the guards and invited the mutiny. . . .

But he is not to be held responsible for the intent, if he was too drunk for a conscious exercise of the will to the particular end, or, in other words, too drunk to entertain the intent, and did not entertain it in fact. If he did entertain it in fact, though but for the intoxication he would not have done so, he is responsible for the intent as well as the acts. . . .

But the Circuit Court held, in effect, that no extent of intoxication could have the effect to disprove the intent, treating the intent as an inference of law for the Court, rather than a question of fact for the jury. In this we think there was error. . . .

NOTE

The proposition that, apart from its relevance on the issue of mens rea or responsibility, defendant's intoxication has no bearing in determining guilt of the crime charged is universally accepted. Is this a sound position? "If a man is punished for doing something when drunk that he would not have done when sober, is he not in plain truth punished for getting drunk?" (G. Williams, Criminal Law: The General Part 564 (2d ed. 1961).)

Compare the following points of view:

J. Hall, General Principles of Criminal Law 556 (1960):

> The principle of mens rea limits penal liability to normal persons who intentionally or recklessly commit harms forbidden by penal law. But since drinking is not usually followed by intoxication, and intoxication does not usually lead to the commission of such harms, it follows that normal persons who commit harms while grossly intoxicated, should not be punished unless, at the time of sobriety and the voluntary drinking, they had such prior experience as to anticipate their intoxication and that they would become dangerous in that condition.

Model Penal Code §2.08, Comment at 3 (Tent. Draft No. 9, 1959):

> This position raises no problem of importance in the ordinary case where drink or drugs have at the most induced a temporary change in personality, impairing judgment or reducing inhibition or control. In such a situation, all of the elements of the offense have been established. The law does no more than to hold that it is not an excuse that the actor might not have committed the offense had he been sober. The infirmity induced by intoxication offers no stronger basis for the actor's exculpation than infirmities produced by other causes.

PEOPLE v. HOOD
Supreme Court of California
1 Cal. 3d 444, 462 P.2d 370 (1969)

Traynor, C.J. [The evidence showed that defendant, who had been drinking heavily, resisted an effort by a police officer to subdue and arrest him and in the course of the struggle seized the officer's gun and shot him in the legs. He was convicted on count 1 of assault with a deadly weapon upon a peace officer, Cal. Penal Code §245. The California Supreme Court reversed because of the failure of the trial court to instruct on the lesser-included offense of simple assault. He was also convicted on count 3 of assault with intent to murder the officer, Cal. Penal Code §217. The supreme court reversed this conviction as well because the trial court gave "hopelessly conflicting instructions on the effect of intoxication." In order to guide the trial court on retrial, the supreme court proceeded to consider the effect of intoxication on the crime of assault with a deadly weapon. The supreme court noted that the California courts of appeal were in conflict on whether simple assault and assault with a deadly weapon were "specific intent" or "general intent" crimes. It then continued:]

The distinction between specific and general intent crimes evolved as a judicial response to the problem of the intoxicated offender. That problem is to reconcile two competing theories of what is just in the treatment of those who commit crimes while intoxicated. On the one hand, the moral culpability of a drunken criminal is frequently less than that of a sober person effecting alike injury. On the other hand, it is commonly felt that a person who voluntarily gets drunk and while in that state commits a crime should not escape the consequences. (See Hall, General Principles of Criminal Law (2d ed. 1960), p. 537.)

Before the nineteenth century, the common law refused to give any effect to the fact that an accused committed a crime while intoxicated. The judges were apparently troubled by this rigid traditional rule, however, for there were a number of attempts during the early part of the nineteenth century to arrive at a more humane, yet workable, doctrine. The theory that these judges explored was that evidence of intoxication could be considered to negate intent, whenever intent was an element of the crime charged. As Professor Hall notes, however, such an exculpatory doctrine could eventually have undermined the traditional rule entirely, since some form of mens rea is a requisite of all but strict liability offenses. (Hall, Intoxication and Criminal Responsibility, 57 Harv. L. Rev. 1045, 1049.) To limit the operation of the doctrine and achieve a compromise between the conflicting feelings of sympathy and reprobation for the intoxicated offender, later courts both in England and this country drew a distinction between so-called specific intent and general intent crimes.

Specific and general intent have been notoriously difficult terms to define and apply, and a number of text writers recommended that they be abandoned altogether. (Hall, General Principles of Criminal Law, supra, p. 142; Williams, Criminal Law — The General Part (2d ed. 1961) §21, p. 49.) Too often the characterization of a particular crime as one of specific or general intent is determined solely by the presence or absence of words describing psychological phenomena —"intent" or "malice," for example — in the statutory language defining the crime. When the definition of a crime consists of only the description of a particular act, without reference to intent to do a further act or achieve a future consequence, we ask whether the defendant intended to do the proscribed act. This intention is deemed to be a general criminal intent. When the definition refers to defendant's intent to do some further act or achieve some additional consequence, the crime is deemed to be one of specific intent. There is no real difference, however, only a linguistic one, between an intent to do an act already performed and an intent to do that same act in the future.

The language of Penal Code section 22, drafted in 1872 when "specific" and "general" intent were not yet terms of art, is somewhat broader than those terms:

> No act committed by a person while in a state of voluntary intoxication is less criminal by reason of his having been in such condition. But whenever the actual existence of any particular purpose, motive, or intent is a necessary element to constitute any particular species or degree of crime, the jury may take into consideration the fact that the accused was intoxicated at the time, in determining the purpose, motive, or intent with which he committed the act.

Even this statement of the relevant policy is no easier to apply to particular crimes. We are still confronted with the difficulty of characterizing the mental element of a given crime as a particular purpose, motive, or intent necessary to constitute the offense, or as something less than that to which evidence of intoxication is not pertinent.

Even if we assume that the presence or absence of words clearly denoting mental activity is a valid criterion for determining the significance of intoxication, our present problem is not resolved. The difficulty with applying such a test to the crime of assault or assault with a deadly weapon is that no word in the relevant code provisions unambiguously denotes a particular mental element, yet the word "attempt" in Penal Code section 240 strongly suggests goal-directed, intentional behavior.[6] This uncertainty accounts for the conflict over whether assault is a crime only of intention or also of recklessness.

We need not reconsider our position in *Carmen* [footnote 6 supra] that an assault cannot be predicated merely on reckless conduct. Even if assault requires an intent to commit a battery on the victim, it does not follow that the crime is one in which evidence of intoxication ought to be considered in determining whether the defendant had that intent. It is true that in most cases specific intent has come to mean an intention to do a future act or achieve a particular result, and that assault is appropriately characterized as a specific intent crime under this definition. An assault, however, is equally well characterized as a general intent crime under the definition of general intent as an intent merely to do a violent act. Therefore, whatever reality the distinction between specific and general intent may have in other contexts, the difference is chimerical in the case of assault with a deadly weapon or simple assault. Since the definitions of both specific intent and general intent cover the requisite intent to commit a battery, the decision whether or not to give effect to evidence of intoxication must rest on other considerations.

A compelling consideration is the effect of alcohol on human behavior. A significant effect of alcohol is to distort judgment and relax the controls on aggressive and anti-social impulses. (Beck and Parker, The Intoxicated Offender — A Problem of Responsibility (1966), 44 Can. Bar Rev. 563, 570-573; Muelberger, Medico-Legal Aspects of Alcohol Intoxication (1956), 45 Mich. State Bar J. 36, 40-41.) Alcohol apparently has less effect on the ability to engage in simple goal-directed behavior, although it may impair the efficiency of that behavior. In other words, a drunk man is capable of forming an intent to do something simple, such as strike another, unless he is so drunk that he has reached the stage of unconsciousness. What he is not as capable as a sober man of doing is exercising judgment about the social consequences of his acts or controlling his impulses toward anti-social acts. He is more likely to act rashly and impulsively and to be susceptible to passion and anger. It would therefore be anomalous to allow evidence of intoxication to relieve a man of responsibility for the crimes of assault with a deadly weapon or simple assault, which are so frequently committed in just such a manner. As the court said in Parker v. United States (D.C. Cir. 1966) 359 F.2d 1009, 1012-1013, "Whatever ambiguities there may be in distinguishing between specific and general intent to determine whether drunkenness constitutes a defense, an offense of this nature is not one which requires an intent that is susceptible to negation through a showing of voluntary intoxication."

Those crimes that have traditionally been characterized as crimes of specific

---

6. Penal Code, section 240 provides: "An assault is an unlawful attempt, coupled with a present ability, to commit a violent injury on the person of another."

It was the strong suggestion of intent in the ordinary usage of the word "attempt" that was at the basis of this court's remark in People v. Carmen, 36 Cal. 2d 768, 775 [228 P.2d 281], that "[o]ne could not very well 'attempt' or try to 'commit' an injury on the person of another if he had no intent to cause any injury to such other person."

intent are not affected by our holding here. The difference in mental activity between formulating an intent to commit a battery and formulating an intent to commit a battery for the purpose of raping or killing may be slight, but it is sufficient to justify drawing a line between them and considering evidence of intoxication in the one case and disregarding it in the other. Accordingly, on retrial the court should not instruct the jury to consider evidence of defendant's intoxication in determining whether he committed assault with a deadly weapon on a peace officer or any of the lesser assaults included therein. . . .

NOTES

1. Pointing to the confusion generated in the lower courts by the decision in People v. Hood, the California Supreme Court in People v. Rocha, 3 Cal. 3d 893, 479 P.2d 372 (1971), announced flatly that assault with a deadly weapon was a general-intent crime as to which the defense of intoxication was irrelevant. For a discussion of the judicial use of the distinction between general and specific intent, see Comment, Rethinking the Specific-General Intent Doctrine in California Criminal Law, 63 Calif. L. Rev. 1352 (1975); Roth, General Versus Specific Intent: A Time for Terminological Understanding in California, 7 Pepperdine L. Rev. 67 (1979).

2. For a decision comparable to *Hood,* see Director of Public Prosecutions v. Majewski, [1977] A.C. 443. A searching criticism may be found in G. Williams, Textbook of Criminal Law 422-430 (1978).

An English committee once proposed the creation of a new offense of dangerous intoxication when the prosecution for a dangerous crime fails for lack of intent due to intoxication. Report of the Committee on Mentally Abnormal Offenders 235 et seq. (Cmnd. 6244, 1975) (the Butler Committee). See Ashworth, The Butler Committee and Criminal Responsibility, [1975] Crim. L. Rev. 687. For a discussion of the Butler Committee recommendation and other alternatives for dealing with the problem, see Criminal Law Revision Committee, Fourteenth Report, Offences against the Person 111-118 (Cmnd. 7844, 1980).

MODEL PENAL CODE

SECTION 2.08.   INTOXICATION

[See Appendix for text of this section.]

COMMENT TO §2.08, AT 7-9 [(TENT. DRAFT NO. 8, 1959)]
Two major problems . . . are presented by the draft.

The first, which seems more readily disposed of, is the question whether intoxication ought to be accorded a significance that is entirely co-extensive with its relevance to disprove purpose or knowledge, when they are the requisite mental elements of a specific crime. We submit that the answer clearly ought to be affirmative; that when the definition of a crime or a degree thereof requires proof of such a state of mind, the legal policy involved will almost certainly obtain whether or not the absence of purpose or knowledge is due to the actor's

self-induced intoxication or to some other cause. For when the purpose or knowledge, as distinguished from recklessness, is made essential for conviction, the
reason very surely is that in the absence of such states of mind the conduct
involved does not present a comparable danger, as in burglary or theft; or
that the actor is not deemed to present as significant a threat, as in treason
and perhaps the first degree of murder; or, finally, that the ends of legal policy
are served by bringing to book or subjecting to graver sanctions those who
consciously defy the legal norm. If the mental state which is the basis of the
law's concern does not exist, the reason for its nonexistence is quite plainly
immaterial. So it is that in the case of crimes of violence against the person,
purpose or knowledge rarely is required to establish liability, though their presence may have weight for sentence; recklessness or even negligence is ordinarily
sufficient.

The second and more difficult question relates to recklessness, where awareness of risk created by the actor's conduct ordinarily is requisite for liability
under Section 2.02. The problem is whether intoxication ought to be accorded
a significance co-extensive with its relevance to disprove such awareness, as in
the case of purpose or of knowledge that has previously been discussed.

It is clear that this is the result that should ensue unless a special rule of
liability is formulated on the subject; and the prevailing law with respect to
"general intent" is, in its most acceptable aspect, precisely such a special rule
upon this point, however unfortunate the terms in which the rule is cast. Whether
it ought to be preserved presents, in our view, the major issue that arises on
this subject.

Those who oppose a special rule for drunkenness in relation to awareness
of the risk in recklessness draw strength initially from this presumptive disfavor
of any special rules of liability. . . . The protagonists of this position draw
further strength from the proposition that it is precisely the awareness of the
risk in recklessness that is the essence of its moral culpability — a culpability
dependent on the magnitude of the specific risk advertently created. When that
risk is greater in degree than that which the actor perceives at the time of
getting drunk, as is frequently the case, the result of a special rule is bound
to be a liability disproportionate to culpability. Hence the solution urged is to
dispense with any special rule, relying rather on the possibility of proving foresight at the time of drinking and, when this cannot be proved, upon a generalized
prohibition of being drunk and dangerous, with sanctions appropriate for such
behavior. To the extent that negligence may establish criminal liability, that
is, of course, a further sanction that may be available without establishing a
special rule.

The case thus made is worthy of respect, but there are strong considerations
on the other side. We mention first the weight of the prevailing law which
here, more clearly than in England, has tended towards a special rule for drunkenness. Beyond this, there is the fundamental point that awareness of the potential consequences of excessive drinking on the capacity of human beings to
gauge the risks incident to their conduct is by now so dispersed in our culture
that we believe it fair to postulate a general equivalence between the risks created
by the conduct of the drunken actor and the risks created by his conduct in
becoming drunk. Becoming so drunk as to destroy temporarily the actor's powers
of perception and of judgment is conduct which plainly has no affirmative social

value to counterbalance the potential danger. The actor's moral culpability lies in engaging in such conduct. Added to this are the impressive difficulties posed in litigating the foresight of any particular actor at the time when he imbibes and the relative rarity of cases where intoxication really does engender unawareness as distinguished from imprudence. These considerations lead us to propose, on balance, that the Code declare that unawareness of a risk of which the actor would have been aware had he been sober be declared immaterial.

STATE v. STASIO

Supreme Court of New Jersey
78 N.J. 467, 396 A.2d 1129 (1979)

SCHREIBER, J. The major issue on this appeal is whether voluntary intoxication constitutes a defense to a crime, one element of which is the defendant's intent. Defendant Stasio was found guilty by a jury of assault with intent to rob, in violation of N.J.S.A. 2A:90-2, and of assault while being armed with a dangerous knife, contrary to N.J.S.A. 2A:151-5. . . . The Appellate Division reversed the convictions and ordered a new trial. . . .

The scene of this incident was the Silver Moon Tavern located at 655 Van Houten Avenue, Clifton. The date was October 7, 1975. The defendant having presented no evidence, what occurred must be discerned from the testimony of three witnesses for the State: Peter Klimek, a part owner of the Silver Moon; Robert Colburn, a patron; and Robert Rowan, a member of the Clifton police force.

Robert Colburn had frequented the Silver Moon Tavern not only for its alcoholic wares but also to engage in pool. On October 7, Colburn arrived at the Tavern about 11:00 A.M. and started to play pool. Sometime before noon the defendant joined him. They stayed together until about 3:00 P.M. when the defendant left the bar. Though the defendant had been drinking during this period, in Colburn's opinion the defendant was not intoxicated upon his departure. Neither the defendant's speech nor his mannerisms indicated drunkenness.

Peter Klimek arrived at the Tavern shortly before 5:00 P.M. and assumed his shift at tending bar. There were about eight customers present when, at approximately 5:40 P.M., the defendant entered and walked in a normal manner to the bathroom. Shortly thereafter he returned to the front door, looked around outside and approached the bar. He demanded that Klimek give him some money. Upon refusal, he threatened Klimek. The defendant went behind the bar toward Klimek and insisted that Klimek give him $80 from the cash register. When Klimek persisted in his refusal, the defendant pulled out a knife. Klimek grabbed the defendant's right hand and Colburn, who had jumped on top of the bar, seized the defendant's hair and pushed his head toward the bar. The defendant then dropped the knife.

Almost immediately thereafter Police Officer Rowan arrived and placed the defendant in custody. He testified that defendant responded to his questions with no difficulty and walked normally. Klimek also stated that defendant did not appear drunk and that he had not noticed any odor of alcohol on defendant's breath.

At the conclusion of the State's case, the defendant elected not to take the stand. He made this decision because of an earlier conference in chambers at which defense counsel had advised the court that his defense would be that defendant had been so intoxicated that he was incapable of forming the intent to rob. The trial court responded by stating that it would charge that "voluntary intoxication was not a defense to any act by the defendant in this matter." The defendant on a voir dire made it clear that his decision not to testify was predicated upon the trial court's position. It might be noted that the defendant had no record of prior convictions.

Holding that the trial court's declaration in view of the defendant's proffer of proof was erroneous, the Appellate Division reversed the convictions and ordered a new trial. The Appellate Division reasoned that specific intent is an essential element of the crime of an assault with intent to rob and that voluntary intoxication may be shown to negate that element of the offense.

This Court last considered the culpability of an individual who had committed an illegal act while voluntarily under the influence of a drug or alcohol in State v. Maik, 60 N.J. 203, 287 A.2d 715 (1972). . . .

A difference of opinion has been expressed in the Appellate Division as to the meaning of Chief Justice Weintraub's discussion of intoxication in *Maik*. In State v. Del Vecchio, 142 N.J. Super. 359, 361 A.2d 579 (1976), a conviction for breaking and entering with intent to steal was reversed on the ground that the jury had improperly been charged that voluntary intoxication was not a defense to a crime requiring a specific intent. The Appellate Division reasoned that, when a specific intent was an element of an offense, voluntary intoxication may negate existence of that intent. . . . In contrast, Judge Allcorn's dissent in State v. Atkins, 151 N.J. Super. 555, 573, 377 A.2d 718 (App. Div. 1977), *rev'd*, 78 N.J. 454, 396 A.2d 1122 (1979), expresses the opinion that *Maik* stands for the proposition that voluntary intoxication is not a defense to any criminal offense irrespective of whether a specific or general intent is an element of the offense.

In our opinion the Chief Justice in *Maik* enunciated a principle applicable generally to all crimes and, unless one of the exceptions to the general rule is applicable, voluntary intoxication will not excuse criminal conduct. The need to protect the public from the prospect of repeated injury and the public policy demanding that one who voluntarily subjects himself to intoxication should not be insulated from criminal responsibility are strongly supportive of this result. We reject the approach adopted by *Del Vecchio* because, although it has surface appeal, it is based on an unworkable dichotomy, gives rise to inconsistencies, and ignores the policy expressed in *Maik*.

Del Vecchio would permit the intoxication defense only when a "specific" as distinguished from a "general" intent was an element of the crime. However, that difference is not readily ascertainable. "The distinction thus made between a 'specific intent' and a 'general intent,'" wrote the Chief Justice in *Maik*, "is quite elusive, and although the proposition [that voluntary intoxication may be a defense if it prevented formation of a specific intent] is echoed in some opinions in our State, . . . it is not clear that any of our cases in fact turned upon it." Professor Hall has deplored the attempted distinction in the following analysis:

"The current confusion resulting from diverse uses of 'general intent' is aggravated by dubious efforts to differentiate that from 'specific intent.' Each crime

. . . has its distinctive mens rea, e.g., intending to have forced intercourse, intending to break and enter a dwellinghouse and to commit a crime there, intending to inflict a battery, and so on. It is evident that there must be as many mentes reae as there are crimes. And whatever else may be said about an intention, an essential characteristic of it is that it is directed towards a definite end. To assert therefore that an intention is 'specific' is to employ a superfluous term just as if one were to speak of a 'voluntary act.' " J. Hall, General Principles of Criminal Law 142 (2d ed. 1960). . . .

Moreover, distinguishing between specific and general intent gives rise to incongruous results by irrationally allowing intoxication to excuse some crimes but not others. In some instances if the defendant is found incapable of formulating the specific intent necessary for the crime charged, such as assault with intent to rob, he may be convicted of a lesser included general intent crime, such as assault with a deadly weapon. In other cases there may be no related general intent offense so that intoxication would lead to acquittal. Thus, a defendant acquitted for breaking and entering with intent to steal because of intoxication would not be guilty of any crime — breaking and entering being at most under certain circumstances the disorderly persons offense of trespass. . . .

Finally, where the more serious offense requires only a general intent, such as rape, . . . intoxication provides no defense, whereas it would be a defense to an attempt to rape, specific intent being an element of that offense. Yet the same logic and reasoning which impels exculpation due to the failure of specific intent to commit an offense would equally compel the same result when a general intent is an element of the offense.

The *Del Vecchio* approach may free defendents of specific intent offenses even though the harm caused may be greater than in an offense held to require only general intent. This course thus undermines the criminal law's primary function of protecting society from the results of behavior that endangers the public safety. This should be our guide rather than concern with logical consistency in terms of any single theory of culpability, particularly in view of the fact that alcohol is significantly involved in a substantial number of offenses. The demands of public safety and the harm done are identical irrespective of the offender's reduced ability to restrain himself due to his drinking. . . .

Until a stuporous condition is reached or the entire motor area of the brain is profoundly affected, the probability of the existence of intent remains. The initial effect of alcohol is the reduction or removal of inhibitions or restraints. But that does not vitiate intent. The loosening of the tongue has been said to disclose a person's true sentiments —"*in vino veritas.*" . . . When a defendant shows that he was comatose and therefore could not have broken and entered into the home or committed some other unlawful activity, such stage of intoxication may be relevant in establishing a general denial. But short of that, voluntary intoxication, other than its employment to disprove premeditation and deliberation in murder, should generally serve as no excuse. In this fashion the opportunities of false claims by defendants may be minimized and misapplication by jurors of the effect of drinking on the defendant's responsibility eliminated. . . .

It might be suggested with some justification that we should adhere to the policy expressed in the new Code of Criminal Justice, effective September 1, 1979, N.J.S.A. 2C:98-4. However, the Deputy Attorney General implied at oral argument that the Legislature would be requested to modify the provisions dealing with intoxication and, in view of the possibility that the Legislature might act, in the interim we prefer to adhere to the principle enunciated in *Maik.* We note that in Arkansas, a law based on the Model Penal Code's provision for a defense of voluntary intoxication was repealed less than two years after it was enacted. Ark. Stat. Ann. §41-207 (1977). The repealing legislation was made effective immediately by a finding of emergency which read in part

> that the defense of voluntary intoxication is detrimental to the welfare and safety of the citizens of this State in that criminals are at times excused from the consequences of their criminal acts merely because of their voluntary intoxication.

1977 Ark. Acts, No. 101, §3. Similarly, Pennsylvania first enacted but then repealed a voluntary intoxication defense which was substantially the same as in the Model Penal Code. 18 Pa. Cons. Stat. Ann. §308 (Purdon Supp. 1978).[a]

The new Code of Criminal Justice provides that a person is not guilty of an offense unless he acted purposely, knowingly, recklessly or negligently, as the law may require. N.J.S.A. 2C:2-2. It also states that intoxication is not a defense "unless it negatives an element of the offense," N.J.S.A. 2C:2-8(a), and that

> [w]hen recklessness established an element of the offense, if the actor, due to self-induced intoxication, is unaware of a risk of which he would have been aware had he been sober, such unawareness is immaterial.

N.J.S.A. 2C:2-8(b). These provisions were taken from the Model Penal Code of the American Law Institute, §2.08 (Prop. Off. Draft 1962). . . .

Purpose or knowledge has been made a component of many offenses so that voluntary intoxication will be an available defense in those situations. Thus, voluntary intoxication may be a defense to aggravated assaults consisting of attempts to cause bodily injury to another with a deadly weapon. Intoxication could exonerate those otherwise guilty of burglaries and criminal trespass. It would be an available defense to arson, robbery, and theft. It could reduce murder to manslaughter, and excuse shoplifting. The Code would also permit the incongruous result of permitting intoxication to be a complete defense to an attempted sexual assault (rape), but not of a completed sexual assault. Whether the Legislature will retain any or all these provisions remains to be seen.

Our holding today does not mean that voluntary intoxication is always irrelevant in criminal proceedings.[7] Evidence of intoxication may be introduced to

---

a. The new Pennsylvania provision states: "Neither voluntary intoxication nor voluntary drugged condition is a defense to a criminal charge, nor may evidence of such conditions be introduced to negative the element of intent of the offense, except that evidence of such intoxication or drugged condition of the defendant may be offered by the defendant whenever it is relevant to reduce murder from a higher degree to a lower degree of murder."— Eds.

7. While we recognize that the rule we announce here is at odds with the rule in a number of other jurisdictions, see Annot., 8 A.L.R.3d 1236 (1966), it is in accord with the holding in several other states. See McDaniel v. State, 356 So. 2d 1151 (Miss. 1978) (armed robbery; court made rule); State v. Vaughan, 268 S.C. 119, 232 S.E.2d 328 (1977) (house-breaking and assault with intent to ravish; court made rule); Commonwealth v. Geiger, 475 Pa. 249, 380 A.2d 338 (1977) (by statute); McKenty v. State, 135 Ga. App. 271, 217 S.E.2d 388 (1975) (by statute); State v. Cornwall, 95 Idaho 680, 518 P.2d 863 (1974) (by statute); Rodriguez v. State, 513 S.W.2d 594 (Tex. Cr. App. 1974) (by statute); State v. Richardson, 495 S.W.2d 435 (Mo. 1973) (second degree

demonstrate that premeditation and deliberation have not been proven so that a second degree murder cannot be raised to first degree murder or to show that the intoxication led to a fixed state of insanity. Intoxication may be shown to prove that a defendant never participated in a crime. Thus it might be proven that a defendant was in such a drunken stupor and unconscious state that he was not a part of a robbery. . . . His mental faculties may be so prostrated as to preclude the commission of the criminal act. Under some circumstances intoxication may be relevant to demonstrate mistake. However, in the absence of any basis for the defense, a trial court should not in its charge introduce that element. A trial court, of course, may consider intoxication as a mitigating circumstance when sentencing a defendant.

Although the evidence in the record demonstrates that the defendant assaulted Klimek while possessed with a knife and that his mental faculties were not prostrated, we are disturbed by the trial court's ruling which precluded the defendant from taking the stand. Defense counsel's proffer of proof that the defendant had been in the tavern between 7:00 A.M. and 5:30 P.M., that he had been drinking most of the day, and that he did not remember anything about the offense could possibly lead to the conclusion that he did not commit the assault. In that event the effect of the voluntary intoxication would demonstrate a denial of the assault. However, if the attack did occur, then the voluntary intoxication would not serve as a defense, even though the defendant could not remember the event. It would have been far better practice for the trial court not to have made its ruling at some unrecorded conference in chambers. The court should have waited until the issue was reached at trial when evidence of intoxication was offered. Permitting defendants to withhold evidence because of an expected jury instruction focuses the trial on appellate review rather than on producing the evidence at the trial. As the Attorney General cogently comments in his brief,

> Any defendant who is dissatisfied with the state of the law could refrain from presenting proofs, take his chance with the verdict and, if found guilty, have a potential defense preserved on appeal.

Under the circumstances here, we are constrained to grant the defendant a new trial.

The judgment of the Appellate Division is affirmed.

PASHMAN, J., concurring in result only and dissenting.

In this and the companion case of State v. Atkins, 78 N.J. 454, 396 A.2d 1122 (1979), the majority rules that a person may be convicted of the crimes of assault *with intent* to rob and breaking and entering *with intent* to steal even though he never, in fact, intended to rob anyone or steal anything. The majority arrives at this anomalous result by holding that voluntary intoxication can never constitute a defense to any crime other than first-degree murder even though, due to intoxication, the accused may not have possessed the mental state specifically required as an element of the offense. This holding not only defies logic

---

murder; court made rule); Chittum v. Commonwealth, 211 Va. 12, 174 S.E.2d 779 (1970) (kidnapping and attempted rape; court made rule). See also Ark. Stat. Ann. §41-207 (1977), discussed supra . . .

and sound public policy, it also runs counter to dictates of prior caselaw and the policies enunciated by our Legislature in the new criminal code. I therefore dissent from that holding although I agree that the defendant is entitled to a new trial. . . .

. . . A person who intentionally commits a bad act is more culpable than one who engages in the same conduct without any evil design. The intentional wrongdoer is also more likely to repeat his offense, and hence constitutes a greater threat to societal repose. A sufficiently intoxicated defendant is thus subject to less severe sanctions not because the law "excuses" his conduct but because the circumstances surrounding his acts have been deemed by the Legislature to be less deserving of punishment.

It strains reason to hold that a defendant may be found guilty of a crime whose definition includes a requisite mental state when the defendant actually failed to possess that state of mind. Indeed, this is the precise teaching of cases allowing the intoxication defense in first-degree murder prosecutions. . . .

Just as the lack of premeditation, willfulness, or deliberation precludes a conviction for first-degree murder, so should the lack of intent to rob or steal be a defense to assault and battery with intent to rob, or breaking and entering with intent to steal. The principle is the same in both situations. If voluntary intoxication negates an element of the offense, the defendant has not engaged in the conduct proscribed by the criminal statute, and hence should not be subject to the sanctions imposed by that statute.

The majority ultimately grounds its conclusions on public policy considerations. It professes to be concerned with protecting society from drunken offenders. There are several problems with this approach. First, the majority's opinion is not even internally consistent. Although intoxication is not to be given the status of a defense, the majority states that it can be considered to "buttress the affirmative defense of reasonable mistake." State v. Atkins, 78 N.J. at 460, 396 A.2d at 1125. It is difficult to comprehend why the public would be less endangered by persons who become intoxicated and, as a result, commit alcohol-induced "mistakes" which would otherwise be criminal offenses, than by persons who get so intoxicated that they commit the same acts without any evil intent. In fact, it appears highly likely that the first group would encompass a larger number of persons and hence constitute a greater menace to society.

Second, the majority's opinion is not likely to deter the commission of alcohol-induced crimes. It is unrealistic to expect that before indulging in intoxicants people will consider the extent of their criminal responsibility for acts they might commit. In this respect, therefore, today's holding will not add to the public's safety.

The most important consideration, however, is that the standards for establishing the defense are extremely difficult to meet. Contrary to the implications contained in the majority opinion, it is not the case that every defendant who has had a few drinks may successfully urge the defense. The mere intake of even large quantities of alcohol will not suffice. Moreover, the defense cannot be established solely by showing that the defendant might not have committed the offense had he been sober. What is required is a showing of such a great prostration of the faculties that the requisite mental state was totally lacking. That is, to successfully invoke the defense, an accused must show that he was so intoxicated that he did not have the intent to commit an offense. Such a state of affairs will likely exist in very few cases. I am confident that our judges and juries will be able to distinguish such unusual instances. . . .

NOTES

1. California is now among the states that have restricted the use of an intoxication defense on the issue whether the defendant had the mens rea required by the crime charged. Cal. Penal Code §22, as amended by Senate Bill 54 (1981), now reads:

> 22. (a) No act committed by a person while in a state of voluntary intoxication is less criminal by reason of his having been in such condition. Evidence of voluntary intoxication shall not be admitted to negate the capacity to form any mental state including, but not limited to, purpose, intent, knowledge, or malice aforethought, with which the accused committed the act.
>
> (b) Whenever the actual existence of any mental state, including, but not limited to, purpose, intent, knowledge, or malice aforethought, is a necessary element to constitute any particular species or degree of crime, evidence that the accused was voluntarily intoxicated at the time of the commission of the crime is admissible on the issue as to whether the defendant actually formed any such mental state.
>
> (c) Voluntary intoxication includes the voluntary ingestion, injection, or taking by any other means of any intoxicating liquor, drug, or other substance.

Note that the statute makes evidence of voluntary intoxication inadmissible on the issue of the defendant's capacity to form the required mental state but admissible on the issue whether the defendant actually formed that mental state. Query: What is the significance of this distinction? How are courts likely to interpret and administer it?

2. Some of the reluctance to give the defendant's intoxication its normal evidentiary significance in rebutting the definitional mens rea elements of the crime charged is suggested by the following data in Moore, Legal Responsibility and Chronic Alcoholism, 122 Am. J. Psychiatry 748, 753 (1966):

> To demonstrate that the association of crime and alcohol is not insignificant, a sampling of a few statistics is enlightening. Of 882 felons arrested in a two-year period in Cincinnati, 64 percent had a urine alcohol level of 0.10 percent or higher. In crimes of violence, the incidence varied from 67 to 88 percent. A four-year study of 588 homicide cases in Philadelphia revealed that one or both parties had been drinking in 64 percent of the cases. In 44 percent of these cases, both parties had been drinking; in 9 percent, the victim only had been drinking and in 11 percent, the offender only had been drinking. In Cincinnati, 84 percent of 225 homicide victims had been drinking and 44 percent had a blood alcohol level of 0.15 percent or higher. So that we are not misled into thinking that the association is between crime and alcohol but not crime and alcoholism, we should consider another study which showed that 43 percent of 223 consecutively admitted male criminals were alcoholics.
>
> This is not an American phenomenon. In Yugoslavia, 60 to 80 percent of all crimes involve intoxication to some degree, with over half of the homicides committed during a state of pathological intoxication. The association of alcohol and crime was lower but not insignificant in Sweden: 39 percent of male offenders

but only 4.2 percent of women offenders were intoxicated at the time of the offense. In Japan, it was found that 36 percent of arsonists, 27 percent of murderers and 18 percent of assaulters had been intoxicated at the time of the crime, and 17.6 percent of all prisoners were intoxicated offenders.

3. The preceding material reveals a variety of approaches to circumscribing the defense of intoxication, all reflected in American law — for example, the general-intent–specific-intent approach, allowing the courts on a crime-by-crime basis to distinguish which crimes do and which do not permit the required mens rea to be drawn into question by evidence of the defendant's intoxication; the statutory exception for crimes requiring recklessness; the flat refusal in all crimes to permit evidence of intoxication to rebut the required mens rea, no matter what it is; and the California modification of this position. Which approach, if any, seems desirable?

STATE v. HALL
Supreme Court of Iowa
214 N.W.2d 205 (1974)

UHLENHUFF J. [Defendant shot and killed a person from whom he had hitched a ride in Oregon. Defendant's version was that shortly before the shooting he took a pill (apparently LSD) given to him by an acquaintance in California who told him it was a "little sunshine" and would make him feel "groovy." The pill induced hallucinations, and the deceased, who was sleeping in the car, seemed to turn into a rabid dog like one defendant's father shot before his eyes as a child. In panic, he seized decedent's gun and shot him. The jury found him sane and convicted him of first-degree murder. He appealed on the ground, inter alia, that the trial court should have instructed that defendant's drug intoxication, if proved, required an acquittal.]

. . . The case is different from the usual one in which the accused contends only that use of alcohol or other drugs prevented him from forming specific intent. Here defendant first contends the drug caused temporary insanity, which constitutes a complete defense. Defendant is right that insanity, if established, is a complete defense. Under our law the test of insanity is "whether the defendant had capacity to know the nature and quality of his acts and [the] distinction between right and wrong." State v. Harkness, 160 N.W.2d 324, 334 (Iowa). In addition to himself as a witness, defendant introduced testimony by two physicians who opined the drug was LSD and answered hypothetical questions about defendant's mental condition. By himself and those witnesses, defendant adduced substantial evidence which would meet the *Harkness* test in an ordinary case of an insanity defense. This evidence assumed the truth of defendant's testimony that he ingested the drug and sustained hallucinations as a result.

Defendant requested an instruction on insanity as a complete defense, tailored to include temporary insanity induced by drugs. The trial court refused it, and instructed that the jury should consider the claimed mental condition in connection with intent, as reducing the offense but not as exonerating it.

This court has held that a temporary mental condition caused by voluntary intoxication from alcohol does not constitute a complete defense. . . . Is the rule the same when the mental condition results from voluntary ingestion of other drugs? We think so, and the cases so hold. Commonwealth v. Campbell, 445 Pa. 488, 495, 284 A.2d 798, 801 ("there should be no legal distinction between the voluntary use of drugs and the voluntary use of alcohol in determining criminal responsibility").

Defendant does not contend that extended use of drugs caused him "settled or established" insanity. . . . He does argue that he did not take the pill voluntarily. . . . But assuming he did take a drug, according to his own testimony no one tricked him into taking it or forced him to do so. . . . Defendant did not take the pill by mistake — thinking, for example, it was candy. If his own testimony is believed, he knew it was a mind-affecting drug. . . . Commonwealth v. Campbell, supra, 445 Pa. at 495, 284 A.2d at 801 (LSD —"nonpredictability of effect on the human body is devoid of any adequate legal justification based upon legal precedent, or reason, or policy considerations for a radical change and departure from our law of criminal responsibility").

We hold that the trial court properly refused the requested instruction. . . . Affirmed.

LeGrand, J. (dissenting). . . . The insanity issue arose at trial because plaintiff testified he had ingested a quantity of LSD shortly before the events in question without knowing what it was and without realizing its possible harmful effects. The majority concedes there was ample medical testimony produced by defendant as to the properties of this hallucinogenic drug to support a finding defendant was suffering from a mental illness or temporary insanity and to require its submission to the jury. However, the majority then deprives defendant of this defense by holding his condition resulted from the voluntary ingestion of drugs, which it equates with voluntary alcoholic intoxication.

I find this portion of the majority opinion unacceptable on two grounds. First, I cannot agree that drug intoxication should be treated the same as that resulting from the use of alcohol. Second, even assuming the two are legally indistinguishable, the evidence here presents a fact question on the voluntariness of defendant's conduct, which should have taken the issue to the jury.

At the outset let me acknowledge that much of defendant's evidence is unlikely, even incredible. However, these are matters of credibility for jury determination. Like the majority, I assume the verity of his testimony for the purposes of this appeal. . . .

My first disagreement with the majority opinion deals with its premise that drug intoxication and alcohol intoxication are legally the same when considering them as a possible defense to the commission of a crime. There is authority to support that view, although not as much as the majority says there is. [Discussion of cases omitted.] . . .

I believe the Pennsylvania court is guilty of serious overstatement in Commonwealth v. Campbell, supra, 284 A.2d at 801, when it says the "overwhelming" view is that there is no distinction between alcoholic intoxication and drug intoxication. The present state of the case law is not nearly so one-sided. . . .

. . . The fallacy in the majority's position is that it puts the issue on a *time* basis rather than an *effect* basis. It says the use of drugs is no defense unless mental illness resulting from long established use is shown because that's what we have said of alcoholic intoxication. But we have said that about alcohol because ordinarily the use of alcohol produces no mental illness except by long continued excessive use. On the other hand that same result can be obtained overnight by the use of modern hallucinatory drugs like LSD.

The reason for our alcohol-intoxication rule disappears when we discuss the use of these drugs. See . . . Comment in 17 DePaul Law Rev., page 365 (1968), "LSD — Its Effect on Criminal Responsibility."

Several quotations from the latter are significant. At page 370 the author says: "LSD can cause a breakdown in the normal functioning of the mind because hallucinations and a complete break with reality is one result of the use of the drug."

At page 371 this appears: "The LSD reaction may be equated, for legal purposes, with delirium tremens. In many ways they have the same effect on the human mind, and it would appear that both should render the subject legally insane."

Our intoxication rationale as applied to alcohol simply does not fit the use of modern hallucinatory drugs; and it was never meant to. It was adopted before such drugs, as we now know them, were in common use. That is why I would say they *are* dissimilar and should be so regarded. . . .

In the case of alcohol, we have long experience which teaches us the usual and ordinary effects of alcohol upon the human mind and body. We are therefore justified in formulating general rules as to alcoholic intoxication, even though they may not operate with precise fairness in every case. We do not yet have the same scientific reliability on the effect of the use of drugs as far as criminal responsibility is concerned. But this should not tempt us to slough the matter off by lumping *all* drugs together with alcohol, where obviously many of them do not belong.

I would adopt a rule which affords a defendant the right to show temporary insanity under the standards announced in State v. Harkness, cited in the majority opinion, even though that condition may have resulted from a voluntary dosage of hallucinatory drugs.

Assuming, however, there is no merit to what I have said . . . there is still another reason why I cannot agree with the majority opinion. Even under that view, it is only *voluntary* intoxication which may not be relied upon as a defense to the commission of a criminal act. . . .

The testimony shows defendant took a pill which he knew to be a drug but which he did not know to be LSD and which he testified he thought to be harmless, although he had been told it would make him feel groovy. There is nothing to indicate he knew it could induce hallucinations or lead to the frightening debilitating effects of mind and body to which the doctors testified. The majority nevertheless holds the defendant's resulting drug intoxication was voluntary. I disagree. . . .

. . . [D]oes voluntary in this context refer to the *mechanical* act of ingesting the pill or does it refer to a willing and intelligent assumption of the possible harmful consequences of that act?

I am convinced voluntary as here used should relate to a knowledgeable acceptance of the danger and risk involved. Applied to the instant case, that rule would demand submission of the issue to a jury. See De Berry v. Commonwealth, (Ky. 1956), 289 S.W.2d 495, 497, where the court held one who commits a crime under the influence of drugs should be held guilty if he takes the drug *knowing the effect it is likely to have.* . . .

In my opinion the trial court erred in holding defendant was not entitled to have the issue of temporary insanity submitted to the jury under proper instruction. I would reverse and remand for a new trial, because of the court's failure to give such an instruction.

NOTES

1. Mental disorder from voluntary intoxication. The principle relied on in the majority opinion has wide acceptance. As stated in State v. Booth, 169 N.W.2d 869, 873 (Iowa 1979):

> Voluntary temporary intoxication does not excuse one for the criminal consequences of his conduct. . . . A distinction is made when prolonged extensive use of alcohol damages the brain and "settled or established" insanity results therefrom. This is treated the same as insanity from any other cause. However, a temporary condition caused by voluntary intoxication, such as is claimed here, does not excuse one from responsibility for his conduct. . . .

As amended in 1979, Conn. Gen. Stat. tit. 53a, §53a-13 provides a definition of the defense of legal insanity but concludes:

> It shall not be a defense under this section if such mental disease or defect was proximately caused by the voluntary ingestion, inhalation or injection of intoxicating liquor or any drug or substance, or any combination thereof, unless such drug was prescribed for the defendant by a licensed practitioner, as defined in section 20-184a, and was used in accordance with the directions of such prescription.

Query: Does this section mean that in Connecticut even a settled condition of legal insanity brought on by a life of excessive drinking is not a defense? How might the statute be more narrowly interpreted?

2. Mental disorder from involuntary intoxication. What should be the situation when defendant's intoxication is not in any sense his or her own fault? The Model Penal Code §2.08(4) provides that involuntary intoxication is a defense only if it so affects the defendant as to leave him, for the time being, in a condition meeting the requirements of the definition of legal insanity; that is, "if by reason of such intoxication the actor at the time of his conduct lacks substantial capacity either to appreciate its criminality or to conform his conduct to the requirements of law." This states the law generally prevailing in the United States.[8]

In support of its position, the Model Penal Code commentary states ((Tent. Draft No. 9, 1959) at 10):

> The actor whose personality is altered by intoxication to a lesser degree is in a position no different from that of others who may have difficulty in conforming to the law and yet are held responsible for violation.

8. See, e.g., Kans. Stat. Ann. ch. 21, §21-3208; Wis. Stat. Ann. tit. 45, §939.42; Torres v. State, 585 S.W.2d 746 (Tex. Crim. App. 1979); State v. Mriglot, 15 Wash. App. 446, 550 P.2d 17 (1977).

Query: If the actor would not have committed the act if sober and if the actor's intoxication is not an intentional act, on what basis can the actor justifiably be held? Compare §68 of the Proposed India Penal Code of 1837 (T. B. Macaulay, A Penal Code Prepared by the Indian Law Commissioners 13-14 (1837)):

> Nothing is an offence which a person does in consequence of being in a state of intoxication, provided that either the substance which intoxicated him was administered to him without his knowledge, or against his will, or that he was ignorant that it possessed any intoxicating quality.

See also State v. Rice, 379 A.2d 140 (Me. 1977).

3. *The test of voluntariness.* On the issue of whether the intoxication of defendant in the *Hall* case was involuntary, as argued by the dissent in that case, compare the Model Penal Code's definition of "self-induced intoxication" in §2.08(5):

> "[S]elf-induced intoxication" means intoxication caused by substances which the actor knowingly introduces into his body, the tendency of which to cause intoxication he knows or ought to know, unless he introduces them pursuant to medical advice or under such circumstances as would afford a defense to a charge of crime.

4. Mental Disorder

a. The Defense of Legal Insanity

(*i*) *Defining the Defense*

M'NAGHTEN'S CASE
House of Lords
10 Cl. & F. 200, 8 Eng. Rep. 718 (1843)

[Defendant was indicted for the murder of Edward Drummond, secretary to the prime minister, Sir Robert Peel. The defense introduced evidence of accused's insanity, particularly his obsession with certain morbid delusions. The presiding judge, Lord Chief Justice Tindal, in his charge to the jury stated:

> The question to be determined is whether at the time the act in question was committed, the prisoner had or had not the use of his understanding, so as to know that he was doing a wrong or wicked act. If the jurors should be of opinion that the prisoner was not sensible, at the time he committed it, that he was violating the laws both of God and man, then he would be entitled to a verdict in his favour: but if, on the contrary, they were of opinion that when he committed the act he was in a sound state of mind, then their verdict must be against him.

The jury returned a verdict of "not guilty, on the ground of insanity." The case attracted considerable attention, and the verdict as well as the general problem of the defense of legal insanity was debated in the House of Lords. As a result, the English judiciary (there were some 15 judges at the time) were invited to attend the House of Lords for the purpose of delivering answers to certain questions propounded to them. The famous *M'Naghten* Rule is found in the answer to the second and third questions delivered by Lord Chief Justice Tindal.]

Your Lordships are pleased to inquire of us, secondly, "What are the proper questions to be submitted to the jury, where a person alleged to be afflicted with insane delusion respecting one or more particular subjects or persons, is charged with the commission of a crime (murder, for example), and insanity is set up as a defence?" And, thirdly, "In what terms ought the question to be left to the jury as to the prisoner's state of mind at the time when the act was committed?" And as these two questions appear to us to be more conveniently answered together, we have to submit our opinion to be, that the jurors ought to be told in all cases that every man is to be presumed to be sane, and to possess a sufficient degree of reason to be responsible for his crimes, until the contrary be proved to their satisfaction; and that to establish a defence on the ground of insanity, it must be clearly proved that, at the time of the committing of the act, the party accused was labouring under such a defect of reason, from disease of the mind, as not to know the nature and quality of the act he was doing; or, if he did know it, that he did not know he was doing what was wrong. The mode of putting the latter part of the question to the jury on these occasions has generally been, whether the accused at the time of doing the act knew the difference between right and wrong: which mode, though rarely, if ever, leading to any mistake with the jury, is not, as we conceive, so accurate when put generally and in the abstract, as when put with reference to the party's knowledge of right and wrong in respect to the very act with which he is charged. If the question were to be put as to the knowledge of the accused solely and exclusively with reference to the law of the land, it might tend to confound the jury, by inducing them to believe that an actual knowledge of the law of the land was essential in order to lead to a conviction; whereas the law is administered upon the principle that every one must be taken conclusively to know it, without proof that he does know it. If the accused was conscious that the act was one which he ought not to do, and if the act was at the same time contrary to the law of the land, he is punishable; and the usual course therefore has been to leave the question to the jury, whether the party accused had a sufficient degree of reason to know that he was doing an act that was wrong: and this course we think is correct, accompanied with such observations and explanations as the circumstances of each particular case may require.

THE KING v. PORTER, 55 Commw. L.R. 182, 186-188 (1933): [Presiding at the trial, Justice Dixon offered the following explication of the *M'Naghten* Rule in his charge to the jury:]

There is a legal standard of disorder of mind which is sufficient to afford a ground of irresponsibility for crime, and a ground for your finding such a verdict as I have indicated [that is, not guilty on the ground of insanity]. It is my duty to explain that standard for you. . . .

Before explaining what that standard actually is, I wish to draw your attention to some general considerations affecting the question of insanity in the criminal law in the hope that by so doing you may be helped to grasp what the law prescribes. The purpose of the law in punishing people is to prevent others from committing a like crime or crimes. Its prime purpose is to deter people from committing offences. It may be that there is an element of retribution in the criminal law, so that when people have committed offences the law considers that they merit punishment, but its prime purpose is to preserve society from the depredations of dangerous and vicious people. Now, it is perfectly useless for the law to attempt, by threatening punishment, to deter people from committing crimes if their mental condition is such that they cannot be in the least influenced by the possibility or probability of subsequent punishment; if they cannot understand what they are doing or cannot understand the ground upon which the law proceeds. The law is not directed, as medical science is, to curing mental infirmities. The criminal law is not directed, as the civil law of lunacy is, to the care and custody of people of weak mind whose personal property may be in jeopardy through someone else taking a hand in the conduct of their affairs and their lives. This is quite a different thing from the question, what utility there is in the punishment of people who, at a moment, would commit acts which, if done when they were in sane minds, would be crimes. What is the utility of punishing people if they be beyond the control of the law for reasons of mental health? In considering that, it will not perhaps, if you have ever reflected upon the matter, have escaped your attention that a great number of people who come into a Criminal Court are abnormal. They would not be there if they were the normal type of average everyday people. Many of them are very peculiar in their dispositions and peculiarly tempered. That is markedly the case in sexual offences. Nevertheless, they are mentally quite able to appreciate what they are doing and quite able to appreciate the threatened punishment of the law and the wrongness of their acts, and they are held in check by the prospect of punishment. It would be very absurd if the law were to withdraw that check on the ground that they were somewhat different from their fellow creatures in mental make-up or texture at the very moment when the check is most needed. You will therefore see that the law, in laying down a standard of mental disorder sufficient to justify a jury in finding a prisoner not guilty on the ground of insanity at the moment of offence, is addressing itself to a somewhat difficult task. It is attempting to define what are the classes of people who should not be punished although they have done actual things which in others would amount to crime. . . . With that explanation I shall tell you what that standard is.

The first thing which I want you to notice is that you are only concerned with the condition of the mind at the time the act complained of was done. . . . The next thing which I wish to emphasize is that his state of mind must have been one of disease, disorder or disturbance. Mere excitability of a normal man, passion, even stupidity, obtuseness, lack of self-control, and impulsiveness, are quite different things from what I have attempted to describe as a state of disease or disorder or mental disturbance arising from some infirmity, temporary or of long standing. If that existed it must then have been of such a character as to prevent him from knowing the physical nature of the act he was doing or of knowing that what he was doing was wrong. . . .

NOTE ON LEGAL INSANITY IN OTHER CONTEXTS

The *M'Naghten* and *Porter* cases deal with the definition of legal insanity insofar as insanity at the time of the act is interposed as a defense at the trial. The law, however, attributes significance to the insanity of the accused for other purposes as well. A person who is insane may not be tried, convicted, or sentenced. Neither may such person be executed if convicted of a capital offense. Further, under many state statutes a person who becomes insane while in prison must be transferred to a mental hospital. Question: Is there reason to assume that the definition of insanity for all of these varied purposes should be the same?

1. Competency to stand trial. So far as concerns insanity for purposes of determining whether an accused may be tried and sentenced, the Model Penal Code states the test in terms generally accepted: "No person who as a result of mental disease or defect lacks capacity to understand the proceedings against him or to assist in his own defense shall be tried, convicted or sentenced for the commission of an offense so long as such incapacity endures." Section 4.04. See, e.g., State ex rel. Davey v. Owen, 133 Ohio St. 96, 104, 12 N.E.2d 144, 148 (1937):

> It is generally recognized that upon such a trial inquiry should be made whether the person indicted has sufficient mental capacity to recall the events of his life so that he can furnish to his counsel facts which ought to be stated and presented to a jury at his trial for the crime charged.

In Dusky v. United States, 362 U.S. 402, 402 (1960), the Supreme Court reversed a finding of competency to stand trial, stating:

> We . . . agree with the suggestion of the Solicitor General that it is not enough for the district judge to find that "the defendant [is] oriented to time and place and [has] some recollection of events," but that the "test must be whether he has sufficient present ability to consult with his lawyer with a reasonable degree of rational understanding — and whether he has a rational as well as factual understanding of the proceedings against him."

Question: If a judge finds that defendant is suffering from total hysterical amnesia concerning the alleged crime but is otherwise in full command of his or her faculties, is a finding of incompetency to stand trial appropriate? The cases are not in accord. See Anno., Amnesia as affecting capacity to commit crime or stand trial, 46 A.L.R.3d 544 (1973); Note, Amnesia, A Case Study in the Limits of Particular Justice, 71 Yale L.J. 109, 115 (1961).

In People v. Francabandera, 33 N.Y.2d 429, 354 N.Y.S.2d 609, 310 N.E.2d 292, 296-297 (1974), the New York Court of Appeals concluded that amnesia concerning the alleged crime does not generally constitute unfitness to proceed under a statute directed to a defendant "who, as a result of a mental disease or defect, lacks capacity to understand the proceedings against him or to assist in his own defense." The statute contemplated a situation, said the court, where "the defendant, because of a current inability to comprehend, or at least a severe impairment to that existing mental state, cannot with a modicum of intelligence assist counsel." However, the court stated that a case-by-case determination of the particular circumstances would be necessary because in some circumstances trial of an amnesiac might result in an unfair trial. In the circumstances presented (where defendant pleaded guilty to reckless endangerment arising out of a drunken exchange of gunfire with police), the court found no unfairness in permitting the prosecution to proceed. The court stated:

The alleged crime was played out in front of an audience and the overwhelming evidence, all of which was available to defendant, pointed to his guilt. From this evidence it could be determined that defendant was probably intoxicated. Had they been willing to risk the consequences, defendant and his counsel might have gone to trial on the question of defendant's inability to form the requisite intent to commit the crimes charged because of intoxication. Coupling the prosecution's evidence on this point with defendant's history of alcoholism, which defendant was perfectly capable of supplying counsel and of course capable, also, of testifying to, would have appeared to be the only course open if the decision to stand trial were made and, indeed, this is argued to us in defendant's brief. It is not explained to us, however, how defendant's lack of memory could actually have crippled his defense in this case in light of the nature of the crime and the evidence possessed by the prosecutor. It cannot be said that the decision to plead guilty to a lesser charge would not have been the most astute decision under these circumstances even had defendant been able to recall the events.

See also Commonwealth v. Barky, 476 Pa. 602, 383 A.2d 526 (1978).

2. Execution. How should insanity be defined for purposes of determining whether a person may be executed? The 1951 Pennsylvania Mental Health Act provided for the transfer to the mental hospital of any person detained in a penal or correctional institution who is mentally ill, and defined mental illness as "an illness which so lessens the capacity of a person to use his customary self-control, judgment and discretion in the conduct of his affairs and social relations as to make it necessary or advisable for him to be under care." In Commonwealth v. Moon, 383 Pa. 18, 117 A.2d 96 (1955), the court held this test applicable to determine whether to stay execution of a convicted murderer, since such a person is "detained" in a penal institution (pending execution) within the meaning of the act. Is the result sound? Why should execution of a person be stayed until the person is able to take proper care of himself or herself while alive?

Under the California Penal Code, a sentenced prisoner may not be executed if a specially impanelled jury of 12 persons finds, after inquiry, that he or she is presently insane. Upon such a finding, the prisoner must be kept in a medical facility of the Department of Corrections "until his reason is restored." §§3701, 3703.[9] Under the same code, a woman may not be executed while pregnant, but the determination of her pregnancy is to be made by three physicians. §§3705, 3706. Question: How can one account for the difference in procedure? Would it make sense to do the reverse — that is, to have 12 jurors determine whether a woman is pregnant and 3 physicians determine whether a person is too insane to be executed? Why not?

What does it mean to require that a condemned prisoner's reason be restored before he may be executed? Can a court decide without a sense of the law's reasons for not executing insane prisoners? What might those reasons be? See Hazard & Louisell, Death, the State and the Insane: Stay of Execution, 9 U.C.L.A.L. Rev. 38 (1962); Note, Insanity and the Condemned, 88 Yale L.J.

---

9. In Solesbee v. Balkom, 339 U.S. 9 (1949), the Supreme Court rejected a due process challenge to a Georgia statute providing that when a person facing execution seeks a stay on grounds of insanity, "the Governor may, within his discretion, have said person examined by such expert physicians as the Governor may choose; and . . . may, if he shall determine that the person convicted has become insane, . . . [stay execution until the person's] sanity shall have been restored."

533 (1979); Comment, The Eighth Amendment and the Execution of the Presently Incompetent, 32 Stan. L. Rev. 765 (1980).

MODEL PENAL CODE
(Tentative Draft No. 4, 1955)

SECTION 4.01. MENTAL DISEASE OR DEFECT EXCLUDING RESPONSIBILITY

(1) A person is not responsible for criminal conduct if at the time of such conduct as a result of mental disease or defect he lacks substantial capacity either to appreciate the criminality of his conduct or to conform his conduct to the requirements of law.

(2) The terms "mental disease or defect" do not include an abnormality manifested only by repeated criminal or otherwise anti-social conduct.

i.e. psychopath

Alternative formulations of paragraph (1):

(a) A person is not responsible for criminal conduct if at the time of such conduct as a result of mental disease or defect his capacity either to appreciate the criminality of his conduct or to conform his conduct to the requirements of law is so substantially impaired that he cannot justly be held responsible.

(b) A person is not responsible for criminal conduct if at the time of such conduct as a result of mental disease or defect he lacks substantial capacity to appreciate the criminality of his conduct or is in such state that the prospect of conviction and punishment cannot constitute a significant restraining influence upon him.

COMMENT TO §4.01 AT 156-160

1. No problem in the drafting of a penal code presents larger intrinsic difficulty than that of determining when individuals whose conduct would otherwise be criminal ought to be exculpated on the ground that they were suffering from mental disease or defect when they acted as they did. What is involved specifically is the drawing of a line between the use of public agencies and public force to condemn the offender by conviction, with resultant sanctions in which there is inescapably a punitive ingredient (however constructive we may attempt to make the process of correction) and modes of disposition in which that ingredient is absent, even though restraint may be involved. To put the matter differently, the problem is to discriminate between the cases where a punitive-correctional disposition is appropriate and those in which a medical-custodial disposition is the only kind that the law should allow.

2. The traditional *M'Naghten* rule resolves the problem solely in regard to the capacity of the individual to know what he was doing and to know that it was wrong. Absent these minimal elements of rationality, condemnation and punishment are obviously both unjust and futile. They are unjust because the individual could not, by hypothesis, have employed reason to restrain the act; he did not and he could not know the facts essential to bring reason into play. On the same ground, they are futile. A madman who believes that he is squeezing lemons when he chokes his wife or thinks that homicide is the command of God is plainly beyond reach of the restraining influence of law; he needs restraint

but condemnation is entirely meaningless and ineffective. Thus the attacks on the *M'Naghten* rule as an inept definition of insanity or as an arbitrary definition in terms of special symptoms are entirely misconceived. The *rationale* of the position is that these are cases in which reason can not operate and in which it is totally impossible for individuals to be deterred. Moreover, the category defined by the rule is so extreme that to the ordinary man the exculpation of the persons it encompasses bespeaks no weakness in the law. He does not identify such persons and himself; they are a world apart.

Jurisdictions in which the *M'Naghten* test has been expanded to include the case where mental disease produces an "irresistible impulse" proceed on the same *rationale*. They recognize, however, that cognitive factors are not the only ones that preclude inhibition; that even though cognition still obtains, mental disorder may produce a total incapacity for self-control. The same result is sometimes reached under *M'Naghten* proper, in the view, strongly put forth by Stephen, that "knowledge" requires more than the capacity to verbalize right answers to a question, it implies capacity to function in the light of knowledge. Stephen, History of English Criminal Law, vol. 2, p. 171. In modern psychiatric terms, the "fundamental difference between verbal or purely intellectual knowledge and the mysterious other kind of knowledge is familiar to every clinical psychiatrist; it is the difference between knowledge divorced from affect and knowledge so fused with affect that it becomes a human reality." Zilboorg, Misconceptions of Legal Insanity, 9 Am. J. Orthopsychiatry 540, 552. The application of *M'Naghten* has been mitigated somewhat, especially in England, by accepting evidence couched in these terms.

3. The draft accepts the view that any effort to exclude the non-deterrables from strictly penal sanctions must take account of the impairment of volitional capacity no less than of impairment of cognition; and that this result should be achieved directly in the formulation of the test, rather than left to mitigation in the application of *M'Naghten*. It also accepts the criticism of the "irresistible impulse" formulation as inept in so far as it may be impliedly restricted to sudden, spontaneous acts as distinguished from insane propulsions that are accompanied by brooding or reflection.

Both the main formulation recommended and alternative (a) deem the proper question on this branch of the inquiry to be whether the defendant was without capacity to conform his conduct to the requirements of law. . . . The application of the principle will call, of course, for a distinction between incapacity, upon the one hand, and mere indisposition on the other. Such a distinction is inevitable in the application of a standard addressed to impairment of volition. We believe that the distinction can be made. . . .

4. One further problem must be faced. In addressing itself to impairment of the cognitive capacity, *M'Naghten* demands that impairment be complete: the actor must *not* know. So, too, the irresistible impulse criterion presupposes a complete impairment of capacity for self-control. The extremity of these conceptions is, we think, the point that poses largest difficulty to psychiatrists when called upon to aid in their administration. The schizophrenic, for example, is disoriented from reality; the disorientation is extreme; but it is rarely total. Most psychotics will respond to a command of someone in authority within the mental hospital; they thus have some capacity to conform to a norm. But this is very different from the question whether they have the capacity to conform

to requirements that are not thus immediately symbolized by an attendant or policeman at the elbow. Nothing makes the inquiry into responsibility more unreal for the psychiatrist than limitation of the issue to some ultimate extreme of total incapacity, when clinical experience reveals only a graded scale with marks along the way. . . .

. . . The law must recognize that when there is no black and white it must content itself with different shades of gray. The draft, accordingly, does not demand *complete* impairment of capacity. It asks instead for *substantial* impairment. This is all, we think, that candid witnesses, called on to infer the nature of the situation at a time that they did not observe, can ever confidently say, even when they know that a disorder was extreme.

If substantial impairment of capacity is to suffice, there remains the question whether this alone should be the test or whether the criterion should state the principle that measures how substantial it must be. To identify the degree of impairment with precision is, of course, impossible both verbally and logically. . . . Alternative (a) proposes to submit the issue squarely to the jury's sense of justice, asking expressly whether the capacity of the defendant "was so substantially impaired that he can not justly be held responsible." Some members of the Council deemed it unwise to present questions of justice to the jury, preferring a submission that in form, at least, confines the inquiry to fact. The proponents of the alternative contend that since the jury normally will feel that it is only just to exculpate if the disorder was extreme, that otherwise conviction is demanded, it is safer to invoke the jury's sense of justice than to rest entirely on the single word "substantial," imputing no specific measure of degree. The issue is an important one and it is submitted for consideration by the Institute. . . .

6. Paragraph (2) of section 4.01 is designed to exclude from the concept of "mental disease or defect" the case of so-called "psychopathic personality." The reason for the exclusion is that, as the Royal Commission put it, psychopathy "is a statistical abnormality; that is to say, the psychopath differs from a normal person only quantitatively or in degree, not qualitatively; and the diagnosis of psychopathic personality does not carry with it any explanation of the causes of the abnormality." While it may not be feasible to formulate a definition of "disease," there is much to be said for excluding a condition that is manifested only by the behavior phenomena that must, by hypothesis, be the result of disease for irresponsibility to be established. Although British psychiatrists have agreed, on the whole, that psychopathy should not be called "disease," there is considerable difference of opinion on the point in the United States. Yet it does not seem useful to contemplate the litigation of what is essentially a matter of terminology; nor is it right to have the legal result rest upon the resolution of a dispute of this kind.

NOTE

For the text of Model Penal Code §4.01 as finally adopted by the American Law Institute, see Appendix to this casebook.

The ALI proposal has been adopted by statute or case law in a very substantial number of American jurisdictions. Two judicial decisions adopting the Model

Penal Code's formulation follow. In People v. Drew, the California Supreme Court adopts the Model Penal Code test in light of the state's unsatisfactory experience with the *M'Naghten* test theretofore prevailing. Many courts have done the same for similar reasons. United States v. Brawner is different. The United States Court of Appeals for the District of Columbia Circuit had earlier abandoned *M'Naghten* in favor of a test (the *Durham* Rule) widely supported by the psychiatric community. In the *Brawner* case the same court adopts the Model Penal Code's test in view of the district's unsatisfactory experience with the *Durham* Rule.

PEOPLE v. DREW

Supreme Court of California, 1978
22 Cal. 3d 333, 583 P.2d 1318

TOBRINER, J. For over a century California has followed the *M'Naghten* test to define the defenses of insanity and idiocy. The deficiencies of that test have long been apparent, and judicial attempts to reinterpret or evade the limitations of *M'Naghten* have proven inadequate. We . . . have concluded that we should discard the *M'Naghten* language, and update the California test of mental incapacity as a criminal defense by adopting the test proposed by the American Law Institute and followed by the federal judiciary and the courts of 15 states. . . .

Despite its widespread acceptance, the deficiencies of *M'Naghten* have long been apparent. Principal among these is the test's exclusive focus upon the cognitive capacity of the defendant, an outgrowth of the then current psychological theory under which the mind was divided into separate independent compartments, one of which could be diseased without affecting the others. . . . Current psychiatric opinion, however, holds that mental illness often leaves the individual's intellectual understanding relatively unimpaired, but so affects his emotions or reason that he is unable to prevent himself from committing the act. . . .

The annals of this court are filled with illustrations . . . : the deluded defendant in People v. Gorshen, 51 Cal. 2d 716, who believed he would be possessed by devilish visions unless he killed his foreman; the schizophrenic boy in People v. Wolff, 61 Cal. 2d 795, who knew that killing his mother was murder but was unable emotionally to control his conduct despite that knowledge; the defendant in People v. Robles (1970) 2 Cal. 3d 205 suffering from organic brain damage, who mutilated himself and killed others in sudden rages. To ask whether such a person knows or understands that his act is "wrong" is to ask a question irrelevant to the nature of his mental illness or to the degree of his criminal responsibility.

Secondly, "*M'Naghten*'s single track emphasis on the cognitive aspect of the personality recognizes no degrees of incapacity. . . . [D]efendant knows right from wrong or he does not. . . . But such a test is grossly unrealistic. . . . As the commentary to the American Law Institute's Model Penal Code observes, 'The law must recognize that when there is no black and white it must content itself with different shades of gray.' "

In short, *M'Naghten* purports to channel psychiatric testimony into the narrow issue of cognitive capacity, an issue often unrelated to the defendant's illness or crime. The psychiatrist called as a witness faces a dilemma: either he can

restrict his testimony to the confines of *M'Naghten,* depriving the trier of fact
of a full presentation of the defendant's mental state, or he can testify that
the defendant cannot tell "right" from "wrong" when that is not really his
opinion because by so testifying he acquires the opportunity to put before the
trier of fact the reality of defendant's mental condition.[a]

Even if the psychiatrist is able to place before the trier of fact a complete
picture of the defendant's mental incapacity, that testimony reaches the trier
of fact weakened by cross-examination designed to show that defendant knew
right from wrong and limited by the *M'Naghten* instruction. As a result, conscientious juries have often returned verdicts of sanity despite plain evidence of
serious mental illness and unanimous expert testimony that the defendant was
insane. (See People v. Wolff, 61 Cal. 2d 795, 812 and cases there cited.)

Conscious of the inadequacies of the *M'Naghten* test, California decisions have
modified that test in two significant respects. First, in People v. Wolff, 61 Cal.
2d 795, we held that the mere capacity to verbalize socially acceptable answers
to questions did not prove sanity; the defendant must not only know but also
"appreciate" or "understand" the nature and wrongfulness of his act. (Pp. 800-
801.) Second, in a series of decisions dating from People v. Wells (1949) 33
Cal. 2d 330 and People v. Gorshen, 51 Cal. 2d 716, we developed the concept
of diminished capacity, under which a defendant can introduce evidence of mental incapacity to negate specific intent, malice, or other subjective elements of
the charged crime. Recently in People v. Cantrell (1973) 8 Cal. 3d 672, we
expressly held that "irresistible impulse" — a concept evolved to supply the volitional element lacking in the *M'Naghten* test — can be utilized to prove diminished capacity. (Pp. 685-686.)

But these innovative modifications to the *M'Naghten* rule fail to cure its basic
defects. . . . The doctrine of diminished capacity, once hailed as a possible
replacement for the defense of insanity (see Diamond, Criminal Responsibility
of the Mentally Ill (1961) 14 Stan. L. Rev. 59), can now be seen to create its
own problems.

The availability of a defense of diminished capacity turns largely on the nature
of the crime charged. If the defendant is charged with a general intent crime,
he cannot raise a defense of diminished capacity regardless of his impaired
mental state. If charged with a specific intent crime, he may be able to reduce
the offense to a lesser included general intent crime. If evidence of diminished
capacity is used to negate criminal intent in a crime which contains no lesser
offense, however, the defendant may secure his outright acquittal and release.
The effectiveness of the defense, and the disposition of the defendant, thus
turn less on the nature and seriousness of the defendant's mental disability
than on the technical structure of the criminal law.

A defendant whose criminal activity arises from mental illness or defect usually
requires confinement and special treatment. Penal Code sections 1026 and 1026a
provide such confinement and treatment for persons acquitted on grounds of
insanity. A successful diminished capacity defense, on the other hand, results
either in the release of the defendant or his confinement as an ordinary criminal
for a lesser term. Because the diminished capacity defense thus fails to identify

a. Query: Why should the court regard a psychiatrist's decision whether to testify truthfully or
falsely as a dilemma worthy of sympathy? — Eds.

the mentally disturbed defendant, it may result in the defendant's not receiving the care appropriate to his condition. Such a defendant, who may still suffer from his mental disturbance, may serve his term, be released and thus permitted to become a danger to the public.

In our opinion the continuing inadequacy of *M'Naghten* as a test of criminal responsibility cannot be cured by further attempts to interpret language dating from a different era of psychological thought, nor by the creation of additional concepts designed to evade the limitations of *M'Naghten.* It is time to recast *M'Naghten* in modern language, taking account of advances in psychological knowledge and changes in legal thought [by adopting] section 4.01 of the American Law Institute's Model Penal Code . . . [which] has won widespread acceptance, having been adopted by every federal circuit except for the first circuit and by 15 states. . . .

. . . [Its] advantages may be briefly summarized. First, the ALI test adds a volitional element, the ability to conform to legal requirements. . . . Second, it avoids the all-or-nothing language of *M'Naghten* and permits a verdict based on lack of substantial capacity. Third, the ALI test is broad enough to permit a psychiatrist to set before the trier of fact a full picture of the defendant's mental impairments and flexible enough to adapt to future changes in psychiatric theory and diagnosis. Fourth, by referring to the defendant's capacity to "appreciate" the wrongfulness of his conduct the test confirms our holding in People v. Wolff, 61 Cal. 2d 795, that mere verbal knowledge of right and wrong does not prove sanity. Finally, by establishing a broad test of nonresponsibility, including elements of volition as well as cognition, the test provides the foundation on which we can order and rationalize the convoluted and occasionally inconsistent law of diminished capacity.

RICHARDSON, J. I respectfully dissent. My objection to the majority's approach may be briefly stated. I believe that a major change in the law of the type contemplated by the majority should be made by the Legislature. . . .

. . . We are not equipped to pick and choose the best among the various alternatives that are available, and we should leave the task to those who are so equipped. . . .

Such a legislative inquiry doubtless will reveal that the ALI test is not without its critics. . . . As simply one illustration, it should be noted that a 1975 study of the British Home Office, Department of Health and Social Security, entitled Report of the Committee on Mentally Abnormal Offenders (hereafter cited as Report) dealt with the specific question of the extent to which mental disorders should constitute defenses to criminal charges. In devising its own proposed test the committee carefully considered but rejected the ALI test for reasons suggesting that it is not, to use the majority's term, the "best criteria currently extant."

The English committee focused on the ALI's use of the term "*mental disease or defect*" and noted that such a vague undefined expression does not help to distinguish between minor and major disorders. The term has been abandoned in Britain for several years. This may be the case in the United States as well. Furthermore the Report notes that the ALI test . . . leaves the interpretation of "mental disease or defect" with "psychiatrists who give evidence to the court.". . .

The committee then opines that the emphasis on capacity "to conform," which appears to be the only attractive portion of the ALI test, presents some very considerable additional problems, saying:

. . ."[T]he test of capacity to conform has to face a well-known philosophical criticism. How can one tell the difference between an impulse which is irresistible and one which is merely not resisted? Let us imagine two patients whose clinical symptoms appear similar, each of whom has been involved with a friend in an argument. Patient *A* flies into a rage and stabs his friend: patient *B* does not. If *A* is prosecuted, a psychiatrist may be ready to testify that by reason of his disease of the mind he was deprived of the capacity to conform to the law, and he will no doubt be influenced by the fact that *A* did not conform to it. Patient *B*, not having assaulted his friend, is not prosecuted, so that no court hears psychiatric evidence about his capacity to conform: but presumably a psychiatrist would say that he had such a capacity, since he did not strike his friend. Some would seek to find a way out of this argument. There are offenders whose lack of self-control shows itself not only in a single offence, but also in their response to everyday temptations or frustrations. If patient *A* had a history of frequent and violent loss of temper, or if under observation after the assault he reacted violently to petty frustrations in the ward, such evidence would support the claim that he is less able than most men to control his temper. If, on the other hand, he was known to be extremely self-controlled, a psychiatrist would be justified in assuming that at normal times he was able to control himself and would have to explain the assault in some other way, for example, by showing that the argument developed in such a way as to give him extreme provocation (as the psychiatric witness did in the California case of [People v.] Gorshen [(1959) 51 Cal. 2d 716]). To this argument the determinist would reply that the fact remains that the man who was normally able to control himself (i.e., who normally conformed) was not able to control himself on the occasion in question, as is shown by the fact that he did not conform. Also, even the psychopath or schizophrenic who is often aggressive is not *always* aggressive, so that aggression on a particular occasion is not completely explained by the psychopathy or schizophrenia. *However this may be, it will generally be agreed that most cases are of the intermediate sort in which neither the circumstances nor the offender's usual behavior provided the obvious explanation; and in such cases it is usually fair to say that the only evidence of incapacity to conform with the law was the act itself.*" (Report, pp. 221-222, italics added.) . . .

Professor Richard Gambino . . . in a current article entitled The Murderous Mind: Insanity v. The Law ((Mar. 18, 1978) Saturday Review, at p. 10) traces the origins of the *M'Naghten* rule, and of various suggested changes in the light of more modern scientific knowledge. Professor Gambino stresses the extreme difficulty in meshing the different disciplines of psychiatry and the law, each possessing as it does its own variant definitions and standards. He emphasizes that "Psychiatry is a healing art. Its function is to understand and cure, not to define moral or legal responsibility or to accomplish justice. In fact, the profession of psychiatry does not use or recognize the terms 'sanity' and insanity. They are strictly legal terms.". . .

The formulation of intelligent rules covering the assertion of insanity as a criminal defense is a very complex problem. This fact underscores the wisdom of judicial restraint. Professor Gambino cites 2 interesting experiments conducted at Stanford University in 1972 which illustrate the disturbing uncertainties which persist 135 years after *M'Naghten*. He reports that "Eight researchers feigned hearing 'voices' and gained admission to 12 different psychiatric hospitals. None of the eight falsified their real life history, except for the voices, nor did any of them have a history of pathological behavior. Yet in 11 of the 12 instances, the researchers were diagnosed as 'schizophrenic,' while in the twelfth, the diagnosis was 'manic depressive.' Although other patients regarded the researchers as normal, no member of the hospitals' staff did. Then, in a follow-up experiment, the staff of a psychiatric hospital were told that one or more fake patients would be sent to them. Although none were actually sent, 41 of 193 patients admitted for treatment in the following period of time were thought to be fakes, in each case by at least one member of the hospital's staff." While the examples may be extreme, they do caution a judicial "go slowly" approach in this area. Assuming, as we may, the validity of the majority's contention that in the 135 years since *M'Naghten* there have been many psychiatric advances, the Legislature is thoroughly justified in taking a very long and careful, indeed skeptical, look before jettisoning the existing and carefully evolved body of law which now composes the California *M'Naghten* rule as illustrated by *Wolff.* (61 Cal. 2d 795). . . .

UNITED STATES v. BRAWNER

United States Court of Appeals, District of Columbia Circuit
471 F.2d 969 (1972)

LEVENTHAL, J. The principal issues raised on this appeal from a conviction for second degree murder and carrying a dangerous weapon relate to appellant's defense of insanity. . . .

. . . We have decided to adopt the ALI rule as the doctrine excluding responsibility for mental disease or defect, for application prospectively to trials begun after this date. . . .

. . . [I]t suffices for our purposes to review a handful of our opinions on the insanity defense.

The landmark opinion was written by Judge Bazelon in Durham v. United States, 214 F.2d 862 (1954). Prior to *Durham* the law of the District of Columbia . . . stated a traditional test of insanity, in terms of right and wrong and irresistible impulse. *Durham* adopted the product rule, pioneered in State v. Pike, 49 N.H. 399, 402 (1869-70), and exculpated from criminal responsibility those whose forbidden acts were the product of a mental disease or defect."

Few cases have evoked as much comment as *Durham*. . . . We view it . . . as the court's effort . . . to alleviate two serious problems with the previous rule.

The first of these was a problem of language which raised an important symbolic issue in the law. We felt that the language of the old right-wrong/irresistible impulse rule for insanity was antiquated, no longer reflecting the community's judgment as to who ought to be held criminally liable for socially destructive acts. We considered the rule as restated to have more fruitful, accurate and

---

a. The precise language of the *Durham* test was "that an accused is not criminally responsible if his unlawful act was the product of mental disease or defect." — EDS.

considered reflection of the sensibilities of the community as revised and expanded in the light of continued study of abnormal human behavior.

The second vexing problem that *Durham* was designed to reach related to the concern of the psychiatrists called as expert witnesses for their special knowledge of the problem of insanity, who often and typically felt that they were obliged to reach outside of their professional expertise when they were asked, under the traditional insanity rule established in 1843 by *M'Naghten's* Case, whether the defendant knew right from wrong. They further felt that the narrowness of the traditional test, which framed the issue of responsibility solely in terms of cognitive impairment, made it impossible to convey to the judge and jury the full range of information material to an assessment of defendant's responsibility. . . .

A difficulty arose under the *Durham* rule in application. The role was devised to facilitate the giving of testimony by medical experts in the context of a legal rule, with the jury called upon to reach a composite conclusion that had medical, legal and moral components.[6] However the pristine statement of the *Durham* rule opened the door to "trial by label." *Durham* did distinguish between "disease," as used "in the sense of a condition which is considered capable of either improving or deteriorating," and "defect," as referring to a condition not capable of such change "and which may be either congenital or the result of injury, or the residual effect of a physical or mental disease." But the court failed to explicate what abnormality of mind was an essential ingredient of these concepts. In the absence of a definition of "mental disease or defect," medical experts attached to them the meanings which would naturally occur to them — medical meanings — and gave testimony accordingly. The problem was dramatically highlighted by the weekend flip flop case, In re Rosenfield, 157 F. Supp. 18 (D.D.C. 1957). The petitioner was described as a sociopath. A St. Elizabeths psychiatrist testified that a person with a sociopathic personality was not suffering from a mental disease. That was Friday afternoon. On Monday morning, through a policy change at St. Elizabeths Hospital, it was determined as an administrative matter that the state of a psychopathic or sociopathic personality did constitute a mental disease.

The concern that medical terminology not control legal outcomes culminated in McDonald v. United States, 312 F.2d 847, 851 (en banc, 1962), where this court recognized that the term, mental disease or defect, has various meanings, depending upon how and why it is used, and by whom. Mental disease means one thing to a physician bent on treatment, but something different, if somewhat overlapping, to a court of law. We provided a legal definition of mental disease or defect, and held that it included "any abnormal condition of the mind which substantially affects mental or emotional processes and substantially impairs behavior controls." "Thus the jury would consider testimony concerning the development, adaptation and functioning of these processes and controls."

While the McDonald standard of mental disease was not without an attribute of circularity, it was useful in the administration of justice because it made

---

6. *Durham* contemplated from the start that the jury would have the guidance of "wider horizons of knowledge" from the medical experts than was available under the prior rule, but that in the last analysis the ultimate question is left to the jury "to perform its traditional function . . . to apply 'our inherited ideas of moral responsibility to individuals prosecuted for crime.' [Juries will] continue to make moral judgments. . . ." 214 F.2d at 876. . . .

plain that clinical and legal definitions of mental disease were distinct, and it helped the jury to sort out its complex task and to focus on the matters given it to decide.

The *Durham* rule also required explication along other lines, notably the resolution of the ambiguity inherent in the formulation concerning actions that were the "product" of mental illness. It was supplemented in Carter v. United States, 252 F.2d 608 at 615-616 (1957): "The simple fact that a person has a mental disease or defect is not enough to relieve him of responsibility for a crime. There must be a relationship between the disease and the criminal act; and the relationship must be such as to justify a reasonable inference that the act would not have been committed if the person had not been suffering from the disease." Thus *Carter* clarified that the mental illness must not merely have entered into the production of the act, but must have played a necessary role. *Carter* identified the "product" element of the rule with the "but for" variety of causation.

The pivotal "product" term continued to present problems, principally that it put expert testimony on a faulty footing. Assuming that a mental disease, in the legal sense, had been established, the fate of the defendant came to be determined by what came to be referred to by the legal jargon of "productivity." On the other hand, it was obviously sensible if not imperative that the experts having pertinent knowledge should speak to the crucial question whether the mental abnormality involved is one associated with aberrant behavior. But since "productivity" was so decisive a factor in the decisional equation, a ruling permitting experts to testify expressly in language of "product" raised in a different context the concern lest the ultimate issue be in fact turned over to the experts rather than retained for the jurors representing the community. . . .

It was in this context that the court came to the decision in Washington v. United States, 390 F.2d 444 (1967), which forbade experts from testifying as to productivity altogether. Chief Judge Bazelon's opinion illuminates the basis of the ruling, as one intended "to help the psychiatrists understand their role in court, and thus eliminate a fundamental cause of unsatisfactory expert testimony," namely, the tendency of the expert to use "concepts [which] can become slogans, hiding facts and representing nothing more than the witness's own conclusion about the defendant's criminal responsibility.". . .

A principal reason for our decision to depart from the *Durham* rule is the undesirable characteristic, surviving even the *McDonald* modification, of undue dominance by the experts giving testimony. . . . The difficulty is rooted in the circumstance that there is no generally accepted understanding, either in the jury or the community it represents, of the concept requiring that the crime be the "product" of the mental disease. . . .

The expert witnesses — psychiatrists and psychologists — are called to adduce relevant information concerning what may for convenience be referred to as the "medical" component of the responsibility issue. But the difficulty — as emphasized in *Washington* — is that the medical expert comes, by testimony given in terms of a non-medical construct ("product"), to express conclusions that in essence embody ethical and legal conclusions. There is, indeed, irony in a situation under which the *Durham* rule, which was adopted in large part to permit experts to testify in their own terms concerning matters within their domain which the jury should know, resulted in testimony by the experts in terms not their own to reflect unexpressed judgments in a domain that is properly not theirs but the jury's. The irony is heightened when the jurymen, instructed under the esoteric "product" standard, are influenced significantly by "product" testimony of expert witnesses really reflecting ethical and legal judgments rather than a conclusion within the witnesses' particular expertise.

It is easier to identify and spotlight the irony than to eradicate the mischief. The objective of *Durham* is still sound — to put before the jury the information that is within the expert's domain, to aid the jury in making a broad and comprehensive judgment. But when the instructions and appellate decisions define the "product" inquiry as the ultimate issue, it is like stopping the tides to try to halt the emergence of this term in the language of those with a central role in the trial — the lawyers who naturally seek to present testimony that will influence the jury who will be charged under the ultimate "product" standard, and the expert witnesses who have an awareness, gained from forensic psychiatry and related disciplines, of the ultimate "product" standard that dominates the proceeding.

. . . The more we have pondered the problem the more convinced we have become that the sound solution lies not in further shaping of the *Durham* "product" approach in more refined molds, but in adopting the ALI's formulation as the linchpin of our jurisprudence.

The ALI's formulation retains the core requirement of a meaningful relationship between the mental illness and the incident charged. The language in the ALI rule is sufficiently in the common ken that its use in the courtroom, or in preparation for trial, permits a reasonable three-way communication — between (a) the law-trained, judges and lawyers; (b) the experts and (c) the jurymen — without insisting on a vocabulary that is either stilted or stultified, or conducive to a testimonial mystique permitting expert dominance and encroachment on the jury's function. There is no indication in the available literature that any such untoward development has attended the reasonably widespread adoption of the ALI rule in the Federal courts and a substantial number of state courts.

Our ruling today includes our decision that in the ALI rule as adopted by this court the term "mental disease or defect" includes the definition of that term provided in our 1962 en banc *McDonald* opinion [312 F.2d at 851], as follows: "[A] mental disease or defect includes any abnormal condition of the mind which substantially affects mental or emotional processes and substantially impairs behavior controls." [b]

We have . . . pondered the suggestion that the jury be instructed that the defendant lacks criminal responsibility if the jury finds that the defendant's mental disease impairs his capacity or controls to such an extent that he cannot "justly be held responsible."

This was the view of a British commission,[23] adapted and proposed in 1955 by Professor Wechsler, the distinguished Reporter for the ALI's Model Penal Code, and sustained by some, albeit a minority, of the members of the ALI's Council. . . .

However, there is a substantial concern that an instruction overtly cast in

b. Note that the ALI formulation contains no definition of "mental disease or defect." — EDS.
23. In 1953 the British Royal Commission on Capital Punishment proposed: "[A person is not responsible for his unlawful act if] at the time of the act the accused was suffering from disease of the mind (or mental deficiency) *to such a degree that he ought not to be held responsible.*"

terms of "justice" cannot feasibly be restricted to the ambit of what may properly be taken into account but will splash with unconfinable and malign consequences. . . .

We are impressed by the observation of Professor Abraham S. Goldstein, one of the most careful students of the problem: "[The] overly general standard may place too great a burden upon the jury. If the law provides no standard, members of the jury are placed in the difficult position of having to find a man responsible for no other reason than their personal feeling about him. Whether the psyches of individual jurors are strong enough to make that decision, or whether the 'law' should put that obligation on them, is open to serious question. It is far easier for them to perform the role assigned to them by legislature and courts if they know — or are able to rationalize — that their verdicts are 'required' by law." [28]

ie, based on "Justice"

Professor Goldstein was referring to the broad "justice" standard recommended by the Royal Commission. But the problems remain acute even with the modifications in the proposal of the ALI Reporter, for that still leads to "justly responsible" as the ultimate and critical term. . . .

It is the sense of justice propounded by those charged with making and declaring the law — legislatures and courts — that lays down the rule that persons without substantial capacity to know or control the act shall be excused. The jury is concerned with applying the community understanding of this broad rule to particular lay and medical facts. Where the matter is unclear it naturally will call on its own sense of justice to help it determine the matter. There is wisdom in the view that a jury generally understands well enough that an instruction composed in flexible terms gives it sufficient latitude so that, without disregarding the instruction, it can provide that application of the instruction which harmonizes with its sense of justice. . . . It is one thing, however, to tolerate and even welcome the jury's sense of equity as a force that affects its application of instructions which state the legal rules that crystallize the requirements of justice as determined by the lawmakers of the community. It is quite another to set the jury at large, without such crystallization, to evolve its own legal rules and standards of justice. . . .

Taking all these considerations into account we conclude that the ALI rule as announced is not productive of injustice, and we decline to proclaim the broad "justly responsible" standard. . . .

Though it provides a general uniformity, the ALI rule leaves room for variations. Thus, we have added an adjustment in the *McDonald* definition of mental disease, which we think fully compatible with both the spirit and text of the ALI rule. In the interest of good administration, we now undertake to set forth, with such precision as the subject will permit, other elements of the ALI rule as adopted by this court.

The two main components of the rule define (1) mental disease, (2) the consequences thereof that exculpate from responsibility.

The first component of our rule, derived from *McDonald*, defines mental disease or defect as an abnormal condition of the mind, and a condition which substantially (a) affects mental or emotional process and (b) impairs behavioral controls. The second component, derived from the Model Penal Code, tells

28. A. Goldstein, The Insanity Defense 81-82 (1967).

which defendant with a mental disease lacks criminal responsibility for particular conduct: it is the defendant who, as a result of this mental condition, at the time of such conduct, either (i) lacks substantial capacity to appreciate that his conduct is wrongful, or (ii) lacks substantial capacity to conform his conduct to the law. . . .

The rule contains a requirement of causality, as is clear from the term "result." Exculpation is established not by mental disease alone but only if "as a result" defendant lacks the substantial capacity required for responsibility. Presumably the mental disease of a kleptomaniac does not entail as a "result" a lack of capacity to conform to the law prohibiting rape.

Under the ALI rule the issue is not whether defendant is so disoriented or void of controls that he is never able to conform to external demands, but whether he had that capacity at the time of the conduct. The question is not properly put in terms of whether he would have capacity to conform in some untypical restraining situation — as with an attendant or policeman at his elbow. The issue is whether he was able to conform in the unstructured condition of life in an open society, and whether the result of his abnormal mental condition was a lack of substantial internal controls. . . .

Section 4.01 of the Model Penal Code as promulgated by ALI contains in subsection (2) what has come to be known as the "caveat paragraph": "(2) The terms 'mental disease or defect' do not include an abnormality manifested only by repeated criminal or otherwise anti-social conduct." The purpose of this provision was to exclude a defense for the so-called "psychopathic personality.". . .

Our own approach is influenced by the fact that our rule already includes a definition of mental disease (from *McDonald*). Under that definition, as we have pointed out, the mere existence of "a long criminal record does not excuse crime." Williams v. United States, 312 F.2d 862, 864 (1962). We do not require the caveat paragraph as an insurance against exculpation of the deliberate and persistent offender. Our *McDonald* rule guards against the danger of misunderstanding and injustice that might arise, say, from an expert's classification that reflects only a conception defining all criminality as reflective of mental illness. There must be testimony to show both that the defendant was suffering from an abnormal condition of the mind and that it substantially affected mental or emotional processes and substantially impaired behavioral controls.

In this context, our pragmatic approach is to adopt the caveat paragraph as a rule for application by the judge, to avoid miscarriage of justice, but not for inclusion in instructions to the jury. . . .

Our adoption of the ALI rule does not depart from the doctrines this court has built up over the past twenty years to assure a broad presentation to the jury concerning the condition of defendant's mind and its consequences. Thus we adhere to our rulings admitting expert testimony of psychologists, as well as psychiatrists, and to our many decisions contemplating that expert testimony on this subject will be accompanied by presentation of the facts and premises underlying the opinions and conclusions of the experts, and that the Government and defense may present, in Judge Blackmun's words, "all possibly revelant evidence" bearing on cognition, volition and capacity. We agree with the amicus submission of the National District Attorneys Association that the law cannot "distinguish between physiological, emotional, social and cultural sources of the impairment" — assuming, of course, requisite testimony establishing exculpation under the pertinent standard — and all such causes may be both referred to by the expert and considered by the trier of fact.

Breadth of input under the insanity defense is not to be confused with breadth of the doctrines establishing the defense. As the National District Attorneys Association brief points out, the latitude for salient evidence of e.g., social and cultural factors pertinent to an abnormal condition of the mind significantly affecting capacity and controls, does not mean that such factors may be taken as establishing a separate defense for persons whose mental condition is such that blame can be imposed. We have rejected a broad "injustice" approach that would have opened the door to expositions of e.g., cultural deprivation, unrelated to any abnormal condition of the mind.

We have recognized that "Many criminologists point out that even normal human behavior is influenced by such factors as training, environment, poverty and the like, which may limit the understanding and options of the individual." King v. United States, 372 F.2d at 388. Determinists may contend that every man's fate is ultimately sealed by his genes and environment, over which he has no control. Our jurisprudence, however, while not oblivious to deterministic components, ultimately rests on a premise of freedom of will. This is not to be viewed as an exercise in philosophic discourse, but as a governmental fusion of ethics and necessity, which takes into account that a system of rewards and punishments is itself part of the environment that influences and shapes human conduct. Our recognition of an insanity defense for those who lack the essential, threshold free will possessed by those in the normal range is not to be twisted, directly or indirectly, into a device for exculpation of those without an abnormal condition of the mind.

Finally, we have not accepted suggestions to adopt a rule that disentangles the insanity defense from a medical model, and announces a standard exculpating anyone whose capacity for control is insubstantial, for whatever cause or reason. There may be logic in these submissions, but we are not sufficiently certain of the nature, range and implications of the conduct involved to attempt an all-embracing unified field theory. The applicable rule can be discerned as the cases arise in regard to other conditions — somnambulism or other automatisms; blackouts due, e.g. to overdose of insulin; drug addiction. Whether these somatic conditions should be governed by a rule comparable to that herein set forth for mental disease would require, at a minimum, a judicial determination, which takes medical opinion into account, finding convincing evidence of an ascertainable condition characterized by "a broad consensus that free will does not exist." Salzman v. United States, 405 F.2d 358, 365 (1968) (concurring opinion of Judge Wright). . . .

BAZELON, C.J., concurring in part and dissenting in part. . . .

The Court's reasoning suggests that our primary goal is to deemphasize the question of productivity or causality. Yet there is strong reason to suspect that adopting the ALI test will not bring us closer to that goal. . . . [P]roductivity in the *Durham* sense — the relationship between the impairment and the act — is not abolished; it is concealed in two questions which are implicit in the test: Could the defendant appreciate the wrongfulness of the particular act he committed? Could he have conformed that particular act to the requirements of law? . . .

The effort to preserve the jury's function from encroachments by the experts must begin with a clear understanding of what that function is. In determining the responsibility issue, a jury has two important tasks: "In the first place it measures the extent to which the defendant's mental and emotional processes and behavior controls were impaired at the time of the unlawful act. The answer to that question is elusive, but no more so than many other facts that a jury must find beyond a reasonable doubt in a criminal trial. . . . The second function is to evaluate that impairment in light of community standards of blameworthiness, to determine whether the defendant's impairment makes it unjust to hold him responsible. The jury's unique qualification for making that determination justifies our unusual deference to the jury's resolution of the issue of responsibility." [47] . . .

Our instruction to the jury should provide that a defendant is not responsible *if at the time of his unlawful conduct his mental or emotional processes or behavior controls were impaired to such an extent that he cannot justly be held responsible for his act.* This test would ask the psychiatrist a single question: what is the nature of the impairment of the defendant's mental and emotional processes and behavior controls? It would leave for the jury the question whether that impairment is sufficient to relieve the defendant of responsibility for the particular act charged.

The purpose of this proposed instruction is to focus the jury's attention on the legal and moral aspects of criminal responsibility, and to make clear why the determination of responsibility is entrusted to the jury and not the expert witnesses. That, plainly, is not to say that the jury should be cast adrift to acquit or convict the defendant according to caprice. The jury would not be instructed to find a defendant responsible if that seems just, and to find him not responsible if that seems just. On the contrary, the instruction would incorporate the very requirements — impairment of mental or emotional processes and behavior controls — that *McDonald* established as prerequisites of the responsibility defense. . . .

. . . A minority of the ALI draftsmen (along with Professor Wechsler, the reporter of the Model Penal Code) proposed a test providing that a person

> is not responsible for criminal conduct if at the time of such conduct as a result of mental disease or defect his capacity either to appreciate the criminality of his conduct or to conform his conduct to the requirements of law is *so substantially impaired that he cannot justly be held responsible.* . . .

The ALI ultimately rejected the minority approach because "[s]ome members of the Council deemed it unwise to present questions of justice to the jury, preferring a submission that *in form, at least,* confines the inquiry to fact." The Court apparently shares this view, and rejects an instruction "overtly cast in terms of 'justice'" on the grounds that such an instruction "cannot feasibly be restricted to the ambit of what may properly be taken into account but will splash with unconfinable and malign consequences.". . .

The Court's . . . objection is apparently that an instruction cast in terms of justice would permit the jury to convict or acquit without regard to legal standard. . . . I take it that in the Court's view the majority version of the ALI

---

47. United States v. Eichberg, 439 F.2d 620, 624-625 (1971) (Bazelon, C.J., concurring).

test offers the jury "legal rules that crystallize the requirements of justice as determined by the lawmakers of the community," and that the minority version sets the jury adrift without such crystallized rules. What, then, are these crystallized rules? . . . Can we seriously maintain that the majority ALI instruction is preferable because its determination that the impairment must be "substantial" reflects a crystallization of the requirements of justice by the lawmakers of the community? Naturally, we would all prefer a rule that could, as a matter of law, draw a bright line between responsible and non-responsible defendants. But the ALI test adopted by this Court is plainly not such a rule. It offers the jury no real help in making the "intertwining moral, legal, and medical judgments" that all of us expect. In fact, because it describes the question as one of fact it may lull the jury into the mistaken assumption that the question of responsibility can best be resolved by experts, leaving the jury at the mercy of the witness who asserts most persuasively that, in his expert judgment, the defendant's capacity was or was not *substantially* impaired. . . .

NOTE ON ADMINISTERING THE DEFENSE OF LEGAL INSANITY

1. May the judge raise the defense? Whether the insanity defense may be forced by the court on an unwilling defendant has proved troublesome. The Model Penal Code decided not to give the trial judge this power on the view that to do so would be "too great an interference with the conduct of the defense." (§4.04, Comment at 194 (Tent. Draft No. 4, 1955).) A leading decision on the subject is Whalem v. United States, 346 F.2d 812 (D.C. Cir. 1965), in which the court concluded that the trial court had the authority to impose the defense over defendant's objection. It was thought that the interests of justice preclude conviction of an obviously mentally irresponsible defendant.

In Frendak v. United States, 408 A.2d 364, 379 (D.C. App. 1979), the court took a more guarded view in response to two United States Supreme Court decisions reinforcing the autonomy of a defendant's choices — North Carolina v. Alford, 400 U.S. 25 (1970), pages 159-161 supra, upholding a guilty plea entered by a defendant who nonetheless insisted on his innocence, and Faretta v. California, 422 U.S. 806 (1975), page 27 supra, upholding the right of defendant to dispense with counsel and to represent himself. The court in *Frendak*, therefore, held that

> Rather than permit a trial judge (as in *Whalem*) to raise an insanity defense whenever there is a sufficient quantum of evidence supporting the defense, we require the judge to respect the choice of a defendant capable of voluntarily and intelligently making that choice. The court will now have the discretion to raise an insanity defense sua sponte only if the defendant is not capable of making, and has not made, an intelligent and voluntary decision.

The court supported its holding by pointing to the "persuasive reasons" why a defendant may prefer to risk being found guilty rather than to be found not guilty by reason of insanity (408 A.2d at 376-377):

First, a defendant may fear that an insanity acquittal will result in the institution of commitment proceedings which lead to confinement in a mental institution for a longer period than the potential jail sentence. . . .

Second, the defendant may object to the quality of treatment or the type of confinement to which he or she may be subject in an institution for the mentally ill. If in need of psychiatric care, the individual may prefer the prospect of receiving whatever treatment is available in the prison. There are, moreover, "numerous restrictions and routines in a mental hospital which differ significantly from those in a prison." Matthews v. Hardy, 420 F.2d 607, 611 (1969). . . . Ms. Frendak, in particular, has indicated that she considers the hospital worse than any prison and, in order to avoid institutionalization there, has gone on hunger strikes, attempted suicide, and refused medication.

Third, a defendant, with good reason, may choose to avoid the stigma of insanity. . . . Although an insanity acquittal officially absolves the defendant of all moral blame, in the eyes of many some element of responsibility may remain. Thus, the insanity acquittee found to have committed criminal acts and labeled insane may well see oneself "twice cursed.". . .

Fourth, other collateral consequences of an insanity acquittal can also follow the defendant throughout his life. . . . In some states, an adjudication of insanity may affect a person's legal rights, for example, the right to vote or serve on a federal jury, and may even restrict his or her ability to obtain a driver's license. Such an adjudication also may adversely affect the defendant in any interaction with the legal system. For instance, it may be used to attack his or her capacity as a trial witness, or could be admissible in a criminal trial to attack the character of a defendant who has put his or her character in issue. Furthermore, the record of such an adjudication would surely be used in any subsequent proceeding for civil commitment.

Finally, a defendant also may oppose the imposition of an insanity defense because he or she views the crime as a political or religious protest which a finding of insanity would denigrate. See [United States v.] Robertson, 507 F.2d at 1165 n. 13 (Wilkey, J., dissenting) (pointing to examples of "horrors" in other countries that might arise here if courts were permitted to raise the insanity defense over the wishes of a competent defendant). In any event, a defendant may choose to forego the defense because of a feeling that he or she is not insane, or that raising the defense would be equivalent to an admission of guilt.

For a review of cases from other jurisdictions and a critical analysis of the subject unsympathetic to judicial raising of the defense, see Singer, The Imposition of the Insanity Defense on an Unwilling Defendant, 41 Ohio St. L.J. 637 (1980). Compare Lord Denning in Bratty v. Attorney-General, [1963] A.C. 386, 411: "The old notion that only the defence can raise a defence of insanity is now gone. The prosecution are entitled to raise it and it is their duty to do so rather than allow a dangerous person to be at large."

2. Raising of defense by defendant. A number of states impose special conditions on a defendant's raising the defense of legal insanity in order to assure adequate opportunity for preparation on the issue by the prosecution. Typically, the defendant is required to notify the prosecution in advance of the trial of his or her intent to raise the defense, to disclose the names of the witnesses he or she intends to call to support the defense, and to submit to a psychiatric examination by experts appointed by the court. The sanction for refusal is the loss of the privilege of presenting expert psychiatric evidence at the trial. The problematic aspect of these requirements is the compulsory psychiatric examination. Does it unconstitutionally infringe the defendant's privilege against self-incrimination? If the defendant does submit, how far may the testimony and report of the examining psychiatrist be used by the prosecution at the trial? See page 57 supra.

A recent, well-considered decision that finds the privilege implicated and therefore imposes a variety of protective conditions on compelling these examinations is Blaisdell v. Commonwealth, 372 Mass. 753, 364 N.E. 191 (1977).

3. *Bifurcated trial.* California and a few other jurisdictions require that the trial of the issue of legal insanity occur only after a trial on the issue of guilt, apart from insanity, has resulted in a verdict of guilty.[10] Commenting on the experience under this system, the California Special Commission on Insanity and Criminal Offenders, First Report 30 (1962), concludes:

> Under present California law . . . the defendant is conclusively presumed sane for the purposes of the first trial. If he is found "guilty" at that trial, then a second trial is held to determine if he is sane or insane. The split trial was introduced in California by legislation adopted in 1927. In the words of the 1925 Commission for the Reform of Criminal Procedure, the purpose of the change was expressed as follows:
> "The abuses of the present system are great. Under a plea of "not guilty" and without any notice to the People that the defense of insanity will be relied upon, defendant has been able to raise the defense upon the trial of the issue as to whether he committed the offense charged. This lack of notice that such defense would be made has very frequently placed the People at a very great disadvantage. An even more serious fault of the present system is that a defendant, when on trial as to whether he committed the offense is able to bring into the case the whole matter of his sanity at the time of the offense charged. This enables him to submit to the jury great masses of evidence having no bearing upon the question whether the offense was committed. This is frequently made the basis of appeals to the sympathy or prejudice of the jury and even though this is not done, often introduces great confusion into the trial."
> We have serious doubts whether these reasons were sound in 1927. In any event, we think they are unsound today.
> The hope that the split trial would simplify the issues at trial on the not guilty plea was destroyed by the *Wells* [33 Cal. 2d 330, 202 P.2d 53 (1949)] and the *Gorshen* [51 Cal. 2d 716, 336 P.2d 492 (1959)] cases. Under the rule of these cases, evidence of defendant's mental condition is, if relevant, admissible at the trial of the issue of his guilt. Moreover, much the same evidence may have to be admitted at the second trial. These complications are increased by the fact that rulings on the admissibility of evidence become highly artificial and difficult to make. In short, the split trial is no longer serving a useful purpose, and we think it should be abandoned. See generally Louisell and Hazard, Insanity as a Defense: The Bifurcated Trial, 49 Calif. L. Rev. 805 (1961).

10. Cal. Penal Code §1026 provides: "When a defendant pleads not guilty by reason of insanity, and also joins with it another plea or pleas, the defendant shall first be tried as if only such other plea or pleas had been entered, and in such trial the defendant shall be conclusively presumed to have been sane at the time the offense is alleged to have been committed. If the jury shall find the defendant guilty, or if the defendant pleads only not guilty by reason of insanity, then the question whether the defendant was sane or insane at the time the offense was committed shall be promptly tried, either before the same jury or before a new jury in the discretion of the court."

It is, of course, generally in the discretion of the trial court, without statutory authorization, to require separate trials when the interests of justice require it, as, for example, when a trial on the issue of guilt which includes the issue of insanity may be unduly prejudicial to the defendant.

4. Instructing the jury on what follows an insanity acquittal. Most courts have held that the jury should not be instructed in the procedures that follow an insanity verdict, on the ground that what will happen to the defendant is not relevant to whether the defendant met the test of legal insanity. See, e.g., Johnson v. State, 265 Ind. 689, 359 N.E.2d 525 (1977). However, some recent decisions are to the contrary. See, e.g., Commonwealth v. Mulgrew, 475 Pa. 271, 380 A.2d 349 (1977); Lyles v. United States, 254 F.2d 725, 728 (D.C. Cir. 1957); Commonwealth v. Mutina, 366 Mass. 810, 323 N.E.2d 294 (1975). In the latter case the court stated (at 301-302):

> If jurors can be entrusted with responsibility for a defendant's life and liberty in such cases as this, they are entitled to know what protection they and their fellow citizens will have if they conscientiously apply the law to the evidence and arrive at a verdict of not guilty by reason of insanity. . . .
>
> The instant case represents a classic example of the injustice which may occur when such information is withheld from the jury. The jury could have had no doubt that the defendant killed Miss Achorn. The jury also heard overwhelmingly persuasive evidence that the defendant was insane at the time of the killing and that, for a long time into the future, he will remain a menace to himself and to society. . . .
>
> Implicit in the jury's guilty verdict was a determination that the Commonwealth had proven the defendant's sanity beyond a reasonable doubt. On the record before us, we have found no rational justification or basis for such a finding, except the jury's understandable concern for the need to confine an insane and still dangerous killer for the protection of society. The jury, lacking knowledge of the commitment necessarily flowing from a verdict of not guilty by reason of insanity, applied their own standards of justice in arriving at a verdict designed to ensure the confinement of the defendant for his own safety and that of the community.

Should the question whether the jury is told the consequences be affected by what those consequences were? Suppose the jurisdiction required mandatory commitment on an insanity verdict? Suppose commitment turned on discretionary civil commitment proceedings?

5. Burden of Proof. (a) *State Law.* All jurisdictions create a presumption of legal sanity at the trial. The effect of this presumption is that, in the absence of evidence on the issue, the sanity of the accused is presumed for all legal purposes. One way of describing this situation is that legal insanity is an affirmative defense. Another is that the defendant has the burden of going forward. American jurisdictions, however, differ on two issues: (1) How much evidence need be presented before the effect of the presumption disappears and the question of the defendant's insanity becomes an issue that must be established by the evidence? (2) Where the issue must be established by the evidence, who bears the burden of persuasion, and how is that burden defined?

As to the first question, some states require only that the defendant present or that there have been presented (for testimony of prosecution witnesses may also suggest evidence of insanity) "some evidence" of legal insanity in order to carry the burden of going forward. Others require more, usually that the evidence raise a reasonable doubt of the sanity of the accused. For citations and further discussion, see Eule, The Presumption of Sanity: Bursting the Bubble, 25 U.C.L.A.L. Rev. 637 (1978); A. Goldstein, The Insanity Defense ch. 8 (1967); Annot., 17 A.L.R.3d 146 (1968); W. LaFave & A. Scott, Criminal Law 313 (1972).

As to the second question, once the defendant has carried his or her burden of going forward, in the federal courts and in most states the prosecution must prove the sanity of the defendant to the satisfaction of the trier of facts beyond a reasonable doubt. See Annot., 17 A.L.R.3d 146, 159 (1968); Lynch v. Overholser, 369 U.S. 705 (1962); Davis v. United States, 160 U.S. 469 (1895). In the remainder of the states, it is the accused who must persuade the trier of facts that he or she was insane, but on the preponderance of the evidence, rather than beyond a reasonable doubt. See Cal. Evidence Code, §522: "The party claiming that any person, including himself, is or was insane has the burden of proof on that issue."

(*b*) *Constitutional requirements.* The constitutionality of placing the burden of going forward on the defendant has never been in doubt. However, the constitutionality of requiring the defendant to carry the burden of proof of his or her insanity has been the subject of some controversy. In Leland v. Oregon, 343 U.S. 790 (1952), an Oregon statute requiring that defendant establish his or her insanity beyond a reasonable doubt was upheld, over a forceful dissent by Justices Frankfurter and Black. The controversy was revived with the Supreme Court's decisions in In re Winship, 397 U.S. 358 (1970), and Mullaney v. Wilbur, 421 U.S. 684 (1975), holding that the due process clause protects the accused against conviction except upon proof beyond a reasonable doubt of every fact necessary to constitute the crime with which he or she is charged. See pages 67-82 supra.

In Rivera v. Delaware, 429 U.S. 877 (1976), the Delaware Supreme Court, relying on *Leland,* had upheld the Delaware law imposing on the defendant the burden of proving insanity by a preponderance of the evidence. The Supreme Court, per curiam, dismissed an appeal as not raising a substantial federal question, thus implying that *Leland* had not been overruled by *Winship* and *Mullaney.* In Patterson v. New York, 432 U.S. 197 (1977), pages 67-75 supra, the Court reaffirmed the *Rivera* holding and thus seemed to settle the constitutionality of requiring the defendant to bear the burden of persuasion on the sanity issue.

For exploration of the constitutional problems remaining after *Patterson*, see page 67 supra.

(*ii*)   *Disposition after Acquittal*

BENHAM v. EDWARDS

United States District Court, N.D. Georgia
501 F. Supp. 1050 (1980)

MURPHY, J. The named plaintiffs in this class action are presently confined in mental hospitals in the State of Georgia following their acquittal of criminal charges by reason of insanity. . . . The plaintiffs challenge the procedures for the commitment and release of persons found not guilty of criminal offenses by reason of insanity (hereinafter "insanity-acquitees") as violative of the due process and equal protection guarantees of the Fourteenth Amendment. The procedures are set out in Ga. Code §27-1503. . . .

Following a finding of not guilty by reason of insanity, the trial court retains jurisdiction over the insanity-acquitee and inquires into the present mental state of the person, and "upon a showing of good cause by the prosecutor" may order such person to be confined to a mental hospital for not less than thirty days. In fact, the commitment is for an indefinite period of time since the State does not initiate a hearing to determine the current mental state of the insanity-acquitee.

To secure release, the erstwhile defendant, now patient, or the hospital, must petition the committing court. A petition cannot be entertained until the initial thirty day period has elapsed, and not within twelve months of any prior petition.

A valid petition will set in motion a hearing at which the sole issue is whether the insanity-acquitee meets the criteria for civil commitment under the Georgia Mental Health Code, Ga. Code Ch. 88-5 or 88-25.[6]

A full panoply of rights are guaranteed the insanity-acquitee: (1) notice of his right to request a hearing; (2) right to counsel, and appointed counsel if the insanity-acquitee cannot afford to retain his own; (3) right to confront and cross-examine witnesses and to offer evidence; (4) right to subpoena witnesses and to require testimony to be given in person or by deposition from any physician upon whose evaluation the decision may rest; (5) right to have established an individualized plan specifically tailored to the person's treatment needs; (6) right to be examined by a physician of his own choosing (at his own expense); and (7) right to have representatives or guardians ad litem appointed in his behalf. These rights are also provided to M.H.C. [Mental Health Code] committees.

The release hearing for insanity-acquitees differs from the commitment and release hearings for M.H.C. committees in a number of ways: (1) insanity-acquitees are presumed to be mentally ill; (2) the burden of proof is cast upon the insanity-acquitee seeking release; (3) the state is not required to prove by clear and convincing evidence that the insanity-acquitee meets the Chapter 88-5 criteria for continued commitment; (4) once an application has been denied, another cannot be filed within one year; (5) the release of an insanity-acquitee must be ordered by the committing court. M.H.C. committees are not encumbered with any of these burdens. The State must prove by clear and convincing evidence and without the aid of a presumption that the M.H.C. committee is mentally ill and in need of treatment. The State must "recommit" the individual within six months of the initial commitment, and at twelve month intervals thereafter. The hospital may release the patient at any time without any judicial approval. . . .

6. Ga. Code Chapter 88-5 pertains to the hospitalization and treatment procedures for the mentally ill. Ga. Code Chapter 88-25 pertains to the mentally retarded. An individual is subject to involuntary commitment under Chapter 88-5 if he is mentally ill and (1) presents a substantial risk of imminent harm to himself or others as manifested by either recent overt acts or recent expressed threats of violence which present a probability of physical injury to himself or other persons, or (2) is so unable to care for his own physical health and safety as to create an imminently life-endangering crisis. Ga. Code §88-501(v).

The criteria for the involuntary commitment of the mentally retarded are scattered throughout numerous provisions of the Ga. Code.

As of 1968, only three states statutorily required a civil commitment hearing prior to the confinement of an insanity-acquitee.[a] . . . In 1968, the Court of Appeals for the District of Columbia decided Bolton v. Harris, 395 F.2d 642 (D.C. Cir. 1968). Chief Judge Bazelon found the D.C. statute by which all acquitees were automatically committed for an indefinite period of time unconstitutional on equal protection grounds: "[P]ersons found not guilty by reason of insanity must be given a judicial hearing with procedures substantially similar to those in civil commitment proceedings."

The equal protection component of the *Bolton* Court's analysis was derived principally from the Supreme Court's decision in Baxstrom v. Herold, 383 U.S. 107 (1966) where a New York statute which provided for the commitment of prisoners to mental hospitals was held unconstitutional. In New York, a convicted prisoner could be transferred to a mental hospital with few of the procedural safeguards which were afforded other committees. The Court acknowledged that there were differences between prisoners and non-prisoners, and that the former's prior criminal conduct was evidence of dangerousness. But the fact that a prisoner had engaged in criminal conduct in the past did not justify diluted procedures for his present commitment: "Classification of mentally ill persons as either insane or dangerously insane of course may be a reasonable distinction for purposes of determining the type of custodial or medical care to be given, but it has no relevance whatever in the context of the opportunity to show whether a person is mentally ill *at all*. . . ."

The fact that insanity-acquitees have been through a trial which determined that they committed an antisocial act, but were not culpable because of their mental state at the time the act was committed, does not obviate the need for a mandatory, state-initiated pre-commitment hearing. First, the lodestar of the *M'Naghten* defense is that the defendant was not accountable "at a particular moment for a particular act." G. Fletcher, Rethinking Criminal Law, §10.4, p. 838 (1978); A. Goldstein, The Insanity Defense, 45-67 (1967). The acquitee's mental state *at the time of trial* is not an issue at the trial. Second, M.H.C. commitment relies on factors which are foreign to the *M'Naghten* defense. The M.H.C. criteria are (1) mental illness and (2) substantial risk of imminent harm as manifested by recent overt acts or threats, or inability to care for oneself creating an imminently life-endangering crisis. The *M'Naghten* test requires only the absence of mental capacity to distinguish between right and wrong in relation to the otherwise criminal act — an act which is not necessarily a manifestation of the likelihood of imminent harm.

Numerous courts have endeavored to rationalize the automatic pre-hearing commitment of insanity-acquitees despite the substantive difference between the insanity defense and the criteria for the commitment of non-insanity-acquitees. In Chase v. Kearns, 278 A.2d 132 (Me. 1971), for example, the Court explained the absence of a hearing prior to commitment as a function of the presumption which operated to the detriment of the insanity-acquitee to the effect that a mental state once proved is presumed to persist. Additionally, the

---

a. At that time, many of the remaining states provided for automatic, mandatory commitment of persons acquitted by reason of insanity. This approach was also adopted in the District of Columbia, in England, and in the proposals of the Model Penal Code (see §4.08, Appendix to this casebook). Other states permitted commitment at the discretion of the trial judge or provided for commitment after a relatively limited hearing. See generally Lynch v. Overholser, 369 U.S. 705, 720, 726-727 (1962) (Clark, J., dissenting). — Eds.

pre-hearing commitment was held to reflect a wise legislative policy which required the insanity-acquitee to be evaluated by the hospital staff prior to his release petition, in the interest of public safety. These rationales also convinced the California Supreme Court in In re Franklin, 7 Cal. 3d 126, 496 P.2d 465 (1972). . . .

The reasoning of these decisions is contaminated with a basic flaw. The presumption of continued insanity is a ubiquitous concept which serves to justify many of the procedures which are the subject of this litigation. Whatever the presumption's validity may be in other contexts, it provides not even a kernel of justification for depriving the insanity-acquitee of his right to a pre-commitment hearing. In short, that which is presumed is insufficient to justify commitment *at all*, to say nothing of commitment without a hearing. What is presumed is the continuity of the mental state earlier established — the mental incapacity to distinguish between right and wrong. In Georgia, this simple finding does not suffice to meet the criteria for M.H.C. commitment.

The second rationale — that the state has an interest in committing the individual to enable psychiatrists to evaluate his current mental state proves too little . . . because the psychiatrists are given an opportunity to evaluate the insanity-acquitee during the thirty-day preliminary period. The plaintiffs have explicitly refrained from challenging the constitutionality of the observation period. When this period elapses, however, the justification vanishes — there is no longer any reason why the State should not initiate a hearing as it does with M.H.C. committees. . . .

On equal protection grounds, then, there is no rational explanation why insanity-acquitees should not be guaranteed a state-initiated hearing to determine their present mental state. People v. McQuillan, 392 Mich. 511, 221 N.W.2d 569 (1974); People v. McNelly, 371 N.Y.S.2d 538 (Sup. Ct. 1975); State v. Krol, 68 N.J. 236, 344 A.2d 289 (1975); State v. Wilcox, 92 Wash. 2d 610, 600 P.2d 561 (1979); State v. Alto, 589 P.2d 402 (Alaska 1979); State v. Clemons, 110 Ariz. 79, 515 P.2d 324 (1973). Two states have held that even the preliminary observation period violates the equal protection clause. Wilson v. State, 259 Ind. 375, 287 N.E.2d 875, 881 (1972) . . . ; State ex rel. Kovach v. Schubert, 64 Wis. 2d 612, 219 N.W.2d 341 (1974). . . . This Court holds only that equal protection requires a hearing when the 30 day observation period ends. . . .

In *Bolton* [also], Chief Judge Bazelon found a due process violation in the D.C. automatic commitment statute. The foundation for the holding was Specht v. Patterson, 386 U.S. 605 (1967) where the Supreme Court held that a defendant convicted under Colorado law for "indecent liberties" could not be given an indeterminate sentence under the Colorado Sex Offenders Act without a full hearing. The fact that the defendant's criminal trial was replete with due process protections was beside the point since commitment under the Sex Offender's Act required distinct findings of fact. Similarly, the commitment of an insanity-acquitee requires distinct findings. *Bolton*, supra, at 650.[13] . . .

___

13. In Clark v. State, 245 Ga. [629,] 645, 266 S.E.2d 466 [1980], the Court attempted to distinguish *Bolton* on the basis that in D.C., the prosecutor [at that time had to] prove beyond a reasonable doubt that the defendant was sane, whereas in Georgia the defendant must prove by a preponderance of the evidence that he was insane in order to avail himself of the defense. But this purported distinction obscures the focus of the *Bolton* decision which was that insanity-acquitees must be granted a hearing to determine *present mental condition*, in spite of the degree of certainty as to his past insanity. It would make no difference if the defendant's insanity at the time of the act was established to a mathematical certainty. . . .

In Fasulo v. Arafeh, 173 Conn. 473, 378 A.2d 553 (1977), the Connecticut Supreme Court invalidated the Connecticut procedure for the release of non-insanity-acquitees. The Court's analysis applies in this situation as well: . . . "[T]hough the Statute provides for annual notice to patients of their right to a hearing, the burden of requesting and, therefore, initiating review remains with the patient. The state seeks to justify this procedure by arguing that allowing the patient to choose whether to have a hearing will avoid unnecessary judicial proceedings. We doubt whether this rationale is adequate since it ignores the practical difficulties of requiring a mental patient to overcome the effects of his confinement, his closed environment, his possible incompetence and the debilitating effects of drugs or other treatment on his ability to make a decision which may amount to the waiver of his constitutional right to a review of his status."

The defendants argue that the "elective" nature of the commitment hearing is reasonable. The failure of an insanity-acquitee to apply for release constitutes a waiver which is not offensive to the Constitution, they contend. This argument fails to address the equal protection implications. Regardless of how reasonable this scheme may be, it is not the procedure which applies to M.H.C. committees. . . . Furthermore, it violates due process to infer a waiver from the patient's inaction. As indicated by the *Fasulo* decision, the patient's circumstances are not conducive to the assertion of his rights. . . .

Like the hapless Daniel M'Naghten, insanity-acquitees may remain in mental hospitals for many years after their acquittal of criminal charges.[15] But unlike M'Naghten, insanity acquitees are entitled to a state-initiated hearing to determine their present mental state following an initial and brief observation period. . . .

[The court next considered what burden of proof was constitutionally mandated at the commitment hearing.]

In Addington v. Texas, 441 U.S. 418 (1979) the Court decided that the "clear and convincing" standard was required by the Due Process Clause of the Fourteenth Amendment in an M.H.C. commitment hearing. Recognizing that the interests of the individual to be free from unwarranted commitment required a standard more rigorous than "a preponderance of the evidence," but that the imprecision of psychiatric diagnosis rendered the "beyond a reasonable doubt" standard impractical, the Court adopted the intermediate standard.

In United States v. Brown, 478 F.2d 606 (D.C. Cir. 1973), the Court upheld the D.C. commitment scheme which arguably imposed a lesser burden of proof on the state in insanity-acquitee commitment hearings than in M.H.C. commitment hearings. The fulcrum of the decision was the finding that "modern standards of the insanity defense, not restricted to those who do not know right from wrong, call for the acquittal of persons who 'may have meaningful elements of responsibility.' ". . . In short, *Brown* held that insanity-acquitees could be punished.

15. In United States ex rel. Schuster v. Herold, 410 F.2d 1071, 1079 (2d Cir. 1969), the Court revealed some "grisly" statistics about the mental hospital population in New York: "Matteawan has 119 inmates who have been confined there since 1935, 29 since 1925, and 4 patients who have been there since at least 1915 — over half a century. . . . [A]s of November 1, 1965, one inmate, then 83 years old, had been at Matteawan since 1901. . . . [A]nother individual was accused of stealing a horse and buggy in 1905 . . . [and] was released 59 years later at the age of 89 because he was no longer a menace to society or other patients. . . . [Another patient] wrongfully [spent] 24 years in Dannemora because he had stolen candy valued at $5.00 at the age of 16.

To punish an insanity-acquitee, or to utilize a procedure which includes a punitive component, runs counter to the overwhelming authority that an insanity-acquitee is not responsible, and not properly subject to punishment. The insanity defense is a recognition that none of the theories which underlie our criminal law — prevention, restraint, rehabilitation, deterrence, education, and retribution — are furthered by punishing the insane. . . .

The reasoning of the Court in *Addington* applies to insanity-acquitees with equal force. . . . In sum, with respect to the commitment of insanity-acquitees, the State must initiate a commitment hearing at which it must sustain the burden of proving, by clear and convincing evidence, that the insanity-acquitee presently meets the criteria for M.H.C. commitment.

[The court proceeded to discuss constitutional requirements respecting release of insanity acquitees once they are validly committed.]

The Court is cognizant that some M.H.C. committees are institutionalized under §88-501(v)(2): "so unable to care for his own physical health and safety as to create an imminently life-endangering crisis." Certainly, they do not pose a threat of physical harm to others, and have not committed any overt act evidencing a risk of inflicting harm on others. But simply because certain members of the class of M.H.C. committees are not dangerous to others does not alter the basic fact that, in general, M.H.C. committees and insanity-acquitees can be distinguished only by the criminal proceedings which were instituted against the latter. Indeed, many insanity-acquitees have evidenced as little likelihood of inflicting harm on others as §88-501(v)(2) committees have. Two of the three named plaintiffs in this case were acquitted of crimes which were entirely non-violent theft crimes.

. . . But there is also one group of insanity-acquitees whose status is substantially different than all M.H.C. committees and all other insanity-acquitees. These are the individuals who have committed acts which are considered violent crimes: murder, rape, armed robbery, arson, aggravated assault, and other offenses of like nature. . . . The equal protection clause does not require that these individuals be treated the same as all others who are involuntarily hospitalized. . . . To obtain release, those insanity-acquitees who were not charged with serious violent crimes must be treated the same as all M.H.C. committees.[28] Those insanity-acquitees who were charged with serious violent crimes may be required to obtain court approval [for release]. . . .

The allocation of the burden of proof, and the standard of proof at a release hearing are particularly troubling issues. . . . It should be remembered that at this point we are dealing solely with insanity-acquitees who were charged with serious violent crimes. . . .

In United States v. Ecker, 543 F.2d 178 (D.C. Cir. 1976), the Court declared that in conditional release hearings, there simply would be no burden of proof assigned: "[P]roceedings involving the care and treatment of the mentally ill

---

28. The procedures for the release and continued hospitalization of M.H.C. committees are set out in §88-506.5 (Supp. 1980). No Court approval is necessary if the chief medical officer of the hospital deems the patient no longer in need of treatment. The patient can be retained if, at twelve month intervals, a "Committee for Continued Hospitalization Review" finds the patient in need of treatment. That determination is reviewed by a Hearing Examiner. The patient is entitled to a full and fair hearing — a hearing which affords the patient all the rights he has at the initial commitment hearing — if he challenges his continued hospitalization.

are not strictly adversary proceedings. . . . These are truly investigatory proceedings in which traditional notions of proof are simply inapplicable. The [court], the hospital, the patient, and the government share an obligation to elucidate and explore all the relevant facts."

The difficulties confronting the parties in a release hearing will be compounded by assigning the burden of proof. In Hill [v. Florida, 358 So. 2d 190 (Fla. App. 1978)], the Court discussed the difficulties confronting a patient who must prove an absence of mental illness and dangerousness: his confinement hampers his ability to prove that he can exist safely in an unconfined environment, and having previously shown himself to be dangerous, it is "all but impossible for him to prove the negative that he is no longer a menace." 358 So. 2d at 203, quoting, Covington v. Harris, 419 F.2d 617, 627 (D.C. Cir. 1969).

In contrast, in People v. Howell, 586 P.2d 27, 30 (Colo. 1978), the Court pointed to the difficulties confronting the State: "Typically one who has already been committed does not have as many opportunities to manifest his dangerousness by acts or threats as were available when he was living unrestrained in the outside world. . . . The absence of overt acts may only reflect successful restraint by the institution and may be no indication of the patient's lack of dangerousness if released from that environment."

. . . This Court holds simply that as a matter of equal protection, if the State must bear the burden in M.H.C. release hearings, then it cannot completely shift that burden to the patient who was acquitted of a serious violent crime by reason of insanity. At most, a shared burden — a mutual effort to construct an adequate record — is permissible. . . .

NOTES AND QUESTIONS

1. Other judicial approaches. As the *Benham* decision indicates, the disposition of persons acquitted by reason of insanity involves important issues relating both to procedures and to substantive criteria, and these issues need to be faced separately for at least three stages in the process — the temporary commitment for observation, the initial decision to require indefinite commitment, and the decision concerning release. Moreover, for each issue the constitutional analysis of equal protection requirements is to some degree distinct from the due process analysis. A multiplicity of legal issues is thus presented. Even if the courts were agreed on the general principles to be applied, some variation in the decisions would necessarily result from the fact that the equal protection analysis is directly linked to the standards and procedures established for civil commitments in the particular state and from the fact that the due process analysis depends (at least in part) on what facts must be established, pursuant to what burden of proof, under the state's rules for presentation of the insanity defense at the criminal trial. The courts are, however, far from agreed even on the question of the general principles to be applied.

(*a*) *The initial commitment decision.* Compare the approach in *Benham* with the following:

Warren v. Harvey, 632 F.2d 925, 931-932 (2d Cir. 1980): The obvious difference between insanity acquittees and other persons facing commitment is the fact that the former have been found, beyond a reasonable doubt, to have committed a criminal act. Insanity acquittees thus have "proved" themselves a danger to society at one time. Non-acquittees, in contrast, have not been found by any factfinder to have harmed society as a result of their mental illness. This difference, we believe, gives rise to considerations which justify a lesser standard of proof to commit insanity acquittees than to commit other persons.

One of the primary objects of any standard of proof is to provide the individual with appropriate protection from the harm that may result from an erroneous decision. . . . Ordinarily, if a person is wrongly committed to a mental institution, he may suffer great harm at the hands of society. He is wrongly deprived of his liberty when he poses no danger to society. Furthermore, he is greatly stigmatized. . . . Therefore, by imposing a more stringent burden of proof, society has sought to "impress the factfinder with the importance of the decision," and thus reduce the chance that a harmless individual will be confined erroneously to an institution. [Addington v. Texas, 441 U.S. 418, 427 (1979)].

The same considerations do not come into play when the person facing commitment is an insanity acquittee. . . . [I]f an insanity acquittee is committed because of an erroneous determination that he is mentally ill, then the odds are high that he may have been found not guilty on insanity grounds because of a similar erroneous determination that he is not sane. While the acquittee therefore may be deprived erroneously of his liberty in the *commitment* process, the liberty he loses is likely to be liberty which society mistakenly had permitted him to retain in the *criminal* process. Concomitantly, while society derives no benefit from erroneously confining ordinary persons who are not in fact mentally ill and dangerous, the erroneous confinement of an insanity acquittee who in fact was not mentally ill at the time of his crime indirectly benefits society by keeping a "sane" criminal off the streets.

. . . [T]he stigma attached to the commitment . . . provides another cogent reason for "weighting" the standard of proof scales in favor of the ordinary individual faced with civil commitment. It is hard to view the insanity acquittee with the same solicitude. Any stigma resulting from the label "mentally ill and dangerous" certainly attached at the time the accused was found not guilty by reason of insanity. . . .

Finally, we cannot ignore the danger of "calculated abuse of the insanity defense." United States v. Brown, 478 F.2d [606, 611 (D.C. Cir. 1973)]. We are reluctant to provide criminal defendants with a loophole at society's expense by enabling those who have committed criminal acts first to escape criminal punishment by pleading insanity and then to escape confinement completely if the government fails to prove by clear and convincing evidence that the defendant will continue to be prone to the very same abnormalities that he sought to establish in his past behavior. . . .

We therefore conclude that . . . [w]hile the due process clause ordinarily requires the strict "clear and convincing" standard of proof in civil commitment proceedings, it does not prohibit the states from providing for the lesser "preponderance of the evidence" standard in commitment hearings for that select group of persons who previously have been tried for criminal acts and found not guilty by reason of insanity. . . .[a]

a. For a thorough analysis of the burden-of-proof issue, reaching a conclusion contrary to that of the above case, see Note, Commitment Following an Insanity Acquittal, 94 Harv. L. Rev. 605 (1981). — Eds.

State v. Krol, 68 N.J. 236, 344 A.2d 289, 295-296 (1975): Commitment following acquittal by reason of insanity is not intended to be punitive, for, although such a verdict implies a finding that defendant has committed the actus reus, it also constitutes a finding that he did so without a criminal state of mind. There is, in effect, no crime to punish. . . . The rationale for involuntarily committing such persons pursuant to N.J.S.A. 2A:163-3 is, rather, to protect society against individuals who, through no culpable fault of their own, pose a threat to public safety. . . .

The anomaly of the procedure established by N.J.S.A. 2A:163-3 is that . . . it does not at any point provide for inquiry by judge or jury into the question of whether the particular defendant involved in fact poses such a risk. The standard for commitment is simply that defendant's "insanity continues." The fact that defendant is presently suffering from some degree of mental illness and that at some point in the past mental illness caused him to commit a criminal act, while certainly sufficient to give probable cause to inquire into whether he is dangerous, does not, in and of itself, warrant the inference that he presently poses a significant threat of harm, either to himself or to others.[2]

. . . The problem is most acute when the offense which defendant has committed is one which, although violating social norms, did not itself involve dangerous behavior. But even where, as in this case, the crime is a violent one,[a] the procedure contains great potential for individual injustice.

. . . Constitutional principles of due process require that any state action bear a reasonable relationship to some legitimate state purpose. . . . Jackson v. Indiana, 406 U.S. 715 (1972). . . . Since N.J.S.A. 2A:163-3 is designed to protect the public against the risk of future dangerous behavior by persons acquitted by reason of insanity who are still suffering from mental illness, the principles of due process enunciated in *Jackson* and like cases require that the standard for commitment must be cast in terms of continuing mental illness and dangerousness to self or others, not in terms of continuing insanity alone. . . .[3]

In establishing a standard for commitment based on dangerousness as well as mental illness, we are cognizant of the difficulties which inhere in such a standard. . . . Dangerousness is a concept which involves substantial elements of vagueness and ambiguity. The practical application of a dangerousness standard is further impeded by the difficulty of making valid and meaningful predictions of the likelihood of future harmful conduct and by the subtle but strong pressures upon decision makers to overpredict dangerousness. To a considerable extent, these are problems which can be dealt with only by trial judges on a case by case basis. An appellate court can only suggest guidelines for analysis.

. . . Dangerous conduct involves not merely violation of social norms enforced by criminal sanctions, but significant physical or psychological injury to persons

2. Empirical studies indicate that, as a group, persons suffering from mental illness are, at most, only slightly more likely to commit harmful acts than the general population. . . .

a. Krol stabbed his wife to death and was found not guilty by reason of insanity on the basis of testimony that he was suffering from an acute schizophrenic condition and acted under the influence of a powerful delusion that his wife was conspiring with his employer to murder him. — EDS.

3. . . . [W]e need not consider whether principles of due process would bar the State in this context from imposing the massive, indefinite curtailment of personal liberty involved in involuntary commitment for any reason less compelling than protection of society against a substantial threat of conduct by the defendant dangerous to himself or others. We note that recent cases indicate a strong trend toward such a construction of the due process clause. . . .

or substantial destruction of property. . . . Personal liberty and autonomy are of too great value to be sacrificed to protect society against the possibility of future behavior which some may find odd, disagreeable, or offensive, or even against the possibility of future non-dangerous acts which would be ground for criminal prosecution if actually committed. Unlike inanimate objects, people cannot be suppressed simply because they may become public nuisances. . . . It is not sufficient that the state establish a possibility that defendant might commit some dangerous acts at some time in the indefinite future. The risk of danger, a product of the likelihood of such conduct and the degree of harm which may ensue, must be substantial within the reasonably foreseeable future. On the other hand, certainty of prediction is not required and cannot reasonably be expected. . . .

(b) The release decision. Compare the approach in *Benham* with the following:

Lublin v. Central Islip Psychiatric Center, 43 N.Y.2d 341, 372 N.E.2d 307, 309-310 (1977): Must a person who has been validly committed as a result of an acquittal by reason of mental defect or disease, and who at a later time seeks release on the claimed ground that he is no longer dangerous to either himself or others, be required to prove by a fair preponderance of the evidence that he may safely be released? We hold that he must. . . . It is beyond doubt that petitioner was both insane and dangerous at the time he murdered his wife and attempted to take his own life. . . . Given the clear existence of this condition, as evidenced by the admitted commission of a violent act, it is appropriate that the condition be presumed to continue until the contrary is proven.

The burden which is placed on petitioner is neither excessive nor novel, for the burden of proof is normally placed upon the party who is seeking affirmative relief. . . . The petitioner is obviously asserting his very strong and basic interest in liberty, for it can no longer be denied that commitment, albeit for treatment, does involve a substantial deprivation of liberty. The State, on the other hand, is asserting both its parens patriae interest in the mentally incompetent, with its concomitant obligation to protect them from harm to either themselves or others, and its responsibility to exercise its police powers to protect its citizenry from an individual who has given proof positive that he is in fact dangerous to both society and himself. We find that in such a case, the State's interest must outweigh that of the individual, and it is the people of the State who must be given the benefit of the doubt. . . . Thus, the applicable standard of proof is that of the normal civil proceeding, and petitioner need only show by a fair preponderance of the credible evidence that he may be discharged or released without danger to himself or others.

Jones v. United States, 411 A.2d 624, 626, 628-629 (D.C. App. 1980), Ferren, J.: [Appellant was charged with petty larceny and found not guilty by reason of insanity. He was thereupon committed indefinitely to St. Elizabeths Hospital pursuant to the District of Columbia procedures applicable following an insanity acquittal. He then sought release. Appellant] argues, in effect, that the §24-301(d) [initial commitment] procedure is to some extent punitive, as evidenced by the less-protective procedures afforded acquitees than civil committees; that *Baxstrom* does not necessarily make that procedure unconstitutional as a means for initially confining acquitees; but that the price of constitutionality is release or civil commitment at the end of the hypothetical maximum prison term, since that is the longest an acquitee can be confined for punitive reasons without a denial of equal protection of the laws.

Appellant derives his argument primarily from United States v. Brown, 155 U.S. App. D.C. 402, 407-08, 478 F.2d 606, 611-12 (1973), in which the United States Court of Appeals for the District of Columbia Circuit acknowledged — and upheld — a partially punitive underpinning to the former §24-301(d) procedure. Specifically, the *Brown* court upheld an instruction . . . that the government had the burden . . . of proving respondent mentally ill and dangerous by a preponderance of the evidence, and further held that this instruction would not violate equal protection even if the government, in a civil commitment proceeding, had the burden of proof beyond a reasonable doubt.

After reviewing numerous cases, we conclude that the courts typically mix evidentiary and punitive rationales in justifying less comprehensive review of acquitees at [initial commitment hearings] than is afforded civil commitees at such proceedings. . . .

Now that we are confronted by the possibility that the criminal commitment procedure can, to some extent, be punitive yet constitutional, we must reconsider the nature of a §24-301(d) confinement. There are three possibilities . . . : (1) it is wholly rehabilitative (i.e., not at all punitive), in which case an acquitee can be committed indefinitely, without regard to a hypothetical maximum prison sentence, subject only to the periodic review afforded civil commitees, . . . (2) it is inherently punitive, in which case the [initial commitment] itself is unconstitutional, . . . or, as appellant urges, (3) it is partially (but perhaps justifiably) punitive at the outset, in which case an acquitee, although lawfully confined for awhile, arguably must be released (or civilly committed) no later than the end of the maximum prison term for which the acquitee could have been sentenced. [12]

. . . [W]e conclude that the difference between criminal and civil commitment procedures cannot be justified on purely evidentiary grounds. It follows, therefore, . . . that there is no basis for confining an acquitee under §24-301(d) beyond the length of the hypothetical maximum prison term, since that term marks the end of society's claim on that individual for any kind of punishment. Any longer confinement must depend, constitutionally, on a de novo civil commitment. . . .

Mack, J., concurring. . . . I concur in the instant holding because the serious reservations that I held about the constitutionality of [our initial commitment] procedures are erased by our choosing to mandate that an acquitee must be released from incarceration at the expiration of the maximum period of possible imprisonment for the criminal charge, subject to the government's right to seek civil commitment.

2. Legislative responses. (a) At the time of the decision in Bolton v. Harris, discussed in the *Benham* case, criminal defendants in the District of Columbia

---

12. We understand appellant to base his argument on the hypothetical maximum prison term to which the acquitee himself could be sentenced, not simply on the maximum sentence for the particular crime involved, without regard to the acquitee's own criminal history. We do not, however, resolve that question here.

were entitled to acquittal on insanity grounds whenever there was a reasonable doubt as to sanity at the time of the offense. Judge Bazelon had stressed this point in holding that due process required the government to bear the burden of proving mental illness in a subsequent commitment proceeding. In 1970 Congress amended the District of Columbia statutes to provide that henceforth at the criminal trial the accused must establish an insanity defense by a preponderance of the evidence. The amendments further provided that following an acquittal on insanity grounds and a temporary commitment for examination, a hearing would be held, but that the person committed would remain confined unless he established by a preponderance of the evidence that he was "entitled to his release." The legislation is discussed in United States v. Brawner, 471 F.2d 966, 997 (D.C. Cir. 1972).

Questions: Is the burden of proof specified for the commitment hearing constitutionally permissible? Does the shift in the burden of proof on the insanity issue at the criminal trial affect the continued validity of the *Bolton* court's analysis with respect to constitutional requirements at the commitment hearing?

(b) Consider the following developments in Michigan as related in Brown & Wittner, Criminal Law (1978 Annual Survey of Michigan Law), 25 Wayne L. Rev. 335, 355-358 (1979):

In 1974, the supreme court decided [in] People v. McQuillan [112] . . . that the statute mandating automatic commitment of a defendant found not guilty by reason of insanity violated due process and equal protection. The court found objectionable that such defendants, unlike persons civilly committed, were not afforded a hearing to determine their mental condition at the time of commitment. . . .

The court made clear that defendants must be released from temporary detention absent a determination that they are mentally ill and dangerous. Finally, the court ruled that the release procedures for defendants who are committed after temporary detention must be similar to those for persons civilly committed.

The new Mental Health Code [119] reflects the *McQuillan* standards; a defendant found not guilty by reason of insanity must be committed to the Department of Mental Health's center for forensic psychiatry for evaluation. This temporary detention may not exceed sixty days. After the evaluation, commitment to a mental institution is permissible only if it is proved at an adversary hearing that he is mentally ill and is dangerous as a result of that illness. The director of the institution must discharge such a person when (1) he is no longer mentally ill or dangerous, and (2) the center for forensic psychiatry evaluates the individual and recommends release.

In practice, these procedures have led to horrifying results. Once a patient's symptoms are brought under control by powerful tranquilizing drugs, the Department of Mental Health no longer considers the patient mentally ill for purposes of continued hospitalization. Thus, the patient is prescribed medicine and released. Problems occur when the patient simply decides to discontinue medication. In many such cases, individuals become "time bombs ready to explode."

The danger is best exemplified by the highly publicized cases of John McGee and Ronald Manlen. Both had been committed following verdicts of not guilty by reason of insanity. While institutionalized, McGee claimed to have previously committed some twenty-five other murders. Both men were released from mental institutions after the center for forensic psychiatry determined that they were no

112. 392 Mich. 511, 221 N.W.2d 569 (1974).
119. Mich. Comp. Laws Ann. §§330.1113-.2102 (Supp. 1978-79).

longer mentally ill and dangerous. One month after his release, McGee kicked his wife to death. Manlen raped two women shortly after his release.

Apparently in response to public outrage over these incidents, the state legislature enacted a statute authorizing the verdict of "guilty but mentally ill" when a defendant raised an insanity defense.[133] The verdict is appropriate when the judge or jury determines that the defendant (1) is guilty of the offense; (2) was mentally ill at the time of the offense; and (3) was not legally insane at the time of the offense. A judge retains the same sentencing powers as in the case of a general guilty verdict. If, however, the court sentences the defendant to prison, treatment "as is psychiatrically indicated for his mental illness" must be given. . . .

The "guilty but mentally ill" verdict has been assailed by members of the defense bar as well as by mental health personnel in the Department of Corrections. Defense lawyers contend that the intended effect of the verdict is to eviscerate the insanity defense. The argument, in essence, is that in those cases where the jurors are afraid that an insane defendant may be set free under the *McQuillan* procedures, they will view the "guilty but mentally ill" verdict as an acceptable compromise. In the eyes of the jurors, the verdict will be "a vehicle for protecting the public's need for security while simultaneously providing for the defendant's individualized treatment." To defense lawyers, of course, the verdict is merely an illegitimate end run of *McQuillan* and an abolition of the mens rea requirement. Mental health practitioners express concern that neither the Department of Corrections nor the Department of Mental Health can provide the "individualized treatment" envisioned by jurors.

3. Questions. Given the emerging requirements of due process and equal protection applicable to the commitment of defendants acquitted by reason of insanity, should changes be made in the insanity defense itself (by shifting the burden of proof, narrowing the scope of the defense, or abolishing it altogether)? Or should changes be made in the laws governing ordinary civil commitment (relaxing the substantive criteria for commitment, the procedures, or the burden of proof)? One answer may be that strict safeguards favoring individual liberty are appropriate in all three areas — criminal prosecutions, commitment following insanity acquittal, and civil commitment. But if some relaxation of such safeguards is considered necessary to insure adequate protection against dangerous, mentally ill persons, which set of procedures should be relaxed, and how? Which kinds of adjustments will most seriously compromise the basic principles of criminal responsibility?

PROBLEM

Similar issues concerning procedures and substantive standards arise with respect to the disposition of persons found incompetent to stand trial. It is by definition inappropriate to try such persons on criminal charges, but it is quite common to confine such persons after an abbreviated hearing and no trial on the criminal charges at all. Does this practice make sense? If such persons should sometimes be confined, what factual showing should be required? Once properly confined, can such persons be held until they regain their competency or should there be some outer limit to the permissible period of confinement? For consider-

133. Mich. Comp. Laws Ann. §768.36 (Supp. 1968-78).

ation of these issues, see Jackson v. Indiana, 406 U.S. 715 (1972) and In re Davis, 8 Cal. 3d 798, 505 P.2d 1018 (1973), holding that constitutional principles of due process and equal protection require that a person institutionalized on a finding of incapacity to stand trial may not be confined more than a reasonable period of time necessary to determine whether there is a substantial likelihood that he will recover that capacity in the foreseeable future. Absent such a finding, the defendant must be released or committed under alternative procedures. See Burt & Morris, A Proposal for the Abolition of the Incompetency Plea, 40 U. Chi. L. Rev. 66 (1972).

b.   Automatism — Sane and Insane

REGINA v. QUICK
Court of Appeal, Criminal Division
[1973] 3 W.L.R. 26

LAWTON, L.J., read the following judgment of the court. On April 19, 1972, at Bristol Crown Court during a trial before Bridge, J., and a jury, the defendant Quick pleaded guilty to count 2 of an indictment which charged him with assault occasioning actual bodily harm. That plea was tendered after a ruling by the trial judge. That ruling is the subject of the appeal in this case. . . . Quick was sentenced to nine months' imprisonment. . . .

In their broadest aspects these appeals raise the question as to what is meant by the phrase "a defect of reason from disease of the mind" within the meaning of the *M'Naughten* Rules. More particularly the question is whether a person who commits a criminal act while under the effects of hypoglycaemia can raise a defence of automatism, as the defendants submitted was possible, or whether such a person must rely on a defence of insanity if he wishes to relieve himself of responsibility for his acts, as Bridge, J., ruled.

The defendant [was a nurse] employed at Farleigh Mental Hospital, Flax Bourton, Somerset. . . . At the trial it was not disputed that at about 4 P.M. on December 27, 1971, one Green, a paraplegic spastic patient, unable to walk, was sitting in Rosemount Ward at the hospital, watching television. Quick was on duty. . . . Half an hour later, Green had sustained two black eyes, a fractured nose, a split lip which required three stitches, and bruising of his arm and shoulders. There was undisputed medical evidence that these injuries could not have been self-inflicted.

The prosecution's case was that Quick had inflicted the injuries on Green. . . . On arraignment Quick pleaded not guilty. At the close of the evidence, following a ruling by the judge as to the effect in law of the evidence relied upon by Quick to support a defence of automatism, he pleaded guilty to count 2 of the indictment. The judge's ruling was to the effect that that evidence could only be relied upon to support a defence of insanity.

The evidence upon which the judge ruled came partly from witnesses for the prosecution and partly from Quick's own evidence and that of a consultant physician, Dr. Cates, who was called on his behalf. The evidence from the prosecution's witnesses included that of one Willerton, a state enrolled nurse, who was on duty in Rosemount Ward at the material time. He said that at about 4

P.M. he had been summoned to the television lounge where he found Green on the floor with injuries to his face and struggling. Quick was sitting astride him. Quick seemed glassy eyed and made no reply when asked what he had done. A patient in the course of his evidence spoke of Quick having collapsed on the floor shortly after he had been involved in the assault on Green. In the course of his own evidence Quick said that he could not remember assaulting Green. He admitted that he had been drinking and that his drinks had included whiskey and a quarter of a bottle of rum. He also said that he was, and had been since the age of seven, a diabetic and that that morning he had taken insulin as prescribed by his doctor. After taking the insulin he had had a very small breakfast and no lunch. Dr. Cates said that on 12 or more occasions Quick had been admitted to hospital either unconscious or semiconscious due to hypoglycaemia, which is a condition brought about when there is more insulin in the bloodstream than the amount of sugar there can cope with. When this imbalance occurs, the insulin has much the same effect as an excess of alcohol in the human body. At the onset of the imbalance the higher functions of the mind are affected. As the effects of the imbalance become more marked, more and more mental functions are upset; and unless an antidote is given (and a lump of sugar is an effective one) the sufferer can relapse into coma. In the later stages of mental impairment a sufferer may become aggressive and violent without being able to control himself or without knowing at the time what he was doing or having any recollection afterwards of what he had done. The following answer by Dr. Cates sums up his evidence about hypoglycaemia and his opinion as to whether Quick could have been doing what he was proved to have been doing in the course of a suggested hypoglycaemic reaction:

> If a patient is going unconscious with a falling blood sugar, for a while he will be aggressive, for a while he will be more than aggressive, for a while he may start being physically violent and then he will be in a semi-conscious state when he could be struggling and resisting people's efforts to give him sugar. Then he may have a fit, then he may stay deeply unconscious for quite a while. It would sound from the evidence that this man developed an increasing effect of a falling blood sugar from some time in the afternoon till when he collapsed after the episode of attack. At least the events fit with that.

Dr. Cates said that on three or four occasions while in hospital under treatment for diabetes Quick had behaved violently when his blood sugar had got too low.

As is well known, insulin is prescribed by doctors in order to ensure that only the requisite amount of sugar is in the patient's bloodstream; but from time to time the sugar level may get too low. Dr. Cates said that there were a number of causes for that. The doctor may have prescribed too much insulin; the patient may have eaten too little or have been over-active. He accepted that on the occasion when Green was attacked, Quick's own conduct that day might well have caused a severe fall in blood sugar.

At the trial and before this court it was accepted by the prosecution that the evidence to which we have referred was enough to justify an issue being left to the jury whether Quick could be held responsible for what he had done to Green. If the jury were to accept the evidence relied on by Quick, what should the verdict be? Quick's counsel submitted, "not guilty"; Sir Joseph Molony on behalf of the Crown submitted that it should be "not guilty by reason of insanity." The judge ruled in favour of the Crown. As Quick did not want to put forward a defence of insanity, after consulting with his counsel, he pleaded guilty to count 2. As that plea had been made as a result of the judge's ruling, it was accepted by the prosecution before this court that if that ruling was adjudged to be wrong it would not be a bar to an appeal by Quick against his conviction. . . .

The question which the judge's ruling raises is one on which it seems that there is no direct English or Commonwealth authority and only a few authorities which bear indirectly upon it. We are grateful to counsel for the depth of their researches.

Our examination of such authorities as there are must start with Bratty v. Attorney-General for Northern Ireland [1963] A.C. 386, because the judge ruled as he did in reliance on that case. Bratty had been accused of the murder of a young girl. He put forward three defences; first, that at the material time he was in a state of automatism by reason of suffering from an attack of psychomotor epilepsy; secondly, that he was guilty only of manslaughter since he was incapable of forming an intent on the ground that his mental condition was so impaired and confused and he was so deficient in reason that he was not capable of forming such intent; and thirdly, that he was insane. The trial judge left the issue of insanity to the jury (which they rejected) but refused to leave the other two issues. The House of Lords adjudged on the evidence in *Bratty*'s case that he had been right to rule as he did, but accepted that automatism as distinct from insanity could be a defence if there was a proper foundation in the evidence for it. In this case, if Quick's alleged condition could have been caused by hypoglycaemia and that condition, like psychomotor epilepsy, was a disease of the mind, then Bridge, J.'s ruling was right. The question remains, however, whether a mental condition arising from hypoglycaemia does amount to a disease of the mind. In Bratty v. Attorney-General for Northern Ireland [1963] A.C. 386, all their Lordships based their speeches on the basis that such medical evidence as there was pointed to Bratty suffering from a "defect of reason from disease of the mind" and nothing else. Lord Denning discussed in general terms what constituted a disease of the mind. He said: "The major mental diseases, which the doctors call psychoses, such as schizophrenia, are clearly diseases of the mind. But in Reg. v. Charlson [1955] 1 W.L.R. 317, Barry, J., seems to have assumed that other diseases such as epilepsy or cerebral tumour are not diseases of the mind, even when they are such as to manifest themselves in violence. I do not agree with this. It seems to me that any mental disorder which has manifested itself in violence and is prone to recur is a disease of the mind. At any rate it is the sort of disease for which a person should be detained in hospital rather than be given an unqualified acquittal." If that opinion is right and there are no restricting qualifications which ought to be applied to it, Quick was setting up a defence of insanity. He may have been at the material time in a condition of mental disorder manifesting itself in violence. Such manifestations had occurred before and might recur. The difficulty arises as soon as the question is asked whether he should be detained in a mental hospital. No mental hospital would admit a diabetic merely because he had a low blood sugar reaction; and common sense is affronted by the prospect of a diabetic being sent to such a hospital, when in most cases the disordered mental condition can be rectified quickly by pushing a lump of sugar or a teaspoonful of glucose into the patient's mouth.

The "affront to common sense" argument, however, has its own inherent weakness. . . . If an accused is shown to have done a criminal act while suffering from a "defect of reason from disease of the mind," it matters not whether the condition of the mind is curable or incurable, transitory or permanent. If the condition is transitory, the Secretary of State may have a difficult problem of disposal; but what happens to those found not guilty by reason of insanity is not a matter for the courts.

In Reg. v. Kemp [1957] 1 Q.B. 399, where the violent act was alleged to have been done during a period of unconsciousness arising from arteriosclerosis, counsel for the accused submitted that his client had done what he had during a period of mental confusion arising from a physical, not a mental, disease. Devlin, J., rejected that argument, saying: "It does not matter, for the purposes of the law, whether the defect of reason is due to a degeneration of the brain or to some other form of mental derangement. That may be a matter of importance medically, but it is of no importance to the law, which merely has to consider the state of mind in which the accused is, not how he got there." Applied without qualification of any kind, Devlin, J.'s statement of the law would have some surprising consequences. Take the not uncommon case of the rugby player who gets a kick on the head early in the game and plays on to the end in a state of automatism. If, while he was in that state, he assaulted the referee, it is difficult to envisage any court adjudging that he was not guilty by reason of insanity. Another type of case which could occur is that of the dental patient who kicks out while coming round from an anaesthetic. The law would be in a defective state if a patient accused of assaulting a dental nurse by kicking her while regaining consciousness could only excuse himself by raising the defence of insanity. . . .

[The court then reviewed the other English decisions relevant to the issue: Hill v. Baxter, [1958] 1 Q.B. 277, and Watmore v. Jenkins, [1962] 2 Q.B. 572, and several commonwealth decisions: Regina v. Cottle, [1958] N.Z.L.R. 999; Regina v. Carter, [1959] Vict. 105; Regina v. Foy, [1960] Queensl. 225.]

In this quagmire of law seldom entered nowadays save by those in desperate need of some kind of defence, Bratty v. Attorney-General for Northern Ireland [, supra,] provides the only firm ground. Is there any discernible path? We think there is. Judges should follow in a common sense way their sense of fairness. This seems to have been the approach of the New Zealand Court of Appeal in Reg. v. Cottle [1958] N.Z.L.R. 999, 1011 and of Sholl, J., in Reg. v. Carter [1959] V.R. 105, 110. In our judgment no help can be obtained by speculating (because that is what we would have to do) as to what the judges who answered the House of Lords' questions in 1843 meant by disease of the mind, still less what Sir Matthew Hale meant in the second half of the 17th century. . . .

. . . Our task has been to decide what the law means now by the words "disease of the mind." In our judgment the fundamental concept is of a malfunctioning of the mind caused by disease. A malfunctioning of the mind of transitory effect caused by the application to the body of some external factor such as violence, drugs, including anaesthetics, alcohol and hypnotic influences cannot fairly be said to be due to disease. Such malfunctioning, unlike that caused by a defect of reason from disease of the mind, will not always relieve an accused from criminal responsibility. A self-induced incapacity will not excuse, nor will one which could have been reasonably foreseen as a result of either doing, or omitting to do something, as, for example, taking alcohol against medical advice after using certain prescribed drugs, or failing to have regular meals while taking insulin. From time to time difficult borderline cases are likely to arise. When they do, the test suggested by the New Zealand Court of Appeal in Reg. v. Cottle [1958] N.Z.L.R. 999, 1011 is likely to give the correct result, viz., can this mental condition be fairly regarded as amounting to or producing a defect of reason from disease of the mind?

In this case Quick's alleged mental condition, if it ever existed, was not caused by his diabetes but by his use of the insulin prescribed by his doctor. Such malfunctioning of his mind as there was, was caused by an external factor and not by a bodily disorder in the nature of a disease which disturbed the working of his mind. It follows in our judgment that Quick was entitled to have his defence of automatism left to the jury and that Bridge, J.'s ruling as to the effect of the medical evidence called by him was wrong. Had the defence of automatism been left to the jury, a number of questions of fact would have had to be answered. If he was in a confused mental condition, was it due to a hypoglycaemic episode or to too much alcohol? If the former, to what extent had he brought about this condition by not following his doctor's instructions about taking regular meals? Did he know that he was getting into a hypoglycaemic episode? If yes, why did he not use the antidote of eating a lump of sugar as he had been advised to do? On the evidence which was before the jury Quick might have had difficulty in answering these questions in a manner which would have relieved him of responsibility for his acts. We cannot say, however, with the requisite degree of confidence, that the jury would have convicted him. It follows that his conviction must be quashed on the ground that the verdict was unsatisfactory.

NOTES

1. Cross, Reflections on Bratty's Case, 78 Law Q. Rev. 236, 239 (1962), writes:

Although they are still comparatively rare, pleas of non-insane automatism are becoming increasingly frequent, and questions may legitimately be raised concerning the sufficiency of the courts' powers. Is it right that someone who has been acquitted on the ground of non-insane automatism should inevitably go free? In R. v. Charlson [39 Crim. App. 37 (1955)] the accused was acquitted on various charges of causing grievous bodily harm to his son because he had acted in a state of automatism which may have been due to a cerebral tumour. It is only natural to feel the deepest sympathy for the accused in such a case, but it is equally natural to question the propriety of an unqualified acquittal. One way of dealing with such problems would be to give the judge power in all cases of a successful plea of automatism, insane or non-insane, to order the detention of the accused pending a medical inquiry, after which the appropriate order could be made. The absence of any such power in cases of non-insane automatism has no doubt contributed to the recent tendencies to define a disease of the mind in broad terms, and to encourage the prosecution to ask for a verdict of "guilty but insane."

2. The earlier American cases are discussed in Fox, Physical Disorder, Consciousness, and Criminal Liability, 63 Colum. L. Rev. 645 (1963). The author points out that relatively few cases have dealt with the question of criminal conduct during various states of sleep. The courts appear to be divided on whether the defense made out by impaired consciousness due to sleep amounts to legal insanity (establishing authority to commit) or absence of a volitional act (leading to outright acquittal). The Model Penal Code has proposed the latter alternative. See §2.01(2)(b), Appendix to this casebook. Reconsider in this connection the *Cogden* case, page 255 supra. Does the Model Penal Code approach make sense as applied to such a case?

Some recent cases have appeared in other jurisdictions. In People v. Grant, 46 Ill. App. 3d 125, 360 N.E.2d 809 (1977), defendant appealed from an aggravated-battery conviction on the ground that the judge gave the usual insanity instruction (Illinois had adopted the Model Penal Code test), when his defense was that he suffered an epileptic psychomotor seizure at the time of the offense. Failure to instruct on the statutory requirement of a voluntary act was urged as error. The court reversed, finding that the issue of automatism should have been decided by the jury. Declining to follow *Bratty*'s case, in which the House of Lords had held that psychomotor epilepsy is a disease of the mind within the meaning of the insanity test, the Illinois court stated (360 N.E.2d at 816):

> [Our] Code provides for the affirmative defense of insanity and requires that every offense be the result of a voluntary act. Our legislature has provided that a person found not guilty of an offense by reason of insanity can be committed to a mental health facility for treatment, although no such provision applies to an alleged offender who commits an involuntary act. . . .
> . . . If the jury finds that the defendant was sane but not responsible for the attack . . . , then he cannot be committed for the offense. We find this course to be mandated by our legislature which only provides for the commitment of persons who are criminally insane.

One judge observed in dissent (id. at 818):

> I share with Lord Denning and the majority of commentators on the subject a belief in the need for protective custody for persons who repeatedly attack others while in a state of automatism. The situation merits an attempt by the legislature to devise a procedure balancing the rights of the public to be protected against the rights of the person subject to automatism to be at liberty and basing any deprivation of that liberty upon the degree of danger presented by that individual.
> . . . I do not agree that the Criminal Code is sufficient. Most of the authority cited by the majority discussing automatism is of comparatively recent origin, and the comments of the drafting committee give no indication of any consideration of the problem by that committee.

3. In State v. Caddell, 287 N.C. 266, 215 S.E.2d 348 (1975), defendant interposed pleas of not guilty and not guilty by reason of insanity to a charge of kidnapping. On the basis of evidence at the trial, the judge instructed the jury on the defenses of both legal insanity and unconsciousness. The jury rejected these defenses, and defendant was convicted. On appeal, defendant contended that the instruction on unconsciousness did not clearly place the burden of

proof on the prosecution. The court affirmed. Overruling a prior decision to the contrary, the court held that while unconsciousness is a defense distinct from insanity, in that it need not result from mental disease and does not subject the defendant to commitment, both are affirmative defenses in which the burden of proof rests on the defendant. The court concluded (215 S.E.2d at 363):

> The same presumption, which casts upon the defendant, claiming insanity, the burden of proving it to the satisfaction of the jury, and thus to negative the presence of mens rea, applies also to the defendant who asserts a temporary mental lapse due to concussion, somnolentia, epilepsy or the like.

In separate opinion the Chief Justice, pointing to the majority of jurisdictions that had held to the contrary, stated (215 S.E.2d at 366):

> . . . [I]f a person is actually unconscious when he does an act which would otherwise be criminal, the absence of consciousness not only excludes the existence of any specific mental state, but also excludes the possibility of a voluntary act without which there can be no criminal liability. Unconsciousness, therefore, can never be an affirmative defense, which imposes the burden of proof upon the defendant, because the State has the burden of proving the essential elements of the offense charged, and "a voluntary act is an absolute requirement for criminal liability." Although the defense of unconsciousness "is sometimes explained on the ground that such a person could not have the requisite mental state for commission of the crime, the better rationale is that the individual has not engaged in a voluntary act."

Query: Is the majority's position unconstitutional under the Supreme Court's burden-of-proof decisions? See Patterson v. New York, 432 U.S. 197 (1977), and related material, pages 67-75 supra.

4. For commentary upon these issues see Leigh, Automatism and Insanity, 5 Crim. L.Q. 160 (1962); Elliott, Responsibility for Involuntary Acts: Ryan v. The Queen, 41 Austl. L.J. 497 (1968); Edwards, Automatism and Social Defense, 8 Crim. L.Q. 258 (1966); Kahn, Automatism: Sane and Insane, [1965] N.Z.L.J. 113, 128; Sim, Involuntary Actus Reus, 25 Mod. L. Rev. 741 (1962); Scoble, Amnesia, Automatism and Insanity, 79 S. Afr. L.J. 338 (1962); Jennings, The Growth and Development of Automatism as a Defense in Criminal Law, 2 Osgoode Hall L. Student J. 370 (1962); William, Automatism, in Essays in Criminal Science 345 (G. Mueller ed. 1961).

For a comment on the *Quick* case, see 37 Mod. L. Rev. 199 (1974).

See also Fingarette, Diminished Mental Capacity as a Criminal Law Defense, 37 Mod. L. Rev. 264 (1974), where the author attempts what he describes as a rational reconstruction of the core doctrine unifying what are at present a congeries of ad hoc defenses: insanity, diminished responsibility, drunkenness, mental defect, automatism, and unconsciousness.

c. Diminished Capacity

UNITED STATES v. BRAWNER [11]

United States Court of Appeals, District of Columbia Circuit
471 F.2d 969 (1972)

LEVENTHAL, J. . . . . Our decision accompanies the redefinition of when a mental condition exonerates a defendant from criminal responsibility with the doctrine that expert testimony as to a defendant's abnormal mental condition may be received and considered, as tending to show, in a responsible way, that defendant did not have the specific mental state required for a particular crime or degree of crime — even though he was aware that his act was wrongful and was able to control it, and hence was not entitled to complete exoneration.

Some of the cases following this doctrine use the term "diminished responsibility," but we prefer the example of the cases that avoid this term, for its convenience is outweighed by its confusion: Our doctrine has nothing to do with "diminishing" responsibility of a defendant because of his impaired mental condition, but rather with determining whether the defendant had the mental state that must be proved as to all defendants.

Procedurally, the issue of abnormal mental condition negativing a person's intent may arise in different ways: For example, the defendant may offer evidence of mental condition not qualifying as mental disease under McDonald [v. United States, 312 F.2d 847 (D.C. Cir. 1962)]. Or he may tender evidence that qualifies under *McDonald,* yet the jury may conclude from all the evidence that defendant has knowledge and control capacity sufficient for responsibility under the ALI rule.

The issue often arises with respect to mental condition tendered as negativing the element of premeditation in a charge of first degree premeditated murder. . . .

An offense like deliberated and premeditated murder requires a specific intent that cannot be satisfied merely by showing that defendant failed to conform to an objective standard. This is plainly established by the defense of voluntary intoxication. In Hopt v. Utah, 104 U.S. 631 (1881), the Court, after stating the familiar rule that voluntary intoxication is no excuse for crime, said: "[W]hen a statute establishing different degrees of murder requires deliberate premeditation in order to constitute murder in the first degree, the question of whether the accused is in such a condition of mind, by reason of drunkenness or otherwise, as to be capable of deliberate premeditation, necessarily becomes a material subject of consideration by the jury. . . ."

Neither logic nor justice can tolerate a jurisprudence that defines the elements of an offense as requiring a mental state such that one defendant can properly argue that his voluntary drunkenness removed his capacity to form the specific intent but another defendant is inhibited from a submission of his contention that an abnormal mental condition, for which he was in no way responsible, negated his capacity to form a particular specific intent, even though the condition did not exonerate him from all criminal responsibility.

In Fisher v. United States, 149 F.2d 28 (1946), the court upheld the trial

---

11. Other portions of this opinion are reprinted at pages 831-839 supra.

court's refusal to instruct the jury that on issues of premeditation and deliberation "it should consider the entire personality of the defendant, his mental, nervous, emotional and physical characteristics as developed by the evidence in the case." Justice Arnold's abbreviated opinion was evidently premised on two factors: (1) that the instruction confused the issue of insanity with the issue of deliberation; (2) that "To give an instruction like the above is to tell the jury they are at liberty to acquit one who commits a brutal crime because he has the abnormal tendencies of persons capable of such crimes." His opinion made no effort to come to terms with the *Hopt* opinion, stressed by Fisher's counsel.

Fisher went to the Supreme Court and there was affirmed, but on the limited ground of disinclination to "force" this court in a choice of legal doctrine for the District of Columbia, 328 U.S. 463 (1946). . . .

Today we . . . are changing the insanity rule, on a prospective basis, to take into account intervening scholarship and court opinions. As a corollary, we deem it appropriate to change the rule of *Fisher* on a prospective basis, and to accept the approach which . . . has been adopted by the overwhelming majority of courts that have recently faced the question. We are convinced by the analysis set forth in the recent opinions of the highest courts of California, Colorado, New Jersey, Iowa, Ohio, Idaho, Connecticut, Nebraska, New Mexico and Nevada. They have joined the states that spoke out before *Fisher* — New York, Rhode Island, Utah, Wisconsin and Wyoming.

The pertinent reasoning was succinctly stated by the Colorado Supreme Court as follows [Battalino v. People, 118 Colo. 587, 199 P.2d 897, 901 (1948)]: "The question to be determined is not whether defendant was insane, but whether the homicidal act was committed with deliberation and premeditation. The evidence offered as to insanity may or may not be relevant to that issue. . . . "'A claim of insanity cannot be used for the purpose of reducing a crime of murder in the first degree to murder in the second degree or from murder to manslaughter. If the perpetrator is responsible at all in this respect, he is responsible in the same degree as a sane man; and if he is not responsible at all, he is entitled to an acquittal in both degrees. However, . . . *evidence of the condition of the mind* of the accused at the time of the crime, together with the surrounding circumstances, may be introduced, not for the purpose of establishing insanity, but to prove that the situation was such that a specific intent was not entertained — that is, *to show absence of any deliberate or premeditated design.*'" (Emphasis in original.)

On the other side of the coin, very few jurisdictions which have recently considered this question have held to the contrary position.

Intervening developments within our own jurisdiction underscore the soundness of a doctrine for consideration of abnormal mental condition on the issue of specific intent. In the *Fisher* opinion of 1946, the court was concerned lest such a doctrine "tell the jury that they are at liberty to acquit one who commits a brutal crime because he has the abnormal tendencies of persons capable of such crimes." That a man's abnormal mental condition short of legal insanity may be material as negativing premeditation and deliberation does not set him "at liberty" but reduces the degree of the criminal homicide. . . .

There has also been a material legislative development since . . . *Fisher*. . . . In 1964, after extensive hearings, Congress enacted the Hospitalization of the Mentally Ill Act, which provides civil commitment for the "mentally ill" who are dangerous to themselves or others. . . . These statutory provisions provide a shield against danger from persons with abnormal mental conditions. . . .

Our rule permits the introduction of expert testimony as to abnormal condition if it is relevant to negative, or establish, the specific mental condition that is an element of the crime. The receipt of this expert testimony to negative the mental condition of specific intent requires careful administration by the trial judge. Where the proof is not offered in the first instance as evidence of exonerating mental disease or defect within the ALI rule the judge may, and ordinarily would, require counsel first to make a proffer of the proof to be adduced outside the presence of the jury. The judge will then determine whether the testimony is grounded in sufficient scientific support to warrant use in the courtroom, and whether it would aid the jury in reaching a decision on the ultimate issues. . . .

NOTES

1. *"Diminished responsibility."* The doctrine exemplified in *Brawner* should be distinguished from what has sometimes been called "diminished responsibility" or "partial responsibility." According to the latter doctrine, quite apart from the definition of the particular crime, the fact that the defendant was mentally disturbed, though to an extent short of that required to establish the defense of legal insanity, has the effect of entitling him to a reduction in the severity of the sentence. Such a doctrine has been recognized by some European countries. For example, the German Criminal Code of 1969 provides in §21 that if a defendant's capacity to appreciate the wrongfulness of his or her act or to act in accordance with such understanding was severely impaired at the time of the act as a result of mental or emotional illness, the defendant is subject to a lesser punishment. StGB, Law of July 4, 1969 (Zweites Gesetz zur Reform des Strafrechts [1969] Bundesgesetzblatt, Pt. 1). In the United Kingdom, a partial-responsibility doctrine has been adopted, applicable solely to murder. The English Homicide Act, 1957, 5 & 6 Eliz. II, ch. II, §2(1) provides:

> Where a person kills or is a party to the killing of another, he shall not be convicted of murder if he was suffering from such abnormality of mind (whether arising from a condition of arrested or retarded development of mind or any inherent causes or induced by disease or injury) as substantially impaired the mental responsibility for acts and omissions in doing or being a party to the killing. . . . A person who but for this section would be liable . . . to be convicted of murder shall be liable instead to be convicted of manslaughter.

While the European doctrine of lessened responsibility is analytically distinct from the diminished-capacity doctrine discussed in *Brawner,* the latter doctrine, of course, tends to serve the purposes of the former — although in a disguised and erratic way. Is there a case to be made for explicit adoption of the kind of lessened responsibility principle common in Europe?

2. *Further reading.* The issue of diminished capacity has generated a lively literature. See Morse, Diminished Capacity: A Moral and Legal Conundrum, 2

Intl. J.L. & Psych. 271 (1979); Arenella, The Diminished Capacity and Diminished Responsibility Defenses: Two Children of a Doomed Marriage, 77 Colum. L. Rev. 827 (1977); Dix, Psychological Abnormality as a Factor in Grading Criminal Liability: Diminished Capacity, Diminished Responsibility, and the Like, 62 J. Crim. L.C. & P.S. 313 (1971).

BETHEA v. UNITED STATES
District of Columbia Court of Appeals
365 A.2d 64 (1976)

HARRIS, J. This is an appeal from a conviction of first-degree murder in which the defense of insanity was unsuccessful. . . .

On June 29, 1973, appellant took a bus to his estranged wife's office. Following an argument there, he shot her five times at close range. Soon thereafter, he was apprehended without significant resistance in an adjoining office. He was charged in a single-count indictment with first-degree murder. Pursuant to a pretrial motion by the government, he was ordered to undergo psychiatric examination at Saint Elizabeths Hospital. The hospital's staff concluded (1) that appellant was suffering from "no mental disorder," (2) that he was competent to stand trial, and (3) that the examination had yielded negative results under both the *Durham* and the *Brawner* tests for criminal exculpability.

Appellant's defense was based on the related assertions that at the time of the shooting his mental condition was such as to amount to insanity, or, in any event, to preclude a finding of the degree of mens rea required for the offense.[4] He did not take the stand, but relied upon the testimony of both lay and expert witnesses to explain his condition and the circumstances leading up to and at the time of the incident. The lay witnesses testified that appellant's behavior on that day appeared somewhat irrational. Dr. Jesse Rubin, a private psychiatrist (who had spent less than three hours with appellant and whose knowledge of the facts was limited to appellant's version thereof), testified that appellant had been under severe emotional stress and suffered from what the doctor diagnosed as a "hysterical neurosis of a dissociative type.[6]

The government sought to rebut the claim of insanity with the testimony of several experts and certain acquaintances and relatives of Eddie and the late Barbara Bethea. Their testimony suggested a more mundane explanation for appellant's behavior. The couple's marital relationship had deteriorated throughout 1972, and even after the separation they continued to have stormy and occasionally violent arguments concerning appellant's financial support of his wife and his suspicions of her infidelity. Drs. Thomas Polley and Robert Robertson challenged Dr. Rubin's diagnosis of "hysterical dissociative reaction," and testified that in any event appellant had not been suffering from any men-

4. Conviction of first-degree murder requires proof that at the time of the killing the perpetrator was of "sound memory and discretion," and commited the act with a purposefulness accompanied by "deliberate and premeditated malice." D.C. Code 1973, §22-24-1.

6. Dr. Rubin explained that dissociative reaction may be described as an "involuntary, psychogenic, that is, emotional" disorder or loss of function. He testified that the illness is characterized by "alterations in the state of consciousness," and may produce symptoms such as amnesia. The condition apparently is directly related to the underlying existence of "severe emotional conflict," and its symptoms might be expected to "begin and end suddenly in emotionally charged situations."

tal disorder which would have significantly impaired his capacity for self-control.[7] . . .

Appellant . . . contends that it was error for the trial court to refuse to instruct the jury "that the testimony introduced on the issue of insanity could be considered on the issues of premeditation, deliberation, and malice." His argument rests upon the circuit court's announcement in United States v. Brawner, that henceforth expert medical testimony concerning a defendant's mental abnormality might be admissible, irrespective of a defense of insanity, for purposes of determining the existence of the mens rea required for the charged offense. We conclude that the trial court was not bound by *Brawner's* concept of diminished responsibility, and that adoption of its principles would be unwarranted.

Prior to *Brawner,* the circuit court in this jurisdiction consistently had rejected the argument that, short of the question of complete exoneration under a defense of insanity, expert medical evidence should be admitted toward negating the mental state requisite for a conviction. . . . [See Fisher v. United States, 149 F.2d 28 (1945).]

. . . In support of the doctrine [of diminished capacity], appellant relies heavily on the rationale of the *Brawner* court's dicta on the subject, the principal theme of which may be characterized as logical relevance. . . . In the abstract, evidence of a mental disease or defect may be as relevant to the issue of mens rea as proof of intoxication or epilepsy, and the logic of consistency could compel a similar evidentiary rule for all such incapacitating conditions. However, . . . we conclude that the argument of logical relevance is insufficient to warrant an abrogation of the *Fisher* rule. . . .

. . . It is true, of course, that the existence of the required state of mind is to be determined subjectively in the sense that the issue must be resolved according to the particular circumstances of a given case. However, this fact may not be allowed to obscure the critical difference between the legal concepts of mens rea and insanity. The former refers to the existence in fact of a "guilty mind"; insanity, on the other hand, connotes a presumption that a particular individual lacks the capacity to possess such a state of mind. It is upon this distinction that the "logic" of the diminished capacity doctrine founders.

. . . The law presumes that all individuals are capable of the mental processes which bear the jurisprudential label "mens rea"; that is, the law presumes sanity. Moreover, for the sake of administrative efficiency and in recognition of fundamental principles of egalitarian fairness, our legal system further presumes that each person is equally capable of the same forms and degrees of intent. The concept of insanity is simply a device the law employs to define the outer limits of that segment of the general population to whom these presumptions concerning the capacity for criminal intent shall not be applied. The line between the sane and the insane for the purposes of criminal adjudication is not drawn

7. Dr. Polley, a clinical psychologist for Saint Elizabeths Hospital, described appellant as emotionally impoverished, but found no indication of dissociative reaction. He concluded that there had been no significant distortion of appellant's thought processes, and that at the time of the shooting appellant had been functioning within the range of a "normal psychological state." Dr. Robertson, a psychiatric consultant to Saint Elizabeths Hospital, explained that there are degrees of dissociative reaction, but testified that the condition should not significantly interfere with behavioral controls. He disputed Dr. Rubin's diagnosis of dissociative reaction, and concluded that at the time of the incident, appellant was not suffering from any mental disorder and was aware of what he was doing.

because for one group the actual existence of the necessary mental state (or lack thereof) can be determined with any greater certainty, but rather because those whom the law declares insane are demonstrably so aberrational in their psychiatric characteristics that we choose to make the assumption that they are incapable of possessing the specified state of mind. Within the range of individuals who are not "insane," the law does not recognize the readily demonstrable fact that as between individual criminal defendants the nature and development of their mental capabilities may vary greatly. . . . By contradicting the presumptions inherent in the doctrine of mens rea, the theory of diminished capacity inevitably opens the door to variable or sliding scales of criminal responsibility. . . .

We recognize that there are exceptions to the basic principle that all individuals are presumed to have a similar capacity for mens rea. The rule that evidence of intoxication may be employed to demonstrate the absence of specific intent figured prominently in the *Brawner* court's advocacy of consistency in the treatment of expert evidence of mental impairment. The asserted analogy is flawed, however, by the fact that there are significant evidentiary distinctions between psychiatric abnormality and the recognized incapacitating circumstances. Unlike the notion of partial or relative insanity, conditions such as intoxication, medication, epilepsy, infancy, or senility are, in varying degrees, susceptible to quantification or objective demonstration, and to lay understanding. As the Ninth Circuit observed in Wahrlich v. Arizona, 479 F.2d 1137, 1138 (9th Cir. 1973): "Exposure to the effects of age and of intoxicants upon state of mind is a part of common human experience which fact finders can understand and apply; indeed, they would apply them even if the state did not tell them they could. The esoterics of psychiatry are not within the ordinary ken."

While the rationale for the diminished capacity dicta in *Brawner* rested heavily upon the concept of logical relevance, the court gave scant attention to the other general prerequisites to the admissibility of evidence, i.e., its reliability and the balance between its probative value and its potential impact upon the other interests which are critical to the adjudicatory mechanism. The responsibility for ascertaining the legal relevance of the proffered medical testimony was left [in *Brawner*] to the trial judge. . . .

Quite apart from our previously expressed reservations concerning the wisdom of burdening the medically-naive court with the administration of such an ad hoc standard, the degree of sophistication of the psychiatric sciences and the validity and reliability of its evidentiary product are not beyond dispute. In Wahrlich v. Arizona, 479 F.2d at 1138, the Ninth Circuit concluded: "[T]he state of the developing art of psychiatry is such that we are not convinced that psychiatric testimony directed to a retrospective analysis of the subtle gradations of specific intent has enough probative value to compel its admission." Criticism of the use of medical proof in the determination of criminal responsibility has not been confined to the case law. One source has identified the problem as: "a) extraneous qualities of psychiatric patients — such as their socio-economic class — may substantially influence psychiatric judgments; b) judges and juries usually defer to psychiatric judgments; c) psychiatric interview procedures are unstandardized; d) it is difficult for judges and juries to evaluate the validity of individual psychiatric judgments; and e) psychiatrists and behavioral scientists who have studied the reliability and validity of psychiatric judgments almost unanimously agree that such judgments are of low reliability and validity." Ennis & Litwack, Psychiatry and the Presumption of Expertise: Flipping Coins in the Courtroom, 62 Cal. L. Rev. 693, 737 (1974). . . .

The potential impact of psychiatric evidence in an area so critically close to the ultimate issue of responsibility cannot be minimized. The post-*Durham* struggle to preserve to the lay trier its full decision-making authority provides a clear indication of the inherent dangers in the unrestrained admission of expert testimony. . . .

The *Brawner* court did indicate that for the time being the admission of psychiatric evidence of diminished capacity would be limited to the trial of offenses involving specific intent. We are not satisfied that the rule could be confined so easily. Assuming the competency of experts to testify as to an accused's capacity for specific intent, we see no logical bar to their observations as to the possible existence or lack of malice or general intent. . . .

The issue is far from inconsequential, for the unrestrained application of the diminished capacity doctrine would have a profound impact upon both the separate defense of insanity and the statutory scheme which governs claims of irresponsibility. In the provisions of D.C. Code 1973, §24-301 [governing commitment and release procedures], Congress struck a careful balance between the interests of the individual and those of the community. While there may be superficial appeal to the idea that the standards of criminal responsibility should be applied as subjectively as possible, the overriding danger of the disputed doctrine is that it would discard the traditional presumptions concerning mens rea without providing for a corresponding adjustment in the means whereby society is enabled to protect itself from those who cannot or will not conform their conduct to the requirements of the law.[56]

Under the present statutory scheme, a successful plea of insanity avoids a conviction, but confronts the accused with the very real possibility of prolonged therapeutic confinement.[58] If, however, psychiatric testimony were generally admissible to cast a reasonable doubt upon whatever degree of mens rea was necessary for the charged offense, thus resulting in outright acquittal, there would be scant reason indeed for a defendant to risk such confinement by arguing the greater form of mental deficiency.[59] Thus, quite apart from the argument

---

56. The government has argued with some persuasiveness that the adoption of the Model Penal Code standard for the insanity defense will reduce the urgency of the diminished capacity argument. [Compare the observations of the California Supreme Court in People v. Drew, supra, on the significance of the adoption of the Model Penal Code test of legal insanity for the issue of the defense of diminished capacity.]

58. Under the provisions of D.C. Code 1973, §§24-301(d) and (e), one who is found not guilty by reason of insanity must be confined until such time as it is shown that he "has recovered his sanity [and] will not in the reasonable future be dangerous to himself or others." In the absence of unopposed certification of such recovery by the appropriate medical authorities, the person so confined must bear the burden of proof by a preponderance of the evidence.

59. . . . [I]t should be noted that although the trial court traditionally has the authority to raise an insanity defense sua sponte, it is unclear whether the consequence of an acquittal on the grounds of insanity would be affected by the defendant's objection to the imposition of the defense. In a recent decision, the circuit court appeared to adopt a construction of the relevant statutes which would have the effect of stripping the community of the protection afforded by the mandatory commitment provisions whenever the defense is initiated by the trial court, irrespective of the defense's response thereto. In light of such uncertainty, the trial court's acknowledged authority to raise the insanity defense would be an unlikely antidote to the defense's use of the diminished capacity doctrine as a strategic ploy.

that the diminished capacity doctrine would result in a considerably greater likelihood of acquittal for those who by traditional standards would be held responsible, the future safety of the offender as well as the community would be jeopardized by the possibility that one who is genuinely dangerous might obtain his complete freedom merely by applying his psychiatric evidence to the threshold issue of intent.

The *Brawner* court expressed satisfaction that the statutory procedures governing civil commitment would "provide a shield against danger from persons with abnormal mental condition." We do not share their optimism. While confinement as a result of either a plea of insanity or a civil petition turns upon the existence of a similar degree of mental impairment, there exist significant procedural differences. . . . The difference between the burden and standards of proof has been justified on the quite logical ground that under normal circumstances civil commitment is directed toward a potential threat to an individual or the community, while in the context of the criminal defense, harm in fact has occurred, and the commission of the act is tacitly acknowledged. . . . We see no justification for thwarting the legitimate policy objectives of the mandatory commitment provisions of §24-301 by reopening the gap between the civil and criminal structures. . . . We conclude that the potential impact of concepts such as diminished capacity or partial insanity — however labeled —is of a scope and magnitude which precludes their proper adoption by an expedient modification of the rules of evidence. If such principles are to be incorporated into our law of criminal responsibility, the change should lie within the province of the legislature. . . .

NOTES AND QUESTIONS

1. The California Supreme Court has played a leading role in developing and extending the doctrine of diminished capacity. The controversy generated by the court's decisions has led to a restrictive statutory intervention in the form of the following two new sections to the Cal. Pen. Code (Senate Bill 54) (1981):

28. (a) Evidence of mental disease, mental defect, or mental disorder shall not be admitted to negate the capacity to form any mental state, including, but not limited to, purpose, intent, knowledge, or malice aforethought, with which the accused committed the act. Evidence of mental disease, mental defect, or mental disorder is admissible on the issue as to whether the criminal defendant actually formed any such mental state.

(b) As a matter of public policy there shall be no defense of diminished capacity, diminished responsibility, or irresistible impulse in a criminal action.

(c) This section shall not be applicable to an insanity hearing pursuant to Section 1026 or 1429.5.

29. In the guilt phase of a criminal action, any expert testifying about a defendant's mental illness, mental disorder, or mental defect shall not testify as to whether the defendant had or did not have the required mental states, which include, but are not limited to, purpose, intent, knowledge, or malice aforethought, for the crimes charged. The question as to whether the defendant had or did not have the required mental states shall be decided by the trier of fact.

Query: What problems are likely to confront the courts in interpreting and applying these new sections? To what extent will they mean the end of diminished capacity in California? How much will it matter that psychiatric evidence on *capacity* to form the required mental state is inadmissible, so long as such evidence is admissible on the issue as to whether the defendant in fact *had* the mental state? To what extent is an answer to this question affected by the statute's prohibition against the psychiatrist's testifying to his or her conclusion as to whether the defendant acted with the required mental state?

2. *Constitutional issues.* In Hughes v. State, 68 Wis. 2d 159, 227 N.W.2d 911 (1975), the Wisconsin Supreme Court, responding to considerations similar to those expressed in the *Bethea* case and reflected in the California statute, sustained a first-degree murder conviction after the trial court had excluded psychiatric testimony offered to rebut the specific intent to kill required for first-degree murder in Wisconsin. The testimony would have been that defendant had an antisocial (or psychopathic) personality, a condition that prevented him from forming the specific intent to. kill. A habeas corpus petition was granted by the federal district court and affirmed by the court of appeals. Hughes v. Mathews, 576 F.2d 1250 (7th Cir. 1976). The court found the Wisconsin conviction unconstitutional in two respects.

First, the jury was instructed that the law presumes that a person intends the natural and probable consequences of his or her own acts, that the presumption may be rebutted, but that in this case, absent circumstances rebutting the presumption, the legal presumption is that death was intended. The court, relying on the United States Supreme Court's burden-of-proof cases, see pages 67-82 supra, held that "by instructing the jury to presume intent if not rebutted, and by excluding psychiatric evidence offered to rebut the presumption, Wisconsin set up a conclusive presumption which unconstitutionally relieved the prosecution of the burden of proving the element of specific intent beyond a reasonable doubt." (Id. at 1255.)

Second, the exclusion of defendant's psychiatric evidence on the issue of specific intent was held to be unconstitutional as a violation of his right under the Sixth and Fourteenth Amendments to present evidence in his behalf. Quoting from a concurring opinion by Justice Harlan, the court stated (at 1258) that this right is violated when "the State has recognized as relevant and competent the testimony of this type of witness, but has arbitrarily barred its use by this defendant." The court concluded that the evidence was relevant in Wisconsin since it met the test of having a tendency to prove (or disprove) a fact in issue and that it was competent there because Wisconsin treated psychiatric evidence as sufficiently trustworthy to allow its use on the issues of legal insanity and competency to stand trial. Finally, as to the policy reason for excluding the evidence — namely, that it would cause judges and juries to find defendants not guilty who are guilty and legally sane — the court said (id. at 1258):

> Whatever validity this argument might have when a finding of no intent would result in no criminal responsibility, it is unpersuasive in the present case where the testimony was offered only to show that a second-degree murder conviction was proper. We expressly leave open the question of whether the State's fear of the "guilty" going free is sufficient justification for excluding psychiatric testimony on the issue of capacity to form intent when there is no lesser included crime of which, absent specific intent, a defendant would be guilty.

3. Problem. Or. Rev. Stat. §161.295 defines legal insanity in the Model Penal Code's language. Section 161.300 provides: "Evidence that the actor suffered from a mental disease or defect is admissible whenever it is relevant to the issue of whether he did or did not have the intent which is an element of the crime." Section 161.305 provides that mental disease or defect excluding responsibility under either §161.295 or §161.300 is an affirmative defense which the defendant must prove by a preponderance of the evidence. Is the latter provision unconstitutional as applied to a defense falling under §161.300? See State v. Stockett, 278 Or. 637, 565 P.2d 739 (1977).

4. Mitigation versus exoneration. In McCarthy v. State, 372 A.2d 180, 183 (Del. 1977), the Delaware Supreme Court held that an instruction on diminished capacity was not appropriate in a prosecution for kidnapping and attempted rape. The court stated:

> [T]he salient aspect of the diminished responsibility doctrine is that it does not relieve the defendant of criminal responsibility. . . . In practice under the doctrine, while conviction for an offense requiring a specific intent was foreclosed, conviction for a lesser-included crime, requiring only a general criminal intent, was not. This specific intent — general intent dichotomy explains not only the application of the doctrine in the first degree murder cases wherein the specific intent element of premeditation and deliberation are negated, . . . but also the seemingly more liberal application of the doctrine in such cases as assault and battery with intent to kill; first degree forgery, requiring specific intent to defraud; . . . and entering a building with intent to commit theft. In each of these instances, the requisite specific intent constituted an aggravating factor to an otherwise general mens rea offense and the doctrine was applied to permit a finding of the lesser offense.
>
> As the above cases illustrate, acceptance of the doctrine requires that there be some lesser-included offense which lacks the requisite specific intent of the greater offense charged. Otherwise, the doctrine of diminished responsibility becomes an impermissible substitute test of criminal responsibility. . . .
>
> In the instant case, there are no such lesser-included offenses within those for which the defendant was charged and tried. The acceptance of the doctrine in this case, therefore, would be inconsistent with the theory's basic purpose.

A different view was taken in People v. Wetmore, 22 Cal. 3d 318, 583 P.2d 1308, 1315 (1978), in which the California Supreme Court observed:

> [A] defense of diminished capacity arising from mental disease or defect extends to all specific intent crimes, whether or not they encompass lesser included offenses. Clearly, if a crime requires specific intent, a defendant who, because of mental disease or defect lacks that intent, cannot commit that crime. The presence or absence of a lesser included offense within the charged crime cannot affect the result. The prosecution must prove all elements of the crime beyond a reasonable doubt; we do not perceive how a defendant who has in his possession evidence which rebuts an element of the crime can logically be denied the right to present that evidence merely because it will result in his acquittal.

The court recognized the practical danger of the defense so interpreted — namely, that mentally disordered persons acquitted on a diminished-capacity defense would be set free, since only persons acquitted on a legal insanity defense are subject to the state's confinement and treatment provisions. It responded (id. at 1315):

> The solution to this problem . . . does not lie in barring the defense of diminished capacity when the charged crime lacks a lesser included offense, but in providing for the confinement and treatment of defendants with diminished capacity arising from mental disease or defect.

The court noted that such task was a legislative problem.

5. *Nature of the testimony.* In United States v. Busic, 592 F.2d 13 (2d Cir. 1978), defendant was convicted of aircraft piracy, defined in 49 U.S.C. §1472(i) to mean "any seizure or exercise of control, by force or violence or threat of force or violence, or by any other form of intimidation, and with wrongful intent, of an aircraft within the special aircraft jurisdiction of the United States."

On appeal, defendant contended that the trial court had improperly excluded psychiatric testimony offered to show that he was incapable of forming the requisite intent to commit the offense. His counsel had offered the testimony of Dr. Bernard L. Diamond, who was prepared to testify as follows (id. at 21):

> Zvanko Busic was in an abnormal mental state on September 10, 1976 when he is alleged to have committed air piracy, homicide, and other criminal acts. . . . It is also my opinion that this abnormal mental state was of such a quality and degree that it prevented the defendant from exercising the ordinary, reasonable and rational powers of free will, choice and decision that constitute the intent required by the definitions of the crimes of which he is charged. Hence, I conclude that Zvanko Busic lacked the capacity for such criminal intent.
>
> I am of the opinion that this abnormal mental state was not caused by mental disease, illness or defect. I do not find the defendant insane or mentally ill in any sense of those terms. . . .
>
> . . . He did what he did out of psychological necessity, not free choice.

The court upheld the exclusion of the testimony on the ground that the availability of such a defense as defendant tendered (id. at 21)

> turns upon whether the offense in question, like deliberated and premeditated murder, requires a specific intent that cannot be satisfied merely by showing that defendant failed to conform to an objective standard. The offense of aircraft piracy, however, requires a showing of general criminal intent, not a showing of specific criminal intent.

Query: Is the court's reason convincing? Suppose that Dr. Diamond was prepared to testify that defendant's abnormal mental state was such that it prevented him from intending to seize the aircraft because he was under a delusion that the aircraft was his own car? Is the difficulty with defendant's position the fact that the crime charged was a general-intent rather than a specific-intent crime, or did the difficulty lie in the nature of the proferred testimony?

In connection with this last question, reconsider the dictum in the *Brawner* decision empowering the trial judge to screen proferred psychiatric testimony for its reliability and its bearing on the legal issues at the trial, page 865 supra, and consider State v. Sikora, which follows.

STATE v. SIKORA

Supreme Court of New Jersey
44 N.J. 453, 210 A.2d 193 (1965)

FRANCIS, J. Defendant Walter J. Sikora shot and killed Douglas Hooey in the early morning of January 15, 1962. Thereafter, on May 15, 1962, a jury found him guilty of murder in the first degree for the killing, and recommended life imprisonment. . . .

On this appeal defendant contends the trial court committed reversible error . . . in refusing to admit certain psychiatric testimony relative to defendant's capacity to premeditate the killing he committed. . . .

[Defendant had an unfortunate childhood. He was an orphan and grew up in a variety of foster homes and orphanages. As an adult he drifted from job to job. He was 36 years old at the time of the killing. Before the killing, he had broken up with a woman with whom he had been living, and she had recently refused to take him back. He was drinking in a tavern where deceased, Hooey, a casual acquaintance, was also present. He testified that Hooey made nasty remarks about his separation from the woman and, with some of his friends, beat him up and threw him out of the tavern. He obtained his old merchant-marine gun, test-fired it, and returned to the tavern, meaning to kill Hooey and, later, the woman. He met and killed Hooey outside the tavern. He then went to the woman's house but found no one there. Police arrested him in his apartment later that morning.]

No defense of insanity was interposed. All the psychiatrists agreed Sikora was legally sane before and at the time of the shooting. Thus it was conceded that he knew the difference between right and wrong; he knew the nature and quality of his act, and he knew that it was wrong to kill.

The error asserted in this Court as requiring reversal of the conviction had its origin in one hypothetical question put by defense counsel to Dr. Noel C. Galen, a psychiatrist produced on behalf of the defendant. . . .

. . . [This question] covered the examination of defendant, his life history, and particularly the events of the several hours preceding the shooting. It concluded with an inquiry as to whether in the doctor's opinion, in view of all those facts and circumstances, Sikora was capable of "premeditating a murder" at the time he killed Hooey. The objection of the State was sustained. No ground was given for the objection. Defense counsel's twice-repeated request to be heard on the law was summarily rejected. On asking the reason for the objection, the court said: "The record is complete. The doctor has testified that the defendant was sane."

We suggest for future guidance in similar situations that the jury be excused and counsel be permitted at least to make a proffer of the proof he expects to adduce by means of the question, and to present his argument with respect to the law claimed to support admissibility. . . .

When the cause reached this Court, we felt the need for enlightenment as to the nature of the evidence sought to be elicited from Dr. Galen by the hypothetical question. Consequently a remand was ordered for the purpose of further testimonial examination of the doctor. . . .

Pursuant to the remand Dr. Galen was recalled and re-examined. . . .

In applying his expertise to this case he reiterated Sikora understood and could differentiate between right and wrong. Also, ordinarily Sikora was able to conceive a design to kill and to deliberate upon it. In fact he was able to do so until a few hours before the homicide occurred. But, because of his individual type of personality disorder, under the stress of certain circumstances which he feels inadequate to cope with, tensions build up within him and his psychological mechanism moves into action which on the surface may seem planned and deliberate but is really in response to unconscious influences and therefore automatic.

According to Dr. Galen, tensions had been building up in Sikora, particularly since his female friend rejected him. When he was humiliated in the tavern by the remarks about her availability for other men because she had broken with him, and then physically beaten by Hooey and his companions, the tensions mounted to the point where they represented a situation in life with which he felt unable to cope. So he began to act in an automatic way; the manner in which a person with his personality inadequacy would characteristically act. He responded to the stress in the way which inevitably would be his way of dealing with that kind of stress. He reacted automatically in the fashion of Dr. Galen's physician friend when he was cut off by another motorist. . . .[a] The beating administered by Hooey in the tavern precipitated the disorganization of his personality to the extent that from then on he probably "acted in at least a semi-automatic way, and probably an automatic way."

The doctor went on to say that from the defendant's course of conduct it could be seen that he was acting in an automatic way "rather than being totally aware of his environment, and the situation. . . ." Although the state was not completely an automatic one there were "strong elements of automatism" present. . . . His personality disorder, the kind of man life had made him, when subjected to that stress prevented him from "seeing reality, or premeditating or forming a rational opinion of what is going on in his life." He had been confronted with a situation and reacted with conduct which was his characteristic way of dealing with the particular kind of stress. As the doctor put it in answer to defense counsel's question:

> You may react to someone cutting you off on the highway in a different way than the Prosecutor may. It has to do with your personality. It has to do with your way of dealing with this kind of stress.

In short the doctor opined that the circumstances to which Sikora had been subjected imposed on his personality disorder a stress that impaired or removed his ability consciously to premeditate or weigh a design to kill. The tension was so great that he could handle it only by an automatic reaction motivated by the predetermined influence of his unconscious. Plainly the doctor meant that Sikora's response was not a voluntary exercise of his free will. The stress

---

a. The court was here referring to the statement of Dr. Galen concerning a physician friend of his who, while driving on a public highway, was cut off by another motorist: "This man who is a professional knows clearly, in a general way, right from wrong, good from evil, if we want to get into that old controversy, but this man chased the car who cut him off and finally cut the car off that cut him off. Now, at this particular time, when he was behaving in this way, which was really endangering his life, endangering the lives of other people, although he was sane at the time, he was acting in an irrational manner with a disturbance of his consciousness; and consciousness is a very difficult thing to define and understand unless one sees it as a dynamic."— EDS.

was such as to distort his mechanisms. During the various actions Sikora took leading up to the killing, which so clearly indicate conception, deliberation and execution of a plan to kill, he was thinking but the thinking was automatic; it was simply subconscious thinking or reaction; it was not conscious thinking. The doctor said Sikora's anxieties at the time were of such a nature that conceivably, his reaction in that automatic way and the commission of the homicide, actually prevented a further disorganization of his personality. The killing, said the doctor, was "a rational murder" but "everything this man did was irrational," and engaged in when he could not conceive the design to kill. . . .

The question now presented is whether psychiatric evidence of the nature described is admissible in first degree murder cases on the issue of premeditation. . . .

In [State v.] Di Paolo, [34 N.J. 279, 168 A.2d 401,] the Chief Justice said that evidence of "any defect, deficiency, trait, condition, or illness which rationally bears upon the question" whether the accused did in fact premeditate is admissible in a first degree murder trial. But he indicated also that if such evidence was unreliable or too speculative or incompetent when tested by concepts established in law for the determination of criminal responsibility, it should not be received on the issue of guilt or innocence or the degree thereof. That is the situation here. . . .

. . . [W]e cannot accept a thesis that responsibility in law for a criminal act perpetrated by a legally sane defendant, can be considered nonexistent or measured by the punishment established for a crime of lower degree, because his act was motivated by subconscious influences of which he was not aware, and which stemmed inevitably from his individual personality structure. . . . A criminal act of that nature is nothing more than the consequence of an impulse that was not resisted. . . .

[Affirmed.]

WEINTRAUB, C.J. (concurring). I join in the opinion of Mr. Justice Francis. . . .

To put the subject in perspective, we must start with the common law's conception of crime. The common law required (1) an evil deed and (2) mens rea — a guilty mind. This conception emerged from man's then understanding of himself. It was felt to be unjust to stigmatize a man a criminal unless his evil deed was accompanied by an evil-meaning mind. Insanity was relevant only insofar as it denied the existence of an evil intent and thus disputed that critical element of the State's charge. It was assumed that all men were able to adhere to the right if they saw the right, and hence insanity was conceived to be such disease of the mind as prevented the accused from understanding the nature of his act and that it was wrong. The law thus separated the sick from the bad upon the basis of a man's capacity to know what was right. Any other imperfection or defect was deemed to be merely a bad trait of character or personality.

The law's conception, resting as it does upon an undemonstrable view of man, is of course vulnerable. But those who attack it cannot offer a view which is demonstrably more authentic. They can tear down the edifice but have nothing better to replace it.

The psychiatric view advanced by Dr. Galen seems quite scientific. It rests upon the elementary concept of cause and effect. The individual is deemed the product of many causes. As a matter of historical fact, he was not the author of any of the formative forces, nor of his capacity or lack of capacity to deal with them. In short, so far as we know, no man is his own maker. I say so far as we know, for man has yet to catch a glimpse of the ultimate truth. The concept of cause-and-effect, satisfying though it may be for most matters, is a dead-end approach to the mystery of our being. . . .

Abstractly, the cause-and-effect thesis could suggest a stultifying determinism whereunder every stroke of a man's pen was ordained when time first stirred. But the psychiatrist, awed by it all, wisely leaves that subject to the philosopher. Besides it is not easy for an inquiring mind to believe it on a string stretching from infinity. Nonetheless the cause-and-effect thesis dominates the psychiatrist's view of his patient. He traces a man's every deed to some cause truly beyond the actor's own making, and says that although the man was aware of his action, he was unaware of assembled forces in his unconscious which decided his course. Thus the conscious is a puppet, and the unconscious the puppeteer.

And so, Dr. Galen, in expounding the psychodynamics of Sikora's murderous exploit, started with the premise that Sikora appreciated the nature of his act and knew it was wrong; that Sikora was aware of the events which indeed he recalled with great detail, but was unaware that his unconscious was so constituted that its reaction to his conscious experience had to be homicidal. The doctor added, as I understand him, that the unconscious probably decided on murder in order to avoid a complete disintegration of the personality.

Now this is interesting, and I will not quarrel with any of it. But the question is whether it has anything to do with the crime of murder. I think it does not.

The witness described Sikora's actions as wholly "automatic." While at times he spoke in other terms, such as that Sikora was really not "fully" conscious of what he was doing despite his "long . . . and rather clear history of what occurred," and although on cross-examination the doctor found himself differentiating between rational and irrational ways of committing murder (a most unscientific discourse, it seems to me), his professional theme remained that the conscious was the unwitting and unsuspecting puppet of the unconscious.

Further, "disease" has nothing to do with this automatic behavior. Although in obeisance to *M'Naghten* the witness said his "diagnosis" of a "personality disorder of a passive dependent type with aggressive features" describes "a mental disorder" listed in the Manual of the American Psychiatric Association, he denied the reality of such classifications. Rather he said mental disturbances or disorders are merely gradients in the range from "essentially normal" to "marked disturbance of the thinking mechanism." The point I stress is that the automatic thesis in nowise depends upon the existence of some "disorder" of the mind. Rather it accounts for all human behavior, whether it be a murder or the retaliatory action of the witness's doctor friend who cut off a motorist who had cut him off, or the raising of one's index finger rather than his pinky, to refer to still another example Dr. Galen gave of the dictatorial control of the unconscious.[1]

Under this psychiatric concept no man could be convicted of anything if the law were to accept the impulses of the unconscious as an excuse for conscious

_____

1. This automaton concept apparently differs from the "irresistible impulse" concept in that it proclaims the conscious is subservient to the unconscious in illness or in health, whereas the irresistible-impulse concept attempts to distinguish between impulses which were not resisted and impulses which could not be resisted because of mental illness.

misbehavior. Although the specific question put to Dr. Galen was whether the defendant was capable of premeditating the murder, his answer would have to be the same if he were asked whether defendant was able to form an intent to do grievous bodily harm or any harm at all. His answer would have to be that the unconscious directed the killing in response to the stimulus of the events preceding the killing. The same explanation would account for the misbehavior of Dr. Galen's motoring friend if he were charged with a violation of the motor vehicle act.

What then shall we do with our fellow automaton whose unconscious directs such antisocial deeds? For one thing, we could say it makes no difference. We could say that in punishing an evil deed accompanied by an evil-meaning mind, the law is concerned only with the existence of a will to do the evil act and it does not matter precisely where within the mind the evil drive resides.

Or we could modify the law's concept of mens rea to require an evil-meaning unconscious. The possibilities here are rich. It would be quite a thing to identify the unconscious drive and then decide whether it is evil for the purpose of criminal liability. For example, if we somehow were satisfied that a man murdered another as an alternative to an unconscious demand for suicide or because the unconscious believed it had to kill to avoid a full-blown psychosis, shall we say there was or was not a good defense? Shall we indict for murder a motorist who kills another because, although objectively he was negligent at the worst, the psychoanalyst assures us that the conscious man acted automatically to fulfill an unconscious desire for self-destruction? All of this is fascinating but much too frothy to support a structure of criminal law.

Finally, we could amend our concept of criminal responsibility by eliminating the requirement of an evil-meaning mind. That is the true thrust of this psychiatric view of human behavior, for while our criminal law seeks to punish only those who act with a sense of wrongdoing and hence excuses those who because of sickness were bereft of that awareness, the psychiatrist rejects a distinction between the sick and the bad. To him no one is personally blameworthy for his make-up or for his acts. To him the law's distinction between a defect of the mind and a defect of character is an absurd invention. . . .

The subject of criminal blameworthiness is so obscure that there is an understandable disposition to let anything in for whatever use the jury may wish to make of it. But it will not do merely to receive testimony upon the automaton thesis, for the jury must be told what its legal effect may be. Specifically, the jury must be told whether a man is chargeable with his unconscious drives.

It seems clear to me that the psychiatric view expounded by Dr. Galen is simply irreconcilable with the basic thesis of our criminal law, for while the law requires proof of an evil-meaning mind, this psychiatric thesis denies there is any such thing. To grant a role in our existing structure to the theme that the conscious is just the innocent puppet of a nonculpable unconscious is to make a mishmash of the criminal law, permitting — indeed requiring — each trier of the facts to choose between the automaton thesis and the law's existing concept of criminal accountability. It would be absurd to decide criminal blameworthiness upon a psychiatric thesis which can find no basis for personal blame. So long as we adhere to criminal blameworthiness, mens rea must be sought and decided at the level of conscious behavior.

5. Changing Patterns of Excuse

ROBINSON v. CALIFORNIA
Supreme Court of the United States
370 U.S. 660 (1962)

MR. JUSTICE STEWART delivered the opinion of the Court.

A California statute makes it a criminal offense for a person to "be addicted to the use of narcotics."[1] This appeal draws into question the constitutionality of that provision of the state law, as construed by the California courts in the present case. . . .

[The prosecution's evidence was principally the testimony of policemen that defendant had scar tissue, discoloration and needle marks which indicated his frequent use of narcotics.]

The judge . . . instructed the jury that the appellant could be convicted under a general verdict if the jury agreed *either* that he was of the "status" *or* had committed the "act" denounced by the statute. "All that the People must show is either that the defendant did use a narcotic in Los Angeles County, or that while in the City of Los Angeles he was addicted to the use of narcotics. . . ."

Under these instructions the jury returned a verdict finding the appellant "guilty of the offense charged." . . .

The broad power of a State to regulate the narcotic drugs traffic within its borders is not here in issue. . . .

Such regulation, it can be assumed, could take a variety of valid forms. A State might impose criminal sanctions, for example, against the unauthorized manufacture, prescription, sale, purchase, or possession of narcotics within its borders. In the interest of discouraging the violation of such laws, or in the interest of the general health or welfare of its inhabitants, a State might establish a program of compulsory treatment for those addicted to narcotics.[7] Such a program of treatment might require periods of involuntary confinement. And penal sanctions might be imposed for failure to comply with established compulsory treatment procedures. Cf. Jacobson v. Massachusetts, 197 U.S. 11. Or a State might choose to attack the evils of narcotics traffic on broader fronts also — through public health education, for example, or by efforts to ameliorate the economic and social conditions under which those evils might be thought

[margin note: alterna-tives]

---

1. The statute is §11721 of the California Health and Safety Code. It provides:

"No person shall use, or be under the influence of, or be addicted to the use of narcotics, excepting when administered by or under the direction of a person licensed by the State to prescribe and administer narcotics. It shall be the burden of the defense to show that it comes within the exception. Any person convicted violating any provision of this section is guilty of a misdemeanor and shall be sentenced to serve a term of not less than 90 days nor more than one year in the county jail. The court may place a person convicted hereunder on probation for a period not to exceed five years and shall in all cases in which probation is granted require as a condition thereof that such person be confined in the county jail for at least 90 days. In no event does the court have the power to absolve a person who violates this section from the obligation of spending at least 90 days in confinement in the county jail."

[The 1963 California Legislature deleted the clause "or be addicted to the use of." 1963 Cal. Stats. ch. 913, §1.]

7. California appears to have established just such a program. . . . The record contains no explanation of why the civil procedures authorized by this legislation were not utilized in the present case.

to flourish. In short, the range of valid choice which a State might make in this area is undoubtedly a wide one, and the wisdom of any particular choice within the allowable spectrum is not for us to decide. Upon that premise we turn to the California law in issue here. . . .

STATUS

This statute [as interpreted by the state court] is not one which punishes a person for the use of narcotics, for their purchase, sale or possession, or for antisocial or disorderly behavior resulting from their administration. It is not a law which even purports to provide or require medical treatment. Rather, we deal with a statute which makes the "status" of narcotic addiction a criminal offense, for which the offender may be prosecuted "at any time before he reforms." California has said that a person can be continuously guilty of this offense, whether or not he has ever used or possessed any narcotics within the State, and whether or not he has been guilty of any antisocial behavior there.

It is unlikely that any State at this moment in history would attempt to make it a criminal offense for a person to be mentally ill, or a leper, or to be afflicted with a venereal disease. A State might determine that the general health and welfare require that the victims of these and other human afflictions be dealt with by compulsory treatment, involving quarantine, confinement, or sequestration. But, in the light of contemporary human knowledge, a law which made a criminal offense of such a disease would doubtless be universally thought to be an infliction of cruel and unusual punishment in violation of the Eighth and Fourteenth Amendments.

We cannot but consider the statute before us as of the same category. In this Court counsel for the State recognized that narcotic addiction is an illness.[8] Indeed, it is apparently an illness which may be contracted innocently or involuntarily.[9] We hold that a state law which imprisons a person thus afflicted as a criminal, even though he has never touched any narcotic drug within the State or been guilty of any irregular behavior there, inflicts a cruel and unusual punishment in violation of the Fourteenth Amendment. To be sure, imprisonment for ninety days is not, in the abstract, a punishment which is either cruel or unusual. But the question cannot be considered in the abstract. Even one day in prison would be a cruel and unusual punishment for the "crime" of having a common cold.

We are not unmindful that the vicious evils of the narcotics traffic have occasioned the grave concern of government. There are, as we have said, countless fronts on which those evils may be legitimately attacked. We deal in this case only with an individual provision of a particularized local law as it has so far been interpreted by the California courts.

Reversed.

MR. JUSTICE DOUGLAS, concurring. . . .

8. In its brief the appellee stated: "Of course it is generally conceded that a narcotic addict, particularly one addicted to the use of heroin, is in a state of mental and physical illness. So is an alcoholic." Thirty-seven years ago this Court recognized that persons addicted to narcotics "are diseased and proper subjects for [medical] treatment." Linder v. United States, 268 U.S. 5, 18.

9. Not only may addiction innocently result from the use of medically prescribed narcotics, but a person may even be a narcotics addict from the moment of his birth. See Schneck, Narcotic Withdrawal Symptoms in the Newborn Infant Resulting from Maternal Addiction, 52 Journal of Pediatrics 584 (1958). . . .

Today we have our differences over the legal definition of insanity. But however insanity is defined, it is in end effect treated as a disease. While afflicted people may be confined either for treatment or for the protection of society, they are not branded as criminals. . . .

We should show the same discernment respecting drug addiction. The addict is a sick person. He may, of course, be confined for treatment or for the protection of society. Cruel and unusual punishment results not from confinement, but from convicting the addict of a crime. The purpose of §11721 is not to cure, but to penalize. Were the purpose to cure, there would be no need for a mandatory jail term of not less than 90 days. . . . A prosecution for addiction, with its resulting stigma and irreparable damage to the good name of the accused, cannot be justified as a means of protecting society, where a civil commitment would do as well. Indeed, in §5350 of the Welfare and Institutions Code, California has expressly provided for civil proceedings for the commitment of habitual addicts. Section 11721 is, in reality, a direct attempt to punish those the State cannot commit civilly.[5] This prosecution has no relationship to the curing of an illness. Indeed, it cannot, for the prosecution is aimed at penalizing an illness, rather than at providing medical care for it. We would forget the teachings of the Eighth Amendment if we allowed sickness to be made a crime and permitted sick people to be punished for being sick. The age of enlightenment cannot tolerate such barbarous action.

MR. JUSTICE HARLAN, concurring.

I am not prepared to hold that on the present state of medical knowledge it is completely irrational and hence unconstitutional for a State to conclude that narcotics addiction is something other than an illness, nor that it amounts to cruel and unusual punishment for the State to subject narcotics addicts to its criminal law. . . . But in this case the trial court's instructions permitted the jury to find the appellant guilty on no more proof than that he was present in California while he was addicted to narcotics. Since addiction alone cannot reasonably be thought to amount to more than a compelling propensity to use narcotics, the effect of this instruction was to authorize criminal punishment for a bare desire to commit a criminal act. . . .

MR. JUSTICE WHITE, dissenting. . . .

The Court clearly does not rest its decision upon the narrow ground that the jury was not expressly instructed not to convict if it believed appellant's use of narcotics was beyond his control. The Court recognizes no degrees of addiction. The Fourteenth Amendment is today held to bar any prosecution for addiction regardless of the degree of frequency of use, and the Court's opinion bristles with indications of further consequences. If it is "cruel and unusual punishment" to convict appellant for addiction, it is difficult to understand why it would be any less offensive to the Fourteenth Amendment to convict him for use on the same evidence of use which proved he was an addict. It is significant that in purporting to reaffirm the power of the States to deal with

---

5. The difference between §5350 and §11721 is that the former aims at treatment of the addiction, whereas §11721 does not. The latter cannot be construed to provide treatment, unless jail sentences, without more, are suddenly to become medicinal. A comparison of the lengths of confinement under the two sections is irrelevant, for it is the purpose of the confinement that must be measured against the constitutional prohibition of cruel and unusual punishments.

the narcotics traffic, the Court does not include among the obvious powers of the State the power to punish for the use of narcotics. I cannot think that the omission was inadvertent.

The Court has not merely tidied up California's law by removing some irritating vestige of an outmoded approach to the control of narcotics. At the very least, it has effectively removed California's power to deal effectively with the recurring case under the statute where there is ample evidence of use but no evidence of the precise location of use. Beyond this it has cast serious doubt upon the power of any State to forbid the use of narcotics under threat of criminal punishment. I cannot believe that the Court would forbid the application of the criminal laws to the use of narcotics under any circumstances. But the States, as well as the Federal Government, are now on notice. They will have to await a final answer in another case. . . .

NOTE

Following the *Robinson* case, the Supreme Court of California upheld an involuntary five-year commitment of a person on a finding that he was a narcotic addict. Examining both the "civil" and "criminal" features of his commitment, the court concluded that the "civil" overtones predominated and that it was therefore not made unconstitutional by *Robinson.* In re De La O, 59 Cal. 2d 128, 378 P.2d 793 (1963). See Note, Civil Commitment of Narcotic Drug Addict Held Constitutional, 8 Utah L. Rev. 367 (1963-1964). In People v. Victor, 62 Cal. 2d 280, 398 P.2d 391 (1965), the supreme court upheld a provision for involuntary commitment of persons "in imminent danger of becoming addicted." See Comment, 64 Mich. L. Rev. 546 (1966).

POWELL v. TEXAS
United States Supreme Court
392 U.S. 514 (1968)

MR. JUSTICE MARSHALL announced the judgment of the Court and delivered an opinion in which the CHIEF JUSTICE, MR. JUSTICE BLACK, and MR. JUSTICE HARLAN join.

In late December 1966, appellant was arrested and charged with being found in a state of intoxication in a public place, in violation of Texas Penal Code, Art. 477 (1952), which reads as follows: "Whoever shall get drunk or be found in a state of intoxication in any public place, or at any private house except his own, shall be fined not exceeding one hundred dollars."

Appellant was tried in the Corporation Court of Austin, Texas, found guilty, and fined $20. He appealed to the County Court at Law No. 1 of Travis County, Texas, where a trial de novo was held. His counsel urged that appellant was "afflicted with the disease of chronic alcoholism," "that his appearance in public [while drunk was]   not of his own volition," and therefore that to punish him criminally for that conduct would be cruel and unusual, in violation of the Eighth and Fourteenth Amendments to the United States Constitution.

The trial judge in the county court, sitting without a jury, made certain findings of fact, . . . but ruled as a matter of law that chronic alcoholism was not a defense to the charge. He found appellant guilty, and fined him $50. There being no further right to appeal within the Texas judicial system, appellant appealed to this Court. . . .

The principal testimony was that of Dr. Davis Wade, a Fellow of the American Medical Association, duly certified in psychiatry. . . . Dr. Wade sketched the outlines of the "disease" concept of alcoholism; noted that there is no generally accepted definition of "alcoholism"; alluded to the ongoing debate within the medical profession over whether alcohol is actually physically "addicting" or merely psychologically "habituating"; and concluded that in either case a "chronic alcoholic" is an "involuntary drinker," who is "powerless not to drink," and who "loses his self-control over his drinking." He testified that he had examined appellant, and that appellant is a "chronic alcoholic," who "by the time he has reached [the state of intoxication] . . . is not able to control his behavior, and [who] . . . has reached this point because he has an uncontrollable compulsion to drink." Dr. Wade also responded in the negative to the question whether appellant has "the willpower to resist the constant excessive consumption of alcohol." He added that in his opinion jailing appellant without medical attention would operate neither to rehabilitate him or lessen his desire for alcohol.

On cross-examination, Dr. Wade admitted that when appellant was sober he knew the difference between right and wrong, and he responded affirmatively to the question whether appellant's act of taking the first drink in any given instance when he was sober was a "voluntary exercise of his will." Qualifying his answer, Dr. Wade stated that

> these individuals have a compulsion, and this compulsion, while not completely overpowering, is a very strong influence, an exceedingly strong influence, and this compulsion, coupled with the firm belief in their mind that they are going to be able to handle it from now on causes their judgment to be somewhat clouded.

Appellant testified concerning the history of his drinking problem. He reviewed his many arrests for drunkenness; testified that he was unable to stop drinking; stated that when he was intoxicated he had no control over his actions and could not remember them later, but that he did not become violent; and admitted that he did not remember his arrest on the occasion for which he was being tried. On cross-examination, appellant admitted that he had had one drink on the morning of the trial and had been able to discontinue drinking. . . .

Evidence in the case then closed. The State made no effort to obtain expert psychiatric testimony of its own, or even to explore with appellant's witness the question of appellant's power to control the frequency, timing, and location of his drinking bouts, or the substantial disagreement within the medical profession concerning the nature of the disease, the efficacy of treatment and the prerequisites for effective treatment. It did nothing to examine or illuminate what Dr. Wade might have meant by his reference to a "compulsion" which was "not completely overpowering," but which was "an exceedingly strong influence," or to inquire into the question of the proper role of such a "compulsion" in constitutional adjudication. Instead, the State concerned itself with a brief argument that appellant had no defense to the charge because he "is legally sane and knows the difference between right and wrong."

Following this abbreviated exposition of the problem before it, the trial court indicated its intention to disallow appellant's claimed defense of "chronic alcoholism." Thereupon defense counsel submitted, and the trial court entered, the following "findings of fact":

> (1) That chronic alcoholism is a disease which destroys the afflicted person's will power to resist the constant, excessive consumption of alcohol.
> (2) That a chronic alcoholic does not appear in public by his own volition but under a compulsion symptomatic of the disease of chronic alcoholism.
> (3) That Leroy Powell, a defendant herein, is a chronic alcoholic who is afflicted with the disease of chronic alcoholism.

Whatever else may be said of them, those are not "findings of fact" in any recognizable, traditional sense in which that term has been used in a court of law; they are the premises of a syllogism transparently designed to bring this case within the scope of this Court's opinion in Robinson v. California, 370 U.S. 660 (1962). Nonetheless, the dissent would have us adopt these "findings" without critical examination; it would use them as the basis for a constitutional holding that "a person may not be punished if the condition essential to constitute the defined crime is part of the pattern of his disease and is occcasioned by a compulsion symptomatic of the disease."

The difficulty with that position, as we shall show, is that it goes much too far on the basis of too little knowledge. In the first place, the record in this case is utterly inadequate to permit the sort of informed and responsible adjudication which alone can support the announcement of an important and wideranging new constitutional principle. We know very little about the circumstances surrounding the drinking bout which resulted in this conviction, or about Leroy Powell's drinking problem, or indeed about alcoholism itself. . . .

Furthermore, the inescapable fact is that there is no agreement among members of the medical profession about what it means to say that "alcoholism" is a "disease." One of the principal works in this field states that the major difficulty in articulating a "disease concept of alcoholism" is that "alcoholism has too many definitions and disease has practically none." This same author concludes that *"a disease is what the medical profession recognizes as such."* In other words, there is widespread agreement today that "alcoholism" is a "disease," for the simple reason that the medical profession has concluded that it should attempt to treat those who have drinking problems. There the agreement stops. Debate rages within the medical profession as to whether "alcoholism" is a separate "disease" in any meaningful biochemical, physiological or psychological sense, or whether it represents one peculiar manifestation in some individuals of underlying psychiatric disorders. . . .

The trial court's "finding" that Powell "is afflicted with the disease of chronic alcoholism," which destroys the afflicted person's will power to resist the constant, excessive consumption of alcohol" covers a multitude of sins. Dr. Wade's testimony that appellant suffered from a compulsion which was an "exceedingly strong influence," but which was "not completely overpowering" is at least

disease ?

more carefully stated, if no less mystifying. Jellinek insists that conceptual clarity can only be achieved by distinguishing carefully between "loss of control" once an individual has commenced to drink and "inability to abstain" from drinking in the first place. Presumably a person would have to display both characteristics in order to make out a constitutional defense, should one be recognized. Yet the "findings" of the trial court utterly fail to make this crucial distinction, and there is serious question whether the record can be read to support a finding of either loss of control or inability to abstain.

Dr. Wade did testify that once appellant began drinking he appeared to have no control over the amount of alcohol he finally ingested. Appellant's own testimony concerning his drinking on the day of the trial would certainly appear, however, to cast doubt upon the conclusion that he was without control over his consumption of alcohol when he had sufficiently important reasons to exercise such control. However that may be, there are more serious factual and conceptual difficulties with reading this record to show that appellant was unable to abstain from drinking. Dr. Wade testified that when appellant was sober, the act of taking the first drink was a "voluntary exercise of his will," but that this exercise of will was undertaken under the "exceedingly strong influence" of a "compulsion" which was "not completely overpowering." Such concepts, when juxtaposed in this fashion, have little meaning. . . .

Compulsion?

It is one thing to say that if a man is deprived of alcohol his hands will begin to shake, he will suffer agonizing pains and ultimately he will have hallucinations; it is quite another to say that a man has a "compulsion" to take a drink, but that he also retains a certain amount of "free will" with which to resist. It is simply impossible, in the present state of our knowledge, to ascribe a useful meaning to the latter statement. This definitional confusion reflects, of course, not merely the undeveloped state of the psychiatric art but also the conceptual difficulties inevitably attendant upon the importation of scientific and medical models into a legal system generally predicated upon a different set of assumptions. . . .

Despite the comparatively primitive state of our knowledge on the subject, it cannot be denied that the destructive use of alcoholic beverages is one of our principal social and public health problems. . . .

There is as yet no known generally effective method for treating the vast number of alcoholics in our society. Some individual alcoholics have responded to particular forms of therapy with remissions of their symptomatic dependence upon the drug. But just as there is no agreement among doctors and social workers with respect to the causes of alcoholism, there is no consensus as to why particular treatments have been effective in particular cases and there is no generally agreed-upon approach to the problem of treatment on a large scale. . . . Thus it is entirely possible that, even were the manpower and facilities available for a full-scale attack upon chronic alcoholism, we would find ourselves unable to help the vast bulk of our "visible"— let alone our "invisible"— alcoholic population.

However, facilities for the attempted treatment of indigent alcoholics are woefully lacking throughout the country. It would be tragic to return large numbers of helpless, sometimes dangerous and frequently unsanitary inebriates to the streets of our cities without even the opportunity to sober up adequately which a brief jail term provides. Presumably no State or city will tolerate such a state of affairs. Yet the medical profession cannot, and does not, tell us with any assurance that, even if the buildings, equipment and trained personnel were made available, it could provide anything more than slightly higher-class jails for our indigent habitual inebriates. Thus we run the grave risk that nothing will be accomplished beyond the hanging of a new sign — reading "hospital"— over one wing of the jailhouse.

One virtue of the criminal process is, at least, that the duration of penal incarceration typically has some outside statutory limit; this is universally true in the case of petty offenses, such as public drunkenness, where jail terms are quite short on the whole. "Therapeutic civil commitment" lacks this feature; one is typically committed until one is "cured." Thus, to do otherwise than affirm might subject indigent alcoholics to the risk that they may be locked up for an indefinite period of time under the same conditions as before, with no more hope than before of receiving effective treatment and no prospect of periodic "freedom."

Faced with this unpleasant reality, we are unable to assert that the use of the criminal process as a means of dealing with the public aspects of problem drinking can never be defended as rational. The picture of the penniless drunk propelled aimlessly and endlessly through the law's "revolving door" of arrest, incarceration, release and re-arrest is not a pretty one. But before we condemn the present practice across-the-board, perhaps we ought to be able to point to some clear promise of a better world for these unfortunate people. Unfortunately, no such promise has yet been forthcoming. . . .

Appellant claims that his conviction on the facts of this case would violate the Cruel and Unusual Punishment Clause of the Eighth Amendment as applied to the States through the Fourteenth Amendment. . . .

. . . [He] seeks to come within the application of the Cruel and Unusual Punishment Clause announced in Robinson v. California, 370 U.S. 660 (1962), which involved a state statute making it a crime to "be addicted to the use of narcotics." This Court held there that "a state statute which imprisons a person thus afflicted [with narcotic addiction] as a criminal, even though he has never touched any narcotic drug within the State or been guilty of any irregular behavior there, inflicts a cruel and unusual punishment. . . ."

On its face the present case does not fall within that holding, since appellant was convicted, not for being a chronic alcoholic, but for being in public while drunk on a particular occasion. The State of Texas thus has not sought to punish a mere status, as California did in Robinson; nor has it attempted to regulate appellant's behavior in the privacy of his own home. Rather, it has imposed upon appellant a criminal sanction for public behavior which may create substantial health and safety hazards, both for appellant and for members of the general public, and which offends the moral and esthetic sensibilities of a large segment of the community. This seems a far cry from convicting one for being an addict, being a chronic alcoholic, being "mentally ill or a leper. . . ."

Robinson so viewed brings this Court but a very small way into the substantive criminal law. And unless Robinson is so viewed it is difficult to see any limiting principle that would serve to prevent this Court from becoming, under the aegis of the Cruel and Unusual Punishment Clause, the ultimate arbiter of the standards of criminal responsibility, in diverse areas of the criminal law, throughout the country.

It is suggested in dissent that *Robinson* stands for the "simple" but "subtle" principle that "[c]riminal penalties may not be inflicted on a person for being in a condition he is powerless to change." . . . In that view, appellant's "condition" of public intoxication was "occasioned by a compulsion symptomatic of the disease" of chronic alcoholism, and thus, apparently, his behavior lacked the critical element of mens rea. Whatever may be the merits of such a doctrine of criminal responsibility, it surely cannot be said to follow from *Robinson*. The entire thrust of *Robinson's* interpretation of the Cruel and Unusual Punishment Clause is that criminal penalties may be inflicted only if the accused has committed some act, has engaged in some behavior, which society has an interest in preventing, or perhaps in historical common law terms, has committed some actus reus. It thus does not deal with the question of whether certain conduct cannot constitutionally be punished because it is, in some sense, "involuntary" or "occasioned by a compulsion."

Likewise, as the dissent acknowledges, there is a substantial definitional distinctional between a "status," as in *Robinson*, and a "condition," which is said to be involved in this case. Whatever may be the merits of an attempt to distinguish between behavior and a condition, it is perfectly clear that the crucial element in this case, so far as the dissent is concerned, is whether or not appellant can legally be held responsible for his appearance in public in a state of intoxication. The only relevance of *Robinson* to this issue is that because the Court interpreted the statute there involved as making a "status" criminal, it was able to suggest that the statute would cover even a situation in which addiction had been acquired involuntarily. 370 U.S., at 667, n. 9. That this factor was not determinative in the case is shown by the fact that there was no indication of how *Robinson* himself had become an addict.

Ultimately, then, the most troubling aspects of this case, were *Robinson* to be extended to meet it, would be the scope and content of what could only be a constitutional doctrine of criminal responsibility. In dissent it is urged that the decision could be limited to conduct which is "a characteristic and involuntary part of the pattern of the disease as it afflicts" the particular individual, and that "it is not foreseeable" that it would be applied "in the case of offenses such as driving a car while intoxicated, assault, theft, or robbery." That is limitation by fiat. In the first place, nothing in the logic of the dissent would limit its application to chronic alcoholics. If Leroy Powell cannot be convicted of public intoxication, it is difficult to see how a State can convict an individual for murder, if that individual, while exhibiting normal behavior in all other respects, suffers from a "compulsion" to kill, which is an "exceedingly strong influence," but "not completely overpowering." Even if we limit our consideration to chronic alcoholics, it would seem impossible to confine the principle within the arbitrary bounds which the dissent seems to envision.

It is not difficult to imagine a case involving psychiatric testimony to the effect that an individual suffers from some aggressive neurosis which he is able to control when sober; that very little alcohol suffices to remove the inhibitions which normally contain these aggressions, with the result that the individual engages in assaultive behavior without becoming actually intoxicated; and that the individual suffers from a very strong desire to drink, which is an "exceedingly strong influence" but "not completely overpowering." Without being untrue to the rationale of this case, should the principles advanced in dissent be accepted here, the Court could not avoid holding such an individual constitutionally unaccountable for his assaultive behavior.

Traditional common-law concepts of personal accountability and essential considerations of federalism lead us to disagree with appellant. We are unable to conclude, on the state of this record or on the current state of medical knowledge, that chronic alcoholics in general, and Leroy Powell in particular, suffer from such an irresistible compulsion to drink and to get drunk in public that they are utterly unable to control their performance of either or both of these acts and thus cannot be deterred at all from public intoxication. And in any event this Court has never articulated a general constitutional doctrine of mens rea.[27]

We cannot cast aside the centuries-long evolution of the collection of interlocking and overlapping concepts which the common law has utilized to assess the moral accountability of an individual for his antisocial deeds. The doctrines of actus reus, mens rea, insanity, mistake, justification, and duress have historically provided the tools for a constantly shifting adjustment of the tension between the evolving aims of the criminal law and changing religious, moral, philosophical, and medical views of the nature of man. This process of adjustment has always been thought to be the province of the States.

Nothing could be less fruitful than for this Court to be impelled into defining some sort of insanity test in constitutional terms. Yet that task would seem to follow inexorably from an extension of *Robinson* in this case. If a person in the "condition" of being a chronic alcoholic cannot be criminally punished as a constitutional matter for being drunk in public, it would seem to follow that a person who contends that, in terms of one test, "his unlawful act was the product of mental disease or mental defect," Durham v. United States, 214 F.2d 862, 875 (C.A.D.C. Cir. 1954), would state an issue of constitutional dimension with regard to his criminal responsibility had he been tried under some different and perhaps lesser standard, e.g., the right-wrong test of *M'Naghten's Case*. . . . But formulating a constitutional rule would reduce, if not eliminate, that fruitful experimentation, and freeze the developing productive dialogue between law and psychiatry into a rigid constitutional mold. It is simply not yet the time to write into the Constitution formulas cast in terms whose meaning, let alone relevance, are not yet clear either to doctors or to lawyers.

Affirmed.

MR. JUSTICE BLACK, whom MR. JUSTICE HARLAN joins, concurring. . . .

I agree with Mr. Justice Marshall that the findings of fact in this case are inadequate to justify the sweeping constitutional rule urged upon us. I could not, however, consider any findings that could be made with respect to "voluntariness" or "compulsion" controlling on the question whether a specific instance of human behavior should be immune from punishment as a constitutional matter. When we say that appellant's appearance in public is caused not by "his own" volition but rather by some other force, we are clearly thinking

27. The Court did hold in Lambert v. California, 355 U.S. 255 (1957), that a person could not be punished for a "crime" of omission, if that person did not know, and the State had taken no reasonable steps to inform him, of his duty to act and of the criminal penalty for failure to do so. It is not suggested either that *Lambert* established a constitutional doctrine of mens rea, see generally Packer, Mens Rea and the Supreme Court, 1962 Sup. Ct. Rev. 107, or that appellant in this case was not fully aware of the prohibited nature of his conduct and of the consequences of taking his first drink.

of a force that is nevertheless "his" except in some special sense.[1] The accused undoubtedly commits the proscribed act and the only question is whether the act can be attributed to a part of "his" personality that should not be regarded as criminally responsible. Almost all of the traditional purposes of the criminal law can be significantly served by punishing the person who in fact committed the proscribed act, without regard to whether his action was "compelled" by some elusive "irresponsible" aspect of his personality. . . . [P]unishment of such a defendant can clearly be justified in terms of deterrence, isolation, and treatment. On the other hand, medical decisions concerning the use of a term such as "disease" or "volition," based as they are on the clinical problems of diagnosis and treatment, bear no necessary correspondence to the legal decision whether the overall objectives of the criminal law can be furthered by imposing punishment. For these reasons, much as I think that criminal sanctions should in many situations be applied only to those whose conduct is morally blameworthy, see Morissette v. United States, 342 U.S. 246 (1951), I cannot think the States should be held constitutionally required to make the inquiry as to what part of a defendant's personality is responsible for his actions and to excuse anyone whose action was, in some complex, psychological sense, the result of a "compulsion." . . .

The rule of constitutional law urged by appellant is not required by Robinson v. California, 370 U.S. 660 (1962). In that case we held that a person could not be punished for the mere status of being a narcotics addict. We explicitly limited our holding to the situation where no conduct of any kind is involved. . . . The argument is made that appellant comes within the terms of our holding in Robinson because being drunk in public is a mere status or "condition." Despite this many-faceted use of the concept of "condition," this argument would require converting Robinson into a case protecting actual behavior, a step we explicitly refused to take in that decision.

A different question, I admit, is whether our attempt in Robinson to limit our holding to pure status crimes, involving no conduct whatever, was a sound one. I believe it was. Although some of our objections to the statute in Robinson are equally applicable to statutes that punish conduct "symptomatic" of a disease, any attempt to explain Robinson as based solely on the lack of voluntariness encounters a number of logical difficulties.[3] Other problems raised by status crimes are in no way involved when the State attempts to punish for conduct, and these other problems were, in my view, the controlling aspects of our decision.

Punishment for a status is particularly obnoxious, and in many instances can reasonably be called cruel and unusual, because it involves punishment for a mere propensity, a desire to commit an offense; the mental element is not simply one part of the crime but may constitute all of it. This is a situation universally

1. If an intoxicated person is actually carried into the street by someone else, "he" does not do the act at all, and of course he is entitled to acquittal. E.g., Martin v. State, 31 Ala. App. 334, 17 So. 2d 427 (1944). [See page 250 supra.]

3. Although we noted in Robinson, 370 U.S., at 667, that narcotics addiction apparently is an illness that can be contracted innocently or involuntarily, we barred punishment for the addiction even when it could be proved that the defendant had voluntarily become addicted. And we compared addiction to the status of having a common cold, a condition that most people can either avoid or quickly cure when it is important enough for them to do so.

sought to be avoided in our criminal law; the fundamental requirement that some action be proved is solidly established even for offenses most heavily based on propensity, such as attempt, conspiracy, and recidivist crimes. . . .

The reasons for this refusal to permit conviction without proof of an act are difficult to spell out, but they are nonetheless perceived and universally expressed in our criminal law. Evidence of propensity can be considered relatively unreliable and more difficult for a defendant to rebut; the requirement of a specific act thus provides some protection against false charges. See 4 Blackstone, Commentaries 21. Perhaps more fundamental is the difficulty of distinguishing, in the absence of any conduct, between desires of the day-dream variety and fixed intentions that may pose a real threat to society; extending the criminal law to cover both types of desire would be unthinkable, since "[t]here can hardly be anyone who has never thought evil. When a desire is inhibited it may find expression in fantasy; but it would be absurd to condemn this natural psychological mechanism as illegal."

In contrast, crimes that require the State to prove that the defendant actually committed some proscribed act involve none of these special problems. In addition, the question whether an act is "involuntary" is, as I have already indicated, an inherently elusive question, and one which the State may, for good reasons, wish to regard as irrelevant. In light of all these considerations, our limitation of our *Robinson* holding to pure status crimes seems to me entirely proper. . . .

The rule of constitutional law urged upon us by appellant would have a revolutionary impact on the criminal law, and any possible limits proposed for the rule would be wholly illusory. If the original boundaries of *Robinson* are to be discarded, any new limits too would soon fall by the wayside and the Court would be forced to hold the States powerless to punish any conduct that could be shown to result from a "compulsion," in the complex, psychological meaning of that term. The result, to choose just one illustration, would be to require recognition of "irresistible impulse" as a complete defense to any crime; this is probably contrary to present law in most American jurisdictions.

The real reach of any such decision, however, would be broader still, for the basic premise underlying the argument is that it is cruel and unusual to punish a person who is not morally blameworthy. I state the proposition in this sympathetic way because I feel there is much to be said for avoiding the use of criminal sanctions in many such situations. See Morissette v. United States [, 342 U.S. 246 (1952), reprinted at pages 324-328 supra.] But the question here is one of constitutional law. The legislatures have always been allowed wide freedom to determine the extent to which moral culpability should be a prerequisite to conviction of a crime. E.g., United States v. Dotterweich, 320 U.S. 277 (1943). The criminal law is a social tool that is employed in seeking a wide variety of goals, and I cannot say the Eighth Amendment's limits on the use of criminal sanctions extend as far as this viewpoint would inevitably carry them.

But even if we were to limit any holding in this field to "compulsions" that are "symptomatic" of a "disease," in the words of the findings of the trial court, the sweep of that holding would still be startling. Such a ruling would make it clear beyond any doubt that a narcotics addict could not be punished for "being" in possession of drugs or, for that matter, for "being" guilty of using them. A wide variety of sex offenders would be immune from punishment if they could show that their conduct was not voluntary but part of the pattern of a disease. More generally speaking, a form of the insanity defense would be made a constitutional requirement throughout the Nation, should the Court now hold it cruel and unusual to punish a person afflicted with any mental disease whenever his conduct was part of the pattern of his disease and occasioned by a compulsion symptomatic of the disease. . . .

MR. JUSTICE WHITE, concurring in the result.

If it cannot be a crime to have an irresistible compulsion to use narcotics, Robinson v. California, 370 U.S. 660, I do not see how it can constitutionally be a crime to yield to such a compulsion. Punishing an addict for using drugs convicts for addiction under a different name. Distinguishing between the two crimes is like forbidding criminal conviction for being sick with flu or epilepsy but permitting punishment for running a fever or having a convulsion. Unless *Robinson* is to be abandoned, the use of narcotics by an addict must be beyond the reach of the criminal law. Similarly, the chronic alcoholic with an irresistible urge to consume alcohol should not be punishable for drinking or for being drunk.

Powell's conviction was for the different crime of being drunk in a public place. Thus even if Powell was compelled to drink, and so could not constitutionally be convicted for drinking, his conviction in this case can be invalidated only if there is a constitutional basis for saying that he may not be punished for being in public while drunk. . . .

The trial court said that Powell was a chronic alcoholic with a compulsion not only to drink to excess but also to frequent public places when intoxicated. Nothing in the record before the trial court supports the latter conclusion, which is contrary to common sense and to common knowledge. The sober chronic alcoholic has no compulsion to be on the public streets; many chronic alcoholics drink at home and are never seen drunk in public. Before and after taking the first drink, and until he becomes so drunk that he loses the power to know where he is or to direct his movements, the chronic alcoholic with a home or financial resources is as capable as the nonchronic drinker of doing his drinking in private, of removing himself from public places and, since he knows or ought to know that he will become intoxicated, of making plans to avoid his being found drunk in public. For these reasons, I cannot say that the chronic who proves his disease and a compulsion to drink is shielded from conviction when he has knowingly failed to take feasible precautions against committing a criminal act, here the act of going to or remaining in a public place. On such facts the alcoholic is like a person with smallpox, who could be convicted for being on the street but not for being ill, or like the epileptic, punishable for driving a car but not for his disease.

MR. JUSTICE FORTAS, with whom MR. JUSTICE DOUGLAS, MR. JUSTICE BRENNAN, and MR. JUSTICE STEWART join, dissenting. . . .

The sole question presented is whether a criminal penalty may be imposed upon a person suffering the disease of "chronic alcoholism" for a condition — being "in a state of intoxication" in public — which is a characteristic part of the pattern of his disease and which, the trial court found, was not the consequence of appellant's volition but of "a compulsion symptomatic of the disease of chronic alcoholism." We must consider whether the Eighth Amendment, made applicable to the States through the Fourteenth Amendment, prohibits the imposition of this penalty in these rather special circumstances as "cruel and unusual punishment." This case does not raise any question as to the right of the police to stop and detain those who are intoxicated in public, whether as a result of the disease or otherwise; or as to the State's power to commit chronic alcoholics for treatment. Nor does it concern the responsibility of an alcoholic for criminal *acts*. We deal here with the mere *condition* of being intoxicated in public.[2]

As I shall discuss, consideration of the Eighth Amendment issue in this case requires an understanding of "the disease of chronic alcoholism" with which, as the trial court found, appellant is afflicted, which has destroyed his "will power to resist the constant excessive consumption of alcohol," and which leads him to "appear in public [not] by his own volition but under a compulsion symptomatic of the disease of chronic alcoholism." . . .

. . . Although there is some problem in defining the concept, its core meaning, as agreed by authorities, is that alcoholism is caused and maintained by something other than the moral fault of the alcoholic, something that, to a greater or lesser extent depending upon the physiological or psychological makeup and history of the individual, cannot be controlled by him. . . .

Authorities have recognized that a number of factors may contribute to alcoholism. Some studies have pointed to physiological influences, such as vitamin deficiency, hormone imbalance, abnormal metabolism, and hereditary proclivity. Other researchers have found more convincing a psychological approach, emphasizing early environment and underlying conflicts and tensions. Numerous studies have indicated the influence of sociocultural factors. It has been shown, for example, that the incidence of alcoholism among certain ethnic groups is far higher than among others.

The manifestations of alcoholism are reasonably well identified. . . . It is well established that alcohol may be habituating and "can be physically addicting." It has been said that "the main point for the nonprofessional is that alcoholism is not within the control of the person involved. He is not willfully drinking." . . .

Robinson stands upon a principle which, despite its subtlety, must be simply stated and respectfully applied because it is the foundation of individual liberty and the cornerstone of the relations between a civilized state and its citizens: Criminal penalties may not be inflicted upon a person for being in a condition he is powerless to change. In all probability, Robinson at some time before his conviction elected to take narcotics. But the crime as defined did not punish this conduct. The statute imposed a penalty for the offense of "addiction" — a condition which Robinson could not control. Once Robinson had become an addict, he was utterly powerless to avoid criminal guilt. He was powerless to choose not to violate the law.

In the present case, appellant is charged with a crime comprised of two ele-

2. It is not foreseeable that findings such as those which are decisive here — namely that the defendant's being intoxicated in public was a part of the pattern of his disease and due to a compulsion symptomatic of that disease — could or would be made in the case of offenses such as driving a car while intoxicated, assault, theft, or robbery. Such offenses require independent acts or conduct and do not typically flow from and are not part of the syndrome of the disease of chronic alcoholism. If an alcoholic should be convicted for criminal conduct which is not a characteristic and involuntary part of the pattern of the disease as it afflicts him, nothing herein would prevent his punishment.

ments — being intoxicated and being found in a public place while in that condition. The crime, so defined, differs from that in *Robinson*. The statute covers more than a mere status. But the essential constitutional defect here is the same as in *Robinson*, for in both cases the particular defendant was accused of being in a condition which he had no capacity to change or avoid. The trial judge sitting as trier of fact found, upon the medical and other relevant testimony, that Powell is a "chronic alcoholic." He defined appellant's "chronic alcoholism" as "a disease which destroys the afflicted person's will power to resist the constant, excessive consumption of alcohol." He also found that "a chronic alcoholic does not appear in public by his own volition but under a compulsion symptomatic of the disease of chronic alcoholism." I read these findings to mean that appellant was powerless to avoid drinking; that having taken his first drink, he had "an uncontrollable compulsion to drink" to the point of intoxication; and that, once intoxicated, he could not prevent himself from appearing in public places. . . .

The findings in this case, read against the background of the medical and sociological data to which I have referred, compel the conclusion that the infliction upon appellant of a criminal penalty for being intoxicated in a public place would be "cruel and inhuman punishment" within the prohibition of the Eighth Amendment. This conclusion follows because appellant is a "chronic alcoholic" who, according to the trier of fact, cannot resist the "constant excessive consumption of alcohol" and does not appear in public by his own volition but under a "compulsion" which is part of his condition.

I would reverse the judgment below.

NOTE

For further consideration of the issues presented in this case see Fingarette, The Perils of *Powell*: In Search of a Factual Foundation for the "Disease Concept of Alcoholism," 83 Harv. L. Rev. 793 (1970); Greenawalt, "Uncontrollable" Actions and the Eighth Amendment: Implications of Powell v. Texas, 69 Colum. L. Rev. 927 (1969).

UNITED STATES v. MOORE

United States Court of Appeals, District of Columbia Circuit
486 F.2d 1139 (1973)

WILKEY, J. This is an appeal from a conviction under two federal statutes for possession of heroin. Appellant contends that his conviction was improper because he is a heroin addict with an overpowering need to use heroin and should not, therefore, be held responsible for being in possession of the drug. After careful consideration, we must reject appellant's contention and affirm the conviction by the trial court. . . .

[The prosecution conceded that Moore was an addict. The evidence was in conflict as to whether he was a trafficking addict. The trial court rejected the defendant's addiction defense by sustaining the indictment, by not permitting defendant's expert witnesses to testify on the nature of defendant's heroin addiction, and by declining to instruct the jury that a nontrafficking addict could not be convicted under the statutes charged.]

We believe it is clear from the evidence that Moore was not a mere nontrafficking addict but was in fact engaged in the drug trade. Yet even if we were to assume that appellant was a simple addict and nothing more, we believe that his conviction must be sustained. . . .

According to appellant this case has one central issue:

> Is the proffered evidence of Appellant's long and intensive dependence on (addiction to) injected heroin, resulting in substantial impairment of his behavior controls and a loss of self-control over the use of heroin, relevant to his criminal responsibility for unlawful possession . . . ?

In other words, is appellant's addiction a defense to the crimes, involving only possession, with which he is charged? Arguing that he has lost the power of self-control with regard to his addiction, appellant maintains that by applying "the broad principles of common law criminal responsibility" we must decide that he is entitled to dismissal of the indictment or a jury trial on this issue. The gist of appellant's argument here is that "the common law has long held that the capacity to control behavior is a prerequisite for criminal responsibility."

It is inescapable that the logic of appellant's argument, if valid, would carry over to all other illegal acts of any type whose purpose was to obtain narcotics for his own use, a fact which is admitted by Judge Wright in his opinion. . . .

LEVENTHAL, J., with whom McGOWAN, J., concurs. . . .

. . . Drug addiction of varying degrees may or may not result in loss of self-control, depending on the strength of character opposed to the drug craving. Under appellant's theory, adopted by the dissenters, only if there is a resulting loss of self-control can there be an absence of *free will* which, under the extension of the common law theory, would provide a valid defense to the addict. If there is a demonstrable absence of free will (loss of self-control), the illegal acts of possession and acquisition cannot be charged to the user of the drugs.

But if it is absence of free will which excuses the mere possessor-acquirer, the more desperate bank robber for drug money has an even more demonstrable lack of free will and derived from precisely the same factors as appellant argues should excuse the mere possessor.

In oral argument appellant maintained that there are different kinds of addicts, that is, some who are able to confine their law violation to possession and acquisition for their own use and some who will commit crimes other than possession or acquisition to feed their habits; and that it is only the latter whom we should punish for their addiction. This position of appellant is, unfortunately, logically untenable, if one accepts appellant's own rationale that we must not punish addicts for possession because of the compulsion under which they act to acquire the drugs.

By definition we have assumed crimes of two classes — first, simple possession and acquisition, or second, greater crimes such as robbery — both motivated by the compulsive need to obtain drugs resulting in loss of self-control. If we punish the second, we can do so only because we find *free will*. If *free will* can exist for the second, it likewise must exist for the first class. . . . In fact, it seems clear that the addict who restrains himself from committing any other crimes except acquisition and possession, assuming he obtains his funds by lawful means, has demonstrated a greater degree of self-control than the addict who in desperation robs a bank to buy at retail. If the addict can restrain himself from committing any other illegal act except purchase and possession, then he is demonstrating a degree of self-control greater than that of the one who robs a pharmacy or a bank, and thus his defense of loss of control and accountability is even less valid than that of the addict who robs the pharmacy or the bank. . . .

All of this points up the wisdom of Justice Black's observation in *Powell*, where he reached the conclusion that questions of "voluntariness" or "compulsion" should not be "controlling on the question [of] whether a specific instance of human behavior should be immune from punishment as a constitutional matter."

. . . Just as Justice Black turned away from the proposed constitutional rule, we spurn the proposed "common law" rule, not only because the recently created statutory scheme of dealing with narcotics addicts stands a reasonable chance of reaching the objectives of "deterrence, isolation, and treatment," but also because the particular nature of the problem of the heroin traffic makes certain policies necessary that should not be weakened by the creation of this defense. There is no compelling policy requiring us to intervene here.

To evaluate the proposed defense in light of the Eighth Amendment we review the case law, in particular, Robinson v. California (1962) and Powell v. Texas (1968). This review demonstrates that the case law simply does not support the position advanced by appellant. [Discussion omitted.]

The broad question raised by this case is whether or when possession of heroin by an addict, though conscious and intentional, lacks elements indispensable to criminality under fundamentals of our system of justice. Appellant contends that his conduct is excusable for lack of ability to control offending behavior, that his "long and intensive dependence on injected heroin stands on the same footing" as "a person forced under threat of death to inject heroin." (Brief at 4). We may fairly assume that a statute contemplates the defense of threat of death, as basic jurisprudence, even though not expressly noted. However, psychic dependence, and a claim of psychic incapacity, did not establish a defense under settled judicial doctrine that Congress may reasonably be said to have contemplated. . . .

Appellant's key defense concepts are impairment of behavioral control and loss of self-control. These have been considered by this court most fully in discussion of the insanity defense, and the philosophy of those opinions is invoked, although appellant disclaims the insanity defense as such. In our 1962 en banc McDonald [v. United States, 312 F.2d 847 (D.C. Cir. 1962)] opinion we required as an essential ingredient of the insanity defense evidence that the crime was the product of a "mental disease or defect"— defined as an "abnormal condition of the mind which substantially affects mental or emotional processes and substantially impairs behavior controls." In our 1972 en banc opinion in *Brawner*, we adopted the test of the ALI's Model Penal Code and required, for exculpation from responsibility for criminal conduct on ground of insanity, evidence from the defendant that as a result of "mental disease or defect," as defined in *McDonald*, he lacked at the time of his conduct "substantial capacity to appreciate the wrongfulness of his conduct or to conform his conduct to the requirements of the law."

Appellant's presentation rests, in essence, on the premise that the "mental disease or defect" requirement of *McDonald* and *Brawner* is superfluous. He discerns a broad principle that excuses from criminal responsibility when conduct results from a condition that impairs behavior control. . . . The broad assertion is that in general the mens rea element of criminal responsibility requires freedom of will, which is negatived by an impairment of behavioral control and loss of self-control.

If drug dependence really negatived mens rea, it would be a defense not only to the offense of possession or purchase of prohibited drugs but to other actions taken under the compulsion of the need to obtain the drug. If there is an impairment and lack of capacity to alter conduct, there is no way in which the line can be drawn in mens rea terms so as to exclude the very large percentage of addicts who must support their habit by engaging in retail sales, or, indeed, committing other crimes in order to satisfy their compulsion for drugs. . . .

. . . It does not follow that because one condition (mental disease) yields an exculpatory defense if it results in impairment of and lack of behavioral controls the same result follows when some other condition impairs behavior controls.

The criminal law expresses the requirements of personal and official discipline needed to protect society. By long tradition of the penal law, an actor's behavior is "involuntary" and there is no criminal responsibility, when he is overwhelmed by force, as when his arm is physically moved by someone else. By long tradition, too, the criminal law reaches only acts that are not only voluntary but also accompanied by a mental element, a "mens rea" (Law latin for guilty mind). Although some modern statutes impose strict liability, statutes defining criminal offenses are generally construed to require a mens rea. . . . However, this mental state may be supplied by proof of knowledge, or even by an objective standard of negligence not dependent on subjective knowledge of the actor. The elements that our basic jurisprudence requires for criminal responsibility — a voluntary act, and a mental state — are plainly fulfilled by an offense of knowing possession of a prohibited article.[62]

The legal conception of criminal capacity cannot be limited to those of unusual endowment or even average powers. A few may be recognized as so far from normal as to be entirely beyond the reach of criminal justice, but in general the criminal law is a means of social control that must be potentially capable of reaching the vast bulk of the population. Criminal responsibility is a concept that not only extends to the bulk of those below the median line of responsibility, but specifically extends to those who have a realistic problem of substantial impairment and lack of capacity due, say, to weakness of intellect that establishes susceptibility to suggestion; or to a loss of control of the mind as a result of passion, whether the passion is of an amorous nature or the result of hate, prejudice or vengeance; or to a depravity that blocks out conscience as an influence on conduct.

The criminal law cannot "vary legal norms with the individual's capacity to meet the standards they prescribe, absent a disability that is both gross and verifiable, such as the mental disease or defect that may establish irresponsibility.

62. See ALI Model Penal Code §§2.01, 2.02 (Proposed Official Draft 1962). Section 2.01(4) states that the requirement of a "voluntary act" embraces possession as an act, "if the possessor knowingly procured or received the thing possessed or was aware of his control thereof for a sufficient period to have been able to terminate his possession."

The most that it is feasible to do with lesser disabilities is to accord them proper weight in sentencing." [65]

Only in limited areas have the courts recognized a defense to criminal responsibility, on the basis that a described condition establishes a psychic incapacity negativing free will in the broader sense. These are areas where the courts have been able to respond to a deep call on elemental justice, and to discern a demarcation of doctrine that keeps the defense within verifiable bounds that do not tear the fabric of the criminal law as an instrument of social control. . . .

In our view, the rule for drug addiction should not be modeled on the rule for mental disease because of crucial distinctions between conditions. The subject of mental disease, though subject to some indeterminacy, and difficulty of diagnosis when extended to volitional impairment as well as cognitive incapacity, has long been the subject of systematic study, and in that framework it is considered manageable to ask psychiatrists to address the distinction, all-important and crucial to the law, between incapacity and indisposition, between those who can't and those who won't, between the impulse irresistible and the impulse not resisted. These are matters as to which the court has accepted the analysis of medicine, medical conditions and symptoms, and on the premise that they can be considered on a verifiable basis, and with reasonable dispatch, the courts have recognized a defense even in conditions not as obvious and verifiable as those covered in the older and limited test of capacity to know right from wrong.

As to the subject of drug dependence and psychic incapacity to refrain from narcotics, even the 1970 Study Draft of the Staff of the National Commission on Reform of Federal Criminal Laws, which favors on balance a drug dependence defense to the crime of possession, for incapacity to refrain from use, candidly recognizes the problems involved. One is "the paradox of jail for the least dangerous possessors (non-addict experimenters and the like) while addicts go free." More important, for present purposes, is the Staff's caution first, that even physical symptoms might "be successfully feigned," and, more broadly, that there is considerable difficulty of verification of the claim of a drug user that he is unable to refrain from use. . . .

The difficulty is sharpened by the appreciable number of narcotic "addicts" who do abandon their habits permanently, and much larger number who reflect their capacity to refrain by ceasing use for varying periods of time. The reasons are not clear but the phenomenon is indisputable. It is noted in the Staff Report, and reported by specialists voicing different approaches to addiction problems.

There is need for reasonable verifiability as a condition to opening a defense to criminal responsibility. The criminal law cannot gear its standards to the individual's capacity "absent a disability that is both gross and verifiable, such as the mental disease or defect that may establish irresponsibility."

That criminal defenses from somatic conditions must hinge on a verifiable predicate has been noted by criminal law specialists most ready to reexamine old dogmas.[88] . . . Not dissimilar considerations undergird the maxim, ignorance

---

65. ALI Model Penal Code §2.09, Comment (Tent. Draft No. 10, 1960), at 6.

88. See, e.g., G. Williams, Criminal Law: The General Part §289, at 888 (2d ed. 1961): courts "peremptorily require medical evidence before considering a defense of automatism" though it is possible that hysterical fugues, epileptic seizures and the like may occur without supporting medical indications. The "possibility of miscarriages of justice must be accepted in order to make the law workable."

of the law is no excuse, which contradicts salient principles underlying mens rea, yet rejects the defense claim in the interest of society. "The plea would be universally made, and would lead to interminable questions incapable of solution." The needs of society require overriding the subjective good faith of the individual as a legal defense, remitting his position to mitigation of punishment and executive clemency. . . .

Our analysis has revealed that there is no broad common law principle of exculpation on ground of lack of control, but rather a series of particular defenses staked out in manageable areas, with the call for justice to the individual confined to ascertainable and verifiable conditions, and limited by the interest of society in control of conduct.[a] . . .

WRIGHT, J., dissenting: . . . I suggest that the development of the common law of mens rea has reached the point where it should embrace a new principle: a drug addict who, by reason of his use of drugs, lacks substantial capacity to conform his conduct to the requirements of the law may not be held criminally responsible for mere possession of drugs for his own use. . . .

The concept of criminal responsibility is, by its very nature, "an expression of the moral sense of the community." United States v. Freeman, 2 Cir., 357 F.2d 606, 615 (1966). In western society, the concept has been shaped by two dominant value judgments — that punishment must be morally legitimate, and that it must not unduly threaten the liberties and dignity of the individual in his relationship to society. As a result, there has historically been a strong conviction in our jurisprudence that to hold a man criminally responsible his actions must have been the product of a "free will." . . . Thus criminal responsibility is assessed only when through "free will" a man elects to do evil, and if he is not a free agent, or is unable to choose or to act voluntarily, or to avoid the conduct which constitutes the crime, he is outside the postulate of the law of punishment.[182]

a. The New York Court of Appeals has also rejected the drug dependence defense in a case of possession. People v. Davis, 33 N.Y.2d 221, 306 N.E.2d 787 (1973). In discussing the reasons of public policy militating against allowing the defense, the court stated (306 N.E.2d at 791):

"Moreover, while it may be that the policy of rehabilitation would be well-served by affording addicts a cruel and unusual punishment and drug dependence defense to possession for their own use, we should not lose sight of the utility of such penalties to law enforcement. For example, these possible penalties may, through the exercise of prosecutorial discretion, enable law enforcement to enlist addict-informers in ferreting out the wholesalers of illicit drugs, thereby facilitating the policy of elimination of the drug traffic. Then, too, punishment may persuade some addicts to undertake rehabilitation through various State or private programs. On the other hand, recognition of the defense might conceivably make the addict the witting or unwitting tool of the drug trafficker."— EDS.

182. Whether premised on the common law concept of mens rea, actus reus, or a combination of the two, the requirement of voluntary action is fundamental to our system of criminal justice. . . .

It should be noted that the Supreme Court's decision in such cases as United States v. Dotterweich, 320 U.S. 277 (1943); United States v. Balint, 258 U.S. 250 (1922); and Shevlin-Carpenter Co. v. Minnesota, 218 U.S. 57 (1910), are by no means inconsistent with the principle set forth. In those cases, the Court refused to interpret statutes creating "regulatory" crimes as requiring "intent" as an element of the offense where the legislature had seen fit not to write such a requirement into the statute. These regulatory offenses are intended to serve an instructive purpose with regard to the general class of persons to which they are addressed. Thus the courts are willing to allow strict liability insofar as mistake of fact is concerned for the accused under such statutes ordinarily is capable of preventing the violation "with no more care than society might reasonably expect and no more exertion than it might reasonably exact from one who has assumed his responsibility." Morissette v. United States, 342 U.S. 246, 256 (1952). . . .

The situation is quite different, however, where the defendant's ability to control his behavior

Despite this general principle, however, it is clear that our legal system does not exculpate all persons whose capacity for control is impaired, for whatever cause or reason. Rather, in determining responsibility for crime, the law assumes "free will" and then recognizes known deviations "where there is a broad consensus that free will does not exist" with respect to the particular condition at issue. . . . The evolving nature of this process is amply demonstrated in the gradual development of such defenses as infancy, duress, insanity, somnambulism and other forms of automatism, epilepsy and unconsciousness, involuntary intoxication, delirium tremens, and chronic alcoholism.

A similar consensus exists today in the area of narcotics addiction. . . .

. . . [I]t can no longer seriously be questioned that for at least some addicts the "overpowering" psychological and physiological need to possess and inject narcotics cannot be overcome by mere exercise of "free will."

Moreover, recognition of a defense of "addiction" for crimes such as possession of narcotics is consistent not only with our historic common law notions of criminal responsibility and moral accountability, but also with the traditional goals of penology — retribution, deterrence, isolation and rehabilitation.

Unlike other goals of penology, the retributive theory of criminal justice looks solely to the past for justification, without regard to considerations of prevention or reformation. . . . Revenge, if it is ever to be legitimate, must be premised on moral blameworthiness, and what segment of our society would feel its need for retribution satisfied when it wreaks vengeance upon those who are diseased because of their disease?

It is of course true that there may have been a time in the past before the addict lost control when he made a conscious decision to use drugs. But imposition of punishment on this basis would violate the long-standing rule that "[t]he law looks to the immediate, and not to the remote cause; to the actual state of the party, and not to the causes, which remotely produced it." . . .

The most widely employed argument in favor of punishing addicts for crimes such as possession of narcotics is that such punishment or threat of punishment has a substantial deterrent effect. Given our present knowledge, however, the merits of this argument appear doubtful. Deterrence presupposes rationality — it proceeds on the assumption that the detriments which would inure to the prospective criminal upon apprehension can be made so severe that he will be dissuaded from undertaking the criminal act. In the case of the narcotic addict, however, the normal sense of reason, which is so essential to effective functioning of deterrence, is overcome by the psychological and physiological compulsions of the disease. As a result, it is widely agreed that the threat of even harsh prison sentences cannot deter the addict from using and possessing the drug.

A similar situation prevails insofar as deterrence of *potential* addicts is concerned. . . . [N]othing in this opinion would in any way affect the criminal responsibility of non-addict users for crimes they may commit — including illegal possession of narcotics. . . .

Moreover, in any discussion of deterrence we must recognize that when an

---

is impaired by some legally recognized disability such as duress, insanity, chronic alcoholism or addiction. Since these persons are *incapable* of conforming to the law no matter what standard of care is required, they cannot be held responsible for violations of even "regulatory statutes."

individual is punished, not for his own good, but to set an example for others, he "suffers not for what he has done but on account of other people's tendency to do likewise." . . . In such situations, the offender serves simply as a tool in the hands of society, and if punishment premised on considerations of deterrence is to be morally legitimate, the punishment meted out must be justifiable in light of the gravity of the offense and the culpability of the offender. See, e.g., Andenaes, The Morality of Deterrence, 37 U. Chi. L. Rev. 649 (1970). Since the addict's possession of narcotics is simply a symptom of his disease and not an act of "free will," however, this conduct cannot properly be deemed "culpable," and it would therefore seem inappropriate for society to utilize him as a mere vehicle through which to deter others. . . .

Shifting our focus now to the goal of isolating the offender, we arrive here at not only a justifiable basis for action but one which, in some cases at least, may be vital to the interests of society. . . .

This does not mean, however, that the goal of isolation justifies infliction of criminal punishment upon the addict. On the contrary, this interest may be fully vindicated through a program of civil commitment with treatment as well as by criminal incarceration. . . .

This, then, brings us to the final and most important goal of modern penology — to rehabilitate the offender. In this age of enlightened correctional philosophy, we now recognize that society has a responsibility to both the individual and the community to treat the offender so that upon his release he may function as a productive, law-abiding citizen. And this is all the more true where, as with the non-trafficking addict possessor, the offender has acted under the compulsion of the disease. . . .

Perhaps the most troublesome question arising out of recognition of the addiction defense I suggest is whether it should be limited only to those acts — such as mere possession for use — which are inherent in the disease itself. It can hardly be doubted that, in at least some instances, an addict may in fact be "compelled" to engage in other types of criminal activity in order to obtain sufficient funds to purchase his necessary supply of narcotics. . . . Nevertheless, I am convinced that Congress has manifested a clear intent to preclude common law extension of the defense beyond those crimes which, like the act of possession, cause direct harm only to the addict himself. . . .

The basic question of criminal responsibility under the addiction defense is a legal, and not a purely medical, determination. Not all drug users are "addicts" and, as with any compulsion, the degree of dependence may vary among different individuals and, indeed, even in a given individual at different stages of his addiction. Thus what we are concerned with here is not an abstract medical or psychiatric definition of addiction which sets forth a clinical checklist of relevant symptoms but, rather, a behavioral model, based upon traditional legal and moral principles, which tests the ability of the defendant to control his behavior. The essential inquiry, then, is simply whether, at the time of the offense, the defendant, as a result of his repeated use of narcotics, lacked substantial capacity to conform his conduct to the requirements of the law.[282]

BAZELON, C.J. (concurring in part and dissenting in part): . . . On the issue of guilt or innocence, Judge Wright's views are closest to my own. I cannot,

---

282. This test of addiction is adapted from the standard for the insanity defense recently announced by this court in United States v. Brawner. . . .

however, accept his view that the addiction/responsibility defense should be limited to the offense of possession. I would also permit a jury to consider addiction as a defense to a charge of, for example, armed robbery or trafficking in drugs, to determine whether the defendant was under such duress or compulsion, because of his addiction, that he was unable to conform his conduct to the requirements of the law. . . .

NOTES

1. In Commonwealth v. Sheehan, 383 N.E.2d 1115 (Mass. 1978), defendant appealed his conviction of robbery of a registered pharmacist on the ground that the trial judge excluded his proffer of expert testimony to show that because of his drug addiction he was not criminally responsible under the Massachusetts test of legal insanity (modeled after the Model Penal Code test). The court affirmed, stating (id. at 1118-1119):

> We reject the defendant's argument that drug addiction itself may qualify as a mental disease or defect which, along with other necessary elements, would warrant a finding of not guilty by reason of insanity under the standards of Commonwealth v. McHoul, 352 Mass. 544, 546-547, 226 N.E.2d 556 (1967). Drug addiction, standing alone, does not qualify as a mental disease or defect which would support a finding of a lack of criminal responsibility under the *McHoul* test. . . .
>
> If the normal consequences of drug addiction are to be accepted as a ground for avoidance of responsibility for criminal conduct, the Legislature is the appropriate body to make that determination. Although the Legislature has dealt with drug dependency and drug addiction in relation to criminal proceedings, it has not adopted the view that drug addiction absolves a defendant of responsibility for his criminal conduct. Indeed, for all crimes other than drug offenses, the Legislature has adopted a procedure which calls for the sentencing of a drug dependent person in the normal course, with the possibility of drug treatment on the order of the judge and with the consent of the defendant. G.L. c. 123, §48. With this expression of public policy by the Legislature, we decline to adopt a general rule of law which absolves one from responsibility for criminal conduct based solely on the consequences of the voluntary use of drugs. Consequently, even if medical experts may undertake to characterize drug addiction in medical terms as a mental disease or defect, we reject drug addiction alone as qualifying as a mental disease or defect for the purpose of applying the *McHoul* test.

2. For commentary on these issues see Fingarette, Addiction and Criminal Responsibility, 84 Yale L.J. 413 (1975); Wald, Alcohol, Drugs, and Criminal Responsibility, 63 Geo. L.J. 69 (1974); Annot., Drug addiction or related mental state as defense to criminal charge, 73 A.L.R.3d 16 (1976).

STATE v. STRASBURG

Supreme Court of Washington
60 Wash. 106, 110 P. 1020 (1910)

PARKER, J. The prosecuting attorney for King county by information charged the defendant with the crime of assault in the first degree. . . . The trial resulted in a verdict of guilty against the defendant. His motion for a new trial being denied, judgment was rendered against him upon the verdict. From this judgment, the defendant has appealed.

The principal grounds relied upon by learned counsel for defendant to secure a reversal of the judgment is that the trial court erred in refusing to admit evidence tending to prove that the defendant at the time charged as the commission of the crime was insane and incapable of understanding the nature and quality of his act; and also that the court erred in instructing the jury

> that, under the laws of this state, it is no defense to a criminal charge that the person charged was at the time of the commission of the offense unable, by reason of his insanity, idiocy or imbecility to comprehend the nature and quality of the act committed, or to understand that it was wrong.

In support of these rulings of the learned trial court, counsel for the state rely upon the provisions of section 7 of our New Criminal Code (section 2259, Rem. & Bal. Code; Laws 1909, p. 891, §7), providing as follows:

> It shall be no defense to a person charged with the commission of a crime that at the time of its commission he was unable, by reason of his insanity, idiocy or imbecility, to comprehend the nature and quality of the act committed, or to understand that it was wrong; or that he was afflicted with a morbid propensity to commit prohibited acts; nor shall any testimony or other proof thereof be admitted in evidence.[a]

It is contended by learned counsel for appellant that this statute withholds from him rights guaranteed by our state Constitution, and particularly those rights guaranteed by the following provisions thereof: Article 1, §3: "No person shall be deprived of life, liberty, or property without due process of law." Article 1, §21: "The right of trial by jury shall remain inviolate." We are then confronted with the novel and grave question: Has the Legislature the power under our Constitution to enact a law taking away from a defendant accused of crime the opportunity to show in his defense the fact that at the time of the commission of the act charged as a crime against him he was insane, and, by reason thereof, was unable to comprehend the nature and quality of the act committed? . . .

. . . [T]he sanity of the accused at the time of committing the act charged against him has always been regarded as much a substantive fact, going to make up his guilt, as the fact of his physical commission of the act. It seems to us the law could as well exclude proof of any other substantive fact going to show his guilt or innocence. If he was insane at the time to the extent that he could not comprehend the nature and quality of the act — in other words, if he had no will to control the physical act of his physical body — how can it in truth be said that the act was his act? To take from the accused the opportunity to offer evidence tending to prove this fact is in our opinion as much a violation of his constitutional right of trial by jury as to take from him the right to offer

---

a. The statute further provided that the trial judge could, after verdict of guilty, order the defendant committed to a state hospital for the insane or to be confined in the insane ward of the penitentiary, if of the view that the defendant, by virtue of his or her insanity, was unable to comprehend the nature and quality of his or her act or to understand that such act was wrong. — Eds

evidence before the jury tending to show that he did not physically commit the act or physically set in motion a train of events resulting in the act. The maxim, "An act done by me against my will is not my act," may, without losing any of its force, be paraphrased to fit our present inquiry as follows: "An act done by me without my will, or in the absence of my will, is not my act." . . .

Finally we will briefly notice the very able and ingenious argument put forward by learned counsel for the state, based upon the seeming assumption that the modern humane treatment of those convicted of crime practically removes them from the realm of punishment, and places them in a position but little different from those other unfortunate members of society which the state is obliged to care for and restrain of their liberty, not because they have committed wrong, but because of their menace to society and themselves without fault of their own — the insane. . . . The argument seems to be in its last analysis that, because of modern humane methods in caring for and treating those convicted of crime, there is no longer any reason for taking into consideration the element of will on the part of those who commit prohibited acts when their guilt is being determined for the purpose of putting them in the criminal class for restraint and treatment. Learned counsel's premise suggests a noble conception, and may give promise of a condition of things towards which the humanitarian spirit of the age is tending; yet the stern and awful fact still remains, and is patent to all men, that the status and condition in the eyes of the world, and under the law, of one convicted of crime, is vastly different from that of one simply adjudged insane. We cannot shut our eyes to the fact that the element of punishment is still in our criminal laws. It is evidenced by the words "shall be punished," found in this very section defining the crime here charged against appellant. It is evidenced by these or similar words characterizing the treatment which the law imposes upon those convicted of crime in practically all parts of our Criminal Code prescribing the fate of the guilty. As long as this is the spirit of our laws, though it may be much mellowed in the treatment of the convicted, as compared with former times, the constitutional rights here invoked must be given full force and effect when an accused person is put upon trial to determine the question of his guilt of crime. . . .

The judgment of the learned trial court is reversed, with direction to grant appellant a new trial.

NOTE

Legislative initiatives to abolish the insanity defense continue today. Montana abolished the defense in 1979. 1979 Montana Laws ch. 713. The new law provides that those convicted defendants who are found to have suffered from a mental disease or defect that would have required their acquittal as legally insane under the prior law must be committed to the state hospital for a term not greater than that provided for the crime committed. The new law also authorizes the acquittal of defendants on the ground that because of a mental disease or defect they could not have a particular state of mind that is an essential element of the offense charged. But these defendants too must be committed to the state hospital. Idaho enacted comparable legislation in 1982. See Idaho Senate Bill No. 1396, 46th Legislature, 2d Sess. (1982).

INSANITY AS A DEFENSE: A PANEL DISCUSSION
Annual Judicial Conference, Second Judicial Circuit of the United States
37 F.R.D. 365, 369-372, 381-383 (1964)

JOSEPH WEINTRAUB, C.J. [N.J. Supreme Court]: . . .

My thesis is that insanity should have nothing to do with the adjudication of guilt but rather should bear upon the disposition of the offender after conviction, and that the contest among *M'Naghten* and its competitive concepts which you have on a paper before you is simply a struggle over an irrelevancy. . . .

I think we all agree that society must be protected from hostile acts and when a forbidden act is done, it must be adjudged that the accused committed it before he may be deprived of his liberty. And so the issue is, shall we employ a criminal process or a civil process to determine that he did the act and to determine society's right to commit him, and as long as we have two processes which may be employed to deal custodially with anti-social conduct, one criminal and the other civil, the test for their application must be blameworthiness or the non-existence of blameworthiness in a very personal sense. And that distinction is supposed to be between the bad and the sick. Now, in separating the bad from the sick, the common law deemed it indisputable that every man has the ability to adhere to the right; psychiatry challenges this basis for a finding of personal blameworthiness. Psychiatry does recognize a volitional apparatus but conceives it to be integrated with the intellect and the emotions, and from its objective view no man can be said to have selected the dimensions of these faculties and hence to be the author of the inadequacy of any of them. And, indeed, the unconscious is deemed to mock and play havoc with the conscious. On that approach, the sick and the wicked must be equally free of blame in a personal sense and there can be no denominator which in terms of justice to the individual will separate one from the other. . . . Upon the psychiatric view the distinction between the sick and the bad is I think an illusion. . . . The thrust of the psychiatric thesis must be to reject insanity as a defense and to deal with all transgressors as unfortunate mortals. In other words, if we could think of the adjudication of guilt as nothing more than a finding that this mortal has demonstrated his capacity to do harm, the need for segregating him or otherwise treating him or dealing with him, I think half the battle would be decided. We then would get to the question of what can we do? How can we best redeem him; recapture whatever there is that can be salvaged? The difficulty I think is that the psychiatry-based critics of *M'Naghten* will not accept the inevitable answer, which, I think, psychiatry gives but rather they urge that *M'Naghten* be abandoned in favor of some other concept of insanity which will excuse and then debate whether the test will be *Durham* . . . or the model code . . . or some refinement of them. And I think that debate just has to be fruitless. It's a quixotic attempt to draw a line that just doesn't exist. No definition of criminal responsibility and hence of legal insanity can be valid unless it truthfully separates the man who is personally blameworthy for his makeup from the man who is not, and I submit to you that there is just no basis in psychiatry to make a differentiation between the two.[a] I would think that if there is anything

---

a. Consider Morris, Psychiatry and the Dangerous Criminal, 41 S. Cal. L. Rev. 514, 519 (1968): "Overwhelmingly, criminal matters are disposed of by pleas of guilty and by bench trials. Only the exceptional case goes to trial by jury. And of these exceptional cases, in only two of every

that would be an anathema to a psychiatrist, it's the concept of blame. I don't think he's interested in that at all and I doubt very much that a psychiatrist would contend that he has any expert information which can give us insight into that real riddle.

PROFESSOR HERBERT WECHSLER: . . .

Chief Justice Weintraub has . . . ventured the suggestion that the whole effort to develop a criterion for determining criminal responsibility as affected by mental disease or defect is a misguided effort. . . . I think it is not a misguided effort. It rests not only on the universal experience of all modern legal systems but I'm tempted to say of all civilized legal systems, though I don't want to beg the question by an epithet. I think, moreover, that there is a solid basis for this phenomenon. I suggest that you think about it not in terms of the effort to do absolute justice to individuals (we must agree with the Chief Justice, this is for God and not for man) but rather in terms of asking ourselves this question: how would you feel about living in a society in which a differentiation of this sort were not attempted?

For example, your elderly father in an advanced arteriosclerotic state is taken to the hospital and while in the hospital experiences a tantrum, a delusion, delusional phase, and knocks over a lamp, with the result that an attendant is killed. Now, would you be satisfied with a legal system in which he could be indicted and convicted of a homicidal crime and his condition regarded as relevant only on the question of what to do with him. Everybody would say no to this. That is why the criterion of responsibility as affected by disease or a defect parallels the traditional mens rea rules in requiring a determination of blameworthiness in the ordinary moral sense, in the sense of working morality, not in the sense of man's responsibility for his nature or his nurture but in the sense that the afflictive sanctions of the law will not be visited on anyone unless he does something which is the product of a choice, unless in traditional jurisprudential terms he performs a juridical act. Now, general confidence that this is so seems to me quite central to the sense of security that is one of the greatest values in a law abiding society. It is a very important thing for all of us to know that if we should be afflicted and in the course of affliction should be the physical agent of harm to others, that the legal system will conduct an inquiry in which the nature of that affliction can be adduced for an estimate of its bearing on blameworthiness in the ordinary sense. We're dealing thus with a proposition which is directly akin to the legal point that accident is not a crime, not punishable, and indeed even to the hesitance of the system to impose criminal liability for negligence, for mere negligence and to the general effort to require at least recklessness and, for ordinary purposes, purposeful wrongdoing. . . .

This brings me to the second part of Chief Justice Weintraub's theme. He spoke of drawing a distinction between civil and criminal roads to commitment,

---

hundred is this defense raised. [Citing Kalven and Zeisel, The American Jury 330 (19660.] Does anyone believe that this percentage measures the actual significance of gross psychopathology to crime? Let him visit the nearest criminal court or penitentiary if he does. Clearly this defense is a sop to our conscience, a comfort for our failure to address the difficult arena of psychopathology and crime. . . ." For a review of the ways mentally disordered offenders are disposed of before trial in the United States, see Goldstein, The Insanity Defense ch. 11, Competing Process and Attrition Before Trial (1967). — EDS.

and that of course is what's involved here. But, again, you must face the question, do you believe in that distinction? And I put it to you that it is vital to believe in that distinction, vital to a healthy society which will use its criminal law to build and buttress self-reliant action on the part of citizens affected by it. And, also, for another reason, namely that an awful lot of sick people in this world have to go to mental institutions who have not engaged in hostile acts of the kind that would ordinarily be crimes. About the toughest problem in dealing with that mental health problem, I should say, is the problem of protecting those people from a deep and scarring stigma, the more so at a time when such commitments seem happily to be relatively brief on the whole and release safe within a short time largely due to the new drugs. Now, how can you safeguard these people from stigma if you merge the process by which they may be committed to a mental institution and the process of dealing with people who have done what the social order condemns, declares to be wrong, if you merge these two types of people and commitments? So I don't think that it's just a question of whether you get sent away and for how long. I rather think that the distinctive feature of the entire criminal process is the element of condemnation that it marshals, of social condemnation. And, indeed, is it not the mark of a healthy society that the criminal law marshal an appropriate moral condemnation?

NOTES AND QUESTIONS

1. In the congressional deliberations over revising the federal criminal code, the Nixon administration proposed a comprehensive bill (Criminal Code Reform Act of 1973, S. 1400, 93d Cong., 1st Sess. (March 17, 1973)). It contained a provision that would abolish legal insanity as a defense to conviction of crime. It reads:

SECTION 501. INSANITY

It is a defense to a prosecution under any federal statute that the defendant, as a result of mental disease or defect, lacked the state of mind required as an element of the offense charged. Mental disease or defect does not otherwise constitute defense.

See Wales, An Analysis of the Proposal to "Abolish" the Insanity Defense in S. 1: Squeezing a Lemon, 124 U. Pa. L. Rev. 687 (1976). Consider, as well, the following comments:

Dershowitz, Abolishing the Insanity Defense: The Most Significant Feature of the Administration's Proposed Criminal Code — An Essay, 9 Crim. L. Bull. 434, 435, 438-439 (1973): The Administration's proposal . . . would mean that a defendant accused, for example, of first-degree murder could be convicted even if he were grossly psychotic, so long as he killed "intentionally" and with "premeditation." (That a grossly psychotic person is capable of intent and premeditation is illustrated by the famous *M'Naughten* case, where the defendant, who was apparently a paranoid schizophrenic, killed an assistant to the Prime Minister of England because he believed he was being persecuted; the murder, which was committed intentionally and with premeditation, would presumably be punishable under the Nixon proposal, even though the defendant was psychotic at the time he pulled the trigger.)

The legislation — characterized by President Nixon as "the most significant feature of the Administration's proposed criminal code"— is designed, according to the President, to curb "unconscionable abuse" of the insanity defense by criminals.

It is not clear to many attorneys what kind of abuse the Administration had in mind: Assistant Attorney General Henry Peterson raised the specter of a hijacker acquitted by reason of insanity walking out of a Washington court and boarding the next plane at Dulles Airport. But the fact is that no such incident has ever occurred (and is unlikely to occur) because most defendants acquitted by reason of insanity are immediately confined in mental hospitals — either state or federal — often for longer than the prison term they would have received if convicted. . . .

The Nixon proposal to abolish the insanity defense may produce some strange bedfellows: Liberal scholars have urged its abolition for years — although for reasons different from those given by the President. Some, such as Professor Joseph Goldstein of the Yale Law School, argue that the insanity "defense" is not really a defense at all, since those acquitted under it are rarely freed but instead sent to mental hospitals to serve indeterminate, and often quite lengthy, "sentences." Others, such as Judge Bazelon, have argued that there is little difference between a compulsion to commit crimes because of psychiatric reasons (which the law recognizes), and an equally strong compulsion grounded in socio-economic conditions (which the law has never recognized). . . .

In the last analysis, it is the jury that decides whether an accused is to be convicted or acquitted. No matter how the law reads, it is a deeply entrenched human feeling that those who are grossly disturbed — whether they are called "madmen," "lunatics," "insane," or "mentally ill"— should not be punished like ordinary criminals. This feeling, which is as old as recorded history, is unlikely to be rooted out by new legislation.

Once before in our Anglo-American legal history, a law was passed calling for the execution of persons convicted of treason even if they were mad. Lord Coke reported that this "cruel and inhumane law lived not long, but was repealed, for . . . it was against the common law."

Goldstein & Katz, Abolish the "Insanity Defense"— Why Not?, 72 Yale L.J. 853, 858-865 (1963): Like self-defense, the insanity defense applies, theoretically at least, only to persons against whom each of the elements of the offense charged could be established. Like defense of self, the defense of insanity, if successfully pleaded, results in "acquittal." But unlike the acquittal of self-defense which means liberty, the acquittal of the insanity defense means deprivation of liberty for an indefinite term in a "mental institution." . . . .

Neither legislative report, nor judicial opinion, nor scholarly comment criticizing or proposing formulations of the insanity defense has faced the crucial questions: "What is the purpose of the defense in the criminal process?" or "What need for an exception to criminal liability is being met and what objectives of the criminal law are being reinforced by the defense?" . . .

In our efforts to understand the suggested relationship between "insanity" and "mens rea" there emerges a purpose for the "insanity defense" which, though there to be seen, has remained of extremely low visibility. That purpose seems to be obscured because thinking about such a relationship has generally been blocked by unquestioning and disarming references to our collective conscience and our religious and moral traditions. Assuming the existence of the suggested relationship between "insanity" and "mens rea," the defense is not to absolve of criminal responsibility "sick" persons who would otherwise be subject to criminal sanction. Rather, its real function is to authorize the state to hold those "who must be found not to possess the guilty mind mens rea," even though the criminal law demands that no person be held criminally responsible if doubt is cast on any material element of the offense charged. . . .

What this discussion indicates, then, is that the insanity defense is not designed, as is the defense of self-defense, to define an exception to criminal liability, but rather to define for sanction an exception from among those who would be free of liability. It is as if the insanity defense were prompted by an affirmative answer to the silently posed question: "Does mens rea or any essential element of an offense exclude from liability a group of persons whom the community wishes to restrain?" If the suggested relationship between mens rea and "insanity" means that "insanity" precludes proof beyond doubt of mens rea then the "defense" is designed to authorize the holding of persons who have committed no crime. So conceived, the problem really facing the criminal process has been how to obtain authority to sanction the "insane" who would be excluded from liability by an overall application of the general principles of the criminal law.

2. *Questions:* Note that the central premise of the argument of Goldstein and Katz is that evidence establishing that the defendant is legally insane necessarily establishes that the material mental elements of the crime have not been proven. Is this true? Where the relevant mental element turns on an objective standard — for example, negligence or recklessness — what is there in any of the tests of legal insanity inconsistent with the defendant's having acted with the required state of mind — for example, negligently or recklessly? Even where the mental element is purpose or knowledge (loosely, "intent"), are all of the tests of legal insanity inconsistent with the defendant's having the required knowledge or purpose? *M'Naghten* requires that the defendant not know the nature and quality of his or her act. To the extent that "knowledge" is broadly interpreted to mean knowledge "charged with effect" or to imply capacity to function in light of knowledge, as it often has been taken to mean (see pages 825, 828 supra), would meeting this test necessarily negate the definitional mens rea of knowledge? *M'Naghten* also requires as an alternative that the defendant not know that what he or she was doing was wrong. If this were true, would it necessarily negate the mens rea of knowledge of the nature and circumstance of the act? The Model Penal Code test (§4.01) requires that the defendant lack "capacity to appreciate the criminality of his conduct or to conform his conduct to the requirement of law." Would a defendant who could not so appreciate or conform necessarily not have the mens rea of purpose or knowledge?

There has been some judicial examination of these questions in connection with statutes establishing a bifurcated procedure under which the issue of guilt must be determined first and the issue of legal insanity determined at a subsequent trial if the defendant is found guilty. The Arizona Supreme Court held this procedure unconstitutional on the ground that a legally insane person could not form an intent. State v. Shaw, 106 Ariz. 103, 471 P.2d 715 (1970). The Wisconsin Supreme Court disagreed. State v. Hebard, 50 Wis. 2d 408, 184 N.W.2d 156 (1971).

3. For further debate on the proposal to abolish the defense of legal insanity and to defer inquiry into the mental condition of the defendant until after conviction, compare Wootton, Crime and the Criminal Law, chs. 2 & 3 (1963), with H. L. A. Hart, The Morality of the Criminal Law 12-29 (1964); and Morris, Psychiatry and the Dangerous Criminal, 41 S. Cal. L. Rev. 514 (1968), with Kadish, The Decline of Innocence, 26 Camb. L.J. 273 (1968). See also Monahan, Abolish the Insanity Defense? — Not Yet, 26 Rutgers L. Rev. 719 (1973).

One should also consider at this point the proposals to do away not simply with particular excuses, such as legal insanity, but with all defenses based on mens rea. These proposals and responses to them were considered in the Note on the Elimination of Mens Rea for All Crimes, page 336 supra.

NOTE ON EXCUSING CONDITIONS GENERALLY

In his essay, Legal Responsibility and Excuses, originally published in Determinism and Freedom (S. Hook ed. 1958), and reprinted in H. L. A. Hart, Punishment and Responsibility 28 (1968) (a more readily available paperback, to which page references will here be made), Professor Hart explores the purpose and importance of excusing conditions in criminal responsibility.

Professor Hart concludes the first part of his discussion as follows (id. at 42):

> One necessary condition of the just application of a punishment is normally expressed by saying that the agent "could have helped" doing what he did, and hence the need to inquire into the "inner facts" is dictated not by the moral principle that only the doing of an *immoral* act may be legally punished, but by the moral principle that no one should be punished who could not help doing what he did. This is a necessary condition (unless strict liability is admitted) for the moral propriety of legal punishment and no doubt also for moral censure; in this respect law and morals are similar. But this similarity as to the one essential condition that there must be a "voluntary" action if legal punishment or moral censure is to be morally permissible does not mean that legal punishment is morally permissible only where the agent had done something morally wrong.

He then discusses another explanation of the centrality of excuses in the law, namely, the "economy of threats" theory of Bentham, holding that where the excusing conditions exist (insanity, coercion, etc.), it is futile to try to induce conformity by the threat of punishment because the actor is by definition beyond the reach of the threat. Therefore, punishment in these cases would not serve to deter, and not punishing in these cases would not weaken the threat against the deterrable. Hart observes (at 42):

> On this theory we inquire into the state of mind of the accused simply to find out whether he belongs to a defined class of persons whose exemption from punishment, if allowed, will not weaken the effect on others of the general threat of punishment made by the law. So there is no question of its being unjust or unfair

to punish a particular criminal or to exempt him from punishment. Once the crime has been committed, the decision to punish or not has nothing to do with any moral claim or right of the criminal to have the features of his case considered, but only with the causal efficacy of his punishment on others.

Hart finds this explanation unacceptable for two reasons: first, because it paradoxically "seems to destroy the entire notion that in punishing we must be just to the particular criminal in front of us and that the purpose of excusing conditions is to protect him from society's claims" (at 43); second, because the argument is based on a non sequitur. It may well be that if the law did not recognize excuses of various kinds, many people who now take a chance in the hope of bringing themselves under these exempting provisions, if discovered, would in fact be deterred. Therefore, maintaining the maximum deterrent efficacy against the deterrable would require maintaining the threat of punishment against all. Hart states:

> It is clear, I think, that if we were to base our views of criminal responsibility on the doctrine of the economy of threats, we should misrepresent altogether the character of our moral preference for a legal system that requires mental conditions of responsibility over a system of total strict liability, or entirely different methods of social control such as hypnosis, propaganda, or conditioning. . . . Recognition of their excusing force may lead to a lower, not a higher, level of efficacy of threats; yet — and this is the point — we would not regard that as sufficient for abandoning the protection of the individual; or if we did, it would be with the recognition that we had sacrificed one principle to another; for more is at stake than the single principle of maintaining the laws at their most efficacious level. (Id. at 44.)

Professor Hart then continues as follows (id. at 44-49):

> What I do mean is that the conception of the law simply as goading individuals into desired courses of behaviour is inadequate and misleading; what a legal system that makes liability generally depend on excusing conditions does is to guide individuals' choices as to behaviour by presenting them with reasons for exercising choice in the direction of obedience, but leaving them to choose.
>
> It is at this point that I would stress the analogy between the mental conditions that excuse from criminal responsibility and the mental conditions that are regarded as invalidating civil transactions such as wills, gifts, contracts, marriages, and the like. These institutions provide individuals with two inestimable advantages in relation to those areas of conduct they cover. These are (1) the advantage to the individual of determining by his choice what the future shall be and (2) the advantage of being able to predict what the future will be. For these institutions enable the individual (1) to bring into operation the coercive forces of the law so that those legal arrangements he has chosen shall be carried into effect and (2) to plan the rest of his life with certainty or at least the confidence (in a legal system that is working normally) that the arrangements he has made will in fact be carried out. By these devices the individual's choice is brought into the legal system and allowed to determine its future operations in various areas thereby giving him a type of indirect coercive control over, and a power to foresee the development of, official life. This he would not have "naturally," that is, apart from these legal institutions.
>
> In brief, the function of these institutions of private law is to render effective the individual's preferences in certain areas. It is therefore clear why in this sphere

the law treats the mental factors of, say, mistake, ignorance of the nature of the transaction, coercion, undue influence, or insanity as invalidating such civil transactions. For a transaction entered into under such conditions will not represent a real choice: the individual might have chosen one course of events and by the transaction procured another (cases of mistake, ignorance, etc.), or he might have chosen to enter the transaction without coolly and calmly thinking out what he wanted (undue influence), or he might have been subjected to the threats of another who had imposed his choices (coercion). . . .

If with this in mind we turn back to criminal law and its excusing conditions, we can regard their function as a mechanism for similarly maximizing within the framework of coercive criminal law the efficacy of the individual's informed and considered choice in determining the future and also his power to predict that future. . . .

. . . [T]he value of these . . . factors can be realized if we conduct the Gedanken-experiment of imagining criminal law operating without excusing conditions. First, our power of predicting what will happen to us will be immeasurably diminished; the likelihood that I shall choose to do the forbidden act (e.g. strike someone) and so incur the sanctions of the criminal law may not be very easy to calculate even under our system: as a basis for this prediction we have indeed only the knowledge of our own character and some estimate of the temptations life is likely to offer us. But if we are also to be liable if we strike someone by accident, by mistake, under coercion, etc., the chances that we shall incur the sanctions are immeasurably increased. From our knowledge of the past career of our body considered as a thing, we cannot infer much as to the chances of its being brought into violent contact with another, and under a system that dispensed with the excusing condition of, say, accident (implying lack of intention) a collision alone would land us in jail. Secondly, our choice would condition what befalls us to a lesser extent. Thirdly, we should suffer sanctions without having obtained any satisfaction. Again, no form of determinism that I, at least, can construct can throw any doubt on, or show to be illusory, the real satisfaction that a system of criminal law incorporating excusing conditions provides for individuals in maximizing the effect of their choices within the framework of coercive law. The choices remain choices, the satisfactions remain satisfactions, and the consequences of choices remain the consequences of choices, even if choices are determined and even if other "determinants" besides our choices condition the satisfaction arising from their being rendered effective in this way by the criminal law. . . .

On this view excusing conditions are accepted as something that may conflict with the social utility of the law's threats; they are regarded as of moral importance because they provide for all individuals alike the satisfactions of a choosing system. Recognition of excusing conditions is therefore seen as a matter of protection of the individual against the claims of society for the highest measure of protection from crime that can be obtained from a system of threats. In this way the criminal law respects the claims of the individual as such, or at least as a *choosing* being, and distributes its coercive sanctions in a way that reflects this respect for the individual. This surely is very central in the notion of justice and is one, though no doubt only one, among the many strands of principle that I think lie at the root of the preference for legal institutions conditioning liability by reference to excusing conditions.

For criticism of Professor Hart's position, see N. Walker, Sentencing in a Rational Society 16-19 (1969); R. Dworkin, Taking Rights Seriously 9-11 (1977).

CHAPTER

10

THEFT OFFENSES

A. THE MEANS OF ACQUISITION

MODEL PENAL CODE

COMMENT TO §223.1 AT 127-132 [AMERICAN LAW INSTITUTE, MODEL PENAL CODE AND COMMENTARIES, PT. II (1980)]

. . . Distinctions among larceny, embezzlement, obtaining by false pretenses, extortion, and the other closely related theft offenses are explicable in terms of a long history of expansion of the role of the criminal law in protecting property. That history begins with a concern for crimes of violence — in the present context, the taking of property by force from the possession of another, i.e., robbery. The criminal law then expanded, by means of the ancient quasi-criminal writ of trespass, to cover all taking of another's property from his possession without his consent, even though no force was used. This misconduct was punished as larceny. The law then expanded once more, through some famous judicial manipulation of the concept of possession, to embrace misappropriation by a person who with the consent of the owner already had physical control over the property, as in the case of servants and even bailees in certain particularly defined situations.

At this point in the chronology of the law of theft, about the end of the 18th century, a combination of circumstances caused the initiative in the further development of the criminal law to pass from the courts to the legislature. . . .

. . . The earliest statutes dealt with embezzlement by such narrowly defined groups as bank clerks. Subsequent laws extended coverage to agents, attorneys, bailees, fiduciaries, public officers, partners, mortgagors in possession, etc., until at last a few American legislatures enacted fraudulent-conversion statutes penalizing misappropriation by anyone who received or had in his possession or control the property of another or property which someone else "is entitled to receive and have." Indeed, some modern embezzlement statutes go so far as to penalize breach of faith without regard to whether anything is misappropriated. Thus, the fiduciary who makes forbidden investments, the official who deposits public funds in an unauthorized depository, the financial advisor who betrays his client into paying more for a property than the market value, may be designated an embezzler. Although this kind of coverage is relatively new for Anglo-American penal law, certain foreign codes have long recognized criminal "breach of trust" as a distinct entity.

The fraud aspects of theft, never regarded with such abhorrence as larceny, begin with the common-law misdemeanor of cheat. This offense required use of false weights or similar "tokens," thus limiting criminal deception to certain special techniques conceived as directed against the public generally. One may suspect that this development was an outgrowth of guild regulation of unfair competition as much as it reflected a desire to protect the buying public. At any rate, the use of false tokens was a technique against which it would be difficult for even a cautious yeoman to guard himself. A mere lie for the purpose of deceiving another in a business transaction did not become criminal until the Statute of 30 Geo. 2, ch. 24 (1757), created the misdemeanor of obtaining property by false pretenses. Even this statute was not at first believed to make mere misrepresentation criminal. Instead, it was thought to require some more elaborate swindling stratagem, such as French law to this day requires. Eventually it was settled in Anglo-American law that false representations of "fact," if "material," would suffice. Today's battleground is over such matters as misrepresentation of "opinion," "law," or "value," as well as "misleading omissions" and "false promises." . . .

. . . If history were the whole explanation of the existence of distinctive theft crimes, there would be little reason to preserve differentiations whose subtleties have occasioned serious procedural difficulties. The problem is not so simple. History has its own logic. The criminal law reached larceny first and embezzlement later because of real distinctions between theft by a stranger and the peculations of a trusted agent. If the move to punish embezzlement was a natural one, it was nevertheless a momentous step when the exceptional liability of servants for stealing from their masters was generalized into fraudulent conversion by anyone who had goods of another in his possession. The ordinary trespass-theft was committed by a stranger, an intruder with no semblance of right even to touch the object taken. The offender was easily recognized by the very taking, surreptitious or forceful, and so set apart from the law-abiding community. No bond of association in joint endeavor linked criminal and victim. In contrast, the embezzler stands always in a lawful as well as in an unlawful relation to the victim and the property. He is respectable; indeed, some tend to identify with him rather than with the bank or insurance company from which he embezzles. The line between lawful and unlawful activity is for the embezzler a question of the scope of his authority, which may be ill-defined. Not every deviation from the authority conferred will be civilly actionable, much less a basis for criminal liability. Sometimes the scope of the authority may be so broad, e.g., as in the case of a revocable inter-vivos trust where the grantor is trustee, as to be hardly distinguishable from ownership. The agent or bailee may actually be part of a co-proprietorship, being entitled to a commission or satisfaction of a lien out of funds in his hands. A man who is psychologically the absolute "owner" may be in the legal position of a bailee with extremely circumscribed freedom to deal with the property, as a result of modern methods of selling consumer goods on credit arrangements involving retention of title by the seller.

The embezzlement problem is complicated further by the necessity of distinguishing between defalcation by one who has "property of another" and failure of a debtor to pay his debts. Modern society is opposed to imprisonment for debt, however committed it may be to punishment for betrayal of trust. Yet when property is entrusted to a dealer for sale, with the expectation that he will receive the proceeds, deduct his commission, and remit the balance, the dealer's criminal liability if he fails to remit may turn on refinements of the civil law of contracts, agency, sales, or trusts. Such refinements, designed to allocate financial risks or to determine priorities among creditors of an insolvent, are hardly a relevant index to the harm done the owner or to the character of the defaulting dealer and thus may be entirely inappropriate as a measure of criminal liability.

It may nevertheless be true that theft by a stranger and a suitably delimited offense of theft by a fiduciary represent similar dangers requiring approximately the same treatment and characterization. . . . To that extent, at least, consolidation conforms to the common understanding of what is substantially the same kind of undesirable conduct. Consolidation also has advantages in the administration of the criminal law if it eliminates procedural problems arising from nice distinctions between closely related types of misbehavior. Differences in the treatment of thieves can be determined on an individual basis by taking into account many factors which are at least as significant as whether fraud or stealth was the means employed to deprive another of his property.

NOTE

Professor George Fletcher has presented a different view of the traditional common law distinctions and technicalities in the law of theft. Fletcher, The Metamorphosis of Larceny, 89 Harv. L. Rev. 469 (1976). His article is worth consulting in connection with the various categories of theft discussed in the following portions of this chapter. The following extract from his introductory comments suggests his general theses (at 469-474):

> The common law of theft strikes most contemporary observers as a maze of arbitrary distinctions. Virtually all the academic writing in the field expresses impatience with the distinctions among larceny, embezzlement, larceny by trick, and obtaining property by false pretenses. Justice Cardozo thought the central distinction between larceny and embezzlement failed to "correspond to an essential difference in the character of the acts"; the technical rules differentiating these two offenses so puzzled Holmes that he dismissed them as the product of "historical accidents." The thrust of the law for the last two centuries has been toward transcendence of these historical "accidents" and the creation of a unified law of theft offenses. . . .
>
> Modern lawyers have obviously lost touch with the style of thought that underlay the rules and distinctions that crystallized prior to the end of the eighteenth century. . . . What we fail to see today is that the way lawyers looked at larceny prior to the end of the eighteenth century represented a coherent system of legal thought . . . that incorporated important substantive values as well as a characteristic style of legal reasoning.
>
> The traditional approach to larceny was built on two structural principles which expressed the distinction between a public sphere of criminal conduct and a private sphere subject at most to regulation by the rules of private law. One of these structural principles, possessorial immunity, was the explicit rule of the courts

that transferring possession of an object conferred immunity from the criminal law on the party receiving possession, for subsequent misuse or misappropriation of the entrusted object. This rule was fundamental in defining the contours of larceny as well as the boundary between larceny and the newer offenses that developed in the eighteenth and nineteenth centuries.

The second structural principle of the common law was the implicit rule that criminal liability should attach to all conduct conforming to a collective image of acting like a thief and only to such conduct. In its expansive aspect, this principle meant that acting like a thief created a prima facie case of liability. In its limiting aspect, the rule meant that objectively unincriminating conduct was not subject to criminal sanctions. Thus, if the actor's intent to steal did not manifest itself in an externally identifiable act of stealing, no larceny could be committed, and, therefore, alternative proof of the actor's criminal intent would be irrelevant.

The premise of the traditional approach to larceny was that it was possible to perceive thievery directly as an event in the world and that the courts should rely on this unanalyzed perception in framing the law of theft. Modern legal theory rejects unanalyzed perceptions as a proper source of law. Today we are inclined to analyze the phenomenon of theft into the twin elements of harm and intent. The harm is the unlicensed acquisition of another's property; the intent is defined derivatively as the intent to effect this harm. The implication of so analyzing the crime of theft is that no particular conduct is necessary in order to prove the required intent. Intent may be established by a variety of means, including confessions, admissions, past criminal conduct, and other circumstantial evidence, all of which presuppose an intrusive and open-ended investigation into the life of the accused.

These two approaches to the law of larceny merit our detailed attention, for they signal two clashing conceptions of the proper scope of the criminal law. The traditional approach reflected a deep commitment to working out the realm of public harms, subject to criminal prosecution, and the realm of private harms, subject only to redress by means of private actions. The view that some harms do not meet the threshold of potentially criminal events remains one of the background assumptions of the legal system. . . . This is reflected in our taking for granted that cheating in the university should not be a crime. The principle of possessorial immunity analogously expressed the privacy of harms that occurred in the context of relationships in which one party entrusted an object to another. Further, the limitation of liability to conduct that appeared manifestly to be thievery exempted another set of deprivations from the scope of the criminal law. . . . Rejecting both possessorial immunity and the principle of objective criminality, the modern law of theft offenses verges on treating every deprivation of property as a public harm.

It is important to realize that an act of thieving might endanger a range of interests other than wealth. In the traditional view, the thief upset the social order not only by threatening property, but by violating the general sense of security and well-being of the community. . . . Similarly, the harm in improper acquisitions by employees, later punished as embezzlement, was traditionally thought to be a breach of trust. Thus, the harm in both larceny and embezzlement was primarily relational: The thief endangered the established order of the community; the embezzler breached a particular relationship of confidence with his employer. The transition to the modern conception of theft witnessed the dissolution of these relational aspects of larceny and embezzlement. Both crimes came to be seen primarily as offenses against property interests. . . . [T]he dishonest displacement of wealth from one person to another therefore becomes a public harm. This transition in the concept of harm and in the nature of theft as a crime lay behind the nineteenth century misunderstanding of the distinctions worked out in the traditional approach to larceny.

See the exchange between Weinreb, Manifest Criminality, Criminal Intent, and the "Metamorphosis of Larceny," 90 Yale L.J. 294 (1980), and Fletcher, Manifest Criminality, Criminal Intent, and the Metamorphosis of Lloyd Weinreb, 90 Yale L.J. 319 (1980).

1. Trespassory Takings

COMMONWEALTH v. TLUCHAK
Superior Court of Pennsylvania
166 Pa. Super. 16, 70 A.2d 657 (1950)

RENO, J. Appellants, husband and wife, separately appealed from convictions for larceny. The court below overruled their motions for new trials and arrest of judgment. The husband was sentenced to pay a fine of $50 and make restitution. Sentence was suspended in the wife's case.

The case arose out of a real estate transaction. By a written instrument appellants agreed to sell their farm to the prosecutor and his wife. The agreement did not include any personal property but it did cover: "All buildings, plumbing, heating, lighting fixtures, screens, storm sash, shades, blinds, awnings, shrubbery and plants." The purchasers took possession on June 14, 1946, and discovered that certain articles which had been on the premises at the time the agreement of sale was executed were missing. They were a commode which had never been attached and lay on the back porch in its shipping crate, an unattached washstand which had been stored in a bedroom, a hay carriage used in the barn, an electric stove cord extending from the switch box in the cellar to the kitchen, and 30 or 35 peach trees. These articles were charged in the indictment as subjects of the larceny.

The Commonwealth contended that the articles which were not covered by the written contract had been sold by an oral agreement between the parties. Appellants denied the oral agreement; denied the sale of the personal property; denied taking the trees; admitted they took the hay carriage; and as to all the articles which they took they contended that they were taken under a claim of right and therefore not feloniously. The jury found against them and, although they contend that the evidence is not sufficient in law to sustain a conviction, we shall assume, for the purpose of this decision, that the testimony established a *sale* of the personal property by appellants to the prosecutor and his wife. That is, that appellants sold but failed or refused to deliver the goods to the purchasers. Are sellers who refuse or fail to deliver goods sold to their purchasers guilty of larceny?

. . . Appellants had possession of the goods, not mere custody of them. The evidence indicates that they were allowed to retain possession without trick or artifice and without fraudulent intent to convert them. Presumably title passed upon payment of the purchase price; nevertheless appellants had lawful possession thereafter. "One who is in lawful possession of the goods or money of another cannot commit larceny by feloniously converting them to his own use, for the reason that larceny, being a criminal trespass on the right of possession,

. . . cannot be committed by one who, being invested with that right, is consequently incapable of trespassing on it." 52 C.J.S., Larceny, §31; and see §1.

An extensive research failed to uncover a Pennsylvania case in which the rule was applied to a factual situation similar to that at bar. But the principle has been recognized; e.g., in Com. v. Quinn, 144 Pa. Super. 400, 408, 19 A.2d 526, 530, this Court approved instructions to a jury wherein it was said:

> But a person may come into possession of somebody else's property in a legal way and if he, being so in possession of the property in a legal way converts it to his own use or withholds it from the owner so that the owner is deprived of the use thereof which he should have, then, though the defendant could not be guilty of larceny because he received it legally, he may be guilty of fraudulent conversion because after having received it he has deprived the owner of his use of it. . . .

As suggested, appellants may have been guilty of fraudulent conversion, or of larceny by bailee *if* the theory is accepted that a vendor retaining possession of goods sold by him becomes constructively a bailee of the purchaser, and criminally culpable for a failure to deliver them to his purchaser. Appellants were indicted for larceny only, and of that they clearly were not guilty. . . .

Judgments and sentences reversed and appellants discharged without delay.

NOTE ON ASPORTATION

Larceny, both at common law and under statutory formulations, requires a carrying away (asportation) as well as a trespassory taking. While courts have substantially minimized the significance of this requirement by holding that any movement of the thing, no matter how slight, is sufficient, problems still may arise. Consider State v. Patton, 364 Mo. 1044, 271 S.W.2d 560 (1954). Defendant purported to sell concrete building blocks, not his own, to an innocent purchaser, who himself carried the blocks away. May defendant be held for larceny? A few courts would answer in the negative because of the absence of an asportation. See, e.g., Ridgell v. State, 110 Ark. 606, 162 S.W. 773 (1914); State v. Laborde, 202 La. 59, 11 So. 2d 404 (1942); People v. Gillis, 6 Utah 84, 21 P. 404 (1889). The majority, however, as in State v. Patton, supra, turn the trick by finding the purchaser to be the innocent agent of the seller and imputing his acts to defendant. See Annot., 144 A.L.R. 1383 (1942). Can this be analytically defended?

The New York Court of Appeals in People v. Alamo, 34 N.Y.2d 453, 358 N.Y.S.2d 375 (1974), dispensed with the requirement of an actual movement of the object in a case where defendant entered a stranger's car, turned on the lights and started the engine. The court upheld the trial court's instruction that the jury might find theft of the car in these circumstances even if defendant had not moved the vehicle (assuming, of course, they found the requisite intent to steal it.) The court read the traditional doctrine requiring an asportation as reflecting a concern that the crucial elements of possession and control were established. Comparing pickpocket cases where some movement of the seized object had been held to be required, the court stated (358 N.Y.S.2d at 379, 381):

The actions needed to gain possession and control over a wallet, including movement of the wallet which, in itself, is merely an element tending to show possession and control, are not necessarily the actions needed to gain possession and control of any automobile. A wallet, or a diamond ring, or a safe are totally inert objects susceptible of movement only by physical lifting or shoving by the thief. An automobile, however, is itself an instrument of transportation and when activated comes within the total possession and control of the operator. In this situation movement or motion is not essential to control. Absent any evidence that the vehicle is somehow fastened or immovable because of a mechanical defect, the thief has taken command of the object of the larceny. He has, in the words of subdivision 1 of section 155.05 of the Penal Law, wrongfully "taken" the property from its owner surely as much so as had the thief in [the pickpocket case]. . . .

The Model Penal Code eliminates the requirement of an asportation and substitutes the requirement that the defendant "exercise unlawful control" over the movable property. Section 223.2(1). The Comment to this section (American Law Institute, Model Penal Code and Commentaries, Pt. II, Comment at 164 (1980)) states:

Since larceny was generally a felony and attempt a misdemeanor, important differences in procedure and punishment turned on the criminologically insignificant fact of slight movement of the object of the theft. Under §5.01 of the Model Code, and in modern criminal law generally, differences in penal consequences between attempt and completed crime are minimized, so that it becomes less important where the line is drawn between them. It is clear, moreover, that similar penalties for the attempt and the completed offense make obsolete any reference to the concept of "asportation"; the same penal consequences follow whether or not an "asportation" has occurred.

Most revised codes follow this lead. Id. at 165.

TOPOLEWSKI v. STATE
Supreme Court of Wisconsin
130 Wis. 244, 109 N.W. 1037 (1906)

[The accused arranged with Dolan, who owed him money and was an employee of the Plankinton Packing Company, to place three barrels of the company's meat on the loading platform, the plan being that accused would load the barrels on his wagon and drive away as if he were a customer. Dolan carried out his end of the plan after informing the company's representatives and receiving their instructions to feign cooperation. Accused took the barrels as planned and was arrested, charged, and convicted of stealing the barrels of meat.]

MARSHALL, J. [after stating the facts.] . . . Did the agreement in legal effect with the accused to place the property of the packing company on the loading platform, where it could be appropriated by the accused, if he was so disposed and was not interfered with in so doing, though his movements in that regard were known to the packing company, and his taking of the property, his efforts to that end being facilitated as suggested, constitute consent to such appropriation?

The case is very near the border line, if not across it, between consent and nonconsent to the taking of the property. Reg. v. Lawrence, 4 Cox C.C. 438, it was held that if the property was delivered by a servant to the defendant by the master's direction the offense cannot be larceny, regardless of the purpose of the defendant. In this case the property was not only placed on the loading platform, as was usual in delivering such goods to customers, with knowledge that the accused would soon arrive, having a formed design to take it, but the packing company's employé in charge of the platform, Ernst Klotz, was instructed that the property was placed there for a man who would call for it. Klotz from such statement had every reason to infer, when the accused arrived and claimed the right to take the property, that he was the one referred to and that it was proper to make delivery to him and he acted accordingly. While he did not physically place the property, or assist in doing so, in the wagon, his standing by, witnessing such placing by the accused, and then assisting him in arranging the wagon, as the evidence shows he did, and taking the order, in the usual way, from the accused as to the disposition of the fourth barrel, and his conduct in respect thereto amounted, practically, to a delivery of the three barrels to the accused.

In Rex v. Egginton, 2 P. & P. 508, we have a very instructive case on the subject under discussion here. A servant informed his master that he had been solicited to aid in robbing the latter's house. By the master's direction the servant opened the house, gave the would-be thieves access thereto and took them to the place where the intended subject of the larceny had been laid in order that they might take it. All this was done with a view to the apprehension of the guilty parties after the accomplishment of their purpose. The servant by direction of the master not only gave access to the house but afforded the would-be thieves every facility for taking the property, and yet the court held that the crime of larceny was complete, because there was no direction to the servant to deliver the property to the intruders or consent to their taking it. They were left free to commit the larceny, as they had purposed doing, and the way was made easy for them to do so, but they were neither induced to commit the crime, nor was any act essential to the offense done by any one but themselves.

. . . We cannot well escape the conclusion that this case falls under the condemnation of the rule that where the owner of property by himself or his agent, actually or constructively, aids in the commission of the offense, as intended by the wrongdoer, by performing or rendering unnecessary some act in the transaction essential to the offense, the would-be criminal is not guilty of all the elements of the offense. . . .

The logical basis for the doctrine above discussed is that there can be no larceny without a trespass. So if one procures his property to be taken by another intending to commit larceny, or delivers his property to such other, the latter purposing to commit such crime, the element of trespass is wanting and the crime not fully consummated however plain may be the guilty purpose of the one possessing himself of such property. That does not militate against a person's being free to set a trap to catch one whom he suspects of an intention to commit the crime of larceny, but the setting of such trap must not go further than to afford the would-be thief the amplest opportunity to carry out his purpose, formed without such inducement on the part of the owner of the property, as to put him in the position of having consented to the taking. If I induce one to come and take my property and then place it before him to be taken, and he takes it with criminal intent, or if knowing that one intends to take my property I deliver it to him and he takes it with such intent, the essential element of trespass involving nonconsent requisite to a completed offense of larceny does not characterize the transaction, regardless of the fact that the moral turpitude involved is no less than it would be if such essential were present. Some writers in treating this subject give so much attention to condemning the deception practiced to facilitate and encourage the commission of a crime by one supposed to have such a purpose in view, that the condemnation is liable to be viewed as if the deception were sufficient to excuse the would-be criminal, or to preclude his being prosecuted; that there is a question of good morals involved as to both parties to the transaction and that the wrongful participation of the owner of the property renders him and the public incapable of being heard to charge the person he has entrapped with the offense of larceny. That is wrong. It is the removal from the completed transaction, which from the mental attitude of the would-be criminal may have all the ingredients of larceny, from the standpoint of the owner of the property of the element of trespass or nonconsent. When such element does not characterize a transaction involving the full offense of larceny so far as concerns the mental purpose of such would-be criminal is concerned, is often not free from difficulty and courts of review should incline quite strongly to support the decision of the trial judge in respect to the matter and not disturb it except in a clear case. It seems that there is such a case before us.

The judgment is reversed, and the cause remanded for a new trial.

NOTES

1. The police had been troubled by a large number of car thefts in a particular locality. An informer approached a police officer and told him that defendant, Jarrott, proposed that he join him in the theft and sale of automobiles. The informer was instructed to play along. Later the informer informed the police officer that Jarrott stated he wanted to get a 1925 coupé and indicated the general time and place that Jarrott, with his ostensible help, planned to steal a car. The police officer thereupon arranged for his own coupé to be present at that time and place. He left it with its parking lights on and with the key in the ignition, concealing himself in the back end. This was known to the informer. Jarrott and the informer later appeared. Jarrott saw the car and proposed they steal it. They entered and drove the car to a car lot, the informer doing the driving on Jarrott's protestation that he could not drive. While Jarrott and the buyer were haggling over the price, the policeman climbed out from the car and made his arrest. Defendant appealed a conviction of larceny on the grounds (1) that the car was never taken from the personal possession of the owner and (2) that the taking occurred with the consent of the owner. What result? Jarrott v. State, 108 Tex. Crim. 427, 1 S.W.2d 619 (1927). Could defendant have also argued that since the informer drove the car it was he who took it and not defendant because the acts of the informer, as a feigned accomplice, could not be attributed to defendant? See State v. Hayes, pages 634-635 supra.

Concerning the defense of entrapment by police agents, which is raised in this Note, see Model Penal Code §2.13, Appendix to this casebook; Annot., Larceny: entrapment or consent, 10 A.L.R.3d 1121 (1966).

2. In United States v. Bryan, 483 F.2d 88 (3d Cir. 1973), the U.S. Lines, on the instruction of the FBI, permitted its agents to deliver a shipment of whiskey to Echols, who was believed to be posing as an agent of the consignee. The court rejected the argument that Echols committed no crime because the U.S. Lines consented to the taking, stating (at 90-92):

> The crime alleged here is violation of 18 U.S.C. §659, which provides penalties for, inter alia, "[w]hoever embezzles, steals, or unlawfully takes, carries away, or conceals . . . from any . . . platform or depot . . . with intent to convert to his own use any goods . . . which constitute an interstate . . . shipment of freight." The crime of stealing under 18 U.S.C. §659 has been given a broad construction, free from the technical requirements of common law larceny. United States v. DeNormand, 149 F.2d 622, 624 (2d Cir. 1945).[1] A trial court instruction that the jury need only find "an unlawful taking of the goods by the defendants," was found sufficient in *DeNormand*. The consent to the removal of the goods by U.S. Lines personnel in this case does not demonstrate the absence of an unlawful taking. In reviewing the record to determine if there was an unlawful taking, the relevant question involves not the state of mind of personnel of U.S. Lines, but rather the state of mind of defendants.
>
> We therefore find no difficulty in reconciling our conclusion that a crime was committed here with the statements in United States v. Cohen, 274 F. 596, 597 (3d Cir. 1921):
>
>> To constitute "stealing" there must be an unlawful taking . . . with intent to convert to the use of the taker and permanently deprive the owner.
>
> and in Vaughn v. United States, 272 F. 451, 452 (9th Cir. 1921), that in a case of larceny, the corpus delicti consists of two elements:
>
>> First, that the property was lost by the owner; and, second, that it was lost by a felonious taking.
>
> Both formulations of the elements of stealing concentrate on the state of mind of the criminal, not upon that of the possessor of the goods taken. In cases where the lawful possessor indicated to the taker that permission was granted for the taking, a finding of commission of a crime would be unlikely. That, however, is not the case sub judice. There is no proof that U.S. Lines led defendants to believe they had permission to take the goods.

3. In the *Topolewski* case, would it have been possible to convict defendant of an attempt to commit larceny? See Regina v. Miller and Page, 49 Crim. App. 241 (1965), holding affirmatively. See The Case of Lady Eldon's French Lace, pages 604-608 supra.

4. See Fletcher, The Metamorphosis of Larceny, 89 Harv. L. Rev. 469, 491-498 (1976), for an interpretation of the *Topolewski* case as a modern survival

---

1. The crime detailed in 18 U.S.C. §659 is therefore different from that detailed in 18 U.S.C. §2113(b), stealing from a bank. The latter statute describes common law larceny and thus requires a "trespassory taking," a taking without consent. Bennett v. United States, 399 F.2d 740, 742 (9th Cir. 1968). While conviction for violation of 18 U.S.C. §2113(b) would be impossible under the consensual circumstances found in the present case, the limitations of the common law do not prevent conviction for violation of 18 U.S.C. §659. See also United States v. Patton, 120 F.2d 73 (3d Cir. 1941).

of the common law commitment to the requirement of "manifest criminality" ("acting like a thief"). The problem in *Topolewski* is also illuminatingly discussed in Williams, Theft, Consent and Illegality: Some Problems, [1977] Crim. L. Rev. 327, 330 et seq.

NOTE ON ROBBERY AND EXTORTION

Note, A Rationale of the Law of Aggravated Theft, 54 Colum. L. Rev. 84-86 (1954): Obviously, larceny may be perpetrated in many ways: a pocket may be picked or a man may be killed to obtain a bankroll. In the former situation, the sole evil is the misappropriation of property; in the latter, bodily injury also results. Consequently, to protect not only against misappropriation but also against injuries which may result from peculiarly dangerous means devised for accomplishing misappropriation, there developed the law of aggravated theft. At common law the only substantive crime embodied within this law was robbery, a larceny accomplished by violence or threat of immediate violence to the person of the victim. In time it was acknowledged that men may be intimidated by threats other than those foreboding bodily harm. As a result, modern legislation has extended the substantive content of aggravated theft, complementing robbery with the crime of extortion. . . .

Entirely a creature of legislative enactment, extortion now exists as a substantive crime in forty-seven states, and in each there is also a robberty statute. The first inquiry, then, concerns the manner in which these crimes differ. The statutory definitions of robbery restate in essence the common law definition: the felonious and forcible taking of property from the person of another or in his presence, against his will, by violence or putting in fear. Extortion statutes are generally of two types. The majority of jurisdictions treat as the substantive crime of extortion the making of certain specified threats for the purpose of obtaining property, but a substantial number require an actual misappropriation with the owner's consent. The differences between the robbery and extortion statutes, therefore, depend to a certain extent on the particular jurisdiction. In jurisdictions following either extortion pattern, robbery requires a taking from the person or in his presence, while for extortion the intimidation is crucial and the place of the taking immaterial. In states which do not require more than the threat for extortion, the fact of misappropriation is relevant only to robbery. And in those states where misappropriation is essential to extortion, there is a distinction based on the factor of consent. The robbery statutes speak of the absence of consent; the extortion statutes require its presence. But the willingness to surrender the property in any case is only an apparent willingness since in both instances the victim must choose between alternative evils, namely, the surrender of his property or the execution of the threat. Only if the taking is accomplished by violence to the person of the victim is this apparent consent precluded, for then the victim is presented with no choice. Thus the definitional distinctions between robbery and extortion are extremely tenuous.[15] . . .

---

15. Often the conviction is for extortion where seemingly the facts constitute robbery. See People v. Jacobsen, 11 Cal. App. 2d 728, 54 P.2d 748 (1936).

California Penal Code: Section 211. Definition. Robbery defined. Robbery is the felonious taking of personal property in the possession of another, from his person or immediate presence, and against his will, accomplished by means of force or fear.

Section 212. Fear Defined. The fear mentioned in Section 211 may be either:

1. The fear of an unlawful injury to the person or property of the person robbed, or of any relative of his or member of his family; or,

2. The fear of an immediate and unlawful injury to the person or property of anyone in the company of the person robbed at the time of the robbery.

Section 518. Definition. Extortion is the obtaining of property from another, with his consent, or the obtaining of an official act of a public officer, induced by a wrongful use of force or fear, or under color of official right.

Section 519. Fear Used to Extort: Threats Inducing. Fear, such as will constitute extortion, may be induced by a threat, either:

1. To do an unlawful injury to the person or property of the individual threatened or of a third person; or,

2. To accuse the individual threatened, or any relative of his, or member of his family, of any crime; or,

3. To expose, or to impute to him or them any deformity, disgrace or crime; or,

4. To expose any secret affecting him or them.

Model Penal Code: Section 222.1. Robbery. [See Appendix for text of this section.]
   Section 223.4. Theft by Extortion.[a] [See Appendix for text of this section.]

2. Misappropriation

NOLAN v. STATE
Maryland Court of Appeals
213 Md. 298, 131 A.2d 851 (1957)

[Defendant was convicted of embezzlement on the following facts. He was the office manager of the Federal Discount Corporation, a finance company engaged in the business of making loans and collections. The evidence showed that he appropriated money from his employer as follows: As payments were received from customers, the payments would be placed in the cash drawer. At the end of the day, an accomplice would prepare a report showing the daily

---

a. American Law Institute, Model Penal Code and Commentaries, Pt. II, Comment to §223.4, at 202 n. 1 (1980) observes: "At common law, robbery included taking not only by force but also by threat of force or even by threat of certain other serious harms. To be guilty of robbery under the Model Penal Code, the defendant must threaten immediate and serious harm. Other coercive deprivation falls under §223.4."

See also id. at 208: "There is no requirement in Section 223.4 that the threatened harm be 'unlawful.' The actor may be privileged or even obligated to inflict the harm threatened; yet, if he employs the threat to coerce a transfer of property for his own benefit, he clearly belongs among those who should be subject to punishment for theft. The case of the policeman who has a duty to arrest illustrates the point. His threat to arrest unless the proposed subject of the arrest pays him money should be treated as extortionate even though the failure to arrest would be dereliction of duty."

cash receipts. Defendant would then appropriate some of the cash from the drawer, and his accomplice would recompute the adding tapes to equal the remaining cash.]

COLLINS, J. . . . The appellant . . . contends that . . . the evidence produced made the crime larceny and not embezzlement, as charged in the indictment.

. . . It is stated in 2 Wharton's Criminal Law, 12th Ed., pgs. 1589, 1590, that, if the case is larceny at common law because the money was taken from the prosecutor's possession, the charge for embezzlement fails. The embezzlement statutes were passed, not to cover any cause within the common law range of larceny, but to cover new cases outside of that range. If the goods were taken from the owner's possession, the crime is larceny, not embezzlement. Goods which have reached their destination are constructively in the owner's possession although he may not yet have touched them and, hence, after such termination of transit, the servant who converts them is guilty of larceny, not of embezzlement. It is there stated at page 1591: "No inconvenience can arise from the maintenance of this distinction, since it is allowable *as well as prudent* to join a count for larceny to that for embezzlement. But great inconvenience would follow from the acceptance of the principle that the embezzlement statutes absorb all cases of larceny by servants." (Italics supplied.) . . .

From the testimony offered by the State, Federal had provided a cash drawer in which the money was deposited as received. Mr. Abrams and Mr. Wolk, officers of the company, also accepted payments and had access to the money drawer in which all the money was placed. The money was not taken by Mr. Nolan until it had been placed in the cash drawer and balanced at the end of the day. When taken by appellant, as alleged, the cash was in the possession of Federal. We must therefore conclude that under the authorities cited and under the testimony in this case there was not sufficient evidence to find the defendant guilty of embezzlement. The case will be remanded for further proceedings in order that the State, if it deems proper, may try the defendant on an indictment for embezzlement and larceny, if such an indictment is returned against the defendant.

PRESCOTT, J. (concurring). It is unfortunate not to be able to concur fully in such an able and carefully prepared opinion as that filed by a majority of this Court. However, as it seems to me that it reestablishes many of the tenuous niceties between larceny and embezzlement with which the early English cases are replete, and that it unnecessarily will embarrass many future prosecutions although the accused palpably may be guilty, I have decided to state the reasons that prevent my complete concurrence.

It seems as though the present case properly can be decided by reference to our present statute on embezzlement alone, without the necessity of the citation of other authorities. . . . Our statute, Art. 27, §154 of the Maryland Code 1951, reads:

> Whosoever being a . . . servant . . . shall fraudulently embezzle any money . . . which . . . . shall be . . . taken into possession by him, for . . . his master or employer, shall be deemed to have feloniously stolen the same from his master or employer, although such money . . . was not received into the possession of such master . . . otherwise than by the actual possession of his . . . servant. . . .

A simple down-to-earth application of the facts presented in the record discloses that every element required in the statute is fully and completely covered. It is conceded that the nature of his employment is within the terms of the statute, and the evidence established to the satisfaction of the jury that the money was taken into his possession for and on behalf of his employer, and that he fraudulently appropriated it to his own use. The statute seems to require no more.

But the majority of the Court feel that the English decisions and other authorities (although apparently there is no Maryland case so ruling) require a holding that because the money went into the drawers before its fraudulent conversion, the offense was larceny and not embezzlement. If this be so, it seems to place the law in an unfortunate and somewhat indefensible position. When a man is in complete charge and control of an office and the law says to him: "If you steal your employer's money before it is placed in a drawer (under your charge and control) you are guilty of embezzlement, but, if you or someone under you places the money in that drawer (still under your charge and control) and then you steal it, you are guilty of larceny, and larceny alone," does it seem right? Could not it be said with just as much reason, logic and justification that if you steal money and place it in your left pocket, you are guilty of embezzlement, but, if you place it in your right pocket, you are guilty of larceny and larceny alone? Would it not be a sounder policy to follow the example of such cases as Calkins v. State, 18 Ohio St. 366. . . . [T]he Ohio Court was requested to make a rather tenuous holding under its embezzlement statute as to whether or not certain property was "under (the) care" of the defendant, but the Court refused to do so, and said: "There is no more reason why courts should allow themselves to be misled by mere names and shadows in the administration of justice in criminal, than in civil cases." . . .

The apprehension that I have concerning the ruling in this case is aptly stated in Komito v. State, 90 Ohio St. 352, 107 N.E. 762, 763, where it is said:

"Courts sometimes indulge in an *ethereal refinement* between larceny and embezzlement that in practical operation very often nullifies these statutes. The only benefit accruing from such a policy results in the rather doubtful advantage of the *criminal escaping his just punishment.*" (Emphasis supplied.)

Thus, we find ourselves in the peculiar position of following the subtle reasoning developed in the English decisions for the purpose of bringing the guilty to the bar of justice; but, in so doing, we directly come to their aid and comfort. Probably the solution of this rather difficult problem lies in the course followed by several of our sister States (and as was done in England) where the legislative power has provided that under an indictment for larceny, or for larceny in one count and embezzlement in another, there may be a conviction of either offense.

NOTE ON EMBEZZLEMENT

The very early conception of larceny as a vi et armis trespassory taking from the possession of the owner invito domino was thought to preclude conviction of persons who physically and lawfully held property of the owner, as, for example, servants, guests, and employees. Since they themselves had "possession" of the owner's goods, their making off with them could not constitute larceny.

This was changed through the course of adjudication by development of the concept of "legal" (or "constructive") possession as distinguished from mere custody. The development was gradual, and there was considerable disputation as to whether, for example, a servant had mere custody or possession when the master entrusted property to him to be taken a distance from the house, as to a market, or when certain property, perhaps jewels, were expressly entrusted to a servant. See Holmes, J., in Commonwealth v. Ryan, 155 Mass. 523, 528, 30 N.E. 364, 365 (1892). Such doubts were resolved by statute in 1529 (21 Hen. VIII, ch. 7) and by later cases so that it soon became established that "a servant, whether at the master's home or elsewhere, never has legal possession of such property of his master as he controls in his capacity as servant." 2 W. O. Russell, Crime 1035 (11th ed., Turner, 1958). A servant, therefore, who made off with his master's goods, committed larceny from the possession of the master. By analogous reasoning, similar results were reached with guests.

But what of the case in which the servant is given goods by a third party for delivery to his master? Could it be said that here as well, when a servant misappropriated the goods, he was taking them from the possession of the master and was hence guilty of larceny? The answer was no, since the master did not have possession and the third party voluntarily gave up possession. See 1 M. Hale, Pleas of the Crown 667.

But a distinction was soon developed where the servant deposited the goods or money so received in a place provided by the master and subject to the master's control prior to the act of misappropriation. In such a case, the possession passed to the master, and the servant retained only custody; hence a dishonest appropriation was larceny. But there was again much disputation as to precisely what manner and place of deposit sufficed to justify such a conclusion. In Nolan v. State, supra, for example, defendant's placement of the receipts in the cash drawer was held to transfer "possession" to the employer. Holmes, J., in Commonwealth v. Ryan, supra, reached a contrary result on similar facts (except that the money was picked up by defendant just a few minutes after he deposited it) and sustained an embezzlement conviction, stating (30 N.E. at 364):

> [T]he judge was right in charging the jury that, if the defendant, before he placed the money in the drawer, intended to appropriate it, and with that intent simply put it in the drawer for his own convenience in keeping it for himself, that would not make his appropriation of it just afterwards larceny. The distinction may be arbitrary, but, as it does not affect the defendant otherwise than by giving him an opportunity, whichever offense he was convicted of, to contend that he should have been convicted of the other, we have the less uneasiness in applying it.

A subsequent statutory development of great importance was precipitated by the decision in Bazeley's Case, 168 Eng. Rep. 517 (1799). Bazeley was a bank teller who pocketed a £1000 note received from a customer for deposit. The court found no larceny since the employer did not acquire possession of the note but only a right to possess it; at the time of the conversion, it was in the legal possession of the teller. It would have been otherwise, it was said, if Bazeley had first deposited the note in a drawer kept for this purpose by the employer. Largely to fill the gap in the law dramatized by this case, the first embezzlement statute was passed in 1799 (39 Geo. III, ch. 85) providing:

if any servant or clerk, or any person employed for the purpose in the capacity of a servant or clerk, to any person or persons whomsoever, or to any body corporate or politick, shall, by virtue, of such employment, receive or take into his possession any money, goods, bond, bill, note, banker's draft, or other valuable security, or effects, for or in the name or on the account of his master or masters, or employer or employers, and shall fraudulently embezzle, secrete, or make away with the same, or any part thereof, every such offender shall be deemed to have feloniously stolen the same.

Modern cases, such as Nolan v. State, supra, are products of and explicable in terms of, if not justified by, this history.

Additional enactments following the original embezzlement statute gradually extended the categories of persons capable of embezzling to others than servants or clerks: brokers, merchants, bankers, attorneys, and other agents in 1812; factors in 1827; trustees under express trusts in 1857; etc. American embezzlement statutes still bear the mark of this piecemeal legislative development. See State v. Riggins, page 935 infra.

STATE v. TAYLOR

Supreme Court of Utah
14 Utah 2d 107, 378 P.2d 352 (1963)

CROCKETT, J. Defendant appeals from a conviction after trial to the court upon the charge that he: on or about the 31st day of October, 1961, committed a felony, to-wit: embezzled money of a value exceeding $50.00 from Utah By-Products Company.

Defendant drove a truck for that company picking up scrap fat, meat and bones from butcher shops and cafes on a daily route. He would give each customer a slip showing the poundage of the items picked up and turn in a copy to the company, which would issue checks to the customers in payment. There was one exception to this procedure. Hill Field Air Force Base required payment in cash rather than by check. So the company would issue a check for the value of scraps, payable to the defendant, who would cash the check and make the required payment.

On October 31, 1961, the defendant made out a slip showing a pickup at Hill Field of bones and scraps totaling $84.25. It is undisputed that he delivered these items to the company, for which he received a check for that amount payable to himself. The difficulty exists because those particular scraps did not come from, and the proceeds of the check were not paid to, the Hill Field account. Inquiry brought forth a confession by the defendant that he had, by issuing shorted weight slips to other customers, accumulated that amount of scrap and turned it in to obtain the money for himself.

No apology can be offered for the defendant's lack of honesty, nor for his disloyalty to his employer. As to transactions where it might be ascertained that he cheated others, he is undoubtedly guilty of wrong. But the manner in which he may be held accountable therefore is not our concern here.

In a criminal proceeding it is not sufficient to show merely that the accused has been dishonest, or that he is a cheater, or otherwise of bad character. He is entitled to be charged with a specific crime so that he may know the "nature and cause of the accusation against him." And the State must prove substantially as charged the offense it relies upon for conviction.

The judgment must stand or fall upon the proof, or lack thereof, of the crime with which the State charged the defendant, essayed to prove, and of which he stands convicted: i.e., that of embezzling $84.25 from the Utah By-Products Company by taking a check for that sum from the company the proceeds of which he was expected to deliver to Hill Field, and failing to do so. It is important to keep in mind that in that transaction the company received the exact items and poundage of scraps its money was intended to pay for; and that Hill Field had no such money coming. It is thus plain that neither lost anything in the transaction so the crime as charged and relied upon for conviction was not proved.

Another significant aspect of this situation is that defendant's only deception or fraud upon the company was in misrepresenting the source from which he obtained the scraps. Fundamental in the nature of embezzlement is the coming into possession of property honestly, "by virtue of one's trust," and then converting it to one's own use in violation of that trust. This is in contrast to situations where, as here, the essential wrong is committed in obtaining possession of the property. Where the intent to take the property of another is formed before the taking, and is coupled with some deception or trick to acquire possession of the property, the crime is not embezzlement. One could not embezzle that which he had already stolen. Since the State did not prove the charge upon which the conviction is grounded, it is reversed.

BURNS v. STATE
Supreme Court of Wisconsin
145 Wis. 373, 128 N.W. 987 (1911)

[A constable upon taking an insane man in charge after pursuit received from another of the pursuers a roll of money that had been thrown away by the man in his flight. The jury, having heard evidence supporting the accusation that the constable had misappropriated the funds, convicted him of larceny by bailee under a Wisconsin statute, which is reproduced in the text of the opinion.]

MARSHALL, J. . . . . Error is assigned because the court instructed the jury to the effect that, if the accused converted to his own use any of Adamsky's money, he did so as bailee. It is suggested that the court should have defined the term "bailee," as used in the statute, and left it to the jury to find the fact as to whether the circumstances satisfied such statute or not.

A court may properly instruct a jury in a criminal case, as well as any other, respecting any fact, or facts, established by the evidence beyond any room for reasonable controversy, and when such evidentiary facts exist establishing, beyond any room for reasonable controversy, an essential of any ultimate conclusion sought, it is not harmful error, if error at all, to treat such essential as having been proven, as the court here did in saying that the accused was a bailee of whatever of Adamsky's money came to his possession.

It seems to be thought that a bailment was not established by the evidence because some sort of contract inter partes was essential thereto. No particular ceremony or actual meeting of minds is necessary to the creation of a bailment. If one, without the trespass which characterizes ordinary larceny, comes into possession of any personalty of another and is in duty bound to exercise some degree of care to preserve and restore the thing to such other or to some person for that other, or otherwise account for the property as that of such other, according to circumstances, — he is a bailee. It is the element of lawful possession, however created, and duty to account for the thing as the property of another, that creates the bailment, regardless of whether such possession is based on contract in the ordinary sense or not.

It is said, generally, in the books, that a bailment is created by delivery of the personalty to one person by another to be dealt with in specie as the property of such other person under a contract, express or implied, but the word "contract" is used in a broad sense. The mutuality essential to the contractual feature may be created by operation of law as well as by the acts of the parties with intention to contract.

So it makes no difference whether the thing be intrusted to a person by the owner, or another, or by some one for the owner or by the law to the same end. Taking possession without present intent to appropriate raises all the contractual elements essential to a bailment. So the person who bona fide recovers the property of another which has been lost, or irresponsibly cast away by an insane man, as in this case, is a bailee as much as if the same property were intrusted to such person by contract inter partes. In the latter case the contract creates the duty. In the former the law creates it. Such a situation is to be distinguished from that where one knowingly receives money paid him by mistake and fraudulently retains it. There the element of bona fide possession may be said not to exist and so the duty accompanied by such possession essential to a bailment not to have been created. . . .

The finder of property who voluntarily bona fide takes it into his possession, immediately, thereupon, has imposed upon him by law the duties of a depositary, the mildest type, as regards degree of duty, of bailee.

So the finder here of the cast-away money was clearly a bailee, and when his duties were voluntarily assumed by the accused he became such, and as there was no controversy in respect to such finding and assumption, the court's reference to the matter was proper.

The next suggestion in behalf of plaintiff in error is that, if the accused was guilty of any offense, it was that of having broken the package and extracted therefrom part of the contents for the purpose of appropriating it to his own use, and executed such purpose, thus committing the offense of larceny, not of conversion by a bailee. It is a sufficient answer thereto that the purpose of the statute [now §943.20(1)(b)] was to abolish the distinction between conversion by a bailee of an entire thing, as a quantity of property in a package of some kind, and the unlawful breaking of the package and conversion of part or all of the contents — whether preceded by the element of breaking bulk with intent to permanently deprive the owner of the thing appropriated or not, — making the latter a statutory class of larcenies, differing only from ordinary larcenies, by absence in the former of the element of trespass in gaining original possession, which is essential to the latter. The meaning of the statute, as indicated, seems very plain:

Whoever being a bailee of any chattel, money or valuable security shall fraudulently take or fraudulently convert the same to his own use or to the use of any person other than the owner thereof, although he shall not break bulk or otherwise determine the bailment, shall be guilty of larceny.

It follows that acquittal of the accused of the offense of larceny is not inconsistent with his conviction of the statute offense of larceny as bailee. . . .

NOTE ON THE MISAPPROPRIATING BAILEE

In the Note following Nolan v. State, supra, we briefly described the development of the possession-custody distinction as a means whereby certain kinds of misappropriation by persons lawfully holding the property of another came to be treated as larceny prior to the enactment of the embezzlement statutes, which eliminated the need for such judicial gap-filling. But just as this distinction proved inadequate to deal with the servant who received goods for his master from a third person, it proved inadequate to deal with the bailee who misappropriated his bailor's property, because the crucial significance of a bailment relation was the transfer of possession and not mere custody. See 5 Words and Phrases, Bailment, 48 (perm. ed.); 2 W. O. Russell, Crime 916 (12th ed., Turner, 1964). The resources of the early common law, however, were up to the task of bringing at least some bailee misappropriations within the scope of larceny. In the Carrier's Case, decided in 1473 (Y.B. 13 Edw. IV, f. 9, pl. 5), a carrier to whom a foreign merchant delivered a shipment for delivery to a consignee broke into the bales and decamped with the contents. The judges of the Star Chamber produced a variety of opinions but apparently reached no conclusion. The case was again argued before the judges in the Exchequer Chamber, who expressed several opinions as to the theory to govern the case. The majority apparently agreed that if the bailment has terminated, the former bailee who then takes the goods may be guilty of larceny. What was unclear was the theory on which defendant should be said to have terminated the bailment. Finally the judges, without stating their reasons, reported that a majority found that in the circumstances defendant committed larceny (2 W. O. Russell, Crime 917-918 (12th ed., Turner, 1964)). As Russell observes (at 918),[1]

Much later we find accepted by the courts the proposition that by breaking bulk the bailee determined [terminated] the bailment and having ceased thereby to be a bailee, in some strange manner lost possession of the property which had been bailed to him and so became a trespasser when he took any portion of the contents.

Stephen observed:

This has always appeared an extraordinary decision, as, to all common apprehension, theft of the whole thing bailed must determine the bailment quite as much as a theft of part of it. I think it obvious from the report that the decision was a

1. See also O. W. Holmes, The Common Law 224 (1946); Beale, The Borderland of Larceny, 6 Harv. L. Rev. 251 (1892); 2 E. H. East, Pleas of the Crown 695.

compromise intended to propitiate the chancellor and perhaps the King. This required a deviation from the common law, which was accordingly made, but was as slight as the judges could make it.

3 J. F. Stephen, History of the Criminal Law 139 (1883). The pragmatic basis for the decision suggested by Stephen was further developed by Professor Hall in his classic study of the case in Theft, Law and Society (2d ed. 1952), where the political, social and economic interests are explored. Hall concludes (at 93):

> On the one hand, the criminal law at the time is clear. On the other hand, the whole complex aggregate of political and economic conditions described above thrusts itself upon the court. The more powerful forces prevailed — that happened which in due course must have happened under the circumstances. The most powerful forces of the time were interrelated very intimately and at many points: the New Monarchy and the nouveau riche — the mercantile class; the business interests of both and the consequent need for a secure carrying trade; the wool and textile industry, the most valuable, by far, in all the realm; wool and cloth, the most important exports; these exports and the foreign trade; this trade and Southampton, chief trading city with the Latin countries for centuries; the numerous and very influential Italian merchants who bought English wool and cloth inland and shipped them from Southampton. The great forces of an emerging modern world, represented in the above phenomena, necessitated the elimination of a formula which had outgrown its usefulness. A new set of major institutions required a new rule. The law, lagging behind the needs of the times, was brought into more harmonious relationship with the other institutions by the decision rendered in the Carrier's Case.

At all events, the breaking-bulk device proved only a stopgap. It left without criminal sanction appropriations without breaking bulk as well as cases where the requirement of breaking was difficult to establish, as where the shipment consisted of separable units.[2] The remedy was again statutory, an act of 1857 (20 & 21 Vict., ch. 54, §4) creating the new crime of larceny by bailee, which placed the dishonest bailee on a par with the dishonest servant. American statutes today either retain similar provisions as a separate crime of larceny by bailee or include misappropriation by a bailee as an instance of embezzlement.

NOTES ON APPROPRIATION OF LOST PROPERTY AND PROPERTY TRANSFERRED BY MISTAKE

Where property dishonestly appropriated by a defendant comes into his or her possession through a mistake of the transferor, as by a mistake in the identity of the transferee, the character of the property, or the quantity being delivered, or through the defendant's finding property which the owner has lost, there is apparently no trespassory interference with possession required for larceny. Neither is there the employee or fiduciary relationship or the element of "entrust-

---

2. The breaking-bulk doctrine was supplemented as a means of dealing with dishonest bailees by the larceny-by-trick doctrine, whereby larceny could be established if the bailee used fraud in obtaining the goods. This is considered in the next section.

ing" required by the usual embezzlement statute.[3] Of what crime, then, may the dishonest accused be convicted?

1. As for lost property, an early partial solution was the distinction between lost property (that property unintentionally placed where found) and mislaid property (that property deliberately placed where found, the owner forgetting where he or she put it). In the latter case, the courts often found that "possession" never left the owner, so that when the finder appropriated it, the finder "took" it from the owner's possession. Regina v. Pierce, 6 Cox Crim. Cas. 117 (1852); State v. Courtsol, 89 Conn. 564, 94 A. 973 (1915). Even as to the former, however, it was eventually determined that the finder took from the constructive possession of the owner, and if at the time the finder appropriated the lost property he or she intended to convert it, knowing or having reason to believe he or she might discover the owner's identity, the finder was guilty of larceny. Penny v. State, 109 Ark. 343, 159 S.W. 1127 (1913); State v. Levy, 23 Minn. 104 (1876). It is generally held, however, that the felonious intent (to appropriate in the face of knowledge or means of knowing the owner's identity) must accompany the original finding and appropriation — otherwise there is no felonious taking. Long v. State, 33 Ala. App. 334, 33 So. 2d 382 (1948); State v. Belt, 125 S.C. 473, 119 S.E. 576 (1923).

Consider the solution to this problem proposed by the Model Penal Code and now adopted by many states. Section 223.5 provides:

> A person who comes into control of property of another that he knows to have been lost, mislaid, or delivered under a mistake as to the nature or amount of the property or the identity of the recipient is guilty of theft if, with purpose to deprive the owner thereof, he fails to take reasonable measures to restore the property to a person entitled to have it.

See American Law Institute, Model Penal Code and Commentaries, Pt. II, Comment to §223.5 at 228 (1980):

> The common-law view of larceny as an infringement of the possession of another required a determination of the actor's state of mind at the moment of finding. . . . The search for an initial fraudulent intent appears to be largely fictional, and in any event poses the wrong question. The realistic objective in this area is not to prevent initial appropriation but to compel subsequent acts to restore to the owner. The section therefore permits conviction even where the original taking was honest in the sense that the actor then intended to restore; if he subsequently changes his mind and determines to keep the property, he will then be guilty of theft.

2. In the case of dishonest appropriation of property delivered by mistake, there is again a twofold problem: first, finding the necessary taking from possession and second, finding a felonious intent coincident with the taking. The solution of the Model Penal Code, also now followed in many states, is §223.5, just quoted. The supporting Commentary states as follows (American Law Insti-

---

3. But in the case of finding, at least, the finder may be held for larceny by bailee or fraudulent conversion under statutes making the misappropriating bailee guilty of crime even where the property was not entrusted to him or her. See Burns v. State, pages 929-931 supra.

tute, Model Penal Code and Commentaries, Pt. II, Comment to §223.5 at 225-226 (1980)):

> [O]ne who accepts a $10 bill knowing that the other person thinks he is handing over a $1 bill acquires it without trespass or false pretense. Moreover, he may not be in any of the employee or fiduciary relations that were enumerated in the typical older embezzlement statutes. Consequently, special legislation or judicial sleight-of-hand was required to reach persons taking advantage of such mistakes.[2] Similarly, if the owner or his agent voluntarily hands the property over to the accused while laboring under a misapprehension as to the identity of the recipient, it requires strenuous manipulation of concepts to disregard the apparent transfer of title as well as possession and to hold that the accused is guilty of larceny because he committed a trespass against the transferor's possession. A prosecution for false pretenses may also be frustrated because the actor may not have created or reinforced the misimpression. Yet the recipient, knowing that the transfer to him is inadvertent, is in a moral and physical situation with respect to the property much like that of the finder of lost property. Moreover, he knows who is rightfully entitled to the property and can easily take steps to restore the property. Accordingly, Section 223.5 imposes theft sanctions against one in this situation who fails to take reasonable measures to restore. Most recent codes and proposals also specifically cover theft of misdelivered property. Some, however, are restricted to theft of lost or mislaid property.
>
> It is necessary to limit the reach of Section 223.5, on the other hand, in order to avoid impinging on certain types of tolerated sharp trading. For example, it is not proposed to punish the purchase of another's property at a bargain price on a mere showing that the buyer was aware that the seller was misinformed regarding the value of what he sold. The language of Section 223.5 is accordingly limited to situations where the mistake is as to "the nature or amount of the property or the identity of the recipient."

Consider, in connection with the last paragraph, Wash. Rev. Code Ann. tit. 9A, §9.54.010:

> Every person who, with intent to deprive or defraud the owner thereof . . . (4) Having received any property by reason of a mistake, shall with knowledge of such mistake secrete, withhold or appropriate the same to his own use or the use of any person other than the true owner or person entitled thereto. . . . Steals such property and shall be guilty of larceny.

Query: Does a sharp buyer commit larceny under this statute when he or she makes a good buy and knows that the seller has mistaken the value of the goods?

---

2. See, e.g., Regina v. Middleton, L.R. 2, C.C.R. 38 (1873), where a defendant making a withdrawal from a bank account knowingly accepted an overpayment from the teller who, looking at the wrong credit document, supposed that the defendant was entitled to a larger amount. A larceny conviction was upheld on grounds which hardly withstand traditional analysis, e.g., that the teller was not authorized or did not "intend" to deliver the larger sum, or to transfer ownership. See Kenny's Outlines of Criminal Law §252 (Turner ed. 1952); Riesman, Possession and the Law of Finders, 52 Harv. L. Rev. 1105 (1939). . . .

PROBLEM

S.F. Chronicle, Nov. 14, 1964, at 4, contained the following story:

MONTGOMERY, Ala. — A man who withdrew $43,000 mistakenly credited to his bank account and refused to give it back was convicted yesterday by a jury in Federal Court.

T. L. (Cotton) Thaggard of Montgomery faces a possible maximum sentence of 10 years in prison and a $5000 fine. He will be sentenced Friday.

It was Thaggard's second trial. The first ended with a deadlocked jury.

Thaggard was tried under a Federal law which prohibits taking anything worth more than $100 from a bank "with intent to steal or purloin."

In his argument to the jury Thursday, defense attorney Calvin Whitesell contended that as far as the defendant knew, the balance in his account was just what the bank told him it was.

"You can't steal what is yours," Whitesell argued.

The dispute began in March 1963 when the Union Bank & Trust Co. erroneously credited a $43,000 deposit to the account of Alabama Motors, a used car business operated by Thaggard. The money belonged to Alabama Power Co.

On March 6, Thaggard asked for his balance, then drew out the $43,000 after the teller had three times verified the amount, at his request.

He finally signed a withdrawal slip and tellers spent 30 minutes counting out the bills and putting them in a brown paper sack.

In the first trial, Thaggard's lawyer, Ira De Ment, contended his client was not guilty of larceny since the money was voluntarily handed over. "I'm not saying he did right. I'm saying he's not guilty of larceny," De Ment said.

U.S. Attorney Ben Hardeman said, "Cotton Thaggard entered that bank with a heart full of larceny and left there with a sack full of money."

Thaggard has spent the time since carrying the bag of money from the bank in and out of jail and court.

He was locked up by a circuit judge on contempt charges when he refused to tell where he put the money, saying he would incriminate himself by answering.

Thaggard was first arrested on a state charge of false pretense. But that charge was dropped when the State Supreme Court ruled that it wasn't false pretense to get the money after three times asking the bank to recheck his balance.

Later, a Federal grand jury indicted Thaggard on a larceny charge involving a bank whose funds were insured by the Federal Deposit Insurance Corporation.

The bank has won a civil judgment against Thaggard in state court and some $10,575 worth of property belonging to him has been sold to satisfy the judgment.

STATE v. RIGGINS
Supreme Court of Illinois
8 Ill. 2d 78, 132 N.E.2d 519 (1956)

HERSHEY, C.J. The defendant, Marven E. Riggins, was indicted in the circuit court of Winnebago County for embezzlement. After a verdict of guilty by a jury, the court sentenced him to a term in the penitentiary of not less than two nor more than seven years. . . .

At the time of the indictment (January, 1955), the defendant was the owner and operator of a collection agency in Rockford, called the Creditors Collection Service, and had been so engaged for about five years. He maintained an office, had both full- and part-time employees, and during 1953 and 1954 had a clientele of some 500 persons and firms for whom he collected delinquent accounts.

In February, 1953, he called on the complaining witness, Dorothy Tarrant, who operated a firm known as Cooper's Music and Jewelry. He said he was in the collection business and asked to collect the firm's delinquent accounts. As a result, they reached an oral agreement whereby the defendant was to undertake the collections.

By this agreement, the defendant was to receive one third on city accounts and one half on out-of-city accounts. It was further agreed that he need not account for the amounts collected until a bill was paid in full, at which time he was to remit by check.

There is a conflict in the evidence as to whether the defendant was to give a check for the whole amount collected and then receive his commission, or whether he was authorized to deduct his commission and account only for the net amount due.

It was further agreed that the defendant would be liable for court costs in the event he chose to file suit on any of the accounts, but the first money collected was to be applied to those costs. If no collection was made, however, the defendant was to stand the loss.

The parties operated under this agreement for almost two years. During that time the complaining witness exercised no control over the defendant as to the time or manner of collecting the accounts, and with her knowledge he commingled funds collected for all his clients in a single bank account. He also used this as a personal account, from which he drew for business, family and personal expenses.

In October, 1954, the complaining witness became aware that the defendant had collected several accounts for her in full, but had not accounted to her. . . . Thereafter, the complaining witness preferred the charges against the defendant which resulted in his indictment and conviction for embezzlement.

To decide whether the defendant, a collection agent, can be guilty of embezzlement in Illinois, it is helpful to consider our embezzlement statutes in the historical context of this crime.

Embezzlement, unknown at common law, is established by statute, and its scope, therefore, is limited to those persons designated therein. . . .

Viewed in their entirety, our laws relating to embezzlement are broad and comprehensive. The following persons are included in those statutes making the crime of embezzlement a felony: "Whoever embezzles or fraudulently converts to his own use" (Ill. Rev. Stat. 1953, chap. 38, par. 207); "a clerk, agent, servant or apprentice of any person" (par. 208); "any banker or broker, or his agent or servant, or any officer, agent or servant of any banking company, or incorporated bank" (par. 209); "any clerk, agent, servant, solicitor, broker, apprentice or officer . . . receiving any money . . . in his fiduciary capacity" (par. 210); "public officers" (par. 214); "administrators, guardians, conservators and other fiduciaries" (par. 216); and certain members and officers of fraternal societies (par. 218). . . .

In this instance we are particularly interested in the general embezzlement statute (par. 208), and the special statute under which defendant was indicted (par. 210). The former, applying to any "clerk, agent, servant or apprentice of any person," was originally enacted in 1827, and has existed in its present

form since 1874. The latter, however, refers to "any clerk, agent, servant, solicitor, broker, apprentice or officer . . . receiving any money, . . . in his fiduciary
capacity" and was not passed until 1919. For present purposes, this latter enactment is very significant, for it also provides as follows: such person

> shall be punished as provided by the criminal statutes of this state for the punish-
> ment of larceny, *irrespective of whether any such* officer, agent, clerk, servant, solicitor,
> broker or apprentice *has or claims to have any commission or interest in such money*,
> substitute for money, or thing of value so received by him.

(Italics added.)

In Commonwealth v. Libbey, 11 Metc., Mass., 64 decided in 1846, it was
held that a collecting agent, who followed that as an independent business and
who had the right to commingle funds, could not be convicted as an "agent"
under a general embezzlement statute. This was predicated on the idea that
he had a joint interest in the property said to be embezzled.

Similarly, a 1903 decision of this court reversed the conviction of an agent
who was employed to solicit subscriptions on commission and who was authorized to deduct her commissions from the amounts collected, for the reason
that she was joint owner with the principal in the amounts collected. McElroy
v. People, 202 Ill. 473, 66 N.E. 1058. . . .

Briefly, then, this was the status of the law in 1919 when the special statute
(par. 210) . . . expressly abrogated the doctrine enunciated in the foregoing
cases and relied upon by the defendant here.[a] . . .

[I]t can hardly be disputed but that the defendant acted as agent for the
complaining witness in collecting her accounts. He undertook the collections
on her behalf by virtue of authority which she delegated to him. He had no
right to collect from anyone except as authorized by her and was required to
render a full account of all matters entrusted to him, the same as any agent.
. . . The prevailing view of the courts in construing embezzlement statutes is
succinctly expressed in 18 Am. Jur., Embezzlement, §30, as follows: "The term
'agent' as used in embezzlement statutes is construed in its popular sense as
meaning a person who undertakes to transact some business or to manage some
affair for another by the latter's authority and to render an account of such
business or affair. . . ."

We conclude that the defendant was an "agent" of the complaining witness,
receiving money in a "fiduciary capacity" and, therefore, within the purview
of said embezzlement statute.

However, the present conviction must be set aside and the cause remanded
for a new trial, because of prejudicial error which intervened at the trial. This
resulted for the most part from improper remarks of the trial court during
defense counsel's closing argument. . . .

Reversed and remanded.

SCHAEFER, J., dissenting. The indictment in this case contains four counts.
Two of them charge that the defendant was the agent of Dorothy Tarrant,

a. Many cases have taken the view (contrary to that of the cases cited by the court) that, even
absent such a specific statutory provision, the fact that a collector is entitled to deduct a commission
out of the funds collected does not preclude an embezzlement conviction for appropriation of
the entire proceeds. See, e.g., Smith v. State, 74 Fla. 44, 76 So. 334 (1917); Commonwealth v.
Hutchins, 232 Mass. 285, 122 N.E. 275 (1919). — EDS.

doing business as Cooper's Jewelry, and two of them charged that he was her servant. It is not contended in this court that the relation of master and servant existed between the complaining witness and the defendant. The critical question is whether the defendant was the agent of the complaining witness. Upon the record it seems to me that he was not. He maintained his own office, had his own employees, and collected accounts for approximately 500 other individuals and firms. He was subject to no control whatsoever by any of his customers in making his collections. His customers knew that he kept all of his collections in a single account. That the defendant was not an agent would be clear, I think, if vicarious liability was sought to be asserted against Dorothy Tarrant on account of the defendant's conduct in the course of his collection activities.

The conclusion of the majority that the defendant was an agent rests upon the assertion that "[t]he term 'agent' as used in embezzlement statutes is construed in its popular sense. . . ." That generalization runs counter to the basic rule that criminal statutes are strictly construed.

More important than generalized statements as to the proper approach to the problem of construction, however, is the language to be construed. The statute under which the defendant was indicted (Ill. Rev. Stat. 1953, chap. 38, par. 210), refers to "any clerk, agent, servant, solicitor, broker, apprentice, or officer." If "agent" has the broad meaning which the majority gives it, each of the other terms is superfluous because all are embraced within the single term "agent." Many of the specific enumerations in the other statutes referred to by the majority likewise become largely, if not entirely, meaningless, for the particular relationships they seek to reach are also swallowed up in the expanded definition of the term "agent."

It is arguable of course that the conduct of the defendant in this case should be regarded as criminal. The General Assembly might wish to make it so. But it might not. It might regard the collection agency as a desirable service enterprise which should not be made unduly perilous. If the defendant in this case, with his little agency, is guilty of one embezzlement, he is guilty of 500. The General Assembly might not want to make the enterprise so hazardous. It has not done so, in my opinion, by the statute before us.[b]

COMMONWEALTH v. STAHL

Superior Court of Pennsylvania
183 Pa. Super. 49, 127 A.2d 786 (1956)

GUNTHER, J. The defendant in this appeal financed the purchase and sale of used cars through the Pottstown Finance Company. In order to obtain money, titles to the vehicles were transferred to the finance company accompanied by judgment notes and bailment leases. When the used car market suffered a setback, the defendant became financially embarrassed and failed to meet his obligations. In the instant case, four cars were involved. He was requested to repay

b. The various statutes relevant to embezzlement at issue in these opinions have all been replaced by §16-1 (Theft and Related Offenses) of the Illinois Revised Criminal Code of 1961, reprinted at page 962 infra. How should this case be decided under the new provisions? — EDS.

the money due or return the cars, but he was unable to do either. It is admitted that the finance company did business with defendant for several years prior to this financial difficulty.

The defendant denies ever having any fraudulent intent; he contends that the practice with reference to the four vehicles was precisely the same as the practice engaged in by the parties for a number of years prior to the decline in the used car market.

The jury found defendant guilty of fraudulent conversion on four bills. Motions for a new trial and in arrest of judgment were filed, argued, and overruled. Defendant was sentenced to serve not less than two (2) months nor more than twenty-three (23) months in the Montgomery County Prison. This appeal followed.

A review of the testimony reveals what were the actual nature and ramifications of the transactions. While the defendant was interested in buying and selling used cars, the prosecutor was interested in lending money on them with notes, car titles, and bailment leases as evidences of indebtedness. The financial arrangement was clearly understood by both parties. Its foundation was credit, and the relationship was that of creditor and debtor. Defendant gave the finance company his personal judgment note in which he obligated himself to pay the loan when it became due. There was no obligation on his part to account for the proceeds from any specific sale or transaction although the loan was secured by paper titles.

It is admitted that the finance company never had ownership of the vehicles involved,[a] that it never had possession of them; and that it never saw them. The record shows that approximately a half million dollars worth of business had been transacted in this manner within a period of over two years. . . .

The crime of fraudulent conversion is committed where the offender receives into his possession money or property of another person and fraudulently withholds, converts, or applies the same to his own use or to the use and benefit of any person other than the one to whom the money or property belonged. If the property so withheld or applied to the defendant's use and benefit did not belong to some other person, but was the defendant's own money or property even though obtained by borrowing the money or by a purchase on credit of the property, the crime has not been committed. . . .

The statute under which this prosecution was brought has no application to a failure by a borrower to fulfil his contract to repay money loaned to him. It is not intended to be used as a substitute for an action at law in collection of a debt.[b]

The evidence, under the circumstances in this case, does not warrant our sustaining a conviction of fraudulent conversion. . . .

The judgment is reversed and the defendant discharged.

a. Note that this conclusion is not inconsistent with the fact, earlier pointed out in the opinion, that titles to the cars were transferred to the finance company. What the finance company obtained were security titles that gave it a lien on the cars good against levying creditors or trustees in bankruptcy. Defendant owned the cars in the sense of being able to convey title to them. — EDS.

b. Cf. Model Penal Code, §223.0(7): "Property in possession of the actor shall not be deemed property of another who has only a security interest therein, even if legal title is in the creditor pursuant to a conditional sales contract or other security agreement." — EDS.

MODEL PENAL CODE

SECTION 223.8. THEFT BY FAILURE TO MAKE REQUIRED DISPOSITIONS OF FUNDS RECEIVED

[See Appendix for text of this section.]

COMMENT TO §223.8 AT 255-262 [AMERICAN LAW INSTITUTE, MODEL PENAL CODE
AND COMMENTARIES, PT. II (1980)]
. . . The challenge is to distinguish default that should be assimilated to theft
from non-performance that should be left to the traditional remedies for breach
of contract.

The difficulty that has troubled courts in the past may be illustrated by the
decisions in Commonwealth v. Mitchneck [1] and State v. Polzin.[2] The *Mitchneck*
case involved a mine operator whose employees signed written authorizations
for him to deduct from their wages the amounts of their grocery bills. Mitchneck
made the deductions but failed to pay the grocer. He was convicted under the
Pennsylvania fraudulent-conversion statute, which at the time covered anyone
who

> having received or having possession, in any capacity or by any means or manner
> whatever, of any money or property, of any kind whatsoever, of or belonging to
> any other person, firm, or corporation, or which any other person, firm, or corpora-
> tion is entitled to receive and have, who fraudulently withholds, converts, or applies
> the same, or any part thereof, . . . to and for his own use and benefit, or to and
> for the use and benefit of any other person.

The conviction was reversed on the ground that Mitchneck did not have in
his possession

> any money *belonging* to his employees. True he owed them money. . . . Defendant's
> liability for the unpaid wages due his employees was, and remained, civil, not
> criminal. His liability for the amount due Vagnoni after his agreement to accept
> or honor the assignments of his employees' wages was likewise civil and not criminal.

If the miners in the *Mitchneck* case had drawn their pay at one window and
passed part of it back to Mitchneck's cashier at the next window, conviction
for embezzlement or fraudulent conversion could have been obtained. The premise of Section 223.8 is that liability should also follow on the facts of the case
as they occurred. The bookkeeping shortcut actually used hardly serves as a
rational basis for exculpating Mitchneck from criminal liability. . . .

The *Polzin* case presents a more complex variation of the same situation.
Polzin was a money lender who took a note from a Mrs. Braseth under an
arrangement by which, instead of paying the cash to her, he agreed to pay off
certain of her creditors. Instead of doing so, he made out a check to a collection
agency which he owned. He then approached the creditors with a proposal to
act for them in collecting their claim from Mrs. Braseth for a 33 percent collection
fee. They accepted the arrangement, after which Polzin paid the creditors and
withheld $19 as his agreed-upon collection fee.

---

1. 130 Pa. Super. 433, 198 A. 463 (1938).
2. 197 Wash. 612, 85 P.2d 1057 (1939).

Polzin was convicted of petty larceny, the jury having evidently taken the view that what was stolen was the $19 fee which Polzin had withheld. The Supreme Court of Washington reversed the conviction. The court held first that there could be no misappropriation of any "property" belonging to Mrs. Braseth, because she never gave Polzin anything other than her note. Since Polzin held no "property" belonging to Mrs. Braseth but had merely promised to make certain payments, he was her debtor rather than her trustee. Second, with respect to the $19 withheld from the creditors, Mrs. Braseth "lost nothing"; the bills had been completely discharged and Polzin had therefore performed his agreement as far as she was concerned.

Section 223.8 was designed in part to provide a theory for reaching cases like *Mitchneck* and *Polzin.* Both were thought to illustrate situations that properly should be assimilated to theft rather than treated as mere breach of contract. . . .

There is a long tradition, deriving to some extent from the harsh days of the debtors' prison and to some extent enshrined in constitutional provisions, against enforcing individual consensual obligations by criminal sanctions. . . . Among the valid objections to the employment of criminal sanctions to enforce debts, as distinct from protecting "ownership" of "property," may be included the following: . . . a feeling that it is up to the contract maker to select his risks and that the invocation of criminal sanctions in cases of non-performance involves the impairment of the incentive to make wise risk selections and thus impairment of the social functions of contract-making . . . ; the unlikelihood of deterring honest insolvency by criminal threats, since insolvency is so often a result of factors beyond the control of the individual; the dangers, in attempting to punish insolvency for which the actor may properly be viewed as at fault, of discouraging the kind of speculation that is properly a part of a free-enterprise system and of securing unjust convictions by hindsight; and the futility, from the creditors' standpoint, of imprisoning a debtor who is unable to pay.

None of the foregoing considerations was thought applicable to cases such as *Mitchneck* and *Polzin.* In neither of those cases was there an ordinary credit transaction or an understanding that involves an assessment of risks at some future date. Mitchneck and Polzin were not supposed to use the funds in any way for their own purposes nor even to retain them for any substantial period. They were merely conduits for the transmission of money to persons designated by the real owner of the money. . . . [A] proprietary use of the money should properly be regarded as theft, much as a guardian may be guilty of embezzlement when he commingles fiduciary funds with his own and reduces the account below the level of his fiduciary obligation in order to satisfy his personal financial needs. . . .

It should be noted, however, that the *Mitchneck* and *Polzin* situations are not free from difficulty even under such a formulation as Section 223.8. The text of the offense requires that the actor "obtain" property from another. The term "obtain" is defined in Section 223.0(5) to mean, in relation to property, "to bring about a transfer or purported transfer of a legal interest in the property, whether to the obtainer or another." The problem in both *Mitchneck* and *Polzin* was that the defendant was not perceived as having "obtained" anything from the victim in this sense, and that perception might be no less applicable to Section 223.8. Indeed, if the property were regarded as having been "obtained" as that term is defined, Section 223.2(1) would be an adequate basis for prosecution. If Mitchneck and Polzin obtained property of another under an understanding and then "exercised unlawful control over" that property, there would seem to be no bar to an ordinary embezzlement prosecution. Even if this is true, however, there may be an important value in addressing a specific formulation to situations of this kind. Convictions of embezzlement are not easily obtained under the broader standards embodied in the general definition of theft.

It is important, nevertheless, to emphasize the point that Section 223.8 must not be construed so broadly that a bright line between theft and breach of contract is obscured. . . . [Consider] credit-card purchases, a practice that has assumed enormous proportions in today's economy. Typically, the purchaser of goods "obtains" property by becoming the drawee-acceptor of a draft, drawn by the merchant in favor of the credit-card company as payee. If unauthorized use of the card is involved, or if forged or stolen cards are used, Section 224.6 is adequate to handle the problem. If the actor intended from the beginning not to pay, Section 223.3 covers the situation. But if the actor is engaged in authorized use and simply cannot pay his bills, it is inappropriate to make him a thief; the risk that he cannot pay is a cost of doing business that credit-card companies should assume. . . .

The path to avoiding such undue extensions of Section 223.8 is to accord proper weight to the limitation embodied in the words "to be reserved," so that Section 223.8 is deemed applicable only in cases of a promise to turn over property actually received in kind or an equivalent sum of money specifically reserved in the sense that a trustee reserves a fiduciary account. It is true that such a construction would seem to limit Section 223.8 to classic instances of embezzlement. . . . [T]here may be some cases beyond ordinary embezzlement to which the provision could be applied by a broad construction of "obtains" to deal with situations where property was not physically exchanged. But in order to eliminate application of the section to cases where civil remedies alone should be permitted, something approaching an explicit agreement to "reserve" would seem to be required.

NOTE

Only some nine states followed the Model Penal Code's lead in this section. See American Law Institute, Model Penal Code and Commentaries, Pt. II, Comment to §223.8 at 266 (1980). What might have been the reasons for the reluctance?

3. Fraud

INTRODUCTORY NOTE

The deposit of history is no less substantial in crimes dealing with the use of fraud to acquire another's property than in crimes dealing with misappropriation by one in lawful possession, previously discussed. In both situations, the common law judges through some remarkable reasoning brought certain species of these nontrespassory takings within the scope of the basic common law crime of larceny, while in parallel developments Parliament expressly dealt with these nontrespassory situations by creating new statutory crimes to cover them. This uncoordinated judicial and legislative development left parallel crimes to cover fundamentally similar kinds of theft. The necessity to distinguish which of these kinds of theft were within the stretched judicial definition of larceny and which within the statutory definitions of new crimes is the legacy of this history.

The early common law, influenced by the ethic of caveat emptor, declined to treat as criminal, situations in which a person acquired another's property through simple deception. The classic justification was given by Holt, C.J., in 1703: "[W]e are not to indict one for making a fool of another." Regina v. Jones, 91 Eng. Rep. 330.[4] But through the development of common law "cheats," the principle was modified as to certain kinds of fraud, which were aimed indiscriminately at any member of the public rather than at a particular person and which were thought to be such that ordinary prudence was an insufficient protection: for example, using a false token, false weights or measures, etc. See Rex v. Wheatley, 97 Eng. Rep. 746, 748 (1761). This common law development was supplemented and amplified by a statute in 1541 that made criminal the acquisition of another's property by deceit in situations doubtfully reached by common law cheats: where accomplished "by colour and means of any [privy] false token or counterfeit letter made in any other man's name." 33 Hen. VIII, ch. 1.

A more far-reaching legislative innovation came in 1757 with the enactment of what subsequently became the prototype false pretense statute, 30 Geo. II, ch. 24, making it a misdemeanor to obtain "money, goods, wares or merchandizes" from any person by false pretenses with intent to cheat or defraud. There originally appeared to be some doubt whether the false pretense statute reached any and all misrepresentations or was to be narrowly read in the light of the common law of cheats and the earlier cheating statutes. It was not until 1789 that the broader meaning was established in Young v. The King, 100 Eng. Rep. 475. See J. Hall, Theft, Law and Society 45-52 (2d ed. 1952); Pearce, Theft by False Promises, 101 U. Pa. L. Rev. 967 (1953). In the meantime the landmark case of The King v. Pear had been decided in 1779, I Leach 211, 168 Eng. Rep. 208, creating the crime of what came to be known as "larceny by trick" as a distinct form of common law larceny. The following report of the case is taken from 168 Eng. Rep. 208:

> The prisoner was indicted for stealing a black horse, the property of Samuel Finch. It appeared in evidence that Samuel Finch was a Livery-Stablekeeper in the Borough; and that the prisoner, on the 2d of July 1779, hired the horse of him to go to Sutton, in the county of Surry, and back again, saying on being asked where he lived, that he lodged at No. 25 in King-street, and should return about eight o'clock the same evening. He did not return; and it was proved that he had sold the horse on the very day he had hired it, to one William Hollist, in Smithfield Market; and that he had no lodging at the place to which he had given the Prosecutor directions.
>
> The learned Judge said: There had been different opinions on the law of this

4. Cf. 1 W. Hawkins, Pleas of the Crown 344 (6th ed. 1788): "[It is] needless to provide severe laws for such mischiefs, against which common prudence and caution may be a sufficient security."

class of cases; that the general doctrine then was that if a horse be let for a particular portion of time, and after that time is expired, the party hiring, instead of returning the horse to its owner, sell it and convert the money to his own use, it is felony, because there is then no privity of contract subsisting between the parties; that in the present case the horse was hired to take a journey into Surry, and the prisoner sold him the same day, without taking any such journey; that there were also other circumstances which imported that at the time of the hiring the prisoner had it in intention to sell the horse, as his saying that he lodged at a place where in fact he was not known. He therefore left it with the Jury to consider, Whether the prisoner meant at the time of the hiring to take such journey, but was afterwards tempted to sell the horse? for if so he must be acquitted; but that if they were of opinion that at the time of the hiring the journey was a mere pretence to get the horse into his possession, and he had no intention to take such journey but intended to sell the horse, they would find that fact specially for the opinion of the Judges.

The Jury found that the facts above stated were true; and also that the prisoner had hired the horse with a fraudulent view and intention of selling it immediately.

The question was referred to the Judges, Whether the delivery of the horse by the prosecutor to the prisoner, had so far changed the possession of the property, as to render the subsequent conversion of it a mere breach of trust, or whether the conversion was felonious?

The Judges differed greatly in opinion on this case; and delivered their opinions seriatim upon it at Lord Chief Justice De Gray's house on 4th February 1780 and on the 22nd of the same month Mr. Baron Perryn delivered their opinion on it. The majority of them thought, That the question, as to the original intention of the prisoner in hiring the horse, had been properly left to the jury; and as they had found, that his view in so doing was fraudulent, the parting with the property had not changed the nature of the possession, but that it remained unaltered in the prosecutor at the time of the conversion; and that the prisoner was therefore guilty of felony.

The reason the judges thought the false pretense statute, 30 Geo. II, was inapplicable to *Pear* appears in the report of the case in 2 E. H. East, Pleas of the Crown 685, 688-689 (1806):

[T]he next question was, Whether this offence were within or at all affected by the statutes of Hen. 8 and Geo. 2. Seven of the Judges were of the opinion, that it was not. That the statute of Hen. 8 was confined to the cases of obtaining goods in other men's names, by false tokens or counterfeit letters, made in any other man's name. The statute of Geo. 2 extended that law to all cases where goods were obtained by false pretences of any kind. But both these statutes were confined to cases where credit was obtained in the name of a third person; and did not extend to cases where a man, on his own account, got goods with an intention to steal them.

Use was made, therefore, of the singular notion that possession never passes to a fraudulent bailee to stretch the concept of larceny to include a species of act thought otherwise unamenable to proper criminal sanction. "Fraud in securing possession joined breaking bulk and custody in servants to extend the definition of larceny far beyond its original traditional meaning." J. Hall, Theft, Law and Society 42 (2d ed. 1952).

When the false pretense statute was subsequently extended to all misrepresentations of fact, regardless of the technique of deception, there were two crimes, larceny by trick (a felony) and statutory false pretenses (only a misdemeanor), covering very much the same kind of criminal conduct. Perhaps the first hint of the theory on which the crimes would be distinguished appears in the *Pear* case itself, as reported in 2 E. H. East, Pleas of the Crown 685, 689 n. (a) (1806):

> On the debate in this case Eyre, B., adverting to these statutes, said he doubted if there was a distinction in this respect between the owner's parting with the possession and with the property in the thing delivered. That where goods were delivered upon a false token, and the owner meant to part with the property absolutely and never expected to have the goods returned again, it might be difficult to reach the case otherwise than through the statutes; aliter, where he parted with the possession only: for there if the possession were obtained by fraud, and not taken according to the agreement; it was on the whole a taking against the will of the owner; and if done animo furandi, it was felony.

Question: Is there any logical reason why "the deceit which eliminated the consent which the owner intended to give when he regarded himself as parting with merely the possession of his chattel would not have the same effect when he regarded himself as parting with something greater, namely, the ownership of it?" 2 W. O. Russell, Crime 1089 (10th ed. 1950).

HUFSTETLER v. STATE
Alabama Court of Appeals
37 Ala. App. 71, 63 So. 2d 730 (1953)

CARR, J. The accused was convicted by the court without a jury on a charge of petit larceny. The property involved was 6½ gallons of gasoline.

The defendant did not testify nor offer any evidence.

The undisputed facts are narrated by a witness [Peter Whorton] as follows.

> . . . I own and operate a store and service station at Forney, Alabama. On March 29, 1952, the defendant drove an automobile up to my gasoline tanks. There were some two or three other men in the car with him, and a man in the back seat got out and started in the store and asked if I had a telephone. When I told him I did not have a telephone, he said he wanted some gasoline and went back and got in the car. I asked him how much and he said "fill it up." I put 6½ gallons of gasoline in the car and this man said to get a quart of oil, and when I went for the oil, the defendant drove off in the automobile together with the man who ordered the gas and the others in the car without paying for the gasoline. This 6½ gallons of gas belonged to me and was of the value of $1.94. . . .

The only question of critical concern is whether, on the basis of the above proof, the judgment of conviction can be sustained.

Appellant's attorney in brief urges that Whorton voluntarily parted with the possession and ownership of the gasoline.

Confusion sometimes arises in an effort to distinguish the kindred criminal offenses of larceny, false pretenses, and embezzlement.

The Massachusetts Supreme Court in Commonwealth v. Barry, 124 Mass. 325, gave a distinction that is clear and comprehensive:

"If a person honestly receives the possession of the goods, chattels or money of another upon any trust, express or implied, and, after receiving them, fraudulently converts them to his own use, he may be guilty of the crime of embezzlement, but cannot be of that of larceny, except as embezzlement is by statute made larceny. If the possession of such property is obtained by fraud, and the owner of it intends to part with his title as well as his possession, the offence is that of obtaining property by false pretenses, provided the means by which they are acquired are such as, in law, are false pretenses. If the possession is fraudulently obtained, with intent on the part of the person obtaining it, at the time he received it, to convert the same to his own use, and the person parting with it intends to part with his possession merely, and not with his title to the property, the offence is larceny." . . .

In the case at bar the circumstances disclose that by the application of the well-known doctrine of aid and abet the appellant secured the possession of the gasoline by a trick or fraud. The obtaining of the property by the consent of the owner under such conditions will not necessarily prevent the taking from being larceny. In other words, an actual trespass is not always required to be proven. The trick or fraud vitiates the transaction, and it will be deemed that the owner still retained the constructive possession.

What we have said related to the possession. It is certainly a logical conclusion that Whorton had no intention of parting with the ownership of the property until he had received pay therefor.

The element of the intent of the appellant is inferable from the factual background. . . .

Affirmed. Remanded for proper sentence.

GRAHAM v. UNITED STATES
United States Court of Appeals, District of Columbia Circuit
187 F.2d 87 (1950)

WASHINGTON, J. The appellant, an attorney, was indicted in two counts for grand larceny under section 2201 of Title 22 of the District of Columbia Code (1940 ed.). He was charged with having stolen money from Francisco Gal in the amounts of $100 and $1,900. He appeals from a judgment and conviction entered upon a verdict of guilty.

The complaining witness, Francisco Gal, consulted appellant in his professional capacity. Gal had been arrested and charged with disorderly conduct, and had forfeited $25 as collateral. He was seeking American citizenship and was apprehensive that the arrest would impede or bar his attainment of that goal. An immigrant employed as a cook, his command of the English language was far from complete. He testified that appellant Graham told him that he wasn't sure what he could do, that Graham would "have to talk to the policeman. You have to pay money for that, because the money is talk." He further testified that Graham told him he would charge him $200 for a fee; that he would have to pay an additional $2,000 for the police; that Graham said "don't mention the money for nobody and for the police either." As a result, Gal testified that he paid the appellant $300 on February 2, 1950 (of which, he said, $200 was paid as a legal fee), and $1,900 on February 3, 1950. The police officer who originally had arrested Gal testified that he came to appellant's office, and after talking with Graham, told Gal that he wasn't in any trouble. Gal testified to substantially the same effect. The officer testified that Graham did not then or at any other time offer or give him money. The appellant testified that the entire payment was intended as a fee for legal services; that he had never mentioned money for the police; that no part of the money was in fact paid to the police or anyone else, but was kept by the appellant.

Appellant's principal contentions are: First, that the evidence supports the proposition that Gal voluntarily gave Graham complete title to the money and therefore appellant is entitled to a directed verdict; and, second, that the trial court's charge to the jury was erroneous in not sufficiently distinguishing between the situation where one obtains complete title to another's property by fraud or trick and the case where possession only is obtained.

Section 2201 of Title 22 of the District of Columbia Code provides as follows:

> Whoever shall feloniously take and carry away anything of value of the amount or value of $50 or upward, including things savoring of the realty, shall suffer imprisonment of not less than one nor more than ten years.

Interpreting this statute, this court has held that "one who obtains money from another upon the representation that he will perform certain service therewith for the latter, intending at the time to convert the money, and actually converting it, to his own use, is guilty of larceny." In classic terminology, "the distinction drawn by the common law is between the case of one who gives up possession of a chattel for a special purpose to another who by converting it to his own use is held to have committed a trespass, and the case of one who, although induced by fraud or trick, nevertheless actually intends that title to the chattel shall pass to the wrongdoer." United States v. Patton, 3 Cir., 1941, 120 F.2d 73, 76.

We now turn to appellant's first contention, that under the evidence in the case the court should have directed a verdict for the defendant. We think this contention without merit. If the jury believed Gal's testimony, and did not believe that of the defendant, it was possible for the jury to conclude beyond a reasonable doubt that the defendant fraudulently induced Gal to give him $2,000 to be used for a special purpose, i.e., to bribe the police, that the defendant did not intend so to use the money, and converted it to his own use. Under the rule stated above, this would be larceny by trick.

Thus, in the *Means* case [Means v. United States, 65 F.2d 206], the defendant was convicted of the crime of larceny under the following circumstances: After the kidnapping of the infant son of Charles Lindbergh, the defendant in an interview with Mrs. McLean persuaded her that he could assist in locating and recovering the kidnapped baby, stating that if Mrs. McLean would give him $100,000 he would use that sum to pay the ransom and secure the return of the child. On the basis of these representations he secured the money from Mrs. McLean. His representations were fraudulent and he intended at the time to convert the money to his own use, and actually so converted it. People v. Edwards, 72 Cal. App. 102, 236 P. 944, provides an even closer precedent. There the defendant took money from the complainant, representing to her that it would be used to bribe officers investigating criminal activities by her husband. The complainant did not know exactly how the defendant was going to use the money but understood that it was going to be used in some manner to corrupt the police. The court, in sustaining a conviction for larceny, held that under these circumstances "title would remain in [the complainant] until the accomplishment of the purpose for which she gave [the defendant] the money, i.e., until its final delivery by [him] to the officers whom she was led to believe were to be bribed." . . .

The judgment of the District Court is affirmed.

NOTES AND QUESTIONS

1. Since on Gal's testimony the money was handed to defendant to be given to the police officer as a bribe, how can the court defend its decision that Gal did not intend to pass his whole interest in the money to defendant, title and all? On the other hand, if the court had held otherwise, thus precluding a larceny-by-trick conviction, could defendant have been convicted of obtaining money by false pretenses? Note that a false promise is generally regarded as inadequate to sustain a false pretense conviction, although it suffices for larceny by trick. See People v. Ashley, pages 951-955 infra.

2. In Bourbonnaise v. State, 96 Okla. Crim. 28, 248 P.2d 640 (1952), defendant bootlegger obtained money from Bean as payment for a bottle of whiskey; he stated he would return with the bottle within 30 minutes after purchasing same from another bootlegger. He never returned. Affirming a conviction of larceny, the court stated (248 P.2d at 642):

> This money was not given the defendant to consummate a purchase of liquor represented by defendant to be in his possession. . . . If such had been the case, then the money would have become defendant's money, and if the defendant had failed to turn over the liquor, then supposed to be in his possession either on his person or somewhere outside, such facts would have supported a charge of obtaining money under false pretense. But here defendant . . . merely agreed to take Bean's money and go purchase the liquor from another bootlegger. The money was not his. He was to pay it over for Bean. It was Bean's money until paid over, and then the whiskey would be Bean's.

3. In Whitmore v. State, 238 Wis. 79, 298 N.W. 194 (1941), defendant bought a car on a conditional sales contract by the terms of which title was reserved to the vendor until the full purchase price was paid. As a down payment, defendant delivered to the vendor a check not covered by sufficient funds. The court affirmed a conviction of obtaining the car by false pretenses, notwithstanding the principle that such a crime is not made out where the defrauded party retains title, stating (298 N.W. at 195):

> Where, however, goods are sold under a conditional sales contract and the legal title is merely retained for purposes of security, the vendee gets a sufficient property interest to support a conviction of obtaining money by false pretenses providing the other requisites of the offense are present. . . . Such a vendee is regarded for most purposes as owner of the property covered by the conditional sales contract. He is variously referred to as beneficial, equitable or substantial owner, there

being outstanding in the vendor only the naked legal title and this temporarily and for security solely. It is our conclusion that the property interest which accompanied delivery of possession to plaintiff in error is sufficient to satisfy the class of the statute.

4. Pearce, Theft by False Promises, 101 U. Pa. L. Rev. 967, 987-989 (1953), writes:

Although some legal scholars have treated larceny by trick as closely related functionally to false pretenses, or even as completely engulfing it, the offenses are respectively aimed at quite different acquisitive techniques. False pretenses is theft by deceit. The misappropriation it punishes must be effected by communication to the owner. Larceny by trick is theft by stealth. It punishes misappropriation effected by unauthorized disposition of the owner's property. The former focuses on defendant's behavior while face to face with the owner: did it amount to a false pretense? The focus of the latter is upon defendant's behavior behind the owner's back: did it amount to an unauthorized appropriation?

One cause of confusion of the offenses is that larceny by trick requires some deceit in addition to the unauthorized disposition of property which is its gravamen. It is thus thought of as a type of theft by fraud. However, the requirement of deceit in larceny by trick stems from its history rather than its function and plays a minor role. . . .

It should be apparent that deceit had little to do with the offensiveness of Pear's behavior. It can hardly be said that being a servant is offensive, yet being a servant plays the same role in larceny by servants as deceit plays in larceny by trick. Each permits a circumvention of the requirement of a "trespassory taking" in order to reach a misappropriation by a person in possession as common law larceny. Fraud for this highly technical purpose need not be subjected to close scrutiny or held to an exacting standard, for there is adequate external evidence of the defendant's antisocial bent in his subsequent misappropriation. Indeed it is true generally, as it was in Pear's Case, that the only substantial evidence of the initial fraud is found in the subsequent unauthorized appropriation.

In contrast, the antisocial act defined by the crime of false pretenses consists entirely of deceit. It consists of so deceiving the owner of the property that he is induced to consent to the defendant's treating the property as his own. This being so, it is unnecessary as well as impossible for the defendant to subsequently misappropriate property which he has stolen by false pretenses. If the behavior by which he induced consent amounts to a false pretense, he has completed his form of theft at the moment the bargain is struck. . . .

Thus it is said that a defendant cannot be convicted of larceny if his deceit induces the owner to transfer his entire interest in the property, whereas he can be if it induces consent merely to his possession or use of the property. This creates the often troublesome paradox that larceny punishes the lesser fraud and exempts the greater. The apparent contradiction disappears with the realization that larceny by trick does not punish *deceit* — it punishes unauthorized appropriation. This functional distinction between larceny and false pretenses suggests a simple test by which specific fact situations can be distributed between the two offenses. If the deceit be eliminated from the transaction by which the property initially came into the defendant's hands, would his subsequent behavior with respect to the property constitute a conversion? If so, the offense may be larceny by trick; it cannot be false pretenses. If not, the offense may be false pretenses; it cannot be larceny by trick.

STATE v. GRIFFEN
Supreme Court of North Carolina
239 N.C. 41, 79 S.E.2d 230 (1953)

[On four occasions defendant, representing himself as a fund raiser for a hospital, elicited money from his victims by assuring them that if they contributed a sum towards the purchase of a car to be raffled off, they would receive their money back with 6 percent interest and the winning raffle ticket. The transactions turned out to be a hollow scheme for the enrichment of defendant. He was indicted on each transaction both for larceny by trick and embezzlement with respect to the same persons, property, and acts. Over his objection, the two indictments on each of the four transactions were consolidated for trial, and the prosecutor was not compelled to elect whether to place defendant on trial for larceny or embezzlement. In each of the four instances he was convicted of both larceny by trick and embezzlement.]

DEVIN, C.J. . . . Generally speaking, to constitute larceny there must be a wrongful taking and carrying away of the personal property of another without his consent, and this must be done with felonious intent; that is, with intent to deprive the owner of his property and to appropriate it to the taker's use fraudulently. It involves a trespass either actual or constructive. The taker must have had the intent to steal at the time he unlawfully takes the property from the owner's possession by an act of trespass. Actual trespass, however, is not a necessary element when possession of the property is fraudulently obtained by some trick or artifice. The embezzlement statute makes criminal the fraudulent conversion of personal property by one occupying some position of trust or some fiduciary relationship as specified in the statute. The person accused must have been entrusted with and received into his possession lawfully the personal property of another, and thereafter with felonious intent must have fraudulently converted the property to his own use. Trespass is not a necessary element. In embezzlement the possession of the property is acquired lawfully by virtue of the fiduciary relationship and thereafter the felonious intent and fraudulent conversion enter in to make the act of appropriation a crime.

In the case at bar, according to the State's evidence, the defendant obtained the property of the witness Stallworth by a trick or fraudulent device. While in a sense it was with his consent, it was only by this trick or fraudulent device that the taking was accomplished, constituting in legal effect a constructive trespass. And the felonious intent necessary to constitute the crime of larceny must have been present and motivating the act at the time of the taking. To constitute embezzlement the defendant must have been the agent, employee or servant of Stallworth and as such entrusted by Stallworth with possession of Stallworth's property for Stallworth, and the defendant must have thereafter fraudulently and with felonious intent converted the property to his own use. Conceding, without deciding, that the evidence is susceptible of either view, it is apparent that both views could not exist at the same time. The defendant could not be guilty of both by the same act. Hence we think the defendant's motion that the solicitor be required to elect whether the defendant be put on trial for larceny or embezzlement should be allowed.

However, it appears that the able judge who presided at the trial of this case was careful to impose on the defendant sentences carrying penalty or punishment only in the cases in which the jury had convicted him of larceny by trick. All the sentences for embezzlement were made to run concurrently with the sentences for larceny. So that the defendant will suffer nothing by reason of the several convictions for embezzlement; nor does it appear that the imposition of the term of 3 to 5 years in prison for all the eight cases was in any respect augmented by the verdicts in those cases. After all it was the same evidence whether tending to show larceny or embezzlement. Hence it would appear that the defendant has no cause for complaint that the court did not require an election. . . .

No error.

BARNHILL, J. (dissenting). The defendant has apparently committed very reprehensible crimes for which, no doubt, he will be punished, either under the former trial and sentence affirmed by this Court or upon a conviction on a new trial. For that reason it is with sincere regret that I enter my dissent to the majority opinion. However, I entertain a deep conviction that no man should suffer the loss of his liberty except upon his conviction in a trial free from substantial error. . . .

In short, the jury found that defendant, in four instances, did steal by trick the property of another. It likewise found that in each of said instances he embezzled the identical property while it was committed to his care as an agent of the prosecuting witness. Thus the jury has found that in each instance the defendant came lawfully into possession of the property involved. At the same time it found that the acquisition of possession was unlawful. This produces an irreconcilable conflict in the verdicts, which, in my opinion, necessitates a new trial. I so vote.[a]

PEOPLE v. ASHLEY
Supreme Court of California
42 Cal. 2d 246, 267 P.2d 271 (1954)

[Defendant, the business manager of a corporation chartered for the purpose of "introducing people," was charged with feloniously taking money from two women and convicted of grand theft under §404 of the California Penal Code. The evidence revealed that defendant obtained a loan of $7,200 from a Mrs. Russ, a woman of 70 years of age, by promising that the loan would be secured by a first mortgage on certain improved property of the corporation and that the money would be used to build a theater on other property owned by the corporation. In fact the corporation leased but did not own the improved property, and no theater was ever built, the money having been used to meet the corporation's operating expenses. After defendant received the money, Mrs.

---

a. Cf. Annot., 146 A.L.R. 532, 594 (1943): "But it is suggested that under many embezzlement statutes, and particularly under statutes defining embezzlement as the fraudulent conversion of property by one to whom it has been intrusted, the offenses of larceny and embezzlement should be considered as overlapping in this respect, so that, consequently, where the money or property was intrusted to the accused and, so far as was apparent to the person so intrusting it to him he received it with the lawful intent to abide by his duty concerning it; the mere fact that when the accused so received the property he harbored a secret intent to subsequently appropriate it to his own purposes should not be a defense to a charge of embezzlement." For cases taking this view see id. at 557-562 — EDS.

Russ frequently quarreled with him over his failure to deliver the promised first mortgage. She finally received a note of the corporation secured by a second trust deed on some unimproved property owned by the corporation. She testified that she accepted this security because defendant had told her to "take that or nothing." She subsequently received four postdated checks in payment of the loan. After it became apparent that these checks would not be paid, defendant requested an extension. Mrs. Russ granted the extension after defendant had threatened to destroy himself if she refused so that she might be paid from the proceeds of his life insurance policies.

[Defendant obtained $13,590 from a Mrs. Neal representing that the corporation intended to use the money to buy the El Patio Theatre. She was initially told that the loan would be secured by a trust deed on the theater building and that she would have good security for her loan because the corporation was worth a half million dollars. However, after obtaining the money, defendant issued Mrs. Neal a note of the corporation for $13,500. Subsequently, she loaned the corporation an additional $4,470 receiving a note for $17,500 in exchange for the previous note. Mrs. Neal testified that when she hesitated in making the additional loan, defendant placed a gun on his desk and said: "Now look here, Mrs. Neal, I don't want no monkey business out of you. Do you understand that?" The corporation did not buy the theater; Mrs. Neal never received the trust deed; and the money was deposited to the corporation's account.

[Evidence was introduced indicating that the corporation was in a strained financial condition and was worth nothing like a half million dollars. There was also evidence showing that the defendant received no salary from the corporation, but that he drove an expensive automobile paid for by the corporation, and that he had drawn numerous checks on corporation funds for the payment of expenses.]

TRAYNOR, J. . . . The case went to the jury with instructions relating to larceny by trick and device and obtaining property by false pretenses. The jurors were instructed that all would have to agree on the type of theft, if any, that was committed. . . .

Although the crimes of larceny by trick and device and obtaining property by false pretenses are much alike, they are aimed at different criminal acquisitive techniques. Larceny by trick and device is the appropriation of property, the possession of which was fraudulently acquired; obtaining property by false pretenses is the fraudulent or deceitful acquisition of both title and possession. In this state, these two offenses, with other larcenous crimes, have been consolidated into the single crime of theft (Pen. Code, §484), but their elements have not been changed thereby. The purpose of the consolidation was to remove the technicalities that existed in the pleading and proof of these crimes at common law. Indictments and informations charging the crime of "theft" can now simply allege an "unlawful taking." Pen. Code, §§951, 952. Juries need no longer be concerned with the technical differences between the several types of theft, and can return a general verdict of guilty if they find that an "unlawful taking" has been proved. The elements of the several types of theft included within section 484 have not been changed, however, and a judgment of conviction of theft, based on a general verdict of guilty, can be sustained only if the evidence discloses the elements of one of the consolidated offenses. In the present case, it is clear from the record that each of the prosecuting witnesses intended to pass both title and possession, and that the type of theft, if any, in each case, was that of obtaining property by false pretenses. . . . [Defendant's] defense was not based on distinctions between title and possession, but rather he contends that there was no unlawful taking of any sort.

To support a conviction of theft for obtaining property by false pretenses, it must be shown that the defendant made a false pretense or representation with intent to defraud the owner of his property, and that the owner was in fact defrauded. It is unnecessary to prove that the defendant benefited personally from the fraudulent acquisition. People v. Jones, 36 Cal. 2d 373, 377, 381, 224 P.2d 353. The false pretense or representation must have materially influenced the owner to part with his property, but the false pretense need not be the sole inducing cause. If the conviction rests primarily on the testimony of a single witness that the false pretense was made, the making of the pretense must be corroborated. Pen. Code, §1110.

The crime of obtaining property by false pretenses was unknown in the early common law, and our statute, like those of most American states, is directly traceable to 30 Geo. 11, ch. 24, section 1. In an early Crown Case Reserved, Rex v. Goodhall, Russ. & Ry. 461 (1821), the defendant obtained a quantity of meat from a merchant by promising to pay at a future day. The jury found that the promise was made without intention to perform. The judges concluded, however, that the defendant's conviction was erroneous because the pretense "was merely a promise of future conduct, and common prudence and caution would have prevented any injury arising from it." Russ. & Ry. at 463. . . . By stating that the "promise of future conduct" was such that "common prudence and caution" could prevent any injury arising therefrom, the new offense was confused with the old common law "cheat." The decision also seems contrary to the plain meaning of the statute, and was so interpreted by two English writers on the law of crimes. Archbold, Pleading and Evidence in Criminal Cases 183 [3d ed. 1828]; Roscoe, Digest of the Law of Evidence in Criminal Cases 418 [2d Amer. ed. 1840]. The opinion of Rex v. Goodhall, supra, was completely misinterpreted in the case of Commonwealth v. Drew, 1837, 19 Pick. 179, 185, 36 Mass. 179, 185, in which the Supreme Judicial Court of Massachusetts declared by way of dictum, that under the statute "naked lies" could not be regarded as "false pretenses." On the basis of these two questionable decisions, Wharton formulated the following generalization: ". . . the false pretense to be within the statute, must relate to a state of things averred to be at the time existing, and not to a state of things thereafter to exist." Wharton, American Criminal Law 542 [1st ed. 1846]. This generalization has been followed in the majority of American cases, almost all of which can be traced to reliance on Wharton or the two cases mentioned above. The rule has not been followed in all jurisdictions, however. Some courts have avoided the problems created by the rule by blurring the distinctions between larceny by trick and device and obtaining property by false pretenses. See generally, Pearce, "Theft by False Promises," 101 U. of Pa. L. Rev. 967.[a] . . . Other courts have repudiated the majority rule. . . .[3]

a. "The technique is to throw the crime of larceny by trick into the breach in the law of theft by fraud which is opened by the promissory fraud rule." Pearce, Theft by False Promises, 101 U. Pa. L. Rev. 967, 987 (1953). See, e.g., Graham v. United States, pages 946-948 supra. — Eds.

3. The majority rule was also rejected by the United States Supreme Court in the construction

. . . The Court of Appeals for the District of Columbia has however, advanced the following reasons in defense of the majority rule: "It is of course true that then [at the time of the early English cases cited by Wharton, supra], as now, the intention to commit certain crimes was ascertained by looking backward from the act and finding that the accused intended to do what he did do. However, where, as here, the act complained of — namely, failure to repay money or use it as specified at the time of borrowing — is as consonant with ordinary commercial default as with criminal conduct, the danger of applying this technique to prove the crime is quite apparent. Business affairs would be materially incumbered by the ever present threat that a debtor might be subjected to criminal penalties if the prosecutor and jury were of the view that at the time of borrowing he was mentally a cheat. The risk of prosecuting one who is guilty of nothing more than a failure or inability to pay his debts is a very real consideration. . . ." Chaplin v. United States, 157 F.2d 697, 698-699.

. . . We do not find this reasoning persuasive. In this state, and in the majority of American states as well as in England, false promises can provide the foundation of a civil action for deceit. In such actions something more than nonperformance is required to prove the defendant's intent not to perform his promise. Nor is proof of nonperformance alone sufficient in criminal prosecutions based on false promises. In such prosecutions the People must, as in all criminal prosecutions, prove their case beyond a reasonable doubt. Any danger, through the instigation of criminal proceedings by disgruntled creditors, to those who have blamelessly encountered "commercial defaults" must, therefore, be predicated upon the idea that trial juries are incapable of weighing the evidence and understanding the instruction that they must be convinced of the defendant's fraudulent intent beyond a reasonable doubt, or that appellate courts will be derelict in discharging their duty to ascertain that there is sufficient evidence to support a conviction. . . .

. . . Moreover, in cases of obtaining property by false pretenses, it must be proved that any misrepresentations of fact alleged by the People were made knowingly and with intent to deceive. If such misrepresentations are made innocently or inadvertently, they can no more form the basis for a prosecution for obtaining property by false pretenses than can an innocent breach of contract. . . .

If false promises were not false pretenses, the legally sophisticated, without fear of punishment, could perpetrate on the unwary fraudulent schemes like that divulged by the record in this case. . . . The inclusion of false promises within sections 484 and 532 of the Penal Code will not "materially encumber" business affairs. . . .

. . . The judgment and the order denying the motion for a new trial are affirmed.

SCHAUER, J. I concur in the judgment solely on the ground that the evidence establishes, with ample corroboration, the making by the defendant of false representations as to existing facts. On that evidence the convictions should be sustained pursuant to long accepted theories of law. . . . Accordingly, I

---

of the federal mail fraud statute, 17 Stat. 283, 323. See Durland v. United States, 161 U.S. 306, 313. On the basis of the *Durland* case, the statute was amended to include specifically false promises, 35 Stat. 1130, 18 U.S.C. §1341 (1946).

dissent from all that portion of the opinion which discusses and pronounces upon the theories which in my view are extraneous to the proper disposition of any issue actually before us. . . .

In a prosecution for obtaining property by the making of a false promise, knowingly and with intent to deceive, the matter to be proved, as to its criminality, is purely subjective. It is not, like the specific intent in such a crime as burglary, a mere element of the crime; it is, in any significant sense, all of the crime. The proof will necessarily be of objective acts, entirely legal in themselves, from which inferences as to the ultimate illegal subjective fact will be drawn. But, whereas in burglary the proof of the subjective element is normally as strong and reliable as the proof of any objective element, in this type of activity the proof of such vital element can almost never be reliable; it must inevitably (in the absence of confession or something tantamount thereto) depend on inferences drawn by creditors, prosecutors, jurors, and judges from facts and circumstances which by reason of their nature cannot possibly exclude innocence with any certainty. . . . Such inferences as proof of the alleged crime have long been recognized as so unreliable that they have been excluded from the category of acceptable proof.

. . . I am unwilling to accept as a premise the scholastic redaction of the majority that rules of proof may be set aside because appellate judges will always know when a jury has been misled and the proof is not sufficient. . . .

The suggestion in the majority opinion that it is inconceivable "that trial juries are incapable of weighing the evidence [impliedly, with omniscient accuracy however inconclusive it be] and understanding the instruction that they must be convinced of the defendant's fraudulent intent beyond a reasonable doubt, or that appellate courts will be derelict [less than omniscient] in discharging their duty" affords no substantial basis for striking down a rule of proof. . . .

With the rule that the majority opinion now enunciates, no man, no matter how innocent his intention, can sign a promise to pay in the future, or to perform an act at a future date, without subjecting himself to the risk that at some later date others, in the light of differing perspectives, philosophies and subsequent events, may conclude that, after all, the accused *should* have known that at the future date he could not perform as he promised — and if he, as a "reasonable" man from the point of view of the creditor, district attorney and a grand or trial jury — *should* have known, then, it may be inferred, he did know. And if it can be inferred that he knew, then this court and other appellate courts will be bound to affirm a conviction. . . .

NEW YORK PENAL LAW

Section 155.05(2)(d)

A person obtains property by false promise when, pursuant to a scheme to defraud, he obtains property of another by means of a representation, express or implied, that he or a third person will in the future engage in particular conduct, and when he does not intend to engage in such conduct or, as the case may be, does not believe that the third person intends to engage in such conduct.

In any prosecution for larceny based upon a false promise, the defendant's intention or belief that the promise would not be performed may not be established by or inferred from the fact alone that such promise was not performed. Such a finding may be based only upon evidence establishing that the facts and circumstances of the case are wholly consistent with guilty intent or belief and wholly inconsistent with innocent intent or belief, and excluding to a moral certainty every hypothesis except that of the defendant's intention or belief that the promise would not be performed. . . .

MODEL PENAL CODE

Section 223.3. Theft by Deception

[See Appendix for text of this section.]

ENGLISH THEFT ACT
chapter 60 (1968)

15. — (1) A person who by any deception dishonestly obtains property belonging to another, with the intention of permanently depriving the other of it shall on conviction or indictment be liable to imprisonment for a term not exceeding ten years. . . .

(3) For purposes of this section "deception" means any deception (whether deliberate or reckless) by words or conduct as to fact or as to law, including a deception as to the present intentions of the persons using the deception or any other person.

NELSON v. UNITED STATES
United States Court of Appeals, District of Columbia Circuit
227 F.2d 21 (1955)

Danaher, J. This is an appeal from a conviction for obtaining goods by false pretenses in violation of D.C. Code §22-1301 (1951). The trial court entered judgment of acquittal on a second count charging grand larceny. Evidence was offered to show that appellant from time to time over a period of months, for purposes of resale, had purchased merchandise from Potomac Distributors of Washington, D.C., Inc. (hereinafter referred to as Potomac Distributors). By September 18, 1952, his account was said to be in arrears more than thirty days. Late that afternoon, appellant sought immediate possession of two television sets and a washing machine, displayed his customers' purchase contracts to support his statement that he had already sold such merchandise and had taken payment therefor, and told one Schneider, secretary-treasurer of Potomac Distributors, "I promised delivery tonight." Appellant was told no further credit could be extended to him because of his overdue indebtedness in excess of $1800, whereupon appellant offered to give security for the desired items as well as for the delinquent account. He represented himself as the owner of a

Packard car for which he had paid $4,260.50, but failed to disclose an outstanding prior indebtedness on the car of $3,028.08 secured by a chattel mortgage in favor of City Bank. Instead, he represented that he owed only one payment of some $55, not then due. Relying upon such representations, Potomac Distributors delivered to appellant two television sets each worth $136, taking in return a demand note for the entire indebtedness, past and present, in the total, $2,047.37, secured by a chattel mortgage on the Packard and the television sets. Appellant promised to make a cash payment on the note within a few days for default of which the holder was entitled to demand full payment. When the promised payment was not forthcoming, Schneider, by telephone calls and a personal visit to appellant's home, sought to locate appellant but learned he had left town. The Packard about that time was in a collision, incurring damage of about $1,000, and was thereupon repossessed in behalf of the bank which held the prior lien for appellant's car purchase indebtedness. . . .

Appellant argues that Potomac Distributors could not have been defrauded for the car on September 18, 1952, "had an equity of between $900 and $1000 and roughly five times the value of the two television sets." That fact is immaterial. . . .

This appellant has sold two television sets, and apparently had taken payment therefor although he had no television sets to deliver to his customers. He could not get the sets from Potomac Distributors without offering security for his past due account as well as for his present purchase. In order to get them he lied. He represented that his car acquired at a cost of more than $4000 required only one further payment of $55. He now complains because his victim believed him when he lied. He argues that the misrepresentations were not material although the victim testified, and the jury could properly find, that he would not have parted with his goods except in reliance upon appellant's statements. . . .

He argues that there was no proof of an intent upon his part to defraud his victim.

> "Wrongful acts knowingly or intentionally committed can neither be justified nor excused on the ground of innocent intent. The intent to injure or defraud is presumed when the unlawful act, which results in loss or injury, is proved to have been knowingly committed. It is a well-settled rule, which the law applies in both criminal and civil cases, that the intent is presumed and inferred from the result of the action."

This quotation from a challenged charge was found by the Supreme Court to be "unexceptionable as matter of law" in Agnew v. United States, 1897, 165 U.S. 36, 53. . . .

Affirmed.

MILLER, J. (dissenting). . . . Nelson did make a false representation; but the question is whether there was evidence from which the jury could properly be permitted to infer that he intended to defraud, and to conclude that Potomac was thereby defrauded. . . .

Differing definitions of the word "defraud" probably cause the difference in opinion between the majority and me. They seem to think it means, in connection with a purchase, to make a false pretense in the process of obtaining goods even though the purchase price is well secured. I think the word means, in connection with a purchase, to make a false pretense as a result of which the seller is deprived of his goods or of the purchase price. The difference is particularly important in a case like this one where a purchaser is charged with defrauding a seller. A purchaser can be said to have defrauded the seller of his goods only if he intended to defraud him of the purchase price for which the seller was willing to exchange them. It seems to me to follow that a purchaser who makes a false statement in buying on credit has not defrauded the seller of his goods if he nevertheless amply secures the debt. . . .

In considering the criminality vel non of the false statement, it must be remembered that the past due indebtedness of $1,697.87 is to play no part. That credit had already been extended generally, and with respect to it Potomac parted with nothing on September 18. Nelson was only charged with defrauding Potomac by obtaining through false pretense the articles then delivered, which had a total value of only $349.50.

What was the actual value on September 18 of the property upon which Potomac took a lien, on the strength of which it parted with property worth $349.50? The bank collection manager, testifying for the Government, said that although on September 18 Nelson still owed the bank $3,028.08, he had on that day an equity in the car worth from $900 to $1,000. The mortgaged television sets were, I suppose, worth their price of $272. Adding to this the minimum equity in the automobile proved by the prosecution, it appears that Potomac had a lien on property worth at least $1,172 to protect a debt of $349.50. The proportion was more than three to one.

Such is the evidence as to what happened September 18, from which the jury was permitted to infer that Nelson then intended to defraud, and to conclude that he then did fraudulently obtain from Potomac the three articles purchased. As to intent, I suggest that it is wholly irrational to presume or infer that one intends to defraud when he buys goods on credit and safeguards that credit by giving more than triple security for it — no matter if he does falsely pretend that the security is even greater. It is equally illogical to conclude that the creditor was thereby defrauded. For that reason, my opinion is that the proof I have outlined — which was the only pertinent proof — did not warrant the trial court in submitting the case to the jury. . . .

As I have said, Nelson was guilty of a moral wrong in falsely and grossly misrepresenting his debt to the bank, but in the circumstances he should not have been indicted and convicted because of it. The District of Columbia statute under which he was prosecuted does not make mere falsehood felonious; it only denounces as criminal a false pretense which was intended to defraud and which in fact had that result. Even a liar is entitled to the full protection of the law. I am afraid a grave injustice has been done in this case.

NOTES AND QUESTIONS

1. Defendant contractor applied to the owner of the house he was in the process of constructing for an advance to meet the weekly payroll. Periodic advances were provided for in the construction contract. Since the owner had just been notified that defendant was indebted to a material-man and requested not to make further advancements, he informed defendant he would make no further payments until the debt was paid. Defendant then assured him that he had that morning discharged the debt (in fact, he had not done so), whereupon the owner paid over the requested advance and defendant paid the employees their wages. May defendant be convicted of obtaining money by false pretenses? See Sanson v. Commonwealth, 313 Ky. 631, 233 S.W.2d 258 (1950); Annot., Obtaining payment by debtor on valid indebtedness by false representation as criminal false pretenses, 20 A.L.R.2d 1266 (1951). Would the prosecutor's case be stronger if defendant's false representation had been that he needed the money to obtain from a carrier a recently arrived shipment of materials for the house? See the material on mens rea, pages 973-986 infra.

2. Cf. Rex v. Clucas, [1949] 2 All E.R. 40, 41-42, per Lord Goddard, C.J.:

> The evidence showed that these two men, who obviously were dishonest, induced bookmakers to bet with them by representing that they were commission agents acting on behalf of a large number of workmen who were making small bets on various races, whereas, in fact, they were making bets in considerable sums of money for themselves alone. The main question which arises . . . can be stated in this way. Does a man who induces a bookmaker to bet with him by making false pretences as to his identity or as to the capacity in which he is making the bets obtain money by false pretences if he is fortunate enough to back a winning horse and so receives money from the bookmaker? In the opinion of the court it is impossible to say that there was here an obtaining of the money by the false pretences which were alleged, because the money was obtained, not by reason of the fact that the accused persons falsely pretended that they were somebody or acting in some capacity which they were not, but because they backed a winning horse as a result of which the bookmaker paid them the sums obtained. No doubt, the bookmaker might never have opened an account with these men if he had known the true facts, but we must distinguish between a contributing cause and the effective cause which led the bookmaker to pay the money, namely, the fact that these men had backed a winning horse.

3. For comments on the *Nelson* case, see 23 U. Chi. L. Rev. 509 (1956); 65 Yale L.J. 887 (1956).

In re CLEMONS
Supreme Court of Ohio
168 Ohio St. 83, 151 N.E.2d 553 (1958)

MATTHIAS, J. The single issue before us is whether the making and issuance, with intent to defraud, of a check signed by the maker with his own name but drawn on a bank in which such maker has no "checking account" constitute a violation of Section 2913.01, Revised Code, i.e., whether the petitioner was convicted of a crime over which the Common Pleas Court of Gallia County had jurisdiction pursuant to the indictment hereinbefore set out.

Section 2913.01, Revised Code, reads in part as follows:

> No person, with intent to defraud, shall falsely make . . . a . . . check . . . or, with like intent, utter or publish as true and genuine such false . . . matter, knowing it to be false. . . .
> Whoever violates this section is guilty of forgery. . . .[a]

a. Punishable by imprisonment from 1 to 20 years. Now Ohio Rev. Code Ann. tit. 29, §2913.31. — EDS.

. . . Although it is true that a check is merely an order to a bank to pay on demand a certain sum, in order for a check to be considered a genuine instrument the maker must have a *right to make such order,* i.e., he must have money in the drawee bank.

It seems perfectly clear to this court that the making of an instrument purporting to be a check, with intent to defraud, drawn on a bank wherein the maker has no "checking account" constitutes the false making of a check within the purview of the statute, regardless of whether the maker signs his own name or that of another, and that such act was intended by the General Assembly to be included in its definition of "forgery" as set out in Section 2913.01, Revised Code.

In fully sustaining the position of the Court of Appeals for Sandusky County, we find that we cannot improve on the following language of explanation used by Judge Fess of that court, in the *Havens* case [91 Ohio App. 578, 109 N.E.2d 49]:

"Forgery at common law is defined by Blackstone as the fraudulent making or altering of a writing to the prejudice of another's right, and by East as the false making or altering, malo animo, of any written instrument for the purposes of fraud and deceit. In 1865, In re Windsor, 6 Best & Smith, 522, Cockburn, C.J., declared that forgery 'by universal acceptation . . . is understood to mean, the making or altering a writing so as to make the writing or alteration purport to be the act of some other person, which it is not.' But in 1869, in Rex v. Ritson, 1 Law Reports, Crown Cases, 200, it was held that forgery is the fraudulent making of an instrument in words purporting to be what they are not, to the prejudice of another's rights. . . . It is apparent that the cases in the United States have departed from the broad common law definition and have followed the more narrow rule pronounced by Cockburn in In re Windsor. In its ordinary sense, forgery is the false signing of another's name, but . . . Section 13083 of the Ohio General Code [Section 2913.01, Revised Code] is much broader and more inclusive than the Cockburn definition. . . ."

Following his lucid explanation, Judge Fess drew this conclusion, which is hereby adopted as the conclusion of the Supreme Court on the subject:

"We, therefore, . . . hold that under Section . . . [2913.01, Revised Code], a person is guilty of the false making of a check where the check is drawn upon a bank in which the maker has no funds or deposit account and is calculated to induce another to give credit to it as genuine and authentic, even though such person signs his own name thereto and likewise that one who utters such a check [with knowledge of its falsity] is guilty of forgery." [b] . . .

Judgment reversed.

TAFT, J. (dissenting). . . . Although the check drawn in the instant case was almost certain to be dishonored by the bank upon which it was drawn, it was exactly what it purported to be, that is, a check drawn by petitioner who signed his own name to it. . . . [O]ur statute by defining a "false making" of a writing as a forgery has not thereby made something a forgery which was not within

---

b. "No case in any other jurisdiction has been found which goes this far." 72 Harv. L. Rev. 566, 568 (1959). The same result would not be possible under Ohio Rev. Code Ann. §§2913.31, 2913.01(G), which supersede the provisions in issue in the principal case. The present bad check statute is Ohio Rev. Code Ann. §2913.11. It embraces the bad check offenses previously defined as forgery and provides for punishment of one to three years' imprisonment. — EDS.

the common-law definition of a forgery. In short, those words were always used in defining the common-law crime of forgery. . . .

NOTES AND QUESTIONS

1. Does the distinction between the making of a false instrument and the making of false statements in an instrument that is what it purports to be — the traditional line between forgery and other fraud crimes — have any criminological significance? What is the point of retaining the crime of forgery, with its separate penalties, distinct from fraud and false pretenses?

2. In the *Clemons* case, could defendant have been convicted of obtaining by false pretenses? Would it make any difference whether something of value was obtained by the bad check? Whether the drawer had an account with the drawee bank but without funds to cover the check or had no account at all? Whether the check was postdated? See State v. Larsen, 76 Idaho 528, 286 P.2d 646 (1955).

3. Compare with the *Clemons* case, Gilbert v. United States, 370 U.S. 650 (1962), holding that a person who endorsed a government check by signing the name of the payee followed by his own, as agent, where he in fact had no such authority, would not be guilty of forgery under the common law, and hence is not guilty under the federal forgery statute, 18 U.S.C. §495. The act was found not to constitute common law forgery because the falsity resided in the misrepresentation of his authority, not in the genuineness of the endorsement.

4. For the Model Penal Code approach, see §224.1, Appendix to this casebook. In England, Regina v. Dodge, [1972] 1 Q.B. 416, reestablished the historic principle that to constitute a forgery the document must not merely contain a lie but tell a lie about itself. See Williams, Forgery and Falsity, [1974] Crim. L. Rev. 71.

4. Consolidation

INTRODUCTORY NOTE

Insofar as the pattern of discrete theft offenses covering fundamentally similar kinds of acquisitive conduct has left gaps in the law — for example, where deliberately false promises are employed to induce another to transfer his property — only legislative or judicial revision of the definitions of criminal conduct can supply an effective remedy. But another and more direct consequence of this condition of the law of theft is procedural in character. A defendant convicted of one of these theft offenses, embezzlement, say, may be able to obtain a reversal on appeal through the curious device of proving that the evidence technically established another offense, say, larceny. See, e.g., Nolan v. State, pages 924-926, and State v. Griffen, pages 950-951 supra. There are some dramatic examples of this tactic succeeding altogether in frustrating conviction of acknowledged thieves. See, e.g., Commonwealth v. O'Malley, 97 Mass. 584 (1867); Nichols

v. People, 17 N.Y. 114 (1858). And in all cases the possibility is a constant threat to the efficient administration of criminal justice. The problem is not with the general principles that a person may not be convicted of a crime with which he or she has not been charged or that a conviction may not stand on appeal where the proof shows the commission of a different crime than the one charged. It is rather that the distinctions between many of the discrete theft offenses (1) are without criminological significance, (2) are so indefinite and intangible that it is often anybody's guess into which theft category some conduct falls in any particular jurisdiction, and (3) turn on highly technical legal characterizations of basically similar fact situations rather than real differences in conduct, so that in these cases a defendant is not likely to be prejudiced (though, of course, he or she may be) by a variance between charge and proof.

The principal means of reform, which has gained widespread acceptance, is to consolidate the variety of common law forms of wrongful acquisition of another's property into one single crime, which might be called "theft" or "larceny," and to deprive the differences in modes of acquisition of any legal significance. Some examples follow.

MODEL PENAL CODE: *Section 223.1.* Consolidation of Theft Offenses; Grading; Provisions Applicable to Theft Generally. [See Appendix for text of this section.]

NEW YORK PENAL LAW: *Section 155.05.* Larceny; Defined. 1. A person steals property and commits larceny when, with intent to deprive another of property or to appropriate the same to himself or to a third person, he wrongfully takes, obtains or withholds such property from an owner thereof.

2. Larceny includes a wrongful taking, obtaining or withholding of another's property, with the intent prescribed in subdivision one of this section, committed in any of the following ways:

(a) By conduct heretofore defined or known as common law larceny by trespassory taking, common law larceny by trick, embezzlement, or obtaining property by false pretenses;

(b) By acquiring lost property. . . .

(c) By committing the crime of issuing a bad check. . . .

(d) By false promise. . . .

(e) By extortion. . . .

Section 155.45. Larceny; Pleading and Proof. 1. Where it is an element of the crime charged that property was taken from the person or obtained by extortion, an indictment for larceny must so specify. In all other cases, an indictment, information or complaint for larceny is sufficient if it alleges that the defendant stole property of the nature or value required for the commission of the crime charged without designating the particular way or manner in which such property was stolen or the particular theory of larceny involved.

2. Proof that the defendant engaged in any conduct constituting larceny as defined in section 155.05 is sufficient to support any indictment, information or complaint for larceny other than one charging larceny by extortion. An indictment charging larceny by extortion must be supported by proof establishing larceny by extortion.

ILLINOIS ANNOTATED STATUTES chapter 38: *Section 16 — 1.* Theft. A person commits theft when he knowingly:

(a) Obtains or exerts unauthorized control over property of the owner; or

(b) Obtains by deception control over property of the owner; or

(c) Obtains by threat control over property of the owner; or

(d) Obtains control over stolen property knowing the property to have been stolen by another, or under such circumstances as would reasonably induce him to believe that the property was stolen, and

(1) Intends to deprive the owner permanently of the use or benefit of the property; or

(2) Knowingly uses, conceals or abandons the property in such manner as to deprive the owner permanently of such use or benefit; or

(3) Uses, conceals, or abandons the property knowing such use, concealment or abandonment probably will deprive the owner permanently of such use or benefit.

CALIFORNIA PENAL CODE: *Section 484.* Every person who shall feloniously steal, take, carry, lead, or drive away the personal property of another, or who shall fraudulently appropriate property which has been entrusted to him, or who shall knowingly and designedly, by any false or fraudulent representation or pretense, defraud any other person of money, labor or real or personal property, . . . is guilty of theft.

Section 952. In charging an offense, each count shall contain, and shall be sufficient if it contains in substance, a statement that the accused has committed some public offense therein specified. . . . In charging theft it shall be sufficient to allege that the defendant unlawfully took the labor or property of another.

B. THE PROPERTY SUBJECT TO THEFT

STATE v. MILLER

Supreme Court of Oregon
192 Or. 188, 233 P.2d 786 (1951)

LUSK, J. [Defendant induced complaining witness to agree to guarantee his indebtedness to another on his false representation that he owned a tractor free of encumbrance and on his executing a chattel mortgage thereto as security. In fact defendant was purchasing the tractor under a conditional sales contract. He was convicted of obtaining property by false pretenses.]

The defendant has appealed from the judgment of conviction, assigning a number of alleged errors, among them the court's overruling of the defendant's motion, interposed at the beginning of the trial, objecting to the introduction of any evidence on the ground that the indictment failed to charge a crime against the defendant. . . .

The statute under which this prosecution is attempted to be maintained is §23-537, O.C.L.A., and, so far as in any way material, reads:

If any person shall, by any false pretenses or by any privity [sic] or false token, and with intent to defraud, obtain or attempt to obtain, from any other person any money or property whatsoever, or shall obtain or attempt to obtain with the like intent the signature of any person to any writing, the false making whereof would be punishable as forgery, such person, upon conviction thereof, shall be punished by imprisonment. . . . The making of a bill of sale, or assignment, or mortgage of personal property, by any person not the owner thereof, for the purpose of obtaining money or credit, or to secure an existing indebtedness, shall be deemed a false pretense within the meaning of this section.

. . . Reduced to its simplest terms, this indictment means that by false pretenses the defendant induced the Hub Lumber Company to agree to pay his indebtedness to the Howard Cooper Corporation if he should fail to pay it. The question is whether this amounts to an allegation that, in the sense of the statute, the defendant obtained "any property" from the Hub Lumber Company. If not, then the indictment does not change a crime. . . . There is no claim that the case falls within the provision of the statute which denounces the making of a bill of sale or assignment or mortgage of personal property by any person not the owner thereof for the purpose of obtaining money or credit or securing an existing indebtedness. Under this latter provision the person in whose favor the false instrument is made must also be the person from whom the money or credit is sought to be obtained or to whom the existing indebtedness is owing. So much is not disputed. . . .

The source of the false pretenses statute in this country is the common law and the statute law of England. State v. Tower, 122 Kan. 165, 251 P. 401. The English courts hold that the thing obtained must be the subject of larceny at common law, and accordingly a conviction for obtaining two dogs by false pretenses was quashed because at common law dog stealing is not larceny, Reg. v. Robinson, 8 Cox's Criminal Law Cases 115 (1859); so likewise of an indictment for obtaining food and lodging by false pretenses. Rex v. Bagley, 17 Cr. App. R. 162 (1923). Under statutes like ours many of the courts of this country take the same view of the law. The California statute covers "money or property." Pen. Code, §532. The court in People v. Cummings, 114 Cal. 437, 46 P. 284, in holding that the word "property" did not include real property, said: "And the offense of false pretenses, under the English statutes, has always been construed as largely analogous to, and closely bordering upon, that of larceny, and as applying only to personal property, which was capable of manual delivery. . . . Real property under the English law was never the subject of the offense either of cheating or of false pretenses." . . .

It should be observed at this point that our statute in respect of the present question is not as broad as those in some of the other states. It reads "any money or property whatsoever." In some of the states, as stated in Burdick [Law of Crime], 481, §640, the statutes, "after enumerating various classes of personal property, conclude the list with what is apparently intended as an all inclusive term, such as 'other things of value,' 'any other valuable thing,' or 'any other valuable thing or effects whatsoever.' " The Kansas statute includes "any money, personal property, right in action, or any other valuable thing or effects whatsoever." G.S. 1949, 21-551. Notwithstanding the comprehensiveness of this provision, the court in State v. Tower, supra, held, in the light of the origin and history of the crime of false pretenses, that obtaining an extension of time in which to pay a matured debt was not a "valuable thing" within the meaning of the section. The term "personal property" was said "to denote personal movable things generally." "Mere pecuniary advantage, devoid of any physical attribute of money, chattel, or valuable security, in the sense of the English statute, was not included."

The Louisiana statute refers to "money or any property." Rev. St. §813. In State v. Eicher, 174 La. 344, 140 So. 498, 499, the defendant was charged with obtaining credit from a bank by falsely representing that a certain note had value and was secured by a chattel mortgage. The indictment was held bad, the court saying that "The privilege of having a note renewed or the time of its payment extended may be and frequently is a valuable one to the debtor. But such privilege or advantage is neither money nor property in the sense those terms are ordinarily used and understood." The court further said: " 'Property,' as that term is used in this statute, means worldly goods or possessions, tangible things, and things which have an exchangeable or commercial value."

These are not isolated holdings, but in their conception of the meaning of the word "property," as used in statutes of this sort, represent the current of authority. . . .

The provisions of the statute which make unlawful the obtaining of the signature of any person with intent to defraud, and the making of a bill of sale or assignment or mortgage of personal property for the purpose of obtaining money or credit or to secure an existing indebtedness, rather definitely indicate that such an intangible thing as credit was not considered by the legislature to be property.

Moreover, this court [has] recognized that "property" under the statute must be something capable of being possessed and the title to which can be transferred. . . . It need hardly be said that the thing which the defendant is charged with obtaining in the present indictment, the guaranty, or, to be more accurate, the benefit of the guaranty which the Hub Lumber Company gave to the Howard Cooper Corporation, could not be possessed, and that there could be no such thing as holding title to it.

Had the indictment alleged that the defendant obtained the signature of the Hub Lumber Company or its agent to a guaranty of the defendant's indebtedness, we would have had an entirely different question. The failure so to allege was not due to an oversight of the pleader but to the facts themselves, for the proof is that no written guaranty was ever executed but merely an oral one. . . .

Even though our statute included "a thing in action," see People v. Ward, 3 N.Y. Cr. R. 483, it would avail the prosecution nothing, for the guaranty was not, so far as the defendant was concerned, a "thing in action." It is doubtless true, as the state's brief asserts, that "a guaranty is a chose in action, a right to indemnity from the guarantor," but it is the right of the creditor who extends credit on the faith of the guaranty, not of the debtor to whom credit is given. The defendant did not receive even a chose in action from the Hub Lumber Company. . . .

. . . The state argues that by the weight of authority the obtaining of a loan by fraud is a violation of the statute and asserts that this is a similar case. But in the loan cases, as the state's brief itself points out, the victim parts with his money. And, while it is true (although not alleged in the indictment) that, just as in the loan cases, the accused obtained credit, he obtained it, not from the victim of his false representations, but from another.

The state's argument of "policy" that the public are entitled to the protection of the law against immoral and reprehensible conduct such as that with which the accused was charged, and of which, no doubt, he was guilty, is appealing, but should be addressed to the legislature, not to the courts. The legislature has not undertaken to make every fraud a crime, but has set boundaries around the crime of false pretenses which the courts must respect and have no authority to pass.

The indictment, in our opinion, does not allege a crime, and the judgment must therefore be reversed and the action dismissed.

NOTES

1. Compare Model Penal Code, §223.0(6):

property means anything of value, including real estate, tangible and intangible personal property, contract rights, choses-in-action and other interests in or claims to wealth, admission or transportation tickets, captured or domestic animals, food and drink, electric or other power.

Or. Rev. Stat. §164.005(5):

any article, substance or thing of value, including, but not limited to, money, tangible and intangible personal property, real property, choses-in-action, evidence of debt or of contract.

2. In Chappell v. United States, 270 F.2d 274 (9th Cir. 1959), defendant, an Air Force sergeant, was convicted of knowingly converting property of the United States by making use of the services and labor of an airman to paint his own private dwellings during the airman's on-duty hours. The statute, 18 U.S.C. §641, the same as that involved in Morissette v. United States, 342 U.S. 246 (1952), pages 324-328, supra, was construed as intending no such revolutionary change in the common law as would be entailed, in the court's view, in holding that an employee's services were property which could be stolen. The conviction was reversed. Cf. People v. Ashworth, 220 A.D. 498, 222 N.Y.S. 24 (1927) (unauthorized use of another's machinery not larceny.) In United States v. Friedman, 445 F.2d 1076 (9th Cir. 1971), doubt was cast on the continued validity of the *Chappell* case.

With respect to theft of services, see Model Penal Code §223.7, Appendix to this casebook; cf. Ill. Ann. Stat. ch. 38, §16-3; N.Y. Penal Law §165.15; Or. Rev. Stat. §164.125.

UNITED STATES v. GIRARD
United States Court of Appeals, 2d Circuit
601 F.2d 69 (1969)

VAN GRAAFEILAND, J. Appellants have appealed from judgments convicting them of the unauthorized sale of government property (18 U.S.C. §641) and of conspiring to accomplish the sale (18 U.S.C. §371). . . .

In May 1977, appellant Lambert was an agent of the Drug Enforcement Administration, and Girard was a former agent. During that month, Girard and one James Bond began to discuss a proposed illegal venture that involved smuggling a planeload of marijuana from Mexico into the United States. Girard told Bond that for $500 per name he could, through an inside source, secure reports from the DEA files that would show whether any participant in the proposed operation was a government informant. Unfortunately for Mr. Girard, Bond himself became an informant and disclosed his conversations with Girard to the DEA. Thereafter, dealings between Bond and Girard were conducted under the watchful eye of the DEA. Bond asked Girard to secure reports on four men whose names were furnished him by DEA agents. DEA records are kept in computerized files, and the DEA hoped to identify the inside source by monitoring access to the four names in the computer bank. In this manner, the DEA learned that Girard's informant was Lambert, who obtained the reports through a computer terminal located in his office. The convictions on Counts One and Two are based on the sale of this information.

Section 641, so far as pertinent, provides that whoever without authority sells any "record . . . or thing of value" of the United States or who "receives . . . the same with intent to convert it to his use or gain, knowing it to have been embezzled, stolen, purloined or converted," shall be guilty of a crime.[a] Appellants contend that the statute covers only tangible property or documents and therefore is not violated by the sale of information. This contention was rejected by District Judge Daly. . . . We agree with the District Judge's decision. . . .

Like the District Judge, we are impressed by Congress' repeated use of the phrase "thing of value" in section 641 and its predecessors. These words are found in so many criminal statutes throughout the United States that they have in a sense become words of art. The word "thing" notwithstanding, the phrase is generally construed to cover intangibles as well as tangibles. For example, amusement is held to be a thing of value under gambling statutes. . . . Sexual intercourse, or the promise of sexual intercourse, is a thing of value under a bribery statute. . . . So also are a promise to reinstate an employee . . . and an agreement not to run in a primary election. . . . The testimony of a witness is a thing of value under 18 U.S.C. §876, which prohibits threats made through the mails with the intent to extort money or any other "thing of value.". . .

Although the content of a writing is an intangible, it is nonetheless a thing of value. The existence of a property in the contents of unpublished writings was judicially recognized long before the advent of copyright laws. . . . Although we are not concerned here with the laws of copyright, we are satisfied, nonetheless, that the Government has a property interest in certain of its private

---

a. The full text of 18 U.S.C. §641 reads as follows: "Whoever embezzles, steals, purloins, or knowingly converts to his use or the use of another, or without authority, sells, conveys or disposes of any record, voucher, money, or thing of value of the United States or of any department or agency thereof, or any property made or being made under contract for the United States or any department or agency thereof, or

"Whoever receives, conceals, or retains the same with intent to convert it to his use or gain, knowing it to have been embezzled, stolen, purloined or converted —

"Shall be fined not more than $10,000 or imprisoned not more than ten years, or both; but if the value of such property does not exceed the sum of $100, he shall be fined not more than $1,000 or imprisoned not more than one year, or both.

"The word 'value' means face, par, or market value, or cost price, either wholesale or retail, whichever is greater." — EDS.

records which it may protect by statute as a thing of value. It has done this by the enactment of section 641. See United States v. Friedman, 445 F.2d 1076, 1087 (9th Cir. 1971) (transcript of grand jury proceedings). Section 641 is not simply a statutory codification of the common law of larceny. See Morissette v. United States, 342 U.S. 246, 269 n.28 (1952). . . . If, as the Court said in *Morissette*, supra, conversion is the "misuse or abuse of property" or its use "in an unauthorized manner," the defendants herein could properly be found to have converted DEA's computerized records.

The District Judge also rejected appellants' constitutional challenge to section 641 based upon alleged vagueness and overbreadth, and again we agree with his ruling. Appellants, at the time of the crime a current and a former employee of the DEA, must have known that the sale of DEA confidential law enforcement records was prohibited. The DEA's own rules and regulations forbidding such disclosure may be considered as both a delimitation and clarification of the conduct proscribed by the statute. . . . Where, as here, we are not dealing with defendants' exercise of a First Amendment freedom, we should not search for statutory vagueness that did not exist for the defendants themselves. . . . Neither should we find a constitutional infirmity simply because the statute might conceivably trespass upon the First Amendment rights of others. In view of the statute's plainly legitimate sweep in regulating conduct, it is not so substantially overbroad that any overbreadth that may exist cannot be cured on a case by case basis.

The judgments . . . are affirmed.

NOTES

1. Mr. Anthony Lewis, of the New York Times, had some harsh things to say about such an interpretation of §641. Speaking about the same theory sanctioned by a federal trial court in another case, he said (International Herald Tribune, June 20, 1978):

> The two men were charged — and convicted — under Section 641 of the federal criminal code, which makes it a crime to steal government property. What was the property? The Justice Department said it was information, and Judge Albert V. Bryan Jr. followed that view of the law when he charged the jury.
>
> "Information may be government property," the judge said, "apart from the document or the sheets of paper themselves." Thus it does not matter if the original government document remains in the files. Anyone who copies it or makes notes from it without official approval has still stolen "property."
>
> For advocates of secrecy, the beauty of that legal theory is that it applies to no matter what kind of government information is involved. National security need not have a thing to do with it. The price of food in the White House mess, the Amtrak deficit — any fact that leaked could be the subject of a criminal prosecution.
>
> In short, the government-property theory of information would give this country an Official Secrets Act. It would be potentially as devastating to the press and public knowledge as Britain's secrecy law, which Americans and a good many Britons have for years condemned.

See Nimmer, National Secrets v. Free Speech: The Issues Left Undecided in the *Ellsberg* Case, 28 Stan. L. Rev. 311 (1974).

2. In United States v. Bottone, 365 F.2d 389, 393-394 (2d Cir. 1966), defendants purchased documents, for ultimate exportation to Europe, from several former employees of Lederle Laboratories, knowing that the employees had temporarily removed and copied the documents. The documents described secret processes for manufacturing antibiotics. The court, per Friendly, J., upheld their conviction of a federal receiving charge, stating (at 393-394):

> The only serious point of law raised by appellants is whether the transportation of papers describing the Lederle processes constituted the transportation in interstate or foreign commerce of "any goods, wares, merchandise, securities or money, of the value of $5,000 or more, knowing the same to have been stolen, converted or taken by fraud." 18 U.S.C. §2314. The problem is not any doubt on our part that papers describing manufacturing procedures are goods, wares, or merchandise, as was held with respect to geophysical maps in United States v. Seagraves, 265 F.2d 876 (3 Cir. 1959), and United States v. Lester, 282 F.2d 750 (3 Cir. 1960). Neither do we have any concern over the value of these papers, since we dismiss out of hand the contentions that secret processes for which European drug manufacturers were willing to pay five and six figures and in whose illicit exploitation appellants eagerly invested a large portion of their time and an appreciable amount of their fortunes were not worth the $5,000 required to subject them to federal prosecution. . . . The serious question is whether, on the facts of this case, the papers showing Lederle processes that were transported in interstate or foreign commerce were "goods" which had been "stolen, converted or taken by fraud" in view of the lack of proof that any of the physical materials so transported came from Lederle's possession. The standard procedure was for Fox and Cancelarich to remove documents from Lederle's files at Pearl River, N.Y., take these to Fox' home within New York state, make photocopies, microfilms or notes, and then restore the purloined papers to the files; only the copies and notes moved or were intended to move in interstate or foreign commerce. The case differs in this respect from the Third Circuit cases of *Seagraves* and *Lester* where, as the records on appeal show, the photostats and tracings delivered by the Gulf Oil geologist were the property of the company, having been made in the company's office, on its paper and with its equipment.
>
> We are not persuaded, however, that a different result should obtain simply because the intangible information that was the purpose of the theft was transformed and embodied in a different physical object. To be sure, where no tangible objects were ever taken or transported, a court would be hard pressed to conclude that "goods" had been stolen and transported within the meaning of §2314; the statute would presumably not extend to the case where a carefully guarded secret formula was memorized, carried away in the recesses of a thievish mind and placed in writing only after a boundary had been crossed.[a] The situation, however, is quite different where tangible goods are stolen and transported and the only obstacle to condemnation is a clever intermediate transcription or use of a photocopy machine. In such a case, when the physical form of the stolen goods is secondary in every respect to the matter recorded in them, the transformation of the information in the stolen papers into a tangible object never possessed by the original owner should be deemed immaterial. It would offend common sense to hold that these defendants fall outside the statute simply because, in efforts to avoid detection, their confederates were at pains to restore the original papers to Lederle's files and transport only copies or notes, although an oversight would have brought them within it.

a. Query: Why not? — Eds.

OXFORD v. MOSS
Divisional Court,
68 Crim. App. 183 (1978)

SMITH, J. This is a prosecutor's Appeal by way of Case stated.

On May 5, 1976, an information was preferred by the prosecutor against the defendant alleging that the defendant stole certain intangible property, namely, confidential information being examination questions for a Civil Engineering Examination to be held in the month of June 1976 at Liverpool University, the information being the property of the Senate of the University, and the allegation being that the Respondent intended permanently to deprive the said Senate of the said property.

The facts . . . are as follows. In May 1976 the defendant was a student at Liverpool University. He was studying engineering. Somehow (and this Court is not concerned precisely how) he was able to acquire the proof of an examination paper for an examination in Civil Engineering to be held in the University during the following month, that is to say June 1976. Without doubt the proof, that is to say the piece of paper, was the property of the University. It was an agreed fact, as set out in the case, that the respondent at no time intended to steal what is described as "any tangible element" belonging to the paper; that is to say it is conceded that he never intended to steal the paper itself.

. . . He was borrowing a piece of paper hoping to be able to return it and not be detected in order that he should acquire advance knowledge of the questions to be set in the examination and thereby, I suppose, he would be enabled to have an unfair advantage as against other students who did not possess the knowledge that he did.

By any standards, it was conduct which is to be condemned, and to the layman it would readily be described as cheating. The question raised is whether it is conduct which falls within the scope of the criminal law.

The learned stipendiary magistrate at Liverpool was of the opinion that, on the facts of the case, confidential information is not a form of intangible property as opposed to the property in the proof examination paper itself, that is the paper and the words printed thereon. He was of the opinion, further, that confidence consisted in the right to control the publication of the proof paper and was a right over property other than a form of intangible property.

Finally, he was of the opinion that by his conduct the respondent had gravely interfered with the owner's right over the paper. He had not permanently deprived the owner of any intangible property. Accordingly, the learned stipendiary magistrate dismissed the charge.

The prosecutor appeals. The question for this Court, shortly put, is whether confidential information can amount to property within the meaning of the Theft Act 1968. By section 1(1) of the statute: "A person is guilty of theft if he dishonestly appropriates property belonging to another with the intention of permanently depriving the other of it. . . . "

By section 4(1): " 'property' includes money and all other property, real or personal, including things in action and other intangible property."

The question for this Court is whether confidential information of this sort falls within that definition contained in section 4(1). We have been referred to a number of authorities emanating from the area of trade secrets and matrimonial secrets. . . .

Those are cases concerned with what is described as the duty to be of good faith. They are clear illustrations of the proposition that, if a person obtains information which is given to him in confidence and then sets out to take an unfair advantage of it, the courts will restrain him by way of an order of injunction or will condemn him in damages if an injunction is found to be inappropriate. . . . [T]hey are of little assistance in the present situation in which we have to consider whether there is property in the information which is capable of being the subject of a charge of theft. In my judgment, it is clear that the answer to that question must be no. Accordingly, I would dismiss the Appeal.

NOTES AND QUESTIONS

1. The "property" in Oxford v. Moss. A comment on the principal case, [1979] Crim. L. Rev. 120, suggests the following argument for treating the action of defendant as a case of theft:

The acquisition of the proof by the defendant might be held to be an assumption of the rights of the owner and therefore an "appropriation," because it was of the essence of the ownership of this particular piece of property that it should be kept out of the sight of unauthorised eyes. The difficulty is one of finding an intention permanently to deprive the owner of the question paper. At first sight, it seems obvious that the defendant did not so intend. However, section 6 of the Theft Act 1968 provides

(1) A person appropriating property belonging to another without meaning the other permanently to lose the thing itself is nevertheless to be regarded as having the intention of permanently depriving the other of it if his intention is to treat the thing as his own to dispose of regardless of the other's rights; and a borrowing or lending of it may amount to so treating if it, but only if, the borrowing or lending is for a period and in circumstances making it equivalent to an outright taking or disposal. . . .

. . . [H]ad not the virtue gone out of the examination paper once it had been seen by unauthorised eyes? If it was rendered thus useless, it appears to be the same in principle as the case of the season ticket [returned after the season] and the dry battery [returned when it is exhausted]; and these are certainly appropriately treated as something more than ordinary borrowings and, indeed, as theft. Thus the best course might have been the bold one of charging theft of the question paper, and arguing that the question paper is more than a piece of paper and that, in the circumstances the borrowing was equivalent to an outright taking or disposal. If the University had to set another paper, it was immaterial whether the defendant took the paper or left it. What he left was of no value. Of course, this argument would depend on evidence being available that circumstances were such that the question paper did indeed become useless to the University and, since it is a question of intention, that the defendant knew of the circumstances which thus made the borrowing equivalent in law to an outright taking and, therefore permanent deprivation.

An answer to this argument might be that the paper became worthless only because the defendant was found out. If he had not been found out, the paper would have been used in the examinations and perhaps no one would have ever known the truth. If that were the only objection, it might be answered by observing that a person would certainly be guilty of theft from *P* if he took *P*'s Rembrandt and replaced it with a copy, even though *P* never realised that the exchange had been made and continued to enjoy the copy as much as he had enjoyed the original until the day of his death.

2. Jointly owned property. Can a partner be convicted of larceny or embezzlement if he or she appropriates partnership funds for personal use? Can a partner be convicted of obtaining property by false pretense if he or she fraudulently induces another partner to transfer such funds to him or her? Most courts answer these questions in the negative. The rationale appears to be that it is "impossible to determine whether or not the defendant partner is in fact indebted to the plaintiff partner until the partnership accounts are settled. . . ." See State v. Quinn, 245 Iowa 846, 64 N.W.2d 323, 329 (1954) (concurring opinion). The Model Penal Code rejects this rule. See §223.0(7), Appendix to this casebook. The Commentary explains that whatever the merits of the rule barring a civil action by one joint owner against another (prior to an accounting of all partnership assets), this rule has no relevance to the criminal law's efforts to deter deprivations of other people's economic interests. See Comment to §206.1(4) (Tent. Draft No. 1, 1953). The Model Penal Code approach has been adopted by judicial interpretation in California. See People v. Sobiek, 30 Cal. App. 3d 458, 106 Cal. Rptr. 519 (1973).

Theft from a spouse raises related problems. In this area, the traditional common law dogmas are rapidly being rejected. See, e.g., People v. Morton, 308 N.Y. 96, 123 N.E.2d 790 (1954); Stewart v. Commonwealth, 252 S.E.2d 329 (Va. 1979). Are there valid reasons for continuing to treat interspousal theft as an exceptional situation? Cf. Model Penal Code §223.1(4):

> It is no defense that theft was from the actor's spouse, except that misappropriation of household and personal effects, or other property normally accessible to both spouses, is theft only if it occurs after the parties have ceased living together.

3. Secured property. In cases where the actual owner of property wrongfully takes it from the possession of another who has a special interest therein, such as a lienor, e.g., People v. Travis, 275 A.D. 444, 90 N.Y.S.2d 848 (1949), or a pledgee, e.g., Rose v. Matt, [1951] 1 All E.R. 361, the prevailing view is that such action constitutes theft. What is the difference between these cases and the partnership and spouse cases?

A somewhat different problem is presented if a person rightfully in possession of goods transfers them with intent to defeat the interests of a secured creditor. For example, someone who purchases an electrical appliance under a conditional sales contract may default on the payments due but conceal the appliance or transfer it to a friend to avoid repossession. Some states have enacted statutes that specifically treat such conduct as theft, at least when certain kinds of security interests are involved. See, e.g., Cal. Penal Code §504a.[5] The Model Penal Code chose to treat these situations not as theft but rather as a separate misdemeanor of defrauding secured creditors. See §§223.0(7), 224.10, Appendix to this case-

5. The section reads: "Every person who shall fraudulently remove, conceal or dispose of any goods, chattels or effects, leased or let to him by any instrument in writing, or any personal property or effects of another in his possession, under a contract of purchase not yet fulfilled, and any person in possession of such goods, chattels, or effects knowing them to be subject to such lease or contract of purchase who shall so remove, conceal or dispose of the same with intent to injure or defraud the lessor or owner thereof, is guilty of embezzlement."

book. The reason for separate treatment of those who impair security interests is stated to be that such conduct "deviates less from social norms than does the conduct of thieves who take property to which they have no claim. Moreover, sellers can guard against this kind of fraud by caution in extending credit." American Law Institute, Model Penal Code and Commentaries, Pt. II, Comment to §224.10 at 347-348 (1980). Query: Is the rationale persuasive? Compare the treatment of theft by deception. Section 223.3, Appendix to this casebook.

4. Unsecured property. Does it follow from the decision to criminalize the defrauding of secured creditors that defrauding unsecured creditors should also be made criminal? See, e.g., Cal. Penal Code §154: "Every debtor who fraudulently removes his property or effects out of this state, or fraudulently sells, conveys, assigns or conceals his property with intent to defraud, hinder or delay his creditors of their rights, claims or demands, is" guilty of a misdemeanor. The Model Penal Code rejected such provisions on the ground that they present a

> problem of punishing conduct that is not itself indicative of any criminal purpose. This problem is analogous to the distinction between preparation and attempt. Section 5.01(2) provides that conduct shall not be held to constitute a substantial step toward completion of the crime, as is required for conviction for attempt, "unless it is strongly corroborative of the actor's criminal purpose." The sale of one's own unencumbered property is itself a neutral and entirely legal act, distinguishable from legitimate business transactions only if intent to defraud creditors can be shown. It is not conduct "strongly corroborative" of any intent to defraud. To permit such interest to be shown in the absence of some corroboration from the act itself comes dangerously close to punishing evil intention alone.

American Law Institute, Model Penal Code and Commentaries, Pt. II, Comment to §224.10 at 346-347 (1980).

C. MENS REA

PEOPLE v. BROWN
Supreme Court of California
105 Cal. 66, 38 P. 518 (1894)

GAROUTE, J. [Appellant, a 17-year-old boy, was convicted of burglary on an information charging that he entered a house with intent to commit larceny. The facts revealed that he entered an acquaintance's house and took a bicycle. He testified: "I took the wheel to get even with the boy, and, of course, I didn't intend to keep it. I just wanted to get even with him. The boy was throwing oranges at me in the evening, and he would not stop when I told him to, and it made me mad. I intended to take it back Sunday night; but, before I got back, they caught me."]

Upon the foregoing state of facts, the court gave the jury the following instruction:

> I think it is not necessary to say very much to you in this case. I may say, generally, that I think counsel for the defense here stated to you in his argument very fairly

the principles of law governing this case, except in one particular. In defining to you the crime of grand larceny, he says it is essential that the taking of it must be felonious. That is true; the taking with the intent to deprive the owner of it; but he adds the conclusion that you must find that the taker intended to deprive him of it permanently. I do not think that is the law. I think in this case, for example, if the defendant took this bicycle, we will say for the purpose of riding twenty-five miles, for the purpose of enabling him to get away, and then left it for another to get it, and intended to do nothing else except to help himself away for a certain distance, it would be larceny, just as much as though he intended to take it all the while. A man may take a horse, for instance, not with the intent to convert it wholly and permanently to his own use, but to ride it to a certain distance, for a certain purpose he may have, and then leave it. He converts it to that extent to his own use and purpose feloniously.

This instruction is erroneous, and demands a reversal of the judgment. If the boy's story be true, he is not guilty of larceny in taking the machine; yet, under the instruction of the court, the words from his own mouth convicted him. The court told the jury that larceny may be committed, even though it was only the intent of the party taking the property to deprive the owner of it temporarily. We think the authorities form an unbroken line to the effect that the felonious intent must be to deprive the owner of the property permanently. The illustration contained in the instruction as to the man taking the horse is too broad in its terms as stating a correct principle of law. Under the circumstances depicted by the illustration, the man might, and again he might not, be guilty of larceny. It would be a pure question of fact for the jury, and dependent for its true solution upon all the circumstances surrounding the transaction. But the test of law to be applied in these circumstances for the purpose of determining the ultimate fact as to the man's guilt or innocence is, did he intend to permanently deprive the owner of his property? If he did not intend so to do, there is no felonious intent, and his acts constitute but a trespass. While the felonious intent of the party taking need not necessarily be an intention to convert the property to his own use, still it must in all cases be an intent to wholly and permanently deprive the owner thereof.

For the foregoing reasons, it is ordered that the judgment and order be reversed, and the cause remanded for a new trial.

NOTE

Some limited exceptions to the requirement of an intent to take permanently have been made judicially and by statute. The courts early found that, where the thing taken was abandoned or recklessly exposed to loss by the taker, this fact was not only evidentiary of an intent to effect a permanent deprivation but would sustain larceny even if a permanent taking was not the object of the defendant's acts. State v. Davis, 38 N.J.L. 176 (1875). See N.Y. Penal Law §155.00(3): "To 'deprive' another of property means . . . (b) to dispose of the property in such manner or under such circumstances as to render it unlikely that an owner will recover such property." Likewise, where the intent to return the thing taken is conditional, as upon receipt of a reward, the requisite mens rea has been found. Slaughter v. State, 113 Ga. 284, 38 S.E. 854 (1901); State

v. Hauptman, 115 N.J.L. 412, 426, 180 A. 809, 819 (1935). The risk of loss rationale has also supported larceny convictions where the defendant intends to pledge, though ultimately to redeem and return, the property taken. Regina v. Phetheon, 9 Car. & P. 552, 173 Eng. Rep. 952 (1840); but cf. Blackburn v. Commonwealth, 28 Ky. 96, 89 S.W. 160 (1905). Many states have long enacted "joy ride" statutes which make criminal the temporary taking of an automobile, and sometimes other vehicles. See, e.g., Cal. Penal Code §499(b).

Question: Why should the law of theft confine itself to cases where the intent of the taker is to effect a permanent deprivation? As Holmes observed (The Common Law 71 (1881)): "A momentary loss of possession is not what has been guarded against with such severe penalties. What the law means to prevent is the loss of it wholly and forever. . . ." But should interference with possession which is more than momentary, though less than permanent, be protected by the law of theft? N.Y. Penal Law §155.00(3), following Model Penal Code §223.0(1), now provides: "To 'deprive' another of property means (a) to withhold it or cause it to be withheld . . . for so extended a period or under such circumstances that the major portion of its economic value or benefit is lost to him. . . ."

For a comparative examination, see Bein, The Theft of Use and the Element of "Intention to Deprive Permanently" in Larceny, 3 Israel L. Rev. 368 (1968).

PROBLEM

In Regina v. Easom, [1971] 2 All E.R. 945, defendant was convicted of stealing a handbag and its contents, consisting of a purse, a notebook, tissues, cosmetics, and a pen. A policewoman went to a cinema and placed her handbag containing these articles on the floor beside her, attached to her wrist by a piece of thread. Defendant sat behind her. The policewoman felt a tug on the thread and heard the sound of rustling and of a handbag being closed. Defendant left his seat. The handbag was found in front of the seat defendant had occupied. Nothing had been taken from it, since defendant, after looking through the handbag, decided it contained nothing worth stealing. The conviction was reversed on appeal on the ground that the facts failed to show a fixed intention to steal the objects.

Presumably if the jury found that defendant intended to steal the bag and its contents when he picked it up, but then later decided to abandon it when discovering that it contained nothing he wanted, a verdict of theft of the bag and its contents would have been proper. But suppose the jury found that when he took up the bag he did so with the purpose of seeing if there was anything in it that was worth stealing, such as money, and, seeing that there was nothing he wanted, he put the bag and its contents back. Would he then be guilty of any crime? Could he be convicted of stealing the bag? Its contents? Of attempt to steal them? Of attempt to steal whatever of value he found in the bag?

Consider also these hypotheticals, suggested in the Comment in [1971] Crim. L. Rev. at 489:

(a) D takes P's ring intending to keep it if the stone is a diamond but otherwise to return it. He takes it to a jeweler who says the stone is paste. D returns the ring to P. Is D guilty of theft?

(b) A dishonest postal sorter picks up a pile of letters, intending to steal any that are registered but, on finding that none of them are, replaces them. Is he guilty of theft of the letters he picked up? Of attempt to steal those letters? Of attempt to steal registered letters?

Consider how the result would be affected if the following provision of the Model Penal Code were in effect: "When a particular purpose is an element of an offense, the element is established although such purpose is conditional, unless the condition negatives the harm or evil sought to be prevented by the law defining the offense." Section 2.02(6).

REGINA v. FEELY

Court of Appeal

[1973] 2 W.L.R. 201

LAWTON, L.J. read the judgment of the court. This defendant, David Feely, appeals by leave of the single judge against his conviction for theft at the Liverpool Crown Court on March 20, 1972. . . .

The appeal raises an important point of law, namely, can it be a defence *in law* for a man charged with theft and proved to have taken money to say that when he took the money he intended to repay it and had reasonable grounds for believing and did believe that he would be able to do so.

[The facts were as follows: Defendant was a branch manager for a firm of bookmakers. In September 1971 the firm sent a circular to all branch managers that the practice of borrowing from tills was to stop. Defendant nevertheless took about £30 from a branch safe on October 4. On October 8 he was transferred to another branch. His successor discovered a cash shortage of about £40, and defendant gave him an IOU for that amount. Though his successor did not report the deficiency, a member of the firm's security staff did and asked defendant for an explanation. Defendant accounted for about £10 by reference to some bets he had paid out, but as to the balance he said that he had taken it because he was "stuck for cash." Defendant stated he borrowed the £30 intending to pay it back and that his employers owed him about £70 from which he wanted them to deduct the money. Trial testimony showed that the firm did owe him that amount. He was convicted of theft of the £30.

[The trial judge directed the jury] that if the defendant had taken the money from either the safe or the till — and it was the prosecution's case and the defendant's own case to start with, that he had taken it from the safe — it was no defence for him to say that he had intended to repay it and that his employers owed him more than enough to cover what he had taken. The trial judge put his direction in stark terms: . . .

> As a matter of law, members of the jury, I am bound to direct you, even if he were prepared to pay back the following day and even if he were a millionaire, it makes no defence in law to this offence. If he took the money, that is the essential matter for you to decide.

At no stage of his summing up did he leave the jury to decide whether the prosecution had proved that the defendant had taken the money dishonestly.

This was because he seems to have thought that he had to decide as a matter of law what amounted to dishonesty and he expressed his concept of dishonesty as follows: ". . . if someone does something deliberately knowing that his employers are not prepared to tolerate it, is that not dishonest?"

Should the jury have been left to decide whether the defendant had acted dishonestly? The search for an answer must start with the Theft Act 1968, under section 1 of which the defendant had been indicted. . . . The design of the new Act is clear; nearly all the old legal terms to describe offences of dishonesty have been left behind; larceny, embezzlement and fraudulent conversion have become theft; receiving stolen goods has become handling stolen goods; obtaining by false pretences has become obtaining pecuniary advantage by deception. Words in everyday use have replaced legal jargon in many parts of the Act. That is particularly noticeable in the series of sections (1 to 6) defining theft.

"Theft" itself is a word known and used by all and is defined . . . as follows: "A person is guilty of theft if he dishonestly appropriates property belonging to another with the intention of permanently depriving the other of it. . . ."

In section 1(1) of the Act of 1968, the word "dishonestly" can only relate to the state of mind of the person who does the act which amounts to appropriation. . . . The Crown did not dispute this proposition, but it was submitted that in some cases (and this, it was said, was such a one) it was necessary for the trial judge to define "dishonestly." . . .

We do not agree that judges should define what "dishonestly" means. This word is in common use whereas the word "fraudulently" which was used in section 1(1) of the Larceny Act 1916 had acquired as a result of case law a special meaning. Jurors, when deciding whether an appropriation was dishonest can be reasonably expected to, and should, apply the current standards of ordinary decent people. . . .

. . . [T]he jury should have been left to decide whether the defendant's alleged taking of the money had been dishonest. They were not, with the result that a verdict of guilty was returned without their having given thought to what was probably the most important issue in the case.

This would suffice for the appeal were it not for . . . two decisions. . . . In Reg. v. Williams [1953] 1 Q.B. 660, the two appellants, who were husband and wife, carried on a general shop, part of which was a sub-post office. The wife was the sub-postmistress. The business of the shop got into difficulties and in order to get out of them the wife, with the knowledge of her husband, took money from the Post Office till to discharge some of the debts of the business. In her evidence, which was supported by that of her husband, she said that she thought she would be able to repay the money out of her salary from the Post Office and from sales from the business. The husband said that he knew it was wrong to do what they had done, but he thought that it would all come right in the end. They were found guilty on a number of counts and in respect of two the jury added a rider that the appellants had intended to repay the money and honestly believed that they would be able to do so, but in respect of three counts, although they intended to repay, they had no honest belief that they would be able to do so. The main ground of the appeal was that the jury had been misdirected as to the word "fraudulently" in section 1(1) of the Larceny Act 1916.

. . . The question in the case which is relevant for the purposes of this appeal was whether the facts found by the jury and recorded in their riders afforded any defence. . . . [The court held they did not, stating]: "They knew that they had no right to take the money which they knew was not their money. The fact that they may have had a hope or expectation in the future of repaying that money is a matter which at most can go to mitigation and does not amount to a defence."

It is possible to imagine a case of taking by an employee in breach of instructions to which no one would, or could reasonably, attach moral obloquy; for example, that of a manager of a shop, who having been told that under no circumstances was he to take money from the till for his own purposes, took 40p from it, having no small change himself, to pay for a taxi hired by his wife who had arrived at the shop saying that she only had a £5 note which the cabby could not change. . . .

If the law drifted off course in Reg. v. Williams [1953] 1 Q.B. 660 because of the strong inference of fraud arising on the facts of that case, it got on to the wrong tack in Reg. v. Cockburn [1968] 1 W.L.R. 281 in which the manager of a shop took money from the till on a Saturday intending, so he said, to replace it with a cheque drawn by his daughter. Before he did so he was dismissed, and when the deficiency of cash was discovered and he was asked by telephone about it, he did not then put forward the explanation which was his defence to a charge of larceny as a servant. At his trial the jury were not directed that it would be a good defence to the charge if the accused were to satisfy them that he intended to replace the money with its currency equivalent. . . . Winn, L.J. delivered the judgment of the court [finding no error and stating] . . . "If coins, half a crown, a 10s. note, a £5 note, whatever it may be, are taken in all the circumstances which I have already indicated with the intention of spending or putting away somewhere those particular coins or notes, albeit not only hoping but intending and expecting reasonably to be able to replace them with their equivalent, nevertheless larceny has been committed because with full appreciation of what is being done, the larcenous person, the person who commits the offence, has taken something which he was not entitled to take, had no claim of right to take, without the consent of the owner, and is in effect trying to force upon the owner a substitution to which the owner has not consented."

We find it impossible to accept that a conviction for stealing, whether it be called larceny or theft, can reveal no moral obloquy. A man so convicted would have difficulty in persuading his friends and neighbours that his reputation had not been gravely damaged. He would be bound to be lowered in the estimation of right thinking people. . . .

If the principle enunciated in Reg. v. Cockburn [1968] 1 W.L.R. 281 was right, there would be a strange divergence between the position of a man who obtains cash by passing a cheque on an account which has no funds to meet it and one who takes money from a till. The man who passes the cheque is deemed in law not to act dishonestly if he genuinely believes on reasonable grounds that when it is presented to the paying bank there will be funds to meet it. . . . But, according to the decision in Reg. v. Cockburn, the man who takes money from a till intending to put it back and genuinely believing on reasonable grounds that he will be able to do so should be convicted of theft.

Lawyers may be able to appreciate why one man should be adjudged to be a criminal and the other not; but we doubt whether anyone else would. People who take money from tills and the like without permission are usually thieves; but if they do not admit that they are by pleading guilty, it is for the jury, not the judge, to decide whether they have acted dishonestly. . . .

For these reasons we allowed the appeal.

PROBLEM

Section 2 of the Theft Act of 1968 deals as follows with the concept of dishonesty:

> (1) A person's appropriation of property belonging to another is not to be regarded as dishonest —
> (a) if he appropriates the property in the belief that he has in law the right to deprive the other of it, on behalf of himself or a third person; or
> (b) if he appropriates the property in the belief that he would have the other's consent if the other knew of the appropriation and the circumstances of it; or
> (c) (except where the property came to him as trustee or personal representative) if he appropriates the property in the belief that the person to whom the property belongs cannot be discovered by taking reasonable steps
> (2) A person's appropriation of property belonging to another may be dishonest notwithstanding that he is willing to pay for the property.

Query: Should the court in the *Feely* case have considered these provisions? What effect should they have on the resolution of the issue?

See the discussion of the *Feely* case in G. Williams, Textbook of Criminal Law 666-670 (1978).

NOTES AND QUESTIONS ON INTENT TO RESTORE OR PAY

1. In State v. Pratt, 114 Kan. 660, 220 P. 505, 506, 507 (1923), defendant was convicted of embezzlement on the following facts:

> [T]he Building & Loan Association purchased $10,000 worth, face value, of the Second Liberty Loan bonds of the United States, which passed into the custody of the appellant as secretary-treasurer of the association. Without any authority to do so, and without the knowledge of the directors and other officers of the association, appellant sold these bonds in January, 1920, in Kansas City. The money was not used for the benefit of the association. In fact, appellant concealed his disposition of these bonds from the association until some time in May or June, 1921. At two or three of the meetings of the board of directors of the association held in the meantime, in which they were checking up the assets of the association, appellant substituted other bonds, which he had taken without authority from the envelopes of private boxes of depositors of the bank of which he was president, and counted those at the board meeting as the bonds of the association.

On appeal defendant contended "that before he could be convicted of the crime of embezzlement the state must prove beyond a reasonable doubt that at the time he wrongfully converted the bonds he had the intent to deprive the owner, not temporarily, but permanently, of its property," and that error was committed in refusing evidence of his intent to restore the bonds or their equivalent and in failing to instruct that such an intent was a good defense. The court affirmed, resting on the weight of authority that "While to constitute . . . embezzlement it is necessary that there be a criminal intent, yet where the money of the principal is knowingly used by the agent in violation of his duty, it is none the less embezzlement because at the time he intended to restore it." Cf. Cal. Penal Code §512 (intent to restore no defense or mitigation in embezzlement if property not restored before indictment or information); §513 (restoration prior to indictment or information mitigates punishment for embezzlement).

Question: Does the holding and reasoning of the court mean that defendant could also have been convicted of embezzlement of the depositors' bonds, which he removed temporarily from the bank of which he was president to cover his misappropriation of the savings and loan association bonds? Why not, if intent to restore is not a defense to embezzlement?

2. The intent to restore is likewise held to be no defense to a false pretense charge. See People v. Weiger, 100 Cal. 352, 34 P. 826 (1893). Defendant obtained goods on credit from the complaining witness on false representations concerning his financial position. The court affirmed a conviction of obtaining by false pretenses, holding immaterial that defendant intended to pay for the goods which he purchased, stating (34 P. at 827):

> In the assumption that it must be held that defendant did not intend to defraud the Sharpless firm if he intended at the time to pay for the goods according to the contract of sale, and truly believed that he was able to do so, I think counsel is in error. Deception, deliberately practiced, for the purpose of gaining an unfair advantage of another, is fraud. Goods obtained by such practices are obtained by fraud. One deprived of his property by such means is defrauded.

Questions: Suppose the goods defendant obtained in the *Weiger* case were a set of law books and that her defense was as follows: Defendant was a young attorney, expecting a visit from a potential client of substance whom she wanted to impress. She obtained the books for this purpose, fully intending to ship them back to the seller after the client's visit. Would it follow from the principle stated in *Weiger* that she would be guilty of obtaining by false pretenses? If so, consider the liability of the young attorney if she took the books from another attorney's office for the same purpose and with the same intent to return them after the client's visit. Would this not be a clear temporary taking inconsistent with larceny? Why is the same defense not available whether she obtained the books by a false representation or by a taking?

3. In connection with the various issues raised in this Note, consider the following observations in Model Penal Code §206.1(2)(c), Comment at 72-73 (Tent. Draft No. 1, 1953):

> As under present law, it is no defense that the actor intends to reimburse the owner later for property presently misappropriated. . . . Deprivation accompanied by an intent to make good later, by payment of money or by the actor's repurchasing an equivalent article for restoration to the owner, is quite different in effect from

the taking of a thing for temporary use of the taker. In the latter situation, the actor's retention of the property offers some assurance of his ability to restore, beyond his general credit. In the former situation, the man who takes money intending to repay or the broker who sells his client's bonds meaning to repurchase and restore the bonds later, substitutes his own credit for the owner's property in hand. Even if the actor carries out his intent to restore, he is simply paying off a liability from his own assets, rather than restoring property which has continued to belong to the owner during the interval of deprivation.

PEOPLE v. BUTLER

Supreme Court of California
55 Cal. Rptr. 511, 421 P.2d 703 (1967)

TRAYNOR, C.J. Defendant was charged by information with the murder of Joseph H. Anderson and with assault with intent to murder William Russell Locklear. A jury convicted defendant of first degree felony murder and of assault with a deadly weapon; it fixed the penalty for the murder at death. This appeal is automatic. (Pen. Code, §1239, subd. (b).)

We have determined that error in the guilt phase of the trial deprived defendant of his primary defense to the charge of first degree felony murder. The judgment of conviction of murder must therefore be reversed. . . .

[There was evidence that defendant, who had been employed by Anderson, the deceased, got into an argument with the latter over his failure to pay him. In the course of the argument, guns were drawn, defendant shot the deceased, and defendant took deceased's wallet.]

No evidence of premeditation or deliberation was adduced by the prosecution. The court instructed the jury that since these elements were not present, it could find first degree murder only if defendant committed the killing in the perpetration of a robbery.

Defendant testified that he did not intend to rob Anderson when he went to the house, but intended only to recover money owed to him. Over his objection, the prosecutor argued to the jury, "If you think a man owes you a hundred dollars, or fifty dollars, or five dollars, or a dollar, and you go over with a gun to try to get his money, it's robbery." And, "If you go into a man's home and merely because he's supposed to owe you some money, you take money from him at gunpoint, you have robbed him." Again objecting to further argument by the prosecutor that a robbery was committed even if defendant believed Anderson owed him money, defendant suggested that a necessary element of theft, the intent to steal, was requisite to robbery, but was overruled by the court.

Defendant's objection was well taken. "Robbery is the felonious taking of personal property in the possession of another, from his person or immediate presence, and against his will, accomplished by means of force or fear." (Pen. Code, §211). An essential element of robbery is the felonious intent or animus furandi that accompanies the taking. Since robbery is but larceny aggravated by the use of force or fear to accomplish the taking of property from the person or presence of the possessor . . . the felonious intent requisite to robbery is the same intent common to those offenses that, like larceny, are grouped in the Penal Code designation of "theft." The taking of property is not theft in the absence of an intent to steal. . . .

Although an intent to steal may ordinarily be inferred when one person takes the property of another, particularly if he takes it by force, proof of the existence of a state of mind incompatible with an intent to steal precludes a finding of either theft or robbery. It has long been the rule in this state and generally throughout the country that a bona fide belief, even though mistakenly held, that one has a right or claim to the property negates felonious intent. . . . A belief that the property taken belongs to the taker . . . or that he had a right to retake goods sold . . . is sufficient to preclude felonious intent. . . .[2]

Defendant testified that in going to Anderson's home "my sole intention was to try to get my money; and that was all." . . . Accordingly, defendant's only defense to robbery-murder was the existence of an honest belief that he was entitled to the money. The trial court's approval of the prosecutor's argument that no such defense exists removed completely from the consideration of the jury a material issue raised by credible, substantial evidence. It precluded any finding that an intent to steal was absent. . . .

[Reversed.]

NOTES AND QUESTIONS

1. For contrary views, see State v. Russell, 217 Kan. 481, 536 P.2d 1392 (1975); Cates v. State, 21 Md. App. 363, 320 A.2d 75 (1974). See also two annotations on this issue: 46 A.L.R.2d 1227 (1956) and 77 A.L.R.3d 1363 (1974).

In some jurisdictions the defendant in a case like *Butler* would have been denied a defense even if he had not used force, since his claim did not go to any particular property of his debtor but to a privilege to appropriate another's property in satisfaction of a debt. See, e.g., Moyers v. State, 186 Ga. 446, 197 S.E. 846 (1938); Commonwealth v. Peakes, 231 Mass. 449, 121 N.E. 420 (1918); Gettinger v. State, 13 Neb. 308, 14 N.W. 403 (1882) ("The law does not permit a creditor to make collection of what is due him by larceny of the debtor's goods"); Edwards v. State, 49 Wis. 2d 105, 181 N.W.2d 383 (1970).

Florida's revised code defines robbery as follows: "Robbery means the taking of money or other property which may be the subject of larceny from the person or custody of another by force, violence, assault, or putting in fear." Fla. Stat. Ann. tit. 44, §812.13. This was interpreted in Bell v. State, 354 So. 2d 1266 (Fla. Dist. App. 1978) to require a result contrary to that reached in the *Butler* case. Do you agree?

2. N.Y. Penal Law §155.15 provides:

1. In any prosecution for larceny committed by trespassory taking or embezzlement, it is an affirmative defense that the property was appropriated under a claim of right made in good faith.

2. Defendant concedes, as he must, that although the offense could not constitute robbery absent an intent to steal, an unprovoked assault accompanying an attempt to collect a debt may be a crime other than robbery. Among the range of offenses that might have been committed are: assault (Pen. Code, §240), assault with a deadly weapon (Pen. Code, §245), assault with intent to commit murder (Pen. Code, §217).

Compare Model Penal Code §223.1(3), which provides:

It is an affirmative defense to prosecution for theft that the actor (a) was unaware that the property or service was that of another; or (b) acted under an honest claim of right to the property or service involved or that he had a right to acquire or dispose of it as he did; or (c) took property exposed for sale, intending to purchase and pay for it promptly, or reasonably believing that the owner, if present, would have consented.

Questions: Would *Butler* be decided differently under these formulations? Note that claim of right is a defense to theft by deception as well as to all other forms of theft under the Model Penal Code formulation, but it is not a defense to larceny by obtaining property by false pretenses under the New York law. What is the case for denying the claim-of-right defense in false-pretenses cases?

PEOPLE v. FICHTNER

New York Supreme Court, Appellate Division, Second Department
281 A.D. 159, 118 N.Y.S.2d 392 (1952)[6]

JOHNSTON, J. Section 850 of the Penal Law provides: "Extortion is the obtaining of property from another . . . , with his consent, induced by a wrongful use of . . . fear. . . ."
Section 851 of the Penal Law provides:

Fear, such as will constitute extortion, may be induced by an oral or written threat: . . . 2. To accuse him, or any relative of his or any member of his family, of any crime; or, 3. To expose, or impute to him, or any of them, any . . . disgrace. . . .

Defendant Fichtner is the manager, and defendant McGuinness the assistant manager, of the Hill Supermarket in Freeport, Nassau County. On January 30, 1951, an indictment was filed against both defendants, charging them in two counts with the crime of extortion in that on January 18, 1951, defendants, aiding and abetting each other, obtained $25 from one Smith, with his consent, which consent defendants induced by a wrongful use of fear by threatening to accuse Smith of the crime of petit larceny, and to expose and impute to him a disgrace unless Smith paid them $25.

Smith testified that on January 18, 1951, he purchased a number of articles in the Hill store for a total of about $12, but left the store without paying for a fifty-three-cent jar of coffee, which he had concealed in his pocket. After Smith left the store he returned at defendant Fichtner's request. Defendants then threatened to call a policeman, to arrest Smith for petit larceny, with resulting publicity in the newspapers and over the radio, unless he paid $75 and signed a paper admitting that during the course of several months he had unlawfully taken merchandise from the store in that amount. Although Smith admitted he had shopped in Hill's Freeport store about sixteen times and in Hill's Merrick store for about two years, he insisted that the only merchandise he had ever

6. *Affirmed without opinion,* 305 N.Y. 864, 114 N.E.2d 212 (1952).

stolen was the fifty-three-cent jar of coffee on the evening in question, and a sixty-five-cent roll of bologna one week previously. However, he finally signed the paper admitting that he had unlawfully taken $50 worth of merchandise from the store during a period of four months. That evening Smith paid $25 in cash and promised to pay the balance in weekly installments of $5. He testified he was induced to sign the paper and make the payment because defendants threatened to accuse him of petit larceny and to expose him to the disgrace of the criminal charge and the resulting publicity. It is not disputed that the $25 taken from Smith was "rung up" on the store register; that the money went into the company funds and that defendants received no part of the money. During the following week Smith reported the incident to the police, and defendants were arrested on January 25, 1951, when Smith, accompanied by a detective, returned to the store and paid the first $5 installment.

Defendants testified that over the course of several weeks, they saw Smith steal merchandise amounting to $5.61, and they honestly believed that during the several months that Smith had been shopping, he had stolen merchandise of the value of $75; that on January 18, 1951, Smith freely admitted that during the four-month period he stole merchandise of the value of $50, and that he voluntarily signed the paper admitting thefts in that amount; that on that date he paid $25 on account and promised to pay the balance in weekly installments.

That the Smith incident was not an isolated one, but rather part of a course of conduct pursued by defendants, even after warning by the police to discontinue the practice, was not only clearly established but admitted by defendant Fichtner. . . .

In my opinion, the verdict is amply supported by the evidence. Implicit in the verdict is a finding that Smith stole only $1.18 in merchandise as he admitted, or at most the $5.61 which defendants claimed they actually saw him steal, and that he was induced to pay the $25 on January 18, 1951, by defendants' threats to accuse him of crime and to expose him to disgrace. By its verdict, the jury rejected defendants' contention that Smith voluntarily admitted having stolen $50 worth of merchandise and that they demanded from Smith only what was rightfully due.

Defendants requested the court to charge that

> if in the judgment of the jury the defendants honestly believed that the amount which the complainant paid or agreed to pay represented the approximate amount of the merchandise which he or they had previously stolen from the Hill Supermarket, then the defendants must be acquitted.

The court refused the request "except as already charged." Although two members of the court are of the opinion that for the reason stated the trial court was justified in refusing to charge as requested, four members of the court are of the further opinion that the request was legally incorrect and, therefore, should have been refused. In other words, we believe that the portion of the main charge to the effect that, under the circumstances of this case, extortion is committed only when one obtains property from another by inducing fear in that other by threatening to accuse him of crime unless he pays an amount over and above what was rightfully due was more favorable to defendants than that which they were entitled to receive. In our opinion, the extortion statutes were intended to prevent the collection of money by the use of fear induced by means of threats to accuse a debtor of crime, and it makes no difference whether the debtor stole any goods, nor how much he stole, and that defendants may properly be convicted even though they believed that the complainant was guilty of the theft of their employer's goods in an amount either equal to or less, or greater than any sum of money obtained from the complainant. Nor is defendants' good faith in thus enforcing payment of the money alleged to be due to their employer a defense. . . .

The law does not authorize the collection of just debts by threatening to accuse the debtor of crime, even though the complainant is in fact guilty of the crime. In my opinion, it makes no difference whether the indebtedness for which a defendant demands repayment is one arising out of the crime for the prosecution of which he threatens the complainant, or is entirely independent and having no connection with the crime which forms the basis of the accusation. The result in both cases is the concealment and compounding of a felony to the injury of the State. It is that result which the extortion statutes were intended to prevent.

[Conviction affirmed.] [a]

WENZEL, J. (dissenting). . . . [T]he jury was permitted to convict defendants of the crime of extortion on proof that they had induced complainant, by the threats alleged, to pay to defendants more than he rightfully owed for goods which he had stolen, even though defendants might have honestly believed that the amount demanded from complainant was the amount which he rightfully owed. In my opinion, although the question is one as to which there is a conflict of authority, if defendants, acting without malice and in good faith, made an honest mistake, they were not guilty of the crime charged. There would then be no criminal intent. The defendants were not acting in their own behalf but in that of their employer, in recovering what they believed to be rightfully due it. . . .

NOTE

New York's statutes have since been changed. N.Y. Penal Law §155.15(2) provides:

> In any prosecution for larceny by extortion committed by instilling in the victim a fear that he or another person would be charged with a crime, it is an affirmative defense that the defendant reasonably believed the threatened charge to be true and that his sole purpose was to compel or induce the victim to take reasonable action to make good the wrong which was the subject of such threatened charge.

Section 215.45 provides:

> 1. A person is guilty of compounding a crime when: (a) He solicits, accepts or agrees to accept any benefit upon an agreement or understanding that he will

a. Accord, People v. Beggs, 178 Cal. 79, 172 P. 152 (1918); In re Sherin, 27 S.D. 232, 130 N.W. 761 (1911); O'Neil v. State, 237 Wis. 391, 296 N.W. 96 (1941). Contra, Mann v. State, 47 Ohio St. 556, 26 N.E. 226 (1890); State v. Burns, 161 Wash. 362, 297 P. 212 (1931). — EDS.

refrain from initiating a prosecution for a crime; or (b) He confers, or offers or agrees to confer, any benefit upon another person upon an agreement or understanding that such other person will refrain from initiating a prosecution for a crime.

2. In any prosecution under this section, it is an affirmative defense that the benefit did not exceed an amount which the defendant reasonably believed to be due as restitution or indemnification for harm caused by the crime.

CHAPTER

11

BUSINESS CRIMES

A. INTRODUCTION

INTRODUCTORY NOTE

The volume and range of criminal law impinging on business are enormous. At the same time, criminal violations by both large and prestigious and smaller corporations have grown to substantial proportions. This situation has given rise to a sharp national debate. Some critics have decried the inadequate use of the criminal law against corporate and other business violators and have urged reform in both the law and in the strategies of prosecution and sentencing. Other observers have expressed grave reservations over the use of criminal prosecutions and sentences in business matters and have urged the use of sanctions other than criminal ones to deal with business misconduct. The purpose of this chapter is to explore these problems.

By *business crimes* we here refer to crimes of varying content having in common that they are committed as part of the process of doing legitimate business. The range of crimes encompassed is great. It may include wholly traditional crimes. For example, manslaughter would be included, if the cause of the death were defective design of a commercial product. So would bribery if done by a business entity in furtherance of its business. Business crimes will also include — indeed principally — crimes expressly formulated to regulate the conduct of business: violations of economic regulatory legislation, for example, like rent and price-control or antitrust legislation; violations of public welfare legislation, like food and drug laws, designed to constrain business or industrial practices which threaten the personal welfare of the consumer or the public interest in environmental protection.

Following this introductory section, we consider the general issue of when it is appropriate to criminalize business conduct as a means of regulation. Just as the proper reach of the criminal law needs to be critically examined when dealing with its use to control deviant sexual practices, drug use, and other so-called victimless crimes, so does it need critical study when dealing with business crimes. For as we saw in our earlier consideration of the problem of criminalization, pages 230-248, the tendency to turn immediately to the criminal law when faced with conduct we disapprove of is as dubious as it is common.

We then consider the subject of criminality within the corporate context, since the extensive use of the corporate form in doing business makes the problems of corporate criminal liability and individual liability of corporate agents central to any consideration of business crimes.

Finally we direct our attention to the varied issues in sentencing the business offender, whether the offender be the corporation itself or an individual acting in the corporation's behalf.

ROSS, HOW LAWLESS ARE BIG COMPANIES?
103 Fortune 57 (Dec. 1, 1980)

[In this article the author sought to assess the extent of corporate delinquency in America during the 1970s by canvassing federal offenses by over 1,000 companies that appeared at some point during that period in Fortune's lists of the 800 largest industrial and nonindustrial corporations. Cases were included if they resulted in convictions, consent decrees, or similar administrative settlements in which the company agreed not to commit the charged offense in the future. Foreign bribes and kickbacks were excluded. Minor cases of corruption far down the chain of command were also excluded: The standard was corporate responsibility at a high level. The report was limited to five crimes — bribery (including kickbacks and illegal rebates), criminal fraud, illegal political contributions, tax evasions, and criminal antitrust violations based on price-fixing and bid-rigging. The study disclosed that 117 corporations, or 11 percent of those canvassed, committed at least one violation in this period. Some were multiple offenders. A total of 163 separate offenses were committed — 98 antitrust violations; 28 cases of kickbacks, bribery, or illegal rebates; 21 instances of illegal political contributions; 11 cases of fraud; and 5 cases of tax evasion.

[Reflecting on this record of substantial criminality by the major corporations of the country, the author states:] Why do some of the largest, most prestigious corporations in America get involved in complex scenarios of illegality that rival the paranoid fantasies of their bitterest critics?

No single answer accounts for the variety of corporate misbehavior. One generalization often invoked plays on the distinction between malum in se — a crime in itself, like the immemorial offenses of the common law — and malum prohibitum — purely statutory crimes that vary with the society. As a celebrated corporate defense counsel recently put it, "These business crimes are perceived by individual actors as victimless. We all grew up in an environment in which we learned that thou shalt not murder, rape, rob, probably not pay off a public official — but not that it was a crime to fix prices."

Most of the economic crimes that fill the lists on the following pages do not bring the social obloquy that attaches to robbery or embezzlement. One chief executive recently boasted to Fortune about how he had once rid his company of some executives who had run afoul of the antitrust laws. "That sent the message to the organization," he said. Ten minutes later, however, he expressed dismay about how his statements would look in print. After all, some years had passed; the men were still living in the community; they had made their peace with the company. Would the same solicitude be accorded a bank robber?

Corrupt practices are certainly not endemic to business, but they do seem endemic to certain situations and certain industries. A persuasive explanation for many violations is economic pressure — the "bottom-line philosophy," as Stanley Sporkin, the SEC's enforcement chief, puts it. "In many instances where people are not lining their own pockets you can only explain corporate crime in terms of 'produce or perish.'"

The common practice of running a company through decentralized profit centers, giving each manager his head but holding him strictly accountable for the results, often provides a setting in which the rules can readily be bent. The temptation comes when heightened competition or a recession squeezes margins.

The pressures that led to criminal behavior in the folding-carton industry were exhaustively described in a 1978 article in the Harvard Business Review by Jeffrey Sonnenfeld and Paul L. Lawrence. Price fixing had long been common in the industry because profit margins were tight, competition was intense, and prices were set at a relatively low level in the corporate hierarchy — a consequence of the many kinds and shapes of boxes ordered. Top management had little control over the impulses of salesmen and junior managers to exchange price information, rig bids, and divvy up customers.

The authors quote the self-exculpatory statement of one executive: "We're not vicious enemies in this industry, but rather people in similar binds. I've always thought of myself as an honorable citizen. We didn't do these things for our own behalf . . . [but] for the betterment of the company." . . .

Competitive pressures can account for kickbacks and other forms of commercial bribery, but perhaps equally significant are industry custom and structure. In trucking, in construction, and on the docks, the pressure of time seems to be the key element. If goods are delayed in transit, or if construction is held up because of the inability to obtain materials or workers, great financial loss can result. Where bribes are not freely offered, they are often extorted.

Companies in regulated industries sometimes violate the law because of the simple fact of regulation. In the beer and liquor industries, for example, both the federal government and the states prohibit or curtail some normal techniques of salesmanship, such as discounts and rebates. The result: illegal rebates and gifts of merchandise to persuade liquor retailers to promote a company's products. . . .

Simple economic incentives explain much illegal behavior: corruption seems to pay, at least in the near term. In industries like folding cartons or corrugated boxes, where antitrust cases were brought, executives perceived an advantage in maintaining price levels, sharing the market, and keeping marginal firms alive. In such a situation, of course, the customers pay and the whole economy suffers from a measure of inefficiency. When a corporation is caught, the shamefaced executives take a drastically different view of the cost-benefit ratio. Some companies might have been better off in the long run if they had followed the alternative, and legal, strategy of expanding their market share by driving their weaker brethren to the wall.

B. CRIMINALIZATION

1. Issues in Choosing Sanctions

F. ALLEN, THE CRIMINAL LAW AS AN INSTRUMENT OF ECONOMIC REGULATION

Intl. Inst. Econ. Research (Orig. Paper 2, 1976)

. . . I am concerned here with . . . the problems created for the law, and especially the *criminal* law, when government delegates to it important functions of economic regulation.

. . . Today the penal law is extensively employed as a device to implement a very wide range of economic regulatory efforts. It has been employed as a sanction in antitrust laws, in connection with the wartime price and rent control legislation, in currency regulation, and in the sale and marketing of securities. Criminal provisions are routinely included in most major pieces of regulatory legislation.

Often this is done thoughtlessly, with no serious consideration being given to such elementary questions as the appropriateness of criminal penalties to the specific regulatory purpose. . . .

. . . It is my contention that in many respects efforts to employ the penal law as a device to advance economic regulation have had a demoralizing effect on the law and the institutions of criminal justice, that the social costs incurred because of this demoralization are significant, and that these costs are entitled to more serious consideration in policy formulation than they have been given in the past.

To approach these questions one needs first to ask, what is the central purpose of the criminal law? The commonsense response to this question is the correct one. The purpose of the criminal law is to prevent or lessen dangerous and disturbing human behavior that destroys or threatens the lives and limbs of members of society and that prevents or interferes with the peaceful enjoyment of their possessions. There are, no doubt, other and subsidiary purposes served by the institutions of criminal justice, but this is the central one.

So important is the preventive function of the criminal law that we, like all other mature societies, have enacted elaborate codes of prohibited behavior, and have delegated to the system of criminal justice various penalties, ranging up to the most rigorous at the command of government. Under the authority of the criminal law, the convicted offender may be deprived of his property (through fines), of his liberty, and even, on occasion, of life itself. The prevalence of those codes and these penalties provides evidence of the high value universally placed on the objectives that the criminal law is intended to achieve.

Yet the very rigor of these penalties, and the stigma associated with their imposition, are the source of other kinds of social concerns. Criminal penalties are a dramatic expression of governmental power. If we know anything it is that governmental power is not always beneficent, that it is prone to abuse. . . .

We are drawn, then, to two conclusions. Effective enforcement of the criminal law is essential to achieving the important benefits of living in an organized society. On the other hand, the containment of the powers of government exercised in criminal law enforcement is an indispensable part of the strategy of freedom. The use of the criminal law for purposes of economic regulation tends to erode those principles primarily relied on in our law to contain the powers of government in the criminal area, a containment essential to the preservation of basic political values.

What are some of these "principles of containment" that the law has devised to channel exercises of government power within specified limits in order to advance rather than destroy our values? There are many, but here we consider only three of the most important. First is the principle that *the penal law should be as clear as possible.* Given the stringency of the stigmatic criminal penalties, everyone would be likely to agree that it is intolerable that men and women should stumble into criminal liability because the law has failed clearly to define what is punishable behavior and what is not. It is intolerable, too, that the law should be so uncertain as to deny guidance and limitation to judicial and administrative officials exercising onerous powers over the lives, liberty, and property of other persons. So fundamental is this principle that it has been raised to the level of a constitutional mandate. "Void for vagueness" is a familiar due process doctrine, and in extreme cases legislation has been invalidated because of the uncertainty of its language.

The second principle may not be so immediately obvious, but on reflection it will be seen to be just as basic as the first. It is that *guilt is personal.* If persons are to be punished, they should be punished because of what they, not someone else, did. There are many instances in the penal law, to be sure, in which criminal defendants are held to be legally accountable for harms perpetrated by other persons. For the most part, however, these are cases in which the defendant has been in complicity with another person; he has, that is, conspired with or directed, encouraged, or assisted the other in the latter's criminal behavior. The moral repugnance that one feels for the practice of shooting innocent hostages when crimes are committed against a totalitarian regime — a practice that disfigures European history in the twentieth century — reflects the basic instinct of justice expressed in the proposition that "guilt is personal."

The third of the principles of containment expresses perhaps most clearly the basic ethical insight that underlies all three, an insight viewed skeptically in an age in which the notion of personal responsibility for behavior is widely rejected. It is the proposition that *criminal penalties should be imposed only on those who deserve to be punished.* This third principle states that the only persons who should be subjected to the stigmatic sanctions of the criminal law are those who are deemed to have intended the harm attributed to them, or who at least were reckless in their behavior. . . .

These, then, are three of the important principles employed by the criminal law to contain the power of the state within constructive and tolerable limits. [E]ach of these principles has come under attack, and has been weakened in those areas of the criminal law directed primarily to objectives of economic regulation.

First, consider the principle of certainty in criminal legislation: persons ought to be able to determine in advance which actions and inactions the law punishes and which it tolerates. . . . Definitions of many economic crimes . . . are characterized by unusual obscurity. The 1890 Sherman Act, the foundation of our national antitrust policy, is illustrative. Section 1 of the Act provides as the criterion of guilt, "restraint of trade and commerce." The concept of "restraint of trade" was known to the law before the Sherman Act was passed, but it had no certain meaning; and it is manifest that Congress had no clear sense of its meaning when it was included in the statute. Ever since, for almost ninety years, judicial interpretation has added new and often unanticipated meanings to the language. . . .

The recurring problems of vagueness in economic regulatory legislation suggest that there may be something inherent in the nature of such regulatory efforts that offend the principle of certainty. . . .

A statute crisply and precisely defining the standards of guilt cannot be drafted when the policy of the statute is not, and perhaps cannot be, crisp and precise. Draftsmen of such legislation have difficulty in articulating the precise harm or conduct sought to be prevented. Such uncertainties do not plague most other areas of serious criminality. . . .

How does the principle that "guilt is personal" fare in the economic cases? One of the leading characteristics of economic regulation through the criminal law is the difficulty encountered in bringing liability to bear on the responsible individual. Most often, the behavior made criminal by such statutes is committed in the context of corporate enterprise. When the responsible corporate officer or agent can be identified, there is ordinarily no theoretical difficulty in imposing criminal liability on him. Often, however, the search for the responsible human party in the corporate hierarchy proves unavailing. Even in the General Electric Equipment cases, brought in the early 1960s, when for the first time substantial criminal penalties were imposed on corporate employees in an antitrust prosecution, the prosecutor was unable to establish the complicity of the officers in the top echelon of the corporation, and penalties were confined to second-level managerial personnel. Often frustrated in his efforts to establish the criminal liability of human agents of the corporation, the prosecutor moves to impose criminal penalties on the corporate body itself, almost always in the form of monetary fines.

But on whom does the burden of the fine fall? Certainly not directly on the guilty party within the corporate structure. On the contrary, it falls directly upon the owners, the stockholders, who ordinarily will have had no part in the commission of the offenses, will have been unaware that criminal acts were being committed, and, even if suspicious of criminal activity, will often have lacked the means to do much about preventing it. . . .

The economic regulation cases have eroded the basic proposition that persons who do not deserve criminal punishment ought not to be found criminally liable. This is perhaps most clearly illustrated in the weakening of the mens rea principle. The proposition that punishment should be limited to those deserving it is fundamental to our conceptions of justice, but it is supportable also on sound utilitarian grounds. . . . A system of law that widely disregards the moral sense of the community may be able to function with reasonable effectiveness for a time, but such a system "lives on capital." The long-term effect is to demoralize the administration of justice and to weaken the community's attachment to the law.

There is a second consideration. The principle of desert defines and limits the scope of criminal regulation. . . . If criminal punishments are limited to behavior perceived by the community to involve some kind of moral dereliction, government is restrained in its persistent tendency to employ the criminal law for whatever purposes it considers desirable or expedient.

In the economic area these restraints tend to break down. . . . Nothing approaching a consensus has been reached on the moral issue in much "economic" behavior, and hence the law is denied the kind of general support necessary for its most effective operation. . . .

. . . Faced by unusual difficulties in enforcing criminal regulatory statutes, the state may wholly relieve the prosecution of obligation to prove that the defendant intended the forbidden conduct or was reckless in his behavior. The state, in other words, may totally reject the principle of desert and create what is known as strict liability. Literally thousands of statutes imposing strict liability have been enacted in the United States. The result is that persons can be and are defined as criminal because of conduct they did not intend, did not know was prohibited, or which, by any standard of prudence and care, could not have avoided.

These, then, are some of the consequences that have resulted from decisions to employ the criminal law as an instrument of economic regulation. Are these consequences worth serious concern? Granted that the kinds of criminality being discussed are not of the most extreme sorts, and, moreover, that they do not result in the law's most drastic penalties, I suggest that they are. But the question is a fair one, and I make two responses to it.

First, even minor criminal penalties (and the sanctions imposed for economic crimes are often far from insignificant) represent a form of social stigmatization. The processes of social moral condemnation that constitute the administration of criminal justice demand for their justification that they be founded on just principles applied with decency and fairness. Second, this is true, not only because justice is an end in itself, but also because unprincipled practices tolerated in one part of the system tend to infect the whole. They cannot be insulated or compartmentalized. . . .

NOTE

To take these issues further, compare the differing analyses in Kadish, Some Observations on the Use of Criminal Sanctions in Enforcing Economic Regulations, 30 U. Chi. L. Rev. 423 (1963), and Ball & Friedman, The Use of Criminal Sanctions in the Enforcement of Economic Legislation: A Sociological View, 17 Stan. L. Rev. 197 (1965).

It is helpful at this point to recall material earlier examined in the law of theft, which also raises the problem of distinguishing accepted business conduct from conduct that should be made criminal. Examples include: (1) the distinction between failure to pay a debt due another and failure to give another money which is his or hers (Commonwealth v. Stahl, pages 938-939 supra, and the Notes following); (2) the early common law refusal to treat as criminal cases instances in which a person acquires another's property through deception and the gradual displacement of that view as the ethic of caveat emptor was itself displaced by a competing ethic (Note, page 942 supra); (3) the distinction between deception about future performance (false promise) and the deception about existing facts (false pretense) (People v. Ashley, pages 951-955 supra).

2. Two Problems

a. Products Liability

STATE v. FORD MOTOR CO.
Indiana Superior Court, Elkhart County, No. 5324 (1979)

THE INDICTMENT

IN THE ELKHART SUPERIOR COURT

INDICTMENT IN FOUR COUNTS CHARGING THREE
COUNTS OF RECKLESS HOMICIDE, A CLASS D FELONY
AND ONE COUNT OF CRIMINAL RECKLESSNESS, A
CLASS A MISDEMEANOR

The Grand Jurors of Elkhart County, State of Indiana, being first duly sworn upon their oaths do present and say:

COUNT I

That Ford Motor Company, a corporation, on or about the 10th day of August, 1978, in the County of Elkhart, State of Indiana, did then and there through the acts and omissions of its agents and employees acting within the scope of their authority with said corporation recklessly cause the death of Judy Ann Ulrich, a human being, to-wit: that the Ford Motor Company, a corporation, did recklessly authorize and approve the design, and did recklessly design and manufacture a certain 1973 Pinto automobile, Serial Number F3T10X298722F, in such a manner as would likely cause said automobile to flame and burn upon rear-end impact; and the said Ford Motor Company permitted said Pinto automobile to remain upon the highways and roadways of Elkhart County, State of Indiana, to-wit: U.S. Highway Number 33, in said County and State; and the said Ford Motor Company did fail to repair and modify said Pinto automobile; and thereafter on said date as a proximate contributing cause of said reckless disregard for the safety of other persons within said automobile, including, the said Judy Ann Ulrich, a rear-end impact involving said Pinto automobile did occur creating fire and flame which did then and there and thereby inflict mortal injuries upon the said Judy Ann Ulrich, and the said Judy Ann Ulrich did then languish and die by incineration in Allen County, State of Indiana, on or about the 11th day of August, 1978.

And so the Grand Jurors aforesaid, upon their oaths aforesaid, do say and charge that the said Ford Motor Company, a corporation, did recklessly cause the death of the said Judy Ann Ulrich, a human being, in the manner and form aforesaid, and contrary to the form of the statutes in such cases made and provided, to-wit: Burns Indiana Statutes, Indiana Code Section 35-42-1-5; [a] and against the peace and dignity of the State of Indiana.

---

a. This section provides: "A person who recklessly kills another human being commits reckless homicide, a Class C felony. However, if the killing results from the operation of a vehicle, the offense is a class D felony." Section 35-40-2-2(c) defines *recklessly* as follows: "A person engages in conduct 'recklessly' if he engages in the conduct in plain, conscious, and unjustifiable disregard of harm that might result and the disregard involves a substantial deviation from acceptable standards of conduct."— EDS.

[Counts II and III repeat the above allegations in connection with the deaths of Donna M. Ulrich and Lynn M. Ulrich, respectively.]

COUNT IV

That Ford Motor Company, a corporation, on or about the 10th day of August, 1978, and diverse days prior thereto, in the County of Elkhart, State of Indiana, did through the acts and omissions of its agents and employees acting within the scope of their authority with said corporation, recklessly create a substantial risk of bodily injury to the persons of Judy Ann Ulrich, Donna M. Ulrich and Lynn M. Ulrich, human beings, and each of them, to-wit: that the Ford Motor Company, a corporation, did recklessly permit a certain 1973 Pinto automobile, Serial Number F3T10X298722F, designed and manufactured by the said Ford Motor Company to remain upon the highways and roadways of Elkhart County, State of Indiana, to-wit: U.S. Highway Number 33 in said County and State; and said Pinto automobile being recklessly designed and manufactured in such a manner as would likely cause said automobile to flame and burn upon rear-end impact; and that the said Ford Motor Company had a legal duty to warn the general public and certain occupants of said Pinto automobile, namely: Judy Ann Ulrich, Donna M. Ulrich and Lynn M. Ulrich of the dangerous tendency of said Pinto automobile to flame and burn upon rear-end impact; and the said Ford Motor Company did fail to repair and modify said Pinto automobile; and that as a proximate contributing cause of said Ford Motor Company's acts, omissions and reckless disregard for the safety of other persons within said Pinto automobile, including the said Judy Ann Ulrich, Donna M. Ulrich and Lynn M. Ulrich, a rear-end impact involving said Pinto automobile did occur on or about August 10, 1978, in Elkhart County, Indiana, creating fire and flame which did then and there and thereby inflict bodily injury upon the persons of the said Judy Ann Ulrich, Donna M. Ulrich and Lynn M. Ulrich, human beings, and each of them.

And so the Grand Jurors aforesaid, upon their oaths aforesaid, do say and charge that the said Ford Motor Company, a corporation, did recklessly create a substantial risk of bodily injury to the persons of Judy Ann Ulrich, Donna M. Ulrich and Lynn M. Ulrich, human beings, and each of them, in the manner and form aforesaid, and contrary to the form of the Statutes in such cases made and provided, to-wit: Burns Indiana Statutes, Indiana Code Section 35-42-2-2,[b] and against the peace and dignity of the State of Indiana.

A TRUE BILL

THE TRIAL (N.Y. TIMES, FEB. 17, 1980, §4, AT 9)

The Ford Pinto trial may go down as a spirited, but defective prototype for trying a new hybrid in American courtrooms — a case in which a manufacturer is tried on criminal charges for an allegedly defective product. . . .

b. This section provides: "(a) A person who recklessly, knowingly, or intentionally performs an act that creates a substantial risk of bodily injury to another person commits criminal recklessness, a Class B misdemeanor. However, the offense is a Class A misdemeanor if the conduct includes the use of a vehicle or deadly weapon. (b) A person who recklessly, knowingly, or intentionally inflicts serious bodily injury on another person commits criminal recklessness, a Class D felony."— EDS.

The state, with the help of volunteer lawyers and law school students, is pursuing its case on a bargain basement budget of $20,000. Ford is spending approximately $1 million on its defense.

Judge Harold R. Staffeldt has insisted from the outset that since this is a criminal case, he would apply "strict construction" rules of evidence. Thus, he will admit only evidence concerning the 1973 Pinto, unless the State lays a "proper foundation" (demonstrating their relevancy) to justify admitting such items as a history of the vehicle's development.

State prosecutors, however, have assumed that [they must] prove recklessness. . . . Critical in this context is what the company knew or should have known before the date of the incident, in addition to information about dates of design and sale.

The 1973 Pinto was the same design as the Pinto sold in 1971 and 1972, prosecutors assert. They argue that crash test results for those models would help demonstrate that their fuel tanks, and thus the 1973 fuel tank, were unsafe and Ford officials knew it.

The State would also like to adduce as evidence hundreds of company documents, from 1960 through 1972, in which the Pinto fuel tank system is discussed. Ford will not authenticate these. But with 20 motions on record to limit admissible evidence, its lawyers have applauded the judge's continued rulings against the State. Its presentation now completed, the prosecution has been barred from introducing 40 percent of its case into the court record. . . .

THE VERDICT (N.Y. TIMES, MAR. 14, 1980, AT 1:A1)

WINAMAC, Ind., March 13 — An Indiana jury today found the Ford Motor Company not guilty on three charges of reckless homicide in connection with the deaths of three young women in a fiery crash in August 1978 involving its Pinto passenger car.

The verdict, delivered just after noon, came after 25 hours of deliberations over a four-day period. It included a session lasting over 14 hours that ended at 3 A.M. today, with the jury foreman reporting to the court that the group of seven men and five women was hopelessly deadlocked. In a session that began at 10 A.M., the jury reached a consensus of not guilty, ending the 10-week trial.

The state charges against Ford led to the first criminal prosecution of an American corporation in a case involving alleged product defects that led to a death. Only monetary penalties were involved, but nonetheless the case was closely watched nationally because of its implications for the enforcement of criminal as well as civil laws against companies accused of manufacturing and selling defective products that subsequently result in death.

The charges arose after the women were killed when their 1973 Pinto burst into flames after it was struck from the rear by a van north of Winamac. The prosecution charged that Ford and its officials knew that gasoline tanks on the once-popular subcompact Pinto model tended to explode when struck from behind, but did nothing to correct the defect after manufacture. Ford denied the charges, arguing that its vehicles are as safe as its competitors'.

There was conflicting testimony about whether the car was moving when it was struck. Prosecution witnesses, including the driver of the van, said the car was moving at about 50 miles per hour, but a hospital attendant testified for the defense that one of the three women, as she was dying, told him that the car was not moving.

After the verdict was announced, jurors discussed their deliberations, and several said that, while they were convinced that the Pinto fuel tank could not withstand a puncture in a rear-end crash at highway speed and was thus unsafe, they had heard insufficient evidence based on the charges in this case.

NOTE, CORPORATE HOMICIDE: A NEW ASSAULT ON CORPORATE DECISION-MAKING
54 Notre Dame Law. 911, 922-924 (1979)

. . . State v. Ford Motor Co. presents issues which transcend those of existing precedents. Prior indictments of corporations for homicide resulted from acts of corporate agents performed within the scope of employment. The engineer recklessly operating the train or a repairman recklessly installing a gas pipe, are examples of the norm. The prosecution of Ford, however, occurs in a completely different setting. Ford's alleged illegal conduct is comprised of three acts: (1) defectively designing the vehicle, (2) defectively manufacturing the vehicle, and (3) allowing the vehicle to remain on the public highways. Each of these acts is the product of a complex business decision. Both the design and manufacture of automobiles are subject to extensive federal regulation. Rigorous testing precedes marketing. Defects discovered after sale to the public may involve recalls, either voluntary or compulsory. Therefore, the Pinto which exploded on August 10, 1978, was the product of many substantial business decisions occurring at various levels of the corporate hierarchy. The deterrent effect of corporate liability for criminal homicide, therefore, must be assessed by the effect of conviction on this decision-making process.

The maximum penalty which can be imposed on a corporation convicted under the Indiana reckless homicide statute is a $10,000 fine. The effectiveness of this sanction as a deterrent to a large, profitable corporation is questionable. . . . Thus, superficially, such indictments appear as futile attempts to impede corporate recklessness when deterrence is the standard of evaluation and "small" fines are the sanction.

The inherent flaw in this analysis is the assumption that the $10,000 fine is the only consequence of conviction. The negative publicity of a criminal conviction is the consequence most likely to deter reckless corporate conduct. A guilty verdict could threaten the fate of a corporation's entire product line by inspiring public mistrust and thereby jeopardizing future revenues. . . . Therefore, the imposition of corporate criminal penalties should deter the instigation of corporate policies that produce incidents such as the Pinto explosion of August 10, 1978, by stimulating greater managerial scrutiny of the design and manufacture of products.

The Pinto case, regardless of its outcome, will also heighten corporate concern regarding recalls. A product designed and manufactured with proper care but subsequently found to be defective may be the basis of a homicide indictment. Thus, a new variable enters decisions concerning the recall of defective products.

Simple cost analysis will no longer suffice because the company must account for potential public animosity in the event of criminal indictment. The net result is increased concern for product safety and consumer protection.

Absent potential criminal responsibility for marketing a defective product, the value of human life is reduced to mere cost analysis. Probability distributions estimating potential consumer deaths and resulting civil liabilities pitted against the cost of adequate safety precautions threatens to become the standard of corporate decision-making. Thus, potential criminal liability provides a prophy-lactic variable likely to weigh heavily in contemporary decision-making models, thereby enhancing corporate responsibility to consumers.

WHEELER, PRODUCTS LIABILITY: MANUFACTURERS, WRONG TARGETS FOR THREAT OF CRIMINAL SANCTIONS? [1]
Natl. L.J. (Dec. 22, 1980)

Even absent the threat of criminal sanctions, manufacturers, in deciding whether to implement any modification affecting product safety, must consider several costs they might incur by producing and selling products that could be made safer. These potential costs include amounts awarded in civil lawsuits for compensatory damages. . . . In any one lawsuit these can total several mil-lions of dollars. . . .

In addition, administrative or judicial proceedings by regulatory agencies to require recalls, warnings or other actions may cost the manufacturer several million dollars. Critical publicized evaluations of the product by government agencies or by private testing entities, such as Consumers' Union, [and adverse publicity about injuries suffered by the product's users] may cause consumers to eschew the particular product and, perhaps, other products made by the manufacturer. . . .

. . . Such a broad array of non-criminal deterrent forces attends few other activities engaged in by members of our society. . . .

. . . [O]ne might contend that even more deterrence is socially desirable and that the additional deterrence can be efficiently achieved by the use of criminal sanctions. . . .

Before deciding whether more deterrence is needed or can efficiently be ob-tained through criminal sanctions, however, one must identify what it is that one wishes to deter.

Since . . . many members of the public seem antipathetic to manufacturers using any cost-benefit safety analysis, one might contend that criminal sanctions are needed to deter the use of any such analysis. That contention would be self-contradictory and unrealistic.

As noted above, the very essence of deterrence theory *requires* that an actor weigh the costs and benefits of contemplated conduct in deciding whether to engage in that conduct. . . .

Also, . . . it is literally impossible to prevent any person from using cost-benefit analysis — except by preventing the person from acting altogether — because the very act of choosing one form of conduct over other forms of conduct necessarily entails a cost-benefit analysis. . . .

---

1. The author was one of the counsel for the defense in the Pinto prosecution.

Alternatively, therefore, one might contend that criminal sanctions are needed to deter manufacturers from quantifying the indisputably necessary cost-benefit analysis — that is, from assigning some dollar value to the societal cost of physical injuries and premature deaths.[63] . . . But both the purpose of trying to provide the public with the mix that it wants and the purpose of enabling courts, juries and regulatory agencies to review the decision-making processes of manufacturers will be better served by encouraging — not deterring — a cost-benefit approach that seeks:

(1) to identify, not lump together, all of the relevant factors;

(2) to ascertain the weight the public would attach to them if the public could be as informed as the scientists, engineers and managers responsible for making the products; and

(3) to design and manufacture products that reflect the public's desires ex ante. . . .

Alternatively, therefore, one might contend that criminal sanctions are needed to deter manufacturers from marketing any product that could be made safer by using current technology, irrespective of the cost consumers might have to pay for the added safety. Costs of additional safety might include higher price, lower reliability, shorter useful life, reduced efficiency, higher maintenance or service costs and many others.

. . . [T]his contention, however, ignores the indisputable fact that the public does not want all technologically feasible safety at any cost. Rather, individual citizens constantly choose to risk their own personal safety and the safety of others, including their loved ones, for a variety of reasons, including price, function, convenience, aesthetics, vanity and pleasure. For example, women wear high-heeled shoes despite the obvious risk of tripping or damaging their Achilles tendons; men undergo hair transplants despite the well-known risk of infection and other injury; men and women undergo face-lifts and other cosmetic surgery, smoke cigarettes, take drugs, drink liquor, drive over the speed limit, play contact sports, shoot guns and engage in innumerable other activities that risk their own safety and the safety of others.

Thus, if criminal sanctions were to be applied to product manufacturers for marketing products that are somewhat less safe, but somewhat cheaper, more reliable, more durable or better in some other respect, criminal sanctions should be applied with equal vigor to Congress for not lowering the speed limit below 55 mph; to state and federal agencies responsible for the construction of highways that have curves, go over hills and have only two lanes (since all such highways are known to result in more highway deaths than straight, multi-lane highways); to drivers who drive at the maximum allowable speed rather than at a lower allowable speed; to parents who do not strap seatbelts onto their children in automobiles; to parents who give their children motorcycles and toys that (like all toys) can injure; to retail stores that sell liquor; to homeowners who burn leaves or use fireplaces; and so forth. Obviously, no sensible person wishes to apply criminal sanctions in that manner.

___

63. It must be emphasized that the relevant cost that society wishes to cause manufacturers to internalize and use in their cost-benefit analyses is the societal cost of human injury, not the "value of human life" as calculated by a particular person whose life is in issue or by a friend or relative of that person. Many, if not most, persons undoubtedly would refuse to give up their own lives or the lives of their loved ones for any sum of money; but society obviously attaches some finite dollar value to human life by allocating only limited resources to police, fire and health programs, among others.

Alternatively, therefore, one might contend that criminal sanctions are needed to deter manufacturers from marketing any product without giving the public the opportunity to exercise an informed choice — that is, without informing the public of every respect in which the product could be made safer, the costs of making each available safety modification and the extent to which safety would be increased by each such modification.

The absurdity of that contention can be seen by considering the implications for almost any product. For example, an automobile has approximately 14,000 parts, each of which can be made safer in at least one way, such as by using higher-grade materials or narrower manufacturing tolerances. To inform the public of each such available modification of the effects on price, comfort, durability, fuel economy and other factors, and of the effect of each modification on the overall safety risk would require a multi-volume buyers' guide that would cost thousands of dollars and go unread by the public.

Alternatively, therefore, one might contend that criminal sanctions are needed to deter manufacturers from marketing products that are less safe than the public wants them to be, all factors considered ex ante. This seems to be the proper, non-paternalistic basis on which to try to justify the application of criminal sanctions under a deterrence theory. . . .

In short, the use of criminal sanctions based on a deterrence theory may be desirable where — because manufacturers have inadequate information, because of high transaction costs in negotiations between buyers and sellers and bystanders, because of a low probability that manufacturers will pay the social costs of marketing products that are less safe than the public wants when all factors are considered or because of any other circumstance — a manufacturer is not sufficiently likely to calculate and internalize accurately the full social costs of manufacturing a particular product.

That, however, serves only to state a theoretical justification for using criminal sanctions to regulate product safety. Several additional questions must be answered before it can sensibly be concluded that such a use of the criminal law is desirable. . . .

Third, . . . a fair and proper review of a manufacturer's past decisions cannot be accomplished without:

(1) Ascribing some dollar value to the social cost of human injury and premature death for use in criminal proceedings;

(2) Adopting some standard of what magnitude of deviation from a socially desirable balance of safety and other costs will constitute criminal recklessness or criminal negligence;

(3) Adopting some set of judicial rules to take account of the fact that the underlying data — such as number of injuries, types of injuries, causes of injuries and costs of implementing design modifications — will always be somewhat fuzzy and subject to different interpretations and inferences by reasonable persons; and

(4) Ascribing some dollar value to the many nonmonetary factors such as durability, reliability, efficiency, serviceability, comfort, convenience and appearance that must be balanced against safety considerations. . . .

. . . [I]f general criminal statutes are to be employed, these questions will have to be answered in the courts.

Fourth, in most instances in which lay juries historically have been called upon to pronounce conduct to be criminally reckless or not, jurors have been able to draw upon their own wealth of first-hand experience to decide whether the conduct substantially deviates from an accepted societal norm. . . .

But in deciding whether a manufacturer acted in a criminally reckless fashion by, for example, making a car more fuel efficient at the cost of a minuscule increase in the risk of whiplash injuries, lay jurors will have neither common experience nor statutory guidance to assist them in judging the propriety of that conduct under general criminal statutes.

Jurors are more likely, therefore, to be influenced in a product case by a gut-level antipathy — inconsistent with their own daily conduct — to the use of cost-benefit safety analysis. Subjecting manufacturers to that irrational antipathy in a civil suit for compensation is one thing; doing it in a criminal proceeding is quite another. . . .

Sixth . . . [t]he deterrent effect of applying general criminal recklessness or criminal negligence laws to product manufacturers is a complete unknown. This is so because the deterring costs depend so greatly upon factors external to the criminal proceedings: the amount of publicity, the accuracy of the reporting, the variety of products sold by the defendant, the public's knowledge of what company manufactures those products and the elasticity of demand for the product in issue, to name a few.

Applying criminal sanctions may therefore result in much more deterrence than is socially desirable. Again, to paint an extreme picture, the result may be that manufacturers will produce ugly, fuel-guzzling, expensive, uncomfortable, slow, cumbersome, inconvenient, short-lived automobiles that are difficult to service.

The public's recent mass move to small, fuel-efficient, more dangerous cars designed to deal better with the world oil situation dramatically demonstrates that maximum safety is not the foremost consideration in product purchases. . . .

Seventh, it is far from clear that it is socially desirable to devote already scarce police, prosecutorial and judicial resources to the criminal prosecution of product manufacturers. Such resources would have to be diverted from the policing and prosecuting of other crimes, or more of the public's resources would have to be used to hire police officers, prosecutors, judges and supporting personnel.

QUESTIONS

1. What principle of law is Wheeler advocating? If current criminal-homicide statutes permit the kind of products-liability prosecution that Wheeler criticizes, what kind of statutory amendment would be necessary to reflect his views?

2. Granted all the ambiguities and difficulties of proof, when there is a really clear case of injury caused by criminal recklessness — that is, by conduct known to involve a substantial and unjustifiable risk — why shouldn't the perpetrator be criminally liable, regardless of whether that perpetrator is an individual driver, a surgeon improperly performing an operation, or a corporate manufacturer distributing a dangerous product? Reconsider at this point the case of **People**

v. Warner-Lambert, 51 N.Y.2d 295, 414 N.E.2d 660 (1980), reprinted at pages
533-535 supra.

3. Does the actual outcome of the Ford Pinto prosecution support or undermine Wheeler's thesis? Consider the following alternative hypotheses suggested
by the episode:

(a) The system "works." In the event of an unwarranted prosecution, the
defense can show that the business decision was a reasonable one, and the
jury will acquit.

(b) The acquittal was a lucky fluke. In a future case the prosecution might
be able to persuade the jury to convict even though the manufacturer's decision
in fact was a reasonable one.

(c) Even with the possibility of products-liability prosecutions, the system still
remains too heavily "tilted" against the prosecution. A manufacturer can over-
whelm the staff of a county prosecutor and secure an acquittal whether or not
the prosecution was well founded.

Can we tell which of the above statements is most plausible? If one of them
seems relatively accurate, what changes (if any) in the law governing products-
liability prosecutions does the statement suggest?

b. Bribery Abroad

GUSTMAN, THE FOREIGN CORRUPT PRACTICES ACT OF 1977:
A TRANSACTIONAL ANALYSIS
13 J. Intl. L. & Econ. 367, 367–377 (1979)

The recent focus on overseas corporate payments is largely a result of the
Watergate Congressional hearings, which revealed a pattern of secret and illegal
domestic political contributions by United States corporations. The Securities
and Exchange Commission (the "SEC") became suspicious of the existence of
"slush funds" disclosed at that time and established a voluntary disclosure
program.[2] As a result, approximately five hundred firms voluntarily acknowledged making secret payments both in the United States and around the world.

Numerous and varied hearings were held by the 94th and 95th Congresses
on the scope of the "sensitive" foreign payments problem and the most expedient
procedure to curb the abuses. The Congressional hearings, coupled with the
SEC voluntary disclosure program, exposed the customary use of secret payments made to secure business abroad. The political ramifications of such disclosures were swift and widespread; at least two foreign leaders apparently resigned
as a result.[6] In light of the pervasive use of bribes to obtain foreign business

2. This became known as the SEC "voluntary compliance and disclosure program." It began
with public statements by SEC Commissioners which indicated that disclosure of past questionable
payments, followed by the establishment of internal corporate procedures to prevent questionable
future payments, would likely prevent the SEC from initiating enforcement actions. For a detailed
analysis of the SEC voluntary disclosure program, see Solomon & Linville, Transnational Conduct
of American Multinational Corporations: Questionable Payments Abroad, 17 B.C. Ind. & Comm.
L. Rev. 303 (1976). . . .

6. Japanese Premier Kakui Tanaka resigned in 1974 after accusations that he had accepted $1.7
million in bribes from Lockheed Corporation. N.Y. Times, Nov. 28, 1974, at 3, col. 5. Recently,
Italian President Giovanni Leone resigned on June 15, 1978, after accusations of tax evasion and
kickbacks, including a $2 million Lockheed bribe. N.Y. Times, June 16, 1978, at 1, col. 3. Lockheed
signed a consent agreement with the SEC promising not to make such payments in the future.

and the political implications of such bribes when made to foreign government officials, the need for legislation became apparent.[7]

Congressional debate concerning the problem of foreign bribery culminated with passage of the Foreign Corrupt Practices Act of 1977 (the "Act"). The Act, which was signed into law and became effective on December 19, 1977, consists of two separate provisions. The first, which applies only to companies subject to the periodic reporting requirements of the Securities Exchange Act of 1934 (the "Exchange Act"), mandates that accurate books and records be maintained and that a system of internal accounting controls be established. The second is essentially a criminal prohibition against the direct or indirect payment of bribes to foreign government officials, foreign political parties and their officials, and candidates for foreign political office. . . .

B.   Provisions of the Act Prohibiting Foreign Corrupt Practices

Sections 103 and 104 of the Act are nearly identical provisions providing criminal penalties for foreign bribery. They differ primarily in their application. Section 103 is applicable to reporting firms under the jurisdiction of the SEC while section 104 covers all other "domestic concerns." The Justice Department is thus provided with exclusive investigative and prosecutorial jurisdiction over corporations and individuals not otherwise within the SEC's jurisdiction. In this way, the dual corporate bribery provisions cover all domestic corporations and individuals regardless of their status with the SEC.

The criminal provisions of the Act prohibit bribery of foreign government decisionmakers, with the exception of "those whose duties are essentially ministerial or clerical." The Act defines foreign bribery as the reporting company's or domestic concern's corrupt use of an instrumentality of interstate commerce in furtherance of an offer, payment, or promise of payment of anything of value for the purpose of influencing a foreign official, political party, or candidate, in order to assist the reporting company or domestic concern in obtaining or retaining business.

The Act provides that upon conviction for a violation of the bribery provisions, a reporting company or domestic concern may be fined up to one million dollars. Officers, directors or stockholders, acting on behalf of such concerns and "willfully" violating the bribery prohibitions, may be fined ten thousand dollars or imprisoned for five years, or both. However, employees or agents of a reporting company or domestic concern may be convicted of violating the criminal provisions of the Act only after a prior conviction of the principal corporation.[40] The Act further prevents the direct or indirect indemnification by the corporation

7. According to the Senate Report: "Recent investigations by the SEC have revealed corrupt foreign payments by over 300 United States companies involving hundreds of millions of dollars. These revelations have had severe adverse effects. Foreign governments friendly to the United States in Japan, Italy and the Netherlands have come under intense pressure from their own people. The image of American democracy abroad has been tarnished. Confidence in the financial integrity of our corporations has been impaired. The efficient functioning of our capital markets has been hampered." S. Rep. No. 114, 95th Cong. 1st Sess. 3 (1977).

40. 15 U.S.C. §78ff(c)(3); 15 U.S.C. §78dd-2(b)(3). "This provision reflects the Committee's concern that in some instances a low level employee or agent of the corporation — perhaps the person who is designated to make the payment — might otherwise be made the scapegoat for the corporation." H.R. Rep. No. 640, 95th Cong., 1st Sess. 11 (1977).

of any fines imposed upon directors, officers, stockholders, employees or agents. Finally, civil injunctive actions may be brought by the SEC, while the Department of Justice is empowered to bring similar actions against domestic concerns and other individuals not subject to SEC jurisdiction.[42]

SOLOMON & GUSTMAN, QUESTIONABLE AND ILLEGAL PAYMENTS BY AMERICAN CORPORATIONS
35 J. Bus. L. 67, 72-74 (1980)

The Act exempts "facilitating" payments and payments made in response to extortion from its coverage. The Act proscribes only those corrupt payments made directly or indirectly to foreign officials for the purpose of obtaining or retaining business or directing business to any other person. Customary facilitating or "grease" payments made to low-level customs officials or other clerical personnel would not be prohibited by the Act for at least three reasons. First, low-level government employees are not foreign officials within the meaning of the Act as the term "does not include any employee of a foreign government or any department, agency, or instrumentality thereof whose duties are essentially ministerial or clerical." Secondly, even if low-level bureaucrats were considered foreign officials within the meaning of the Act, any payments made to such officials would be exempt if they were not made to obtain or retain business. This "business purpose" test was added to assure exclusion of just such facilitating or "grease payments" from the scope of the Act. Finally, the language of the Act is cast in terms which differentiate between corrupt and facilitating or "grease" payments. By use of the word "corruptly," Congress intended to distinguish between payments made to influence the decision-making process of a foreign official and those made merely to move a particular matter to an eventual end.

The Act also exempts payments made in response to extortion. Although criminal liability under the Act does not turn on who first suggested payment, the Act prohibits only "corrupt" payments, thus requiring an evil motive on behalf of the payor. . . .

Business entertainment poses unique problems under the criminal provisions of the Act. Neither the specific language of the Act nor the applicable legislative history addresses the issue of whether entertainment of foreign government officials could be violative of the Act. The Act prohibits the "payment . . . of anything of value" for the "purpose of . . . influencing any act or decision of such foreign official . . . in order to assist such domestic concern in obtaining or retaining business." Since the Act contains no de minimis exception, strictly construed it would appear to prohibit even reasonable expenditures for entertainment of foreign government officials, provided it could be shown that such expenditures were made in order to obtain or retain business. In view of the common use of entertainment expenditures in the business world, it is possible that the courts, when presented with this issue, will develop a "reasonable level"

---

42. The Department of Justice, however, lacks civil investigative apparatus for determining whether there has been a violation of the Act. Justice is therefore confined to the use of criminal investigatory aids such as the grand jury, subpoena, and search warrants in order to obtain sufficient information for the purpose of determining whether criminal prosecution or civil injunctive action is necessary. Only if the investigation fails to turn up insufficient criminal criteria will a civil injunctive action be considered. . . .

test to determine acceptable entertainment expenditures. However, in the absence of that interpretation and the wording in the Act appearing to encompass payments of anything of value, it is likely that the Department of Justice and the SEC will strictly construe the provisions of the Act, especially with respect to excessive entertainment expenditures.

ESTEY & MARSTON, PITFALLS (AND LOOPHOLES) IN THE FOREIGN BRIBERY LAW, 98 Fortune 182, 188 (1978): [Enforcement] does not mean, however, that a new and more honorable day has dawned for Americans who do business aboard. The FCPA may well turn out to be about as effective as Prohibition was against booze. Companies that never indulged in bribery will say how evil it is. Those that could take it or leave it will leave it — and already there have been public testimonials about how good it feels to stop. Even those really hooked, the corporations that have to grease palms to get foreign business, will probably proclaim public temperance while privately trying to figure out how to continue business as usual. Some are simply converting themselves into subcontractors overseas, depending on their foreign prime contractors to deal with local officials. Enforcement may be vigorous but in the long run it may do more to conceal foreign bribery than to eradicate it.

In the end, the impact of the FCPA will depend largely on the answer to a question barely considered during legislative debate: Why did so many presumably prudent, otherwise law-abiding businessmen spend hard-earned corporate cash on payments now labeled unnecessary and repugnant? If it was because of a moral blind spot, the FCPA may be a cure. But if they paid because the economics of international competition demand it, then the sinner will go right on sinning, while keeping a sharp eye out for all those policemen around the corner.

QUESTIONS

1. Why should bribery of officials by American firms overseas be a proper object of American criminal law? Is it enough that the practice does not comport with American standards of ethical business conduct? Are there tangible harms threatened by this conduct, other than its moral affront, which justify a legal effort to control it? What bearing does the exclusion of "grease payments" have on these two questions?

2. If foreign bribery is, in principle, a proper concern of American law, is the use of the *criminal* law a prudent alternative in the circumstances? What are the practical considerations which favor and disfavor the use of the criminal sanction for this purpose?

3. In debates about the Foreign Corrupt Practices Act, some supporters of that legislation happened to be among those who opposed criminalization of the use of marijuana. Are these two positions consistent? Conversely, is it consistent to oppose the foreign-bribery statute while supporting criminal punishment for marijuana use? What principles could be invoked to support the foreign-bribery statute while opposing criminal punishment for marijuana use and possession?

4. For arguments pro and con on the Foreign Corrupt Practices Act, see

American Enterprise Institute for Public Policy Research, Criminalization of Payments to Influence Foreign Governments (1977). See also Unlawful Corporate Payments Act of 1977: Hearings Before the Subcommittee on Consumer Protection and Finance of the Comm. on Interstate and Foreign Commerce, House of Representatives, 95th Cong., 1st Sess. (1977); Hearings before the Subcomm. on Multinational Corporations, United States Senate, 94th Congress, 1st Sess. Pt. 12 (1975); Hearings before the Comm. on Banking, Housing and Urban Affairs, United States Senate, 94th Cong., 2d Sess. (1976); Solomon & Linville, Transnational Conduct of American Multinational Corporations: Questionable Payments Abroad, 17 B.C. Indus. and Com. L. Rev. 303 (1976); United States Department of Commerce, Report of the President on Export Promotion Functions and Potential Export Disincentives (1980); Estey & Marston, Pitfalls (and Loopholes) in the Foreign Bribery Law, 98 Fortune 182 (1978).

C.   CRIMINAL LIABILITY FOR CORPORATE CONDUCT [2]

The two main problems of corporate criminality with which these materials deal are: (1) For whose acts is the corporation to be bound? (2) On what ground may higher-up corporate officials be individually held for acts of lesser employees?

The first problem involves the rationale of corporate punishment as a supplement or substitute for punishment of the individual actors; it also involves the legal criteria for determining which of the actions of which of its employees and officials the corporation is to be held criminally liable for.

The second problem deals with the personal criminal liability of individual employees and officials who act for the corporation. The lesser employees present no special issue; the normal legal doctrines of personal and accomplice liability suffice. The major issue is the individual liability of high officials of corporations who may be accountable in some sense for the actions of lower-echelon employees but may not be liable under the rigorous requirements of purpose or knowledge imposed by the usual doctrines of accomplice liability.

1.   Liability of the Corporate Entity

NEW YORK CENTRAL & HUDSON RIVER RAILROAD CO. v. UNITED STATES

United States Supreme Court
212 U.S. 481 (1909)

MR. JUSTICE DAY delivered the opinion of the court.

This is a writ of error to the Circuit Court of the United States for the Southern

---

2. For recent writing on the subject, see C. Stone, Where the Law Ends — The Social Control of Corporate Behavior (1975); Friedman, Some Reflections on the Corporations as Criminal Defendant, 55 Notre Dame Law. 173 (1979); Miller, Corporate Criminal Liability: A Principle Extended to Its Limits, 38 Fed. B.J. 49 (1979); Coffee, Beyond the Shut-Eyed Sentry: Toward a Theoretical View of Corporate Misconduct and an Effective Legal Response, 63 Va. L. Rev. 1099 (1977); Elkins, Corporations and the Criminal Law: An Uneasy Alliance, 65 Ky. L.J. 73 (1976); Leigh, The Criminal Liability of Corporations and Other Groups, 9 Ottawa L. Rev. 247, especially 266 et seq. (1977).

District of New York, sued out by the New York Central and Hudson River Railroad Company, plaintiff in error. In the Circuit Court the railroad company and Fred L. Pomeroy, its assistant traffic manager, were convicted for the payment of rebates to the American Sugar Refining Company and others, upon shipments of sugar from the city of New York to the city of Detroit, Michigan. . . .

The facts are practically undisputed. . . . It was shown that the established, filed and published rate between New York and Detroit was 23 cents per 100 pounds on sugar, except during the month of June, 1904, when it was 21 cents per 100 pounds.

The sugar refining companies were engaged in selling and shipping their products in Brooklyn and Jersey City, and W. H. Edgar & Son were engaged in business in Detroit, Michigan, where they were dealers in sugar. By letters between Palmer, in charge of the traffic of the sugar refining companies and of procuring rates for the shipment of sugar, and the general and assistant traffic managers of the railroad company, it was agreed that Edgar & Son should receive a rate of 18 cents per 100 pounds from New York to Detroit. It is unnecessary to quote from these letters, from which it is abundantly established that this concession was given to Edgar & Son to prevent them from resorting to transportation by the water route between New York and Detroit, thereby depriving the roads interested of the business, and to assist Edgar & Son in meeting the severe competition with other shippers and dealers. . . .

. . . . The principal attack in this court is upon the constitutional validity of certain features of the Elkins act. 32 Stat. 847. That act, among other things, provides:

> (1) That anything done or omitted to be done by a corporation common carrier subject to the act to regulate commerce, and the acts amendatory thereof, which, if done or omitted to be done by any director or officer thereof, or any receiver, trustee, lessee, agent or person acting for or employed by such corporation, would constitute a misdemeanor under said acts, or under this act, shall also be held to be a misdemeanor committed by such corporation, and upon conviction thereof it shall be subject to like penalties as are prescribed in said acts, or by this act, with reference to such persons, except as such penalties are herein changed. . . .
>
> In construing and enforcing the provisions of this section, the act, omission or failure of any officer, agent or other person acting for or employed by any common carrier, acting within the scope of his employment, shall in every case be also deemed to be the act, omission or failure of such carrier, as well as of that person.

It is contended that these provisions of the law are unconstitutional because Congress has no authority to impute to a corporation the commission of criminal offenses, or to subject a corporation to a criminal prosecution by reason of the things charged. The argument is that to thus punish the corporation is in reality to punish the innocent stockholders, and to deprive them of their property without opportunity to be heard, consequently without due process of law. . . . As no action of the board of directors could legally authorize a crime, and as indeed the stockholders could not do so, the arguments come to this: that owing to the nature and character of its organization and the extent of its power and authority, a corporation cannot commit a crime of the nature charged in this case.

Some of the earlier writers on common law held the law to be that a corporation could not commit a crime. . . . In Blackstone's Commentaries, chapter 18, §12, we find it stated: "A corporation cannot commit treason, or felony, or other crime in its corporate capacity, though its members may in their distinct individual capacities." The modern authority, universally, so far as we know, is the other way. In considering the subject, Bishop's New Criminal Law, §417, devotes a chapter to the capacity of corporations to commit crime, and states the law to be: "Since a corporation acts by its officers and agents their purposes, motives, and intent are just as much those of the corporation as are the things done. If, for example, the invisible, intangible essence of air, which we term a corporation, can level mountains, fill up valleys, lay down iron tracks, and run railroad cars on them, it can intend to do it, and can act therein as well viciously as virtuously.". . .

It is now well established that in actions for tort the corporation may be held responsible for damages for the acts of its agent within the scope of his employment.

And this is the rule when the act is done by the agent in the course of his employment, although done wantonly or recklessly or against the express orders of the principal. In such cases the liability is not imputed because the principal actually participates in the malice or fraud, but because the act is done for the benefit of the principal, while the agent is acting within the scope of his employment in the business of the principal, and justice requires that the latter shall be held responsible for damages to the individual who has suffered by such conduct. . . .

It is true that there are some crimes, which in their nature cannot be committed by corporations. But there is a large class of offenses, of which rebating under the Federal statutes is one, wherein the crime consists in purposely doing the things prohibited by statute. In that class of crimes we see no good reason why corporations may not be held responsible for and charged with the knowledge and purposes of their agents, acting within the authority conferred upon them. . . .

It is a part of the public history of the times that statutes against rebates could not be effectually enforced so long as individuals only were subject to punishment for violation of the law, when the giving of rebates or concessions inured to the benefit of the corporations of which the individuals were but the instruments. This situation, developed in more than one report of the Interstate Commerce Commission, was no doubt influential in bringing about the enactment of the Elkins Law, making corporations criminally liable. . . .

We see no valid objection in law, and every reason in public policy, why the corporation which profits by the transaction, and can only act through its agents and officers, shall be held punishable by fine because of the knowledge and intent of its agents to whom it has intrusted authority to act in the subject-matter of making and fixing rates of transportation, and whose knowledge and purposes may well be attributed to the corporation for which the agents act. . . .

UNITED STATES v. HILTON HOTELS CORP.

United States Court of Appeals, 9th Circuit
467 F.2d 1000 (1972)

BROWNING, J. This is an appeal from a conviction under an indictment charging a violation of section 1 of the Sherman Act, 15 U.S.C. §1.

Operators of hotels, restaurants, hotel and restaurant supply companies, and other businesses in Portland, Oregon, organized an association to attract conventions to their city. To finance the association, members were asked to make contributions in predetermined accounts. Companies selling supplies to hotels were asked to contribute an amount equal to one per cent of their sales to hotel members. To aid collections, hotel members, including appellant, agreed to give preferential treatment to suppliers who paid their assessments, and to curtail purchases from those who did not.

The jury was instructed that such an agreement by the hotel members, if proven, would be a per se violation of the Sherman Act. Appellant argues that this was error.

We need not explore the outer limits of the doctrine that joint refusals to deal constitute per se violations of the Act, for the conduct involved here was of the kind long held to be forbidden without more. . . . [The court's discussion of substantive antitrust law under the Sherman Act is omitted.]

Appellant's president testified that it would be contrary to the policy of the corporation for the manager of one of its hotels to condition purchases upon payment of a contribution to a local association by the supplier. The manager of appellant's Portland hotel and his assistant testified that it was the hotel's policy to purchase supplies solely on the basis of price, quality, and service. They also testified that on two occasions they told the hotel's purchasing agent that he was to take no part in the boycott. The purchasing agent confirmed the receipt of these instructions, but admitted that, despite them, he had threatened a supplier with loss of the hotel's business unless the supplier paid the association assessment. He testified that he violated his instructions because of anger and personal pique toward the individual representing the supplier.

Based upon this testimony, appellant requested certain instructions bearing upon the criminal liability of a corporation for the unauthorized acts of its agents. These requests were rejected by the trial court. The court instructed the jury that a corporation is liable for the acts and statements of its agents "within the scope of their employment," defined to mean "in the corporation's behalf in performance of the agent's general line of work," including "not only that which has been authorized by the corporation, but also that which outsiders could reasonably assume the agent would have authority to do." The court added:

> A corporation is responsible for acts and statements of its agents, done or made within the scope of their employment, even though their conduct may be contrary to their actual instructions or contrary to the corporation's stated policies.

Appellant objects only to the court's concluding statement.

Congress may constitutionally impose criminal liability upon a business entity for acts or omissions of its agents within the scope of their employment. Such liability may attach without proof that the conduct was within the agent's actual authority, and even though it may have been contrary to express instructions.

The intention to impose such liability is sometimes express, New York Central & Hudson R.R. Co. v. United States, 212 U.S. 481, but it may also be implied. The text of the Sherman Act does not expressly resolve the issue. For the reasons that follow, however, we think the construction of the Act that best achieves its purpose is that a corporation is liable for acts of its agents within the scope of their authority even when done against company orders. . . .

Legal commentators have argued forcefully that it is inappropriate and ineffective to impose criminal liability upon a corporation, as distinguished from the human agents who actually perform the unlawful acts. . . . But it is the legislative judgment that controls, and "the great mass of legislation calling for corporate criminal liability suggests a widespread belief on the part of legislators that such liability is necessary to effectuate regulatory policy." ALI Model Penal Code, Comment on §2.07, Tentative Draft No. 4, p. 149 (1956). Moreover, the strenuous efforts of corporate defendants to avoid conviction, particularly under the Sherman Act, strongly suggests that Congress is justified in its judgment that exposure of the corporate entity to potential conviction may provide a substantial spur to corporate action to prevent violations by employees.

Because of the nature of Sherman Act offenses and the context in which they normally occur, the factors that militate against allowing a corporation to disown the criminal acts of its agents apply with special force to Sherman Act violations.

Sherman Act violations are commercial offenses. They are usually motivated by a desire to enhance profits.[4] They commonly involve large, complex, and highly decentralized corporate business enterprises, and intricate business processes, practices, and arrangements. More often than not they also involve basic policy decisions, and must be implemented over an extended period of time.

Complex business structures, characterized by decentralization and delegation of authority, commonly adopted by corporations for business purposes, make it difficult to identify the particular corporate agents responsible for Sherman Act violations. At the same time, it is generally true that high management officials, for whose conduct the corporate directors and stockholders are the most clearly responsible, are likely to have participated in the policy decisions underlying Sherman Act violations, or at least to have become aware of them.

Violations of the Sherman Act are a likely consequence of the pressure to maximize profits that is commonly imposed by corporate owners upon managing agents and, in turn, upon lesser employees. In the face of that pressure, generalized directions to obey the Sherman Act, with the probable effect of foregoing profits, are the least likely to be taken seriously. And if a violation of the Sherman Act occurs, the corporation, and not the individual agents, will have realized the profits from the illegal activity.

In sum, identification of the particular agents responsible for a Sherman Act violation is especially difficult, and their conviction and punishment is peculiarly ineffective as a deterrent. At the same time, conviction and punishment of the business entity itself is likely to be both appropriate and effective.

---

4. A purpose to benefit the corporation is necessary to bring the agent's acts within the scope of his employment. Standard Oil Co. v. United States, 307 F.2d 120, 128-129 (5th Cir. 1962).

For these reasons we conclude that as a general rule a corporation is liable under the Sherman Act for the acts of its agents in the scope of their employment, even though contrary to general corporate policy and express instructions to the agent.

Thus the general policy statements of appellant's president were no defense. Nor was it enough that appellant's manager told the purchasing agent that he was not to participate in the boycott. The purchasing agent was authorized to buy all of appellant's supplies. Purchases were made on the basis of specifications, but the purchasing agent exercised complete authority as to source. He was in a unique position to add the corporation's buying power to the force of the boycott. Appellant could not gain exculpation by issuing general instructions without undertaking to enforce those instructions by means commensurate with the obvious risks. . . . Affirmed.

NOTES

1. The traditional view. Though some cases have imposed more restrictive doctrines,[3] the respondeat superior doctrine announced in the foregoing *New York Central* case and developed in the *Hilton Hotels* case represents the prevailing view of corporate liability in the United States. The requirements of liability have been summarized as follows in Note, Developments in the Law — Corporate Crime: Regulating Corporate Behavior through Criminal Sanctions, 92 Harv. L. Rev. 1227, 1247-1251 (1979):

> . . . Under the doctrine of respondeat superior, a corporation may be held criminally liable for the acts of any of its agents if an agent (1) commits a crime (2) within the scope of employment (3) with the intent to benefit the corporation.
>
> First, it must be proved that an illegal act was committed by an agent of the corporation, and that the agent acted with the specific intent required by the governing statute. Proving specific intent should be the same for a corporation as for an individual defendant, because under respondeat superior, the intent of the offending agent is imputed directly to the corporation. However, since the corporation is perceived as an aggregation of its agents, it is not necessary to prove that a specific person acted illegally, only that *some* agent of the corporation committed the crime. Thus, proving that a corporate defendant committed the illegal act is in practice substantially easier than an individual prosecution.
>
> Courts have also found the requirement of corporate criminal intent satisfied where no agent's criminal intent has been shown. Corporations have been convicted of crimes requiring knowledge on the basis of the "collective knowledge" of the employees as a group, even though no single employee possessed sufficient information to know that the crime was being committed. For example, in United States v. T.I.M.E.-D.C., Inc.,[24] a trucking company was found guilty of knowingly violating an ICC regulation which forbade truckers from driving when ill. One employee, a dispatcher, knew that the driver in question had telephoned to say he could not work, and then changed his mind after learning of the company's new absentee policy. Corporate officers, the court found, knew that the harsh new policy was likely to encourage truckers to drive despite being ill. Through the collective knowl-

3. E.g., People v. Canadian Fur Trappers Corp., 248 N.Y. 159, 161 N.E. 445 (1925). See Note, 50 Geo. L.J. 547 (1962).
24. 381 F. Supp. 730 (W.D. Va. 1974).

edge of the dispatcher and the officers, the corporation was found to have known that the driver was unfit to drive under the ICC regulation. . . .

Second, to establish corporate liability under the doctrine of respondeat superior, the prosecution must show that the illegal act was committed within the agent's scope of employment. The traditional agency definition limits scope of employment to conduct that is authorized, explicitly or implicitly, by the principal or that is similar or incidental to authorized conduct. However, courts generally find conduct to fall within the scope of employment even if it was specifically forbidden by a superior and occurred despite good faith efforts on the part of the corporation to prevent the crime. Thus, scope of employment in practice means little more than that the act occurred while the offending employee was carrying out a job-related activity. This extension is essential, for if scope of employment were limited to authorized conduct under the doctrine of respondeat superior, a corporation could too easily evade criminal liability. . . .

Third, it must be proved that the agent committed the crime with the intent to benefit the corporation. The corporation may be held criminally liable even if it received no actual benefit from the offense, although the existence or absence of benefit is relevant as evidence of an intent to benefit.[a]

The requirements of scope of employment and intent to benefit the corporation can also be met through ratification. When an employee commits a crime with no intent to benefit the corporation, or while acting outside the scope of his employment, subsequent approval of the act by his supervisor will be sufficient to hold the corporation liable for the employee's criminal act. In a sense, under the doctrine of ratification, a corporation is culpable for approving the criminal act, rather than committing it.[38]

2. *Relationship to tort standards.* (a) Is the test of respondeat superior applied in criminal cases the same as that applied in tort suits for compensatory damages? Should it be stricter?

(b) What test of respondeat superior should apply in civil suits against corporations where punitive (exemplary) damages are sought, in addition to compensatory ones? (Courts usually require a showing of outrageous intentional misconduct or at least reckless or wanton disregard of the rights of others for a punitive-damage award.) Some courts apply the same respondeat superior standards for both compensatory and punitive damages. See Morris, Punitive Damages in Personal Injury Cases, 21 Ohio St. L.J. 216, 220 (1960). A large number, however, apply a stricter standard and require that superior corporate officers either order or ratify the misconduct (id. at 221). See Restatement (Second) of Torts §909 (1965).

On what grounds can a distinction be made between criminal liability and punitive liability in a civil suit? Does it matter that while a criminal penalty is

---

a. "But while benefit is not essential in terms of result, the purpose to benefit the corporation is decisive in terms of equating the agent's action with that of the corporation. For it is an elementary principle of agency that 'an act of a servant is not within the scope of employment if it is done with no intention to perform it as a part of or incident to a service on account of which he is employed.' Restatement of the Law of Agency (2d) §235. . . . Thus the taking in or paying out of money by a bank teller, while certainly one of his regular functions, would hardly cast the corporation for criminal liability if in such 'handling' the faithless employee was pocketing the funds as an embezzler or handing them over to a confederate under some ruse." Standard Oil Co. of Texas v. United States, 307 F.2d 120, 128 (5th Cir. 1962). — EDS.

38. This notion conflicts with the traditional criminal law principle that one is generally not criminally liable for an act merely because he approved of it after the fact. See generally Sayre, Criminal Responsibility for the Acts of Another, 43 Harv. L. Rev. 689, 708 (1930).

imposed just once, punitive damages may be awarded to a multiplicity of injured plaintiffs, as, for example, in a products-liability case? See the opinion of Judge Friendly in Roginsky v. Richardson-Merrell, Inc., 378 F.2d 832 (2d Cir. 1967). See Annot., 29 A L.R.3d 1021 (1968).

3. *The case for corporate liability.* Should corporations be subject to criminal liability, which, in effect, means criminal fines? Is such a penalty fair, in view of the fact that the loss is suffered by shareholders? On another level, can punishing the corporation add distinctively to the deterrent effect of punishing the individual corporate actors?

The Commentary to Model Penal Code §2.07 ((Tent. Draft No. 4), 1955 at 148-151) offers the following observations on these and related issues:

> In approaching the analysis of corporate criminal capacity, it will be observed initially that the imposing of criminal penalties on corporate bodies results in a species of vicarious criminal liability. The direct burden of a corporate fine is visited on the shareholders of the corporation. In most cases, the shareholders have not participated in the criminal conduct and lack the practical means of supervision of corporate management to prevent misconduct by corporate agents. This is not to say, of course, that all the considerations of policy which are involved in imposing vicarious responsibility on the human principal are present in the same degree in the corporate cases. Two fundamental distinctions should be noted. First, the very fact that the corporation is the party nominally convicted means that the individual shareholders escape the oppobrium and incidental disabilities which normally follow a personal conviction or those which may result even from being named in an indictment. Second, the shareholder's loss is limited to his equity in the corporation. His personal assets are not ordinarily subject to levy and the conviction of the corporation will not result in loss of liberty to the stockholders. Nevertheless, the fact that the direct impact of corporate fines is felt by a group ordinarily innocent of criminal conduct underscores the point that such fines ought not to be authorized except where they clearly may be expected to accomplish desirable social purposes. To the extent that shareholders participate in criminal conduct, they may be reached directly through application of the ordinary principles of criminal liability.
>
> It would seem that the ultimate justification of corporate criminal responsibility must rest in large measure on an evaluation of the deterrent effects of corporate fines on the conduct of corporate agents. Is there reason for anticipating a substantially higher degree of deterrence from fines levied on corporate bodies than can fairly be anticipated from proceeding directly against the guilty officer or agent or from other feasible sanctions of a non-criminal character?
>
> It may be assumed that ordinarily a corporate agent is not likely to be deterred from criminal conduct by the prospect of corporate liability when, in any event, he faces the prospect of individually suffering serious criminal penalties for his own act. If the agent cannot be prevented from committing an offense by the prospect of personal liability, he ordinarily will not be prevented by the prospect of corporate liability.
>
> Yet the problem cannot be resolved so simply. For there are probably cases in which the economic pressures within the corporate body are sufficiently potent to tempt individuals to hazard personal liability for the sake of company gain, especially where the penalties threatened are moderate and where the offense does not involve behavior condemned as highly immoral by the individual's associates. This tendency may be particularly strong where the individual knows that his guilt may be difficult to prove or where a favorable reaction to his position by a jury

may be anticipated even where proof of guilt is strong. A number of appellate opinions reveal situations in which juries have held the corporate defendant criminally liable while acquitting the obviously guilty agents who committed the criminal acts. . . .

This may reflect more than faulty or capricious judgment on the part of the juries. It may represent a recognition that the social consequences of a criminal conviction may fall with a disproportionately heavy impact on the individual defendants where the conduct involved is not of a highly immoral character. It may also reflect a shrewd belief that the violation may have been produced by pressures on the subordinates created by corporate managerial officials even though the latter may not have intended or desired the criminal behavior and even though the pressures can only be sensed rather than demonstrated. Furthermore, the great mass of legislation calling for corporate criminal liability suggests a widespread belief on the part of legislators that such liability is necessary to effectuate regulatory policy. In some cases, such as the Elkins Act, legislatures have added corporate liability to the criminal penalties on the belief founded on experience, that such additional sanctions are necessary. N.Y. Central R.R. v. United States, 212 U.S. 481, 494-495 (1909).

The case so made out, however, does not demonstrate the wisdom of corporate fines generally. Rather, it tends to suggest that such liability can best be justified in cases in which penalties directed to the individual are moderate and where the criminal conviction is least likely to be interpreted as a form of social moral condemnation. This indicates a general line of distinction between the "malum prohibitum" regulatory offenses, on the one hand, and more serious offenses, on the other. . . .

In surveying the case law on the subject of corporate criminal liability one may be struck at how few are the types of common-law offenses which have actually resulted in corporate criminal responsibility. They are restricted for the most part to thefts (including frauds) and involuntary manslaughter. . . . No cases have been found in which a corporation was sought to be held criminally liable for such crimes as murder, treason, rape or bigamy. In general, such offenses may be effectively punished and deterred by prosecutions directed against the guilty individuals. . . .

The burden of this analysis may suggest the conclusion that corporate criminal responsibility should be withheld from serious crimes defined by the Model Penal Code. There are considerations, however, which indicate the prudence of retaining responsibility on a more restricted basis for these crimes. As noted above, the acquisitive offenses, both common-law crimes and those defined by special legislation such as the Federal Mail Fraud Act, traditionally have constituted one of the major categories of corporate crime. In a rough way, also, corporate fines in these cases may be employed to deprive a corporation of an unjust enrichment resulting from the commission of offenses by its agents. Moreover, there may be situations in which it is highly desirable to retain a degree of corporate responsibility for the Code offenses as when the crime is committed in the State by a foreign corporation but where the guilty individual agent is outside the jurisdiction and hence not amenable to prosecution in the State.

4. The Model Penal Code alternative. The Model Penal Code provisions, which have influenced the legislation of several states,[4] represent an attempt to cut back on the traditional scope of corporate liability. See Model Penal Code §2.07,

---

4. See, e.g., Ill. Rev. Stat. ch. 38, §5-4; N.Y. Penal Law §20.20; Pa. Cons. Stat. Ann. §307; Tex. Penal Code tit. 2, §7.22.

Appendix to this casebook. (Consider whether the *Hilton Hotels* case would have been decided the same way if the Model Penal Code standards had been applicable?) The following excerpt may be helpful in penetrating the rather complex language of the Model Penal Code formulation and in offering a basis for its critical assessment.

NOTE, DEVELOPMENTS IN THE LAW — CORPORATE CRIME:
REGULATING CORPORATE BEHAVIOR THROUGH
CRIMINAL SANCTIONS
92 Harv. L. Rev. 1227, 1251-1257 (1979)

. . . Adopted by the American Law Institute in 1962, the Model Penal Code offers a complex, multifaceted approach which includes three distinct systems of corporate criminal liability. The first system applies to crimes of intent where no "legislative purpose to impose liability on corporations plainly appears"; [39] this includes crimes which are usually committed by individuals, such as mail fraud, larceny, and manslaughter, but does not cover crimes generally involving corporations, such as price-fixing and securities fraud. Under this first system, a corporation can be held liable for a crime committed by an agent only if the offense was performed, authorized, or recklessly tolerated by the board of directors or a high managerial official. [41] As with respondeat superior, the corporation is liable only when a director or managerial offical acts "in behalf of the corporation" and "within the scope of his office or employment." But unlike respondeat superior, only the intent of top officials and not that of subordinates is imputed to the corporation. The Model Penal Code defines a "high managerial agent" as an officer or other agent of the corporation "having duties of such responsibility that his conduct may fairly be assumed to represent the policy of the corporation. . . ." [44]

The second system of corporate liability also concerns crimes of intent, but it deals with crimes for which the legislature has plainly intended to impose liability on corporations. [45] Like respondeat superior, this second system holds a corporation criminally responsible for the crime of any agent committed within the scope of employment and with an intent to benefit the corporation. But the draftsmen of the Model Penal Code, believing that the primary purpose of holding corporations accountable for the acts of lower-level employees is to encourage diligent supervision by managerial officials, added an affirmative defense: the corporation can escape liability under the second system by proving by a preponderance of the evidence that the high managerial agent with supervisory responsibility over the subject matter of the offense acted with "due diligence" to prevent it. [48]

39. Model Penal Code §2.07(1)(a), (c) (1962).
41. Model Penal Code §2.07(1)(c) (1962).
44. Model Penal Code §2.07(4)(c) (1962). The framers of the Model Penal Code intended that corporate liability not be imposed for the unauthorized conduct "of a foreman in a large plant or of an insignificant branch manager. . . ." Model Penal Code §2.07, Comment at 151 (Tent. Draft No. 4, 1955).
45. Model Penal Code §2.07(1)(a) (1962). . . .
48. Id. §2.07(5) (1962). However, a due diligence defense is not permitted if it is "plainly inconsistent with the legislative purpose in defining the particular offense." Id.

The third system created by the Model Penal Code applies only to strict liability crimes; it assumes a legislative purpose to impose liability on corporations for these crimes "unless the contrary plainly appears." [49] The principles of respondeat superior apply to this system, but since only strict liability crimes are involved, neither evidence of specific intent to commit a crime nor intent to benefit the corporation is required to find corporate liability.[50] The defense of due diligence is not available.[51] Imposing liability on the corporation for strict liability crimes has the effect of punishing stockholders for offenses they could not have prevented, but this is justified, as with any strict liability crime, by the pressing need to prevent the injury caused by the offense.

The Code also sets forth a small category of offenses based on the failure to discharge a "specific duty of affirmative performance" imposed by law on corporations.[54] "Specific duty" refers to narrowly defined tasks set forth by statute or regulation, such as a duty to file a report with an administrative agency; it does not encompass any generally imposed obligations, such as the duty of reasonable care.[55] This standard of corporate liability should be considered a part of the third system, since resting corporate guilt solely on the failure to discharge a specific duty is one form of strict liability. With both strict liability and duty to act offenses, liability focuses solely on the results of corporate action or inaction; the position in the corporate hierarchy of the person who acted and the intent with which he acted are irrelevant to the determination of liability. . . .

The doctrine of respondeat superior and the three systems presented in the Model Penal Code must be compared in terms of the dual purposes of the corporate criminal law — deterrence and just deserts. Two factors which affect the degree of deterrence differ substantially among the various systems of corporate criminal liability. The first factor, ease of evasion, reflects the ability of a corporation to benefit from an illegal act by an employee but still not be legally subject to liability for it. The second factor, difficulty of detection and proof, is based on the assumption that the corporate defendant is legally subject to liability, and focuses on the evidentiary burden the prosecution must carry in order to win a conviction.

Corporate criminal liability is most easily evaded under the first Model Penal Code system. This is the only system where liability rests solely on the conduct of top corporate officials. Consequently, liability can be evaded whenever illegal activity occurs without the authorization or reckless toleration of top officials. Since an executive cannot authorize or recklessly tolerate an offense unless he knows about it, a corporation can escape liability under this system as long as high officials remain ignorant of illegal activity. Superiors can preserve their ignorance by conveying to employees the understanding that they do not wish to be told of information which may subject the corporation to liability. Alternatively, they can protect themselves from knowledge — and the corporation from liability — simply by delegating to subordinates full responsibility for those activities which might result in criminal violations. Corporate liability is more difficult

---

49. Id. §2.07(2) (1962).
50. Compare id. §2.07(2) with id. §2.07(1)(a).
51. Id. §2.07(5).
54. Model Penal Code §2.07(1)(b) (1962).
55. Id. §2.07, Status of Section at 38.

to evade under the other three systems, because under each the corporation is responsible for the acts of every agent, not merely those of high managerial officials. . . .

The first Model Penal Code system has an additional drawback in that large corporations can more easily evade liability than small ones. Larger, multidivisional organizations generally maintain a layer of top managers who reserve their own energies for policymaking, coordination, and program evaluation, and delegate responsibility for day to day operations to middle-level employees. . . . [T]he top officials whose conduct would subject the corporations to liability are often too far removed from daily operations to be charged with authorizing or recklessly tolerating criminal activity at lower levels.

The first Model Penal Code system also presents greater difficulties of proof than the other three systems of corporate criminal liability. To establish liability under this system, the prosecutor must undertake a two part investigation into the inner workings of the corporation. First, he must discover the persons who performed, authorized, or recklessly tolerated the crime. . . . [E]ven when subordinates believe their illegal conduct was ordered or condoned by top executives, they may actually have misinterpreted lawful orders which became distorted as they passed down the chain of command. The second part of the prosecutor's investigation requires him to ascertain whether the persons who commanded, authorized, or recklessly tolerated the crime are high managerial officials within the meaning of the Model Penal Code. While it is clear under this system that the involvement of an officer subjects a corporation to criminal liability, no criteria yet exist for determining which other, lower ranking employees should be considered "high managerial agents."

Corporate criminal liability is less difficult to prove under the other three systems since none demand so extensive an investigation into the inner workings of the corporation. . . .

Like deterrence, the other major purpose of the corporate criminal law, just deserts, is approached differently by the various systems of corporate liability. Underlying the respondeat superior and corporate strict liability systems is the moral theory which holds a corporation responsible for the acts of every one of its agents. The first Model Penal Code system is based on the retributive theory which considers a corporation blameworthy solely for the acts of its top officials. Only the Model Penal Code system of respondeat superior with a due diligence defense focuses at all on the reasonableness of corporate efforts to prevent illegal behavior. This system, though, differs critically from the moral theory based on the reasonableness of corporate practices and procedures; the defense the second system offers relates to the due diligence employed by the supervisor of the agent who committed the illegal act rather than to the care undertaken by the corporation as a whole. Thus, if the responsible supervisor failed to act with due diligence, the second Model Penal Code system could theoretically impose corporate criminal liability even though the corporation's overall efforts to prevent regulatory violations were reasonable.

A new system of corporate liability based on the reasonableness of the corporation's practices and procedures to avert illegal conduct would better reflect the blameworthiness of the corporation as an entity. Under this new system, a corporation could be held criminally liable, as under respondeat superior, when an agent acting within the scope of employment commits a crime on behalf of the corporation. But the corporation could rebut this presumption of liability by proving by a preponderance of the evidence that it, as an organization, exercised due diligence to prevent the crime. Since the acts of top officials are likely to represent the practices and procedures of the corporation, the involvement of policy-making officials in corporate criminal activity should almost always refute a due diligence defense. Effective deterrence can be achieved under this system only if, in order to establish the affirmative defense of due diligence, a corporation must adopt stringent procedures to combat illegal activity. The corporation should be required to demonstrate that it employed two kinds of precautions: first, that the illegal conduct had been clearly and convincingly forbidden, and second, that reasonable safeguards designed to prevent corporate crimes had been developed and implemented, including regular procedures for evaluation, detection, and remedy. Proper evaluation assures on a continuing basis that the safeguards adopted are adequate to prevent violations through such procedures as periodic assessments of price-setting policies. Detection procedures, such as outside audits and regular compliance reports, bring dangerous conditions and ongoing violations to the attention of top management. Adequate remedies include disciplining wrongdoers and insuring prompt repair of conditions conducive to future violations.

A system of liability based on the absence of reasonable efforts to prevent corporate crime would rest criminal responsibility on the blameworthiness of the corporation, yet effectively deter corporate crime. For these reasons, Congress should adopt the due diligence defense for all corporate crimes in its revision of the federal criminal code. Even if Congress merely codifies the now predominant respondeat superior doctrine, federal courts could on their own develop corporate due diligence as an affirmative defense. The traditional criminal law principle that sanctions should rest on blameworthiness justifies courts in providing corporate defendants with the opportunity to establish the absence of blameworthiness by proving the reasonableness of corporate practices and procedures.

COMMONWEALTH v. BENEFICIAL FINANCE CO.

Supreme Judicial Court of Massachusetts
360 Mass. 188, 275 N.E.2d 33 (1971)

SPIEGEL, J. [The opinion in this case decided appeals from two separate trials. The individual and corporate defendants in both trials were charged with bribery or conspiring to engage in bribery. Both trials involved bribery schemes devised by several finance companies in Massachusetts to obtain favorable treatment from the state Small Loans Regulatory Board or the state Commissioner of Banks. Although the conspiracies charged in the two trials were both extensive and interrelated, the following excerpts from the opinion concern only the first trial and only the conviction of Beneficial Finance Company.

[In addition to Beneficial, two other corporations (Household Finance Corp. and Liberty Loan Corp.) were convicted at the first trial, as were several employees of these corporations, including Farrell and Glynn, both employees of Beneficial Management Co., a wholly-owned subsidiary of the Beneficial Finance Co., and Hanley and Garfinkle, both members of the Small Loans Regulatory Board.

The purpose of the conspiracy charged in the first trial was to influence the Board to set a high maximum interest rate on certain loans within its jurisdiction. To this end, Hanley and Garfinkle received bribes. Glynn participated in the conspiracy by acting as a direct contact with the bribed officials. Farrell supervised Glynn's activities in furtherance of the conspiracy; he also chaired the intercorporate meeting at which the bribery plan was eventually adopted.]

The defendants and the Commonwealth have proposed differing standards upon which the criminal responsibility of a corporation should be predicated. The defendants argue that a corporation should not be held criminally liable for the conduct of its servants or agents unless such conduct was performed, authorized, ratified, adopted or tolerated by the corporations' directors, officers or other "high managerial agents" who are sufficiently high in the corporate hierarchy to warrant the assumption that their acts in some substantial sense reflect corporate policy. This standard is that adopted by the American Law Institute Model Penal Code, approved in May, 1962. Section 2:07 of the Code provides that, except in the case of regulatory offences and offences consisting of the omission of a duty imposed on corporations by law, a corporation may be convicted of a crime if "the commission of the offence was authorized, requested, commanded, performed or recklessly tolerated by the board of directors or by a high managerial agent acting in behalf of the corporation within the scope of his office or employment." The section proceeds to define "high managerial agent" as "an officer of a corporation . . . or any other agent . . . having duties of such responsibility that his conduct may fairly be assumed to represent the policy of the corporation."

The Commonwealth, on the other hand, argues that the standard applied by the judge in his instructions to the jury was correct. These instructions, which prescribe a somewhat more flexible standard than that delineated in the Model Penal Code, state in part, as follows:

[T]he Commonwealth does not have to prove that the individual who acted criminally was expressly requested or authorized in advance by the corporation to do so, nor must the Commonwealth prove that the corporation expressly ratified or adopted that criminal conduct on the part of that individual or those individuals. *It does not mean that the Commonwealth must prove that the individual who acted criminally was a member of the corporation's board of directors, or that he was a high officer in the corporation, or that he held any office at all.* If the Commonwealth did prove that an individual for whose act it seeks to hold a corporation criminally liable was an officer of the corporation, the jury should consider that. *But more important than that, it should consider what the authority of that person was as such officer in relation to the corporation.* The mere fact that he has a title is not enough to make the corporation liable for his criminal conduct. The Commonwealth must prove that the individual for whose conduct it seeks to charge *the corporation criminally was placed in a position by the corporation where he had enough power, duty, responsibility and authority to act for and in behalf of the corporation to handle the particular business or operation or project of the corporation in which he was engaged at the time that he committed the criminal act, with power of decision as to what he would or would not do while acting for the corporation, and that he was acting for and in behalf of the corporation in the accomplishment of that particular business or operation or project,* and that he committed a criminal act while so acting. . . .

The difference between the judge's instructions to the jury and the Model Penal Code lies largely in the latter's reference to a "high managerial agent" and in the Code requirement that to impose corporate criminal liability, it at least must appear that its directors or high managerial agent "authorized . . . or recklessly tolerated" the allegedly criminal acts. The judge's instructions focus on the authority of the corporate agent in relation to the *particular* corporate business in which the agent was engaged. The Code seems to require that there be authorization or reckless inaction by a corporate representative having some relation to framing corporate policy, or one "having duties of such responsibility that his conduct may fairly be assumed to represent the policy of the corporation." Close examination of the judge's instructions reveals that they preserve the underlying "corporate policy" rationale of the Code by allowing the jury to infer "corporate policy" from the *position* in which the corporation placed the agent in commissioning him to handle the particular corporate affairs in which he was engaged at the time of the criminal act. We need not deal with the Model Penal Code in greater detail. . . .

[The court then analyzed prior Massachusetts cases concerning criminal liability of corporations and vicarious criminal liability. As to the latter, the court found "a long line of decisions in this Commonwealth holding that before criminal responsibility can be imposed on the master, based on a master-servant relationship under the doctrine of respondeat superior, actual participation in, or approval of, the servant's criminal act must be shown." The court also noted that this rule was applied both to mala in se and mala prohibita offences.]

The thrust of each of the cases cited above involving a human principal is that it is fundamental to our criminal jurisprudence that for more serious offences guilt is personal and not vicarious. "One is punished for his own blameworthy conduct, not that of others." Commonwealth v. Stasiun, 349 Mass. 38, 48, 206 N.E.2d 672, 679, citing Perkins, Criminal Law, 550, and Sayre, Criminal Responsibility for the Acts of Another, 43 Harv. L. Rev. 689. . . .

As alluded to by Professor Sayre, and pointed out by the Commonwealth in its brief, the very nature of a corporation as a "person" before the law renders it impossible to equate the imposition of vicarious liability on a human principal with the imposition of vicarious liability on a corporate principal. "A corporation can act only through its agents. . . . [C]orporate criminal liability is necessarily vicarious." . . . Thus, the issue is not whether vicarious liability should be imposed on a corporation under the "direct participation and assent rule" of the master-servant cases cited above, but rather, whether the acts and intent of natural persons, be they officers, directors or employees, can be treated as the acts and intent of the corporation itself. For the foregoing reasons, despite the strenuous urging of the defendants, we are unconvinced that the standard for imposing criminal responsibility on a human principal adequately deals with the evidentiary problems which are inherent in ascribing the acts of individuals to a corporate entity.

Since we have exhausted our review of Massachusetts cases in point, we turn to cases in other jurisdictions discussing the problem of corporate criminal responsibility. We note, however, that in view of the fact that the crimes alleged here, namely, conspiracy and the substantive offences of bribery, are mala in se, we necessarily exclude discussion of those cases which clearly involve "public welfare" offences by a corporation, unless such cases cast some insight into the question before us. Generally, these cases concern public nuisances resulting from the nonperformance of a nondelegable duty, rather than the rule of respondeat superior. . . .

Household argues that the *New York Central* case [212 U.S. 481, pages 1006-1008 supra] is one in which Congress clearly dispensed with the necessity of proving corporate intent and is therefore distinguishable from the case before us. While we agree that the thrust of the opinion in that case is addressed to the constitutionality of the statutory imputation of the agent's acts to the corporation, we think that the case falls outside the class of offences generally denominated as "public welfare" offences and . . . serves as precedent for the proposition that a corporation may be held criminally responsible for the acts of one who is neither a director, officer nor "high managerial agent" of the corporation. In this regard, the case illustrates the public policy rationale for imposing vicarious liability upon a corporation and thus warranting the treatment of corporations in a manner different from that of individuals for the acts of their agents. This rationale was subsequently developed and applied in lower Federal court cases which dealt with crimes requiring specific intent. . . .

Another Federal case applying the above standard is C.I.T. Corp. v. United States, 150 F.2d 85 (9th Cir). This case is significant in that a large national money lending corporation was held criminally responsible for the criminal acts of a minor branch manager. The corporation was convicted of conspiracy to make false credit statement applications to the Federal Housing Administration, a crime which under the statute specifically required the element of knowledge. On appeal, the corporation argued that the branch manager was too low in the corporate hierarchy and that he had no corporate power to commit the acts complained of with the criminal intent imputable to the corporate entity. In refuting this argument the court said: "We do not agree. It is the function delegated to the corporate officer or agent which determines his power to engage the corporation in a criminal transaction." . . .

The standard applied in the above cases clearly focused on the scope of authority of the agents to act in the narrow sphere of corporate business relating to the criminal act. This essential consideration was succinctly set forth in somewhat different terms in the case of United States v. Nearing, 252 F. 223, 231 (S.D.N.Y.) wherein Judge Learned Hand stated that "the criminal liability of a corporation is to be determined by the *kinship of the act to the powers of the officials, who commit it*" (emphasis supplied). . . .

Household, Beneficial and Liberty all vigorously attack these cases in an attempt to distinguish them from the cases before us. The thrust of their argument is that all of these cases fall into 1 of 2 categories; either they involve public welfare and regulatory statute crimes in which intent was not an element, or if the crimes did include intent as a necessary element, then they assert that the corporations were only held liable if one high in the corporate hierarchy directed, approved or acquiesced in the agent's criminal act. . . .

We think that the answer to these contentions is twofold. First, the defendants' attempted categorization of the above cases into two neat little groups greatly oversimplifies the complex and multifaceted issues which confronted the various courts in the cases we have cited. The principal cases of . . . *C.I.T.* and *Nearing* . . . entail prosecutions for the crimes of conspiracy, a crime requiring specific intent. . . . Secondly, the argument that only high corporate officers were involved has no basis in fact. In the *C.I.T.* case, a minor branch manager was involved, and in [another] case, a salesman. . . .

Household argues that in applying the foregoing standard of corporate criminal responsibility, we are merely applying the rule of respondeat superior as it is applied in civil cases. . . .

It may be that the theoretical principles underlying this standard are, in general, the same as embodied in the rule of respondeat superior. Nevertheless, as we observed at the outset, the judge's instructions, as a whole and in context, required a greater quantum of proof in the practical application of this standard than is required in a civil case. In focusing on the "kinship" between the authority of an individual and the act he committed, the judge emphasized that the jury must be satisfied "beyond a reasonable doubt" that the act of the individual "*constituted*" the act of the corporation. Juxtaposition of the traditional criminal law requirement of ascertaining guilt beyond a reasonable doubt (as opposed to the civil law standard of the preponderance of the evidence), with the rule of respondeat superior, fully justifies application of the standard enunciated by the judge to a criminal prosecution against a corporation for a crime requiring specific intent.

The foregoing is especially true in view of the particular circumstances of this case. In order to commit the crimes charged in these indictments, the defendant corporations either had to offer to pay money to a public official or conspire to do so. The disbursal of funds is an act peculiarly within the ambit of corporate activity. These corporations by the very nature of their business are constantly dealing with the expenditure and collection of moneys. It could hardly be expected that any of the individual defendants would conspire to pay, or would pay, the substantial amount of money here involved, namely $25,000, out of his own pocket. The jury would be warranted in finding that the disbursal of such an amount of money would come from the corporate treasury. A reasonable inference could therefore be drawn that the payment of such money by the corporations was done as a matter of corporate policy and as a reflection of corporate intent, thus comporting with the underlying rationale of the Model Penal Code, and probably with its specific requirements.

Moreover, we do not think that the Model Penal Code standard really purports to deal with the evidentiary problems which are inherent in establishing the quantum of proof necessary to show that the directors or officers of a corporation authorize, ratify, tolerate, or participate in the criminal acts of an agent when such acts are apparently performed on behalf of the corporation. Evidence of such authorization or ratification is too easily susceptible of concealment. As is so trenchantly stated by the judge: "Criminal acts are not usually made the subject of votes of authorization or ratification by corporate Boards of Directors; and the lack of such votes does not prevent the act from being the act of the corporation." . . .

Additional factors of importance are the size and complexity of many large modern corporations which necessitate the delegation of more authority to lesser corporate agents and employees. As the judge pointed out: "There are not enough seats on the Board of Directors, nor enough offices in a corporation, to permit the corporation engaged in widespread operations to give such a title or office to every person in whom it places the power, authority, and responsibility for decision and action." This latter consideration lends credence to the view that the title or position of an individual in a corporation should not be conclusively determinative in ascribing criminal responsibility. In a large corporation, with many numerous and distinct departments, a high ranking corporate officer or agent may have no authority or involvement in a particular sphere of corporate activity, whereas a lower ranking corporate executive might have much broader power in dealing with a matter peculiarly within the scope of his authority. Employees who are in the lower echelon of the corporate hierarchy often exercise more responsibility in the *everyday operations* of the corporation than the directors or officers. Assuredly, the title or office that the person holds may be considered, but it should not be the decisive criterion upon which to predicate corporate responsibility. . . .

Considering everything we have said above, we are of opinion that the quantum of proof necessary to sustain the conviction of a corporation for the acts of its agents is sufficiently met if it is shown that the corporation has placed the agent in a position where he has enough authority and responsibility to act for and in behalf of the corporation in handling the *particular* corporate business, operation or project in which he was engaged at the time he committed the criminal act. The judge properly instructed the jury to this effect and correctly stated that this standard does not depend upon the responsibility or authority which the agent has with respect to the entire corporate business, but only to his position with relation to the particular business in which he was serving the corporation. Some of the factors that the jury were entitled to consider in applying the above test, although perhaps not in themselves decisive, are the following: (1) the extent of control and authority exercised by the individual over and within the corporation,[62] (2) the extent and manner to which corporate funds were used in the crime, (3) a repeated pattern of criminal conduct tending to indicate corporate toleration or ratification of the agent's acts. . . .

[The court then considered whether, under the legal standards it enunciated, the conduct of Farrell and Glynn and their relationship to Beneficial sufficed to support the conviction of Beneficial. The conduct of these two individuals presented a problem since neither was formally an employee of Beneficial: Farrell was an officer and director of Beneficial Management Co. (a wholly-owned subsidiary) and Glynn, although he "reported" to Farrell, was on the payroll of a third company, Industrial Bankers (also a wholly-owned subsidiary of Beneficial). The court, after examining the interlocking relationships and the functional identity of the corporate operations (Beneficial and its subsidiaries were all part of the "Beneficial Finance System," a term used by Beneficial to describe its overall operations) concluded that there was "sufficient evidence to support a finding that there existed between defendants Farrell and Glynn and the corporation Beneficial Management a relationship of agency with the corporation Beneficial which empowered Farrell and Glynn to act on behalf of Beneficial in dealing with Hanley in his official capacity and also in connection with the Rate Board proceedings."]

---

62. With regard to a small closely held corporation, in which the individual *is* the corporation, this factor may be considered somewhat decisive.

2. *Liability of Corporate Agents*

INTRODUCTORY NOTE

Personal liability of corporate officers and agents has not been much affected by the conceptual concerns that hindered development of criminal liability of the corporate entity. One argument against criminal liability was that corporate agents should not be criminally liable for their actions when they acted for the corporation in a representative capacity. But this argument never drew much support in the case law. See 3A W. Fletcher, Encyclopedia of the Law of Private Corporations §1348, at 630 (1975); Note, Individual Liability of Agents for Corporate Crime under the Proposed Federal Criminal Code, 31 Vand. L. Rev. 965, 971 (1978).

The general law of accomplice liability (see Chapter 8 Section A supra) governs the liability of persons for crimes committed within a corporate setting as well as elsewhere. The special problems derive from the bureaucratic arrangement of corporate activities, with lower employees responsible to higher-level employees in a hierarchy leading up to the highest officers, and the difficulty of establishing the liability of higher officers under doctrines generally governing the liability of one person for the acts of another (for example, aiding, authorizing, commanding, with intent, etc.). How to find a means of holding superior officers liable in appropriate cases without embracing a doctrine of vicarious liability is the central issue presented by the materials in this subsection. See generally, Note, supra, 31 Vand. L. Rev. 965 (1978); Note, Developments in the Law — Corporate Crime: Regulating Corporate Behavior through Criminal Sanctions, 91 Harv. L. Rev. 1227, 1259-1275 (1979).

GORDON v. UNITED STATES
United States Court of Appeals, 10th Circuit
203 F.2d 248 (1953), rev'd, 347 U.S. 909 (1954)

[Defendant partners in a sewing-machine and appliance business were convicted of violating the Defense Production Act by selling sewing machines on credit terms prohibited by that act and regulations issued thereunder. Section 601 provided that any person who "willfully" violated its provisions or any regulation or order issued thereunder should upon conviction be punished as therein specified. The case was not submitted to the jury on the question whether the partners had actual notice of the transactions. Instead, it was tried and submitted on the theory that knowledge of one partner regarding the transactions was "imputable, attributable and chargeable" to the other and that the knowledge and acts of the salespeople who made the sales and kept the records while acting in the course of their employment were imputable and chargeable to the employing partners. On the "very perplexing question whether the partners can be held criminally responsible for the knowledge and acts of their agents and employees, who the evidence shows, while acting in the course of their employment, actually made the sales without having collected the required down payment," the court, per MURRAH, J., answered in the affirmative, stating:]

Deeply rooted in our criminal jurisprudence is the notion that criminal guilt is personal to the accused; that wilfulness or a guilty mind is an essential ingredient of a punishable offense, and that one cannot intend an act in which he did not consciously participate, acquiesce, or have guilty knowledge. Morissette v. United States, 342 U.S. 246.

Amenable to this notion, the courts have been reluctant to hold the master or the employer criminally responsible for the acts of his agent or employee which he did not authorize, counsel, advise, approve or ratify. It is only in the so-called public welfare offenses usually involving police regulation of food, drink and drugs that the courts have relaxed the necessity for proof of a wilful intent.

In our case wilfulness is specifically made a prerequisite to guilt. Indeed it is the gist of the offenses charged in all of the counts in the information. And the trial court instructed the jury that in every crime or public offense there must be a "union or joint operation of act and intent" but "that the intent or intention is manifest by the circumstances connected with the offense as well as by direct testimony."

What the court did in effect was to make wilfulness an essential element of the offenses charged in the information, and to charge the employers with the guilty knowledge and acts of the employees in determining the question of wilfulness. In so doing, it had recent precedent in this court. In Inland Freight Lines v. United States, 10 Cir., 191 F.2d 313, the defendant was charged with the wilful violation of a regulatory statute in keeping and preserving false records of which it had knowledge only through its agents and employees. In determining the question of wilfulness the defendant was charged with the knowledge of its employees, and we reversed only because the jury was permitted to infer wilfulness from mere negligence on the part of the employer in failing to investigate the integrity of records which it was charged with the duty of preparing and keeping. See also Inland Freight Lines v. United States, 10 Cir., 202 F.2d 169.

The effect of this is not to dispense with wilfulness or guilty knowledge as an element of the offense. It is to charge the employer with knowledge of records he is required to keep and acts he is required or forbidden to do, and which he necessarily keeps, does or omits to do by and through his agents and employees. To be sure, the knowledge with which he is charged is not direct; it is constructive. If it be called vicarious responsibility, it is nevertheless a responsibility of him on whom the law places the duty. It is permissible proof of a wilfulness which in its proper context denotes more than mere negligence but less than bad purpose or evil motive. It connotes a course of conduct which may be construed by the triers of facts as deliberate and voluntary, hence intentional; or it may be construed as negligent, inadvertent and excusable. The act or omission itself is not inexorably penalized. The ultimate question of guilt is left to the ameliorating influence of those who sit in judgment. Considered in this light, we do not think the instructions of the court fall short of the traditional standards for guilt.

HUXMAN, J. dissenting: . . . The partners denied intent to violate the law or any knowledge that their employees were violating it. They were entitled to have their testimony weighed and evaluated under proper instructions by the court together with all other revelant evidence. They were entitled to have the jury told that they were not criminally liable for the acts of their employees, although committed within the scope of their employment, unless they directed such activities or had guilty knowledge thereof. It is a principle embedded in the English law from time immemorial that the sins of the father shall not be visited upon the son merely because the father is the agent of the son and his unlawful acts were committed within the scope of his employment, under a criminal statute making wilfulness an element of the offense when the son had no knowledge of or part in such violations.

Strong reliance is placed upon Inland Freight Lines v. United States, 191 F.2d 313, by this court. But that case is clearly distinguishable. There the sole defendant was the corporation charged with keeping false records and it was held that the knowledge of its agents was the knowledge of the corporation. That is the well established principle of criminal law as applied in the case of a corporation. It is, as the law recognizes, the only way a corporation can be held criminally responsible for violations of penal statutes. While a corporation is recognized as a separate legal entity, such separate entity is a pure fiction of the law. As a separate entity and aside from its agents and employees a corporation can do nothing. It has no conscience, will, or power of thought. It acts only through its agents. Their acts are the only acts it can commit and their knowledge of necessity is the only knowledge it can have.

The only cases in which a principal without actual intent or knowledge of criminal acts of wrong-doing by his employees has been held criminally responsible for such acts arose under welfare statutes such as the Pure Food and Drug Laws, Liquor Laws and Weight and Measure Acts. But under all of these acts where a principal was held guilty because of the acts of his agents without knowledge or intent on his part wilfulness was not an element of the offense and the statute made the doing of the act the offense.

NOTE

The United States Supreme Court granted certiorari and reversed the Tenth Circuit's decision in *Gordon* in the following per curiam opinion (347 U.S. 909, 909 (1954)):

> Petitioners are business partners in the sale of appliances. They were convicted under Section 603 of the Defense Production Act of 1950 . . . which provides that "Any person who willfully violates" regulations promulgated under the Act shall be guilty of crime. The jury was instructed that the knowledge of petitioners' employees was chargeable to petitioners in determining petitioners' wilfulness. Because of the instruction, the government has confessed error. We agree, and accordingly reverse the judgment and remand the case to the district court for retrial.

Four years later, the Supreme Court held a partnership liable for the "knowing and willful" violation of the Motor Carrier Act, 18 U.S.C. §835, 49 U.S.C. §322(a), based on the conduct of an employee, and distinguished *Gordon* by explaining, "here the government does not seek to hold the individual partners, but only the partnership as an entity." United States v. A & P Trucking Co., 358 U.S. 121, 126 (1958).

UNITED STATES v. PARK

Supreme Court of the United States
421 U.S. 658 (1975)

Mr. Chief Justice Burger delivered the opinion of the Court. . . .

Acme Markets, Inc., is a national retail food chain with approximately 36,000 employees, 874 retail outlets, 12 general warehouses, and four special warehouses. Its headquarters, including the office of the president, respondent Park, who is chief executive officer of the corporation, are located in Philadelphia, Pa. In a five-count information filed in the United States District Court for the District of Maryland, the Government charged Acme and respondent with violations of the Federal Food, Drug, and Cosmetic Act. Each count of the information alleged that the defendants had received food that had been shipped in interstate commerce and that, while the food was being held for sale in Acme's Baltimore warehouse following shipment in interstate commerce, they caused it to be held in a building accessible to rodents and to be exposed to contamination by rodents. These acts were alleged to have resulted in the food's being adulterated within the meaning of 21 U.S.C. §§342(a) (3) and (4),[1] in violation of 21 U.S.C. §331(k).[2]

Acme pleaded guilty to each count of the information. Respondent pleaded not guilty. The evidence at trial demonstrated that in April 1970 the Food and Drug Administration (FDA) advised respondent by letter of insanitary conditions in Acme's Philadelphia warehouse. In 1971 the FDA found that similar conditions existed in the firm's Baltimore warehouse. An FDA consumer safety officer testified concerning evidence of rodent infestation and other insanitary conditions discovered during a 12-day inspection of the Baltimore warehouse in November and December 1971. He also related that a second inspection of the warehouse had been conducted in March 1972. On that occasion the inspectors found that there had been improvement in the sanitary conditions, but that "there was still evidence of rodent activity in the building and in the warehouses and we found some rodent-contaminated lots of food items."

The Government also presented testimony by the Chief of Compliance of the FDA's Baltimore office, who informed respondent by letter of the conditions at the Baltimore warehouse after the first inspection.[6] There was testimony by

---

1. Section 402 of the Act, 21 U.S.C. §342, provides in pertinent part:
"A food shall be deemed to be adulterated —
"(a) . . . (3) if it consists in whole or in part of any filthy, putrid, or decomposed substance, or if it is otherwise unfit for food; or (4) if it has been prepared, packed, or held under insanitary conditions whereby it may have become contaminated with filth, or whereby it may have been rendered injurious to health. . . ."
2. Section 301 of the Act, 21 U.S.C. §331, provides in pertinent part:
"The following acts and the causing thereof are prohibited: . . .
"(k) The alteration, mutilation, destruction, obliteration, or removal of the whole or any part of the labeling of, or the doing of any other act with respect to, a food, drug, device, or cosmetic, if such act is done while such article is held for sale (whether or not the first sale) after shipment in interstate commerce and results in such article being adulterated or misbranded."
6. The letter, dated January 27, 1972, included the following:
"We note with much concern that the old and new warehouse areas used for food storage were actively and extensively inhabited by live rodents. Of even more concern was the observation that such reprehensible conditions obviously existed for a prolonged period of time without any detection, or were completely ignored. . . .
"We trust this letter will serve to direct your attention to the seriousness of the problem and formally advise you of the urgent need to initiate whatever measures are necessary to prevent recurrence and ensure compliance with the law."

Acme's Baltimore division vice president, who had responded to the letter on behalf of Acme and respondent and who described the steps taken to remedy the insanitary conditions discovered by both inspections. The Government's final witness, Acme's vice president for legal affairs and assistant secretary, identified respondent as the president and chief executive officer of the company and read a bylaw prescribing the duties of the chief executive officer.[7] He testified that respondent functioned by delegating "normal operating duties," including sanitation, but that he retained "certain things, which are the big, broad, principles of the operation of the company," and had "the responsibility of seeing that they all work together.". . .

Respondent was the only defense witness. He testified that, although all of Acme's employees were in a sense under his general direction, the company had an "organizational structure for responsibilities for certain functions" according to which different phases of its operation were "assigned to individuals who, in turn, have staff and departments under them." He identified those individuals responsible for sanitation, and related that upon receipt of the January 1972 FDA letter, he had conferred with the vice president for legal affairs, who informed him that the Baltimore division vice president "was investigating the situation immediately and would be taking corrective action and would be preparing a summary of the corrective action to reply to the letter." Respondent stated that he did not "believe there was anything [he] could have done more constructively than what [he] found was being done."

On cross-examination, respondent conceded that providing sanitary conditions for food offered for sale to the public was something that he was "responsible for in the entire operation of the company," and he stated that it was one of many phases of the company that he assigned to "dependable subordinates." Respondent was asked about and, over the objections of his counsel, admitted receiving, the April 1970 letter addressed to him from the FDA regarding insanitary conditions at Acme's Philadelphia warehouse. He acknowledged that, with the exception of the division vice president, the same individuals had responsibility for sanitation in both Baltimore and Philadelphia. Finally, in response to questions concerning the Philadelphia and Baltimore incidents, respondent admitted that the Baltimore problem indicated the system for handling sanitation "wasn't working perfectly" and that as Acme's chief executive officer he was responsible for "any result which occurs in our company."

At the close of the evidence, respondent's renewed motion for a judgment of acquittal was denied. The relevant portion of the trial judge's instructions to the jury challenged by respondent is set out in the margin.[9] Respondent's

---

7. The bylaw provided in pertinent part:

"The Chairman of the board of directors or the president shall be the chief executive officer of the company as the board of directors may from time to time determine. He shall, subject to the board of directors, have general and active supervision of the affairs, business, offices and employees of the company. . . .

"He shall, from time to time, in his discretion or at the order of the board, report the operations and affairs of the company. He shall also perform such other duties and have such other powers as may be assigned to him from time to time by the board of directors."

9. "In order to find the Defendant guilty on any count of the Information, you must find beyond a reasonable doubt on each count. . . .

"Thirdly, that John R. Park held a position of authority in the operation of the business of Acme Markets, Incorporated.

"However, you need not concern yourselves with the first two elements of the case. The main

counsel objected to the instructions on the ground that they failed fairly to reflect our decision in United States v. Dotterweich, [320 U.S. 277 (1943)], and to define " 'responsible relationship.' " The trial judge overruled the objection. The jury found respondent guilty on all counts of the information, and he was subsequently sentenced to pay a fine of $50 on each count.[10]

The Court of Appeals reversed the conviction and remanded for a new trial. That court viewed the Government as arguing "that the conviction may be predicated solely upon a showing that . . . [respondent] was the President of the offending corporation," and it stated that as "a general proposition, some act of commission or omission is an essential element of every crime." It reasoned that, although our decision in United States v. Dotterweich had construed the statutory provisions under which respondent was tried to dispense with the traditional element of " 'awareness of some wrongdoing,' " the Court had not construed them as dispensing with the element of "wrongful action." The Court of Appeals concluded that the trial judge's instructions "might well have left the jury with the erroneous impression that Park could be found guilty in the absence of 'wrongful action' on his part," and that proof of this element was required by due process. It . . . directed that on retrial the jury be instructed as to "wrongful action," which might be "gross negligence and inattention in discharging . . . corporate duties and obligations or any of a host of other acts of commission or omission which would 'cause' the contamination of food.". . . .

The question presented by the Government's petition for certiorari in United States v. Dotterweich, supra, and the focus of this Court's opinion, was whether "the manager of a corporation, as well as the corporation itself, may be prosecuted under the Federal Food, Drug, and Cosmetic Act of 1938 for the introduction of misbranded and adulterated articles into interstate commerce." In Dotterweich, a jury had disagreed as to the corporation, a jobber purchasing drugs from manufacturers and shipping them in interstate commerce under its own label, but had convicted Dotterweich, the corporation's president and general manager. The Court of Appeals reversed the conviction on the ground that only the drug dealer, whether corporation or individual, was subject to the criminal provisions of the Act, and that where the dealer was a corporation, an individual connected therewith might be held personally only if he was operating the corporation "as his 'alter ego.' "

In reversing the judgment of the Court of Appeals and reinstating Dotter-

---

issue for your determination is only with the third element, whether the Defendant held a position of authority and responsibility in the business of Acme Markets. . . .

"The statute makes individuals, as well as corporations, liable for violations. An individual is liable if it is clear, beyond a reasonable doubt, that the elements of the adulteration of the food as to travel in interstate commerce are present. As I have instructed you in this case, they are, and that the individual had a responsible relation to the situation, even though he may not have participated personally.

"The individual is or could be liable under the statute, even if he did not consciously do wrong. However, the fact that the Defendant is pres[id]ent and is a chief executive officer of the Acme Markets does not require a finding of guilt. Though, he need not have personally participated in the situation, he must have had a responsible relationship to the issue. The issue is, in this case, whether the Defendant, John R. Park, by virtue of his position in the company, had a position of authority and responsibility in the situation out of which these charges arose."

10. Sections 303 (a) and (b) of the Act, 21 U.S.C. §§333(a) and (b), provide:

"(a) Any person who violates a provision of section 331 of this title shall be imprisoned for not more than one year or fined not more than $1,000, or both. . . ."

weich's conviction, this Court looked to the purposes of the Act and noted that they "touch phases of the lives and health of people which, in the circumstances of modern industrialism, are largely beyond self-protection." It observed that the Act is of "a now familiar type" which "dispenses with the conventional requirement for criminal conduct — awareness of some wrongdoing. In the interest of the larger good it puts the burden of acting at hazard upon a person otherwise innocent but standing in responsible relation to a public danger."

Central to the Court's conclusion that individuals other than proprietors are subject to the criminal provisions of the Act was the reality that "the only way in which a corporation can act is through the individuals who act on its behalf.". . .

At the same time, however, the Court was aware of the concern which was the motivating factor in the Court of Appeals' decision, that literal enforcement "might operate too harshly by sweeping within its condemnation any person however remotely entangled in the proscribed shipment." A limiting principle, in the form of "settled doctrines of criminal law" defining those who "are responsible for the commission of a misdemeanor," was available. In this context, the Court concluded, those doctrines dictated that the offense was committed "by all who . . . have . . . a responsible share in the furtherance of the transaction which the statute outlaws."

The Court recognized that, because the Act dispenses with the need to prove "consciousness of wrongdoing," it may result in hardship even as applied to those who share "responsibility in the business process resulting in" a violation. It regarded as "too treacherous" an attempt "to define or even to indicate by way of illustration the class of employees which stands in such a responsible relation." The question of responsibilty, the Court said, depends "on the evidence produced at the trial and its submission — assuming the evidence warrants it — to the jury under appropriate guidance." The Court added: "In such matters the good sense of prosecutors, the wise guidance of trial judges, and the ultimate judgment of juries must be trusted.". . .

Dotterweich and the cases which have followed reveal that in providing sanctions which reach and touch the individuals who execute the corporate mission — and this is by no means necessarily confined to a single corporate agent or employee — the Act imposes not only a positive duty to seek out and remedy violations when they occur but also, and primarily, a duty to implement measures that will insure that violations will not occur. The requirements of foresight and vigilance imposed on responsible corporate agents are beyond question demanding, and perhaps onerous, but they are no more stringent than the public has a right to expect of those who voluntarily assume positions of authority in business enterprises whose services and products affect the health and well-being of the public that supports them. Cf. Wasserstrom, Strict Liability in the Criminal Law, 12 Stan. L. Rev. 731, 741-745 (1960).

The Act does not, as we observed in *Dotterweich*, make criminal liability turn on "awareness of some wrongdoing" or "conscious fraud." The duty imposed by Congress on responsible corporate agents is, we emphasize, one that requires the highest standard of foresight and vigilance, but the Act, in its criminal aspect, does not require that which is objectively impossible. The theory upon which responsible corporate agents are held criminally accountable for "causing" violations of the Act permits a claim that a defendant was "powerless" to prevent or correct the violation to "be raised defensively at a trial on the merits." United States v. Wiesenfeld Warehouse Co., 376 U.S. 86, 91 (1964). If such a claim is made, the defendant has the burden of coming forward with evidence, but this does not alter the Government's ultimate burden of proving beyond a reasonable doubt the defendant's guilt, including his power, in light of the duty imposed by the Act, to prevent or correct the prohibited condition. Congress has seen fit to enforce the accountability of responsible corporate agents dealing with products which may affect the health of consumers by penal sanctions cast in rigorous terms, and the obligation of the courts is to give them effect so long as they do not violate the Constitution.

We cannot agree with the Court of Appeals that it was incumbent upon the District court to instruct the jury that the Government had the burden of establishing "wrongful action" in the sense in which the Court of Appeals used that phrase. The concept of a "reasonable relationship" to, or a "reasonable share" in, a violation of the Act indeed imports some measure of blameworthiness; but it is equally clear that the Government establishes a prima facie case when it introduces evidence sufficient to warrant a finding by the trier of the facts that the defendant had, by reason of his position in the corporation, responsibility and authority either to prevent in the first instance, or promptly to correct, the violation complained of, and that he failed to do so. . . .

Reading the entire charge satisfies us that the jury's attention was adequately focused on the issue of respondent's authority with respect to the conditions that formed the basis of the alleged violations. Viewed as a whole, the charge did not permit the jury to find guilt solely on the basis of respondent's position in the corporation. . . .

Reversed.

MR. JUSTICE STEWART, with whom MR. JUSTICE MARSHALL and MR. JUSTICE POWELL join, dissenting.

Although agreeing with much of what is said in the Court's opinion, I dissent from the opinion and judgment, because the jury instructions in this case were not consistent with the law as the Court today expounds it.

As I understand the Court's opinion, it holds that in order to sustain a conviction under §301(k) of the Federal Food, Drug, and Cosmetic Act the prosecution must at least show that by reason of an individual's corporate position and responsibilities, he had a duty to use care to maintain the physical integrity of the corporation's food products. A jury may then draw the inference that when the food is found to be in such condition as to violate the statute's prohibitions, that condition was "caused" by a breach of the standard of care imposed upon the responsible official. This is the language of negligence, and I agree with it.

To affirm this conviction, however, the Court must approve the instructions given to the members of the jury who were entrusted with determining whether the respondent was innocent or guilty. Those instructions did not conform to the standards that the Court itself sets out today.

The trial judge instructed the jury to find Park guilty if it found beyond a reasonable doubt that Park "had a responsible relation to the situation. . . . The issue is, in this case, whether the Defendant, John R. Park, by virtue of his position in the company, had a position of authority and responsibility in the situation out of which these charges arose." Requiring, as it did, a verdict of guilty upon a finding of "responsibility," this instruction standing alone could have been construed as a direction to convict if the jury found Park "responsible" for the condition in the sense that his position as chief executive officer gave him formal responsibility within the structure of the corporation. But the trial judge went on specifically to caution the jury not to attach such a meaning to his instruction, saying that "the fact that the Defendant is pres[id]ent and is a chief executive officer of the Acme Markets does not require a finding of guilt." "Responsibility" as used by the trial judge therefore had whatever meaning the jury in its unguided discretion chose to give it.

The instructions, therefore, expressed nothing more than a tautology. They told the jury: "You must find the defendant guilty if you find that he is to be held accountable for this adulterated food." In other words: "You must find the defendant guilty if you conclude that he is guilty.". . .

To be sure, "the day [is] long past when [courts] . . . parsed instructions and engaged in nice semantic distinctions," Cool v. United States, 409 U.S. 100, 107 (Rehnquist, J., dissenting). But this Court has never before abandoned the view that jury instructions must contain a statement of the applicable law sufficiently precise to enable the jury to be guided by something other than its rough notions of social justice. And while it might be argued that the issue before the jury in this case was a "mixed" question of both law and fact, this has never meant that a jury is to be left wholly at sea, without any guidance as to the standard of conduct the law requires. . . .

The *Dotterweich* case stands for two propositions, and I accept them both. First, "any person" within the meaning of 21 U.S.C. §333 may include any corporate officer or employee "standing in responsible relation" to a condition or transaction forbidden by the Act. 320 U.S., at 281. Second, a person may be convicted of a criminal offense under the Act even in the absence of "the conventional requirement for criminal conduct — awareness of some wrongdoing." Ibid.

But before a person can be convicted of a criminal violation of this Act, a jury must find — and must be clearly instructed that it must find — evidence beyond a reasonable doubt that he engaged in wrongful conduct amounting at least to common-law negligence. There were no such instructions, and clearly, therefore, no such finding in this case. . . .

NOTES

1. The federal courts have been slow to recognize situations in which the corporate agents found it "objectively impossible" to avoid the harm. See United States v. Starr, 535 F.2d 512 (9th Cir. 1976); United States v. Y. Heta Ltd., 535 F.2d 508 (9th Cir. 1976).

2. Is *Park* just another instance of vicarious criminal liability? Consider Note, Developments in the Law — Corporate Crime: Regulating Corporate Behavior through Criminal Sanctions, 92 Harv. L. Rev. 1227, 1262 n. 102:

It should be stressed that holding corporate officials criminally responsible for causing strict liability violations is not imposing vicarious liability. In *Park* and *Dotterweich*, corporate executives were culpable for their own failure to exercise the quality of care needed to prevent violations within the realms of their own authority; their guilt was not vicariously imputed from the guilt of their subordinates.

3. The *Park* case involved violation of a strict-liability statute. Where the subordinate employee commits an offense with mens rea requirements (knowledge, for example), the standards developed in that case would not seem applicable. Given the principle on which the *Gordon* case, pages 1024-1026 supra, rested, the superior employee could not be convicted of a crime requiring knowledge of some circumstance unless he or she can be proven to have had it. Where a superior directs or authorizes a subordinate employee to do an act, the basis of liability is clear. Problems arise over establishing knowledge in less clear instances. Consider the following observations in Note, Developments in the Law — Corporate Crime: Regulating Corporate Behavior through Criminal Sanctions, 92 Harv. L. Rev. 1227, 1276-1277 (1979):

> A corporate official can be held liable for acquiescing in the crimes of his subordinates only when he had the power and the obligation to control the behavior. . . . However, treating acquiescence as willful complicity does not stretch the net of potential liability too broadly since proof that the defendant knew of the offense remains an essential element of liability. And an official who knows of an offense need only make a good faith effort to correct it. This duty can easily be fulfilled by ordering an end to the illegal activity or by instituting new procedures designed to make such violations less likely to recur. . . .
>
> The primary limitation on the deterrent effectiveness of the acquiescence standard lies in the need to prove that the defendant knew of his subordinate's crime. Such knowledge is often difficult to prove even when officials do know of criminal conduct. Furthermore, because of the nature of the corporate bureaucracy, top executives often will not know of crimes by their subordinates. Top officials have too little time to learn of all that goes on at lower levels of the company and their employees tend to shield them from knowledge of criminal activity, both to protect the superiors from taint and the subordinates from embarrassment. Indeed, executives may take pains *not* to learn of subordinates' offenses once they recognize that they can escape criminal liability so long as they remain ignorant.
>
> Government enforcement agencies can often reduce the difficulty of proving knowledge by notifying responsible corporate officials of ongoing violations. The problem of proving knowledge is also mitigated to some extent by the rule that willful blindness is equivalent to knowledge. Found throughout the criminal law, this rule permits courts to hold liable under a specific intent statute an individual who "willfully and intentionally remain[s] ignorant of a fact, important and material to his conduct." [138] Despite these alternative means of proving knowledge, the knowledge requirement places an inherent limitation on the potential deterrent effectiveness of specific intent statutes.

138. Griego v. United States, 298 F.2d 845, 849 (10th Cir. 1962). . . .

NATIONAL COMMISSION ON REFORM OF FEDERAL
CRIMINAL LAWS, WORKING PAPERS
Vol. 1, 200-201, 185-188 (1970)

[C]ompany policy with respect to compliance with regulatory standards or requirements is usually set not at the level of actual compliance or noncompliance, but rather at the highest managerial or supervisory level. There seems to be a general belief that many individual employees who violate these regulatory statutes do so because they are under pressure, although not necessarily stated pressure, from higher levels to increase profits in any way possible. In such cases, it seems distasteful to prosecute inferior officials or employees "who are the tools rather than the responsible originators of the violative conduct." [110] Thus it has been noted, with respect to the electrical equipment cases, that "the high policymakers of General Electric and other companies involved escaped personal accountability for a criminal conspiracy of lesser officials that extended over several years to the profit of the corporations, despite the belief of the trial judge and most observers that these higher officials either knew of and condoned these activities or were willfully ignorant of them." [111] In addition, it has been noted that in many cases violation by a lower echelon employee "may have been produced by pressures on the subordinates created by corporate managerial officials even though the latter may not have intended or even desired the criminal behavior and even though the pressures can only be sensed rather than demonstrated." [112] In either case the problem is essentially one involving the difficulties of locating and proving participation in the offense by such high-level policy formulators.

There are several possibilities with respect to controlling conduct in furtherance of a corporate enterprise indirectly, by placing responsibility for such conduct upon persons in the corporate structure other than the person actually engaging in the conduct. . . .

There are two possibilities with respect to the corporation's managers. First, the managers of the corporation could be held vicariously responsible for the criminal conduct of the employees of the corporation. The most extreme application of this possibility would be to authorize a fine and/or jail term for the directors for all types of offenses committed by all employees of the corporation: the directors would be held responsible (a) even though they have no direct means of controlling the conduct of the employees, and (b) regardless of (i) whether they had knowledge of the fact the conduct was taking place, or (ii) whether the officers appointed by them were involved in the conduct; each of the executive officers could be held similarly responsible without regard to whether the offense occurred within his particular line of duty or was committed by an employee under his supervision. A more limited application of the vicarious

110. Kadish, Some Observations on the Use of Criminal Sanctions in Enforcing Economic Regulations, 30 U. Chi. L. Rev. 423, 431 (1963). . . . This thought may have been behind the Supreme Court's statement in United States v. New York Central & Hudson R. R.R., 212 U.S. 481, 495 (1909), that history had shown that the "statutes against rebates could not be effectively enforced so long as individuals only were subject to punishment for violation of the law, when the giving of rebates or concessions inured to the benefit of the corporations of which the individuals were but the instruments," and that criminal liability of the *corporations* was therefore required to control the subject matter and correct the abuses aimed at.
111. Kadish, supra, at 431.
112. Model Penal Code, §2.07, Comment at 149 (Tent. Draft No. 4, 1955).

responsibility possibility would be to restrict managerial responsibility on a line of duty basis — the directors would be responsible only for offenses occurring in connection with corporate activities requiring board approval and offenses in which elected officers were involved; and each of the executive officers would be held for offenses occurring within his sphere of authority and for offenses committed by employees under his supervision. Vicarious responsibility could be further restricted by eliminating directorial liability and limiting responsibility of the officers to those offenses within their jurisdiction over which no other person had the final signoff power. Finally, vicarious liability of the officers and directors could be limited to strict liability offenses.[69]

The second possibility with respect to the officers and directors would be to pin their responsibility upon their own fault; they could be held responsible for offenses which they could have prevented had they properly performed their duties of management and supervision. No existing Federal statute has been found which so provides, and such liability would not seem to exist under the decisional law in the Federal courts. But the suggestion has been made at various times that such a duty be statutorily created. Thus, . . . hearings were held in 1961 on a bill which would have amended section 14 of the Clayton Act to impose liability on corporate executives for "ratifying" acts constituting a violation of the act, defining "ratification" as the possession of knowledge or reasonable cause to believe that the corporation is engaging in a violation, the possession of authority to stop or prevent the violation or to report it to someone with such authority, and the failure to exercise such authority. And the possibility of imposing a duty on corporate officers "to learn of and control the activities of their employees" was suggested in the recent critique of the Federal Trade Commission prepared by several Yale Law School students under the direction of Ralph Nader.

Finally, it has been suggested that such a duty could be imposed generally upon all corporate executives with respect to all types of criminal conduct occurring on behalf of their corporations.[73] Liability for failure to perform the duty (i.e., to exercise one's authority to prevent the offense) . . . would probably have to depend upon negligence, or, perhaps recklessness. The imposition of such a duty, enforced through criminal sanctions directed to the managers, would tend to decrease the incidence of conduct constituting the actual offense by applying a threat to those actually having control over the actors (compulsory self-policing), as well as by stepping up the deterrent impact upon the actor — he is now threatened not only with detection and prosecution by law enforcement officials but with an increased possibility of detection and punishment administered within the corporation for which he works.

---

69. Corporate officers may be said to be vicariously responsible for strict liability offenses under existing law (United States v. Dotterweich, 320 U.S. 277 (1934) . . . because the basis for such responsibility is their position in the corporation. (This liability is not "vicarious" in the derivative sense because the officer's liability does not depend upon the commission of the offense by a particular employee; it is a *result* which is the basis of liability rather than an act.)

73. See, e.g., Comment, Increasing Community Control Over Corporate Crime — A Problem in the Law of Sanctions, 71 Yale L.J. 280, 303-304 (1961); Davids, Penology and Corporate Crime, 58 J. Crim. L.C. & P.S. 524, 530 (1967), and authorities there cited; Kadish, Some Observations on the Use of Criminal Sanctions in Enforcing Economic Regulations, 30 U. Chi. L. Rev. 423, 430-433 (1963), noting the difficulties with respect to defining the extent to which an official of a nationwide corporation must be aware of its far-flung operations.

CRIMINAL CODE REFORM BILL, S. 1437, 95th Cong., 2d Sess. (1978): *Section 403.* (a) CONDUCT ON BEHALF OF AN ORGANIZATION. — Except as otherwise expressly provided, a person is criminally liable for an offense based upon conduct that he engages in or causes in the name of an organization or on behalf of an organization to the same extent as if he engaged in or caused the conduct in his own name or on his own behalf.

(b) OMISSION TO PERFORM A DUTY OF AN ORGANIZATION. — Except as otherwise expressly provided, whenever a duty to act is imposed upon an organization by a statute, or by a regulation, rule, or order issued pursuant thereto, an agent of the organization having significant responsibility for the subject matter to which the duty relates is criminally liable for an offense based upon an omission to perform the duty, if he has the state of mind required for the commission of the offense, to the same extent as if the duty were imposed upon him directly.

(c) RECKLESS FAILURE TO SUPERVISE CONDUCT OF AN ORGANIZATION. — Except as otherwise expressly provided, a person responsible for supervising particular activites on behalf of an organization who, by his reckless failure to supervise adequately those activities, permits or contributes to the commission of an offense by the organization is criminally liable for the offense, except that if the offense committed by the organization is a felony the person is liable under this subsection only for a Class A misdemeanor.

NOTE, INDIVIDUAL LIABILITY OF AGENTS FOR CORPORATE CRIMES UNDER THE PROPOSED FEDERAL CRIMINAL CODE
31 Vand. L. Rev. 965, 991-1004 (1978)

Section 403 . . . states three general principles of individual liability for crime in the corporate setting. Section 403 applies when a corporation commits an offense defined elsewhere in the Proposed Code or in any other statute and the statute or Code provision defining the offense does not specify the individuals within the organization who should bear the criminal responsibility.

A.   SECTION 403(a) — CONDUCT ON BEHALF OF AN ORGANIZATION

. . . . The primary purpose of section 403(a) appears to be merely the codification of the rule that individuals are responsible for their conduct even when acting in a representative capacity. Section 403(a) offers little guidance in deciding how high in the corporate hierarchy criminal responsibility should be imposed or how to identify responsible senior officials.

B.   SECTION 403(b) — FAILURE TO PERFORM A DUTY OF AN ORGANIZATION

. . . The language of the subsection resembles the *Park* Court's [421 U.S. 658, pages 1027-1032 supra] articulation of *Dotterweich* [320 U.S. 277 (1945)] liability, which emphasized that the culpability of responsible corporate managers rests upon their violation of a statutory duty to discover and remedy violations of the law within the corporation. Section 403(b) thus serves to identify those corporate officials who are not the immediate criminal actors but who should nonetheless bear criminal responsibility for certain corporate violations contemplated by the subsection. . . .

Section 403(b) applies only when "a duty to act is imposed upon an organization by a statute, or by a regulation, rule, or order issued pursuant thereto.". . . A statute or regulation may prescribe explicitly the duty of the corporation (and, by virtue of section 403(b), of the individual agent) to act, such as a duty to file a report or income tax return. *Dotterweich* and its progeny, however, clearly indicate that a statute can impose duties without expressly stating so. . . . *Park* . . . relied on the Food and Drug Act's imposition of a "positive duty to seek out and remedy violations . . . and . . . a duty to implement measures that will insure that violations will not occur." However, the Food and Drug Act makes no mention of any such specific duties. . . .

. . . This . . . reflects the current notion that strict liability regulatory offenses impose upon the corporation and its officers the duty to insure the quality of corporate products and activities and to refrain from conduct that would endanger public health, safety, or welfare.

Agencies regulating corporate activities may insure the availability of section 403(b) for future prosecutions by issuing regulations explicitly describing the circumstances in which corporations have a duty to act. . . . The Senate Judiciary Committee admits that the "phrase is designedly rather amorphous, in order to leave to prosecutors, judges, and juries the basic task of defining the class of persons who stand in such a relation to an organization that criminal responsibility for its actions may rightfully be imposed upon them.". . . .

Section 403(b) further requires that the individual have significant responsibility "for the subject matter to which the duty relates." Thus the prosecution must demonstrate a connection between the corporate duty and the defendant's individual area of responsibility. This language reflects the concern in *Park* that the defendant have some responsibility for the offense beyond the mere fact of his position within the corporation. In United States v. H. B. Gregory Co. [502 F.2d 700 (7th Cir. 1974)] the offense arose from rodent infestation of a warehouse. The individual defendant, who was president and treasurer of the company, had general responsibility for the operation of the warehouse, but at trial the government presented testimony emphasizing that the corporation specifically charged the defendant with responsibility for rodent control problems. Such evidence clearly is helpful in identifying the proper defendants.

C. SECTION 403(c) — RECKLESS FAILURE TO SUPERVISE CONDUCT OF AN ORGANIZATION

Sections 403(a) and 403(b) substantially codify present case laws by punishing individual conduct on behalf of the corporation and by identifying proper defendants when a corporation fails to perform an act required by law. Section 403(c), however, establishes a basis for inculpating more corporate officials for more types of corporate offenses than presently exists in federal criminal law.[199] . . .

The Senate Judiciary Committee remarked that criminal liability based on a failure to supervise is new to federal law and is a "modest extension" of federal

---

199. Section 403(c), unlike §403(b), does not require the existence of a corporate duty to act.

criminal liability;[200] in fact, such liability has been an unarticulated influence in both state and federal cases dealing with individual liability for corporate crime. The Committee intends section 403(c) to "place an affirmative duty to exercise reasonable supervision on responsible supervisory personnel" to punish the "do it but don't tell me about it" attitude of senior officials, and to establish "a basis for punishment of those who could and should control the illegal activities of their subordinates but choose instead to condone those activities."

. . . Section 403(c) does not refer to individuals with "primary" or "significant" responsibility, however, and the pool of possible defendants culpable for a particular corporate offense is apparently larger under section 403(c) than under section 403(b). In addition, when a statute imposes a duty on the corporation that is not discharged, which invokes section 403(b), liability for that offense could extend not only to the manager possessing significant responsibility but also to the lower echelon supervisors responsible under 403(c) for employees in that area of corporate activity. Furthermore, the culpability of any individual defendant under the provisions of sections 403(a), (b), or (c) automatically could implicate that defendant's supervisor under section 403(c) for inadequate supervision of the lower echelon defendants. . . .

Section 403(c) translates the civil liability of directors for breach of a duty of adequate supervision owed to the corporation into criminal liability for breach of a duty owed to the general public. Indicia of a tortious failure to supervise gleaned from civil cases, however, cannot be applied uncritically in prosecutions under section 403(c). Both the language of section 403(c) and the legislative history of the Proposed Code emphasizes that criminal liability requires a neglect greater than that producing civil liability. Section 403(c) requires a "reckless" failure to supervise adequately. Section 302(c) of the Proposed Code defines "reckless" as an awareness and disregard of a risk that a circumstance exists or that a result of conduct will occur. This risk, in turn, "must be of such a nature and degree that to disregard it constitutes a gross deviation from the standard of care that a reasonable person would exercise in such a situation." The standard of recklessness in section 403(c) indicates that the prosecution's burden is heavy, and fears expressed in the legislative hearings concerning the expansiveness of such liability seem unfounded. . . .

Unlike sections 403(a) and (b), section 403(c) does not require that the individual defendant possessed the culpable state of mind necessary in the underlying offense. For example, subordinate agents might commit a serious felony requiring an intentional state of mind, but prosecution of their supervisor under section 403(c) would require only a showing of his recklessness rather than intent. However, section 403(c) imposes only misdemeanor sanctions upon corporate supervisors, even though the underlying corporate offense resulting from the defendants' failure to supervise might be a felony. This ameliorative sentencing provision is intended to reduce any harsh results that might flow from section 403(c) and indicates a congressional reluctance to impose the most severe felony penalties on the basis of a liability new to the law and as yet unclear in impact.

---

200. Opponents of the subsection called it a "dangerous experiment of uncertain consequences." Subcommittee Hearings, pt. III, subpt. B, at 1782 (statement of the National Association of Manufacturers).

NOTE

For a less sanguine assessment of §403, see American Bar Association, Ad Hoc Committee of the Section of Corporations, Banking and Business Law, Report on Proposed Federal Criminal Code, 34 Bus. Law. 725, 763-771 (1979).

D. SENTENCING THE BUSINESS OFFENDER

UNITED STATES v. BERGMAN
United States District Court, S.D.N.Y.
416 F. Supp. 490 (1976)

[For the opinion in this case, see page 211 supra.]

BROWDER v. UNITED STATES
United States District Court, C.D. Or.
398 F. Supp. 1042 (1975)

[For the opinion in this case, see page 219 supra.]

POSNER, OPTIMAL SENTENCES FOR WHITE-COLLAR CRIMINALS
17 Am. Crim. L. Rev. 409, 410-411, 413-416 (1980)

. . . [W]hite-collar crimes are those more likely to be committed by the affluent than by the poor criminal — crimes that involve fraud, monopoly, and breach of faith rather than violence. The white-collar criminal is the affluent perpetrator of those crimes.

The point I wish to argue in this article, an application of the economic analysis of crime and punishment pioneered by Gary Becker,[2] can now be stated simply: the white-collar criminal as I have defined him should be punished only by monetary penalties — by fines (where civil damages or penalties are inadequate or inappropriate) rather than by imprisonment or other "afflictive" punishments (save as they may be necessary to coerce payment of the monetary penalty). In a social cost-benefit analysis of the choice between fining and imprisoning the white-collar criminal, the cost side of the analysis favors fining because, as we shall see, the cost of collecting a fine from one who can pay it (an important qualification) is lower than the cost of imprisonment. On the benefit side, there is no difference in principle between the sanctions. The fine for a white-collar crime can be set at whatever level imposes the same disutility on the defendant, and thus yield the same deterrence, as the prison sentence that would have been imposed instead. Hence, fining the affluent offender is preferable to impris-

2. See Becker, Crime and Punishment: An Economic Approach, 76 J. Pol. Econ. 169 (1968); for a nontechnical discussion, see R. Posner, Economic Analysis of Law 164-72 (2d ed. 1977). Becker argues that the use of fines as punishment minimizes the social loss resulting from crime.

oning him from society's standpoint because it is less costly and no less efficacious.

The reason that the fine is the cheaper sanction is that, unlike imprisonment,
it is a transfer payment. Because the dollars collected from the criminal as a
fine show up on the benefit side of the social ledger, the net social cost is
limited to the costs of collecting the fine. A term of imprisonment, on the other
hand, yields no comparable social revenue if we disregard the negligible, and
nowadays usually zero, output of the prisoner. On the contrary, to the social
costs of imprisonment must be added the considerable sums spent on maintaining prisoners. To be sure, for a middle-class offender, a short prison term might
be the deterrent equivalent of a large fine. But it would not follow that the
social costs of the short prison term were correspondingly low, because the
greater one's income, the greater is the cost of imprisonment in lost earnings.
As long as these are earnings in legitimate occupations, their loss is a social
cost similar to the cost of the prison guards. The large fine avoids these costs.

I anticipate relatively little disagreement with the proposition that fines are
cheaper to society than imprisonment when the offender can pay the fine. I
expect great resistance, however, to the proposition that the social *benefits* of
punishment are no greater when punishment takes the form of imprisonment
than when it takes the form of a fine. It will be argued that there is no money
equivalent to the pain of imprisonment, perhaps especially to the affluent, educated, "sensitive" person — the white-collar criminal — that would be within
his power to pay. (The offender here is necessarily an individual: a corporation
or other "artificial" person cannot, of course, be punished by imprisonment.)
But whether this is so depends . . . on the severity of the prison sentences
actually imposed for white-collar crimes. . . . [I]t is no doubt true that very
few people would consider a fine of any size to be as severe a punishment as
death, or imprisonment for life, or, perhaps, imprisonment for twenty years.
Thus, if these are optimal punishments (putting aside the consideration that
imprisonment is more costly to administer), it might indeed be difficult to find
a monetary equivalent. Perhaps these are optimal punishments for some white-
collar crimes. If so, my proposal to substitute fines for prison for white-collar
criminals is in serious difficulty — but only in a rather academic sense. For whatever may be theoretically optimal, white-collar criminals, at least in this country,
are not punished by death or long prison terms. . . . [T]he prison sentences
for white-collar crimes — when prison sentences are imposed on the perpetrators
of such crimes — barely exceed two years. Even this figure greatly exaggerates
the actual time served behind bars, which is shortened by parole and time off
for good behavior.

Perhaps, as I have suggested, these prison terms are too short given the
gravity of the crimes and the difficulty of detecting them. That is a large question
that I do not propose to investigate here. I shall instead treat the existing level
of imprisonment for white-collar crime as part of the background of the analysis.
Given that level, it is highly improbable that there is *no* fine equivalent to a
prison sentence in the amount of disutility it imposes on the offender. An individual who has the boldness, the effrontery, to commit a crime — even of
the white-collar variety — will have the capacity and inclination to consider realistic trade-offs between 90 days, or even a year or two, in one of the federal
system's minimal security prisons and a hefty fine. If he would be deterred by

the threat of such a prison sentence, he would be equally deterred by the threat of a $50,000 or $100,000 or $250,000 fine. (And fines could be indexed to prevent inflation from reducing their bite.) . . .

If it is objected that the schedule of prison-fine equivalences cannot in fact be calculated, there are two replies. The first is that a nice calculation is not required; the prison sentences imposed in white-collar cases — or in any other cases for that matter — are not themselves the product of any nice calculation of the amount of disutility imposed by the sentence on the offender, but are only the roughest of guesses. The second and more interesting reply is that there are in fact methods, imperfect ones to be sure, of empirically tracing out the curve of indifference between fine and imprisonment. . . .

Professor Coffee, in his contribution to this symposium, offers [several] reasons why the threat of imprisonment is inherently greater than that of a fine.[9] One is that the optimal fine may exceed the offender's ability to pay. While this is certainly possible, it is no reason to prefer imprisonment to fines in cases where offenders *can* pay the fines. All I am arguing in this paper is that fines are preferable to imprisonment where the fines are collectible.

Second, Coffee, following Block and Lind, argues that in order to be sure that an offender will pay whatever fine is levied, he must be threatened with a prison sentence that is more severe than the fine. If there is no difference in severity, the offender will be indifferent between the two forms of punishment. This point is correct but does not support Coffee's position. The purpose of imprisonment in Block and Lind's analysis is not to deter the offender but to coerce collection of the fine. The very premise of their proposal is thus the superior economic efficiency of fines to imprisonment as a method of punishment. . . .

. . . If it is true, for whatever reason, that imprisonment is unpleasant relative to fines — because of a "stigma" effect, or because prison guards are brutal, or because imprisonment interferes with an offender's predilection for taking risks more than fines do — this affects simply the exchange rate between dollars of fine and days of imprisonment and not the choice of which method of punishment to use. If we think that the term of imprisonment for a crime provides the correct amount of deterrence, then in computing the fine equivalent we will want to be sure that we take account of all of the factors that make imprisonment a source of disutility. The fine equivalent is still the cheaper punishment method, however, as long as the fine can be collected from the offender.

I turn now to what seems a separate, but is really the same, objection to substituting fines for imprisonment in white-collar crimes: namely, that a system in which poor offenders were usually imprisoned and rich offenders usually fined would be a system that discriminated against poor people. This argument is just a variant of the fallacy that imprisonment is inherently more punitive than fines. It gains some plausibility only from the ridiculous "rates of exchange" that used to be commonplace in crimes where the criminal had the option of paying a fine or going to jail, a practice that has been invalidated by the Supreme Court under the Equal Protection Clause of the fourteenth amendment.[16] The

---

9. See Coffee, Corporate Crime and Punishment: A Non-Chicago View of the Economics of Criminal Sanctions, 17 Am. Crim. L. Rev. 419 (1980).

16. The practice has been invalidated in those cases in which the defendant's indigency is a determining factor in his imprisonment. See Tate v. Short, 401 U.S. 395 (1971) (inability to pay

assumption behind this argument, however, is false. For every prison sentence there is some fine equivalent; if the fine is so large that it cannot be collected, then the offender should be imprisoned. How then are the rich favored under such a system?

A possible answer is that the rich could "buy" more crime under a fine system than under an imprisonment system. Suppose that the expected cost to society of a crime is $100, the probability of apprehension and conviction is 10 percent, and therefore the fine is set at $1,000 so that expected punishment cost will be equal to the expected social cost. A rich man would not be deterred from committing this crime as long as the expected benefits to him were greater than $1000. But now suppose that instead of a fine of $1000, a prison term of one month is imposed for this crime based on a study which shows that the disutility of a month in prison to an average person is $1,000. Since the disutility of imprisonment rises with income, this form of punishment will deter the rich man more than the poor one. Stated differently, a nominally uniform prison term has the effect of price discrimination based on income.

But this is not to say that a system of fines discriminates against the poor. It is rather that a *uniform* prison term discriminates against the rich compared with a *uniform* fine. If we want to discriminate against the rich through a fine system, that is easily done by progressively varying the fine with the offender's income. If we want not to discriminate against the rich through an imprisonment system, we can make the length of the sentence inverse to the offender's income. In either case the choice to discriminate is independent of the form of the punishment.

Where fines are trivial, it is natural to suppose that only substantial jail sentences will carry a "stigma" effect which adds to deterrence. Yet even if, improbably, imprisonment produced a stigma effect which no magnitude of fine could duplicate, only the rate of exchange between fine and imprisonment, and not the principle of equivalence, would be affected. The fine equivalent would then be higher than if a fine carried a stigma as well. But, in fact, the presence of stigma is an argument for fines rather than for prison sentences. Most students of the criminal process locate the source of the stigma in the fact of conviction rather than the form of the sentence. The more punishment society obtains simply from the stigmatizing effect of conviction, the smaller the fine that must be imposed to produce the optimal severity of punishment; and the smaller the fine, the less likely it is to exceed the white-collar criminal's ability to pay. . . .

. . . If the criminal sanction is to be retained in this area, then, as I have argued in this article, fines should be substituted for prison sentences when the optimal fine is within the power of the offender to pay. In principle, this position could, and I think should, be extended beyond the white-collar domain to include the non-white-collar crimes that the affluent occasionally commit. . . .

---

fine resulting from traffic offense cannot justify imprisonment if affluent offender not subject to possible imprisonment); Williams v. Illinois, 399 U.S. 235 (1970) (defendant sentenced to fine and imprisonment may not be imprisoned for period greater than statutory maximum because of his inability to pay the fine). In *Williams*, the choice was a $500 fine or 100 days in jail. Putting aside all other costs to the individual of imprisonment, and ignoring taxes, someone who earned $5 a day was better off paying the fine than going to prison, and for an affluent offender there was no semblance of equivalence between the fine and the prison sentence. . . .

NOTE

The article referred to by Professor Posner, Coffee, Corporate Crime and Punishment: A Non-Chicago View of the Economics of Criminal Sanctions, 17 Am. Crim. L. Rev. 419 (1980), uses the tools of economic analysis to reach quite different conclusions. A reading of the whole article will be rewarding for those wishing to pursue these matters further. Professor Coffee introduces his article with the following comments (id. at 420-423):

Modern efforts to develop an economic theory for the optimal use of criminal sanctions essentially began with the work of University of Chicago Professor Gary Becker. In essence, Becker has propounded a "cost minimization" model that recognizes three general types of costs associated with crime: (1) the social costs that result from the illegal conduct; (2) the punishment costs that result from the imposition of a sanction upon the offender; and (3) the transaction costs to the judicial system that are associated with apprehending and punishing offenders.[4] . . . [F]rom this definition of the relevant costs the Becker model can proceed to its basic assertion: an optimal system of criminal justice reduces the aggregate of these costs to a minimum. Inherently, such a model requires trade-offs, because reducing one type of cost (e.g., the cost to the victim) will not reduce the aggregate cost if in so doing another cost component is increased by a more than corresponding margin.

From such a perspective focused on getting the "biggest bang for the buck," a number of trade-offs become evident: some forms of criminal sanctions may be more expensive than others; it may be more costly to achieve a high apprehension rate than to punish severely those few who are apprehended; the harmful effects of some crimes may be less than the enforcement costs necessary to deter them. The temptation arises to draw some fairly obvious policy conclusions from the Becker model and proclaim them the fruit of economic reasoning. Indeed, although Professor Becker has surrounded his own conclusions with a number of careful qualifications, his disciples have begun to treat his model as a set of policy prescriptions which are ready for implementation. As so modified, this theory for the optimal use of criminal sanctions — which this article will call the Free Market Model — has three basic tenets, each of which contradicts the conventional wisdom which both criminal lawyers and criminologists have long shared:

1. The Preferred Form of Sanction: Fines are seen as the optimal form of criminal sanction, superior to incarceration, because imprisonment wastes both society's resources and the offender's productive capacity. . . .

2. The Appropriate Cost-Bearer: When crimes are committed on behalf of an organization, the organization, rather than the individual who actually engages in the criminal act, should pay the fine. . . .

3. The Certainty-Severity Trade-Off: In general, high penalties are favored over more vigorous law enforcement. That is, it is asserted to be more cost efficient to raise the severity of the sanction than the probability of conviction, because society can incarcerate more cheaply than it can apprehend additional offenders.

It is an understatement to call such a model counter-intuitive. More accurately, it is a profound attack on traditional criminal law scholarship, one that almost seems to gain a perverse delight in reversing assumptions that have stood since the times of Bentham and Beccaria. No doubt, the practical lawyer is inclined to respond to such contentions in the manner of Dickens' Mr. Bumble, but the consis-

4. G. Becker, The Economic Approach to Human Behavior 77 (1976).

tent response of the Chicago school to its critics has been that the test of a model is its ability to predict, not the plausibility of its premises.

Cogent as this claim may seem, the present state of empirical knowledge does not permit either side to claim more than fragmentary evidence in its favor. Thus, in the absence of unambiguous data (a situation likely to persist), it is necessary to focus on the internal logic of the Free Market Model. . . . The . . . objective of this inquiry . . . will be to demonstrate that the Free Market Model is not *the* economic theory of criminal sanctions, but only *an* economic theory. Moreover, it is an economic theory which seems flawed once we introduce both traditional elements of economic analysis (such as uncertainty) and non-economic factors that are deeply embedded in the structure of our criminal justice system (such as the tendency toward nullification of extreme penalties). These factors, however, can be introduced into a rational-actor model for the "criminal choice" decision. Once this is done, the method of economic analysis seems to lead to policy conclusions quite different from those of the Free Market Model.

. . . From a starting point only marginally different from that of the Free Market Model, this article will assert that economic analysis tends to support the following propositions: (1) the threat of incarceration typically will have a greater deterrent value than the threat of a fine; (2) more deterrence is generated by penalties focused on an individual than on an organization; and, (3) the *certainty* of a sanction is, within the context discussed, more important than its *severity*.

NOTES ON SANCTIONING CORPORATE OFFENDERS

1. Corporations charged with criminal violations often find it useful to plead nolo contendere (or no contest). By entering such a plea, the corporation gives notice that it does not wish to contest the charge against it, yet avoids the onus of a guilty plea. Pleading nolo carries a double benefit: First, a judgment rendered on the basis of a nolo plea cannot serve as the basis of collateral estoppel against the corporation by a subsequent plaintiff in a suit for civil damages; second, in cases where punishment for the violation is limited to a modest statutory fine, a nolo plea can get the corporation out of a controversy quickly and with a minimum of expense.

One way to counter this tactic, as well as add to the force of the sanction, is for the sentencing court to impose conditions of probation and suspend the statutory fine. For example, in a case involving a nolo plea entered in response to charges of violation of pollution-control statutes, the judge required, as a condition of probation, that the offending corporation initiate and administer a program designed to end the charged pollution, failing which the court would oversee operations of the company with its own appointed trustee.[5]

Query: What difficulties attach to the use of probation? Can a court do any more than impose the punishment it originally withheld (that is, the fine) if the corporation violates the conditions? It has been suggested that courts should receive authorization to hold companies in contempt if probation conditions are not followed.[6] Would this policy be desirable? Is it proper or feasible for

5. United States v. Atlantic Richfield Co., 465 F.2d 58 (7th Cir. 1972). On appeal the Court of Appeals reversed because the conditions were found to be unreasonable. For a defense of the use of probation, see Note: Structural Crime and Rehabilitation; A New Approach to Corporate Sanctions, 89 Yale L.J. 353 (1979).

6. C. Stone, Where the Law Ends, The Social Control of Corporate Behavior 188 (1975).

the corporation to be subjected to having its business affairs and operations overseen by the court through conditions or probation? Are courts competent to take such action? In Coffee, "No Soul to Damn: No Body to Kick"; An Unscandalized Inquiry into the Problem of Corporate Punishment, 79 Mich. L. Rev. 386, 448-459 (1981), the author examines probation and other preventive techniques in corporate sentencing.

2. The Model Penal Code proposes charter forfeiture as a possible criminal sanction for corporate crime. Section 6.04, Appendix to this casebook, authorizes a court to order forfeiture on a finding that a high managerial agent in behalf of the corporation has purposely engaged in a persistent course of criminal conduct and that prevention of future criminal conduct requires the order be granted.

Query: What difficulties attend the use of this sanction? Is it too extreme to be taken seriously? Can it reasonably be expected to be used against large corporations employing many people?

3. The National Commission on Reform of Federal Criminal Laws, in its Final Report (1971), proposed two innovative sanctions against corporate criminal offenders: §3007 required notice or publicity to the public affected; §3502 provided for disqualification of corporate officers. The terms of these provisions were as follows:

SECTION 3007. SPECIAL SANCTION FOR ORGANIZATIONS
When an organization is convicted of an offense, the court may require the organization to give notice of its conviction to the persons or class of persons ostensibly harmed by the offense, by mail or by advertising in designated areas or by designated media or otherwise.

SECTION 3007. SPECIAL SANCTION FOR ORGANIZATIONS
[When an organization is convicted of an offense, the court may require the organization to give appropriate publicity to the conviction by notice to the class or classes of persons or sector of the public interested in or affected by the conviction, by advertising in designated areas or by designated media or otherwise.]

SECTION 3502. DISQUALIFICATION FROM EXERCISING ORGANIZATION FUNCTIONS
An executive officer or other manager of an organization convicted of an offense committed in furtherance of the affairs of the organization may, as part of the sentence, be disqualified from exercising similar functions in the same or other organizations for a period not exceeding five years, if the court finds the scope or willfulness of his illegal actions make it dangerous for such functions to be entrusted to him.

Query: What is the theory of the publicity sanction? Insofar as it involves financial hurt to an offending corporation, what advantages does it have over a fine calculated to inflict a comparable financial hurt? For a thoughtful examination of the uses and limits of publicity as a sanction against corporate criminality, see Coffee, "No Soul to Damn: No Body to Kick"; An Unscandalized Inquiry into the Problem of Corporate Punishment, 79 Mich. L. Rev. 386, 424-434 (1981).

4. Judge Charles Renfrew, while he was a United States District Court judge in San Francisco, imposed an unusual sentence on five corporate executives

convicted of a Sherman Act price-fixing conspiracy. Along with suspended jail
sentences and fines, he required as a special condition of probation that each
defendant "make an oral presentation before twelve business, civic or other
groups about the circumstances of this case and his participation therein" and
"submit a written report to the Court giving details of each such appearance,
the composition of the group, the import of the presentation, and the response
thereto." He then sought to assess the effect of this sentence by obtaining responses from those who heard the defendants speak and from others in the
business and legal community. He recounts this experience in The Paper Label
Sentences: An Evaluation, 86 Yale L.J. 590 (1977). Critiques of his experiment
by attorneys follow his article.

CHAPTER
12

DISPOSITION OF CONVICTED OFFENDERS

The sentencing decision is of enormous consequence. It is the culminating stage of an elaborate system of procedural and substantive criminal law whose ultimate rationale is the efficient and reliable identification of persons who have committed crimes. At the sentencing stage the decision must finally be made about what to do with the convicted offender, a decision whose total social impact is equalled only by its import to the individual, whose life and liberty are at stake.

Attitudes about sentencing and about the procedural and institutional arrangements appropriate for it are presently undergoing fundamental change. As we indicated in Chapter 3, nearly all American jurisdictions, until very recently, delegated broad unstructured powers to the trial judge, who was expected to tailor the sentence to the circumstances of the individual offender, giving particular weight to the offender's prospects for successful rehabilitation. That approach probably still obtains, at this writing, in a majority of American jurisdictions, but a growing minority are enacting reforms designed to curb judicial discretion and to provide a greater measure of "determinacy" in the sentencing process.

To facilitate study of this complex and rapidly changing picture, we examine first the institutions and procedures of sentencing as they currently function under the traditional "indeterminate" approach characterized by broad judicial discretion and individualized sentencing decisions. We then consider the reform movement, characterized by tighter restrictions on discretion, and explore the new generation of problems that this approach has spawned.

Our classification is at best imperfect, because as we shall see, sentencing procedure in the indeterminate systems has not escaped the influence of the reform movement and its pressure for greater procedural safeguards. The "traditional" approach thus embodies many quite modern elements and is itself in a state of flux. Even the apparent trend away from discretion and indeterminacy may not be a permanent one; signs of a return to the traditional approach are beginning to be seen in some jurisdictions. The reader will need to keep in mind these caveats about the immediate state of the law, but the basic problems that these materials address are of course anything but transitory. The debate about who should hold or share the authority to determine punishment, how that authority should be exercised, and how it should be controlled seems likely to remain of intense interest to prosecuting and defense counsel, criminal justice officials, legislators, and the general public throughout the foreseeable future.

A. THE TRADITIONAL SENTENCING STRUCTURE

1. The Distribution of Sentencing Authority

ZIMRING, MAKING THE PUNISHMENT FIT THE CRIME: A CONSUMER'S GUIDE TO SENTENCING REFORM
Hastings Center Rep. 13-14 (Dec. 1976)

The best single phrase to describe the allocation of sentencing power in state and federal criminal justice is "multiple discretion." Putting aside the enormous power of the police to decide whether to arrest, and to select initial charges, there are four separate institutions that have the power to determine criminal sentences — the legislature, the prosecutor, the judge, and the parole board or its equivalent.

The *legislature* sets the range of sentences legally authorized after conviction for a particular criminal charge. Criminal law in the United States is noted for extremely wide ranges of sentencing power, delegated by legislation to discretionary agents, with extremely high maximum penalties and very few limits on how much less than the maximum can be imposed. In practice, then, most legislatures delegate their sentencing powers to other institutions. For example, second-degree murder in Pennsylvania, prior to 1973, was punishable by "not more than 20 years" in the state penitentiary. Any sentence above twenty years could not be imposed; any sentence below twenty years — including probation — was within the power of the sentencing judge.

The *prosecutor* is not normally thought of as an official who has, or exercises, the power to determine punishment. In practice, however, the prosecutor is the most important institutional determinant of a criminal sentence. He has the legal authority to drop criminal charges, thus ending the possibility of punishment. He has the legal authority in most systems to determine the specific offense for which a person is to be prosecuted, and this ability to select a charge can also broaden or narrow the range of sentences that can be imposed upon conviction. In congested urban court systems (and elsewhere) he has the absolute power to reduce charges in exchange for guilty pleas and to recommend particular sentences to the court as part of a "plea bargain"; rarely will his recommendation for a lenient sentence be refused in an adversary system in which he is supposed to represent the punitive interests of the state.

The *judge* has the power to select a sentence from the wide range made available by the legislature for any charge that produces a conviction. His powers are discretionary — within this range of legally authorized sanctions his selection cannot be appealed, and is not reviewed. Thus, under the Pennsylvania system we studied, a defendant convicted of second-degree murder can be sentenced to probation, one year in the penitentiary, or twenty years. On occasion, the legislature will provide a mandatory minimum sentence, such as life imprisonment for first-degree murder, that reduces the judge's options once a defendant has been convicted of that particular offense. In such cases the prosecutor and judge retain the option to charge or convict a defendant for a lesser offense in order to retain their discretionary power. More often the judge has a wide range of sentencing choices and, influenced by the prosecutor's recommendation, will select either a single sentence (such as two years) or a minimum and maximum sentence (not less than two nor more than five years) for a particular offender.

The *parole* or *correctional authority* normally has the power to modify judicial sentences to a considerable degree. When the judge pronounces a single sentence, such as two years, usually legislation authorizes release from prison to parole after a specified proportion of the sentence has been served. When the judge has provided for a minimum and maximum sentence, such as two to five years, the relative power of the correctional or parole authority is increased, because it has the responsibility to determine at what point in a prison sentence the offender is to be released. The parole board's decision is a discretionary one, traditionally made without guidelines or principles of decision.

This outline of our present sentencing system necessarily misses the range of variation among jurisdictions in the fifty states and the federal system, and oversimplifies the complex interplay among institutions in each system. It is useful, however, as a context in which to consider specific proposed reforms; it also helps to explain why the labyrinthine status quo has few articulate defenders. . . .

NOTE ON LEGAL NORM AND DISCRETION IN THE SENTENCING PROCESS[1]

The administration of criminal justice is marked at the same time by as elaborate a structure of limitations on the exercise of governmental power and as free an exercise of discretionary judgment as will be found in our legal system. In that part of the criminal process from accusation to conviction and appeal, the two root principles of the rule of law — legality and due process — have their historical origins and their fullest expression. The principle of *nulla poena sine lege* imposes formidable restraints on the definition of criminal conduct. Standards of conduct must meet stringent tests of specificity and clarity, may act only prospectively, and must be strictly construed in favor of the accused. Further, defining criminal conduct has largely come to be regarded as a legislative function, thereby precluding the judiciary from devising new crimes. The public-mischief doctrine and the sometimes over-generalized "ends" of criminal conspiracy are usually regarded as anomalous departures from this main stream. The cognate principle of procedural regularity and fairness, in short, due process of law, commands that the legal standard be applied to the individual with scrupulous fairness in order to minimize the chances of convicting the innocent, to protect against abuse of official power, and to generate an atmosphere of impartial justice. As a consequence, a complex network of procedural requirements embodied variously in constitutional, statutory, or judge-made law is im-

---

1. This Note is adapted from Kadish, Legal Norm and Discretion in the Police and Sentencing Process, 75 Harv. L. Rev. 904, 905, 915-919 (1962).

posed on the criminal adjudicatory process — public trial, unbiased tribunal, legal representation, open hearing, confrontation, and related concomitants of procedural justice.

On the other hand, after conviction, these principles become subordinated in favor of a wide-ranging freedom of officials to make decisions within the area of their competence.

The individualization of penal dispositions, principally through the institutions of the indeterminate sentence, probation, and parole, is a development whose value was long taken for granted. Nevertheless, the new penology resulted in vesting in judges and parole and probation agencies the greatest degree of uncontrolled power over the liberty of human beings that one can find in the legal system.

Consider the sentencing and probation decision made by courts and the related decisions about when and whether to release on parole made by parole agencies. The discretion of the judge and agency in these matters is virtually free of substantive control or guidance. The probation and parole decision is usually confined solely by legislative exclusion of certain classes of offenders and crimes and by a general directive to grant parole or probation when satisfied of a reasonable likelihood that the offender will be law-abiding and that the public welfare will be furthered.

There is a comparable legal relaxation in the adjudicative process. During judicial sentencing, a hearing and counsel are normally available. However, the use of the confidential and ex parte presentence report, which is often unavailable to offenders or their counsel, tends to deprive hearings of much of their significance. In parole-release proceedings, there is often no right to a hearing beyond what is granted by statute, and even where statutes provide for a hearing the obligation is usually interpreted as requiring no more than an attenuated interview, permission to have counsel and to present evidence being solely at the discretion of the board and often denied.[2]

When one seeks reasons for the deliberate abandonment of the legal norm after conviction, the answers appear to lie in two principal conceptions: that the discretion exercised entails solely the dispensing of leniency which an offender may receive as a matter of grace, but never as a matter of right; and that the exercise of the discretion turns on a purely professional diagnostic judgment by experts, rendering substantive and procedural restraints inappropriate, destructive, and unnecessary.

2.   The Judicial Sentencing Decision

[See pages 210-230 supra.]

NOTE

The above materials can usefully be read (or reviewed) at this point. In Chapter 3 we focused on the substantive problem of determining what punishment was

---

2. In Greenholtz v. Inmates of Nebraska Penal & Correctional Complex, 439 U.S. 817 (1979) (pages 1088-1093 infra), the Supreme Court held that the due process clause applied in parole-release proceedings only when state statutes create a reasonable expectation of release based on more than the "possibility" or "mere hope" of regaining liberty.

most appropriate for a given case and postponed detailed consideration of procedural and institutional concerns. In reexamining the particular cases presented
in Chapter 3, consider how the nature of the sentencing decision bears on
the choice of appropriate procedures and on the allocation of decisionmaking
authority. Given the kinds of factors that need to be considered in reaching
sentencing judgments, are highly formalized procedures unsuitable, or does
the importance of elusive, relatively subjective factors suggest the need for particularly careful procedural safeguards? Are the kinds of decisions involved most
appropriately entrusted to judges, or should sentencing authority be exercised
by officials who have special training or involvement in penology (a parole board,
for example)? If expertise should not be the primary criterion, should a greater
degree of sentencing authority be entrusted to the community at large (through
the jury, for example, or through the legislature)? These issues are not far in
the background of the cases in Chapter 3, and they can usefully be considered
as well in connection with the material that follows.

3. Procedure at Sentencing

a. Constitutional Requirements

WILLIAMS v. NEW YORK
Supreme Court of the United States
337 U.S. 241 (1949)

Mr. Justice Black delivered the opinion of the Court.

A jury in a New York state court found appellant guilty of murder in the
first degree. The jury recommended life imprisonment, but the trial judge imposed sentence of death. In giving his reasons for imposing the death sentence
the judge discussed in open court the evidence upon which the jury had convicted
stating that this evidence had been considered in the light of additional information obtained through the court's "Probation Department, and through other
sources." . . .

The Court of Appeals of New York affirmed the conviction and sentence
over the contention that as construed and applied the controlling penal statutes
are in violation of the due process clause of the Fourteenth Amendment of
the Constitution of the United States "in that the sentence of death was based
upon information supplied by witnesses with whom the accused had not been
confronted and as to whom he had no opportunity for cross-examination or
rebuttal." . . .

The narrow contention here makes it unnecessary to set out the facts at length.
The record shows a carefully conducted trial lasting more than two weeks in
which appellant was represented by three appointed lawyers who conducted
his defense with fidelity and zeal. The evidence proved a wholly indefensible
murder committed by a person engaged in a burglary. The judge instructed
the jury that if it returned a verdict of guilty as charged, without recommendation
for life sentence, "The Court must impose the death penalty," but if such recommendation was made, "the Court may impose a life sentence." The judge went
on to emphasize that "the Court is not bound to accept your recommendation."

About five weeks after the verdict of guilty with recommendation of life imprisonment, and after a statutory pre-sentence investigation report to the judge, the defendant was brought to court to be sentenced. Asked what he had to say, the appellant protested his innocence. After each of his three lawyers had appealed to the court to accept the jury's recommendation of a life sentence, the judge gave reasons why he felt that the death sentence should be imposed. He narrated the shocking details of the crime as shown by the trial evidence, expressing his own complete belief in appellant's guilt. He stated that the pre-sentence investigation revealed many material facts concerning appellant's background which though relevant to the question of punishment could not properly have been brought to the attention of the jury in its consideration of the question of guilt. He referred to the experience appellant "had had on thirty other burglaries in and about the same vicinity" where the murder had been committed. The appellant had not been convicted of these burglaries although the judge had information that he had confessed to some and had been identified as the perpetrator of some of the others. The judge also referred to certain activities of appellant as shown by the probation report that indicated appellant possessed "a morbid sexuality" and classified him as a "menace to society." The accuracy of the statements made by the judge as to appellant's background and past practices was not challenged by appellant or his counsel, nor was the judge asked to disregard any of them or to afford appellant a chance to refute or discredit any of them by cross-examination or otherwise.

The case presents a serious and difficult question. The question relates to the rules of evidence applicable to the manner in which a judge may obtain information to guide him in the imposition of sentence upon an already convicted defendant. Within limits fixed by statutes, New York judges are given a broad discretion to decide the type and extent of punishment for convicted defendants. Here, for example, the judge's discretion was to sentence to life imprisonment or death. To aid a judge in exercising this discretion intelligently the New York procedural policy encourages him to consider information about the convicted person's past life, health, habits, conduct, and mental and moral propensities. The sentencing judge may consider such information even though obtained outside the courtroom from persons whom a defendant has not been permitted to confront or cross-examine. It is the consideration of information obtained by a sentencing judge in this manner that is the basis for appellant's broad constitutional challenge to the New York statutory policy.

Appellant urges that the New York statutory policy is in irreconcilable conflict with the underlying philosophy of a second procedural policy grounded in the due process of law clause of the Fourteenth Amendment. That policy as stated in In re Oliver, 333 U.S. 257, 273, is in part that no person shall be tried and convicted of an offense unless he is given reasonable notice of the charges against him and is afforded an opportunity to examine adverse witnesses. That the due process clause does provide these salutary and time-tested protections where the question for consideration is the guilt of a defendant seems entirely clear from the genesis and historical evolution of the clause. See, e.g., Chambers v. Florida, 309 U.S. 227, 326. . . .

Tribunals passing on the guilt of a defendant always have been hedged in by strict evidentiary procedural limitations. But both before and since the American colonies became a nation, courts in this country and in England practiced a policy under which a sentencing judge could exercise a wide discretion in the sources and types of evidence used to assist him in determining the kind and extent of punishment to be imposed within limits fixed by law. Out-of-court affidavits have been used frequently, and of course in the smaller communities sentencing judges naturally have in mind their knowledge of the personalities and backgrounds of convicted offenders. . . .

In addition to the historical basis for different evidentiary rules governing trial and sentencing procedures there are sound practical reasons for the distinction. In a trial before verdict the issue is whether a defendant is guilty of having engaged in certain criminal conduct of which he has been specifically accused. Rules of evidence have been fashioned for criminal trials which narrowly confine the trial contest to evidence that is strictly relevant to the particular offense charged. These rules rest in part on a necessity to prevent a time consuming and confusing trial of collateral issues. They were also designed to prevent tribunals concerned solely with the issue of guilt of a particular offense from being influenced to convict for that offense by evidence that the defendant had habitually engaged in other misconduct. A sentencing judge, however, is not confined to the narrow issue of guilt. His task within fixed statutory or constitutional limits is to determine the type and extent of punishment after the issue of guilt has been determined. Highly relevant — if not essential — to his selection of an appropriate sentence is the possession of the fullest information possible concerning the defendant's life and characteristics. And modern concepts individualizing punishment have made it all the more necessary that a sentencing judge not be denied an opportunity to obtain pertinent information by a requirement of rigid adherence to restrictive rules of evidence properly applicable to the trial.

Undoubtedly the New York statutes emphasize a prevalent modern philosophy of penology that the punishment should fit the offender and not merely the crime. The belief no longer prevails that every offense in a like legal category calls for an identical punishment without regard to the past life and habits of a particular offender. This whole country has traveled far from the period in which the death sentence was an automatic and commonplace result of convictions — even for offenses today deemed trivial. Today's philosophy of individualizing sentences makes sharp distinctions for example between first and repeated offenders. Indeterminate sentences, the ultimate termination of which are sometimes decided by non-judicial agencies have to a large extent taken the place of the old rigidly fixed punishments. The practice of probation which relies heavily on non-judicial implementation has been accepted as a wise policy. Execution of the United States parole system rests on the discretion of an administrative parole board. . . . Retribution is no longer the dominant objective of the criminal law. Reformation and rehabilitation of offenders have become important goals of criminal jurisprudence.

Modern changes in the treatment of offenders make it more necessary now than a century ago for observance of the distinctions in the evidential procedure in the trial and sentencing processes. For indeterminate sentences and probation have resulted in an increase in the discretionary powers exercised in fixing punishments. In general, these modern changes have not resulted in making the lot of offenders harder. On the contrary a strong motivating force for the changes has been the belief that by careful study of the lives and personalities of convicted offenders many could be less severely punished and restored sooner to complete freedom and useful citizenship. This belief to a large extent has been justified.

Under the practice of individualizing punishments, investigational techniques have been given an important role. Probation workers making reports of their investigations have not been trained to prosecute but to aid offenders. Their reports have been given a high value by conscientious judges who want to sentence persons on the best available information rather than on guess-work and inadequate information. To deprive sentencing judges of this kind of information would undermine modern penological procedural policies that have been cautiously adopted throughout the nation after careful consideration and experimentation. We must recognize that most of the information now relied upon by judges to guide them in the intelligent imposition of sentences would be unavailable if information were restricted to that given in open court by witnesses subject to cross-examination. And the modern probation report draws on information concerning every aspect of a defendant's life.[15] The type and extent of this information make totally impractical if not impossible open court testimony with cross-examination. Such a procedure could endlessly delay criminal administration in a retrial of collateral issues.

The considerations we have set out admonish us against treating the due-process clause as a uniform command that courts throughout the Nation abandon their age-old practice of seeking information from out-of-court sources to guide their judgment toward a more enlightened and just sentence. New York criminal statutes set wide limits for maximum and minimum sentences. Under New York statutes a state judge cannot escape his grave responsibility of fixing sentence. In determining whether a defendant shall receive a one-year minimum or a twenty-year maximum sentence, we do not think the Federal Constitution restricts the view of the sentencing judge to the information received in open court. The due-process clause should not be treated as a device for freezing the evidential procedure of sentencing in the mold of trial procedure. So to treat the due-process clause would hinder if not preclude all courts — state and federal — from making progressive efforts to improve the administration of criminal justice. . . . We hold that appellant was not denied due process of law.[18]

Affirmed.

MR. JUSTICE RUTLEDGE dissents.

MR. JUSTICE MURPHY, dissenting. . . .

Due process of law includes at least the idea that a person accused of crime shall be accorded a fair hearing through all the stages of the proceedings against him. I agree with the Court as to the value and humaneness of liberal use of probation reports as developed by modern penologists, but, in a capital case,

---

15. A publication circulated by the Administrative Office of the United States Courts contains a suggested form for all United States probation reports and serves as an example of the type of information contained in the reports. This form consists of thirteen "marginal headings" (1) Offenses; (2) Prior Record; (3) Family History; (4) Home and Neighborhood; (5) Education; (6) Religion; (7) Interests and Activities; (8) Health (physical and mental); (9) Employment; (10) Resources; (11) Summary; (12) Plan; and (13) Agencies Interested. Each of the headings is further broken down into sub-headings. The form represents a framework into which information can be inserted to give the sentencing judge a composite picture of the defendant. Administrative Office of the United States Courts, The Presentence Investigation Report, Pub. No. 101 (1943).

18. What we have said is not to be accepted as a holding that the sentencing procedure is immune from scrutiny under the due-process clause. See Townsend v. Burke, 334 U.S. 736.

against the unanimous recommendation of a jury, where the report would concededly not have been admissible at the trial, and was not subject to examination by the defendant, I am forced to conclude that the high commands of due process were not obeyed.

NOTE, DUE PROCESS AND LEGISLATIVE STANDARDS IN SENTENCING, 101 U. Pa. L. Rev. 257, 276-277 (1952): The practical problem which is posed is not that of admissibility but the utilization of procedural devices to ensure accuracy and allow argument on the relevancy of the disclosed information to the particular circumstances of the case. The presentence probation report in Williams v. New York illustrates this problem. The probation department there concluded that Williams was a "psychopathic liar" whose ideas "revolve around a morbid sexuality," that he was "a full time burglar," "emotionally unstable," "suffers no remorse," and was deemed to be "a menace to society." His criminal record, confined to a charge of theft when he was 11 years old and a conviction as a wayward minor, did not support such generalizations. The conclusions of the probation department were apparently based upon (1) stolen goods found in his room, (2) identification of Williams by a woman whose apartment he allegedly burglarized and a seven year old girl he had allegedly raped, (3) allegations that he had committed "about 30 burglaries," and (4) "there was information" that he had acted as a "pimp" and had been observed taking indecent photographs of young children. Aside from the truth or falsity of these statements or their adequacy as a basis for a death sentence, in this case life or death turned upon conclusions drawn by probation officers from hearsay and from unproven allegations. Such information is highly relevant to the question of sentence, but its accuracy depends upon the ability and fairness of the probation officer, who must weigh evidence, judge the credibility of the informants and be zealous in closely examining them and probing for what Wigmore calls "the possible (and usual) remainder." Where probation officers are "experienced professional men, habitually inquiring day after day into the same limited class of facts," the necessary skills may often be applied; but at best this method of ascertaining facts has serious deficiences because it relies for cross-interrogation and cross-investigation upon one "who has neither the strong interest nor the full knowledge that are required," and which usually only the defendant can provide.

NOTE ON CONSTITUTIONAL DEVELOPMENTS SINCE WILLIAMS

1. The sentencing stage, or a separate proceeding? Specht v. Patterson, 386 U.S. 605 (1967), involved a Colorado Sex Offenders Act that permitted imposition of an indeterminate sentence of one day to life, even after conviction on a charge normally carrying a shorter maximum sentence, if the judge found that the defendant "at large, constitutes a threat of bodily harm to members of the public, or is an habitual offender and mentally ill." The Court held that in the proceeding leading to such a finding, defendant was entitled to "the full panoply of the relevant protections which due process guarantees in state criminal proceedings," including notice, counsel, the right to present evidence, the right to confront the witnesses against him and the right to cross-examine.[3] The Court said (id. at 608):

> We adhere to Williams v. New York, supra; but we decline the invitation to extend it to this radically different situation. . . . The Sex Offenders Act does not make the commission of an enumerated crime the basis for sentencing. It makes one conviction the basis for commencing another proceeding under another Act to determine whether a person constitutes a threat of bodily harm to the public, or is an habitual offender and mentally ill. That is a new finding of fact that was not an ingredient of the offense charged.

Does *Specht* apply whenever a legislature attempts to guide judicial sentencing discretion by specifying the facts that must be found prior to imposition of a long-term prison sentence? Consider 18 U.S.C. §3575, which provides that if a convicted defendant is found to be a "dangerous special offender,"[4] the court may sentence him to "an appropriate term not to exceed twenty-five years and not disproportionate in severity to the maximum term otherwise authorized by law for such felony." Virtually every state has analogous legislation providing for enhanced punishment for some specially defined category such as "habitual offenders." See American Bar Association, Standards for Criminal Justice, Sentencing Alternatives and Procedures §18-6.5, Commentary at 18·469 (2d ed. 1980). Does *Specht* require the "full panoply" of due process safeguards, on the ground that such statutes require a "new finding of fact"? Or should *Specht* be limited to statutes that charge a different and more severe offense, so that it would not apply to statutes that regulate sentencing within the permissible range for a given offense? Note that if *Specht* is applicable, a legislature could avoid its impact by deleting all references to specific factual findings and instead entrusting application of the enhanced term to the judge's unguided discretion. Does it make sense to afford *fewer* procedural safeguards under that type of statutory structure? If not, is there something fundamentally unsound about *Specht* (or about *Williams*)?[5]

3. The Court did not explicitly mention the rights to jury trial and to proof beyond a reasonable doubt; at the time of the *Specht* decision these rights had not yet been held essential components of due process in state criminal proceedings. See In re Winship, 397 U.S. 358 (1970), pages 64-65 supra; Duncan v. Louisiana, 391 U.S. 145 (1968), pages 94-96 supra.

4. 18 U.S.C. §3575(e) defines a "special offender" as a person either (1) previously convicted of two or more serious offenses, previously imprisoned at least once, whose crime is committed less than five years after release from prison or (2) who commits the offense as part of a pattern of criminal conduct constituting "a substantial source of his income, and in which he manifested special skill or expertise" or (3) who organized or directed a conspiracy of three or more persons in connection with the offense. Section 3575(f) provides that an offender is deemed "dangerous" if a period of confinement longer than that provided for the underlying felony "is required for the protection of the public from further criminal conduct by the defendant."

5. The applicability of *Specht* to §3575 is still a subject of disagreement among the federal courts. Compare United States v. Bowdach, 561 F.2d 1160 (5th Cir. 1977)(*Specht* may govern because §3575 could be considered a separate proceeding) with United States v. Stewart, 531 F.2d 326, 332 (6th Cir. 1976)(*Specht* is inapplicable because §3575 merely identifies aggravating circumstances and "does not create a new and distinct criminal charge"). See generally Note, The Constitutionality of Statutes Permitting Increased Sentences for Habitual or Dangerous Criminals, 89 Harv. L. Rev. 356 (1975).

The apparent anomaly suggested by *Specht* — that informal procedures may be acceptable so long as the legislature provides no substantive standards for decision — recurs in many other problems of procedural due process. Compare the law on burden of proof, where the legislature can make conduct criminal whether or not circumstance X (for example, intent) is present, but if the legislature chooses to make X an element of the offense, that element must be proved beyond a reasonable doubt. See pages 77-81 supra.

2. Constitutional requirements at the sentencing stage. In Gardner v. Florida, 430 U.S. 349 (1977), defendant had been convicted of murder, and the jury had recommended life imprisonment, but the judge, relying on a confidential presentence report, had sentenced defendant to death. Although the facts were thus virtually identical to those that had appeared dispositive in *Williams,* the Court found the procedure constitutionally defective and vacated the death sentence. A plurality opinion by Justice Stevens, joined by Justices Stewart and Powell, first distinguished *Williams* as a case in which the facts contained in the presentence report had been "described in detail" by the sentencing judge and never actually challenged by the defense. The plurality then emphasized that two constitutional developments since *Williams* mandated closer scrutiny of sentencing procedure than *Williams* had contemplated. The first was heightened sensitivity to capital sentencing; the second independent development was the recognition in intervening decisions that (id. at 358):

> the sentencing process, as well as the trial itself, must satisfy the requirements of the Due Process Clause. Even though the defendant has no substantive right to a particular sentence within the range authorized by statute, the sentencing is a critical stage of the criminal proceeding at which he is entitled to the effective assistance of counsel.

Writing separately, Justices Brennan and Marshall both agreed that the failure to disclose the presentence report was impermissible in the context of death penalty sentencing. Chief Justice Burger and Justices White, Blackmun, and Rehnquist concurred in the result.

Does *Gardner* suggest that notice, confrontation, cross-examination, and other elements of procedural due process will (or should) be extended to sentencing procedure in noncapital cases? The materials that follow indicate the many dimensions of this question.

b. Disclosure of the Presentence Report

AMERICAN BAR ASSOCIATION, STANDARDS FOR CRIMINAL JUSTICE,
SENTENCING ALTERNATIVES AND PROCEDURES
§18-5.4, Commentary at 18·366-369 (2d ed. 1980)

Among the states, by statute, court rule, or judicial decision, the movement has been toward making disclosure of the presentence report mandatory in most instances. At least thirty-one states have established some mandatory requirement for disclosure of all or a portion of the report. The majority of these statutes either make no provision for exclusion or have been interpreted by judicial decision or court rule to require complete disclosure. The remainder typically exempt disclosures of information obtained from confidential sources and, less frequently, diagnostic opinions or other evaluative material and recommendations. Finally, a few states continue to make disclosure discretionary with the court. A few states lack any express provision, but in no jurisdiction has a statute, rule, or court decision been found forbidding the court to make disclosure.

On the federal level, rule 32(c) of the Federal Rules of Criminal Procedure was amended by Congress in 1975 to require disclosure, except where disclosure would (1) reveal "diagnostic opinion which might seriously disrupt a program of rehabilitation," (2) compromise "sources of information obtained upon a promise of confidentiality," or (3) "result in harm, physical or otherwise, to the defendant or other persons." Even in these cases, rule 32(c)(3)(B) requires the court to provide "a summary of the factual information contained therein to be relied on in determining sentence." . . . ª

Although the federal rule contains relatively broader exceptions to its disclosure requirement than most states have enacted, case law since the 1975 amendments has begun to narrow the latitude of these exceptions. In United States v. Long, a federal district court directed that before any of the exceptions in rule 32(c) are to be invoked, several less drastic alternatives should be considered: (1) summarization of "the excluded portions of the report in such a way as to protect informants, the defendant or third persons," (2) "submission of the presentence report without the excluded material to another judge for sentence in order to foreclose any possible reliance on the excluded portions," and (3)

---

a. Fed. R. Crim. P. 32(c) (as amended through Aug. 1, 1979) provides as follows:

(c) PRESENTENCE INVESTIGATION

(*1*) *When made.* The probation service of the court shall make a presentence investigation and report to the court before the imposition of sentence or the granting of probation unless, with the permission of the court, the defendant waives a presentence investigation and report, or the court finds that there is in the record information sufficient to enable the meaningful exercise of sentencing discretion, and the court explains this finding on the record.

The report shall not be submitted to the court or its contents disclosed to anyone unless the defendant has pleaded guilty or nolo contendere or has been found guilty, except that a judge may, with the written consent of the defendant, inspect a presentence report at any time.

(*2*) *Report.* The report of the presentence investigation shall contain any prior criminal record of the defendant and such information about his characteristics, his financial condition and the circumstances affecting his behavior as may be helpful in imposing sentence or in granting probation or in the correctional treatment of the defendant, and such other information as may be required by the court.

(*3*) *Disclosure.*

(A) Before imposing sentence the court shall upon request permit the defendant, or his counsel if he is so represented, to read the report of the presentence investigation exclusive of any recommendation as to sentence, but not to the extent that in the opinion of the court the report contains diagnostic opinion which might seriously disrupt a program of rehabilitation, sources of information obtained upon a promise of confidentiality, or any other information which, if disclosed, might result in harm, physical or otherwise, to the defendant or other persons; and the court shall afford the defendant or his counsel an opportunity to comment thereon and, at the discretion of the court, to introduce testimony or other information relating to any alleged factual inaccuracy contained in the presentence report.

(B) If the court is of the view that there is information in the presentence report which should not be disclosed under subdivision (c)(3)(A) of this rule, the court in lieu of making the report or part thereof available shall state orally or in writing a summary of the factual information contained therein to be relied on in determining sentence, and shall give the defendant or his counsel an opportunity to comment thereon. The statement may be made to the parties in camera.

(C) Any material disclosed to the defendant or his counsel shall also be disclosed to the attorney for the government.

(D) Any copies of the presentence investigation report made available to the defendant or his counsel and the attorney for the government shall be returned to the probation officer immediately following the imposition of sentence or the granting of probation, unless the court, in its discretion otherwise directs.

(E) The reports of studies and recommendations contained therein made by the Director of the Bureau of Prisons or the Parole Commission pursuant to 18 U.S.C. §§4205(c), 4252, 5010(e), or 5037(c) shall be considered a presentence investigation within the meaning of subdivision (c)(3) of this rule.

disclosure to counsel "under a protective order requiring that counsel not divulge the material to his client."[14] . . . A Fifth Circuit decision, United States v. Woody, has similarly tightened the summarization requirement in rule 32(c)(3)(B), ruling that "the summary should, in a manner as specific as the facts permit, inform the defendant of the nature of the information."[16] Generally, *Woody* indicated that the summary should relate "the precise nature of any behavioral characteristics or instances of illegal conduct detailed in the report." A pro forma statement that the defendant had a poor reputation with law enforcement authorities was found deficient in that case for failure to give "notice of the nature of the reputation or the underlying allegations supporting the reputation."

NOTE ON "MANDATORY" DISCLOSURE IN PRACTICE

A thorough analysis of disclosure practice under the new federal Rule 32(c)(3) appears in Fennell & Hall, Due Process at Sentencing: An Empirical and Legal Analysis of the Disclosure of Presentence Reports in Federal Courts, 93 Harv. L. Rev. 1613 (1980). The authors noted several significant respects in which the rule in practice fails to achieve full and meaningful disclosure:

(1) The rule does not provide for automatic disclosure, but only for disclosure on request by the defendant, and the rule does not require that the defendant be informed of the right to disclosure. As a result, although most federal judges do disclose the reports in the bulk of their cases, a substantial minority (17 percent) disclosed the report in no more than 50 percent of their cases.

(2) The rule does not explicitly detail the when, where, and how of disclosure. In 30 percent of the federal districts, disclosure occurs only on the day of sentencing, and 21 percent of the federal judges permitted access to the report only in their chambers or in the courtroom. Only 42 percent of the districts permitted defense counsel to obtain a copy of the report; in the rest counsel were required to take notes from the report.

(3) Information designated "confidential" was included in 17 percent of the presentence reports. The resort to confidentiality appears to vary widely among probation officers; 28 percent of the probation officers accounted for 84 percent of the reports using confidential information.

(4) Of the judges surveyed, 21 percent followed a standard practice of making no disclosure of their reliance on confidential information, and another 10 percent made no disclosure for at least one type of confidential information (family background, psychiatric reports, or law enforcement information). Moreover, an additional 12 percent of the judges merely indicated receipt of confidential information without disclosing its nature. Thus, at least 43 percent of the judges did not provide adequate summaries of the undisclosed information, despite the clear command to the contrary in Rule 32(c)(3)(B).

14. 411 F. Supp. 1203, 1207 (E. D. Mich. 1976).
16. 567 F.2d 1353, 1361 (5th Cir. 1978). . . .

c. Challenging the Presentence Report

UNITED STATES v. WESTON
United States Court of Appeals, 9th Circuit
448 F.2d 626 (1971)

DUNIWAY, J. Weston, also known as Wallace, appeals from her conviction by a jury of violating 21 U.S.C. §174, receiving, concealing and facilitating the transportation of 537.11 grams of heroin, knowing that it had been imported contrary to law. . . .

After the verdict was received, the court indicated that it felt that the minimum mandatory sentence, five years, would be appropriate. Government counsel demurred and asked that a presentence report be obtained. Before sentencing, the report was read by Weston's retained counsel.

The most damaging information contained in it is the following:

> This officer interviewed Narcotic Agents of the Federal Bureau of Narcotics and Dangerous Drugs who have been investigating Mrs. Wallace's involvement in narcotics since about February of this year. They advised that in their opinion Mrs. Wallace is a very intelligent and clever dealer in heroin. They feel that she has never used the drug but has been the chief supplier to the Western Washington area.
>
> According to their investigation Mrs. Wallace traveled to Mexico or Arizona periodically to obtain approximately $60,000.00 worth of heroin. She then would distribute the drug to various dealers in Western Washington earning approximately $140,000.00 profit on the $60,000.00 investment. Narcotic agents felt that she might have made such trips as frequently as every two weeks. They feel fortunate in obtaining sufficient evidence to bring Mrs. Wallace to court.
>
> Narcotic agents advised that four of Mrs. Wallace's distributors have been apprehended and two have already been sentenced. . . .
>
> *Defendant's Version:* Mrs. Wallace refused to participate in the presentence investigation. She did explain that she feels bitter and dissatisfied with the jury verdict of guilty in the current offense and with the Prosecuting Attorney's refusal to allow her to plea [sic] to a lesser offense. Due to her unwillingness to discuss herself, the offense and other pertinent background information, this report is limited in scope.
>
> Mrs. Wallace states that she sees no reason to submit to a presentence study since there is no possibility of probation and she fails to see how a presentence report might help her. At this point her attitude toward the offense is one of denial with regard to her extensive involvement in drug sales.

The report also shows a series of 9 vagrancy and shoplifting charges against Weston, in Spokane, Portland, Seattle, Renton, Pasco and Tacoma, between 1963 and 1969. The first and last were marked "no disposition," or "stricken." She was convicted once in Portland in 1964, fined $75.00 and sentenced to 90 days suspended, and once in Tacoma in 1969 and fined $150. In each other case she forfeited bail — $100. That is substantially all that the report contains.

At the sentencing hearing, the court asked counsel to comment on the information indicating that Weston was a large-scale heroin dealer. Counsel replied that "she says it's just not true," that making $140,000 profit every two weeks was beyond counsel's imagination, and that he had never seen Weston display any sign of wealth. . . .

The court then summarized its views:

> Well, . . . this court has great respect for the probation service in this and other districts, and I believe as a whole they are a group of officers who are extremely objective, very concerned with the welfare of the defendants, who they report upon, and also are attentive to their duties as officers of the Court.
>
> And when statements are made categorically as they are made here, the Court has no alternative, in the face of contrary factual information, rather than simply a vehement denial, but to accept as true the information furnished the Court which in turn was obtained by the probation officer from the officers of the Federal Bureau of Narcotics and Dangerous Drugs.
>
> However, officers can be in error; mistakes can be made. . . .
>
> . . . So I'm going to advise you, I'm sure you're already aware of it, that Rule 35 of the Federal Rules of Criminal Procedure provides that within 120 days after imposition of sentence the Court may reduce or otherwise modify the sentence imposed. And I invite you to conduct your own investigation, and if you feel that you can obtain facts that contradict the factual statements that are so damaging here to this defendant, and to her co-defendant to a lesser degree, the Court will welcome the submission to it. . . .

The colloquy then continued:

> *Mr. Kempton:* Yes, your Honor. . . . [L]et's say we have one narcotics agent on the streets that tells Mr. *Levy* of the Probation Department, "We think she's the biggest dealer in the Western states," I can't conceive of what type of investigation I can do to come back and say that she isn't.
>
> *The Court:* Well, I can't do any more than I've done to point out this remedy to you. I recognize that the problem could be a difficult one. But I think you can appreciate the Court's position: to choose between a flat denial of the defendant and a factual matter reliably represented to the Court by the Bureau of Narcotics and Dangerous Drugs through the probation officer, who tacitly, at least indicates, that this information is correct.
>
> Very well.
>
> Mrs. Weston, again, do you have anything further to say before sentence is pronounced?
>
> *The Defendant:* This is not true. And I have no way — if they have any way of proving this is true, why don't they bring the evidence that this is true, that I was going out of town and doing all of this stuff? They can not have any evidence of it because this is not true. . . .

The court then imposed the maximum sentence, 20 years, and continued:

> Now, in addition to what I've said, that Rule 35 affords counsel an opportunity to move for reduction of sentence, I'm going to direct the United States to do something I've never directed before. I'm going to direct them to submit to me in camera factual material that support the conclusions set forth in the report. I can well understand that the Bureau of Narcotics and Dangerous Drugs would be reluctant to reveal the sources of their information. But in view of the severity of the sentence just imposed on Mrs. Weston, which I think is a proper sentence if these be the facts, I want to have a second look at it. So if you will obtain that information in due course and submit it to me in camera, it can be contained in a sealed envelope and mailed to me. . . .

. . . I will go over the matter carefully, and on my own motion, if I'm satisfied there's some doubt, if I determine that there's a reasonable doubt that these statements made are factual, have a factual basis, I will on my own motion modify the sentence within the time prescribed.

On November 2, 1970, the court filed an order reciting the material about Weston's dealing in narcotics that we have quoted from the pre-sentence report, stating that a report prepared by the Bureau of Narcotics and Dangerous Drugs had been submitted to the court in camera, and that "the conclusions . . . of the pre-sentence report . . . are supported by the facts detailed in the confidential report. The Court is satisfied that it imposed the appropriate sentence. . . ."

The confidential report has been forwarded to us under seal. It is an unsworn memorandum from agent Wilson to his superior. It does little to corroborate the charge in the probation report. Instead of showing, as that report indicates, that Weston made trips "periodically" to Mexico, "as frequently as every two weeks," it quotes a named informant, described only as "previously identified as a reliable cooperating individual," who indicates that on one occasion such a trip was about to be made, not even that it was in fact made. It does use the $300 an ounce figure for the Mexican price, and $1000 as the resale price.

The report next details the events leading to this case, and a later search of Jackson's house, where 2 ounces of heroin and 2 ounces of cocaine were found, in packages identical to those seized in this case. The report finally quotes the informer as saying that Weston was distributing quantities of heroin to Jackson for delivery to select customers.

That is all there is. To say that it corroborates the very broad charges contained in the pre-sentence report is an over-statement. Moreover, it contains nothing to show, rather than to assert, that the informant was reliable, or otherwise to verify the very serious charge made against Weston. . . .

In essence, then, what we have is a conviction at a trial providing all of the safeguards required by the Constitution, of an offense warranting, in the opinion of the trial judge, the minimum sentence of five years. This is followed by a determination, based on unsworn evidence detailing otherwise unverified statements of a faceless informer that would not even support a search warrant or an arrest, and without any of the constitutional safeguards, that Weston is probably guilty of additional and far more serious crimes, for which she is then given an additional sentence of fifteen years. Cf. Specht v. Patterson, 1967, 386 U.S. 605. . . . To us, there is something radically wrong with a system of justice that can produce such a result. The problem is, what, if anything, can be done about it.

It has long been the rule in this circuit that this court "has no authority to review the sentence so long as it falls within the statutory limits." . . .

Moreover, in Williams v. New York, 1949, 337 U.S. 241, the Supreme Court held that due process does not require that information relied upon in sentencing must be "restricted to that given in open court by witnesses subject to cross-examination." . . .

The government argues, in substance, that the rule against review of sentences, taken together with the rule in *Williams,* require affirmance of the sentence here.

Weston's case, however, is different from *Williams.* She vigorously denied the accuracy of the charges and objected to the judge's consideration of them without more substantiation of them than appeared in the probation report. Williams apparently did neither. . . . Furthermore, Williams' constitutional attack was much broader. He challenged the use of any hearsay information whatsoever in sentencing unless a trial-type hearing were held complete with due process safeguards and standard rules of evidence. . . . Weston's case does not present that issue. . . .

Two arguments can be made in support of the proposition that the court properly relied upon the report. The first is that Williams v. New York permits it. A number of courts, including this court, have frequently cited *Williams* for the general proposition that evidence of other criminal conduct not resulting in a conviction may be considered in imposing sentence. . . . We would not repudiate this rule if we could.[1] . . . But that does not solve our present problem. Here the other criminal conduct charged was very serious, and the factual basis for believing the charge was almost nil. . . .

It can be argued that there were a number of things that Weston might have done to refute the charge beside denying it: (a) The probation report named four persons, two of whom had been convicted and two of whom were charged with narcotics offenses, as Weston's distributors. This, it is said, provided a fertile field for investigation of probation reports, files, interviewing witnesses, defendants, etc. . . .

(b) The report indicated that Weston had made trips to Mexico as frequently as every two weeks. It is argued that she was in a position to supply information, if true, that she had not traveled, that she had lived continuously in the area, information as to where she was at various times during the preceding several months, etc.

(c) In view of the amount of profit alleged in the transaction, Weston had available to her a showing as to what monies or properties she had. . . .

This will not do. . . . In addition to the difficulty of "proving a negative," we think it a great miscarriage of justice to expect Weston or her attorney to assume the burden and expense of proving to the court that she is not the large scale dealer that the anonymous informant says that she is.

In Townsend v. Burke, supra, the Supreme Court made it clear that a sentence cannot be predicated on false information. We extend it but little in holding that a sentence cannot be predicated on information of so little value as that here involved. A rational penal system must have some concern for the probable accuracy of the informational inputs in the sentencing process.

The conviction is valid, but the sentence must be vacated. On resentencing, the District Court may not rely upon the information contained in the presen-

---

1. There is a trend on the part of some authorities toward excluding this type of information at sentencing.

The Advisory Committee on Sentencing and Review of the American Bar Association has recognized that arrests and other dispositions short of an adjudication can be misleading and would not provide for their inclusion in the presentence report. ABA Project on Standards for Criminal Justice, Probation 37 (approved draft), 1970.

In Baker v. United States, 4 Cir., 1968, 388 F.2d 931, 934, n. 4, the Fourth Circuit, setting down minimum disclosure rules for presentence reports, recently stated that "[n]o conviction or criminal charge should be included in the report, or considered by the court, unless referable to an official record."

We do not go so far.

tence report unless it is amplified by information such as to be persuasive of the validity of the charge there made. . . .

UNITED STATES v. FATICO

United States Court of Appeals, 2d Circuit
579 F.2d 707 (1978)

OAKES, J. This is an unusual interlocutory appeal by the United States from a unique order excluding evidence sought to be introduced at a sentencing hearing. . . .

Carmine and Daniel Fatico were indicted in connection with a series of truck hijackings. After a mistrial was declared due to a jury deadlock,[1] they pleaded guilty to and were convicted of one count of conspiracy to possess a quantity of furs stolen from a foreign shipment. They face maximum sentences of five years' imprisonment and $10,000 fines. 18 U.S.C. §371. Prior to sentencing, defendants objected to statements in the presentence reports identifying them as "made" members of the Gambino organized crime family and important figures in the upper echelon of organized crime activity. The Government then offered to support its allegations at a sentencing hearing by the testimony of the former head of the FBI's Organized Crime section in the New York office, based upon information furnished to him by a reliable confidential informant, allegedly a member of the Gambino Family. The Government objected to disclosure of the confidential source for the obvious reasons that both his life and usefulness as an informant would be jeopardized. However, the Government proffered additional evidence to corroborate the informant, consisting of the testimony of two coconspirators who turned Government's evidence in the trial and who are under the Government witness protection program, as well as other evidence set forth in the margin.[4]

The district court took judicial notice that major hijacking gangs have been preying on Kennedy Airport, and acknowledged that there was substantial evidence of organized crime's involvement because sophisticated fencing techniques are utilized in these operations. It stated that membership in and ties to profes-

---

1. This trial was for armed hijacking of a truck containing fur pelts. . . .
4. The memorandum continues: "The Faticos' association with Aniello Dellacroce and the 'Gambino family' will be further supported by independent observations of police officers. On November 23, 1966, officers of the New York Police Department arrested Carmine Fatico together with Aniello Dellacroce and other Gambino family members such as Paul Costellano and Joseph N. Gallo during a raid at a 'social club' on Mulberry Street. Fatico, Dellacroce and nine others were charged with consorting with known criminals.

"Subsequently in 1976, at the time of the death of the 'boss of bosses,' Carlo Gambino, police officers surverlling [sic] the Gambino funeral services observed Carmine and Daniel Fatico, together with other 'family members' being admitted to the funeral home, while scores of other individuals were refused entry.

"Finally, the defendants [sic] ties to organized crime are underscored by their activities over the years. Both Carmine and Daniel Fatico have lengthy records dating back to the 1930's. Carmine Fatico has been convicted of grand larcey [sic], bookmaking and felonious assault. His brother Daniel has an extensive arrest record for such organized crime activities as burglary, bookmaking, policy, illicit manufacture of alcohol and running a disorderly house. Daniel has been covicted [sic] of assault, unlawful entry and conspiracy to posses [sic] an unregistered still. By their instant pleas, the Faticos have admitted participation in conspiracies involving armed truck hijackings and the fencing of truckloads of stolen goods. Such activities are clearly those of organized crime."

sional criminal groups are material facts that should be considered in sentencing, and it noted that the rules of evidence, other than those involving privileges, do not apply in sentencing proceedings. The district court further recognized that the Government cannot and will not reveal informers' identities because of past murders of informants who implicate organized crime members. Nevertheless, Judge Weinstein concluded that the Fifth Amendment right to due process and the Sixth Amendment right of confrontation would both be violated by introduction of the FBI agent's testimony since the credibility of the informant and the reliability of his information could not be meaningfully attacked through extrinsic evidence or cross-examination. . . .

As the court below correctly stated, the Federal Rules of Evidence, except those relating to privileges, do not apply to sentencing proceedings. The statute, 18 U.S.C. §3577, moreover, requires that "[n]o limitation" be placed on "the information concerning the background, character, and conduct of a person convicted of an offense . . . for the purpose of imposing an appropriate sentence." Thus any exclusion must be based not merely upon the hearsay nature of the evidence but on its Due Process or Confrontation Clause implications.

The Due Process Clause is plainly implicated at sentencing. E.g., Gardner v. Florida, 430 U.S. 349 (1977) (plurality); Williams v. New York, 337 U.S. 241, 252 n. 18 (1949); Townsend v. Burke, 334 U.S. 736, 740-41 (1948); see Note, Procedural Due Process at Judicial Sentencing for Felony, 81 Harv. L. Rev. 821, 825, 826 (1968). It does not necessarily follow, however, that all of the procedural safeguards and strict evidentiary limitations of a criminal trial proper are required. The Supreme Court has held quite to the contrary, specifically on the issue of hearsay in a presentence report. Williams v. New York, supra, held that it was not a denial of due process in sentencing to rely on information supplied by witnesses whom the accused could neither confront nor cross-examine.[10]

Williams does not hold that all hearsay information must be considered. Indeed, it is well recognized that materially false information used in sentencing may invalidate the sentence imposed. E.g., United States v. Tucker, 404 U.S. 443, 447 (1972); Townsend v. Burke, supra. Additionally, a significant possibility of misinformation justifies the sentencing court in requiring the Government to verify the information. See United States v. Weston, 448 F.2d 626, 634 (9th Cir. 1971). . . .

The thrust of . . . *Weston* is that the reliability of evidence that is difficult to challenge must be ensured through cross-examination or otherwise, by demanding certain guarantees of reliability. Here, once the defendants challenged the truth of the hearsay statement, the district court correctly called for additional corroboration by the Government. But such corroboration was available by testi-

---

10. Contrary to the district court's intimations, Williams v. New York has not been overruled by Gardner v. Florida. *Gardner* held that a defendant cannot be sentenced to death based on secret information in a presentence investigation report which he cannot dispute or explain because it is not disclosed to him. The Court noted that *Williams'* holding was not "directly applicable" because in *Williams* the facts contained in the report upon which the trial court relied were revealed to counsel in open court. In this case, as in *Williams,* the defendant was apprised of all information proffered by the Government. Additionally, even if *Gardner* is interpreted as having qualified *Williams,* see 430 U.S. at 356-58, 362, (opinion of Stevens, J.), there can be no doubt that its holding is strictly limited to due process guarantees in *capital* cases. See id. at 356, 359, 360; id. at 363-64 (opinion of White, J.). . . .

mony of two coconspirators, the nature of the crime itself, and the testimony of those who observed appellees with members of the Gambino family. See note 4 supra. Sufficient reliability is apparent; the proffered corroborating evidence was adequate.

We hold, therefore, that Due Process does not prevent use in sentencing of out-of-court declarations by an unidentified informant where there is good cause for the nondisclosure of his identity and there is sufficient corroboration by other means. Thus, the trial court erred in excluding the agent's testimony about the informer's declaration once the Government represented that it would produce the specified corroboration.[14]

While it is not clear whether, or to what extent, the Confrontation Clause of the Sixth Amendment is implicated at sentencing . . . or to what extent that Clause overlaps with the hearsay rule and Due Process guarantees when statements of out-of-court declarants cannot be refuted by cross-examination, for present purposes it is unnecessary to differentiate between the requirements of the Due Process Clause of the Fifth Amendment and the Confrontation Clause of the Sixth. . . . [F]or the same reasons which counsel rejection of a due process attack, we conclude that admission of an unidentified informant's corroborated declarations in a sentencing proceeding where there is good cause for not disclosing his identity is not barred by the Confrontation Clause.

Judgment reversed.[17]

NOTES

1. The proceedings on remand from the Court of Appeals' decision in *Fatico* are reported in United States v. Fatico, 458 F. Supp. 388 (E.D.N.Y. 1978). Judge Weinstein held an evidentiary hearing, at which seven law-enforcement agents testified for the government that 17 different informants independently had told them that defendant was a "made" member of the Gambino "family." Defendant called no witnesses, and, as Judge Weinstein noted, his inability to cross-examine any of the 17 informants made it difficult for him to defend against their accusations.

Since the absence of effective cross-examination left the judge with "lingering doubts" about the reliability of the hearsay evidence (458 F. Supp. at 398-399), it became necessary to determine the applicable burden of proof. Judge Weinstein held that where the sentencing court will give a matter only slight weight, a "preponderance of the evidence" standard might be suitable. However, he deemed that standard inappropriate for resolving factual disputes when the matter at issue (such as membership in organized crime) will result in a much harsher sentence.

---

14. Of course, the weight given to the informer's declarations and the assessment of credibility are matters for the sentencing court. . . .

17. While we express no views on the sentence ultimately to be imposed, we do not understand the statement in the trial court's opinion that "[a]t stake, is the difference between freedom and up to five years in prison." Why the district court suggests that the defendants may go free despite their conviction if the agent's testimony is excluded, but will receive sentences of five years if it is allowed, is not readily apparent. . . . The proffered testimony on organized crime ties does not appear to alter significantly the picture already on the record of the type of crime involved, the role of defendants as revealed at the trial and their prior conduct.

Three alternative standards were considered: "clear and convincing evidence" (which the court deemed equivalent to a 70-percent probability); "clear, unequivocal, and convincing evidence" (roughly 80-percent probability); and "beyond a reasonable doubt" (roughly 95-percent probability). Judge Weinstein held that under the circumstances, the "beyond a reasonable doubt" standard was not mandated but that any standard lower than that of "clear, unequivocal, and convincing evidence" would be unacceptable. He then found that the testimony offered by the government satisfied the latter standard. Defendant was sentenced to a four-year term, to be served consecutively to a three-year sentence previously imposed for a gambling conviction.

2. On appeal from Judge Weinstein's decision imposing sentence, the Court of Appeals affirmed the holding that the "beyond a reasonable doubt" standard was not applicable; held that the testimony was sufficient to establish Fatico's organized crime involvement by any of the lesser standards discussed by the district judge; and upheld the sentence imposed, "by no means, however, endorsing all the rules of the district court." United States v. Fatico, 603 F.2d 1053, 1056 (2d Cir. 1979). In a footnote the Court of Appeals observed (id. at 1057 n. 9):

> We note the Government's request, even though it did not file a cross-appeal, that we reject not only the burden of proof standard that the district judge utilized but also the entire concept of a hearing, which apparently is now called in the criminal bar a *"Fatico* hearing," in sentencing matters altogether. We decline as unnecessary to this decision to adopt any standard of proof or reject any standard except "proof beyond a reasonable doubt." And although we do not believe that a sentencing hearing will be necessary every time a defendant disputes facts or statements in the presentence report, we certainly would not hold it an abuse of discretion on the part of a district judge to hold such a hearing where there is reason to question the reliability of material facts having in the judge's view direct bearing on the sentence to be imposed, especially where those facts are essentially hearsay. . . .

3. For further discussion of the burden-of-proof problem, including the related issue of allocating the burden of production on sentencing issues, see Note, A Hidden Issue of Sentencing: Burdens of Proof for Disputed Allegations in Presentence Reports, 66 Geo. L.J. 1515 (1978); American Bar Association, Standards for Criminal Justice, Sentencing Alternatives and Procedures, §§18-6.4, 18-6.5, Commentary at 18·462-467, 18·479-482 (2d ed. 1980).

4. Appellate Review

AMERICAN BAR ASSOCIATION, STANDARDS FOR CRIMINAL JUSTICE, APPELLATE REVIEW OF SENTENCES, §§20-1.1, 20-1.2, Commentary at 20·7, 20·14-16 (2d ed. 1980): The number of jurisdictions in this country in which appellate review of sentences is available is steadily growing. Over half of the states now permit review of the merits of sentences in some circumstances. The principle that there ought to be appellate review of sentences, particularly of sentences imposed in serious cases, is now widely accepted. . . . Many jurisdictions still lack a system for effective appellate review of sentences, more likely because of inertia than rejection of the principle. . . .

. . . It is intolerable to operate on an assumption that each sentencing authority can properly select a sentence within a wide range of statutorily authorized sanctions in the unfettered discretion of a single person. No other country in the free world permits this condition to exist.

Much of the literature on appellate review of sentences is concerned with intolerable disparities in sentences imposed for the same offense. Even the most generous allowance for the notion that a sentence should be appropriate to the offender as well as to the offense would not explain, much less justify, the perceived pattern of unevenness. The criminal justice system in most jurisdictions is greatly fragmented at the trial court level, with judges of dissimilar attitudes, burdensome caseloads, and few coordinating mechanisms. At the same time, criminal codes tend to permit a very wide range of possible sentences for each offense. The results, which have been described many times, are a broad disparity of sentences for persons whose offenses are essentially identical and whose backgrounds and future prospects are markedly similar. One purpose of appellate review of sentences is to correct instances of injustice involving excessive sentences. It can provide a method to counter the personal idiosyncrasies or errors of judgment on the part of sentencing judges. It can reduce inequality of judgments where the differences cannot be explained on rational grounds. Thus, the first object of appellate review is the correction of sentences that are excessive in length.

Elimination of gross disparities is not the full justification for appellate review of sentences. Conceivably, other means could be employed to that end. The essence of the appellate process is the refinement and articulation of a body of legal doctrines through the collegial process of a multijudge court. Throughout the long period in which there has been little or no appellate review of sentences, there has been little success in attaining a set of well-developed criteria for sentencing policies. Trial courts normally have not been expected or required to give explanations for their sentence choices. Thus, jurisprudence has not developed evenly among those judges carrying the burden of initial sentence decisions. Neither have trial judges had the opportunity to stand back and reflect upon a whole range of issues arising from a multiplicity of decisions. This can come only from the relatively detached position of appellate courts. As with other issues of criminal law and procedure that come before appellate tribunals, the issues pertaining to criminal sentences can be brought within a coherent body of general principles, and corollaries of those principles, that carry out the fundamental aims of substantive criminal law.

Appellate review of sentences cannot be expected to eliminate all difficulties associated with the use of criminal sanctions. What should occur is an improvement, extremely valuable with each step forward, in the understanding of the purposes and limits of criminal law in our society. . . . At the same time, the whole process would become more comprehensible to the individual offender. . . . A more principled procedure for sentencing, along with the opportunity for appellate review of sentences, should further the goal of rehabilitation of some offenders by reducing inmates' hostility toward what they may see as an arbitrary system.

NOTE

For a study of appellate review in two states, see Zeisel & Diamond, The Search for Sentencing Equity: Sentence Review in Massachusetts and Connecticut, [1977] Am. B. Foundation Research J. 881. The authors report that hopes for the evolution of a jurisprudence of sentencing do not seem supported by experience in either state. In Massachusetts, the sentencing review board does not issue reasons for its decisions; in Connecticut, where reasons are required (id. at 888):

> opinions could become precedents, leading to guidelines. As presently written, the opinions seldom serve that purpose. More often than not they fail to articulate the reasons for rejecting or allowing the appeal, most probably because such articulation is difficult.

Zeisel and Diamond also report that the contribution of appellate review to a reduction in sentencing disparities has been at best minimal (id. at 889):

> There are too few reductions per judge and there is hardly any effort to establish general guidelines from which the judges could learn. . . . The rare direct contacts of the trial judge with the decisions of the review board and the lack of specificity of reasoning in these cases make it improbable that messages are received by the trial judge that will change his future sentencing pattern.

GAVIN v. COMMONWEALTH
Supreme Judicial Court of Massachusetts
367 Mass. 331, 327 N.E.2d 707 (1971)

KAPLAN, J. These three cases launch a renewed attack on one feature of the statute, G.L. c. 278, §§28A-28D, laying down a procedure for appellate review of certain criminal sentences. When there is a sentence to the State prison or a sentence to the reformatory for women for a term of more than five years, the person sentenced is promptly notified of his right to appeal for a review of the sentence, and he may lodge such an appeal in the Appellate Division of the Superior Court. . . . The division may consider an appeal with or without affording a hearing, but "no sentence shall be increased without giving the defendant an opportunity to be heard." §28B.[3] The division's jurisdiction is limited to a review of the judgment only so far as it relates to the sentence imposed; it may let that part of the judgment stand or amend it by substituting "a different appropriate sentence . . . or any other disposition of the case which could have been made at the time of the imposition of the sentence . . . under review. . . ." . . .

The present cases attack again the failure of the Appellate Division to give a statement of reasons for increase of sentence. The facts may be recited briefly. On his pleas of guilty Gavin was sentenced by the trial judge on January 20,

---

3. Part at least of the purpose of permitting increase of sentence is to discourage frivolous appeals. . . .

1972, to a term of five to seven years in State prison on an indictment for armed robbery (masked) and to a like term on an indictment for assault and robbery (masked), the terms to run concurrently. He appealed the sentences and appeared with counsel and was heard by the Appellate Division on November 1, 1972, in a proceeding which customarily takes between fifteen and thirty minutes and of which no stenographic record is kept. The division modified the judgment by ordering the two sentences to be served consecutively rather than concurrently, with effects, among other things, on the date of Gavin's eligibility for discretionary early parole. The division did not state reasons for the modification (nor, so far as appears, did the appellant request it to do so). . . .

[Discussion of proceedings involving the other appellants is omitted.]

1. The appellants argue that when the statute (§28B) guarantees to appellants "an opportunity to be heard" in case of an increase of sentence, a statement of reasons by the deciding body is necessarily implied as a matter of sound statutory construction. This contention . . . is not buttressed by anything more than an enumeration of the claimed advantages of providing such a statement. . . . It seems to us that in ordinary parlance and practical experience "opportunity to be heard" does not comprehend any particular understanding about the style of decision. . . .

2. Next, the appellants base an argument on North Carolina v. Pearce, 395 U.S. 711 (1969). . . . The *Pearce* case started from the agreed proposition that a criminal sentence actuated by a judge's vindictiveness is a sentence without due process. When a criminal conviction is upset on appeal or by collateral attack for error of the trial judge, and the defendant is retried, and again convicted, and a sentence is then imposed upon him by the judge more severe than that originally set, there may be possible ground for suspicion — so the Supreme Court thought — that vindictiveness, pique at the "wasted" time and effort or the like, even though subconscious, may in some degree have motivated the resentence. Yet such motivation would ordinarily be hard to establish by positive proof. To prevent injustice to the individual or an improper "chilling" effect for the future on prospective appellants, the *Pearce* case in the name of due process requires the judge at the time of the stepped-up resentence to make express findings directed to absolving himself of the possible reproach. . . .[7] But in the *Walsh* cases[a] our court as well as the Court of Appeals thought the *Pearce* case inapplicable to the resentencing procedure under §§28A-28D. . . . Quite apart from the fact that §28A bars the original sentencing judge from participating as a member of the Appellate Division in the reexamination of his own judgments, it is hard to see in the routine reviews of sentences under our statute any likely chances for the arousal of base passions of retaliation

---

7. "[W]henever a judge imposes a more severe sentence upon a defendant after a new trial, the reasons for his doing so must affirmatively appear. Those reasons must be based upon objective information concerning identifiable conduct on the part of the defendant occurring after the time of the original sentencing proceeding. And the factual data upon which the increased sentence is based must be made part of the record, so that the constitutional legitimacy of the increased sentence may be fully reviewed on appeal." 395 U.S. at 726 (1969).

a. In Walsh v. Commonwealth, 358 Mass. 193, 260 N.E.2d 911 (1970), the Massachusetts Supreme Judicial Court had rejected the precise claim reasserted in *Gavin* — that it would be unconstitutional to increase the sentence on appeal without giving reasons. In subsequent habeas corpus proceedings, a divided panel of the United States Court of Appeals had also rejected the claim. Walsh v. Picard, 446 F.2d 1209 (1st Cir. 1970). — Eds.

in any panel member that suggests a need for anything on the order of the *Pearce* type of prophylactic statement. . . . The fact that few sentences have been in fact increased on such review over the years, when compared with the number of sentences reviewed or with the number of sentences reduced, also strongly suggests to us . . . that *Pearce* statements have no proper place even if they could be altered in their form to suit the occasion. . . .

3. . . . [A]ppellants turn to another and broader due process contention. . . . Goldberg v. Kelly, 397 U.S. 254 (1970), had been but recently decided when the *Walsh* cases were handed down and its implications had not yet been explored. *Goldberg* speaks of the process minimally required by the Constitution when an individual confronts the government in a matter of consequence. The process "due" is variable, a resultant of the forces intrinsic to particular situations, as illustrated by the court's remark that "[t]he extent to which procedural due process must be afforded . . . is influenced by the extent to which . . . [the person] may be 'condemned to suffer grievous loss,' . . . and depends upon whether the . . . [person's] interest in avoiding that loss outweighs the governmental interest in summary adjudication." . . .

In the present case we are surely dealing with a significant interest of the individual. In weighing his minimal entitlement to procedural protection, we must note that at present, . . . he gets notice of his opportunity to appeal, help of counsel in deciding whether to appeal with its attendant risk, availability of a record and possible resort to the views of the trial judge, appearance before the tribunal with assistance of counsel, and ultimate collegial rather than individual judgment. Does the constitutional minimum in the particular situation require, in addition, a statement of reasons by the tribunal?

On the affirmative side, it may be suggested that the preparation of such a statement would provide a test for the judges themselves, and for the prisoner also of the soundness of the judges' reasoning. We can recognize that there is more than mere sentimental attractiveness in the idea that an explanation is "owed" to the prisoner on whom a harsher sentence has been imposed after he has pleaded for a reduction; if the explanation would not help materially in his rehabilitation, it would at least symbolize that he was being treated as a person rather than a cipher. A statement of reasons might usually be more easily written by the Appellate Division for revising a sentence than by the trial judge for imposing the original sentence, since the former would be a more focused analysis looking to correction of possible misjudgment embodied in the sentence reviewed rather than to the formation of an original judgment. And in view of the [infrequency of increases on appeal], it cannot be said that a heavy administrative burden would be cast on the division by a requirement that it give reasons for increasing sentences.

On the other side, we may recall that . . . our sentencing conforms to the old and still conventional model . . . that allows very wide discretion to the trial judge. Thus an explanatory statement at the time of sentencing would serve no sharp analytic purpose, and in all events it has not been required. See Williams v. New York, 337 U.S. 241, 252 (1949). Appellate review under our statute has to some extent the character of an extension, without precise litigious formalities, of the trial judge's effort to attain a just sentence. Through the combined experience of its members, the Appellate Division may know better than the single judge what is the usual range of the sentences for the grade of offense; it may have less of a sense than the trial judge of the characteristics and potentialities of the individual; but discretion permeates decision making on both levels. . . . If the inveterate habits of our judicial system as a whole bear on claims of constitutional right, then we must note that though appellate courts customarily — yet not invariably — write something in justification of their modifications of decisions appealed from, our system by and large does not insist that judges explain all their consequential decisions. . . .

On the whole, weighing the nature of review by our Appellate Division, we believe the *Goldberg* case and decisions emanating from it do not oblige us to alter the constitutional position taken in the *Walsh* cases, although, as noted, the constitutional question cannot be considered free from doubt.

4. Although we are persuaded that the omission of the Appellate Division to state reasons for increase of sentence does not cause the procedure to fall below the minimal standard of fairness required by the Constitution, this does not preclude the question whether the practice should be changed in the interests of the "proper administration of criminal justice." If an inquiry on this line is to be undertaken, it should in the first instance be done by the Superior Court with a view to possible rule making under §28B. . . .[15]

Judgments affirmed.

NOTES

1. The power to increase the sentence on appeal. With or without a statement of reasons, why should an appellate court ever be permitted to impose a *higher* sentence than the trial judge had pronounced? The problem arises in two distinct settings.

(*a*) *Increases authorized when only the defendant appeals.* Consider the following comment:

Low, Special Offender Sentencing, 8 Am. Crim. L.Q. 70, 82-85 (1970): The arguments in favor of power in the appellate court to increase a sentence if the defendant appeals basically come down to two: that in principle it is not sound to place limitations on a reviewing court which may prevent the doing of justice in a concrete case; and that without some deterrent to appeals against sentence, a defendant with nothing to lose will automatically appeal, thereby flooding the courts with appeals, most of which will be without merit anyway.

The second contention is the easiest to answer. . . . [I]t is erroneous in principle because it reflects the adoption of a remedy that has nothing to do with the problem which is sought to be cured. . . . The kind of appeal that is sought

---

15. The relevant jurisdictions having appellate review of sentences by a special tribunal, apart from ordinary review of the trial merits, stand as follows. Maine does not require a statement by the tribunal, but trial judges are required to give reasons at original sentencing. Connecticut, Montana, and Maryland (the latter, apparently, by rule) require statements of reasons in all cases appealed.

In Connecticut there is provision for publishing those statements of reasons that the Reporter considers will be useful as precedents and will serve the public interest.

The ABA Standards [American Bar Association, Standards Relating to Appellate Review of Sentences (Approved Draft 1968)], which recommend that review of sentences be by the regular appellate courts, suggest that statements be discretionary, but that they should normally be given in cases where sentences are modified by increase or reduction. Standard 3.1(b), with commentary at 48.

to be deterred is the frivolous appeal, the appeal that is without merit and that therefore is thought to take up the court's time without purpose. But the solution of permitting an increase is just as likely to deter the meritorious appeal as it is the appeal that is without merit; it operates with equal force as a deterrent to good appeals as well as bad ones. If too many frivolous appeals is the problem, other methods of attack — more streamlined appellate court procedures, for example — should be tried before resort is had to overkill.

The deterrence theory also suffers from another serious defect. To say on the one hand that our conceptions of justice require that decisions be subject to a reviewing process, and on the other that we are so afraid that defendants will take advantage of the process that we must build in serious incentives not to take advantage of it, reflects a kind of hypocrisy which I think we could well do without. The image of justice is not advanced by our present practice of permitting a single individual to make a decision of enormous consequence — often involving a range of choice between probation and twenty or thirty years — and at the same time taking the position that he need not state his reasons and that no one can undo the decision he has made. To correct this image by saying that we will provide a check against abuse only if the defendant is willing to take the risk that his sentence will be doubled seems to me to compound rather than cure the genuine issues of fairness which I see in this situation. . . .

This is not an answer, however, to the contention that if justice in the particular case at the appellate level indicates that an increase is in order, the court should be empowered to go ahead and impose one. I admit that there is force to this contention, and it seems clear to me that it is on this point — not deterrence — that the issue should turn.

My response to this justification for authorizing an increase in the sentence is that I think the issue more properly addressed is one of whether the prosecution should be entitled to appeal. . . . [T]here is an element of unfairness in responding to a request to reduce by imposing an increase. There is no other context in which this is permitted. . . . If the prosecutor wants an increase, then he should ask for it, and should put the defendant on notice that he will have to defend himself against an increase. If there are reasons why the prosecutor should not be entitled to take an appeal against the sentence — as I believe there are — then those same reasons seem equally convincing to me in the situation where the defendant alone has appealed.[a]

(b) *Increases authorized when the prosecution appeals.* Compare the following viewpoints:

American Bar Association, Minimum Standards for Criminal Justice, Standards Relating to Appellate Review of Sentences, §3.4, Commentary at 56-57 (1967): There are two major arguments in support of allowing an appeal by the state to increase the too-lenient sentence. The first concedes that the interests of the defendant deserve protection by a review provision, but at the same time argues that the

a. In connection with the American Bar Association's 1967 Project on Minimum Standards for Criminal Justice, the Advisory Committee on Standards Relating to Appellate Review of Sentences recommended against appellate authority to increase sentence when only the defendant appeals, but the ABA House of Delegates approved an amendment that had been supported on the grounds mentioned, and criticized, by Professor Low in the excerpt above. — EDS.

interests of the state need the same protection. Justice demands correction of the too-lenient sentence as well as the sentence that is too severe. The second argument is closely related. The product of the fact that many sentences are either too low or too high is the much discussed disparity problem. Providing an appeal by both the state and the defendant will open both sides of this problem to review and should contribute significantly to its resolution.

In spite of some sympathy for the position supported by these arguments, the Advisory Committee has concluded that the state should not be permitted an appeal that could result in an increase of the sentence. . . .

There are two basic reasons which lead the Committee to this view. In the first place, there is the prospect of serious constitutional difficulties if an increase is allowed on an appeal by the state.[a] . . .

The second reason why the Committee opposes an appeal by the state in this context is that it is not sufficiently clear that such a provision would make a significant contribution to the objectives sought by those who favor it. . . . [T]he guilty-plea bargainers — who are undoubtedly the chief beneficiaries of the too-lenient sentence — would surely exact as part of the bargain that no appeal of their sentence would be taken. . . . In the second place, a much more serious problem could be created by giving the state the power to seek an increase on appeal. The existence of such power could well have the effect of preventing the defendant from appealing even on the merits of his conviction. The ability to seek an increase could be a powerful club, the very existence of which — even assuming its good faith use — might induce a defendant to leave well enough alone.

American Bar Association, Standards for Criminal Justice, Appellate Review of Sentences, §20-1.1, Commentary at 20 · 8-9 (2d ed. 1980): After constitutional doubts have been removed, substantial arguments can be marshaled to support limited government appeal from sentences. . . . [I]t is as appropriate to correct an excessively low sentence as it is to correct an excessively high one. The position of the original [ABA] standards, authorizing increase in a sentence even though only the defendant had appealed, was admittedly not completely satisfactory. However, given the premise that all sentence appeals must be on defendants' initiative [because a prosecutor's appeal was thought vulnerable to double jeopardy objections], there would be no other way to provide even partial implementation of the desideratum of evenhandedness in appellate review. These difficulties are resolved if prosecution appeals are permitted. Plainly, it is preferable to restrict the power of appellate courts to increase sentences to those cases in which the government has taken an appeal.

Government appeal is sometimes challenged as unsound because it may tend to deter some defendants from appealing their convictions on claims of errors unrelated to sentence. This contention assumes that the government may be inclined to take a cross-appeal from sentence because a defendant has appealed on the merits of the conviction. . . . Even the possibility of a retaliatory cross-appeal by the government on the sentence could create an undesirable cloud

---

a. In United States v. DiFrancesco, 101 U.S. 426 (1980), the United States Supreme Court ruled that an increase in sentence, after appeal by the prosecutor, would not violate the double jeopardy clause. — EDS.

on a defendant's decision whether to seek review of the conviction. Thus, the standard provides that the power to authorize a prosecution appeal should be placed in an officer with statewide responsibility rather than in a local prosecutor. The proposed Federal Criminal Code, for example, would allow the United States to appeal only if the Attorney General or his designee permit it in a particular case.[a]

2. *The obligation to give reasons for the sentence.* (a) *The trial judge's obligation to give reasons.* Very few jurisdictions require that the trial court state its reasons at the time sentence is imposed. Is there any good explanation for the prevailing practice? The preparation of such statements would impose additional, burdensome duties on busy judges. But if we want thoughtfully individualized sentences and expect judges to take seriously their obligation to perform this function, is this a burden that judges should be asked to bear?

Even if considerations of convenience or efficiency might be thought to warrant dispensing with reasons, the absence of reasons raises serious problems of fairness to the defendant. Recall, for example, that the defendant has a constitutional right to challenge a sentence if he can show that it is based in significant part on inaccurate or unreliable information. See pages 1060-1066 supra. How can a defendant show this when the basis for the sentence is not disclosed? Where appellate review is authorized, the defendant can set aside a sentence shown to be excessive, but can he or she show this effectively if the reasons for the judge's choice of a severe sentence can be left to speculation? At least one state supreme court has required its trial judges to state their reasons in order to facilitate appellate review. See Commonwealth v. Riggins, 474 Pa. 115, 377 A.2d 140 (1977).[6]

In the context of parole administration, the United States Supreme Court has held that when a parole board seeks to reincarcerate a parolee for violation of parole conditions, due process requires "a written statement by the factfinders as to the evidence relied on and the reasons for revoking parole." See Morrissey v. Brewer, pages 1076-1081 infra. But the same requirement has not been imposed with respect to the sentencing judge's decision to commit the offender to prison in the first instance. Should it be? The constitutional issues are canvassed in Berkowitz, The Constitutional Requirement for a Written Statement of Reasons and Facts in Support of the Sentencing Decision: A Due Process Proposal, 60 Iowa L. Rev. 205 (1974).

(b) *The appellate court's obligation to give reasons.* Reconsider the various purposes of appellate review of sentencing, as described by the ABA at page 1074 supra. To what extent can these purposes be achieved if the reviewing court provides no reasons for its decision?

It can be argued that reasons should be given on all appeals, but the case for a reasons requirement is particularly strong whenever the appellate court sets aside the trial court's sentence and even stronger when, as in *Gavin,* the appellate court orders that the sentence be *increased.* As Justice Kaplan notes, it has become increasingly common in civil cases for appellate courts to decide

---

a. Does this restriction effectively eliminate the danger? — Eds.

6. In Maine a similar requirement has been adopted by statute. Me. Rev. Stat. Ann. tit. 15, §§2141-2144. Maryland requires statements of reasons in all appealed cases. Md. Ann. Code art. 27, §§645JA-645JG, rule 762.

appeals without giving reasons, at least when the decision is to affirm or dismiss. How often is an appellate court likely to *reverse*, even in a routine civil case, without providing some hint as to its reasons? In criminal cases, an additional complication is the defendant's constitutional right under North Carolina v. Pearce, pages 1070-1071 supra, to be protected against vindictive sanctions for having exercised his right to appeal. Is there not a serious danger of vindictiveness in the Massachusetts scheme? Can the court's conclusion to the contrary be reconciled with its observation, in footnote 3 of the opinion, that "[p]art at least of the purpose of permitting increase of sentence is to discourage frivolous appeals"?

5. Parole

The parole system raises significant problems concerning the initial decision whether to release on parole, concerning the fairness and effectiveness of supervision by parole officers after release, and concerning revocation of parole and reincarceration of the parolee for violation of the release conditions. A useful description and analysis of current parole practice can be found in A. von Hirsch & K. Hanrahan, The Question of Parole (1979).

It would be natural to examine parole problems in the order they normally arise, by considering the release decision first and the problems of supervision and revocation subsequently. Doctrinal developments, however, have proceeded according to a different logic. The parole-revocation decision, involving the deprivation of a liberty currently enjoyed, came under scrutiny first. Later cases then confronted the question whether the principles established with respect to revocation should also be applied to the threshold decision about parole release. To facilitate understanding of this evolution, we follow a parallel order, considering the revocation decision at this point and the parole-release decision subsequently.

a. Parole Revocation

MORRISSEY v. BREWER
Supreme Court of the United States
408 U.S. 471 (1972)

MR. CHIEF JUSTICE BURGER delivered the opinion of the Court.

We granted certiorari in this case to determine whether the Due Process Clause of the Fourteenth Amendment requires that a State afford an individual some opportunity to be heard prior to revoking his parole.

Petitioner Morrissey was convicted of false drawing or uttering of checks in 1967 pursuant to his guilty plea, and was sentenced to not more than seven years' confinement. He was paroled from the Iowa State Penitentiary in June 1968. Seven months later, at the direction of his parole officer, he was arrested in his home town as a parole violator and incarcerated in the county jail. One week later, after review of the parole officer's written report, the Iowa Board of Parole revoked Morrissey's parole and he was returned to the penitentiary located about 100 miles from his home. Petitioner asserts he received no hearing prior to revocation of his parole.

The parole officer's report on which the Board of Parole acted shows that petitioner's parole was revoked on the basis of information that he had violated the conditions of parole by buying a car under an assumed name and operating it without permission, giving false statements to police concerning his address and insurance company after a minor accident, and obtaining credit under an assumed name and failing to report his place of residence to his parole officer. The report states that the officer interviewed Morrissey, and that he could not explain why he did not contact his parole officer despite his effort to excuse this on the ground that he had been sick. Further, the report asserts that Morrissey admitted buying the car and obtaining credit under an assumed name and also admitted being involved in the accident. The parole officer recommended that his parole be revoked because of "his continual violating of his parole rules." . . .

[After exhausting state remedies, Morrissey filed a habeas corpus petition. The federal district court held that no hearing on the matter of parole revocation was required. The Court of Appeals for the Fourth Circuit agreed.]

Before reaching the issue of whether due process applies to the parole system, it is important to recall the function of parole in the correctional process.

During the past 60 years, the practice of releasing prisoners on parole before the end of their sentences has become an integral part of the penological system. Note, Parole Revocation in the Federal System, 56 Geo. L.J. 705 (1968). Rather than being an ad hoc exercise of clemency, parole is an established variation on imprisonment of convicted criminals. Its purpose is to help individuals reintegrate into society as constructive individuals as soon as they are able, without being confined for the full term of the sentence imposed. It also serves to alleviate the costs to society of keeping an individual in prison. The essence of parole is release from prison, before the completion of sentence, on the condition that the prisoner abide by certain rules during the balance of the sentence. . . .

To accomplish the purpose of parole, those who are allowed to leave prison early are subjected to specified conditions for the duration of their terms. These conditions restrict their activities substantially beyond the ordinary restrictions imposed by law on an individual citizen. Typically parolees are forbidden to use liquor or to have associations or correspondence with certain categories of undesirable persons. Typically also they must seek permission from their parole officers before engaging in specified activities, such as changing employment or living quarters, marrying, acquiring or operating a motor vehicle, traveling outside the community and incurring substantial indebtedness. Additionally, parolees must regularly report to the parole officer to whom they are assigned and sometimes they must make periodic written reports of their activities. . . .

The parole officers are part of the administrative system designed to assist parolees and to offer them guidance. The conditions of parole serve a dual purpose; they prohibit, either absolutely or conditionally, behavior which is deemed dangerous to the restoration of the individual into normal society. And through the requirement of reporting to the parole officer and seeking guidance and permission before doing many things, the officer is provided with information about the parolee and an opportunity to advise him. The combination puts the parole officer into the position in which he can try to guide the parolee into constructive development.

The enforcement leverage which supports the parole conditions derives from the authority to return the parolee to prison to serve out the balance of his sentence if he fails to abide by the rules. In practice not every violation of parole conditions automatically leads to revocation. Typically a parolee will be counseled to abide by the conditions of parole, and the parole officer ordinarily does not take steps to have parole revoked unless he thinks that the violations are serious and continuing so as to indicate that the parolee is not adjusting properly and cannot be counted on to avoid antisocial activity. The broad discretion accorded the parole officer is also inherent in some of the quite vague conditions, such as the typical requirement that the parolee avoid "undesirable" associations or correspondence. . . . Yet revocation of parole is not an unusual phenomenon, affecting only a few parolees. It has been estimated that 35-45% of all parolees are subjected to revocation and return to prison. Sometimes revocation occurs when the parolee is accused of another crime; it is often preferred to a new prosecution because of the procedural ease of recommitting the individual on the basis of a lesser showing by the State.

Implicit in the system's concern with parole violations is the notion that the parolee is entitled to retain his liberty as long as he substantially abides by the conditions of his parole. The first step in a revocation decision thus involves a wholly retrospective factual question: whether the parolee has in fact acted in violation of one or more conditions of his parole. Only if it is determined that the parolee did violate the conditions does the second question arise: should the parolee be recommitted to prison or should other steps be taken to protect society and improve chances of rehabilitation? The first step is relatively simple; the second is more complex. The second question involves the application of expertise by the parole authority in making a prediction as to the ability of the individual to live in society without committing antisocial acts. This part of the decision, too, depends on facts, and therefore it is important for the Board to know not only that some violation was committed but also to know accurately how many and how serious the violations were. Yet this second step, deciding what to do about the violation once it is identified, is not purely factual but also predictive and discretionary.

If a parolee is returned to prison, he often receives no credit for the time "served" on parole. Thus the returnee may face a potential of substantial imprisonment.

We begin with the proposition that the revocation of parole is not part of a criminal prosecution and thus the full panoply of rights due a defendant in such a proceeding does not apply to parole revocations. . . . Revocation deprives an individual not of the absolute liberty to which every citizen is entitled, but only of the conditional liberty properly dependent on observance of special parole restrictions.

We turn therefore to the question whether the requirements of due process in general apply to parole revocations. As Mr. Justice Blackmun has written recently, "This Court has rejected the concept that constitutional rights turn upon whether a governmental benefit is characterized as a 'right' or as a 'privilege.'" Graham v. Richardson, 403 U.S. 365, 374. Whether any procedural protections are due depends on the extent to which an individual will be "condemned to suffer grievous loss." Joint Anti-Fascist Refugee Committee v. McGrath, 341 U.S. 123, 168 (1951) (Frankfurter, J., concurring), quoted in Goldberg v. Kelly, 397 U.S. 154, 163 (1970). The question is not merely the "weight" of the individual's interest, but whether the nature of the interest is one within the contemplation of the "liberty or property" language of the Fourteenth Amendment. . . . Once it is determined that due process applies, the question remains what process is due. It has been said so often by this Court and others as not to require citation of authority that due process is flexible and calls for such procedural protections as the particular situation demands. . . .

. . . [T]he liberty of a parolee, although indeterminate, includes many of the core values of unqualified liberty and its termination inflicts a "grievous loss" on the parolee and often on others. It is hardly useful any longer to try to deal with this problem in terms of whether the parolee's liberty is a "right" or a "privilege." By whatever name the liberty is valuable and must be seen as within the protection of the Fourteenth Amendment. Its termination calls for some orderly process, however informal.

Turning to the question what process is due, we find that the State's interests are several. The State has found the parolee guilty of a crime against the people. That finding justifies imposing extensive restrictions on the individual's liberty. Release of the parolee before the end of his prison sentence is made with the recognition that with many prisoners there is a risk that they will not be able to live in society without committing additional antisocial acts. Given the previous conviction and the proper imposition of conditions, the State has an overwhelming interest in being able to return the individual to imprisonment without the burden of a new adversary criminal trial if in fact he has failed to abide by the conditions of his parole.

Yet the State has no interest in revoking parole without some informal procedural guarantees. Although the parolee is often formally described as being "in custody," the argument cannot even be made here that summary treatment is necessary as it may be with respect to controlling a large group of potentially disruptive prisoners in actual custody. Nor are we persuaded by the argument that revocation is so totally a discretionary matter that some form of hearing would be administratively intolerable. A simple factual hearing will not interfere with the exercise of discretion. Serious studies have suggested that fair treatment on parole revocation will not result in fewer grants of parole.

This discretionary aspect of the revocation decision need not be reached unless there is first an appropriate determination that the individual has in fact breached the conditions of parole. The parolee is not the only one who has a stake in his conditional liberty. Society has a stake in whatever may be the chance of restoring him to normal and useful life within the law. Society thus has an interest in not having parole revoked because of erroneous information or because of an erroneous evaluation of the need to revoke parole, given the breach of parole conditions. . . . And society has a further interest in treating the parolee with basic fairness: fair treatment in parole revocations will enhance the chance of rehabilitation by avoiding reactions to arbitrariness. . . .

. . . In analyzing what is due, we see two important stages in the typical process of parole revocation.

(a) Arrest of Parolee and Preliminary Hearing. The first stage occurs when the parolee is arrested and detained, usually at the direction of his parole officer.

The second occurs when parole is formally revoked. There is typically a substantial time lag between the arrest and the eventual determination by the parole board whether parole should be revoked. Additionally, it may be that the parolee is arrested at a place distant from the state institution, to which he may be returned before the final decision is made concerning revocation. Given these factors, due process would seem to require that some minimal inquiry be conducted at or reasonably near the place of the alleged parole violation or arrest and as promptly as convenient after arrest while information is fresh and sources are available. . . . Such an inquiry should be seen as in the nature of a "preliminary hearing" to determine whether there is probable cause or reasonable grounds to believe that the arrested parolee has committed acts which would constitute a violation of parole conditions. . . .

In our view due process requires that after the arrest, the determination that reasonable grounds exist for revocation of parole should be made by someone not directly involved in the case. . . .

This independent officer need not be a judicial officer. The granting and revocation of parole are matters traditionally handled by administrative officers. . . . It will be sufficient . . . in the parole revocation context, if an evaluation of whether reasonable cause exists to believe that conditions of parole have been violated is made by someone such as a parole officer other than the one who has made the report of parole violations or has recommended revocation. . . .

The hearing officer shall have the duty of making a summary, or digest, of what transpires at the hearing in terms of the responses of the parolee and the substance of the documents or evidence given in support of parole revocation and of the parolee's position. Based on the information before him, the officer should determine whether there is probable cause to hold the parolee for the final decision of the parole board on revocation. Such a determination would be sufficient to warrant the parolee's continued detention and return to the state correctional institution pending the final decision. . . .

[Chief Justice Burger also affirmed that the hearing officer should state his reasons and the evidence relied upon.]

(b) The Revocation Hearing. There must also be an opportunity for a hearing, if it is desired by the parolee, prior to the final decision on revocation by the parole authority. . . . The revocation hearing must be tendered within a reasonable time after the parolee is taken into custody. A lapse of two months, as the State suggests occurs in some cases, would not appear to be unreasonable.

We cannot write a code of procedure; that is the responsibility of each State. Most States have done so by legislation, others by judicial decision usually on due process grounds. Our task is limited to deciding the minimum requirements of due process. They include (a) written notice of the claimed violations of parole; (b) disclosure to the parolee of evidence against him; (c) opportunity to be heard in person and to present witnesses and documentary evidence; (d) the right to confront and cross-examine adverse witnesses (unless the hearing officer specifically finds good cause for not allowing confrontation); (e) a "neutral and detached" hearing body such as a traditional parole board, members of which need not be judicial officers or lawyers; and (f) a written statement by the factfinders as to the evidence relied on and reasons for revoking parole. We emphasize there is no thought to equate this second stage of parole revocation to a criminal prosecution in any sense; it is a narrow inquiry; the process should be flexible enough to consider evidence including letters, affidavits, and other material that would not be admissible in an adversary criminal trial.

We do not reach or decide the question whether the parolee is entitled to the assistance of retained counsel or to appointed counsel if he is indigent.

. . . Obviously a parolee cannot relitigate issues determined against him in other forums, as in the situation presented when the revocation is based on conviction of another crime. . . .

We reverse and remand to the Court of Appeals for further proceedings consistent with this opinion. . . .

LEE & ZUCKERMAN, REPRESENTING PAROLE VIOLATORS, 11 Crim. L. Bull. 327 (1975): * [A]lmost three years after the decision in Morrissey v. Brewer, growing numbers of parolees are represented by lawyers at parole revocation hearings. But judicial decisions and the occasional presence of lawyers have not transformed parole revocation hearings into models of due process. . . .

Some of the problems in representing parolees involve the [New York] parole board's failure to comply fully with the procedural requirements set out in Morrissey v. Brewer. . . . Other problems stem from basic characteristics of the parole system in New York, and elsewhere, which remain unaffected by the procedural requirements established by Morrissey v. Brewer. . . .

Assuming for the moment that accurate predictions about an individual's future social behavior can be made and that the persons constituting the New York State Board of Parole possess the training and experience required to make such determinations . . . parole revocation determinations in New York remain unreliable because the parole board members are asked to perform the impossible task of being judge, jury, and prosecutor. . . . A typical parole revocation hearing begins with the presiding commissioner reading the charges to the parolee, asking him whether he understands them, whether he has consulted with his counsel about them, and how he wishes to plead to each charge. Following any preliminary applications by the parolee's counsel, the presiding commissioner offers in evidence the report of violation of parole prepared by the parole officer who supervised the parolee in question. Almost invariably, counsel objects (usually on hearsay grounds) to receipt in evidence of all or part of the report. Almost invariably, too, counsel's objection is overruled or merely "noted." Thus, at the very outset of the hearing, the supposedly objective and dispassionate parole board finds itself in the conflicting roles of judge (or jury) and prosecutor.

The board begins, in the role of judge, by reading the charges, . . . rapidly switches to the prosecutorial function as it seeks to introduce the violation report, only to reappear with the speed of the Ghost of Christmas Present, swathed once again in judicial robes, to rule upon objections to the very report it has sought to introduce. The commissioners continue to play the judicial role, making rulings on evidence, for example, until it is time to switch to prosecutor again for the cross-examination of the defendant-parolee and his witnesses, if any.

* Editor's Note [by the editor of the Criminal Law Bulletin]: This article is written out of the authors' direct experience with revocation hearings in New York. . . .

Only two of the twelve members of the board of parole are attorneys. Even if all twelve members were legally trained and possessed the wisdom of Solomon and the patience of Job, they would be unable to resolve the conflicting roles impressed upon them by the Supreme Court and the New York court of appeals. . . . The obvious solution is to recognize the adversary nature of the final revocation hearing and, accordingly, to have the State Department of Correctional Services represented by counsel, while the parole board members function as closely as possible to the "neutral and detached magistrates" envisioned by the *Morrissey* court.

In spite of the Supreme Court's admonition in *Morrissey* that the minimum requirements of due process at a final parole revocation hearing include "the right to confront and cross-examine adverse witnesses," the parole board never produces any witnesses, other than parole officers, even though it has the power to subpoena witnesses. The parole officer's testimony usually contains substantial amounts of hearsay, and violation charges are not infrequently sustained, solely or in large part, on the basis of hearsay. . . .

Morrissey requires "a written statement by the factfinders as to the evidence relied on and reasons for revoking parole." The parole board's response to this requirement is a set formula: "Parole violations sustained. Parole revoked. Held — months. Reasons: parole violation report, admissions, credible testimony of Parole Officer." There is no effort to state what particular evidence was relied on to sustain particular violations, or to explain what factors influenced the decision as to how long to hold the parolee or even the decision to reincarcerate him at all. Nor is there ever any explanation why a proposed alternative to reincarceration has been rejected. Parole board noncompliance with *Morrissey* in this respect prevents parolees and lawyers from knowing what criteria the board uses, frustrates judicial review, and protects the parole board's capacity to act arbitrarily.

Perhaps the most basic problem in representing parolees is the kind of violations that serve as the basis for parole revocation and reincarceration. . . . Parolees are frequently unaware of all the conditions with which they are required to comply. But even if a parolee is aware of all the rules and tries to comply, he can, at virtually any time, be charged with violating his parole because the conditions are so broad and vague that a parole officer so disposed can always find a violation, e.g., failing to "make every effort to secure . . . gainful employment." Parolees are frequently charged with violations to which the real defense is that whatever occurred (if anything) does not justify revocation of parole.

Legislative and administrative reforms limiting parole conditions to a few specific requirements and restricting the discretion of parole officers to charge parolees with violations are essential if the parole system is to take on a semblance of fairness.

NOTES ON THE RIGHT TO COUNSEL

1. In Gagnon v. Scarpelli, 411 U.S. 778 (1973), the Supreme Court held that an indigent offender facing revocation of probation or parole was not automatically entitled to the assistance of appointed counsel at the revocation hearing. The Court reaffirmed its holding in *Morrissey* that because revocation of parole entails a serious deprivation of liberty, the hearing must satisfy due process. But the Court concluded that due process does not invariably require the assistance of counsel. The Court stressed first that affording counsel would adversely affect the nature of the revocation hearing (id. at 787-788):

> The role of the hearing body itself, aptly described in *Morrissey* as being "predictive and discretionary" as well as fact-finding, may become more akin to that of a judge at a trial, and less attuned to the rehabilitative needs of the individual probationer or parolee.

Although recognizing that these costs must be borne when fair resolution of an issue requires a trained advocate, the Court said that revocation hearings often involve no serious factual dispute: "[i]n most cases, the probationer or parolee has been convicted of committing another crime or has admitted the charges . . . , [and] mitigating evidence . . . is often not susceptible of proof or is so simple as not to require either investigation or exposition by counsel." Id. at 787. Moreover, the Court reasoned, the need for counsel is further diminished by the facts that: (1) a revocation hearing, unlike a criminal trial, does not involve formal rules of evidence; (2) the state is represented not by a prosecutor but by a parole officer whose "function is not so much to compel conformance to a strict code of behavior as to supervise a course of rehabilitation, [and who] has been entrusted traditionally with broad discretion to judge the progress of rehabilitation in individual cases" (id. at 784); and (3) the decisionmakers are trained specialists rather than untrained jurors.

Although the Court thus rejected the claim of a constitutional right to appointed counsel in all revocation cases, it did indicate that under some circumstances counsel would be necessary to satisfy due process requirements. As to this question, no specific guidelines were provided, but the Court suggested that counsel presumably should be provided when the parolee requesting counsel denies the alleged violation of parole conditions or when he or she claims that there are complex circumstances that justify or mitigate the violation and make revocation inappropriate.

2. Compare Kadish, The Advocate and the Expert: Counsel in the Peno-Correctional Process, 45 Minn. L. Rev. 803, 833 (1961):

> [T]he determination to revoke and recommit because of conduct in violation of the conditions on which release was granted, involves, if not exclusively, then at least centrally, the fairly narrowly focused issue of what the conduct of the releasee actually was and whether it constituted a violation of a stated condition, entitling the court or agency to consider whether revocation is thereby indicated. Given the character of the issue to be determined and the fact that the continued liberty of a person depends on the outcome, it is difficult to understand the view sometimes expressed that a lawyer has no proper business in these matters. The central task of ascertaining whether the prisoner has committed the acts alleged, and measuring the acts proven against a standard to which he was obliged to conform is precisely the business of the criminal trial itself where the right to the assistance of counsel has been recognized as one of the "immutable principles of justice." Indeed, in many contested revocation proceedings, the conduct charged actually constitutes the commission of a criminal act. No doubt it is simpler and faster for a court or a board to make the determination by whatever means seem to it sufficient to

persuade — whether it be an informal talk with the parole officer or a brief interview with the prisoner or a written report by an investigator. But it would seem patently at war with the central concept of procedural justice to deny to a person with his liberty at stake the opportunity to hear and meet the specific charge against him with the benefit of counsel.

See also American Bar Association, Standards for Criminal Justice, Sentencing Alternatives and Procedures, §18-7.5, Commentary at 18·531-532 (2d ed. 1980).

STANDLEE v. RHAY

United States Court of Appeals, 9th Circuit
557 F.2d 1303 (1977)

CARTER, J. . . . . Appellee was paroled on September 28, 1970, from his 1959 conviction for rape. In January 1971, he was arrested and charged with two counts of second degree criminal assault. Subsequently, he was charged with six parole violations based on the same acts for which he was criminally charged: two counts of abduction, two counts of second degree assault, one count of attempted rape, and one count of sexual molestation.

Prior to his trial on the two criminal charges, a parole revocation hearing was held on March 11, 1971, at which appellee was represented by counsel. At that time, appellee testified that he was in another state and had an alibi but refused to name the people who could testify to this fact. He was found guilty of all six violations, but the hearing was continued until after the conclusion of his trial.

The criminal trial was held in King County Superior Court, Washington. Appellee pleaded not guilty and again presented an alibi defense. Two witnesses testified that he had been in Portland at the time the assault took place. One of the witnesses was apparently a girl friend. The second witness, Mrs. Merrill, was a friend of the girl friend. The trial judge, sitting without a jury, believed the testimony of Mrs. Merrill led to a reasonable doubt about appellee's guilt. He stated:

[T]he testimony of Mrs. Merrill impressed me, not only her testimony but her appearance and demeanor upon the witness stand. . . . [T]o me her testimony is the one that weighed the scales of balance, whichever way they would fall. . . . [S]he left a reasonable doubt in my mind as to whether or not this defendant was the man who committed the offense.

Appellee therefore was acquitted.

The parole revocation was re-opened on June 17, 1971. The question of appellee's guilt was reexamined, with the same defense testimony presented except that Mrs. Merrill did not personally testify.[1] The hearing officer independently weighed the evidence and concluded on a preponderance of the evidence that appellee was guilty of the six parole violations.

Appellee then sought habeas relief in the Washington courts. The Supreme

---

1. Appellee claims that he could not afford to pay Mrs. Merrill's travel costs and witness fees. A transcript of her trial testimony was reviewed, however.

Court of Washington denied relief. . . . Having exhausted his state remedies, appellee filed a petition for a writ of habeas corpus with the district court. The petition was granted and appellee released. His present whereabouts is unknown.

Appellee argues that the doctrine of collateral estoppel prohibits the parole board from finding him guilty of violations when the issue of guilt for the same acts had been resolved in his favor by the trial court. Collateral estoppel is embodied in the fifth amendment guarantee against double jeopardy, Ashe v. Swenson, 397 U.S. 436 (1970), and is applicable to the states through the fourteenth amendment's due process clause, Benton v. Maryland, 395 U.S. 784 (1969). The Supreme Court noted that collateral estoppel means "simply that when an issue of ultimate fact has once been determined by a valid and final judgment, that issue cannot again be litigated between the same parties in any future lawsuit." Ashe v. Swenson, supra, 397 U.S. at 443. . . .

The difference in the burdens of proof in criminal and civil proceedings usually precludes application of collateral estoppel. . . . Because of this difference in burdens of proof, an adjudication of the issues in a criminal case "does not constitute an adjudication on the preponderance-of-the-evidence burden applicable in civil proceedings." One Lot Emerald Cut Stones v. United States, 409 U.S. 232, 235 (1971).

The nature of the sanction imposed by a proceeding also is determinative of whether collateral estoppel applies. Thus, an "acquittal on a criminal charge is not a bar to a civil action by the Government, *remedial in its nature,* arising out of the same facts on which the criminal proceeding was based. . . ." Helvering v. Mitchell, [303 U.S. 391, 397 (1938)] (emphasis added). Where, however, a punitive sanction results from a "civil" action, a prior acquittal in a criminal proceeding will bar the subsequent civil action. See Coffey v. United States, 116 U.S. 436 (1886).

This distinction is illustrated by cases involving forfeiture proceedings instigated subsequent to acquittals in criminal proceedings. . . . One Lot Emerald Cut Stones v. United States, supra. There the Court held that a forfeiture proceeding pursuant to 19 U.S.C. §1497 was not barred by an earlier acquittal of criminal charges stemming from the same acts. It reasoned that both the differences in burdens of proof and in types of sanctions prevented the operation of collateral estoppel. We believe this reasoning controls here.

It is well established that parole revocation is not part of a criminal prosecution. Morrissey v. Brewer, 408 U.S. 471, 480 (1972). Revocation of parole is remedial rather than punitive, since it seeks to protect the welfare of parolees and the safety of society. Gagnon v. Scarpelli, 411 U.S. 778, 783-84 (1973); Morrissey v. Brewer, supra, 408 U.S. at 477. The termination of parole results in a deprivation of liberty and thus is a grievous loss to the parolee. But the harshness of parole revocation does not alter its remedial nature. . . .

The district court concluded that parole revocation is a punitive rather than remedial sanction. It based this conclusion on two grounds. First, the parole provisions of the State of Washington are found in Title 9 of the Revised Code of Washington, entitled "Crimes and Punishments." Second, the courts have extended several procedural safeguards to parole revocation hearings which indicate their quasi-criminal nature. We believe the district court was in error in reaching this conclusion.

While the location of a statute in a code may be relevant in interpreting that statute, the district court overemphasized this factor while giving no deference to the courts of Washington. The location of the statute is not dispositive. . . .

It is true that the Supreme Court has extended certain procedural safeguards to parole revocation proceedings. See Gagnon v. Scarpelli, supra, 411 U.S. at 782; Morrissey v. Brewer, supra, 408 U.S. at 489. But similar procedural safeguards have been extended to forfeiture proceedings without changing their remedial nature. . . . The extension of certain constitutional rights to a *proceeding* does not of itself change the nature of the *sanction* which results from that proceeding. The district court also did not recognize the lower standard of proof in a parole revocation proceeding. . . . It follows that collateral estoppel does not bar a subsequent parole revocation hearing after a criminal acquittal. The sanctions imposed and the burdens of proof are different. . . .

Appellee contends that he was denied due process because his key alibi witness, Mrs. Merrill, was not present at the final revocation hearing. Instead, her testimony was read from the trial transcript. As we have stated, however, parole revocation proceedings are not part of the criminal process and are not protected by the full panoply of due process rights. Indeed, the use of transcripts has been expressly approved by the Supreme Court: "While in some cases there is simply no adequate alternative to live testimony, we emphasize that we did not in *Morrissey* intend to prohibit use where appropriate of the conventional substitutes for live testimony, including affidavits, depositions, and documentary evidence." Gagnon v. Scarpelli, supra, 411 U.S. at 783, n. 5.

At the very least, therefore, appellee would have to show prejudice resulting from the use of the transcript. The burden is on the parolee to demonstrate that the failure to provide a particular safeguard was under the circumstances of his case so prejudicial as to be a denial of due process.

In this case, appellee was represented by an attorney at every stage of the proceeding. It was appellee's attorney himself who moved for the introduction of the transcript as evidence. The hearing officer knew of the weight of Mrs. Merrill's testimony in the criminal trial and could balance it against the live testimony he heard. We think it is clear that the reason for the finding of guilt is the lesser standard of proof in the parole revocation proceeding. No prejudice resulted. . . .

The judgment of the district court is reversed and the case remanded with instructions to deny the petition for writ of habeas corpus.

NOTES

1. The burden of proof. Was the court justified in assuming that a "preponderance of the evidence" standard satisfies due process requirements in the parole revocation context? Consider first whether that standard would be acceptable in resolving a disputed rape allegation in a *sentencing* proceeding. See United States v. Fatico, pages 1064-1066 supra. Second, even if that standard would be acceptable for sentencing, are there reasons why a higher standard nevertheless should be required for revocation of parole. See American Bar Association, Standards for Criminal Justice, Sentencing Alternatives and Procedures, §18-7.5, Commentary at 18·532-533 (2d ed. 1980):

> Various standards of proof currently apply to the revocation hearing. The dominant federal rule is "preponderance of the evidence." In several states, however, a "reasonable doubt" standard must be met, at least where the violation itself involves a crime. [The ABA] standards take the intermediate position that the fact of a violation should be proven by "clear and convincing" evidence. Underlying this position is the premise that a liberty interest should not be sacrificed simply on the "preponderance" standard, which is normally applicable only to civil trials. Otherwise, an unfortunate incentive might arise to use the revocation hearing as a substitute for a criminal prosecution with its higher standard of proof. Even where this incentive is not present, the focus of the law should be on the precipitating event that is said to justify the loss of present liberty. Where the original crime did not require incarceration, proven subsequent behavior that is considered sufficient to justify confinement should be established under a standard that approaches providing the same assurance of factual accuracy that a criminal trial does.

2. *The special significance of a prior acquittal.* Even if a "preponderance of the evidence" standard is acceptable for resolving issues not previously litigated, should an acquittal in formal criminal proceedings nevertheless receive special deference? Contrary to Standlee v. Rhay, supra, some courts hold that an acquittal bars parole revocation based on related charges. See, e.g., People v. Grayson, 58 Ill. 2d 260, 319 N.E.2d 43, 45-46 (1974):

> While . . . violations of conditions of probation need be proved by only a preponderance of the evidence, we believe [that] differences [between a criminal trial and a probation revocation hearing] cannot fairly serve to permit relitigation of the identical issue upon the same evidence. . . . The acquittal of defendant on the charge of armed robbery was, under the evidence in this case, a determination that he was not one of the robbers. Once the ultimate and only disputed fact of identity had been determined by a final and valid judgment, the State could not constitutionally hale defendant before a new court in a criminal proceeding or a probation revocation proceeding and litigate that issue again.

3. *Procedural rights at the hearing.* Was there adequate justification for the refusal to summon defendant's alibi witness under the circumstances presented in *Standlee*? *Morrissey* explicitly guarantees the right to confront adverse witnesses (subject to a "good cause" exception[7]), but it says nothing about a right to compulsory process for obtaining *favorable* witnesses, a right specifically guaranteed by the Sixth Amendment in "criminal prosecutions." Why should the latter right be denied recognition in the parole-revocation context? Consider, for example, whether it would be permissible to impose the burden of persuasion on defendant on the alibi issue, either in parole-revocation proceedings or for that matter in a criminal prosecution.[8] If defendant should not have to bear the burden

---

7. On the scope of this "good cause" exception, see cases collected in Note, Revocation of Conditional Liberty for the Commission of a Crime: Double Jeopardy and Self-Incrimination Limitations, 74 Mich. L. Rev. 525, 527 & n. 13 (1976).

8. The allocation of the burden of persuasion on alibi claims in criminal prosecutions is considered at page 77 supra.

of persuasion, is it sound to require him to bear the risk of inability to produce the crucial witnesses?

Assuming that a right to compulsory process should be recognized in general, what circumstances would provide "good cause" for restricting the right? Are distance and expense relevant? What should be the bearing of the fact that, as in *Standlee,* the witness has already testified in related criminal proceedings; does the availability of the transcript of those proceedings make the witness's presence less essential, or does the confirmed importance of the credibility issue make the witness's presence even more essential?

b. The Parole-Release Decision

GREENHOLTZ v. INMATES OF NEBRASKA PENAL & CORRECTIONAL
COMPLEX

Supreme Court of the United States
442 U.S. 1 (1979)

[A group of Nebraska prisoners brought suit against the state parole board, claiming that state statutes and board procedures denied them procedural due process. The statutes provided that prisoners become eligible for release on parole after serving their minimum term, less good-time credits. Each prisoner (whether or not eligible for release) was granted an "initial parole review hearing" at least once a year. This procedure involved board review of the prisoner's file, followed by an informal interview with the prisoner. If the Board decided to deny parole at this point, it would inform the inmate why release was deferred and make recommendations designed to help the inmate correct any deficiencies observed; if the board decided that the prisoner was a likely candidate for release, a "final hearing" would be scheduled. At the final hearing, the inmate could present evidence, call witnesses, and be represented by private counsel of his choice. However, the inmate was not permitted to cross-examine any adverse witnesses or even to hear their testimony. If parole was denied, the board would provide a written statement of reasons for denial within 30 days.

[The United States Court of Appeals held that the prisoners had a constitutionally protected interest in "conditional liberty" under Morrissey v. Brewer, 408 U.S. 471 (1972), and that the board's procedures fell short of those required by due process. The court of appeals required, among other things, that each prisoner eligible for parole receive a full formal hearing, with the right to advance notice of the date of the hearing, the right to appear in person and present written evidence (though not the right to call witnesses in his behalf), and the right, if parole is denied, to a written statement of both the facts relied upon and the reasons for denying parole. The Supreme Court granted review.]

MR. CHIEF JUSTICE BURGER delivered the opinion of the Court. . . .

The Due Process Clause applies when government action deprives a person of liberty or property. . . . This has meant that to obtain a protectible right "a person clearly must have more than an abstract need or desire for it. He must have more than a unilateral expectation of it. He must, instead, have a legitimate claim of entitlement to it." . . . [Board of Regents v. Roth, 408 U.S. 564, 577 (1972)].

There is no constitutional or inherent right of a convicted person to be conditionally released before the expiration of a valid sentence. The natural desire of an individual to be released is indistinguishable from the initial resistance to being confined. But the conviction, with all its procedural safeguards, has extinguished that liberty right: "[G]iven a valid conviction, the criminal defendant has been constitutionally deprived of his liberty." Meachum v. Fano, 427 U.S. 215, 224 (1977).

Decisions of the Executive Branch, however serious their impact, do not automatically invoke due process protection; there simply is no constitutional guarantee that all executive decisionmaking must comply with standards that assure error-free determinations. This is especially true with respect to the sensitive choices presented by the administrative decision to grant parole release.

. . . In parole releases, like its siblings probation release and institution rehabilitation, few certainties exist. In each case, the decision differs from the traditional mold of judicial decisionmaking in that the choice involves a synthesis of record facts and personal observation filtered through the experience of the decisionmaker and leading to a predictive judgment as to what is best both for the individual inmate and for the community. . . . The entire inquiry is, in a sense, an "equity" type judgment that cannot always be articulated in traditional findings.

Respondents suggest two theories to support their view that they have a constitutionally protected interest in a parole determination which calls for the process mandated by the Court of Appeals. First, they claim that a reasonable entitlement is created whenever a state provides for the *possibility* of parole. Alternatively, they claim that the language in Nebraska's statute, Neb. Rev. Stat. §83-1,114(1), creates a legitimate expectation of parole, invoking due process protections.

In support of their first theory, respondents rely heavily on Morrissey v. Brewer, supra, where we held that a parole revocation determination must meet certain due process standards. . . . The fallacy in respondents' position is that parole *release* and parole *revocation* are quite different. There is a crucial distinction between being deprived of a liberty one has, as in parole, and being denied a conditional liberty that one desires. The parolees in *Morrissey* . . . were at liberty and as such could "be gainfully employed and [were] free to be with family and friends and to form the other enduring attachments of normal life." 408 U.S., at 482. The inmates here, on the other hand, are confined and thus subject to all of the necessary restraints that inhere in a prison.

A second important difference between discretionary parole *release* from confinement and *termination* of parole lies in the nature of the decision that must be made in each case. . . . The parole release decision . . . is more subtle and depends on an amalgam of elements, some of which are factual but many of which are purely subjective appraisals by the Board members based upon their experience with the difficult and sensitive task of evaluating the advisability of parole release. . . . The decision turns on a "discretionary assessment of a multiplicity of imponderables, entailing primarily what a man is and what he may become rather than simply what he has done." Kadish, The Advocate and the Expert — Counsel in the Peno-Correctional Process, 45 Minn. L. Rev. 803, 813 (1961).

That the state holds out the *possibility* of parole provides no more than a mere hope that the benefit will be obtained, . . . a hope which is not protected by due process.

Respondents' second argument is that the Nebraska statutory language itself creates a protectible expectation of parole. They rely on the section which provides in part:

> Whenever the Board of Parole considers the release of a committed offender who is eligible for release on parole, it shall order his release unless it is of the opinion that his release should be deferred because:
>
> (a) There is a substantial risk that he will not conform to the conditions of parole;
>
> (b) His release would depreciate the seriousness of his crime or promote disrespect for law;
>
> (c) His release would have a substantially adverse effect on institutional discipline; or
>
> (d) His continued correctional treatment, medical care, or vocational or other training in the facility will substantially enhance his capacity to lead a law-abiding life when released at a later date. Neb. Rev. Stat. §83-1,114(1).[5]

Respondents emphasize that the structure of the provision together with the use of the word "shall" binds the Board of Parole to release an inmate unless any one of the four specifically designated reasons are found. . . .

. . . We can accept respondent's view that the expectancy of release provided in this statute is entitled to some measure of constitutional protection. However, we emphasize that this statute has unique structure and language and thus whether any other state statute provides a protectible entitlement must be decided on a case-by-case basis. We therefore turn to an examination of the statutory procedures to determine whether they provide the process that is due in these circumstances.

. . . No ideal, error-free way to make parole release decisions has been developed; the whole question has been and will continue to be the subject of experimentation involving analysis of psychological factors combined with fact evaluation guided by the practical experience of the actual parole decisionmakers in predicting future behavior. Our system of federalism encourages this state experimentation. If parole determinations are encumbered by procedures that states regard as burdensome and unwarranted, they may abandon or curtail parole. . . .

Procedures designed to elicit specific facts, such as those required in *Morrissey* . . . are not necessarily appropriate to a Nebraska parole determination. . . . Two procedures mandated by the Court of Appeals are particularly challenged by the Board:[6] the requirement that a formal hearing be held for every inmate,

---

5. The statute also provides a list of 14 explicit factors and one catch-all factor that the Board is obligated to consider in reaching a decision. Neb. Rev. Stat. §83-1,114(2)(a)-(n). . . .

6. The Board also objects to the Court of Appeals' order that it provide written notice reasonably in advance of the hearing together with a list of factors that might be considered. At present the Board informs the inmate in advance of the month during which the hearing will be held, thereby allowing time to secure letters or statements; on the day of the hearing it posts notice of the exact time. There is no claim that either the timing of the notice or its substance seriously prejudices the inmate's ability to prepare adequately for the hearing. The present notice is constitutionally adequate.

and the requirement that every adverse parole decision include a statement of the evidence relied upon by the Board.

The requirement of a hearing as prescribed by the Court of Appeals in all cases would provide at best a negligible decrease in the risk of error. See D. Stanley, Prisoners Among Us 43 (1976). . . . At the Board's initial interview hearing, the inmate is permitted to appear before the Board and present letters and statements on his own behalf. He is thereby provided with an effective opportunity to insure, first, that the records before the Board are in fact the records relating to his case; and second, to present any special considerations demonstrating why he is an appropriate candidate for parole. Since the decision is one that must be made largely on the basis of the inmate's files, this procedure adequately safeguards against serious risks of error and thus satisfies due process.

Next, . . . [t]o require the parole authority to provide a summary of the evidence would tend to convert the process into an adversary proceeding and to equate the Board's parole release determination with a guilt determination. . . . The Board's decision is much like a sentencing judge's choice — provided by many states — to grant or deny probation following a judgment of guilt, a choice never thought to require more than what Nebraska now provides for the parole release determination. Cf. Dorszynski v. United States, 418 U.S. 424 (1974). The Nebraska procedure affords an opportunity to be heard and when parole is denied it informs the inmate in what respects he falls short of qualifying for parole; this affords the process that is due under these circumstances. . . .

Reversed.

Mr. Justice Powell, concurring in part and dissenting in part.

I agree with the Court that the respondents have a right under the Fourteenth Amendment to due process in the consideration of their release on parole. I do not believe, however, that the applicability of the Due Process Clause to parole release determinations depends upon the particular wording of the statute governing the deliberations of the parole board. . . . Nothing in the Constitution requires a State to provide for probation or parole. But when a State adopts a parole system that applies general standards of eligibility, prisoners justifiably expect that parole will be granted fairly and according to law whenever those standards are met. This is so whether the governing statute states, as here, that parole "shall" be granted unless certain conditions exist, or provides some other standard for making the parole decision. Contrary to the Court's conclusion, I am convinced that the presence of a parole system is sufficient to create a liberty interest, protected by the Constitution, in the parole release decision.

The Court correctly concludes, in my view, that the Court of Appeals erred in ordering that a formal hearing be held for every inmate and that every adverse parole decision include a statement of the evidence relied upon by the Board. . . . I do not agree, however, with the Court's decision that the present notice afforded to prisoners scheduled for final hearings . . . is constitutionally adequate. . . . [A]lthough a prisoner is allowed "[to] present evidence, call witnesses and be represented by private counsel," at the final hearing, his ability to do so necessarily is reduced or nullified completely by the State's refusal to give notice of the hearing more than a few hours in advance. . . .

Mr. Justice Marshall, with whom Mr. Justice Brennan and Mr. Justice Stevens join, dissenting in part. . . .

A criminal offender's interest in securing release on parole is . . . directly comparable to the liberty interests we recognized in *Morrissey*. . . . [T]he Court finds a difference of constitutional dimension between a deprivation of liberty one has and a denial of liberty one desires. While there is obviously some difference, it is not one relevant to the established constitutional inquiry. . . . As the Court of Appeals for the Second Circuit has recognized, "[w]hether the immediate issue be release or revocation, the stakes are the same: conditional freedom versus incarceration." United States ex rel. Johnson v. Chairman of New York State Board of Parole, 500 F.2d 925, 928 (CA2 1974). . . .

The Court's second justification for distinguishing between parole release and parole revocation is based on the "nature of the decision that must be made in each case." But even assuming the subjective nature of the decisionmaking process were relevant to due process analysis in general, this consideration does not adequately distinguish the processes of granting and revoking parole. . . . *Morrissey* . . . makes clear that the parole revocation decision includes a decisive subjective component. Moreover, to the extent parole release proceedings hinge on predictive determinations, those assessments are necessarily predicated on findings of fact. Accordingly, the presence of subjective considerations is a completely untenable basis for distinguishing the interests at stake here from the liberty interest recognized in *Morrissey*.

The Court also concludes that the existence of a parole system by itself creates "no more than a mere hope that the benefit will be obtained," and thus does not give rise to a liberty interest. . . . [T]he available evidence belies the majority's broad assumptions concerning inmate expectations, at least with respect to the federal system, and there is no suggestion that experience in other jurisdictions is significantly different.[10]

I also cannot subscribe to the Court's assessment of the procedures necessary to safeguard respondents' liberty interest. . . . [The Court] assumes existing procedures adequately reduce the likelihood that an inmate's files will contain incorrect information which could lead to an erroneous decision. No support is cited for this assumption, and the record affords none. In fact, researchers and courts have discovered many substantial inaccuracies in inmate files, and evidence in the instant case revealed similar errors. . . .

Finally, apart from avoiding the risk of actual error, this Court has stressed the importance of adopting procedures that preserve the appearance of fairness and the confidence of inmates in the decisionmaking process. The Chief Justice recognized in *Morrissey* that "fair treatment in parole revocations will enhance the chance of rehabilitation by avoiding reactions to arbitrariness." . . . As Justice Frankfurter argued in Joint Anti-Fascist Refugee Committee v. McGrath, 341 U.S. 123, 171-172 (1951) (concurring): "The validity and moral authority of a conclusion largely depend on the mode by which it was reached. Secrecy is not congenial to truth-seeking and self-righteousness gives too slender an assurance of rightness. No better instrument has been devised for arriving at truth than to give a person in jeopardy of serious loss notice of the case against him and opportunity to meet it. Nor has a better way been found for generating the feeling, so important to a popular government, that justice has been done."

---

10. The New York State Parole Board, for example, granted parole in 75.4% of the cases it considered during 1972. . . .

In my judgment, the need to assure the appearance, as well as the existence, of fairness supports a requirement that the Parole Board advise inmates of the specific dates for their hearings, the criteria to be applied, and the reasons and essential facts underlying adverse decisions. . . .

While the question is close, I agree with the majority that a formal hearing is not always required when an inmate first becomes eligible for discretionary parole. . . . The Court of Appeals directed the Parole Board to conduct such a formal hearing as soon as an inmate becomes eligible for parole, even where the likelihood of a favorable decision is negligible, but the court required no hearing thereafter. From a practical standpoint, this relief offers no appreciable advantage to the inmates. . . . I believe the Board's current practice of combining both formal and informal hearings is constitutionally sufficient. . . .

[However,] I would require the Board to provide a statement of the crucial evidence on which it relies in denying parole. . . . [I]t is difficult to believe that subsequently disclosing the factual justification for a decision will render the proceeding more adversarial, especially when the Board already provides a general statement of reasons. Such a requirement would direct the Board's focus to the relevant statutory criteria and promote more careful consideration of the evidence. It would also enable inmates to detect and correct inaccuracies that could have a decisive impact.[23]

. . . I respectfully dissent.

NOTE

Connecticut Board of Pardons v. Dumschat, 101 S. Ct. 2460 (1981), involved a challenge to Connecticut procedures affecting inmates sentenced to life imprisonment. Those inmates were required to serve a minimum term (20 years in most cases), but state law established a Board of Pardons empowered to reduce the minimum term and thus accelerate eligibility for parole. Evidence showed that at least 75 percent of those serving life sentences received such a reduction from the Board of Pardons before completing the minimum term and that virtually all of the inmates benefiting from such a reduction were promptly paroled. The chairman of the Board of Parole testified that "no more than 10 or 15 percent" of the state's life inmates serve their 20-year minimum terms.

The United States Court of Appeals held that although the Connecticut statutes, unlike those considered in *Greenholtz*, did not contain a presumption in favor of early release or any list of specific factors to be considered, nevertheless the "overwhelming likelihood that Connecticut life inmates will be pardoned and released before they complete their minimum terms gives them a constitutionally protected liberty interest in pardon proceedings." 618 F.2d 216, 220 (2d Cir. 1980).

---

23. The preprinted list of reasons for denying parole is unlikely to disclose these types of factual errors. Out of 375 inmates denied parole during a six-month period, the only reason given 285 of them was: "Your continued correctional treatment, vocational, education, or job assignment in the facility will substantially enhance your capacity to lead a law-abiding life when released at a later date." Although the denial forms also include a list of six "recommendations for correcting deficiencies," such as "exhibit some responsibility and maturity," the evidence at trial showed that all six items were checked on 370 of the 375 forms, regardless of the facts of the particular case.

The Supreme Court, by a 7 – 2 vote, reversed. Chief Justice Burger, writing for the majority, said (id. at 2464):

> . . . In terms of the Due Process Clause, a Connecticut felon's expectation that a lawfully imposed sentence will be commuted or pardoned is no more substantial than an inmate's expectation, for example, that he will not be transferred to another prison; it is simply a unilateral hope. . . . No matter how frequently a particular form of clemency has been granted, the statistical probabilities standing alone generate no constitutional protections; a contrary conclusion would trivialize the Constitution. The ground for a constitutional claim, if any, must be found in statutes or other rules defining the obligations of the authority charged with exercising clemency.

Justices Brennan and White wrote concurring opinions. Justice Brennan said (id. at 2465):

> [A] statistical likelihood . . . is not enough to create a protectible liberty interest. Rather, respondents must also show — by reference to statute, regulation, administrative practice, contractual arrangement or other mutual understanding — that particularized standards or criteria guide the State's decisionmakers. The *structure* of the State's decisionmaking process is thus as significant as the likely *result* of that process. Respondents have not shown that the Board is required to base its decisions on objective and defined criteria. As in Meachum v. Fano, 427 U.S. 215, 228 (1976), the decisionmaker can deny the requested relief for any constitutionally permissible reason or for no reason at all. Accordingly, I agree that respondents have no protectible liberty interest in a pardon.

Justices Stevens and Marshall dissented.

6. Guilty Plea Sentencing

INTRODUCTORY NOTE

In Chapter 2, pages 147-168 supra, we examined the plea bargaining system as a means of ascertaining guilt and considered the factors that have led the Supreme Court to approve more lenient treatment for defendants who plead guilty. The present section examines the plea bargaining system as a means of influencing or determining the punishment imposed.

S. SCHULHOFER, PROSECUTORIAL DISCRETION AND FEDERAL SENTENCING REFORM 8-12 (Federal Judicial Center 1979): [The] "normal" procedure for determining sentences applies, of course, only in a small minority of cases, since about eighty to ninety percent of all federal convictions are obtained by plea of guilty (or nolo contendere) rather than by trial. Who determines punishment in a guilty plea case? Under the Federal Rules of Criminal Procedure,[a] there are four distinct routes to the imposition of sentence:

---

a. The applicable provisions are contained in Rule 11(e), reprinted at page 153 supra. — Eds.

1. The defendant may plead guilty to all of the original charges, with hopes for leniency but no official assurances
2. The defendant may plead guilty to only some of the initial charges, in exchange for the prosecutor's agreement to dismiss the remainder (rule 11(e)(1)(A))
3. The defendant may plead guilty (either to all or some of the charges) in exchange for the prosecutor's agreement to make a nonbinding recommendation on sentence (rule 11(e)(1)(B))
4. The defendant may plead guilty pursuant to an agreement specifying the sentence that must be imposed if the guilty plea is accepted (rule 11(e)(1)(C)).

In the first instance, the mix of prosecutorial, judicial, and Parole Commission roles is identical to that in contested cases. In the other three situations, it becomes difficult to generalize; solid empirical evidence concerning the distribution of sentencing power is virtually nonexistent. In a charge-reduction agreement (item 2.), the prosecutor controls the outer boundaries of sentencing, but since the judge will generally have the option to impose substantial prison terms even after charge reduction, the determination whether the defendant will go to prison, and if so, for how long, remains largely under judicial control.[b]

In an agreement for a recommended sentence (item 3.), the judge is, in theory, free to disregard the recommendation and impose any sentence within statutory limits. In practice, the judge cannot exercise this prerogative very often without eliminating defendants' willingness to tender this type of plea. Government recommendations therefore are probably accepted in most instances. It cannot be assumed, however, that the prosecution in fact controls the sentencing decision here. A few judicial decisions rejecting recommended sentences can suffice to communicate the court's preferences, and thereafter recommendations will normally conform to what the judge will accept — they must do so if the prosecutor is to retain the credibility of this inducement to plead. Thus a process of mutual accommodation between prosecutors and judges may determine the actual level of sentences imposed in "recommendation" cases. And even if the prosecutor plays the dominant role in practice, he can retain control over sentencing only with the court's continued acquiescence.

The plea agreement for a definite sentence (item 4.) appears to involve the greatest limitation upon the judicial role. Since rejection of the disposition contemplated by the agreement entitles the defendant to withdraw his plea, the court may exercise this prerogative less readily than it would in the case of a nonbinding recommendation. Even so, the court's ability to influence dispositions remains significant. Rejection of the plea in a given case may be followed quickly by a new agreement more acceptable to the judge; if not, subsequent agreements may, as in recommendation cases, tend to conform more closely to judicial preferences. Even in binding agreement cases, therefore, the ultimate pattern of sentences depends on the judge to a great degree, and prosecutorial control can predominate only with the court's express or tacit acquiescence.

---

b. In most jurisdictions the judge can exercise even greater control by refusing to approve the reduction of charges. See page 1100 infra. In that event the defendent is entitled to withdraw his guilty plea, but he or she then must either plead guilty to the original charges or face trial and the possibility of conviction on the original charges. — Eds.

SANTOBELLO v. NEW YORK
Supreme Court of the United States
404 U.S. 257 (1971)

MR. CHIEF JUSTICE BURGER delivered the opinion of the Court.

We granted certiorari in this case to determine whether the State's failure to keep a commitment concerning the sentence recommendation on a guilty plea required a new trial.

The facts are not in dispute. The State of New York indicted petitioner in 1969 on two felony counts, Promoting Gambling in the First Degree, and Possession of Gambling Records in the First Degree, N.Y. Penal Law §§225.10, 225.20. Petitioner first entered a plea of not guilty to both counts. After negotiations, the Assistant District Attorney in charge of the case agreed to permit petitioner to plead guilty to a lesser-included offense, Possession of Gambling Records in the Second Degree, N.Y. Penal Law §225.15, conviction of which would carry a maximum prison sentence of one year. The prosecutor agreed to make no recommendation as to the sentence.

On June 16, 1969, petitioner accordingly withdrew his plea of not guilty and entered a plea of guilty to the lesser charge. Petitioner represented to the sentencing judge that the plea was voluntary and that the facts of the case, as described by the Assistant District Attorney, were true. The court accepted the plea and set a date for sentencing. A series of delays followed. . . . On January 9 petitioner appeared before a different judge. . . . [A]nother prosecutor had replaced the prosecutor who had negotiated the plea. The new prosecutor recommended the maximum one-year sentence. In making this recommendation, he cited petitioner's criminal record and alleged links with organized crime. Defense counsel immediately objected on the ground that the State had promised petitioner before the plea was entered that there would be no sentence recommendation by the prosecution. He sought to adjourn the sentence hearing in order to have time to prepare proof of the first prosecutor's promise. The second prosecutor, apparently ignorant of his colleague's commitment, argued that there was nothing in the record to support petitioner's claim of a promise, but the State, in subsequent proceedings, has not contested that such a promise was made.

The sentencing judge ended discussion, with the following statement, quoting extensively from the presentence report:

> Mr. Aronstein [Defense Counsel], I am not at all influenced by what the District Attorney says, so that there is no need to adjourn the sentence, and there is no need to have any testimony. It doesn't make a particle of difference what the District Attorney says he will do, or what he doesn't do.
>
> I have here, Mr. Aronstein, a probation report. I have here a history of a long, long serious criminal record. I have here a picture of the life history of this man. . . .
>
> Under the plea, I can only send him to the New York City Correctional Institution for men for one year, which I am hereby doing.

The judge then imposed the maximum sentence of one year. . . .

This record represents another example of an unfortunate lapse in orderly prosecutorial procedures, in part, no doubt, because of the enormous increase in the workload of the often understaffed prosecutor's offices. The heavy workload may well explain these episodes, but it does not excuse them. The disposition of criminal charges by agreement between the prosecutor and the accused, sometimes loosely called "plea bargaining," is an essential component of the administration of justice. Properly administered, it is to be encouraged. . . .

This phase of the process of criminal justice, and the adjudicative element inherent in accepting a plea of guilty, must be attended by safeguards to insure the defendant what is reasonably due in the circumstances. Those circumstances will vary, but a constant factor is that when a plea rests in any significant degree on a promise or agreement of the prosecutor, so that it can be said to be part of the inducement or consideration, such promise must be fulfilled. . . . It is now conceded that the promise to abstain from a recommendation was made, and at this stage the prosecution is not in a good position to argue that its inadvertent breach of agreement is immaterial. The staff lawyers in a prosecutor's office have the burden of "letting the left hand know what the right hand is doing" or has done. That the breach of agreement was inadvertent does not lessen its impact.

We need not reach the question whether the sentencing judge would or would not have been influenced had he known all the details of the negotiations for the plea. He stated that the prosecutor's recommendation did not influence him and we have no reason to doubt that. Nevertheless, we conclude that the interests of justice and appropriate recognition of the duties of the prosecution in relation to promises made in the negotiation of pleas of guilty will be best served by remanding the case to the state courts for further consideration. The ultimate relief to which petitioner is entitled we leave to the discretion of the state court, which is in a better position to decide whether the circumstances of this case require only that there be specific performance of the agreement on the plea, in which case petitioner should be resentenced by a different judge, or whether, in the view of the state court, the circumstances require granting the relief sought by petitioner, i.e., the opportunity to withdraw his plea of guilty. . . .

The judgment is vacated and the case is remanded for reconsideration not inconsistent with this opinion.

MR. JUSTICE DOUGLAS, concurring. . . .

Where the "plea bargain" is not kept by the prosecutor, the sentence must be vacated and the state court will decide in light of the circumstances of each case whether due process requires (a) that there be specific performance of the plea bargain or (b) that the defendant be given the option to go to trial on the original charges. One alternative may do justice in one case, and the other in a different case. In choosing a remedy, however, a court ought to accord a defendant's preference considerable, if not controlling, weight inasmuch as the fundamental rights flouted by a prosecutor's breach of a plea bargain are those of the defendant, not of the State.

[A separate opinion by JUSTICE MARSHALL, joined by JUSTICES BRENNAN and STEWART, is omitted.]

NOTES

1. The source of the obligation to honor plea commitments. The *Santobello* obligation to honor promises made to induce a guilty plea seems self-evidently just. But what is the constitutional basis for this principle? Consider the following alternative explanations and their divergent implications for the scope of the rights recognized in *Santobello*.

(*a*) *The prerequisties of a valid plea.* Once a guilty plea has been made, shouldn't the appropriate sentence be determined by a neutral assessment of the punishment warranted by the offense rather than by negotiation? Perhaps part of the answer is that the plea itself is not valid unless it represents a voluntary and intelligent waiver of the right to trial. See page 150 supra. But precisely how does a prosecutor's breach of promise defeat these requirements? If the choice to plead guilty is voluntary when made, it is hard to see how that choice could be rendered involuntary retrospectively by a prosecutor's failure to perform the promise. If the choice is based on an assumption of full performance, then the failure to perform could indeed be seen as rendering the plea decision "unintelligent." But this problem could be avoided either by the *Santobello* solution, guaranteeing full performance, or by a clear announcement that there is a risk of nonperformance, which defendants must weigh in their decisions. Why did the *Santobello* court take the former route? Does the Court's choice reflect recognition that defendant's actual expectations are not likely to adjust to technical provisos and subtle risks of nonperformance? If so, does *Santobello* in effect suggest that the "intelligence" of the waiver and thus the validity of the plea depend on fulfillment of defendant's good faith expectations (at least when "reasonable"), regardless of whether the prosecutor technically guaranteed the expected results? What (if anything) would be wrong with such a standard?[9]

(*b*) *The principle of governmental fair dealing.* If *Santobello* cannot be satisfactorily explained as an effort to protect the good faith, subjective expectations of the defense, does it reflect instead a notion that government should be held to standards of honesty and reliability in its dealings? An argument to this effect is developed in Westen & Westin, A Constitutional Law of Remedies for Broken Plea Bargains, 66 Calif. L. Rev. 471 (1978).

Does this notion have constitutional roots? Consider, for example, whether the constitution should require New York to honor an unauthorized commitment to buy supplies made by an employee in a state purchasing agency. Should the commitment be binding even if the seller has not yet relied on it to its detriment? If not, should the principle of fair dealing nonetheless have greater force in the plea bargaining context? A formal guarantee of governmental reliability undoubtedly enhances the smooth functioning of the plea bargaining system. But does the constitution require that New York's plea bargaining system be an efficient one? Is New York required to permit plea bargaining at all?

If the principle of fair dealing is necessary to account for *Santobello*, what remedy is called for in the event of governmental misconduct? Should a breach of promise generate only a right to withdraw the plea? If the defendant has already suffered detrimental reliance (for example, by testifying against coconspirators or by serving a portion of his or her sentence on the plea), it may be impossible to restore the status quo ante, and specific performance may be the only equitable alternative. But suppose that the defendant has not yet begun to serve his or her sentence and that the status quo ante can be fully restored

---

9. Consider whether cases such as United States v. Miller, page 1099 infra, and United States v. Needles, page 1100 infra, are consistent with this standard. If not, which approach is preferable?

by vacating the conviction. Should the defendant nevertheless be entitled to insist that his or her expectations be fulfilled, that is, that specific performance of the bargain be ordered? What (if anything) would be wrong with such a requirement?[10]

In reviewing the materials that follow, consider the extent to which the primary objective of the decisions should be to protect the legitimate expectations of the defense, to enforce standards of fair dealing by the government, or to permit the widest latitude for the choice of a suitable sentence by the judge.

2. *Determining the scope of the bargain.* How should courts determine the precise nature of the plea commitments made? Consider these situations:

(a) *Making or withholding recommendations.* In United States v. Crusco, 536 F.2d 21 (3d Cir. 1976), a defendant indicted on two drug charges agreed to plead guilty to one count, carrying a 15-year maximum sentence. In return, the prosecution promised "to take no position on sentencing." At the sentencing hearing, the defense attorney pleaded for leniency, citing defendant's integrity and claiming that "by no stretch of the imagination is he a heavy weight or a person in a position to deal in large quantities of drugs." The government then responded by pointing to facts tending to suggest that defendant held a high position in the organized crime hierarchy. The Court of Appeals held this to be a breach of the bargain and allowed defendant to withdraw his plea. The court rejected the government's claim that its factual comments did not amount to a "position on sentencing" and also rejected its claim that misrepresentations by the defense attorney had opened the way for the prosecutor to set the record straight. Thus, despite the "hyperbole" of the defense argument, the government's promise to "take no position" barred it from making a response.

United States v. Miller, 565 F.2d 1273 (3d Cir. 1977), involved a similar episode of defense pleas for leniency, followed by government rebuttal of the defense assertions. In this instance, however, the government had promised in connection with the plea bargain, "to make no recommendation as to sentence." The Court of Appeals held that this promise was not violated by the remarks made at sentencing and distinguished *Crusco* on the ground that the promise in that case "to take no position" was broader than a promise "to make no recommendation." One judge dissented, viewing the case as indistinguishable from *Crusco.*

Questions: (i) Does the result in *Miller* depend on the fact that the defense had made arguably inaccurate factual claims. If the commitment "to make no recommendation" has no more meaning than the *Miller* court seems to give it, can the prosecutor stress derogatory facts regardless of what the defense might say? Is this fair to the defense?

(ii) Given the *Crusco* decision, careful prosecutors are unlikely to extend a commitment "to take no position." But suppose that defense counsel does succeed in getting such a promise. How much "hyperbole" may defense counsel

---

10. Consider the rules previously mentioned, to the effect that plea agreements contemplating dismissal of charges or imposition of a definite sentence are subject to judicial approval and that if approval is denied, the defendant is entitled to withdraw the plea. See page 1095 supra. If the defendant could compel enforcement of the prosecutor's promise, would judges lose their capacity to influence the propriety and consistency of punishments imposed in guilty plea cases? If so, would the overall fairness of the guilty plea system be enhanced or diminished?

ethically employ in pleading for leniency? Conversely, suppose that a prosecutor finds it tactically advantageous to extend a *Crusco*-type commitment. Is it ethical or fair to the sentencing court for a prosecutor to make that kind of a promise?

(iii) Should the scope of such prosecutorial promises be broadly construed in order to protect legitimate defense expectations, or should their scope be narrowly construed, in order to avoid trapping the prosecution in an unintended commitment? Which approach facilitates the smooth and reliable functioning of the plea negotiation system? Which approach provides the better basis for penologically sound sentencing decisions?

(*b*) *Dismissal of charges.* (*i*) *The court's prerogative to reject dismissals.* Frequently a guilty plea is offered in exchange for a prosecutor's commitment to dismiss a portion of the charges. In nearly all jurisdictions such dismissals are subject to court approval, because they can affect the scope of the court's sentencing discretion.[11] If the court refuses to approve the dismissal, the defendant must, of course, be permitted to withdraw his or her plea. But if *Santobello* is read to protect bargaining expectations created by prosecutorial officials and to require specific performance of commitments made, would the defendant then have the right to insist on his or her plea and to compel judicial acquiescence in the charge dismissal? Would this approach be sound?

(*ii*) *The court's prerogatives after acceptance of a charge dismissal.* Consider United States v. Needles, 472 F.2d 652 (2d Cir. 1973):

Needles entered his guilty plea before Judge Zavatt on December 29, 1971. At the time, appellant faced an indictment that charged him with 30 separate violations of the Gun Control Act. Appellant was represented by competent counsel, who apparently negotiated an understanding with the Assistant United States Attorney in charge of the case to move to dismiss the remaining 29 counts of the indictment after appellant pleaded guilty to, and was sentenced on, one. . . .

[On the day of sentencing, Needles moved to withdraw his guilty plea because he claimed that the presentence report was replete with inaccurate and derogatory information, notably information relating to the other 29 counts.]

The only issue touching on the guilty plea as to which the alleged errors in the pre-sentence report might arguably be relevant is a defendant's understanding of the "consequences" of his plea when he made it. See Fed. R. Crim. P. 11. The principal "consequence," of course, is the possibility of imprisonment, but this was explained to appellant at the December 29 hearing. We realize that it is the probability of imprisonment, not merely the possibility, that is of crucial interest to a defendant. Nonetheless, "consequence" in this context does not mean a defendant's expectation of leniency, unless it was induced by a government promise; no such promise was made here by the prosecutor, the judge or anyone else. Needles was told only that the Government would move to dismiss the remaining 29 counts of the indictment. This promise was kept at a substantial advantage to defendant, since his potential term of imprisonment was reduced considerably. Appellant's only claim of misrepresentation is that he believed that the prosecutor would make no recommendation as to sentence, that the information contained in the report could only have come from the prosecutor, and that this amounted to bad faith.[2] No such argument was made at the time to the district court. More

11. The issue is discussed in Schulhofer, Due Process of Sentencing, 128 U. Pa. L. Rev. 733, 773-778 (1980).

2. On this point, appellant cites Santobello v. New York, 404 U.S. 257 (1971), a case manifestly inapplicable on its facts.

significantly, no defendant can reasonably expect the probation office to refrain from seeking whatever information the prosecutor may have regarding the case then before the court or any other case involving that defendant. In fact, failure to so inquire or refusal to respond accurately would be a breach of duty. What appellant's argument is reduced to, in the last analysis, is that the information that led to a 30-count indictment should have been hidden from the sentencing judge and that appellant could reasonably have so expected. The argument falls of its own weight.

Schulhofer, Due Process of Sentencing, 128 U. Pa. L. Rev. 733, 757-758 (1980): Available evidence suggests that criminal sentencing decisions . . . are based heavily upon actual offense behavior as distinguished from the formal offense of conviction. Empirical studies of judicial sentencing indicate that in many jurisdictions prosecutorial decisions to reduce pending charges appear to have little or no impact on the sentence ultimately imposed.[97] Efforts to study the same phenomenon by interviewing and other nonstatistical techniques confirm the impression that many judges currently disregard charge-reduction agreements and treat the defendant much the same as if he or she had been convicted on the initial charges. Parole boards have long been suspected of following the same practice.

This process of real-offense sentencing provides a means through which the prosecutor's formally uncontrolled sentencing powers can, to some degree, be held in check. But the broad judicial and parole board discretion that currently afford the opportunity for real-offense judgments serve at the same time to obscure the very existence of this practice, as well as its many potentially unfair effects. A judge's or parole official's impressions about the seriousness of the actual offense behavior need not be made explicit and rarely can be challenged in a way that would ensure their reliability. Defendants and defense counsel unaware of the practice or uncertain about its precise extent may greatly overestimate the advantages of a charge-reduction plea agreement. In current practice, real-offense sentencing thus neutralizes part of the threat to fair process posed by untrammeled prosecutorial powers, but it creates new problems of fairness at least as serious as those it seeks so crudely and unsystematically to remedy.

COOPER v. UNITED STATES
United States Court of Appeals, 4th Circuit
594 F.2d 12 (1979)

PHILLIPS, J. Cooper appeals his jury trial conviction on two counts of bribery of a witness, 18 U.S.C. §201(e), and two counts of obstruction of justice, 18 U.S.C. §1503. He assigns errors in the . . . refusal of the district court to compel enforcement of a proposal made to him by the government in plea discussions. . . .

---

97. See, e.g., J. Eisenstein & H. Jacob, Felony Justice: An Organizational Analysis of Criminal Courts 131-34, 160, 279-83 (1977); Rhodes, Plea Bargaining: Who Gains? Who Loses?, at V-8 to V-10 (1978); Wilkins, Kress, Gottfredson, Caplin, & Gelman, Sentencing Guidelines: Structuring Judicial Discretion 88 (1976). Contra, Shin, Do Lesser Pleas Pay?: Accommodations in the Sentencing and Parole Processes, 1 J. Crim. Just. 27, 34-35 (1973). [For critical analysis of the data, see Alschuler, The Changing Plea-Bargaining Debate, 69 Calif. L. Rev. 652, 654-656 n. 7 (1981).]

About two months before Cooper's trial, at around 11:00 A.M. on May 11, 1977, an Assistant United States Attorney and Cooper's then defense counsel met to discuss a possible plea bargain. After some initial negotiations, the government attorney proposed a plea agreement under which defendant would (a) be removed from the Witness Protection Program, (b) remain incarcerated, (c) continue to cooperate with the federal authorities, (d) plead guilty to one count of obstruction of justice, and (e) testify on three occasions in the on-going narcotics trials, while the government would (a) bring defendant's cooperation to the sentencing judge's attention, and (b) dismiss all other counts of the indictment. Defense counsel agreed to communicate the proposal to defendant, who was then incarcerated, and to get back to the government promptly.

Defense counsel immediately visited Cooper and obtained his agreement to the proposal. Beginning at approximately noon on May 11, defense counsel attempted to call the Assistant United States Attorney and notify him of Cooper's acceptance but could not reach him. At 1:30 P.M. on May 11, the Assistant United States Attorney met with his superior, the United States Attorney for the District of Maryland, and was instructed by the latter to withdraw the proposal. When the Assistant United States Attorney and defense counsel finally made telephone contact later that afternoon between 2:30 and 3:30 P.M., Cooper's counsel was notified at the outset that the offer had been withdrawn. Defense counsel protested that this was not acceptable practice, and that Cooper had agreed to accept the proposal. When his protests were unavailing, he requested and received permission to carry his objection to the United States Attorney. This was done, but again to no avail. Defendant then moved to compel enforcement of the proposal, and at a pretrial hearing this motion was denied by the district court. Cooper's conviction on four counts, sentencing to a total of fifteen years imprisonment, and appeal followed.

In giving formal approval to plea bargaining as an essential and desirable practice in the administration of criminal justice, the Supreme Court in Santobello v. New York, 404 U.S. 257 (1971), made only brief allusion to the substantive principles that should control the practice. . . . [T]he precise source and specific content of the right recognized and given protection in that case were not developed, but it was plain in context that the source was constitutional.

Both before and since *Santobello,* the courts have understandably drawn heavily on the ready analogies of substantive and remedial contract law to supply the body of doctrine necessary to order plea bargaining practices and to afford relief to defendants aggrieved in the negotiating process. To the extent therefore that there has evolved any general body of "plea bargain law," it is heavily freighted with these contract law analogies.[4] When *Santobello* made it plain, however, that the core concept here is the existence of a constitutional right in the defendant to be treated with "fairness" throughout the process, this presaged inevitably the question of the extent to which contract law may be drawn upon to define the limits of this constitutional right. That is the precise issue presented in this case, where we are asked to find and enforce a right probably lying beyond any provided by contract law analogy.

In each of the earlier cases in which this court has found violations of defendants' plea negotiation rights, the defendant had entered a guilty plea and in

---

4. The cases are exhaustively collected and analyzed in these terms in P. Westen & D. Westin, A Constitutional Law of Remedies for Broken Plea Bargains, 66 Calif. L. Rev. 471 (1978).

some instances performed other obligations of a struck plea agreement before the government reneged on some element of its undertaking. . . . Therefore, in each of these cases a specific agreement had clearly been reached and the defendant had fully or substantially performed his side of the bargain before asserting any denial of right by the government's failure fully to perform its side. Accordingly, it was possible in each to view the defendant's situation as one perfectly analogous to that of any party aggrieved by the breach of an express commercial contract or by the failure of another to perform a promise upon which the party had relied to his tangible detriment, and to give an appropriate remedy — specific performance or rescission — again drawn from remedial contract law.

This is not the situation here. In this case we are asked to find a right and provide a remedy for a defendant whose attempted acceptance of a plea proposal was preceded by an asserted withdrawal of the proposal, so that in classic contract law there had arisen no right to be violated by the government and enforced by the courts. The alternative of "promissory estoppel" would seem no more available because of the lack of any tangible "detrimental reliance" by the defendant, who at this point had been able to do no more than form the subjective intent to accept the offer and experience whatever expectations of benefit had been created by anticipation of its fulfillment. Obviously analyzing the claim of right and violation essentially in these terms, the district court found no merit in it and accordingly denied the relief sought.

While we agree that within classic contract doctrine the defendant here could probably claim no right and hence show no violation, we nonetheless conclude that right and violation of right was shown, and that relief must be given. This, of course, means that we find the constitutional right to "fairness" to be wider in scope than that defined by the law of contract. . . . In quite general terms, analogies from contract law will usually provide a reliable inclusive test for the existence of constitutional right and violation, but not an equally reliable exclusive test. Conduct by government prosecutors that in the market place would constitute breach of contract or give rise to promissory estoppel will practically always reflect constitutionally unfair conduct in transactions between sovereign and citizen in matters of liberty and punishment. But the obverse of this does not follow. Just because the elements of express contract or promissory estoppel have not been realized in particular plea negotiations cannot mean conclusively that there has been no unfairness in the constitutional sense. This is primarily because contract law is not concerned solely with fairness. . . . [C]ontract law also contains many elements of an essentially neutral moral and ethical cast. Some of these reflect merely a pragmatic necessity to force certainty of consequences in complicated negotiation exchanges, . . . such [as] mechanical rules . . . dictating the consequences of particular sequences in the transmission and receipt of contract offers, acceptances, withdrawals, etc. . . . These are all well and good for contract law, but constitutional decisions cannot be made to turn in favor of the government on the fortuities of communications or on a refusal to accord any substantive value to reasonably induced expectations that government will honor its firmly advanced proposals. . . .

We begin by noting that two distinct sources of constitutional right are involved here: most obviously and directly, the right to fundamental fairness embraced within substantive due process guarantees; less directly perhaps, but nonetheless importantly, the Sixth Amendment right to effective assistance of counsel. The general relevance of the former is too plain to require discussion. That of the latter can be readily stated. Because prosecutors are required to conduct plea negotiations through defense counsel, the government's positions and communications in plea discussions are necessarily mediated to the defendant through his counsel. For this reason, not only the credit and integrity of the government but those of his counsel are involved in a defendant's perception of the process. . . . To the extent that the government attempts through defendant's counsel to change or retract positions earlier communicated, a defendant's confidence in his counsel's capability and professional responsibility, as well as in the government's reliability, are necessarily jeopardized and the effectiveness of counsel's assistance easily compromised.[9] . . .

Within this general constitutional framework of substantive due process, here given an added dimension by the necessary implication of the right to effective assistance of counsel, we conclude that the defendant's constitutional rights were here violated by the government's failure to honor its plea proposal. . . . When, as here, such a proposal — specific, unambiguous and not unreasonable on its face — is offered by the government to a defendant through his counsel, constitutional fairness requires that it be fulfilled if within a reasonable time the defendant unequivocally communicates his assent to it, and unless in the interval extenuating circumstances affecting the propriety of the proposal that were unknown to and not reasonably discoverable by the government when the proposal was made have supervened or become known. This necessarily means that once presented, such a proposal may not be withdrawn in the face of proffered acceptance for no other reason than that a superior disagrees with an apparently authorized subordinate's judgment in making it.

We conclude this analysis of constitutional right and violation by looking at the practical consequences on the one hand of recognizing the right, and on the other, of failing to recognize it. . . . Ready means of safeguarding the right here recognized while protecting every legitimate governmental and public interest involved in plea bargaining plainly lie with the Department of Justice and the several offices of the United States Attorneys. First off, no right can arise in a defendant until plea discussions are voluntarily entered into by authorized government agents; there is no constitutional right in defendants to have the government "bargain" in the first instance. Once plea discussions are underway, it clearly lies with these agencies of government, among other things, to keep the left hand informed of the right's doing;[11] to withhold or limit the actual, and circumscribe the apparent, authority of subordinates if this be considered necessary; to incorporate reservations relating to higher level approval routinely in all proposals or specially in some; and, if thought necessary, to protect against perjured testimony of the making and acceptance of proposals by routine require-

9. A subtle point perhaps, but one certainly familiar to every lawyer who has had to take to his client bad news respecting his settlement negotiations with the other side, particularly when these involve unfavorable changes of earlier positions. In the instant case there is indeed a strong indication of just such a loss of confidence. Defense counsel who was involved in the plea negotiations was replaced before trial.

11. Episodic failures of communication and the lack of established procedures to ensure inter and intra-office consistency of plea bargain positions recur in the cases as causes of broken plea bargain promises. . . . Just such a failure of communication or understanding underlay the difficulty here. Government can avoid these; defendants have no control over them.

ments of signed memoranda. We cannot believe such simple and obvious precautions unreasonable or even significantly burdensome from an administrative standpoint. . . .

Reasonableness of the right's recognition is equally compelled by a consideration of the unreasonableness of permitting the indiscriminate withdrawal of plea proposals at the stage attempted in this case. There is no suggestion in this record of deliberate abuse of the assumed opportunity freely to make and withdraw plea proposals as a means of testing the wills and confidence of defendants and their counsel or of deliberate harassment. We must recognize, however, that our failure to find constitutional right and violation in this case would necessarily give judicial approval to a practice whose possibilities for easy abuse, or at least the appearance of abuse, are abundantly clear.

There remains the question of the appropriate remedy for correcting on remand the constitutional error here found. Obviously the only remedy available is specific enforcement of the plea proposal, to the extent that is now possible. Events occurring both in and out of court since the district court declined to enforce the proposal as made have so far compromised the situation that full enforcement may only be approximated now. . . . While it can be assumed that defendant will elect to plead guilty as proposed upon remand, since his conviction must otherwise stand, we can of course only give that as an option; we cannot direct it. Though it is conceivable that defendant might still be held to some aspects of the other obligations of the proposal, we think the situation so far compromised now by the lapse of time and intervening circumstance that this must simply be disregarded on remand. By like token, the government should be now considered relieved of any reciprocal obligations respecting sentencing recommendations. This leaves the proposal to dismiss all other charges, which of course may now be enforced contingent upon the entering of the proposed guilty plea.

Accordingly, we vacate the judgment and remand with instructions that the defendant be now allowed to enter a plea of guilty to one of the counts of obstruction of justice upon which he was convicted. If he does so, the indictment should be dismissed as to all remaining counts; otherwise the judgment may be reinstated. Further proceedings should be conducted by a district judge who has not participated in the prior proceedings, and in the course of any further proceedings the government is relieved of any obligations respecting sentencing recommendations that were included in the original plea proposal. . . .

QUESTIONS

1. What is the basis for the constitutional obligation of specific performance recognized under the circumstances in *Cooper?* Reconsider the possible sources of the *Santobello* principle, discussed in Note 1, page 1097 supra. Do these principles justify: (1) recognition of a constitutionally binding obligation under circumstances that would not give rise to a legal obligation under the ordinary law of contract and (2) a remedy of specific performance even in the absence of detrimental reliance by the defendant?

2. To what extent does the right to specific performance, as recognized by the court in *Cooper,* bind not only the prosecution but also the judge? Note that the plea agreement contemplated dismissal of all but one count and the court ordered that this be done if defendant chose to plead guilty. Does this mean that in order to protect expectations which crystallize when the government makes a plea proposal, the trial judge *must* accept a defendant's voluntary plea and that the constitution forbids the exercise of judicial discretion to reject plea agreements calling for an inappropriate disposition or sentence? Would such a principle serve to enhance the overall fairness of plea bargaining? If the judge's control over plea agreements should be preserved, even at some risk to a defendant's expectations, then do similar considerations suggest preserving control by the supervising prosecutor as well?

3. In *Cooper* the court draws additional support from the Sixth Amendment right to counsel. The point is, as the court indicates, quite "subtle." See page 1104 footnote 9 supra. What are the implications of the court's view of Sixth Amendment requirements?

B.   THE DETERMINATE-SENTENCE MOVEMENT

1.   *The Case for Reform*

F. ALLEN, THE BORDERLAND OF CRIMINAL JUSTICE
32-36 (1964)

. . . [A]n idea once propagated and introduced into the active affairs of life undergoes change. . . . The application of the rehabilitative ideal to the institutions of criminal justice presents a striking example of such a development. . . . [T]he rehabilitative ideal has been debased in practice and . . . the consequences resulting from this debasement are serious and, at times, dangerous.

This proposition may be supported, first, by the observation that, under the dominance of the rehabilitative ideal, the language of therapy is frequently employed, wittingly or unwittingly, to disguise the true state of affairs that prevails in our custodial institutions and at other points in the correctional process. . . . Too often the vocabulary of therapy has been exploited to serve a public-relations function. Recently, I visited an institution devoted to the diagnosis and treatment of disturbed children. The institution had been established with high hopes and, for once, with the enthusiastic support of the state legislature. Nevertheless, fifty minutes of an hour's lecture, delivered by a supervising psychiatrist before we toured the building, were devoted to custodial problems. This fixation on problems of custody was reflected in the institutional arrangements which included, under a properly euphemistic label, a cell for solitary confinement. Even more disturbing was the tendency of the staff to justify these custodial measures in therapeutic terms. Perhaps on occasion the requirements of institutional security and treatment coincide. But the inducements to self-deception in such situations are strong and all too apparent. In short, the language of therapy has frequently provided a formidable obstacle to a realistic analysis of the conditions that confront us. . . .

There is a second kind of unintended consequence that results from the application of the rehabilitative ideal to the practical administration of criminal justice.

Surprisingly enough, the rehabilitative ideal has often led to increased severity of penal measures. . . . The tendency of proposals for wholly indeterminate sentences, a clearly identifiable fruit of the rehabilitative ideal, is unmistakably in the direction of lengthened periods of imprisonment. . . . This reference to the tendency of the rehabilitative ideal to encourage increasingly long periods of incarceration brings me to my final proposition. It is that the rise of the rehabilitative ideal has often been accompanied by attitudes and measures that conflict, sometimes seriously, with the values of individual liberty and volition. . . .

   [A] study of criminal justice is fundamentally a study in the exercise of political power. No such study can properly avoid the problem of the abuse of power. The obligation of containing power within the limits suggested by a community's political values has been considerably complicated by the rise of the rehabilitative ideal. For the problem today is one of regulating the exercise of power by men of good will, whose motivations are to help not to injure, and whose ambitions are quite different from those of the political adventurer so familiar to history. There is a tendency for such persons to claim immunity from the usual forms of restraint and to insist that professionalism and a devotion to science provide sufficient protection against unwarranted invasion of individual rights. This attitude is subjected to mordant criticism by Aldous Huxley in his book Brave New World Revisited. Mr. Huxley observes: "There seems to be a touching belief among certain Ph.D's in sociology that Ph.D's in sociology will never be corrupted by power. Like Sir Galahad's, their strength is the strength of ten because their heart is pure — and their heart is pure because they are scientists and have taken six thousand hours of social studies." I suspect that Mr. Huxley would have been willing to extend his point to include professional groups other than sociologists.

   . . . Measures which subject individuals to the substantial and involuntary deprivation of their liberty contain an inescapable punitive element, and this reality is not altered by the facts that the motivations that prompt incarceration are to provide therapy or otherwise contribute to the person's well-being or reform. As such, these measures must be closely scrutinized to insure that power is being applied consistently with those values of the community that justify interference with liberty for only the most clear and compelling reasons. . . .

AMERICAN FRIENDS SERVICE COMMITTEE,
THE STRUGGLE FOR JUSTICE
39-45 (1971)

   While opposition to "mollycoddling" prisoners still exists, the basic thrust of the [individualized treatment] model has been accepted by almost all liberals, reformers of all persuasions, the scientific community, probably a majority of judges, and those of law-and-order persuasion who perceive the model's repressive potential.

   How has the model united such a motley collection of supporters? Its conceptual simplicity and scientific aura appeal to the pragmatism of a society confident that American know-how can reduce any social problem to manageable proportions. Its professed repudiation of retribution adds moral uplift and an inspirational aura. At the same time, the treatment model is sufficiently vague in concept and flexible in practice to accommodate both the traditional and utilitarian objectives of criminal law administration. . . . Even the proponents of retribution, although denied entry through the front door, soon discovered that harsh sentences could be accommodated within the treatment model as long as they were rationalized in terms of public protection or the necessity for prolonged regimes of reeducation. . . .

When one probes beneath the surface of the treatment model, one finds not only untenable factual assumptions, but also disturbing value judgments . . . :

1. [This] model of criminal justice . . . rests on the proposition that at least in large measure crime is a problem of individual pathology. . . . To the extent that it is also acknowledged that social and environmental factors, such as slums, poverty, unemployment, and parental guidance or the lack of it, also "cause" crime, a program of individualized treatment is inadequate. . . .

2. At the level of individual pathology, treatment ideology assumes that we know something about the individual causes of crime. If it is to have any scientific basis, such knowledge must be based on the study of representative samples both of criminals and of control groups of noncriminals. . . . We have libraries full of criminological research on the etiology of crime, but most of it has been conducted without control groups and therefore tells us nothing about causation. . . .

3. Even if the existence, significance, and characteristics of an individual criminal pathology are unknown, one might in theory still evolve treatment methods that turned criminals into noncriminals. It has been a frequent occurrence in medicine to stumble upon treatments that worked despite ignorance about the cause of the disease or the reasons for the treatment's success. . . . Most research fails . . . [the minimum methodological standards for investigating this possibility.] . . . [T]he apparently insoluble problem of such research is the . . . necessity of establishing indicators to distinguish success from failure. This is true even if one proceeds at the most superficial level, defining failure as recidivism, the commission of another crime following treatment. We have no way of determining the real rate of recidivism because most criminals are undetected and most suspected criminals do not end up being convicted. . . .

4. In the absence of credible scientific data on the causation or treatment of crime, the content of the correctional treatment program rests largely on speculation or on assumptions unrelated to criminality. Thus one finds that accepted correctional practice is dominated by indoctrination in white Anglo-Saxon middle-class values. In institutions this means learning a trade, establishing work habits through the therapy of labor, keeping clean and clean-shaven, minding your own business, and acquiring such basic or supplemental educational skills and religious training as the institution might provide and the parole board might think relevant. . . . Without debating the merits of these ingredients of the good life — those of us not being corrected are free to take them or leave them — the fact that the correlation between such Puritan virtues and crime causation is speculative or nonexistent would, one might suppose, have raised some troubling questions. . . .

5. . . . [A]lthough treatment ideology purports to look beyond the criminal's

crime to the whole personality, and bases its claims to sweeping discretionary power on this rationale, it measures its success against the single factor of an absence of reconviction for a criminal act. Whether or not the subject of the treatment process has acquired greater self-understanding, a sense of purpose and power in his own destiny, or a new awareness of his relatedness to man and the universe is not subject to statistical study and so is omitted from the evaluation.

It will make a critical difference . . . [whether treatment processes instead] tend to stunt the human potential by training programs that, as with animals, condition their subjects to an unthinking conformity to inflexible, externally imposed rules. In studying the criminal justice system we have found few things to be thankful for, but the ineffectiveness of correctional treatment may well be one of those few. . . . If such correctional methods really did work, it might be more success than a free society could endure. . . .

M. FRANKEL, CRIMINAL SENTENCES: LAW WITHOUT ORDER
5, 9-11, 17-23, 98-102 (1973)

. . . [T]he almost wholly unchecked and sweeping powers we give to judges in the fashioning of sentences are terrifying and intolerable for a society that professes devotion to the rule of law. . . .

The . . . problem of excessive judicial power reflects a congeries of causes, advertent and accidental. To look only at the most important and positive of these, the prevalent thesis of the last hundred years or so has been that the treatment of criminals must be "individualized." The Mikado's boast, we have proudly thought, was silly; the punishment in a civilized society must fit the unique criminal, not the crime. . . . The ideal of individualized justice is by no means an unmitigated evil, but it must be an ideal of justice *according to law.* This means we must reject individual distinctions — discriminations, that is — unless they can be justified by relevant tests capable of formulation and application with sufficient objectivity to ensure that the results will be more than the idiosyncratic ukases of particular officials, judges or others. I think an approach to such a standard is possible.[a] . . . [H]owever, if we had to choose between our status quo and a system of narrow "tariffs" for each category of crime, only my prejudiced belief that many judges are humane would make me pause in preferring the latter.

a. Elaborating on this point, Judge Frankel writes (at 98-102): "It is not my claim that rehabilitation is always and everywhere impossible. Nor do I argue that an indeterminate sentence could never be wise and fair. The great evil in current thinking is the pair of false assumptions that (1) rehabilitation is *always* possible and (2) indeterminate sentences are *always* desirable. I urge that the shoe belongs on the other foot. . . . [An indeterminate sentence] may be suitable upon detailed showings in specific cases involving (1) demonstrated needs for rehabilitation and incapacitation and (2) rationally organized means for serving those needs. Otherwise, and for the great majority of cases, sentences ought to be stated with maximum certainty, based almost entirely upon factors known on the day of sentencing, and determined with the nearest approach we can make to objective, equal, and 'impersonal' evaluation of the relevant qualities of both the criminal and the crime." For further development of principles to guide rehabilitation programs in the prison context, after the premises of the individualized-treatment model are rejected, see N. Morris, The Future of Imprisonment 28-57 (1974). — EDS.

Having said that, let me flee from the appearance of undue complacency about the judges. The judges simply are not good enough — nobody could be — to redress the fundamental absurdities of the system. . . .

. . . [S]weeping penalty statutes allow sentences to be "individualized" not so much in terms of defendants but mainly in terms of the wide spectrums of character, bias, neurosis, and daily vagary encountered among occupants of the trial bench. It is no wonder that wherever supposed professionals in the field — criminologists, penologists, probation officers, and, yes, lawyers and judges — discuss sentencing, the talk inevitably dwells upon the problem of "disparity." Some writers have quibbled about the definitiveness of the evidence showing disparity. It is among the least substantial of quibbles. The evidence is conclusive that judges of widely varying attitudes on sentencing, administering statutes that confer huge measures of discretion, mete out widely divergent sentences where the divergences are explainable only by the variations among the judges, not by material differences in the defendants or their crimes. Even in our age of science and skepticism, the conclusion would seem to be among those still acceptable as self-evident. What would require proof of a weighty kind, and something astonishing in the way of theoretical explanation, would be the suggestion that assorted judges, subject to little more than their own unfettered wills, could be expected to impose consistent sentences. In any event, if proof were needed that sentences vary simply because judges vary, there is plenty of it. . . .

[T]he tragic state of disorder in our sentencing practices is not attributable to any unique endowments of sadism or bestiality among judges as a species. Without claiming absolute detachment, I am prepared to hypothesize that judges in general, if only because of occupational conditioning, may be somewhat calmer, more dispassionate, and more humane than the average of people across the board. But nobody has the experience of being sentenced by "judges in general." The particular defendant on some existential day confronts a specific judge. The occupant of the bench on that day may be punitive, patriotic, self-righteous, guilt-ridden, and more than customarily dyspeptic. The vice in our system is that all such qualities have free rein as well as potentially fatal impact upon the defendant's finite life.

Such individual, personal powers are not evil only, or mainly, because evil people may come to hold positions of authority. The more pervasive wrong is that a regime of substantially limitless discretion is by definition arbitrary, capricious, and antithetical to the rule of law. . . .

TWENTIETH CENTURY FUND, TASK FORCE ON CRIMINAL SENTENCING, FAIR AND CERTAIN PUNISHMENT 33 (1976): [T]he vagaries of sentencing — one convicted robber being sentenced to life and another being placed on probation — have seriously affected the deterrent value of criminal sanctions. For many convicted offenders, there is what amounts to amnesty. And for other offenders, often undistinguishable from the first group in terms of past record, current crime, or future dangerousness, there is the injustice of the exemplary sentence. The judge, aware that most persons who commit the particular crime are not sentenced to prison, determines to make an example of this offender and thus sentences him to an unfairly long term.

Such haphazard sentencing does little to increase the deterrent impact of the criminal law, since the potential criminal is likely to calculate his potential sentence by reference to what most similarly situated offenders receive. And the sad fact today is that most criminals do not receive any or very little punishment for their crimes.

This fact presents another kind of danger, mentioned by President Ford in his speech to the California legislature. "There is a temptation," he said, "to call for a massive crackdown on crime and to advocate throwing every convicted felon in jail and throwing the key away." But this temptation must be resisted, as the President cautioned, if for no other reason than that unrealistically high penalties are counterproductive. Because juries refuse to convict, the result is often less, rather than more, imprisonment. And, as the President also pointed out in proposing mandatory sentencing for certain offenses, sentences "need not be severe. It is the certainty of confinement that is presently lacking."

NOTE

Notice that, although critics of indeterminate sentencing share many common perceptions, there are important differences of emphasis among them. Some reject rehabilitation as a goal because it has not proved successful. Others seem concerned because rehabilitation possibly *will* be successful and for that reason will intrude on the individual dignity of the offender. Some critics focus on side effects that a system aimed at rehabilitation may produce (for example, disparity, severity), whether or not it achieves its rehabilitative goal.

Are all of these objections compatible, or is it important to choose among them? Consider, for example, the significance of recent evidence showing that some prison programs may be more effective in reducing recidivism than was previously thought. (See page 209 supra.) Does such evidence strengthen or weaken the case against indeterminacy (or is it beside the point)? Consider the significance of the view, held by some historians of criminal justice, that discretion and indeterminacy in sentencing have functioned to reduce the severity of sanctions. (See page 1053 supra.) If this view is accurate, would it require critics to reassess their assault on rehabilitation, or would the most important objections remain?

Consider which of the various objections is paramount for each of the critics above. Which of these objections (if any) seem important and persuasive to you?

A. VON HIRSCH, DOING JUSTICE: THE CHOICE OF PUNISHMENTS
66, 69-81, 84-90 (1976)

If one asks how severely a wrongdoer deserves to be punished, a familiar principle comes to mind: *Severity of punishment should be commensurate with the seriousness of the wrong.* Only grave wrongs merit severe penalties; minor misdeeds deserve lenient punishments. Disproportionate penalties are undeserved — severe sanctions for minor wrongs or vice versa. This principle has variously been called a principle of "proportionality" or "just deserts"; we prefer to call it *commensurate deserts.* . . .

The principle of commensurate deserts, in our opinion, is a requirement of justice; thus: . . .

The principle ensures, as no utilitarian criterion of allocation can, that the rights of the person punished not be unduly sacrificed for the good of others. When speaking earlier of the general justification of punishment, we argued that the social benefits of punishing do not alone justify depriving the convicted offender of his rights: it is also necessary that the deprivation be deserved. A similar argument holds for allocation. . . . A utilitarian theory of allocation (one based on deterrence, for instance) could lead to punishing the offender more severely than he deserves if the net benefits of so doing were to outweigh the costs. The excess in severity may be useful for society, but that alone should not justify the added intrusion into the rights of the person punished. . . .

Equity is sacrificed when the principle is disregarded, even when done for the sake of crime prevention. Suppose there are two kinds of offenses, A and B, that are of approximately equal seriousness; but that offense B can more effectively be deterred through the use of a severe penalty. Notwithstanding the deterrent utility of punishing offense B more severely, the objection remains that the perpetrators of that offense are being treated as though they are more blameworthy than the perpetrators of offense A — and that is not so if the crimes are of equivalent gravity.

It is sometimes suggested that the principle of commensurate deserts sets only an upper limit on severity — *no more* than so much punishment. We disagree. Imposing only a slight penalty for a serious offense treats the offender as *less* blameworthy than he deserves. Understating the blame depreciates the values that are involved: disproportionately lenient punishment for murder implies that human life — the victim's life — is not worthy of much concern; excessively mild penalties for official corruption denigrate the importance of an equitable political process. The commensurateness principle, in our view, bars disproportionate leniency as well as disproportionate severity.

Norval Morris has recently suggested that the principle sets only broad upper and lower limits — and that, within those limits, the sentence should be determined on utilitarian grounds (e.g., deterrence).[a] Again, we do not agree. . . . If A and B commit a burglary under circumstances suggesting similar culpability, they deserve similar punishments; imposing unequal sanctions on them for utilitarian ends — even within the outer bounds of proportionality Morris proposes — still unjustly treats one as though he were more to blame than the other. . . .

It has also been objected . . . that applying the principle in sentencing decisions would aggravate disparities, given judges' divergent views of the seriousness of offenses. But that holds true only if, as in current practice, the assessment of seriousness is left to the discretion of the individual judge. The principle has to be consistently applied; and consistent application requires . . . the articulation of standards and the placing of limits on individual decision-makers' discretion. . . .

We think that the commensurate-deserts principle should have priority over other objectives in decisions about how much to punish. . . .

In giving the principle this priority, we need not claim the priority to be

a. The reference is to N. Morris, The Future of Imprisonment 60, 74 (1974). — EDS.

absolute: perhaps . . . there are some unusual cases where it will be necessary to vary from the deserved sentence. But the principle derives its force from the fact that it applies *unless* special reasons for departing from it are shown: the burden rests on him who would deviate from the commensurate sentence. . . .

Having argued that the severity of the penalty should depend on the seriousness of the offense, we face the question: How should "seriousness" be judged?

. . . In gauging seriousness, one should ordinarily look to the harm characteristically done or risked by the act of a *single* offender, rather than the totality of damage caused by behavior of that kind. (Shoplifting is a minor crime because the harm done by a single act of shoplifting is relatively trivial, although the total economic harm done by all acts of shoplifting may well be substantial.) This focus on the single act is based on notions of culpability: the individual may be held responsible for the risks or consequences of his own acts, but not for the cumulated damage done by others who happen to commit the same crime, since he has no control over their actions.* . . .

PRIOR CRIMINAL RECORD

The seriousness of "the offense," to which the commensurate-deserts principle looks, embraces the defendant's prior criminal record: the number of his previous convictions and the seriousness of the crimes involved. A first offense, in our view, is deserving of less punishment than a second or third.

In the American criminal justice system, and in most others with which we are familiar, an offender's record of previous convictions considerably influences the severity with which he is punished. The first offender can expect more lenient treatment that the repeater. But why so?

Grounds other than commensurate deserts could account for this practice. One theory is predictive: the more often someone has offended in the past, the more likely he is to do it again — and hence, arguably, the greater reason for restraining him. Another theory has to do with deterrence: having continued to commit crimes despite previous punishments, repeaters might as a class require a greater penalty to induce them to desist. But such explanations would not suffice, given the preeminence we have accorded commensurate deserts. Unless the repeater *deserves* it, he could not, in our theory, be punished any differently from the first offender.

The reason for treating the first offense as less serious is, we think, that repetition alters the degree of culpability that may be ascribed to the offender. In assessing a first offender's culpability, it ought to be borne in mind that he was, at the time he committed the crime, only one of a large audience to whom the law impersonally addressed its prohibitions. His first conviction, however, should call dramatically and personally to his attention that the behavior is condemned. A repetition of the offense following that conviction may be re-

---

* Some conduct (e.g., an environmental offense such as littering) is prohibited primarily because of its aggregate effects, rather than because of the consequences of a single violation. But even here one should, in assessing the seriousness of a single violation, discount the aggregate harm in some approximate way to reflect the fact that *this* offender's contribution to the harm was minuscule.

garded as more culpable, since he persisted in the behavior after having been forcefully censured for it through his prior punishment.

Our view of the first infraction as less culpable is reinforced when the evidentiary problems confronting the sentencer are considered. With an instrument as crude as the fact-finding process of the criminal law, the degree of culpability of the defendant is a judgment in which one seldom can have great confidence in any single instance. Did the defendant really intend the harm (or was intent merely imputed to him because the criminal law presumes persons to intend the natural and probable consequences of their acts)? Was there any contributory fault on the part of the victim? If the crime implicated several persons, was the defendant a central or only a peripheral participant? It is hard to be certain in a single situation, but with each repetition, the ascription of culpability can be made with a little more confidence. That the offender could have been provoked, for example, is ordinarily less believable on the third occasion he assaults someone than on the first.

Our view of repetition has an important collateral advantage of parsimony in inflicting pain. Penalties for first offenses can be kept on the low side, reflecting the doubts just mentioned about the extent of the offender's culpability. More severe penalties would be reserved mainly for offenders who had offended and been punished before. . . .

Since a record of prior offenses bears both on the offender's deserts and on the likelihood of recidivism, what practical difference does it make which theory is adopted? The difference is this. The commensurate-deserts principle looks only to the seriousness of the offender's prior crimes. A theory of predictive restraint, by contrast, allows one to consider not only his criminal record but *anything else* that bears on his likelihood of offending again: matters of the offender's social status having nothing to do with his blameworthiness — e.g., his lack of a fixed abode, a steady job, or a high school diploma — could warrant a longer sentence to the extent that they indicated a higher statistical likelihood of recidivism. It is this attention to matters of status that we find objectionable. Perhaps jobless offenders are, on average, more likely to recidivate than those with steady jobs; but it is still offensive to punish a criminal more severely, irrespective of the gravity of the crimes he has perpetrated, on the grounds that he happens to have no job. The commensurate-deserts principle, while taking prior crimes into account, would exclude these other factors. . . .

SEVERITY OF PUNISHMENTS

. . . The principle of commensurate deserts calls for maintenance of a "proportion" between the seriousness of the crime and the severity of the penalty. . . .

The assessment of severity, as the assessment of the harmfulness of the offense, should be standardized: the focus should be on how unpleasant the punishment *characteristically* is. Such standardization is necessary as a limit on discretion. . . . It is also needed as a safeguard against class justice. Judges sometimes impose different penalties on persons convicted of similar crimes, in the hope of producing equivalent amounts of discomfort: the middle-class person is put on probation and the ghetto youth jailed for the same infraction, on the theory that the former's sensitivities are greater. More drastic measures thus come to be imposed chiefly on those of lower status who are deemed to have "less to lose" — but only because they have lost so much already through their deprived social situation. . . .

G. FLETCHER, RETHINKING CRIMINAL LAW 460, 466 (1978): If the argument were that recidivists were particularly dangerous and punishment ought to be inflicted in proportion to the offender's dangerousness, we could at least try to argue against the proposition on empirical grounds. There might be some data that one could use to argue that some recidivists are no more dangerous than comparable categories of persons never punished. But this is precisely the type of unethical, repressive use of governmental power that von Hirsch seeks to avoid. . . .

. . . von Hirsch's argument is not that recidivism renders the actor personally more culpable for the same act of wrongdoing, but rather that persistent violation expresses a rejection of established authority. This is an additional wrong that arguably raises the level of wrongdoing and justifies an increased penalty. Yet this view of authority and defiance clashes with the basic premises of a society based upon formally defined offices. In a society of free and responsible adults, organized to live by the rule of formal authority, the defiant offender is punished according to what he or she does, not according to the implied threat of further disobedience.

The contemporary pressure to consider prior convictions in setting the level of the offense and of punishment reflects a theory of social protection rather than a theory of deserved punishment. The rule of thumb is that recidivists are more dangerous and that society will be better served if the recidivists are isolated for longer terms. This view raises empirical and methodological issues in gauging the dangerousness of recidivists and it poses serious ethical issues in punishing a person more severely on the basis of past crimes already once punished. These are issues that must be confronted directly, with no illusions about the camouflage offered by the concepts of retribution and desert.

GALLIGAN, GUIDELINES AND JUST DESERTS: A CRITIQUE OF RECENT TRENDS IN SENTENCING REFORM, [1981] Crim. L. Rev. 297, 303-306: For practical purposes the key concept in the deserts approach is the seriousness of the offence. This involved an assessment of the degree of wrongdoing combined with the culpability of the offender. . . . Of course judges are required to make these evaluations as part of their daily business, and I am not suggesting that because they are difficult to make, one should not attempt them. What is clear is that in practice we accept that evaluations of seriousness are inherently broad and approximate rather than precise. So an approach to sentencing which seems to depend upon a precise assessment of comparative seriousness begins on a shaky foundation.

Furthermore it is not at all clear that a presumptive sentencing system which restricts the judge's decision to a limited number of factors will produce more accurate assessments of seriousness than a system which leaves the matter largely to the judge's own evaluation. The reformer faces a dilemma: (i) if he gives the judge a wide discretion to decide the degree of seriousness and therefore deserts, then there is a risk of uncontrollable subjective assessments; (ii) if however he stipulates the factors that count towards seriousness and limits the judge to them, then there is a risk of the resulting assessments being crude and approximate. The tendency amongst reformers is to go for (ii); this makes sentencing easier, it reduces discretion and ensures a good level of uniformity. But the cost is clear: resulting assessments of deserts are necessarily broad and approximate, when it is basic to just deserts that they be fine and precise. This problem is exacerbated in those systems which do not even allow the judge to weigh up for himself the given factors, but which simply allot a score to each objectively defined factor.

There is an even more fundamental problem: what counts towards seriousness? . . . Take past convictions: almost all just deserts proponents consider past convictions to be relevant to deserts. But the relevance of past convictions is deeply equivocal. . . .

In short, what counts towards deserts is by no means settled, but there is a tendency for just deserts proponents to get the best of both worlds. By characterising all factors in terms of deserts, they get the moral advantage of doing to the offender only what is deserved; at the same time they get the forward-looking, utilitarian advantages related to deterrence, rehabilitation and social protection which in principle are improper considerations on a just deserts approach.

In any event is a sentencing system based solely on deserts desirable? . . . The argument for distribution according to deserts is the principle of fairness, but let us be clear about the consequences of basing distribution of punishment on strict deserts:

(a) Sentences at the top of the range for any category of offence will be uniform, so those who have committed the same offence in roughly the same circumstances will get the same sentence. There will be no room for passing a more severe protective penalty on an offender who might be classified as dangerous. But there is a great risk that this concern with uniformity will have the effect of keeping the range of penalties within the system high, so that the dangerous offender will be adequately covered anyhow. The point is that a lot of non-dangerous offenders will therefore get longer sentences in the interests of consistency. . . . In short, a rigid rule of consistency in sentencing may work against a general reduction of the normal penalty scales.

(b) A just deserts approach also has the effect of levelling-up at the bottom of the penalty range. In many sentencing systems at present, . . . there is usually a discretion in the sentencer to treat offenders towards the bottom of the offence category more leniently than their deserts might require, in the hope that they might be diverted from a life of crime and incarceration. This discretion is perhaps most important when the sentencer has to decide whether to send an offender to prison for the first time. A rigorous just deserts approach, however, would remove that discretion and require the application of a reasonably fixed penalty. The risk is that this would mean imposing prison sentences in situations where non-custodial measures might have been applied previously. Thus the effect of just deserts may be to increase significantly the prison population.[10] . . .

These considerations are all aspects of the one central problem: within a

10. For research on this point: J. Petersilia and P. W. Greenwood, "Mandatory Prison Sentences: Projected Effect on Crime and Prison" (1978) 69 J. of Crim. Law and Criminology 604.

given penalty range, is equal treatment based on deserts really so important that it always trumps other goals and values? . . .

NOTE

For further discussion of these issues, see Bedau, Retribution and the Theory of Punishment, 75 J. Philos. 601 (1978); von Hirsch, Desert and Previous Convictions in Sentencing, 65 Minn. L. Rev. 591 (1981).

2. *Implementing Reform*

SCHULHOFER, DUE PROCESS OF SENTENCING, 128 U. Pa. L. Rev. 733, 736-740 (1980): [The traditional] sentencing process is "indeterminate" in several respects. Crucial decisions are made by prosecutors, judges, and parole officials. In each instance the decisionmaker's power is broad and unstructured, and although the effect of a sentencing decision by one kind of official may be tempered by the decisions of others, the decision itself is not subject to any form of appeal. Finally, the sentence is not only indeterminate in terms of legal standards and controls but also indeterminate in time. Even after sentence is pronounced by the judge, the actual date of release in the case of imprisonment depends upon parole board action, and the critical decision may be years away. Indeed, after release the parolee remains subject to reimprisonment under the original sentence if he or she violates the conditions of release.

Many reform proposals focus upon this delay in determining the actual sentence, with its result of prolonged and cruel suspense for the prisoners affected. These proposals accordingly contemplate either abolition of parole or a requirement that the parole release date be fixed very early in the prisoner's term; the sentence established at the outset will then represent "flat time," the term of imprisonment that will actually be served. The most extreme version of this type of "determinate" sentencing is that enacted in 1975 in Maine, under which parole is abolished and trial judges select flat-time sentences from within broad statutory ranges at the time of conviction.[15] This system provides certainty for the offender entering prison, but of course does nothing to make the critical decisions more uniform or predictable and, in fact, aggravates the problems of broad judicial discretion by removing the countervailing power of the parole board.

More commonly, reform proposals treat broad judicial discretion as the principal evil. . . . Legislation recently enacted in California specifies within very narrow limits the sentence to be imposed for each offense.[19] . . . But the variety and complexity of criminal conduct render specification of precise statutory penalties a prodigious task and render the resulting statutes exceedingly cumbersome. . . . As a solution to these difficulties, [such] legislation commonly author-

---

15. Me. Rev. Stat. Ann. tit. 17A, §§1151-1254 (1979).
19. Cal. Penal Code §§1170, 3000, 3040 (West Supp. 1979).

izes some residuum of judicial discretion,[21] but the disease of excessive detail typically remains, while the attempted cure creates a loophole that could conceivably defeat the entire enterprise.[22]

Legislative specification of punishment poses another problem that most reformers consider even more serious — the enactment of increasingly severe penalties. . . . The case for short sentences rests, of course, upon much more controversial values than does the case for consistent sentences. . . . [But] any proponent of greater consistency in sentencing must recognize that pursuit of this goal through legislatively prescribed sentences may mean sentences much longer than those currently imposed, aggravation of the already severe overcrowding in prisons, and increased likelihood of nullification — never a very orderly or consistent phenomenon — by police, prosecutors, juries, trial and appellate judges, prison administrators, parole boards (if any), and those charged with dispensing executive clemency. These factors, together with the difficulties of achieving adequate specificity without excessive detail, render troublesome and potentially self-defeating any approach relying, as does the California statute, upon narrow, legislatively prescribed penalty ranges.

An alternative approach, which could alleviate these difficulties, is to preserve relatively broad statutory ranges of punishment and to entrust the development of narrower penalty ranges and more precise categories of offenses to a "sentencing commission," an administrative agency exercising power delegated by the legislature. A sentencing commission would have the time and resources to deal with the complex array of sentencing problems and, though ultimately accountable to the legislature, would be insulated to a degree from the most immediate political pressures. . . . The sentencing commission approach has now been adopted in Illinois, Minnesota, and Pennsylvania, and it has been included in several bills introduced in Congress, including S. 1437, the proposed federal criminal code passed by the Senate in 1978. . . .

TWENTIETH CENTURY FUND, TASK FORCE ON CRIMINAL SENTENCING, FAIR AND CERTAIN PUNISHMENT
12-25 (1976)

A sentencing system that achieves certainty of sentence with justice must avoid the evils of the present system and of the proposals to remedy it — of untrammeled discretion on the one hand and of total inflexibility on the other. The

---

21. See, e.g., Cal. Penal Code §1170(a)(2) (West Supp. 1979) (authorizing court, in its discretion, to impose fine, probation, or county jail term in lieu of mandated state prison terms).

22. The sentencing reform legislation recently enacted in Indiana provides a striking example of this danger. The new statute specifies a single "presumptive sentence" for each of five grades of felonies, but authorizes substantial adjustments to the presumptive sentence when the trial judge finds an aggravating or mitigating circumstance. The vagueness of many of these circumstances provides the judge with discretion to choose a sentence of, for example, two-to-eight years' imprisonment for a Class C felony or six-to-twenty years' imprisonment for a Class B felony. Ind. Code Ann. §§35-50-1-1 to 35-50-6-6 (Burns Supp. 1979); see Lagoy, Hussey, & Kramer, A Comparative Assessment of Determinate Sentencing in Four Pioneer States, 24 Crime & Delinquency 385, 391-94 (1978).

present discretion of the sentencing judge and parole board must be considerably limited and firmly guided; yet they must remain able to adapt the sentence reasonably to the particular circumstances of the crime and the peculiar characteristics of the criminal.

The Task Force proposes a system under which the legislature would retain the power to make those broad policy decisions that can be wisely and justly made about crime and do not involve the particulars of specific crimes and criminals. The sentencing judge would have some degree of guided discretion to consider and weigh those pertinent factors that cannot be wisely evaluated in the absence of the particular crime and criminal. And the parole board would have some degree of guided discretion to consider and weigh factors that were unavailable at the time of sentencing so that it could tailor its decision regarding release to the needs of the prisoner and society.

We call our proposal "presumptive sentencing." The underlying presumption here is that a finding of guilty of committing a crime would predictably incur a particular sentence unless specific mitigating or aggravating factors are established.

The process should start with the legislature (or legislative commission or judicial body), which would break crimes down into several subcategories. *For each subcategory of crime, we propose that the legislature, or a body it designates, adopt a presumptive sentence that should generally be imposed on typical first offenders who have committed the crime in the typical fashion.*

The legislature also would determine how much the presumptive first-offender sentence ought to be increased for each succeeding conviction according to a formula based on a predetermined percentage. The theory behind this approach is that sentences for first offenders should be relatively low but that they should increase — rather sharply — with each succeeding conviction. Thus, we have suggested a geometric progression as the appropriate increment for more serious offenses: 50 percent "enhancement" for the second armed robbery, 100 percent for the third, 200 percent for the fourth, etc. The rise would, however, be less steep for petty offenders: 10 percent for the second-time pickpocket, 20 percent for the third, 30 percent for the fourth, etc.

The Task Force recommends that the legislature, or the body it designates, also define specific aggravating or mitigating factors, again based on frequently recurring characteristics of the crime and the criminal. If aggravating factors outweighed the mitigating factors, the judge could impose a sentence that exceeded the presumptive by a specified percentage. If mitigating factors outweighed aggravating factors, the judge could impose a sentence that fell below the presumptive, again by a specified percentage. . . .

In imposing sentences, judges normally consider a wide variety of factors. Some of these, such as the defendant's race, appearance, or sex, are clearly improper; others, such as whether the defendant pleaded guilty or "cooperated" with the authorities, are debatable. . . . [D]ifferent judges — acting without legislative or appellate court guidance — have different views as to whether a given factor is appropriately considered in sentencing. It is our conclusion that these issues should be openly debated, that, in situations where the factors are fairly typical and frequently recurring, the legislature (or delegated body) should decide whether these factors should be considered in sentencing.

Only in truly extraordinary and unanticipated circumstances would the judge be permitted to deviate from the presumptive sentence *beyond* the narrow range permitted by an ordinary finding of aggravating or mitigating factors. Any deviation would have to be justified in a reasoned opinion subject to a searching review on appeal. . . .

The parole board or releasing agency would have more limited authority than at present. . . . The board could decide on release, but only within a previously fixed range and on the basis of relevant information (as defined by the legislature) that was not available to the sentencing judge. The justification for early release would be to facilitate the prisoner's transition to the outside community or because of compelling medical need. As a support to prison discipline, good time should also be a reason for releasing a prisoner somewhat earlier than the date prescribed by his judicially imposed sentence. Good time would be calculated by a formula set by the legislature, for example, three days of vested good time for every month without an infraction.

In effect, we propose a complete restructuring of the functions of the releasing agency. Today, it serves primarily to determine the actual sentence to be served, which, in our view, is properly a legislative and judicial function. The vitally important function on which the releasing agency should concentrate is aiding prisoners in their difficult transition from prison routine to the outside society. . . .

How presumptive sentencing might work in actuality can be illustrated briefly by the ways in which several different offenders would be punished after committing armed robbery involving the display or threatened use of a loaded gun. We will assume that the legislature has prescribed a 2-year presumptive sentence for a crime of this sort, with no minimum and a 10-year maximum.

A typical first offender convicted of a typical armed robbery, with no aggravating or mitigating circumstances, would generally receive a sentence of two years' imprisonment. But what if the judge were to find considerable aggravating factors, such as the robbing of a blind newsstand operator or some other particularly vulnerable victim? We will assume that the legislature had decided that a 50 percent increase could be imposed where aggravating factors substantially exceeded the mitigating ones. Thus, the sentence would be three years.

Assuming that the legislature had applied a 50 percent enhancement over the presumptive sentence for second offenses, a typical second offender convicted of the same armed robbery would receive a sentence of three years. If the aggravating circumstances were found to outweigh mitigating circumstances, then the sentence would be three years plus 50 percent more, or four and a half years.

But let us assume that this same offender had mercilessly taunted and threatened his extremely vulnerable victims by firing several shots into the air, cocking the hammer of the pistol at their heads, and promising that the next bullet was for them. In such circumstances, if the trial judge thought it was warranted, he would then write a reasoned decision for a sentence of up to eight years — beyond the addition for aggravating factors but within the legislatively prescribed maximum. . . . The extraordinary nature of a case calling for a sentence *beyond* the established range of deviation for specified factors would have to be demonstrated by the sentencing judge's opinion, which would be subject to close appellate scrutiny. . . .

ZIMRING, MAKING THE PUNISHMENT FIT THE CRIME:
A CONSUMER'S GUIDE TO SENTENCING REFORM
Hastings Center Rep. 13, 15-17 (Dec. 1976)

The Twentieth Century Fund scheme of "presumptive sentences," because it is the most sophisticated attempt to date, will serve as an illustration of the formidable collection of problems that confront a system of "fair and certain" legislatively determined punishments. . . .

I agree with the aims and priorities of the report, at the same time that I suspect the introduction of this (or many other) reform proposals into the legislative process might do more harm than good.

Why so skeptical? Consider a few of the obstacles to making the punishment fit the crime:

1. *The incoherence of the criminal law.* Any system of punishment that attaches a single sanction to a particular offense must define offenses with a morally persuasive precision that present laws do not possess. . . . But can we be precise? The Task Force tried, providing illustrative definitions of five different kinds of nighttime housebreaking with presumptive sentences from two years (for armed burglary, where the defendant menaces an occupant) through six months' probation. The Task Force did not attempt to deal with daylight or nonresidential burglary.

The problem is not simply that any such penal code will make our present statutes look like Reader's Digest Condensed Books; we lack the capacity to define into formal law the nuances of situation, intent, and social harm that condition the seriousness of particular criminal acts. . . .

Rape, an offense that encompasses a huge variety of behaviors, is graded into three punishments: six years (when accompanied by an assault that causes bodily injury); three years (when there is no additional bodily harm); and six months (when committed on a previous sex partner, with no additional bodily harm). Two further aggravating conditions are also specified. Put aside for a moment the fact that prior consensual sex reduces the punishment by a factor of six and the problem that rape with bodily harm has a "presumptive sentence" one year longer than intentional killing. Have we really defined the offense into its penologically significant categories? Can we rigorously patrol the border between forcible rape without additional bodily harm and that with further harm — when that distinction can mean the difference between six months and six years in the penitentiary?

I am not suggesting that these are problems of sloppy drafting. Rather, we may simply lack the ability to comprehensively define in advance those elements of an offense that should be considered in fixing a criminal sentence.

2. *The paradox of prosecutorial power.* . . . The long list of different offenses proposed in the report provides the basis for the exercise of prosecutorial discretion: the selection of initial charges and the offer to reduce charges (charge-bargaining) are more important in a fixed-price system precisely because the charge at conviction determines the sentence. The prosecutor files a charge of "premeditated" killing (ten years) and offers to reduce the charge to "intentional" killing (five years) in exchange for a guilty plea. . . .

This means that the disparity between sentences following a guilty plea and those following jury trial are almost certain to remain. Similarly, disparity between different areas and different prosecutors will remain, because one man's "premeditation" can always be another's "intention." It is unclear whether total disparity will decrease, remain stable, or increase under a regime of determinate sentences. It is certain that disparities will remain.

The paradox of prosecutorial power under determinate sentencing is that exorcising discretion from two of the three discretionary agencies in criminal sentencing does not necessarily reduce either the role of discretion in sentence determination or the total amount of sentence disparity. Logically, three discretions may be better than one. The practical lesson is that no serious program to create a rule of law in determining punishment can ignore the pivotal role of the American prosecutor.

3. *The legislative law-and-order syndrome.* Two members of the Twentieth Century Fund Task Force express doubts that a legislature will endorse six-month sentences for burglary, even if it could be shown that six months is above or equal to the present sentence served. I share their skepticism. When the legislature determines sentencing ranges, it is operating at a level of abstraction far removed from individual case dispositions, or even the allocation of resources to courts and correctional agencies. At that level of abstraction the symbolic quality of the criminal sanction is of great importance. The penalty provisions in most of our criminal codes are symbolic denunciations of particular behavior patterns, rather than decisions about just sentences. This practice has been supported by the multiple ameliorating discretions in the present system.

It is the hope of most of the advocates of determinate sentencing that the responsibilities thrust on the legislature by their reforms will educate democratically elected officials to view their function with realism and responsibility — to recognize the need for priorities and moderation in fixing punishment. This is a hope, not firmly supported by the history of penal policy and not encouraged by a close look at the operation and personnel of the state legislatures.

Yet reallocating power to the legislature means gambling on our ability to make major changes in the way elected officials think, talk, and act about crime. Once a determinate sentencing bill is before a legislative body, it takes only an eraser and pencil to make a one-year "presumptive sentence" into a six-year sentence for the same offense. The delicate scheme of priorities in any well-conceived sentencing proposal can be torpedoed by amendment with ease and political appeal. . . .

4. *The lack of consensus and principle.* But what if we could trade disparity for high mandatory sentences beyond those merited by utilitarian or retributive demands of justice? Would it be a fair trade? It could be argued that a system which treats some offenders unjustly is preferable to one in which all are treated unjustly. Equality is only one, not the exclusive, criterion for fairness.

The last point leads to a more fundamental concern about the link between structural reform and achieving justice. The Task Force asks the question with eloquent simplicity: "How long is too long? How short is too short?" The question is never answered in absolute terms; indeed, it is unanswerable. . . . Yet how can we mete out fair punishment without agreeing on what is fair? How can we do justice before we define it? . . .

NOTES ON THE IMPLICATIONS OF REFORM

1. Severity. Recall that indeterminate sentencing has been attacked for its tendency to increase the time prisoners actually serve. The movement away from indeterminacy now is attacked on precisely the same ground. In general, which approach does have the greater potential for producing unduly harsh sentencing policy? In the particular political climate of your own state, which approach is more likely to generate more severe sentences? Several studies have attempted to measure the impact of determinate-sentence schemes on the size of prison populations and on average time served, but the effort to separate the effect of new legislation from other changes that may be occurring simultaneously is fraught with methodological problems. A large-scale effort to ascertain the impact of the new California sentencing scheme is now nearing completion. For earlier studies in other states, see, e.g., Clear, Hewitt & Regoli, Discretion and the Determinate Sentence: Its Distribution, Control and Effect on Time Served, 24 Crime & Delinquency 428 (1978); Petersilia & Greenwood, Mandatory Prison Sentences: Their Projected Effects on Crime and Prison Populations, 69 J. Crim. L. & Criminology 604 (1978).

If it is true that sentencing reform will lead to longer prison terms, can this fairly be counted as an objection? On what basis? Consider the comments of Judge Frankel in Symposium, Developments in Judicial Administration, 80 F.R.D. 147, 156-157 (1978):

> S. 1437[a] makes sentencing policies and decisions explicit and visible, and allocates responsibility in similar fashion. The Sentencing Commission will publish the standards. The judges will either follow the standards or deviate, explaining themselves in either case. A judge disposed to appear draconian for the media will know he or she is *being* draconian, and will not have the secret belief (or illusion) that everything will be quietly set to rights down the road a way by the parole authority. There will be some disasters, as there now are. How much these are actually repaired today by parole remains still a matter of guesswork. . . .
>
> . . . "Responsibility is the great developer of men," Brandeis said when he protested the intrusions of the judges upon administrators' domains. The point is no less apt in reverse. Let the judges judge and be held accountable. . . . Unless the democratic faith is a total illusion, the people can be led to understand that a five-year sentence, served in full, is not different from a fifteen-year sentence of which only a third need be served. If the people have had to be fooled to settle even for the barbaric sentences we now impose — if they'll demand still longer sentences when they understand the facts — I'd vote with Holmes and everybody else who supports the right of the people to go to hell if that is their preference. I confess at the same time to a hope that an enlightened Commission, reasonably articulate, will be able to sell as well as formulate "an effective, humane, and rational sentencing policy. . . ."

For further exploration of the severity problem, see Foote, Deceptive Determinate Sentencing, in National Institute of Law Enforcement and Criminal Justice, Determinate Sentencing: Reform or Regression? 133-140 (1978); Schulhofer,

---

a. The reference is to the sentencing provisions of the proposed federal criminal code, as passed by the United States Senate in 1978. S. 1437, 95th Cong., 2d Sess. (1978). — Eds.

Due Process of Sentencing, 128 U. Pa. L. Rev. 733, 801-813 (1980). The latter article argues that a sentencing commission should, to a degree, be insulated from political pressures, and that this technique for deflecting popular demands for severity is not inconsistent with principles of democratic government.

2. *The content of "equal" treatment.* What kinds of facts about the offender and the offense should be used to define the principal sentencing categories under a presumptive- or determinate-sentence scheme? What kinds of facts should count as permissible aggravating or mitigating circumstances? Consider, for example, the relevance of drug addiction. Are two defendants convicted of the same offense "similarly situated" if one is an addict and the other is not? Should the addiction be treated as a mitigating factor (because it created a strong temptation to commit the crime) or as an aggravating factor (because it indicates a greater likelihood of recidivism)? In part, the answer may depend on whether the sentencing scheme adopts a "just deserts" model, focusing only on the seriousness of the offense, or whether it seeks to structure discretion in the pursuit of a variety of goals, including incapacitation. A commitment to "consistency" or "equal treatment" does not resolve these substantive questions, and it may even make them more troublesome by putting a specific, highly visible price on membership in the affected category — "drug addicts" serve eight months more than others for the same offense.

Consider also the dangers of discrimination (or the appearance of discrimination) against racial minorities and the poor. Presumably no responsible sentencing commission would treat minority status or poverty as an explicit aggravating factor, even if statistics indicated some apparent correlation between these characteristics and recidivism. But what if such a commission chose to give favorable "points" for having a high school diploma or a stable marriage. (The United States Parole Commission for a time followed such a policy). Persons lacking these characteristics may well be more likely to commit new offenses, but they are also likely to include disproportionately large numbers of the poor. Should the use of such characteristics therefore be impermissible? Of course, characteristics such as those mentioned are probably given considerable weight by many judges today, but a presumptive-sentence system, rather than eliminating such unseemly appearances, might only make them more visible, and again place an explicit price on the favored characteristics — eight months off for being "middle class."

How can such problems be avoided? Should social and economic variables be excluded in constructing the categories (with the resulting danger that larger numbers of offenders will be presumed "high-risk" and subjected to long periods of confinement)? Over the long run it may prove possible to develop more discriminating (and less discriminatory) techniques for identifying the most dangerous offenders. But to some, attempts to categorize offenders by a relatively mechanical process based on a few, predetermined criteria will seem offensive and "inhuman" no matter what the criteria employed. Is it preferable to avoid categories completely and leave sentencing power totally unstructured? For discussion of these problems, see Coffee, Repressed Issues of Sentencing: Accountability, Predictability and Equality in the Era of the Sentencing Commission, 66 Geo. L.J. 975 (1978).

3. *Plea bargaining.* As Professor Zimring indicates, presumptive sentencing could actually increase discretion and disparities in sentencing by removing

the ability of judges and parole boards to check the powers exercised by prosecutors in connection with plea bargaining. It is difficult, however, to assess just how much the existing difficulties of plea bargaining would be enhanced and to assess the extent to which any such costs would be offset by the gains that presumably would be realized through the greater consistency and predictability of sentencing in cases going to trial. The problem is explored in Alschuler, Sentencing Reform and Prosecutorial Power: A Critique of Recent Proposals for "Fixed" and "Presumptive Sentencing," 126 U. Pa. L. Rev. 550 (1978); Schulhofer, Due Process of Sentencing, 128 U. Pa. L. Rev. 733, 742-755 (1980). It seems likely that in many jurisdictions, presumptive sentencing will aggravate the problems of discretion by transferring additional sentencing power to prosecutors who are typically much younger and less experienced than judges, whose actions are more likely to be affected by personal and professional considerations unrelated to the merits, and whose decisions are made in much less visible fashion.

What can be done about this problem? Is it preferable to give judges the greatest possible flexibility in sentencing, so that they can counteract prosecutorial power? Or is there some way to control the discretion of *both* judges and prosecutors?

One device often suggested for preserving judicial control is called "real offense" sentencing. This technique contemplates that in determining offense seriousness in a presumptive- or guidelines-sentence system, the judge would simply ignore the formal offense of conviction (often determined by plea negotiation) and instead make an independent determination of the seriousness of the crime actually committed. In this way the prosecutor and defense counsel presumably would lose their ability to control the sentence by stipulating the offense to which the plea will be entered. A form of real-offense sentencing has been adopted by the United States Parole Commission in applying its parole-release guidelines and has been upheld by the courts. See, e.g., Billiteri v. U.S. Board of Parole, 541 F.2d 938 (2d Cir. 1976).

If real-offense sentencing worked as intended and therefore successfully offset the effects of charge bargaining by the parties, why would defendants plead guilty? Part of the answer may be that they would not fully understand how the real-offense system worked. If so, would judges be obliged to explain the system to them, or could the pleas be considered valid despite the defendants' misplaced hopes for leniency? (Consider whether the misimpressions would be any worse than those held by many guilty plea defendants under indeterminate-sentence systems today). Another reason why defendants might continue to plead guilty is that resourceful attorneys might continue finding ways to manipulate the guidelines and thus to subvert efforts to preserve judicial control. In either event, real-offense sentencing could create difficulties much more troublesome than those it purports to solve. See Schulhofer, supra at 757-772.

Another possible approach for controlling prosecutorial discretion in the context of presumptive- or guidelines-sentencing is to regulate the prosecutorial charging decision, either by guidelines within the prosecutor's office or by judicial control over charge bargaining. Again, it will be difficult to assure that such controls prove effective in practice. And again, if such controls do prove effective, how will the perceived need to encourage guilty pleas be satisfied? Here the answer probably has to be a guideline provision granting an explicit, predetermined sentence concession in return for the guilty plea (or perhaps a sentence concession for waiving a jury and accepting a bench trial). But would the Supreme Court (*should* the Supreme Court) permit states to establish a specific statutory price for exercising the right to trial? Isn't the present system of unpredictable and haphazardly (or invidiously) distributed guilty plea concessions even worse than that? For discussion of these problems and related issues affecting the control of prosecutorial charging and sentencing power, see Schulhofer, supra at 772-798; Vorenberg, Decent Restraint of Prosecutorial Power, 94 Harv. L. Rev. 1521 (1981).

4. Parole. The same considerations that have prompted restrictions on judicial sentencing discretion have led to narrowing the early-release powers of parole boards. For example, the United States Parole Commission has established formal Guidelines for Decision-Making, which include a detailed table setting forth expected release dates for various combinations of offense behavior and recidivism risk (the latter being determined by a "Salient Factor Score" computed from various personal characteristics such as number of prior convictions, employment plans, and history of drug abuse). See 28 U.S.C. §2.20 (1979). Although the actual release date can be modified in the event of misbehavior in prison, the factors necessary to compute the normally expected release date under the "Guideline Table" all can be determined on the date the inmate enters prison. For discussion of the new Parole Commission guidelines system, see Project, Parole Release Decision-Making and the Sentencing Process, 84 Yale L.J. 810 (1975).

Once parole-release decisions are structured in terms of narrow criteria essentially unrelated to rehabilitative progress in prison, why should the parole system be retained at all? See A. von Hirsch & K. Hanrahan, The Question of Parole 88-100 (1979).

The question whether parole should be retained or abolished continues to divide reformers who in other respects agree on the adoption of presumptive- or determinate-sentence schemes. At least six states — California, Illinois, Indiana, Maine, Minnesota, and New Mexico — have abolished the early-release functions of the parole board.[12] Both Oregon and Pennsylvania have recently adopted extensive sentencing reforms that contemplate retention of the parole-release function.[13] In the sentencing provisions of the proposed federal criminal code, the parole-release issue was a major source of disagreement between the House and Senate versions of the bill.[14]

---

12. In both Maine and New Mexico, the revised statutes leave the trial judge to select the sentence from a rather wide range. They therefore provide for a system in which the time to be served is "determinate" once sentence is pronounced, but they do not attempt to create greater uniformity or predictability in the decisions that sentencing judges make. See Me. Rev. Stat. Ann. tit. 17A, §§1151-1254; 1977 N.M. Laws ch. 216; Note, Definite Sentencing in New Mexico: The 1977 Sentencing Act, 9 N.M.L. Rev. 131 (1979). The remaining four states not only abolish parole but also seek greater uniformity in decisions at the judicial level, through a system of presumptive sentences established either by the legislature or a sentencing commission. See Cal. Penal Code §§1170, 3000, 3040; Ill. Ann. Stat. ch. 38, §§1003-1108; Ind. Code Ann. §§35-50-1-1 to 35-50-6-6; 1978 Minn. Laws ch. 723.

13. See Or. Rev. Stat. §§144.110-144.125; 144.775-144.790; Pa. Stat. Ann. §§1381-1386.

14. The bill approved by the Senate Judiciary Committee abolished early release on parole. See S. 1722, 96th Cong., 1st Sess. (1979). The House Judiciary Committee approved a bill that provided for retention of parole release. See H.R. 6233, 96th Cong., 2d Sess. (1980).

APPENDIX

AMERICAN LAW INSTITUTE MODEL PENAL CODE OFFICIAL DRAFT, 1962

PART I. GENERAL PROVISIONS

Contents

PART II. DEFINITION OF SPECIFIC CRIMES
Offenses Involving Danger to the Person

Contents

PART I.   GENERAL PROVISIONS

Article 1.   Preliminary

SECTION 1.01.   TITLE AND EFFECTIVE DATE [Omitted.]

SECTION 1.02.   PURPOSES; PRINCIPLES OF CONSTRUCTION

(1) The general purposes of the provisions governing the definition of offenses are:

(a) to forbid and prevent conduct that unjustifiably and inexcusably inflicts or threatens substantial harm to individual or public interests;

(b) to subject to public control persons whose conduct indicates that they are disposed to commit crimes;

(c) to safeguard conduct that is without fault from condemnation as criminal;

(d) to give fair warning of the nature of the conduct declared to constitute an offense;

(e) to differentiate on reasonable grounds between serious and minor offenses.

(2) The general purposes of the provisions governing the sentencing and treatment of offenders are:

(a) to prevent the commission of offenses;

(b) to promote the correction and rehabilitation of offenders;

(c) to safeguard offenders against excessive, disproportionate or arbitrary punishment;

(d) to give fair warning of the nature of the sentences that may be imposed on conviction of an offense;

(e) to differentiate among offenders with a view to a just individualization in their treatment;

(f) to define, coordinate and harmonize the powers, duties and functions of the courts and of administrative officers and agencies responsible for dealing with offenders;

(g) to advance the use of generally accepted scientific methods and knowledge in the sentencing and treatment of offenders;

(h) to integrate responsibility for the administration of the correctional system in a State Department of Correction [or other single department or agency].

(3) The provisions of the Code shall be construed according to the fair import of their terms but when the language is susceptible of differing constructions it shall be interpreted to further the general purposes stated in this Section and the special purposes of the particular provision involved. The discretionary powers conferred by the Code shall be exercised in accordance with the criteria stated in the Code and, insofar as such criteria are not decisive, to further the general purposes stated in this Section.

SECTION 1.03.   TERRITORIAL APPLICABILITY

(1) Except as otherwise provided in this Section, a person may be convicted under the law of this State of an offense committed by his own conduct or the conduct of another for which he is legally accountable if:

(a) either the conduct which is an element of the offense or the result which is such an element occurs within this State; or

(b) conduct occurring outside the State is sufficient under the law of this State to constitute an attempt to commit an offense within the State; or

(c) conduct occurring outside the State is sufficient under the law of this State to constitute a conspiracy to commit an offense within the State and an overt act in furtherance of such conspiracy occurs within the State; or

(d) conduct occurring within the State establishes complicity in the commission of, or an attempt, solicitation or conspiracy to commit, an offense in another jurisdiction which also is an offense under the law of this State; or

(e) the offense consists of the omission to perform a legal duty imposed by the law of this State with respect to domicile, residence or a relationship to a person, thing or transaction in the State; or

(f) the offense is based on a statute of this State which expressly prohibits conduct outside the State, when the conduct bears a reasonable relation to a legitimate interest of this State and the actor knows or should know that his conduct is likely to affect that interest.

(2) Subsection (1)(a) does not apply when either causing a specified result or a purpose to cause or danger of causing such a result is an element of an offense and the result occurs or is designed or likely to occur only in another jurisdiction where the conduct charged would not constitute an offense, unless a legislative purpose plainly appears to declare the conduct criminal regardless of the place of the result.

(3) Subsection (1)(a) does not apply when causing a particular result is an element of an offense and the result is caused by conduct occurring outside the State which would not constitute an offense if the result had occurred there, unless the actor purposely or knowingly caused the result within the State.

(4) When the offense is homicide, either the death of the victim or the bodily impact causing the death constitutes a "result," within the meaning of Subsection (1)(a) and if the body of the homicide victim is found within the State, it is presumed that such result occurred within the State.

(5) This State includes the land and water and the air space above such land and water with respect to which the State has legislative jurisdiction.

SECTION 1.04. CLASSES OF CRIMES; VIOLATIONS

(1) An offense defined by this Code or by any other statute of this State, for which a sentence of [death or of] imprisonment is authorized, constitutes a crime. Crimes are classified as felonies, misdemeanors or petty misdemeanors.

(2) A crime is a felony if it is so designated in this Code or if persons convicted thereof may be sentenced [to death or] to imprisonment for a term which, apart from an extended term, is in excess of one year.

(3) A crime is a misdemeanor if it is so designated in this Code or in a statute other than this Code enacted subsequent thereto.

(4) A crime is a petty misdemeanor if it is so designated in this Code or in a statute other than this Code enacted subsequent thereto or if it is defined by a statute other than this Code which now provides that persons convicted thereof may be sentenced to imprisonment for a term of which the maximum is less than one year.

(5) An offense defined by this Code or by any other statute of this State constitutes a violation if it is so designated in this Code or in the law defining the offense or if no other sentence than a fine, or fine and forfeiture or other civil penalty is authorized upon conviction or if it is defined by a statute other than this Code which now provides that the offense shall not constitute a crime. A violation does not constitute a crime and conviction of a violation shall not give rise to any disability or legal disadvantage based on conviction of a criminal offense.

(6) Any offense declared by law to constitute a crime, without specification of the grade thereof or of the sentence authorized upon conviction, is a misdemeanor.

(7) An offense defined by any statute of this State other than this Code shall be classified as provided in this Section and the sentence that may be imposed upon conviction thereof shall hereafter be governed by this Code.

SECTION 1.05. ALL OFFENSES DEFINED BY STATUTE; APPLICATION OF GENERAL PROVISIONS
              OF THE CODE

(1) No conduct constitutes an offense unless it is a crime or violation under this Code
or another statute of this State.

(2) The provisions of Part I of the Code are applicable to offenses defined by other
statutes, unless the Code otherwise provides.

(3) This Section does not affect the power of a court to punish for contempt or to
employ any sanction authorized by law for the enforcement of an order or a civil judgment
or decree.

SECTION 1.06. TIME LIMITATIONS

(1) A prosecution for murder may be commenced at any time.

(2) Except as otherwise provided in this Section, prosecutions for other offenses are
subject to the following periods of limitation:

(a) a prosecution for a felony of the first degree must be commenced within six
years after it is committed;

(b) a prosecution for any other felony must be commenced within three years after
it is committed;

(c) a prosecution for a misdemeanor must be commenced within two years after it
is committed;

(d) a prosecution for a petty misdemeanor or a violation must be commenced within
six months after it is committed.

(3) If the period prescribed in Subsection (2) has expired, a prosecution may nevertheless be commenced for:

(a) any offense a material element of which is either fraud or a breach of fiduciary
obligation within one year after discovery of the offense by an aggrieved party or by
a person who has legal duty to represent an aggrieved party and who is himself not
a party to the offense, but in no case shall this provision extend the period of limitation
otherwise applicable by more than three years; and

(b) any offense based upon misconduct in office by a public officer or employee at
any time when the defendant is in public office or employment or within two years
thereafter, but in no case shall this provision extend the period of limitation otherwise
applicable by more than three years.

(4) An offense is committed either when every element occurs, or, if a legislative
purpose to prohibit a continuing course of conduct plainly appears, at the time when
the course of conduct or the defendant's complicity therein is terminated. Time starts
to run on the day after the offense is committed.

(5) A prosecution is commenced either when an indictment is found [or an information
filed] or when a warrant or other process is issued, provided that such warrant or process
is executed without unreasonable delay.

(6) The period of limitation does not run:

(a) during any time when the accused is continuously absent from the State or has
no reasonably ascertainable place of abode or work within the State, but in no case
shall this provision extend the period of limitation otherwise applicable by more than
three years; or

(b) during any time when a prosecution against the accused for the same conduct
is pending in this State.

SECTION 1.07. **METHOD OF PROSECUTION WHEN CONDUCT CONSTITUTES MORE THAN ONE OFFENSE**

(1) *Prosecution for Multiple Offenses; Limitation on Convictions.* When the same conduct of a defendant may establish the commission of more than one offense, the defendant may be prosecuted for each such offense. He may not, however, be convicted of more than one offense if:

(a) one offense is included in the other, as defined in Subsection (4) of this Section; or

(b) one offense consists only of a conspiracy or other form of preparation to commit the other; or

(c) inconsistent findings of fact are required to establish the commission of the offenses; or

(d) the offenses differ only in that one is defined to prohibit a designated kind of conduct generally and the other to prohibit a specific instance of such conduct; or

(e) the offense is defined as a continuing course of conduct and the defendant's course of conduct was uninterrupted, unless the law provides that specific periods of such conduct constitute separate offenses.

(2) *Limitation on Separate Trials for Multiple Offenses.* Except as provided in Subsection (3) of this Section, a defendant shall not be subject to separate trials for multiple offenses based on the same conduct or arising from the same criminal episode, if such offenses are known to the appropriate prosecuting officer at the time of the commencement of the first trial and are within the jurisdiction of a single court.

(3) *Authority of Court to Order Separate Trials.* When a defendant is charged with two or more offenses based on the same conduct or arising from the same criminal episode, the Court, on application of the prosecuting attorney or of the defendant, may order any such charge to be tried separately, if it is satisfied that justice so requires.

(4) *Conviction of Included Offense Permitted.* A defendant may be convicted of an offense included in an offense charged in the indictment [or the information]. An offense is so included when:

(a) it is established by proof of the same or less than all the facts required to establish the commission of the offense charged; or

(b) it consists of an attempt or solicitation to commit the offense charged or to commit an offense otherwise included therein; or

(c) it differs from the offense charged only in the respect that a less serious injury or risk of injury to the same person, property or public interest or a lesser kind of culpability suffices to establish its commission.

(5) *Submission of Included Offense to Jury.* The Court shall not be obligated to charge the jury with respect to an included offense unless there is a rational basis for a verdict acquitting the defendant of the offense charged and convicting him of the included offense.

SECTION 1.08. **WHEN PROSECUTION BARRED BY FORMER PROSECUTION FOR THE SAME OFFENSE** [Omitted.]

SECTION 1.09. **WHEN PROSECUTION BARRED BY FORMER PROSECUTION FOR DIFFERENT OFFENSE** [Omitted.]

SECTION 1.10. **FORMER PROSECUTION IN ANOTHER JURISDICTION: WHEN A BAR** [Omitted.]

SECTION 1.11. **FORMER PROSECUTION BEFORE COURT LACKING JURISDICTION OR WHEN FRAUDULENTLY PROCURED BY THE DEFENDANT** [Omitted.]

SECTION 1.12.   PROOF BEYOND A REASONABLE DOUBT; AFFIRMATIVE DEFENSES; BURDEN
OF PROVING FACT WHEN NOT AN ELEMENT OF AN OFFENSE; PRESUMPTIONS

(1) No person may be convicted of an offense unless each element of such offense is proved beyond a reasonable doubt. In the absence of such proof, the innocence of the defendant is assumed.

(2) Subsection (1) of this Section does not:

(a) require the disproof of an affirmative defense unless and until there is evidence supporting such defense; or

(b) apply to any defense which the Code or another statute plainly requires the defendant to prove by a preponderance of evidence.

(3) A ground of defense is affirmative, within the meaning of Subsection (2)(a) of this Section, when:

(a) it arises under a section of the Code which so provides; or

(b) it relates to an offense defined by a statute other than the Code and such statute so provides; or

(c) it involves a matter of excuse or justification peculiarly within the knowledge of the defendant on which he can fairly be required to adduce supporting evidence.

(4) When the application of the Code depends upon the finding of a fact which is not an element of an offense, unless the Code otherwise provides:

(a) the burden of proving the fact is on the prosecution or defendant, depending on whose interest or contention will be furthered if the finding should be made; and

(b) the fact must be proved to the satisfaction of the Court or jury, as the case may be.

(5) When the Code establishes a presumption with respect to any fact which is an element of an offense, it has the following consequences:

(a) when there is evidence of the facts which give rise to the presumption, the issue of the existence of the presumed fact must be submitted to the jury, unless the Court is satisfied that the evidence as a whole clearly negatives the presumed fact; and

(b) when the issue of the existence of the presumed fact is submitted to the jury, the Court shall charge that while the presumed fact must, on all the evidence, be proved beyond a reasonable doubt, the law declares that the jury may regard the facts giving rise to the presumption as sufficient evidence of the presumed fact.

(6) A presumption not established by the Code or inconsistent with it has the consequences otherwise accorded it by law.

SECTION 1.13.   GENERAL DEFINITIONS

In this Code, unless a different meaning plainly is required:

(1) "statute" includes the Constitution and a local law or ordinance of a political subdivision of the State;

(2) "act" or "action" means a bodily movement whether voluntary or involuntary;

(3) "voluntary" has the meaning specified in Section 2.01;

(4) "omission" means a failure to act;

(5) "conduct" means an action or omission and its accompanying state of mind, or, where relevant, a series of acts and omissions;

(6) "actor" includes, where relevant, a person guilty of an omission;

(7) "acted" includes, where relevant, "omitted to act";

(8) "person," "he" and "actor" include any natural person and, where relevant, a corporation or an unincorporated association;

(9) "element of an offense" means (i) such conduct or (ii) such attendant circumstances or (iii) such a result of conduct as

(a) is included in the description of the forbidden conduct in the definition of the offense; or

(b) establishes the required kind of culpability; or

(c) negatives an excuse or justification for such conduct; or

(d) negatives a defense under the statute of limitations; or

(e) establishes jurisdiction or venue;

(10) "material element of an offense" means an element that does not relate exclusively to the statute of limitations, jurisdiction, venue or to any other matter similarly unconnected with (i) the harm or evil, incident to conduct, sought to be prevented by the law defining the offense, or (ii) the existence of a justification or excuse for such conduct;

(11) "purposely" has the meaning specified in Section 2.02 and equivalent terms such as "with purpose," "designed" or "with design" have the same meaning;

(12) "intentionally" or "with intent" means purposely;

(13) "knowingly" has the meaning specified in Section 2.02 and equivalent terms such as "knowing" or "with knowledge" have the same meaning;

(14) "recklessly" has the meaning specified in Section 2.02 and equivalent terms such as "recklessness" or "with recklessness" have the same meaning;

(15) "negligently" has the meaning specified in Section 2.02 and equivalent terms such as "negligence" or "with negligence" have the same meaning;

(16) "reasonably believes" or "reasonable belief" designates a belief which the actor is not reckless or negligent in holding.

Article 2. General Principles of Liability

SECTION 2.01. REQUIREMENT OF VOLUNTARY ACT; OMISSION AS BASIS OF LIABILITY; POSSESSION AS AN ACT

(1) A person is not guilty of an offense unless his liability is based on conduct which includes a voluntary act or the omission to perform an act of which he is physically capable.

(2) The following are not voluntary acts within the meaning of this Section:

(a) a reflex or convulsion;

(b) a bodily movement during unconsciousness or sleep;

(c) conduct during hypnosis or resulting from hypnotic suggestion;

(d) a bodily movement that otherwise is not a product of the effort or determination of the actor, either conscious or habitual.

(3) Liability for the commission of an offense may not be based on an omission unaccompanied by action unless:

(a) the omission is expressly made sufficient by the law defining the offense; or

(b) a duty to perform the omitted act is otherwise imposed by law.

(4) Possession is an act, within the meaning of this Section, if the possessor knowingly procured or received the thing possessed or was aware of his control thereof for a sufficient period to have been able to terminate his possession.

SECTION 2.02. GENERAL REQUIREMENTS OF CULPABILITY

(1) *Minimum Requirements of Culpability.* Except as provided in Section 2.05, a person is not guilty of an offense unless he acted purposely, knowingly, recklessly or negligently, as the law may require, with respect to each material element of the offense.

(2) *Kinds of Culpability Defined.*

(a) *Purposely.*

A person acts purposely with respect to a material element of an offense when:

(i) if the element involves the nature of his conduct or a result thereof, it is his conscious object to engage in conduct of that nature or to cause such a result; and

(ii) if the element involves the attendant circumstances, he is aware of the existence of such circumstances or he believes or hopes that they exist.

(b) *Knowingly.*

A person acts knowingly with respect to a material element of an offense when:

(i) if the element involves the nature of his conduct or the attendant circumstances, he is aware that his conduct is of that nature or that such circumstances exist; and

(ii) if the element involves a result of his conduct, he is aware that it is practically certain that his conduct will cause such a result.

(c) *Recklessly.*

A person acts recklessly with respect to a material element of an offense when he consciously disregards a substantial and unjustifiable risk that the material element exists or will result from his conduct. The risk must be of such a nature and degree that, considering the nature and purpose of the actor's conduct and the circumstances known to him, its disregard involves a gross deviation from the standard of conduct that a law-abiding person would observe in the actor's situation.

(d) *Negligently.*

A person acts negligently with respect to a material element of an offense when he should be aware of a substantial and unjustifiable risk that the material element exists or will result from his conduct. The risk must be of such a nature and degree that the actor's failure to perceive it, considering the nature and purpose of his conduct and the circumstances known to him, involves a gross deviation from the standard of care that a reasonable person would observe in the actor's situation.

(3) *Culpability Required Unless Otherwise Provided.* When the culpability sufficient to establish a material element of an offense is not prescribed by law, such element is established if a person acts purposely, knowingly or recklessly with respect thereto.

(4) *Prescribed Culpability Requirement Applies to All Material Elements.* When the law defining an offense prescribes the kind of culpability that is sufficient for the commission of an offense, without distinguishing among the material elements thereof, such provision shall apply to all the material elements of the offense, unless a contrary purpose plainly appears.

(5) *Substitutes for Negligence, Recklessness and Knowledge.* When the law provides that negligence suffices to establish an element of an offense, such element also is established if a person acts purposely, knowingly or recklessly. When recklessness suffices to establish an element, such element also is established if a person acts purposely or knowingly. When acting knowingly suffices to establish an element, such element also is established if a person acts purposely.

(6) *Requirement of Purpose Satisfied if Purpose Is Conditional.* When a particular purpose is an element of an offense, the element is established although such purpose is conditional, unless the condition negatives the harm or evil sought to be prevented by the law defining the offense.

(7) *Requirement of Knowledge Satisfied by Knowledge of High Probability.* When knowledge of the existence of a particular fact is an element of an offense, such knowledge is established if a person is aware of a high probability of its existence, unless he actually believes that it does not exist.

(8) *Requirement of Wilfulness Satisfied by Acting Knowingly.* A requirement that an offense be committed wilfully is satisfied if a person acts knowingly with respect to the material elements of the offense, unless a purpose to impose further requirements appears.

(9) *Culpability as to Illegality of Conduct.* Neither knowledge nor recklessness or negligence as to whether conduct constitutes an offense or as to the existence, meaning or application

of the law determining the elements of an offense is an element of such offense, unless the definition of the offense or the Code so provides.

(10) *Culpability as Determinant of Grade of Offense.* When the grade or degree of an offense depends on whether the offense is committed purposely, knowingly, recklessly or negligently, its grade or degree shall be the lowest for which the determinative kind of culpability is established with respect to any material element of the offense.

SECTION 2.03. CAUSAL RELATIONSHIP BETWEEN CONDUCT AND RESULT; DIVERGENCE BETWEEN RESULT DESIGNED OR CONTEMPLATED AND ACTUAL RESULT OR BETWEEN PROBABLE AND ACTUAL RESULT

(1) Conduct is the cause of a result when:

(a) it is an antecedent but for which the result in question would not have occurred; and

(b) the relationship between the conduct and result satisfies any additional causal requirements imposed by the Code or by the law defining the offense.

(2) When purposely or knowingly causing a particular result is an element of an offense, the element is not established if the actual result is not within the purpose or the contemplation of the actor unless:

(a) the actual result differs from that designed or contemplated, as the case may be, only in the respect that a different person or different property is injured or affected or that the injury or harm designed or contemplated would have been more serious or more extensive than that caused; or

(b) the actual result involves the same kind of injury or harm as that designed or contemplated and is not too remote or accidental in its occurrence to have a [just] bearing on the actor's liability or on the gravity of his offense.

(3) When recklessly or negligently causing a particular result is an element of an offense, the element is not established if the actual result is not within the risk of which the actor is aware or, in the case of negligence, of which he should be aware unless:

(a) the actual result differs from the probable result only in the respect that a different person or different property is injured or affected or that the probable injury or harm would have been more serious or more extensive than that caused; or

(b) the actual result involves the same kind of injury or harm as the probable result and is not too remote or accidental in its occurrence to have a [just] bearing on the actor's liability or on the gravity of his offense.

(4) When causing a particular result is a material element of an offense for which absolute liability is imposed by law, the element is not established unless the actual result is a probable consequence of the actor's conduct.

SECTION 2.04. IGNORANCE OR MISTAKE

(1) Ignorance or mistake as to a matter of fact or law is a defense if:

(a) the ignorance or mistake negatives the purpose, knowledge, belief, recklessness or negligence required to establish a material element of the offense; or

(b) the law provides that the state of mind established by such ignorance or mistake constitutes a defense.

(2) Although ignorance or mistake would otherwise afford a defense to the offense charged, the defense is not available if the defendant would be guilty of another offense had the situation been as he supposed. In such case, however, the ignorance or mistake of the defendant shall reduce the grade and degree of the offense of which he may be convicted to those of the offense of which he would be guilty had the situation been as he supposed.

(3) A belief that conduct does not legally constitute an offense is a defense to a prosecution for that offense based upon such conduct when:

(a) the statute or other enactment defining the offense is not known to the actor and has not been published or otherwise reasonably made available prior to the conduct alleged; or

(b) he acts in reasonable reliance upon an official statement of the law, afterward determined to be invalid or erroneous, contained in (i) a statute or other enactment; (ii) a judicial decision, opinion or judgment; (iii) an administrative order or grant of permission; or (iv) an official interpretation of the public officer or body charged by law with responsibility for the interpretation, administration or enforcement of the law defining the offense.

(4) The defendant must prove a defense arising under Subsection (3) of this Section by a preponderance of evidence.

SECTION 2.05. WHEN CULPABILITY REQUIREMENTS ARE INAPPLICABLE TO VIOLATIONS AND TO OFFENSES DEFINED BY OTHER STATUTES; EFFECT OF ABSOLUTE LIABILITY IN REDUCING GRADE OF OFFENSE TO VIOLATION

(1) The requirements of culpability prescribed by Sections 2.01 and 2.02 do not apply to:

(a) offenses which constitute violations, unless the requirement involved is included in the definition of the offense or the Court determines that its application is consistent with effective enforcement of the law defining the offense; or

(b) offenses defined by statutes other than the Code, insofar as a legislative purpose to impose absolute liability for such offenses or with respect to any material element thereof plainly appears.

(2) Notwithstanding any other provision of existing law and unless a subsequent statute otherwise provides:

(a) when absolute liability is imposed with respect to any material element of an offense defined by a statute other than the Code and a conviction is based upon such liability, the offense constitutes a violation; and

(b) although absolute liability is imposed by law with respect to one or more of the material elements of an offense defined by a statute other than the Code, the culpable commission of the offense may be charged and proved, in which event negligence with respect to such elements constitutes sufficient culpability and the classification of the offense and the sentence that may be imposed therefor upon conviction are determined by Section 1.04 and Article 6 of the Code.

SECTION 2.06. LIABILITY FOR CONDUCT OF ANOTHER; COMPLICITY

(1) A person is guilty of an offense if it is committed by his own conduct or by the conduct of another person for which he is legally accountable, or both.

(2) A person is legally accountable for the conduct of another person when:

(a) acting with the kind of culpability that is sufficient for the commission of the offense, he causes an innocent or irresponsible person to engage in such conduct; or

(b) he is made accountable for the conduct of such other person by the Code or by the law defining the offense; or

(c) he is an accomplice of such other person in the commission of the offense.

(3) A person is an accomplice of another person in the commission of an offense if:

(a) with the purpose of promoting or facilitating the commission of the offense, he

(i) solicits such other person to commit it; or

(ii) aids or agrees or attempts to aid such other person in planning or committing it; or

(iii) having a legal duty to prevent the commission of the offense, fails to make proper effort so to do; or

(b) his conduct is expressly declared by law to establish his complicity.

(4) When causing a particular result is an element of an offense, an accomplice in the conduct causing such result is an accomplice in the commission of that offense, if he acts with the kind of culpability, if any, with respect to that result that is sufficient for the commission of the offense.

(5) A person who is legally incapable of committing a particular offense himself may be guilty thereof if it is committed by the conduct of another person for which he is legally accountable, unless such liability is inconsistent with the purpose of the provision establishing his incapacity.

(6) Unless otherwise provided by the Code or by the law defining the offense, a person is not an accomplice in an offense committed by another person if:

(a) he is a victim of that offense; or

(b) the offense is so defined that his conduct is inevitably incident to its commission; or

(c) he terminates his complicity prior to the commission of the offense and

(i) wholly deprives it of effectiveness in the commission of the offense; or

(ii) gives timely warning to the law enforcement authorities or otherwise makes proper effort to prevent the commission of the offense.

(7) An accomplice may be convicted on proof of the commission of the offense and of his complicity therein, though the person claimed to have committed the offense has not been prosecuted or convicted or has been convicted of a different offense or degree of offense or has an immunity to prosecution or conviction or has been acquitted.

SECTION 2.07.   LIABILITY OF CORPORATIONS, UNINCORPORATED ASSOCIATIONS AND PERSONS ACTING, OR UNDER A DUTY TO ACT, IN THEIR BEHALF

(1) A corporation may be convicted of the commission of an offense if:

(a) the offense is a violation or the offense is defined by a statute other than the Code in which a legislative purpose to impose liability on corporations plainly appears and the conduct is performed by an agent of the corporation acting in behalf of the corporation within the scope of his office or employment, except that if the law defining the offense designates the agents for whose conduct the corporation is accountable or the circumstances under which it is accountable, such provisions shall apply; or

(b) the offense consists of an omission to discharge a specific duty of affirmative performance imposed on corporations by law; or

(c) the commission of the offense was authorized, requested, commanded, performed or recklessly tolerated by the board of directors or by a high managerial agent acting in behalf of the corporation within the scope of his office or employment.

(2) When absolute liability is imposed for the commission of an offense, a legislative purpose to impose liability on a corporation shall be assumed, unless the contrary plainly appears.

(3) An unincorporated association may be convicted of the commission of an offense if:

(a) the offense is defined by a statute other than the Code which expressly provides for the liability of such an association and the conduct is performed by an agent of the association acting in behalf of the association within the scope of his office or employment, except that if the law defining the offense designates the agents for whose conduct the association is accountable or the circumstances under which it is accountable, such provisions shall apply; or

(b) the offense consists of an omission to discharge a specific duty of affirmative performance imposed on associations by law.

(4) As used in this Section:

(a) "corporation" does not include an entity organized as or by a governmental agency for the execution of a governmental program;

(b) "agent" means any director, officer, servant, employee or other person authorized to act in behalf of the corporation or association and, in the case of an unincorporated association, a member of such association;

(c) "high managerial agent" means an officer of a corporation or an unincorporated association, or, in the case of a partnership, a partner, or any other agent of a corporation or association having duties of such responsibility that his conduct may fairly be assumed to represent the policy of the corporation or association.

(5) In any prosecution of a corporation or an unincorporated association for the commission of an offense included within the terms of Subsection (1)(a) or Subsection (3)(a) of this Section, other than an offense for which absolute liability has been imposed, it shall be a defense if the defendant proves by a preponderance of evidence that the high managerial agent having supervisory responsibility over the subject matter of the offense employed due diligence to prevent its commission. This paragraph shall not apply if it is plainly inconsistent with the legislative purpose in defining the particular offense.

(6) (a) A person is legally accountable for any conduct he performs or causes to be performed in the name of the corporation or an unincorporated association or in its behalf to the same extent as if it were performed in his own name or behalf.

(b) Whenever a duty to act is imposed by law upon a corporation or an unincorporated association, any agent of the corporation or association having primary responsibility for the discharge of the duty is legally accountable for a reckless omission to perform the required act to the same extent as if the duty were imposed by law directly upon himself.

(c) When a person is convicted of an offense by reason of his legal accountability for the conduct of a corporation or an unincorporated association, he is subject to the sentence authorized by law when a natural person is convicted of an offense of the grade and the degree involved.

SECTION 2.08. INTOXICATION

(1) Except as provided in Subsection (4) of this Section, intoxication of the actor is not a defense unless it negatives an element of the offense.

(2) When recklessness establishes an element of the offense, if the actor, due to self-induced intoxication, is unaware of a risk of which he would have been aware had he been sober, such unawareness is immaterial.

(3) Intoxication does not, in itself, constitute mental disease within the meaning of Section 4.01.

(4) Intoxication which (a) is not self-induced or (b) is pathological is an affirmative defense if by reason of such intoxication the actor at the time of his conduct lacks substantial capacity either to appreciate its criminality [wrongfulness] or to conform his conduct to the requirements of law.

(5) *Definitions.* In this Section unless a different meaning plainly is required:

(a) "intoxication" means a disturbance of mental or physical capacities resulting from the introduction of substances into the body;

(b) "self-induced intoxication" means intoxication caused by substances which the actor knowingly introduces into his body, the tendency of which to cause intoxication he knows or ought to know, unless he introduces them pursuant to medical advice or under such circumstances as would afford a defense to a charge of crime;

(c) "pathological intoxication" means intoxication grossly excessive in degree, given the amount of the intoxicant, to which the actor does not know he is susceptible.

Section 2.09. Duress

(1) It is an affirmative defense that the actor engaged in the conduct charged to constitute an offense because he was coerced to do so by the use of, or a threat to use, unlawful force against his person or the person of another, which a person of reasonable firmness in his situation would have been unable to resist.

(2) The defense provided by this Section is unavailable if the actor recklessly placed himself in a situation in which it was probable that he would be subjected to duress. The defense is also unavailable if he was negligent in placing himself in such a situation, whenever negligence suffices to establish culpability for the offense charged.

(3) It is not a defense that a woman acted on the command of her husband, unless she acted under such coercion as would establish a defense under this Section. [The presumption that a woman, acting in the presence of her husband, is coerced is abolished.]

(4) When the conduct of the actor would otherwise be justifiable under Section 3.02, this Section does not preclude such defense.

Section 2.10. Military Orders

It is an affirmative defense that the actor, in engaging in the conduct charged to constitute an offense, does no more than execute an order of his superior in the armed services which he does not know to be unlawful.

Section 2.11. Consent

(1) *In General.* The consent of the victim to conduct charged to constitute an offense or to the result thereof is a defense if such consent negatives an element of the offense or precludes the infliction of the harm or evil sought to be prevented by the law defining the offense.

(2) *Consent to Bodily Harm.* When conduct is charged to constitute an offense because it causes or threatens bodily harm, consent to such conduct or to the infliction of such harm is a defense if:

(a) the bodily harm consented to or threatened by the conduct consented to is not serious; or

(b) the conduct and the harm are reasonably foreseeable hazards of joint participation in a lawful athletic contest or competitive sport; or

(c) the consent establishes a justification for the conduct under Article 3 of the Code.

(3) *Ineffective Consent.* Unless otherwise provided by the Code or by the law defining the offense, assent does not constitute consent if:

(a) it is given by a person who is legally incompetent to authorize the conduct charged to constitute the offense; or

(b) it is given by a person who by reason of youth, mental disease or defect or intoxication is manifestly unable or known by the actor to be unable to make a reasonable judgment as to the nature or harmfulness of the conduct charged to constitute the offense; or

(c) it is given by a person whose improvident consent is sought to be prevented by the law defining the offense; or

(d) it is induced by force, duress or deception of a kind sought to be prevented by the law defining the offense.

SECTION 2.12. DE MINIMIS INFRACTIONS

The Court shall dismiss a prosecution if, having regard to the nature of the conduct charged to constitute an offense and the nature of the attendant circumstances, it finds that the defendant's conduct:

(1) was within a customary license or tolerance, neither expressly negatived by the person whose interest was infringed nor inconsistent with the purpose of the law defining the offense; or

(2) did not actually cause or threaten the harm or evil sought to be prevented by the law defining the offense or did so only to an extent too trivial to warrant the condemnation of conviction; or

(3) presents such other extenuations that it cannot reasonably be regarded as envisaged by the legislature in forbidding the offense.

The Court shall not dismiss a prosecution under Subsection (3) of this Section without filing a written statement of its reasons.

SECTION 2.13. ENTRAPMENT

(1) A public law enforcement official or a person acting in cooperation with such an official perpetrates an entrapment if for the purpose of obtaining evidence of the commission of an offense, he induces or encourages another person to engage in conduct constituting such offense by either:

(a) making knowingly false representations designed to induce the belief that such conduct is not prohibited; or

(b) employing methods of persuasion or inducement which create a substantial risk that such an offense will be committed by persons other than those who are ready to commit it.

(2) Except as provided in Subsection (3) of this Section, a person prosecuted for an offense shall be acquitted if he proves by a preponderance of evidence that his conduct occurred in response to an entrapment. The issue of entrapment shall be tried by the Court in the absence of the jury.

(3) The defense afforded by this Section is unavailable when causing or threatening bodily injury is an element of the offense charged and the prosecution is based on conduct causing or threatening such injury to a person other than the person perpetrating the entrapment.

Article 3.   General Principles of Justification

SECTION 3.01. JUSTIFICATION AN AFFIRMATIVE DEFENSE; CIVIL REMEDIES UNAFFECTED

(1) In any prosecution based on conduct which is justifiable under this Article, justification is an affirmative defense.

(2) The fact that conduct is justifiable under this Article does not abolish or impair any remedy for such conduct which is available in any civil action.

SECTION 3.02. JUSTIFICATION GENERALLY: CHOICE OF EVILS

(1) Conduct which the actor believes to be necessary to avoid a harm or evil to himself or to another is justifiable, provided that:

(a) the harm or evil sought to be avoided by such conduct is greater than that sought to be prevented by the law defining the offense charged; and

(b) neither the Code nor other law defining the offense provides exceptions or defenses dealing with the specific situation involved; and

(c) a legislative purpose to exclude the justification claimed does not otherwise plainly appear.

(2) When the actor was reckless or negligent in bringing about the situation requiring a choice of harms or evils or in appraising the necessity for his conduct, the justification afforded by this Section is unavailable in a prosecution for any offense for which recklessness or negligence, as the case may be, suffices to establish culpability.

SECTION 3.03. EXECUTION OF PUBLIC DUTY

(1) Except as provided in Subsection (2) of this Section, conduct is justifiable when it is required or authorized by:

(a) the law defining the duties or functions of a public officer or the assistance to be rendered to such officer in the performance of his duties; or

(b) the law governing the execution of legal process; or

(c) the judgment or order of a competent court or tribunal; or

(d) the law governing the armed services or the lawful conduct of war; or

(e) any other provision of law imposing a public duty.

(2) The other sections of this Article apply to:

(a) the use of force upon or toward the person of another for any of the purposes dealt with in such sections; and

(b) the use of deadly force for any purpose, unless the use of such force is otherwise expressly authorized by law or occurs in the lawful conduct of war.

(3) The justification afforded by Subsection (1) of this Section applies:

(a) when the actor believes his conduct to be required or authorized by the judgment or direction of a competent court or tribunal or in the lawful execution of legal process, notwithstanding lack of jurisdiction of the court or defect in the legal process; and

(b) when the actor believes his conduct to be required or authorized to assist a public officer in the performance of his duties, notwithstanding that the officer exceeded his legal authority.

SECTION 3.04. USE OF FORCE IN SELF-PROTECTION

(1) *Use of Force Justifiable for Protection of the Person.* Subject to the provisions of this Section and of Section 3.09, the use of force upon or toward another person is justifiable when the actor believes that such force is immediately necessary for the purpose of protecting himself against the use of unlawful force by such other person on the present occasion.

(2) *Limitations on Justifying Necessity for Use of Force.*

(a) The use of force is not justifiable under this Section:

(i) to resist an arrest which the actor knows is being made by a peace officer, although the arrest is unlawful; or

(ii) to resist force used by the occupier or possessor of property or by another person on his behalf, where the actor knows that the person using the force is doing so under a claim of right to protect the property, except that this limitation shall not apply if:

(1) the actor is a public officer acting in the performance of his duties or a person lawfully assisting him therein or a person making or assisting in a lawful arrest; or

(2) the actor has been unlawfully dispossessed of the property and is making a re-entry or recaption justified by Section 3.06; or

(3) the actor believes that such force is necessary to protect himself against death or serious bodily harm.

(b) The use of deadly force is not justifiable under this Section unless the actor believes that such force is necessary to protect himself against death, serious bodily harm, kidnapping or sexual intercourse compelled by force or threat; nor is it justifiable if:

(i) the actor, with the purpose of causing death or serious bodily harm, provoked the use of force against himself in the same encounter; or

(ii) the actor knows that he can avoid the necessity of using such force with complete safety by retreating or by surrendering possession of a thing to a person asserting a claim of right thereto or by complying with a demand that he abstain from any action which he has no duty to take, except that:

(1) the actor is not obliged to retreat from his dwelling of place or work, unless he was the initial aggressor or is assailed in his place of work by another person whose place of work the actor knows it to be; and

(2) a public officer justified in using force in the performance of his duties or a person justified in using force in his assistance or a person justified in using force in making an arrest or preventing an escape is not obliged to desist from efforts to perform such duty, effect such arrest or prevent such escape because of resistance or threatened resistance by or on behalf of the person against whom such action is directed.

(c) Except as required by paragraphs (a) and (b) of this Subsection, a person employing protective force may estimate the necessity thereof under the circumstances as he believes them to be when the force is used, without retreating, surrendering possession, doing any other act which he has no legal duty to do or abstaining from any lawful action.

(3) *Use of Confinement as Protective Force.* The justification afforded by this Section extends to the use of confinement as protective force only if the actor takes all reasonable measures to terminate the confinement as soon as he knows that he safely can, unless the person confined has been arrested on a charge of crime.

SECTION 3.05.   USE OF FORCE FOR THE PROTECTION OF OTHER PERSONS

(1) Subject to the provisions of this Section and of Section 3.09, the use of force upon or toward the person of another is justifiable to protect a third person when:

(a) the actor would be justified under Section 3.04 in using such force to protect himself against the injury he believes to be threatened to the person whom he seeks to protect; and

(b) under the circumstances as the actor believes them to be, the person whom he seeks to protect would be justified in using such protective force; and

(c) the actor believes that his intervention is necessary for the protection of such other person.

(2) Notwithstanding Subsection (1) of this Section:

(a) when the actor would be obliged under Section 3.04 to retreat, to surrender the possession of a thing or to comply with a demand before using force in self-protection, he is not obliged to do so before using force for the protection of another person, unless he knows that he can thereby secure the complete safety of such other person; and

(b) when the person whom the actor seeks to protect would be obliged under Section 3.04 to retreat, to surrender the possession of a thing or to comply with a demand if he knew that he could obtain complete safety by so doing, the actor is obliged to try to cause him to to do so before using force in his protection if the actor knows that he can obtain complete safety in that way; and

(c) neither the actor nor the person whom he seeks to protect is obliged to retreat when in the other's dwelling or place of work to any greater extent than in his own.

SECTION 3.06. USE OF FORCE FOR THE PROTECTION OF PROPERTY

(1) *Use of Force Justifiable for Protection of Property.* Subject to the provisions of this Section and of Section 3.09, the use of force upon or toward the person of another is justifiable when the actor believes that such force is immediately necessary:

(a) to prevent or terminate an unlawful entry or other trespass upon land or a trespass against or the unlawful carrying away of tangible, movable property, provided that such land or movable property is, or is believed by the actor to be, in his possession or in the possession of another person for whose protection he acts; or

(b) to effect an entry or re-entry upon land or to retake tangible movable property, provided that the actor believes that he or the person by whose authority he acts or a person from whom he or such other person derives title was unlawfully dispossessed of such land or movable property and is entitled to possession, and provided, further, that:

(i) the force is used immediately or on fresh pursuit after such dispossession; or

(ii) the actor believes that the person against whom he uses force has no claim of right to the possession of the property and, in the case of land, the circumstances, as the actor believes them to be, are of such urgency that it would be an exceptional hardship to postpone the entry or re-entry until a court order is obtained.

(2) *Meaning of Possession.* For the purposes of Subsection (1) of this Section:

(a) a person who has parted with the custody of property to another who refuses to restore it to him is no longer in possession, unless the property is movable and was and still is located on land in his possession;

(b) a person who has been dispossessed of land does not regain possession thereof merely by setting foot thereon;

(c) a person who has a license to use or occupy real property is deemed to be in possession thereof except against the licensor acting under claim of right.

(3) *Limitations on Justifiable Use of Force.*

(a) *Request to Desist.* The use of force is justifiable under this Section only if the actor first requests the person against whom such force is used to desist from his interference with the property, unless the actor believes that:

(i) such request would be useless; or

(ii) it would be dangerous to himself or another person to make the request; or

(iii) substantial harm will be done to the physical condition of the property which is sought to be protected before the request can effectively be made.

(b) *Exclusion of Trespasser.* The use of force to prevent or terminate a trespass is not justifiable under this Section if the actor knows that the exclusion of the trespasser will expose him to substantial danger of serious bodily harm.

(c) *Resistance of Lawful Re-entry or Recaption.* The use of force to prevent an entry or re-entry upon land or the recaption of movable property is not justifiable under this Section, although the actor believes that such re-entry or recaption is unlawful, if:

(i) the re-entry or recaption is made by or on behalf of a person who was actually dispossessed of the property; and

(ii) it is otherwise justifiable under paragraph (1)(b) of this Section.

(d) *Use of Deadly Force.* The use of deadly force is not justifiable under this Section unless the actor believes that:

(i) the person against whom the force is used is attempting to dispossess him of his dwelling otherwise than under a claim of right to its possession; or

(ii) the person against whom the force is used is attempting to commit or consummate arson, burglary, robbery or other felonious theft or property destruction and either:

(1) has employed or threatened deadly force against or in the presence of the actor; or

(2) the use of force other than deadly force to prevent the commission or the consummation of the crime would expose the actor or another in his presence to substantial danger of serious bodily harm.

(4) *Use of Confinement as Protective Force.* The justification afforded by this Section extends to the use of confinement as protective force only if the actor takes all reasonable measures to terminate the confinement as soon as he knows that he can do so with safety to the property, unless the person confined has been arrested on a charge of crime.

(5) *Use of Device to Protect Property.* The justification afforded by this Section extends to the use of a device for the purpose of protecting property only if:

(a) the device is not designed to cause or known to create a substantial risk of causing death or serious bodily harm; and

(b) the use of the particular device to protect the property from entry or trespass is reasonable under the circumstances, as the actor believes them to be; and

(c) the device is one customarily used for such a purpose or reasonable care is taken to make known to probable intruders the fact that it is used.

(6) *Use of Force to Pass Wrongful Obstructor.* The use of force to pass a person whom the actor believes to be purposely or knowingly and unjustifiably obstructing the actor from going to a place to which he may lawfully go is justifiable, provided that:

(a) the actor believes that the person against whom he uses force has no claim of right to obstruct the actor; and

(b) the actor is not being obstructed from entry or movement on land which he knows to be in the possession or custody of the person obstructing him, or in the possession or custody of another person by whose authority the obstructor acts, unless the circumstances, as the actor believes them to be, are of such urgency that it would not be reasonable to postpone the entry or movement on such land until a court order is obtained; and

(c) the force used is not greater than would be justifiable if the person obstructing the actor were using force against him to prevent his passage.

SECTION 3.07. USE OF FORCE IN LAW ENFORCEMENT

(1) *Use of Force Justifiable to Effect an Arrest.* Subject to the provisions of this Section and of Section 3.09, the use of force upon or toward the person of another is justifiable when the actor is making or assisting in making an arrest and the actor believes that such force is immediately necessary to effect a lawful arrest.

(2) *Limitations on the Use of Force.*

(a) The use of force is not justifiable under this Section unless:

(i) the actor makes known the purpose of the arrest or believes that it is otherwise known by or cannot reasonably be made known to the person to be arrested; and

(ii) when the arrest is made under a warrant, the warrant is valid or believed by the actor to be valid.

(b) The use of deadly force is not justifiable under this Section unless:

(i) the arrest is for a felony; and

(ii) the person effecting the arrest is authorized to act as a peace officer or is assisting a person whom he believes to be authorized to act as a peace officer; and

(iii) the actor believes that the force employed creates no substantial risk of injury to innocent persons; and

(iv) the actor believes that:

(1) the crime for which the arrest is made involved conduct including the use or threatened use of deadly force; or

(2) there is a substantial risk that the person to be arrested will cause death or serious bodily harm if his apprehension is delayed.

(3) *Use of Force to Prevent Escape from Custody.* The use of force to prevent the escape of an arrested person from custody is justifiable when the force could justifiably have been employed to effect the arrest under which the person is in custody, except that a guard or other person authorized to act as a peace officer is justified in using any force, including deadly force, which he believes to be immediately necessary to prevent the escape of a person from a jail, prison, or other institution for the detention of persons charged with or convicted of a crime.

(4) *Use of Force by Private Person Assisting an Unlawful Arrest.*

(a) A private person who is summoned by a peace officer to assist in effecting an unlawful arrest, is justified in using any force which he would be justified in using if the arrest were lawful, provided that he does not believe the arrest is unlawful.

(b) A private person who assists another private person in effecting an unlawful arrest, or who, not being summoned, assists a peace officer in effecting an unlawful arrest, is justified in using any force which he would be justified in using if the arrest were lawful, provided that (i) he believes the arrest is lawful, and (ii) the arrest would be lawful if the facts were as he believes them to be.

(5) *Use of Force to Prevent Suicide or the Commission of a Crime.*

(a) The use of force upon or toward the person of another is justifiable when the actor believes that such force is immediately necessary to prevent such other person from committing suicide, inflicting serious bodily harm upon himself, committing or consummating the commission of a crime involving or threatening bodily harm, damage to or loss of property or a breach of the peace, except that:

(i) any limitations imposed by the other provisions of this Article on the justifiable use of force in self-protection, for the protection of others, the protection of property, the effectuation of an arrest or the prevention of an escape from custody shall apply notwithstanding the criminality of the conduct against which such force is used; and

(ii) the use of deadly force is not in any event justifiable under this Subsection unless:

(1) the actor believes that there is a substantial risk that the person whom he seeks to prevent from committing a crime will cause death or serious bodily harm to another unless the commission or the consummation of the crime is prevented and that the use of such force presents no substantial risk of injury to innocent persons; or

(2) the actor believes that the use of such force is necessary to suppress a riot or mutiny after the rioters or mutineers have been ordered to disperse and warned, in any particular manner that the law may require, that such force will be used if they do not obey.

(b) The justification afforded by this Subsection extends to the use of confinement as preventive force only if the actor takes all reasonable measures to terminate the confinement as soon as he knows that he safely can, unless the person confined has been arrested on a charge of crime.

Section 3.08.   **Use of Force by Persons with Special Responsibility for Care, Discipline or Safety of Others**

The use of force upon or toward the person of another is justifiable if:

(1) the actor is the parent or guardian or other person similarly responsible for the general care and supervision of a minor or a person acting at the request of such parent, guardian or other responsible person and:

    (a) the force is used for the purpose of safeguarding or promoting the welfare of the minor, including the prevention or punishment of his misconduct; and

    (b) the force used is not designed to cause or known to create a substantial risk of causing death, serious bodily harm, disfigurement, extreme pain or mental distress or gross degradation; or

(2) the actor is a teacher or a person otherwise entrusted with the care or supervision for a special purpose of a minor and:

    (a) the actor believes that the force used is necessary to further such special purpose, including the maintenance of reasonable discipline in a school, class or other group, and that the use of such force is consistent with the welfare of the minor; and

    (b) the degree of force, if it had been used by the parent or guardian of the minor, would not be unjustifiable under Subsection (1)(b) of this Section; or

(3) the actor is the guardian or other person similarly responsible for the general care and supervision of an incompetent person; and:

    (a) the force is used for the purpose of safeguarding or promoting the welfare of the incompetent person, including the prevention of his misconduct, or, when such incompetent person is in a hospital or other institution for his care and custody, for the maintenance of reasonable discipline in such institution; and

    (b) the force used is not designed to cause or known to create a substantial risk of causing death, serious bodily harm, disfigurement, extreme or unnecessary pain, mental distress, or humiliation; or

(4) the actor is a doctor or other therapist or a person assisting him at his direction, and:

    (a) the force is used for the purpose of administering a recognized form of treatment which the actor believes to be adapted to promoting the physical or mental health of the patient; and

    (b) the treatment is administered with the consent of the patient or, if the patient is a minor or an incompetent person, with the consent of his parent or guardian or other person legally competent to consent in his behalf, or the treatment is administered in an emergency when the actor believes that no one competent to consent can be consulted and that a reasonable person, wishing to safeguard the welfare of the patient, would consent; or

(5) the actor is a warden or other authorized official of a correctional institution, and:

    (a) he believes that the force used is necessary for the purpose of enforcing the lawful rules or procedures of the institution, unless his belief in the lawfulness of the rule or procedure sought to be enforced is erroneous and his error is due to ignorance or mistake as to the provisions of the Code, any other provision of the criminal law or the law governing the administration of the institution; and

    (b) the nature or degree of force used is not forbidden by Article 303 or 304 of the Code; and

    (c) if deadly force is used, its use is otherwise justifiable under this Article; or

(6) the actor is a person responsible for the safety of a vessel or an aircraft or a person acting at his direction, and

(a) he believes that the force used is necessary to prevent interference with the operation of the vessel or aircraft or obstruction of the execution of a lawful order, unless his belief in the lawfulness of the order is erroneous and his error is due to ignorance or mistake as to the law defining his authority; and

(b) if deadly force is used, its use is otherwise justifiable under this Article; or

(7) the actor is a person who is authorized or required by law to maintain order or decorum in a vehicle, train or other carrier or in a place where others are assembled, and:

(a) he believes that the force used is necessary for such purpose; and

(b) the force used is not designed to cause or known to create a substantial risk of causing death, bodily harm, or extreme mental distress.

SECTION 3.09. MISTAKE OF LAW AS TO UNLAWFULNESS OF FORCE OR LEGALITY OF ARREST; RECKLESS OR NEGLIGENT USE OF OTHERWISE JUSTIFIABLE FORCE; RECKLESS OR NEGLIGENT INJURY OR RISK OF INJURY TO INNOCENT PERSONS

(1) The justification afforded by Sections 3.04 to 3.07, inclusive, is unavailable when:

(a) the actor's belief in the unlawfulness of the force or conduct against which he employs protective force or his belief in the lawfulness of an arrest which he endeavors to effect by force is erroneous; and

(b) his error is due to ignorance or mistake as to the provisions of the Code, any other provision of the criminal law or the law governing the legality of an arrest or search.

(2) When the actor believes that the use of force upon or toward the person of another is necessary for any of the purposes for which such belief would establish a justification under Sections 3.03 to 3.08 but the actor is reckless or negligent in having such belief or in acquiring or failing to acquire any knowledge or belief which is material to the justifiability of his use of force, the justification afforded by those Sections is unavailable in a prosecution for an offense for which recklessness or negligence, as the case may be, suffices to establish culpability.

(3) When the actor is justified under Sections 3.03 to 3.08 in using force upon or toward the person of another but he recklessly or negligently injures or creates a risk of injury to innocent persons, the justification afforded by those Sections is unavailable in a prosecution for such recklessness or negligence towards innocent persons.

SECTION 3.10. JUSTIFICATION IN PROPERTY CRIMES

Conduct involving the appropriation, seizure or destruction of, damage to, intrusion on or interference with property is justifiable under circumstances which would establish a defense of privilege in a civil action based thereon, unless:

(1) the Code or the law defining the offense deals with the specific situation involved; or

(2) a legislative purpose to exclude the justification claimed otherwise plainly appears.

SECTION 3.11. DEFINITIONS

In this Article, unless a different meaning plainly is required:

(1) "unlawful force" means force, including confinement, which is employed without

the consent of the person against whom it is directed and the employment of which constitutes an offense or actionable tort or would constitute such offense or tort except for a defense (such as the absence of intent, negligence, or mental capacity; duress; youth; or diplomatic status) not amounting to a privilege to use the force. Assent constitutes consent, within the meaning of this Section, whether or not it otherwise is legally effective, except assent to the infliction of death or serious bodily harm.

(2) "deadly force" means force which the actor uses with the purpose of causing or which he knows to create a substantial risk of causing death or serious bodily harm. Purposely firing a firearm in the direction of another person or at a vehicle in which another person is believed to be constitutes deadly force. A threat to cause death or serious bodily harm, by the production of a weapon or otherwise, so long as the actor's purpose is limited to creating an apprehension that he will use deadly force if necessary, does not constitute deadly force;

(3) "dwelling" means any building or structure, though movable or temporary, or a portion thereof, which is for the time being the actor's home or place of lodging.

Article 4. Responsibility

SECTION 4.01. MENTAL DISEASE OR DEFECT EXCLUDING RESPONSIBILITY

(1) A person is not responsible for criminal conduct if at the time of such conduct as a result of mental disease or defect he lacks substantial capacity either to appreciate the criminality [wrongfulness] of his conduct or to conform his conduct to the requirements of law.

(2) As used in this Article, the terms "mental disease or defect" do not include an abnormality manifested only by repeated criminal or otherwise anti-social conduct.

SECTION 4.02. EVIDENCE OF MENTAL DISEASE OR DEFECT ADMISSIBLE WHEN RELEVANT TO ELEMENT OF THE OFFENSE; [MENTAL DISEASE OR DEFECT IMPAIRING CAPACITY AS GROUND FOR MITIGATION OF PUNISHMENT IN CAPITAL CASES]

(1) Evidence that the defendant suffered from a mental disease or defect is admissible whenever it is relevant to prove that the defendant did or did not have a state of mind which is an element of the offense.

[(2) Whenever the jury or the Court is authorized to determine or to recommend whether or not the defendant shall be sentenced to death or imprisonment upon conviction, evidence that the capacity of the defendant to appreciate the criminality [wrongfulness] of his conduct or to conform his conduct to the requirements of law was impaired as a result of mental disease or defect is admissible in favor of sentence of imprisonment.]

SECTION 4.03. MENTAL DISEASE OR DEFECT EXCLUDING RESPONSIBILITY IS AFFIRMATIVE DEFENSE; REQUIREMENT OF NOTICE; FORM OF VERDICT AND JUDGMENT WHEN FINDING OF IRRESPONSIBILITY IS MADE

(1) Mental disease or defect excluding responsibility is an affirmative defense.

(2) Evidence of mental disease or defect excluding responsibility is not admissible unless the defendant, at the time of entering his plea of not guilty or within ten days thereafter or at such later time as the Court may for good cause permit, files a written notice of his purpose to rely on such defense.

(3) When the defendant is acquitted on the ground of mental disease or defect excluding responsibility, the verdict and the judgment shall so state.

Section 4.04. Mental Disease or Defect Excluding Fitness to Proceed

No person who as a result of mental disease or defect lacks capacity to understand the proceedings against him or to assist in his own defense shall be tried, convicted or sentenced for the commission of an offense so long as such incapacity endures.

Section 4.05. Psychiatric Examination of Defendant with Respect to Mental Disease or Defect

(1) Whenever the defendant has filed a notice of intention to rely on the defense of mental disease or defect excluding responsibility, or there is reason to doubt his fitness to proceed, or reason to believe that mental disease or defect of the defendant will otherwise become an issue in the cause, the Court shall appoint at least one qualified psychiatrist or shall request the Superintendent of the _____ Hospital to designate at least one qualified psychiatrist, which designation may be or include himself, to examine and report upon the mental condition of the defendant. The Court may order the defendant to be committed to a hospital or other suitable facility for the purpose of the examination for a period of not exceeding sixty days or such longer period as the Court determines to be necessary for the purpose and may direct that a qualified psychiatrist retained by the defendant be permitted to witness and participate in the examination.

(2) In such examination any method may be employed which is accepted by the medical profession for the examination of those alleged to be suffering from mental disease or defect.

(3) The report of the examination shall include the following: (a) a description of the nature of the examination; (b) a diagnosis of the mental condition of the defendant; (c) if the defendant suffers from a mental disease or defect, an opinion as to his capacity to understand the proceedings against him and to assist in his own defense; (d) when a notice of intention to rely on the defense of irresponsibility has been filed, an opinion as to the extent, if any, to which the capacity of the defendant to appreciate the criminality [wrongfulness] of his conduct or to conform his conduct to the requirements of law was impaired at the time of the criminal conduct charged; and (e) when directed by the Court, an opinion as to the capacity of the defendant to have a particular state of mind which is an element of the offense charged.

If the examination can not be conducted by reason of the unwillingness of the defendant to participate therein, the report shall so state and shall include, if possible, an opinion as to whether such unwillingness of the defendant was the result of mental disease or defect.

The report of the examination shall be filed [in triplicate] with the clerk of the Court, who shall cause copies to be delivered to the district attorney and to counsel for the defendant.

Section 4.06. Determination of Fitness to Proceed; Effect of Finding of Unfitness; Proceedings if Fitness is Regained [; Post-Commitment Hearing]

(1) When the defendant's fitness to proceed is drawn in question, the issue shall be determined by the Court. If neither the prosecuting attorney nor counsel for the defendant contests the finding of the report filed pursuant to Section 4.05, the Court may make the determination on the basis of such report. If the finding is contested, the Court shall hold a hearing on the issue. If the report is received in evidence upon such hearing, the party who contests the finding thereof shall have the right to summon and to cross-examine the psychiatrists who joined in the report and to offer evidence upon the issue.

(2) If the Court determines that the defendant lacks fitness to proceed, the proceeding

against him shall be suspended, except as provided in Subsection (3) [Subsections (3) and (4)] of this Section, and the Court shall commit him to the custody of the Commissioner of Mental Hygiene [Public Health or Correction] to be placed in an appropriate institution of the Department of Mental Hygiene [Public Health or Correction] for so long as such unfitness shall endure. When the Court, on its own motion or upon the application of the Commissioner of Mental Hygiene [Public Health or Correction] or the prosecuting attorney, determines, after a hearing if a hearing is requested, that the defendant has regained fitness to proceed, the proceeding shall be resumed. If, however, the Court is of the view that so much time has elapsed since the commitment of the defendant that it would be unjust to resume the criminal proceeding, the Court may dismiss the charge and may order the defendant to be discharged or, subject to the law governing the civil commitment of persons suffering from mental disease or defect, order the defendant to be committed to an appropriate institution of the Department of Mental Hygiene [Public Health].

(3) The fact that the defendant is unfit to proceed does not preclude any legal objection to the prosecution which is susceptible of fair determination prior to trial and without the personal participation of the defendant.

[Alternative: (3) At any time within ninety days after commitment as provided in Subsection (2) of this Section, or at any later time with permission of the Court granted for good cause, the defendant or his counsel or the Commissioner of Mental Hygiene [Public Health or Correction] may apply for a special post-commitment hearing. If the application is made by or on behalf of a defendant not represented by counsel, he shall be afforded a reasonable opportunity to obtain counsel, and if he lacks funds to do so, counsel shall be assigned by the Court. The application shall be granted only if the counsel for the defendant satisfies the Court by affidavit or otherwise that as an attorney he has reasonable grounds for a good faith belief that his client has, on the facts and the law, a defense to the charge other than mental disease or defect excluding responsibility.

[(4) If the motion for a special post-commitment hearing is granted, the hearing shall be by the Court without a jury. No evidence shall be offered at the hearing by either party on the issue of mental disease or defect as a defense to, or in mitigation of, the crime charged. After hearing, the Court may in an appropriate case quash the indictment or other charge, or find it to be defective or insufficient, or determine that it is not proved beyond a reasonable doubt by the evidence, or otherwise terminate the proceedings on the evidence or the law. In any such case, unless all defects in the proceedings are promptly cured, the Court shall terminate the commitment ordered under Subsection (2) of this Section and order the defendant to be discharged or, subject to the law governing the civil commitment of persons suffering from mental disease or defect, order the defendant to be committed to an appropriate institution of the Department of Mental Hygiene [Public Health].]

Section 4.07.   Determination of Irresponsibility on Basis of Report; Access to Defendant by Psychiatrist of His Own Choice; Form of Expert Testimony When Issue of Responsibility Is Tried

(1) If the report filed pursuant to Section 4.05 finds that the defendant at the time of the criminal conduct charged suffered from a mental disease or defect which substantially impaired his capacity to appreciate the criminality [wrongfulness] of his conduct or to conform his conduct to the requirements of law, and the Court, after a hearing if a hearing is requested by the prosecuting attorney or the defendant, is satisfied that such impairment was sufficient to exclude responsibility, the Court on motion of the defendant shall enter judgment of acquittal on the ground of mental disease or defect excluding responsibility.

(2) When, notwithstanding the report filed pursuant to Section 4.05, the defendant wishes to be examined by a qualified psychiatrist or other expert of his own choice, such examiner shall be permitted to have reasonable access to the defendant for the purposes of such examination.

(3) Upon the trial, the psychiatrists who reported pursuant to Section 4.05 may be called as witnesses by the prosecution, the defendant or the Court. If the issue is being tried before a jury, the jury may be informed that the psychiatrists were designated by the Court or by the Superintendent of the _____ Hospital at the request of the Court, as the case may be. If called by the Court, the witness shall be subject to cross-examination by the prosecution and by the defendant. Both the prosecution and the defendant may summon any other qualified psychiatrist or other expert to testify, but no one who has not examined the defendant shall be competent to testify to an expert opinion with respect to the mental condition or responsibility of the defendant, as distinguished from the validity of the procedure followed by, or the general scientific propositions stated by, another witness.

(4) When a psychiatrist or other expert who has examined the defendant testifies concerning his mental condition, he shall be permitted to make a statement as to the nature of his examination, his diagnosis of the mental condition of the defendant at the time of the commission of the offense charged and his opinion as to the extent, if any, to which the capacity of the defendant to appreciate the criminality [wrongfulness] of his conduct or to conform his conduct to the requirements of law or to have a particular state of mind which is an element of the offense charged was impaired as a result of mental disease or defect at that time. He shall be permitted to make any explanation reasonably serving to clarify his diagnosis and opinion and may be cross-examined as to any matter bearing on his competency or credibility or the validity of his diagnosis or opinion.

SECTION 4.08. LEGAL EFFECT OF ACQUITTAL ON THE GROUND OF MENTAL DISEASE OR DEFECT EXCLUDING RESPONSIBILITY; COMMITMENT; RELEASE OR DISCHARGE

(1) When a defendant is acquitted on the ground of mental disease or defect excluding responsibility, the Court shall order him to be committed to the custody of the Commissioner of Mental Hygiene [Public Health] to be placed in an appropriate institution for custody, care and treatment.

(2) If the Commissioner of Mental Hygiene [Public Health] is of the view that a person committed to his custody, pursuant to paragraph (1) of this Section, may be discharged or released on condition without danger to himself or to others, he shall make application for the discharge or release of such person in a report to the Court by which such person was committed and shall transmit a copy of such application and report to the prosecuting attorney of the county [parish] from which the defendant was committed. The Court shall thereupon appoint at least two qualified psychiatrists to examine such person and to report within sixty days, or such longer period as the Court determines to be necessary for the purpose, their opinion as to his mental condition. To facilitate such examination and the proceedings thereon, the Court may cause such person to be confined in any institution located near the place where the Court sits, which may hereafter be designated by the Commissioner of Mental Hygiene [Public Health] as suitable for the temporary detention of irresponsible persons.

(3) If the Court is satisfied by the report filed pursuant to paragraph (2) of this Section and such testimony of the reporting psychiatrists as the Court deems necessary that the committed person may be discharged or released on condition without danger to himself or others, the Court shall order his discharge or his release on such conditions as the Court determines to be necessary. If the Court is not so satisfied, it shall promptly

order a hearing to determine whether such person may safely be discharged or released. Any such hearing shall be deemed a civil proceeding and the burden shall be upon the committed person to prove that he may safely be discharged or released. According to the determination of the Court upon the hearing, the committed person shall thereupon be discharged or released on such conditions as the Court determines to be necessary, or shall be recommitted to the custody of the Commissioner of Mental Hygiene [Public Health], subject to discharge or release only in accordance with the procedure prescribed above for a first hearing.

(4) If, within [five] years after the conditional release of a committed person, the Court shall determine, after hearing evidence, that the conditions of release have not been fulfilled and that for the safety of such person or for the safety of others his conditional release should be revoked, the Court shall forthwith order him to be recommitted to the Commissioner of Mental Hygiene [Public Health], subject to discharge or release only in accordance with the procedure prescribed above for a first hearing.

(5) A committed person may make application for his discharge or release to the Court by which he was committed, and the procedure to be followed upon such application shall be the same as that prescribed above in the case of an application by the Commissioner of Mental Hygiene [Public Health]. However, no such application by a committed person need be considered until he has been confined for a period of not less than [six months] from the date of the order of commitment, and if the determination of the Court be adverse to the application, such person shall not be permitted to file a further application until [one year] has elapsed from the date of any preceding hearing on an application for his release or discharge.

SECTION 4.09. STATEMENTS FOR PURPOSES OF EXAMINATION OR TREATMENT INADMISSIBLE EXCEPT ON ISSUE OF MENTAL CONDITION

A statement made by a person subjected to psychiatric examination or treatment pursuant to Sections 4.05, 4.06 or 4.08 for the purposes of such examination or treatment shall not be admissible in evidence against him in any criminal proceeding on any issue other than that of his mental condition but it shall be admissible upon that issue, whether or not it would otherwise be deemed a privileged communication [, unless such statement constitutes an admission of guilt of the crime charged].

SECTION 4.10. IMMATURITY EXCLUDING CRIMINAL CONVICTION; TRANSFER OF PROCEEDINGS TO JUVENILE COURT

(1) A person shall not be tried for or convicted of an offense if:
(a) at the time of the conduct charged to constitute the offense he was less than sixteen years of age [, in which case the Juvenile Court shall have exclusive jurisdiction]; or
(b) at the time of the conduct charged to constitute the offense he was sixteen or seventeen years of age, unless:
(i) the Juvenile Court has no jurisdiction over him, or,
(ii) the Juvenile Court has entered an order waiving jurisdiction and consenting to the institution of criminal proceedings against him.
(2) No court shall have jurisdiction to try or convict a person of an offense if criminal proceedings against him are barred by Subsection (1) of this Section. When it appears that a person charged with the commission of an offense may be of such an age that criminal proceedings may be barred under Subsection (1) of this Section, the Court shall hold a hearing thereon, and the burden shall be on the prosecution to establish

to the satisfaction of the Court that the criminal proceeding is not barred upon such grounds. If the Court determines that the proceeding is barred, custody of the person charged shall be surrendered to the Juvenile Court, and the case, including all papers and processes relating thereto, shall be transferred.

Article 5. Inchoate Crimes

SECTION 5.01. CRIMINAL ATTEMPT

(1) *Definition of Attempt.* A person is guilty of an attempt to commit a crime if, acting with the kind of culpability otherwise required for commission of the crime, he:

(a) purposely engages in conduct which would constitute the crime if the attendant circumstances were as he believes them to be; or

(b) when causing a particular result is an element of the crime, does or omits to do anything with the purpose of causing or with the belief that it will cause such result without further conduct on his part; or

(c) purposely does or omits to do anything which, under the circumstances as he believes them to be, is an act or omission constituting a substantial step in a course of conduct planned to culminate in his commission of the crime.

(2) *Conduct Which May Be Held Substantial Step Under Subsection (1)(c).* Conduct shall not be held to constitute a substantial step under Subsection (1)(c) of this Section unless it is strongly corroborative of the actor's criminal purpose. Without negativing the sufficiency of other conduct, the following, if strongly corroborative of the actor's criminal purpose, shall not be held insufficient as a matter of law:

(a) lying in wait, searching for or following the contemplated victim of the crime;

(b) enticing or seeking to entice the contemplated victim of the crime to go to the place contemplated for its commission;

(c) reconnoitering the place contemplated for the commission of the crime;

(d) unlawful entry of a structure, vehicle or enclosure in which it is contemplated that the crime will be committed;

(e) possession of materials to be employed in the commission of the crime, which are specially designed for such unlawful use or which can serve no lawful purpose of the actor under the circumstances:

(f) possession, collection or fabrication of materials to be employed in the commission of the crime, at or near the place contemplated for its commission, where such possession, collection or fabrication serves no lawful purpose of the actor under the circumstances;

(g) soliciting an innocent agent to engage in conduct constituting an element of the crime.

(3) *Conduct Designed to Aid Another in Commission of a Crime.* A person who engages in conduct designed to aid another to commit a crime which would establish his complicity under Section 2.06 if the crime were committed by such other person, is guilty of an attempt to commit the crime, although the crime is not committed or attempted by such other person.

(4) *Renunciation of Criminal Purpose.* When the actor's conduct would otherwise constitute an attempt under Subsection (1)(b) or (1)(c) of this Section, it is an affirmative defense that he abandoned his effort to commit the crime or otherwise prevented its commission, under circumstances manifesting a complete and voluntary renunciation of his criminal purpose. The establishment of such defense does not, however, affect the liability of an accomplice who did not join in such abandonment or prevention.

Within the meaning of this Article, renunciation of criminal purpose is not voluntary if it is motivated, in whole or in part, by circumstances, not present or apparent at the inception of the actor's course of conduct, which increase the probability of detection or apprehension or which make more difficult the accomplishment of the criminal purpose. Renunciation is not complete if it is motivated by a decision to postpone the criminal conduct until a more advantageous time or to transfer the criminal effort to another but similar objective or victim.

SECTION 5.02. CRIMINAL SOLICITATION

(1) *Definition of Solicitation.* A person is guilty of solicitation to commit a crime if with the purpose of promoting or facilitating its commission he commands, encourages or requests another person to engage in specific conduct which would constitute such crime or an attempt to commit such crime or which would establish his complicity in its commission or attempted commission.

(2) *Uncommunicated Solicitation.* It is immaterial under Subsection (1) of this Section that the actor fails to communicate with the person he solicits to commit a crime if his conduct was designed to effect such communication.

(3) *Renunciation of Criminal Purpose.* It is an affirmative defense that the actor, after soliciting another person to commit a crime, persuaded him not to do so or otherwise prevented the commission of the crime, under circumstances manifesting a complete and voluntary renunciation of his criminal purpose.

SECTION 5.03. CRIMINAL CONSPIRACY

(1) *Definition of Conspiracy.* A person is guilty of conspiracy with another person or persons to commit a crime if with the purpose of promoting or facilitating its commission he:

(a) agrees with such other person or persons that they or one or more of them will engage in conduct which constitutes such crime or an attempt or solicitation to commit such crime; or

(b) agrees to aid such other person or persons in the planning or commission of such crime or of an attempt or solicitation to commit such crime.

(2) *Scope of Conspiratorial Relationship.* If a person guilty of conspiracy, as defined by Subsection (1) of this Section, knows that a person with whom he conspires to commit a crime has conspired with another person or persons to commit the same crime, he is guilty of conspiring with such other person or persons, whether or not he knows their identity, to commit such crime.

(3) *Conspiracy With Multiple Criminal Objectives.* If a person conspires to commit a number of crimes, he is guilty of only one conspiracy so long as such multiple crimes are the object of the same agreement or continuous conspiratorial relationship.

(4) *Joinder and Venue in Conspiracy Prosecutions.*

(a) Subject to the provisions of paragraph (b) of this Subsection, two or more persons charged with criminal conspiracy may be prosecuted jointly if:

(i) they are charged with conspiring with one another; or

(ii) the conspiracies alleged, whether they have the same or different parties, are so related that they constitute different aspects of a scheme of organized criminal conduct.

(b) In any joint prosecution under paragraph (a) of this Subsection:

(i) no defendant shall be charged with a conspiracy in any county [parish or district] other than one in which he entered into such conspiracy or in which an overt act pursuant to such conspiracy was done by him or by a person with whom he conspired; and

(ii) neither the liability of any defendant nor the admissibility against him of evidence of acts or declarations of another shall be enlarged by such joinder; and

(iii) the Court shall order a severance or take a special verdict as to any defendant who so requests, if it deems it necessary or appropriate to promote the fair determination of his guilt or innocence, and shall take any other proper measures to protect the fairness of the trial.

(5) *Overt Act.* No person may be convicted of conspiracy to commit a crime, other than a felony of the first or second degree, unless an overt act in pursuance of such conspiracy is alleged and proved to have been done by him or by a person with whom he conspired.

(6) *Renunciation of Criminal Purpose.* It is an affirmative defense that the actor, after conspiring to commit a crime, thwarted the success of the conspiracy, under circumstances manifesting a complete and voluntary renunciation of his criminal purpose.

(7) *Duration of Conspiracy.* For purposes of Section 1.06(4):

(a) conspiracy is a continuing course of conduct which terminates when the crime or crimes which are its object are committed or the agreement that they be committed is abandoned by the defendant and by those with whom he conspired; and

(b) such abandonment is presumed if neither the defendant nor anyone with whom he conspired does any overt act in pursuance of the conspiracy during the applicable period of limitation; and

(c) if an individual abandons the agreement, the conspiracy is terminated as to him only if and when he advises those with whom he conspired of his abandonment or he informs the law enforcement authorities of the existence of the conspiracy and of his participation therein.

Section 5.04. Incapacity, Irresponsibility or Immunity of Party to Solicitation or Conspiracy

(1) Except as provided in Subsection (2) of this Section, it is immaterial to the liability of a person who solicits or conspires with another to commit a crime that:

(a) he or the person whom he solicits or with whom he conspires does not occupy a particular position or have a particular characteristic which is an element of such crime, if he believes that one of them does; or

(b) the person whom he solicits or with whom he conspires is irresponsible or has an immunity to prosecution or conviction for the commission of the crime.

(2) It is a defense to a charge of solicitation or conspiracy to commit a crime that if the criminal object were achieved, the actor would not be guilty of a crime under the law defining the offense or as an accomplice under Section 2.06(5) or 2.06(6)(a) or (b).

Section 5.05. Grading of Criminal Attempt, Solicitation and Conspiracy; Mitigation in Cases of Lesser Danger; Multiple Convictions Barred

(1) *Grading.* Except as otherwise provided in this Section, attempt, solicitation and conspiracy are crimes of the same grade and degree as the most serious offense which is attempted or solicited or is an object of the conspiracy. An attempt, solicitation or conspiracy to commit a [capital crime or a] felony of the first degree is a felony of the second degree.

(2) *Mitigation.* If the particular conduct charged to constitute a criminal attempt, solicitation or conspiracy is so inherently unlikely to result or culminate in the commission of

a crime that neither such conduct nor the actor presents a public danger warranting the grading of such offense under this Section, the Court shall exercise its power under Section 6.12 to enter judgment and impose sentence for a crime of lower grade or degree or, in extreme cases, may dismiss the prosecution.

(3) *Multiple Convictions.* A person may not be convicted of more than one offense defined by this Article for conduct designed to commit or to culminate in the commission of the same crime.

SECTION 5.06. POSSESSING INSTRUMENTS OF CRIME; WEAPONS

(1) *Criminal Instruments Generally.* A person commits a misdemeanor if he possesses any instrument of crime with purpose to employ it criminally. "Instrument of crime" means:

(a) anything specially made or specially adapted for criminal use; or

(b) anything commonly used for criminal purposes and possessed by the actor under circumstances which do not negative unlawful purpose.

(2) *Presumption of Criminal Purpose from Possession of Weapon.* If a person possesses a firearm or other weapon on or about his person, in a vehicle occupied by him, or otherwise readily available for use, it shall be presumed that he had the purpose to employ it criminally, unless:

(a) the weapon is possessed in the actor's home or place of business;

(b) the actor is licensed or otherwise authorized by law to possess such weapon; or

(c) the weapon is of a type commonly used in lawful sport.

"Weapon" means anything readily capable of lethal use and possessed under circumstances not manifestly appropriate for lawful uses which it may have; the term includes a firearm which is not loaded or lacks a clip or other component to render it immediately operable, and components which can readily be assembled into a weapon.

(3) *Presumptions as to Possession of Criminal Instruments in Automobiles.* Where a weapon or other instrument of crime is found in an automobile, it is presumed to be in the possession of the occupant if there is but one. If there is more than one occupant, it shall be presumed to be in the possession of all, except under the following circumstances:

(a) where it is found upon the person of one of the occupants;

(b) where the automobile is not a stolen one and the weapon or instrument is found out of view in a glove compartment, car trunk, or other enclosed customary depository, in which case it shall be presumed to be in the possession of the occupant or occupants who own or have authority to operate the automobile;

(c) in the case of a taxicab, a weapon or instrument found in the passengers' portion of the vehicle shall be presumed to be in the possession of all the passengers, if there are any, and, if not, in the possession of the driver.

SECTION 5.07. PROHIBITED OFFENSIVE WEAPONS

A person commits a misdemeanor if, except as authorized by law, he makes, repairs, sells, or otherwise deals in, uses or possesses any offensive weapon. "Offensive weapon" means any bomb, machine gun, sawed-off shotgun, firearm specially made or specially adapted for concealment or silent discharge, any blackjack, sandbag, metal knuckles, dagger, or other implement for the infliction of serious bodily injury which serves no common lawful purpose. It is a defense under this Section for the defendant to prove by a preponderance of evidence that he possessed or dealt with the weapon solely as a curio or in a dramatic performance, or that he possessed it briefly in consequence of having found it or taken it from an aggressor, or under circumstances similarly negativing any purpose or likelihood that the weapon would be used unlawfully. The presumptions provided in Section 5.06(3) are applicable to prosecutions under this Section.

Article 6. Authorized Disposition of Offenders

SECTION 6.01. DEGREES OF FELONIES

(1) Felonies defined by this Code are classified, for the purpose of sentence, into three degrees, as follows:
  (a) felonies of the first degree;
  (b) felonies of the second degree;
  (c) felonies of the third degree.
A felony is of the first or second degree when it is so designated by the Code. A crime declared to be a felony, without specification of degree, is of the third degree.

(2) Notwithstanding any other provision of law, a felony defined by any statute of this State other than this Code shall constitute for the purpose of sentence a felony of the third degree.

SECTION 6.02. SENTENCE IN ACCORDANCE WITH CODE; AUTHORIZED DISPOSITIONS

(1) No person convicted of an offense shall be sentenced otherwise than in accordance with this Article.

[(2) The Court shall sentence a person who has been convicted of murder to death or imprisonment, in accordance with Section 210.6.]

(3) Except as provided in Subsection (2) of this Section and subject to the applicable provisions of the Code, the Court may suspend the imposition of sentence on a person who has been convicted of a crime, may order him to be committed in lieu of sentence, in accordance with Section 6.13, or may sentence him as follows:
  (a) to pay a fine authorized by Section 6.03; or
  (b) to be placed on probation [, and, in the case of a person convicted of a felony or misdemeanor to imprisonment for a term fixed by the Court not exceeding thirty days to be served as a condition of probation]; or
  (c) to imprisonment for a term authorized by Sections 6.05, 6.06, 6.07, 6.08, 6.09, or 7.06; or
  (d) to fine and probation or fine and imprisonment, but not to probation and imprisonment [, except as authorized in paragraph (b) of this Subsection].

(4) The Court may suspend the imposition of sentence on a person who has been convicted of a violation or may sentence him to pay a fine authorized by Section 6.03.

(5) This Article does not deprive the Court of any authority conferred by law to decree a forfeiture of property, suspend or cancel a license, remove a person from office, or impose any other civil penalty. Such a judgment or order may be included in the sentence.

SECTION 6.03. FINES

A person who has been convicted of an offense may be sentenced to pay a fine not exceeding:
  (1) $10,000, when the conviction is of a felony of the first or second degree;
  (2) $5,000, when the conviction is of a felony of the third degree;
  (3) $1,000, when the conviction is of a misdemeanor;

(4) $500, when the conviction is of a petty misdemeanor or a violation;

(5) any higher amount equal to double the pecuniary gain derived from the offense by the offender;

(6) any higher amount specifically authorized by statute.

SECTION 6.04. PENALTIES AGAINST CORPORATIONS AND UNINCORPORATED ASSOCIATIONS; FORFEITURE OF CORPORATE CHARTER OR REVOCATION OF CERTIFICATE AUTHORIZING FOREIGN CORPORATION TO DO BUSINESS IN THE STATE

(1) The Court may suspend the sentence of a corporation or an unincorporated association which has been convicted of an offense or may sentence it to pay a fine authorized by Section 6.03.

(2) (a) The [prosecuting attorney] is authorized to institute civil proceedings in the appropriate court of general jurisdiction to forfeit the charter of a corporation organized under the laws of this State or to revoke the certificate authorizing a foreign corporation to conduct business in this State. The Court may order the charter forfeited or the certificate revoked upon finding (i) that the board of directors or a high managerial agent acting in behalf of the corporation has, in conducting the corporation's affairs, purposely engaged in a persistent course of criminal conduct and (ii) that for the prevention of future criminal conduct of the same character, the public interest requires the charter of the corporation to be forfeited and the corporation to be dissolved or the certificate to be revoked.

(b) When a corporation is convicted of a crime or a high managerial agent of a corporation, as defined in Section 2.07, is convicted of a crime committed in the conduct of the affairs of the corporation, the Court, in sentencing the corporation or the agent, may direct the [prosecuting attorney] to institute proceedings authorized by paragraph (a) of this Subsection.

(c) The proceedings authorized by paragraph (a) of this Subsection shall be conducted in accordance with the procedures authorized by law for the involuntary dissolution of a corporation or the revocation of the certificate authorizing a foreign corporation to conduct business in this State. Such proceedings shall be deemed additional to any other proceedings authorized by law for the purpose of forfeiting the charter of a corporation or revoking the certificate of a foreign corporation.

SECTION 6.05. YOUNG ADULT OFFENDERS

(1) *Specialized Correctional Treatment.* A young adult offender is a person convicted of a crime who, at the time of sentencing, is sixteen but less than twenty-two years of age. A young adult offender who is sentenced to a term of imprisonment which may exceed thirty days [alternatives: (1) ninety days; (2) one year] shall be committed to the custody of the Division of Young Adult Correction of the Department of Correction, and shall receive, as far as practicable, such special and individualized correctional and rehabilitative treatment as may be appropriate to his needs.

(2) *Special Term.* A young adult offender convicted of a felony may, in lieu of any other sentence of imprisonment authorized by this Article, be sentenced to a special term of imprisonment without a minimum and with a maximum of four years, regardless of the degree of the felony involved, if the Court is of the opinion that such special term is adequate for his correction and rehabilitation and will not jeopardize the protection of the public.

[(3) *Removal of Disabilities; Vacation of Conviction.*

(a) In sentencing a young adult offender to the special term provided by this Section or to any sentence other than one of imprisonment, the Court may order that so long as he is not convicted of another felony, the judgment shall not constitute a conviction for the purposes of any disqualification or disability imposed by law upon conviction of a crime.

(b) When any young adult offender is unconditionally discharged from probation or parole before the expiration of the maximum term thereof, the Court may enter an order vacating the judgment of conviction.]

[(4) *Commitment for Observation.* If, after pre-sentence investigation, the Court desires additional information concerning a young adult offender before imposing sentence, it may order that he be committed, for a period not exceeding ninety days, to the custody of the Division of Young Adult Correction of the Department of Correction for observation and study at an appropriate reception or classification center. Such Division of the Department of Correction and the [Young Adult Division of the] Board of Parole shall advise the Court of their findings and recommendations on or before the expiration of such ninety-day period.]

SECTION 6.06. SENTENCE OF IMPRISONMENT FOR FELONY; ORDINARY TERMS

A person who has been convicted of a felony may be sentenced to imprisonment, as follows:

(1) in the case of a felony of the first degree, for a term the minimum of which shall be fixed by the Court at not less than one year nor more than ten years, and the maximum of which shall be life imprisonment;

(2) in the case of a felony of the second degree, for a term the minimum of which shall be fixed by the Court at not less than one year nor more than three years, and the maximum of which shall be ten years;

(3) in the case of a felony of the third degree, for a term the minimum of which shall be fixed by the Court at not less than one year nor more than two years, and the maximum of which shall be five years.

ALTERNATE SECTION 6.06. SENTENCE OF IMPRISONMENT FOR FELONY; ORDINARY TERMS

A person who has been convicted of a felony may be sentenced to imprisonment, as follows:

(1) in the case of a felony of the first degree, for a term the minimum of which shall be fixed by the Court at not less than one year nor more than ten years, and the maximum at not more than twenty years or at life imprisonment;

(2) in the case of a felony of the second degree, for a term the minimum of which shall be fixed by the Court at not less than one year nor more than three years, and the maximum at not more than ten years;

(3) in the case of a felony of the third degree, for a term the minimum of which shall be fixed by the Court at not less than one year nor more than two years, and the maximum at not more than five years.

No sentence shall be imposed under this Section of which the minimum is longer than one-half the maximum, or, when the maximum is life imprisonment, longer than ten years.

SECTION 6.07. SENTENCE OF IMPRISONMENT FOR FELONY; EXTENDED TERMS

In the cases designated in Section 7.03, a person who has been convicted of a felony may be sentenced to an extended term of imprisonment, as follows:

(1) in the case of a felony of the first degree, for a term the minimum of which shall be fixed by the Court at not less than five years nor more than ten years, and the maximum of which shall be life imprisonment;

(2) in the case of a felony of the second degree, for a term the minimum of which shall be fixed by the Court at not less than one year nor more than five years, and the maximum of which shall be fixed by the Court at not less than ten nor more than twenty years;

(3) in the case of a felony of the third degree, for a term the minimum of which shall be fixed by the Court at not less than one year nor more than three years, and the maximum of which shall be fixed by the Court at not less than five nor more than ten years.

SECTION 6.08. SENTENCE OF IMPRISONMENT FOR MISDEMEANORS AND PETTY MISDEMEANORS; ORDINARY TERMS

A person who has been convicted of a misdemeanor or a petty misdemeanor may be sentenced to imprisonment for a definite term which shall be fixed by the Court and shall not exceed one year in the case of a misdemeanor or thirty days in the case of a petty misdemeanor.

SECTION 6.09. SENTENCE OF IMPRISONMENT FOR MISDEMEANORS AND PETTY MISDEMEANORS; EXTENDED TERMS

(1) In the cases designated in Section 7.04, a person who has been convicted of a misdemeanor or a petty misdemeanor may be sentenced to an extended term of imprisonment, as follows:

(a) in the case of a misdemeanor, for a term the minimum of which shall be fixed by the Court at not more than one year and the maximum of which shall be three years;

(b) in the case of a petty misdemeanor, for a term the minimum of which shall be fixed by the Court at not more than six months and the maximum of which shall be two years.

(2) No such sentence for an extended term shall be imposed unless:

(a) the Director of Correction has certified that there is an institution in the Department of Correction, or in a county, city [or other appropriate political subdivision of the State] which is appropriate for the detention and correctional treatment of such misdemeanants or petty misdemeanants, and that such institution is available to receive such commitments; and

(b) the [Board of Parole] [Parole Administrator] has certified that the Board of Parole is able to visit such institution and to assume responsibility for the release of such prisoners on parole and for their parole supervision.

SECTION 6.10. FIRST RELEASE OF ALL OFFENDERS ON PAROLE; SENTENCE OF IMPRISONMENT INCLUDES SEPARATE PAROLE TERM; LENGTH OF PAROLE TERM; LENGTH OF RECOMMITMENT AND REPAROLE AFTER REVOCATION OF PAROLE; FINAL UNCONDITIONAL RELEASE

(1) *First Release of All Offenders on Parole.* An offender sentenced to an indefinite term of imprisonment in excess of one year under Section 6.05, 6.06, 6.07, 6.09 or 7.06

shall be released conditionally on parole at or before the expiration of the maximum of such term, in accordance with Article 305.

(2) *Sentence of Imprisonment Includes Separate Parole Term; Length of Parole Term.* A sentence to an indefinite term of imprisonment in excess of one year under Section 6.05, 6.06, 6.07, 6.09 or 7.06 includes as a separate portion of the sentence a term of parole or of recommitment for violation of the conditions of parole which governs the duration of parole or recommitment after the offender's first conditional release on parole. The minimum of such term is one year and the maximum is five years, unless the sentence was imposed under Section 6.05(2) or Section 6.09, in which case the maximum is two years.

(3) *Length of Recommitment and Reparole After Revocation of Parole.* If an offender is recommitted upon revocation of his parole, the term of further imprisonment upon such recommitment and of any subsequent reparole or recommitment under the same sentence shall be fixed by the Board of Parole but shall not exceed in aggregate length the unserved balance of the maximum parole term provided by Subsection (2) of this Section.

(4) *Final Unconditional Release.* When the maximum of his parole term has expired or he has been sooner discharged from parole under Section 305.12, an offender shall be deemed to have served his sentence and shall be released unconditionally.

SECTION 6.11. PLACE OF IMPRISONMENT

(1) When a person is sentenced to imprisonment for an indefinite term with a maximum in excess of one year, the Court shall commit him to the custody of the Department of Correction [or other single department or agency] for the term of his sentence and until release in accordance with law.

(2) When a person is sentenced to imprisonment for a definite term, the Court shall designate the institution or agency to which he is committed for the term of his sentence and until released in accordance with law.

SECTION 6.12. REDUCTION OF CONVICTION BY COURT TO LESSER DEGREE OF FELONY OR TO MISDEMEANOR

If, when a person has been convicted of a felony, the Court, having regard to the nature and circumstances of the crime and to the history and character of the defendant, is of the view that it would be unduly harsh to sentence the offender in accordance with the Code, the Court may enter judgment of conviction for a lesser degree of felony or for a misdemeanor and impose sentence accordingly.

SECTION 6.13. CIVIL COMMITMENT IN LIEU OF PROSECUTION OR OF SENTENCE

(1) When a person prosecuted for a [felony of the third degree,] misdemeanor or petty misdemeanor is a chronic alcoholic, narcotic addict [or prostitute] or person suffering from mental abnormality and the Court is authorized by law to order the civil commitment of such person to a hospital or other institution for medical, psychiatric or other rehabilitative treatment, the Court may order such commitment and dismiss the prosecution. The order of commitment may be made after conviction, in which event the Court may set aside the verdict or judgment of conviction and dismiss the prosecution.

(2) The Court shall not make an order under Subsection (1) of this Section unless it is of the view that it will substantially further the rehabilitation of the defendant and will not jeopardize the protection of the public.

Article 7.   Authority of Court in Sentencing

SECTION 7.01. CRITERIA FOR WITHHOLDING SENTENCE OF IMPRISONMENT AND FOR PLACING DEFENDANT ON PROBATION

(1) The Court shall deal with a person who has been convicted of a crime without imposing sentence of imprisonment unless, having regard to the nature and circumstances of the crime and the history, character and condition of the defendant, it is of the opinion that his imprisonment is necessary for protection of the public because:

(a) there is undue risk that during the period of a suspended sentence or probation the defendant will commit another crime; or

(b) the defendant is in need of correctional treatment that can be provided most effectively by his commitment to an institution; or

(c) a lesser sentence will depreciate the seriousness of the defendant's crime.

(2) The following grounds, while not controlling the discretion of the Court, shall be accorded weight in favor of withholding sentence of imprisonment:

(a) the defendant's criminal conduct neither caused nor threatened serious harm;

(b) the defendant did not contemplate that his criminal conduct would cause or threaten serious harm;

(c) the defendant acted under a strong provocation;

(d) there were substantial grounds tending to excuse or justify the defendant's criminal conduct, though failing to establish a defense;

(e) the victim of the defendant's criminal conduct induced or facilitated its commission;

(f) the defendant has compensated or will compensate the victim of his criminal conduct for the damage or injury that he sustained;

(g) the defendant has no history of prior delinquency or criminal activity or has led a law-abiding life for a substantial period of time before the commission of the present crime;

(h) the defendant's criminal conduct was the result of circumstances unlikely to recur;

(i) the character and attitudes of the defendant indicate that he is unlikely to commit another crime;

(j) the defendant is particularly likely to respond affirmatively to probationary treatment;

(k) the imprisonment of the defendant would entail excessive hardship to himself or his dependents.

(3) When a person who has been convicted of a crime is not sentenced to imprisonment, the Court shall place him on probation if he is in need of the supervision, guidance, assistance or direction that the probation service can provide.

SECTION 7.02. CRITERIA FOR IMPOSING FINES

(1) The Court shall not sentence a defendant only to pay a fine, when any other disposition is authorized by law, unless having regard to the nature and circumstances of the crime and to the history and character of the defendant, it is of the opinion that the fine alone suffices for protection of the public.

(2) The Court shall not sentence a defendant to pay a fine in addition to a sentence of imprisonment or probation unless:

(a) the defendant has derived a pecuniary gain from the crime; or

(b) the Court is of opinion that a fine is specially adapted to deterrence of the crime involved or to the correction of the offender.

(3) The Court shall not sentence a defendant to pay a fine unless:

(a) the defendant is or will be able to pay the fine; and

(b) the fine will not prevent the defendant from making restitution or reparation to the victim of the crime.

(4) In determining the amount and method of payment of a fine, the Court shall take into account the financial resources of the defendant and the nature of the burden that its payment will impose.

SECTION 7.03. CRITERIA FOR SENTENCE OF EXTENDED TERM OF IMPRISONMENT; FELONIES

The Court may sentence a person who has been convicted of a felony to an extended term of imprisonment if it finds one or more of the grounds specified in this Section. The finding of the Court shall be incorporated in the record.

(1) The defendant is a persistent offender whose commitment for an extended term is necessary for protection of the public.

The Court shall not make such a finding unless the defendant is over twenty-one years of age and has previously been convicted of two felonies or of one felony and two misdemeanors, committed at different times when he was over [insert Juvenile Court age] years of age.

(2) The defendant is a professional criminal whose commitment for an extended term is necessary for protection of the public.

The Court shall not make such a finding unless the defendant is over twenty-one years of age and:

(a) the circumstances of the crime show that the defendant has knowingly devoted himself to criminal activity as a major source of livelihood; or

(b) the defendant has substantial income or resources not explained to be derived from a source other than criminal activity.

(3) The defendant is a dangerous, mentally abnormal person whose commitment for an extended term is necessary for protection of the public.

The Court shall not make such a finding unless the defendant has been subjected to a psychiatric examination resulting in the conclusions that his mental condition is gravely abnormal; that his criminal conduct has been characterized by a pattern of repetitive or compulsive behavior or by persistent aggressive behavior with heedless indifference to consequences; and that such condition makes him a serious danger to others.

(4) The defendant is a multiple offender whose criminality was so extensive that a sentence of imprisonment for an extended term is warranted.

The Court shall not make such a finding unless:

(a) the defendant is being sentenced for two or more felonies, or is already under sentence of imprisonment for felony, and the sentences of imprisonment involved will run concurrently under Section 7.06; or

(b) the defendant admits in open court the commission of one or more other felonies and asks that they be taken into account when he is sentenced; and

(c) the longest sentences of imprisonment authorized for each of the defendant's crimes, including admitted crimes taken into account, if made to run consecutively would exceed in length the minimum and maximum of the extended term imposed.

SECTION 7.04. CRITERIA FOR SENTENCE OF EXTENDED TERM OF IMPRISONMENT; MISDEMEANORS AND PETTY MISDEMEANORS.

The Court may sentence a person who has been convicted of a misdemeanor or petty misdemeanor to an extended term of imprisonment if it finds one or more of the grounds specified in this Section. The finding of the Court shall be incorporated in the record.

(1) The defendant is a persistent offender whose commitment for an extended term is necessary for protection of the public.

The Court shall not make such a finding unless the defendant has previously been convicted of two crimes, committed at different times when he was over [insert Juvenile Court age] years of age.

(2) The defendant is a professional criminal whose commitment for an extended term is necessary for protection of the public.

The Court shall not make such a finding unless:

(a) the circumstances of the crime show that the defendant has knowingly devoted himself to criminal activity as a major source of livelihood; or

(b) the defendant has substantial income or resources not explained to be derived from a source other than criminal activity.

(3) The defendant is a chronic alcoholic, narcotic addict, prostitute or person of abnormal mental condition who requires rehabilitative treatment for a substantial period of time.

The Court shall not make such a finding unless, with respect to the particular category to which the defendant belongs, the Director of Correction has certified that there is a specialized institution or facility which is satisfactory for the rehabilitative treatment of such persons and which otherwise meets the requirements of Section 6.09, Subsection (2).

(4) The defendant is a multiple offender whose criminality was so extensive that a sentence of imprisonment for an extended term is warranted.

The Court shall not make such a finding unless:

(a) the defendant is being sentenced for a number of misdemeanors or petty misdemeanors or is already under sentence of imprisonment for crimes of such grades, or admits in open court the commission of one or more such crimes and asks that they be taken into account when he is sentenced; and

(b) maximum fixed sentences of imprisonment for each of the defendant's crimes, including admitted crimes taken into account, if made to run consecutively, would exceed in length the maximum period of the extended term imposed.

SECTION 7.05.   FORMER CONVICTION IN ANOTHER JURISDICTION; DEFINITION AND PROOF OF CONVICTION; SENTENCE TAKING INTO ACCOUNT ADMITTED CRIMES BARS SUBSEQUENT CONVICTION OF SUCH CRIMES

(1) For purposes of paragraph (1) of Section 7.03 or 7.04, a conviction of the commission of a crime in another jurisdiction shall constitute a previous conviction. Such conviction shall be deemed to have been of a felony if sentence of death or of imprisonment in excess of one year was authorized under the law of such other jurisdiction, of a misdemeanor if sentence of imprisonment in excess of thirty days but not in excess of a year was authorized and of a petty misdemeanor if sentence of imprisonment for not more than thirty days was authorized.

(2) An adjudication by a court of competent jurisdiction that the defendant committed a crime constitutes a conviction for purposes of Sections 7.03 to 7.05 inclusive, although sentence or the execution thereof was suspended, provided that the time to appeal has expired and that the defendant was not pardoned on the ground of innocence.

(3) Prior conviction may be proved by any evidence, including fingerprint records made in connection with arrest, conviction or imprisonment, that reasonably satisfies the Court that the defendant was convicted.

(4) When the defendant has asked that other crimes admitted in open court be taken

into account when he is sentenced and the Court has not rejected such request, the sentence shall bar the prosecution or conviction of the defendant in this State for any such admitted crime.

Section 7.06. Multiple Sentences; Concurrent and Consecutive Terms

(1) *Sentences of Imprisonment for More Than One Crime.* When multiple sentences of imprisonment are imposed on a defendant for more than one crime, including a crime for which a previous suspended sentence or sentence of probation has been revoked, such multiple sentences shall run concurrently or consecutively as the Court determines at the time of sentence, except that:

(a) a definite and an indefinite term shall run concurrently and both sentences shall be satisfied by service of the indefinite term; and

(b) the aggregate of consecutive definite terms shall not exceed one year; and

(c) the aggregate of consecutive indefinite terms shall not exceed in minimum or maximum length the longest extended term authorized for the highest grade and degree of crime for which any of the sentences was imposed; and

(d) not more than one sentence for an extended term shall be imposed.

(2) *Sentences of Imprisonment Imposed at Different Times.* When a defendant who has previously been sentenced to imprisonment is subsequently sentenced to another term for a crime committed prior to the former sentence, other than a crime committed while in custody:

(a) the multiple sentences imposed shall so far as possible conform to Subsection (1) of this Section; and

(b) whether the Court determines that the terms shall run concurrently or consecutively, the defendant shall be credited with time served in imprisonment on the prior sentence in determining the permissible aggregate length of the term or terms remaining to be served; and

(c) when a new sentence is imposed on a prisoner who is on parole, the balance of the parole term in the former sentence shall be deemed to run during the period of the new imprisonment.

(3) *Sentence of Imprisonment for Crime Committed While on Parole.* When a defendant is sentenced to imprisonment for a crime committed while on parole in this State, such term of imprisonment and any period of reimprisonment that the Board of Parole may require the defendant to serve upon the revocation of his parole shall run concurrently, unless the Court orders them to run consecutively.

(4) *Multiple Sentences of Imprisonment in Other Cases.* Except as otherwise provided in this Section, multiple terms of imprisonment shall run concurrently or consecutively as the Court determines when the second or subsequent sentence is imposed.

(5) *Calculation of Concurrent and Consecutive Terms of Imprisonment.*

(a) When indefinite terms run concurrently, the shorter minimum terms merge in and are satisfied by serving the longest minimum term and the shorter maximum terms merge in and are satisfied by discharge of the longest maximum term.

(b) When indefinite terms run consecutively, the minimum terms are added to arrive at an aggregate minimum to be served equal to the sum of all minimum terms and the maximum terms are added to arrive at an aggregate maximum equal to the sum of all maximum terms.

(c) When a definite and an indefinite term run consecutively, the period of the definite term is added to both the minimum and maximum of the indefinite term and both sentences are satisfied by serving the indefinite term.

(6) *Suspension of Sentence or Probation and Imprisonment; Multiple Terms of Suspension and*

Probation. When a defendant is sentenced for more than one offense or a defendant already under sentence is sentenced for another offense committed prior to the former sentence:

(a) the Court shall not sentence to probation a defendant who is under sentence of imprisonment [with more than thirty days to run] or impose a sentence of probation and a sentence of imprisonment [, except as authorized by Section 6.02(3)(b)]; and

(b) multiple periods of suspension or probation shall run concurrently from the date of the first such disposition; and

(c) when a sentence of imprisonment is imposed for an indefinite term, the service of such sentence shall satisfy a suspended sentence on another count or a prior suspended sentence or sentence to probation; and

(d) when a sentence of imprisonment is imposed for a definite term, the period of a suspended sentence on another count or a prior suspended sentence or sentence to probation shall run during the period of such imprisonment.

(7) *Offense Committed While Under Suspension of Sentence or Probation.* When a defendant is convicted of an offense committed while under suspension of sentence or on probation and such suspension or probation is not revoked:

(a) if the defendant is sentenced to imprisonment for an indefinite term, the service of such sentence shall satisfy the prior suspended sentence or sentence to probation; and

(b) if the defendant is sentenced to imprisonment for a definite term, the period of the suspension or probation shall not run during the period of such imprisonment; and

(c) if sentence is suspended or the defendant is sentenced to probation, the period of such suspension or probation shall run concurrently with or consecutively to the remainder of the prior periods, as the Court determines at the time of sentence.

SECTION 7.07. PROCEDURE ON SENTENCE; PRE-SENTENCE INVESTIGATION AND REPORT; REMAND FOR PSYCHIATRIC EXAMINATION; TRANSMISSION OF RECORDS TO DEPARTMENT OF CORRECTION

(1) The Court shall not impose sentence without first ordering a pre-sentence investigation of the defendant and according due consideration to a written report of such investigation where:

(a) the defendant has been convicted of a felony; or

(b) the defendant is less than twenty-two years of age and has been convicted of a crime; or

(c) the defendant will be [placed on probation or] sentenced to imprisonment for an extended term.

(2) The Court may order a pre-sentence investigation in any other case.

(3) The pre-sentence investigation shall include an analysis of the circumstances attending the commission of the crime, the defendant's history of delinquency or criminality, physical and mental condition, family situation and background, economic status, education, occupation and personal habits and any other matters that the probation officer deems relevant or the Court directs to be included.

(4) Before imposing sentence, the Court may order the defendant to submit to psychiatric observation and examination for a period of not exceeding sixty days or such longer period as the Court determines to be necessary for the purpose. The defendant may be remanded for this purpose to any available clinic or mental hospital or the Court may appoint a qualified psychiatrist to make the examination. The report of the examination shall be submitted to the Court.

(5) Before imposing sentence, the Court shall advise the defendant or his counsel of

the factual contents and the conclusions of any pre-sentence investigation or psychiatric examination and afford fair opportunity, if the defendant so requests, to controvert them. The sources of confidential information need not, however, be disclosed.

(6) The Court shall not impose a sentence of imprisonment for an extended term unless the ground therefor has been established at a hearing after the conviction of the defendant and on written notice to him of the ground proposed. Subject to the limitation of Subsection (5) of this Section, the defendant shall have the right to hear and controvert the evidence against him and to offer evidence upon the issue.

(7) If the defendant is sentenced to imprisonment, a copy of the report of any pre-sentence investigation or psychiatric examination shall be transmitted forthwith to the Department of Correction [or other state department or agency] or, when the defendant is committed to the custody of a specific institution, to such institution.

SECTION 7.08. COMMITMENT FOR OBSERVATION; SENTENCE OF IMPRISONMENT FOR FELONY DEEMED TENTATIVE FOR PERIOD OF ONE YEAR; RE-SENTENCE ON PETITION OF COMMISSIONER OF CORRECTION

(1) If, after pre-sentence investigation, the Court desires additional information concerning an offender convicted of a felony or misdemeanor before imposing sentence, it may order that he be committed, for a period not exceeding ninety days, to the custody of the Department of Correction, or, in the case of a young adult offender, to the custody of the Division of Young Adult Correction, for observation and study at an appropriate reception or classification center. The Department and the Board of Parole, or the Young Adult Divisions thereof, shall advise the Court of their findings and recommendations on or before the expiration of such ninety-day period. If the offender is thereafter sentenced to imprisonment, the period of such commitment for observation shall be deducted from the maximum term and from the minimum, if any, of such sentence.

(2) When a person has been sentenced to imprisonment upon conviction of a felony, whether for an ordinary or extended term, the sentence shall be deemed tentative, to the extent provided in this Section, for the period of one year following the date when the offender is received in custody by the Department of Correction [or other state department or agency].

(3) If, as a result of the examination and classification by the Department of Correction [or other state department or agency] of a person under sentence of imprisonment upon conviction of a felony, the Commissioner of Correction [or other department head] is satisfied that the sentence of the Court may have been based upon a misapprehension as to the history, character or physical or mental condition of the offender, the Commissioner, during the period when the offender's sentence is deemed tentative under Subsection (2) of this Section shall file in the sentencing Court a petition to re-sentence the offender. The petition shall set forth the information as to the offender that is deemed to warrant his re-sentence and may include a recommendation as to the sentence to be imposed.

(4) The Court may dismiss a petition filed under Subsection (3) of this Section without a hearing if it deems the information set forth insufficient to warrant reconsideration of the sentence. If the Court is of the view that the petition warrants such reconsideration, a copy of the petition shall be served on the offender, who shall have the right to be heard on the issue and to be represented by counsel.

(5) When the Court grants a petition filed under Subsection (3) of this Section, it shall re-sentence the offender and may impose any sentence that might have been imposed originally for the felony of which the defendant was convicted. The period of his imprisonment prior to re-sentence and any reduction for good behavior to which he is entitled shall be applied in satisfaction of the final sentence.

(6) For all purposes other than this Section, a sentence of imprisonment has the same finality when it is imposed that it would have if this Section were not in force.

(7) Nothing in this Section shall alter the remedies provided by law for vacating or correcting an illegal sentence.

SECTION 7.09.   CREDIT FOR TIME OF DETENTION PRIOR TO SENTENCE; CREDIT FOR IMPRISONMENT UNDER EARLIER SENTENCE FOR THE SAME CRIME

(1) When a defendant who is sentenced to imprisonment has previously been detained in any state or local correctional or other institution following his [conviction of] [arrest for] the crime for which such sentence is imposed, such period of detention following his [conviction] [arrest] shall be deducted from the maximum term, and from the minimum, if any, of such sentence. The officer having custody of the defendant shall furnish a certificate to the Court at the time of sentence, showing the length of such detention of the defendant prior to sentence in any state or local correctional or other institution, and the certificate shall be annexed to the official records of the defendant's commitment.

(2) When a judgment of conviction is vacated and a new sentence is thereafter imposed upon the defendant for the same crime, the period of detention and imprisonment theretofore served shall be deducted from the maximum term, and from the minimum, if any, of the new sentence. The officer having custody of the defendant shall furnish a certificate to the Court at the time of sentence, showing the period of imprisonment served under the original sentence, and the certificate shall be annexed to the official records of the defendant's new commitment.

PART II.   DEFINITION OF SPECIFIC CRIMES

Offenses Involving Danger to the Person

Article 210.   Criminal Homicide

SECTION 210.0.   DEFINITIONS

In Articles 210-213, unless a different meaning plainly is required:
    (1) "human being" means a person who has been born and is alive;
    (2) "bodily injury" means physical pain, illness or any impairment of physical condition;
    (3) "serious bodily injury" means bodily injury which creates a substantial risk of death or which causes serious, permanent disfigurement, or protracted loss or impairment of the function of any bodily member or organ;
    (4) "deadly weapon" means any firearm, or other weapon, device, instrument, material or substance, whether animate or inanimate, which in the manner it is used or is intended to be used is known to be capable of producing death or serious bodily injury.

SECTION 210.1.   CRIMINAL HOMICIDE

(1) A person is guilty of criminal homicide if he purposely, knowingly, recklessly or negligently causes the death of another human being.
    (2) Criminal homicide is murder, manslaughter or negligent homicide.

SECTION 210.2. MURDER

(1) Except as provided in Section 210.3(1)(b), criminal homicide constitutes murder when:

(a) it is committed purposely or knowingly; or

(b) it is committed recklessly under circumstances manifesting extreme indifference to the value of human life. Such recklessness and indifference are presumed if the actor is engaged or is an accomplice in the commission of, or an attempt to commit, or flight after committing or attempting to commit robbery, rape or deviate sexual intercourse by force or threat of force, arson, burglary, kidnapping or felonious escape.

(2) Murder is a felony of the first degree [but a person convicted of murder may be sentenced to death, as provided in Section 210.6].

SECTION 210.3. MANSLAUGHTER

(1) Criminal homicide constitutes manslaughter when:

(a) it is committed recklessly; or

(b) a homicide which would otherwise be murder is committed under the influence of extreme mental or emotional disturbance for which there is reasonable explanation or excuse. The reasonableness of such explanation or excuse shall be determined from the viewpoint of a person in the actor's situation under the circumstances as he believes them to be.

(2) Manslaughter is a felony of the second degree.

SECTION 210.4. NEGLIGENT HOMICIDE

(1) Criminal homicide constitutes negligent homicide when it is committed negligently.

(2) Negligent homicide is a felony of the third degree.

SECTION 210.5. CAUSING OR AIDING SUICIDE

(1) *Causing Suicide as Criminal Homicide.* A person may be convicted of criminal homicide for causing another to commit suicide only if he purposely causes such suicide by force, duress or deception.

(2) *Aiding or Soliciting Suicide as an Independent Offense.* A person who purposely aids or solicits another to commit suicide is guilty of a felony of the second degree if his conduct causes such suicide or an attempted suicide, and otherwise of a misdemeanor.

[SECTION 210.6. SENTENCE OF DEATH FOR MURDER; FURTHER PROCEEDINGS TO DETERMINE SENTENCE*

(1) *Death Sentence Excluded.* When a defendant is found guilty of murder, the Court shall impose sentence for a felony of the first degree if it is satisfied that:

(a) none of the aggravating circumstances enumerated in Subsection (3) of this Section was established by the evidence at the trial or will be established if further proceedings are initiated under Subsection (2) of this Section; or

* . . . The brackets are meant to reflect the fact that the Institute took no position on the desirability of the death penalty. . . .

(b) substantial mitigating circumstances, established by the evidence at the trial, call for leniency; or

(c) the defendant, with the consent of the prosecuting attorney and the approval of the Court, pleaded guilty to murder as a felony of the first degree; or

(d) the defendant was under 18 years of age at the time of the commission of the crime; or

(e) the defendant's physical or mental condition calls for leniency; or

(f) although the evidence suffices to sustain the verdict, it does not foreclose all doubt respecting the defendant's guilt.

(2) *Determination by Court or by Court and Jury.* Unless the Court imposes sentence under Subsection (1) of this Section, it shall conduct a separate proceeding to determine whether the defendant should be sentenced for a felony of the first degree or sentenced to death. The proceeding shall be conducted before the Court alone if the defendant was convicted by a Court sitting without a jury or upon his plea of guilty or if the prosecuting attorney and the defendant waive a jury with respect to sentence. In other cases it shall be conducted before the Court sitting with the jury which determined the defendant's guilt or, if the Court for good cause shown discharges that jury, with a new jury empanelled for the purpose.

In the proceeding, evidence may be presented as to any matter that the Court deems relevant to sentence, including but not limited to the nature and circumstances of the crime, the defendant's character, background, history, mental and physical condition and any of the aggravating or mitigating circumstances enumerated in Subsections (3) and (4) of this Section. Any such evidence not legally privileged, which the Court deems to have probative force, may be received, regardless of its admissibility under the exclusionary rules of evidence, provided that the defendant's counsel is accorded a fair opportunity to rebut any hearsay statements. The prosecuting attorney and the defendant or his counsel shall be permitted to present argument for or against sentence of death.

The determination whether sentence of death shall be imposed shall be in the discretion of the Court, except that when the proceeding is conducted before the Court sitting with a jury, the Court shall not impose sentence of death unless it submits to the jury the issue whether the defendant should be sentenced to death or to imprisonment and the jury returns a verdict that the sentence should be death. If the jury is unable to reach a unanimous verdict, the Court shall dismiss the jury and impose sentence for a felony of the first degree.

The Court, in exercising its discretion as to sentence, and the jury, in determining upon its verdict, shall take into account the aggravating and mitigating circumstances enumerated in Subsections (3) and (4) and any other facts that it deems relevant, but it shall not impose or recommend sentence of death unless it finds one of the aggravating circumstances enumerated in Subsection (3) and further finds that there are no mitigating circumstances sufficiently substantial to call for leniency. When the issue is submitted to the jury, the Court shall so instruct and also shall inform the jury of the nature of the sentence of imprisonment that may be imposed, including its implication with respect to possible release upon parole, if the jury verdict is against sentence of death.

Alternative formulation of Subsection (2):

(2) *Determination by Court.* Unless the Court imposes sentence under Subsection (1) of this Section, it shall conduct a separate proceeding to determine whether the defendant should be sentenced for a felony of the first degree or sentenced to death. In the proceeding, the Court, in accordance with Section 7.07, shall consider the report of the presentence investigation and, if a psychiatric examination has been ordered, the report of such examination. In addition, evidence may be presented as to any matter that the Court deems relevant to sentence, including but not limited to the nature and circumstances of the crime, the defendant's character, background, history, mental and physical

condition and any of the aggravating or mitigating circumstances enumerated in Subsections (3) and (4) of this Section. Any such evidence not legally privileged, which the Court deems to have probative force, may be received, regardless of its admissibility under the exclusionary rules of evidence, provided that the defendant's counsel is accorded a fair opportunity to rebut any hearsay statements. The prosecuting attorney and the defendant or his counsel shall be permitted to present argument for or against sentence of death.

The determination whether sentence of death shall be imposed shall be in the discretion of the Court. In exercising such discretion, the Court shall take into account the aggravating and mitigating circumstances enumerated in Subsections (3) and (4) and any other facts that it deems relevant but shall not impose sentence of death unless it finds one of the aggravating circumstances enumerated in Subsection (3) and further finds that there are no mitigating circumstances sufficiently substantial to call for leniency.

(3) *Aggravating Circumstances.*

(a) The murder was committed by a convict under sentence of imprisonment.

(b) The defendant was previously convicted of another murder or of a felony involving the use or threat of violence to the person.

(c) At the time the murder was committed the defendant also committed another murder.

(d) The defendant knowingly created a great risk of death to many persons.

(e) The murder was committed while the defendant was engaged or was an accomplice in the commission of, or an attempt to commit, or flight after committing or attempting to commit robbery, rape or deviate sexual intercourse by force or threat of force, arson, burglary or kidnapping.

(f) The murder was committed for the purpose of avoiding or preventing a lawful arrest or effecting an escape from lawful custody.

(g) The murder was committed for pecuniary gain.

(h) The murder was especially heinous, atrocious or cruel, manifesting exceptional depravity.

(4) *Mitigating Circumstances.*

(a) The defendant has no significant history of prior criminal activity.

(b) The murder was committed while the defendant was under the influence of extreme mental or emotional disturbance.

(c) The victim was a participant in the defendant's homicidal conduct or consented to the homicidal act.

(d) The murder was committed under circumstances which the defendant believed to provide a moral justification or extenuation for his conduct.

(e) The defendant was an accomplice in a murder committed by another person and his participation in the homicidal act was relatively minor.

(f) The defendant acted under duress or under the domination of another person.

(g) At the time of the murder, the capacity of the defendant to appreciate the criminality [wrongfulness] of his conduct or to conform his conduct to the requirements of law was impaired as a result of mental disease or defect or intoxication.

(h) The youth of the defendant at the time of the crime.]

Article 211. Assault; Reckless Endangering; Threats

Section 211.0. Definitions

In this Article, the definitions given in Section 210.0 apply unless a different meaning plainly is required.

SECTION 211.1. ASSAULT

(1) *Simple Assault.* A person is guilty of assault if he:
   (a) attempts to cause or purposely, knowingly or recklessly causes bodily injury to another; or
   (b) negligently causes bodily injury to another with a deadly weapon; or
   (c) attempts by physical menace to put another in fear of imminent serious bodily injury.
Simple assault is a misdemeanor unless committed in a fight or scuffle entered into by mutual consent, in which case it is a petty misdemeanor.
(2) *Aggravated Assault.* A person is guilty of aggravated assault if he:
   (a) attempts to cause serious bodily injury to another, or causes such injury purposely, knowingly or recklessly under circumstances manifesting extreme indifference to the value of human life; or
   (b) attempts to cause or purposely or knowingly causes bodily injury to another with a deadly weapon.
Aggravated assault under paragraph (a) is a felony of the second degree; aggravated assault under paragraph (b) is a felony of the third degree.

SECTION 211.2. RECKLESSLY ENDANGERING ANOTHER PERSON

A person commits a misdemeanor if he recklessly engages in conduct which places or may place another person in danger of death or serious bodily injury. Recklessness and danger shall be presumed where a person knowingly points a firearm at or in the direction of another, whether or not the actor believed the firearm to be loaded.

SECTION 211.3. TERRORISTIC THREATS

A person is guilty of a felony of the third degree if he threatens to commit any crime of violence with purpose to terrorize another or to cause evacuation of a building, place of assembly, or facility of public transportation, or otherwise to cause serious public inconvenience, or in reckless disregard of the risk of causing such terror or inconvenience.

Article 212.   Kidnapping and Related Offenses; Coercion

SECTION 212.0. DEFINITIONS

In this Article, the definitions given in Section 210.0 apply unless a different meaning plainly is required.

SECTION 212.1. KIDNAPPING

A person is guilty of kidnapping if he unlawfully removes another from his place of residence or business, or a substantial distance from the vicinity where he is found, or if he unlawfully confines another for a substantial period in a place of isolation, with any of the following purposes:
   (a) to hold for ransom or reward, or as a shield or hostage; or
   (b) to facilitate commission of any felony or flight thereafter; or

(c) to inflict bodily injury on or to terrorize the victim or another; or

(d) to interfere with the performance of any governmental or political function.

Kidnapping is a felony of the first degree unless the actor voluntarily releases the victim alive and in a safe place prior to trial, in which case it is a felony of the second degree. A removal or confinement is unlawful within the meaning of this Section if it is accomplished by force, threat or deception, or, in the case of a person who is under the age of 14 or incompetent, if it is accomplished without the consent of a parent, guardian or other person responsible for general supervision of his welfare.

Section 212.2. Felonious Restraint

A person commits a felony of the third degree if he knowingly:

(a) restrains another unlawfully in circumstances exposing him to risk of serious bodily injury; or

(b) hold another in a condition of involuntary servitude.

Section 212.3. False Imprisonment

A person commits a misdemeanor if he knowingly restrains another unlawfully so as to interfere substantially with his liberty.

Section 212.4. Interference with Custody

(1) *Custody of Children.* A person commits an offense if he knowingly or recklessly takes or entices any child under the age of 18 from the custody of its parent, guardian or other lawful custodian, when he has no privilege to do so. It is an affirmative defense that:

(a) the actor believed that his action was necessary to preserve the child from danger to its welfare; or

(b) the child, being at the time not less than 14 years old, was taken away at its own instigation without enticement and without purpose to commit a criminal offense with or against the child.

Proof that the child was below the critical age gives rise to a presumption that the actor knew the child's age or acted in reckless disregard thereof. The offense is a misdemeanor unless the actor, not being a parent or person in equivalent relation to the child, acted with knowledge that his conduct would cause serious alarm for the child's safety, or in reckless disregard of a likelihood of causing such alarm, in which case the offense is a felony of the third degree.

(2) *Custody of Committed Persons.* A person is guilty of a misdemeanor if he knowingly or recklessly takes or entices any committed person away from lawful custody when he is not privileged to do so. "Committed person" means, in addition to anyone committed under judicial warrant, any orphan, neglected or delinquent child, mentally defective or insane person, or other dependent or incompetent person entrusted to another's custody by or through a recognized social agency or otherwise by authority of law.

Section 212.5. Criminal Coercion

(1) *Offense Defined.* A person is guilty of criminal coercion if, with purpose unlawfully to restrict another's freedom of action to his detriment, he threatens to:

(a) commit any criminal offense; or

(b) accuse anyone of a criminal offense; or

(c) expose any secret tending to subject any person to hatred, contempt or ridicule, or to impair his credit or business repute; or

(d) take or withhold action as an official, or cause an official to take or withhold action.

It is an affirmative defense to prosecution based on paragraphs (b), (c) or (d) that the actor believed the accusation or secret to be true or the proposed official action justified and that his purpose was limited to compelling the other to behave in a way reasonably related to the circumstances which were the subject of the accusation, exposure or proposed official action, as by desisting from further misbehavior, making good a wrong done, refraining from taking any action or responsibility for which the actor believes the other disqualified.

(2) *Grading.* Criminal coercion is a misdemeanor unless the threat is to commit a felony or the actor's purpose is felonious, in which cases the offense is a felony of the third degree.

Article 213. Sexual Offenses

SECTION 213.0. DEFINITIONS

In this Article, unless a different meaning plainly is required:

(1) the definitions given in Section 210.0 apply;

(2) "Sexual intercourse" includes intercourse per os or per anum, with some penetration however slight; emission is not required;

(3) "Deviate sexual intercourse" means sexual intercourse per os or per anum between human beings who are not husband and wife, and any form of sexual intercourse with an animal.

SECTION 213.1. RAPE AND RELATED OFFENSES

(1) *Rape.* A male who has sexual intercourse with a female not his wife is guilty of rape if:

(a) he compels her to submit by force or by threat of imminent death, serious bodily injury, extreme pain or kidnapping, to be inflicted on anyone; or

(b) he has substantially impaired her power to appraise or control her conduct by administering or employing without her knowledge drugs, intoxicants or other means for the purpose of preventing resistance; or

(c) the female is unconscious; or

(d) the female is less than 10 years old.

Rape is a felony of the second degree unless (i) in the course thereof the actor inflicts serious bodily injury upon anyone, or (ii) the victim was not a voluntary social companion of the actor upon the occasion of the crime and had not previously permitted him sexual liberties, in which cases the offense is a felony of the first degree. Sexual intercourse includes intercourse per os or per anum, with some penetration however slight; emission is not required.

(2) *Gross Sexual Imposition.* A male who has sexual intercourse with a female not his wife commits a felony of the third degree if:

(a) he compels her to submit by any threat that would prevent resistance by a woman of ordinary resolution; or

(b) he knows that she suffers from a mental disease or defect which renders her incapable of appraising the nature of her conduct; or

(c) he knows that she is unaware that a sexual act is being committed upon her or that she submits because she mistakenly supposes that he is her husband.

Section 213.2. Deviate Sexual Intercourse by Force or Imposition

(1) *By Force or Its Equivalent.* A person who engages in deviate sexual intercourse with another person, or who causes another to engage in deviate sexual intercourse, commits a felony of the second degree if:

(a) he compels the other person to participate by force or by threat of imminent death, serious bodily injury, extreme pain or kidnapping, to be inflicted on anyone; or

(b) he has substantially impaired the other person's power to appraise or control his conduct, by administering or employing without the knowledge of the other person drugs, intoxicants or other means for the purpose of preventing resistance; or

(c) the other person is unconscious; or

(d) the other person is less than 10 years old.

Deviate sexual intercourse means sexual intercourse per os or per anum between human beings who are not husband and wife, and any form of sexual intercourse with an animal.

(2) *By Other Imposition.* A person who engages in deviate sexual intercourse with another person, or who causes another to engage in deviate sexual intercourse, commits a felony of the third degree if:

(a) he compels the other person to participate by any threat that would prevent resistance by a person of ordinary resolution; or

(b) he knows that the other person suffers from a mental disease or defect which renders him incapable of appraising the nature of his conduct; or

(c) he knows that the other person submits because he is unaware that a sexual act is being committed upon him.

Section 213.3. Corruption of Minors and Seduction

(1) *Offense Defined.* A male who has sexual intercourse with a female not his wife, or any person who engages in deviate sexual intercourse or causes another to engage in deviate sexual intercourse, is guilty of an offense if:

(a) the other person is less than [16] years old and the actor is at least [4] years older than the other person; or

(b) the other person is less than 21 years old and the actor is his guardian or otherwise responsible for general supervision of his welfare; or

(c) the other person is in custody of law or detained in a hospital or other institution and the actor has supervisory or disciplinary authority over him; or

(d) the other person is a female who is induced to participate by a promise of marriage which the actor does not mean to perform.

(2) *Grading.* An offense under paragraph (a) of Subsection (1) is a felony of the third degree. Otherwise an offense under this section is a misdemeanor.

Section 213.4. Sexual Assault

A person who has sexual contact with another not his spouse, or causes such other to have sexual conduct with him, is guilty of sexual assault, a misdemeanor, if:

(1) he knows that the contact is offensive to the other person; or

(2) he knows that the other person suffers from a mental disease or defect which renders him or her incapable of appraising the nature of his or her conduct; or

(3) he knows that the other person is unaware that a sexual act is being committed; or

(4) the other person is less than 10 years old; or

(5) he has substantially impaired the other person's power to appraise or control his or her conduct, by administering or employing without the other's knowledge drugs, intoxicants or other means for the purpose of preventing resistance; or

(6) the other person is less than [16] years old and the actor is at least [four] years older than the other person; or

(7) the other person is less than 21 years old and the actor is his guardian or otherwise responsible for general supervision of his welfare; or

(8) the other person is in custody of law or detained in a hospital or other institution and the actor has supervisory or disciplinary authority over him.

Sexual contact is any touching of the sexual or other intimate parts of the person for the purpose of arousing or gratifying sexual desire.

SECTION 213.5. INDECENT EXPOSURE

A person commits a misdemeanor if, for the purpose of arousing or gratifying sexual desire of himself or of any person other than his spouse, he exposes his genitals under circumstances in which he knows his conduct is likely to cause affront or alarm.

SECTION 213.6. PROVISIONS GENERALLY APPLICABLE TO ARTICLE 213

(1) *Mistake as to Age.* Whenever in this Article the criminality of conduct depends on a child's being below the age of 10, it is no defense that the actor did not know the child's age, or reasonably believed the child to be older than 10. When criminality depends on the child's being below a critical age other than 10, it is a defense for the actor to prove by a preponderance of the evidence that he reasonably believed the child to be above the critical age.

(2) *Spouse Relationships.* Whenever in this Article the definition of an offense excludes conduct with a spouse, the exclusion shall be deemed to extend to persons living as man and wife, regardless of the legal status of their relationship. The exclusion shall be inoperative as respects spouses living apart under a decree of judicial separation. Where the definition of an offense excludes conduct with a spouse or conduct by a woman, this shall not preclude conviction of a spouse or woman as accomplice in a sexual act which he or she causes another person, not within the exclusion, to perform.

(3) *Sexually Promiscuous Complainants.* It is a defense to prosecution under Section 213.3. and paragraphs (6), (7) and (8) of Section 213.4 for the actor to prove by a preponderance of the evidence that the alleged victim had, prior to the time of the offense charged, engaged promiscuously in sexual relations with others.

(4) *Prompt Complaint.* No prosecution may be instituted or maintained under this Article unless the alleged offense was brought to the notice of public authority within [3] months of its occurrence or, where the alleged victim was less than [16] years old or otherwise incompetent to make complaint, within [3] months after a parent, guardian or other competent person specially interested in the victim learns of the offense.

(5) *Testimony of Complainants.* No person shall be convicted of any felony under this Article upon the uncorroborated testimony of the alleged victim. Corroboration may be circumstantial. In any prosecution before a jury for an offense under this Article,

the jury shall be instructed to evaluate the testimony of a victim or complaining witness with special care in view of the emotional involvement of the witness and the difficulty of determining the truth with respect to alleged sexual activities carried out in private.

Offenses Against Property

Article 220.   Arson, Criminal Mischief, and Other Property Destruction

SECTION 220.1.   ARSON AND RELATED OFFENSES

(1) *Arson.* A person is guilty of arson, a felony of the second degree, if he starts a fire or causes an explosion with the purpose of:

(a) destroying a building or occupied structure of another; or

(b) destroying or damaging any property, whether his own or another's, to collect insurance for such loss. It shall be an affirmative defense to prosecution under this paragraph that the actor's conduct did not recklessly endanger any building or occupied structure of another or place any other person in danger of death or bodily injury.

(2) *Reckless Burning or Exploding.* A person commits a felony of the third degree if he purposely starts a fire or causes an explosion, whether on his own property or another's, and thereby recklessly:

(a) places another person in danger of death or bodily injury; or

(b) places a building or occupied structure of another in danger of damage or destruction.

(3) *Failure to Control or Report Dangerous Fire.* A person who knows that a fire is endangering life or a substantial amount of property of another and fails to take reasonable measures to put out or control the fire, when he can do so without substantial risk to himself, or to give a prompt fire alarm, commits a misdemeanor if:

(a) he knows that he is under an official, contractual, or other legal duty to prevent or combat the fire; or

(b) the fire was started, albeit lawfully, by him or with his assent, or on property in his custody or control.

(4) *Definitions.* "Occupied structure" means any structure, vehicle or place adapted for overnight accommodation of persons, or for carrying on business therein, whether or not a person is actually present. Property is that of another, for the purposes of this section, if anyone other than the actor has a possessory or proprietory interest therein. If a building or structure is divided into separately occupied units, any unit not occupied by the actor is an occupied structure of another.

SECTION 220.2.   CAUSING OR RISKING CATASTROPHE

(1) *Causing Catastrophe.* A person who causes a catastrophe by explosion, fire, flood, avalanche, collapse of building, release of poison gas, radioactive material or other harmful or destructive force or substance, or by any other means of causing potentially widespread injury or damage, commits a felony of the second degree if he does so purposely or knowingly, or a felony of the third degree if he does so recklessly.

(2) *Risking Catastrophe.* A person is guilty of a misdemeanor if he recklessly creates a risk of catastrophe in the employment of fire, explosives or other dangerous means listed in Subsection (1).

(3) *Failure to Prevent Catastrophe.* A person who knowingly or recklessly fails to take reasonable measures to prevent or mitigate a catastrophe commits a misdemeanor if:

(a) he knows that he is under an official, contractual or other legal duty to take such measures; or

(b) he did or assented to the act causing or threatening the catastrophe.

SECTION 220.3. CRIMINAL MISCHIEF

(1) *Offense Defined.* A person is guilty of criminal mischief if he:

(a) damages tangible property of another purposely, recklessly, or by negligence in the employment of fire, explosives, or other dangerous means listed in Section 220.2(1); or

(b) purposely or recklessly tampers with tangible property of another so as to endanger person or property; or

(c) purposely or recklessly causes another to suffer pecuniary loss by deception or threat.

(2) *Grading.* Criminal mischief is a felony of the third degree if the actor purposely causes pecuniary loss in excess of $5,000, or a substantial interruption or impairment of public communication, transportation, supply of water, gas or power, or other public service. It is a misdemeanor if the actor purposely causes pecuniary loss in excess of $100, or a petty misdemeanor if he purposely or recklessly causes pecuniary loss in excess of $25. Otherwise criminal mischief is a violation.

Article 221. Burglary and Other Criminal Intrusion

SECTION 221.0. DEFINITIONS

In this Article, unless a different meaning plainly is required:

(1) "occupied structure" means any structure, vehicle or place adapted for overnight accommodation of persons, or for carrying on business therein, whether or not a person is actually present.

(2) "night" means the period between thirty minutes past sunset and thirty minutes before sunrise.

SECTION 221.1. BURGLARY

(1) *Burglary Defined.* A person is guilty of burglary if he enters a building or occupied structure, or separately secured or occupied portion thereof, with purpose to commit a crime therein, unless the premises are at the time open to the public or the actor is licensed or privileged to enter. It is an affirmative defense to prosecution for burglary that the building or structure was abandoned.

(2) *Grading.* Burglary is a felony of the second degree if it is perpetrated in the dwelling of another at night, or if, in the course of committing the offense, the actor:

(a) purposely, knowingly or recklessly inflicts or attempts to inflict bodily injury on anyone; or

(b) is armed with explosives or a deadly weapon.

Otherwise, burglary is a felony of the third degree. An act shall be deemed "in the course of committing" an offense if it occurs in an attempt to commit the offense or in flight after the attempt or commission.

(3) *Multiple Convictions.* A person may not be convicted both for burglary and for the offense which it was his purpose to commit after the burglarious entry or for an attempt to commit that offense, unless the additional offense constitutes a felony of the first or second degree.

Section 221.2. Criminal Trespass

(1) *Buildings and Occupied Structures.* A person commits an offense if, knowing that he is not licensed or privileged to do so, he enters or surreptitiously remains in any building or occupied structure, or separately secured or occupied portion thereof. An offense under this Subsection is a misdemeanor if it is committed in a dwelling at night. Otherwise it is a petty misdemeanor.

(2) *Defiant Trespasser.* A person commits an offense if, knowing that he is not licensed or privileged to do so, he enters or remains in any place as to which notice against trespass is given by:

(a) actual communication to the actor; or

(b) posting in a manner prescribed by law or reasonably likely to come to the attention of intruders; or

(c) fencing or other enclosure manifestly designed to exclude intruders.

An offense under this Subsection constitutes a petty misdemeanor if the offender defies an order to leave personally communicated to him by the owner of the premises or other authorized person. Otherwise it is a violation.

(3) *Defenses.* It is an affirmative defense to prosecution under this Section that:

(a) a building or occupied structure involved in an offense under Subsection (1) was abandoned; or

(b) the premises were at the time open to members of the public and the actor complied with all lawful conditions imposed on access to or remaining in the premises; or

(c) the actor reasonably believed that the owner of the premises, or other person empowered to license access thereto, would have licensed him to enter or remain.

Article 222. Robbery

Section 222.1. Robbery

(1) *Robbery Defined.* A person is guilty of robbery if, in the course of committing a theft, he:

(a) inflicts serious bodily injury upon another; or

(b) threatens another with or purposely puts him in fear of immediate serious bodily injury; or

(c) commits or threatens immediately to commit any felony of the first or second degree.

An act shall be deemed "in the course of committing a theft" if it occurs in an attempt to commit theft or in flight after the attempt or commission.

(2) *Grading.* Robbery is a felony of the second degree, except that it is a felony of the first degree if in the course of committing the theft the actor attempts to kill anyone, or purposely inflicts or attempts to inflict serious bodily injury.

Article 223. Theft and Related Offenses

Section 223.0. Definitions

In this Article, unless a different meaning plainly is required:

(1) "deprive" means: (a) to withhold property of another permanently or for so extended a period as to appropriate a major portion of its economic value, or with intent to restore only upon payment of reward or other compensation; or (b) to dispose of the property so as to make it unlikely that the owner will recover it.

(2) "financial institution" means a bank, insurance company, credit union, building and loan association, investment trust or other organization held out to the public as a place of deposit of funds or medium of savings or collective investment.

(3) "government" means the United States, any State, county, municipality, or other political unit, or any department, agency or subdivision of any of the foregoing, or any corporation or other association carrying out the functions of government.

(4) "movable property" means property the location of which can be changed, including things growing on, affixed to, or found in land, and documents although the rights represented thereby have no physical location. "Immovable property" is all other property.

(5) "obtain" means: (a) in relation to property, to bring about a transfer or purported transfer of a legal interest in the property, whether to the obtainer or another; or (b) in relation to labor or service, to secure performance thereof.

(6) "property" means anything of value, including real estate, tangible and intangible personal property, contract rights, choses-in-action and other interests in or claims to wealth, admission or transportation tickets, captured or domestic animals, food and drink, electric or other power.

(7) "property of another" includes property in which any person other than the actor has an interest which the actor is not privileged to infringe, regardless of the fact that the actor also has an interest in the property and regardless of the fact that the other person might be precluded from civil recovery because the property was used in an unlawful transaction or was subject to forfeiture as contraband. Property in possession of the actor shall not be deemed property of another who has only a security interest therein, even if legal title is in the creditor pursuant to a conditional sales contract or other security agreement.

SECTION 223.1. CONSOLIDATION OF THEFT OFFENSES; GRADING; PROVISIONS APPLICABLE TO THEFT GENERALLY

(1) *Consolidation of Theft Offenses.* Conduct denominated theft in this Article constitutes a single offense. An accusation of theft may be supported by evidence that it was committed in any manner that would be theft under this Article, notwithstanding the specification of a different manner in the indictment or information, subject only to the power of the Court to ensure fair trial by granting a continuance or other appropriate relief where the conduct of the defense would be prejudiced by lack of fair notice or by surprise.

(2) *Grading of Theft Offenses.*

(a) Theft constitutes a felony of the third degree if the amount involved exceeds $500, or if the property stolen is a firearm, automobile, airplane, motorcycle, motorboat or other motor-propelled vehicle, or in the case of theft by receiving stolen property, if the receiver is in the business of buying or selling stolen property.

(b) Theft not within the preceding paragraph constitutes a misdemeanor, except that if the property was not taken from the person or by threat, or in breach of a fiduciary obligation, and the actor proves by a preponderance of the evidence that the amount involved was less than $50, the offense constitutes a petty misdemeanor.

(c) The amount involved in a theft shall be deemed to be the highest value, by any reasonable standard, of the property or services which the actor stole or attempted to steal. Amounts involved in thefts committed pursuant to one scheme or course of conduct, whether from the same person or several persons, may be aggregated in determining the grade of the offense.

(3) *Claim of Right.* It is an affirmative defense to prosecution for theft that the actor:

(a) was unaware that the property or service was that of another; or

(b) acted under an honest claim of right to the property or service involved or that he had a right to acquire or dispose of it as he did; or

(c) took property exposed for sale, intending to purchase and pay for it promptly, or reasonably believing that the owner, if present, would have consented.

(4) *Theft from Spouse.* It is no defense that theft was from the actor's spouse, except that misappropriation of household and personal effects, or other property normally accessible to both spouses, is theft only if it occurs after the parties have ceased living together.

SECTION 223.2. THEFT BY UNLAWFUL TAKING OR DISPOSITION

(1) *Movable Property.* A person is guilty of theft if he unlawfully takes, or exercises unlawful control over, movable property of another with purpose to deprive him thereof.

(2) *Immovable Property.* A person is guilty of theft if he unlawfully transfers immovable property of another or any interest therein with purpose to benefit himself or another not entitled thereto.

SECTION 223.3. THEFT BY DECEPTION

A person is guilty of theft if he purposely obtains property of another by deception. A person deceives if he purposely:

(1) creates or reinforces a false impression, including false impressions as to law, value, intention or other state of mind; but deception as to a person's intention to perform a promise shall not be inferred from the fact alone that he did not subsequently perform the promise; or

(2) prevents another from acquiring information which would affect his judgment of a transaction; or

(3) fails to correct a false impression which the deceiver previously created or reinforced, or which the deceiver knows to be influencing another to whom he stands in a fiduciary or confidential relationship; or

(4) fails to disclose a known lien, adverse claim or other legal impediment to the enjoyment of property which he transfers or encumbers in consideration for the property obtained, whether such impediment is or is not valid, or is or is not a matter of official record.

The term "deceive" does not, however, include falsity as to matters having no pecuniary significance, or puffing by statements unlikely to deceive ordinary persons in the group addressed.

SECTION 223.4. THEFT BY EXTORTION

A person is guilty of theft if he obtains property of another by threatening to:

(1) inflict bodily injury on anyone or commit any other criminal offense; or

(2) accuse anyone of a criminal offense; or

(3) expose any secret tending to subject any person to hatred, contempt or ridicule, or to impair his credit or business repute; or

(4) take or withhold action as an official, or cause an official to take or withhold action; or

(5) bring about or continue a strike, boycott or other collective unofficial action, if the property is not demanded or received for the benefit of the group in whose interest the actor purports to act; or

(6) testify or provide information or withhold testimony or information with respect to another's legal claim or defense; or

(7) inflict any other harm which would not benefit the actor.

It is an affirmative defense to prosecution based on paragraphs (2), (3) or (4) that the property obtained by threat of accusation, exposure, lawsuit or other invocation of official action was honestly claimed as restitution or indemnification for harm done in the circumstances to which such accusation, exposure, lawsuit or other official action relates, or as compensation for property or lawful services.

SECTION 223.5. THEFT OF PROPERTY LOST, MISLAID, OR DELIVERED BY MISTAKE

A person who comes into control of property of another that he knows to have been lost, mislaid, or delivered under a mistake as to the nature or amount of the property or the identity of the recipient is guilty of theft if, with purpose to deprive the owner thereof, he fails to take reasonable measures to restore the property to a person entitled to have it.

SECTION 223.6. RECEIVING STOLEN PROPERTY

(1) *Receiving.* A person is guilty of theft if he purposely receives, retains, or disposes of movable property of another knowing that it has been stolen, or believing that it has probably been stolen, unless the property is received, retained, or disposed with purpose to restore it to the owner. "Receiving" means acquiring possession, control or title, or lending on the security of the property.

(2) *Presumption of Knowledge.* The requisite knowledge or belief is presumed in the case of a dealer who:

(a) is found in possession or control of property stolen from two or more persons on separate occasions; or

(b) has received stolen property in another transaction within the year preceding the transaction charged; or

(c) being a dealer in property of the sort received, acquires it for a consideration which he knows is far below its reasonable value.

"Dealer" means a person in the business of buying or selling goods including a pawn-broker.

SECTION 223.7. THEFT OF SERVICES

(1) A person is guilty of theft if he purposely obtains services which he knows are available only for compensation, by deception or threat, or by false token or other means to avoid payment for the service. "Services" includes labor, professional service, transportation, telephone or other public service, accommodation in hotels, restaurants or elsewhere, admission to exhibitions, use of vehicles or other movable property. Where compensation for service is ordinarily paid immediately upon the rendering for such service, as is the case of hotels and restaurants, refusal to pay or absconding without payment or offer to pay gives rise to a presumption that the service was obtained by deception as to intention to pay.

(2) A person commits theft if, having control over the disposition of services of others, to which he is not entitled, he knowingly diverts such services to his own benefit or to the benefit of another not entitled thereto.

SECTION 223.8. THEFT BY FAILURE TO MAKE REQUIRED DISPOSITION OF FUNDS RECEIVED

A person who purposely obtains property upon agreement, or subject to a known legal obligation, to make specified payment or other disposition, whether from such property or its proceeds or from his own property to be reserved in equivalent amount, is guilty of theft if he deals with the property obtained as his own and fails to make the required payment or disposition. The foregoing applies notwithstanding that it may be impossible to identify particular property as belonging to the victim at the time of the actor's failure to make the required payment or disposition. An officer or employee of the government or of a financial institution is presumed: (i) to know any legal obligation relevant to his criminal liability under this Section, and (ii) to have dealt with the property as his own if he fails to pay or account upon lawful demand, or if an audit reveals a shortage or falsification of accounts.

SECTION 223.9. UNAUTHORIZED USE OF AUTOMOBILES AND OTHER VEHICLES

A person commits a misdemeanor if he operates another's automobile, airplane, motor-cycle, motorboat, or other motor-propelled vehicle without consent of the owner. It is an affirmative defense to prosecution under this Section that the actor reasonably believed that the owner would have consented to the operation had he known of it.

Article 224. Forgery and Fraudulent Practices

SECTION 224.0 DEFINITIONS

In this Article, the definitions given in Section 223.0 apply unless a different meaning plainly is required.

SECTION 224.1. FORGERY

(1) *Definition.* A person is guilty of forgery if, with purpose to defraud or injure anyone, or with knowledge that he is facilitating a fraud or injury to be perpetrated by anyone, the actor:

(a) alters any writing of another without his authority; or

(b) makes, completes, executes, authenticates, issues or transfers any writing so that it purports to be the act of another who did not authorize that act, or to have been executed at a time or place or in a numbered sequence other than was in fact the case, or to be a copy of an original when no such original existed; or

(c) utters any writing which he knows to be forged in a manner specified in paragraphs (a) or (b).

"Writing" includes printing or any other method of recording information, money, coins, tokens, stamps, seals, credit cards, badges, trade-marks, and other symbols of value, right, privilege, or identification.

(2) *Grading.* Forgery is a felony of the second degree if the writing is or purports to be part of an issue of money, securities, postage or revenue stamps, or other instruments issued by the government, or part of an issue of stock, bonds or other instruments representing interests in or claims against any property or enterprise. Forgery is a felony of the third degree if the writing is or purports to be a will, deed, contract, release, commercial instrument, or other document evidencing, creating, transferring, altering, terminating, or otherwise affecting legal relations. Otherwise forgery is a misdemeanor.

Section 224.2. Simulating Objects of Antiquity, Rarity, Etc.

A person commits a misdemeanor if, with purpose to defraud anyone or with knowledge that he is facilitating a fraud to be perpetrated by anyone, he makes, alters or utters any object so that it appears to have value because of antiquity, rarity, source, or authorship which it does not possess.

Section 224.3. Fraudulent Destruction, Removal or Concealment of Recordable Instruments

A person commits a felony of the third degree if, with purpose to deceive or injure anyone, he destroys, removes or conceals any will, deed, mortgage, security instrument or other writing for which the law provides public recording.

Section 224.4. Tampering with Records

A person commits a misdemeanor if, knowing that he has no privilege to do so, he falsifies, destroys, removes or conceals any writing or record, with purpose to deceive or injure anyone or to conceal any wrongdoing.

Section 224.5. Bad Checks

A person who issues or passes a check or similar sight order for the payment of money, knowing that it will not be honored by the drawee, commits a misdemeanor. For the purposes of this Section as well as in any prosecution for theft committed by means of a bad check, an issuer is presumed to know that the check or order (other than a postdated check or order) would not be paid, if:

   (1) the issuer had no account with the drawee at the time the check or order was issued; or

   (2) payment was refused by the drawee for lack of funds, upon presentation within 30 days after issue, and the issuer failed to make good within 10 days after receiving notice of that refusal.

Section 224.6. Credit Cards

A person commits an offense if he uses a credit card for the purpose of obtaining property or services with knowledge that:

   (1) the card is stolen or forged; or

   (2) the card has been revoked or cancelled; or

   (3) for any other reason his use of the card is unauthorized by the issuer.

It is an affirmative defense to prosecution under paragraph (3) if the actor proves by a preponderance of the evidence that he had the purpose and ability to meet all obligations to the issuer arising out of his use of the card. "Credit card" means a writing, or other evidence of an undertaking to pay for property or services delivered or rendered to or upon the order of a designated person or bearer. An offense under this Section is a felony of the third degree if the value of the property or services secured or sought to be secured by means of the credit card exceeds $500; otherwise it is a misdemeanor.

SECTION 224.7. DECEPTIVE BUSINESS PRACTICES

A person commits a misdemeanor if in the course of business he:

(1) uses or possesses for use a false weight or measure, or any other device for falsely determining or recording any quality or quantity; or

(2) sells, offers or exposes for sale, or delivers less than the represented quantity of any commodity or service; or

(3) takes or attempts to take more than the represented quantity of any commodity or service when as buyer he furnishes the weight or measure, or

(4) sells, offers or exposes for sale adulterated or mislabeled commodities. "Adulterated" means varying from the standard of composition or quality prescribed by or pursuant to any statute providing criminal penalties for such variance, or set by established commercial usage. "Mislabeled" means varying from the standard of truth or disclosure in labeling prescribed by or pursuant to any statute providing criminal penalties for such variance, or set by established commercial usage; or

(5) makes a false or misleading statement in any advertisement addressed to the public or to a substantial segment thereof for the purpose of promoting the purchase or sale of property or services; or

(6) makes a false or misleading written statement for the purpose of obtaining property or credit; or

(7) makes a false or misleading written statement for the purpose of promoting the sale of securities, or omits information required by law to be disclosed in written documents relating to securities.

It is an affirmative defense to prosecution under this Section if the defendant proves by a preponderance of the evidence that his conduct was not knowingly or recklessly deceptive.

SECTION 224.8. COMMERCIAL BRIBERY AND BREACH OF DUTY TO ACT DISINTERESTEDLY

(1) A person commits a misdemeanor if he solicits, accepts or agrees to accept any benefit as consideration for knowingly violating or agreeing to violate a duty of fidelity to which he is subject as:

(a) partner, agent or employee of another;

(b) trustee, guardian, or other fiduciary;

(c) lawyer, physician, accountant, appraiser, or other professional adviser or informant;

(d) officer, director, manager or other participant in the direction of the affairs of an incorporated or unincorporated association; or

(e) arbitrator or other purportedly disinterested adjudicator or referee.

(2) A person who holds himself out to the public as being engaged in the business of making disinterested selection, appraisal, or criticism of commodities or services commits a misdemeanor if he solicits, accepts or agrees to accept any benefit to influence his selection, appraisal or criticism.

(3) A person commits a misdemeanor if he confers, or offers or agrees to confer, any benefit the acceptance of which would be criminal under this Section.

SECTION 224.9. RIGGING PUBLICLY EXHIBITED CONTEST

(1) A person commits a misdemeanor if, with purpose to prevent a publicly exhibited contest from being conducted in accordance with the rules and usages purporting to govern it, he:

(a) confers or offers or agrees to confer any benefit upon, or threatens any injury to a participant, official or other person associated with the contest or exhibition; or

(b) tampers with any person, animal or thing.

(2) *Soliciting or Accepting Benefit for Rigging.* A person commits a misdemeanor if he knowingly solicits, accepts or agrees to accept any benefit the giving of which would be criminal under Subsection (1).

(3) *Participation in Rigged Contest.* A person commits a misdemeanor if he knowingly engages in, sponsors, produces, judges, or otherwise participates in a publicly exhibited contest knowing that the contest is not being conducted in compliance with the rules and usages purporting to govern it, by reason of conduct which would be criminal under this Section.

SECTION 224.10. DEFRAUDING SECURED CREDITORS

A person commits a misdemeanor if he destroys, removes, conceals, encumbers, transfers or otherwise deals with property subject to a security interest with purpose to hinder enforcement of that interest.

SECTION 224.11. FRAUD IN INSOLVENCY

A person commits a misdemeanor if, knowing that proceedings have been or are about to be instituted for the appointment of a receiver or other person entitled to administer property for the benefit of creditors, or that any other composition or liquidation for the benefit of creditors has been or is about to be made, he:

(a) destroys, removes, conceals, encumbers, transfers, or otherwise deals with any property with purpose to defeat or obstruct the claim of any creditor, or otherwise to obstruct the operation of any law relating to administration of property for the benefit of creditors; or

(b) knowingly falsifies any writing or record relating to the property; or

(c) knowingly misrepresents or refuses to disclose to a receiver or other person entitled to administer property for the benefit of creditors, the existence, amount or location of the property, or any other information which the actor could be legally required to furnish in relation to such administration.

SECTION 224.12. RECEIVING DEPOSITS IN A FAILING FINANCIAL INSTITUTION

An officer, manager or other person directing or participating in the direction of a financial institution commits a misdemeanor if he receives or permits the receipt of a deposit, premium payment or other investment in the institution knowing that:

(1) due to financial difficulties the institution is about to suspend operations or go into receivership or reorganization; and

(2) the person making the deposit or other payment is unaware of the precarious situation of the institution.

SECTION 224.13. MISAPPLICATION OF ENTRUSTED PROPERTY AND PROPERTY OF GOVERNMENT OR FINANCIAL INSTITUTION

A person commits an offense if he applies or disposes of property that has been entrusted to him as a fiduciary, or property of the government or of a financial institution, in a manner which he knows is unlawful and involves substantial risk of loss or detriment to the owner of the property or to a person for whose benefit the property was entrusted. The offense is a misdemeanor if the amount involved exceeds $50; otherwise it is a petty misdemeanor. "Fiduciary" includes trustee, guardian, executor, administrator, receiver and any person carrying on fiduciary functions on behalf of a corporation or other organization which is a fiduciary.

SECTION 224.14. SECURING EXECUTION OF DOCUMENTS BY DECEPTION

A person commits a misdemeanor if by deception he causes another to execute any instrument affecting, purporting to affect, or likely to affect the pecuniary interest of any person.

Offenses Against the Family

Article 230. Offenses Against the Family

SECTION 230.1. BIGAMY AND POLYGAMY

(1) *Bigamy.* A married person is guilty of bigamy, a misdemeanor, if he contracts or purports to contract another marriage, unless at the time of the subsequent marriage:
    (a) the actor believes that the prior spouse is dead; or
    (b) the actor and the prior spouse have been living apart for five consecutive years throughout which the prior spouse was not known by the actor to be alive; or
    (c) a Court has entered a judgment purporting to terminate or annul any prior disqualifying marriage, and the actor does not know that judgment to be invalid; or
    (d) the actor reasonably believes that he is legally eligible to remarry.
(2) *Polygamy.* A person is guilty of polygamy, a felony of the third degree, if he marries or cohabits with more than one spouse at a time in purported exercise of the right of plural marriage. The offense is a continuing one until all cohabitation and claim of marriage with more than one spouse terminates. This section does not apply to parties to a polygamous marriage, lawful in the country of which they are residents or nationals, while they are in transit through or temporarily visiting this State.
(3) *Other Party to Bigamous or Polygamous Marriage.* A person is guilty of bigamy or polygamy, as the case may be, if he contracts or purports to contract marriage with another knowing that the other is thereby committing bigamy or polygamy.

SECTION 230.2. INCEST

A person is guilty of incest, a felony of the third degree, if he knowingly marries or cohabits or has sexual intercourse with an ancestor or descendant, a brother or sister of the whole or half blood [or an uncle, aunt, nephew or niece of the whole blood]. "Cohabit" means to live together under the representation or appearance of being married. The relationships referred to herein include blood relationships without regard to legitimacy, and relationship of parent and child by adoption.

SECTION 230.3. ABORTION [Omitted.]

SECTION 230.4.   ENDANGERING WELFARE OF CHILDREN

A parent, guardian, or other person supervising the welfare of a child under 18 commits a misdemeanor if he knowingly endangers the child's welfare by violating a duty of care, protection or support.

SECTION 230.5.   PERSISTENT NON-SUPPORT

A person commits a misdemeanor if he persistently fails to provide support which he can provide and which he knows he is legally obliged to provide to a spouse, child or other dependent.

Offenses Against Public Administration

Article 240.   Bribery and Corrupt Influence [Omitted.]

Article 241.   Perjury and Other Falsification in Official Matters [Omitted.]

Article 242.   Obstructing Governmental Operations; Escapes [Omitted.]

Article 243.   Abuse of Office [Omitted.]

Offenses Against Public Order and Decency

Article 250.   Riot, Disorderly Conduct, and Related Offenses

SECTION 250.1.   RIOT; FAILURE TO DISPERSE

(1) *Riot.* A person is guilty of riot, a felony of the third degree, if he participates with [two] or more others in a course of disorderly conduct:
    (a) with purpose to commit or facilitate the commission of a felony or misdemeanor;
    (b) with purpose to prevent or coerce official action; or
    (c) when the actor or any other participant to the knowledge of the actor uses or plans to use a firearm or other deadly weapon.
(2) *Failure of Disorderly Persons to Disperse Upon Official Order.* Where [three] or more persons are participating in a course of disorderly conduct likely to cause substantial harm or serious inconvenience, annoyance or alarm, a peace officer or other public servant engaged in executing or enforcing the law may order the participants and others in the immediate vicinity to disperse. A person who refuses or knowingly fails to obey such an order commits a misdemeanor.

SECTION 250.2.   DISORDERLY CONDUCT

(1) *Offense Defined.* A person is guilty of disorderly conduct if, with purpose to cause public inconvenience, annoyance or alarm, or recklessly creating a risk thereof, he:
    (a) engages in fighting or threatening, or in violent or tumultuous behavior; or
    (b) makes unreasonable noise or offensively coarse utterance, gesture or display, or addresses abusive language to any person present; or

(c) creates a hazardous or physically offensive condition by any act which serves no legitimate purpose of the actor.

"Public" means affecting or likely to affect persons in a place to which the public or a substantial group has access; among the places included are highways, transport facilities, schools, prisons, apartment houses, places of business or amusement, or any neighborhood.

(2) *Grading.* An offense under this section is a petty misdemeanor if the actor's purpose is to cause substantial harm or serious inconvenience, or if he persists in disorderly conduct after reasonable warning or request to desist. Otherwise disorderly conduct is a violation.

SECTION 250.3. FALSE PUBLIC ALARMS

A person is guilty of a misdemeanor if he initiates or circulates a report or warning of an impending bombing or other crime or catastrophe, knowing that the report or warning is false or baseless and that it is likely to cause evacuation of a building, place of assembly, or facility of public transport, or to cause public inconvenience or alarm.

SECTION 250.4. HARASSMENT

A person commits a petty misdemeanor if, with purpose to harass another, he:
(1) makes a telephone call without purpose of legitimate communication; or
(2) insults, taunts or challenges another in a manner likely to provoke violent or disorderly response; or
(3) makes repeated communications anonymously or at extremely inconvenient hours, or in offensively coarse language; or
(4) subjects another to an offensive touching; or
(5) engages in any other course of alarming conduct serving no legitimate purpose of the actor.

SECTION 250.5. PUBLIC DRUNKENNESS; DRUG INCAPACITATION

A person is guilty of an offense if he appears in any public place manifestly under the influence of alcohol, narcotics or other drugs, not therapeutically administered, to the degree that he may endanger himself or other persons or property, or annoy persons in his vicinity. An offense under this Section constitutes a petty misdemeanor if the actor has been convicted hereunder twice before within a period of one year. Otherwise the offender constitutes a violation.

SECTION 250.6. LOITERING OR PROWLING

A person commits a violation if he loiters or prowls in a place, at a time, or in a manner not usual for lawabiding individuals under circumstances that warrant alarm for the safety of persons or property in the vicinity. Among the circumstances which may be considered in determining whether such alarm is warranted is the fact that the actor takes flight upon appearance of a peace officer, refuses to identify himself, or manifestly endeavors to conceal himself or any object. Unless flight by the actor or other circumstance makes it impracticable, a peace officer shall prior to any arrest for an offense under this section afford the actor an opportunity to dispel any alarm which would otherwise be warranted, by requesting him to identify himself and explain his presence and conduct. No person shall be convicted of an offense under this Section if the peace officer did not comply with the preceding sentence, or if it appears at trial that the explanation given by the actor was true and, if believed by the peace officer at the time, would have dispelled the alarm.

SECTION 250.7. OBSTRUCTING HIGHWAYS AND OTHER PUBLIC PASSAGES

(1) A person, who, having no legal privilege to do so, purposely or recklessly obstructs any highway or other public passage, whether alone or with others, commits a violation, or, in case he persists after warning by a law officer, a petty misdemeanor. "Obstructs" means renders impassable without unreasonable inconvenience or hazard. No person shall be deemed guilty of recklessly obstructing in violation of this Subsection solely because of a gathering of persons to hear him speak or otherwise communicate, or solely because of being a member of such a gathering.

(2) A person in a gathering commits a violation if he refuses to obey a reasonable official request or order to move:

(a) to prevent obstruction of a highway or other public passage; or

(b) to maintain public safety by dispersing those gathered in dangerous proximity to a fire or other hazard.

An order to move, addressed to a person whose speech or other lawful behavior attracts an obstructing audience, shall not be deemed reasonable if the obstruction can be readily remedied by police control of the size or location of the gathering.

SECTION 250.8. DISRUPTING MEETINGS AND PROCESSIONS

A person commits a misdemeanor if, with purpose to prevent or disrupt a lawful meeting, procession or gathering, he does any act tending to obstruct or interfere with it physically, or makes any utterance, gesture or display designed to outrage the sensibilities of the group.

SECTION 250.9. DESECRATION OF VENERATED OBJECTS [Omitted.]

SECTION 250.10. ABUSE OF CORPSE [Omitted.]

SECTION 250.11. CRUELTY TO ANIMALS [Omitted.]

SECTION 250.12. VIOLATION OF PRIVACY [Omitted.]

Article 251.   Public Indecency

SECTION 251.1. OPEN LEWDNESS

A person commits a petty misdemeanor if he does any lewd act which he knows is likely to be observed by others who would be affronted or alarmed.

SECTION 251.2. PROSTITUTION AND RELATED OFFENSES

(1) *Prostitution.* A person is guilty of prostitution, a petty misdemeanor, if he or she:

(a) is an inmate of a house of prostitution or otherwise engages in sexual activity as a business; or

(b) loiters in or within view of any public place for the purpose of being hired to engage in sexual activity.

"Sexual activity" includes homosexual and other deviate sexual relations. A "house of prostitution" is any place where prostitution or promotion of prostitution is regularly carried on by one person under the control, management or supervision of another. An "inmate" is a person who engages in prostitution in or through the agency of a house of prostitution. "Public place" means any place to which the public or any substantial group thereof has access.

(2) *Promoting Prostitution.* A person who knowingly promotes prostitution of another commits a misdemeanor or felony as provided in Subsection (3). The following acts shall, without limitation of the foregoing, constitute promoting prostitution:

(a) owning, controlling, managing, supervising or otherwise keeping, alone or in association with others, a house of prostitution or a prostitution business; or

(b) procuring an inmate for a house of prostitution or a place in a house of prostitution for one who would be an inmate; or

(c) encouraging, inducing, or otherwise purposely causing another to become or remain a prostitute; or

(d) soliciting a person to patronize a prostitute; or

(e) procuring a prostitute for a patron; or

(f) transporting a person into or within this state with purpose to promote that person's engaging in prostitution, or procuring or paying for transportation with that purpose; or

(g) leasing or otherwise permitting a place controlled by the actor, alone or in association with others, to be regularly used for prostitution or the promotion of prostitution, or failure to make reasonable effort to abate such use by ejecting the tenant, notifying law enforcement authorities, or other legally available means; or

(h) soliciting, receiving, or agreeing to receive any benefit for doing or agreeing to do anything forbidden by this Subsection.

(3) *Grading of Offenses Under Subsection (2).* An offense under Subsection (2) constitutes a felony of the third degree if:

(a) the offense falls within paragraph (a), (b) or (c) of Subsection (2); or

(b) the actor compels another to engage in or promote prostitution; or

(c) the actor promotes prostitution of a child under 16, whether or not he is aware of the child's age; or

(d) the actor promotes prostitution of his wife, child, ward or any person for whose care, protection or support he is responsible.

Otherwise the offense is a misdemeanor.

(4) *Presumption from Living off Prostitutes.* A person, other than the prostitute or the prostitute's minor child or other legal dependent incapable of self-support, who is supported in whole or substantial part by the proceeds of prostitution is presumed to be knowingly promoting prostitution in violation of Subsection (2).

(5) *Patronizing Prostitutes.* A person commits a violation if he hires a prostitute to engage in sexual activity with him, or if he enters or remains in a house of prostitution for the purpose of engaging in sexual activity.

(6) *Evidence.* On the issue whether a place is a house of prostitution the following shall be admissible evidence: its general repute; the repute of the persons who reside in or frequent the place; the frequency, timing and duration of visits by non-residents. Testimony of a person against his spouse shall be admissible to prove offenses under this Section.

SECTION 251.3.   LOITERING TO SOLICIT DEVIATE SEXUAL RELATIONS

A person is guilty of a petty misdemeanor if he loiters in or near any public place for the purpose of soliciting or being solicited to engage in deviate sexual relations.

SECTION 251.4.   OBSCENITY [Omitted.]

PART III.   TREATMENT AND CORRECTION [Omitted.]

PART IV.   ORGANIZATION OF CORRECTION [Omitted.]

TABLE OF CASES

Italics indicate principal cases. Asterisked page references indicate location
where a case is quoted from or discussed at some length.

BIBLIOGRAPHIC REFERENCES

This table lists books, articles, reports, and other secondary authorities extracted or referred to in the casebook. Student notes and comments follow alphabetical listing by author.

Materials of General Import

American Law Institute, Model Penal Code and Commentaries (1981).
J. Andenaes, The General Part of the Criminal Law of Norway (1965).
P. Brett, An Inquiry into Criminal Guilt (1963).
G. Fletcher, Rethinking Criminal Law (1978).
L. Fuller, The Morality of Law (1964).
J. Hall, General Principles of Criminal Law (1960).
H. L. A. Hart, The Morality of the Criminal Law (1964).
H. L. A. Hart, Punishment and Responsibility (1968).
O. W. Holmes, The Common Law (1881).
W. LaFave & A. Scott, Criminal Law (1972).
T. B. Macaulay, A Penal Code Prepared by the Indian Law Commissioners (1837).
National Commission on Reform of Federal Criminal Laws, Working Papers (1970).
H. Packer, The Limits of the Criminal Sanction (1968).
R. Perkins, Criminal Law (2d ed. 1969).
President's Commission on Law Enforcement and the Administration of Justice, The Challenge of Crime in a Free Society (1967).
J. F. Stephen, A History of the Criminal Law of England (1883).
J. F. Stephen, Digest of the Criminal Law (5th ed. 1894).
F. Wharton, Criminal Law (12th ed. 1932).
G. Williams, Criminal Law: The General Part (2d ed. 1961).
G. Williams, Textbook of Criminal Law (1978).

Chapter 1
The Structure of the Criminal Justice System

American Bar Foundation, Criminal Justice in the United States (1967).
Federal Bureau of Investigation, Uniform Crime Reports — 1979 (1980).
J. Goldkamp, Two Classes of Accused: A Study of Bail and Detention in American Justice (1979).

G. Kelling et al., The Kansas City Preventive Patrol Experiment: A Technical Report (1974).

President's Commission on Law Enforcement and the Administration of Justice: The Challenge of Crime in a Free Society (1967).

U.S. Dept. of Justice, Sourcebook of Criminal Justice Statistics — 1980 (1981).

P. Wice, Bail and Its Reform: A National Survey (1973).

Chapter 2
How Guilt Is Established

R. Allen, The Restoration of In re Winship: A Comment on Burdens of Persuasion after Patterson v. New York, 76 Mich. L. Rev. 30 (1977).

R. Allen, Structuring Jury Decisionmaking in Criminal Cases: A Unified Constitutional Approach to Evidentiary Devices, 94 Harv. L. Rev. 321 (1980).

Alschuler, The Changing Plea-Bargaining Debate, 69 Calif. L. Rev. 652 (1981).

Alschuler, The Defense Attorney's Role in Plea Bargaining, 84 Yale L.J. 1179 (1975).

Alschuler, The Prosecutor's Role in Plea Bargaining, 36 U. Chi. L. Rev. 50 (1968).

Alschuler, The Supreme Court, The Defense Attorney, and the Guilty Plea, 47 U. Colo. L. Rev. 1 (1975).

American Bar Association, Code of Professional Responsibility (1970).

American Bar Association, Standards for Criminal Justice, Discovery and Procedure before Trial (1980).

American Bar Association, Standards for Criminal Justice, Providing Defense Services (1980).

Angel, Substantive Due Process and the Criminal Law, 9 Loy. Chi. L.J. 61 (1977).

Arenella, Reforming the Federal Grand Jury and the State Preliminary Hearing to Prevent Conviction without Adjudication, 78 Mich. L. Rev. 463 (1980).

Aronson, Should the Privilege against Self-Incrimination Apply to Compelled Psychiatric Examinations?, 26 Stan. L. Rev. 55 (1973).

Ashford & Risinger, Presumptions, Assumptions, and Due Process in Criminal Cases: A Theoretical Overview, 79 Yale L.J. 165 (1969).

Ayer, The Fifth Amendment and the Inference of Guilt from Silence: Griffin v. California after Fifteen Years, 78 Mich. L. Rev. 841 (1980).

Bazelon, The Defective Assistance of Counsel, 42 U. Cin. L. Rev. 1 (1973).

Bazelon, The Realities of Gideon and Argersinger, 64 Geo. L.J. 811 (1976).

Bermant, McGuire, McKinley & Salo, The Logic of Simulation in Jury Research, 1 Crim. J. & Behavior 224 (1974).

S. Bing & S. Rosenfeld, The Quality of Justice in the Lower Criminal Courts of Metropolitan Boston (1970).

Bradley, Griffin v. California: Still Viable after All These Years, 79 Mich. L. Rev. 1290 (1981).

Bress, Professional Ethics in Criminal Trials: A View of Defense Counsel's Responsibility, 64 Mich. L. Rev. 1493 (1966).

Broeder, The Functions of the Jury — Facts or Fictions?, 21 U. Chi. L. Rev. 386 (1947).

Burger, Some Further Reflections on the Problems of Adequacy of Trial Counsel, 49 Fordham L. Rev. 1 (1980).

Burger, The Special Skills of Advocacy: Are Specialized Training and Certification of Advocates Essential to Our System of Justice?, 42 Fordham L. Rev. 227 (1973).

Burger, Standards of Conduct for Prosecution and Defense Personnel: A Judge's Viewpoint, 5 Am. Crim. L.Q. 11 (1966).

J. Casper, American Criminal Justice: The Defendant's Perspective (1972).

Charrow & Charrow, Making Legal Language Understandable: A Psycholinguistic Study of Jury Instructions, 79 Colum. L. Rev. 1306 (1979).

Cornish & Sealy, Juries and the Rules of Evidence, [1973] Crim. L. Rev. 208.

Damaška, Evidentiary Barriers to Conviction and Two Models of Criminal Procedure, 121 U. Pa. L. Rev. 506 (1973).

Damaška, Presentation of Evidence and Factfinding Precision, 123 U. Pa. L. Rev. 1083 (1975).

Damaška, Structures of Authority and Comparative Criminal Procedure, 84 Yale L.J. 480 (1975).

Dauer & Leff, Correspondence: The Lawyer as Friend, 86 Yale L.J. 573 (1977).

Dutile, The Burden of Proof in Criminal Cases: A Comment on the *Mullaney-Patterson* Doctrine, 55 Notre Dame Law. 380 (1980).

Eisenberg, Private Ordering through Negotiation: Dispute-Settlement and Rulemaking, 89 Harv. L. Rev. 637 (1976).

Enker, Perspectives on Plea Bargaining, in President's Commission on Law Enforcement and the Administration of Justice, Task Force Report: The Courts (1967).

Fairman, Does the Fourteenth Amendment Incorporate the Bill of Rights?, 2 Stan. L. Rev. 5 (1949).

Fletcher, Two Kinds of Legal Rules: A Comparative Study of Burden-of-Persuasion Practices in Criminal Cases, 77 Yale L.J. 880 (1968).

Forston, Judge's Instructions: A Quantitative Analysis of Juror's Listening Comprehension, 18 Today's Speech 34 (1970).

Frankel, The Search for Truth: An Umpireal View, 123 U. Pa. L. Rev. 1031 (1975).

M. Freedman, Lawyers' Ethics in an Adversary System (1975).

Freedman, Professional Responsibility of the Criminal Defense Lawyer: The Three Hardest Questions, 64 Mich. L. Rev. 1469 (1966).

Fried, The Lawyer as Friend: The Moral Foundation of the Lawyer-Client Relation, 85 Yale L.J. 1060 (1976).

M. Friedland, Double Jeopardy (1969).

Friendly, The Bill of Rights as a Code of Criminal Procedure, 53 Calif. L. Rev. 929 (1965).

Friendly, The Fifth Amendment Tomorrow: The Case for Constitutional Change, 37 U. Cin. L. Rev. 671 (1968).

Gerbasi, Zuckerman & Reis, Justice Needs a New Blindfold: A Review of Mock Jury Research, 84 Psych. Bull. 323 (1977).

A. Goldman, The Moral Foundations of Professional Ethics (1980).

Goldstein & Marcus, The Myth of Judicial Supervision in Three "Inquisitorial Systems": France, Italy, and Germany, 87 Yale L.J. 240 (1977).

Griffiths, Ideology in Criminal Procedure or a Third "Model" of the Criminal Process, 79 Yale L.J. 359 (1970).

E. Griswold, The Fifth Amendment Today (1955).

Haney & Lowy, Bargain Justice in an Unjust World: Good Deals in the Criminal Courts, 13 L. & Socy. Rev. 633 (1979).

Harris, Annals of Law: In the Criminal Court I, The New Yorker, April 14, 1973, at 45.

M. Heumann, Plea Bargaining (1978).

Jeffries & Stephan, Defenses, Presumptions and Burdens of Proof in the Criminal Law, 88 Yale L.J. 1325 (1979).

Johnson, Importing Justice, 87 Yale L.J. 406 (1977).

Kadish, Methodology and Criteria in Due Process Adjudication — A Survey and Criticism, 66 Yale L.J. 319 (1975).

M. Kadish & S. Kadish, Discretion to Disobey (1973).

M. Kadish & S. Kadish, On Justified Rule Departures by Officials, 59 Calif. L. Rev. 905 (1971).

H. Kalven & H. Zeisel, The American Jury (1966).

Langbein, Torture and Plea Bargaining, 46 U. Chi. L. Rev. 3 (1978).

Langbein & Weinreb, Continental Criminal Procedure: "Myth" and Reality, 87 Yale L.J. 1549 (1978).

Lefstein, The Criminal Defendant Who Proposes Perjury, 6 Hofstra L. Rev. 665 (1978).

Levin & Cohen, The Exclusionary Rules in Nonjury Criminal Cases, 119 U. Pa. L. Rev. 905 (1971).

L. Levy, Origins of the Fifth Amendment (1968).

L. Mayers, Shall We Amend the Fifth Amendment? (1959).

McKay, Self-Incrimination and the New Privacy, [1967] Sup. Ct. Rev. 193.

McLane, The Burden of Proof in Criminal Cases: *Mullaney* and *Patterson* Compared, 15 Crim. L. Bull. 346 (1979).

H. Miller, W. McDonald & J. Cramer, Plea Bargaining in the United States (1977).

National Study Commission on Defense Services, Guidelines for Legal Defense Systems in the United States (1976).

Nesson, Reasonable Doubt and Permissive Inferences: The Value of Complexity, 92 Harv. L. Rev. 1187 (1979).

D. Newman, Conviction, The Determination of Guilt or Innocence without Trial (1966).

Noonan, The Purposes of Advocacy and the Limits of Confidentiality, 64 Mich. L. Rev. 1485 (1966).

Orkin, Defence of One Known to Be Guilty, 1 Crim. L.Q. 170 (1958).

Reed, Jury Simulation: The Impact of Judge's Instructions and Attorney Tactics on Decisionmaking, 71 J. Crim. L. & Criminology 68 (1980).

Rubenstein & White, Plea Bargaining: Can Alaska Live without It?, 62 Judicature 266 (1979).

B. Sales, A. Elwork & J. Alfini, Making Jury Instructions Understandable (1981).

Saltzburg, The Unnecessarily Expanding Role of the American Trial Judge, 64 Va. L. Rev. 1 (1978).

Scheflin, Jury Nullification: The Right to Say "No," 45 S. Cal. L. Rev. 168 (1972).

Scheflin & Van Dyke, Jury Nullification: The Contours of a Controversy, 43 L. & Contemp. Prob. 51 (1980).

Schlesinger, Comparative Criminal Procedure: A Plea for Utilizing Foreign Experience, 26 Buffalo L. Rev. 361 (1977).

Schulhofer, Due Process of Sentencing, 128 U. Pa. L. Rev. 733 (1980).

Schwartzer, Communicating with Juries: Problems and Remedies, 69 Calif. L. Rev. 731 (1981).

Schwartzer, Dealing with Incompetent Counsel — The Trial Judge's Role, 93 Harv. L. Rev. 633 (1980).

Simon, The Effects of Newspapers on the Verdicts of Potential Jurors, in R. Simon, The Sociology of Law (1968).

Simon, Homo Psychologicus: Notes on a New Legal Formalism, 32 Stan. L. Rev. 487 (1980).

Simon, The Ideology of Advocacy, [1978] Wis. L. Rev. 29.

R. Simon, The Jury and the Defense of Insanity (1967).

Simon & Mahan, Quantifying Burdens of Proof, 5 L. & Socy. Rev. 319 (1971).

Simpson, Jury Nullification in the American System: A Skeptical View, 64 Tex. L. Rev. 488 (1976).

Strawn & Buchanan, Jury Confusion: A Threat to Justice, 59 Judicature 478 (1976).

Sue, Smith & Caldwell, Effects of Inadmissible Evidence on the Decisions of Simulated Jurors: A Moral Dilemma, 3 J. Applied Soc. Psych. 345 (1973).

Underwood, The Thumb on the Scales of Justice: Burdens of Persuasion in Criminal Cases, 86 Yale L.J. 1299 (1977).

Van Alstyne, The Demise of the Right-Privilege Distinction in Constitutional Law, 81 Harv. L. Rev. 1439 (1968).

Van Dyke, Comment, Jury Nullification in Historical Perspective: Massachusetts as a Case Study, 12 Suffolk U.L. Rev. 968 (1978).

Van Dyke, The Jury as a Political Institution, The Center Magazine, 17-26 (Mar.-Apr. 1970).

Walsh, The American Jury: A Reassessment, 79 Yale L.J. 142 (1969).

Wax, Inconsistent and Repugnant Verdicts in Criminal Trials, 24 N.Y.L. Sch. L. Rev. 713 (1979).

Wasserstrom, Lawyers as Professionals: Some Moral Issues, 5 Human Rights 1 (1975).

Wesson, The Privilege against Self-Incrimination in Civil Commitment Proceedings, [1980] Wis. L. Rev. 697.

Wilkerson, Public Defenders as Their Clients See Them, 1 Am. J. Crim. L. 141 (1972).

G. Williams, The Proof of Guilt (1963).

Wyzanski, A Trial Judge's Freedom and Responsibility, 65 Harv. L. Rev. 1281 (1952).

Zeisel, The Offer That Cannot Be Refused, in F. Zimring & R. Frase, The Criminal Justice System (1980).

Zeisel, Reflections on Experimental Techniques in the Law, 2 J. Legal Stud. 107 (1973).

Client Service in a Defender Organization, 117 U. Pa. L. Rev. 448 (1969).

The Constitutionality of Affirmative Defenses after Patterson v. New York, 78 Colum. L. Rev. 655 (1978).

Improper Evidence in Nonjury Trials: Basis for Reversal?, 79 Harv. L. Rev. 407 (1965).

Inconsistent Verdicts in a Federal Criminal Trial, 60 Colum. L. Rev. 999 (1960).

The Indigent's Right to an Adequate Defense: Expert and Investigational Assistance in Criminal Proceedings, 55 Cornell L. Rev. 632 (1970).

The Unconstitutionality of Statutory Criminal Presumptions, 22 Stan. L. Rev. 341 (1970).

Chapter 3
The Justification of Punishment

H. B. Acton, The Philosophy of Punishment (1969).

American Bar Association, Standards for Criminal Justice, Sentencing Alternatives and Procedures (2d ed. 1980).

Andenaes, General Prevention, 43 J. Crim. L.C. & P.S. 176 (1952).

Andenaes, The General Preventive Effects of Punishment, 114 U. Pa. L. Rev. 949 (1960).

Armstrong, The Retributivist Hits Back, 70 Mind 471 (1961).

Beale, Consent in the Criminal Law, 8 Harv. L. Rev. 317 (1895).

California Assembly Committee on Criminal Procedure, Progress Report, Deterrent Effects of Criminal Sanctions (May 1968).

Cohen, Moral Aspects of the Criminal Law, 49 Yale L.J. 987 (1940).

P. Devlin, The Enforcement of Morals (1959).

E. Durkheim, The Division of Labor in Society (G. Simpson trans. 1933).

Dworkin, Lord Devlin and the Enforcement of Morals, 75 Yale L.J. 986 (1966).

A. C. Ewing, The Morality of Punishment (1929).

G. Ezorsky, Philosophical Perspectives on Punishment (1972).

R. Gerber & P. McAnany, Contemporary Punishment: Views, Explanations and Justifications (1972).

Gerber & McAnany, Punishment: Current Survey of Philosophy and Law, 11 St. Louis U.L.J. 491 (1967).

Gussfield, On Legislating Morals: The Symbolic Process of Designating Deviancy, 56 Calif. L. Rev. 54 (1968).

H. L. A. Hart, Law, Liberty, and Morality (1963).

H. L. A. Hart, Punishment and Responsibility (1968).

Hart, Social Solidarity and the Enforcement of Morality, 35 U. Chi. L. Rev. 1 (1967).

Home Office, Scottish Home Department, Report of the Committee on Homosexual Offenses and Prostitution (Wolfenden Report) (1957).

Hughes, Morals and the Criminal Law, 71 Yale L.J. 662 (1962).

Junker, Criminalization and Criminogenesis, 19 U.C.L.A.L. Rev. 694 (1972).

Kadish, The Crisis of Overcriminalization, 374 Annals 156 (1967).

Kadish, More on Overcriminalization: A Reply to Professor Junker, 19 U.C.L.A.L. Rev. 719 (1972).

I. Kant, The Metaphysical Elements of Justice (J. Ladd trans. 1965).

Mabbot, Punishment, 48 Mind 152 (1932).

Mallin, In Warm Blood: Some Historical and Procedural Aspects of Regina v. Dudley and Stephens, 34 U. Chi. L. Rev. 387 (1967).

Martinson, New Findings, New Views: A Note of Caution Regarding Sentencing Reform, 7 Hofstra L. Rev. 243 (1979).

Martinson, What Works? — Questions and Answers about Prison Reform, 36 Pub. Interest 22 (1974).

B. Mitchell, Law, Morality, and Religion in a Secular Society (1967).

H. Morris, The Future of Imprisonment (1974).

H. Morris, On Guilt and Innocence (1976).

Morris, Persons and Punishment, 52 Monist 475 (1968).

H. Morris (ed.), Freedom and Responsibility (1961).

N. Morris & G. Hawkins, The Honest Politician's Guide to Crime Control (1970).

Murphy, Marxism and Retribution, 2 Philosophy & Pub. Aff. 217 (1973).

National Research Council, Deterrence and Incapacitation: Estimating the Effects of Criminal Sanctions on Crime Rates (1978).

E. Pincoffs, The Rationale of Legal Punishment (1966).

President's Commission on Law Enforcement and the Administration of Justice, Task Force Report: Corrections (1967).

Puttkamer, Consent in Criminal Assault, 19 Ill. L. Rev. 617 (1925).

Radzinowicz & Turner, A Study of Punishment I: Introductory Essay, 21 Canadian B. Rev. 91 (1943).

Rivera, Our Straight-Laced Judges: The Legal Position of Homosexual Persons in the United States, 30 Hastings L.J. 799 (1979).

E. Rostow, The Sovereign Prerogative (1962).

Sellin, The Law and Some Aspects of Criminal Conduct, in Aims and Methods of Legal Research 113 (A. Conrad ed. 1955).

Simpson, Cannibals at Common Law, 77 U. Chi. L. Sch. Rec. 3 (1981).

Skolnick, Criminalization and Criminogenesis: A Reply to Professor Junker, 19 U.C.L.A.L. Rev. 715 (1972).

A. von Hirsch, Doing Justice (1976).

Walker, The Efficacy and Morality of Deterrents, [1979] Crim. L. Rev. 129.

R. Wasserstrom, Philosophy and Social Issues (1980).

Williams, Consent and Public Policy, [1962] Crim. L. Rev. 74.

F. Zimring & G. Hawkins, Deterrence: The Legal Threat in Crime Control (1973).

Chapter 4
Defining Criminal Conduct —
The Elements of Just Punishment

Bolgar, The Present Function of the Maxim Ignorantia Juris Neminem Excusat — A Comparative Study, 52 Iowa L. Rev. 626 (1967).

Brady, Strict Criminal Offenses: A Justification, 8 Crim. L. Bull. 217 (1973).

Brett, Mistake of Law as a Criminal Defense, 5 Melb. U.L. Rev. 179 (1966).

Budd & Lynch, Voluntariness, Causation and Strict Liability, [1978] Crim. L. Rev. 74.

Campbell, A Strict Accountability Approach to Criminal Responsibility, 29 Fed. Prob. 333 (1965).

Clark, Accident — or What Became of *Kilbride* and *Lake,* in Essays on Criminal Law in New Zealand 47 (1971).

A. T. Denning, Freedom under the Law (1949).

G. Dworkin & G. Blumenfeld, Punishment for Intentions, 75 Mind 396 (1966).

Ewing, A Study of Punishment II: Punishment as Viewed by the Philosopher, 21 Canadian B. Rev. 102 (1943).

Fletcher, The Theory of Criminal Negligence, 119 U. Pa. L. Rev. 401 (1971).

Foote, Vagrancy Type Law and Its Administration, 104 U. Pa. L. Rev. 603 (1956).

W. Friedmann, Law in a Changing Society (1964).

Goldstein, Conspiracy to Defraud the United States, 68 Yale L.J. 405 (1959).

Goodhart, Possession of Drugs and Absolute Liability, 84 L.Q. Rev. 382 (1968).

Hall & Seligman, Mistake of Law and Mens Rea, 8 U. Chi. L. Rev. 641 (1941).

H. L. A. Hart, Book Review (Wootton, Crime and the Criminal Law), 74 Yale L.J. 1325 (1965).

H. L. A. Hart, Law, Liberty and Morality (1963).

H. L. A. Hart, The Morality of the Criminal Law (1965).

H. L. A. Hart & A. Honoré, Causation in the Law (1959).

H. M. Hart, The Aims of the Criminal Law, 23 L. & Contemp. Prob. 401 (1958).

Houlgate, Ignorantia Juris: A Plea for Justice, 78 Ethics 32 (1967).

Hughes, Criminal Omissions, 67 Yale L.J. 590 (1958).

Hughes, Criminal Responsibility, 16 Stan. L. Rev. 470 (1964).

Kadish, The Decline of Innocence, 26 Cambridge L.J. 273 (1968).

Kennedy, Switching Off Life Support Machines: The Legal Implications, [1977] Crim. L. Rev. 443.

Lanham, *Larsonneur* Revisited, [1976] Crim. L. Rev. 276.

J. Marshall, Intention — in Law and Society (1968).

Morris, An Australian News Letter, [1955] Crim. L. Rev. 290.

Morris, Somnambulistic Homicide: Ghosts, Spiders, and North Koreans, 5 Res Judicatae 29 (1951).

Murphy, Involuntary Acts and Criminal Liability, 51 Ethics 332 (1971).

Perkins, Ignorance and Mistake in Criminal Law, 88 U. Pa. L. Rev. 35 (1939).

Reiter, Antisocial or Criminal Acts and Hypnosis: A Case Study, 46 A.B.A.J. 81 (1960).

Sayre, Public Welfare Offenses, 33 Colum. L. Rev. 55 (1933).

Schwartz, Reform of the Federal Criminal Laws: Issues, Tactics and Prospects, [1977] Duke L.J. 171.

Smith, The Heilbron Report, [1976] Crim. L. Rev. 97.

J. F. Stephen, Law, Equality, Fraternity (1967).

Wasserstrom, Strict Liability in the Criminal Law, 12 Stan. L. Rev. 731 (1960).

Wechsler & Michael, A Rationale of the Law of Homicide, 37 Colum. L. Rev. 701 (1937).

Weinrib, The Case for a Duty to Rescue, 90 Yale L.J. 247 (1980).

Williams, Euthanasia, 41 Medico-Legal J. 14 (1973).

B. Wootton, Crime and the Criminal Law (1963).

Applying Estoppel Principles in Criminal Cases, 78 Yale L.J. 1046 (1969).

Criminal Liability without Fault: A Philosophical Perspective, 75 Colum. L. Rev. 1517 (1975).

Hypnotism and the Law, 14 Vand. L. Rev. 1509 (1961).

Reliance on Apparent Authority as a Defense to Criminal Prosecution, 77 Colum. L. Rev. 775 (1977).

United States v. Barker: Misapplication of the Reliance on an Official Interpretation of the Law Defense, 66 Calif. L. Rev. 809 (1978).

Chapter 5
Rape

Berger, Man's Trial, Woman's Tribulation: Rape Cases in the Courtroom, 77 Colum. L. Rev. 1 (1977).

Clarke, Corroboration in Sexual Cases, [1980] Crim. L. Rev. 362.

Geis, Rape-in-Marriage: Law and Law Reform in England, the United States, and Sweden, 6 Adel. L. Rev. 284 (1978).

Puttkammer, Consent in Rape, 19 Ill. L. Rev. 410 (1925).

Tanford & Bocchino, Rape Victim Shield Laws and the Sixth Amendment, 128 U. Pa. L. Rev. 544 (1980).

The Rape Corroboration Requirement: Repeal Not Reform, 81 Yale L.J. 1365 (1972).

Recent Statutory Developments in the Definition of Forcible Rape, 61 Va. L. Rev. 1500 (1975).

Towards a Consent Standard in the Law of Rape, 43 U. Chi. L. Rev. 613 (1976).

Chapter 6
Homicide

Baldus & Cole, A Comparison of the Work of Thorsten Sellin & Isaac Ehrlich on the Deterrent Effect of Capital Punishment, 85 Yale L.J. 170 (1975).

Barzun, In Favor of Capital Punishment, 31 Am. Scholar 181 (1962).

H. Bedau, The Case against the Death Penalty (1977).

H. Bedau, The Courts, the Constitution, and Capital Punishment (1977).

H. Bedau, The Death Penalty in America (1964).

W. Berns, For Capital Punishment (1979).

C. Black, Capital Punishment: The Inevitability of Caprice and Mistake (1981).

Bowers & Pierce, The Illusion of Deterrence in Isaac Ehrlich's Research on Capital Punishment, 85 Yale L.J. 187 (1975).

Cardozo, What Medicine Can Do for Law, in B. Cardozo, Law and Literature and Other Essays and Addresses (1931).

Collings, Negligent Murder — Some Stateside Footnotes to D.P.P. v. Smith, 49 Calif. L. Rev. 254 (1961).

Devlin, Criminal Responsibility and Punishment: Functions of Judge and Jury, [1954] Crim. L. Rev. 661.

Ehrlich, Deterrence: Evidence and Inference, 85 Yale L.J. 209 (1975).

Ehrlich, The Deterrent Effect of Capital Punishment: A Question of Life and Death, 65 Am. Econ. Rev. 397 (1975).

J. Frank & B. Frank, Not Guilty (1957).

H. L. A. Hart, The Morality of the Criminal Law (1965).

Hogan, The Killing Ground, [1974] Crim. L. Rev. 387.

Johnson, Foreword: The Accidental Decision and How It Happens, 65 Calif. L. Rev. 231 (1977).

Judson et al., A Study of the California Penalty Jury in First-Degree-Murder Cases, 21 Stan. L. Rev. 1297 (1969).

Lempert, Desert and Deterrence: An Assessment of the Moral Bases of the Case for Capital Punishment, 79 Mich. L. Rev. 1177 (1981).

T. B. Macaulay, A Penal Code Prepared by the Indian Law Commissioners (1837).

M. Meltsner, Cruel and Unusual: The Supreme Court and Capital Punishment (1973).

Michael & Wechsler, A Rationale of the Law of Homicide, 37 Colum. L. Rev. 1261 (1937).

Morse, Diminished Capacity: A Moral and Legal Conundrum, 2 Intl. J.L. & Psych. 271 (1979).

Passell, The Deterrent Effect of the Death Penalty: A Statistical Test, 28 Stan. L. Rev. 61 (1975).

Peck, The Deterrent Effect of Capital Punishment: Ehrlich and His Critics, 85 Yale L.J. 359 (1976).

Schulhofer, Harm and Punishment: A Critique of Emphasis on the Results of Conduct in the Criminal Law, 122 U. Pa. L. Rev. 1497 (1974).

T. Sellin, The Death Penalty, A Report for the Model Penal Code Project of the American Law Institute (1955).

Smith, The Element of Chance in Criminal Liability, [1971] Crim. L. Rev. 63.

Wechsler, The Challenge of a Model Penal Code, 65 Harv. L. Rev. 1097 (1952).

van den Haag, On Deterrence and the Death Penalty, 60 J. Crim. L.C. & P.S. 141 (1969).

E. van den Haag, Punishing Criminals (1975).

Williams, Provocation and the Reasonable Man, [1954] Crim. L. Rev. 740.

Zeisel, Race Bias in the Administration of the Death Penalty: The Florida Experience, 95 Harv. L. Rev. 456 (1981).

The California Supreme Court Assaults the Felony-Murder Rule, 22 Stan. L. Rev. 1059 (1970).

Merger and the California Felony-Murder Rule, 20 U.C.L.A.L. Rev. 250 (1972).

Provocation: The Reasonableness of the Reasonable Man, 106 U. Pa. L. Rev. 102 (1958).

Report of the Royal Commission on Capital Punishment, 1949-1953 (1953).

Chapter 7
The Significance of Resulting Harm

Arnold, Criminal Attempts — The Rise and Fall of an Abstraction, 40 Yale L.J. 53 (1930).

Dutile & Moore, Mistake and Impossibility: Arranging a Marriage between Two Difficult Partners, 74 Nw. U.L. Rev. 166 (1979).

G. Dworkin & G. Blumenfeld, Punishment for Intention, 75 Mind 396 (1966).

Enker, Mens Rea and Criminal Attempt, [1977] Am. B. Found. Research J. 845.

Greenawalt, Speech and Crime, [1980] Am. B. Found. Research J. 645.

Guthrie, Brain Death and Criminal Liability, 15 Crim. L. Bull. 40 (1979).

H. L. A. Hart & A. Honoré, Causation in the Law (1958).

Hughes, One Further Footnote on Attempting the Impossible, 42 N.Y.U.L. Rev. 1005 (1967).

Keedy, Criminal Attempts at Common Law, 102 U. Pa. L. Rev. 464 (1954).

Lanham, Murder by Instigating Suicide, [1980] Crim. L. Rev. 213.

Mack, Bad Samaritanism and the Causation of Harm, 9 Philosophy & Pub. Aff. 230 (1980).

Morris, Punishment for Thoughts, 49 Monist 342 (1965).

Perkins, An Analysis of Assault and Attempts to Assault, 47 Minn. L. Rev. 71 (1962).

Perkins, Criminal Attempt and Related Problems, 2 U.C.L.A.L. Rev. 319 (1955).

Sayre, Criminal Attempts, 41 Harv. L. Rev. 821 (1928).

Schulhofer, Harm and Punishment: A Critique of Emphasis on the Results of Conduct in the Criminal Law, 122 U. Pa. L. Rev. 1497 (1974).

Smith, The Element of Chance in Criminal Liability, [1971] Crim. L. Rev. 63.

Smith, Two Problems in Criminal Attempts, 70 Harv. L. Rev. 422 (1957).

Stuart, Mens Rea, Negligence and Attempts, [1968] Crim. L. Rev. 647.

J. Waite, The Prevention of Repeated Crime (1943).

Weigend, Why Lady Eldon Should Be Acquitted: The Social Harm in Attempting the Impossible, 27 DePaul L. Rev. 231 (1979).

Comment on *Stephenson*, 31 Mich. L. Rev. 659 (1933).

Chapter 8
Group Criminality

Blakey & Goldstock, "On the Waterfront": RICO and Labor Racketeering, 17 Am. Crim. L. Rev. 341 (1980).

Burgman, Unilateral Conspiracy: Three Critical Perspectives, 29 DePaul L. Rev. 75 (1979).

Cousens, Agreement as an Element of Conspiracy, 23 Va. L. Rev. 898 (1937).

Hogan, Victims as Parties to Crime, [1962] Crim. L. Rev. 683.

Johnson, The Unnecessary Crime of Conspiracy, 61 Calif. L. Rev. 1137 (1973).

Marcus, Conspiracy: The Criminal Agreement in Theory and Practice, 65 Geo. L.J. 925 (1977).

Marcus, Co-Conspirators Declarations: The Federal Rules of Evidence and Other Recent Developments, from a Criminal Law Perspective, 7 Am. J. Crim. L. 287 (1979).

Rahl, Conspiracy and the Anti-Trust Laws, 44 Ill. L. Rev. 743 (1950).

Remington & Joseph, Charging, Convicting, and Sentencing the Multiple Criminal Offender, [1961] Wis. L. Rev. 528.

Sayre, Criminal Responsibility for the Acts of Another, 43 Harv. L. Rev. 689 (1930).

Turner, The Definition of Agreement under the Sherman Act: Conscious Parallelism and Refusals to Deal, 75 Harv. L. Rev. 655 (1962).

Wechsler, Jones & Korn, The Treatment of Inchoate Crimes in the Model Penal Code of the American Law Institute: Attempt, Solicitation and Conspiracy, 68 Colum. L. Rev. 957 (1968).

An Analysis of Wharton's Rule, 71 Nw. U.L. Rev. 547 (1976).

The Co-Conspirator's Exception to the Hearsay Rule: Bootstrapping in the New Procedure from the First Circuit, 50 Colo. L. Rev. 93 (1978).

Complicity in a Conspiracy as an Approach to Conspiratorial Liability, 16 U.C.L.A.L. Rev. 155 (1968).

Conspiracy: Statutory Reform since the Model Penal Code, 75 Colum. L. Rev. 1122 (1975).

Developments in the Law — Criminal Conspiracy, 72 Harv. L. Rev. 920 (1959).

Elliott v. United States: Conspiracy Law and the Judicial Pursuit of Organized Crime through RICO, 65 Va. L. Rev. 109 (1978).

The Hearsay Exception for Co-Conspirator's Declaration, 25 U. Chi. L. Rev. 530 (1958).

Reconstructing the Independent Evidence Requirement of the Co-Conspirator Hearsay Exception, 127 U. Pa. L. Rev. 143 (1979).

Chapter 9A
Exculpation — Principles of Justification

B. Babcock, A. Freedman, E. Norton & S. Ross, Sex Discrimination and the Law: Causes and Remedies (1975).

E. Bochnak, Women's Self-Defense Cases (1981).

S. Brownmiller, Against Our Will: Men, Women and Rape (1975).

B. Cardozo, Law and Literature (1930).

Chevigny, The Right to Resist an Unlawful Arrest, 78 Yale L.J. 1128 (1969).

Day, Shooting the Fleeing Felon: State of the Law, 14 Crim. L. Bull. 285 (1978).

Fletcher, Proportionality and the Psychotic Aggressor: A Vignette in Comparative Criminal Theory, 8 Israel L. Rev. 367 (1973).

Fletcher, Should Intolerable Conditions Generate a Justification or an Excuse for Escape?, 26 U.C.L.A.L. Rev. 1355 (1979).

Fuller, The Case of the Speluncean Explorers, 62 Harv. L. Rev. 616 (1949).

Gardner, The Defense of Necessity and the Right to Escape from Prison, 49 S. Calif. L. Rev. 110 (1975).

Glazebrook, The Necessity Plea in English Criminal Law, 30 Cambridge L.J. 87 (1972).

F. Hicks, Human Jettison (1927).

Kadish, Respect for Life and Regard for Rights in the Criminal Law, 64 Calif. L. Rev. 861 (1976).

Mitchell, Does Wife Abuse Justify Homicide?, 24 Wayne L. Rev. 1705 (1978).

Murphy, The Killing of the Innocent, 56 Monist 527 (1973).

R. Nozick, Anarchy, State and Utopia (1974).

L. Schwartz, Reform of the Federal Criminal Laws, [1977] Duke L.J. 171, 217.

Taurek, Should the Numbers Count?, 6 Philosophy & Pub. Aff. 293 (1977).

Tiffany & Anderson, Legislating the Necessity Defense in Criminal Law, 52 Den. L.J. 839 (1975).

Vandenbraak, Limits on the Use of Defensive Force to Prevent Intramarital Assaults, 10 Rut.-Cam. L.J. 643 (1979).

Williams, A Commentary on R. v. Dudley and Stephens, 8 Cambrian L. Rev. 94 (1977).

Williams, (2) Necessity, [1978] Crim. L. Rev. 128.

From Duress to Intent: Shifting the Burden in Prison-Escape Prosecutions, 127 U. Pa. L. Rev. 1142 (1979).

Intolerable Conditions as a Defense to Prison Escapes, 26 U.C.L.A.L. Rev. 1126 (1979).

Justification: The Impact of the Model Penal Code on State Law Reform, 75 Colum. L. Rev. 914 (1975).

Justifiable Use of Force under Article 35 of the Penal Law of New York, 18 Buffalo L. Rev. 285 (1969).

The Law of Necessity as Applied in the Bisbee Deportation Case, 13 Ariz. L. Rev. 264 (1961).

Medical Necessity as a Defense to Criminal Liability: United States v. Randall, 46 Geo. Wash. L. Rev. 273 (1978).

Necessity as a Defense to a Charge of Criminal Trespass in an Abortion Clinic, [1979] Crim. L. Rev. 501, 506.

The Necessity Defense in Prison Escape after United States v. Bailey, 65 Va. L. Rev. 359 (1979).

Chapter 9B
Exculpation — Principles of Excuse

Andenaes, The Morality of Deterrence, 37 U. Chi. L. Rev. 649 (1970).

Arenella, The Diminished Capacity and Diminished Responsibility Defenses: Two Children of a Doomed Marriage, 77 Colum. L. Rev. 827 (1977).

Ashworth, The Butler Committee and Criminal Responsibility, [1975] Crim. L. Rev. 687.

Austin, A Plea for Excuses, 56 Proc. Aristotelian Socy. 1 (1956-57).

Beck & Parker, The Intoxicated Offender — A Problem of Responsibility, 44 Canadian B. Rev. 563 (1966).

Brown and Wittner, Criminal Law (1978 Annual Survey of Michigan Law), 25 Wayne L. Rev. 335 (1979).

Burt & Morris, A Proposal for the Abolition of the Incompetency Plea, 40 U. Chi. L. Rev. 66 (1972).

California Special Commission on Insanity and Criminal Offenders, First Report (1962).

Cross, Reflections on *Bratty's* Case, 78 L.Q. Rev. 236 (1962).

Delgado, Ascription of Criminal States of Mind: Toward a Defense Theory for the Coercively Persuaded ("Brainwashed") Defendant, 63 Minn. L. Rev. 1 (1978).

Dershowitz, Abolishing the Insanity Defense: The Most Significant Feature of the Administration's Proposed Criminal Code — An Essay, 9 Crim. L. Bull. 424 (1973).

Diamond, Criminal Responsibility of the Mentally Ill, 14 Stan. L. Rev. 59 (1961).

Dix, Psychological Abnormality as a Factor in Grading Criminal Liability: Diminished Capacity, Diminished Responsibility, and the Like, 62 J. Crim. L.C. & P.S. 313 (1971).

R. Dworkin, Taking Rights Seriously, ch. 1 (1977).

Edwards, Automatism and Social Defense, 8 Crim. L.Q. 258 (1966).

Elliot, Responsibility for Involuntary Acts: Ryan v. The Queen, 41 Austl. L.J. 497 (1968).

Ennis & Litwack, Psychiatry and the Presumption of Expertise: Flipping Coins in the Courtroom, 62 Calif. L. Rev. 693 (1974).

Eule, The Presumption of Sanity: Bursting the Bubble, 25 U.C.L.A.L. Rev. 637 (1978).

Fingarette, Addiction and Criminal Responsibility, 84 Yale L.J. 413 (1975).

Fingarette, Diminished Mental Capacity as a Criminal Law Defense, 37 Mod. L. Rev. 264 (1974).

Fingarette, The Perils of *Powell:* In Search of a Factual Foundation for the "Disease Concept of Alcoholism," 83 Harv. L. Rev. 793 (1970).

Fletcher, The Individualization of Excusing Conditions, 47 S. Calif. L. Rev. 1269 (1974).

Fox, Physical Disorder, Consciousness, and Criminal Liability, 63 Colum. L. Rev. 645 (1963).

Gambino, The Murderous Mind: Insanity v. the Law, Saturday Review, March 1978.

A. Goldstein, The Insanity Defense (1967).

Goldstein & Katz, Abolish the "Insanity Defense"— Why Not?, 73 Yale L.J. 853 (1963).

Greenawalt, "Uncontrollable" Actions and the Eighth Amendment; Implications of Powell v. Texas, 69 Colum. L. Rev. 927 (1969).

Hazard & Louisell, Death, the State and the Insane: Stay of Execution, 9 U.C.L.A.L. Rev. 38 (1962).

Jennings, The Growth and Development of Automatism as a Defense in Criminal Law, 2 Osgoode Hall L. Student J. 370 (1962).

Kadish, The Decline of Innocence, 26 Cambridge L.J. 273 (1968).

Kahn, Automatism: The Sane and Insane, [1965] N.Z.L.J. 113.

Kalven & Zeisel, The American Jury (1960).

Leigh, Automatism and Insanity, 5 Crim. L.Q. 160 (1962).

Louisell & Hazard, Insanity as a Defense: The Bifurcated Trial, 49 Calif. L. Rev. 805 (1961).

Lunde & Wilson, Brainwashing as a Defense to Criminal Liability: Patty Hearst Revisited, 13 Crim. L. Bull. 341 (1977).

Milgram, Obedience to Authority (1974).

Monohan, Abolish the Insanity Defense? — Not Yet, 26 Rutgers L. Rev. 719 (1973).

Moore, Legal Responsibility and Chronic Alcoholism, 122 Am. J. Psychiatry 748 (1966).

Morris, Psychiatry and the Dangerous Criminal, 41 S. Calif. L. Rev. 514 (1968).

Morse, Diminished Capacity: A Moral and Legal Conundrum, 2 Intl. J.L. & Psych. 271 (1979).

Muelberger, Medico-Legal Aspects of Alcohol Intoxication, 45 Mich. State B.J. 36 (1956).

Newman & Weitzer, Duress, Free Will and the Criminal Law, 30 S. Calif. L. Rev. 313 (1957).

O'Regan, Duress and Murder, 35 Mod. L. Rev. 596 (1972).

Roth, General versus Specific Intent: A Time for Terminological Understanding in California, 7 Pepperdine L. Rev. 67 (1979).

Sim, Involuntary Actus Reus, 25 Mod. L. Rev. 741 (1962).

Singer, The Imposition of the Insanity Defense on an Unwilling Defendant, 41 Ohio St. L.J. 637 (1980).

Wald, Alcohol, Drugs, and Criminal Responsibility, 63 Geo. L.J. 69 (1974).

Wales, An Analysis of the Proposal to "Abolish" the Insanity Defense in S. 1: Squeezing a Lemon, 124 U. Pa. L. Rev. 687 (1976).

N. Walker, Sentencing in a Rational Society (1969).

Williams, Automatism, in Essays in Criminal Science 345 (G. Mueller ed. 1961).

B. Wootton, Crime and the Criminal Law (1963).

Amnesia, A Case Study in the Limits of Particular Justice, 61 Yale L.J. 109 (1961).

The Eighth Amendment and the Execution of the Presently Incompetent, 32 Stan. L. Rev. 765 (1980).

Insanity and the Condemned, 88 Yale L.J. 533 (1979).

Rethinking the Specific-General Intent Doctrine in California Criminal Law, 63 Calif. L. Rev. 1352 (1975).

Chapter 10
Theft Offenses

Beale, The Borderland of Larceny, 6 Harv. L. Rev. 251 (1892).

Bein, The Theft of Use and the Element of "Intention to Deprive Permanently" in Larceny, 3 Israel L. Rev. 368 (1968).

Fletcher, The Metamorphosis of Larceny, 89 Harv. L. Rev. 469 (1976).

J. Hall, Theft, Law and Society (2d ed. 1952).

Lowe, Larceny by a Trick and Contract, [1957] Crim. L. Rev. 28.

Nimmer, National Secrets v. Free Speech: The Issues Left Undecided in the *Ellsberg* Case, 26 Stan. L. Rev. 311 (1974).

Pearce, Theft by False Promises, 101 U. Pa. L. Rev. 967 (1953).

Riesman, Possession and the Law of Finders, 52 Harv. L. Rev. 1105 (1939).

Williams, Theft, Consent and Illegality: Some Problems, [1977] Crim. L. Rev. 327.

A Rationale of the Law of Aggravated Theft, 54 Colum. L. Rev. 84 (1954).

Chapter 11
Business Crimes

F. Allen, The Criminal Law as an Instrument of Economic Regulation, Intl. Inst. Econ. Research (Orig. Paper #2, 1976).

Ball & Friedman, The Use of Criminal Sanctions in the Enforcement of Economic Legislation: A Sociological View, 17 Stan. Rev. 197 (1965).

Coffee, Beyond the Shut-Eyed Sentry: Toward a Theoretical View of Corporate Misconduct and an Effective Legal Response, 63 Va. L. Rev. 1099 (1977).

Coffee, Corporate Crime and Punishment: A Non-Chicago View of the Economics of Criminal Sanctions, 17 Am. Crim. L. Rev. 419 (1980).

Coffee, "No Soul to Damn, No Body to Kick": An Unscandalized Inquiry into the Problem of Corporate Punishment, 79 Mich. L. Rev. 386 (1981).

Davids, Penology and Corporate Crime, 58 J. Crim. L.C. & P.S. 524 (1967).

Elkins, Corporations and the Criminal Law: An Uneasy Alliance, 65 Ky. L.J. 73 (1976).

Estey & Marston, Pitfalls (and Loopholes) in the Foreign Bribery Law, 98 Fortune 182 (1978).

Friedman, Some Reflections on the Corporation as Criminal Defendant, 55 Notre Dame Law. 173 (1979).

Gustman, The Foreign Corrupt Practices Act of 1977: A Transactional Analysis, 13 J. Intl. L. & Econ. 367 (1979).

Kadish, Some Observations on the Use of Criminal Sanctions in Enforcing Economic Regulations, 30 U. Chi. L. Rev. 423 (1963).

Miller, Corporate Criminal Liability: A Principle Extended to Its Limits, 38 Fed. B.J. 29 (1979).

C. Morris, Punitive Damages in Personal Injury Cases, 21 Ohio St. L.J. 216 (1960).

Posner, Optimal Sentences for White-Collar Criminals, 17 Am. Crim. L. Rev. 409 (1980).

Renfrew, The Paper Label Sentences: An Evaluation, 86 Yale L.J. 590 (1977).

Ross, How Lawless Are Big Companies?, 103 Fortune 56 (1980).

Sayre, Criminal Responsibility for the Acts of Another, 43 Harv. L. Rev. 689 (1930).

Solomon & Gustman, Questionable and Illegal Payments by American Corporations, 35 J. Bus. L. 67 (1980).

Solomon & Linville, Transnational Conduct of American Multinational Corporations: Questionable Payments Abroad, 17 B.C. Ind. & Comm. L. Rev. 303 (1976).

C. Stone, Where the Law Ends — The Social Control of Corporate Behavior (1975).

Wasserstrom, Strict Liability in the Criminal Law, 12 Stan. L. Rev. 731 (1960).

Wheeler, Products Liability: Manufacturers, Wrong Targets for Threat of Criminal Sanctions?, Natl. L.J. (Dec. 22, 1980).

Corporate Homicide: A New Assault on Corporate Decision-Making, 56 Notre Dame Law. 911 (1979).

Developments in the Law — Corporate Crime: Regulating Corporate Behavior through Criminal Sanctions, 92 Harv. L. Rev. 1227 (1979).

Increasing Community Control over Corporate Crime — A Problem in the Law of Sanctions, 71 Yale L.J. 280 (1961).

Individual Liability of Agents for Corporate Crime under the Proposed Federal Criminal Code, 31 Vand. L. Rev. 965 (1978).

Structural Crime and Rehabilitation: A New Approach to Corporate Sanctions, 89 Yale L.J. 535 (1979).

Chapter 12
Disposition of Convicted Offenders

F. Allen, The Borderland of Criminal Justice (1964).

American Bar Association, Standards for Criminal Justice, Appellate Review of Sentences (2d ed. 1980).

American Friends Service Committee, The Struggle for Justice (1971).

Alschuler, The Changing Plea-Bargaining Debate, 69 Calif. L. Rev. 652 (1981).

Alschuler, Sentencing Reform and Prosecutorial Power: A Critique of Recent Proposals for "Fixed" and "Presumptive Sentencing," 126 U. Pa. L. Rev. 550 (1978).

Bedau, Retribution and the Theory of Punishment, 75 J. Philosophy 601 (1978).

Clear, Hewitt & Regoli, Discretion and the Determinate Sentence: Its Distribution, Control and Effect on Time Served, 24 Crime & Delinquency 428 (1978).

Coffee, Repressed Issues of Sentencing: Accountability, Predictability and Equality in the Era of the Sentencing Commission, 66 Geo. L.J. 975 (1978).

J. Eisenstein & H. Jacob, Felony Justice: An Organizational Analysis of Criminal Courts (1977).

M. Frankel, Criminal Sentences: Law without Order (1973).

Foote, Deceptive Determinate Sentencing, in National Institute of Law Enforcement and Criminal Justice, Determinate Sentencing: Reform or Regression? (1978).

Frankel, Symposium, Developments in Judicial Administration, 80 F.R.D. 147 (1978).

Galligan, Guidelines and Just Deserts: A Critique of Recent Trends in Sentencing Reform, [1981] Crim. L. Rev. 297.

Kadish, The Advocate and the Expert: Counsel in the Peno-Correctional Process, 45 Minn. L. Rev. 803 (1961).

Kadish, Legal Norm and Discretion in the Police and Sentencing Process, 75 Harv. L. Rev. 904 (1962).

Lagoy, Hussey & Kramer, A Comparative Assessment of Determinate Sentencing in Four Pioneer States, 24 Crime & Delinquency 385 (1978).

Lee & Zuckerman, Representing Parole Violators, 11 Crim. L. Bull. 327 (1975).

Low, Special Offender Sentencing, 8 Am. Crim. L.Q. 70 (1970).

N. Morris, The Future of Imprisonment (1974).

Petersilia & Greenwood, Mandatory Prison Sentences: Their Projected Effects on Crime and Prison Populations, 69 J. Crim. L. & Criminology 604 (1978).

Rhodes, Plea Bargaining: Who Gains? Who Loses? (1978).

Schulhofer, Due Process of Sentencing, 128 U. Pa. L. Rev. 733 (1980).

Schulhofer, Prosecutorial Discretion and Federal Sentencing Reform (Federal Judicial Center 1979).

Shin, Do Lesser Pleas Pay? Accommodations in the Sentencing and Parole Processes, 1 Crim. Just. 27 (1973).

Twentieth Century Fund, Task Force on Criminal Sentencing, Fair and Certain
    Punishment (1976).
A. von Hirsch, Doing Justice: The Choice of Punishments (1976).
A. von Hirsch & K. Hanrahan, The Question of Parole (1979).
Vorenberg, Decent Restraint of Prosecutorial Power, 94 Harv. L. Rev. 1521
    (1981).
Westen & Westin, A Constitutional Law of Remedies for Broken Plea Bargains,
    66 Calif. L. Rev. 471 (1978).
Wilkins, Kress, Gottfredson, Caplin, & Gelman, Sentencing Guidelines:
    Structuring Judicial Discretion 88 (1976).
Zeisel & Diamond, The Search for Sentencing Equity: Sentence Review in
    Massachusetts and Connecticut, [1977] Am. B. Found. Research J. 881.
Zimring, Making the Punishment Fit the Crime: A Consumer's Guide to
    Sentencing Reform, Hastings Center Rep. (Dec. 1976).

The Constitutionality of Statutes Permitting Increased Sentences for Habitual
    or Dangerous Criminals, 89 Harv. L. Rev. 356 (1975).
Due Process and Legislative Standards in Sentencing, 101 U. Pa. L. Rev. 257
    (1952).
A Hidden Issue of Sentencing: Burdens of Proof for Disputed Allegations in
    Presentence Reports, 66 Geo. L.J. 1515 (1978).
Parole Release Decision-Making and the Sentencing Process, 84 Yale L.J. 810
    (1975).
Parole Revocation in the Federal System, 56 Geo. L.J. 705 (1968).
Revocation of Conditional Liberty for the Commission of a Crime: Double
    Jeopardy and Self-Incrimination Limitations, 74 Mich. L. Rev. 525 (1976).

INDEX